For more resources, visit the Web site for

The American Promise

bedfordstmartins.com/roark

FREE Online Study Guide

Get instant feedback on your progress with

- Chapter self-tests
- Key terms review
- Map quizzes
- Timeline activities
- Note-taking outlines

FREE History research and writing help

Refine your research skills and find plenty of good sources with

- Suggested references for each chapter compiled by the textbook authors
- A database of useful images, maps, documents, and more at *Make History*
- A guide to online sources for history
- Help with writing history papers
- A tool for building a bibliography
- Tips on avoiding plagiarism

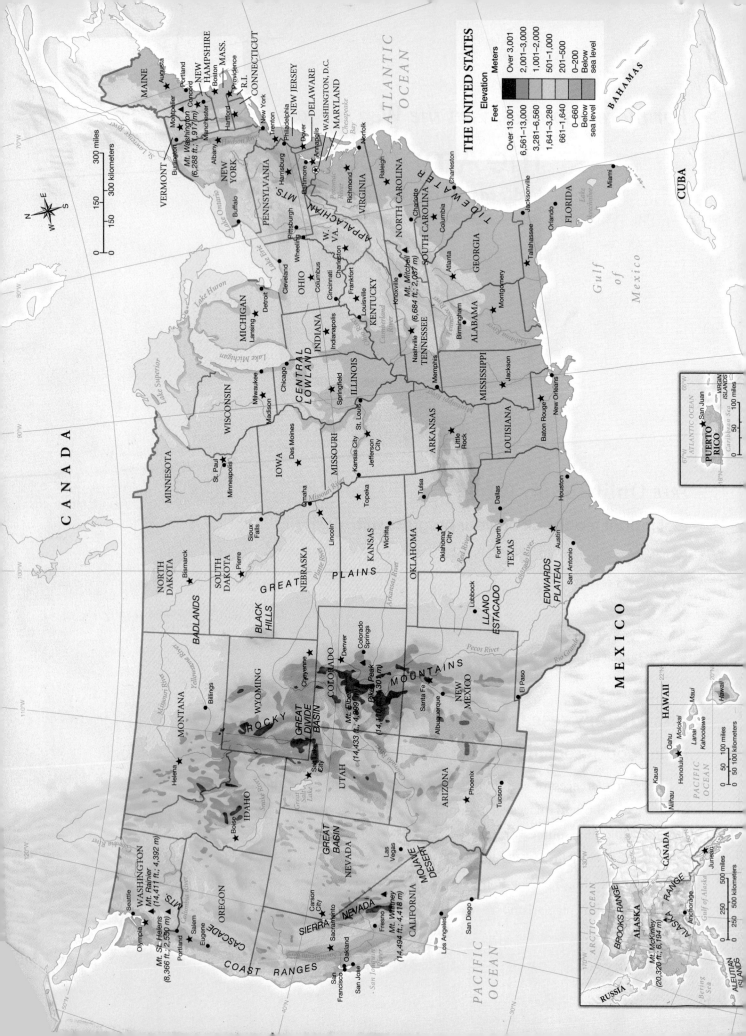

THE UNITED STATES

Elevation

Feet	Meters
Over 13,001	Over 3,001
6,561–13,000	2,001–3,000
3,281–6,560	1,001–2,000
1,641–3,280	501–1,000
661–1,640	201–500
0–660	0–200
Below sea level	Below sea level

CANADA

MAINE
Augusta
NEW HAMPSHIRE
Portland
Montpelier
VERMONT
Mt. Washington (6,288 ft.; 1,917 m)
Concord
Manchester
Boston
MASS.
Providence
R.I.
CONNECTICUT
Hartford
New York
Burlington
Albany
Buffalo
NEW YORK
Lake Ontario
PENNSYLVANIA
NEW JERSEY
Harrisburg
Philadelphia
Trenton
DELAWARE
Dover
WASHINGTON, D.C.
MARYLAND
Annapolis
Baltimore
Chesapeake Bay
Norfolk
Richmond
VIRGINIA
W. VA.
Charleston
Wheeling
Pittsburgh
Columbus
OHIO
Cincinnati
Frankfort
KENTUCKY
Louisville
Raleigh
NORTH CAROLINA
Charlotte
Columbia
SOUTH CAROLINA
Charleston
Mt. Mitchell (6,684 ft.; 2,037 m)
Knoxville
TIDEWATER
Jacksonville
GEORGIA
Atlanta
Montgomery
ALABAMA
Birmingham
Nashville
TENNESSEE
Memphis
APPALACHIAN MTS.
Lake Erie
Cleveland
Detroit
Lansing
MICHIGAN
Lake Huron
Lake Michigan
Lake Superior
Milwaukee
WISCONSIN
Madison
Chicago
CENTRAL LOWLAND
INDIANA
Indianapolis
ILLINOIS
Springfield
St. Louis
Tallahassee
Orlando
FLORIDA
Lake Okeechobee
Miami
ATLANTIC OCEAN
BAHAMAS
CUBA
Gulf of Mexico
MISSISSIPPI
Jackson
LOUISIANA
Baton Rouge
New Orleans
ARKANSAS
Little Rock
MISSOURI
Jefferson City
Kansas City
Topeka
Tulsa
OKLAHOMA
Oklahoma City
Wichita
KANSAS
Des Moines
IOWA
St. Paul
Minneapolis
MINNESOTA
Sioux Falls
NORTH DAKOTA
Bismarck
SOUTH DAKOTA
Pierre
BADLANDS
BLACK HILLS
NEBRASKA
Lincoln
Omaha
Platte River
Missouri River
GREAT PLAINS
Houston
Dallas
Fort Worth
TEXAS
San Antonio
Austin
Lubbock
LLANO ESTACADO
EDWARDS PLATEAU
Colorado River
Red River
Arkansas River
Fort Worth
El Paso
Rio Grande
Pecos River
MEXICO
ROCKY MOUNTAINS
Santa Fe
Albuquerque
NEW MEXICO
Pikes Peak (14,110 ft.; 4,301 m)
Colorado Springs
Denver
COLORADO
Mt. Elbert (14,433 ft.; 4,399 m)
Cheyenne
WYOMING
GREAT DIVIDE BASIN
Billings
MONTANA
Helena
Yellowstone River
Missouri River
IDAHO
Boise
Snake River
Salt Lake City
Great Salt Lake
UTAH
GREAT BASIN
ARIZONA
Phoenix
Tucson
NEVADA
Carson City
Las Vegas
MOJAVE DESERT
CALIFORNIA
Los Angeles
San Diego
Sacramento
Fresno
San Jose
Oakland
San Francisco
Mt. Whitney (14,494 ft.; 4,418 m)
SIERRA NEVADA
San Joaquin River
COAST RANGES
CASCADE MTS.
Salem
Eugene
OREGON
Portland
Mt. St. Helens (8,366 ft.; 2,550 m)
Olympia
Seattle
WASHINGTON
Mt. Rainier (14,411 ft.; 4,392 m)
Columbia River
PACIFIC OCEAN

St. Lawrence River
Hudson River
Potomac River
Cumberland River
Mississippi River
Alabama River

300 miles
300 kilometers
150
150
0

N E
W
S

PUERTO RICO
San Juan
ATLANTIC OCEAN
VIRGIN ISLANDS
Caribbean Sea
100 miles
50
0
100

HAWAII
Kauai
Nihau
Oahu
Honolulu
Molokai
Lanai
Maui
Kahoolawe
Hawaii
PACIFIC OCEAN
100 miles
50
0
50
100 kilometers

ALASKA
BROOKS RANGE
ALASKA RANGE
Mt. McKinley (20,320 ft.; 6,194 m)
Juneau
Anchorage
Gulf of Alaska
CANADA
ARCTIC OCEAN
Bering Sea
RUSSIA
ALEUTIAN ISLANDS
500 miles
250
0
250
500 kilometers

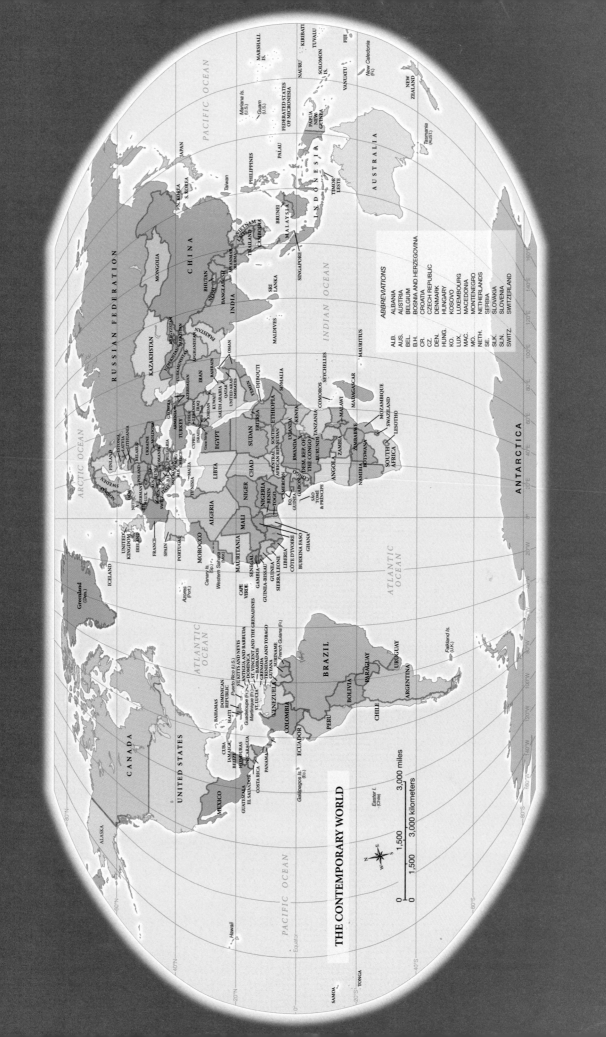

THE CONTEMPORARY WORLD

The American Promise

A History of the United States

FIFTH EDITION

The
American
Promise

A History of the United States

FIFTH EDITION
VOLUME 2: FROM 1865

James L. Roark
Emory University

Michael P. Johnson
Johns Hopkins University

Patricia Cline Cohen
University of California, Santa Barbara

Sarah Stage
Arizona State University

Susan M. Hartmann
The Ohio State University

BEDFORD/ST. MARTIN'S
BOSTON ◆ NEW YORK

FOR BEDFORD/ST. MARTIN'S

Publisher for History: Mary Dougherty
Executive Editor for History: William J. Lombardo
Director of Development for History: Jane Knetzger
Developmental Editor: Michelle McSweeney
Senior Production Editor: Bridget Leahy
Assistant Production Manager: Joe Ford
Senior Marketing Manager for U.S. History: Amy Whitaker
Editorial Assistants: Jennifer Jovin and Laura Kintz
Production Assistants: Elise Keller and Victoria Royal
Copy Editor: Linda McLatchie
Indexer: Leoni Z. McVey
Photo Researchers: Pembroke Herbert and Sandi Rygiel, Picture Research Consultants, Inc.
Permissions Manager: Kalina K. Ingham
Senior Art Director: Anna Palchik
Text Designer: Tom Carling, Carling Design, Inc.
Cover Designer: Billy Boardman
Cover Photo: Gulf War Troops in Parade. Troops walk down the "Canyon of Heroes," on Broadway in Manhattan,
     as part of their welcome home parade. June 10, 1991. © Najlah Feanny/CORBIS SABA
Cartography: Mapping Specialists Limited
Composition: Cenveo Publisher Services
Printing and Binding: RR Donnelley and Sons

President: Joan E. Feinberg
Editorial Director: Denise B. Wydra
Director of Marketing: Karen R. Soeltz
Director of Production: Susan W. Brown
Associate Director, Editorial Production: Elise S. Kaiser
Managing Editor: Elizabeth M. Schaaf

Library of Congress Control Number: 2011939422

7   6   5   4   3   2
f   e   d   c   b   a

For information, write: Bedford/St. Martin's, 75 Arlington Street, Boston, MA 02116 (617-399-4000)

ISBN: 978–0–312–66312-4 (Combined Edition)
ISBN: 978–0–312–56953-2 (Loose-leaf Edition)
ISBN: 978–0–312–66313-1 (Vol. 1)
ISBN: 978–0–312–56948-8 (Loose-leaf Edition)
ISBN: 978–0–312–66314-8 (Vol. 2)
ISBN: 978–0–312–56946-4 (Loose-leaf Edition)
ISBN: 978–0–312–56954-9 (Vol. A)
ISBN: 978–0–312–56947-1 (Vol. B)
ISBN: 978–0–312–56944-0 (Vol. C)

As authors, we continue to be deeply gratified that *The American Promise* is one of the most widely adopted texts for the U.S. history survey, reaching students at all levels and helping instructors in all classroom environments. We know from years of firsthand experience that the survey course is the most difficult to teach and the most difficult to take, and we remain committed to making this book the most teachable and readable introductory American history text available. In creating this fifth edition, we set out to develop a resource that is both recognizable and new.

Our experience as teachers continues to inform every aspect of our text, beginning with its framework. We have found that students need *both* the structure a political narrative provides *and* the insights gained from examining social and cultural experience. To write a comprehensive, balanced account of American history, we focus on the public arena — the place where politics intersects social and cultural developments — to show how Americans confronted the major issues of their day and created far-reaching historical change. To engage students in the American story and to portray fully the diversity of the American experience, we stitch into our narrative the voices of hundreds of contemporaries, provide a vivid and compelling art program, and situate American history in the global world in which students live. To help students read, understand, and remember American history, we provide the best in pedagogical aids. While this edition rests solidly on our original goals and premises, the book has also changed, largely in response to adopters who helped us see new ways that the book could work for their students.

Users of past editions have emphasized the central role that *The American Promise* plays in their introductory courses — both as an in-class tool for them to teach from and as a resource for students to study from independently. Our goal in this fifth edition was to make our text even more successful for all students and instructors, whether they are using it in class or at home, whether in print or online. Within the book's

covers, we added more contemporary voices to enliven the narrative, more visuals that promote analytical skills, and more pedagogy to facilitate independent study and class discussion. In an effort to assist instructors to help their students meet specific learning objectives, our new pedagogy highlights historical interrelationships and causality, underscores the importance of global contexts in U.S. history, and models historical thinking.

To extend the text, our array of multimedia and print supplements has never been more abundant or more impressive. A range of options — from video clips to lecture kits on CD-ROM and much more — offers instructors endless combinations to tailor *The American Promise* to fit the needs of their classroom. (See pages xii–xv.) Students of all learning styles have more ways than ever to enhance their traditional textbook experience and make history memorable. The e-book, for example, allows students to zoom in on and more closely examine the text's hundreds of historical photographs and artifacts. The book companion site links to even more primary documents, including images, texts, and audiovisual files, and its Online Study Guide provides Web-based self tests, map exercises, and visual activities. By seamlessly connecting our text to its rich storehouse of digital resources, these supplements help students better understand the people whose ideas and actions shaped their times and whose efforts still affect our lives.

Our title, *The American Promise*, reflects our agreement with playwright Arthur Miller's conviction that the essence of America has been its promise. For millions, the nation has held out the promise of a better life, unfettered worship, equality before the law, representative government, democratic politics, and other freedoms seldom found elsewhere. But none of these promises has come with guarantees. As we see it, much of American history is a continuing struggle over the definition and realization of the nation's promise. Who are we, and what do we want to be? Abraham Lincoln, in the midst of what he termed the "fiery trial" of the Civil

War, pronounced the nation "the last best hope of Earth." Kept alive by countless sacrifices, that hope has been marred by compromises, disappointments, and denials, but it still lives. We believe that our new edition of *The American Promise,* with its increased attention to human agency, will continue to show students that American history is an unfinished story and to make them aware of the legacy of hope bequeathed to them by generations of Americans stretching back more than four centuries, a legacy that is theirs to preserve and build on.

Features

We know that a history survey textbook may be unfamiliar or challenging for many students. The benefit of this full-length format is that we have room to give students *everything* they need to succeed. Our book is designed to pique students' interest and to assist them in every way in their reading, reviewing, and studying for exams. We are pleased to draw your attention to three aspects of our textbook that make *The American Promise* stand out from the crowd — our visual program, pedagogical support, and special features.

Visuals. From the beginning, readers have proclaimed this textbook a visual feast, richly illustrated in ways that extend and reinforce the narrative. The fifth edition offers more than eight hundred contemporaneous **illustrations** — one-third of them new — along with innovative techniques for increasing visual literacy. Twelve new **Visualizing History** features show students how to examine the evidence through a wide spectrum of historic objects, including archaeological artifacts, furniture, paintings, photographs, advertisements, clothing, and political cartoons. In addition, one picture in each chapter includes a special **visual activity caption** that reinforces the skill of image analysis. More than three hundred **artifacts** — from dolls and political buttons to guns and sewing machines — emphasize the importance of material culture in the study of the past and make the historical account tangible.

Our highly regarded and thoroughly redesigned **map program,** with more than 170 maps in all, rests on the old truth that "History is not intelligible without geography." Each chapter offers, on average, four **full-size maps** showing major developments in the narrative and two or three **spot maps** embedded in the narrative that emphasize an area of detail from the discussion. To help students think critically about the role of geography in American history, we include **two critical-thinking map exercises** per chapter. Revised maps in the fifth edition illustrate new scholarship on topics such as the Comanche empire in the American Southwest and highlight recent events in the Middle East. Another unique feature is our brief **Atlas of the Territorial Growth of the United States,** a series of full-color maps at the end of each volume that reveals the changing cartography of the nation.

Throughout the text, a host of tables, figures, and other graphics enhance and reinforce the content. **Thematic chronologies** summarize complex events and highlight key points in the narrative. To support our emphasis on the global context of U.S. history, **Global Comparison figures** showcase data with a focus on transnational connections. In addition, occasional **Promise of Technology** illustrations examine the ramifications — positive and negative — of technological developments in American society and culture.

Pedagogy. As part of our ongoing efforts to make *The American Promise* the most teachable and readable survey text available, we paid renewed attention to imaginative and effective pedagogy. Each chapter begins with a concise but colorful **opening vignette** that invites students into the narrative with lively accounts of individuals or groups who embody the central themes of the chapter. New vignettes in this edition include the Grimké sisters speaking out against slavery, Frederick Jackson Turner proclaiming his frontier hypothesis, migrant mother Frances Owens struggling to survive in the Great Depression, and the experience of Vietnam War veteran Frederick Downs Jr. Each vignette ends with a **narrative overview** of all of the chapter's main topics. Major sections within each chapter have **introductory paragraphs** that preview the subsections that follow and conclude with **review questions** to help students check their comprehension of main ideas. **Running heads** with dates and topical headings remind students of chronology, and **callouts** draw attention to interesting quotations from a wide range of American voices. In addition, **key terms,** set in boldface type and grouped together at the end of the chapter, highlight important people, events, and concepts. All chapters culminate in a **conclusion,** which reexamines central ideas and provides a bridge to the next chapter, and a **Selected Bibliography,** which lists important books to jump-start student research and to show students that our narrative comes from scholarship.

The two-page **Reviewing the Chapter** section at the end of each chapter provides a thorough review guide to ensure student success. A list of **Key Terms**, grouped according to chapter headings, provides a starting point for self study and suggests important relationships among major topics, while an illustrated chapter **Timeline** gives clear chronological overviews of key events. Three sets of questions prompt students to think critically and to make use of the facts they have mastered. **Review Questions,** repeated from within the narrative, focus on a specific topic or event, and **Making Connections** questions prompt students to think about broad developments within the chapter. An **all-new set of Linking to the Past** questions cross-reference developments in earlier chapters, encouraging students to make comparisons, see causality, and understand change over longer periods of time. **Online Study Guide cross-references** at the end of the review section point students to free self-assessment quizzes and other study aids.

Special Features. We have been delighted to learn that students and instructors alike use and enjoy our special features. Many instructors use them for class discussion or homework, and students report that even when the special features are not assigned, they read these features on their own because they find them interesting, informative, and exceptional entry points back into the narrative text itself. Each boxed feature concentrates on a historical thinking skill or a habit of mind. We include features that focus on analyzing written or visual primary source evidence, and other features that pose intriguing questions about the past or America's relation to the world and thereby model historical inquiry, the curiosity at the heart of our discipline. For this edition, we have added a **new Visualizing History** feature to many chapters. Images such as Native American weaponry, Puritan furniture, nineteenth-century paintings, photographs by progressive reformers, early-twentieth-century advertisements, and twenty-first-century political cartoons are all presented as sources for examination. By stressing the importance of historical context and asking critical questions, each of these new features shows students how to mine visual documents for evidence in order to reach conclusions about the past.

Fresh topics and the addition of questions in our four enduring special features further enrich this edition. Each biographical **Seeking the American Promise** essay explores a different promise of America — the promise of home ownership or the promise of higher education, for example — while recognizing that the promises fulfilled for some have meant promises denied to others. New subjects in this edition include indentured servant Anne Orthwood and her struggle in colonial America, progressive reformer Alice Hamilton, World War I servicewoman Nora Saltonstall, Chinese scientist Qian Xuesen and his encounter with anticommunism in America, and Vietnamese immigrant-turned-politician Joseph Cao. In addition to these new topics, all Seeking the American Promise features now conclude with a **new set of Questions for Consideration** that help students explore the subject further and understand its significance within the chapter and the book as a whole.

Each **Documenting the American Promise** feature juxtaposes three or four primary documents to show varying perspectives on a topic or an issue and to provide students with opportunities to build and practice their skills of historical interpretation. Feature introductions and document headnotes contextualize the sources, and **Questions for Analysis and Debate** promote critical thinking about primary sources. New topics in this edition are rich with human drama and include "Hunting Witches in Salem, Massachusetts," "Mill Girls Stand Up to Factory Owners," and "The Press and the Pullman Strike."

Historical Questions essays pose and interpret specific questions of continuing interest in order to demonstrate various methods and perspectives of historical thinking. **New question sets** accompanying each of these features focus on a particular mode of inquiry: **Thinking about Evidence, Thinking about Beliefs and Values,** and **Thinking about Cause and Effect.** New to this edition is the feature "How Did America's First Congress Address the Question of Slavery?"

Beyond America's Borders features consider the reciprocal connections between the United States and the wider world and challenge students to think about the effects of transnational connections over time. With the goal of widening students' perspectives and helping students see that this country did not develop in isolation, these features are enhanced by new end-of-feature questions, **America in a Global Context.** New essays in this edition include "European Nations and the Peace of Paris, 1783" and "Global Prosperity in the 1850s."

Updated Scholarship

We updated the fifth edition in myriad ways to reflect our ongoing effort to offer a comprehensive text that braids all Americans into the national narrative and to frame that national narrative in a more global perspective. To do so, we have paid particular attention to the most recent scholarship and, as always, appreciated and applied many suggestions from our users that keep the book fresh, accurate, and organized in a way that works best for students.

In Volume One, we focused our attention on Native Americans, especially in the West, because of the publication of exciting new scholarship. In Chapter 6, we have incorporated into the narrative more coverage of Indians and their roles in various conflicts between the British and the colonists before the Revolution. Chapter 9 expands the coverage of American conflicts with Indians in the Southwest, adding new material on Creek chief Alexander McGillivray. Chapter 10 greatly increases the coverage of Indians in the West, with a new section devoted to the Osage territory and the impressive Comanche empire known as Comanchería. In addition, several new Visualizing History features — on ancient tools used in Chaco Canyon, on Aztec weaponry and its weaknesses in the face of Spanish steel, on Mohawk clothing and accessories, and on gifts exchanged between Anglos and Indians on the Lewis and Clark trail — highlight the significance of Native American material culture over the centuries.

Volume Two also includes expanded attention to Native Americans — particularly in Chapter 17, where we improved our coverage of Indian schools, assimilation techniques used by whites, and Indian resistance strategies — but our main effort for the fifth edition in the second half of the book has been to do more of what we already do best, and that is to give even more attention to women, African Americans, and the global context of U.S. history. In the narrative, we have added coverage of women as key movers in the rise of the Lost Cause after the Civil War, and we consider the ways in which the GI Bill disproportionately benefited white men after World War II. New features and opening vignettes focus on widely recognized as well as less well-known women who both shaped and were shaped by the American experience: the depression-era struggle of Florence Owens (the face of the famous Dorothea Lange photograph *Migrant Mother*), the workplace reforms set in motion by progressive activist Alice Hamilton, and the World War I service of overseas volunteer Nora Saltonstall. Chapter 16 includes new coverage of the Colfax massacre, arguably the single worst incidence of brutality against African Americans during the Reconstruction era. Chapter 27 provides new coverage of civil rights activism and resistance in northern states, and Chapter 28 increases coverage of black power and urban rebellions across the country. A new Visualizing History feature in Chapter 16 examines the Winslow Homer painting *A Visit from the Old Mistress*.

Because students live in an increasingly global world and need help making connections with the world outside the United States, we have continued our efforts to incorporate the global context of American history throughout the fifth edition. This is particularly evident in Volume Two, where we have expanded coverage of transnational issues in recent decades, such as the 1953 CIA coup in Iran, the U.S. bombing campaign in Vietnam, and U.S. involvement in Afghanistan.

In addition to the many changes noted above, in both volumes we have updated, revised, and improved the fifth edition in response to both new scholarship and requests from instructors. New and expanded coverage areas include, among others, taxation in the pre-Revolutionary period and the early Republic, the Newburgh Conspiracy of the 1780s, the overbuilding of railroads in the West during the Gilded Age, the 1918–1919 global influenza epidemic, finance reform in the 1930s, post–World War II considerations of universal health care, the economic downturn of the late 2000s, the Obama presidency, and the most recent developments in the Middle East.

Acknowledgments

We gratefully acknowledge all of the helpful suggestions from those who have read and taught from previous editions of *The American Promise*, and we hope that our many classroom collaborators will be pleased to see their influence in the fifth edition. In particular, we wish to thank the talented scholars and teachers who gave generously of their time and knowledge to review this book: Patricia Adams, *Chandler-Gilbert Community College*; Susan Agee, *Truckee Meadows Community College*; Jennifer Bertolet, *George Washington University*; Michael Bryan, *Greenville Technical College*; Kim Burdick, *Delaware Technical and Community College*; Monica Butler, *Seminole State College, Sanford*; Andria Crosson, *University of Texas San Antonio*; Lawrence Devaro, *Rowan University and Camden County College*;

Space, puts the online resources available with this textbook in one convenient and completely customizable course space. There you and your students can access an interactive e-book and primary sources reader; maps, images, documents, and links; chapter review quizzes; interactive multimedia exercises; and research and writing help. In HistoryClass you can get all our premium content and tools and assign, rearrange, and mix them with your own resources. For more information, visit **yourhistoryclass.com**.

Bedford Coursepack for Blackboard, WebCT, Desire2Learn, Angel, Sakai, or Moodle. We have free content to help you integrate our rich content into your course management system. Registered instructors can download coursepacks with no hassle and no strings attached. Content includes our most popular free resources and book-specific content for *The American Promise*. Visit **bedfordstmartins.com/coursepacks** to see a demo, find your version, or download your coursepack.

Instructor's Resource Manual. The instructor's manual offers both experienced and first-time instructors tools for preparing lectures and running discussions. It includes chapter review material, teaching strategies, and a guide to chapter-specific supplements available for the text.

Guide to Changing Editions. Designed to facilitate an instructor's transition from the previous edition of *The American Promise* to the current edition, this guide presents an overview of major changes as well as of changes in each chapter.

Computerized Test Bank. The test bank includes a mix of fresh, carefully crafted multiple-choice, matching, short-answer, and essay questions for each chapter. It also contains the Historical Question, Documenting the American Promise, Seeking the American Promise, and Beyond America's Borders questions from the textbook and model answers for each. The questions appear in Microsoft Word format and in easy-to-use test bank software that allows instructors to easily add, edit, re-sequence, and print questions and answers. Instructors can also export questions into a variety of formats, including WebCT and Blackboard.

***The Bedford Lecture Kit*: Maps, Images, Lecture Outlines, and i>clicker Content.** Look good and save time with *The Bedford Lecture Kit*. These presentation materials are downloadable individually from the Instructor Resources tab at **bedfordstmartins.com/roark/catalog** and are available on *The Bedford Lecture Kit* Instructor's Resource CD-ROM. They provide ready-made and fully customizable PowerPoint multimedia presentations that include lecture outlines with embedded maps, figures, and selected images from the textbook and extra background for instructors. Also available are maps and selected images in JPEG and PowerPoint formats; content for i>clicker, a classroom response system, in Microsoft Word and PowerPoint formats; the *Instructor's Resource Manual* in Microsoft Word format; and outline maps in PDF format for quizzing or handing out. All files are suitable for copying onto transparency acetates.

***Make History* — Free Documents, Maps, Images, and Web Sites.** *Make History* combines the best Web resources with hundreds of maps and images, to make it simple to find the source material you need. Browse the collection of thousands of resources by course or by topic, date, and type. Each item has been carefully chosen and helpfully annotated to make it easy to find exactly what you need. Available at **bedfordstmartins.com/makehistory**.

***Reel Teaching: Film Clips for the U.S. History Survey*.** This DVD provides a large collection of short video clips for classroom presentation. Designed as engaging "lecture launchers" varying in length from 1 to 15 or more minutes, the 59 documentary clips were carefully chosen for use in both semesters of the U.S. survey course. The clips feature compelling images, archival footage, personal narratives, and commentary by noted historians.

***America in Motion: Video Clips for U.S. History*.** Set history in motion with *America in Motion*, an instructor DVD containing dozens of short digital movie files of events in twentieth-century American history. From the wreckage of the battleship *Maine*, to FDR's Fireside Chats, to Oliver North testifying before Congress, *America in Motion* engages students with dynamic scenes from key events and challenges them to think critically. All files are classroom-ready, edited for brevity, and easily integrated with PowerPoint or other presentation software for electronic lectures or assignments. An accompanying guide provides each clip's historical context, ideas for use, and suggested questions.

***The American Promise* via Dallas Tele-Learning Distance Learning Courses.** *The

American Promise has been selected as the textbook for the award-winning U.S. history video-based courses *Shaping America: U.S. History to 1877* and *Transforming America: U.S. History since 1877* by Dallas TeleLearning at the LeCroy Center for Educational Telecommunications, Dallas County Community College District. Guides for students and instructors fully integrate the narrative of *The American Promise* into each course. For more information on these distance-learning opportunities, visit the Dallas TeleLearning Web site at **http://telelearning.dcccd.edu**, email **learn@dcccd.edu**, or call 972-669-6650.

Videos and Multimedia. A wide assortment of videos and multimedia CD-ROMs on various topics in U.S. History is available to qualified adopters through your Bedford/St. Martin's sales representative.

Package and Save Your Students Money

For information on free packages and discounts up to 50%, visit **bedfordstmartins.com/roark/catalog**, or contact your local Bedford/St. Martin's sales representative.

Bedford e-Book. The e-book for this title, described above, can be packaged with the print text at a discount.

***Reading the American Past,* Fifth Edition.** Edited by Michael P. Johnson, one of the authors of *The American Promise*, and designed to complement the textbook, *Reading the American Past* provides a broad selection of over 150 primary source documents, as well as editorial apparatus to help students understand the sources. Available free when packaged with the print text.

Reading the American Past e-Book. The reader is also available as an e-book. When packaged with the print or electronic version of the textbook, it is available for free.

The Bedford Series in History and Culture. More than one hundred fifty titles in this highly praised series combine first-rate scholarship, historical narrative, and important primary documents for undergraduate courses. Each book is brief, inexpensive, and focused on a specific topic or period. For a complete list of titles, visit **bedfordstmartins.com/history/series**. Package discounts are available.

Rand McNally Atlas of American History. This collection of more than eighty full-color maps illustrates key events and eras from early exploration, settlement, expansion, and immigration to U.S. involvement in wars abroad and on U.S. soil. Introductory pages for each section include a brief overview, timelines, graphs, and photos to quickly establish a historical context. Available for $3.00 when packaged with the print text.

Maps in Context: A Workbook for American History. Written by historical cartography expert Gerald A. Danzer (University of Illinois at Chicago), this skill-building workbook helps students comprehend essential connections between geographic literacy and historical understanding. Organized to correspond to the typical U.S. history survey course, *Maps in Context* presents a wealth of map-centered projects and convenient pop quizzes that give students hands-on experience working with maps. Available free when packaged with the print text.

The Bedford Glossary for U.S. History. This handy supplement for the survey course gives students historically contextualized definitions for hundreds of terms—from *abolitionism* to *zoot suit*—that they will encounter in lectures, reading, and exams. Available free when packaged with the print text.

U.S. History Matters: A Student Guide to World History Online. This resource, written by Alan Gevinson, Kelly Schrum, and the late Roy Rosenzweig (all of George Mason University), provides an illustrated and annotated guide to 250 of the most useful Web sites for student research in U.S. history as well as advice on evaluating and using Internet sources. This essential guide is based on the acclaimed "History Matters" Web site developed by the American Social History Project and the Center for History and New Media. Available free when packaged with the print text.

Trade Books. Titles published by sister companies Hill and Wang; Farrar, Straus and Giroux; Henry Holt and Company; St. Martin's Press; Picador; and Palgrave Macmillan are available at a 50% discount when packaged with Bedford/St. Martin's textbooks. For more information, visit **bedfordstmartins.com/tradeup**.

A Pocket Guide to Writing in History. This portable and affordable reference tool by Mary Lynn Rampolla provides reading, writing, and

Contents

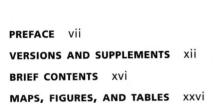

CHAPTER 16

Reconstruction,
1863–1877   498

CHAPTER 17
The Contested West,
1865–1900   534

CHAPTER 18
Business and Politics in the Gilded Age,
1865–1900   568

CHAPTER 19
The City and Its Workers, 1870–1900 602

CHAPTER 20
Dissent, Depression, and War, 1890–1900 638

CHAPTER 27
The Politics and Culture of Abundance, 1952–1960   896

CHAPTER 28
Reform, Rebellion, and Reaction, 1960–1974   930

Maps, Figures, and Tables

Maps

Figures and Tables

Special Features

The
American
Promise

A History of
the United States

FIFTH EDITION

CARPETBAG

A carpetbag was
a nineteenth-century
suitcase made from carpet, often
brightly colored. Applied first to wildcat
bankers on the western frontier, the term "carpetbagger"
was a derogatory name for rootless and penniless adventurers who
could carry everything they owned in a single bag. Critics of Republican administrations in the
South hurled the name "carpetbaggers" at white Northerners who moved South during
Reconstruction and became active in politics. The background image of bombed-out Richmond
provides a reminder that one of the central tasks of the Reconstruction governments was the
rebuilding of the South's battered cities and devastated agricultural economy.

Carpetbag: Nancy Gewirz/Antique Textile Resource; background: Library of Congress.

16

Reconstruction
1863–1877

IN 1856, JOHN RAPIER, A FREE BLACK BARBER IN FLORENCE, ALABAMA, urged his four freeborn sons to flee the increasingly repressive and dangerous South. Searching for a color-blind society, the brothers scattered around the world. James T. Rapier chose Canada, where he went to live with his uncle in a largely black community and studied Greek and Latin in a log schoolhouse. After his conversion at a Methodist revival, James wrote to his father: "I have not thrown a card in 3 years[,] touched a woman in 2 years[,] smoked nor drunk any Liquor in going on 2 years." He vowed, "I will endeavor to do my part in solving the problems [of African Americans] in my native land."

The Union victory in the Civil War gave James Rapier the opportunity to redeem his pledge. In 1865, after more than eight years of exile, the twenty-seven-year-old Rapier returned to Alabama, where he presided over the first political gathering of former slaves in the state. Alabama freedmen produced a petition that called on the federal government to thoroughly reconstruct the South, to guarantee suffrage, free schools, and equal rights for all men, regardless of color.

Rapier soon discovered that Alabama's whites found it agonizingly difficult to accept defeat and black freedom. They responded to the revolutionary changes under the banner "White Man — Right or Wrong — Still the White Man!" In 1868, when Rapier and other Alabama blacks vigorously supported the Republican presidential candidate, former Union general Ulysses S. Grant, the recently organized Ku Klux Klan went on a bloody rampage of whipping, burning, and shooting. A mob of 150 outraged whites scoured Rapier's neighborhood seeking four black politicians they claimed were trying to "Africanize Alabama." They caught and hanged three, but the "nigger carpetbagger from Canada" escaped. Rapier considered fleeing the state, but he decided to stay and fight.

By the early 1870s, Rapier had emerged as Alabama's most prominent black leader. Demanding that the federal government end the violence against ex-slaves, guarantee their civil rights, and give them land, he won election in 1872 to the House of Representatives, where he joined six other black congressmen. Defeated for reelection in 1874 in a campaign marked by white violence and ballot-box stuffing, Rapier turned to cotton farming, generously giving thousands of dollars of his profits to black schools and churches.

But persistent black poverty and unrelenting racial violence convinced Rapier that blacks could never achieve equality and prosperity in the South. He purchased land in Kansas and urged Alabama's blacks to escape with

James T. Rapier

Black suffrage sent fourteen African American congressmen to Washington, D.C., during Reconstruction, among them James T. Rapier of Alabama. Temporarily at least, he and his black colleagues helped shape post-emancipation society. In 1874, when Rapier spoke on behalf of a civil rights bill, he described the humiliation of being denied service at inns all along his route from Montgomery to Washington. Elsewhere in the world, he said, class and religion were invoked to defend discrimination. In Europe, "they have princes, dukes, lords"; in India, "brahmans or priests, who rank above the sudras or laborers." But in America, "our distinction is color." Alabama Department of Archives and History.

him. In 1883, however, before he could leave Alabama, Rapier died of tuberculosis at the age of forty-five.

In 1865, Union general Carl Schurz had foreseen many of the troubles Rapier would encounter in the postwar South. Schurz concluded that the Civil War was "a revolution but half accomplished." Northern victory had freed the slaves, he observed, but it had not changed former slaveholders' minds about blacks' unfitness for freedom. Left to themselves, whites would "introduce some new system of forced labor, not perhaps exactly slavery in its old form but something similar to it." To defend their freedom, Schurz concluded, blacks would need federal protection, land of their own, and voting rights. Until whites "cut loose from the past, it will be a dangerous experiment to put Southern society upon its own legs."

As Schurz discovered, the end of the war did not mean peace. The United States was one of only two societies in the New World in which slavery ended in a bloody war. (The other was Haiti.) Not surprisingly, racial turmoil continued in the South after the armies quit fighting in 1865. The nation entered one of its most chaotic and conflicted eras — Reconstruction, a violent period that would define the defeated South's status within the Union and the meaning of freedom for ex-slaves.

The place of the South within the nation and the extent of black freedom were determined not only in Washington, D.C., where the federal government played an active role, but also in the state legislatures and county seats of the South, where blacks eagerly participated in the process. Moreover, on farms and plantations from Virginia to Texas, ex-slaves struggled to become free workers while ex-slaveholders clung to the Old South. A small band of white women joined in the struggle for racial equality, and soon their crusade broadened to include gender equality. Their attempts to secure voting rights for women were thwarted, however.

Reconstruction witnessed a gigantic struggle to determine the consequences of Confederate defeat and emancipation. In the end, white Southerners prevailed. Their New South was a different South from the one to which most whites wished to return but also vastly unlike the one of which James Rapier dreamed.

▶ Wartime Reconstruction

Reconstruction did not wait for the end of war. As the odds of a northern victory increased, thinking about reunification quickened. Immediately, a question arose: Who had authority to devise a plan for reconstructing the Union? President Abraham Lincoln firmly believed that reconstruction was a matter of executive responsibility. Congress just as firmly asserted its jurisdiction. Fueling the argument were significant differences about the terms of reconstruction. Lincoln's primary aim was the restoration of national unity, which he sought through a program of speedy, forgiving political reconciliation. Congress feared that the president's program meant restoring the old southern ruling class to power. It wanted assurances of white loyalty and guarantees of black rights.

In their eagerness to formulate a plan for political reunification, neither Lincoln nor Congress gave much attention to the South's land and labor problems. But as the war rapidly eroded slavery and traditional plantation agriculture, Yankee military commanders in the Union-occupied areas of the Confederacy had no choice but to oversee the emergence of a new labor system.

"To Bind Up the Nation's Wounds"

On March 4, 1865, in his second inaugural address, President Lincoln surveyed the history of the war and then looked ahead to peace. "With malice toward none; with charity for all; with firmness in the right, as God gives us to see the right," Lincoln said, "let us strive on to finish the work we are in; to bind up the nation's wounds . . . to do all which may achieve and cherish a just, and a lasting peace." Lincoln had contemplated reunion for nearly two years. While deep compassion for the enemy guided his thinking about peace, his plan for reconstruction aimed primarily at shortening the war and ending slavery.

Lincoln's Proclamation of Amnesty and Reconstruction in December 1863 set out his terms. He offered a full pardon, restoring property (except slaves) and political rights, to rebels willing to renounce secession and to accept emancipation. His offer excluded only high-ranking Confederate military and political officers and a few other groups. When 10 percent of a state's voting population had taken an oath of allegiance, the state could organize a new government and be readmitted into the Union. Lincoln's plan did not require ex-rebels to extend social or political rights to ex-slaves, nor did it anticipate a program of long-term federal assistance to freedmen. Clearly, the president looked forward to the rapid, forgiving restoration of the broken Union.

Lincoln's easy terms enraged abolitionists such as Wendell Phillips of Boston, who charged that the president "makes the negro's freedom a mere sham." He "is willing that the negro should be free but seeks nothing else for him." He compared Lincoln to the most passive of the Civil War generals: "What McClellan was on the battlefield — 'Do as little hurt as possible!' — Lincoln is in civil affairs — 'Make as little change as possible!'" Phillips and other northern radicals called instead for a thorough overhaul of southern society. Their ideas proved to be too drastic for most Republicans during the war years, but Congress agreed that Lincoln's plan was inadequate.

In July 1864, Congress put forward a plan of its own. Congressman Henry Winter Davis of Maryland and Senator Benjamin Wade of Ohio jointly sponsored a bill that demanded that at least half of the voters in a conquered rebel state take the oath of allegiance before reconstruction could begin. The **Wade-Davis bill** also banned all ex-Confederates from participating in the drafting of new state constitutions. Finally, the bill guaranteed the equality of freedmen before the law. Congress's reconstruction would be neither as quick nor as forgiving as Lincoln's. When Lincoln refused to sign the bill and let it die, Wade and Davis charged the president with usurpation of power. They warned Lincoln to confine himself to "his executive duties — to obey and execute, not make the laws — to suppress by arms armed rebellion, and leave political organization to Congress."

Undeterred, Lincoln continued to nurture the formation of loyal state governments under his own plan. Four states — Louisiana, Arkansas, Tennessee, and Virginia — fulfilled the president's requirements, but Congress refused to seat representatives from the "Lincoln states." In his last public address in April 1865, Lincoln defended his plan but for the first time expressed publicly his endorsement of suffrage for southern blacks, at least "the very intelligent, and . . . those who serve our cause as soldiers." The announcement demonstrated that Lincoln's thinking about reconstruction was still evolving. Four days later, he was dead.

"Take it quietly UNCLE ABE and I will draw it closer than ever!"

"A few more stitches ANDY and the good old UNION will be mended!"

Wartime Reconstruction

This cartoon from the presidential campaign of 1864 shows the "Rail Splitter" Abraham Lincoln leveraging the broken nation back together while his running mate, Andrew Johnson, who once was a tailor by trade, stitches the Confederate states securely back into the Union. Optimism that the task of reconstructing the nation after the war would be both quick and easy shines through the cartoon. The Granger Collection, NY.

Land and Labor

Of all the problems raised by the North's victory in the war, none proved more critical than the South's transition from slavery to free labor. As federal armies invaded and occupied the Confederacy, hundreds of thousands of slaves became free workers. In addition, Union armies controlled vast territories in the South where legal title to land had become unclear. The Confiscation Acts passed during the war punished "traitors" by taking away their property. The question of what to do with federally occupied land and how to organize labor on it engaged former slaves, former slaveholders, Union military commanders, and federal government officials long before the war ended.

> "What's the use of being free if you don't own land enough to be buried in?"
>
> — A former slave

In the Mississippi valley, occupying federal troops announced a new labor code. It required slaveholders to sign contracts with ex-slaves and to pay wages. It obligated employers to provide food, housing, and medical care. It outlawed whipping, but it reserved to the army the right to discipline blacks who refused to work. The code required black laborers to enter into contracts, work diligently, and remain subordinate and obedient. Military leaders clearly had no intention of promoting a social or economic revolution. Instead, they sought to restore plantation agriculture with wage labor. The effort resulted in a hybrid system that one contemporary called "compulsory free labor," something that satisfied no one.

Planters complained because the new system fell short of slavery. Blacks could not be "transformed by proclamation," a Louisiana sugar planter declared. Yet under the new system, blacks "are expected to perform their new obligations without coercion, & without the fear of punishment which is essential to stimulate the idle and correct the vicious." Without the right to whip, he argued, the new labor system did not have a chance. Either Union soldiers must "*compel* the negroes to work," planters insisted, or the planters themselves must "be authorized and sustained in using force."

African Americans found the new regime too reminiscent of slavery to be called free labor. Its chief deficiency, they believed, was the failure to provide them with land of their own. Freedmen believed they had a moral right to land because they and their ancestors had worked it without compensation for more than two centuries. "What's the use of being free if you don't own land enough to be buried in?" one man asked. Several wartime developments led freedmen to believe that the federal government planned to undergird black freedom with landownership.

In January 1865, General William Tecumseh Sherman set aside part of the coast south of Charleston for black settlement. He devised the plan to relieve himself of the burden of thousands of impoverished blacks who trailed desperately behind his army. By June 1865, some 40,000 freedmen sat on 400,000 acres of "Sherman land." In addition, in March 1865, Congress passed a bill establishing the Bureau of Refugees, Freedmen, and Abandoned Lands. The **Freedmen's Bureau**, as it was called, distributed food and clothing to destitute Southerners and eased the transition of blacks from slaves to free persons. Congress also authorized the agency to divide abandoned and confiscated land into 40-acre plots, to rent them to freedmen, and eventually to sell them "with such title as the United States can convey." By June 1865, the bureau had situated nearly 10,000 black families on a half million acres abandoned by fleeing planters. Other ex-slaves eagerly anticipated farms of their own.

Despite the flurry of activity, wartime reconstruction failed to produce agreement about whether the president or Congress had the authority to devise policy or what proper policy should be.

The African American Quest for Autonomy

Ex-slaves never had any doubt about what they wanted from freedom. They had only to contemplate what they had been denied as slaves. (See "Documenting the American Promise," page 504.) Slaves had to remain on their plantations; freedom allowed blacks to see what was on the other side of the hill. Slaves had to be at work in the fields by dawn; freedom permitted blacks to sleep through a sunrise. Freedmen also tested the etiquette of racial subordination. "Lizzie's maid passed me today when I was coming from church *without speaking to me*," huffed one plantation mistress.

To whites, emancipation looked like pure anarchy. Blacks, they said, had reverted to their natural condition: lazy, irresponsible, and wild. Without the discipline of slavery, whites predicted, blacks would go the way of "the Indian and the buffalo." Actually, former slaves were experimenting with freedom, but they could not long afford to roam the countryside, neglect work, and casually provoke whites. Soon, most were back at work in whites' kitchens and fields.

But other items on ex-slaves' agenda of freedom endured. They continued to dream of land and economic independence. "The way we can best take care of ourselves is to have land," one former slave declared in 1865, "and turn it and till it by our own labor." Freedmen also wanted to learn to read and write. Many black soldiers had become literate in the Union army, and they understood the value of the pen and book. "I wishes the Childern all in School," one black veteran asserted. "It is beter for them then to be their Surveing a mistes [mistress]."

The restoration of broken families was another persistent black aspiration. Thousands of freedmen took to the roads in 1865 to look for kin who had been sold away or to free those who were being held illegally as slaves. A black soldier from Missouri wrote his daughters that he was coming for them. "I will have you if it cost me my life," he declared. "Your Miss Kitty said that I tried to steal you," he told them. "But I'll let her know that god never intended for a man to steal his own flesh and blood." And he swore that "if she meets me with ten thousand soldiers, she [will] meet her enemy."

Independent worship was another continuing aspiration. African Americans greeted freedom with a mass exodus from white churches, where they had been required to worship when slaves. Some joined the newly established southern branches of all-black northern churches, such as the African Methodist Episcopal Church. Others formed black versions of the major southern denominations, Baptists and Methodists. Freedmen interpreted the events of the Civil War and reconstruction as Christian people. One

DOCUMENTING THE AMERICAN PROMISE

The Meaning of Freedom

The Emancipation Proclamation states that "all persons held as slaves" within the states still in rebellion on January 1, 1863, "are, and henceforward shall be, free." Although the proclamation in and of itself did not free any slaves, it transformed the character of the war. Despite often intolerable conditions, black people focused on the possibilities of freedom.

DOCUMENT 1
Letter from John Q. A. Dennis to Edwin M. Stanton, July 26, 1864

John Q. A. Dennis, formerly a slave in Maryland, wrote to ask Secretary of War Edwin M. Stanton for help in reuniting his family.

BOSTON. Dear Sir I am Glad that I have the Honour to Write you a few line I have been in troble for about four yars my Dear wife was taken from me Nov 19th 1859 and left me with three Children and I being a Slave At the time Could Not do Anny thing for the poor little Children for my master it was took me Carry me some forty mile from them So I Could Not do for them and the man that they live with half feed them and half Cloth them & beat them like dogs & when I was admitted to go to see them it use to brake my heart & Now I say again I am Glad to have the honour to write to you to see if you Can Do Anny thing for me or for my poor little Children I was keap in Slavy untell last Novr 1863. then the Good lord sent the Cornel borne [federal colonel William Birney?] Down their in Marland in worsester Co So as I have been recently freed I have but letle to live on but I am Striveing Dear Sir but what I went too know of you Sir is it possible for me to go & take my Children from those men that keep them in Savery if it is possible will you pleas give me a permit from your hand then I think they would let them go. . . .

Hon sir will you please excuse my Miserable writeing & answer me as soon as you can I want get the little Children out of Slavery, I being Criple would like to know of you also if I Cant be permited to rase a Shool Down there & on what turm I Could be admited to Do so No more At present Dear Hon Sir

SOURCE: *Freedom: A Documentary History of Emancipation, 1861–1867*, ser. 1, vol. 1, *The Destruction of Slavery*, 386, edited by Ira Berlin, Joseph P. Reidy, and Leslie S. Rowland. Copyright © 1985. Reprinted with the permission of Cambridge University Press.

DOCUMENT 2
Report from Reverend A. B. Randall, February 28, 1865

A. B. Randall, the white chaplain of a black regiment stationed in Little Rock, Arkansas, affirmed the importance of legal marriage to freed slaves and emphasized their conviction that emancipation was only the first step toward full freedom.

Weddings, just now, are very popular, and abundant among the Colored People. They have just learned, of the Special Order No. 15. of Gen Thomas [Adjutant General Lorenzo Thomas] by which, they may not only be lawfully married, but have their Marriage Certificates, Recorded; in a book furnished by the Government. This is most desirable. . . . Those who were captured . . . at Ivy's Ford, on the 17th of January, by Col Brooks, had their Marriage Certificates, taken from them; and destroyed; and then were roundly cursed, for having such papers in their posession. I have married, during the month, at this Post; Twenty five couples; mostly, those, who have families; & have been living together for years. I try to dissuade single men, who are soldiers, from marrying, till their time of enlistment is out: as that course seems to me, to be most judicious. The Colord People here, generally consider, this war not only; their exodus, from bondage; but the road, to Responsibility; Competency; and an honorable Citizenship — God grant that their hopes and expectations may be fully realized.

WARTIME RECONSTRUCTION **505**

SOURCE: *Freedom: A Documentary History of Emancipation, 1861–1867*, ser. 2, vol. 1, *The Black Military Experience*, 712, edited by Ira Berlin, Joseph P. Reidy, and Leslie S. Rowland. Copyright © 1982. Reprinted with the permission of Cambridge University Press.

DOCUMENT 3
Petition "to the Union Convention of Tennessee Assembled in the Capitol at Nashville," January 9, 1865

In January 1865, black Tennesseans petitioned a convention of white Unionists debating the reorganization of state government.

We the undersigned petitioners, American citizens of African descent, natives and residents of Tennessee, and devoted friends of the great National cause, do most respectfully ask a patient hearing of your honorable body in regard to matters deeply affecting the future condition of our unfortunate and long suffering race.

First of all, however, we would say that words are too weak to tell how profoundly grateful we are to the Federal Government for the good work of freedom which it is gradually carrying forward; and for the Emancipation Proclamation which has set free all the slaves in some of the rebellious States, as well as many of the slaves in Tennessee. . . .

We claim freedom, as our natural right, and ask that in harmony and co-operation with the nation at large, you should cut up by the roots the system of slavery, which is not only a wrong to us, but the source of all the evil which at present afflicts the State. For slavery, corrupt itself, corrupted nearly all, also, around it, so that it has influenced nearly all the slave States to rebel against the Federal Government, in order to set up a government of pirates under which slavery might be perpetrated.

In the contest between the nation and slavery, our unfortunate people have sided, by instinct, with the former. We have little fortune to devote to the national cause, for a hard fate has hitherto forced us to live in poverty, but we do devote to its success, our hopes, our toils, our whole heart, our sacred honor, and our lives. We will work, pray, live, and, if need be, die for the Union, as cheerfully as ever a white patriot died for his country. The color of our skin does not lessen in the least degree, our love either for God or for the land of our birth. . . .

We know the burdens of citizenship, and are ready to bear them. We know the duties of the good citizen, and are ready to perform them cheerfully, and would ask to be put in a position in which we can discharge them more effectually. . . .

This is a democracy — a government of the people. It should aim to make every man, without regard to the color of his skin, the amount of his wealth, or the character of his religious faith, feel personally interested in its welfare. Every man who lives under the Government should feel that it is his property, his treasure, the bulwark and defence of himself and his family. . . .

This is not a Democratic Government if a numerous, law-abiding, industrious, and useful class of citizens, born and bred on the soil, are to be treated as aliens and enemies, as an inferior degraded class, who must have no voice in the Government which they support, protect and defend, with all their heart, soul, mind, and body, both in peace and war. . . .

The possibility that the negro suffrage proposition may shock popular prejudice at first sight, is not a conclusive argument against its wisdom and policy. No proposition ever met with more furious or general opposition than the one to enlist colored soldiers in the United States army. The opponents of the measure exclaimed on all hands that the negro was a coward; that he would not fight; that one white man, with a whip in his hand could put to flight a regiment of them. . . . Yet the colored man has fought so well, on almost every occasion, that the rebel government is prevented, only by its fears and distrust of being able to force him to fight for slavery as well as he fights against it, from putting half a million of negroes into its ranks.

The Government has asked the colored man to fight for its preservation and gladly has he done it. It can afford to trust him with a vote as safely as it trusted him with a bayonet.

SOURCE: *Freedom: A Documentary History of Emancipation, 1861–1867*, ser. 2, vol. 1, *The Black Military Experience*, 811–16, edited by Ira Berlin, Joseph P. Reidy, and Leslie S. Rowland. Copyright © 1982. Reprinted with the permission of Cambridge University Press.

Questions for Analysis and Debate

1. How does John Q. A. Dennis interpret his responsibility as a father?

2. Why do you think ex-slaves wanted their marriages legalized?

3. Why, according to petitioners to the Union Convention of Tennessee, did blacks deserve voting rights?

AML. DOVE wishes to know of the whereabouts of his mother, Areno, his sisters Maria, Neziah, and Peggy, and his brother Edmond, who were owned by Geo. Dove, of Rockingham county, Shenandoah Valley, Va. Sold in Richmond, after which Saml. and Edmond were taken to Nashville, Tenn., by Joe Mick; Areno was left at the Eagle Tavern, Richmond
                    Respectfully yours,
                              SAML. DOVE.
Utica, New York, Aug. 5, 1865–3m
                    U. S. CHRISTIAN COMMISSION,
                    NASHVILLE, TENN., July 19, 1865.

Harry Stephens and Family, 1866, and Samuel Dove Ad, 1865
Dressed in their Sunday best, this Virginia family sits proudly for a photograph. Many black families were not as fortunate as the Stephens family. Separated by slavery or war, former slaves desperately sought news of missing family members through newspaper advertisements like the one posted by Samuel Dove in August 1865. We do not know whether he succeeded in locating his mother, brother, and sisters. Ad: Chicago Historical Society; Family: The Metropolitan Museum of Art, Gilman Collection, Purchase, The Horace W. Goldsmith Foundation Gift, 2005 (2005.100.277)/Art Resource, NY.

black woman thanked Lincoln for the Emancipation Proclamation, declaring, "When you are dead and in Heaven, in a thousand years that action of yours will make the Angels sing your praises I know it."

> **REVIEW** Why did Congress object to Lincoln's wartime plan for reconstruction?

▶ Presidential Reconstruction

Abraham Lincoln died on April 15, 1865, just hours after John Wilkes Booth shot him at a Washington, D.C., theater. Chief Justice Salmon P. Chase immediately administered the oath of office to Vice President **Andrew Johnson** of

Tennessee. Congress had adjourned in March and would not reconvene until December. Throughout the summer and fall, the "accidental president" made critical decisions about the future of the South without congressional advice. With dizzying speed, he drew up and executed a plan of reconstruction.

Congress returned to the capital in December to find that, as far as the president and former Confederates were concerned, reconstruction was completed. Most Republicans, however, thought Johnson's puny demands of ex-rebels made a mockery of the sacrifice of Union soldiers. Instead of honoring the dead by insisting on "a new birth of freedom," as Lincoln had promised in his 1863 speech at Gettysburg, Johnson had acted as midwife to the rebirth of the Old South and the stillbirth of black liberty. They proceeded to dismantle Johnson's program and substitute a program of their own.

***A Pastoral Visit*, 1881**
Freedom from bondage permitted blacks to flee white ministers and churches, to "come out from under the yoke," as one ex-slave put it. In *A Pastoral Visit*, Virginia-born artist Richard Norris Brooke portrays a dignified elderly black minister seated at a table with a family of his parishioners. In this sympathetic and respectful depiction, the poor family shares what it has. It is safe to say that no white minister had ever sat down for a meal in this humble northern Virginia cabin. In the Collection of the Corcoran Gallery of Art, Washington, D.C.

Johnson's Program of Reconciliation

Born in 1808 in Raleigh, North Carolina, Andrew Johnson was the son of illiterate parents. Self-educated and ambitious, Johnson moved to Tennessee, where he worked as a tailor, accumulated a fortune in land, acquired five slaves, and built a career in politics championing the South's common white people and assailing its "illegitimate, swaggering, bastard, scrub aristocracy." The only senator from a Confederate state to remain loyal to the Union, Johnson held the planter class responsible for secession. Less than two weeks before he became president, he announced what he would do to planters if he ever had the chance: "I would arrest them — I would try them — I would convict them and I would hang them."

Despite such statements, Johnson was no friend of the Republicans. A Democrat all his life, Johnson occupied the White House only because the Republican Party in 1864 had needed a vice presidential candidate who would appeal to loyal, Union-supporting Democrats. Johnson vigorously defended states' rights (but not secession) and opposed Republican efforts to expand the power of the federal government. A steadfast supporter of slavery, Johnson had owned slaves until 1862, when Tennessee rebels, angry at his Unionism, confiscated them. When he grudgingly accepted emancipation, it was more because he hated planters than sympathized with slaves. "Damn the negroes," he said. "I am fighting those traitorous aristocrats, their masters." At a time when the nation confronted the future of black Americans, the new president harbored unshakable racist convictions. Africans, Johnson said, were "inferior to the white man in point of intellect — better calculated in physical structure to undergo drudgery and hardship."

> "Damn the negroes. I am fighting those traitorous aristocrats, their masters."
> — President ANDREW JOHNSON

Like Lincoln, Johnson stressed the rapid restoration of civil government in the South. Like Lincoln, he promised to pardon most, but not all, ex-rebels. Johnson recognized the state governments created by Lincoln but set out his own requirements for restoring the other rebel states to the Union. All that the citizens of a state had to do was to renounce the right of secession, deny that the debts of the Confederacy were legal and binding, and ratify the Thirteenth Amendment abolishing slavery, which became part of the Constitution in December 1865.

Johnson's eagerness to restore relations with southern states and his lack of sympathy for blacks also led him to return to pardoned ex-Confederates all confiscated and abandoned land, even if it was in the hands of freedmen. Reformers were shocked. They had expected the president's hatred of planters to mean the permanent confiscation of the South's plantations and the distribution of the land to loyal freedmen. Instead, his instructions canceled the promising beginnings made by General Sherman and the Freedmen's Bureau to settle blacks on land of their own. As one freedman observed, "Things was hurt by Mr. Lincoln getting killed."

White Southern Resistance and Black Codes

In the summer of 1865, delegates across the South gathered to draw up the new state constitutions required by Johnson's plan of reconstruction. Rather than take their medicine, delegates choked on even the president's mild requirements. Refusing to renounce secession, the South Carolina and Georgia conventions merely "repudiated" their secession ordinances, preserving in principle their right to secede. South Carolina and Mississippi refused to disown their Confederate war debts. Mississippi rejected the Thirteenth Amendment outright, and Alabama rejected it in part. Despite these defiant acts, Johnson did nothing. White Southerners began to think that by standing up for themselves they — not victorious Northerners — would shape reconstruction.

In the fall of 1865, newly elected southern legislators across the South adopted a series of laws known as **black codes**, which made a travesty of black freedom. The codes sought to keep ex-slaves subordinate to whites by subjecting them to every sort of discrimination. Several states made it illegal for blacks to own a gun. Mississippi made insulting gestures and language

by blacks a criminal offense. The codes barred blacks from jury duty. Not a single southern state granted any black the right to vote.

At the core of the black codes, however, lay the matter of labor. Faced with the death of slavery, legislators sought to hustle freedmen back to the plantations. Whites were almost universally opposed to black landownership. Whitelaw Reid, a northern visitor to the South, found that the "man who should sell small tracts to them would be in actual personal danger." South Carolina attempted to limit blacks to either farmwork or domestic service by requiring them to pay annual taxes of $10 to $100 to work in any other occupation. Mississippi declared that blacks who did not possess written evidence of employment could be declared vagrants and be subject to involuntary plantation labor. Under so-called apprenticeship laws, courts bound thousands of black children — orphans and others whose parents they deemed unable to support them — to work for planter "guardians."

Johnson refused to intervene. A staunch defender of states' rights, he believed that the citizens of every state should be free to write their own constitutions and laws. Moreover, Johnson was as eager as other white Southerners to restore white supremacy and black subordination. As he remarked in 1865, "White men alone must manage the South."

But Johnson also followed the path that he believed offered him the greatest political return. A conservative Tennessee Democrat at the head of a northern Republican Party, he began to look southward for political allies. Despite tough talk about punishing traitors, he personally pardoned fourteen thousand wealthy or high-ranking ex-Confederates. By pardoning powerful whites, by accepting governments even when they failed to satisfy his minimal demands, and by acquiescing in the black codes, he won useful southern friends.

In the fall elections of 1865, white Southerners dramatically expressed their mood. To represent them in Congress, they chose former Confederates. Of the eighty senators and representatives they sent to Washington, fifteen had served in the Confederate army, ten of them as generals. Another sixteen had served in civil and judicial posts in the Confederacy. Nine others had served in the Confederate Congress. One — Alexander Stephens — had been vice president of the Confederacy. As one Georgian remarked, "It looked as though Richmond had moved to Washington."

The Black Codes
Titled "Selling a Freeman to Pay His Fine at Monticello, Florida," this 1867 drawing from a northern magazine equates black codes with the reinstitution of slavery. The laws stopped short of reenslavement but sharply restricted blacks' freedom. In Florida, as in other southern states, certain acts, such as breaking a labor contract, were made criminal offenses, the penalty for which could be involuntary plantation labor for a year. The Granger Collection, NYC.

Expansion of Federal Authority and Black Rights

Southerners had blundered monumentally. They had assumed that what Andrew Johnson was willing to accept, Republicans would accept as well. But southern intransigence compelled even moderates to conclude that ex-rebels were a "generation of vipers," still untrustworthy and dangerous. So angry were Republicans with the rebels that the federal government refused to supply artificial limbs to disabled Southerners, as they did for Union veterans.

The black codes became a symbol of southern intentions to "restore all of slavery but its name." Northerners were hardly saints when it came to racial justice, but black freedom had become a hallowed war aim. "We tell the white men of Mississippi," the *Chicago Tribune* roared, "that the men of the North will convert the State of Mississippi into a frog pond before they will allow such laws to disgrace one foot of the soil in which the bones of our soldiers sleep and over which the flag of freedom waves."

The moderate majority of the Republican Party wanted only assurance that slavery and treason were dead. They did not champion black equality, the confiscation of plantations, or black voting, as did the radical minority within the party. But southern obstinacy had succeeded in forging unity (at least temporarily) among Republican factions. In December 1865, exercising

Congress's right to determine the qualifications of its members, Republicans refused to seat the southern representatives elected in the fall elections. Rather than accept Johnson's claim that the "work of restoration" was done, Congress challenged his executive power.

Republican senator Lyman Trumbull declared that the president's policy meant that an ex-slave would "be tyrannized over, abused, and virtually reenslaved without some legislation by the nation for his protection." Early in 1866, the moderates produced two bills that strengthened the federal shield. The first, the Freedmen's Bureau bill, prolonged the life of the agency established by the previous Congress. It had distributed food, supervised labor contracts, and sponsored schools for freedmen. Arguing that the Constitution never contemplated a "system for the support of indigent persons," President Andrew Johnson vetoed the bill. Congress failed by a narrow margin to override the president's veto.

The moderates designed their second measure, what would become the **Civil Rights Act of 1866**, to nullify the black codes by affirming African Americans' rights to "full and equal benefit of all laws and proceedings for the security of person and property as is enjoyed by white citizens." The act boldly required the end of racial discrimination in state laws and represented an extraordinary expansion of black rights and federal authority. The president argued that the civil rights bill amounted to "unconstitutional invasion of states' rights" and vetoed it. In essence, he denied that the federal government possessed the authority to protect the civil rights of blacks.

In April 1866, an incensed Republican Party again pushed the civil rights bill through Congress and overrode the presidential veto. In July, it passed another Freedmen's Bureau bill and overrode Johnson's veto. For the first time in American history, Congress had overridden presidential vetoes of major legislation. As a worried South Carolinian observed, Johnson had succeeded in uniting the Republicans and probably touched off "a fight this fall such as has never been seen."

REVIEW How did the North respond to the passage of black codes in the southern states?

▶ Congressional Reconstruction

By the summer of 1866, President Andrew Johnson and Congress had dropped their gloves and stood toe-to-toe in a bare-knuckle contest unprecedented in American history. Johnson made it clear that he would not budge on either constitutional issues or policy. Moderate Republicans responded by amending the Constitution. But the obstinacy of Johnson and white Southerners pushed Republican moderates ever closer to the radicals and to acceptance of additional federal intervention in the South. Congress also voted to impeach the president for the first time since the nation was formed. In time, Congress debated whether to make voting rights color-blind, while women sought to make voting sex-blind as well.

The Fourteenth Amendment and Escalating Violence

In June 1866, Congress passed the **Fourteenth Amendment** to the Constitution, and two years later it gained the necessary ratification of three-fourths of the states. The most important provisions of this complex amendment made all native-born or naturalized persons American citizens and prohibited states from abridging the "privileges and immunities" of citizens, depriving them of "life, liberty, or property without due

Reconstruction Cartoon
Most white southerners had difficulty adjusting to defeat, but no one defied and damned the Yankees like white women. This 1865 cartoon pokes fun at two Richmond ladies as they pass by a Union officer on their way to receive free government rations. One says sourly to the other, "Don't you think that Yankee must feel like shrinking into his boots before such high-toned Southern ladies as we?" Just a step behind the white women is a smiling black woman, who obviously views the Yankee through different eyes. Miriam and Ira D. Wallach Division of Art, Prints and Photographs, The New York Public Library. Astor, Lenox and Tilden Foundations.

process of law," and denying them "equal protection of the laws." By making blacks national citizens, the amendment provided a national guarantee of equality before the law. In essence, it protected blacks against violation by southern state governments.

The Fourteenth Amendment also dealt with voting rights. It gave Congress the right to reduce the congressional representation of states that withheld suffrage from some of its adult male population. In other words, white Southerners could either allow black men to vote or see their representation in Washington slashed. Whatever happened, Republicans stood to benefit from the Fourteenth Amendment. If southern whites granted voting rights to freedmen, Republicans would gain valuable black votes. If whites refused, the representation of southern Democrats would plunge.

The Fourteenth Amendment's suffrage provisions ignored the small band of politicized women who had emerged from the war demanding "the ballot for the two disenfranchised classes, negroes and women." Founding the **American Equal Rights Association** in 1866, **Susan B. Anthony** and **Elizabeth Cady Stanton** lobbied for "a government by the people, and the whole people; for the people and the whole people." They felt betrayed when their old antislavery allies refused to work for their goals. "It was the Negro's hour," Frederick Douglass explained. Senator Charles Sumner suggested that woman suffrage could be "the great question of the future."

The Fourteenth Amendment provided for punishment of any state that excluded voters on the basis of race but not on the basis of sex. The amendment also introduced the word *male* into the Constitution when it referred to a citizen's right to vote. Stanton predicted that "if that word 'male' be inserted, it will take us a century at least to get it out."

Tennessee approved the Fourteenth Amendment in July, and Congress promptly welcomed the state's representatives and senators back. Had President Johnson counseled other southern states to ratify this relatively mild amendment and warned them that they faced the fury of an outraged Republican Party if they refused, they might have listened. Instead, Johnson advised Southerners to reject the Fourteenth Amendment and to rely on him to trounce the Republicans in the fall congressional elections.

Johnson had decided to make the Fourteenth Amendment the overriding issue of the 1866 elections and to gather its white opponents into

Elizabeth Cady Stanton and Susan B. Anthony, 1870
Outspoken suffragists Elizabeth Cady Stanton (left) and Susan B. Anthony (right) were veteran reformers who advocated, among other things, better working conditions for labor, married women's property rights, liberalization of divorce laws, and women's admission into colleges and trade schools. Their passion for other causes led some conservatives to oppose women's political rights because they equated the suffragist cause with radicalism in general. Women could not easily overcome such views, and the long struggle for the vote eventually drew millions of women into public life. ©Bettmann/Corbis.

a new conservative party, the National Union Party. The president's strategy suffered a setback when whites in several southern cities went on rampages against blacks. When a mob in New Orleans assaulted delegates to a black suffrage convention, thirty-four blacks died. In Memphis, white mobs killed at least forty-six people. The slaughter shocked Northerners and renewed skepticism about Johnson's claim that southern whites could be trusted. "Who doubts that the Freedmen's Bureau ought to be abolished forthwith," a New Yorker observed sarcastically, "and the blacks remitted to the paternal care of their old masters, who 'understand the nigger, you know, a great deal better than the Yankees can.'"

The 1866 elections resulted in an overwhelming Republican victory. Johnson had bet that Northerners would not support federal protection of black rights and that a racist backlash would blast the Republican Party. But the war was still fresh in northern minds, and as one Republican explained, southern whites "with all their intelligence were traitors, the blacks with all their ignorance were loyal."

> "If that word 'male' be inserted [in the Fourteenth Amendment], it will take us a century at least to get it out."
> — ELIZABETH CADY STANTON

Memphis Riots, May 1866

On May 1, 1866, two carriages, one driven by a white man and the other by a black man, collided on a busy street in Memphis, Tennessee. This minor incident led to three days of bloody racial violence in which dozens of blacks and two whites died. South Memphis, pictured in this lithograph from *Harper's Weekly*, was a shantytown where the families of black soldiers stationed at nearby Fort Pickering lived. The army commander refused to send troops to protect soldiers' families and property, and white mobs ran wild. The Granger Collection, NYC.

Radical Reconstruction and Military Rule

When Johnson continued to urge Southerners to reject the Fourteenth Amendment, every southern state except Tennessee voted it down. "The last one of the sinful ten," thundered Representative James A. Garfield of Ohio, "has flung back into our teeth the magnanimous offer of a generous nation." After the South rejected the moderates' program, the radicals seized the initiative.

Each act of defiance by southern whites had boosted the standing of the radicals within the Republican Party. Except for freedmen themselves, no one did more to make freedom the "mighty moral question of the age." Radicals such as Massachusetts senator Charles Sumner and Pennsylvania representative Thaddeus Stevens did not speak with a single voice, but they united in demanding civil and political equality. Southern states were "like clay in the hands of the potter," Stevens declared in January 1867, and he called on Congress to begin reconstruction all over again.

In March 1867, Congress overturned the Johnson state governments and initiated military rule of the South. The **Military Reconstruction Act** (and three subsequent acts) divided the ten unreconstructed Confederate states into five military districts. Congress placed a Union general in charge of each district and instructed him to "suppress insurrection, disorder, and violence" and to begin political reform. After the military had completed voter registration, which would include black men, voters in each state would elect delegates to conventions that would draw up new state constitutions. Each constitution would guarantee black suffrage. When the voters of each state had approved the constitution and the state legislature had ratified the Fourteenth Amendment, the state could submit its work to Congress. If Congress approved, the state's senators and representatives could be seated, and political reunification would be accomplished.

Reconstruction Military Districts, 1867

Radicals proclaimed the provision for black suffrage "a prodigious triumph," for it extended far beyond the limited suffrage provisions of the Fourteenth Amendment. Republicans now believed that only the voting power of ex-slaves could bring about a permanent revolution in the South. When combined with the disfranchisement of thousands of ex-rebels, it promised to cripple any neo-Confederate resurgence and guarantee Republican state governments in the South.

Despite its bold suffrage provision, the Military Reconstruction Act of 1867 disappointed those who also advocated the confiscation of southern plantations and their redistribution to ex-slaves. Thaddeus Stevens agreed with the freedman who said, "Give us our own land and we take care of ourselves, but without land, the old masters can hire us or starve us, as they please." But most Republicans believed they had provided blacks with what they needed: equal legal rights and the ballot. If blacks were to get land, they would have to gain it themselves.

Declaring that he would rather sever his right arm than sign such a formula for "anarchy and chaos," Andrew Johnson vetoed the Military Reconstruction Act. Congress overrode his veto the very same day, dramatizing the shift in power from the executive to the legislative branch of government. With the passage of the Reconstruction Acts of 1867, congressional reconstruction was virtually completed. Congress left whites owning most of the South's land but, in a departure that justified the term "radical reconstruction," had given black men the ballot. In 1867, the nation began an unprecedented experiment in interracial democracy — at least in the South, for Congress's plan did not touch the North. But before the spotlight swung away from Washington to the South, the president and Congress had one more scene to play.

Impeaching a President

Despite his defeats, Andrew Johnson had no intention of yielding control of reconstruction. In a dozen ways, he sabotaged Congress's will and encouraged southern whites to resist. He issued a flood of pardons, waged war against the

---

Andrew Johnson Cartoon

Appearing in 1868 during President Andrew Johnson's impeachment trial, this cartoon includes captions that read: "This little boy would persist in handling books above his capacity" and "And this was the disastrous result." The cartoonist's portrait of Johnson being crushed by the Constitution refers to the president's flouting of the Tenure of Office Act, which caused Republicans to vote for his impeachment. The cartoon's celebration of Johnson's destruction proved premature, however. The Granger Collection, NYC.

THIS LITTLE BOY WOULD PERSIST IN HANDLING BOOKS ABOVE HIS CAPACITY.

AND THIS WAS THE DISASTROUS RESULT.

Freedmen's Bureau, and replaced Union generals eager to enforce Congress's Reconstruction Acts with conservative officers eager to defeat them. Johnson claimed that he was merely defending the "violated Constitution." At bottom, however, the president subverted congressional reconstruction to protect southern whites from what he considered the horrors of "Negro domination."

When Congress realized that overriding Johnson's vetoes did not ensure that it got its way, it looked for other ways to exert its will. According to the Constitution, the House of Representatives can impeach and the Senate can try any federal official for "treason, bribery, or other high crimes and misdemeanors." Radicals argued that Johnson's abuse of constitutional powers and his failure to fulfill constitutional obligations to enforce the law were impeachable offenses. But moderates interpreted the constitutional provision to mean violation of criminal statutes. As long as Johnson refrained from breaking the law, impeachment (the process of formal charges of wrongdoing against the president or other federal official) remained stalled.

Then, in August 1867, Johnson suspended Secretary of War Edwin M. Stanton from office. The Tenure of Office Act, which had been passed earlier in the year, demanded the approval of the Senate for the removal of any government official who had been appointed with Senate approval. As required by the act, the president requested the Senate to consent to Stanton's dismissal. When the Senate balked, Johnson removed Stanton anyway. "Is the President crazy, or only drunk?" asked a dumbfounded Republican moderate. "I'm afraid his doings will make us all favor impeachment."

News of Johnson's open defiance of the law convinced every Republican in the House to vote for a resolution impeaching the president. Supreme Court chief justice Salmon Chase presided over the Senate trial, which lasted from March until May 1868. Chase refused to allow Johnson's opponents to raise broad issues of misuse of power and forced them to argue their case exclusively on the narrow legal grounds of Johnson's removal of Stanton. Johnson's lawyers argued that the president had not committed a criminal offense, that the Tenure of Office Act was unconstitutional, and that in any case it did not apply to Stanton, who had been appointed by Lincoln. When the critical vote came, thirty-

Major Reconstruction Legislation, 1865–1875

1865

Thirteenth Amendment (ratified 1865)	Abolishes slavery.

1865 and 1866

Freedmen's Bureau Acts	Establish the Freedmen's Bureau to distribute food and clothing to destitute Southerners and help freedmen with labor contracts and schooling.
Civil Rights Act of 1866	Affirms the rights of blacks to enjoy "full and equal benefit of all laws and proceedings for the security of person and property as is enjoyed by white citizens" and effectively requires the end of legal discrimination in state laws.
Fourteenth Amendment (ratified 1868)	Makes native-born blacks citizens and guarantees all citizens "equal protection of the laws." Threatens to reduce representatives of a state that denies suffrage to any of its male inhabitants.

1867

Military Reconstruction Acts	Impose military rule in the South, establish rules for readmission of ex-Confederate states to the Union, and require those states to guarantee the vote to black men.

1869

Fifteenth Amendment (ratified 1870)	Prohibits racial discrimination in voting rights in all states in the nation.

1875

Civil Rights Act of 1875	Outlaws racial discrimination in transportation, public accommodations, and juries.

five senators voted guilty and nineteen not guilty. The impeachment forces fell one vote short of the two-thirds needed to convict.

After his trial, Johnson called a truce, and for the remaining ten months of his term, congressional reconstruction proceeded unhindered by presidential interference. Without interference from Johnson, Congress revisited the suffrage issue.

The Fifteenth Amendment and Women's Demands

In February 1869, Republicans passed the **Fifteenth Amendment** to the Constitution, which prohibited states from depriving any citizen of the right to vote because of "race, color, or previous condition of servitude." The Reconstruction Acts of 1867 already required black suffrage in the South; the Fifteenth Amendment extended black voting nationwide. Partisan advantage played an important role in the amendment's passage. Gains by northern Democrats in the 1868 elections worried Republicans, and black voters now represented the balance of power in several northern states. By giving the ballot to northern blacks, Republicans could lessen their own political vulnerability. As one Republican congressman observed, "Party expediency and exact justice coincide for once."

Some Republicans, however, found the final wording of the Fifteenth Amendment "lame and halting." Rather than absolutely guaranteeing the right to vote, the amendment merely prohibited exclusion on grounds of race. The distinction would prove to be significant. In time, white Southerners would devise tests of literacy and property and other apparently nonracial measures that would effectively disfranchise blacks yet not violate the Fifteenth Amendment. But an amendment that fully guaranteed the right to vote courted defeat outside the South. Rising antiforeign sentiment — against the Chinese in California and European immigrants in the Northeast — caused states to resist giving up total control of suffrage requirements. In March 1870, after three-fourths of the states had ratified it, the Fifteenth Amendment became part of the Constitution. Republicans generally breathed a sigh of relief, confident that black suffrage was "the last great point that remained to be settled of the issues of the war."

Woman suffrage advocates, however, were sorely disappointed with the Fifteenth Amendment's failure to extend voting rights to women. The amendment denied states the right to forbid suffrage only on the basis of race. Elizabeth Cady Stanton and Susan B. Anthony condemned the Republicans' "negro first" strategy and pointed out that women remained "the only class of citizens wholly unrepresented in the government." Stanton wondered aloud why ignorant black men should legislate for educated and cultured white women. Increasingly, activist women concluded that woman "must not put her trust in man." The Fifteenth Amendment severed the early feminist movement from its abolitionist roots. Over the next several decades, feminists established an independent suffrage crusade that drew millions of women into political life.

Republicans took enough satisfaction in the Fifteenth Amendment to promptly scratch the "Negro question" from the agenda of national politics. Even that steadfast crusader for equality Wendell Phillips concluded that the black man now held "sufficient shield in his own hands. . . . Whatever he suffers will be largely now, and in future, his own fault." Northerners had no idea of the violent struggles that lay ahead.

REVIEW Why did Johnson urge the southern states to reject the Fourteenth Amendment?

▶ The Struggle in the South

Northerners believed they had discharged their responsibilities with the Reconstruction Acts and the amendments to the Constitution, but Southerners knew that the battle had just begun. Black suffrage established the foundation for the rise of the Republican Party in the South. Gathering together outsiders and outcasts, southern Republicans won elections, wrote new state constitutions, and formed new state governments.

Challenging the established class for political control was dangerous business. Equally dangerous were the confrontations that took place on southern farms and plantations, where blacks sought to give economic meaning to their newly won legal and political equality. Ex-masters had their own ideas about the labor system that should replace slavery. Freedom remained contested territory, and Southerners fought pitched battles with one another to determine the contours of their new world.

What Did the Ku Klux Klan Really Want?

In 1866, six Confederate veterans in Pulaski, Tennessee, founded the Ku Klux Klan for fun and fellowship. But by 1868, when congressional reconstruction went into effect, the Klan had spread across the South, and members had shifted to more serious matters.

According to former Confederate general and Georgia Democratic politician John B. Gordon, the Klan owed its popularity to the "instinct of self-preservation . . . the sense of insecurity and danger, particularly in those neighborhoods where the Negro population largely predominated." Everywhere whites looked, he said, they saw "great crime." Republican politicians marched ignorant freedmen to the polls, where they blighted honest government. Ex-slaves drove overseers from plantations and claimed the land for themselves. Black rapists made white women cower behind barred doors. It was necessary, Gordon declared, "in order to protect our families from outrage and preserve our own lives, to have something that we could regard as a brotherhood — a combination of the best men of the country, to act purely in self-defense."

Behind the Klan's high-minded and self-justifying rhetoric, however, lay another agenda. It was revealed in their actions, not their words. Klansmen embarked on a campaign to reverse history. Garbed in robes and hoods, they engaged in guerrilla warfare against free labor, civil equality, and political democracy. They aimed to terrorize their enemies — ex-slaves and white Republicans — into submission. Changes in four particular areas of southern life proved flash points for Klan violence: racial etiquette, education, labor, and politics.

The Klan punished those blacks and whites who broke the Old South's racial code. The Klan considered "impudence" a punishable offense. Asked to define "impudence" before a congressional investigating committee, one white man responded: "Well, it is considered impudence for a negro not to be polite to a white man — not to pull off his hat and bow and scrape to a white man, as was done formerly." Klansmen whipped blacks for speaking disrespectfully, refusing to yield the sidewalk, and dressing well. Black women who "dress up and fix up like ladies" risked a midnight visit from the Klan. The Klan sought to restore racial subordination in every aspect of private and public life.

Klansmen also took aim at black education. White men found the sight of blacks in classrooms hard to stomach. Schools were easy targets, and scores of them went up in flames. Teachers, male and female, were flogged, or worse. Klansmen drove northern-born teacher Alonzo B. Corliss from North Carolina for "teaching niggers and making them like white men." In Cross Plains, Alabama, the Klan hanged an Irish-born teacher along with four black men. Planters wanted ex-slaves back in the fields, not at desks. In 1869, an Alabama newspaper announced that the burning of a black school should be "a warning for them to stick hereafter to 'de shovel and de hoe,' and let their dirty-backed primers go."

Planters turned to the Klan as part of their effort to preserve plantation agriculture. An Alabama white admitted that in his area the Klan was "intended principally for the negroes who failed to work." Hooded bands "punished Negroes whose landlords had complained of them." Sharecroppers who disputed their share at "settling up time" risked a visit from the night riders. It was dangerous for freedmen to consider changing employers. "If we got out looking for some other place to go," an ex-slave from Texas remembered, "them KKK they would tend to Mister negro good and plenty."

Above all, the Klan terrorized Republicans. Klansmen became the military arm of the Democratic Party. They drove blacks from the polls on election day and assaulted Republican officeholders. Klansmen gave Andrew Flowers, a black politician in Chattanooga, a brutal beating and told him that they "did not intend any nigger to hold office in the United States." Jack Dupree, president of the Republican Club in Monroe County, Mississippi, a man known to "speak his mind," had his throat cut and was disemboweled while his wife was forced to watch.

Political violence reached astounding levels. Arkansas experienced nearly three hundred political killings in the three months before the fall elections

Freedmen, Yankees, and Yeomen

African Americans made up the majority of southern Republicans. After gaining voting rights in 1867, nearly all eligible black men registered to vote as Republicans, grateful to the party that had freed them and granted them the franchise.

"It is the hardest thing in the world to keep a negro away from the polls," observed an Alabama white man. Black women, like white women, remained disfranchised, but they mobilized along with black men. In the 1868 presidential election, they bravely wore buttons supporting the Republican candidate, Ulysses S. Grant. Southern blacks did not all have identical political priorities, but they

Ku Klux Klan Rider in Tennessee about 1868 and Klan Banner

The white robes that we associate with the Ku Klux Klan are a twentieth-century phenomenon. During Reconstruction, Klansmen wore robes of various designs and colors. Hooded horses added another element to the Klan's terror. The Klansman holds a flag that looks very much like the satanic dragon on the colorful Klan banner shown here, which contains a Latin motto from Saint Augustine's definition of Catholic truth: "that which [has been believed] always, everywhere, by all." Among Klansmen, this motto was likely to refer to the truth of white supremacy.

Rider: Tennessee State Museum Collection; banner: Chicago Historical Society.

in 1868. Louisiana was even bloodier, suffering more than one thousand killings in the same year. In Georgia, the Klan murdered three scalawag members of the legislature and drove ten others from their homes. As one Georgia Republican commented after a Klan attack: "We don't call them [D]emocrats, we call them southern murderers."

It proved hard to arrest Klansmen and harder still to convict them. "If a white man kills a colored man in any of the counties of this State," observed a Florida sheriff, "you cannot convict him." Federal intervention — in the Ku Klux Klan Acts of 1870 and 1871— signaled an end to much of the Klan's power but not to counterrevolutionary violence in the South. Other groups continued the terror in the cause of white supremacy.

QUOD SEMPER, QUOD UBIQUE, QUOD ABOMNIBUS.

Thinking about Beliefs and Attitudes

1. What changes during Reconstruction particularly provoked the Klan? Why do you think these issues were so important to Klansmen?

2. Why did Klansmen believe that their actions were justified? Why do you think they hid their identities?

3. What southern traditions did the Klan seek to perpetuate?

united in their desire for education and equal treatment before the law.

Northern whites who made the South their home after the war were a second element of the South's Republican Party. Conservative white Southerners called them **carpetbaggers**, men so poor that they could stuff all their earthly belongings in a single carpet-sided suitcase and swoop southward like buzzards to "fatten on our misfortunes." But most Northerners who moved south were young men who looked upon the South as they did the West — as a promising place to make a living. Northerners in the southern Republican Party consistently supported programs that encouraged vigorous economic development along the lines of the northern free-labor model.

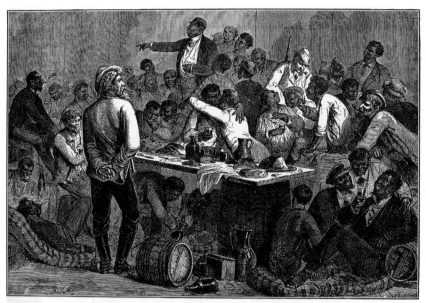

A Southern Legislature in the Carpet-Bagger Days
This late-nineteenth-century wood engraving reveals the southern Democratic view of Republican state governments during Reconstruction. It drips with prejudice and misinformation. Contrary to fact, the legislators are depicted as overwhelmingly black. Rather than serious men, they are lazy, drunk, and disorderly. While some lie about on cushions, others have literally drunk themselves under the table, which is spread with food rather than legislative documents. The white man in the foreground who calmly observes the circus is probably meant to be a manipulative carpetbagger, while the white man in the rear with the hat, pipe, and rifle slung over his shoulder is probably a treasonous scalawag. The Granger Collection, NYC.

Southern whites made up the third element of the South's Republican Party. Approximately one out of four white Southerners voted Republican. The other three condemned the one who did as a traitor to his region and his race and called him a **scalawag**, a term for runty horses and low-down, good-for-nothing rascals. Yeoman farmers accounted for the majority of southern white Republicans. Some were Unionists who emerged from the war with bitter memories of Confederate persecution. Others were small farmers who wanted to end state governments' favoritism toward plantation owners. Yeomen supported initiatives for public schools and for expanding economic opportunity in the South.

The South's Republican Party, then, was made up of freedmen, Yankees, and yeomen — an improbable coalition. The mix of races, regions, and classes inevitably meant friction as each group maneuvered to define the party. But Reconstruction represents an extraordinary moment in American politics: Blacks and whites joined together in the Republican Party to pursue political change. Formally, of course, only men participated in politics — casting ballots and holding offices — but white and black women

also played a part in the political struggle by joining in parades and rallies, attending stump speeches, and even campaigning.

Reconstruction politics was not for cowards. Most whites in the South condemned southern Republicans as illegitimate and felt justified in doing whatever they could to stamp them out. Violence against blacks — the "white terror" — took brutal institutional form in 1866 with the formation in Tennessee of the **Ku Klux Klan**, a social club of Confederate veterans that quickly developed into a paramilitary organization supporting Democrats. The Klan went on a rampage of whipping, hanging, shooting, burning, and throat-cutting to defeat Republicans and restore white supremacy. (See "Historical Question," page 516.) Rapid demobilization of the Union army after the war left only twenty thousand troops to patrol the entire South. Without effective military protection, southern Republicans had to take care of themselves.

Republican Rule

In the fall of 1867, southern states held elections for delegates to state constitutional conventions, as required by the Reconstruction Acts. About 40 percent of the white electorate stayed home because they had been disfranchised or because they had decided to boycott politics. Republicans won three-fourths of the seats. About 15 percent of the Republican delegates to the conventions were Northerners who had moved south, 25 percent were African Americans, and 60 percent were white Southerners. As a British visitor observed, the delegate elections reflected "the mighty revolution that had taken place in America." But Democrats described the state conventions as zoos of "baboons, monkeys, mules . . . and other jackasses." In fact, the conventions brought together serious, purposeful men who hammered out the legal framework for a new order.

The reconstruction constitutions introduced two broad categories of changes in the South: those that reduced aristocratic privilege and increased democratic equality and those that expanded the state's responsibility for the general welfare. In the first category, the constitutions adopted universal male suffrage, abolished property qualifications for holding office, and made more offices elective and fewer appointed. In the second category, they enacted prison reform; made the state responsible for caring for orphans, the insane, and the deaf and mute; and exempted debtors' homes from seizure.

To Democrats, however, the new state constitutions looked like wild revolution. They were blind to the fact that no constitution confiscated and redistributed land, as virtually every former slave wished, or disfranchised ex-rebels wholesale, as most southern Unionists advocated. And Democrats were convinced that the new constitutions initiated "Negro domination" in politics. In fact, although four out of five Republican voters were black men, more than four out of five Republican officeholders were white. Southerners sent fourteen black congressmen and two black senators to Washington, but only 6 percent of Southerners in Congress during Reconstruction were black (Figure 16.1). The sixteen black men in Congress included exceptional men, such as Representative **James T. Rapier** of Alabama (see pages 499–500) and Mississippi senator Blanche K. Bruce, who was born a slave in Virginia and became a local school superintendent in Mississippi, a position that paved his way to the Senate. No state legislature experienced "Negro rule," despite black majorities in the populations of some states.

FIGURE 16.1 Southern Congressional Delegations, 1865–1877
The statistics contradict the myth of black domination of congressional representation during Reconstruction.

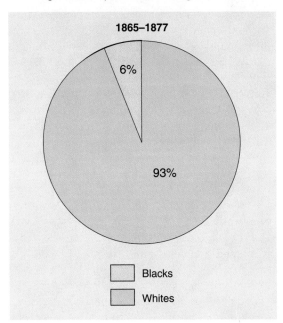

1865–1877

6%

93%

☐ Blacks
☐ Whites

Southern voters ratified the new constitutions and swept Republicans into power. When the former Confederate states ratified the Fourteenth Amendment, Congress readmitted them. Southern Republicans then turned to a staggering array of problems. Wartime destruction — burned cities, shattered bridges, broken levees, devastated railroads — littered the landscape. The South's share of the nation's wealth had fallen from 30 percent to only 12 percent. Manufacturing, always a small contributor to the southern economy, limped along at a fraction of prewar levels, and once-powerful agricultural production remained anemic. Without the efforts of the Freedmen's Bureau, black and white Southerners would have starved. Making matters worse, racial harassment and reactionary violence dogged Southerners who sought reform. In this desperate context, Republicans struggled to breathe life into the region.

Activity focused on three areas — education, civil rights, and economic development. Every state inaugurated a system of public education. Before the Civil War, whites had deliberately kept slaves illiterate, and planter-dominated governments rarely spent tax money to educate the children of yeomen. By 1875, half of Mississippi's and South Carolina's eligible children (the majority of whom were black) were attending school. Although schools were underfunded, literacy rates rose sharply. Public schools were racially segregated, but education remained for many blacks a tangible, deeply satisfying benefit of freedom and Republican rule.

State legislatures also attacked racial discrimination and defended civil rights. Republicans especially resisted efforts to segregate blacks from whites in public transportation. Mississippi levied fines of up to $1,000 and three years in jail for owners of railroads and steamboats that pushed blacks into "smoking cars" or to lower decks. Well-off blacks took particular aim at hotels and theaters that denied "full and equal rights." But passing color-blind laws was one thing; enforcing them was another. A Mississippian complained: "Education amounts to nothing, good behavior counts for nothing, even money cannot buy for a colored man or woman decent treatment and the comforts that white people claim and can obtain." Despite the laws, segregation — later called Jim Crow — developed at white insistence and became a feature of southern life long before the end of the Reconstruction era.

Republican governments also launched ambitious programs of economic development. They envisioned a South of diversified agriculture, roaring factories, and booming towns. State legislatures chartered scores of banks and industrial companies, appropriated funds to fix ruined levees and drain swamps, and went on a railroad-building binge. These efforts fell far short of solving the South's economic troubles, however. In addition, Republican spending to stimulate economic growth meant rising taxes and enormous debt that siphoned funds from schools and other programs.

The southern Republicans' record, then, was mixed. To their credit, the biracial party adopted an ambitious agenda to change the South, even though money was scarce, the Democrats continued their harassment, and factionalism threatened the Republican Party from within. However, corruption infected Republican governments in the South. Public morality reached new lows everywhere in the nation after the Civil War, and the chaos of the postwar South proved fertile soil for bribery, fraud, and influence peddling. Despite shortcomings, however, the Republican Party made headway in its efforts to purge the South of aristocratic privilege and racist oppression. Republican governments had less success in overthrowing the long-established white oppression of black farm laborers in the rural South.

Students at a Freedmen's School in Virginia, ca. 1870s, and a One-Cent Primer
"The people are hungry and thirsty after knowledge," a former slave observed immediately after the Civil War. African American leader Booker T. Washington remembered "a whole race trying to go to school." The students at this Virginia school stand in front of their log-cabin classroom reading books, but more common were eight-page primers that cost a penny. These simple readers offered ex-slaves the elements of literacy. For people long forbidden to learn to read and write, literacy symbolized freedom. Literacy also allowed those who were deeply religious to experience the joy of reading the Bible for themselves and those who were merely practical to understand labor contracts and participate knowledgeably in politics. Primer: Gladstone Collection; students: Valentine Museum, Cook Collection.

Black Woman in Cotton Fields, Thomasville, Georgia
Few images of everyday black women during the Reconstruction era survive. Taken in 1895, this photograph nevertheless goes to the heart of the labor struggle following the Civil War, when white landlords wanted emancipated slaves to continue working in the fields. Freedom allowed some women to escape field labor, but not this Georgian, who probably worked to survive. The photograph reveals a strong person with a clear sense of who she is. Though worn to protect her head and body from the fierce heat, her intricately wrapped headdress dramatically expresses her individuality. Her bare feet also reveal something about her life. Courtesy, Georgia Department of Archives and History, Atlanta, GA.

White Landlords, Black Sharecroppers

Ex-slaves who wished to escape slave labor and ex-masters who wanted to reinstitute old ways clashed repeatedly. Except for having to pay subsistence wages, planters had not been required to offer many con-cessions to emancipation. They continued to believe that African Americans would not work without coercion. Whites moved quickly to restore the antebellum (pre–Civil War) world of work gangs, white overseers, field labor for black women and children, clustered cabins, minimal personal freedom, and even whipping whenever they could get away with it.

Ex-slaves resisted every effort to turn back the clock. They argued that if any class could be described as "lazy," it was the planters, who, as one former slave noted, "lived in idleness all their lives on stolen labor." Ex-slaves believed that land of their own would anchor their economic independence and end planters' interference in their personal lives. They could then, for example, make their own decisions about whether women and children would labor in the fields. Indeed, within months after the war, perhaps one-third of black women abandoned field labor to work on chores in their own cabins just as poor white women did. Hundreds of thousands of black children enrolled in school. But without their own land, ex-slaves had little choice but to work on plantations, and they feared that their return to the planters' fields would undermine their independence.

Freedmen resisted efforts by ex-masters to restore slavelike conditions on plantations. Instead of working for wages, David Golightly Harris of South Carolina observed, "the negroes all seem disposed to rent land," which increased their independence from whites. By rejecting wage labor, by striking, and by abandoning the most reactionary employers, blacks sought to force concessions. Out of this tug-of-war between white landlords and black laborers emerged a new system of southern agriculture.

Sharecropping was a compromise that offered something to both ex-masters and ex-slaves but satisfied neither. Under the new system, planters divided their cotton plantations into small farms that freedmen rented, paying with a share of each year's crop, usually half. Sharecropping gave blacks more freedom than the system of wages and labor gangs and released them from day-to-day supervision by whites. Black families abandoned the old slave quarters and scattered over plantations, building separate cabins for themselves on the patches of land they rented (Map 16.1). Black families now decided who would work, for how long, and how hard. Black women negotiated with ex-mistresses about work the white women wanted done

A Post-Slavery Encounter

A Visit from the Old Mistress, 1876

Winslow Homer, one of the nation's foremost painters, was widely recognized for his ability to convey drama and emotion on canvas. Homer typically sketched and painted ordinary people in their everyday lives. During the Civil War, Homer worked as an illustrator for *Harper's Weekly*, depicting scenes of the war for curious Northerners. In 1875, he traveled from his home in New York City to Virginia, where he observed firsthand the transformation of relationships between former slaves and their former owners.

A Visit from the Old Mistress captures the moment when a white woman arrives in the humble cabin of former slaves and encounters three black women, one of whom holds a toddler. Homer typically said

little about his paintings, and there is much we don't know about the story being told in this work. Why has the old mistress come? We can imagine that she has come to talk about work she wants done in the big house. If so, she would have come asking, not commanding, for the end of slavery meant that ex-slaves had control over their own labor and negotiated what they would be paid and the conditions under which they would work.

Notice the way Homer has arranged the subjects of his painting, with the former slaves on one side of the room and the former mistress on the other. What does the generous space between them suggest? How do the two sides compare? Look particularly at the women's clothing and their stance. What does the white

woman's posture suggest? How are the three black women positioned, and what does this say about their attitude toward the old mistress? What do you detect in the facial expressions of the people in this image?

The end of slavery required wrenching readjustments in the lives of Southerners, black and white. Do you think Homer's simple domestic scene reveals an opinion about what the artist witnessed, or does *A Visit from the Old Mistress* try merely to capture truthfully a complex moment? How might this painting have looked different if it had been created before emancipation?

SOURCE: Smithsonian American Art Museum, Washington, D.C./Art Resource, NY.

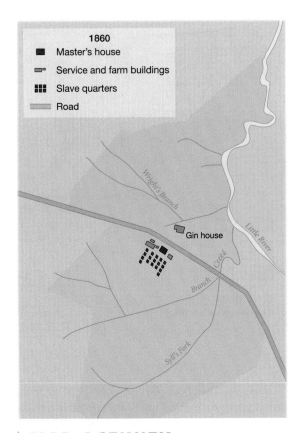

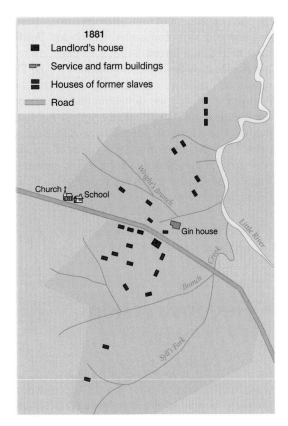

MAP ACTIVITY

Map 16.1   A Southern Plantation in 1860 and 1881

These maps of the Barrow plantation in Georgia illustrate some of the ways in which ex-slaves expressed their freedom. Freedmen and freedwomen deserted the clustered living quarters behind the master's house, scattered over the plantation, built family cabins, and farmed rented land. The former Barrow slaves also worked together to build a school and a church.

READING THE MAP: Compare the number and size of the slave quarters in 1860 with the homes of the former slaves in 1881. How do they differ? Which buildings were prominently located along the road in 1860, and which could be found along the road in 1881?

CONNECTIONS: How might the former master feel about the new configuration of buildings on the plantation in 1881? In what ways did the new system of sharecropping replicate the old system of plantation agriculture? In what ways was it different?

in the big house. (See "Visualizing History," page 522.) Still, most black families remained dependent on white landlords, who had the power to evict them at the end of each growing season. For planters, sharecropping offered a way to resume agricultural production, but it did not allow them to restore the old slave plantation.

Sharecropping introduced a new figure — the country merchant — into the agricultural equation. Landlords supplied sharecroppers with land, mules, seeds, and tools, but blacks also needed credit to obtain essential food and clothing before they harvested their crops. Thousands of small crossroads stores sprang up to offer credit. Under an arrangement called a **crop lien**, a merchant would advance goods to a sharecropper in exchange for a *lien*, or legal claim, on the farmer's future crop. Some merchants charged exorbitant rates of interest, as much as 60 percent, on the goods they sold. At the end of the growing season, after the landlord had taken half of the farmer's crop for rent, the merchant took most of the rest. Sometimes, the farmer's debt to the merchant exceeded the income he received from his remaining half of the crop, and the farmer would have no choice but to borrow more from the merchant and begin the cycle all over again.

An experiment at first, sharecropping spread quickly and soon dominated the cotton South. Lien merchants forced tenants to plant cotton, which was easy to sell, instead of food crops. The result was excessive production of cotton and falling cotton prices, developments that cost thousands of small white farmers their land and pushed them into the great army of sharecroppers. The new sharecropping system of agriculture took shape just as the political power of Republicans in the South began to buckle under Democratic pressure.

REVIEW   What brought the elements of the South's Republican coalition together?

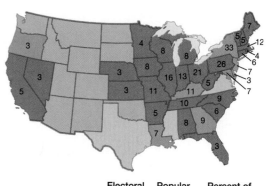

Candidate	Electoral Vote	Popular Vote	Percent of Popular Vote
Ulysses S. Grant (Republican)	214	3,012,833	52.7
Horatio Seymour (Democrat)	80	2,703,249	47.3
Nonvoting states (Reconstruction)			

MAP 16.2
The Election of 1868

▶ Reconstruction Collapses

By 1870, after a decade of war and reconstruction, Northerners wanted to put "the southern problem" behind them. Increasingly, practical, business-minded men came to the forefront of the Republican Party, replacing the band of reformers and idealists who had been prominent in the 1860s. While northern commitment to defend black freedom eroded, southern commitment to white supremacy intensified. Without northern protection, southern Republicans were no match for the Democrats' economic coercion, political fraud, and bloody violence. One by one, Republican state governments fell in the South. The election of 1876 both confirmed and completed the collapse of reconstruction.

> "His imperturbability is amazing. I am in doubt whether to call it greatness or stupidity."
> — Congressman JAMES A. GARFIELD, speaking of President Grant

Grant's Troubled Presidency

In 1868, the Republican Party's presidential nomination went to **Ulysses S. Grant**, the North's favorite general. Hero of the Civil War and a supporter of congressional reconstruction, Grant was the obvious choice. His Democratic opponent, Horatio Seymour of New York, ran on a platform that blasted congressional reconstruction as "a flagrant usurpation of power . . . unconstitutional, revolutionary, and void." The Republicans answered by **"waving the bloody shirt"** — that is, they reminded voters that the

Democrats were "the party of rebellion." During the campaign, the Ku Klux Klan erupted in a reign of terror across the South, murdering hundreds of Republicans. Fear of violence cost Grant votes, but he gained a narrow 309,000-vote margin in the popular vote and a substantial victory (214 votes to 80) in the electoral college (Map 16.2).

Grant was not as good a president as he was a general. The talents he had demonstrated on the battlefield — decisiveness, clarity, and resolution — were less obvious in the White House. He hoped to forge a policy that secured both justice for blacks and sectional reconciliation, but he took office at a time when a majority of white Northerners had grown weary of the "Southern Question" and were increasingly willing to let southern whites manage their own affairs. Moreover, Grant surrounded himself with fumbling kinfolk and old friends from his army days. He made a string of dubious appointments that led to a series of damaging scandals. Charges of corruption tainted his vice president, Schuyler Colfax, and brought down two of his cabinet officers. Though never personally implicated in any scandal, Grant was aggravatingly naive and blind to the rot that filled his administration. Republican congressman James A. Garfield declared: "His imperturbability is amazing. I am in doubt whether to call it greatness or stupidity."

In 1872, anti-Grant Republicans bolted and launched the Liberal Party. To clean up the graft and corruption,

I BEG TO REPEAT THAT THESE FRAUDS ON THE GOVERNMENT SHALL BE PROBED TO THE VERY BOTTOM.

Liberals proposed ending the spoils system, by which victorious parties rewarded loyal workers with public office, and replacing it with a nonpartisan civil service commission that would oversee competitive examinations for appointment to office (as discussed in chapter 18). Liberals also demanded that the federal government remove its troops from the South and restore "home rule" (southern white control). Democrats liked the Liberals' southern policy and endorsed the Liberal presidential candidate, Horace Greeley, the longtime editor of the *New York Tribune*. The nation, however, still felt enormous affection for the man who had saved the Union and reelected Grant with 56 percent of the popular vote.

Grant's ambitions for his administration extended beyond reconstruction, but not even foreign affairs could escape the problems of the South. Grant coveted Santo Domingo (present-day Dominican Republic) in the Caribbean and argued that the acquisition of this tropical land would permit the United States to expand its trade and would also provide a new home for the South's blacks, who were so desperately harassed by the Klan. Aggressive foreign policy had not originated with the Grant administration. Lincoln's and Johnson's secretary of state, William H. Seward, had thwarted French efforts to set up a puppet empire under Maximilian in Mexico, and his purchase of Alaska ("Seward's Ice Box") from Russia in 1867 for only $7 million fired Grant's imperialist ambition. But in the end, Grant could not convince Congress to approve

the treaty annexing Santo Domingo. The South preoccupied Congress and undermined Grant's initiatives.

Northern Resolve Withers

Although Grant genuinely wanted to see blacks' civil and political rights protected, he understood that most Northerners had grown weary of reconstruction and were increasingly willing to let southern whites manage their own affairs. Citizens wanted to shift their attention to other issues, especially after the nation slipped into a devastating economic depression in 1873. More than eighteen thousand businesses collapsed, leaving more than a million workers on the streets. Northern businessmen wanted to invest in the South but believed that recurrent federal intrusion was itself a major cause of instability in the region. Republican leaders began to question the wisdom of their party's alliance with the South's lower classes — its small farmers and sharecroppers. One member of Grant's administration proposed allying with the "thinking and influential native southerners . . . the intelligent, well-to-do, and controlling class."

Congress, too, wanted to leave reconstruction behind, but southern Republicans made that

Grant's Proposed Annexation of Santo Domingo

difficult. When the South's Republicans begged for federal protection from Klan violence, Congress enacted three laws in 1870 and 1871 that were intended to break the back of white terrorism. The severest of the three, the **Ku Klux Klan Act** (1871), made interference with voting rights a felony. Federal marshals arrested thousands of Klansmen and came close to destroying the Klan, but they did not end all terrorism against blacks. Congress also passed the **Civil Rights Act of 1875**, which boldly outlawed racial discrimination in transportation, public accommodations, and juries. But federal authorities never enforced the law aggressively, and segregated facilities remained the rule throughout the South.

By the early 1870s, the Republican Party had lost its leading champions of African American rights to death or defeat at the polls. Other Republicans concluded that the quest for black equality was mistaken or hopelessly naive. In May 1872, Congress restored the right of office-holding to all but three hundred ex-rebels. Many Republicans had come to believe that traditional white leaders offered the best hope for honesty, order, and prosperity in the South.

Underlying the North's abandonment of reconstruction was unyielding racial prejudice. Northerners had learned to accept black freedom during the war, but deep-seated prejudice prevented many from accepting black equality. Even the actions they took on behalf of blacks often served partisan political advantage. Northerners generally supported Indiana senator Thomas A. Hendricks's harsh declaration that "this is a white man's Government, made by the white man for the white man."

The U.S. Supreme Court also did its part to undermine reconstruction. The Court issued a series of decisions that significantly weakened the federal government's ability to protect black Southerners. In the *Slaughterhouse* cases (1873), the Court distinguished between national and state citizenship and ruled that the Fourteenth Amendment protected only those rights that stemmed from the federal government, such as voting in federal elections and interstate travel. Since the Court decided that most rights derived from the states, it sharply curtailed the federal government's authority to defend black citizens. Even more devastating, the *United States v. Cruikshank* ruling (1876) said that the reconstruction amendments gave Congress the power to legislate against discrimination only by states, not by individuals. The "suppression of ordinary crime," such as assault, remained a state responsibility. The Supreme Court did not declare

reconstruction unconstitutional but eroded its legal foundation.

The mood of the North found political expression in the election of 1874, when for the first time in eighteen years the Democrats gained control of the House of Representatives. As one Republican observed, the people had grown tired of the "negro question, with all its complications, and the reconstruction of Southern States, with all its interminable embroilments." Reconstruction had come apart. The people were tired of it. Grant grew increasingly unwilling to enforce it. Congress gradually abandoned it. And the Supreme Court denied the constitutionality of significant parts of it. Rather than defend reconstruction from its southern enemies, Northerners steadily backed away from the challenge. By the early 1870s, southern Republicans faced the forces of reaction largely on their own.

White Supremacy Triumphs

Reconstruction was a massive humiliation to most white Southerners. Republican rule meant intolerable insults: Black militiamen patrolled town streets, black laborers negotiated contracts with former masters, black maids stood up to former mistresses, black voters cast ballots, and black legislators such as James T. Rapier enacted laws. Whites resisted the consequences of their defeat in the Civil War by making it clear that military failure did not discredit their "civilization." They expressed their devotion to all that was good in the South — racial hierarchy, honor, vigorous masculinity — by making an idol of Robert E. Lee, the embodiment of the southern gentleman. They celebrated the "great Confederate cause," or **Lost Cause**, by extolling the deeds of their soldiers, "the noblest band of men who ever fought or ever took pen to record." Southern women took the lead in erecting monuments to the Confederate dead and, with pageantry, oratory, and flowers, in keeping alive the memory of the Lost Cause throughout the old Confederacy.

But the most important way white Southerners responded to the humiliation of reconstruction was their assault on Republican governments in the South, which attracted more hatred than did any other political regimes in American history. The northern retreat from reconstruction permitted southern Democrats to harness white rage to politics. Taking the name **Redeemers**, Democrats in the South promised to replace "bayonet rule" (a few federal troops continued to be stationed in the South) with "home rule." They branded Republican governments a carnival of extravagance, waste, and fraud and promised that honest, thrifty Democrats would supplant the irresponsible tax-and-spend Republicans. Above all, Redeemers swore to save southern civilization from a descent into "African barbarism." As one man put it, "We must render this either a white man's government, or convert the land into a Negro man's cemetery."

Southern Democrats adopted a multipronged strategy to overthrow Republican governments. First, they sought to polarize the parties around color. They went about gathering all the South's white voters into the Democratic Party, leaving the Republicans to depend on blacks, who made up a minority of the population in almost every southern state. To dislodge whites from the Republican Party, Democrats fanned the flames of racial prejudice. A South Carolina Democrat crowed that his party appealed to the "proud Caucasian race, whose sovereignty on earth God has proclaimed." Local newspapers published the names of whites who kept company with blacks, and neighbors ostracized offenders. One victim proclaimed, "No white man can live in the South in the future and act with any other than the Democratic party unless he is willing and prepared to live a life of social isolation."

Democrats also exploited the severe economic plight of small white farmers by blaming it on Republican financial policy. Government spending soared during reconstruction, and small farmers saw their tax burden skyrocket. "This is tax time," a South Carolinian reported. "We are nearly all on our head about them. They are so high &

"White Man's Country"
White supremacy emerged as a central tenet of the Democratic Party before the Civil War, and Democrats kept up a vicious racist attack on Republicans throughout Reconstruction. This silk ribbon from the 1868 presidential campaign between Republican Ulysses S. Grant and his Democratic opponent, New York governor Horatio Seymour, openly declares the Democrats' racial goal. During the campaign, Democratic vice presidential nominee Francis P. Blair Jr. promised that a Seymour victory would restore "white people" to power by declaring the reconstruction governments in the South "null and void." Collection of Janice L. and David J. Frent.

so little money to pay with" that farmers were "selling every egg and chicken they can get." In 1871, Mississippi reported that one-seventh of the state's land — 3.3 million acres — had been forfeited for nonpayment of taxes. The small farmers' economic distress had a racial dimension. Because few freedmen succeeded in acquiring land, they rarely paid taxes. In Georgia in 1874, blacks made up 45 percent of the population but paid only 2 percent of the taxes. From the perspective of a small white farmer, Republican rule meant that he was paying more taxes and paying them to aid blacks.

"Of Course He Wants to Vote the Democratic Ticket"
This Republican cartoon from the October 21, 1876, issue of *Harper's Weekly* comments sarcastically on the possibility of honest elections in the South. The caption reads: "You're free as air, ain't you? Say you are or I'll blow yer black head off." The cartoon demonstrates not only some Northerners' concern that violence would deliver the election to the Democrats but also the perception that white Southerners were crude, drunken, ignorant brutes. The Granger Collection, NY.

If racial pride, social isolation, and financial hardship proved insufficient to drive yeomen from the Republican Party, Democrats turned to terrorism. "Night riders" targeted white Republicans as well as blacks for murder and assassination. Whether white or black, a "dead Radical is very harmless," South Carolina Democratic leader Martin Gary told his followers.

But the primary victims of white violence were black Republicans, especially local leaders. Emanuel Fortune, whom the Klan drove from Jackson County, Florida, declared: "The object of it is to kill out the leading men of the republican party." But violence targeted all black voters, not just leaders. And it escalated to an unprecedented ferocity on Easter Sunday in 1873 in tiny Colfax, Louisiana. The black majority in the area had made Colfax a Republican stronghold until 1872, when Democrats turned to intimidation and fraud to win the local election. Republicans refused to accept the result and eventually occupied the courthouse in the middle of the town. After three weeks, 165 white men attacked. They overran the Republicans' defenses and set the courthouse on fire. When the blacks tried to surrender, the whites murdered them. At least 81 black men were slaughtered that day. Although the federal government indicted the attackers, the Supreme Court ruled that it did not have the right to prosecute. And since local whites would not prosecute neighbors who killed blacks, the defendants in the **Colfax massacre** went free.

Even before adopting the all-out white supremacist tactics of the 1870s, Democrats had taken control of the governments of Virginia, Tennessee, and North Carolina. The new campaign brought fresh gains. The Redeemers retook Georgia in 1871, Texas in 1873, and Arkansas and Alabama in 1874. Mississippi became a scene of open, unrelenting, and often savage intimidation of black voters and their few remaining white allies. As the state election approached in 1876, Governor Adelbert Ames appealed to Washington for federal troops to control the violence, only to hear from the attorney general that the "whole public are tired of these annual autumnal outbreaks in the South." Abandoned, Mississippi Republicans succumbed to the Democratic onslaught in the fall elections. By 1876, only three Republican state governments survived in the South (Map 16.3).

MAP ACTIVITY

Map 16.3   The Reconstruction of the South
Myth has it that Republican rule of the former Confederacy was not only harsh but long. In most states, however, conservative southern whites stormed back into power in months or just a few years. By the election of 1876, Republican governments could be found in only three states, and they soon fell.

READING THE MAP: List in chronological order the readmission of the former Confederate states to the Union. Which states reestablished conservative governments most quickly?
CONNECTIONS: What did the former Confederate states need to do in order to be readmitted to the Union? How did reestablished conservative governments react to reconstruction?

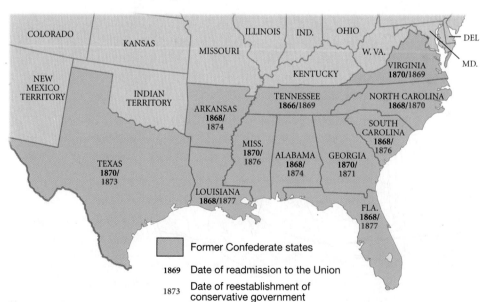

An Election and a Compromise

The centennial year of 1876 witnessed one of the most tumultuous elections in American history. Its chaos and confusion provided a fitting conclusion to the experiment known as reconstruction. The election took place in November, but not until March 2 of the following year did the nation know who would be inaugurated president on March 4. The Democrats nominated New York's governor, **Samuel J. Tilden**, who immediately targeted the corruption of the Grant administration and the "despotism" of Republican reconstruction. The Republicans put forward **Rutherford B. Hayes**, governor of Ohio. Privately, Hayes considered "bayonet rule" a mistake but concluded that waving the bloody shirt — reminding voters that the Democrats were the "party of rebellion" — remained the Republicans' best political strategy.

On election day, Tilden tallied 4,288,590 votes to Hayes's 4,036,000. But in the all-important electoral college, Tilden fell one vote short of the majority required for victory. The electoral votes of three states — South Carolina, Louisiana, and Florida, the only remaining Republican governments in the South — remained in doubt because both Republicans and Democrats in those states claimed victory. To win, Tilden needed only one of the nineteen contested votes. Hayes had to have all of them.

Congress had to decide who had actually won the elections in the three southern states and thus who would be president. The Constitution provided no guidance for this situation. Moreover, Democrats controlled the House, and Republicans controlled the Senate. Congress created a special electoral commission to arbitrate the disputed returns. All of the commissioners voted their party affiliation, giving every state to the Republican Hayes and putting him over the top in electoral votes (Map 16.4).

Some outraged Democrats vowed to resist Hayes's victory. Rumors flew of an impending coup and renewed civil war. But the impasse was broken when negotiations behind the scenes resulted in an informal understanding known as the **Compromise of 1877**. In exchange for a Democratic promise not to block Hayes's inauguration and to deal fairly with the freedmen, Hayes vowed to refrain from using the army to uphold the remaining Republican regimes in the South and to provide the South with substantial federal subsidies for railroads. Two days later, the nation celebrated Hayes's peaceful inauguration.

Stubborn Tilden supporters bemoaned the "stolen election" and damned "His Fraudulency," Rutherford B. Hayes. Old-guard radicals such as William Lloyd Garrison denounced Hayes's bargain as a "policy of compromise, of credulity, of weakness, of subserviency, of surrender." But the nation as a whole celebrated, for the country had weathered a grave crisis. The last three Republican state governments in the South fell quickly once Hayes abandoned them and withdrew the U.S. Army. Reconstruction came to an end.

REVIEW How did the Supreme Court undermine the Fourteenth and Fifteenth Amendments?

MAP 16.4
The Election of 1876

Candidate	Electoral Vote	Popular Vote	Percent of Popular Vote
Rutherford B. Hayes (Republican)	185*	4,036,298	47.9**
Samuel J. Tilden (Democrat)	184	4,288,590	51.0

*19 electoral votes were disputed.

**Percentages do not total 100 because some popular votes went to other parties.

▶ Conclusion: "A Revolution But Half Accomplished"

In 1865, when General Carl Schurz visited the South, he discovered "a revolution but half accomplished." White Southerners resisted the passage from slavery to free labor, from white racial despotism to equal justice, and from white political monopoly to biracial democracy. The old elite wanted to get "things back as near to slavery as possible," Schurz reported, while African Americans such as James T. Rapier and some whites were eager to exploit the revolutionary implications of defeat and emancipation.

The northern-dominated Republican Congress pushed the revolution along. Although it refused to provide for blacks' economic welfare, Congress employed constitutional amendments to require ex-Confederates to accept legal equality and share political power with black men. Congress was not willing to extend such power to women, however. Conservative southern whites fought ferociously to recover their power and privilege. When Democrats regained control of politics, whites used both state power and private violence to wipe out many of the gains of Reconstruction, leading one observer to conclude that the North had won the war but the South had won the peace.

The Redeemer counterrevolution, however, did not mean a return to slavery. Northern victory in the Civil War ensured that ex-slaves no longer faced the auction block and could send their children to school, worship in their own churches, and work independently on their own rented farms. Sharecropping, with all its hardships, provided more autonomy and economic welfare than bondage had. It was limited freedom, to be sure, but it was not slavery.

The Civil War and emancipation set in motion the most profound upheaval in the nation's history, and nothing reactionary whites did entirely erased its revolutionary impact. War destroyed the largest slave society in the New World. The world of masters and slaves succumbed to that of landlords and sharecroppers, a world in which white racial dominance continued, though with greater freedom for blacks. War also gave birth to a modern nation-state, and Washington increased its role in national affairs. When the South returned to the Union, it did so as a junior partner. The victorious North set the nation's compass toward the expansion of industrial capitalism and the final conquest of the West.

Despite massive changes, however, the Civil War remained only a "half accomplished" revolution. By not fulfilling the promises the nation seemed to hold out to black Americans at war's end, Reconstruction represents a tragedy of enormous proportions. The failure to protect blacks and guarantee their rights had enduring consequences. Almost a century after Reconstruction, the nation would embark on what one observer called a "second reconstruction." The solid achievements of the Thirteenth, Fourteenth, and Fifteenth Amendments to the Constitution would provide a legal foundation for the renewed commitment. It is worth remembering, though, that it was only the failure of the first reconstruction that made the modern civil rights movement necessary.

▶ Selected Bibliography

General Works

Michael W. Fitzgerald, *Splendid Failure: Postwar Reconstruction in the American South* (2007).
Eric Foner, *Reconstruction: America's Unfinished Revolution* (1988).
James M. McPherson, *Ordeal by Fire: The Civil War and Reconstruction* (3rd ed., 2000).

The Meaning of Freedom

Ira Berlin et al., eds., *Freedom: A Documentary History of Emancipation, 1861–1867*, 5 vols. to date (1982–).
John Hope Franklin and Loren Schweninger, *In Search of the Promised Land: A Slave Family in the Old South* (2006).
Thavolia Glymph, *Out of the House of Bondage: The Transformation of the Plantation Household* (2008).
Leon F. Litwack, *Been in the Storm So Long: The Aftermath of Slavery* (1979).
Susan Eva O'Donovan, *Becoming Free in the Cotton South* (2007).
Howard N. Rabinowitz, *Race Relations in the Urban South, 1865–1890* (1978).
Roger L. Ransom and Richard Sutch, *One Kind of Freedom: The Economic Consequences of Emancipation* (1977).
Loren Schweninger, *James T. Rapier and Reconstruction* (1978).
Clarence E. Walker, *A Rock in a Weary Land: The African Methodist Episcopal Church during the Civil War and Reconstruction* (1982).

The Politics of Reconstruction

Richard F. Bensel, *Yankee Leviathan: The Origins of Central State Authority in America, 1859–1877* (1990).
Philip Dray, *Capitol Men: The Epic Story of Reconstruction through the Lives of the First Black Congressmen* (2008).
Ellen Carol DuBois, *Feminism and Suffrage: The Emergence of an Independent Women's Movement in America, 1848–1869* (1978).
Richard L. Hume and Jerry B. Gough, *Blacks, Carpetbaggers, and Scalawags: The Constitutional Conventions of Radical Reconstruction* (2008).
Heather Cox Richardson, *The Death of Reconstruction: Race, Labor, and Politics in the Post–Civil War North, 1865–1901* (2001).
Leslie A. Schwalm, *Emancipation's Diaspora: Race and Reconstruction in the Upper Midwest* (2009).
Brooks D. Simpson, *The Reconstruction Presidents* (1998).
Mark Wahlgren Summers, *A Dangerous Stir: Fear, Paranoia, and the Making of Reconstruction* (2009).

C. Vann Woodward, *Reunion and Reaction: The Compromise of 1877 and the End of Reconstruction* (1951).

The Struggle in the South

James Alex Baggett, *The Scalawags: Southern Dissenters in the Civil War and Reconstruction* (2003).

Nancy D. Bercaw, *Gendered Freedoms: Race, Rights, and the Politics of Household in the Delta, 1861–1875* (2003).

Stephen Budiansky, *The Bloody Shirt: Terror after the Civil War* (2008).

Jane Turner Censer, *The Reconstruction of White Southern Womanhood, 1865–1895* (2003).

Paul A. Cimbala, *Under the Guardianship of the Nation: The Freedmen's Bureau and the Reconstruction of Georgia, 1865–1870* (1997).

Jane E. Dailey, *Before Jim Crow: The Politics of Race in Post-Emancipation Virginia* (2000).

Laura F. Edwards, *Gendered Strife and Confusion: The Political Culture of Reconstruction* (1997).

Sarah E. Gardner, *Blood and Irony: Southern White Women's Narratives of the Civil War, 1861–1937* (2004).

Stephen Kantrowitz, *Ben Tillman and the Reconstruction of White Supremacy* (2000).

Charles Lane, *The Day Freedom Died: The Colfax Massacre, the Supreme Court, and the Betrayal of Reconstruction* (2008).

George C. Rable, *But There Was No Peace: The Role of Violence in the Politics of Reconstruction* (1984).

James L. Roark, *Masters without Slaves: Southern Planters in the Civil War and Reconstruction* (1977).

Hyman Rubin III, *South Carolina Scalawags* (2006).

Peter Wallenstein, *From Slave South to New South: Public Policy in Nineteenth-Century Georgia* (1987).

▶ **FOR MORE BOOKS ABOUT TOPICS IN THIS CHAPTER,** see the Online Bibliography at **bedfordstmartins.com/roark.**

▶ **FOR ADDITIONAL PRIMARY SOURCES FROM THIS PERIOD,** see Michael Johnson, ed., *Reading the American Past*, Fifth Edition.

▶ **FOR WEB SITES, IMAGES, AND DOCUMENTS RELATED TO TOPICS AND PLACES IN THIS CHAPTER,** visit Make History at **bedfordstmartins.com/roark.**

Reviewing Chapter 16

KEY TERMS

Explain each term's significance.

Wartime Reconstruction
    Wade-Davis bill (p. 501)
    Freedmen's Bureau (p. 503)

Presidential Reconstruction
    Andrew Johnson (p. 506)
    black codes (p. 508)
    Civil Rights Act of 1866 (p. 510)

Congressional Reconstruction
    Fourteenth Amendment (p. 510)
    American Equal Rights Association
      (p. 511)
    Susan B. Anthony (p. 511)
    Elizabeth Cady Stanton (p. 511)
    Military Reconstruction Act (p. 512)
    Fifteenth Amendment (p. 515)

The Struggle in the South
    carpetbagger (p. 517)
    scalawag (p. 518)
    Ku Klux Klan (p. 518)
    James T. Rapier (p. 519)
    sharecropping (p. 521)
    crop lien (p. 523)

Reconstruction Collapses
    Ulysses S. Grant (p. 524)
    "waving the bloody shirt" (p. 524)
    Ku Klux Klan Act (p. 526)
    Civil Rights Act of 1875 (p. 526)
    Slaughterhouse cases (p. 526)
    United States v. Cruikshank (p. 526)
    Lost Cause (p. 526)
    Redeemers (p. 526)
    Colfax massacre (p. 528)
    Samuel J. Tilden (p. 529)
    Rutherford B. Hayes (p. 529)
    Compromise of 1877 (p. 529)

REVIEW QUESTIONS

Use key terms and dates to support your answer.

1. Why did Congress object to Lincoln's wartime plan for reconstruction? (pp. 501–506)

2. How did the North respond to the passage of black codes in the southern states? (pp. 506–510)

3. Why did Johnson urge the southern states to reject the Fourteenth Amendment? (pp. 510–515)

4. What brought the elements of the South's Republican coalition together? (pp. 515–524)

5. How did the Supreme Court undermine the Fourteenth and Fifteenth Amendments? (pp. 524–529)

MAKING CONNECTIONS

Draw on key terms, the timeline, and review questions.

1. Reconstruction succeeded in advancing black civil rights but failed to secure them over the long term. Why and how did the federal government retreat from defending African Americans' civil rights in the 1870s? In your answer, cite specific actions by Congress and the Supreme Court.

2. Why was distributing plantation land to former slaves such a controversial policy? In your answer, discuss why landownership was important to freedmen and why Congress rejected redistribution as a general policy.

3. At the end of the Civil War, it remained to be seen exactly how emancipation would transform the South. How did emancipation change political and labor organization in the region? In your answer, discuss how ex-slaves exercised their new freedoms and how white Southerners attempted to limit them.

4. The Republican Party shaped Reconstruction through its control of Congress and state legislatures in the South. How did the identification of the Republican Party with Reconstruction policy affect the party's political fortunes in the 1870s? In your answer, be sure to address developments on the federal and state levels.

LINKING TO THE PAST

Link events in this chapter to earlier events.

1. In what ways did the attitudes and actions of President Johnson increase northern resolve to reconstruct the South and the South's resolve to resist reconstruction?

2. White women, abolitionists, and blacks all had hopes for a brighter future that were in some ways dashed during the turmoil of reconstruction. What specific goals of these groups slipped away? What political allies abandoned their causes, and why?

▶ **FOR PRACTICE QUIZZES AND OTHER STUDY TOOLS,** see the Online Study Guide at bedfordstmartins.com/roark.

TIMELINE 1863–1877

1863	• Proclamation of Amnesty and Reconstruction.
1864	• Lincoln refuses to sign Wade-Davis bill.
1865	• Freedmen's Bureau established.
	• President Abraham Lincoln shot; dies on April 15; succeeded by Andrew Johnson.
	• Black codes enacted.
	• Thirteenth Amendment becomes part of Constitution.
1866	• Congress approves Fourteenth Amendment.
	• Civil Rights Act.
	• American Equal Rights Association founded.
	• Ku Klux Klan founded.
1867	• Military Reconstruction Act.
	• Tenure of Office Act.
1868	• Impeachment trial of President Johnson.
	• Republican Ulysses S. Grant elected president.
1869	• Congress approves Fifteenth Amendment.
1871	• Ku Klux Klan Act.
1872	• Liberal Party formed.
	• President Grant reelected.
1873	• Economic depression sets in for remainder of decade.
	• *Slaughterhouse* cases.
	• Colfax massacre.
1874	• Democrats win majority in House of Representatives.
1875	• Civil Rights Act.
1876	• *United States v. Cruikshank.*
1877	• Republican Rutherford B. Hayes assumes presidency; Reconstruction era ends.

LAKOTA VEST

This Lakota vest demonstrates how Native Americans adopted Euro-American articles of clothing and decorative motifs while employing materials that perpetuated native traditions. The vest belonged to Thomas American Horse, who had his initials worked into the beads at the neck. The American flag, as the vest demonstrates, figured frequently as a design in Indian art. The coming of the American flag, and with it the railroads and the slaughter of the buffalo pictured on the cover of *Leslie's Weekly* in 1871, points to the great changes that Indians faced in the struggle to control the vast land and resources of the American West.

Vest: Private Collection, photograph American Hurrah Archive, NYC; background: Library of Congress.

17

The Contested West
1865–1900

TO CELEBRATE THE FOUR HUNDREDTH ANNIVERSARY OF COLUMBUS'S voyage to the New World, Chicago hosted the World's Columbian Exposition in 1893. Architects and landscapers created a magical White City on the shores of Lake Michigan, complete with a Midway Plaisance where the first Ferris wheel awed and delighted the four million fairgoers.

Among the organizations vying to hold meetings in the White City was the American Historical Association, whose members — dedicated to the advancement of historical studies — gathered on a warm July evening to hear Frederick Jackson Turner deliver his landmark essay "The Significance of the Frontier in American History." Turner began by noting that the 1890 census could no longer discern a clear frontier line. His tone was elegiac: "The existence of an area of free land, its continuous recession, and the advance of settlement westward," he observed, "explained American development."

Of course, *west* has always been a comparative term in American history. Until the gold rush focused attention on California, the West for settlers lay beyond the Appalachians and east of the Mississippi in lands drained by the Ohio River, a part of the country now known as the Old Northwest. But by the second half of the nineteenth century, with the end of the Mexican-American War, the West now stretched from Canada to Mexico, from the Mississippi River to the Pacific Ocean.

Turner, who had originally studied the old frontier east of the Mississippi, viewed the West as a process as much as a place. The availability of land provided a "safety valve," releasing social tensions and providing opportunities for social mobility that worked to Americanize Americans. The West demanded strength and nerve, fostered invention and adaptation, and produced self-confident, individualistic Americans. Turner's theory underscored the exceptionalism of America's history, highlighting its difference from the rest of the world. His "frontier thesis" would earn him a professorship at Harvard and a permanent place in American history.

Yet the historians who applauded Turner in Chicago had short memories. That afternoon, they had crossed the midway to attend Buffalo Bill Cody's Wild West extravaganza, which featured exhibitions of riding, shooting, and roping and presented dramatic reenactments of great moments in western lore. Part circus, part theater, the show included 100 cowboys, 97 Indians,

535

180 horses, and 18 American bison. The troupe performed the "Attack on the Settler's Cabin" and their own version of "Custer's Last Stand," ending with Buffalo Bill galloping to the rescue through a cloud of dust only to mouth the words "Too late." The historians cheering in the stands that July afternoon no doubt dismissed Buffalo Bill's history as amateur, but he made a point that Turner's thesis ignored: The West was neither free nor open. The story of the country was a story of fierce and violent contest for land and resources.

In the decades following the Civil War, the United States pursued empire in the American West in Indian wars that lasted until 1890. Pushed off their land and onto reservations, Native Americans resisted as they faced waves of miners and settlers and the transformation of the environment by railroads, mines, barbed wire, and mechanized agriculture. The pastoral agrarianism Turner celebrated in his frontier thesis belied the urban, industrial West already emerging on the Comstock Lode in Nevada and in the commercial farms of California.

Buffalo Bill's mythic West, with its heroic cowboys and noble savages, obscured the complex reality of the West as a fiercely contested terrain. Competing groups of Anglos, Hispanics, former slaves, Chinese, and a host of others arrived seeking the promise of land and riches, while the Indians who inhabited the vast territory struggled to preserve their sovereignty and their cultural identity. And, with its emphasis on the rugged individualism of white men pioneering the frontier, Turner's vision of the West overlooked racial diversity and failed to acknowledge the role of women in community building.

Yet in the waning decade of the nineteenth century, as history blurred with nostalgia, Turner's evocation of the frontier as a crucible for American identity hit a nerve in a population facing rapid changes. A major depression started in May 1893, even before the Columbian Exposition opened its doors. Americans already worried about the economy, immigration, and urban industrialism found in Turner's message a new cause for concern. Would America continue to be America now that the frontier was closed? As they struggled with the question, it became clear that the West did not exist out of place and time. Nor was it particularly exceptional. The problems confronting the United States at the turn of the twentieth century — the exploitation of land and labor, the consolidation of capital, and vicious ethnic and racial rivalries — all played themselves out under western skies.

Buffalo Bill Poster
Buffalo Bill Cody used colorful posters to publicize his Wild West show during the 1880s and 1890s. One of his most popular features was the reenactment of Custer's Last Stand, which he performed for Queen Victoria in London and at the World's Columbian Exposition in Chicago. Sitting Bull, who fought at the Battle of the Little Big Horn, toured with the company in 1885 and traveled to England with the show. Cody's romantic depictions of western history helped create the myth of the Old West. Buffalo Bill Historical Center, Cody, Wyoming.

▶ Conquest and Empire in the West

While the European powers expanded their authority and wealth through imperialism and colonialism, establishing far-flung empires in Asia, Africa, and South America, the United States focused its attention on the West. As posited by **Frederick Jackson Turner**, American exceptionalism stressed how the history of the United States differed from that of European nations, citing America's western frontier as a case in point. Yet recent historians have argued that the process by which the United States expanded its borders in the nineteenth century can best be understood in the global context of imperialism and colonialism — language applied to European powers in this period that makes explicit how expansion in the American West involved the conquest, displacement, and rule over native peoples. (See "Beyond America's Borders," page 542.)

The federal government, through chicanery and conquest, pushed the Indians off their lands (Map 17.1) and onto designated Indian territories or reservations. The Indian wars that followed the Civil War depleted the Native American population and handed the lion's share of Indian land over to white settlers. The decimation of the bison herds inevitably pushed the Plains Indians onto reservations, where they lived as wards of the state. Through the lens of colonialism, we can see how the United States, with its commitment to an imperialist, expansionist ideology, colonized the West.

Indian Removal and the Reservation System

Beginning in the early days of the Republic, the government advocated a policy of **Indian removal**. With plenty of land open in the West, the army removed eastern tribes — often against their will — to territory west of the Mississippi. In the 1830s, President Andrew Jackson pushed the Five Civilized Tribes — the Cherokee, Choctaw, Chickasaw, Creek, and Seminole peoples — off their land in the southern United States. Jackson's Indian removal forced thousands of men, women, and children to leave their homes in Georgia and Tennessee and walk hundreds of miles west. So many died of hunger, exhaustion, and disease along the way that the Cherokees called their path "the trail on which we cried." At the end of this trail of tears stood land set aside as Indian Territory (present-day Oklahoma). Here, the government promised, the Indians could remain "as long as grass shall grow." But hunger for western land soon negated that promise.

Manifest destiny — the belief that the United States had a "God-given" right to aggressively spread the values of white civilization and expand the nation from ocean to ocean — dictated U.S. policy. In the name of manifest destiny, Americans forced the removal of the Five Civilized Tribes to Oklahoma; colonized Texas and won its independence from Mexico in 1836; conquered California, Arizona, New Mexico, and parts of Utah and Colorado in the Mexican-American War of 1846–1848; and invaded Oregon in the mid-1840s.

By midcentury, western land no longer seemed inexhaustible, and instead of removing Indians to the west, the government sought to take control of Indian lands and promised in return to pay annuities and put the Indians on lands reserved for their use — **reservations**. In 1851, some ten thousand Plains Indians came together at Fort Laramie in Wyoming to negotiate a treaty that ceded a wide swath of their land to allow passage of wagon trains headed west. In return, the government promised that the rest of the Indian land would remain inviolate.

The Indians who "touched the pen" to the 1851 **Treaty of Fort Laramie** hoped to preserve their culture in the face of the white onslaught, which had already decimated their population and despoiled their environment. White invaders cut down trees, miners polluted streams, and hunters killed off bison and small game. Whites brought alcohol, guns, and something even more deadly — disease. Smallpox was the biggest killer of Native Americans in the West. Epidemics spread from Mexico up to Canada. Between 1780 and 1870, the population of the Plains tribes declined by half. Cholera, diphtheria, measles, scarlet fever, and other contagious diseases also took their toll. "If I could see this thing, if I knew where it came from, I would go there and fight it," a Cheyenne warrior anguished. Disease shifted the balance of power on the plains from Woodland agrarian tribes like the Mandan and Hidatsa (who died at the rate of 79 percent) to the Lakota (Western) Sioux, who fled the contagion of villages to take up life as equestrian (horse-riding) nomads on the western plains. As the Sioux pushed west, they displaced weaker tribes.

In the Southwest, the Navajo people, like the Cherokee, endured a forced march called the "Long Walk" from their homeland to the desolate Bosque Redondo Reservation in New Mexico in 1864. "This ground we were brought on, it is not productive," complained the Navajo leader Barboncito. "We plant but it does not yield. All the stock we brought here have nearly all died."

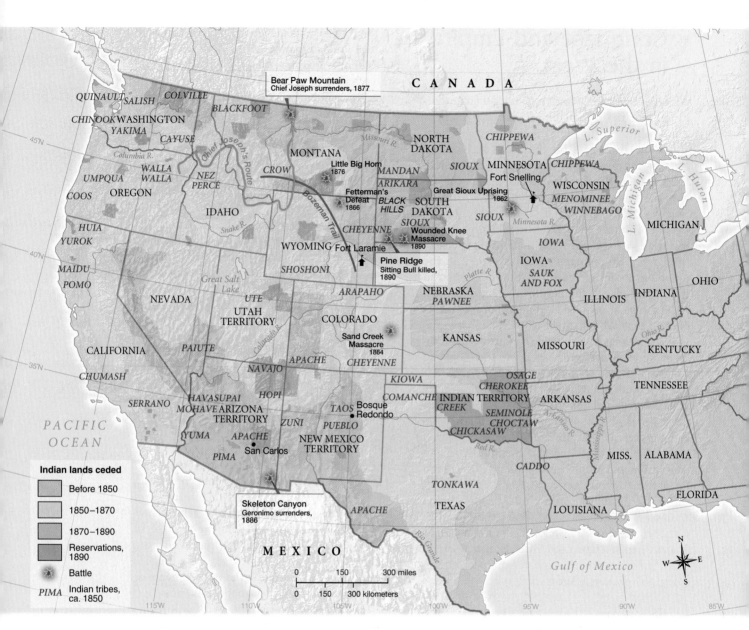

MAP ACTIVITY

Map 17.1 The Loss of Indian Lands, 1850–1890

By 1890, western Indians were isolated on small, scattered reservations. Native Americans had struggled to retain their land in major battles, from the Santee Uprising in Minnesota in 1862 to the massacre at Wounded Knee, South Dakota, in 1890.

READING THE MAP: Where was the largest reservation located in 1890? Which states on this map show no reservations in 1890? Compare this map to Map 17.3, Federal Land Grants to Railroads and the Development of the West.

CONNECTIONS: Why did the federal government force Native Americans onto reservations? What developments prompted these changes?

Poverty and starvation stalked the reservations. Confined by armed force, the Indians eked out an existence on stingy government rations. These once proud peoples found themselves dependent on government handouts and the assistance of Indian agents who, in the words of

Paiute Sarah Winnemucca, did "nothing but fill their pockets." Winnemucca launched a lecture campaign in the United States and Europe denouncing the government's reservation policy.

Styled as stepping-stones on the road to "civilization," Indian reservations closely resembled

Waiting for Rations on the Reservation
Indians who agreed to give up land and go onto reservations received food and clothing rations from the local Indian agency. Here a group of Lakota Sioux gather to receive their goods at the Standing Rock Reservation in 1881. On the right is a ration card from the Rosebud reservation. Indian agencies were notorious for their paltry provisions. Often Indians outwitted the government by taking rations during the winter, when they were hungry, only to leave the reservation to resume their nomadic hunting life during the summer season. The decimation of the great bison herds drove them permanently onto the reservations in the 1880s. Photograph: National Anthropological Archives, Smithsonian Institution, Washington, D.C.; ration ticket: National Museum of the American Indian, Smithsonian Institution (239391), Washington, D.C. Photos by Photo Services.

colonial societies where native populations, ruled by outside bureaucrats, saw their culture assaulted, their religious practices outlawed, their children sent away to school, and their way of life attacked in the name of progress and civilization. Self-styled "friends of the Indians," many of them easterners with little experience in the West, maintained that reservations would provide a classroom of civilization where Indians could be taught to speak English, to worship a Christian god, to give up hunting for farming, and to reject tribal ways.

To Americans raised on theories of racial superiority, the Indians constituted, in the words of one Colorado militia major, "an obstacle to civilization . . . [and] should be exterminated." This attitude pervaded the military, and the cavalry annihilated entire villages with ruthless efficiency. In November 1864 at the Sand Creek massacre in Colorado Territory, Colonel John M. Chivington and his Colorado militia descended on a village of Cheyenne, mostly women and children. Their leader, Black Kettle, raised a white flag and an American flag to signal surrender, but the charging cavalry

ignored his signal and butchered 270 Indians. Chivington watched as his men scalped and mutilated their victims and later justified the killing of Indian children with the terse remark, "Nits make lice." The city of Denver treated Chivington and his men as heroes, but a congressional inquiry castigated the soldiers for their "fiendish malignity" and condemned the "savage cruelty" of the massacre.

The Decimation of the Great Bison Herds

In the centuries following the arrival of the first European settlers, the great herds of buffalo (American bison), once numbering as many as thirty million, fell into serious decline. A host of environmental and human factors contributed to the destruction of the bison. The dynamic ecology of the Great Plains, with its droughts, fires, and blizzards, combined with the ecological imperialism of humans (Indian buffalo-robe traders as well as whites and their cattle), put increasing pressure on the bison. By the 1850s,

SLAUGHTERED FOR THE HIDE.—[See Page 1002.]

VISUAL ACTIVITY

"Slaughtered for the Hide"

In 1874, *Harper's Weekly* featured this cover with its illustration of a buffalo hide hunter skinning a carcass on the southwestern plains. By 1872, the Santa Fe railroad reached Kansas, making Dodge City the center for the shipment of buffalo hides to the East, where they were made into leather belting used to run the nation's machinery. In a matter of months, hunters decimated the great southern bison herds. City father Colonel Richard Dodge wrote of the carnage, "The air was foul with sickening stench, and the vast plain which only a short twelve months before teemed with animal life, was a dead, solitary putrid desert." Dodge estimated that hunters slaughtered more than three million bison between 1872 and 1874. The grim reality of the trade makes the magazine's subtitle, "A Journal of Civilization," highly ironic. Library of Congress.

READING THE IMAGE: What virtues and stereotypes of the West does this magazine cover extol?

CONNECTIONS: How might the notion of "civilization" have differed according to the Native American perspective?

a combination of drought and commerce had driven the great herds onto the far western plains.

After the Civil War, the accelerating pace of industrial expansion brought about the near extinction of the bison. Industrial demand for heavy leather belting used in machinery and the development of larger, more accurate rifles combined to hasten the slaughter of the bison. At the same time, the nation's growing transcontinental rail system cut the range in two and divided the herds. For the Sioux and other nomadic tribes of the plains, the buffalo constituted a way of life — a source of food, fuel, and shelter and a central part of their religion and rituals. To the railroads, the bison were a nuisance, at best a cheap source of meat for their workers and a target for sport. "It will not be long before all the buffaloes are extinct near and between the railroads," Ohio senator John Sherman predicted in 1868.

In the end, the army took credit for the conquest of the Plains Indians, but victory came about largely as a result of the decimation of the great bison herds. General Philip Sheridan acknowledged as much when he applauded white hide hunters for "destroying the Indians' commissary." With their food supply gone, Indians had to choose between starvation and the reservation. "A cold wind blew across the prairie when the last buffalo fell," the great Sioux leader **Sitting Bull** lamented, "a death wind for my people."

On the southern plains in 1867, more than five thousand warring Comanches, Kiowas, and Southern Arapahos gathered at Medicine Lodge Creek in Kansas to negotiate a treaty. Satak, or Sitting Bear, a prominent Kiowa chief and medicine man, explained why the Indians sought peace: "In the far-distant past . . . the world seemed large enough for both the red man and the white man." But, he observed, "its broad plains seem now to contract, and the white man grows jealous of his red brother." To preserve their land from white encroachment, the Indians signed the Treaty of Medicine Lodge, agreeing to move to a reservation. Yet they continued to leave the reservation's confines to hunt during the summer months. After 1870, hide hunters poured into the region, and within a decade they had nearly exterminated the southern bison herds. Luther Standing Bear recounted the sight and stench: "I saw the bodies of hundreds of dead buffalo lying about, just wasting, and the odor was terrible. . . . They were letting our food lie on the plains to rot." With the buffalo gone, the Indians faced starvation and reluctantly moved to the reservations.

Indian Wars and the Collapse of Comanchería

The Indian wars in the West marked the last resistance of a Native American population devastated by disease and demoralized by the removal policy pursued by the federal government. More accurately called "settlers' wars" (since they began with "peaceful settlers," often miners, overrunning Native American land), the wars flared up again only a few years after the signing of the Fort Laramie treaty. The Dakota Sioux in Minnesota went to war in 1862. For years, under the leadership of Chief Little Crow, the Dakota, also known as the Santee, had pursued a policy of accommodation, ceding land in return for the promise of annuities. But with his people on the verge of starvation (the local Indian agent told the hungry Dakota, "Go and eat grass"), Little Crow reluctantly led his angry warriors in a desperate campaign against the intruders, killing more than 1,000 settlers. American troops quelled what was called the Great Sioux Uprising (also called the Santee Uprising) and marched 1,700 Sioux to Fort Snelling, where 400 Indians were put on trial for murder and 38 died in the largest mass execution in American history.

After the Civil War, President Ulysses S. Grant faced the prospect of protracted Indian war on the Great Plains. Reluctant to spend more money and sacrifice more lives in battle, Grant adopted a "peace policy" designed to segregate and control the Indians while opening up land to white settlers. This policy won the support of both friends of the Indians, who feared for their survival, and Indian haters, who coveted their land and wished to confine them to the least desirable areas in the West. General William Tecumseh Sherman summed up the new Indian policy succinctly: "Remove all to a safe place and then reduce them to a helpless condition." The army herded the Indians onto reservations (see Map 17.1), where the U.S. Bureau of Indian Affairs supposedly ministered to their needs. But peace in the West remained elusive.

The great Indian empire of **Comanchería**, which in the eighteenth century stretched from the Canadian plains to Mexico, by 1865 numbered fewer than five thousand Comanches, who ranged from west Texas north to Oklahoma. Through decades of dealings with the Spanish and French, the Comanches had built a complex empire based on trade in horses, hides, guns, and captives. Expert equestrians, the Comanches inaugurated the horse-centered way of life that eventually came to characterize the Plains Indians.

In 1871, Grant's peace policy in the West gave way to all-out warfare as the U.S. Army dispatched three thousand soldiers to wipe out the remains of the Comanche empire. Comanchería had been greatly reduced, but Comanche raiding parties took a toll in lives and livestock and virtually obliterated white settlements in west Texas. To defeat the Indians, the army adopted the tactics General William Sherman had used in his march through Confederate Georgia during the Civil War. At the decisive battle of Palo Duro Canyon in 1874, only three Comanche warriors died in battle, but U.S. soldiers took the Indians' camp, burning more than two hundred tepees, hundreds of robes and blankets, and thousands of pounds of winter supplies and shooting more than a thousand horses. Coupled with the decimation of the bison, the army's scorched-earth policy led to the final collapse of the Comanche people — more an economic than a military defeat. Crippled by poverty, malnutrition, and the loss of their trading-raiding economy, the surviving Indians of Comanchería, now numbering fewer than 1,500, reluctantly retreated to the reservation at Fort Sill.

The Fight for the Black Hills

On the northern plains, the fever for gold fueled the conflict between Indians and Euro-Americans. In 1866, the Cheyenne united with the Sioux in Wyoming to protect their hunting grounds in the Powder River valley, which were threatened by the construction of the Bozeman Trail connecting Fort Laramie with the goldfields in Montana. Captain William Fetterman, who had boasted that with eighty men he could ride through the Sioux nation, was killed along with all of his troops in an Indian attack. The Sioux's impressive victories led to the second **Treaty of Fort Laramie** in 1868, in which the United States agreed to abandon the Bozeman Trail and guaranteed the Indians control of the **Black Hills**, land sacred to the Lakota Sioux.

The second Treaty of Fort Laramie was full of contradictions — in one breath promising to preserve Indian land and in the next forcing the tribes to relinquish all territory outside their reservations. A controversial provision of the treaty guaranteed the Indians access to their traditional hunting grounds "so long as the buffalo may range thereon in such numbers as to justify the chase." With the bison facing extermination, the provision was ominous. Yet the government's fork-tongued promises induced some of the tribes to accept the treaty. The great Sioux chief Red Cloud led many of his people onto the reservation. Red Cloud soon

Imperialism, Colonialism, and the Treatment of the Sioux and the Zulu

Viewed through the lens of colonialism, the British war with the Zulu in South Africa offers a compelling contrast to the United States' war against the Lakota Sioux. The Zulu, like the Sioux, came to power as a result of devastating intertribal warfare. In the area that is today the KwaZulu-Natal province of the Republic of South Africa, the Zulu king Shaka united his empire by 1826 with an army of more than twenty thousand. And like the Sioux, the Zulu earned a formidable reputation as brave warriors who fought to protect their land from white encroachment.

In 1806, the British seized the Cape of Good Hope to secure shipping interests, leading to conflicts with Dutch-speaking settlers there known as the Boers, who had inhabited the southern tip of Africa since the seventeenth century. Clashes between Britons and Boers eventually resulted in the Great Trek, the migration of nearly twelve thousand Boers northeastward beginning in 1835. There they claimed land and established the South African Republic (the Transvaal) in 1853 and the Orange Free State in 1854, both independent of British rule. But the Great Trek brought the Boers into Zululand, where they met with bloody resistance.

The Zulu lived in a highly complex society, with all the young men organized into *amabutho*, regiments of warriors arranged by age and bound to local chiefs under the supreme command of the Zulu king, who demanded obedience and bravery. During his harsh reign, Shaka inspected his regiments after each battle, picking out cowards and putting them to death on the spot. Young men could not start their own households without the local chief's permission, thus ensuring an ample stock of warriors and making the Zulu army, in the words of one English observer, "a celibate, man-slaying machine." The Boer settlers repeatedly faced the wrath of the Zulu, who slaughtered the first trekkers to arrive in Zululand and raided Boer settlements to steal cattle.

The British entered the fray in 1879, sparking the Anglo-Zulu War, which a recent historian has condemned as being "as unnecessary as it was unjust." Sir Theophilus Shepstone, British secretary for native affairs, hinted at Britain's motive when he wrote in 1878, "Had [its] 30,000 warriors been in time changed to labourers working for wages, Zululand would have been a prosperous peaceful country instead of what it is now, a source of perpetual danger to itself and its neighbors."

With aims of both placating the Boers and securing a source of labor for British economic expansion — made paramount by the discovery of diamonds in the region — British troops under Lord Chelmsford invaded Zululand. Leading soldiers armed with the latest rifles and artillery, Chelmsford — with a confidence reminiscent of that of George Armstrong Custer — expected to subdue the Zulu easily. But in January 1879, at the battle of Isandhlwana, the Zulu army of

Zululand and Cape Colony, 1878

British
Boer Republics

KALAHARI DESERT
TRANSVAAL
ORANGE FREE STATE
ZULULAND
Isandlwana
CAPE COLONY
ATLANTIC OCEAN
INDIAN OCEAN
Cape Town

---

regretted his decision. "Think of it!" he told a visitor to the Pine Ridge Reservation. "I, who used to own . . . country so extensive that I could not ride through it in a week . . . must tell Washington when I am hungry. I must beg for that which I own." Several Sioux chiefs, among them **Crazy Horse** of the Oglala band and Sitting Bull of the Hunkpapa, refused to sign the treaty. Crazy Horse said that he wanted no part of the "piecemeal penning" of his people.

In 1874, the discovery of gold in the Black Hills of the Dakotas led the government to break its promise to Red Cloud. Miners began pouring into the region, and the Northern Pacific Railroad made plans to lay track. Lieutenant Colonel **George Armstrong Custer**, whose troopers found gold in the area, trumpeted news of the strike. At first, the government offered to purchase the Black Hills. But to the Lakota Sioux, the Black Hills were sacred — "the heart of everything that is." They refused to sell. The army responded by issuing an ultimatum ordering all Lakota Sioux and Northern Cheyenne bands onto the Pine Ridge Reservation and threatening to hunt down those who refused.

more than 25,000 surprised a British encampment. In less than two hours, more than 4,000 Zulu and British were killed. Only a handful of British soldiers managed to escape, and Chelmsford lost 1,300 officers and men.

When news of Isandhlwana reached London, commentators compared the massacre to Custer's defeat at the Little Big Horn three years earlier and noted that native forces armed with spears had defeated a modern army. The military disaster shocked and outraged the nation, damaging the British military's reputation of invincibility.

Vowing that the Zulu would "pay dearly for their triumph of a day," the British immediately launched unconditional war against the Zulu. In the ensuing battles, neither side took prisoners. The Zulu beat the British twice more, but after seven months the British finally routed the Zulu army and abandoned Zululand to its fate — partition, starvation, and civil war.

Historians would later compare the British victory to the U.S. Army's defeat of the Sioux in the American West, but the Zulu and Sioux met different economic fates. As Shepstone hinted in 1878, the British goal had been to subdue the Zulu and turn them into cheap labor. Compared to the naked economic exploitation of the Zulu, the U.S. policy toward the Sioux, with its forced assimilation on reservations and its misguided attempts to turn the nomadic tribes into sedentary, God-fearing farmers, may seem less exploitative if no less ruthless in its cultural imperialism.

Zulu Warriors

Chief Ngoza (center) poses with Zulu men in full war dress. Their distinctive cowhide shields date to the reign of King Shaka. Each warrior also carried two or three throwing spears and an *ikwa*, or flat-bladed stabbing spear used in close combat. Zulu warriors marched at the double and could cover up to fifty miles a day. Campbell Collections of the University of KwaZulu-Natal.

Both the Little Big Horn and Isandhlwana became legends that spawned a romantic image of the "noble savage": fierce in battle, honored in defeat. Describing this myth, historian James Gump, who has chronicled the subjugation of the Sioux and the Zulu, observed, "Each western culture simultaneously dehumanized and glamorized the Sioux and Zulu," and noted that the noble savage mythology was "a product of the racist ideologies of the late nineteenth century as well as the guilt and compassion associated with the bloody costs of empire building."

Imperial powers, both Britain and the United States defeated indigenous rivals and came to dominate their lands (and, in the case of the Zulu, their labor) in the global expansion that marked the nineteenth century.

America in a Global Context

1. How was the British war with the Zulu similar to and different from the American war with the Sioux?

2. Compare the fate of the defeated Zulu with that of the Sioux.

In the summer of 1876, the army launched a three-pronged attack led by Custer, General **George Crook**, and Colonel John Gibbon. Crazy Horse stopped Crook at the Battle of the Rosebud. Custer, leading the second prong of the army's offensive, divided his troops and ordered an attack. On June 25, he spotted signs of the Indians' camp. Crying "Hurrah Boys, we've got them," he led 265 men of the Seventh Cavalry into the largest Indian camp ever assembled on the Great Plains, more than 8,000 Indians. Nomadic bands of Sioux, Cheyenne, and Arapaho had come together for a summer buffalo hunt and camped along the banks of the Greasy Grass River (whites called it the Little Big Horn). Indian warriors led by Sitting Bull and Crazy Horse set upon Custer and his men and quickly annihilated them. "It took us about as long as a hungry man to eat his dinner," the Cheyenne chief Two Moons recalled. Gibbon arrived two days later to discover the carnage.

"Custer's Last Stand," as the **Battle of the Little Big Horn** was styled in myth, turned out to be the last stand for the Sioux. The Indians'

Crazy Horse at the Little Big Horn
This pictograph by Amos Bad Heart Bull, an Oglala Sioux from the Pine Ridge Reservation, pictures Crazy Horse at the center of the battle of the Little Big Horn. Although the artist was only seven years old in 1876, he based his pictures on the recollections of his uncle and other Oglala elders. Crazy Horse ritually prepared for battle by painting hail stones on his body, wearing a small stone tied behind one ear, and placing a single eagle feather in his hair. According to one of the Arapaho warriors who fought beside him against Custer, Crazy Horse "was the bravest man he ever saw." The Granger Collection, New York.

nomadic way of life meant they could not remain a combined force for long. The bands that had massed at the Little Big Horn scattered, and the army hunted them down. "Wherever we went," wrote the Oglala holy man Black Elk, "the soldiers came to kill us." In 1877, Crazy Horse was captured and killed. Four years later, in 1881, Sitting Bull surrendered. The government took the Black Hills and confined the Lakota to the Great Sioux Reservation. The Sioux never accepted the loss of the Black Hills. In 1923, they filed suit, demanding the return of the land illegally taken from them. After a protracted court battle lasting nearly sixty years, the U.S. Supreme Court ruled in 1980 that the government had illegally abrogated the Treaty of Fort Laramie and upheld an award of $122.5 million in compensation to the tribes. The Sioux refused the settlement and continue to press for the return of the Black Hills.

> **REVIEW** How did the slaughter of the bison contribute to the Plains Indians' removal to reservations?

▶ Forced Assimilation and Resistance Strategies

More than two hundred years of contact with whites utterly transformed Native American societies. The indigenous peoples Christopher Columbus had mistakenly dubbed "Indians" included more than five hundred distinct tribal entities with different languages, myths, religions, and physical appearance. According to the census of 1900, the Indian population in the continental United States stood at 250,000 (admittedly an undercount), down from estimates as high as 15 million at the time of first contact with Europeans. Not only had the population been decimated by war, disease, and the obliteration of the bison, but Indian lands had shrunk so much that by 1890 Euro-Americans controlled 97.5 percent of the territory formerly occupied by Native Americans.

Imperialistic attitudes of whites toward Indians continued to evolve in the late nineteenth century. To "civilize" the Indians, the U.S. government sought to force assimilation on their children. Reservations, once designed as stepping-stones to civilization, became increasingly unpopular among whites who coveted Indian land. A new policy of allotment gained favor. It promised to put Indians on parcels of land, forcing them into farming, and then to redistribute the rest of the land to settlers. In the face of this ongoing assault on their way of life, Indians actively resisted, contested, and adapted to colonial rule.

Indian Schools and the War against Indian Culture

Indian schools constituted the cultural battleground of the Indian wars in the West, their avowed purpose being "to destroy the Indian in him and save the man." In 1877, Congress appropriated funds for Indian education, reasoning that "it was less expensive to educate Indians than to kill them." Virginia's Hampton Institute, created in 1868 to school newly freed slaves, accepted its first Indian students in 1878. Although many Indian schools operated on the reservations, authorities much preferred boarding facilities that isolated students from the "contamination" of tribal values.

Many Native American parents resisted sending their children away. When all else failed, the military kidnapped the children and sent them off to school. An agent at the Mescalero Apache Agency in Arizona Territory reported in 1886 that "it became necessary to visit the camps unexpectedly with a detachment of police, and seize such children as were proper and take them away to school, willing or unwilling." The parents put up a struggle. "Some hurried their children off to the mountains or hid them away in camp, and the police had to chase and capture them like so many wild rabbits," the agent observed. "This unusual proceeding created quite an outcry. The men were sullen and muttering, the women loud in their lamentations and the children almost out of their wits with fright." Once at school, the children were stripped and scrubbed, their clothing and belongings were confiscated, and their hair was hacked off and doused with kerosene to kill lice. Issued stiff new uniforms, shoes, and what one boy recalled as the "torture" of woolen long underwear, the children often lost not only their possessions but also their names: Hehakaavita (Yellow Elk) became Thomas Goodwood; Polingaysi Qoyawayma became Elizabeth White.

Hampton Pageant, 1892
The Indian students in this picture are dressed for Columbia's Roll Call, a pageant at Hampton Institute honoring the nation's heroes on Indian Citizen Day, 1892. Among others portrayed are Christopher Columbus, Pocahontas, George Washington, and, in the center, a student dressed as Columbia, symbol of the Republic, draped in the American flag. There was no mention of Crazy Horse, Sitting Bull, or Geronimo, all Indians who resisted white encroachment and appropriation of their land in the West. Courtesy of Hampton University Archives.

The curriculum featured agricultural and manual arts for boys and domestic skills for girls, training designed to make Indians "willing workers" who would no longer be a burden to the government. The **Carlisle Indian School** in Pennsylvania, founded in 1879, became the model for later institutions. To encourage assimilation, Carlisle pioneered the "outing system" — sending students to live with white families during summer vacations. The policy reflected the school's slogan: "To civilize the Indian, get him into civilization. To keep him civilized, let him stay."

Merrill Gates, a member of the Board of Indian Commissioners, summed up the goal of Indian education: "To get the Indian out of the blanket and into trousers, — and trousers with a pocket in them, *and with a pocket that aches to be filled with dollars!*" Gates's faith in the "civilizing" power of the dollar reflected the unabashed materialism of the Gilded Age. But the cultural annihilation that Gates cheerfully predicted did not prove so easy.

The Dawes Act and Indian Land Allotment

In the 1880s, the practice of rounding up Indians and herding them onto reservations lost momentum in favor of allotment — a new policy designed to encourage assimilation through farming and the ownership of private property. Americans vowing to avenge Custer urged the government to get tough with the Indians. Reservations, they argued, took up too much good land that white settlers could put to better use. At the same time, people sympathetic to the Indians were appalled at the desperate poverty on the reservations and feared for the Indians' survival. Helen Hunt Jackson, in her classic work *A Century of Dishonor* (1881), convinced many readers that the Indians had been treated unfairly. "Our Indian policy," the *New York Times* concluded, "is usually spoliation behind the mask of benevolence."

> "Our Indian policy is usually spoliation behind the mask of benevolence"
>
> — The *New York Times*

The Indian Rights Association, a group of mainly white easterners formed in 1882, campaigned for the dismantling of the reservations, now viewed as obstacles to progress. To "cease to treat the Indian as a red man and treat him as a man" meant putting an end to tribal communalism and fostering individualism. "Selfishness," declared Senator Henry Dawes of Massachusetts, "is at the bottom of civilization." Dawes called for "allotment in severalty" — the institution of private property.

In 1887, Congress passed the **Dawes Allotment Act**, dividing up reservations and allotting parcels of land to individual Indians as private property. Each unmarried Indian man and woman as well as married men and children (married women were excluded) became eligible to receive 160 acres of land from reservation property. Indians who took allotments earned U.S. citizenship. To protect Indians from land speculators, the government held most of the allotted land in trust, and the Indians could not sell it for twenty-five years. Since Indian land far surpassed the acreage needed for allotments, the government reserved the right to sell the "surplus" to white settlers.

The Dawes Act effectively reduced Indian land from 138 million acres to a scant 48 million. The legislation, in the words of one critic, worked "to despoil the Indians of their lands and to make them vagabonds on the face of the earth." The Dawes Act completed the dispossession of the western Indian peoples and dealt a crippling blow to traditional tribal culture. Amended in 1891 and again in 1906, it remained in effect until 1934, when the United States restored the right of Native Americans to own land communally (as discussed in chapter 24).

Indian Resistance and Survival

Faced with the extinction of their entire way of life, different groups of Indians responded in different ways in the waning decades of the nineteenth century. In the 1870s, Comanche and Kiowa raiding parties frustrated the U.S. Army by using the reservation at Fort Sill as an asylum, knowing that troops could not pursue them onto reservation land. They brazenly used the reservations as a seasonal supply base during the winter months, taking the meager annuities doled out by the Indian agents, only to resume their nomadic ways when spring came. Soon other tribes followed their lead.

Some tribes, including the Crow, Arikara, Pawnee, and Shoshoni, chose to fight alongside the army against their old enemies, the Sioux. The Crow chief Plenty Coups explained why he allied with the United States: "Not because we loved the white man . . . or because we hated the Sioux . . . but because we plainly saw that this course was the only one which might save our beautiful country for us." The Crow and Shoshoni got to stay in their homelands and avoided the fate of other tribes shipped to reservations far away.

Indians who refused to stay on reservations risked being hunted down — a clear indication that reservations were intended to keep Indians in, not to keep whites out, as the friends of the Indians had intended. The Nez Percé war of 1877 is perhaps the most harrowing example of the army's policy. In 1863, the government dictated a treaty drastically reducing Nez Percé land. Most of the chiefs refused to sign the treaty and did not move to the reservation. In 1877, the army issued an ultimatum — come in to the reservation or be hunted down. Some eight hundred Nez Percé people, many of them women and children, fled across the mountains of Idaho, Wyoming, and Montana, heading for the safety of Canada. At the end of their 1,300-mile trek, 50 miles from freedom, they stopped to rest in the snow. The army's Indian scouts spotted their tepees, and the soldiers attacked. Yellow Wolf recalled their plight: "Children crying with cold. No fire. There could be no light. Everywhere the crying, the death wail." After a five-day siege, the Nez Percé leader, **Chief Joseph**, surrendered.

Chief Joseph
Chief Joseph came to symbolize the heroic resistance of the Nez Percé. General Nelson Miles promised the Nez Percé that they could return to their homeland if they surrendered. But he betrayed them, as he would betray the Apache people seven years later. The Nez Percé were shipped off to Indian Territory (Oklahoma). In 1879, Chief Joseph traveled to Washington, D.C., to speak for his people. "Let me be a free man," he pleaded, "free to choose my own teachers, free to follow the religion of my fathers, free to think and talk and act for myself — and I will obey every law." National Anthropological Archives, Smithsonian Institution, Washington, D.C. (#2906).

His speech, reported by a white soldier, would become famous. "I am tired of fighting," he said as he surrendered his rifle. "Our chiefs are killed. It is cold and we have no blankets. The little children are freezing to death. . . . I am tired.

My heart is sick and sad. From where the sun now stands, I will fight no more forever."

In the Southwest, the Apaches resorted to armed resistance. They roamed the Sonoran Desert of southern Arizona and northern Mexico, perfecting a hit-and-run guerrilla warfare that terrorized white settlers and bedeviled the army in the 1870s and 1880s. General George Crook combined a policy of dogged pursuit with judicious diplomacy. Crook relied on Indian scouts to track the raiding parties, recruiting nearly two hundred, including Apaches, Navajos, and Paiutes. By 1882, Crook had succeeded in persuading most of the Apaches to settle on the San Carlos Reservation in Arizona Territory. A desolate piece of desert inhabited by scorpions and rattlesnakes, San Carlos, in the words of one Apache, was "the worst place in all the great territory stolen from the Apaches."

Geronimo, a respected shaman (medicine man) of the Chiricahua Apache, refused to stay at San Carlos and repeatedly led raiding parties in the early 1880s. His warriors attacked ranches to obtain ammunition and horses. Among Geronimo's band was **Lozen**, a woman who rode with the warriors, armed with a rifle and a cartridge belt. The sister of a great chief who described her as being as "strong as a man, braver than most, and cunning in strategy," Lozen never married and remained a warrior in Geronimo's band even after her brother's death. In the spring of 1885, Geronimo and his followers, including Lozen, went on a ten-month offensive, moving from the Apache sanctuary in the Sierra Madre to raid and burn ranches and towns on both sides of the Mexican border. General Crook caught up with Geronimo in the fall and persuaded him to return to San Carlos, only to have him slip away on the way back to the reservation. Chagrined, Crook resigned his post. General **Nelson Miles**, Crook's replacement, adopted a policy of hunt and destroy.

Geronimo's band of thirty-three Apaches, including women and children, managed to elude Miles's troops for more than five months. In the end, this small band fought two thousand soldiers to a stalemate. After months of pursuit, Lieutenant Leonard Wood, a member of Miles's spit-and-polish cavalry, discarded his horse and most of his clothes until he was reduced to wearing nothing "but a pair of canton flannel drawers, and an old blue blouse, a pair of moccasins and a hat without a crown."

Eventually, Miles's scouts cornered Geronimo in 1886 at Skeleton Canyon. Caught between Mexican regulars and the U.S. Army, Geronimo agreed to march north with the soldiers and negotiate a settlement. "We have not slept for six months," he admitted, "and we are worn out." Although fewer than three dozen Apaches had been considered "hostile," when General Miles induced them to surrender, the government rounded up nearly five hundred Apaches, including the scouts who had helped track Geronimo, and sent them as prisoners to Florida. By 1889, more than a quarter of them had died, some as a result of illnesses contracted in the damp lowland climate and some by suicide. Their plight roused public opinion, and in 1892 they were moved to Fort Sill in Oklahoma and later to New Mexico.

Geronimo lived to become something of a celebrity. He appeared at the St. Louis Exposition in 1904, and he rode in President Theodore Roosevelt's inaugural parade in 1905. In a newspaper interview, he confessed, "I want to go to my old home before I die. . . . Want to go back to the mountains again. I asked the Great White Father to allow me to go back, but he said no." None of the Apaches were permitted to return to Arizona; when Geronimo died in 1909, he was buried in Oklahoma.

On the plains, many tribes turned to a nonviolent form of resistance — a compelling new religion called the **Ghost Dance**. The Paiute shaman Wovoka, drawing on a cult that had developed in the 1870s, combined elements of Christianity and traditional Indian religion to found the Ghost

Dance religion in 1889. Wovoka claimed that he had received a vision in which the Great Spirit spoke through him to all Indians, prophesying that if they would unite in the Ghost Dance ritual, whites would be destroyed in an apocalypse. The shaman promised that Indian warriors slain in battle would return to life and that buffalo once again would roam the land unimpeded. This religion, born of despair and with a message of hope, spread like wildfire over the plains. The Ghost Dance was performed in Idaho, Montana, Utah, Wyoming, Colorado, Nebraska, Kansas, the Dakotas, and Indian Territory by tribes as diverse as the Sioux, Arapaho, Cheyenne, Pawnee, and Shoshoni. Dancers often went into hypnotic trances, dancing until they dropped from exhaustion.

The Ghost Dance was nonviolent, but it frightened whites, especially when the Sioux taught that wearing a white ghost shirt made Indians immune to soldiers' bullets. Soon whites began to fear an uprising. "Indians are dancing in the snow and are wild and crazy," wrote the Bureau of Indian Affairs agent at the Pine Ridge Reservation in South Dakota. Frantic, he pleaded for reinforcements. "We are at the mercy of these dancers. We need protection, and we need it now." President Benjamin Harrison dispatched several thousand federal troops to Sioux country to handle any outbreak.

Ghost Dancers
Arapaho women at the Darlington Agency in Indian Territory (Oklahoma) participate in the Ghost Dance. Different tribes performed variations of the dance, but generally dancers formed a circle and danced until they reached the trancelike state shown here. The ceremonial drum (right) features a drawing of a thunderbird. Whites feared the dancers and demanded that the army dispatch troops to subdue them. The result was the killing of Sitting Bull and the massacre at Wounded Knee.
Ghost Dance: National Anthropological Archives, Smithsonian Institution, Washington, D.C. (#81-9626); Drum: Collection of Charles Stoneroad, Courtesy of the Oakland Museum of California.

In December 1890, when Sitting Bull joined the Ghost Dance, he was killed by Indian police as they tried to arrest him at his cabin on the Standing Rock Reservation. His people, fleeing the scene, joined with a larger group of Miniconjou Sioux, who were apprehended by the Seventh Cavalry, Custer's old regiment, near Wounded Knee Creek, South Dakota. As the Indians laid down their arms, a soldier attempted to take a rifle from a deaf Miniconjou man, and the gun went off. The soldiers opened fire. In the ensuing melee, Indian men, women, and children were mowed down in minutes by the army's brutally efficient Hotchkiss rapid-fire guns. Caught in the crossfire, one Indian recounted, "I saw my friends sinking about me, and heard the whine of many bullets." In a matter of minutes, eighty-three Indian men lay dead. The cavalry then hunted down women and children attempting to flee into the bluffs and canyons. The next day, more than two hundred Sioux lay dead or dying in the snow.

Settler Jules Sandoz surveyed the scene the day after the massacre at **Wounded Knee**. "Here in ten minutes an entire community was as the buffalo that bleached on the plains," he wrote. "There was something loose in the world that hated joy and happiness as it hated brightness and color, reducing everything to drab agony and gray." It had taken Euro-Americans 250 years to wrest control of the eastern half of the United States from the Indians. It took them less than 40 years to take the western half. The subjugation of the American Indians marked the first chapter in a national mission of empire that would presage overseas imperialistic adventures in Asia, Latin America, the Caribbean, and the Pacific islands.

REVIEW In what ways did different Indian groups defy and resist colonial rule?

▶ Gold Fever and the Mining West

Mining stood at the center of the United States' quest for empire in the West. The California gold rush of 1849 touched off the frenzy. The four decades following witnessed equally frenetic rushes for gold and other metals, most notably on the **Comstock Lode** in Nevada and later in New Mexico, Colorado, the Dakotas, Montana, Idaho, Arizona, and Utah. Each rush built on the last, producing new mining technologies and innovations in financing as hordes of miners,

eager to strike it rich, moved from one boomtown to the next. Mining in the West, however, was a story not only of boom and bust but also of community building and the development of territories into states (Map 17.2).

At first glance, the mining West may seem much different from the East, but by the 1870s the term *urban industrialism* described Virginia City, Nevada, as accurately as it did Pittsburgh or Cleveland. A close look at mining on the Comstock Lode indicates some of the patterns and paradoxes of western mining. The diversity of peoples drawn to the West by the promise of mining riches and land made the region the most cosmopolitan in the nation, as well as the most contested. And a look at territorial government uncovers striking parallels with the corruption and cupidity in politics east of the Mississippi.

Mining on the Comstock Lode

By 1859, refugees from California's played-out goldfields flocked to the Washoe basin in Nevada. There prospectors found the gold they sought mired in blackish sand they called "that blasted blue stuff." Eventually, an enterprising miner had the stuff assayed, and it turned out that the Washoe miners had stumbled on the richest vein of silver ore on the continent — the legendary Comstock Lode, named for prospector Henry Comstock.

To exploit even potentially valuable silver claims required capital and expensive technology well beyond the means of the prospector. An active San Francisco stock market sprang up to finance operations on the Comstock. Shrewd businessmen soon recognized that the easiest way to get rich was not to mine at all but to sell their claims or to form mining companies and sell shares of stock. The most unscrupulous mined the wallets of gullible investors by selling shares in bogus mines. Speculation, misrepresentation, and outright thievery ran rampant. In twenty years, more than $300 million poured from the earth in Nevada alone. A little stayed in Virginia City, but a great deal more went to speculators in California, some of whom got rich without ever leaving San Francisco.

The promise of gold and silver drew thousands to the mines of the West, the honest as well as the unprincipled. As author Mark Twain observed in Virginia City's *Territorial Enterprise*, "All the peoples of the earth had representative adventures in the Silverland." Irish, Chinese, Germans, English, Scots, Welsh, Canadians, Mexicans, Italians, Scandinavians, French, Swiss,

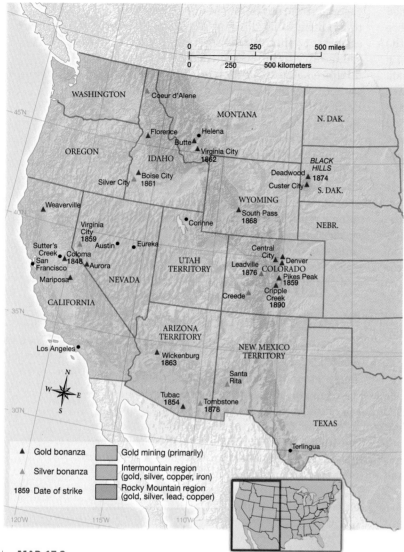

MAP 17.2
Western Mining, 1848–1890
Rich deposits of gold, silver, copper, lead, and iron larded the mountains of the West, from the Sierra Nevada of California to the Rockies of Colorado and the Black Hills of South Dakota. Beginning with the gold strike on Sutter's Creek in California in 1848 and continuing through the rush for gold in Cripple Creek, Colorado, in 1890, miners from all over the world flocked to the West. Few struck it rich, but many stayed on as paid workers in the increasingly mechanized corporate mines.

became Nevada, as many as 30 percent of the people came from outside the United States, compared to 25 percent in New York and 21 percent in Massachusetts.

Irish immigrants formed the largest ethnic group in the mining district. In Virginia City, fully one-third of the population claimed at least one parent from Ireland. Irish and Irish American women constituted the largest group of women on the Comstock. As servants, boardinghouse owners, and washerwomen, they made up a significant part of the workforce. By contrast, the Chinese community, numbering 642 in 1870, remained overwhelmingly male. Virulent anti-Chinese sentiment barred the men from work in the mines, but despite the violent anti-Asian rhetoric, the mining community came to depend on Chinese labor. Many boardinghouses and affluent homes employed a Chinese cook or servant along with an Irish parlor maid.

As was so often the case in the West, where Euro-American ambitions clashed with Native American ways, the discovery of precious metals on the Comstock spelled disaster for the Indians. No sooner had the miners struck pay dirt than they demanded that army troops "hunt Indians" and establish forts to protect transportation to and from the diggings. This sudden and dramatic intrusion left Nevada's native tribes — the Northern Paiute and Bannock Shoshoni — exiles in their own land. At first they resisted, but over time they made peace with the invaders and developed resourceful strategies to adapt and preserve their culture and identity despite the havoc wreaked by western mining and settlement.

In 1873, Comstock miners uncovered a new vein of ore, a veritable cavern of gold and silver. This "Big Bonanza" speeded the transition from small-scale industry to corporate oligopoly, creating a radically new social and economic environment. The Comstock became a laboratory for new mining technology. Huge stamping mills pulverized rock with pistonlike hammers driven by steam engines. Enormous Cornish pumps sucked water from the mine shafts, and huge ventilators circulated air in the underground chambers. No backwoods mining camp, Virginia City was an industrial center with more than 1,200 stamping mills working on average a ton of ore every day. Almost 400 men worked in milling, nearly 300 labored in manufacturing

Chileans, and other South and Central Americans came to share in the bonanza. With them came a sprinkling of Russians, Poles, Greeks, Japanese, Spaniards, Hungarians, Portuguese, Turks, Pacific Islanders, and Moroccans, as well as other North Americans, African Americans, and American Indians. This polyglot population, typical of mining boomtowns, made Virginia City in the 1870s more cosmopolitan than New York or Boston. In the part of Utah Territory that eventually

industries, and roughly 3,000 toiled in the mines. The Gould and Curry mine covered sixty acres. Most of the miners who came to the Comstock ended up as laborers for the big companies.

New technology eliminated some of the dangers of mining but often created new ones. In the hard-rock mines of the West, accidents in the 1870s disabled one out of every thirty miners and killed one in eighty. Ross Moudy, who worked as a miner in Cripple Creek, Colorado, recalled how a stockholder visiting the mine nearly fell to his death. The terrified visitor told the miner next to him that "instead of being paid $3 a day, they ought to have all the gold they could take out." Moudy's biggest worry was carbon dioxide, which often filled the tunnels because of poor ventilation. "Many times," he confessed, "I have been carried out unconscious." Those who avoided accidents still breathed air so dangerous that respiratory diseases eventually disabled them.

After a year on the job, Moudy joined a labor union "because I saw it would help me to keep in work and for protection in case of accident or sickness." The union provided good sick benefits and hired nurses, "so if one is alone and sick he is sure to be taken care of." On the Comstock Lode, because of the difficulty of obtaining skilled labor, the richness of the ore, and the need for a stable workforce, labor unions formed early and held considerable bargaining power. Comstock miners commanded $4 a day, the highest wage in the mining West.

The mining towns of the "Wild West" are often portrayed as lawless outposts, filled with saloons and rough gambling dens and populated almost exclusively by men, except for the occasional dance-hall floozy. The truth is more complex, as Virginia City's development attests. An established urban community built to serve an industrial giant, Virginia City in its first decade boasted

"Mining on the Comstock"
This illustration, made at Gold Hill, Nevada, in 1876, shows a sectional view of a mine, highlighting the square-set timber method, an innovation in mining that assembled prefabricated timbers into cubes stacked on cubes that could support virtually any underground chasm. Note also the tunnels, incline, cooling-off room, blower, and air shaft, along with a collection of miner's tools. Mines like the one pictured here honeycombed the hills of Gold City and neighboring Virginia City on the Comstock Lode in Nevada. University of California at Berkeley, Bancroft Library.

churches, schools, theaters, an opera house, and hundreds of families. By 1870, women composed 30 percent of the population, and 75 percent of the women listed their occupation in the census as housekeeper. Mary McNair Mathews, a widow from Buffalo, New York, who lived on the Comstock in the 1870s, worked as a teacher, nurse, seamstress, laundress, and lodging-house operator. She later published a book on her adventures.

By 1875, Virginia City boasted a population of 25,000 people, making it one of the largest cities between St. Louis and San Francisco. A must-see stop on the way west, the "Queen of the Comstock" hosted American presidents as well as legions of lesser dignitaries. No rough outpost of the Wild West, Virginia City represented, in the words of a recent chronicler, "the distilled essence of America's newly established course — urban, industrial, acquisitive, and materialistic, on the move, 'a living polyglot' of cultures that collided and converged."

The Diverse Peoples of the West

The West of the late nineteenth century was indeed a polyglot place, as much so as the big cities of the East. The sheer number of peoples who mingled in the West produced a complex blend of racism and prejudice. One historian has noted, not entirely facetiously, that there were at least eight oppressed "races" in the West — Indians, Latinos, Chinese, Japanese, blacks, Mormons, strikers, and radicals.

African Americans who ventured out to the territories faced hostile settlers determined to keep the West "for whites only." In response, they formed all-black communities such as Nicodemas, Kansas. That settlement, founded by thirty black Kentuckians in 1877, grew to a community of seven hundred by 1880. Isolated and often separated by great distances, small black settlements grew up throughout the West, in Nevada, Utah, and the Pacific Northwest, as well as in Kansas. Black soldiers who served in the West during the Indian wars often stayed on as settlers. Called **buffalo soldiers** because Native Americans thought their hair resembled that of the bison, these black troops numbered up to 25,000. In the face of discrimination, poor treatment, and harsh conditions, the buffalo soldiers served with distinction and boasted the lowest desertion rate in the army.

Hispanic peoples had lived in Texas and the Southwest since Juan de Oñate led pioneer settlers up the Rio Grande in 1598. Hispanics had occupied the Pacific coast since San Diego was founded in 1769. Overnight, they were reduced to a "minority"

after the United States annexed Texas in 1845 and took land stretching to California after the Mexican-American War ended in 1848. At first, the Hispanic owners of large *ranchos* in California, New Mexico, and Texas greeted conquest as an economic opportunity — new markets for their livestock and buyers for their lands. But racial prejudice soon ended their optimism. Californios (Mexican residents of California), who had been granted American citizenship by the Treaty of Guadalupe Hidalgo (1848), faced discrimination by Anglos who sought to keep them out of California's mines and commerce. Whites illegally squatted on *rancho* land while protracted litigation over Spanish and Mexican land grants forced the Californios into court. Although the U.S. Supreme Court eventually validated most of their claims, it took so long — seventeen years on average — that many Californios sold their property to pay taxes and legal bills. The city of Oakland, California, sits on what was once a 19,000-acre ranch owned by the Peralta family, who lost the land to Anglos.

Swindles, chicanery, and intimidation dispossessed scores of Californios. Many ended up segregated in urban barrios (neighborhoods) in their own homeland. Their percentage of California's population declined from 82 percent in 1850 to 19 percent in 1880 as Anglos migrated to the state. In New Mexico and Texas, Mexicans remained a majority of the population but became increasingly impoverished as Anglos dominated business and took the best jobs. Skirmishes between Hispanics and whites in northern New Mexico over the fencing of the open range lasted for decades. Groups of Hispanics with names such as *Las Manos Negras* (the Black Hands) cut fences and burned barns. In Texas, violence along the Rio Grande pitted Tejanos (Mexican residents of Texas) against the Texas Rangers, who saw their role as "keeping Mexicans in their place."

Even more than the Mexicans, the Chinese suffered brutal treatment at the hands of employers and other laborers. Drawn by the promise of gold, more than 20,000 Chinese had joined the rush to California by 1852. Miners determined to keep "California for Americans" succeeded in passing prohibitive foreign license laws to keep the Chinese out of the mines. But Chinese immigration continued. In the 1860s, when white workers moved on to find riches in the bonanza mines of Nevada, Chinese laborers took jobs abandoned by the whites. Railroad magnate Charles Crocker hired Chinese gangs to work on the Central Pacific, reasoning that "the race that built the Great Wall" could lay tracks across the treacherous Sierra Nevada. Some 12,000

Buffalo Soldiers to the Rescue in Colorado
In this painting, artist Frederic Remington portrays the bravery of African American "buffalo soldiers." In 1879 the Ute went on the warpath in Colorado when an Indian agent threatened to destroy their ponies to force them into farming. The Ute killed the whites, and the soldiers pursuing them soon found themselves pinned down and under siege. Captain Francis Dodge and his troop of thirty-five buffalo soldiers rode twenty-three hours to the rescue. Remington's picture is imagined — painted well after the fact. Although Remington spent a stint tracking Geronimo in Arizona for *Harper's Magazine*, he returned to the East and there gained renown for his depictions of the mythic Old West. The Granger Collection, New York.

Chinese, representing 90 percent of Crocker's workforce, completed America's first transcontinental railroad in 1869.

By 1870, more than 63,000 Chinese immigrants lived in America, 77 percent of them in California. A 1790 federal statute that limited naturalization to "white persons" was modified after the Civil War to extend naturalization to blacks ("persons of African descent"). But the Chinese and other Asians continued to be denied access to citizenship. As perpetual aliens, they constituted a reserve army of transnational laborers that many saw as a threat to American labor. For the most part, the Chinese did not displace white workers but instead found work as railroad laborers, cooks, servants, and farmhands while white workers sought out more lucrative fields. In the 1870s, when California and the rest of the nation weathered a major economic depression, the Chinese became easy scapegoats. California workingmen rioted and fought to keep Chinese workers out of the state, claiming they were "coolie labor" — involuntary contract laborers recruited by business interests determined to keep wages at rock bottom.

In 1876, the Workingmen's Party formed to fight for Chinese exclusion. Racial and cultural animosities stood at the heart of anti-Chinese agitation. Denis Kearney, the fiery San Francisco leader of the movement, made clear this racist bent when he urged legislation to "expel every one of the moon-eyed lepers." Nor was California alone in its anti-immigrant nativism. As the country confronted growing ethnic and racial diversity with the rising tide of global immigration in the decades following the Civil War, many questioned the principle of racial equality at the same time they argued against the assimilation of "nonwhite" groups. In this climate, Congress passed the **Chinese Exclusion Act** in 1882, effectively barring Chinese immigration and setting a precedent for further immigration restrictions.

> **"Expel every one of the moon-eyed lepers."**
> — San Francisco leader DENIS KEARNEY, speaking of Chinese immigrants

Chinese Workers
Chinese section hands, wearing their distinctive conical hats, are shown here in 1898 shoveling dirt for the North Pacific Coast Railroad in Corte Madera, California. Charles Crocker was the first railroad executive to hire Chinese laborers to work on the Central Pacific railroad in the 1860s, reasoning that the race that built the Great Wall could build tracks through the Sierra Nevada. California Historical Society, FN-25345.

The Chinese Exclusion Act led to a sharp drop in the Chinese population — from 105,465 in 1880 to 89,863 in 1900 — because Chinese immigrants, overwhelmingly male, did not have families to sustain their population. Eventually, Japanese immigrants, including women as well as men, replaced the Chinese, particularly in agriculture. As "nonwhite" immigrants, they could not become naturalized citizens, but their children born in the United States claimed the rights of citizenship. Japanese parents, seeking to own land, purchased it in their children's names. Although anti-Asian prejudice remained strong in California and elsewhere in the West, Asian immigrants formed an important part of the economic fabric of the western United States.

The Mormons, who had fled west to Utah Territory in 1844 to avoid religious persecution, established Salt Lake City, a thriving metropolis of more than 150,000 residents by 1882. To counter criticism of the Mormon practice of polygamy (church leader Brigham Young had twenty-seven wives), the Utah territorial legislature gave women the right to vote in 1870, the first universal woman suffrage act in the nation. (Wyoming had granted suffrage to white women in 1869.) Although woman's rights advocates argued that the newly enfranchised women would "do away with the horrible institution of polygamy," it remained in force. Not until 1890 did the church hierarchy

yield to pressure and renounce polygamy. The fierce controversy over polygamy postponed statehood for Utah until 1896.

Territorial Government

The federal government practiced a policy of benign neglect when it came to territorial government in the West. The president appointed a governor, a secretary, and two to four judges, along with an attorney and a marshal. In Nevada Territory, that meant that a handful of officials governed an area the size of New England. Originally a part of the larger Utah Territory, Nevada, propelled by mining interests, moved on the fast track to statehood, entering the Union in 1864, long before its population or its development merited statehood.

More typical were the territories extant in 1870 — New Mexico, Utah, Washington, Colorado, Dakota, Arizona, Idaho, Montana, and Wyoming. These areas remained territories for inordinately long periods ranging from twenty-three to sixty-two years. While awaiting statehood, they were subject to territorial governors who were underpaid, often unqualified, and largely ignored in Washington. Most territorial governors won their posts because of party loyalty and had little knowledge of the areas they served, little notions of their duties, and limited ability to perform them.

In theory, territorial governors received adequate salaries, as high as $3,500 in an era when the average workingman earned less than $500 a year. In practice, the funds rarely arrived in a timely fashion, and more than one governor found that he had to pay government expenses out of his own pocket. As one cynic observed, "Only the rich or those having 'no visible means of support,' can afford to accept office." John C. Frémont, the governor of Arizona Territory, complained he was so poor that he could not inspect the Grand Canyon because he didn't have money to keep a horse.

Territorial governors with fewer scruples accepted money from special interests — mine owners and big ranchers. Nearly all territorial appointees tried to make ends meet by maintaining business connections with the East or by taking advantage of investment opportunities in the West. Distance and the lack of funds made it difficult to summon officers from Washington to investigate charges of corruption. Officials who ventured west to look into such charges often felt intimidated by gun-packing westerners. One judge sent to New Mexico Territory in 1871 reported that he "stayed three days, made up his mind that it would be dangerous to do any investigating, . . . and returned to his home without any action." Underfunded and overlooked, victims of political cronyism, and prey to special interests, territorial governments were rife with conflicts of interest and corruption, mirroring the self-serving political and economic values of the country as a whole in the rush for riches that followed the Civil War.

REVIEW How did industrial technology change mining in Nevada?

► Land Fever

In the three decades following 1870, more land was settled than in all the previous history of the country. Americans by the hundreds of thousands packed up and moved west, goaded if not by the hope of striking gold, then by the promise of owning land. The agrarian West shared with the mining West a persistent restlessness, an equally pervasive addiction to speculation, and a penchant for exploiting natural resources and labor.

Two factors stimulated the land rush in the trans-Mississippi West. The **Homestead Act of 1862** promised 160 acres free to any citizen or

Admission of States in the Trans-Mississippi West

Year	State	Year	State
1821	Missouri	1889	North Dakota
1836	Arkansas	1889	South Dakota
1845	Texas	1889	Montana
1846	Iowa	1889	Washington
1850	California	1890	Idaho
1858	Minnesota	1890	Wyoming
1859	Oregon	1896	Utah
1861	Kansas	1907	Oklahoma
1864	Nevada	1912	New Mexico
1867	Nebraska	1912	Arizona
1876	Colorado		

prospective citizen, male or female, who settled on the land for five years. Even more important, **transcontinental railroads** opened up new areas and actively recruited settlers. After the completion of the first transcontinental railroad in 1869, homesteaders abandoned the covered wagon, and by the 1880s they could choose from four competing rail lines and make the trip west in a matter of days.

Although the country was rich in land and resources, not all who wanted to own land achieved their goal. During the transition from the family farm to large commercial farming, small farms gave way to vast spreads worked by migrant labor or paid farmworkers. Just as industry corporatized and consolidated in the East, the period from 1870 to 1900 witnessed corporate consolidation in mining, ranching, and agriculture.

Moving West: Homesteaders and Speculators

A Missouri homesteader remembered packing as her family pulled up stakes and headed west to Oklahoma in 1890. "We were going to God's Country," she wrote. "You had to work hard on that rocky country in Missouri. I was glad to be leaving it. . . . We were going to a new land and get rich."

Norwegian Immigrant and Sod House
Norwegian immigrant Beret Olesdater sits in front of her sod house in Lac qui Parle, Minnesota, in 1896. On the plains, where trees were scarce and lumber was often prohibitively expensive, settlers built with the materials at hand. The dugout was the most primitive dwelling, carved into a hillside. Huts cut from blocks of sod, like the one pictured here, marked a step up. Life for women on the plains proved especially lonely and hard. © Minnesota Historical Society/ Corbis.

People who ventured west searching for "God's Country" faced hardship, loneliness, and deprivation. To carve a farm from the raw prairie of Iowa, the plains of Nebraska, or the forests of the Pacific Northwest took more than fortitude and backbreaking toil. It took luck. Blizzards, tornadoes, grasshoppers, hailstorms, drought, prairie fires, accidental death, and disease were only a few of the catastrophes that could befall even the best farmer. Homesteaders on free land still needed as much as $1,000 for a house, a team of farm animals, a well, fencing, and seed.

Poor farmers called "sodbusters" did without even these basics, living in dugouts carved into hillsides and using muscle instead of machinery.

"Father made a dugout and covered it with willows and grass," one Kansas girl recounted. When it rained, the dugout flooded, and "we carried the water out in buckets, then waded around in the mud until it dried." Rain wasn't the only problem. "Sometimes the bull snakes would get in the roof and now and then one would lose his hold and fall down on the bed. . . . Mother would grab the hoe . . . and after the fight was over Mr. Bull Snake was dragged outside." The sod house, a step up from the dugout, had walls cut from blocks of sod and a roof of sod, lumber, or tin. (See "Documenting the American Promise," page 558.)

For women on the frontier, obtaining simple daily necessities such as water and fuel meant backbreaking labor. Out on the plains, where water was scarce, women often had to trudge to the nearest creek or spring. "A yoke was made to place across [Mother's] shoulders, so as to carry at each end a bucket of water," one daughter recollected, "and then water was brought a half mile from spring to house." Gathering fuel was another heavy chore. Without ready sources of coal or firewood, settlers on the plains turned to what substitutes they could scavenge — twigs, tufts of grass, corncobs, sunflower stalks. But by far the most prevalent fuel was "chips" — chunks of dried cattle and buffalo dung, found in abundance on the plains.

Despite the hardships, some homesteaders succeeded in building comfortable lives. The sod hut made way for a more substantial house; the log cabin yielded to a white clapboard home with a porch and a rocking chair. For others, the promise of the West failed to materialize. Already by the 1870s, much of the best land had been taken. Too often, homesteaders found that only the least desirable tracts were left — poor land, far from markets, transportation, and society. "There is plenty of land for sale in California," one migrant complained in 1870, but "the majority of the available lands are held by speculators, at prices far beyond the reach of a poor man." The railroads, flush from land grants provided by the state and federal governments, owned huge swaths of land in the West and actively recruited settlers. Altogether, the land grants totaled approximately 180 million acres — an area almost one-tenth the size of the United States (Map 17.3). Of the 2.5 million farms established between 1860 and 1900,

Midwestern Settlement before 1862

homesteading accounted for only one in five; the vast majority of farmland sold for a profit.

As land grew scarce on the prairie in the 1870s, farmers began to push farther west, moving into western Kansas, Nebraska, and eastern Colorado — the region called the **Great American Desert** by settlers who had passed over it on their way to California and Oregon. Many agricultural experts warned that the semiarid land (where less than twenty inches of rain fell annually) would not support a farm on the 160 acres allotted to homesteaders. But their words of caution were drowned out by the extravagant claims of western promoters, many employed by the railroads to sell off their land grants. "Rain follows the plow" became the slogan of western boosters, who insisted that cultivation would alter the climate of the region and bring more rainfall. Instead, drought followed the plow. Droughts were a cyclical fact of life on the Great Plains. Plowed up, the dry topsoil blew away in the wind. A period of relatively good rainfall in the early 1880s encouraged farming; then a protracted drought in the late 1880s and early 1890s sent starving farmers reeling back from the plains. Thousands left, some in wagons carrying the slogan "In God we trusted, in Kansas we busted."

Fever for fertile land set off a series of spectacular land runs in Oklahoma. When two million acres of land in former Indian Territory opened for settlement in 1889, thousands of homesteaders massed on the border. At the opening pistol shot, "with a shout and a yell the swift riders shot out, then followed the light buggies or wagons," a reporter wrote. "Above all, a great cloud of dust hover[ed] like smoke over a battlefield." By nightfall, Oklahoma boasted two tent cities with more than ten thousand residents. In the last frenzied land rush on Oklahoma's Cherokee strip in 1893, several settlers were killed in the stampede, and nervous men guarded their claims with rifles. As public land grew scarce, the hunger for land grew fiercer for both farmers and ranchers.

Ranchers and Cowboys

Cattle ranchers followed the railroads onto the plains, establishing a cattle kingdom from Texas to Wyoming between 1865 and 1885. Cowboys drove huge herds, as many as three thousand

Railroad Locomotive
In the years following the Civil War, the locomotive replaced the covered wagon, enabling settlers to travel from Chicago or St. Louis to the West Coast in two days. By the 1890s, more than 72,000 miles of track stretched west of the Mississippi River. The first transcontinental railroad, completed in 1869, soon led to the creation of competing systems, so that by the 1880s travelers going west could choose from four railroad lines. In this photograph, men and women perched on a locomotive celebrate the completion of a section of track. Library of Congress.

head of cattle that grazed on public lands as they followed cattle tracks like the Chisholm Trail from Texas to railheads in Kansas. More than 1.5 million Texas longhorns went to market before the range began to close in the 1880s.

Barbed wire revolutionized the cattle business and sounded the death knell for the open range. In 1874, Joseph F. Glidden, an Illinois sheriff, invented and patented barbed wire. Gambler and promoter John "Bet a Million" Gates made his fortune by corralling a herd of Texas longhorns in downtown San Antonio, proving the merit of the flimsy-looking wire he went on to market profitably. As the largest ranches in Texas began to fence, nasty fights broke out between big ranchers and "fence cutters," who resented the end of the free

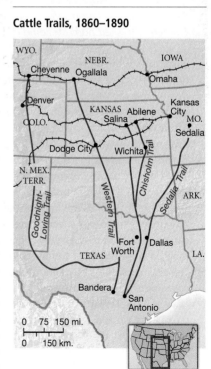

Cattle Trails, 1860–1890

Young Women Homesteaders and the Promise of the West

"Young men! Poor men! Widows! Resolve to have a home of your own!" urged New York editor Horace Greeley. "If you are able to buy and pay for one in the East, very well; if not, make one in the broad and fertile West!" In his exhortation to go west, Greeley did not speak to men alone. Many women, and not just widows, heeded the call. The Homestead Act of 1862 allowed unmarried women and female heads of households to claim free land. Many did. The number of women establishing homesteads in the West ranged from 5 percent of homesteaders in the early settlements to more than 20 percent after 1900.

Among the women homesteaders were Clara and Mary Troska and their two cousins Helen and Christine Sonnek, who headed to North Dakota. "Mary, Helen, Christine and I packed our suitcases," Clara wrote. "I took my mandolin, Christine took hers and her rifle. . . . We were on our way to Minot." Young women like Clara between the ages of twenty-one and twenty-five constituted the largest percentage of women (53 percent) taking up claims in the Dakotas.

Like Christine Sonnek, who took her mandolin along with her rifle, homesteading women prepared to enjoy their new environment despite its challenges. Their letters, diaries, and reminiscences reveal not only the hardships they faced but also the sense of promise that lured them west. Adventurous, resourceful, and exuberant, many of these young homesteading women seemed to relish their experiences.

DOCUMENT 1
The Varied Activities of a Woman Homesteader

Dakota homesteader Bess Cobb's letter to a friend reveals the optimism and high spirits that energized the young women who filed homesteading claims.

Suppose you girls are saying "poor Bess" and feeling dreadfully sorry for me out here in the wild and wooly uncivilized regions of America. But really time just seems to fly. I haven't done half I had planned and I am afraid winter will be here before we are ready for it. I've sewed some, done a little fancy-work and lots of darning and mending but most of my time has been spent out of doors digging in the garden and riding. . . . You can see a team miles away — up one valley we can see ten miles, up to the Cannon Ball river — so when any one starts to our shack, if we see them in time we can comb our hair, change our gowns and get a good meal in running order before they arrive. You see Dakota has some redeeming qualities. Wish you could come out, but I suppose you think I am too far away. I have the neatest little shack I've ever seen and "my crops" are tip top. I know you would enjoy our camp life for a short time.

SOURCE: "Excerpts from a letter written by Bess Cobb, Guide to Manuscripts 1364, State Historical Society, North Dakota Heritage Center, Bismarck," from pages 140–41 in *Land in Her Own Name: Women as Homesteaders in North Dakota* by H. Elaine Lindgren. Copyright © 1996. Reprinted with permission of University of Oklahoma Press.

DOCUMENT 2
A Hard Winter

Lucy Goldthorpe, a young schoolteacher, came from Iowa to Dakota in 1905. Here she describes to a reporter her survival during the winter and contrasts her childhood fantasies with homestead reality.

There were many long, cold days and nights in my little homestead shack that winter! The walls were only single board thickness, covered with tar paper on the outside. I'd spent money sparingly, because I didn't have much, but I had worked hard all during summer and fall in an effort to winterize the structure. Following the pattern used by many of the settlers, I covered the interior walls with a blue building paper. Everything was covered, including the ceiling, and the floor. To help seal out the cold I'd added layers of gunny sacks over the paper on the floor and then the homemade wool rugs I'd shipped from home.

Regardless of what I did the cold crept in through the thin walls. With no storm entry at the door and only single windows my little two-lid laundry stove with oven attached to the pipe had a real struggle to keep the place livable. . . .

A neighbor family returning to their claim "from the outside" brought me fresh vegetables. They were such a prized addition to my meals that I put the bag in bed with me at night to keep them from freezing. Night after night I stored food and my little alarm clock in the stove pipe oven; that was the only way I could keep the clock running and be sure of a non-frozen breakfast.

Each day brought new, unexpected challenges and at times I wondered if I would be able to stay with it until the land was mine. Could any land be worth the lonely hours and hardships? The howling wind and driving snow, the mournful wail of coyotes searching the tormented land for food did nothing to make the winter any more pleasant. . . .

As a child I had enjoyed hearing my father tell of the hardships of the early days. They seemed so exciting to me as I listened in the warmth and security of our well built, fully winterized Iowa home. Like most youngsters I'd wished for the thrill of those other days. Little did I think that an opportunity for just that would come through homesteading alone, far out in the windswept, unsettled land. Believe me, it wasn't nearly as glamorous as the imagination would have it!

SOURCE: Roberta M. Starry, "Petticoat Pioneer." Excerpt from page 48 in *The West* 7, no. 5, October 1967. Copyright © 1967. Reprinted with permission.

DOCUMENT 3
Socializing and Entertainment

Homesteading wasn't all hard times. Young, single homesteaders found time for fun. Here Effie Vivian Smith describes a "shack party" during the winter of 1906 on her Dakota claim.

I never enjoyed myself better in my life than I have this winter. We go some place or some one is here from 1 to 4 times a week. A week ago last Fri. a load of 7 drove out to my claim. Cliff, Clara, David, and I had gone out the Wed. before and such a time as we had. My shack is 10 feet 3 inches by 16 feet and I have only 2 chairs and a long bench for seats, a table large enough for 6, a single bed, and only 3 knives so 2 of them ate with paring knives & 1 with the butcher knife. We had two of them sit on the bed and moved the table up to them. . . . We played all the games we could think of both quiet and noisy and once all but Clara went out & snowballed. They brought a

bu[shel] of apples, & a lot of nuts, candy, & gum & we ate all night. . . .

We have just started a literary society in our neighborhood. Had our first debate last Fri. The question was Resolved that city life is better than country life. All the judges decided in the negative. . . . Tomorrow our crowd is going to a literary [society] 6 or 7 miles from here, and the next night to a dance at the home of one of our bachelor boys. We always all go in our sleigh. I am learning to dance this winter but don't attend any except the ones we get up ourselves and they are just as nice & just as respectable as the parties we used to have at Ruthven [Iowa]. I just love to dance. . . .

SOURCE: H. Elaine Lindgren, "Letter to her cousin, written on January 9, 1906." From pages 177–78 in *Land in Her Own Name: Women as Homesteaders in North Dakota.* Copyright © 1996 University of Oklahoma Press. Reprinted with permission.

DOCUMENT 4
Homesteading Pays Off

Homesteading proved rewarding for many women, not only economically but also because of the sense of accomplishment they experienced. Here Theona Carkin tells how the sale of her Dakota homestead helped finance her university degree.

Life in general was dotted with hardships but there were many good times also. I have always felt that my efforts on my homestead were very worthwhile and very rewarding, and I have always been proud of myself for doing it all.

By teaching off and on . . . and upon selling the homestead, I was able to pay all my own college expenses.

SOURCE: "99-Year-Old U Graduate Recalls Early Childhood." From page 5 in *Alumni Review*, June 1985. Published by the University of North Dakota, Grand Forks.

Questions for Analysis and Debate

1. What sorts of hardships did the young women homesteaders encounter in the Dakotas?

2. How did their youth affect how they reacted to hardship?

3. What did the young women find particularly appealing about their experiences as homesteaders?

4. What did they wish to convey about their experiences?

5. How did homesteading benefit women who chose not to remain on the land?

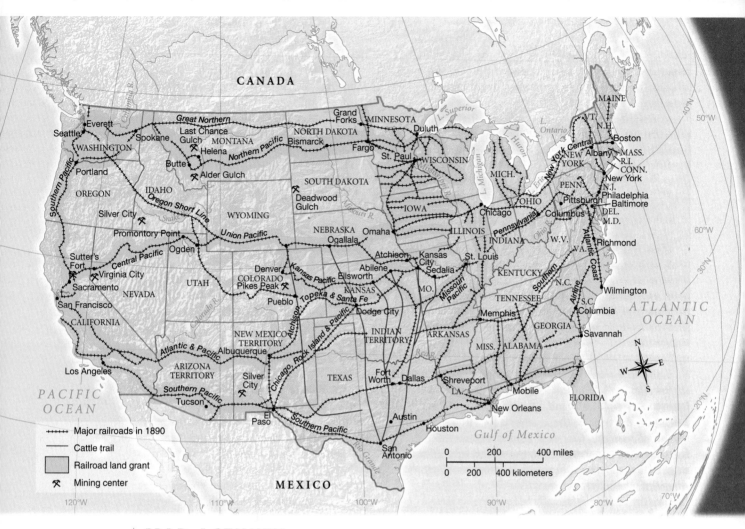

MAP ACTIVITY

Map 17.3   Federal Land Grants to Railroads and the Development of the West, 1850–1900
Generous federal land grants meant that railroads could sell the desirable land next to the track at a profit or hold it for speculation. Railroads received more than 180 million acres, an area as large as Texas. Built well ahead of demand, the western railroads courted settlers, often onto land not fit for farming.

READING THE MAP: Which mining cities and towns were located directly on a railroad line? Which towns were located at the junction of more than one line or railroad branch?
CONNECTIONS: In what ways did the growth of the railroads affect the population of the West? What western goods and products did the railroads help bring east and to ports for shipping around the world?

range. One old-timer observed, "Those persons, Mexicans and Americans, without land but who had cattle were put out of business by fencing." Fencing forced small-time ranchers who owned land but could not afford to buy barbed wire or sink wells to sell out for the best price they could get. The displaced ranchers, many of them Mexicans, ended up as wageworkers on the huge spreads owned by Anglos or by European syndicates.

On the range, the cowboy gave way to the cattle king and, like the miner, became a wage laborer. Many cowboys were African Americans (as many as five thousand in Texas alone). Writers of western literature chose to ignore the presence of black cowboys like Deadwood Dick (Nat Love), who was portrayed as a white man in the dime novels of the era.

By 1886, cattle overcrowded the range. Severe blizzards during the winter of 1886–87 decimated the herds. "A whole generation of cowmen," wrote

THE PROMISE OF TECHNOLOGY

Barbed Wire

The original working model of Joseph Glidden's barbing machine, patented in 1874, consisted of an old-fashioned coffee mill with its casing cut away and its grinder altered to cut and coil small lengths of wire. The barbs were strung by hand between strands of plain wire. Despite its flimsiness, barbed wire could contain cattle, as master promoter John "Bet a Million" Gates demonstrated by corralling a herd of Texas longhorns in downtown San Antonio in 1879. How did barbed wire transform cattle ranching in the West? Ellwood House Museum, De Kalb, IL.

one chronicler, "went dead broke." Fencing worsened the situation. During blizzards, cattle stayed alive by keeping on the move. But when they ran up against barbed wire fences, they froze to death. In the aftermath of the "Great Die Up," new labor-intensive forms of cattle ranching replaced the open-range model.

Tenants, Sharecroppers, and Migrants

In the post–Civil War period, as agriculture became a big business tied by the railroads to national and global markets, an increasing number of laborers worked land that they would never own. In the southern United States, farmers labored under particularly heavy burdens. The Civil War wiped out much of the region's capital, which had been invested in slaves, and crippled the plantation economy. Newly freed slaves rarely obtained land of their own and often ended up as farm laborers. "The colored folks stayed with the old boss man and farmed and worked on the plantations," a black Alabama sharecropper observed bitterly. "They were still slaves, but they were free slaves." Some freed-people did manage to pull together enough resources to go west. In 1879, more than fifteen thousand black **Exodusters** moved from Mississippi and Louisiana to take up land in Kansas.

California's Mexican cowboys, or *vaqueros*, commanded decent wages throughout the Southwest. Skilled horsemen, the vaqueros boasted that five of them could do the work of

thirty Anglo cowboys. The vocabulary of ranching, with words such as *rodeo, lasso,* and *lariat,* testified to the centrality of the vaqueros' place in the cattle industry. But by 1880, as the coming of the railroads ended the long cattle drives and as large feedlots began to replace the open range, the value of their skills declined. Many vaqueros ended up as migrant laborers, often on land their families had once owned. Similarly, in Texas, Tejanos found themselves displaced. After the heyday of cattle ranching ended in the late 1880s, cotton production rose in the southeastern regions of the state. Ranchers turned their pastures into sharecroppers' plots and hired displaced cowboys, most of them Mexicans, as seasonal laborers for as little as seventy-five cents a day, thereby creating a growing army of agricultural wageworkers.

Land monopoly and large-scale farming fostered tenancy and migratory labor on the West Coast. By the 1870s, less than 1 percent of California's population owned half the state's available agricultural land. The rigid economics of large-scale commercial agriculture and the seasonal nature of the crops spawned a ragged army of migratory agricultural laborers. Derisively labeled "blanket men" or "bindle stiffs," these transients worked the fields in the growing season and wintered in the flophouses of San Francisco. Most farm laborers were Chinese immigrants. After passage of the Chinese Exclusion Act of 1882, Mexicans, Filipinos, and Japanese immigrants filled the demand for migratory workers.

A Vaquero
Rafael "Chappo" Remudas is pictured here in Burns, Oregon, around 1890. He came as a vaquero to the high desert in 1872 and became boss of the P Ranch, handing down his skills to a new generation of white "buckaroos," who replaced the vaqueros. Chappo proudly sits his horse, surrounded by the tools of his trade: his lasso wound tightly around his saddle horn, his kerchief tied at his neck, *tapederos* (covered stirrups to protect his feet), heavy leggings, a flat-crowned sombrero, and his silver-mounted bridle.
Photo courtesy of the Harney County Historical Society, Burns, OR.

Commercial Farming and Industrial Cowboys

In the late nineteenth century, the population of the United States remained overwhelmingly rural. The 1870 census showed that nearly 80 percent of the nation's people lived on farms and in villages of fewer than 8,000 inhabitants. By 1900, the figure had dropped to 66 percent (Figure 17.1). At the same time, the number of farms rose. Rapid growth in the West increased the number of the nation's farms from 2 million in 1860 to more than 5.7 million in 1900.

Despite the hardships individual farmers experienced, new technology and farming techniques revolutionized American farm life. Mechanized farm machinery halved the time and labor cost of production and made it possible to cultivate vast tracts of land. Meanwhile, urbanization provided farmers with expanding markets for their produce, and railroads carried crops to markets thousands of miles away. Even before the start of the twentieth century, American agriculture had entered the era of what would come to be called agribusiness — farming as a big business — with the advent of huge commercial farms.

As farming moved onto the prairies and plains, mechanization took command. Steel plows, reapers, mowers, harrows, seed drills, combines, and threshers replaced human muscle. Horse-drawn implements gave way to steam-powered machinery. By 1880, a single combine could do the work of twenty men, vastly increasing the acreage a farmer could cultivate. Mechanization spurred the growth of bonanza wheat farms, some more than 100,000 acres, in California and

FIGURE 17.1   Changes in Rural and Urban Populations, 1870–1900
Between 1870 and 1900, both the number of urban dwellers and the number of farms increased, even as the number of rural inhabitants fell. Mechanization made it possible to farm with fewer hands, fueling the exodus from farm to city throughout the second half of the nineteenth century.

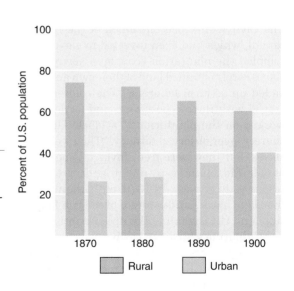

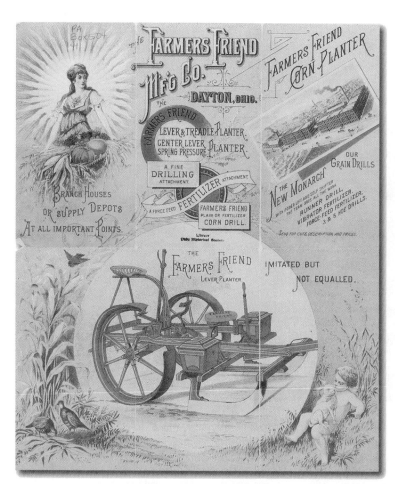

Mechanical Corn Planter
Mechanical planters came into use in the 1860s. The Farmers Friend Manufacturing Company of Dayton, Ohio, advertised its lever and treadle corn planter in the early 1880s. Although this planter, which featured attachments for grain drilling and fertilizing, appears to have been designed to be drawn by farm animals, steam-powered farm implements would soon replace animal power. Notice how the female figure on the left, symbolizing the bucolic farm life, is offset by the company's impressive factory in Dayton on the right.
Ohio Historical Society.

the Red River Valley of North Dakota and Minnesota. This agricultural revolution meant that Americans raised more than four times the corn, five times the hay, and seven times the wheat and oats they had before the Civil War.

Like cotton farmers in the South, western grain and livestock farmers increasingly depended on foreign markets for their livelihood. A fall in global market prices meant that a farmer's entire harvest went to pay off debts. In the depression that followed the panic of 1893, many heavily mortgaged farmers lost their land to creditors. As a Texas cotton farmer complained, "By the time the World Gets their Liveing out of the Farmer as we have to Feed the World, we the Farmer has nothing Left but a Bear Hard Liveing." Commercial farming, along with mining, represented another way in which the West developed its own brand of industrialism. The far West's industrial economy sprang initially from California gold and the vast territory that came under American control following the Mexican-American War. In the ensuing rush on land and resources, environmental factors interacted with economic

and social forces to produce enterprises as vast in scale and scope as anything found in the East.

Two Alsatian immigrants, Henry Miller and Charles Lux, pioneered the West's mix of agriculture and industrialism. Beginning as meat wholesalers, Miller and Lux quickly expanded their business to encompass cattle, land, and land reclamation projects such as dams and irrigation systems. With a labor force of migrant workers, a highly coordinated corporate system, and large sums of investment capital, the firm of **Miller & Lux** became one of America's industrial behemoths. Eventually, these "industrial cowboys" grazed a herd of 100,000 cattle on 1.25 million acres of company land in California, Oregon, and Nevada and employed more than 1,200 migrant laborers on their corporate ranches. Miller & Lux dealt with the labor problem by offering free meals to migratory workers, thus keeping wages low while winning goodwill among an army of unemployed who competed for the work. When the company's Chinese cooks rebelled at washing the dishes resulting from the free meals, the migrant laborers were forced to eat

Loggers in Washington, 1890
Loggers pose on and beside one huge felled tree. The loggers worked in all-male crews with a "faller" cutting down the tree, "buckers" cutting it into manageable pieces, and "whistle punks" relaying information. By 1890, loggers using only axes and handsaws had harvested over one billion board feet of timber in the state of Washington alone. The massive deforestation continued and picked up speed as steam power replaced brawn and horse-power. Loggers lived a hard, dirty life in remote migratory camps, working long hours and sometimes wearing the same clothes for months on end. ©Bettmann/Corbis.

after the ranch hands and use their dirty plates. By the 1890s, more than eight hundred migrants a year followed what came to be known as the "Dirty Plate Route" on Miller & Lux ranches throughout California.

Since the days of Thomas Jefferson, agrarian life had been linked with the highest ideals of a democratic society. Now agrarianism itself had been transformed. The farmer was no longer a self-sufficient yeoman but often a businessman or a wage laborer tied to a global market. And even as farm production soared, industrialization outstripped it. More and more farmers left the fields for urban factories or found work in the "factories in the fields" of the new industrialized agribusiness. Now that the future seemed to lie not with the small farmer but with industrial enterprises, was democracy itself at risk? This question would ignite a farmers' revolt in the 1880s and dominate political debate in the 1890s.

REVIEW Why did many homesteaders find it difficult to acquire good land in the West?

▶ Conclusion: The West in the Gilded Age

In 1871, author Mark Twain published *Roughing It*, a chronicle of his days spent in mining towns in California and Nevada. There he found corrupt politics, vulgar display, and mania for speculation, the same cupidity he later skewered in *The Gilded Age* (1873), his biting satire of greed and corruption in the nation's capital. Far from being an antidote to the meretricious values of the East — an innocent idyll out of place and time — the American West, with its get-rich-quick ethos and its addiction to gambling and speculation, helped set the tone for the Gilded Age.

Twain's view countered that of Frederick Jackson Turner and perhaps better suited a West that witnessed the overbuilding of railroads, the consolidation of business in mining and ranching; the rise of commercial farming; corruption and a penchant for government handouts; racial animosity, whether in the form of Indian wars or Chinese exclusion; the exploitation of labor and natural resources, which led to the decimation of the great bison herds, the pollution of rivers with mining wastes, and the overgrazing of the plains; and the beginnings of an imperial policy that would provide a template for U.S. adventures abroad. Turner, intent on promoting what was unique about the frontier, failed to note that the same issues that came to dominate debate east of the Mississippi — the growing power of big business, the exploitation of land and labor, corruption in politics, and ethnic and racial tensions exacerbated by colonial expansion and unparalleled immigration — took center stage in the West at the end of the nineteenth century.

▶ Selected Bibliography

General

Najia Aarin-Heriot, *Chinese Immigrants, African Americans, and Racial Anxiety in the United States, 1848–1882* (2003).

Robert V. Hine and John Mack Faragher, *The American West: A New Interpretive History* (2000).

Patricia Nelson Limerick, *Something in the Soil: Legacies and Reckonings in the New West* (2000).

Valerie Matsumoto and Blake Allmendinger, eds., *Over the Edge: Remapping the American West* (1999).

Louis S. Warren, *Buffalo Bill's America: William Cody and the Wild West Show* (2005).

Richard White, *"It's Your Misfortune and None of My Own": A New History of the American West* (1991).

Richard White, *Railroaded: The Transcontinentals and the Making of Modern America* (2011).

David M. Wrobel, *Promised Lands: Promotion, Memory, and the Creation of the American West* (2002).

Indians

David Wallace Adams, *Education for Extinction: American Indians and the Boarding School Experience, 1875–1928* (1995).

Gary Clayton Anderson, *The Conquest of Texas: Ethnic Cleansing in the Promised Land, 1820–1875* (2005).

Stuart Banner, *How the Indians Lost Their Land: Law and Power on the Frontier* (2005).

Ned Blackhawk, *Violence over the Land: Indian Empires in the Early American West* (2006).

Colin Calloway, *First Peoples: A Documentary Survey of American Indian History* (3rd ed., 2008).

James O. Gump, *The Dust Rose like Smoke: The Subjugation of the Zulu and the Sioux* (1994).

Pekka Hamalainen, *The Comanche Empire* (2008).

Andrew C. Isenberg, *The Destruction of the Bison: An Environmental History, 1730–1920* (2000).

Edward Lazarus, *Black Hills, White Justice: The Sioux Nation versus the United States, 1775 to the Present* (1991).

Jeffrey Ostler, *The Plains Sioux and U.S. Colonialism from Lewis and Clark to Wounded Knee* (2004).

Nathaniel Philbrick, *The Last Stand: Custer, Sitting Bull, and the Battle of the Little Bighorn* (2010).

Francis Paul Prucha, *The Great Father: The United States Government and the American Indian* (1986).

Charles M. Robinson III, *A Good Year to Die: The Story of the Great Sioux War* (1995).

Alan Trachtenberg, *Shades of Hiawatha: Staging Indians, Making Americans, 1880–1930* (2004).

Mining, Ranching, and Farming

Suchen Chan, *This Bittersweet Soil: The Chinese in American Agriculture, 1860–1919* (1986).

Suchen Chan, Douglas Henry Daniels, Mario T. Garcia, and Terry P. Wilson, *Peoples of Color in the American West* (1994).

Roger Daniels, *Asian American: Chinese and Japanese in the United States since 1850* (1997).

Deborah Fitzgerald, *Every Farm a Factory: The Industrial Ideal in American Agriculture* (2003).

Manuel G. Gonzales, *Mexicanos: A History of Mexicans in the United States* (1999).

J. S. Holliday, *Rush for Riches: Gold Fever and the Making of California* (1999).

David Igler, *Industrial Cowboys: Miller & Lux and the Transformation of the Far West, 1850–1920* (2001).

Andrew C. Isenberg, *Mining California: An Ecological History* (2005).

Ronald M. James, *The Roar and the Silence: The History of Virginia City and the Comstock Lode* (1998).

William Loren Katz, *Black West: A Documentary and Pictorial History of the African American Role in the Westward Expansion of the United States* (2005).

Karen R. Merrill, *Public Lands and Political Meaning: Ranchers, the Government, and the Property between Them* (2002).

Rodman Wilson Paul, *Mining Frontiers of the Far West, 1848–1880* (rev. ed., 2001).

William G. Robbins, *Colony and Empire: The Capitalist Transformation of the American West* (1994).

Steven Stoll, *Larding the Lean Earth: Soil and Society in Nineteenth-Century America* (2002).

FOR MORE BOOKS ABOUT TOPICS IN THIS CHAPTER, see the Online Bibliography at **bedfordstmartins.com/roark.**

FOR ADDITIONAL PRIMARY SOURCES FROM THIS PERIOD, see Michael Johnson, ed., *Reading the American Past*, Fifth Edition.

FOR WEB SITES, IMAGES, AND DOCUMENTS RELATED TO TOPICS AND PLACES IN THIS CHAPTER, visit Make History at **bedfordstmartins.com/roark.**

Reviewing Chapter 17

KEY TERMS

Explain each term's significance.

Conquest and Empire in the West
- Frederick Jackson Turner (p. 537)
- Indian removal (p. 537)
- reservations (p. 537)
- Treaty of Fort Laramie (1851) (p. 537)
- Sitting Bull (p. 540)
- Comanchería (p. 541)
- Treaty of Fort Laramie (1868) (p. 541)
- Black Hills (p. 541)
- Crazy Horse (p. 542)
- George Armstrong Custer (p. 542)
- George Crook (p. 543)
- Battle of the Little Big Horn (p. 543)

Forced Assimilation and Resistance Strategies
- Carlisle Indian School (p. 545)
- Dawes Allotment Act (p. 546)
- Chief Joseph (p. 546)
- Geronimo (p. 547)
- Lozen (p. 547)
- Nelson Miles (p. 547)
- Ghost Dance (p. 548)
- Wounded Knee (p. 549)

Gold Fever and the Mining West
- Comstock Lode (p. 549)
- buffalo soldiers (p. 552)
- Chinese Exclusion Act (p. 553)

Land Fever
- Homestead Act of 1862 (p. 555)
- transcontinental railroad (p. 555)
- Great American Desert (p. 557)
- Exodusters (p. 561)
- Miller & Lux (p. 563)

REVIEW QUESTIONS

Use key terms and dates to support your answer.

1. How did the slaughter of the bison contribute to the Plains Indians' removal to reservations? (pp. 537–544)

2. In what ways did different Indian groups defy and resist colonial rule? (pp. 544–559)

3. How did industrial technology change mining in Nevada? (pp. 549–555)

4. Why did many homesteaders find it difficult to acquire good land in the West? (pp. 555–564)

MAKING CONNECTIONS

Draw on key terms, the timeline, and review questions.

1. Westward migration brought settlers into conflict with Native Americans. What was the U.S. government's policy toward Indians in the West, and how did it evolve over time? How did the Indians resist and survive white encroachment? In your answer, discuss the cultural and military features of the conflict.

2. The economic and industrial developments characteristic of the East after the Civil War also made their mark on the West. How did innovations in business and technology transform mining and agriculture in the West? In your answer, be sure to consider effects on production and the consequences for the lives of miners and agricultural laborers.

3. Settlers from all over the world came to the American West seeking their fortunes but found that opportunity was not equally available to all. In competition for work and land, why did Anglo-American settlers usually have the upper hand? How did legal developments contribute to this circumstance?

4. Railroads had a profound impact on the development of the western United States. What role did railroads play in western settlement, industrialization, and agriculture? How did railroads affect Indian populations in the West?

Link events in this chapter to earlier events.

1. In what ways were the goals of migrants to the West similar to those of the northerners who moved to the South after the Civil War? How did they differ? (See chapter 16.)

2. How did the racism of the West compare with the racist attitudes against African Americans in the Reconstruction South? (See chapter 16.)

TIMELINE 1851–1900

1851	• First Treaty of Fort Laramie.
1862	• Homestead Act. • Great Sioux Uprising (Santee Uprising).
1864	• Sand Creek massacre.
1867	• Treaty of Medicine Lodge.
1868	• Second Treaty of Fort Laramie.
1869	• First transcontinental railroad completed.
1870	• Hunters begin to decimate bison herds.
1873	• "Big Bonanza" discovered on Comstock Lode.
1874	• Discovery of gold in Black Hills.
1876	• Battle of the Little Big Horn.
1877	• Chief Joseph surrenders. • Crazy Horse arrested and killed.
1878	• Indian students enroll at Hampton Institute in Virginia.
1879	• Carlisle Indian School opens in Pennsylvania. • More than fifteen thousand Exodusters move to Kansas.
1881	• Sitting Bull surrenders.
1882	• Chinese Exclusion Act. • Indian Rights Association formed.
1886	• Geronimo surrenders.
1886 –1888	• Severe blizzards decimate cattle herds.
1887	• Dawes Allotment Act.
1889	• Rise of Ghost Dance. • Two million acres in Oklahoma opened for settlement.
1890	• Sitting Bull killed. • Massacre at Wounded Knee, South Dakota.
1893	• Last land rush takes place in Oklahoma Territory. • Frederick Jackson Turner presents "frontier thesis."
1900	• Census finds 66 percent of population lives in rural areas, compared to 80 percent in 1870.

▶ **FOR PRACTICE QUIZZES AND OTHER STUDY TOOLS**, visit the Online Study Guide at **bedfordstmartins.com/roark**.

CAMPAIGN PINS

These gilt campaign pins depicting James G. Blaine thumbing his nose at rival Grover Cleveland proved ironic—the Democrat Cleveland won the presidency in 1884 by campaigning for honest government. Public concern about the lucrative partnership of government and business made Thomas Kepler's 1889 cartoon, "The Bosses of the Senate," a defining symbol of the Gilded Age. The trusts are caricatured as bloated moneybags who dominate the Senate chambers. The motto "This is a Senate of the Monopolists, by the Monopolists, and for the Monopolists" hangs prominently on the wall.

Pins: Collection of Janice L. and David J. Frent; background: Library of Congress.

18

Business and Politics in the Gilded Age
1865–1900

ONE NIGHT OVER DINNER, AUTHORS MARK TWAIN AND CHARLES Dudley Warner teased their wives about the sentimental novels they read. When the two women challenged them to write something better, they set to work. Warner supplied the melodrama, while Twain "hurled in the facts." The result was a runaway best seller, a savage satire of the "get-rich-quick" era that would forever carry the book's title, *The Gilded Age* (1873).

Twain left no one unscathed in the novel — political hacks, Washington lobbyists, Wall Street financiers, small-town boosters, and the "great putty-hearted public" that tolerated the plunder. Underneath the glitter of the Gilded Age lurked vulgarity, crass materialism, and political corruption. Twain had witnessed the crooked partnership of business and politics in the administration of Ulysses S. Grant. Here he describes how a lobbyist finagled to get a bill through Congress:

> Why the matter is simple enough. A Congressional appropriation costs money.... A majority of the House Committee, say $10,000 apiece — $40,000; a majority of the Senate Committee, the same each — say $40,000; a little extra to one or two chairmen of one or two such committees, say $10,000 each — $20,000; and there's $100,000 of the money gone, to begin with. Then, seven male lobbyists, at $3,000 each — $21,000; one female lobbyist, $3,000; a high moral Congressman or Senator here and there — the high moral ones cost more, because they give tone to a measure — say ten of these at $3,000 each, is $30,000; then a lot of small fry country members who won't vote for anything whatever without pay — say twenty at $500 apiece, is $10,000 altogether; lot of jimcracks for Congressmen's wives and children — those go a long way — you can't spend too much money in that line — well, those things cost in a lump, say $10,000 — along there somewhere; — and then comes your printed documents.... [W]ell, never mind the details, the total in clean numbers foots up $118,254.42 thus far!

In Twain's satire, Congress is for sale to the highest bidder. The corrupt interplay of business and politics raised serious questions about the health of American democracy.

The Gilded Age seemed to tarnish all who touched it. No one would learn that better than Twain, who, even as he attacked it as an "era of incredible rottenness," fell prey to its enticements. Born Samuel Langhorne Clemens, he grew up in a rough Mississippi River town, where he became a

569

Mark Twain and *The Gilded Age*
Popular author Mark Twain (Samuel Langhorne Clemens) wrote acerbically about the excesses of the Gilded Age in his novel of that name written with Charles Dudley Warner and published in 1873. No one knew the meretricious lure of the era better than Twain, who succumbed to a get-rich-quick scheme that led him to the brink of bankruptcy. Photo: Beinecke Rare Book and Manuscript Library, Yale University; book: Newberry Library.

riverboat pilot. Taking the pen name Mark Twain, he gained fame chronicling western mining booms. In 1866, he came east to launch a career as an author, public speaker, and itinerant humorist. Twain played to packed houses, but his work was judged too vulgar for the genteel tastes of the time because he wrote about common people using common language. His masterpiece, *The Adventures of Huckleberry Finn*, was banned in Boston when it appeared in 1884.

Huck Finn's creator eventually stormed the citadels of polite society, hobnobbing with the wealthy and living in increasingly lavish style. Succumbing to the money fever of his age, Twain plunged into a scheme in the hope of making millions. By the 1890s, he faced bankruptcy and began a dogged climb out of debt.

Twain's tale was common in an age when the promise of wealth led as many to ruin as to riches. In the Gilded Age, fortunes were made and lost with dizzying frequency. Those who pursued riches, whether in the mines of the West or in the stock market, found many rocks in their path. Wall Street panics in 1873 and 1893 periodically interrupted the boom times and plunged the country into economic depression. But with railroad overbuilding and industry expanding on every level, the mood of the country remained buoyant.

The rise of industrialism in the United States and the interplay of business and politics strike the key themes in the Gilded Age. From 1870 to 1890, the transition from a rural, agricultural economy to urban industrialism, global in its reach, transformed American society. The growth of old industries and the creation of new ones, along with the rise of big business, signaled the coming of age of industrial capitalism. Economic issues increasingly shaped party politics, although old divisions engendered by sectionalism and slavery by no means disappeared. Meanwhile, new concerns over lynchings, temperance, and suffrage propelled women into more active roles in society.

Perhaps nowhere were the hopes and fears that industrialism inspired more evident than in the public's attitude toward the business moguls of the day. Men like Andrew Carnegie, John D. Rockefeller, and J. P. Morgan sparked the popular imagination as the heroes and villains in the high drama of industrialization. And as concern grew over the power of big business and the growing chasm between rich and poor, many Americans looked to the government for solutions.

▶ Old Industries Transformed, New Industries Born

In the years following the Civil War, the American economy underwent a transformation. Where once wealth had been measured in tangible assets — property, livestock, buildings — the economy now ran on money and the new devices of business — paper currency, securities, and anonymous corporate entities. Wall Street, the heart of the country's financial system, increasingly affected Main Street. The scale and scope of American industry expanded dramatically. Old industries like iron transformed into modern industries typified by the behemoth U.S. Steel. Discovery and invention stimulated new industries, from oil refining to electric light and power. The expansion of the nation's rail system in the decades after the Civil War played the key role in the transformation of the American economy.

Jay Gould, Andrew Carnegie, John D. Rockefeller, and other business leaders pioneered new strategies to seize markets and consolidate power in the rising railroad, steel, and oil industries. Always with an eye to the main chance, these business tycoons set the tone in the get-rich-quick era of freewheeling capitalism that came to be called the **Gilded Age**.

Railroads: America's First Big Business

The military conquest of America's inland empire and the dispossession of Native Americans (see chapter 17) relied on an elaborate new railroad system, which allowed businesses to expand on a nationwide scale. The first transcontinental railroad, completed in 1869, linked new markets in the West to the nation's eastern and midwestern farms and cities. Between 1870 and 1880, overbuilding doubled the amount of track in the country and it nearly doubled again in the following decade. By 1900, the nation boasted more than 193,000 miles of railroad track — more than in all of Europe and Russia combined (Map 18.1). The railroads had become America's first big business. Privately owned but publicly financed by enormous land grants from the federal government and the states, the railroads epitomized the insidious nexus of business and politics in the Gilded Age.

To understand how the railroads came to dominate American life, there is no better place to start than with the career of **Jay Gould**, who pioneered the expansion of America's railway system and became the era's most notorious speculator. Jason "Jay" Gould bought his first railroad before he turned twenty-five. It was only sixty-two miles long, in bad repair, and on the brink of failure, but within two years he sold it at a profit of $130,000.

Gould, by his own admission, knew little about railroads and cared less about their operation. The secretive Gould operated in the stock market like a shark, looking for vulnerable railroads, buying enough stock to take control, and threatening to undercut his competitors until they bought him out at a high profit. The railroads that fell into his hands fared badly and often went bankrupt. Gould's genius lay not in providing transportation, but in cleverly buying and selling railroad stock on Wall Street, the nerve center of the new economy.

> ## "The most hated man in America."
> — Railroad tycoon JAY GOULD, speaking of himself

JUSTICE IN THE WEB.

Jay Gould as a Spider
In this 1885 political cartoon titled "Justice in the Web," artist Fredrick Burr Opper portrays Jay Gould as a hideous spider whose web, formed by Western Union telegraph lines, has entrapped "justice" through its monopoly of the telegraph industry. The telegraph, by transmitting coded messages across electric wire, formed the nervous system of the new industrial order. Gould, who controlled Western Union as well as the Erie and the Union Pacific Railroads, made his fortune by stock speculation. Images like this one fueled the public's distaste for Gould and made him, in his own words, "the most hated man in America." Granger Collection.

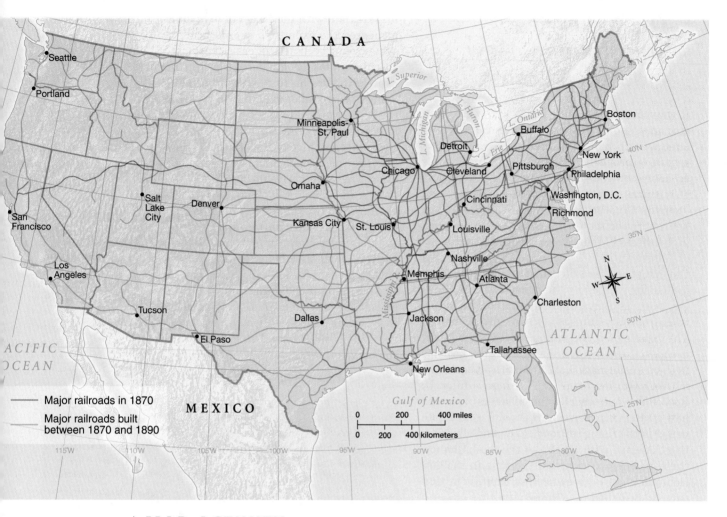

MAP ACTIVITY

MAP 18.1   Railroad Expansion, 1870–1890

Railroad mileage nearly quadrupled between 1870 and 1890, with the greatest growth occurring in the trans-Mississippi West. The western railroads — the Great Northern, Northern Pacific, Southern Pacific, and Atlantic and Pacific — were completed in the 1880s. Fueled by speculation and built ahead of demand, the western railroads made fortunes for individual speculators. But they rarely paid for themselves and often left disaster in their wake. At the same time, they fed a culture of insider dealing and political corruption.

READING THE MAP: Where were most of the railroad lines located in 1870? By 1890, how many railroads reached the west coast? What was the end point of the only western route?

CONNECTIONS: Why were so many rails laid between 1870 and 1890? How did the railroads affect the nation's economy?

The New York Stock Exchange, dating back to 1792, expanded as the volume of stock increased sixfold between 1869 and 1901. Where on one sleepy day in 1830 only thirty-one stocks traded, by 1886 more than a million shares a day changed hands. As the scale and complexity of the financial system increased, the line between investment and speculation blurred, causing many Americans to question if the concern with paper profits fueled the boom and bust cycles that led to panic and depression, putting hardworking Americans out of jobs. Yet however crass their motives, millionaire speculators like Jay Gould built America's rail system. In the 1880s, Gould moved to put together a second transcontinental railroad. His competitors had little choice but to adopt his strategy of expansion and consolidation, which in turn encouraged overbuilding and stimulated a national market.

The dramatic growth of the railroads created the country's first big business. Before the Civil War, even the largest textile mill in New England employed no more than 800 workers. By contrast, the Pennsylvania Railroad by the 1870s boasted a payroll of more than 55,000 workers. Capitalized at more than $400 million, the Pennsylvania Railroad constituted the largest private enterprise in the world.

The big business of railroads bestowed enormous riches on a handful of tycoons. Both Gould and his competitor "Commodore" Cornelius Vanderbilt amassed fortunes estimated at $100 million. Such staggering wealth eclipsed that of upper-class Americans from previous generations and left a legacy of lavish spending for an elite crop of ultrarich heirs. (See "Visualizing History," page 574.)

The Republican Party, firmly entrenched in Washington, worked closely with business interests, subsidizing the transcontinental railroad system with land grants of a staggering 100 million acres of public land and $64 million in tax incentives and direct aid. States and local communities joined the railroad boom, knowing that only those towns and villages along the tracks would grow and flourish. The combined federal and state land giveaway amounted to more than 180 million acres, an area larger than Texas.

A revolution in communication accompanied and supported the growth of the railroads. The telegraph, developed by Samuel F. B. Morse, marched across the continent alongside the railroad. By transmitting coded messages along electrical wire, the telegraph formed the "nervous system" of the new industrial order. Telegraph service quickly replaced Pony Express mail carriers in the West and transformed business by providing instantaneous communication. Again Jay Gould took the lead. In 1879, through stock manipulation, he seized control of Western Union, the company that monopolized the telegraph industry. By the end of the century, the telegraph carried 63 million messages a year and made it possible to move money around the world. Financiers in London and New York could follow the markets on ticker tape and transfer funds by wire.

The railroads soon fell on hard times. Already by the 1870s, lack of planning led to overbuilding. Across the nation, railroads competed fiercely for business. A manufacturer in an area served by competing railroads could get substantially reduced shipping rates in return for promises of steady business. Because railroad owners lost money through this kind of competition, they tried to set up agreements, or "pools," to end cutthroat competition by dividing up territory and setting rates. But these informal gentlemen's agreements invariably failed because men like Jay Gould, intent on undercutting all competitors, refused to play by the rules.

Novelist Charles Dudley Warner described how the rail speculators operated:

> [They fasten upon] some railway that is prosperous, pays dividends, pays a liberal interest on its bonds, and has a surplus. They contrive to buy, no matter at what the cost, a controlling interest in it. . . . Then they absorb its surplus; let it run down so that it pays no dividends and by-and-by cannot even pay its interest; then they squeeze the bondholders, who may be glad to accept anything that is offered out of the wreck, and perhaps then they throw the property into the hands of a receiver, or consolidate it with some other road at a value enormously greater than it cost them in stealing it. Having in one way or another sucked it dry, they look around for another road.

The public's alarm at the control wielded by the new railroad magnates and the tactics they employed provided a barometer of attitudes toward big business itself. When Gould died in 1892, the press described him as "the world's richest man." Rival Cornelius Vanderbilt judged Gould "the smartest man in America." But to the public, he was, as he himself admitted shortly before his death, "the most hated man in America."

Andrew Carnegie, Steel, and Vertical Integration

If Jay Gould was the man Americans loved to hate, **Andrew Carnegie** became one of America's heroes. Unlike Gould, for whom speculation was the game and wealth the goal, Carnegie turned his back on speculation and worked to build something enduring — Carnegie Steel, the biggest steel business in the world during the Gilded Age.

The growth of the steel industry proceeded directly from railroad building. The first railroads ran on iron rails, which cracked and broke with alarming frequency. Steel, both stronger and more flexible than iron, remained too expensive for use in rails until Englishman Henry Bessemer developed a way to make steel more cheaply from pig iron. Andrew Carnegie, among the first to champion the new "King Steel," came to dominate the emerging industry.

The Vanderbilts and the Gilded Age

Nothing represented the Gilded Age better than the Gold Room of Marble House, the "cottage" Alva Vanderbilt opened in Newport, Rhode Island, in 1892. William K. Vanderbilt, Alva's husband, was the grandson of Cornelius Vanderbilt, the founder of the New York Central Railway and the richest man of his era. His sons doubled his wealth, and his grandsons spent it lavishly. Alva, who enjoyed building houses, judged Marble House her triumph and liked to describe it as "Versailles improved." Modeled after Marie Antoinette's château, the Petit Trianon, on the grounds of Versailles, the mansion suited Alva's ambition to bring French culture to America. Designed by Richard Morris Hunt, the architect of the plutocracy, Marble House replicated the glory of the seventeenth-century French royal palaces Alva had admired when she visited France in her youth. Why might Alva have chosen to model her Newport home after a French queen's château?

The Gold Room, Alva's miniature version of Versailles's Hall of Mirrors, is a riot of neoclassical exuberance, with panels of Greek gods and goddesses adorning the walls. Above the striated black-and-white marble mantelpiece, bronze figures bear a vast candelabra, while cupids cavort and cherubs blow

Marble House: The Vanderbilt Mansion in Newport, Rhode Island

The Gold Room in Marble House

Carnegie, a Scottish immigrant, landed in New York in 1848 at the age of twelve. He rose from a job cleaning bobbins in a textile factory to become one of the richest men in America. Before he died, he gave away more than $300 million, most notably to public libraries. His generosity, combined with his own rise from poverty, burnished his public image.

When Carnegie was a teenager, his skill as a telegraph operator caught the attention of Tom Scott, superintendent of the Pennsylvania Railroad. Scott hired Carnegie, soon promoted him, and lent him the money for his first foray into Wall Street investment. As a result of this crony capitalism, Carnegie became a millionaire before his thirtieth birthday. At that point, Carnegie turned

trumpets on the walls and ceilings. Why do you think the Vanderbilts chose classical figures for their decoration? The enormous chandeliers and wood panels painted in red, green, and gold are multiplied in their dazzling magnificence by vast mirrors hung over the four doors, above the mantelpiece, and on the south wall. Critics charged that Marble House, with its Gold Room, was "a symbol of the heartless, glittering emptiness of the Gilded Age." What did they mean by this criticism?

The Vanderbilts' wealth and their lavish spending made it hard for old-money New Yorkers, living in their staid brownstones, to compete. Alva and William's Fifth Avenue mansion in New York City had a ballroom that could accommodate 1,600 guests. At their legendary costume ball in 1883, the Vanderbilts released live doves to astound their guests.

Alva Vanderbilt, pictured right at her famous costume ball dressed as a Venetian princess, flouted convention by divorcing William in 1895. Her indomitable will, her quest for recognition, and her fearless defiance of convention led her to the women's rights cause. She would become a principal supporter of the National Woman's Party and serve as its president.

In 1909, Alva organized two highly successful suffrage meetings at Marble House and prevailed upon her old friends to give to the cause. Many bought tickets to the meetings just to have the opportunity to tour the mansion. Crowds of more than five hundred thronged the grounds. In 1932, shortly before she died, Alva sold Marble House with the

Alva Vanderbilt Releasing the Doves

assurance that it would be kept as she had designed it. In the 1960s, the Preservation Society of Newport County took over the house, and today it is a National Historic Landmark open to the public. Alva Vanderbilt no doubt felt a deep pride in her creation, once describing it as "like a fourth child," and she had no trouble opening it to raise funds for the suffragist cause.

How might she feel about paying visitors wandering the rooms of Marble House today?

SOURCE: Marble House: © Dave G. Houser/Corbis; Gold Room: © Kelly-Mooney Photography/Corbis; Alva Vanderbilt: photo courtesy of The Preservation Society of Newport County.

away from speculation and struck out on his own to reshape the iron and steel industry. "My preference was always manufacturing," he wrote. "I wished to make something tangible." By applying the lessons of cost accounting and efficiency that he had learned from twelve years with the Pennsylvania Railroad, Carnegie turned steel into the nation's first manufacturing big business.

In 1872, Andrew Carnegie acquired one hundred acres in Braddock, Pennsylvania, on the outskirts of Pittsburgh, convenient to two railroad lines and fronted by the Monongahela River, a natural highway to Pittsburgh and the Ohio River and to the coal and iron mines farther north. There Carnegie built the largest, most up-to-date Bessemer steel plant in the world. At

Andrew Carnegie in 1894
"The man who dies rich . . . dies disgraced," asserted Andrew Carnegie. A classic rags-to-riches hero, Carnegie gave away more than $300 million before he died in 1919. Public libraries were among his favorite philanthropies; he contributed to the building of more than 2,500. But Carnegie was not so benign to his workers, whom he drove mercilessly, demanding a twelve-hour day, six days a week.
©Bettmann/Corbis.

that time, steelmakers produced about 70 tons a week. Within two decades, Carnegie's blast furnaces poured out an incredible 10,000 tons a week. He soon cut the cost of making rails by more than half, from $58 to $25 a ton. His formula for success was simple: "Cut the prices, scoop the market, run the mills full; watch the costs and profits will take care of themselves."

To guarantee the lowest costs and the maximum output, Carnegie pioneered a system of business organization called **vertical integration**. All aspects of the business were under Carnegie's control — from the mining of iron ore, to its transport on the Great Lakes, to the production of steel. Vertical integration, in the words of one observer, meant that "from the moment these crude stuffs were dug out of the earth until they flowed in a stream of liquid steel in the ladles, there was never a price, profit, or royalty paid to any outsider."

Always Carnegie kept his eyes on the account books, looking for ways to cut costs. The great productivity Carnegie encouraged came at a high price. He deliberately pitted his managers against one another, firing the losers and rewarding the winners with a share in the company. Workers achieved the output Carnegie demanded by enduring low wages, dangerous working conditions, and twelve-hour days six days a week. One worker, commenting on the contradiction between Carnegie's generous philanthropy in endowing public libraries and his tightfisted labor policy, observed, "After working twelve hours, how can a man go to a library?"

By 1900, Andrew Carnegie had become the best-known manufacturer in the nation, and

FIGURE 18.1   Iron and Steel Production, 1870–1900
Iron and steel production in the United States grew from nearly none in 1870 to 10 million tons a year by 1900. The secrets to the great increase in steel production were the use of the Bessemer process and vertical integration, pioneered by Andrew Carnegie. By 1900, Carnegie's mills alone produced more steel than all of Great Britain. With corporate consolidation after 1900, the rate of growth in steel proved even more spectacular.

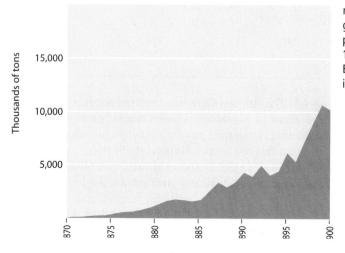

the age of iron had yielded to an age of steel. Steel from Carnegie's mills supported the elevated trains in New York and Chicago, formed the skeleton of the Washington Monument, supported the first steel bridge to span the Mississippi, and girded America's first skyscrapers. Carnegie steel armored the naval fleet that helped make the United States a world military power. As a captain of industry, Carnegie's only rival was the titan of the oil industry, John D. Rockefeller.

John D. Rockefeller, Standard Oil, and the Trust

Edwin Drake's discovery of oil in Pennsylvania in 1859 sent thousands rushing to the oil fields in search of "black gold." In the days before the automobile and gasoline, crude oil was refined into lubricating oil for machinery and kerosene for lamps, the major source of lighting in nineteenth-century houses before the invention of gas lamps and electric lighting. The amount of capital needed to buy or build an oil refinery in the 1860s and 1870s remained relatively low — less than $25,000, or roughly what it cost to lay one mile of railroad track. With start-up costs so low, the new petroleum industry experienced riotous competition among many small refineries. Ultimately, **John D. Rockefeller** and his Standard Oil Company succeeded in controlling nine-tenths of the oil-refining business.

Rockefeller grew up the son of a shrewd Yankee who peddled quack cures for cancer. Under his father's rough tutelage, he learned how to drive a hard bargain. "I trade with the boys and skin 'em and just beat 'em every time I can," "Big Bill" Rockefeller boasted. "I want to make 'em sharp." John D. learned his lessons well. In 1865, at the age of twenty-five, he controlled the largest oil refinery in Cleveland. Like a growing number of business owners, Rockefeller abandoned partnership or single proprietorship to embrace the corporation as the business structure best suited to maximize profit and minimize personal liability. In 1870, he incorporated his oil business, founding the Standard Oil Company, a behemoth so huge that it served as the precursor not only of today's ExxonMobil but also of Amoco, Chevron, Sunoco, and ConocoPhillips.

As the largest refiner in Cleveland, Rockefeller demanded secret rebates from the railroads in exchange for his steady business. Rebates enabled Rockefeller to drive out his competitors through predatory pricing.

The railroads, facing the pressures of cutthroat competition, needed Rockefeller's business so badly that they gave him a share of the rates that his competitors paid. A Pennsylvania Railroad official later confessed that Rockefeller extracted such huge rebates that the railroad, which could not risk losing his business, sometimes ended up paying him to transport Standard's oil. Secret deals, predatory pricing, and rebates enabled Rockefeller to undercut his competitors and pressure competing refiners to sell out or face ruin.

To gain legal standing for Standard Oil's secret deals, Rockefeller in 1882 pioneered a new form of corporate structure — the **trust**. The trust differed markedly from Carnegie's vertical approach in steel. Instead of attempting to control all aspects of the oil business, from the well to the consumer, Rockefeller used horizontal integration to control the refining process. Several trustees held stock in various refinery companies "in trust" for Standard's stockholders. This elaborate stock swap allowed the trustees to coordinate policy among the refineries, giving Rockefeller a virtual monopoly on the oil-refining business. The Standard Oil trust, valued at more than $70 million, paved the way for trusts in sugar, whiskey, matches, and many other products.

When the federal government responded to public pressure to outlaw the trust as a violation of free trade, Standard Oil changed tactics and reorganized as a holding company. Instead of stockholders in competing companies acting through trustees to set prices and determine territories, the holding company simply brought competing companies under one central administration. No longer technically separate businesses, they could act in concert without violating antitrust laws that forbade companies from forming "combinations in restraint of trade." As Standard Oil's empire grew, Rockefeller ended the independence of the refinery operators and closed inefficient plants. Next he moved to control sources of crude oil and took charge of the transportation and marketing of petroleum products. By the 1890s, Standard Oil ruled more than 90 percent of the oil business, employed 100,000 people, and was the biggest, richest, most feared, and most admired business organization in the world.

John D. Rockefeller enjoyed enormous success in business, but he was not well liked by the public. Before he died in 1937 at the age of ninety-eight, Rockefeller had become the country's first billionaire. But despite his modest habits, his pious Baptist

VISUAL ACTIVITY

"What a Funny Little Government"

The power wielded by John D. Rockefeller and the Standard Oil Company is captured in this political cartoon by Horace Taylor, which appeared in the January 22, 1900, issue of the *Verdict*. Rockefeller is pictured holding the White House and the Treasury Department in the palm of his hand, while in the background the U.S. Capitol has been converted into an oil refinery. Rockefeller and the company he ran held so much power that many feared democracy itself was threatened in the Gilded Age. Collection of the New-York Historical Society.

READING THE IMAGE: According to Horace Taylor, what kind of relationship did John D. Rockefeller have with the federal government? What benefits did he accrue from it?

CONNECTIONS: How much influence did industrialists such as Rockefeller exert over the national government in the late nineteenth century?

faith, and his many charitable gifts, he never shared in the public affection that Carnegie enjoyed. Editor and journalist Ida M. Tarbell's "History of the Standard Oil Company," which ran for three years (1902–1905) in serial form in *McClure's Magazine*, largely shaped the public's harsh view of Rockefeller.

Ida M. Tarbell had grown up in the Pennsylvania oil region, and her father had owned one of the small refineries gobbled up by Standard Oil. Her devastatingly thorough history chronicled the methods Rockefeller had used to take over the oil industry. Publicly, Rockefeller refused to respond to her allegations, although in private he dubbed her "Miss Tarbarrel." "If I step on that worm I will call attention to it," he explained. "If I ignore it, it will disappear." Yet by the time

Tarbell finished publishing her story, Rockefeller slept with a loaded revolver by his bed in fear of would-be assassins. Standard Oil and the man who created it had become the symbol of heartless monopoly.

New Inventions: The Telephone and Electricity

The second half of the nineteenth century was an age of invention. Men like Thomas Alva Edison and Alexander Graham Bell became folk heroes. But no matter how dramatic the inventors or the inventions, the new electric and telephone industries pioneered by Edison and Bell soon eclipsed their inventors and fell under the control of bankers and industrialists.

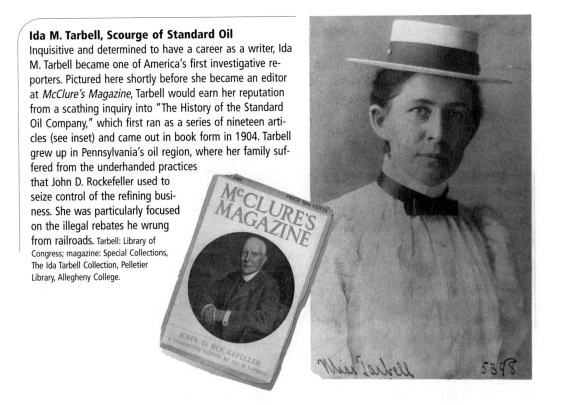

Ida M. Tarbell, Scourge of Standard Oil
Inquisitive and determined to have a career as a writer, Ida M. Tarbell became one of America's first investigative reporters. Pictured here shortly before she became an editor at *McClure's Magazine*, Tarbell would earn her reputation from a scathing inquiry into "The History of the Standard Oil Company," which first ran as a series of nineteen articles (see inset) and came out in book form in 1904. Tarbell grew up in Pennsylvania's oil region, where her family suffered from the underhanded practices that John D. Rockefeller used to seize control of the refining business. She was particularly focused on the illegal rebates he wrung from railroads. Tarbell: Library of Congress; magazine: Special Collections, The Ida Tarbell Collection, Pelletier Library, Allegheny College.

Alexander Graham Bell came to America from Scotland at the age of twenty-four with a passion to find a way to teach the deaf to speak (his wife and mother were deaf). Instead, he developed a way to transmit voice over wire — the telephone. Bell's invention astounded the world when he demonstrated it at the Philadelphia Centennial Exposition in 1876. Dumbfounded by the display, the emperor of Brazil cried out, "My God, it talks!"

In 1880, Bell's company, American Bell, pioneered "long lines" (long-distance telephone service), creating American Telephone and Telegraph (AT&T) as a subsidiary. In 1900, AT&T became the parent company of the system as a whole, controlling Western Electric, which manufactured and installed the equipment, and coordinating the Bell regional divisions. This complicated organizational structure meant that Americans could communicate not only locally but also across the country. And unlike a telegraph message, which had to be written out and taken to a telegraph station, sent over the wire, and then delivered by hand to the recipient, the telephone connected both parties immediately and privately. Bell's invention proved a boon to business, contributing to speed and efficiency. The number of telephones soared, reaching 310,000 in 1895 and more than 1.5 million in 1900.

Notable American Inventions 1865–1899

1865	Railroad sleeping car
1867	Typewriter
1868	Railroad refrigerator car
1870	Stock ticker
1874	Barbed wire
1876	Telephone
1877	Phonograph
1879	Incandescent lightbulb
1882	Electric fan
1885	Adding machine
1886	Coca-Cola
1888	Kodak camera
1890	Electric chair
1891	Zipper
1895	Safety razor
1896	Electric stove
1899	Tape recorder

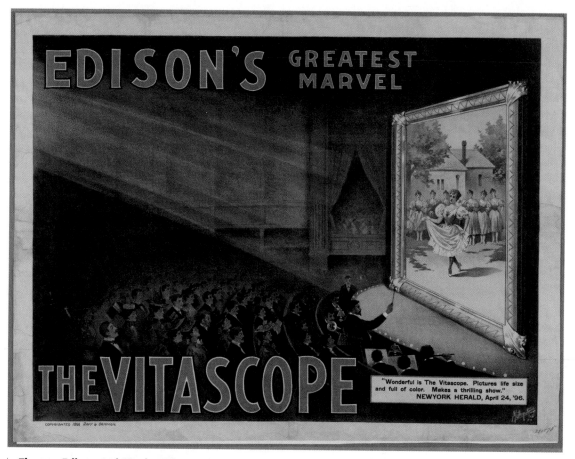

Thomas Edison and Moving Pictures
Edison's "greatest marvel," the Vitascope, was actually not his own invention. Edison was slow to develop a projection system, but the market for a machine that would project films for large audiences led him to acquire the Vitascope, pictured here in a postcard, from Thomas Armat and C. Francis Jenkins. The first theatrical exhibition took place in New York City in 1896. The Vitascope became a popular attraction in variety and vaudeville theaters, where rapt audiences like the one pictured here dressed up and enjoyed moving pictures accompanied by a live orchestra. Library of Congress.

Even more than Alexander Graham Bell, inventor **Thomas Alva Edison** embodied the old-fashioned virtues of Yankee ingenuity and rugged individualism that Americans most admired. A self-educated dynamo, he worked twenty hours a day in his laboratory in Menlo Park, New Jersey, vowing to turn out "a minor invention every ten days and a big thing every six months or so." He almost made good on his promise. At the height of his career, he averaged a patent every eleven days and invented such "big things" as the phonograph, the motion picture camera, and the filament for the incandescent lightbulb.

Edison, in competition with George W. Westinghouse, pioneered the use of electricity as an energy source. By the late nineteenth century, electricity had become a part of American urban life. It powered trolley cars and lighted factories, homes, and office buildings. Indeed, electricity became so prevalent in urban life that it symbolized the city, whose bright lights contrasted with rural America, left largely in the dark because private enterprise judged it not profitable enough to run electric lines to outlying farms and ranches.

While Americans thrilled to the new electric cities and the changes wrought by inventors, the day of the inventor quietly yielded to the heyday of the corporation. In 1892, the electric industry consolidated. Reflecting a nationwide trend in business, Edison General Electric dropped the name of its inventor, becoming simply General Electric (GE). For years, an embittered Edison

THE PROMISE OF TECHNOLOGY

Electrifying America

This 1889 cartoon was part of a campaign Thomas Edison waged against George Westinghouse in what came to be known as the "war of the currents." With the system of how best to provide electric current to the nation at stake, Edison launched a massive public relations campaign to discredit the high-voltage alternating current (AC) favored by Westinghouse. In the cartoon, innocent pedestrians are electrocuted by the wires as a policeman runs for help. The skull in the wires attached to the electric lightbulb warns that this new technology can be deadly. Although the direct current (DC) Edison championed was less dangerous to handle, it could reach only a one-mile radius from a power station. Despite his campaign to discredit Westinghouse, Edison lost the war of the currents. Cities that wanted electric lighting found Westinghouse's alternating current, despite the dangers of high voltage, less expensive and better suited to their needs. Was Edison taking a risk in trying to discredit alternating current? Granger Collection.

AN UNRESTRAINED DEMON.

refused to set foot inside a GE building. General Electric could afford to overlook the slight. A prime example of the trend toward business consolidation taking place in the 1890s, GE soon dominated the market.

> **REVIEW**   What devices did John D. Rockefeller use to gain control of 90 percent of the oil-refining business by 1890?

▶ From Competition to Consolidation

Even as Rockefeller and Carnegie built their empires, the era of the "robber barons," as they were dubbed by their detractors, was drawing to a close. Increasingly, businesses replaced partnerships and sole proprietorships with the anonymous corporate structure that would come to dominate the twentieth century. At the same time, mergers led to the creation of huge new corporations.

Banks and financiers played a key role in this consolidation, so much so that the decades at the turn of the twentieth century can be characterized as a period of **finance capitalism** — investment sponsored by banks and bankers. When the depression that followed the panic of 1893 bankrupted many businesses, bankers stepped in to bring order and to reorganize major industries. During these years, a new social philosophy based on the theories of naturalist Charles Darwin helped to justify consolidation and to inhibit state or federal regulation of business. A conservative Supreme Court further frustrated attempts to control business by consistently declaring unconstitutional legislation designed to regulate railroads or to outlaw trusts and monopolies.

J. P. Morgan and Finance Capitalism

John Pierpont Morgan, the preeminent finance capitalist of the late nineteenth century, loathed competition and sought whenever possible to eliminate it by substituting consolidation and

J. P. Morgan, Photograph by Edward Steichen
Few photographs of J. P. Morgan exist. Morgan, who
suffered from a skin condition that left him with a
misshapen strawberry of a nose, rarely allowed his
picture to be taken. But it was his eyes that people
remembered — eyes so piercing that Edward Steichen,
who took this photograph, observed that "meeting his
gaze was a little like confronting the headlights of an
express train." George Eastman House. Reprinted with permission
of Joanna T. Steichen.

central control. Morgan's passion for order made
him the architect of business mergers. The son
of a prominent banker, **J. P. Morgan** inherited
along with his wealth the stern business code of
the old-fashioned merchant bankers, men who
valued character and reputation. Aloof and silent,
Morgan looked down on the climbers and the
speculators with a haughtiness that led his rivals
to call him "Jupiter," after the ruler of the Roman
gods. At the turn of the twentieth century, he
dominated American banking, exerting an influence so powerful that his critics charged he controlled a vast "money trust" even more insidious
than Rockefeller's Standard Oil.

Morgan acted as a power broker in the reorganization of the railroads and the creation of
industrial giants such as General Electric and
U.S. Steel. When the railroads fell on hard times
in the 1890s, he used his access to capital to
rescue embattled, wrecked, and ruined companies.
Morgan quickly took over the struggling railroads

and moved to eliminate competition by creating
what he called "a community of interest" among
the managers he handpicked. By the time he
finished "Morganizing" the railroads, a handful
of directors controlled two-thirds of the nation's
track.

Banker control of the railroads helped to
coordinate the industry. But reorganization came
at a high price. To keep investors happy and to
guarantee huge profits from the sale of stock,
Morgan heavily "watered" the stock of the railroads, issuing more shares than the assets of
the company warranted. J. P. Morgan & Co.
made millions of dollars from commissions and
from blocks of stock acquired through
reorganization. The flagrant overcapitalization
created by the watered stock hurt the railroads
in the long run, saddling them with enormous
debt. Equally harmful was the management style
of the Morgan directors. Bankers, not railroad
men, they aimed at short-term profit and discouraged the continued technological and organizational innovation needed to run the railroads
effectively.

In 1898, Morgan moved into the steel industry, directly challenging Andrew Carnegie. Morgan
supervised the mergers of several smaller steel
companies, which soon expanded from the manufacture of finished goods to compete head-to-
head with Carnegie in steel production. The
pugnacious Carnegie cabled his partners in the
summer of 1900: "Action essential: crisis has
arrived . . . have no fear as to the result; victory
certain." The press trumpeted news of the impending fight between the feisty Scot and the haughty
Wall Street banker, but what the papers called
the "battle of the giants" in the end proved little
more than the wily maneuvering of two businessmen so adept that even today it is difficult to
say who won. For all his belligerence, the sixty-
six-year-old Carnegie yearned to retire to Skibo
Castle, his home in Scotland. He may well have
welcomed Morgan's bid for power. Morgan, who
disdained haggling, agreed to pay Carnegie's
asking price, $480 million (the equivalent of
about $10 billion in today's currency). According
to legend, when Carnegie later teased Morgan,
saying that he should have asked $100 million
more, Morgan replied, "You would have got it if
you had."

Morgan's acquisition of Carnegie Steel signaled the passing of the old entrepreneurial
order personified by Andrew Carnegie and the
arrival of a new, anonymous corporate world.
The banker quickly moved to pull together
Carnegie's chief competitors to form a huge new

Homestead Steelworks
The Homestead steelworks, outside Pittsburgh, is pictured shortly after J. P. Morgan bought out Andrew Carnegie and created U.S. Steel, the precursor of today's USX. Try to count the smokestacks in the picture. Air pollution on this scale posed a threat to the health of citizens and made for a dismal landscape. Workers complained that trees would not grow in Homestead. Hagley Museum & Library.

corporation, United States Steel, known today as USX. Created in 1901 and capitalized at $1.4 billion, U.S. Steel was the largest corporation in the world. Yet for all its size, it did not hold a monopoly in the steel industry. Significant small competitors, such as Bethlehem Steel, remained independent, creating a competitive system called an oligopoly, in which several companies control production. The smaller manufacturers simply followed the lead of U.S. Steel in setting prices and dividing the market so that each company held a comfortable share. Although oligopoly did not entirely eliminate competition, it did effectively blunt it.

When J. P. Morgan died in 1913, his estate totaled $68 million, not counting an estimated $50 million in art treasures. Andrew Carnegie, who gave away more than $300 million before his death six years later, is said to have quipped, "And to think he was not a rich man!" But Carnegie's gibe missed the mark. The quest for power, not wealth, had motivated J. P. Morgan, and his power could best be measured not in the millions he owned but in the billions he controlled. Even more than Carnegie or Rockefeller, Morgan left his stamp on the twentieth century and formed the model for corporate consolidation

that economists and social scientists soon justified with a new social theory known as social Darwinism.

Social Darwinism, Laissez-Faire, and the Supreme Court

John D. Rockefeller Jr., the son of the founder of Standard Oil, once remarked to his Baptist Bible class that the Standard Oil Company, like the American Beauty rose, resulted from "pruning the early buds that grew up around it." The elimination of smaller, inefficient units, he said, was "merely the working out of a law of nature and a law of God." The comparison of the business world to the natural world gave rise to a theory of society paralleling the relatively new notion of evolution formulated by the British naturalist Charles Darwin. In his monumental work *On the Origin of Species* (1859), Darwin theorized that in the struggle for survival, adaptation to the environment triggered among species a natural selection process that led to

> "The drunkard in the gutter is just where he ought to be, according to the fitness and tendency of things. . . . Millionaires are the product of natural selection."
> — Social Darwinist
> **WILLIAM GRAHAM SUMNER**

Social Darwinism: Did Wealthy Industrialists Practice What They Preached?

Darwinism, with its emphasis on tooth-and-claw competition, seemed ideally suited to the get-rich-quick mentality of the Gilded Age. By placing the theory of evolution in an economic context, social Darwinism argued against government intervention in business while at the same time insisting that reforms to ameliorate the evils of urban industrialism would only slow evolutionary progress. Most of the wealthy industrialists of the day probably never read Charles Darwin or the exponents of social Darwinism. Nevertheless, the catchphrases of social Darwinism larded the rhetoric of business in the Gilded Age.

Andrew Carnegie, alone among the American business moguls, not only championed social Darwinism but also avidly read the works of its primary exponent, the British social philosopher Herbert Spencer. Significantly, Spencer, not Darwin, coined the catchphrase "survival of the fittest." Carnegie spoke of his indebtedness to Spencer in terms usually reserved for religious conversion: "Before Spencer, all for me had been darkness, after him, all had become light — and right." In his autobiography, Carnegie wrote, "I had found the truth of evolution. 'All is well since all grows better' became my motto, my true source of comfort."

Not content to worship Spencer from afar, Carnegie assiduously worked to make his acquaintance and then would not rest until he had convinced the reluctant Spencer to come to America. In Pittsburgh, Carnegie promised, Spencer could best view his evolutionary theories at work in the world of industry. Clearly, Carnegie viewed his steelworks as the apex of America's new industrial order, a testimony to the playing out of evolutionary theory in the economic world.

In 1882, Spencer undertook an American tour. Carnegie personally invited him to Pittsburgh, squiring him through the Braddock steel mills. But Spencer failed to appreciate Carnegie's achievement. The heat, noise, and pollution of Pittsburgh reduced Spencer to near collapse, and he could only choke out, "Six months' residence here would justify suicide." Carnegie must have been devastated.

How well Carnegie actually understood the principles of social Darwinism is debatable. In his 1900 essay "Popular Illusions about Trusts," Carnegie spoke of the "law of evolution that moves from the heterogeneous to the homogeneous," citing Spencer as his source. Spencer, however, had written of the movement "from an indefinite incoherent homogeneity to a definite coherent heterogeneity." Instead of acknowledging that the history of human evolution moved from the simple to the more complex, Carnegie seemed to insist that evolution moved from the complex to the simple. This confusion of the most basic evolutionary theory calls into question Carnegie's grasp of Spencer's ideas or indeed of Darwin's. Other business leaders too busy making money to read no doubt understood even less about the working of evolutionary theory and social Darwinism, which they so often claimed as their own.

---

evolution. Herbert Spencer in Britain and William Graham Sumner in the United States developed the theory of **social Darwinism**. The social Darwinists concluded that societal progress came about as a result of relentless competition in which the strong survived and the weak died out.

In social terms, the idea of the "survival of the fittest," coined by Herbert Spencer, had profound significance, as Sumner, a professor of political economy at Yale University, made clear in his book *What Social Classes Owe to Each Other* (1883). "The drunkard in the gutter is just where he ought to be, according to the fitness and tendency of things," Sumner insisted. Conversely, "millionaires are the product of

natural selection," and although "they get high wages and live in luxury," Sumner claimed, "the bargain is a good one for society."

Social Darwinists equated wealth and power with "fitness" and believed that the unfit should be allowed to die off to advance the progress of humanity. Any efforts by the rich to aid the poor would only tamper with the rigid laws of nature and slow down evolution. Social Darwinism acted to curb social reform while at the same time glorifying great wealth. In an age when Rockefeller and Carnegie amassed hundreds of millions of dollars (billions in today's currency) and the average worker earned $500 a year, social Darwinism justified economic inequality (See "Historical Question," above.)

The distance between preachment and practice is boldly evident in the example of William Graham Sumner, America's foremost social Darwinist. Ironically, Sumner, who often sounded like an apologist for the rich, aroused the wrath of the very group he championed. The problem was that strict social Darwinists like Sumner insisted absolutely that the government ought not to meddle in the economy. The purity of Sumner's commitment to laissez-faire led him to adamantly oppose the protective tariffs the pro-business Republicans enacted to inflate the prices of manufactured goods produced abroad so that U.S. businesses could compete against foreign rivals. Sumner outspokenly attacked the tariff and firmly advocated free trade from his chair in political economy at Yale University. In 1890, the same year Congress passed the McKinley tariff, Sumner's fulminations against this highest tariff in the nation's history so outraged Yale's wealthy alumni that they mounted a campaign (unsuccessful) to have him fired.

Inconsistency never seemed to trouble Andrew Carnegie, who did not acknowledge a contradiction between his worship of Spencer and his strong support for the tariff. The comparison of Carnegie's position and Sumner's underscores the reality that although in theory laissez-faire constrained the government from playing an active role in business affairs, in practice industrialists fought for government favors — whether tariffs, land grants, or subsidies — that worked to their benefit. Only when legislatures proposed taxes or regulation did business leaders cry foul and invoke the "natural laws" of social Darwinism and its corollary, laissez-faire.

Herbert Spencer
The British writer and philosopher Herbert Spencer became a hero to industrialist Andrew Carnegie, who orchestrated Spencer's trip to America in 1882. The sage of social Darwinism proved a great disappointment to Carnegie. A cautious hypochondriac, Spencer guarded himself zealously against any painful contact with that teeming competitive world that he extolled. Once on American soil, Spencer spurned Carnegie's offer of hospitality during his visit to Pittsburgh and insisted on staying in a hotel. And when Carnegie eagerly demonstrated the wonders of the world's most modern steel mill to his guest, the tour reduced Spencer to a state of near collapse. Hulton Archives/Getty Images.

Thinking about Beliefs and Attitudes

1. In what ways did American business moguls think that the notion of evolution applied to them?

2. Why were most industrialists inconsistent in invoking the principles of social Darwinism?

Andrew Carnegie softened some of the harshness of social Darwinism in his essay "The Gospel of Wealth," published in 1889. The millionaire, Carnegie wrote, acted as a "mere trustee and agent for his poorer brethren, bringing to their service his superior wisdom, experience, and ability to administer, doing for them better than they could or would do for themselves." Carnegie preached philanthropy and urged the rich to "live unostentatious lives" and "administer surplus wealth for the good of the people." His **gospel of wealth** earned much praise but won few converts. Most millionaires followed the lead of J. P. Morgan, who contributed to charity but hoarded private treasures in his marble library.

Social Darwinism nicely suited an age in which the gross inequalities accompanying industrialization seemed to cry out for action. Assuaging the nation's conscience, social Darwinism justified neglect of the poor in the name of "race progress." With so many of the poor coming from different races and ethnicities, social Darwinism fueled racism. A new "scientific racism" purported to prove "Anglo-Saxons" superior to all other groups. Social Darwinism buttressed the status quo and reassured comfortable, white Americans that all was as it should be. Even the gospel of wealth, which mitigated the harshest dictates of social Darwinism, insisted that Americans lived in the best of all possible worlds and that the rich were the natural rulers.

With its emphasis on the free play of competition and the survival of the fittest, social Darwinism encouraged the economic theory of **laissez-faire** (French for "let it alone"). Business argued that government should not meddle in economic affairs, except to protect private property. A conservative Supreme Court agreed. During the 1880s and 1890s, the Court increasingly reinterpreted the Constitution to protect business from taxation, regulation, labor organization, and antitrust legislation.

In a series of landmark decisions, the Court used the Fourteenth Amendment, originally intended to protect freed slaves from state laws violating their rights, to protect corporations. Defining corporations as "persons," the Court reiterated the amendment's language, that no state can "deprive any person of life, liberty, or property, without due process of law." In 1886 in *Santa Clara County v. Southern Pacific Railroad*, the Court reasoned that legislation designed to regulate the railroad deprived the corporation of "due process." Using the same reasoning, the Court struck down state laws regulating railroad rates, declared income tax unconstitutional, and judged labor unions a "conspiracy in restraint of trade." The Court's elevation of the rights of property over other rights stemmed from the conservatism of its justices. According to Justice Stephen J. Field, the Constitution "allows no impediments to the acquisition of property." Field, born into a wealthy New England family, spoke with the bias of the privileged class to whom property rights were sacrosanct. Imbued with this ideology, the Court refused to impede corporate consolidation and did nothing to curb the excesses of big business or promote the humane treatment of workers. Only in the arena of politics did Americans tackle the issues raised by corporate capitalism.

REVIEW Why did the ideas of social Darwinism appeal to many Americans in the late nineteenth century?

▶ Politics and Culture

For many Americans, politics provided a source of identity, a means of livelihood, and a ready form of entertainment. No wonder voter turnout averaged a hefty 77 percent (compared to 57 percent in the 2008 presidential election). A variety of factors contributed to the complicated interplay of politics and culture. Patronage provided an economic incentive for voter participation, but ethnicity, religion, sectional loyalty, race, and gender all influenced the political life of the period.

Political Participation and Party Loyalty

Patronage proved a strong motivation for party loyalty among many voters. Political parties in power doled out federal, state, and local government jobs to their loyal supporters. With hundreds of thousands of jobs to be filled, the choice of party affiliation could mean the difference between a paycheck and an empty pocket. Money greased the wheels of this system of patronage, dubbed the **spoils system** from the adage "to the victor go the spoils." With their livelihoods tied to their party identity, government employees in particular had an incentive to vote in great numbers.

Political affiliation provided a powerful sense of group identity for many voters proud of their loyalty to the Democrats or the Republicans.

Hayes Campaign Lantern, 1876
Republicans carried this lantern in the presidential campaign of 1876. Designed for nighttime rallies, the lantern featured paper transparencies that allowed light to shine through the stars and illuminate the portrait of the candidate, Rutherford B. Hayes. Marching men with lighted lanterns held aloft must have been a dramatic sight in small towns across the country, where politics constituted a major form of entertainment in the nineteenth century. Collection of Janice L. and David J. Frent.

Democrats, who traced the party's roots back to Thomas Jefferson, called theirs "the party of the fathers." The Republican Party, founded in the 1850s, still claimed strong loyalties in the North as a result of its alignment with the Union during the Civil War. Republicans proved particularly adept at evoking Civil War loyalty, using a tactic called "waving the bloody shirt" — reminding voters which side they had fought for in the Civil War. Noting the power of old sectional loyalties, one of the party faithful observed, "Iowa will go Democratic when Hell goes Methodist."

Religion and ethnicity also played a significant role in politics. In the North, Protestants from the old-line denominations, particularly Presbyterians and Methodists, flocked to the Republican Party, which championed a series of moral reforms, including local laws requiring businesses to close in observance of the Sabbath. In the burgeoning cities, the Democratic Party courted immigrants and working-class Catholic and Jewish voters, charging, rightly, that Republican moral crusades often masked attacks on immigrant culture.

Sectionalism and the New South

After the end of Reconstruction, most white voters in the former Confederate states remained loyal Democrats, voting for Democratic candidates in every presidential election for the next seventy years. Labeling the Republican Party the agent of "Negro rule," Democrats urged white southerners to "vote the way you shot." Yet the so-called solid South proved far from solid on the state and local levels. The economic plight of the South led to shifting political alliances and to third-party movements that challenged Democratic attempts to define politics along race lines and maintain the Democratic Party as the white man's party.

The South's economy, devastated by the war, foundered at the same time the North experienced an unprecedented industrial boom. Soon an influential group of southerners called for a **New South** modeled on the industrial North. Henry Grady, the ebullient young editor of the *Atlanta Constitution*, used his paper's influence (it boasted the largest circulation of any weekly in the country) to extol the virtues of a new industrial South. Part bully, part booster, Grady exhorted the South to use its natural advantages — cheap labor and abundant natural resources — to go head-to-head in competition with northern industry.

Grady's message fell on receptive ears. Many southerners, men and women, black and white, joined the national migration from farm to city, leaving the old plantations to molder and decay. With the end of military rule in 1877, southern Democrats took back state governments, calling themselves "Redeemers." Yet rather than restore the economy of the old planter class, they embraced northern promoters who promised prosperity and profits.

The railroads came first, opening up the region for industrial development. Southern railroad mileage grew fourfold from 1865 to 1890. The number of cotton spindles also soared as textile mill owners abandoned New England in search of the cheap labor and proximity to raw materials promised in the South. By 1900, the South had become the nation's leading producer of cloth, and more than 100,000 southerners, many of them women and children, worked in the region's textile mills.

The New South prided itself most on its iron and steel industry, which grew up in the area surrounding Birmingham, Alabama. During this period, the smokestack replaced the white-pillared plantation as the symbol of the New South. Andrew Carnegie toured the region in 1889 and observed, "The South is Pennsylvania's most formidable industrial enemy." But southern industry remained controlled by northern investors, who had no intention of letting the South beat the North at its own game. Elaborate mechanisms rigged the price of southern steel, inflating it, as one northern insider confessed, "for the purpose of protecting the Pittsburgh mills and in turn the Pittsburgh steel users." Similarly, in the lumber and mining industries, investors in the North and abroad, not southerners, reaped the lion's share of the profits.

In only one industry did the South truly dominate — tobacco. Capitalizing on the invention of a machine for rolling cigarettes, the American Tobacco Company, founded by the Duke family of North Carolina, eventually dominated the industry. As cigarettes replaced chewing tobacco in popularity at the turn of the twentieth century, a booming market developed for Duke's "ready mades." Soon the company sold 400,000 cigarettes a day.

In practical terms, the industrialized New South proved an illusion. Much of the South remained agricultural, caught in the grip of the insidious crop lien system (see chapter 16). White

> "Iowa will go Democratic when Hell goes Methodist."
> — A Northern Republican

southern farmers, desperate to get out of debt, sometimes joined with African Americans to pursue their goals politically. Between 1865 and 1900, voters in every state south of the Mason-Dixon line experimented with political alliances that crossed the color line and threatened the status quo.

Gender, Race, and Politics

Gender — society's notion of what constitutes acceptable masculine or feminine behavior — influenced politics throughout the nineteenth century. From the early days of the Republic, citizenship had been defined in male terms. Citizenship and its prerogatives (voting and officeholding) served as a badge of manliness and rested on its corollary, patriarchy — the power and authority men exerted over their wives and families. With the advent of universal (white) male suffrage in the early nineteenth century, gender eclipsed class as the defining feature of citizenship; men's dominance over women provided the common thread that knit all white men together politically. The concept of **separate spheres** dictated political participation for men only. Once the public sphere of political participation became equated with manhood, women found themselves increasingly restricted to the private sphere of home and hearth.

Women were not alone in their limited access to the public sphere. Though Reconstruction legislation had guaranteed their freedom, blacks continued to face discrimination, especially in the New South. Segregation, commonly practiced under the rubric of **Jim Crow** laws (as discussed in chapter 21), prevented ex-slaves from riding in the same train cars as whites, from eating in the same restaurants, or from using the same toilet facilities.

Amid the turmoil of the post-Reconstruction South, some groups struck cross-racial alliances in search of political might. In Virginia, the "Readjusters," a coalition of blacks and whites determined to "readjust" (lower) the state debt and spend more money on public education, captured state offices from 1879 to 1883. Groups like the Readjusters rested on the belief that universal political rights (voting, officeholding, patronage) could be extended to black males in the public sphere while maintaining racial segregation in the private sphere. Democrats, for their part, fought back by trying to convince voters that black voting would inevitably lead

to miscegenation (racial mixing). Black male political power and sexual power, they warned, went hand in hand. Ultimately, their arguments prevailed, and many whites returned to the Democratic fold to protect "white womanhood" and with it white supremacy.

The notion that black men threatened white southern womanhood reached its most vicious form in the practice of lynching — the killing and mutilation of black men by white mobs. By 1892, the practice had become so prevalent that a courageous black editor, **Ida B. Wells**, launched an antilynching movement. That year, a white mob lynched a friend of Wells's whose grocery store competed too successfully with a white-owned store. Wells shrewdly concluded that lynching served "as an excuse to get rid of Negroes who were acquiring wealth and property and thus keep the race terrorized." She began to collect data on lynching and discovered that in the decade between 1882 and 1892 lynching rose in the South by an overwhelming 200 percent, with more than 241 black people killed. The vast increase in lynching testified to the retreat of the federal government following Reconstruction and to white southerners' determination to maintain supremacy through terrorism and intimidation.

In the face of this carnage, Wells struck back. As the first salvo in her attack, she put to rest the "old threadbare lie that Negro men assault white women." As she pointed out, violations of black women by white men, which were much more frequent than black attacks on white women, went unnoticed and unpunished. Wells articulated lynching as a problem of race and gender. She insisted that the myth of black attacks on white southern women masked the reality that mob violence had more to do with economics and the shifting social structure of the South than with rape. She demonstrated in a sophisticated way how the southern patriarchal system, having lost its control over blacks with the end of slavery, used its control over white women to circumscribe the liberty of black men.

Wells's strong stance immediately resulted in reprisal. While she was traveling in the North, vandals ransacked her office in Tennessee and destroyed her printing equipment. Yet the warning that she would be killed on sight if she ever returned to Memphis only stiffened her resolve. As she wrote in her autobiography, *Crusade for Justice* (1928), "Having lost my paper, had a price put on my life and been made an exile . . . , I felt that I owed it to myself and to my race to

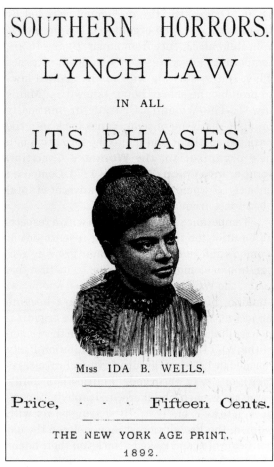

SOUTHERN HORRORS.

LYNCH LAW

IN ALL

ITS PHASES

Miss IDA B. WELLS.

Price,   · · ·   Fifteen Cents.

THE NEW YORK AGE PRINT,
1892.

Ida B. Wells
Ida B. Wells began her antilynching campaign in 1892 after a friend's murder led her to examine the problem of lynching in the South. She spread her message in lectures and pamphlets like this one, distributed for fifteen cents. Wells brought the horror of lynching to a national and international audience and mobilized other African American women to undertake social action under the auspices of the National Association of Colored Women. She later became a founding member of the National Association for the Advancement of Colored People (NAACP). Manuscript, Archives and Rare Books Division, Schomburg Center for Research in Black Culture, The New York Public Library, Astor, Lenox, and Tilden Foundations.

tell the whole truth now that I was where I could do so freely." As a reporter, first for the *New York Age* and later for the *Chicago Inter-Ocean*, she used every opportunity to hammer home her message. Beginning in 1894 and continuing for decades, antilynching bills were introduced in Congress, only to be defeated by southern opposition.

Lynching did not end during Ida B. Wells's lifetime, but Wells's forceful voice brought the

issue to national and international prominence. At her funeral in 1931, black leader W. E. B. Du Bois eulogized Wells as the woman who "began the awakening of the conscience of the nation." Wells's determined campaign against lynching provided just one example of women's political activism during the Gilded Age. The suffrage and temperance movements, along with the growing popularity of women's clubs, dramatized how women refused to be relegated to a separate sphere that kept them out of politics.

Women's Activism

No one better recognized the potency of the gendered notion of political rights than Elizabeth Cady Stanton, who lamented the introduction of the word *male* into the Fourteenth Amendment (see chapter 16). The explicit linking of manhood with citizenship and voting rights in the Constitution marked a major setback for reformers who supported the vote for women. In 1869, Stanton along with Susan B. Anthony formed the National Woman Suffrage Association, the first independent woman's rights organization in the United States (discussed in chapter 20). Women found ways to act politically long before they voted and cleverly used their moral authority as wives and mothers to move from the domestic sphere into the realm of politics.

The extraordinary activity of women's clubs in the period following the Civil War provides just one example. Women's clubs proliferated from the 1860s to the 1890s, often in response to the exclusionary policies of men's organizations. In 1868, newspaper reporter Jane Cunningham Croly (pen name Jennie June) founded the Sorosis Club in New York City after the New York Press Club denied entry to women journalists wishing to attend a banquet honoring the British author Charles Dickens. In 1890, Croly brought state and local clubs together under the umbrella of the **General Federation of Women's Clubs** (GFWC). Not wanting to alienate southern women, the GFWC barred black women's clubs from joining, despite their vehement objections. Women's clubs soon abandoned literary pursuits to devote themselves to "civic usefulness," endorsing an end to child labor, supporting the eight-hour workday, and helping pass pure food and drug legislation.

The temperance movement (the movement to end drunkenness) attracted by far the largest number of organized women in the late nineteenth century. By the late 1860s and the

"Woman's Holy War"
This political cartoon from 1874 styles the temperance campaign as "Woman's Holy War" and shows a woman knight in armor (demurely seated sidesaddle on her charger), wielding a battle-ax and trampling on barrels of liquor. The image of temperance women as ax-wielding Amazons proved a popular satiric image. The temperance movement experienced a resurgence in the 1870s after Bible-toting women marched to shut down saloons from New York to Michigan. Their activism led to the creation of the Woman's Christian Temperance Union in 1874.
Picture Research Consultants & Archives.

1870s, the liquor business was flourishing, with about one saloon for every fifty males over the age of fifteen. During the winter of 1873–74, temperance women adopted a radical new tactic. Armed with Bibles and singing hymns, they marched on taverns and saloons and refused to leave until the proprietors signed a pledge to quit selling liquor. Known as the Woman's Crusade, the movement spread like a prairie fire through small towns in Ohio, Indiana, Michigan, and Illinois and soon moved east into New York, New England, and Pennsylvania. Before it was over, more than 100,000 women had marched in more than 450 cities and towns.

The women's tactics may have been new, but the temperance movement dated back to the 1820s. Originally, the movement was led by Protestant men who organized clubs to pledge voluntary abstinence from liquor. By the 1850s, temperance advocates won significant victories when states, starting with Maine, passed laws to prohibit the sale of liquor (known as "Maine laws"). The Woman's Crusade dramatically brought the issue of temperance back into the national spotlight and led to the formation of a new organization, the **Woman's Christian Temperance Union** (WCTU) in 1874. Composed entirely of women, the WCTU advocated total abstinence from alcohol.

Temperance provided women with a respectable outlet for their increasing resentment of women's inferior status and their growing recognition of women's capabilities. In its first five years, the WCTU relied on education and moral suasion, but when Frances Willard became president in 1879, she politicized the organization (as discussed in chapter 20). When the women of the WCTU joined with the Prohibition Party (formed in 1869 by a group of evangelical clergymen), one wag observed, "Politics is a man's game, an' women, childhern, and prohyibitionists do well to keep out iv it." By sharing power with women, the Prohibitionist men violated the old political rules and risked attacks on their honor and manhood.

Even though they could not yet vote, women found ways to affect the political process. Like men, they displayed strong party loyalties and rallied around traditional Republican and Democratic candidates. Third parties courted women, recognizing that their volunteer labor and support could be key assets in party building. Nevertheless, despite growing political awareness among women, politics, particularly presidential politics, remained an exclusively male prerogative.

REVIEW   How did race and gender influence politics?

▶ Presidential Politics

The presidents of the Gilded Age, from Rutherford B. Hayes (1877–1881) to William McKinley (1897–1901), are largely forgotten men, primarily because so little was expected of them. In wartime, Lincoln had expanded the power of the presidency, but following the war, even as the nation addressed western expansion, economic transformation, and nascent urban industrialism, the power of the presidency waned. The dominant creed of laissez-faire, coupled with the dictates of social Darwinism, warned the president and the government to leave business alone. Still, presidents in the Gilded Age grappled with corruption and party strife and struggled toward the creation of new political ethics designed to replace patronage with a civil service system that promised to award jobs on the basis of merit, not party loyalty.

Corruption and Party Strife

The political corruption and party factionalism that characterized the administration of Ulysses S. Grant (1869–1877) (see chapter 16) continued to trouble the nation in the 1880s. The spoils system — awarding jobs for political purposes — remained the driving force in party politics at all levels of government in the Gilded Age. Pro-business Republicans generally held a firm grip on the White House, while Democrats had better luck in Congress. Both parties relied on patronage to cement party loyalty. Corruption was rampant, with senators and representatives, and sometimes members of the executive branch, on the payrolls of business interests. The notion of "conflict of interest" did not exist; nor did a standard of accepted ethical behavior. Reformers eager to end corruption and the replace the spoils system with a merit-based civil service system faced an uphill battle.

A small but determined group of reformers championed a new ethics that would preclude politicians from getting rich from public office. The selection of U.S. senators particularly concerned them. Under the Constitution, senators were selected by state legislatures, not directly elected by the voters. Powerful business interests often contrived to control state legislatures and through them U.S. senators. As journalist Henry Demarest Lloyd quipped, Standard Oil "had done everything to the Pennsylvania legislature except to refine it." Nothing prevented a senator from collecting a paycheck from any of the great corporations. So many did so that political cartoonists often portrayed senators as huge money bags labeled with the names of the corporations they served. In this climate, a constitutional amendment calling for the direct election of senators faced stiff opposition from entrenched interests.

Republican president **Rutherford B. Hayes**, whose disputed election in 1876 signaled the end of Reconstruction in the South, tried to steer a middle course between spoilsmen and reformers. Although the Democratic press ridiculed him as "Rutherfraud" because he had not been popularly elected (see chapter 16), Hayes proved a hardworking, well-informed executive who wanted peace, prosperity, and an end to party strife. Yet the Republican Party remained divided into factions led by strong party bosses who boasted that they could make or break any president.

Foremost among the Republican bosses in the Senate stood Roscoe Conkling of New York, a master spoilsman who ridiculed civil service as "snivel service." He and his followers, called the "Stalwarts," represented the Grant faction of the party. Conkling's archrival, Senator James G. Blaine of Maine, led the "Half Breeds." Not as openly corrupt as the Grant wing of the party, the Half Breeds and their champion were nevertheless tainted with charges of corruption. A third group, called the "Mugwumps," consisted primarily of reform-minded Republicans from Massachusetts and New York who deplored the spoils system and advocated **civil service reform**. The name "Mugwump" came from the Algonquian word for "chief," but critics used the term derisively, punning that the Mugwumps straddled the fence on issues of party loyalty, "with their mug on one side and wump on the other."

President Hayes's middle course pleased no one, and he soon managed to alienate all factions of his party. No one was surprised when he announced that he would not seek reelection in 1880. To avoid choosing among its factions, the Republican Party in 1880 nominated a dark-horse candidate, Representative **James A. Garfield** of Ohio. To foster party unity, they picked Stalwart Chester A. Arthur as the vice presidential candidate. The Democrats made an attempt to overcome sectionalism and establish a national party by selecting as their presidential standard-bearer an old Union general, Winfield Scott Hancock. But as one observer noted, "It is a peculiarly constituted party that sends rebel brigadiers to Congress because of their rebellion, and then nominates a Union General as its candidate for president because of his loyalty." Hancock garnered only lukewarm support, receiving just 155 electoral votes to Garfield's 214, although the popular vote was less lopsided.

> "[Standard Oil] had done everything to the Pennsylvania legislature except to refine it."
> — Journalist **HENRY DEMAREST LLOYD**

Garfield's Assassination and Civil Service Reform

"My God," Garfield swore after only a few months in office, "what is there in this place that a man should ever want to get into it?" Garfield, like Hayes, faced the difficult task of remaining independent while pacifying the party bosses and placating the reformers. As the federal bureaucracy grew to nearly 150,000 jobs, thousands of office seekers swarmed to the nation's capital, each clamoring for a position. In the days before Secret Service protection, the White House door stood open to all comers. Garfield took a fatalistic view. "Assassination," he told a friend, "can no more be guarded against than death by lightning, and it is best not to worry about either."

On July 2, 1881, less than four months after taking office, Garfield was shot. His assailant,

Civil Service Exams
In this 1890s photograph, prospective police officers in Chicago take the written civil service exam. Civil service meant that politicians and party bosses could no longer use jobs in the government to reward the party faithful. Many people worried that merit examinations would favor the educated elite at the expense of immigrant groups such as the Irish, who had made a place for themselves in the political system by the late nineteenth century. Chicago Historical Society.

Charles Guiteau, though clearly insane, turned out to be a disappointed office seeker who claimed to be motivated by political partisanship. He told the police officer who arrested him, "I did it; I will go to jail for it; Arthur is president, and I am a Stalwart." Throughout the hot summer, the country kept a deathwatch as Garfield lingered. When he died in September, Chester A. Arthur became president. The press almost universally condemned Republican factionalism for creating the political climate that produced Guiteau and led to the second political assassination in a generation.

Stalwart Roscoe Conkling saw his hopes for the White House dashed. Attacks on the spoils system increased, and the public joined the chorus calling for reform. Both parties claimed credit for passage of the Pendleton Civil Service Act of 1883, which established a permanent Civil Service Commission consisting of three members appointed by the president. Some fourteen thousand jobs came under a merit system that required examinations for office and made it impossible to remove jobholders for political reasons. The new law also prohibited federal jobholders from contributing to political campaigns, thus drying up the major source of the party bosses' revenue. Soon, business interests stepped in to replace officeholders as the nation's chief political contributors. Ironically, civil service reform thus gave business an even greater influence in political life.

Reform and Scandal: The Campaign of 1884

With Conkling's downfall, James G. Blaine assumed leadership of the Republican Party and at long last captured the presidential nomination in 1884. A magnetic Irish American, Blaine inspired such devotion that his supporters called themselves Blainiacs. But Mugwumps like editor Carl Schurz insisted that Blaine "wallowed in spoils like a rhinoceros in an African pool." They bolted the party and embraced the Democrats' presidential nominee, the stolid **Grover Cleveland**, reform governor of New York. The burly, beer-drinking Cleveland distinguished himself from an entire generation of politicians by the simple motto "A public office is a public trust." First as mayor of Buffalo and later as governor of New York, he built a reputation for honesty, economy, and administrative efficiency. The Democrats, who had not won the presidency since 1856, had high hopes for his candidacy,

"Another Voice for Cleveland"
This political cartoon ran in the magazine *Judge* in the fall of 1884 during the presidential campaign. Grover Cleveland, the Democratic candidate, is pictured cringing from the cries of a babe in arms — an allusion to his admission that he had fathered an illegitimate child. Despite the lurid publicity, Cleveland won the election. Library of Congress.

especially after the Mugwumps threw their support to Cleveland. As the Mugwumps insisted, "The paramount issue this year is moral rather than political."

The Mugwumps soon regretted their words. The 1884 contest degenerated so far into scandal and nasty mudslinging that one disgusted journalist styled it "the vilest campaign ever waged." In July, Cleveland's hometown paper, the *Buffalo Telegraph*, dropped the bombshell that the candidate had fathered an illegitimate child in an affair with a local widow. Cleveland, a bachelor, stoically accepted responsibility for the child. Crushed by the scandal, the Mugwumps lost much of their enthusiasm. At public rallies, Blaine's partisans taunted Cleveland, chanting, "Ma, Ma, where's my Pa?" Silent but fuming, Cleveland waged his campaign in the traditional fashion by staying home.

Blaine set a new campaign style by launching a whirlwind national tour. On a last-minute stop in New York City, the exhausted candidate committed a misstep that may have cost him the election. He overlooked a remark by a supporter, a local clergyman who cast a slur on Catholic voters by styling the Democrats as the party of "Rum, Romanism, and Rebellion." Linking drinking (rum) and Catholicism (Romanism) offended Irish Catholic voters, whom Blaine had counted on to desert the Democratic Party and support him because of his Irish background.

With less than a week to go until the election, Blaine had no chance to recover from the negative publicity. He lost New York State by fewer than 1,200 votes and with it the election. In the final tally, Cleveland defeated Blaine by a scant 23,005 votes nationwide but won with

Candidate	Electoral Vote	Popular Vote	Percent of Popular Vote
Grover Cleveland (Democrat)	219	4,874,986	48.5*
James G. Blaine (Republican)	182	4,851,981	48.3

*Percentages do not total 100 because some popular votes went to other parties.

MAP 18.2
The Election of 1884

219 electoral votes to Blaine's 182 (Map 18.2), ending twenty-four years of Republican control of the presidency. Cleveland's followers had the last word. To the chorus of "Ma, Ma, where's my Pa?" they retorted, "Going to the White House, ha, ha, ha."

REVIEW   How did the question of civil service reform contribute to divisions within the Republican Party?

▶ Economic Issues and Party Realignment

Four years later, in the election of 1888, fickle voters turned Cleveland out, electing Republican Benjamin Harrison, the grandson of President William Henry Harrison. Then, in the only instance in American history when a president once defeated at the polls returned to office, the voters brought Cleveland back in the election of 1892. What factors account for such a surprising turnaround? The 1880s witnessed a remarkable political realignment as a set of economic concerns replaced appeals to Civil War sectional loyalties. The tariff, federal regulation of the railroads and trusts, and the campaign for free silver restructured American politics. A Wall Street panic in 1893 set off a major depression that further fed political unrest.

The Tariff and the Politics of Protection

The tariff became a potent political issue in the 1880s. The concept of a protective tariff to raise the price of imported goods and stimulate American industry dated back to Alexander Hamilton in the founding days of the Republic. The Republicans turned the tariff to political ends in 1861 by enacting a measure that both raised revenues for the Civil War and rewarded their industrial supporters, who wanted protection from foreign competition. After the war, the pro-business Republicans continued to revise and enlarge the tariff. Manufactured goods such as steel and textiles, and some agricultural products, including sugar and wool, benefited from protection. Most farm products, notably wheat and cotton, did not. By the 1880s, the tariff produced more than $2.1 billion in revenue. Not only did the high tariff pay off the nation's Civil War debt and fund pensions for Union soldiers, but it also created a huge surplus that sat idly in the Treasury's vaults while the government argued about how (or even whether) to spend it.

To many Americans, particularly southern and midwestern farmers who sold their crops in a world market but had to buy goods priced artificially high because of the protective tariff, the answer was simple: Reduce the tariff. Advocates of free trade and moderates agitated for tariff reform. But those who benefited from the tariff — industrialists insisting that America's "infant industries" needed protection and some westerners producing protected raw materials such as wool, hides, and lumber — firmly opposed lowering the tariff. Many argued that workers, too, benefited from high tariffs that protected American wages by giving American products an edge over imported goods.

The Republican Party seized on the tariff question to forge a new national coalition. "Fold up the bloody shirt and lay it away," Blaine advised a colleague in 1880. "It's of no use to us. You want to shift the main issue to protection." By encouraging an alliance among industrialists, labor, and western producers of raw materials — groups seen to benefit from the tariff — Blaine hoped to solidify the North, Midwest, and West against the solidly Democratic South. Although the tactic failed for Blaine in the presidential election of 1884, it worked for the Republicans four years later.

Cleveland, who had straddled the tariff issue in the election of 1884, startled the nation in 1887 by calling for tariff reform. Cleveland attacked the tariff as a tax levied on American consumers by powerful industries. And he pointed out that high tariffs impeded the expansion of American markets abroad at a time when American industries needed to expand if they were to keep growing. The Republicans countered by arguing that "tariff tinkering" would only unsettle prosperous industries, drive down wages, and shrink the farmers' home market. Republican Benjamin Harrison, who supported the high tariff, ousted Cleveland from the White House in 1888, carrying all the western and northern states except Connecticut and New Jersey.

Back in power, the Republicans brazenly passed the highest tariff in the nation's history in 1890. The new tariff, sponsored by Republican representative William McKinley of Ohio and signed into law by Harrison, stirred up a hornet's nest of protest across the United States. The American people had elected Harrison to preserve protection but not to enact a higher tariff. Democrats condemned the **McKinley tariff** and labeled the Republican Congress that passed it the "Billion Dollar Congress" for its carnival of spending, which depleted the nation's surplus by enacting a series of pork barrel programs shamelessly designed to bring federal money to congressmen's own constituents. In the congressional election of 1890, angry voters swept the hapless Republicans, including tariff sponsor McKinley, out of office. Two years later, Harrison himself was defeated. Grover Cleveland, whose call for tariff revision had cost him the election in 1888, triumphantly returned to the White House vowing to lower the tariff. Such were the changes in the political winds whipped up by the tariff issue.

Controversy over the tariff masked deeper divisions in American society. Conflict between workers and farmers on the one side and bankers and corporate giants on the other erupted throughout the 1880s and came to a head in the 1890s. Both sides in the tariff debate spoke to concern over class conflict when they insisted that their respective plans, whether McKinley's high tariff or Cleveland's tariff reform, would bring prosperity and harmony. For their part, many working people shared the sentiment voiced by one labor leader that the tariff was "only a scheme devised by the old parties to throw dust in the eyes of laboring men."

Railroads, Trusts, and the Federal Government

American voters may have divided on the tariff, but increasingly they agreed on the need for federal regulation of the railroads and federal legislation to curb the power of the "trusts" (a term loosely applied to all large business combinations). As early as the 1870s, angry farmers in the Midwest who suffered from the unfair shipping practices of the railroads organized to fight for railroad regulation. The Patrons of Husbandry, or the Grange, founded in 1867 as a social and educational organization for farmers, soon became an independent political movement. By electing Grangers to state office, farmers made it possible for several midwestern states to pass laws in the 1870s and 1880s regulating the railroads. At first, the Supreme Court ruled in favor of state regulation (*Munn v. Illinois*, 1877). But in 1886, the Court reversed itself, ruling that because railroads crossed state boundaries, they fell outside state jurisdiction (*Wabash v. Illinois*). With more than three-fourths of railroads crossing state lines, the Supreme Court's decision effectively quashed the states' attempts at railroad regulation.

Anger at the *Wabash* decision finally led to the first federal law regulating the railroads, the Interstate Commerce Act, passed in 1887 during Cleveland's first administration. The act established the nation's first federal regulatory agency, the **Interstate Commerce Commission (ICC)**, to oversee the railroad industry. In its early years, the ICC was never strong enough to pose a serious threat to the railroads. For example, it could not end rebates to big shippers. In its early decades, the ICC proved more important as a precedent than effective as a watchdog.

Concern over the growing power of the trusts led Congress to pass the **Sherman Antitrust Act** in 1890. The act outlawed pools and trusts, ruling that businesses could no longer enter into agreements to restrict competition. It did nothing to restrict huge holding companies such as Standard Oil, however, and proved to be a weak sword against the trusts. In the following decade, the government successfully struck down only six trusts but used the law four times against labor by outlawing unions as a "conspiracy in restraint of trade." In 1895, the conservative Supreme Court dealt the antitrust law a crippling

> "[The tariff is] only a scheme devised by the old parties to throw dust in the eyes of laboring men."
> — A labor leader

blow in *United States v. E. C. Knight Company.* In its decision, the Court ruled that "manufacture" did not constitute "trade." This semantic quibble drastically narrowed the law, in this case allowing the American Sugar Refining Company, which had bought out a number of other sugar companies (including E. C. Knight) and controlled 98 percent of the production of sugar, to continue its virtual monopoly.

Both the ICC and the Sherman Antitrust Act testified to the nation's concern about corporate abuses of power and to a growing willingness to use federal measures to intervene on behalf of the public interest. As corporate capitalism became more and more powerful, public pressure toward government intervention grew. Yet not until the twentieth century would more active presidents sharpen and use these weapons effectively against the large corporations.

The Fight for Free Silver

While the tariff and regulation of the trusts gained many backers, the silver issue stirred passions like no other issue of the day. On one side stood those who believed that gold constituted the only honest money. Although other forms of currency circulated, notably paper money such as banknotes and greenbacks, the government's support of the gold standard meant that anyone could redeem paper money for gold. Many who supported the gold standard were eastern creditors who did not wish to be paid in devalued dollars. On the opposite side stood a coalition of western silver barons and poor farmers from the West and South who called for **free silver**. The mining interests, who had seen the silver bonanza in the West drive down the price of the precious metal, wanted the government to buy silver and mint silver dollars. Farmers from the West and South who had suffered from deflation during the 1870s and 1880s hoped that increasing the money supply with silver dollars, thus causing inflation, would give them some debt relief by enabling them to pay off their creditors with cheaper dollars.

During the depression following the panic of 1873, critics of hard money organized the Greenback Labor Party, an alliance of farmers and urban wage laborers. The Greenbackers favored issuing paper currency not tied to the gold supply, citing the precedent of the greenbacks issued during the Civil War. The government had the right to define what constituted legal tender, the Greenbackers reasoned: "Paper is equally money, when . . . issued according to law." They proposed that the nation's currency be based on its wealth — land, labor, and capital — and not simply on its reserves of gold. The Greenback Labor Party captured more than a million votes and elected fourteen members to Congress in 1878. Although conservatives considered the Greenbackers dangerous cranks, their views eventually prevailed in the 1930s, when the country abandoned the gold standard.

After the Greenback Labor Party collapsed, proponents of free silver came to dominate the monetary debate in the 1890s. Advocates of free silver pointed out that until 1873 the country had enjoyed a system of bimetallism — the minting of both silver and gold into coins. In that year, at the behest of those who favored gold, the Republican Congress had voted to stop buying and minting silver, an act silver supporters denounced as the "crime of '73." By sharply contracting the money supply at a time when the nation's economy was burgeoning, the Republicans had enriched bankers and investors at the expense of cotton and wheat farmers and industrial wageworkers. In 1878 and again in 1890, with the Sherman Silver Purchase Act, Congress took steps to ease the tight money policy and appease advocates of silver by passing legislation requiring the government to buy silver and issue silver certificates. Though good for the mining interests, the laws did little to promote the inflation desired by farmers. Soon monetary reformers began to call for "the free and unlimited coinage of silver," a plan whereby nearly all the silver mined in the West would be minted into coins circulated at the rate of sixteen ounces of silver — equal in value to one ounce of gold.

By the 1890s, the silver issue crossed party lines. The Democrats hoped to use it to achieve a union between western and southern voters. Unfortunately for them, Democratic president Grover Cleveland remained a staunch conservative in money matters and supported the gold standard as vehemently as any Republican. After a panic on Wall Street in the spring of 1893, Cleveland called a special session of Congress and bullied the legislature into repealing the Silver Purchase Act because he believed it threatened economic confidence. Repeal proved disastrous for Cleveland, not only economically but also politically. It did nothing to bring prosperity and dangerously divided the country. Angry farmers, furious at the president's harsh monetary policy, warned Cleveland not to travel west of the Mississippi River if he valued his life.

U.S. Currency
Gold remained the nation's standard currency, but silver supporters, including farmers and western mining interests, demanded the minting of silver dollars and the issuance of silver certificates like the one above. On the left is a dollar gold piece. The American Numismatic Association; Picture Research Consultants & Archives.

Panic and Depression

President Cleveland had scarcely begun his second term in office in 1893 when the country faced the worst depression it had yet seen. In the face of economic disaster, Cleveland clung to the economic orthodoxy of the gold standard. In the winter of 1894–95, the president walked the floor of the White House, sleepless over the prospect that the United States might go bankrupt. Individuals and investors, rushing to trade in their banknotes for gold, strained the country's monetary system. The Treasury's gold reserves dipped so low that unless they could be buttressed, the unthinkable might happen: The U.S. Treasury might not be able to meet its obligations.

At this juncture, J. P. Morgan stepped in and suggested a plan. A group of bankers would purchase $65 million in U.S. government bonds, paying in gold. Cleveland knew that such a scheme would unleash a thunder of protest, yet to save the gold standard, the president had no choice but to accept Morgan's help. A storm of controversy erupted over the deal. The press claimed that Cleveland had lined his own pockets and rumored that Morgan had made $8.9 million. Neither allegation was true. Cleveland had not profited a penny, and Morgan made far less than the millions his critics claimed.

But if President Cleveland's action managed to salvage the gold standard, it did not save the country from hardship. The winter of 1894–95 was one of the worst times in American history. People faced unemployment, cold, and hunger. A firm believer in limited government, Cleveland insisted that nothing could be done to help: "I do not believe that the power and duty of the General Government ought to be extended to the relief of individual suffering which is in no manner properly related to the public service or benefit." Nor did it occur to Cleveland that his great faith in the gold standard prolonged the depression, favored creditors over debtors, and caused immense hardship for millions of Americans.

REVIEW   Why were Americans split on the question of the tariff and currency?

▶ Conclusion: Business Dominates an Era

The gold deal between J. P. Morgan and Grover Cleveland underscored a dangerous reality: The federal government was so weak that its solvency depended on a private banker. This lopsided power relationship signaled the dominance of business in the era Mark Twain satirically but accurately characterized as the Gilded Age. Perhaps no other era in American history spawned greed, corruption, and vulgarity on so grand a scale — an era when speculators like Jay Gould not only built but wrecked railroads to turn paper profits; an era when the get-rich-quick ethic of the western prospector infused the whole continent; and an era when business boasted openly of buying politicians, who in turn lined their pockets at the public's expense.

Nevertheless, the Gilded Age was not without its share of solid achievements, many inextricably linked to its empire in the West (see chapter 17). Where dusty roads and cattle trails once sprawled across the continent, steel rails now bound the country together, creating a national market that enabled America to make the leap into the industrial age. Factories and refineries poured out American steel and oil at unprecedented rates. Businessmen like Carnegie, Rockefeller, and Morgan developed new strategies to consolidate American industry. New inventions, including the telephone and electric light and power, changed Americans' everyday lives. By the end of the nineteenth century, the country had achieved industrial maturity. It boasted the largest, most innovative, most productive economy in the world. No other era in the nation's history witnessed such a transformation.

Yet the changes that came with these developments worried many Americans and gave rise to the era's political turmoil. Race and gender profoundly influenced American politics, leading to new political alliances. Fearless activist Ida B. Wells fought racism in its most brutal form — lynching. Women's organizations championed causes, notably suffrage and temperance, and challenged prevailing views of woman's proper sphere. Reformers fought corruption by instituting civil service. And new issues — the tariff, the regulation of the trusts, and currency reform — restructured the nation's politics.

The Gilded Age witnessed a nation transformed. Fueled by expanding industry, cities grew exponentially, not only with new inhabitants from around the globe but also with new bridges, subways, and skyscrapers. The frenzied growth of urban America brought wealth and opportunity, but also the exploitation of labor, racism toward newcomers, and social upheaval that lent a new urgency to calls for social reform.

▶ Selected Bibliography

General Works

Charles W. Calhoun, ed., *The Gilded Age: Essays on the Origins of Modern America* (1996).
Sean Dennis Cashman, *America in the Gilded Age: From the Death of Lincoln to the Rise of Theodore Roosevelt* (1993).
Rebecca Edwards, *New Spirits: Americans in the Gilded Age, 1865–1905* (2006).
Jackson Lears, *Rebirth of a Nation: The Making of Modern America, 1877–1920* (2009).
Richard While, *Railroaded: The Transcontinentals and the Making of Modern America* (2011).

Business

Kathleen Brady, *Ida Tarbell: Portrait of a Muckraker* (1984).
Edward Chancellor, *Devil Take the Hindmost: A History of Financial Speculation* (1999).
Ron Chernow, *Titan: The Life of John D. Rockefeller, Sr.* (1998).
Steve Fraser, *Every Man a Speculator: A Cultural History of Wall Street in America* (2005).
Morton J. Horowitz, *The Transformation of American Law, 1870–1960* (1992).
Walter Licht, *Industrializing America* (1995).
David Nasaw, *Andrew Carnegie* (2006).
T. J. Stiles, *The First Tycoon: The Epic Life of Cornelius Vanderbilt* (2009).
Jean Strouse, *Morgan: American Financier* (1999).
Viviana A. Zelizer, *The Social Meaning of Money* (1994).

Politics

Paula Baker, *The Moral Framework of Public Life* (1991).
Richard F. Bensel, *The Political Economy of American Industrialization, 1877–1900* (2000).
Ruth Bordin, *Women and Temperance: The Quest for Power and Liberty, 1873–1900* (1990).
Alyn Brodsky, *Grover Cleveland: A Study in Character* (2000).
Robert W. Cherny, *American Politics in the Gilded Age, 1868–1900* (1997).
Jane Dailey, Glenda Elizabeth Gilmore, and Bryant Simon, eds., *Jumpin' Jim Crow: Southern Politics from the Civil War to Civil Rights* (2000).

Rebecca Edwards, *Angels in the Machinery: Gender in American Party Politics from the Civil War to the Progressive Era* (1997).

Dana Frank, *Buy American: The Untold Story of Economic Nationalism* (1999).

Paula Giddings, *Ida, a Sword among Lions: Ida B. Wells and the Campaign against Lynching* (2008).

Steven Hahn, *A Nation under Our Feet: Black Political Struggles in the Rural South from Slavery to the Great Migration* (2003).

Darlene Clark Hine and Kathleen Thompson, *A Shining Thread of Hope: The History of Black Women in America* (1998).

Ari Hoogenboom, *Rutherford B. Hayes: Warrior and President* (1995).

H. Paul Jeffers, *An Honest President: The Life and Presidencies of Grover Cleveland* (2000).

Ross Evans Paulson, *Liberty, Equality, and Justice: Civil Rights, Women's Rights, and the Regulation of Business, 1865–1932* (1997).

Dorothy Salem, *To Better Our World: Black Women in Organized Reform, 1890–1920* (1990).

Ian Tyrell, *Woman's World, Woman's Empire: The Woman's Christian Temperance Union in International Perspective, 1880–1930* (1991).

LeeAnn Whites, *Gender Matters: Civil War, Reconstruction, and the Making of the New South* (2005).

Culture

Judy Arlene Hilkey, *Character Is Capital: Success Manuals and Manhood in Gilded Age America* (1997).

Jane H. Hunter, *How Young Ladies Became Girls: The Victorian Origins of American Girlhood* (2002).

Paulette D. Kilmer, *The Fear of Sinking: The American Success Formula in the Gilded Age* (1996).

Alan Trachtenberg, *The Incorporation of America: Culture and Society in the Gilded Age* (anniversary edition, 2009).

FOR MORE BOOKS ABOUT TOPICS IN THIS CHAPTER, see the Online Bibliography at bedfordstmartins.com/roark.

FOR ADDITIONAL PRIMARY SOURCES FROM THIS PERIOD, see Michael Johnson, ed., *Reading the American Past*, Fifth Edition.

FOR WEB SITES, IMAGES, AND DOCUMENTS RELATED TO TOPICS AND PLACES IN THIS CHAPTER, visit Make History at bedfordstmartins.com/roark.

Reviewing Chapter 18

KEY TERMS

Explain each term's significance.

Old Industries Transformed, New Industries Born

Gilded Age (p. 571)

Jay Gould (p. 571)

Andrew Carnegie (p. 573)

vertical integration (p. 576)

John D. Rockefeller (p. 577)

trust (p. 577)

Ida M. Tarbell (p. 578)

Thomas Alva Edison (p. 580)

From Competition to Consolidation

finance capitalism (p. 581)

J. P. Morgan (p. 582)

social Darwinism (p. 584)

gospel of wealth (p. 585)

laissez-faire (p. 586)

Politics and Culture

spoils system (p. 586)

New South (p. 587)

separate spheres (p. 588)

Jim Crow (p. 588)

Ida B. Wells (p. 588)

General Federation of Women's Clubs (GFWC) (p. 589)

Woman's Christian Temperance Union (WCTU) (p. 590)

Presidential Politics

Rutherford B. Hayes (p. 591)

civil service reform (p. 591)

James A. Garfield (p. 591)

Grover Cleveland (p. 592)

Economic Issues and Party Realignment

McKinley tariff (p. 595)

Interstate Commerce Commission (ICC) (p. 595)

Sherman Antitrust Act (p. 595)

free silver (p. 596)

REVIEW QUESTIONS

Use key terms and dates to support your answer.

1. What devices did John D. Rockefeller use to gain control of 90 percent of the oil-refining business by 1890? (pp. 571–581)

2. Why did the ideas of social Darwinism appeal to many Americans in the late nineteenth century? (pp. 581–586)

3. How did race and gender influence politics? (pp. 586–590)

4. How did the question of civil service reform contribute to divisions within the Republican Party? (pp. 590–594)

5. Why were Americans split on the question of the tariff and currency? (pp. 594–597)

MAKING CONNECTIONS

Draw on key terms, the timeline, and review questions.

1. How did the railroads contribute to the growth of American industry? In your answer, discuss the drawbacks and benefits of these developments.

2. Late-nineteenth-century industrialization depended on developments in technology and business strategy. What were some of the key innovations in both arenas? How did they facilitate the maturation of American industry?

3. By the 1870s, several new concerns had displaced slavery as the defining question of American politics. What were these new issues, and how did they shape new regional, economic, and racial alliances and rivalries? In your answer, consider the part that political parties played in this process.

4. Energetic political activity characterized Gilded Age America, both within and beyond formal party politics. How did the activism of women denied the vote contribute to the era's electoral politics? In your answer, be sure to cite specific examples of political action.

5. The U.S. Congress and the Supreme Court facilitated the concentration of power in the hands of private business concerns during the Gilded Age. Citing specific policies and court decisions, discuss how government helped augment the power of big business in the late nineteenth century.

LINKING TO THE PAST

Link events in this chapter to earlier events.

1. In what ways did the military conquest of the trans-Mississippi West, with its dislocation of Native Americans, play a significant role in the industrial boom of the Gilded Age? (See chapter 17.)

2. In what ways did the rampant get-rich-quick mentality of western miners and land speculators help set the tone for the Gilded Age? Is the West the herald of the Gilded Age, or must we look to New York and Washington? (See chapter 17.)

▶ FOR PRACTICE QUIZZES AND OTHER STUDY TOOLS, visit the Online Study Guide at bedfordstmartins.com/roark.

TIMELINE 1869–1901

1869	• First transcontinental railroad completed.
	• National Woman Suffrage Association founded.
1870	• John D. Rockefeller incorporates Standard Oil Company.
1872	• Andrew Carnegie builds the largest, most up-to-date Bessemer steel plant in the world.
1873	• Wall Street panic leads to major economic depression.
1874	• Woman's Christian Temperance Union (WCTU) founded.
1876	• Alexander Graham Bell demonstrates telephone.
1877	• Republican Rutherford B. Hayes sworn in as president.
	• "Redeemers" come to power in South.
	• *Munn v. Illinois.*
1880	• Republican James A. Garfield elected president.
1881	• Garfield assassinated; Vice President Chester A. Arthur becomes president.
1882	• John D. Rockefeller develops the trust.
1883	• Pendleton Civil Service Act.
1884	• Democrat Grover Cleveland elected president.
1886	• *Wabash v. Illinois.*
1887	• Interstate Commerce Act.
1888	• Republican Benjamin Harrison elected president.
1890	• McKinley tariff.
	• General Federation of Women's Clubs (GFWC) founded.
	• Sherman Antitrust Act.
1892	• Ida B. Wells launches antilynching campaign.
1893	• Wall Street panic touches off national depression.
1895	• J. P. Morgan bails out U.S. Treasury.
1901	• U.S. Steel incorporated and capitalized at $1.4 billion.

BROOKLYN BRIDGE FAN
Advertisers used images of the Brooklyn Bridge to sell everything from patent medicine to soap. The front side of this colorful commemorative fan celebrates the opening of the bridge on May 24, 1883; the reverse side promotes a furniture company. The background photograph shows the wooden platforms that connected the gothic towers as the huge cables went into place high over the East River. It took fourteen years and cost the lives of twenty-seven men to complete the bridge.
Fan: Museum of the City of New York; background: ©Bettmann/Corbis.

19

The City and its Workers
1870–1900

"A TOWN THAT CRAWLED NOW STANDS ERECT, AND WE WHOSE BACKS
were bent above the hearths know how it got its spine," boasted a steelworker surveying New York City. Where once wooden buildings stood
rooted in the mire of unpaved streets, cities of stone and steel sprang up in
the last decades of the nineteenth century. The labor of millions of workers,
many of them immigrants, laid the foundations for urban America.

No symbol better represented the new urban landscape than the
Brooklyn Bridge, opened in May 1883. The great bridge soared over the
East River in a single mile-long span. Begun in 1869, the bridge was the
dream of builder John Roebling, who died in a freak accident almost as
soon as construction began.

Building the Brooklyn Bridge took fourteen years and cost the lives of
twenty-seven men. Nearly three hundred workers labored around the clock
in three shifts, six days a week, most for $2 a day. To sink the foundation
deep into the riverbed, common laborers tunneled down through mud and
debris, working in reinforced wooden boxes called caissons, which were
open at the bottom and pressurized to keep the water from flooding in.
Before long, the workers experienced a mysterious malady they called
"bends" because it left them doubled over in pain after they came to the
surface. Scientists later discovered that nitrogen bubbles trapped in the
bloodstream caused the condition and that it could be prevented if the men
came up slowly to allow for decompression.

The first death occurred when the caissons reached a depth of seventy-
one feet. On April 22, 1872, a heavyset German immigrant named John
Meyers complained that he did not feel well and headed home to his
boardinghouse. Before he could reach his bed, he collapsed and died. Eight
days later, another man dropped dead, and the entire workforce in the caissons went out on strike. Conditions had become so hazardous and terrifying that the workers demanded a higher wage for fewer hours of work.

One worker, Frank Harris, remembered the men's fear of working in the
caissons. As a scrawny sixteen-year-old from Ireland, Harris started to work
a few days after landing in America. He described his experience:

> The six of us were working naked to the waist in the small iron chamber
> with the temperature of about 80 degrees Fahrenheit: In five minutes the

603

sweat was pouring from us, and all the while we were standing in icy water that was only kept from rising by the terrific pressure. No wonder the headaches were blinding.

By the fifth day, Harris experienced terrible shooting pains in his ears, and fearing he might go deaf, he quit. Like Harris, many immigrant workers walked off the job, often as many as a hundred a week. But a ready supply of immigrants meant that the work never slowed or stopped; new workers eagerly entered the caissons, where they could earn in a day more than they made in a week in Ireland or Italy.

Washington Roebling, who took over as chief engineer after his father's death, routinely worked twelve to fourteen hours six days a week. Soon he, too, fell victim to the bends and ended up an invalid, directing the completion of the bridge through a telescope from his window in Brooklyn Heights. His wife, Emily Warren Roebling, acted as site superintendent and general engineer of the project. At the dedication of the bridge, Roebling turned to his wife and said, "I want the world to know that you, too, are one of the Builders of the Bridge."

At the end of the nineteenth century, the Brooklyn Bridge stood as a symbol of many things: the industrial might of the United States; the labor of the nation's immigrants; the ingenuity and genius of its engineers and inventors; the rise of iron and steel; and, most of all, the ascendancy of urban America. Poised on the brink of the twentieth century, the nation was shifting inexorably from a rural, agricultural society to an urban, industrial nation. In the burgeoning cities, tensions would erupt into conflict as workers squared off to fight for their rights to organize into labor unions and to demand safer working conditions, shorter hours, and better pay. And the explosive growth of the cities would foster political corruption as unscrupulous bosses and entrepreneurs cashed in on the building boom. Immigrants, political bosses, middle-class managers, poor laborers, and the very rich populated the nation's cities, crowding the streets, laboring in the stores and factories, and taking their leisure at the new ballparks, amusement parks, dance halls, and municipal parks that dotted the urban landscape. As the new century dawned, the city and its workers moved to center stage in American life.

Workers in the Caissons

In 1870 *Frank Leslie's Illustrated Weekly* ran an article on the construction of the Brooklyn Bridge. Illustrations show the workers inside the caissons below the East River. Crews entered through a cylindrical airlock that took them down more than seventy feet. There in the wooden caissons they worked with pick and shovel to break up the big boulders and haul the rock away. "What with the flaming lights, the deep shadows, the confusing noise of hammer, drills, and chains, the half-naked forms flitting about," wrote one reporter, the scene resembled hell. The hot, dangerous work fell primarily to Irish immigrant workers. Library of Congress.

▶ The Rise of the City

"We cannot all live in cities, yet nearly all seem determined to do so," New York editor Horace Greeley complained. The last three decades of the nineteenth century witnessed an urban explosion. Cities and towns grew more than twice as rapidly as the total population. Among the fastest-growing cities, Chicago expanded at a meteoric rate, doubling its population each decade. The number of cities with more than 100,000 inhabitants jumped from eighteen in 1870 to thirty-eight in 1900. Most of the nation's largest cities were east of the Mississippi, although St. Louis and San Francisco both ranked among the top ten urban areas. By 1900, the United States boasted three cities with more than a million inhabitants — New York, Chicago, and Philadelphia.

Patterns of **global migration** contributed to the rise of the city. In the port cities of the East Coast, more than fourteen million people arrived, many from southern and eastern Europe, and huddled together in dense urban ghettos. The word *slum* entered the American vocabulary along with a growing concern over the rising tide of newcomers. In the city, the widening gap between rich and poor became more visible, exacerbated by changes in the city landscape brought about by advances in transportation and technology.

The Urban Explosion: A Global Migration

The United States grew up in the country and moved to the city, or so it seemed by the end of the nineteenth century. Between 1870 and 1900, eleven million people moved into cities. Burgeoning industrial centers such as Pittsburgh, Chicago, New York, and Cleveland acted as giant magnets, attracting workers from the countryside. But rural Americans were by no means the only ones migrating to cities. Worldwide in scope, the movement from rural areas to urban industrial centers attracted millions of immigrants to American shores in the waning decades of the nineteenth century.

By the 1870s, the world could be conceptualized as three interconnected geographic regions (Map 19.1). At the center stood an industrial core bounded by Chicago and St. Louis in the west; Toronto, Glasgow, and Berlin in the north; Warsaw in the east; and Milan, Barcelona, Richmond, and Louisville in the south.

Surrounding this industrial core lay a vast agricultural domain encompassing Canada, much of Scandinavia, Russia and Poland, Hungary, Greece, Italy and Sicily, southern Spain, the South and the western plains of America, central and northern Mexico, the hinterlands of northern China, and the southern islands of Japan. Capitalist development in the late nineteenth century shattered traditional patterns of economic activity in this rural periphery. As old patterns broke down, these rural areas exported, along with other raw materials, new recruits for the industrial labor force.

> "We cannot all live in cities, yet nearly all seem determined to do so."
> — New York editor
> **HORACE GREELEY**

Beyond this second circle lay an even larger third world including the Caribbean, Central and South America, the Middle East, Africa, India, and most of Asia. Ties between this part of the world and the industrial core strengthened in the late nineteenth century, but most of the people living there stayed put. They worked on plantations and railroads, and in mines and ports, as part of a huge export network managed by foreign powers that staked out spheres of influence and colonies in this vast region.

In the 1870s, railroad expansion and low steamship fares gave the world's peoples a newfound mobility, enabling industrialists to draw on a global population for cheap labor. When Andrew Carnegie opened his first steel mill in 1872, his superintendent hired workers he called "buckwheats" — young American boys just off the farm. By the 1890s, however, Carnegie's workforce was liberally sprinkled with other rural boys, Hungarians and Slavs who had migrated to the United States, willing to work for low wages.

Altogether, more than 25 million immigrants came to the United States between 1850 and 1920. They came from all directions: east from Asia, south from Canada, north from Latin America, and west from Europe (Map 19.2). Part of a worldwide migration, immigrants traveled to South America and Australia as well as to the United States. Yet more than 70 percent of all European immigrants chose North America as their destination.

The largest number of immigrants to the United States came from the British Isles and from German-speaking lands (Figure 19.1). The vast majority of immigrants were white; Asians accounted for fewer than one million immigrants, and other people of color numbered even fewer. Yet ingrained racial prejudices

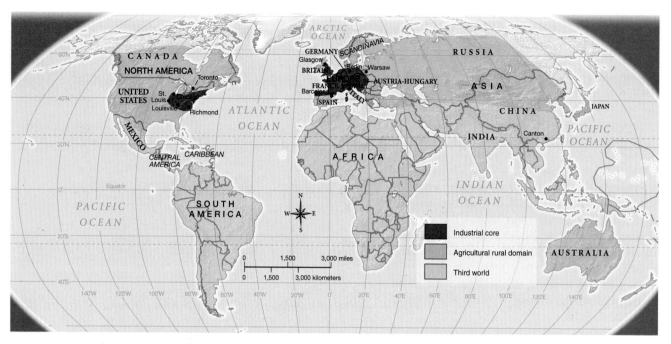

MAP ACTIVITY

Map 19.1   Economic Regions of the World, 1890s

The global nature of the world economy at the turn of the twentieth century is indicated by three interconnected geographic regions. At the center stands the industrial core — western Europe and the northeastern United States. The second region — the agricultural periphery — supplied immigrant laborers to the industries in the core. Beyond these two regions lay a vast area tied economically to the industrial core by colonialism.

READING THE MAP: What types of economic regions were contained in the United States in this period? Which continents held most of the industrial core? Which held most of the agricultural rural domain? Which held the greatest portion of the third world?

CONNECTIONS: Which of these three regions provided the bulk of immigrant workers to the United States? What major changes prompted the global migration at the end of the nineteenth century?

increasingly influenced the country's perception of immigration patterns. One of the classic formulations of the history of European immigration divided immigrants into two distinct waves that have been called the "old" and the "new" immigration. According to this theory, before 1880 the majority of immigrants came from northern and western Europe, with Germans, Irish, English, and Scandinavians making up approximately 85 percent of the newcomers. After 1880, the pattern shifted, with more and more ships carrying passengers from southern and eastern Europe. Italians, Hungarians, eastern European Jews, Turks, Armenians, Poles, Russians, and other Slavic peoples accounted for more than 80 percent of all immigrants by 1896 (Figure 19.2). Implicit in the distinction was an invidious comparison between "old" pioneer settlers and "new" unskilled laborers. Yet this sweeping general-ization spoke more to perception than to reality. In fact, many of the earlier immigrants from Ireland, Germany, and Scandinavia came not as settlers or farmers, but as wageworkers, and they were met with much the same disdain as the Italians and Slavs who followed them.

The "new" immigration resulted from a number of factors. Improved economic conditions in western Europe coupled with increased immigration to Australia and Canada slowed the flow of immigrants coming into the United States from northern and western Europe. At the same time, economic depression in southern Italy, the persecution of Jews in eastern Europe, and a general desire to avoid conscription into the Russian army led many people from southern and eastern Europe to move to the United States. The need of America's industries for cheap, unskilled labor during prosperous years also stimulated immigration.

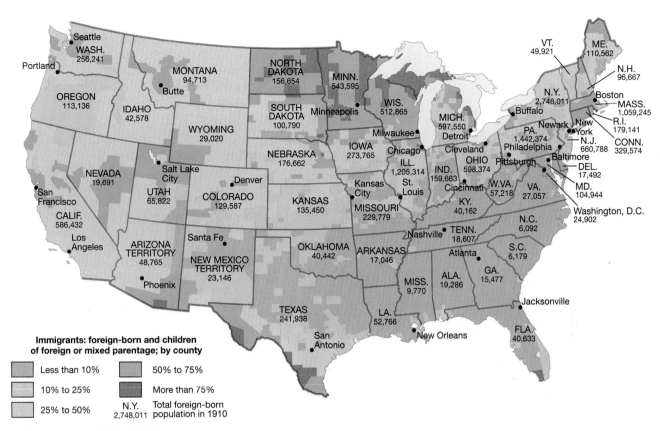

Immigrants: foreign-born and children
of foreign or mixed parentage; by county

- Less than 10%
- 10% to 25%
- 25% to 50%
- 50% to 75%
- More than 75%
- N.Y. 2,748,011 Total foreign-born population in 1910

MAP ACTIVITY

Map 19.2   The Impact of Immigration, to 1910

Immigration flowed in all directions — south from Canada, north from Mexico and Latin America, east from Asia, and west from Europe.

READING THE MAP: Which states had high percentages of immigrants? Which cities attracted the most immigrants? Which cities attracted the fewest?

CONNECTIONS: Why did most immigrants gravitate toward the cities? Why do you think the South drew such a low percentage of immigrants?

Steamship companies courted immigrants — a highly profitable, self-loading cargo. By the 1880s, the price of a ticket from Liverpool had dropped to less than $25. Would-be immigrants eager for information about the United States relied on letters from friends and relatives, advertisements, and word of mouth — sources that were not always dependable or truthful. Even photographs proved deceptive: Workers dressed in their Sunday best looked more prosperous than they actually were to relatives in the old country, where only the very wealthy wore white collars or silk dresses. No wonder people left for the United States believing, as one Italian immigrant observed, "that if they were ever fortunate enough to reach America, they would fall into a pile of manure and get up brushing the diamonds out of their hair."

Most of the newcomers stayed in the nation's cities. By 1900, almost two-thirds of the country's immigrant population resided in cities, many of the immigrants too poor to move on. (The average laborer immigrating to the United States carried only about $21.50.) Although the foreign-born population rarely outnumbered the native-born population, taken together immigrants and their American-born children did constitute a majority in some areas, particularly in the nation's largest cities: Philadelphia, 55 percent; Boston, 66 percent; Chicago, 75 percent; and New York City, an amazing 80 percent in 1900.

Not all the newcomers came to stay. Perhaps eight million European immigrants — most of them young men — worked for a year or a season and then returned to their homelands. Immigration officers called these immigrants,

Russian Immigrant Family
A Russian immigrant family is shown leaving Ellis Island in 1900. Notice the white slips of paper pinned to their coats indicating that they have been processed. The family is well dressed, but the paucity of their possessions testifies to the struggles they face. She carries her belongings in a white cloth sack, and he has a suitcase in one hand and bedding draped over his arm. An immigration official in uniform stands on the left. Keystone-Mast Collection, UCR/California Museum of Photography, University of California, Riverside.

many of them Italians, "birds of passage" because they followed a regular pattern of migration to and from the United States. By 1900, almost 75 percent of the new immigrants were young, single men.

Women generally had less access to funds for travel and faced tighter family control. Because the traditional sexual division of labor relied on women's unpaid domestic labor and care of the very young and the very old, women most often came to the United States as wives, mothers, or daughters, not as single wage laborers. Only among the Irish did women immigrants outnumber men by a small margin from 1871 to 1891.

Jews from eastern Europe most often came with their families and came to stay. Beginning in the 1880s, a wave of violent **pogroms**, or persecutions, in Russia and Poland prompted the departure of more than a million Jews in the next two decades. (See "Seeking the American

Promise," page 610.) Most of the Jewish immigrants settled in the port cities of the East, creating distinct ethnic enclaves, like Hester Street in the heart of New York City's Lower East Side, which rang with the calls of pushcart peddlers and vendors hawking their wares, from pickles to feather beds.

Racism and the Cry for Immigration Restriction

Ethnic diversity and racism played a role in dividing skilled workers (those with a craft or specialized ability) from the globe-hopping proletariat of unskilled workers (those who supplied muscle or tended machines). As industrialists mechanized to replace skilled workers with lower-paid unskilled labor, they drew on recent immigrants, particularly those from southern and eastern Europe, who had come to the United States in the hope of bettering their lives. Skilled workers, frequently members of older immigrant groups, criticized the newcomers. One Irish worker complained, "There should be a law . . . to keep all the Italians from comin' in and takin' the bread out of the mouths of honest people."

The Irish worker's resentment brings into focus the impact of racism on America's immigrant laborers. Throughout the nineteenth century and into the twentieth, members of the educated elite as well as the uneducated viewed ethnic and even religious differences as racial characteristics, referring to the Polish or the Jewish "race." Americans judged "new" immigrants of southern and eastern European "races" as inferior. Each wave of newcomers was deemed somehow inferior to the established residents. The Irish who criticized the Italians so harshly had themselves been stigmatized as a lesser "race" a generation earlier.

Immigrants not only brought their own religious and racial prejudices to the United States but also absorbed the popular prejudices of American culture. Social Darwinism, with its strongly racist overtones, decreed that whites stood at the top of the evolutionary ladder. But who was "white"? Skin color supposedly served as a marker for the "new" immigrants — "swarthy" Italians; dark-haired, olive-skinned Jews. But even blond, blue-eyed Poles were not considered white. The social construction of "race" is nowhere more apparent than in the testimony of an Irish dockworker who boasted that he hired only "white men," a category that he insisted excluded "Poles and Italians." For the new immigrants, Americanization and assimilation would prove inextricably part of becoming "white."

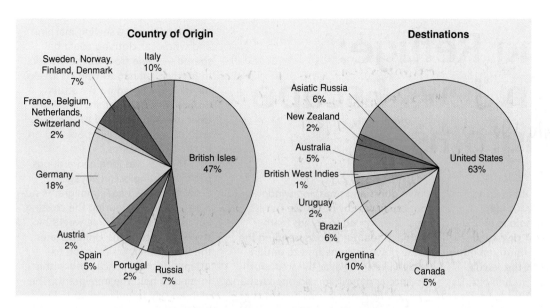

FIGURE 19.1 GLOBAL COMPARISON: European Emigration, 1870–1890
A look at European emigration between 1870 and 1890 shows that emigrants from Germany, Austria, and the British Isles (including England, Ireland, Scotland, and Wales) formed the largest group of out-migrants during those decades. After 1890, the origin of European emigrants tilted south and east, with Italians and eastern Europeans growing in number (see Figure 19.2). The United States, by far the most popular destination for global emigrants in this period, took in nearly two-thirds of the Europeans who left their homelands. What factors might account for the United States being the most popular destination for European emigrants?

For African Americans, the cities of the North promised not just economic opportunity but an escape from institutionalized segregation and persecution. Throughout the South, Jim Crow laws — restrictions that segregated blacks — became common in the decades following Reconstruction. Intimidation and lynching terrorized blacks. "To die from the bite of frost is far more glorious than

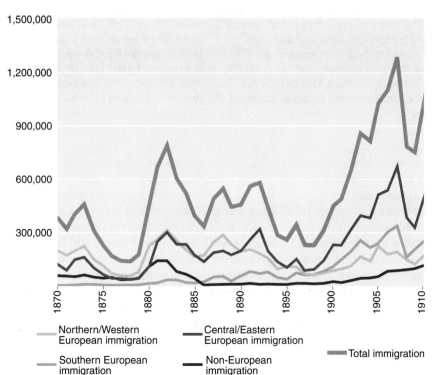

FIGURE 19.2 European Immigration, 1870–1910
Before 1880, more than 85 percent of U.S. immigrants came from northern and western Europe—Germany, Ireland, England, and the Scandinavian countries. After 1880, 80 percent of the "new" immigrants came from Italy, Turkey, Hungary, Armenia, Poland, Russia, and other Slavic countries.

Seeking Refuge: Russian Jews Escape the Pogroms

Fifteen-year-old Abraham Bisno recalled running for his life. "I hid myself in a clay hole in an old brickyard on a hillside," he remembered. "I witnessed the mob coming down the hill to assault the Jewish settlement. I saw children and old people beaten — buildings burned — I heard women screaming."

Violent pogroms — deadly riots against Jews — erupted in Russia in 1881 in the wake of the assassination of Czar Alexander II, sparked by rumors that he had been murdered by Jews. Kiev, where Abraham Bisno lived with his parents, became the scene of a pogrom in late April. "For days on end," Bisno wrote, "entire neighborhoods were looted and largely destroyed by crowds estimated at over four thousand." Fanatical priests fed anti-Semitism (hatred of Jews) by denouncing the Jews as heartless "Christ-killers" who used the blood of Christian children in their rituals. The government failed to move quickly to put down the violence, even after only one of the ten who plotted the czar's assassination turned out to be Jewish.

Bands of Russians swarmed through the Jewish quarters, breaking down doors and smashing windows, looting or destroying all the furnishings. They ripped to shreds feather beds and feather pillows, sending the white down into the breeze until it settled like snow over the scenes of violence and mayhem. No one knows precisely how many Jews died at the hands of the mob, but estimates range as high as five hundred. "The building we lived in and the place we worked in were assaulted at the same time," Bisno recalled. "Mother ran for her life while we struggled for ours; we were all separated by the mob — the shop was destroyed, the goods carried away."

These and subsequent pogroms and persecutions prompted a great wave of Jewish migration. Between 1880 and 1914, more than 2.7 million Jews sought refuge from religious persecution, the vast majority of them heading to the United States. Among the first to emigrate were Abraham Bisno and his family. When the Bisnos learned that Jewish groups in Europe and America had raised money to help Russian Jews emigrate, they scraped together forty rubles to get from Kiev to Brody in Galicia, where the refugees gathered.

"Our family sold a sewing machine and whatever clothing could be spared — some from our very backs." In Brody, they had to wait six weeks, begging for bread on the streets, before they received aid to pay for their passage overland to Hamburg and from there to Liverpool and on to the United States.

The trip was long and arduous, particularly the ocean voyage. Crowded in steerage, immigrants suffered seasickness during the crossing, which took two to three weeks by steamer. Once in the United States, the Bisno family was sent on to Atlanta by an American committee formed to help the immigrants. The men quickly found work as tailors. Bisno struck out on his own, moving to Chattanooga, where he apprenticed to an English-speaking tailor and quickly picked up the language by reading signs and advertisements. But the Bisnos were unhappy in the South. Abraham's mother complained that she could not find a butcher who sold kosher meat, and his father fretted that there was no Orthodox synagogue in the neighborhood. So after nine months, the family moved to a larger Jewish community in Chicago.

The slums of the nation's big cities, where many of the Jewish immigrants ended up, were far from a "promised land." The Bisnos lived in a dilapidated shack above a stable with a yard "full of rags, junk, rats, and vermin." Other Jewish immigrants voiced their disappointment at the conditions they encountered in the United States. "The dirt, the noise, the confusion, the swarming hurrying crowds!" Goldie

at the hands of a mob," proclaimed the *Defender*, Chicago's largest African American newspaper. In the 1890s, many blacks moved north, settling for the most part in the growing cities. Racism relegated them to poor jobs and substandard living conditions, but by 1900 New York, Philadelphia, and Chicago had the largest black communities in the nation. Although the most significant African American migration out of the South would occur during and after World War I, the great exodus was already under way.

On the West Coast, Asian immigrants became scapegoats of the changing economy. After California's gold rush, many Chinese who had come to work "on the gold mountain" found jobs on the country's transcontinental railroads. When the railroad work ended, they took work other groups shunned, including domestic service. But hard times in the 1870s made them a target for disgruntled workers. Prohibited from owning land, the Chinese migrated to the cities. In 1870, San Francisco housed a Chinese population

Stone exclaimed. "My heart sank. This was all so different from what I had expected or dreamed."

Bad as conditions were, the immigrant Jews appreciated the safe haven the United States afforded. And although the sweatshops where Bisno and other Jewish immigrants labored were dark and bleak, for most Jews the slums proved a temporary prison. The United States provided not only a refuge but also a chance to start over and prosper. Bisno watched as many of his friends and relatives, after saving or borrowing a little money, opened small businesses of their own. "All had to begin in a very small way," he recalled. "With a hundred or two hundred dollars they were able to start grocery stores, markets, cigar stores." Bisno quickly moved up in his trade, becoming a contractor in a sweatshop by the time he reached the age of sixteen. But then his life took a different course. Moved by the Haymarket martyrs, he converted to socialism in 1886, joined the Knights of Labor, and went on to become a labor organizer. The first president of the Chicago Cloak Makers' Union, he worked until his death in 1929 to improve the lot of garment workers.

Jewish Refugees from the Pogroms
In this colorful depiction, Liberty, dressed in the Stars and Stripes, opens the gates of the country to a Jewish immigrant couple and their children fleeing the pogroms in Russia. Abraham Bisno and his family were among the first group of immigrants to flee Kiev after the pogroms of 1881 and to seek refuge in the United States. Yivo Institute for Jewish Research.

Questions for Consideration

1. Compare the Jewish immigrants from Russia with other immigrant groups discussed in this chapter. What attracted each group to America? What were their expectations? How did each group fare?

2. What aspects of Bisno's life in America led him to join the labor movement? How may his childhood in Russia have influenced him in this direction?

---

estimated at 12,022, and it continued to grow until passage of the Chinese Exclusion Act in 1882 (see chapter 17). For the first time in the nation's history, U.S. law excluded an immigrant group on the basis of race.

Huang Zunxian came to San Francisco in 1882 as Chinese consul general. Disillusioned with the anti-Chinese violence he saw all around him, he wrote a series of angry poems that took Americans to task for their hypocrisy. One of them read:

They have sealed the gates tightly
Door after door with guards beating alarms.
Anyone with a yellow-colored face
Is beaten even if guiltless.
The American eagle strides the heavens soaring
With half of the globe clutched in his claw.
Although the Chinese arrived later,
Couldn't you leave them a little space?

Despite the Chinese Exclusion Act, some Chinese managed to come to America using a loophole that allowed relatives to join their

Rags to Riches
The formulaic novels of popular author Horatio Alger feature fatherless young men who, through the right combination of "pluck and luck," move ahead in the world. Alger's message of rags to riches fueled the dreams of countless young people in the late nineteenth century. Yet despite the myth, few Americans rose from rags to riches. Even Alger's heroes, such as his popular character Ragged Dick, pictured here, more often traded their rags for respectability, not for great wealth. Picture Research Consultants & Archives.

Give me your tired, your poor,
Your huddled masses yearning to breathe free,
The wretched refuse of your teeming shore,
Send these, the homeless, tempest-tost to me,
I lift my lamp beside the golden door!

The tide of immigrants to New York City soon swamped the immigration office at Castle Garden in lower Manhattan. After the federal government took over immigration in 1890, it built a facility on **Ellis Island** in New York harbor, opened in 1892. After a fire gutted the wooden building, an imposing new brick edifice replaced it in 1900. Its overcrowded halls became the gateway to the United States for millions.

To many Americans, the "new" immigrants seemed uneducated, backward, and uncouth — impossible to assimilate. "These people are not Americans," editorialized the popular journal *Public Opinion*, "they are the very scum and offal of Europe." Terence V. Powderly, head of the broadly inclusive Knights of Labor, complained that the newcomers "herded together like animals and lived like beasts." Blue-blooded Yankees led by Senator Henry Cabot Lodge of Massachusetts formed an unlikely alliance with leaders of organized labor — who feared that immigrants would drive down wages — to press for immigration restrictions. Lodge and his supporters championed a literacy test as a requirement for immigration, knowing that the vast majority of Italian and Slavic peasants could neither read nor write. In 1896, Congress approved a literacy test for immigrants, but President Grover Cleveland promptly vetoed it. "It is said," the president reminded Congress, "that the quality of recent immigration is undesirable. The time is quite within recent memory when the same thing was said of immigrants, who, with their descendants, are now numbered among our best citizens." Cleveland's veto forestalled immigration restriction but did not stop anti-immigrant forces from seeking to close the gates. They would continue to press for restrictions until they achieved their goal in the 1920s (as discussed in chapter 23).

The Social Geography of the City

During the Gilded Age, cities experienced demographic and technological changes that greatly altered the social geography of the city. Cleveland, Ohio, provides a good example. In the 1870s, Cleveland was a small city in both population and area. Oil magnate John D. Rockefeller could, and often did, walk from his large brick house on Euclid Avenue to his office downtown. On his

families. By contrast, the nation's small Japanese community of about 3,000 expanded rapidly after 1890, until pressures to keep out all Asians led in 1910 to the creation of an immigration station at Angel Island in San Francisco Bay. Asian immigrants were detained there, sometimes for months, and many were deported as "undesirable." Their sad stories can be read in the graffiti on the barracks walls.

On the East Coast, the volume of immigration from Europe in the last two decades of the century proved unprecedented. In 1888 alone, more than half a million Europeans landed in America, 75 percent of them in New York City. The Statue of Liberty, a gift from the people of France erected in 1886, stood sentinel in the harbor. The verse inscribed at Liberty's base was penned by a young Jewish woman named Emma Lazarus:

Knife and Scissors Sharpener Pushcart
Joseph Antonucci, an Italian immigrant, used this knife and scissors sharpener cart on Chicago's West Side in 1900. After a day's work, Antonucci usually parked the cart in a fire station or a customer's stable and then took the train home. Sometimes he pushed his cart for miles to ply his trade beyond the city limits in towns such as Hammond, Indiana. For poor immigrants who could not afford rent, pushcarts provided a cheap and portable means of livelihood. The cries of street peddlers, vendors, and scissors sharpeners like Antonucci added to the cacophony of the urban streets. Chicago Historical Society.

organized by ethnicity and income. First the horse car in the 1870s and then the electric streetcar in the 1880s made it possible for those who could afford the five-cent fare to work downtown and flee after work to the "cool green rim" of the city, with its single-family homes, lawns, gardens, and trees. Social segregation — the separation of rich and poor, and of ethnic and old-stock Americans — was one of the major social changes engendered by the rise of the industrial metropolis, evident not only in Cleveland but in cities across the nation.

Race and ethnicity affected the way cities evolved. Newcomers to the nation's cities faced hostility and not surprisingly sought out their kin and country folk as they struggled to survive. Distinct ethnic neighborhoods often formed around a synagogue or church. African Americans typically experienced the greatest residential segregation, but every large city had its ethnic enclaves — Little Italy, Chinatown, Bohemia Flats, Germantown — where English was rarely spoken.

Poverty, crowding, dirt, and disease constituted the daily reality of New York City's immigrant poor — a plight documented by photojournalist **Jacob Riis** in his best-selling book *How the Other Half Lives* (1890). By taking his camera into the hovels of the poor, Riis opened the nation's eyes to conditions in the city's slums (see chapter 21, "Visualizing History," page 688). Riis invited his readers into a Bottle Street tenement:

> One, two, three beds are there, if the old boxes and heaps of foul straw can be called by that name; a broken stove with a crazy pipe from which the smoke leaks at every joint; a table of rough boards propped up on boxes, piles of rubbish in the corner. The closeness and smell are appalling.

While Riis's audience shivered at his revelations about the "other half," many middle-class Americans worried equally about the excesses of the wealthy. They feared the class antagonism fueled by the growing chasm between rich and poor so visible in the nation's cities, and shared Riis's view that "the real danger to society comes not only from the tenements, but from the ill-spent wealth which reared them."

The excesses of the Gilded Age's newly minted millionaires were nowhere more visible than in the lifestyle of the Vanderbilts. "Commodore"

way, he passed the small homes of his clerks and other middle-class families. Behind these homes ran miles of alleys crowded with the dwellings of Cleveland's working class. Farther out, on the shores of Lake Erie, close to the factories and foundries, clustered the shanties of the city's poorest laborers.

Within two decades, the Cleveland that Rockefeller knew no longer existed. The coming of mass transit transformed the walking city. In its place emerged a central business district surrounded by concentric rings of residences

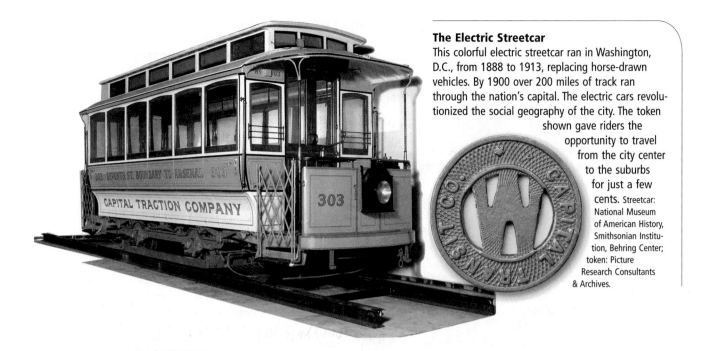

The Electric Streetcar
This colorful electric streetcar ran in Washington, D.C., from 1888 to 1913, replacing horse-drawn vehicles. By 1900 over 200 miles of track ran through the nation's capital. The electric cars revolutionized the social geography of the city. The token shown gave riders the opportunity to travel from the city center to the suburbs for just a few cents. Streetcar: National Museum of American History, Smithsonian Institution, Behring Center; token: Picture Research Consultants & Archives.

Cornelius Vanderbilt, an uncouth ferryman who built the New York Central Railroad, died in 1877, leaving his son $90 million. William Vanderbilt doubled that sum, and his two sons proceeded to spend lavishly on Fifth Avenue mansions and "cottages" in Newport, Rhode Island, that sought to rival the palaces of Europe (see chapter 18, "Visualizing History," page 574). In 1883, Alva (Mrs. William) Vanderbilt launched herself into New York society by throwing a costume party so opulent that not even old New York society, which turned up its nose at the nouveau riche, could resist an invitation. Dressed as a Venetian princess, the hostess greeted her twelve hundred guests. But her sister-in-law Alice Vanderbilt stole the show by appearing as that miraculous new invention, the electric light, resplendent in a white satin evening dress studded with diamonds. The *New York World* speculated that Alva Vanderbilt's party cost more than a quarter of a million dollars (more than $4 million today).

Such ostentatious displays of wealth became especially alarming when they were coupled with disdain for the well-being of ordinary people. When a reporter in 1882 asked William Vanderbilt whether he considered the public good when running his railroads, he shot back, "The public be damned." The fear that America had become a plutocracy — a society ruled by the rich — gained credence from the fact that the wealthiest 1 percent of the population owned more than half the real and personal property

in the country. As the new century dawned, reformers would form a progressive movement to address the problems of urban industrialism and the substandard living and working conditions it produced.

REVIEW Why did American cities experience explosive growth in the late nineteenth century?

▶ At Work in Industrial America

The number of industrial wageworkers in the United States exploded in the second half of the nineteenth century, more than tripling from 5.3 million in 1860 to 17.4 million in 1900. More than half of the country's men, women, and children made up the laboring class that performed manual work for wages. These workers toiled in a variety of settings. Many skilled workers and artisans still earned a living in small workshops. But with the rise of corporate capitalism, large factories, mills, and mines increasingly dotted the landscape. Sweatshops and outwork — the contracting of piecework, including finishing garments by hand, to be performed in the home — provided work experiences different from those of factory operatives and industrial workers. Pick-and-shovel labor, whether on the railroads or in the building trades, constituted yet another kind of work. Managers, as well as women "typewriters" and salesclerks, formed a new white-collar segment of America's workforce.

America's Diverse Workers

Common laborers formed the backbone of the American labor force. They built the railroads and subways, tunneled under New York's East River to anchor the Brooklyn Bridge, and helped lay the foundation of industrial America. These "human machines" stood at the bottom of the country's economic ladder and generally came from the most recent immigrant groups. Initially, the Irish wielded the picks and shovels that built American cities, but by the turn of the century, as the Irish bettered their lot, Slavs and Italians took up their tools.

At the opposite end of labor's hierarchy stood skilled craftsmen like iron puddler James J. Davis, a Welsh immigrant who worked in the Pennsylvania mills. Using brains along with brawn, puddlers took up the melted pig iron in the heat of the furnace and, with long, heavy "spoons" (poles), formed the cooling metal into 200-pound balls, relying on eye and intuition to make each ball uniform. Davis likened his work to baking bread: "I am like some frantic baker in the inferno. . . . My spoon weighs twenty-five pounds, my porridge is pasty iron, and the heat of my kitchen is so great that if my body was not hardened to it the ordeal would drop me in my tracks."

Possessing such a skill meant earning good wages. Davis made up to $7 a day, when there was work. But most industry and manufacturing work in the nineteenth century remained seasonal; few workers could count on year-round pay. In addition, two major depressions only twenty years apart, beginning in 1873 and 1893, spelled unemployment and hardship. In an era before unemployment insurance, workers' compensation, or old-age pensions, even the best worker could not guarantee security for his family. "The fear of ending in the poor-house is one of the terrors that dog a man through life," Davis confessed.

Skilled workers like Davis wielded power on the shop floor. Employers attempted to limit workers' control by replacing people with machines, breaking down skilled work into ever-smaller tasks that could be performed by unskilled factory operatives. New England's textile mills provide a classic example of the effects of mechanized factory labor in the nineteenth century. Mary, a weaver at the mills in Fall River, Massachusetts, went to work in the 1880s at the age of twelve. By then, mechanization of the

Sweatshop Worker
Sweatshop workers endured crowded and often dangerous conditions. Most were young women, like the one shown here sewing pants in New York City. Young working women earned little money but prided themselves on their independence. Notice the young woman's stylish hairdo, white shirt-waist, and necklace (an indication that she did not turn over all the money in her pay envelope to her father, as was often the case). George Eastman House.

looms had reduced the job of the weaver to watching for breaks in the thread. "At first the noise is fierce, and you have to breathe the cotton all the time, but you get used to it," Mary told a reporter from *Independent* magazine. "When the bobbin flies out and a girl gets hurt, you can't hear her shout — not if she just screams, you can't. She's got to wait, 'till you see her. . . . Lots of us is deaf."

During the 1880s, the number of foreign-born mill workers almost doubled. At Fall River, Mary and her Scots-Irish family resented the new immigrants. "The Polaks learn weavin' quick," she remarked, using a common derogatory term to identify a rival group. "They just as soon live on nothin' and work like that. But it won't do 'em much good for all they'll make out of it." Employers encouraged racial and ethnic antagonism because it inhibited labor organization.

The majority of factory operatives in the textile mills were young, unmarried women like Mary. They worked from six in the morning to six at night six days a week, and they took home about $1 a day. The seasonal nature of the work also drove wages down. "Like as not your mill will 'shut down' three months," and "some weeks you only get two or three days' work," Mary recounted. After twenty years of working in the mill, Mary's family had not been able to scrape together enough money to buy a house: "We saved some, but something always comes."

Mechanization transformed the garment industry as well. With the introduction of the foot-pedaled sewing machine in the 1850s and the use of mechanical cloth-cutting knives in the 1870s, independent tailors were replaced with workers hired by contractors to sew pieces of cloth into suits and dresses. Working in **sweatshops**, small rooms hired for the season or even in the contractor's own tenement, women and children formed an important segment of garment workers. Discriminated against in the marketplace, where they earned less than men, women generally worked for wages for only eight to ten years, until they married.

Sadie Frowne, a sixteen-year-old Polish Jew, went to work in a Brooklyn sweatshop in the 1890s. Frowne sewed for eleven hours a day in a 20-by-14-foot room containing fourteen machines. "The machines go like mad all day, because the faster you work the more money you get," she recalled. Paid by the piece, she earned about $4.50 a week and, by rigid economy, tried to save $2. Young and single, Frowne typified the woman wage earner in the late nineteenth century. In 1890, the average workingwoman was twenty-two and had been working since the age of fifteen, laboring twelve hours a day six days a week and earning less than $6 a week. Only marriage delivered women from dead-end jobs. No wonder single working women scrimped to buy ribbons and finery to make themselves attractive to young men.

The Family Economy: Women and Children

In 1900, the typical male worker in manufacturing earned $435 a year, about $12,000 in today's dollars. Many working-class families, whether native-born or immigrant, lived in or near poverty, their economic survival dependent on the contributions of all family members, regardless of sex or age. "Father," asked one young immigrant girl, "does everybody in America live like this? Go to work early, come home late, eat and go to Sleep? And the next day again work, eat, and sleep?" Most workers did. The **family economy** meant that everyone needed to contribute to maintain even the most meager household. Children dutifully turned over their wages to their fathers and kept only a tiny portion for themselves. One statistician estimated that in 1900 as many as 64 percent of working-class families relied on income other than the husband's wages to make ends meet. The paid and unpaid work of women and children proved essential for family survival, let alone economic advancement.

In the cities, boys as young as six years old plied their trades as bootblacks and newsboys. Often working under an adult contractor, these children earned as little as fifty cents a day. Many of them were homeless — orphaned or

Bootblacks
The faces and hands of the two bootblacks shown here with a third boy on a New York City street in 1896 testify to their grimy trade. Boys as young as six years old found work on city streets as bootblacks and newsboys. Often they worked for contractors who took a cut of their meager earnings. When families could no longer afford to feed their children, boys often headed out on their own at a young age. For these child workers, even free education was a luxury they could not afford. Alice Austin photo, Staten Island Historical Society.

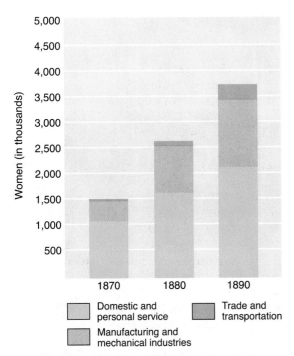

FIGURE 19.3   Women and Work, 1870–1890
In 1870, close to 1.5 million women worked in nonagricultural occupations. By 1890, that number had more than doubled to 3.7 million. More and more women sought work in manufacturing and mechanical industries, although domestic service still constituted the largest employment arena for women.

working class, rarely worked for wages outside the home. In 1890, only 3 percent were employed. Nevertheless, working-class married women found ways to contribute to the family economy. In many Italian families, for example, piecework such as making artificial flowers allowed married women to contribute to the family economy without leaving their homes. Black women, married and unmarried, worked for wages in much greater numbers. The 1890 census showed that 25 percent of married African American women were employed, often as domestics in the houses of white families.

> "Father, does everybody in America live like this? Go to work early, come home late, eat and go to Sleep? And the next day again work, eat, and sleep?"
> — A young immigrant girl

White-Collar Workers: Managers, "Typewriters," and Salesclerks

In the late nineteenth century, business expansion and consolidation led to a managerial revolution, creating a new class of white-collar workers who worked in offices and stores. As skilled workers saw their crafts replaced by mechanization, some moved into management positions. "The middle class is becoming a salaried class," a writer for the *Independent* magazine observed, "and is rapidly losing the economic and moral independence of former days." As large business organizations consolidated, corporate development separated management from ownership, and the job of directing the firm became the province of salaried executives and managers, the majority of whom were white men drawn from the 8 percent of Americans who held high school diplomas.

cast off by their families. "We wuz six, and we ain't got no father," a child of twelve told reporter Jacob Riis. "Some of us had to go."

Child labor increased decade by decade after 1870. The percentage of children under fifteen engaged in paid labor did not drop until after World War I. The 1900 census estimated that 1,750,178 children ages ten to fifteen were employed, an increase of more than a million over thirty years. Children in this age range constituted more than 18 percent of the industrial labor force. Many younger children not counted by the census worked beside their older siblings in mills, in factories, and on the streets.

In the late nineteenth century, the number of women workers also rose sharply, with their most common occupations changing slowly from domestic service to factory work and then to office work. In 1870, the census listed 1.5 million women working for wages in nonagricultural occupations. By 1890, the number had more than doubled, with 3.7 million women working for pay (Figure 19.3). Women's working patterns varied considerably according to race and ethnicity. White married women, even among the

Until late in the century, when engineering schools began to supply recruits, many skilled workers moved from the shop floor to positions of considerable responsibility. William "Billy" Jones, the son of a Welsh immigrant, was one such worker. Beginning as an apprentice at the age of ten, Jones rose through the ranks to become plant superintendent at Andrew Carnegie's Pittsburgh steelworks in 1872. By all accounts, Jones was the best steel man in the industry, and Carnegie rewarded him with a "hell of a big salary," $25,000 — the same salary as the president of the United States. Most middle managers averaged far less, $1,100 a year being counted as a good salary. Senior executives, generally recruited from the college-educated elite, took home $4,000 or more, and a company's general manager could earn as much as $15,000 a year, approximately 30 times what the average worker earned. (Today's top CEOs on average earn 550 times more than the average worker receives.) At the top of the economic pyramid, the great industrialists amassed fortunes that rank John D. Rockefeller, Andrew Carnegie, and Cornelius Vanderbilt among the top ten richest men in American history, easily outpacing today's billionaires.

The new white-collar workforce also included women **"typewriters"** and salesclerks. In the decades after the Civil War, as businesses became larger and more far-flung, the need for more elaborate and exact records, as well as the greater volume of correspondence, led to the hiring of more office workers. Mechanization transformed business as it had industry and manufacturing. The adding machine, the cash register, and the typewriter came into general use in the 1880s. Employers seeking literate workers soon turned to nimble-fingered women. Educated men had many other career choices, but for middle-class white women, secretarial work constituted one of the very few areas where they could put their literacy to use for wages.

Sylvie Thygeson was typical of the young women who went to work as secretaries. Thygeson grew up in an Illinois prairie town and went to work as a country schoolteacher after graduating high school in 1884. Realizing that teaching school did not pay a living wage, she mastered typing and stenography and found work as a secretary to help support her family. According to her account, she made "a fabulous sum of money" (possibly $25 a month). Nevertheless, she gave up her job after a few years when she met and married her husband.

Called "typewriters," women workers like Thygeson were seen as indistinguishable from the machines they operated. Far from viewing their jobs as dehumanizing, women typewriters took pride in their work and relished the economic independence it afforded them. But the entry of women into the workplace challenged traditional gender roles. Society distinguished between "ladies" (who stayed at home) and "working girls" (by definition lower-class women and a term often used for prostitutes). When white middle-class women entered offices as court reporters, typewriters, and stenographers, issues of class and gender clashed. Could a "lady" work? And if she did, did her economic independence threaten men and marriage? Some of this ambivalence can be seen in a poem published in 1896 in the

Clerical Worker
A stenographer takes dictation in an 1890s office. Notice that the apron, a symbol of feminine domesticity, has accompanied women into the workplace. In the 1880s, with the invention of the typewriter, many women put their literacy skills to use in the nation's offices. Brown Brothers.

Boston *Courier*. The poet waxes eloquent on his attraction to the "typewriter":

> The click of the keys, as her fingers fly,
>   And the ring of the silvery bell,
> I hardly hear, though I sit quite near,
>   Enchained by her magic spell.

After several verses, however, he ruefully abandons his ardor in the face of her modesty and professional manner. And, more telling, he acknowledges that the independent working woman may not need him at all.

> So, to her of my love I shall never speak,
>   Twould be vain I can clearly see.
> Why, she gets sixteen dollars a week.
>   And what does she want of me?

As Sylvie Thygeson's story shows, most women chose marriage and the home over the office, despite concerns to the contrary. But by the 1890s, secretarial work was the overwhelming choice of native-born, single white women, who constituted more than 90 percent of the female clerical force. Not only considered more genteel than factory work or domestic labor, office work also meant more money for shorter hours. In 1883, Boston's clerical workers on average made more than $6 a week, compared with less than $5 for women working in manufacturing.

As a new consumer culture came to dominate American urban life in the late nineteenth century, department stores offered another employment opportunity for women in the cities. Boasting ornate facades, large plate-glass display windows, and marble and brass fixtures, stores such as Macy's in New York, Wanamaker's in Philadelphia, and Marshall Field in Chicago stood as monuments to the material promise of the era. Within these palaces of consumption, cash girls, stock clerks, and wrappers earned as little as $3 a week, while at the top of the scale, buyers like Belle Cushman of the fancy goods department at Macy's earned $25 a week, an unusually high salary for a woman in the 1870s. Salesclerks counted themselves a cut above factory workers. Their work was neither dirty nor dangerous, and even when they earned less than factory workers, they felt a sense of superiority.

REVIEW How did business expansion and consolidation change workers' occupations in the late nineteenth century?

▶ Workers Organize

By the late nineteenth century, industrial workers were losing ground in the workplace. In the fierce competition to reduce prices and cut costs, industrialists, led by Andrew Carnegie, invested heavily in new machinery that replaced skilled workers with unskilled labor. The erosion of skills and the redefinition of labor as mere "machine tending" left the worker with a growing sense of individual helplessness that served as a spur to collective action. In 1877, in the midst of a depression that left many workers destitute, labor flexed its muscle in the Great Railroad Strike and showed the power of collective action. This and other strikes underscored the tensions produced by rapid industrialization.

In the 1870s and 1880s, labor organizations grew, and the Knights of Labor and the American Federation of Labor attracted workers. Convinced of the inequity of the wage-labor system, labor organizers spoke eloquently of abolishing class privileges and monopoly. Their rhetoric as well as the violence often associated with strikes frightened many middle-class Americans and caused them to equate the labor movement with the specter of class war and anarchism.

The Great Railroad Strike of 1877

Economic depression following the panic of 1873 threw as many as three million people out of work. Those who were lucky enough to keep their jobs watched as pay cuts eroded their wages until they could no longer feed their families. In the summer of 1877, the Baltimore and Ohio (B&O) Railroad announced a 10 percent wage cut at the same time it declared a 10 percent dividend to its stockholders. Angry brakemen in West Virginia, whose wages had already fallen from $70 to $30 a month, walked out on strike. One B&O worker described the hardship that drove him to take such desperate action: "We eat our hard bread and tainted meat two days old on the sooty cars up the road, and when we come home, find our wives complaining that they cannot even buy hominy and molasses for food."

The West Virginia brakemen's strike touched off the **Great Railroad Strike** of 1877, a nationwide uprising that spread rapidly to Pittsburgh and Chicago, St. Louis and San Francisco (Map 19.3). Within a few days, nearly 100,000 railroad workers walked off the job. The spark of rebellion soon led an estimated 500,000 laborers to join the train workers. In Reading, Pennsylvania, militiamen refused to fire on the strikers, saying, "We may be militiamen, but we are workmen first." Rail traffic ground to a halt; the nation lay paralyzed.

Violence erupted as the strike spread. In Pittsburgh, strikers clashed with militia brought in from Philadelphia, who arrogantly boasted

Strike activity

MAP 19.3

The Great Railroad Strike of 1877

Starting in West Virginia and Pennsylvania, the strike spread as far north as Albany, New York, and as far west as San Francisco, bringing rail traffic to a standstill. Called the Great Uprising, the strike heralded the beginning of a new era of working-class protest and trade union organization.

they would clean up "the workingmen's town." Charging with bayonets leveled, the troops opened fire on the crowds, killing twenty people.

Angry workers retaliated by reducing an area two miles long beside the tracks to smoldering rubble. Before the day ended, twenty more workers had been shot, and the railroad had sustained millions of dollars' worth of property damage. Nothing like the Pittsburgh riots had ever happened in American history. Armed workers had chased the Philadelphia militia out of town. Now business pressured the federal government to step in.

> **"The railroad strikers, as a rule, are good men, sober, intelligent, and industrious."**
>
> — President
> RUTHERFORD B. HAYES

Within eight days, the governors of nine states, acting at the prompting of the railroad owners and managers, defined the strike as an "insurrection" and called for federal troops. President Rutherford B. Hayes, after hesitating briefly, called out the army. By the time the troops arrived, the violence had run its course. Federal troops did not shoot a single striker in 1877. But they struck a blow against labor by acting as strikebreakers — opening rail traffic, protecting nonstriking train crews (known by the derogatory term "scabs"), and maintaining peace along the line. In three weeks, the strike was over.

Although many middle-class Americans initially sympathized with the conditions that led to the strike, they condemned the strikers for the violence and property damage that occurred. The *New York Times* editorialized about the "dangerous classes," and the *Independent* magazine offered the following advice on how to deal with "rioters": "If the club of a policeman, knocking out the brains of the rioter, will answer then well and good; but if it does not promptly meet the exigency, then bullets and bayonets . . . constitutes [*sic*] the one remedy and one duty of the hour."

"The strikes have been put down by force," President Hayes noted in his diary on August 5. "But now for the real remedy. Can't something be done by education of the strikers, by judicious control of the capitalists, by wise general policy

Destruction from the Great Railroad Strike of 1877
Pictures of the devastation caused in Pittsburgh during the strike shocked many Americans. When militiamen fired on striking workers, killing more than twenty strikers, the mob retaliated by destroying a two-mile area along the track, reducing it to a smoldering rubble. Property damage totaled $2 million. Curious pedestrians came out to view the destruction. Carnegie Library of Pittsburgh.

to end or diminish the evil? The railroad strikers, as a rule, are good men, sober, intelligent, and industrious." While Hayes acknowledged the workers' grievances, most businessmen and industrialists did not and fought the idea of labor unions, arguing that workers and employers entered into contracts as individuals and denying the right of unions to bargain collectively for their workers. For their part, workers quickly recognized that they held little power individually and flocked to join unions. As labor leader Samuel Gompers noted, the nation's first national strike dramatized the frustration and unity of the workers and served as an alarm bell to labor "that sounded a ringing message of hope to us all."

The Knights of Labor and the American Federation of Labor

The **Knights of Labor**, the first mass organization of America's working class, proved the chief beneficiary of labor's newfound consciousness. The Noble and Holy Order of the Knights of Labor had been founded in 1869 by Uriah Stephens, a Philadelphia garment cutter. A secret society of workers, the Knights envisioned a "universal brotherhood" of all workers, from common laborers to master craftsmen. The organization's secrecy and ritual served to bind Knights together at the same time that it discouraged company spies and protected members from reprisals.

Although the Knights played no active role in the 1877 railroad strike, membership swelled as a result of the growing interest in labor organizing that followed the strike. In 1878, the Knights abandoned secrecy and launched an ambitious campaign to organize workers, attempting to bridge the boundaries of ethnicity, gender, ideology, race, and occupation in a badly fragmented society. **Leonora Barry** served as general investigator for women's work from 1886 to 1890, helping the Knights recruit teachers, waitresses, housewives, and domestics along with factory and sweatshop workers. Women composed perhaps 20 percent of the membership. The Knights also made good on its vow to include African Americans, organizing more than 95,000 black workers. That the Knights of Labor often fell short of its goals to unify the working class proved less surprising than the scope of its efforts.

Under the direction of Grand Master Workman **Terence V. Powderly**, the Knights became the dominant force in labor during the 1880s. The organization advocated a kind of workers' democracy that embraced reforms including public ownership of the railroads, an income tax, equal pay for women workers, and the abolition of child labor. A loose mix of ideology, unionism, culture, fraternalism, and mysticism, the Knights called for one big union to create a cooperative commonwealth that would supplant the wage system and remove class distinctions. Only the "parasitic" members of society — gamblers, stockbrokers, lawyers, bankers, and liquor dealers — were denied membership.

In theory, the Knights of Labor opposed strikes. Powderly championed arbitration and preferred to use boycotts. But in practice, much of the organization's appeal came from the Knights' sweeping victory against railroad tycoon Jay Gould in the Great Southwest Strike of 1885. Despite the reservations of its leadership, the Knights became a militant labor organization that won passionate support from working people with the slogan "An injury to one is the concern of all."

The Knights of Labor was not without rivals. Many skilled workers belonged to craft unions organized by trade. Among the largest and richest of these unions stood the Amalgamated Association of Iron and Steel Workers, founded in 1876 and counting twenty thousand skilled workers as members. Trade unionists spurned the broad reform goals of the Knights and focused on workplace issues. **Samuel Gompers**, a cigar maker born in London of Dutch Jewish ancestry, promoted what he called "pure and simple" unionism. Gompers founded the Organized Trades and Labor Unions in 1881 and reorganized it in 1886 into the **American Federation of Labor (AFL)**, which coordinated the activities of craft unions throughout the United States. His plan was simple: organize skilled workers such as machinists and locomotive engineers — those with the most bargaining power — and use strikes to gain immediate objectives such as higher pay and better working conditions. Gompers at first drew few converts. The AFL had only 138,000 members in 1886, compared with 730,000 for the Knights of Labor. But events soon brought down the Knights, and Gompers's brand of unionism came to prevail.

Haymarket and the Specter of Labor Radicalism

While the AFL and the Knights of Labor competed for members, more radical labor groups, including socialists and anarchists, believed that reform was futile and called instead for social revolution. Both the socialists and the anarchists, sensitive to criticism that they preferred revolution in theory to improvements here and now, rallied around the popular issue of the eight-hour day.

Since the 1840s, labor had sought to end the twelve-hour workday, which was standard in industry and manufacturing. By the mid-1880s, it seemed clear to many workers that labor shared too little in the new prosperity of the decade, and pressure mounted for the eight-hour day. Labor championed the popular issue and launched major rallies in cities across the nation. Supporters of the movement set May 1, 1886, as the date for a nationwide general strike in support of the eight-hour workday.

All factions of the nascent labor movement came together in Chicago on May Day for what was billed as the largest demonstration to date. A group of labor radicals led by anarchist Albert Parsons, a *Mayflower* descendant, and August Spies, a German socialist, spearheaded the eight-hour movement in Chicago. Chicago's Knights of Labor rallied to the cause even though Terence Powderly and the union's national leadership, worried about the increasing activism of the rank and file, refused to endorse the movement for shorter hours. Samuel Gompers was on hand, too, to lead the city's trade unionists, although he privately urged the AFL assemblies not to participate in the general strike.

Gompers's skilled workers were labor's elite. Many still worked in small shops where negotiations between workers and employers took place in an environment tempered by personal relationships. Well dressed in their frock coats and starched

A RECORD OF THE
Terrible Scenes of May 4, 1886.

Chicago and New York:
BELFORD, CLARKE & CO.,
1886.

VISUAL ACTIVITY

"The Chicago Riot"

Inflammatory pamphlets like this one, published in the wake of the Haymarket bombing, presented a one-sided view of the incident and stirred public passion. In this charged atmosphere, the anarchist speakers at the rally were tried and convicted for the bombing even though witnesses testified that none of them had thrown the bomb. The identity of the bomb thrower remains uncertain. Chicago Historical Society.

READING THE IMAGE: What does the cover suggest about the views of the author of the pamphlet?

CONNECTIONS: In what ways does this pamphlet reflect the public climate following the Haymarket bombing?

shirts, the AFL's skilled workers stood in sharp contrast to the dispossessed workers out on strike across town at Chicago's huge McCormick reaper works. There strikers watched helplessly as the company brought in strikebreakers to take their jobs and marched the "scabs" to work under the protection of the Chicago police and security guards supplied by the Pinkerton Detective Agency. Cyrus McCormick Jr., son of the inventor of the mechanical reaper, viewed labor organization as a threat to his power as well as to his profits; he was determined to smash the union.

During the May Day rally, 45,000 workers paraded peacefully down Michigan Avenue in support of the eight-hour day, many singing the song that had become the movement's anthem:

> We want to feel the sunshine;
> We want to smell the flowers,
> We're sure that God has willed it,
> And we mean to have eight hours.
> Eight hours for work, eight hours for rest,
> eight hours for what we will!

Trouble came two days later, when strikers attacked strikebreakers outside the McCormick works and police opened fire, killing or wounding six men. Angry radicals rushed out a circular urging workers to "arm yourselves and appear in full force" at a rally in Haymarket Square.

On the evening of May 4, the turnout at Haymarket was disappointing. No more than two or three thousand gathered in the drizzle to hear Spies, Parsons, and the other speakers. Mayor Carter Harrison, known as a friend of labor, mingled conspicuously in the crowd, pronounced the meeting peaceable, and went home to bed. Sometime later, police captain John "Blackjack" Bonfield, who had made his reputation cracking skulls, marched his men into the crowd, by now fewer than three hundred people, and demanded that it disperse. Suddenly, someone threw a bomb into the police ranks. After a moment of stunned silence, the police drew their revolvers. "Fire and kill all you can," shouted a police lieutenant. When the melee ended, seven policemen and an unknown number of other people lay dead. An additional sixty policemen and thirty or forty civilians suffered injuries.

News of the "Haymarket riot" provoked a nationwide convulsion of fear, followed by blind rage directed at anarchists, labor unions, strikers, immigrants, and the working class in general. Eight men, including Parsons and Spies, went on trial in Chicago, although witnesses testified that none of them had thrown the bomb. "Convict these men," thundered the state's attorney, Julius S. Grinnell, "make examples of them, hang them, and you save our institutions." Although the state could not link any of the defendants to the **Haymarket bombing**, the jury nevertheless found them all guilty. Four were executed, one committed suicide, and three received prison sentences. On the gallows, Spies spoke for the Haymarket martyrs: "The time will come when our silence will be more powerful than the voices you throttle today."

The bomb blast at Haymarket had lasting repercussions. To commemorate the death of the Haymarket martyrs, labor made May 1 an annual international celebration of the worker. But the Haymarket bomb, in the eyes of one observer, proved "a godsend to all enemies of the labor movement." It effectively scotched the eight-hour-day movement and dealt a blow to the Knights of Labor, already wracked by internal divisions. With the labor movement everywhere under attack, many skilled workers turned to the American Federation of Labor. Gompers's narrow economic strategy made sense at the time and enabled one segment of the workforce — the skilled — to organize effectively and achieve tangible gains. But the nation's unskilled workers remained untouched by the AFL's brand of trade unionism. The vast majority of America's workers would have to wait another forty years before a mainstream labor union, the Congress of Industrial Organizations (CIO), moved to organize the unskilled (as discussed in chapter 24).

REVIEW Why did the fortunes of the Knights of Labor rise in the late 1870s and decline in the 1890s?

Maids and Domestics

These Swedish immigrant women were working as maids in the Merchant's Hotel in Black River Falls, Wisconsin, when they posed for this picture in 1890. Each carries a tool of her trade—broom and dustpan, iron, potato peeler, dishcloth, pie plate, serving tray. The women, young and well dressed, have similar collars, but no clear uniform. Domestic work could be hard and lonely. Only the largest private house would have so many women employed. Wisconsin Historical Society (WHi (V22d) 1386).

▶ At Home and at Play

The growth of urban industrialism not only dramatically altered the workplace but also transformed home and family life and gave rise to new forms of commercialized leisure. Industrialization redefined the very concepts of work and home. Increasingly, men went out to work for wages, while most white married women stayed home, either working in the home without pay — cleaning, cooking, and rearing children — or supervising paid domestic servants who did the housework.

Domesticity and "Domestics"

The separation of the workplace and the home that marked the shift to industrial society redefined the home as a "haven in the heartless world," presided over by a wife and mother who made the household her separate sphere. The growing separation of workplace and home led to a new ideology, one that sentimentalized the home and women's role in it. The cultural ideology that dictated woman's place in the home began to develop in the early 1800s and has been called the **cult of domesticity**, a phrase used to prescribe an ideal of middle-class, white womanhood that dominated the period from 1820 to the end of the nineteenth century.

The cult of domesticity and the elaboration of the middle-class home led to a major change in patterns of hiring household help. The live-in servants, or **domestics**, became a fixture in the North, replacing the hired girl of the previous century. In American cities by 1870, 15 to 30 percent of all households included live-in domestic servants, more than 90 percent of them women. Earlier in the mid-nineteenth century, native-born women increasingly took up other work and left domestic service to immigrants. In the East, the maid was so often Irish that "Bridget" became a generic term for female domestics. (The South continued to rely on black female labor, first slave and later free.)

Servants by all accounts resented the long hours and lack of privacy. "She is liable to be rung up at all hours," one study of domestics reported. "Her very meals are not secure from interruption, and even her sleep is not sacred." No wonder tension between domestic servants and their female employers proved endemic. Domestic service became the occupation of last resort, a "hard and lonely life" in the words of one female servant.

For women of the white middle class, domestics were a boon, freeing them from household drudgery and giving them more time to spend with their children or to pursue club work or reform. Thus, while domestic service supported the cult of domesticity, it created for those women who could afford it opportunities that expanded their horizons outside the home in areas such as women's clubs and the temperance and suffrage movements.

Such benefits of middle-class respectability contrasted sharply with the austerity of the working-class home. Reformer Margaret Byington recounted her visit with the family of a Slavic worker in Homestead, the Carnegie mill town outside Pittsburgh. The family lived in a two-room dwelling, and Byington found the young mother doing the family laundry in a big washtub set on a chair in the middle of the downstairs room, struggling to keep her two babies from tumbling into the scalding water. Further describing the congested home, Byington noted the room's single large bed and "the inevitable cook

stove upon which in the place of honor was simmering the evening's soup. Upstairs in a second room, a boarder and the man of the house were asleep. Soon they would get up and turn their beds over to two more boarders, who were out at work." In the eyes of Byington and many middle-class reformers, the Slavs' crowded tenement, with its lack of privacy, scarcely qualified as a "home."

Cheap Amusements

Growing class divisions manifested themselves in patterns of leisure as well as in work and home life. The poor and working class took their leisure, when they had any, not in the crowded tenements that housed their families, but increasingly in the cities' new dance halls, music houses, ballparks, and amusement arcades, which by the 1890s formed a familiar part of the urban landscape.

The growing anonymity of urban industrial society posed a challenge to traditional rituals of courtship. Young workingwomen no longer

Beach Scene at Coney Island

Coney Island became a symbol of commercialized leisure and mechanical excitement at the turn of the twentieth century. This fanciful rendering captures the frenetic goings-on. Men and women, along with costumed clowns, frolic in the waves. Notice the woolen bathing outfits, with their leggings, modest skirts and blouses, and bathing hats. Men box and play ball, a woman flies on a parachute, while a uniformed policeman wades into the fray, brandishing his billy club. On the shore are the rides — with the Ferris wheel dominating the skyline — and the famous hotel in the shape of an elephant. Sunday crowds on the island reportedly reached 100,000. Beach scene: Library of Congress; Sand pail: Private Collection.

met prospective husbands only through their families. Fleeing crowded tenements, the young sought each other's company in dance halls and other commercial retreats. Scorning proper introductions, working-class youths "picked up" partners at dance halls, where drinking was part of the evening's entertainment. Young workingwomen, who rarely could afford more than trolley fare when they went out, counted on being "treated" by men, a transaction that often implied sexual payback. Young women's need to negotiate sexual encounters if they wished to participate in commercial amusements blurred the line between respectability and promiscuity and made the dance halls a favorite target of reformers who feared they lured teenaged girls into prostitution.

For men, baseball became a national pastime in the 1870s — then, as now, one force in urban life capable of uniting a city across class lines. Cincinnati mounted the first entirely paid team, the Red Stockings, in 1869. Soon professional teams proliferated in cities across the nation, and Mark Twain hailed baseball as "the very symbol, the outward and visible expression, of the drive and push and rush and struggle of the raging, tearing, booming nineteenth century."

The increasing commercialization of entertainment in the late-nineteenth-century city was best seen at **Coney Island**. A two-mile stretch of sand nine miles from Manhattan by trolley or steamship, Coney Island in the 1870s and 1880s attracted visitors to its beaches, dance pavilions, and penny arcades, where they consumed treats ranging from oysters to saltwater taffy. In the 1890s, Coney Island was transformed into the site of some of the largest and most elaborate amusement parks in the country. Promoter George Tilyou built Steeplechase Park in 1897, advertising "10 hours of fun for 10 cents." With its mechanical thrills and fun-house laughs, the amusement park encouraged behavior that one schoolteacher aptly described as "everyone with the brakes off." By 1900, as many as a million New Yorkers flocked to Coney Island on any given weekend, making the amusement park the unofficial capital of a new mass culture.

"Everyone with the brakes off."
— A schoolteacher's description of behavior at Coney Island's Steeplechase Amusement park

REVIEW   How did urban industrialism shape the world of leisure?

▶ City Growth and City Government

Private enterprise, not planners, built the cities of the United States. Boosters, builders, businessmen, and politicians all had a hand in creating the modern metropolis. With a few notable exceptions, such as Washington, D.C., and Savannah, Georgia, there was no such thing as a comprehensive city plan. Cities simply mushroomed, formed by the dictates of profit and the exigencies of local politics. With the rise of the city came the need for public facilities, transportation, and services that would tax the imaginations of America's architects and engineers and set the scene for the rough-and-tumble of big-city government, politics, and politicians.

Building Cities of Stone and Steel

Skyscrapers and mighty bridges dominated the imagination and the urban landscape. Less imposing but no less significant were the paved streets, the parks and public libraries, and the subways and sewers. In the late nineteenth century, Americans rushed to embrace new technology of all kinds, making their cities the most modern in the world.

Structural steel made enormous advances in building possible. A decade after the completion of the **Brooklyn Bridge** (see pages 603–604), engineers used the new technology to construct the Williamsburg Bridge just to the north. More prosaic and utilitarian than its neighbor, the new bridge was never as acclaimed, but it was longer by four feet and completed in half the time. It became the model for future building as the age of steel supplanted the age of stone and iron.

Chicago, not New York, gave birth to the modern skyscraper. Rising from the ashes of the Great Fire of 1871, which destroyed three square miles and left eighteen thousand people homeless, Chicago offered a generation of skilled architects and engineers the chance to experiment. Commercial architecture became an art form at the hands of a skilled group of architects who together constituted the "Chicago school." Men of genius such as Louis Sullivan gave Chicago some of the world's finest commercial buildings. Employing the dictum "Form follows

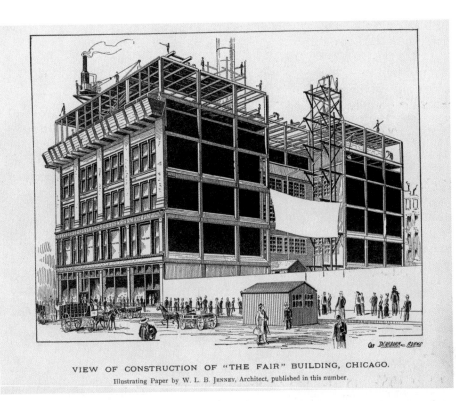

VIEW OF CONSTRUCTION OF "THE FAIR" BUILDING, CHICAGO.
Illustrating Paper by W. L. B. JENNEY, Architect, published in this number.

Chicago Skyscraper Going Up
With the advent of structural steel, skyscrapers like this one in progress in Chicago in 1891 became prominent features of the American urban landscape. This architect's rendering of the Fair Building, a department store designed by William Le Baron Jenney, shows a modern skyscraper whose foundations supported the structural steel skeleton so that the walls could simply "hang" on the outside of the building, because they no longer had to support the structure. Newberry Library (*Inland Architect*, Nov. 1891).

function," they built startlingly modern structures. A fitting symbol of modern America, the skyscraper expressed the domination of corporate power.

Alongside the skyscrapers rose new residential apartments for the rich and the middle class. The "French flat" — apartments with the latest plumbing and electricity — gained popularity in the 1880s as affluent city dwellers overcame their distaste for multifamily housing (which carried the stigma of the tenement) and gave in to "flat fever." "Housekeeping isn't fun," cried one New York woman. "Give us flats!" In 1883 alone, more than one thousand new apartments went up in Chicago.

Across the United States, municipal governments undertook public works on a scale never before seen. They paved streets, built sewers and water mains, replaced gas lamps with electric lights, ran trolley tracks on the old horsecar lines, and dug underground to build subways, tearing down the unsightly elevated tracks that had clogged city streets. In San Francisco, Andrew Smith Hallidie mastered the city's hills, building a system of cable cars in 1873. Boston completed the nation's first subway system in 1897, and New York and Philadelphia soon followed.

Cities became more beautiful with the creation of urban public parks to complement the new buildings that quickly filled city lots. Much of the credit for America's greatest parks goes to one man — landscape architect **Frederick Law Olmsted**. The indefatigable Olmsted designed parks in Atlanta, Boston, Brooklyn, Hartford, Detroit, Chicago, and Louisville, as well as the grounds for the U.S. Capitol. But he is best remembered for the creation of New York City's Central Park. Completed in 1873, it became the first landscaped public park in the United States. Olmsted and his partner, Calvert Vaux, directed the planting of more than five million trees, shrubs, and vines to transform the eight hundred acres between 59th and 110th streets into an oasis for urban dwellers. "We want a place," he wrote, where people "may stroll for an hour, seeing, hearing, and feeling nothing of the bustle and jar of the streets."

American cities did not overlook the mind in their efforts at improvement. They created a comprehensive free public school system that educated everyone from the children of the middle class to the sons and daughters of immigrant workers. Yet the exploding urban population strained the system and led to crowded

The Boston Public Library

When the first public library in the country moved to its new site in Boston's Copley Square in 1895, the best artists and architects of the day lent their talents to build "a palace for the people." Architect Charles F. McKim designed the library around a cloistered courtyard in the style of a Renaissance palazzo. Sculptor Augustus Saint-Gaudens modeled the Sienna marble lions that guard the grand stairway. French muralist Puvis de Chavannes contributed the allegorical mural representing literature and learning. A frolicking nude Bacchante by Frederick MacMonnies graced the courtyard fountain for a few days until scandalized Bostonians demanded its removal. Today it has been restored to its place. Library photograph: ©Richard Cheek for the Boston Public Library; statue: image copyright ©The Metropolitan Museum of Art/Art Resource, NY.

and inadequate facilities. In 1899, more than 544,000 pupils attended school in New York's five boroughs. Municipalities across the United States provided free secondary school education for all who wished to attend, even though only 8 percent of Americans completed high school.

To educate those who couldn't go to school, American cities created the most extensive free public library system in the world. In 1895, the Boston Public Library opened its bronze doors under the inscription "Free to All." Designed in the style of a Renaissance palazzo, with more than 700,000 books on the shelves ready to be checked out, the library earned the description "a palace of the people."

Despite the Boston Public Library's legend "Free to All," the poor did not share equally in the advantages of city life. The parks, the libraries, and even the subways and sewers benefited some city dwellers more than others. Few library cards were held by Boston's laborers, who worked six days a week and found the library closed on Sunday. And in the 1890s, there was nothing central about New York's Central Park. It was a four-mile walk from the tenements of Hester Street to the park's entrance at 59th Street and Fifth Avenue. Then, as now, the comfortable majority, not the indigent minority, reaped a disproportionate share of the benefits in the nation's big cities.

Any story of the American city, it seems, must be a tale of two cities — or, given the cities' great diversity, a tale of many cities within each metropolis. At the turn of the twentieth century, a central paradox emerged: The enduring monuments of America's cities — the bridges, skyscrapers, parks, and libraries — stood as the undeniable achievements of the same system of municipal government that reformers dismissed as boss-ridden, criminal, and corrupt.

City Government and the "Bosses"

The physical growth of the cities required the expansion of public services and the creation of entirely new facilities: streets, subways, elevated trains, bridges, docks, sewers, and public utilities. There was work to be done and money to be made. The professional politician — the colorful big-city boss — became a phenomenon of urban growth and **bossism** a national phenomenon. Though corrupt and often criminal, the boss saw to the building of the city and provided needed social services for the new residents. Yet not even the big-city boss could be said to rule the unruly city. The governing of America's cities resembled more a tug-of-war than boss rule.

The most notorious of all the city bosses was **William Marcy "Boss" Tweed** of New York. At midcentury, Boss Tweed's Democratic Party "machine" held sway. A machine was really no more than a political party organized at the grassroots level. Its purpose was to win elections and reward its followers, often with jobs on the city's payroll. New York's citywide Democratic machine, **Tammany Hall**, commanded an army of party functionaries. At the bottom were district captains. In return for votes, they provided services for their constituents, everything from a scuttle of coal in the winter to housing for an evicted family. At the top were powerful ward bosses who distributed lucrative franchises for subways and streetcars. They formed a shadow government more powerful than the city's elected officials.

As chairman of the Tammany general committee, Tweed kept the Democratic Party together and ran the city through the use of bribery and graft. "As long as I count the votes," he shamelessly boasted, "what are you going to do about

Tammany Bank
This cast-iron bank, a campaign novelty, bears the name of the New York City Democratic machine. It conveys its political reform message graphically: When you put a penny in the politician's hand, he puts it in his pocket. Tammany Hall dominated city politics for more than a century, dispensing contracts and franchises worth millions of dollars. Some of those dollars invariably found their way into the pockets of Tammany politicians. Collection of Janice L. and David J. Frent.

it?" The excesses of the Tweed ring soon led to a clamor for reform and cries of "Throw the rascals out." Cartoonist Thomas Nast pilloried Tweed in the pages of *Harper's Weekly*. His cartoons, easily understood even by those who could not read, did the boss more harm than hundreds of outraged editorials. Tweed's rule ended in 1871. Eventually, he was tried and convicted and later died in jail.

New York was not the only city to experience bossism and corruption. The British visitor James Bryce concluded in 1888, "There is no denying that the government of cities is the one conspicuous failure of the United States." More than 80 percent of the nation's thirty largest cities experienced some form of boss rule in the decades around the turn of the twentieth century. However, infighting among powerful ward bosses often meant that no single boss enjoyed exclusive power in the big cities.

"As long as I count the votes, what are you going to do about it?"
— New York's BOSS TWEED

Urban reformers and proponents of good government (derisively called "goo goos" by their rivals) challenged machine rule and sometimes succeeded in electing reform mayors. But the reformers rarely managed to stay in office for long. Their detractors called them "mornin' glories," observing that they "looked lovely in the mornin' and withered up in a short time." The bosses enjoyed continued success largely because the urban political machine helped the cities' immigrants and poor, who remained the bosses' staunchest allies. "What tells in holding your district," a Tammany ward boss observed, "is to go right down among the poor and help them in the different ways they need help. It's philanthropy, but it's politics, too — mighty good politics." Saloons were the epicenter of

ward politics. They played a crucial role in workers' lives and often served informally as political headquarters, as well as employment agencies and union halls.

A few reform mayors managed to achieve success and longevity by following the bosses' model. **Hazen S. Pingree** of Detroit exemplified the successful reform mayor. A businessman who went into politics in the 1890s, Pingree, like most good-government candidates, promised to root out dishonesty and inefficiency. But when the depression of 1893 struck, Pingree emerged as a champion of the working class and the poor. He hired the unemployed to build schools, parks, and public baths. By providing jobs and needed services, he built a powerful political organization based on working-class support. Detroit's

Chicago's White City

This painting by H. D. Nichols captures the monumental architecture of the White City built for the World's Columbian Exposition in 1893. In the foreground, the central Court of Honor features a Frederick MacMonnies fountain, with Christopher Columbus at the prow of his ship. In the distance is Daniel Chester French's sixty-foot gilded statue *Republic*. Monumental, harmonious, and pristine, the White City was designed by Daniel Burnham and Frederick Law Olmsted to awe and overwhelm fairgoers. And so it did, drawing millions of visitors from America and abroad, who eagerly snapped up souvenirs, such as the playing cards pictured here, to commemorate their visit. Painting: Chicago Historical Society; Cards: Compliments of Columbus Antique Mall & Museum.

voters kept him in the mayor's office for four terms and then helped elect him governor twice.

The big-city boss, through the skillful orchestration of rewards, exerted powerful leverage and lined up support for his party from a broad range of constituents, from the urban poor to wealthy industrialists. In 1902, when journalist **Lincoln Steffens** began "The Shame of the Cities," a series of articles exposing city corruption, he found that business leaders who fastidiously refused to mingle socially with the bosses nevertheless struck deals with them. "He is a self-righteous fraud, this big businessman," Steffens concluded. "I found him buying boodlers [bribers] in St. Louis, defending grafters in Minneapolis, originating corruption in Pittsburgh, sharing with bosses in Philadelphia, deploring reform in Chicago, and beating good government with corruption funds in New York."

The complexity of big-city government, apparent in the many levels of corruption that Steffens uncovered, pointed to one conclusion: For all the color and flamboyance of the big-city boss, he was simply one of many actors in the drama of municipal government. Old-stock aristocrats, new professionals, saloonkeepers, pushcart peddlers, and politicians all fought for their interests in the hurly-burly of city government. They didn't much like each other, and they sometimes fought savagely. But they learned to live with one another. Compromise and accommodation — not boss rule — best characterized big-city government by the turn of the twentieth century, although the cities' reputation for corruption left an indelible mark on the consciousness of the American public.

White City or City of Sin?

Americans have always been of two minds about the city. They like to boast of its skyscrapers and bridges, its culture and sophistication, and they pride themselves on its bigness and bustle. At the same time, they fear it as the city of sin, the home of immigrant slums, the center of vice and crime. Nowhere did the divided view of the American city take form more graphically than in Chicago in 1893. In that year, Chicago hosted the **World's Columbian Exposition**, the grandest world's fair in the nation's history. (See "Beyond America's Borders," page 632.) The fairground on Lake Michigan offered a lesson in what Americans on the eve of the twentieth century imagined a city might be. Only five miles down the shore from downtown Chicago, the White City, as the fairground became known,

seemed light-years away from Chicago, with its stockyards, slums, and bustling terminals. Frederick Law Olmsted and architect Daniel Burnham supervised the transformation of a swampy wasteland into a pristine paradise of lagoons, fountains, wooded islands, gardens, and imposing buildings.

"Sell the cookstove if necessaray and come," novelist Hamlin Garland wrote to his parents on the farm. And come they did, in spite of the panic and depression that broke out only weeks after the fair opened in May 1893. In six months, fairgoers purchased more than 27 million tickets, turning a profit of nearly a half million dollars for promoters. Visitors from home and abroad strolled the elaborate grounds and visited the exhibits — everything from a model of the Brooklyn Bridge carved in soap to the latest goods and inventions. Half carnival, half culture, the great fair offered something for everyone. On the Midway Plaisance, crowds thrilled to the massive wheel built by Mr. Ferris and watched agog as Little Egypt danced the hootchy-kootchy.

In October, the fair closed its doors in the midst of the worst depression the country had yet seen. During the winter of 1894, Chicago's unemployed and homeless took over the grounds, vandalized the buildings, and frightened the city's comfortable citizens out of their wits. When reporters asked Daniel Burnham what should be done with the moldering remains of the White City, he responded, "It should be torched." And it was. In July 1894, in a clash between federal troops and striking railway workers, incendiaries set fires that leveled the fairgrounds.

In the end, the White City remained what it had always been, a dreamscape. Buildings that looked like marble were actually constructed of staff, a plaster substance that began to crumble even before fire destroyed the fairgrounds. Perhaps it was not so strange, after all, that the legacy of the White City could be found on Coney Island, where two new amusement parks, Luna and Dreamland, sought to combine, albeit in a more tawdry form, the beauty of the White City and the thrill of the Midway Plaisance. More enduring than the White City itself was what it represented: the emergent industrial might of the United States, at home and abroad, with its inventions, manufactured goods, and growing consumer culture.

REVIEW How did municipal governments respond to the challenges of urban expansion?

The World's Columbian Exposition and Nineteenth-Century World's Fairs

The 1893 World's Columbian Exposition in Chicago and the other great world's fairs of the nineteenth century represented a unique phenomenon of industrial capitalism and a testament to the expanding global market economy. The Chicago fair, named to celebrate the four hundredth anniversary of Columbus's arrival in the New World, offered a cornucopia of international exhibits testifying to growing international influences ranging from cultural to technological exchange.

Great cities vied to host world's fairs, as much to promote commercial growth as to demonstrate their cultural refinement. Each successive fair sought to outdo its predecessor. Chicago's fair followed on the great success of the 1889 Universal Exposition in Paris. The Paris Exposition featured as its crowning glory the 900-foot steel tower constructed by Alexandre-Gustav Eiffel. How could Chicago, a prairie upstart, top that?

The answer was the creation of the White City, with its monumental architecture, landscaped grounds, and first Ferris wheel. The White City celebrated the classicism of the French Beaux Arts school, which borrowed heavily from the massive geometric styling and elaborate detailing of Greek and Renaissance architecture. Beneath its Renaissance facade, the White City acted as an enormous emporium dedicated to the unabashed materialism of the Gilded Age. Fairgoers could view virtually every kind of manufactured product in the world inside the imposing Manufactures and Liberal Arts Building, including Swiss glassware and clocks, Japanese lacquerware and bamboo, British woolen products, and French perfumes and linens. The German pavilion displayed fine wooden furniture as well as tapestries, porcelain, and jewelry belonging to the ruling family.

As suited an industrial age, manufactured products and heavy machinery drew the largest crowds. Displays introduced visitors to the latest mechanical and technological innovations, many the result of international influences. For five cents, fairgoers could put two hard rubber tubes into their ears and listen for the first time to a Gramophone playing the popular tune "The Cat Came Back." The Gramophone, which signaled the beginning of the recorded music industry, was itself the work of a German immigrant, Emile Berliner (Thomas Edison later claimed credit for a similar invention, calling it the phonograph).

Such international influences were evident throughout the Columbian Exposition. At the Tiffany pavilion, one of the most popular venues at the fair, visitors oohed and aahed over the display of lamps, ornamental metalwork, and fine jewelry that Louis Comfort Tiffany credited to the influence of Japanese art forms. Juxtaposed with Tiffany's finery stood a display of firearms in the Colt gallery. An American company since 1836, Colt had opened a factory in England in 1851, and its revolvers enjoyed an international reputation — the best-known firearms not only in America but also in Canada, Mexico, and many European countries. Colt's new automatic weapon, the machine gun, would soon play a major role on the world stage in both the Boxer uprising in China and the Spanish-American War.

All manner of foodstuffs — teas from India, Irish whiskey, and pastries and other confectionery from Germany and France — tempted fairgoers. American food products such as Shredded Wheat, Aunt Jemima syrup, and Juicy Fruit gum debuted at the fair, where they competed for ribbons. Winners such as Pabst "Blue Ribbon" Beer used the award in advertisements. And the fair introduced two new foods — carbonated soda and the hamburger — destined to become America's best-known contributions to international cuisine.

The Columbian Exposition also served as a testimony to American technological achievement and progress. By displaying technology in action, the White City tamed it and made it accessible to American and world consumers. The fair helped promote new technologies, particularly electric light and power. With 90,000 electric lights, 5,100 arc lamps, electric fountains, an electric elevated railroad, and electric launches plying the lagoons, the White City provided a glowing advertisement for electricity. In the Electricity Building, fairgoers visited the Bell Telephone Company exhibit,

"All Nations Are Welcome"
Uncle Sam, flanked by the city of Chicago, welcomes representatives carrying the flags of many nations to the World's Columbian Exposition in 1893. In the background are the fairgrounds on the shores of Lake Michigan. More than one hundred nations participated in the fair by sending exhibits and mounting pavilions to showcase their cultures and products. Chicago Historical Society.

marveled at General Electric's huge dynamo (electric generator), and gazed into the future at the all-electric home and model demonstration kitchen.

Consumer culture received its first major expression and celebration at the Columbian Exposition. Not only did this world's fair anticipate the mass marketing, packaging, and advertising of the twentieth century, but the vast array of products on display also cultivated the urge to consume. Thousands of concessionaires with products for sale sent a message that tied enjoy-ment inextricably to spending money and purchasing goods, both domestic and foreign. The Columbian Exposition set a pattern for the twentieth-century world's fairs that followed, making a powerful statement about the possibilities of urban life in an industrial age and encouraging the rise of a new middle-class consumer culture. As G. Brown Goode, head of the Smithsonian Institution observed, the Columbian Exposition was in many ways "an illustrated encyclopedia of civilization."

America in a Global Context

1. Would you describe the Columbian Exposition as a commercial venture, a cultural display, or an entertainment? Why?

2. What role did the fair play in popularizing new technologies?

3. What was meant by the observation that the fair was "an illustrated encyclopedia of civilization"?

4. How did the international flavor of the White City compare with the reality of global migration into America's fast-growing cities?

► Conclusion: Who Built the Cities?

As much as the great industrialists and financiers, as much as eminent engineers like John and Washington Roebling, common workers, most of them immigrants, built the nation's cities. The unprecedented growth of urban, industrial America resulted from the labor of millions of men, women, and children who toiled in workshops and factories, in sweatshops and mines, on railroads and construction sites across America.

America's cities in the late nineteenth century teemed with life. Immigrants and blue bloods, poor laborers and millionaires, middle-class managers and corporate moguls, secretaries, salesgirls, sweatshop laborers, and society matrons lived in the cities and contributed to their growth. Town houses and tenements jostled for space with skyscrapers and great department stores, while parks, ball fields, amusement arcades, and public libraries provided the city masses with recreation and entertainment.

Municipal governments, straining to build the new cities, experienced the rough-and-tumble of machine politics as bosses and their constituents looked to profit from city growth. Reformers deplored the graft and corruption that accompanied the rise of the cities. But they were rarely able to oust the party bosses for long because they failed to understand the services the political machines provided for their largely immigrant and poor constituents; nor did reformers account for the ties between city politicians and wealthy businessmen who sought to benefit from franchises and contracts.

For America's workers, urban industrialism along with the rise of big business and corporate consolidation drastically changed the workplace. Industrialists replaced skilled workers with new machines that could be operated by cheaper unskilled labor. And during hard times, employers did not hesitate to cut workers' already meager wages. As the Great Railroad Strike of 1877 demonstrated, when labor united, it could bring the nation to attention. Organization held out the best hope for the workers; first the Knights of Labor and later the American Federation of Labor won converts among the nation's working class.

The rise of urban industrialism challenged the American promise, which for decades had been dominated by Jeffersonian agrarian ideals. Could such a promise exist in the changing world of cities, tenements, immigrants, and huge corporations? In the great depression that came in the 1890s, mounting anger and frustration would lead farmers and workers to join forces and create a grassroots movement to fight for change under the banner of a new People's Party.

► Selected Bibliography

Immigration

John Bodnar, *The Transplanted: A History of Immigration in Urban America* (1985).

Vincent J. Cannato, *American Passage: The History of Ellis Island* (2010).

Roger Daniels, *Guarding the Golden Door: American Immigration Policy and Immigrants since 1882* (2004).

Martha Gardner, *The Qualities of a Citizen: Women, Immigration, and Citizenship, 1870–1965* (2005).

Dirk Hoerder, *Cultures in Contact: World Migrations in the Second Millennium* (2002).

Matthew Frye Jacobson, *Whiteness of a Different Color: European Immigrants and the Alchemy of Race* (1998).

David M. Reimers, *Unwelcome Strangers* (1998).

David R. Roediger, *Working toward Whiteness: How America's Immigrants Became White* (2005).

Ronald Takaki, *Strangers from a Different Shore: A History of Asian Americans* (1998).

Workers and Unions

Susan Porter Benson, *Counter Cultures: Saleswomen, Managers, and Customers in American Department Stores, 1890–1940* (1986).

Ileen A. DeVault, *United Apart: Gender and the Rise of Craft Unionism* (2004).

Hasia Diner, *Lower East Side Memories: A Jewish Place in America* (2000).

Leon Fink, *Workingman's Democracy: The Knights of Labor and American Politics* (1983).

James Green, *Death in the Haymarket: A Story of Chicago, the First Labor Movement, and the Bombing That Divided Gilded Age America* (2006).

Hamilton Hold, ed., *The Life Stories of Undistinguished Americans as Told by Themselves* (2000).

Jacqueline Jones, *American Work: Four Centuries of Black and White Labor* (1998).

Jackson Lears, *Rebirth of a Nation: The Making of Modern America, 1877–1920* (2009).

Susan Levine, *Labor's True Women: Carpet Weavers, Industrialization, and Labor Reform in the Gilded Age* (1984).

David Montgomery, *The Fall of the House of Labor: The Workplace, the State, and American Labor Activism, 1865–1925* (1987).

Roy Rosenzweig, *Eight Hours for What We Will: Workers and Leisure in an Industrial City, 1870–1920* (1983).

Timothy Spears, *Chicago Dreaming: Midwesterners and the City, 1871–1919* (2005).

Carole Srole, *Transcribing Class and Gender: Masculinity and Femininity in Nineteenth Century Courts and Offices* (2009).

Sharon Hartman Strom, *Beyond the Typewriter: Gender, Class, and the Origins of Modern American Office Work, 1900–1930* (1992).

Robert E. Weir, *Knights Unhorsed: Internal Conflict in a Gilded Age Social Movement* (2000).

The City and Its Amusements

LeRoy Ashby, *With Amusement for All: A History of American Popular Culture since 1830* (2006).

Sven Beckert, *The Monied Metropolis: New York City and the Consolidation of the American Bourgeoisie, 1850–1896* (2001).

Gary S. Cross and John K. Walton, *The Playful Crowd: Pleasure Places in the Twentieth Century* (2005).

Sarah Deutsch, *Women and the City: Gender, Space, and Power in Boston, 1870–1940* (2000).

Nan Enstad, *Ladies of Labor, Girls of Adventure: Working Women, Popular Culture, and Labor Politics at the Turn of the Twentieth Century* (1999).

Margaret Garb, *City of American Dreams: A History of Home Ownership and Housing Reform in Chicago, 1871–1919* (2005).

Richard Haw, *The Brooklyn Bridge: A Cultural History* (2005).

Elizabeth Hawes, *New York, New York: How the Apartment House Transformed Life in the City, 1869–1930* (1993).

Kathy Peiss, *Cheap Amusements: Working Women and Leisure in Turn-of-the-Century New York* (1986).

Roy Rosenzweig and Elizabeth Blackmar, *The Park and the People: A History of Central Park* (1992).

Witold Rybczynski, *A Clearing in the Distance: Frederick Law Olmsted and America in the Nineteenth Century* (1999).

Jules Tygiel, *Past Time: Baseball as History* (2000).

▶ **FOR MORE BOOKS ABOUT TOPICS IN THIS CHAPTER,** see the Online Bibliography at **bedfordstmartins.com/roark.**

▶ **FOR ADDITIONAL PRIMARY SOURCES FROM THIS PERIOD,** see Michael Johnson, ed., *Reading the American Past*, Fifth Edition.

▶ **FOR WEB SITES, IMAGES, AND DOCUMENTS RELATED TO TOPICS AND PLACES IN THIS CHAPTER,** visit Make History at **bedfordstmartins.com/roark.**

Reviewing Chapter 19

KEY TERMS

Explain each term's significance.

The Rise of the City
>global migration (p. 605)
>pogroms (p. 608)
>Ellis Island (p. 612)
>Jacob Riis (p. 613)

At Work in Industrial America
>sweatshops (p. 616)
>family economy (p. 616)
>"typewriters" (p. 618)

Workers Organize
>Great Railroad Strike (p. 619)
>Knights of Labor (p. 621)
>Leonora Barry (p. 622)
>Terence V. Powderly (p. 622)
>Samuel Gompers (p. 622)
>American Federation of Labor (p. 622)
>Haymarket bombing (p. 623)

At Home and at Play
>cult of domesticity (p. 624)
>domestics (p. 624)
>Coney Island (p. 626)

City Growth and City Government
>Brooklyn Bridge (p. 626)
>Frederick Law Olmsted (p. 627)
>bossism (p. 629)
>William Marcy "Boss" Tweed (p. 629)
>Tammany Hall (p. 629)
>Hazen S. Pingree (p. 630)
>Lincoln Steffens (p. 631)
>World's Columbian Exposition (p. 631)

REVIEW QUESTIONS

Use key terms and dates to support your answer.

1. Why did American cities experience explosive growth in the late nineteenth century? (pp. 605–614)

2. How did business expansion and consolidation change workers' occupations in the late nineteenth century? (pp. 614–619)

3. Why did the fortunes of the Knights of Labor rise in the late 1870s and decline in the 1890s? (pp. 619–624)

4. How did urban industrialism shape the world of leisure? (pp. 624–626)

5. How did municipal governments respond to the challenges of urban expansion? (pp. 626–633)

MAKING CONNECTIONS

Draw on key terms, the timeline, and review questions.

1. Americans expressed both wonder and concern at the nation's mushrooming cities. Why did cities provoke such divergent responses? In your answer, discuss the dramatic demographic, environmental, and political developments associated with urbanization.

2. Why did patterns of immigration to the United States in the late nineteenth century change? How did Americans respond to the immigrants who arrived late in the century? In your answer, consider how industrial capitalism, nationally and globally, contributed to these developments.

3. How did urban industrialization affect Americans' lives outside of work? Describe the impact of late-nineteenth-century economic developments on home life and leisure. In your answer, consider how class, race, gender, and ethnicity contributed to diverse urban experiences.

4. When workers began to embrace organization in the late 1870s, what did they hope to accomplish? Were they successful? Why or why not? In your answer, discuss both general conditions and specific events that shaped these developments.

LINKING TO THE PAST

Link events in this chapter to earlier events.

1. Compare the lives of migrant workers and industrial cowboys in the West to workers in the nation's cities. What are the major similarities? (See chapter 17.)

2. You have already looked at the development of America's industries in the nineteenth century from the vantage point of moguls such as Andrew Carnegie and John D. Rockefeller. How does your view of industrialism change when the focus is shifted to the nation's workers? (See chapter 18.)

▶ **FOR PRACTICE QUIZZES AND OTHER STUDY TOOLS,** visit the Online Study Guide at **bedfordstmartins.com/roark.**

TIMELINE 1869–1897

1869	• Knights of Labor founded.
	• Cincinnati mounts first paid baseball team, the Red Stockings.
1871	• Boss Tweed's rule in New York ends.
	• Chicago's Great Fire.
1873	• Panic on Wall Street touches off depression.
	• San Francisco's cable car system opens.
1877	• Great Railroad Strike.
1880s	• Immigration from southern and eastern Europe rises.
1882	• Chinese Exclusion Act.
1883	• Brooklyn Bridge opens.
1886	• American Federation of Labor (AFL) founded.
	• Haymarket bombing.
1890s	• African American migration from the South begins.
1890	• Jacob Riis publishes *How the Other Half Lives.*
1892	• Ellis Island opens in New York harbor to process immigrants.
1893	• World's Columbian Exposition.
	• Panic on Wall Street touches off major economic depression.
1895	• Boston Public Library opens.
1896	• President Grover Cleveland vetoes immigrant literacy test.
1897	• Steeplechase Park opens on Coney Island.
	• Nation's first subway system opens in Boston.

637

IN THE OLD
PARTIES WE TRUSTED
untill FINANCIALLY WE ARE BUSTED

And if we would
our rights regain
We must nominate
Honest Men

It is the best that
We can do
And elect them
all in 92

DOWN WITH
MONOPOLY

PEOPLE'S PARTY BANNER

This buffalo banner from the 1892 Populist
convention declares "In the Old Parties We Trusted
until Financially we are Busted" and promises to
elect "Honest Men." In the background some of
those men stand, along with women and children,
on the steps of the capitol in Topeka in 1893, after
being elected to the Kansas House of
Representatives. Perhaps taking the buffalo as a
mascot was a poor choice for the new party, for
just as the great herds on the western plains had
been decimated in the 1880s, the People's (or
Populist) Party would go down to defeat in 1896.
Banner: Nebraska State Historical Society; background: Kansas State
Historical Society.

Dissent, Depression, and War 1890–1900

FRANCES WILLARD TRAVELED TO ST. LOUIS IN FEBRUARY 1892 WITH high hopes. Political change was in the air, and Willard was there to help fashion a new reform party, one that she hoped would embrace her two passions — temperance and woman suffrage. As head of the Woman's Christian Temperance Union, an organization with members in every state and territory in the nation, Willard wielded considerable clout. At her invitation, twenty-eight of the country's leading reformers had already met in Chicago to draft a set of principles to bring to St. Louis. Always expedient, Willard had settled for a statement condemning the saloon rather than an endorsement for a stronger measure to prohibit the sale of alcohol. But at the convention, she hoped to press the case for woman suffrage and prohibition. Willard knew it would not be easy, but in the heady atmosphere of 1892 she determined to try. No American woman before her had played such a central role in a political movement. At the height of her political power, Willard took her place among the leaders on the podium in St. Louis.

Exposition Music Hall presented a colorful spectacle. "The banners of the different states rose above the delegates throughout the hall, fluttering like the flags over an army encamped," wrote one reporter. The fiery orator Ignatius Donnelly attacked the money kings of Wall Street. Mary Elizabeth Lease, a veteran campaigner from Kansas known for exhorting farmers to "raise less corn and more hell," added her powerful voice to the cause. Terence V. Powderly, head of the Knights of Labor, called on workers to join hands with farmers against the "nonproducing classes." Frances Willard urged the crowd to outlaw the liquor traffic and give the vote to women. Between speeches, the crowd sang labor songs like "Hurrah for the Toiler" and "All Hail the Power of Laboring Men."

Over the next few days, delegates hammered out a series of demands, breathtaking in their scope. They tackled the tough questions of the day — the regulation of business, the need for banking and currency reform, the right of labor to organize and bargain collectively, and the role of the federal government in regulating business, curbing monopoly, and guaranteeing democracy. But the new party determined to stick to economic issues and

639

Frances Willard

Frances Willard, the forward-thinking leader of the Woman's Christian Temperance Union, learned to ride a bicycle at age fifty-three. The bicycle became hugely popular in the 1890s, even though traditionalists fulminated that it was unladylike for women to straddle a bike and immodest for them to wear the divided skirts that allowed them to pedal. Shown here in 1895, Willard declared bicycling a "harmless pleasure" that encouraged "clear heads and steady hands." Willard brought her progressive ideas to the People's Party 1892 convention, where she shared a place on the platform with the new party's leaders. Photo: Courtesy of the Frances E. Willard Memorial Library and Archives (WCTU).

resisted endorsing either temperance or woman suffrage. As a member of the platform committee, Willard fought for both and complained of the "crooked methods . . . employed to scuttle these planks." Outmaneuvered in committee, she brought the issues to the floor of the convention, only to go down to defeat by a vote of 352 to 238.

Despite Willard's disappointment, the convention ended its work amid a chorus of cheers. According to one eyewitness, "Hats, paper, handkerchiefs, etc., were thrown into the air; . . . cheer after cheer thundered and reverberated through the vast hall reaching the outside of the building where thousands who had been waiting the outcome joined in the applause till for blocks in every direction the exultation made the din indescribable."

What was all the shouting about? The cheering crowd was celebrating the birth of a new political party, officially named the People's Party. Fed up with the Democrats and Republicans, a broad coalition of groups came together in St. Louis to fight for change. They resolved to reconvene in Omaha in July to nominate candidates for the upcoming presidential election. Defeated but not willing to abandon the new party, Willard resolved to work for the nomination of a presidential candidate committed to temperance and suffrage.

The St. Louis gathering marked an early milestone in one of the most turbulent decades in U.S. history. Unrest, agitation, agrarian revolt, labor strikes, a severe financial panic and depression, and a war of expansion shook the 1890s. As the decade opened, Americans dissatisfied with the two major political parties were already flocking to organizations including the Farmers' Alliance, the American Federation of Labor, and the Woman's Christian Temperance Union, and they worked together to create the political alliance that gave birth to the People's (or Populist) Party. In a decade of unrest and uncertainty, the People's Party countered laissez-faire economics by insisting that the federal government play a more active role to ensure greater economic equity in industrial America.

This challenge to the status quo culminated in 1896 in one of the most hotly contested presidential elections in the nation's history. At the close of the tumultuous decade, the Spanish-American War helped to bring the country together, with Americans rallying to support the troops. But disagreement over American imperialism and overseas expansion raised questions about the nation's role on the world stage as the United States stood poised to enter the twentieth century.

▶ The Farmers' Revolt

Hard times in the 1880s and 1890s created a groundswell of agrarian revolt. A bitter farmer wrote from Minnesota, "I settled on this Land in good Faith Built House and Barn. Broken up Part of the Land. Spent years of hard Labor in grubbing fencing and Improving." About to lose his farm to foreclosure, he lamented, "Are they going to drive us out like trespassers . . . and give us away to the Corporations?"

Crop prices for the nation's six million farmers fell decade after decade, even as their share of the world market grew (Figure 20.1). In parts of Kansas, wheat sold for so little that angry farmers burned their crops for fuel rather than take them to market. At the same time, consumer prices soared (Figure 20.2). Farmers couldn't make ends meet. In Kansas alone, almost half the farms had fallen into the hands of the banks by 1894 through foreclosure.

The Farmers' Alliance

At the heart of the farmers' problems stood a banking system dominated by eastern commercial banks committed to the gold standard, a railroad rate system that was capricious and unfair, and rampant speculation that drove up the price of land. In the West, farmers rankled under a system that allowed railroads to charge them exorbitant freight rates while granting rebates to large shippers (see chapter 18). In the South, lack of currency and credit drove farmers to the stopgap credit system of the crop lien, turning the entire region into "a vast pawn shop." Determined to do something, farmers banded together to fight for change.

Farm protest was not new. In the 1870s, farmers had supported the Grange and the Greenback Labor Party. As the farmers' situation grew more desperate, they organized, forming regional alliances. The first **Farmers' Alliance** came together in Lampasas County, Texas, to fight "landsharks and horse thieves." During the 1880s, the movement spread rapidly. In frontier farmhouses in Texas, in log cabins in the backwoods of Arkansas, and in the rural parishes of Louisiana, separate groups of farmers formed similar alliances for self-help.

As the movement grew, farmers' groups consolidated into two regional alliances: the Northwestern Farmers' Alliance, active in Kansas, Nebraska, and other midwestern Granger states; and the more radical Southern Farmers' Alliance. In the 1880s, traveling lecturers preached the Alliance message. Worn-out men and careworn women did not need to be convinced that something was wrong. By 1887, the Southern Farmers' Alliance had grown to more than 200,000 members, and by 1890 it counted more than 3 million members.

> "We are going to get out of debt and be free and independent people once more."
> — A Georgia farmer, on the effects of the Alliance movement

Kansas Farm Family Forced Off Their Farm
Hard times in the 1880s sent farmers reeling back from the plains. In 1894, almost half the farmers in Kansas lost their land because they could not make mortgage payments. The Owens family of Greeley County, pictured here, were among the defeated, forced to pack up their belongings and head east. The simple writing on their wagon tells the chronology of their retreat. Kansas State Historical Society.

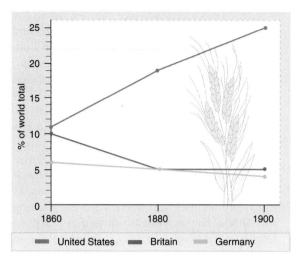

FIGURE 20.1   GLOBAL COMPARISON: Share of the World Wheat Market, 1860–1900

Although many countries produced wheat for home use, Britain, Germany, and the United States were among the largest wheat exporters. Exporting wheat worldwide became viable in the United States only after the completion of the transcontinental railroad in 1869. The resulting growth of the railroads, coupled with the development of improved mechanical reapers throughout the second half of the century, led to the mechanization of U.S. agriculture, allowing wheat farmers to harvest ever-larger crops. From 1860 to 1900, the United States' percentage of world wheat production more than doubled, while Germany's declined and Britain's was cut in half as a result of its growing emphasis on industrialization. What was the impact of entering a world market for U.S. wheat farmers?

Radical in its inclusiveness, the Southern Alliance reached out to African Americans, women, and industrial workers. Through cooperation with the **Colored Farmers' Alliance**, an African American group founded in Texas in the 1880s, blacks and whites attempted to make common cause. As Georgia's Tom Watson, a Southern Alliance stalwart, pointed out, "The colored tenant is in the same boat as the white tenant, . . . and . . . the accident of color can make no difference in the interests of farmers, croppers, and laborers."

The political culture of the Alliance encouraged the inclusion of women and children and used the family as its defining symbol. Women rallied to the Alliance banner along with their menfolk, drawn to meetings that combined picnic, parade, revival, country fair, and political convention. "I am going to work for prohibition, the Alliance, and for Jesus as long as I live," swore one woman.

In wagon trains, men and women in the thousands thronged to Alliance meetings to listen to speeches and to debate and discuss the issues of the day. The Alliance leaders aimed to do more than exhort their followers; they aimed to educate them. The Farmers' Alliance produced and distributed "a perfect avalanche of literature" — speeches, newspapers, books, and tracts — full of damning details about the political collusion between business and politics, along with detailed analyses of the securities and commodities markets, the tariff and international trade, and credit and currency. Alliance lecturers reached out to the illiterate, often speaking for hours under the broiling sun to educate their rapt audiences on the fine points of economics and politics.

At the heart of the Alliance movement stood a series of farmers' cooperatives. By "bulking" their cotton —

FIGURE 20.2   Consumer Prices and Farm Income, 1865–1910

Around 1870, consumer prices and farm income were about equal. During the 1880s and 1890s, however, farmers suffered great hardships as prices for their crops steadily declined and the cost of consumer goods continued to rise.

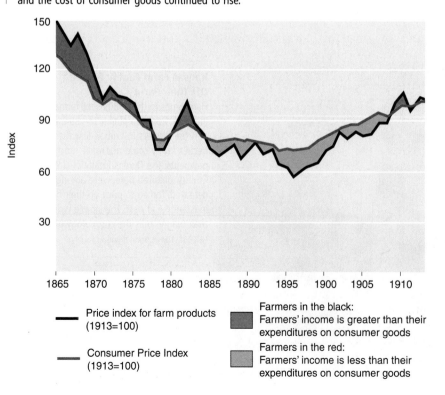

Price index for farm products (1913=100)

Consumer Price Index (1913=100)

Farmers in the black: Farmers' income is greater than their expenditures on consumer goods

Farmers in the red: Farmers' income is less than their expenditures on consumer goods

that is, selling it together — farmers could negotiate a better price. And by setting up trade stores and exchanges, they sought to escape the grasp of the merchant/creditor. Through the cooperatives, the Farmers' Alliance promised to change the way farmers lived. "We are going to get out of debt and be free and independent people once more," exulted one Georgia farmer.

Cooperatives sprang up throughout the South and West. But the Alliance faced insurmountable difficulties in running successful cooperatives. Opposition by merchants, bankers, wholesalers, and manufacturers made it impossible for the cooperatives to get credit. As the cooperative movement died, the Farmers' Alliance moved toward direct political action. Confounded by the failure of the Democrats and Republicans to break with commercial interests and support the farmers, Alliance leaders moved, often reluctantly, toward the formation of a third party.

The Populist Movement

In the earliest days of the Alliance movement, a leader of the Southern Farmers' Alliance insisted, "The Alliance is a strictly white man's nonpolitical, secret business association." But by 1892, it was none of those things. Advocates of a third party carried the day at the convention of laborers, farmers, and common folk in 1892 in St. Louis, where the Farmers' Alliance gave birth to the **People's Party** and launched the Populist movement. "There is something at the back of all this turmoil more than the failure of crops or the scarcity of ready cash," a journalist observed in 1892.

The same spirit of religious revival that animated the Farmers' Alliance infused the People's Party. The Populists built on the work of the Alliance to mount a critique of industrial society and a call for action. Convinced that the money and banking systems worked to the advantage of the wealthy few, they demanded economic democracy. To help farmers get the credit they needed at reasonable rates, southern farmers hit on the ingenious idea of a **subtreasury** — a plan that would allow farmers to store their nonperishable crops until prices rose and to receive commodity credit from the federal government to obtain needed supplies. The subtreasury promised to get rid of the crop lien system once and for all. Although the idea would be enacted piecemeal in progressive and New Deal legislation in the twentieth century, conservatives in the 1890s dismissed it as far-fetched "corn tassel communism."

Mary Elizabeth Lease
This painting of Lease, taken in 1895 at the height of her political activities in Kansas, shows a well-dressed, mild-eyed woman — belying her reputation as a hell-raiser who supposedly exhorted Kansas farmers to "raise less corn and more hell." Lease's admirers styled her "The People's Joan of Arc." But in the eyes of her detractors, who attacked not only her speeches but also the propriety of a woman who dared to pursue a career as a public speaker, she was "a lantern-jawed, google-eyed nightmare" and "a petticoated smut-mill." Kansas State Historical Society.

To the western farmer, the Populists promised land reform, championing a plan that would claim excessive land granted to railroads or sold to foreign investors. The Populists' boldest proposal called for government ownership of the railroads and the telegraph system to put an end to discriminatory rates. Citing examples of how the powerful railroads had corrupted the political system, the Populists did not shrink from advocating what their opponents branded state socialism.

The Populists also demanded currency reform. Farmers in all sections rallied to the cry for cheaper currency, calling for free silver and greenbacks — attempts to increase the nation's tight money supply and thus make credit easier to obtain. And to empower the common people, the Populist platform called for the direct election of senators (then chosen by state legislatures) and for other electoral reforms, including the secret ballot and the right to initiate legislation, to recall elected officials, and to submit issues to the people by means of a referendum. Because the Populists shared common cause with labor against corporate interests, they also supported the eight-hour workday and an end to contract labor.

The sweeping array of Populist reforms enacted in the Populist platform changed the agenda of politics for decades to come. More than just a response to hard times, Populism presented an alternative vision of American economic democracy.

> **REVIEW**   Why did American farmers organize alliances in the late nineteenth century?

▶ The Labor Wars

While farmers united to fight for change, industrial laborers fought their own battles in a series of bloody strikes so fiercely waged on both sides that historians have called them the "labor wars." Industrial workers felt increasingly threatened as businesses combined into huge corporations, and in the 1890s labor took a stand. At issue was the right of workers to organize and to speak through unions to bargain collectively and fight for better working conditions, higher wages, shorter hours, and greater worker control in the face of increased mechanization.

Three major conflicts of the period — the lockout of steelworkers in Homestead, Pennsylvania, in 1892; the miners' strike in Cripple Creek, Colorado, in 1894; and the Pullman strike in Illinois that same year — raised fundamental questions about the rights of labor and the sanctity of private property.

The Homestead Lockout

In 1892, steelworkers in Pennsylvania squared off against Andrew Carnegie in a decisive struggle over the right to organize in the Homestead steel mills. Carnegie was unusual among industrialists as a self-styled friend of labor. In 1886, he had written, "The right of the workingmen to combine and to form trade unions is no less sacred than the right of the manufacturer to enter into associations and conferences with his fellows."

> "If we undertake to resist the seizure of our jobs, we will be shot down like dogs."
>
> — A Homestead striker

Yet as much as he cherished his liberal beliefs, Carnegie cherished his profits more. In 1892, Carnegie resolved to crush the Amalgamated Iron and Steel Workers, one of the largest and richest craft unions in the American Federation of Labor (AFL). When the Amalgamated attempted to renew its contract at Carnegie's Homestead mill, its leaders were told that since "the vast majority of our employees are Non union, the Firm has decided that the minority must give place to the majority." While it was true that only 800 skilled workers belonged to the elite Amalgamated, the union had long enjoyed the support of the plant's 3,000 non-union workers. Slavs, who did much of the unskilled work, made common cause with the Welsh, Scottish, and Irish skilled workers who belonged to the union. Never before had the Amalgamated been denied a contract.

Carnegie preferred not to be directly involved in the union busting that lay on the horizon, so that spring he sailed to Scotland and left **Henry Clay Frick**, the toughest antilabor man in the industry, in charge of the Homestead plant. By summer, a strike looked inevitable. Frick prepared by erecting a fifteen-foot fence around the plant and topping it with barbed wire. Workers aptly dubbed it "Fort Frick." To defend his fort and protect strikebreakers, Frick hired 316 mercenaries from the Pinkerton National Detective Agency at the rate of $5 per day, more than double the wage of the average Homestead worker.

The Pinkerton Agency, founded before the Civil War, came into its own in the 1880s as a private security force for hire. Pinkerton agents were a motley crew, recruited from all levels of society, from urban thugs to college boys. The "Pinks" earned the hatred of workers by protecting strikebreakers and acting as company spies.

On June 28, the **Homestead lockout** began when Frick locked the workers out of the mills and prepared to bring in strikebreakers, whom the workers derogatorily referred to as "scabs." Hugh O'Donnell, the young Irishman who led the union, vowed to prevent scabs from entering the plant. On July 6 at 4 a.m., a lookout spotted two barges moving up the Monongahela River in the fog. Frick was attempting to smuggle Pinkertons into Homestead.

Workers sounded the alarm, and within minutes a crowd of more than a thousand, hastily armed with rifles, hoes, and fence posts, rushed to the riverbank to meet the enemy. When the Pinkertons attempted to come ashore, gunfire broke out, and more than a dozen Pinkertons and some thirty strikers fell, killed or wounded. The Pinkertons retreated to the barges. For twelve hours, the workers, joined by their family members, threw everything they had at the barges, from fireworks to dynamite. Finally, the

Pinkertons hoisted a white flag and arranged with O'Donnell to surrender. With three workers dead and scores wounded, the crowd, numbering perhaps ten thousand, was in no mood for conciliation. As the hated "Pinks" came up the hill, they were forced to run a gantlet of screaming, cursing men, women, and children. When a young guard dropped to his knees, weeping for mercy, a woman used her umbrella to poke out his eye. One Pinkerton had been killed in the siege on the barges. In the grim rout that followed their surrender, not one avoided injury.

The "battle of Fort Frick" ended in a dubious victory for the workers. They took control of the plant and elected a council to run the community. At first, public opinion favored their cause. Newspapers urged Frick to negotiate or submit to arbitration. A congressman castigated Carnegie for "skulking in his castle in Scotland." Populists, meeting in St. Louis, condemned the use of "hireling armies."

The action of the Homestead workers struck at the heart of the capitalist system, pitting the workers' right to their jobs against the rights of private property. The workers' insistence that "we are not destroying the property of the company — merely protecting our rights" did not prove as compelling to the courts and the state as the property rights of the mill owners. Four days after the confrontation, Pennsylvania's governor, who sympathized with the workers, nonetheless yielded to pressure from Frick and ordered eight thousand National Guard troops into Homestead to protect Carnegie's property. The strikers, thinking they had nothing to fear from the militia, welcomed the troops with a brass band. But they soon understood the reality. The troops' ninety-five-day occupation not only protected Carnegie's property but also enabled Frick to reopen the mills and bring in strikebreakers. "We have been deceived," one worker complained bitterly. "We have stood idly by and let the town be occupied by soldiers who come here, not as our protectors, but as the protectors of non-union men. . . . If we undertake to resist the seizure of our jobs, we will be shot down like dogs."

Then, in a misguided effort to ignite a general uprising, **Alexander Berkman**, a Russian immigrant and anarchist, attempted to assassinate Frick. Berkman bungled his attempt. Shot twice and stabbed with a dagger, Frick survived and showed considerable courage, allowing a doctor to remove the bullets but refusing to leave his desk until the day's work

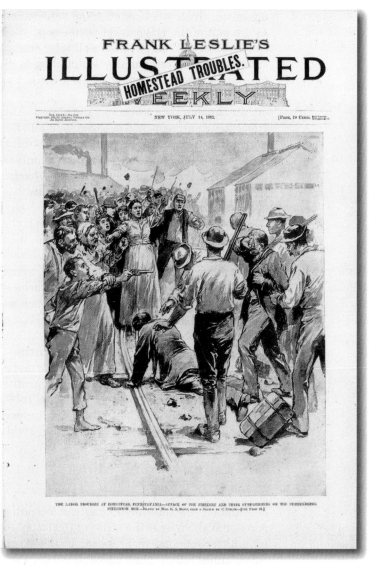

Homestead Workers Attack the Pinkertons

The nation's attention was riveted on labor strife at the Homestead steel mill in the summer of 1892. *Frank Leslie's Illustrated Weekly* ran a cover story on the violence that Pinkerton agents faced from a crowd of men, women, and children armed with clubs, guns, and ax handles.

The workers, who had been locked out by Henry Clay Frick, were enraged that Frick had hired the Pinkertons to bring in strikebreakers. Overwhelmed by the strikers, the Pinkertons surrendered. Although the mob was armed (note the boy with a gun in the foreground), not one of the Pinkertons was shot as they ran the gantlet. All, however, were beaten. The New York Society Library.

was completed. "I do not think that I shall die," Frick remarked coolly, "but whether I do or not, the Company will pursue the same policy and it will win." After the assassination attempt, public opinion turned against the workers.

Berkman was quickly tried and sentenced to prison. Although the Amalgamated and the AFL denounced his action, the incident linked anarchism and unionism, already associated in the public mind as a result of the Haymarket bombing in 1886 (see chapter 19). Hugh O'Donnell later wrote, "The bullet from Berkman's pistol, failing in its foul intent, went straight through the heart of the Homestead strike."

In the end, the workers capitulated. The Homestead mill reopened in November, and the men returned to work, except for the union leaders, now blacklisted in every steel mill in the country. With the owners firmly in charge, the company slashed wages, reinstated the twelve-hour day, and eliminated five hundred jobs.

In the drama of events at Homestead, the significance of what occurred often remained obscured: The workers at Homestead had been taught a lesson. They would never again, in the words of the National Guard commander, "believe the works are their's [sic] quite as much as Carnegie's." Another forty-five years would pass before steelworkers, unskilled as well as skilled, successfully unionized. In the meantime, Carnegie's production tripled, even in the midst of a depression. "Ashamed to tell you profits these days," Carnegie wrote a friend in 1899. And no wonder: Carnegie's profits had grown from $4 million in 1892 to $40 million in 1900.

The Cripple Creek Miners' Strike of 1894

Less than a year after the Homestead lockout, a panic on Wall Street in the spring of 1893 touched off a bitter economic depression. In the West, silver mines fell on hard times, leading to the **Cripple Creek miners' strike of 1894**. When mine owners moved to lengthen the workday from eight to ten hours, the newly formed Western Federation of Miners (WFM) vowed to hold the line in Cripple Creek, Colorado. In February 1894, the WFM threatened to strike all mines working more than eight-hour shifts. The mine owners divided: Some quickly settled with the WFM; others continued to demand ten hours, provoking a strike.

The striking miners received help from many quarters. Working miners paid $15 a month to a strike fund, and miners in neighboring districts sent substantial contributions. The miners enjoyed the support and assistance of local businesses and grocers, who provided credit to the strikers. With these advantages, the Cripple Creek strikers could afford to hold out for their demands.

Even more significant, Governor Davis H. Waite, a Populist elected in 1892, had strong ties to the miners and refused to use the power of the state against the strikers. Governor Waite asked the strikers to lay down their arms and demanded that the mine owners disperse their hired deputies. The miners agreed to arbitration and selected Waite as their sole arbitrator. By May, the recalcitrant mine owners capitulated, and the union won an eight-hour day.

Governor Waite's intervention demonstrated the pivotal power of the state in the nation's labor wars. Having a Populist in power made a difference. A decade later, in 1904, with Waite out of office, mine owners relied on state troops to take back control of the mines, defeating the WFM and blacklisting all of its members. In retrospect, the Cripple Creek miners' strike of 1894 proved the exception to the rule of state intervention on the side of private property. More typical was the outcome of another strike in 1894 in Pullman, Illinois.

Eugene V. Debs and the Pullman Strike

The economic depression that began in 1893 swelled the ranks of the unemployed to three million, almost half of the working population. "A fearful crisis is upon us," wrote a labor publication. Nowhere were workers more demoralized than in the model town of Pullman, on the outskirts of Chicago.

In the wake of the Great Railroad Strike of 1877, **George M. Pullman**, the builder of Pullman railroad cars, had moved his plant and workers away from the "snares of the great city." In 1880, he purchased 4,300 acres nine miles south of Chicago and built a model town. The town of Pullman boasted parks, fountains, playgrounds, an auditorium, a library, a hotel, shops, and markets, along with 1,800 units of housing. Noticeably absent was a saloon.

The housing in Pullman was clearly superior to that in neighboring areas, but workers paid a high price to live in the model town. George M. Pullman expected a 6 percent return on his investment. As a result, Pullman's rents ran 10 to 20 percent higher than housing costs in nearby communities. And a family in Pullman could never own its own home. George Pullman refused to "sell an acre under any circumstances." As long as he controlled the town absolutely, he held the powerful whip of eviction over his employees and could quickly get rid of "troublemakers." Although observers at first praised the beauty and orderliness of the town, critics by the 1890s compared Pullman's model town to a "gilded cage" for workers.

The depression brought hard times to Pullman. Workers saw their wages slashed five times between May and December 1893, with cuts totaling at least 28 percent. At the same time, Pullman refused to lower the rents in his model town, insisting that "the renting of the dwellings and the employment of workmen at Pullman are in no way tied together." When workers went to the bank to cash their paychecks, they found that the rent had been taken out. One worker discovered only forty-seven cents in his pay envelope for two weeks' work. When the bank teller asked him whether he wanted to apply it to his back rent, he retorted, "If Mr. Pullman needs that forty-seven cents worse than I do, let him have it." At the same time, Pullman continued to pay his stockholders an 8 percent dividend, and the company accumulated a $25 million surplus.

At the heart of the labor problems at Pullman lay not only economic inequity but also the company's attempt to control the work process, substituting piecework for day wages and undermining skilled craftsworkers. The Pullman workers rebelled. During the spring of 1894, Pullman's desperate workers, seeking help, flocked to the ranks of the **American Railway Union** (ARU), led by the charismatic **Eugene V. Debs**. The ARU, unlike the skilled craft unions of the AFL, pledged to organize all railway workers — from engineers to engine wipers. "It has been my life's desire," wrote Debs, "to unify railroad employees and to eliminate the aristocracy of labor, which unfortunately exists, and organize them so all will be on an equality." The ARU's belief in industrial democracy, however, was not matched by a commitment to racial equality; by a narrow margin, union members voted to exclude African American workers.

George Pullman responded to union organization at his plant by firing three of the union's leaders the day after they led a delegation to protest wage cuts. Angry men and women walked off the job in disgust. What began as a spontaneous protest in May 1894 quickly blossomed into a strike that involved more than 90 percent of Pullman's 3,300 workers. "We do not know what the outcome will be, and in fact we do not much care," one worker confessed. "We know that we are working for less wages than will maintain ourselves and families in the necessaries of life, and on that proposition we refuse to work any longer." Pullman countered by shutting down the plant.

A Pullman Craftsworker
Pullman Palace cars were known for their luxurious details. Here, a painter working in the 1890s applies elaborate decoration to the exterior of a Pullman car. In the foreground is an intricately carved door, an example of fine hand-detailing. The Pullman workers' strike in 1894 stemmed in part from the company's efforts to undermine the status of craftsworkers by reducing them to low-paid piecework. Control of the workplace, as much as issues related to wages and hours, fueled the labor wars of the 1890s. Chicago Historical Society.

In June, the Pullman strikers appealed to the ARU to come to their aid. Debs hesitated to commit his fledgling union to a major strike in the midst of a depression. He pleaded with the workers to find

The Press and the Pullman Strike: Framing Class Conflict

Press coverage of the 1894 Pullman strike and the subsequent American Railway Union boycott was extensive and usually partisan. How newspapers covered the Pullman strike provides a window into the way the press framed class conflict in the United States in the 1890s. The *Chicago Times*, for example, clearly supported the ARU, as was evident in its coverage of events. By contrast, the *Chicago Tribune* and most other Chicago newspapers sided with George M. Pullman and the General Managers Association. Nellie Bly, the era's most colorful investigative reporter, wrote a personal account of her experience with ARU members for the *New York World*.

DOCUMENT 1
Chicago Tribune, May 12, 1894

PULLMAN MEN OUT
Discharges the Cause

Two thousand employees in the Pullman car works struck yesterday, leaving 800 others at their posts. This was not enough to keep the works going, so a notice was posted on the big gates at 6 o'clock . . . saying: "These shops closed until further notice."

Mr. Pullman said last night he could not tell when work would be resumed. The American Railway Union, which has been proselytizing for a week among the workmen, announces that it will support the strikers . . . [intimating] that the trainmen on the railways on which are organized branches of the union might refuse to handle any of the Pullman rolling stock.

DOCUMENT 2
Chicago Times, May 12, 1894

PULLMAN MEN OUT
Firing Three Men Starts It

Almost the entire force of men employed in the Pullman shops went on strike yesterday. Out of the 4,800 men and women employed in the various departments there were probably not over 800 at work at 6 o'clock last evening. The immediate cause of the strike was the discharge or laying off of three men in the iron machine shop. The real but remote cause is the question of wages over which the men have long been dissatisfied and on account of which they had practically resolved to strike a month ago. . . .

The position of the company is that no increase in wages is possible. . . . President George M. Pullman told the committee that the company was doing business at a

loss even at the reduced wages paid the men and offered to show his books in support of his assertion.

DOCUMENT 3
Chicago Times, May 15, 1894

SKIMS OFF THE FAT
Pullman Company Declares a Dividend Today

Full Pockets Swallow $600,000 While Honest Labor Is Starving

Today the Pullman Company will declare a quarterly dividend of 2 per cent on its capital stock of $30,000,000 and President George M. Pullman is authority for the statement that his company owes no man a cent. This despite the assertion of Mr. Pullman that the works have been run at a loss for eight months. Six hundred thousand dollars to shareholders, while starvation threatens the workmen.

DOCUMENT 4
Chicago Tribune, July 1, 1894

MOBS BENT ON RUIN
Men Who Attempt to Work Are Terrorized and Beaten

Continued and menacing lawlessness marked the progress yesterday of Dictator Debs and those who obey his orders in their efforts at coercing the railroads of the country into obeying the mandates of the American Railway Union. The Rock Island was the chief sufferer from the mob spirit which broke loose the moment its men struck. . . . At 10 o'clock the officials threw up their hands and discontinued service for the night. At Blue Island, anarchy reigned. The Mayor and police force of that town could do nothing to repress the riotous strikers and they did their own sweet will. . . .

On the Illinois Central it was the same old story of destruction of the company's property without interference from the police. . . . Dictator Debs was as blatant as ever yesterday. He asserted . . . that the fight against Pullman was now a thing of the past. He is waging his warfare against the General Managers, who had committed the sin of combining against him.

DOCUMENT 5
Chicago Tribune, July 7, 1894

YARDS FIRE SWEPT
Rioters Prevent Firemen from Saving the Property

From Brighton Park to Sixty-First Street the yards of the Pan-Handle road were last night put to the torch by the rioters. Between 600 and 700 freight cars have been destroyed, many of them loaded. Miles and miles of costly track are in a snarled tangle of heat-twisted rails. Not less than $750,000 — possibly a whole $1,000,000 of property — has been sacrificed to the caprice of a mob of drunken Anarchists and rebels. That is the record of the night's work by the Debs strikers in the Stock-Yards District.

DOCUMENT 6
Chicago Times, July 7, 1894

MEN NOT AWED BY SOLDIERS
Railway Union Is Confident of Winning against Armed Capital

Despite the presence of United States troops and the mobilization of five regiments of state militia, despite threats of martial law and total extermination of the strikers by bullet and bayonet, the great strike inaugurated by the American Railway Union holds three-fourths of the roads running out of Chicago in its strong fetters, and last night traffic was more fully paralyzed than at any time since the inception of the tie-up. . . . With the exception of an occasional car or two moved by the aid of the military, not a wheel is turning. . . .

If the soldiers are sent to this district, bloodshed and perhaps death will follow today, for this is the most lawless element in the city, as is shown by their riotous work yesterday. . . . But the perpetrators are not American Railway Union men. The people engaged in this outrageous work of destruction are not strikers, most of them are not even grown men. The persons who set the fires yesterday on the authority of the firemen and police are young hoodlums. . . . The setting fire to the cars yesterday was done openly where anyone could see it and when the slightest effort would have resulted in the apprehension of the guilty ones, but no such effort was made. The firemen were overwhelmed with the work of attending to a dozen different fires and could not, and the police on the scene apparently didn't care to or would not make arrests.

DOCUMENT 7
New York World, July 14, 1894

CHEERS FOR NELLIE BLY
Nellie Bly Covers the Strike

I found in my mail this morning an earnest request from the Pullman A. R. U. for me to be present at a meeting which was to be held in the Turner Hall, Kensington. . . .

Several of the workmen made speeches this afternoon trying to cheer the spirits of their hungry and disheartened brothers. I was introduced and asked to say a few words to the men. . . .

So I took my nerves in hand and my place before the table near where the speakers sat. I don't intend to repeat what I said, but I told them several truths. They were especially amused when I told them that I had come to Chicago very bitterly set against the strikers; that so far as I understood the question, I thought the inhabitants of the model town of Pullman hadn't a reason on earth to complain. With this belief I visited the town, intending in my articles to denounce the riotous and bloodthirsty strikers. Before I had been half a day in Pullman I was the most bitter striker in the town.

That is true. I've [flip]flopped, as they call it, and I am brave enough to confess it. If ever men and women had cause to strike, those men and women are in Pullman. I also said to these men, sitting so quietly and peaceably before me, hungry for a word of sympathy or a word of hope, that if any of them wished to make any statements to me I would be glad to have them do so. After the meeting I was besieged. If I attempted to tell half the tales of wrong I've listened to I could fill an entire copy of *The World*.

Questions for Analysis and Debate

1. How do the *Tribune* and *Times* articles differ in their portrayal of events and actors in the strike?

2. Which version of the strike do you think most middle-class readers, who tended to be sympathetic to the strikers but fearful of violence, would find most compelling?

3. Which version of the strike do you think was favored by business owners, who provided advertising revenue to the newspapers?

4. Do you think readers found Nellie Bly's article persuasive? Why or why not?

another solution. But when George Pullman ada-mantly refused arbitration, the ARU membership voted to boycott all Pullman cars. Beginning on June 29, switchmen across the United States refused to handle any train that carried Pullman cars.

The conflict escalated quickly. The General Managers Association (GMA), an organization of managers from twenty-four different railroads, acted in concert to quash the **Pullman boycott**. Determined to kill the ARU, they recruited strike-breakers and fired all the protesting switchmen. Their tactics set off a chain reaction. Entire train crews walked off the job in a show of solidarity with the Pullman workers. In a matter of days, the boy-cott/strike spread to more than fifteen railroads and affected twenty-seven states and territories. By July 2, rail lines from New York to California lay paralyzed. Even the GMA was forced to concede that the railroads had been "fought to a standstill."

The boycott remained surprisingly peaceful. In contrast to the Great Railroad Strike of 1877, no major riots broke out, and no serious property damage occurred. Debs, in a whirlwind of activ-ity, fired off telegrams to all parts of the country advising his followers to avoid violence and respect law and order. But the nation's newspapers, fed press releases by the GMA, distorted the issues and misrepresented the strike. Across the coun-try, papers ran headlines like "Wild Riot in Chicago" and "Mob Is in Control." (See "Documenting the American Promise," page 648.)

In Washington, Attorney General Richard B. Olney, a lawyer with strong ties to the railroads, determined to put down the strike. In his way stood the governor of Illinois, John Peter Altgeld, who, observing that the boycott remained peace-ful, refused to call out troops. To get around Altgeld, Olney convinced President Grover Cleveland that federal troops had to intervene to protect the mails. To further cripple the boycott, two conservative Chicago judges issued an injunction so sweeping that it prohibited Debs from speaking in public. By issuing the injunction, the court made the boycott a crime punishable by a jail sentence for contempt of court, a civil process that did not require a jury trial. Even the conservative *Chicago Tribune* judged the injunction "a menace to liberty . . . a weapon ever ready for the capitalist." Furious, Debs risked jail by refusing to honor it.

Olney's strategy worked. President Grover Cleveland called out the army. On July 5, nearly 8,000 troops marched into Chicago. The GMA was jubilant. "It has now become a fight between the United States Government and the American Railway Union," a spokesman observed, "and we shall leave them to fight it out." Violence

Nellie Bly in Her Traveling Clothes, 1890
The journalist Elizabeth Jane Cochran took the pen name Nellie Bly (from a popular song by composer Stephen Foster) when she began her career writing for the *Pittsburg Dispatch* in 1880. Best known for her vow to travel around the world in fewer than 80 days, she is shown here in her travel costume. Her dispatches to the *New York World* documenting her trip made her an international celebrity. But some of her best writing involved gritty stories about society's poor and outcast. In 1894 she interviewed striking workers at the Pullman Palace Car company. In direct defiance of her editor, Joseph Pulitzer, Bly declared her allegiance with the strikers. Library of Congress.

immediately erupted. In one day, troops killed 25 workers and wounded more than 60. In the face of bullets and bayonets, the strikers held firm. "Troops cannot move trains," Debs reminded his followers, a fact that was borne out as the railroads remained paralyzed despite the mil-itary intervention. But if the army could not put down the boycott, the injunction could and did. Debs was arrested and imprisoned for con-tempt of court. With its leader in jail, its head-quarters raided and ransacked, and its members demoralized, the ARU was defeated along with

National Guard Occupying Pullman, Illinois
After President Grover Cleveland called out the troops to put down the Pullman strike in 1894, the National Guard occupied the town of Pullman to protect George M. Pullman's property. Here, guardsmen ring the Arcade building, the town shopping center, while curious men and women look on. The intervention of troops at Homestead and Pullman enabled the owners to bring in strikebreakers and defeat the unions. In Cripple Creek, Colorado, where a Populist governor used the militia to keep the peace and not fight the strikers, the miners won the day in 1894. Chicago Historical Society.

the boycott. Pullman reopened his factory, hiring new workers to replace many of the strikers and leaving 1,600 workers without jobs.

In the aftermath of the strike, a special commission investigated the events at Pullman, taking testimony from 107 witnesses, from the lowliest workers to George M. Pullman himself. Stubborn and self-righteous, Pullman spoke for the business orthodoxy of his era, steadfastly affirming the right of business to safeguard its interests through confederacies such as the GMA and at the same time denying labor's right to organize. "If we were to receive these men as representatives of the union," he stated, "they could probably force us to pay any wages which they saw fit."

From his jail cell, Eugene Debs reviewed the events of the Pullman strike. With the courts and the government ready to side with industrialists in the interest of defending private property, Debs realized that labor had little recourse. Strikes seemed futile, and unions remained helpless; workers would have to take control of the state itself. Debs went into jail a

trade unionist and came out six months later a socialist. At first, he turned to the Populist Party, but after its demise he formed the Socialist Party in 1900 and ran for president on its ticket five times. Debs's dissatisfaction with the status quo was shared by another group even more alienated from the political process — women.

> **REVIEW** What tactics led to the defeat of the strikers in the 1890s? Where were they able to succeed and why?

▶ Women's Activism

"Do everything," **Frances Willard** urged her followers in 1881 (see pages 639–40). The new president of the Woman's Christian Temperance Union (WCTU) meant what she said. The WCTU followed a trajectory that was common for women in the late nineteenth century. As women organized to deal with issues that touched their homes and families, they moved into politics, lending new urgency to the cause of woman suffrage. Urban industrialism dislocated women's lives no less than men's. Like men, women sought political change and organized to promote issues central to their lives, campaigning for temperance and woman suffrage.

Frances Willard and the Woman's Christian Temperance Union

A visionary leader, Frances Willard spoke for a group left almost entirely out of the U.S. electoral process. In 1890, only one state, Wyoming, allowed women to vote in national elections. But lack of the franchise did not mean that women were apolitical. The WCTU demonstrated the breadth of women's political activity in the late nineteenth century.

Women supported the temperance movement because they felt particularly vulnerable to the effects of drunkenness. Dependent on men's wages, women and children suffered when money went for drink. The drunken, abusive husband epitomized the evils of a nation in which women remained second-class citizens. The WCTU, composed entirely of women, viewed all women's interests as essentially the same and therefore did not hesitate to use the singular *woman* to emphasize gender solidarity. Although mostly white and middle-class, WCTU members resolved to speak for their entire sex.

Woman's Christian Temperance Union Postcards
The Woman's Christian Temperance Union distributed postcards like these to attack the liquor trade. These cards are typical in their portrayal of saloon backers as traitors to the nation. In the top card, notice the man trampling on the American flag as he casts his ballot—a sly allusion to the need for woman suffrage. The second card shows a saloon keeper recruiting an "army of drunkards." Collection of Joyce M. Tice.

> **"All this work has tended more toward the liberation of women than it has toward the extinction of the saloon."**
>
> — FRANCES WILLARD, on the activities of the WCTU

When Frances Willard became president in 1879, she radically changed the direction of the organization. Social action replaced prayer as women's answer to the threat of drunkenness. Viewing alcoholism as a disease rather than a sin and poverty as a cause rather than a result of drink, the WCTU became involved in labor issues, joining with the Knights of Labor to press for better working conditions for women workers. Describing workers in a textile mill, a WCTU member wrote in the organization's *Union Signal* magazine, "It is dreadful to see these girls, stripped almost to the skin . . . and running like racehorses from the beginning to the end of the day." She concluded, "The hard slavish work is drawing the girls into the saloon."

Willard capitalized on the cult of domesticity as a shrewd political tactic to move women into public life and gain power to ameliorate social problems. Using "home protection" as her watchword, she argued as early as 1884 that women needed the vote to protect home and family. By the 1890s, the WCTU's grassroots network of local unions had spread to all but the most isolated rural areas of the country. Strong and rich, with more than 200,000 dues-paying members, the WCTU was a formidable group.

Willard worked to create a broad reform coalition in the 1890s, embracing the Knights of Labor, the People's Party, and the Prohibition Party. Until her death in 1898, she led, if not a woman's rights movement, then the first organized mass movement of women united around a women's issue. By 1900, thanks largely to the WCTU, women could claim a generation of experience in political action — speaking, lobbying, organizing, drafting legislation, and running private charitable institutions. As Willard observed, "All this work has tended more toward the liberation of women than it has toward the extinction of the saloon."

Elizabeth Cady Stanton, Susan B. Anthony, and the Movement for Woman Suffrage

Unlike the WCTU, the organized movement for woman suffrage remained small and relatively weak in the late nineteenth century. The U.S. woman's rights movement was begun by **Elizabeth Cady Stanton** at the first woman's rights convention in the United States, at Seneca Falls, New York, in 1848. Women's rights advocates split in 1867 over whether the Fourteenth and Fifteenth Amendments, which granted voting rights to African American males, should have extended the vote to women as well. Stanton and her ally, **Susan B. Anthony**, launched the National Woman Suffrage Association in 1869, demanding the vote for women (see chapter 18). A more conservative group, the American Woman Suffrage Association (AWSA), formed the same year. Composed of men as well as women, the AWSA believed that women should vote in local but not national elections.

By 1890, the split had healed, and the newly united **National American Woman Suffrage Association** (NAWSA) launched campaigns on the state level to gain the vote for women. Twenty years had made a great change. Woman suffrage, though not yet generally supported, was no longer considered a crackpot idea. Thanks to the WCTU's support of the "home protection" ballot, suffrage had become accepted as a means to an end even when it was not embraced as a woman's natural right. The NAWSA honored Elizabeth Cady Stanton by electing her its first president, but Susan B. Anthony, who took the helm in 1892, emerged as the leading figure in the new united organization.

Stanton and Anthony, both in their seventies, were coming to the end of their public careers. Since the days of the Seneca Falls

Campaigning for Woman Suffrage
In 1896, women voted in only four states — Wyoming, Colorado, Idaho, and Utah. The West led the way in the campaign for woman suffrage, with Wyoming Territory granting women the vote as early as 1869. Sparse population meant that only sixteen votes were needed in the state's territorial legislature to obtain passage of woman suffrage. The poster calls on Nebraska to join the suffrage column, while the flag illustrates the number of states in which women could vote. Poster: Nebraska State Historical Society; Flag: Smithsonian Institution, Washington, D.C.

WOMEN VOTE
FOR
PRESIDENT
And for All Other Officers in All Elections on the Same Terms as Men in
Wyoming, Colorado, Utah and Idaho
WHY NOT
IN
NEBRASKA?

woman's rights convention, they had worked for reforms for their sex, including property rights, custody rights, and the right to education and gainful employment. But the prize of woman suffrage still eluded them. Suffragists won victories in Colorado in 1893 and Idaho in 1896. One more state joined the suffrage column in 1896 when Utah entered the Union. But women suffered a bitter defeat in a California referendum on woman suffrage that same year. Never losing faith, Susan B. Anthony remarked in her last public appearance, in 1906, "Failure is impossible." It would take until 1920 for all women to gain the vote with the ratification of the Nineteenth Amendment, but the unification of the two woman suffrage groups in 1890 signaled a new era in women's fight for the vote, just as Frances Willard's place on the platform in 1892 in St. Louis symbolized women's growing role in politics and reform.

> **REVIEW**   How did women's temperance activism contribute to the cause of woman suffrage?

▶ Depression Politics

The depression that began in the spring of 1893 and lasted for more than four years put nearly half of the labor force out of work, a higher percentage than during the Great Depression of the 1930s (as discussed in chapters 23 and 24). The human cost of the depression was staggering. "I Take my pen in hand to let you know that we are Starving to death," a Kansas farm woman wrote to the governor in 1894. "Last cent gone," wrote a young widow in her diary. "Children went to work without their breakfasts." The burden of feeding and sheltering the unemployed and their families fell to private charity, city government, and some of the stronger trade unions. Following the harsh dictates of social Darwinism and laissez-faire, the majority of America's elected officials believed that it was inappropriate for the government to intervene. But the scope of the depression made it impossible for local agencies to supply sufficient relief, and increasingly Americans called on the federal government to take action. Armies of the unemployed marched on Washington to demand relief, and the Populist Party experienced a surge of support as the election of 1896 approached.

> **"I Take my pen in hand to let you know that we are Starving to death."**
>
> —A Kansas farm woman in 1894

Coxey's Army

Masses of unemployed Americans marched to Washington, D.C., in the spring of 1894 to call attention to their plight and to urge Congress to enact a public works program to end unemployment. Jacob S. Coxey of Massilon, Ohio, led the most publicized contingent. Convinced that men could be put to work building badly needed roads for the nation, Coxey proposed a scheme to finance public works through non-interest-bearing bonds. "What I am after," he maintained, "is to try to put this country in a condition so that no man who wants work shall be obliged to remain idle." His plan won support from the AFL and the Populists.

Starting out from Ohio with one hundred men, **Coxey's army**, as it was dubbed, swelled as it marched east through the spring snows of the Alleghenies. In Pennsylvania, Coxey recruited several hundred from the ranks of those left unemployed by the Homestead lockout. Called by Coxey the Commonweal of Christ, the army advanced to the tune of "Marching through Georgia":

> We are not tramps nor vagabonds,
>   that's shirking honest toil,
> But miners, clerks, skilled artisans,
>   and tillers of the soil
> Now forced to beg our brother worms
>   to give us leave to toil,
> While we are marching with Coxey.
> Hurrah! hurrah! for the unemployed's appeal
> Hurrah! hurrah! for the marching commonweal!

On May 1, Coxey's army arrived in Washington. When Coxey defiantly marched his men onto the Capitol grounds, police set upon the demonstrators with nightsticks, cracking skulls and arresting Coxey and his lieutenants. Coxey went to jail for twenty days and was fined $5 for "walking on the grass."

Those who had trembled for the safety of the Republic heaved a sigh of relief after Coxey's arrest, hoping that it would halt the march on Washington. But other armies of the unemployed, totaling possibly as many as five thousand people, were still on their way. Too poor to pay for railway tickets, they rode the rails as "freeloaders." The more daring contingents commandeered entire trains, stirring fears of revolution. Journalists who covered the march did little to quiet the nation's fears. They delighted in military terminology, describing themselves as "war correspondents." To boost newspaper sales, they gave to the episode a tone of urgency and heightened the sense of a nation imperiled.

Coxey's Army

A contingent of Coxey's army stops to rest on its way to Washington, D.C. A "petition in boots," Coxey's followers were well dressed, as evidenced by the men in this photo wearing white shirts, vests, neckties, and bowler hats. Music was an important component of the march, including the anthem "Marching with Coxey," sung to the tune of "Marching through Georgia." Band members are pictured on the right with their instruments. Despite their peaceful pose, the marchers stirred the fears of many conservative Americans, who predicted an uprising of the unemployed. Instead, Coxey and a contingent of his marchers were arrested and jailed for "walking on the grass" when they reached the nation's capital. Ohio Historical Society.

By August, the leaderless, tattered armies dissolved. Although the "On to Washington" movement proved ineffective in forcing federal relief legislation, Coxey's army dramatized the plight of the unemployed and acted, in the words of one participant, as a "living, moving object lesson." Like the Populists, Coxey's army called into question the underlying values of the new industrial order and demonstrated how ordinary citizens turned to means outside the regular party system to influence politics in the 1890s.

The People's Party and the Election of 1896

Even before the depression of 1893 gave added impetus to their cause, the Populists had railed against the status quo. "We meet in the midst of a nation brought to the verge of moral, political, and material ruin," Ignatius Donnelly had declared in his keynote address at the creation of the People's Party in St. Louis in 1892. "The fruits of the toil of millions are boldly stolen to build up colossal fortunes for a few. . . . From the same prolific

womb of governmental injustice we breed the two great classes — tramps and millionaires."

The fiery rhetoric frightened many who saw in the People's Party a call not to reform but to revolution. Throughout the country, the press denounced the Populists as "cranks, lunatics, and idiots." When one self-righteous editor dismissed them as "calamity howlers," Populist governor Lorenzo Lewelling of Kansas shot back, "If that is so I want to continue to howl until those conditions are improved."

The People's Party captured more than a million votes in the presidential election of 1892, a respectable showing for a new party (Map 20.1). But increasingly, sectional and racial animosities threatened its unity. In the South, the Populists' willingness to form common cause with black farmers made them anathema. Realizing that race prejudice obscured the common economic interests of black and white farmers, **Tom Watson** of Georgia openly courted African Americans, appearing on platforms with black speakers and promising "to wipe out the color line." When angry Georgia whites threatened to

Candidate	Electoral Vote	Popular Vote	Percent of Popular Vote
Grover Cleveland (Democrat)	277	5,555,426	46.1
Benjamin Harrison (Republican)	145	5,182,690	43.0
James B. Weaver (People's)	22	1,029,846	8.5

MAP 20.1
The Election of 1892

lynch a black Populist preacher, Watson rallied two thousand gun-toting Populists to the man's defense. Although many Populists remained racist in their attitudes toward African Americans, the spectacle of white Georgians riding through the night to protect a black man from lynching was symbolic of the enormous changes the Populist Party promised in the South.

As the presidential election of 1896 approached, the depression intensified cries for reform not only from the Populists but also throughout the electorate. Depression worsened the tight money problem caused by the deflationary pressures of the gold standard. Once again, proponents of free silver stirred rebellion in the ranks of both the Democratic and the Republican parties. When the Republicans nominated Ohio governor **William McKinley** on a platform pledging the preservation of the gold standard, western advocates of free silver representing miners and farmers walked out of the convention. Open rebellion also split the Democratic Party as vast segments in the West and South repudiated President Grover Cleveland because of his support for gold. In South Carolina, Benjamin Tillman won his race for Congress by promising, "Send me to Washington and I'll stick my pitchfork into [Cleveland's] old ribs!"

The spirit of revolt animated the Democratic National Convention in Chicago in the summer of 1896. **William Jennings Bryan** of Nebraska, the thirty-six-year-old "boy orator from the Platte," whipped the convention into a frenzy with his passionate call for free silver. In his speech in favor of the silver plank in the party's platform, Bryan masterfully cataloged the grievances of farmers and laborers, closing his dramatic speech with a ringing exhortation: "Do not crucify mankind upon a cross of gold." Pandemonium broke loose as delegates stampeded to nominate Bryan, the youngest candidate ever to run for the presidency.

The juggernaut of free silver rolled out of Chicago and on to St. Louis, where the People's Party met a week after the Democrats adjourned. Smelling victory, many western Populists urged the party to ally with the Democrats and endorse Bryan. A major obstacle in the path of fusion, however, was Bryan's running mate, Arthur M. Sewall. A Maine railway director and bank president, Sewall, who had been placed on the ticket to appease conservative Democrats, embodied everything the Populists detested.

Populism's regional constituencies remained as divided over tactics as they were uniform in their call for change. Western Populists, including a strong coalition of farmers and miners in states such as Idaho and Colorado, championed free silver. In these largely Republican states, Populists had joined forces with Democrats in previous elections and saw no problem with becoming "Popocrats" once Bryan led the Democratic ticket on a free silver platform. Similarly in the Midwest, a Republican stronghold, Populists who had used fusion with the Democrats as a tactic to win elections had little trouble backing Bryan. But in the South, where Democrats had resorted to fraud and violence to steal elections from the Populists in 1892 and 1894, support for a Democratic ticket proved especially hard to swallow. Die-hard southern Populists wanted no part of fusion.

All of these tactical differences emerged as the Populists met in St. Louis in 1896 to nominate a candidate for president. To show that they remained true to their principles, delegates first voted to support all the planks of the 1892 platform, added to it a call for public works projects for the unemployed, and only narrowly defeated a plank for woman suffrage. To deal with the problem of fusion, the convention selected the vice presidential candidate first. The nomination of Tom Watson undercut opposition to Bryan's candidacy. And although Bryan quickly sent a telegram to protest that he would not drop Sewall as his running mate, mysteriously his message never reached the convention floor. Fusion triumphed. Watson's vice presidential nomination

Gold Elephant Campaign Button and Silver Ribbon from St. Louis, 1896
Mechanical elephant badges that opened to show portraits of William McKinley and his running mate, Garret Hobart, were popular campaign novelties in the election of 1896. The elephant, the mascot of the Republican Party, is gilded to indicate the party's support of the gold standard. By contrast, the delegate ribbon from the St. Louis National Silver Convention in 1896 features a silver eagle and fringe testifying to the power of free silver as a campaign issue. The Democrats nominated William Jennings Bryan on a free-silver platform, and the Populists put him on their ticket as well. Elephant: Collection of Janice L. and David J. Frent; ribbon: Nebraska State Historical Society.

paved the way for the selection of Bryan by a lopsided vote. The Populists did not know it, but their cheers for Bryan signaled not a chorus of victory but the death knell for the People's Party.

Few contests in the nation's history have been as fiercely fought and as full of emotion as the presidential election of 1896. On one side stood Republican William McKinley, backed by the wealthy industrialist and party boss Mark Hanna. Hanna played on the business community's fears of Populism to raise a Republican war chest more than double the amount of any previous campaign. On the other side, William Jennings Bryan, with few assets beyond his silver tongue, struggled to make up in energy and eloquence what his party lacked in campaign funds, crisscrossing the country in a whirlwind tour, traveling more than eighteen thousand miles and delivering more than six hundred speeches in three months. According to his own reckoning, he visited twenty-seven states and spoke to more than five million Americans.

As election day approached, the silver states of the Rocky Mountains lined up solidly for Bryan. The Northeast stood solidly for McKinley. Much of the South, with the exception of the border states, abandoned the Populists and returned to the Democratic "party of the fathers," leaving Tom Watson to lament that

"[Populists] play Jonah while [Democrats] play the whale." The Midwest hung in the balance. Bryan intensified his campaign in Illinois, Michigan, Ohio, and Indiana. But midwestern farmers proved less receptive than western voters to the blandishments of free silver.

In the cities, Democrats charged the Republicans with mass intimidation. "Men, vote as you please," the head of New York's Steinway Piano Company reportedly announced to his workers on the eve of the election, "but if Bryan is elected tomorrow the whistle will not blow

"Swallowed!"
This political cartoon from 1900 shows William Jennings Bryan as a python swallowing the Democratic Party's donkey mascot. Bryan, who ran unsuccessfully in 1896, won the Democratic nomination again in 1900 and in 1908. Ironically, it was not the Democratic party so much as the Populist party that Bryan swallowed. By nominating the Democrat Bryan on their ticket in 1896, the Populist Party lost its identity. The Granger Collection, New York.

Wednesday morning." Intimidation alone did not explain the failure of urban labor to rally to Bryan. Republicans repeatedly warned workers that if the Democrats won, the inflated silver dollar would be worth only fifty cents. However much farmers and laborers might insist that they were united as producers against the non-producing bosses, it was equally true that inflation did not offer the boon to urban laborers that it did to western farmers.

On election day, four out of five voters went to the polls in an unprecedented turnout. In the critical midwestern states, as many as 95 percent of the eligible voters cast their ballots. In the end, the election hinged on between 100 and 1,000 votes in several key states, including Wisconsin, Iowa, and Minnesota. Although McKinley won twenty-three states to Bryan's twenty-two, the electoral vote showed a lopsided 271 to 176 in McKinley's favor (Map 20.2).

The biggest losers in 1896 turned out to be the Populists. On the national level, they polled fewer than 300,000 votes, a million less than in 1894. In the clamor to support Bryan, Populists in the South, determined to beat McKinley at any cost, swallowed their differences and drifted back to the Democratic Party. The People's Party was crushed, and with it the agrarian revolt.

But if Populism proved unsuccessful at the polls, it nevertheless set the domestic political agenda for the United States in the next decades, highlighting issues such as railroad regulation, banking and currency reform, electoral reforms, and an enlarged role for the federal government in the economy. Meanwhile, as the decade ended,

the bugle call to arms turned America's attention to foreign affairs and effectively drowned out the trumpet of reform. The struggle for social justice gave way to a war for empire as the United States asserted its power on the world stage.

REVIEW   Why was the People's Party unable to translate national support into victory in the 1896 election?

▶ The United States and the World

Throughout much of the second half of the nineteenth century, U.S. interest in foreign policy took a backseat to territorial expansion in the American West. The United States stood aloof while Great Britain, France, Germany, Spain, Belgium, and an increasingly powerful Japan competed for empires in Asia, Africa, Latin America, and the Pacific. Between 1870 and 1900, European nations colonized more than 20 percent of the world's landmass and 10 percent of the world's population.

At the turn of the twentieth century, the United States pursued a foreign policy consisting of two currents—isolationism and expansionism. Although the determination to remain detached from European politics had been a hallmark of U.S. foreign policy since the nation's founding, Americans simultaneously believed in manifest destiny—the "obvious" right to expand the nation from ocean to ocean. With its own inland empire secured, the United States looked outward. Determined to protect its sphere of influence in the Western Hemisphere and to expand its trading in Asia, the nation moved away from isolationism and toward a more active role on the world stage. The push for commercial expansion joined with a sense of Christian mission and led both to the strengthening of the Monroe Doctrine in the Western Hemisphere and to a more assertive policy in Asia. All of these trends were in evidence during the Spanish-American War and the debates that followed.

Markets and Missionaries

The depression of the 1890s provided a powerful impetus to American commercial expansion. As markets weakened at home, American businesses looked abroad for profits. As early as 1890, Captain Alfred Thayer Mahan, leader of a growing group of American expansionists, prophesied, "Whether

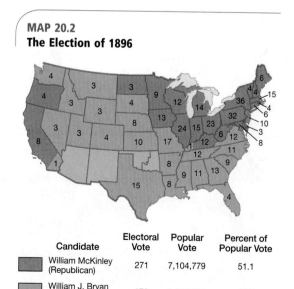

MAP 20.2
The Election of 1896

Candidate	Electoral Vote	Popular Vote	Percent of Popular Vote
William McKinley (Republican)	271	7,104,779	51.1
William J. Bryan (Democrat-People's)	176	6,502,925	47.7

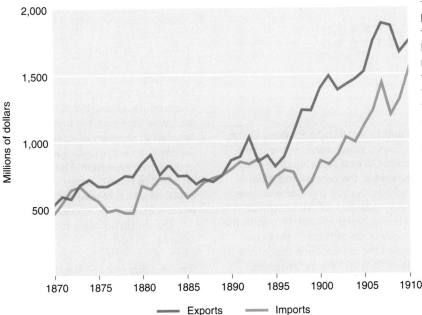

FIGURE 20.3 **Expansion in U.S. Trade, 1870–1910**
Between 1870 and 1910, American exports more than tripled. Imports generally rose, but they were held in check by the high protective tariffs championed by Republican presidents from Ulysses S. Grant to William Howard Taft. A decline in imports is particularly noticeable after the passage of the prohibitive McKinley tariff in 1890.

they will or not, Americans must now begin to look outward. The growing production of the country requires it." As the depression deepened, one diplomat warned that Americans "must turn [their] eyes abroad, or they will soon look inward upon discontent."

Exports constituted a small but significant percentage of the profits of American business in the 1890s (Figure 20.3). And where American interests led, businessmen expected the government's power and influence to follow to protect their investments. Companies like Standard Oil actively sought to use the U.S. government as their agent, often putting foreign service employees on the payroll. "Our ambassadors and ministers and consuls," wrote John D. Rockefeller appreciatively, "have aided to push our way into new markets and to the utmost corners of the world." Whether "our" referred to the United States or to Standard Oil remained ambiguous; in practice, the distinction was of little importance in late-nineteenth-century foreign policy.

America's foreign policy often appeared little more than a sidelight to business development. In Hawai'i (first called the Sandwich Islands), American sugar interests fomented a rebellion in 1893, toppling the increasingly independent Queen Lili'uokalani. (See

"Beyond America's Borders," page 660.) They pushed Congress to annex the islands, which would allow planters to avoid the high McKinley tariff on sugar. When President Cleveland learned that Hawai'ians opposed annexation, he withdrew the proposal from Congress. But expansionists still coveted the islands and continued to look for an excuse to push through annexation.

However compelling the economic arguments about overseas markets proved, business interests alone did not account for the new expansionism that seized the nation during the 1890s. As Mahan confessed, "Even when material interests are the original exciting cause, it is the sentiment to which they give rise, the moral tone which emotion takes that constitutes the greater

Mei Foo Lamp
The Standard Oil Company sold more than a million Mei Foo ("beautiful companion") lamps in China during the 1890s to promote the sale of kerosene in the China market. The first oil tankers were square-rigged kerosene clipper ships that plied the Pacific beginning in 1892 as the petroleum industry rushed to capture the China trade. Standard Oil ads admonished, "If a person wishes to have luck, longevity, health and peace, he or she must live in a world of light." Courtesy of ExxonMobil Corporation.

Regime Change in Hawai'i

Queen Lili'uokalani came to the throne in Hawai'i in 1891 determined to take back power for her monarchy and her people. As a member of Hawai'i's native royalty, or *ali'i*, she had received a first-rate education in missionary school. As a young woman, she converted to Christianity, adopted the English name Lydia, and married the white (*haole*) governor of Maui. Yet she maintained a reverence for traditional Hawai'ian ways and resented the treatment of her people by the white minority. Her brother, King Kalakaua, had proven a weak leader, coerced by the white elite into signing the "Bayonet Constitution," which put the government squarely in the hands of the whites. Determined to rule, not simply to reign, Lili'uokalani moved ahead with plans to wrest power from the minority she referred to as Hawai'i's "guests."

American missionaries first came to Hawai'i in 1820. Some intermarried with their Christian converts, creating a group of *hapa haole* (half whites), as well as a growing number of children born in Hawai'i to white parents. The temptations of wealth led many missionaries, like Amos Starr Cooke, to acquire land and take up sugar planting. In 1851, he founded Castle & Cooke, which became one of the world's largest sugar producers. By the end of the century, missionaries and planters had blended into one ruling class and gained control of extensive tracts of land. Thanks to the "Bayonet Constitution," they controlled the islands, even though native Hawai'ians and the Japanese and Chinese "coolie" laborers imported to work on the sugar plantations outnumbered them ten to one.

Sugar became a booming business in Hawai'i as a result of favorable reciprocity treaties with the United States. But hard times came to the islands with the passage of the McKinley tariff in 1890. The tariff wiped out the advantage Hawai'ian sugar had enjoyed in the American market, with devastating results. Within two years, the value of Hawai'ian sugar exports plummeted from $13 million to $8 million.

One way to avoid the tariff was by incorporating Hawai'i into the United States through annexation. Foremost among those who championed this scheme was Lorrin Thurston, the thirty-five-year-old grandson of American missionaries. Thurston, born in Hawai'i and educated in the United States, was zealous in his belief that Hawai'i should be ruled by "the intelligent part of the community" — white Americans and their children. In 1892, he founded the secret Annexation Club and traveled to Washington, D.C., where he won the support of Republican secretary of state James G. Blaine, an enthusiastic supporter of American expansion. Thurston returned to Hawai'i armed with the knowledge that annexation had influential friends in Washington.

Queen Lili'uokalani picked Saturday, January 14, 1893, as the day to promulgate her new constitution. Her aim was to return Hawai'i to Hawai'ians by allowing only those with native ancestry the right to vote. Learning of her intentions, Thurston quickly hatched a plot to overthrow the monarchy. Thurston's daring plan could work only with the cooperation of the United States. So late that night, he called on John L. Stevens, the American minister to Hawai'i. Laying out his plan, he urged Stevens, a staunch annexationist, to support the overthrow of the queen and to pledge U.S. support for Thurston's actions. Without hesitating, Stevens promised to land Marines from the USS *Boston* "to protect American lives and property."

Two days later, 162 American Marines and sailors marched into Honolulu armed with carbines, howitzers (small cannons), and Gatling guns. The next day, Thurston and 17

force." Much of that moral tone was set by American missionaries intent on spreading the gospel of Christianity to the "heathen." No area on the globe constituted a greater challenge than China.

An 1858 agreement, the Tianjin (Tientsin) treaty admitted foreign missionaries to China. Although Christians converted only 100,000 in a population of 400 million, the Chinese nevertheless resented the interference of missionaries in village life. Opposition to foreign missionaries took the form of antiforeign secret societies, most notably the Boxers, whose Chinese name translated to "Righteous Harmonious Fist." No simple boxing club, the Boxers in 1899 began to hunt down and kill Chinese Christians and missionaries in northwestern Shandong (Shan-tung) Province. With the tacit support of China's Dowager Empress, the Boxers became bolder. Under the slogan "Uphold the Ch'ing Dynasty, Exterminate the Foreigners," they marched on the cities. Their rampage eventually led to the massacre of some 30,000 Chinese converts and 250 foreign nuns, priests, and missionaries along with their families. In August 1900, 2,500 U.S. troops joined an international

of his confederates seized control of a government building and proclaimed themselves a "provisional government." Minister Stevens promptly recognized the revolutionaries as the legitimate government of Hawai'i.

To avoid bloodshed, Queen Lili'uokalani agreed to step aside. But in a masterstroke, she composed a letter addressed not to her enemies in the provisional government, but to the U.S. government. Protesting her overthrow, she yielded her authority "until such time as the Government of the United States, shall, upon the facts being presented to it, undo the action of its representatives and reinstate me in the authority which I claim as the constitutional sovereign of the Hawai'ian Islands." The action now shifted to Washington, where Grover Cleveland, a Democrat skeptical of America's adventures abroad, quickly squelched plans for annexation and supported the Hawai'ian queen. The provisional government, however, enjoyed the support of Republicans in Congress and refused to step down, biding its time, waiting for the Republicans to take back the White House.

In 1898, as the taste for empire swept the United States in the wake of the Spanish-American War, President William McKinley quietly signed a treaty annexing Hawai'i. His action pleased not only Hawai'i's sugar growers but also American expansionists, who judged Hawai'i strategically important in expanding U.S. trade with China.

"Hawai'i is ours," Grover Cleveland wrote sadly. "As I look back upon the first steps in this miserable business, and as I contemplate the means used to complete the outrage, I am ashamed of the whole affair."

Queen Lili'uokalani (1838–1917)

An accomplished woman who straddled two cultures, Lydia Kamakaeha Dominis, or Queen Lili'uokalani, spoke English as easily as her native Hawai'ian and was fluent in French and German as well. She traveled widely in Europe and the United States. Despite President Cleveland's belief that the monarchy should be restored, Lili'uokalani never regained her throne. In 1898, she published *Hawai'i's Story by Hawai'i's Queen*, outlining her version of the events that had led to her downfall. In 1993, on the one hundredth anniversary of the revolution that deposed her, Congress passed and President Bill Clinton signed a resolution offering an apology to native Hawai'ians for the overthrow of their queen. Courtesy of the Lili'uokalani Trust.

America in a Global Context

1. How did economic issues on the mainland affect the status of Hawai'i?

2. What role did party politics play in the annexation of Hawai'i?

force sent to rescue the foreigners and put down the uprising in the Chinese capital of Beijing (Peking). The European powers imposed the humiliating Boxer Protocol in 1901, giving themselves the right to maintain military forces in Beijing and requiring the Chinese government to pay an exorbitant indemnity of $333 million for the loss of life and property resulting from the **Boxer uprising**.

In the aftermath of the uprising, missionaries voiced no concern at the paradox of bringing Christianity to China

at gunpoint. "It is worth any cost in money, worth any cost in bloodshed," argued one bishop, "if we can make millions of Chinese true and intelligent Christians." Merchants and missionaries alike shared such moralistic reasoning. Indeed, they worked hand in hand; trade and Christianity marched into Asia together. "Missionaries," admitted the American clergyman Charles Denby, "are the pioneers of trade and commerce. . . . The missionary, inspired by holy zeal, goes everywhere and by degrees foreign commerce and trade follow."

VISUAL ACTIVITY

The Open Door

The trade advantage gained by the United States through the Open Door policy, enunciated by Secretary of State John Hay in 1900, is portrayed graphically in this political cartoon. Uncle Sam stands prominently in the "open door," while representatives of the other great powers seek admittance to the "Flowery Kingdom" of China. Uncle Sam holds the golden key of "American diplomacy," while the Chinese man on the other side of the door beams with pleasure. In fact, the Open Door policy promised equal access for all powers to the China trade, not U.S. preeminence as the cartoon implies. Culver Pictures.

READING THE IMAGE: How does the cartoon portray the United States' role in international diplomacy?
CONNECTIONS: In what ways does this image misrepresent the reality of American and European involvement in China and of the Open Door policy?

The Monroe Doctrine and the Open Door Policy

The emergence of the United States as a world power pitted the nation against other colonial powers, particularly Germany and Japan, which posed a threat to the twin pillars of America's expansionist foreign policy — one dating back to President James Monroe in the 1820s, the other formalized in 1900 under President William McKinley. The first, the **Monroe Doctrine**, came to be interpreted as establishing the Western Hemisphere as an American "sphere of influence" and warned European powers to stay away or

risk war. The second, the Open Door, dealt with maintaining market access to China.

American diplomacy actively worked to buttress the Monroe Doctrine, with its assertion of American hegemony (domination) in the Western Hemisphere. In the 1880s, Republican secretary of state James G. Blaine promoted hemispheric peace and trade through Pan-American cooperation but at the same time used American troops to intervene in Latin American border disputes. In 1895, President Cleveland risked war with Great Britain to enforce the Monroe Doctrine when a conflict developed between Venezuela and British Guiana. After American saber rattling, the British backed down and accepted U.S. mediation in the area despite their territorial claims in Guiana.

In Central America, American business triumphed in a bloodless takeover that saw French and British interests routed by behemoths such as the United Fruit Company of Boston. United Fruit virtually dominated the Central American nations of Costa Rica and Guatemala, while an importer from New Orleans turned Honduras into a "banana republic" (a country run by U.S. business interests). Thus, by 1895, the United States, through business as well as diplomacy, had successfully achieved hegemony in Latin America and the Caribbean, forcing even the British to concur with the secretary of state that "the infinite resources [of the United States] combined with its isolated position render it master of the situation and practically invulnerable as against any or all other powers."

At the same time that American foreign policy warned European powers to stay out of the Western Hemisphere, the United States competed for trade in the Eastern Hemisphere. As American interests in China grew, the United States became more aggressive in defending its presence in Asia and the Pacific. The United States risked war with Germany in 1889 to guarantee the U.S. Navy access to Pago Pago in the Samoan Islands, a port for refueling on the way to Asia. Germany, seeking dominance over the islands, challenged the United States by sending warships to the region. But before fighting broke out, a great typhoon destroyed the German and American ships. Acceding to the will of nature, the potential combatants later divided the islands amicably in the 1899 Treaty of Berlin.

The biggest prize in Asia remained the China market. In the 1890s, China, weakened by years of internal warfare, was beginning to be partitioned into spheres of influence by Britain, Japan, Germany, France, and Russia. Concerned about the integrity of China and no less about American trade, Secretary of State John Hay in 1899–1900 wrote a series of notes calling for an "open door" policy that would ensure trade access to all and maintain

Chinese sovereignty. The notes — sent to Britain, Germany, and Russia and later to France, Japan, and Italy — were greeted by the major powers with polite evasion. Nevertheless, Hay skillfully managed to maneuver the major powers into doing his bidding, and in 1900 he boldly announced the Open Door as international policy. The United States, by insisting on the **Open Door policy**, managed to secure access to Chinese markets, expanding its economic power while avoiding the problems of maintaining a far-flung colonial empire on the Asian mainland. But as the Spanish-American War soon demonstrated, Americans found it hard to resist the temptations of overseas empire.

"A Splendid Little War"

The **Spanish-American War** began as a humanitarian effort to free Cuba from Spain's colonial grasp and ended with the United States itself acquiring territory overseas and fighting a dirty guerrilla war with Filipino nationalists who, like the Cubans, sought independence. Behind the contradiction stood the twin pillars of American foreign policy: The Monroe Doctrine made Spain's presence in Cuba unacceptable, and U.S. determination to keep open the door to Asia made the Philippines attractive as a stepping-stone to China. Precedent for the nation's imperial adventures also came from the recent Indian wars in the American West, which provided a template for the subjugation of native peoples in the name of civilization.

Looking back on the Spanish-American War of 1898, Secretary of State John Hay judged it "a splendid little war; begun with the highest motives, carried on with magnificent intelligence and spirit, favored by that fortune which loves the brave." At the close of a decade marred by bitter depression, social unrest, and political upheaval, the war offered Americans a chance to wave the flag and march in unison. War fever proved as infectious as the tune of a John Philip Sousa march. Few argued the merits of the conflict until it was over and the time came to divide the spoils.

The war began with moral outrage over the treatment of Cuban revolutionaries, who had

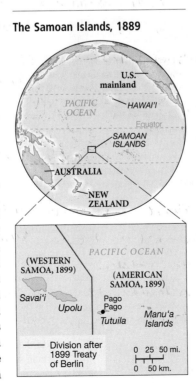

The Samoan Islands, 1889

U.S. mainland

PACIFIC OCEAN

HAWAI'I

Equator

SAMOAN ISLANDS

AUSTRALIA

NEW ZEALAND

PACIFIC OCEAN

(WESTERN SAMOA, 1899)

(AMERICAN SAMOA, 1899)

Savai'i

Upolu

Pago Pago

Tutuila

Manu'a Islands

— Division after 1899 Treaty of Berlin

0   25 50 mi.

0   50 km.

launched a fight for independence against the Spanish colonial regime in 1895. In an attempt to isolate the guerrillas, the Spanish general Valeriano Weyler herded Cubans into crowded and unsanitary concentration camps, where thousands died of hunger, disease, and exposure. Starvation soon spread to the cities. Tens of thousands of Cubans died, and countless others were left without food, clothing, or shelter. By 1898, fully a quarter of the island's population had perished in the Cuban revolution.

> **"You furnish the pictures and I'll furnish the war."**
> — Newspaper owner,
> WILLIAM RANDOLPH HEARST

As the Cuban rebellion dragged on, pressure for American intervention mounted. American newspapers fueled public outrage at Spain. A fierce circulation war raged in New York City between William Randolph Hearst's *Journal* and Joseph Pulitzer's *World*. Their competition provoked what came to be called **yellow journalism**, named for the colored ink used in a popular comic strip. Practitioners of yellow journalism pandered to the public's appetite for sensationalism. The Cuban war provided

a wealth of dramatic copy. Newspapers fed the American people a daily diet of "Butcher" Weyler and Spanish atrocities. Hearst sent artist Frederic Remington to document the horror, and when Remington wired home, "There is no trouble here. There will be no war," Hearst shot back, "You furnish the pictures and I'll furnish the war."

American interests in Cuba were, in the words of the U.S. minister to Spain, more than "merely theoretical or sentimental." American business had more than $50 million invested in Cuban sugar, and American trade with Cuba, a brisk $100 million a year before the rebellion, had dropped to near zero. Nevertheless, the business community balked, wary of a war with Spain. When industrialist Mark Hanna, the Republican kingmaker and senator from Ohio, urged restraint, a hotheaded **Theodore Roosevelt** exploded, "We will have this war for the freedom of Cuba, Senator Hanna, in spite of the timidity of commercial interests."

To expansionists like Roosevelt, more than Cuban independence was at stake. War with

Yellow Journalism
Most cartoonists followed the lead of Hearst and Pulitzer in promoting war with Spain. Cartoonist Grant Hamilton drew this cartoon for *Judge* magazine in March 1898. It shows a brutish Spain (the "Devil's Deputy") with bloody hands trampling on a sailor from the *Maine*. Cuba is prostrate, and a pile of skulls represents civilians "starved to death by Spain." Such vicious representations of Spain became common in the American press in the weeks leading up to the Spanish-American War. What does the cartoon say about American attitudes toward race? Collection of the New-York Historical Society.

Spain opened up the prospect of expansion into Asia as well, since Spain controlled not only Cuba and Puerto Rico but also Guam and the Philippine Islands. Appointed assistant secretary of the navy in April 1897, Roosevelt took the helm in the absence of his boss and audaciously ordered the U.S. fleet to Manila in the Philippines. In the event of conflict with Spain, Roosevelt would have the navy in a position to capture the islands and gain an entry point to China.

President McKinley slowly moved toward intervention. In a show of American force, he dispatched the battleship *Maine* to Cuba. On the night of February 15, 1898, a mysterious explosion destroyed the *Maine*, killing 267 crew members. The source of the explosion remained unclear, but inflammatory stories in the press enraged Americans, who immediately blamed the Spanish government. (See "Historical Question," page 666.) Rallying to the cry "Remember the *Maine*," Congress declared war on Spain in April. In a surge of patriotism, more than a million men rushed to enlist. War brought with it a unity of purpose and national harmony that ended a decade of political dissent and strife. "In April, everywhere over this good fair land, flags were flying," wrote Kansas editor William Allen White. "At the stations, crowds gathered to hurrah for the soldiers, and to throw hats into the air, and to unfurl flags."

Soon they had something to cheer about. Five days after McKinley signed the war resolution, a U.S. Navy squadron commanded by Admiral George Dewey destroyed the Spanish fleet in Manila Bay (Map 20.3). Dewey's stunning victory caught the United States by surprise. Although naval strategists including Theodore Roosevelt had been orchestrating the move for some time,

MAP ACTIVITY

Map 20.3   The Spanish-American War, 1898
The Spanish-American War was fought in two theaters, the Philippine Islands and Cuba. Five days after President William McKinley called for a declaration of war, Admiral George Dewey captured Manila without the loss of a single American sailor. The war lasted only eight months. Troops landed in Cuba in mid-June and by mid-July had taken Santiago and Havana and destroyed the Spanish fleet.

READING THE MAP: Which countries held imperial control over countries and territories immediately surrounding the Philippine Islands and Cuba?
CONNECTIONS: What role did American newspapers play in the start of the war? How did the results of the war serve American aims in both Asia and the Western Hemisphere?

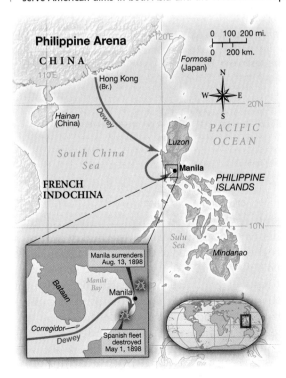

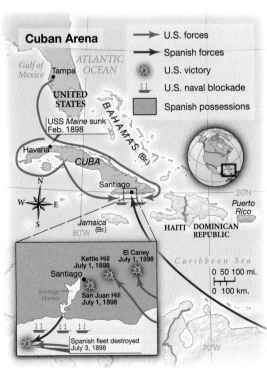

Did Terrorists Sink the *Maine*?

At 9:40 p.m. on the evening of February 15, 1898, the U.S. battleship *Maine* blew up in Havana harbor. "The shock threw us backward," reported one eyewitness. "From the deck forward of amidships shot a streak of fire as high as the tall buildings on Broadway. Then the glare of light widened out like a funnel at the top, and down through this bright circle fell showers of wreckage and mangled sailors." In all, 267 sailors drowned or burned to death in one of the worst naval catastrophes to occur during peacetime.

Captain Charles Dwight Sigsbee, the last man to leave the burning ship, filed a terse report saying that the *Maine* had blown up and "urging [that] public opinion should be suspended until further report." But the yellow press, led by William Randolph Hearst's *New York Journal*, ran banner headlines proclaiming, "The War Ship *Maine* Was Split in Two by an Enemy's Secret Infernal Machine!"

Public opinion quickly divided between those who suspected foul play and those who believed the explosion had been an accident. Foremost among the accident theorists was the Spanish government, along with U.S. business interests who hoped to avoid war. The "jingoes," as proponents of war were

called, rushed to blame Spain. Even before the details were known, Assistant Secretary of the Navy Theodore Roosevelt wrote, "The *Maine* was sunk by an act of dirty treachery on the part of the Spaniards I believe; though we shall never find out definitely, and officially it will go down as an accident."

In less than a week, the navy formed a court of inquiry, and divers inspected the wreckage. The panel reported on March 25, 1898, that a mine had exploded under the bottom of the ship, igniting gunpowder in the forward magazine. The panel could not determine whether the mine had been planted by the Spanish government or by recalcitrant followers of Valeriano Weyler. The infamous Weyler had been ousted after the American press dubbed him "the Butcher" for his harsh treatment of the Cubans.

As time passed, however, more people came to view the explosion of the *Maine* as an accident. European experts concluded that the *Maine* had exploded accidentally, from a fire in the coal bunker adjacent to the reserve gunpowder. Perhaps poor design, not treachery, had sunk the *Maine*.

In 1910, New York congressman William Sultzer put it succinctly:

"The day after the ship was sunk, you could hardly find an American who did not believe that she had been foully done to death by a treacherous enemy. Today you can hardly find an American who believes Spain had anything to do with it." The *Maine* still lay in the mud of Havana harbor, a sunken tomb containing the remains of many sailors. The Cuban government asked for the removal of the wreck, and veterans demanded a decent burial for the sailors. So in March 1910, Congress voted to raise the *Maine* and reinvestigate.

The "Final Report on Removing the Wreck of Battleship *Maine* from the Harbor of Habana, Cuba" appeared in April 1913. This report confirmed that the original naval inquiry was in error, but it ruled out the accident theory by concluding that the nature of the initial explosion indicated a homemade bomb — once again casting suspicion on Weyler's fanatic followers. Following the investigation and removal of human remains, the wreckage of the *Maine* was towed out to sea and, with full funeral honors, sunk in six hundred fathoms of water.

Controversy over the *Maine* proved harder to sink. In the Vietnam era, when faith in the "military establishment" plummeted, Admiral Hyman Rickover launched yet another investigation. Viewing the 1913 "Final Report" as a cover-up, he complained that the ship had been sunk so deep "that there will be no chance of the true facts being revealed." Rickover, a maverick who held the naval brass

few Americans had ever heard of the Philippines. Even McKinley confessed that he could not immediately locate the archipelago on the map. He nevertheless recognized the strategic importance of the Philippines and dispatched U.S. troops to secure the islands.

The war in Cuba ended almost as quickly as it began. The first troops landed on June 22, and after a handful of battles the Spanish forces surrendered on July 17. The war lasted just long

enough to elevate Theodore Roosevelt to the status of bona fide war hero. Roosevelt resigned his navy post and formed the Rough Riders, a regiment composed of a sprinkling of Ivy League polo players and a number of western cowboys. Roosevelt admired horsemanship and had gained the cowboys' respect during his stint as a cattle rancher in the Dakotas. While the troops languished in Tampa awaiting their orders, Roosevelt and his men staged rodeos for the press, with

in low esteem, blamed "the warlike atmosphere in Congress and the press, and the natural tendency to look for reasons for the loss that did not reflect on the Navy." Judging the sinking an accident, Rickover warned, "We must make sure that those in 'high places' do not without more careful consideration of the consequences, exert our prestige and might."

Two decades later, the pendulum swung back. A 1995 study of the *Maine* published by the Smithsonian Institution concluded that zealot followers of General Weyler sank the battleship: "They had the opportunity, the means, and the motivation, and they blew up the *Maine* with a small low-strength mine they made themselves." According to this theory, the terrorists' homemade bomb burst the *Maine*'s hull, triggering a massive explosion. And in 1998 *National Geographic* employed computer models to show that an external explosion (bomb) was capable of sinking the *Maine*.

Thinking about Evidence

1. How have explanations for the sinking of the *Maine* changed over time? Has the evidence changed, or have interpretations of the evidence shifted?

2. What does the word *terrorism* suggest about how our understanding of the event may have changed in the twenty-first century?

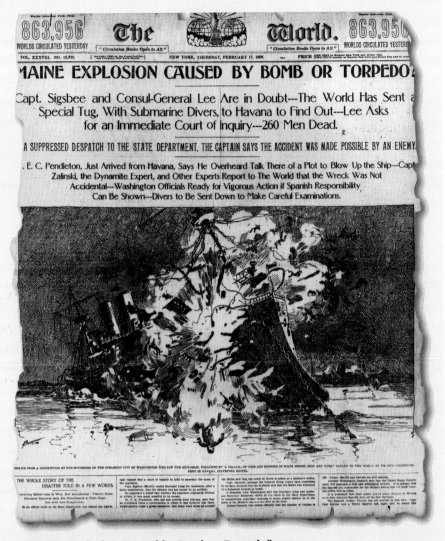

"Maine Explosion Caused by Bomb or Torpedo"
The yellow press wasted no time claiming foul play in the explosion of the *Maine*. The front page of the New York *World* on February 17, 1898, two days after the blast, trumpeted the news and graphically portrayed the destruction of the ship. The text hinted at a plot to blow up the *Maine* and insisted that the explosion was not accidental, although there was no evidence to back up the assertion. The extent of the destruction and the deaths of 267 sailors fueled war fever. ©Collection of the New-York Historical Society.

the likes of New York socialite William Tiffany busting broncos in competition with Dakota cowboy Jim "Dead Shot" Simpson. When the Rough Riders shipped out to Cuba, journalists fought for a berth with the colorful regiment. The Rough Riders' charge up Kettle Hill and Roosevelt's role in the decisive battle of San Juan Hill made front-page news. Overnight, Roosevelt became the most famous man in America. By the time he sailed home from Cuba, a coalition of independent Republicans was already plotting his political future.

The Debate over American Imperialism

After a few brief campaigns in Cuba and Puerto Rico brought the Spanish-American War to an end, the American people woke up in possession of an empire that stretched halfway around the globe. As part of the spoils of war, the United States acquired Cuba, Puerto Rico, Guam, and the Philippines. Yielding to pressure from American sugar growers, President McKinley expanded the empire further, annexing Hawai'i in July 1898.

Contemptuous of the Cubans, whom General William Shafter declared "no more fit for self-government than gun-powder is for hell," the U.S. government directed the writing of a new Cuban constitution in 1900 and refused to give up military control of the island until the Cubans accepted the so-called Platt Amendment — a series of provisions that granted the United States the right to intervene to protect Cuba's "independence," as well as the power to oversee Cuban debt so that European creditors would not find an excuse for intervention. For good measure, the United States gave itself a ninety-nine-year lease on a naval base at Guantánamo. In return, McKinley promised to implement an extensive sanitation program to clean up the island, making it more attractive to American investors.

MAP ACTIVITY

Map 20.4   U.S. Overseas Expansion through 1900

The United States extended its interests abroad with a series of territorial acquisitions. Although Cuba was granted independence, the Platt Amendment kept the new nation firmly under U.S. control. In the wake of the Spanish-American War, the United States woke up to find that it held an empire extending halfway around the globe.

READING THE MAP: Does the map indicate that more territory was acquired by purchase or by war, occupation, or unilateral decision? How many purchases of land outside the continental United States did the government make?
CONNECTIONS: What foreign policy developments occurred in the 1890s? How did American political leaders react to them? Where was U.S. expansion headed and why?

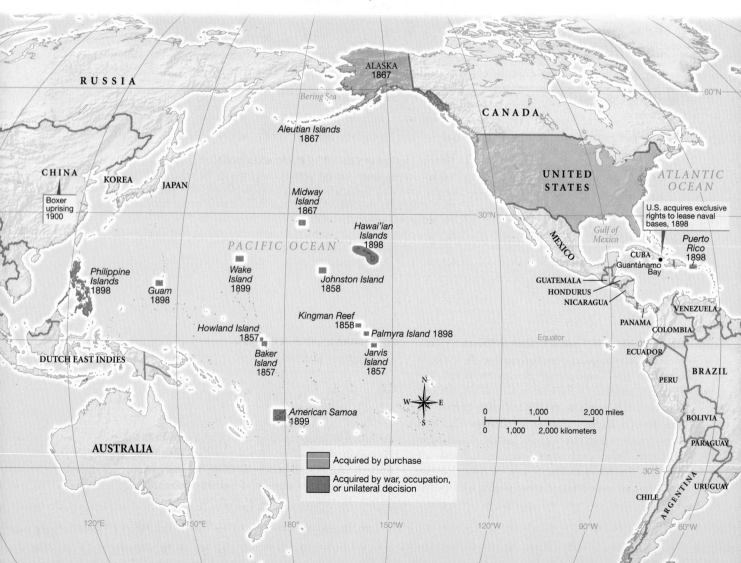

Columbia's Easter Bonnet
The United States, symbolized by the female figure of Columbia, tries on "World Power" in this cartoon from *Puck* that appeared in 1901 after the Spanish-American War left the United States in control of Spain's former colonies in Guam, the Philippines, and Puerto Rico. The bonnet, in the shape of an American battleship, indicates the key role the U.S. Navy played in the conflict. "Expansion," spelled out in the smoke from the ship's smokestack, points to a new overseas direction for American foreign policy at the turn of the twentieth century. Library of Congress.

In the formal Treaty of Paris (1898), Spain ceded the Philippines to the United States along with the former Spanish colonies of Puerto Rico and Guam (Map 20.4). Empire did not come cheap. When Spain initially balked at these terms, the United States agreed to pay an indemnity of $20 million for the islands. Nor was the cost measured in money alone. Filipino revolutionaries under **Emilio Aguinaldo**, who had greeted U.S. troops as liberators, bitterly fought the new masters. It would take seven years and 4,000 American dead — almost ten times the number killed in Cuba — not to mention an estimated 20,000 Filipino casualties, to defeat Aguinaldo and secure American control of the Philippines, America's coveted stepping-stone to China.

At home, a vocal minority, mostly Democrats and former Populists, resisted the country's foray into overseas empire, judging it unwise,

immoral, and unconstitutional. William Jennings Bryan, who enlisted in the army but never saw action, concluded that American expansionism only distracted the nation from problems at home. Pointing to the central paradox of the war, Representative Bourke Cockran of New York admonished, "We who have been the destroyers of oppression are asked now to become its agents." Mark Twain, lending his bitter eloquence to the cause of anti-imperialism, lamented that the United States had become "yet another Civilized Power, with its banner of the Prince of Peace in one hand and its loot-basket and its butcher-knife in the other."

The anti-imperialists were soon drowned out by cries for empire. As Senator Knute Nelson of Minnesota assured his colleagues, "We come as ministering angels, not as despots." Fresh from the conquest of Native Americans in the West, the nation largely embraced the heady mixture of racism and missionary zeal that fueled American adventurism abroad. The *Washington Post* trumpeted, "The taste of empire is in the mouth of the people," thrilled at the prospect of "an imperial policy, the Republic renascent, taking her place with the armed nations."

REVIEW Why did the United States largely abandon its isolationist foreign policy in the 1890s?

▶ Conclusion: Rallying around the Flag

A decade of domestic strife ended amid the blare of martial music and the waving of flags. The Spanish-American War drowned out the calls for social reform that had fueled the Populist politics of the 1890s. During that decade, angry farmers facing hard times looked to the Farmers' Alliance to fight for their vision of economic democracy, workers staged bloody battles across the country to assert their rights, and women attacked drunkenness and the conditions that fostered it and mounted a suffrage movement to secure their basic political rights. In St. Louis in 1892, Frances Willard joined with other disaffected Americans to form a new People's Party to fight for change.

The bitter depression that began in 1893 led to increased labor strife. The Pullman boycott brutally dramatized the power of property and the conservatism of the laissez-faire state. Even the miners' victory in Cripple Creek,

Colorado, in 1894 proved short-lived. But workers' willingness to confront capitalism on the streets of Chicago, Homestead, Cripple Creek, and a host of other sites across America eloquently testified to labor's growing determination, unity, and strength.

As the depression deepened, the sight of Coxey's army of unemployed marching on Washington to demand federal intervention in the economy signaled a growing shift in the public mind against the stand-pat politics of laissez-faire personified by President William McKinley. The call for the government to take action to better the lives of workers, farmers, and the dispossessed manifested itself in the fiercely fought presidential campaign of William Jennings Bryan in 1896. With the outbreak of the Spanish-American War in 1898, the decade ended on a harmonious note with patriotic Americans rallying around the flag. Few questioned America's foray into overseas empire. The United States took its place on the world stage, buttressing its hemispheric domination with the Monroe Doctrine and employing the Open Door policy, which promised access to the riches of China. But even though Americans basked in patriotism and contemplated empire, old grievances had not been laid to rest. The People's Party had been beaten, but the Populist spirit lived on in the demands for greater government involvement in the economy, expanded opportunities for direct democracy, and a more equitable balance of profits and power between the people and the big corporations. This reform agenda would be taken up by a new generation of progressive reformers in the first decades of the twentieth century.

▶ Selected Bibliography

The Farmers Alliance, the Labor Wars, and Women's Activism

Peter H. Argersinger, *The Limits of Agrarian Radicalism: Western Populism and American Politics* (1995).

Jean H. Baker, *Sisters: The Lives of America's Suffragists* (2005).

Ruth Bordin, *Frances Willard: A Biography* (1986).

Ellen Carol DuBois, *Woman Suffrage and Women's Rights* (1998).

Michel Lewis Goldberg, *An Army of Women: Gender and Politics in Gilded Age Kansas* (1997).

Steven Hahn, *A Nation under Our Feet: Black Political Struggles in the Rural South from Slavery to the Great Migration* (2003).

Elizabeth Jameson, *All That Glitters: Class, Conflict, and Community in Cripple Creek* (1998).

Michael Kazin, *The Populist Persuasion: An American History* (rev. ed., 1998).

Paul Krause, *The Battle for Homestead, 1880–1892* (1992).

Jackson Lears, *The Rebirth of a Nation: The Making of Modern America, 1877–1920* (2009).

Connie L. Lester, *Up from the Mudsills of Hell: The Farmers' Alliance, Populism, and Progressive Agriculture in Tennessee, 1870–1915* (2006).

Michael McGerr, *A Fierce Discontent: The Rise and Fall of the Progressive Movement in America* (2005).

David Nasaw, *Andrew Carnegie* (2006).

Charles Postel, *The Populist Vision (2007).*

Nick Salvatore, *Eugene V. Debs: Citizen and Socialist* (1982).

Depression and the Election of 1896

Steve Fraser, *Every Man a Speculator: A Cultural History of Wall Street in America* (2005).

Stephen Kantrowitz, *Ben Tillman and the Reconstruction of White Supremacy* (2000).

Michael Kazin, *A Godly Hero: The Life of William Jennings Bryan* (2006).

Kenneth L. Kusmer, *Down and Out, on the Road: The Homeless in American History* (2002).

Gretchen Ritter, *Goldbugs and Greenbacks: The Antimonopoly Tradition in the Politics of Finance in America* (1997).

Troy Rondinone, *The Great Industrial War: Framing Class Conflict in the Media, 1865–1950* (2010).

Carol A. Schwantes, *Coxey's Army: An American Odyssey* (1985).

Douglas Steeples and David O. Whitten, *Democracy in Desperation: The Depression of 1893* (1998).

U.S. Foreign Policy and the Spanish-American War

Fred Anderson and Andrew Cayton, *The Domination of War: Empire and Liberty in North America, 1500–2000* (2005).

Kristin Hoganson, *Fighting for American Manhood: How Gender Politics Provoked the Spanish-American and Philippine-American Wars* (1998).

Matthew Frye Jacobson, *Barbarian Virtues: The United States Encounters Foreign Peoples at Home and Abroad, 1876–1917* (2000).

Amy Kaplan, *The Anarchy of Empire in the Making of U.S. Culture* (2002).

Stephen Kinzer, *Overthrow: America's Century of Regime Change from Hawaii to Iraq* (2006).

Walter LaFeber, *The American Search for Opportunity, 1865–1913* (1994).

Brian Linn, *The Philippine War, 1899–1902* (2000).

Paul T. McCartney, *Power and Progress: American National Identity, the War of 1898, and the Rise of American Imperialism* (2006).

Ivan Musicant, *Empire by Default: The Spanish American War and the Dawn of the American Century* (1998).

Diana Preston, *Besieged in Peking: The Story of the 1900 Boxer Uprising* (1999).

Margaret Strobel, *Gender, Sex, and Empire* (1993).

Evan Thomas, *The War Lovers: Roosevelt, Lodge, Hearst, and the Rush to Empire, 1898* (2010).

▶ **FOR MORE BOOKS ABOUT TOPICS IN THIS CHAPTER,** see the Online Bibliography at **bedfordstmartins.com/roark.**

▶ **FOR ADDITIONAL PRIMARY SOURCES FROM THIS PERIOD,** see Michael Johnson, ed., *Reading the American Past*, Fifth Edition.

▶ **FOR WEB SITES, IMAGES, AND DOCUMENTS RELATED TO TOPICS AND PLACES IN THIS CHAPTER,** visit Make History at **bedfordstmartins.com/roark.**

Reviewing Chapter 20

KEY TERMS

Explain each term's significance.

The Farmers' Revolt
>   Farmers' Alliance (p. 641)
>   Colored Farmers' Alliance (p. 642)
>   People's Party (Populist Party) (p. 643)
>   subtreasury (p. 643)

The Labor Wars
>   Henry Clay Frick (p. 644)
>   Homestead lockout (p. 644)
>   Alexander Berkman (p. 645)
>   Cripple Creek miners' strike of 1894
>   (p. 646)
>   George M. Pullman (p. 646)
>   American Railway Union (ARU) (p. 647)
>   Eugene V. Debs (p. 647)
>   Pullman boycott (p. 650)

Women's Activism
>   Frances Willard (p. 651)
>   Elizabeth Cady Stanton (p. 653)
>   Susan B. Anthony (p. 653)
>   National American Woman Suffrage
>   Association (NAWSA) (p. 653)

Depression Politics
>   Coxey's army (p. 654)
>   Tom Watson (p. 655)
>   William McKinley (p. 656)
>   William Jennings Bryan (p. 656)

The United States and the World
>   Boxer uprising (p. 661)
>   Monroe Doctrine (p. 662)
>   Open Door policy (p. 663)
>   Spanish-American War (p. 663)
>   yellow journalism (p. 664)
>   Theodore Roosevelt (p. 664)
>   Emilio Aguinaldo (p. 669)

REVIEW QUESTIONS

Use key terms and dates to support your answer.

1. Why did American farmers organize alliances in the late nineteenth century? (pp. 641–644)

2. What tactics led to the defeat of the strikers in the 1890s? Where were they able to succeed and why? (pp. 644–651)

3. How did women's temperance activism contribute to the cause of woman suffrage? (pp. 651–654)

4. Why was the People's Party unable to translate national support into victory in the 1896 election? (pp. 654–658)

5. Why did the United States largely abandon its isolationist foreign policy in the 1890s? (pp. 658–669)

MAKING CONNECTIONS

Draw on key terms, the timeline, and review questions.

1. In the late nineteenth century, Americans clashed over the disparity of power brought about by industrial capitalism. Why did many farmers and urban workers look to the government to help advance their vision of economic justice? In your answer, discuss specific reforms working-class Americans pursued and the strategies they employed.

2. In the 1890s, workers mounted labor protests and strikes. What circumstances gave rise to these actions? How did they differ from earlier strikes, such as the Great Railroad Strike of 1877? In your answer, discuss specific actions, being sure to consider how local and national circumstances contributed to their ultimate resolution.

3. How did women's activism in the late nineteenth century help advance the cause of woman suffrage? In your answer, discuss specific gains made in the late nineteenth century, as well as shifts in reformers' strategies.

4. Given the farmers' unrest in the 1890s, why did the Populist Party fail to defeat Republican William McKinley in the election of 1896? What coalitions failed to come together?

Link events in this chapter to earlier events.

1. How did the conquest of Native Americans in the West foreshadow U.S. expansion abroad? In what ways did the assumptions of racial superiority evident in U.S. Indian policy affect the treatment of Cubans and Filipinos? (See chapter 17.)

2. Why in the midst of burgeoning growth did the United States experience a major depression in the 1890s? Draw on your knowledge of the development of U.S. industries such as the railroads. (See chapter 18.)

▶ **For practice quizzes and other study tools,** visit the Online Study Guide at bedfordstmartins.com/roark.

TIMELINE 1884–1901

1884	• Frances Willard, head of Woman's Christian Temperance Union, calls for woman suffrage.
1890	• National American Woman Suffrage Association (NAWSA) formed.
	• Wyoming only state allowing women to vote in national elections.
	• Southern Farmers' Alliance numbers three million members.
1892	• People's (Populist) Party founded.
	• Homestead lockout.
1893	• Stock market crash touches off severe economic depression.
	• President Grover Cleveland nixes attempt to annex Hawai'i.
1894	• Miners' strike in Cripple Creek, Colorado.
	• Coxey's army marches to Washington, D.C.
	• Federal troops and court injunction crush Pullman boycott.
1895	• President Grover Cleveland enforces Monroe Doctrine in border dispute between British Guiana and Venezuela.
1896	• Democrats and Populists support William Jennings Bryan for president.
	• Republican William McKinley elected president.
1898	• U.S. battleship *Maine* explodes in Havana harbor.
	• Congress declares war on Spain.
	• Admiral George Dewey destroys Spanish fleet in Manila Bay, the Philippines.
	• U.S. troops defeat Spanish forces in Cuba.
	• Treaty of Paris ends war with Spain and cedes Philippines, Puerto Rico, and Guam to the United States.
	• United States annexes Hawai'i.
1899–1900	• Secretary of State John Hay enunciates Open Door policy in China.
	• Boxer uprising in China.
1901	• Boxer Protocol imposed on Chinese government.

THE PROGRESSIVE PARTY

BORN 1912

PROGRESSIVE PARTY SOUVENIR BANDANA
This colorful bandana from the 1912 presidential race celebrates the Progressive Party and its candidate, Theodore Roosevelt. The progressive reform movement began at the grassroots, growing out of the crises of the 1890s to emerge full-blown in 1900. The appalling conditions in New York's tenements, documented by Jacob Riis in photographs like this one of a Baxter Street courtyard, goaded reformers to action. Roosevelt would become the Progressives' champion, challenging laissez-faire liberalism and arguing for government action to ensure greater social justice. In 1912 Roosevelt's followers broke with Republicans to form the new Progressive Party, demanding "We Want Our Teddy Back."
Bandana: Collection of Janice L. and David J. Frent; background: The Jacob A. Riis Collection, #108, Museum of the City of New York.

21

Progressivism from the Grass Roots to the White House
1890–1916

IN THE SUMMER OF 1889, JANE ADDAMS LEASED TWO FLOORS OF A dilapidated mansion on Chicago's West Side. Her Italian and Russian Jewish neighbors must have scratched their heads, wondering why this well-dressed woman, who surely could afford a better house in a better neighborhood, chose to live on South Halsted Street. Yet the house, built by Charles Hull, precisely suited Addams's needs.

Personal action marked the first step in Addams's search for solutions to the social problems created by urban industrialism. Her object was twofold: She wanted to help her immigrant neighbors, and she wanted to offer an opportunity for educated women like herself to find meaningful work. Addams's emphasis on the reciprocal relationship between the social classes made Hull House different from other philanthropic enterprises. She wished to do things with, not just for, Chicago's poor.

In the next decade, Hull House expanded from two rented floors in the old brick mansion wedged between a saloon and an undertaker to some thirteen buildings housing a remarkable variety of activities. Addams converted the basement bathroom into public baths, opened a restaurant for workingwomen too tired to cook after their long shifts, and sponsored a nursery and kindergarten. Hull House offered classes, lectures, art exhibits, musical instruction, and college extension courses. It boasted a gymnasium, a theater, a manual training workshop, a labor museum, and the first public playground in Chicago.

From the first, Hull House attracted an extraordinary set of reformers. Some stayed for decades, as did Julia Lathrop before she went to Washington, D.C., in 1912 to head the Children's Bureau. Others, like Gerard Swope, who later became president of the General Electric Company, came for only a short time. Hull House residents pioneered the scientific investigation of urban ills. Armed with statistics, they launched campaigns to improve housing, end child labor, fund playgrounds, mediate between labor and management, and lobby for laws to protect workers.

Jane Addams

Jane Addams was twenty-nine years old when she founded Hull House on South Halsted Street in Chicago. She and her college roommate, Ellen Gates Starr, established America's premier social settlement. Her desire to live among the poor and her insistence that settlement house work benefited educated women such as herself as well as her immigrant neighbors separated her from the charity workers who had come before her and marked the distance from philanthropy to progressive reform. Her autobiographical *Twenty Years at Hull-House*, published in 1910, is shown in the inset. Photo: Jane Addams Memorial Collection (JAMC neg. 14), Special Collections, University of Illinois at Chicago, photographer: Max Platz; Book: Newberry Library.

Addams quickly learned that it was impossible to deal with urban problems without becoming involved in political action. Her determination to clean up the garbage on Halsted Street led her into politics. Piles of decaying garbage overflowed the street's wooden trash bins, breeding flies and disease. Investigation revealed that the local ward boss got a kickback from a contractor who didn't bother to provide adequate service. To end the graft, Addams got herself appointed garbage inspector. Out on the streets at six in the morning, she rode atop the garbage wagon to make sure it made its rounds. Eventually, her struggle to aid the urban poor led her not only to city hall but on to the state capitol and to Washington, D.C., as well.

Under Jane Addams's leadership, Hull House became a "spearhead for reform," part of a broader movement that contemporaries called progressivism. The transition from personal action to political activism that Addams personified became one of the hallmarks of this reform period, which lasted from the 1890s to World War I.

By the 1890s, many Americans recognized that the laissez-faire approach of government toward business no longer worked. The classical liberalism of the nation's Founders, which opposed the tyranny of centralized government, had not foreseen the enormous private wealth and power of the Gilded Age's business giants. As the gap between rich and poor widened in the 1890s, progressive reformers began demanding government intervention to guarantee a more equitable society. The willingness to use the government to promote change and to counterbalance the power of private interests redefined liberalism in the twentieth century.

Faith in activism in both the political and the private realms united an otherwise diverse group of progressive reformers. A sense of Christian mission inspired some. Others, fearing social upheaval, sought to remove some of the worst evils of urban industrialism — tenements, child labor, and harsh working conditions. A belief in technical expertise and scientific management infused progressivism and made the cult of efficiency part and parcel of the movement.

Progressives shared a growing concern about the power of wealthy individuals and corporations and a strong dislike of the trusts, but they were not immune to the prejudices of the era. Although they pressed for direct democracy, many progressives sought to restrict the rights of African Americans, Asians, and even the women who formed the backbone of the movement.

All of these elements — uplift and efficiency, social justice and social control, direct democracy and discrimination — came together in the Progressive Era both at the grassroots level in the cities and states and in the presidencies of Theodore Roosevelt and Woodrow Wilson.

▶ Grassroots Progressivism

Much of progressive reform began at the grassroots level and percolated upward into local, state, and eventually national politics as reformers attacked the social problems fostered by urban industrialism. Although **progressivism** flourished in many different settings across the country, urban problems inspired the progressives' greatest efforts. In their zeal to "civilize the city," reformers founded settlement houses, professed a new Christian social gospel, and campaigned against vice and crime in the name of "social purity." Allying with the working class, they sought to better the lot of sweatshop garment workers and to end child labor. Their reform efforts often began on the local level but ended up being debated in state legislatures and in the U.S. Congress.

Civilizing the City

Progressives attacked the problems of the city on many fronts. The settlement house movement attempted to bridge the distance between the classes. The social gospel called for churches to play a new role in social reformation. And the social purity movement campaigned to clean up vice, particularly prostitution.

The **settlement house** movement, which began in England, came to the United States in 1886 with the opening of the University Settlement House in New York City. The needs of poor urban neighborhoods provided the impetus for these social settlements. In 1893, Lillian Wald, a nurse attending medical school in New York, went to care for a woman living in a dilapidated tenement. The experience led Wald to leave medical school and recruit several other nurses to move to New York City's Lower East Side "to live in the neighborhood as nurses, identify ourselves with it socially, and . . . contribute to it our citizenship." Wald's Henry Street settlement expanded in 1895, pioneering public health nursing. Although Wald herself was Jewish, she insisted that the settlement remain independent of religious ties, making it different from the avowedly religious settlements in England.

Women, particularly college-educated women like **Jane Addams** and Lillian Wald, formed the backbone of the settlement house movement and

---

Children Playing at Hull House
A young settlement house worker leads neighborhood children in a circle game in this photograph taken at Hull House at the turn of the twentieth century. Jane Addams recognized early on that Chicago's working mothers needed safe, reliable child care. Hull House filled the need by providing day nurseries. Older children, like the boys and girls pictured here in their short pants and pinafores, could find at Hull House a snack and a place to play after school. Adena Rich Miller Scrapbook (JAMC neg. 435b), Special Collection, University Library, University of Illinois at Chicago.

Making the Workplace Safer: Alice Hamilton Explores the Dangerous Trades

Nothing in Alice Hamilton's middle-class, midwestern upbringing hinted at the leading role she would play in the progressive movement as a pioneer in the field of occupational health and safety. Yet at an early age, she resolved to become a doctor, because, as she wrote, "as a doctor I could go anywhere I pleased — to the far-off lands or to city slums — and be quite sure that I could be of use anywhere."

This desire to be of use prompted Hamilton to earn a medical degree at the University of Michigan and to study bacteriology in Germany and at Johns Hopkins University. In September 1897, she fulfilled a longtime dream by moving into Hull House, where she, like most of the residents, worked a day job (at Northwestern University's Medical School) and participated in settlement activities in the evenings and on weekends. Hamilton soon focused on the area of public health, particularly the link between occupation and illness.

Through her work, Hamilton came to believe that the poor health of many immigrants resulted from unsafe conditions and noxious chemicals, especially lead dust, in the industrial workplace. Employers insisted that lead poisoning resulted from workers' failure to wash their hands before they ate, or they blamed workers' ill health on alcoholism, but Hamilton disagreed. As she noted, the United States was far behind Europe in the field of industrial toxicology and in the regulation of dangers in the workplace. "The employers [here] could, if they wished, shut their eyes to the dangers their workmen faced," Hamilton observed, "for nobody held them responsible, while the workers [largely immigrants] accepted the risks with fatalistic submissiveness as part of the price one must pay for being poor."

In 1910, at the age of thirty-two, Hamilton was appointed to the newly created Occupational Disease Commission of Illinois, the first investigative body of its kind in the United States. For the next decade, she relied primarily on "shoe leather epidemiology" to explore the dangerous trades. With her assistants, she visited factories, read hospital records, and interviewed workers in their homes to discover instances of lead poisoning. "No young doctor," she wrote, "can hope for work as exciting and rewarding." Lead poisoning builds up slowly in the body, leading to colic and convulsions. Lead harms the nervous system, causing paralysis and wristdrop, a condition in which the hands and fingers cannot be extended. In cases of chronic lead poisoning, victims suffer from weight loss, constipation, high blood pressure, anemia, abdominal pain, fatigue, and premature senility. One of Hamilton's case studies tells the grim story.

A Hungarian, thirty-six years old, worked for seven years grinding lead paint. During this time he had three attacks of colic, with vomiting and headache. I saw him in the hospital, a skeleton of a man, looking almost twice his age, his limbs soft and flabby, his muscles wasted. He was extremely emaciated, his color was a dirty grayish yellow, his eyes dull and expressionless. He lay in an apathetic condition, rousing when spoken to and answering rationally but slowly, with often an appreciable delay, then sinking back into apathy.

In 1911, Hamilton prepared a report making clear the connection

stood in the vanguard of the progressive movement. Settlement houses gave college-educated women eager to use their knowledge a place to put their talents to work in the service of society and to champion progressive reform. (See "Seeking the American Promise," above.) Largely because of women's efforts, settlements like Hull House grew in number from six in 1891 to more than four hundred in 1911. In the process, settlement house women created a new profession — social work — and stimulated the new reform movement of progressivism.

For their part, churches confronted urban social problems by enunciating a new **social gospel**, one that saw its mission as not simply to reform individuals but to reform society. The social gospel offered a powerful corrective to social Darwinism and the gospel of wealth,

between occupation and illness, leading to needed reforms in Illinois. In 1913, the U.S. commissioner of labor asked her to undertake a national study. "I had, as a Federal agent," she wrote, "no right to enter any establishment — that depended on the courtesy of the employer. I must discover for myself where the plants were, and the method of investigation to be followed. . . . Nobody would keep tabs on me, I should not even receive a salary." Using her intelligence and charm, she was rarely denied entry, and her experience at Hull House led her directly to the workers in their homes when she wanted the facts. Her powers of persuasion prompted several employers to institute reforms in their plants to cut down on lead dust.

By 1915, Hamilton had become the foremost American authority on lead poisoning and one of a handful of prominent specialists in industrial disease. When the Harvard Medical School began a program in industrial hygiene in 1916, Hamilton became the first woman invited to join the faculty. Until her retirement in 1935, she alternated a semester of teaching at Harvard with her field work "exploring the dangerous trades." In her long retirement (she lived to be 101), she continued to blend her commitment to social justice and civil rights, political activism, and concern for the poorest workers. Hamilton died on September 22, 1970, three months before Congress passed the Occupational Safety and Health Act, institutionalizing the reforms she had fought for her whole life.

Alice Hamilton
This picture of Alice Hamilton was taken the year she graduated from the University of Michigan medical school in 1893. A resident of Hull House, she pioneered the field of occupational health and safety. Schlesinger Library, Radcliffe Institute for Advanced Study, Harvard University.

Questions for Consideration

1. What was the importance of Hull House in Alice Hamilton's career?

2. Hamilton observed that regulation of industry was much more advanced in Europe than in the United States, where, as she put it, the "subject was tainted with Socialism or with feminine sentimentality for the poor." In her own work, how did she overcome this attitude?

which fostered the belief that riches somehow signaled divine favor (see chapter 18). Washington Gladden, a prominent social gospel minister, challenged that view when he urged Congregationalists to turn down a gift from John D. Rockefeller, arguing that it was "tainted money." In place of the gospel of wealth, progressive clergy exhorted their congregations to put Christ's teachings to work in their daily lives.

Charles M. Sheldon's popular book *In His Steps* (1898) called on men and women to Christianize capitalism by asking the question "What would Jesus do?"

Ministers also played an active role in the **social purity movement**, the campaign to attack vice. The Reverend Charles H. Parkhurst shocked his Madison Square congregation in the 1890s by donning a disguise and touring

New York City's brothels to uncover the links between political corruption and urban vice. Armed with eyewitness accounts and affidavits, he demanded reform. To end the "social evil," as reformers delicately referred to prostitution, the social purity movement brought together ministers who wished to stamp out sin, doctors concerned about the spread of venereal disease, and women reformers determined to fight the double standard that made premarital and extramarital sex acceptable for men but demanded chastity of women. Advanced progressive reformers linked prostitution to poverty and championed higher wages for women. "Is it any wonder," asked the Chicago vice commission, "that a tempted girl who receives only six dollars per week working with her hands sells her body for twenty-five dollars per week when she learns there is a demand for it and men are willing to pay the price?"

Attacks on alcohol went hand in hand with the push for social purity. In the early twentieth century, the Anti-Saloon League, formed in 1895 under the leadership of Protestant clergy, added to the efforts of the Woman's Christian Temperance Union in campaigning to end the sale of liquor. Reformers pointed to links between drinking, prostitution, wife and child abuse, unemployment, and industrial accidents. The powerful liquor lobby fought back, spending liberally in election campaigns, fueling the charge that liquor corrupted the political process.

An element of nativism (dislike of foreigners) ran through the movement for prohibition, as it did in a number of progressive reforms. The Irish, the Italians, and the Germans were among the groups stigmatized by temperance reformers for their drinking. Even though most workers toiled six days a week and had only Sunday for recreation and relaxation, some progressives campaigned on the local level to enforce the Sunday closing of taverns, stores, and other commercial establishments. To further deny the working class access to alcohol, these progressives pushed for state legislation to outlaw the sale of liquor. By 1912, seven states were "dry."

Progressives' efforts to civilize the city demonstrated their willingness to take action; their belief that environment, not heredity alone, determined human behavior; and their optimism that conditions could be corrected through government action without radically altering America's economy or institutions. All of these attitudes characterized the progressive movement.

Progressives and the Working Class

Day-to-day contact with their neighbors made settlement house workers particularly sympathetic to labor unions. When Mary Kenney O'Sullivan complained that her bookbinders' union met in a dirty, noisy saloon, Jane Addams invited the union to meet at Hull House. And during the Pullman strike in 1894 (see chapter 20, "Documenting the American Promise," page 648), Hull House residents organized strike relief. "Hull-House has been so unionized," grumbled one Chicago businessman, "that it has lost its usefulness and become a detriment and harm to the community." But to the working class, the support of middle-class reformers marked a significant gain.

Attempts to forge a cross-class alliance became institutionalized in 1903 with the creation of the **Women's Trade Union League** (WTUL). The WTUL brought together women workers and middle-class "allies." Its goal was to organize workingwomen into unions under the auspices of the American Federation of Labor (AFL). However, as one workingwoman confided, "The men think that the girls should not get as good work as the men and should not make half as much money as a man." Samuel Gompers, president of the AFL, endorsed the principle of equal pay for equal work, shrewdly observing that it would help male workers more than women, since many employers hired women precisely because they could be paid less.

Although the alliance between workingwomen, primarily immigrants and daughters of immigrants, and their middle-class allies was not without tension, the WTUL helped workingwomen achieve significant gains. Its most notable success came in 1909 in the "uprising of the twenty thousand," when hundreds of women employees of the Triangle Shirtwaist Company in New York City went on strike to protest low wages, dangerous working conditions, and management's refusal to recognize their union, the International Ladies' Garment Workers Union. In support, an estimated twenty thousand garment workers, most of them teenage girls and many of them Jewish and Italian immigrants, stayed out on strike through the winter, picketing in the bitter cold. By the time the strike ended in February 1910, the workers had won important demands in many shops. The solidarity shown by the women workers proved to be the strike's greatest achievement. As Clara Lemlich, one of the strike's leaders, exclaimed, "They used to say that you couldn't even organize women. They wouldn't come to union meetings. They were 'temporary' workers. Well we showed them!"

The WTUL made enormous contributions to the strike. It provided volunteers for the picket lines, posted more than $29,000 in bail, protested police brutality, organized a parade of ten thousand strikers, took part in the arbitration conference, appealed for funds, and generated publicity for the strike. Under the leadership of the WTUL, women from every class of society, from J. P. Morgan's daughter Anne to socialists on New York's Lower East Side, joined the strikers in a dramatic display of cross-class alliance.

But for all its success, the uprising of the twenty thousand failed fundamentally to change conditions for women workers, as the tragic Triangle fire dramatized in 1911. A little over a year after the shirtwaist makers' strike ended, fire alarms sounded at the Triangle Shirtwaist factory. The ramshackle building, full of lint and combustible cloth, burned to rubble in half an hour. A WTUL member described the scene below on the street: "Two young girls whom I knew to be working in the vicinity came rushing toward me, tears were running from their eyes and they were white and shaking as they caught me by the arm. 'Oh,' shrieked one of them, 'they are jumping. Jumping from ten stories up! They are going through the air like bundles of clothes.'"

The terrified Triangle workers had little choice but to jump. Flames blocked one exit, and the other door had been locked to prevent workers from pilfering. The flimsy, rusted fire escape collapsed under the weight of fleeing workers, killing dozens. Trapped, 54 workers on the top floors jumped to their deaths. Of 500 workers, 146 died and scores of others were injured. The owners of the Triangle firm went to trial for negligence, but they avoided conviction when authorities determined that the fire had been started by a careless smoker. The Triangle Shirtwaist Company reopened in another firetrap within a matter of weeks.

Outrage and a sense of futility overwhelmed Rose Schneiderman, a leading WTUL organizer, who made a bitter speech at the memorial service for the dead Triangle workers. "I would be a traitor to those poor burned bodies if I came here to talk good fellowship," she told her audience. "We have tried you good people of the public and we have found you wanting. . . . I know from my experience it is up to the working people to save themselves . . . by a strong working class movement." The Triangle fire severely tested the bonds

> ## "They used to say that you couldn't even organize women. . . . Well we showed them!"
> — Strike leader
> **CLARA LEMLICH**

Women Strikers
Throughout the bitter winter of 1909, garment workers led a strike demanding union representation, shorter hours, better working conditions, and higher wages. The strikers, primarily young women from the Jewish and Italian immigrant communities, joined the International Ladies' Garment Workers Union and proved that women could be unionized and mount an effective strike. The Women's Trade Union League, a cross-class alliance of working women and middle-class "allies," contributed money and offered moral support to the strikers. The women pictured here claim 30,000 are on strike, but historically the strike has been called the "uprising of the 20,000." With their tailored dress and fancy hats, the workers could easily be mistaken for their middle-class WTUL "allies." The illustration on the right urges consumers to fight sweatshops by buying only garments that carry the union label. Strikers: Brown Brothers; ad: Picture Research Consultants & Archives.

14.   Viewing the unfortunates at the Morgue

Triangle Fire Morgue
After the Triangle fire on March 26, 1911, New York City set up a makeshift morgue at the end of Manhattan's Charities Pier. There, the remains of more than a hundred young women and two dozen young men were laid out in coffins for their friends and relatives to identify. Those trapped in the building were burned beyond recognition. A ring, a charred shoe, a melted hair comb often provided the only clues to the identity of a sister, a daughter, or a sweetheart. Artist John Sloan created the striking image, with its dark triangle representing the capitalist triumvirate of Rent, Profit, and Interest. A bloated businessman weeps over his lost profits while a young woman worker lies burning on the pavement and a leering skeleton poses on the left. Photo: Hadwin Collection, Kheel Center, Cornell University, Ithaca, NY; illustration: Granger Collection.

of the cross-class alliance. Schneiderman and other WTUL leaders determined that organizing and striking were no longer enough, particularly when the AFL paid so little attention to women workers. Increasingly, the WTUL turned its efforts to lobbying for protective legislation — laws that would limit hours and regulate women's working conditions.

Advocates of protective legislation won a major victory in 1908 when the U.S. Supreme Court, in *Muller v. Oregon*, reversed its previous rulings and upheld an Oregon law that limited to ten the hours women could work in a day. A mass of sociological evidence put together by Florence Kelley of the National Consumers' League and Josephine Goldmark of the WTUL demonstrated the ill effects of long hours on the health and safety of women. The data convinced the Court that long hours endangered women and therefore the entire human race. The Court's ruling set a precedent, but one that separated the well-being of women workers from that of men by arguing that women's reproductive role

justified special treatment. Later generations of women fighting for equality would question the effectiveness of this strategy and argue that it ultimately closed good jobs to women. The WTUL, however, greeted protective legislation as a first step in the attempt to ensure the safety of all workers.

The **National Consumers' League** (NCL), like the WTUL, fostered cross-class alliance. When Florence Kelley took over the leadership of the NCL in 1899, she urged middle-class women to boycott stores and exert pressure for decent wages and working conditions for women employees, primarily saleswomen. The league published a "white list" of stores that met its standards. Like the WTUL, the NCL increasingly promoted protective legislation to better working conditions for women. Frustrated by the reluctance of the private sector to respond to the need for reform, progressives turned to government at all levels. Aware that European governments had assumed a social role, providing regulation of industries and benefits to workers, American progressives wanted their own state and federal governments to help level the playing field between workers and industrialists. Critics would later charge that the progressives assumed too easily that government regulation could best solve social problems.

Reform also fueled the fight for woman suffrage. For women like Jane Addams and Florence Kelley, involvement in social reform led inevitably to support for woman suffrage. These new suffragists emphasized the reforms that could be accomplished if women had the vote. Addams insisted that in an urban, industrial society, a good housekeeper could not be sure the food she fed her family or the water and milk they drank were pure unless she became involved in politics and wielded the ballot — and not just the broom — to protect her family. The concept of **municipal housekeeping** encouraged women to put their talents to work in the service of society.

> **REVIEW** What types of people were drawn to the progressive movement, and what motivated them?

▶ Progressivism: Theory and Practice

Progressive reformers developed a theoretical basis for their activist approach by countering social Darwinism with a dynamic new reform Darwinism. The progressives emphasized action and experimentation. Dismissing the view that humans should leave progress to the dictates of natural selection, progressive reform Darwinists argued that human intelligence could shape change and improve society. In their zeal for action, progressives often showed an unchecked admiration for speed and efficiency that promoted scientific management and a new cult of efficiency. These varied strands of progressive theory found practical application in state and local politics, where reformers challenged traditional laissez-faire government.

Reform Darwinism and Social Engineering

The active, interventionist approach of the progressives directly challenged social Darwinism, with its insistence that the world operated on the principle of survival of the fittest and that human beings stood powerless in the face of the law of natural selection. Without abandoning the evolutionary framework of Darwinism, a new group of sociologists argued that evolution could be advanced more rapidly if men and women used their intellects to alter the environment. Sociologist Lester Frank Ward put it clearly in his book *Dynamic Sociology* (1883). "I insist that the time must soon come," he wrote, "when control of blind natural forces in society must give way to human foresight." Dubbed **reform Darwinism**, the new sociological theory condemned the laissez-faire approach, insisting that the liberal state should play a more active role in solving social problems.

Efficiency and *expertise* became watchwords in the progressive vocabulary. In *Drift and Mastery* (1914), journalist and critic Walter Lippmann called for skilled "technocrats" to use scientific techniques to control social change, substituting social engineering for aimless drift. Progressive reformers' emphasis on expertise inevitably fostered a kind of elitism. Unlike the Populists, who advocated a greater voice for the masses, progressives, for all their interest in social justice, insisted that experts be put in charge.

At its extreme, the application of expertise and social engineering took the form of **scientific management**, whose mechanized routine alienated the working class. Frederick Winslow Taylor pioneered "systematized shop management." After dropping out of Harvard, Taylor went to work as a machinist at Midvale Steel in Philadelphia in the 1880s. Obsessed with making humans and machines produce more and faster, he earned a master's of engineering degree in 1885 and went back to Midvale to restructure the workplace. With a stopwatch in his hand, he meticulously timed workers and attempted to break down their work into its simplest components, one repetitious action after another, on the theory that productivity would increase if tasks could be simplified. An advocate of piecework, quotas, and pay incentives for productivity, Taylor insisted that unions were unnecessary. As a consulting engineer, he spread his gospel of efficiency and won many converts among corporate managers. Workers hated the monotony of systematized shop management and argued that it led to the speedup — pushing workers to produce more in less time and for less pay. But many progressives applauded the increased productivity and efficiency of Taylor's system.

> "I insist that the time must soon come when control of blind natural forces in society must give way to human foresight."
>
> — Sociologist **LESTER FRANK WARD**

Progressive Government: City and State

The politicians who became premier progressives were generally the followers, not the leaders, in a movement already well advanced at the grassroots level. Yet they left their stamp on the movement. Tom Johnson made Cleveland a model of progressive reform, Robert M. La Follette turned Wisconsin into a laboratory for progressivism, and Hiram Johnson ended the domination of the Southern Pacific Railroad in California politics.

Progressivism burst forth at every level of government in 1900, but nowhere more forcefully than in Cleveland with the election of Democrat **Thomas Loftin Johnson** as mayor. A self-made millionaire by age forty, Johnson moved to Cleveland in 1899, where he began his career in politics. During his mayoral campaign, he pledged to reduce the streetcar fare from five cents to three cents. His election touched off a seven-year war between Johnson and the streetcar moguls, who argued that they couldn't meet costs with the lower fare. To get his three-cent fare, Johnson had the city buy the streetcar system, a tactic of municipal ownership progressives called "gas and water socialism." Under Johnson's administration, Cleveland became, in the words of journalist Lincoln Steffens, the "best governed city in America." Reelected four times, Johnson fought for fair taxation and championed greater democracy through the use

of the initiative, referendum, and recall — devices that allowed voters to have a direct say in legislative and judicial matters.

In Wisconsin, Republican **Robert M. La Follette** converted to the progressive cause early in the 1900s. An astute politician, La Follette capitalized on the grassroots movement for reform to launch his long political career as governor (1901–1905) and U.S. senator (1906–1925). A graduate of the University of Wisconsin, La Follette brought scientists and professors into his administration and used the university, just down the street from the statehouse in Madison, as a resource in drafting legislation.

As governor, La Follette lowered railroad rates, raised railroad taxes, improved education, preached conservation, established factory regulation and workers' compensation, instituted the first direct primary in the country, and inaugurated the first state income tax. Under his leadership, Wisconsin earned the title "laboratory of democracy." A fiery orator, "Fighting Bob" La Follette united his supporters around issues that transcended party loyalties. This emphasis on reform characterized progressivism, which attracted followers from both major parties. Democrats like Tom Johnson and Republicans like Robert La Follette could lay equal claim to the label "progressive." Democrats and Republicans alike crossed party lines to work for reform.

West of the Rockies, progressivism arrived somewhat later and found a champion in Republican **Hiram Johnson** of California, who served as governor from 1911 to 1917 and later as a U.S. senator. Since the 1870s, California

Tom Johnson

Tom Johnson, the reform mayor of Cleveland from 1901 to 1909, is shown here campaigning in Cleveland's Wade Park in 1908. For more than seven years, Mayor Johnson fought for a three-cent streetcar fare, winning the support of the working class and angering the businessmen who ran the city's streetcars. To get this low fare, Johnson finally instituted municipal ownership of the transit system. The Western Reserve Historical Society, Cleveland, OH.

politics had been dominated by the Southern Pacific Railroad, a corporation so rapacious that novelist Frank Norris styled it *The Octopus* (1901). Johnson ran for governor in 1910 on the promise to "kick the Southern Pacific out of politics." With the support of the reform wing of the Republican Party and the promise "to return the government to the people," he handily won. As governor, he introduced the direct primary; supported the initiative, referendum, and recall; strengthened the state's railroad commission; supported conservation; and signed an employer's liability law.

REVIEW How did progressives justify their demand for more activist government?

▶ Progressivism Finds a President: Theodore Roosevelt

On September 6, 1901, President William McKinley was shot by Leon Czolgosz, an anarchist, while attending the Pan-American Exposition in Buffalo, New York. Eight days later, McKinley died. When news of his assassination reached his friend and political mentor Mark Hanna, Hanna is said to have growled, "Now that damned cowboy is president." He was speaking of Vice President Theodore Roosevelt, the colorful hero of the battle of San Juan Hill, who had indeed punched cattle in the Dakotas in the 1880s.

In the first hours of his presidency, Roosevelt reassured the shocked nation that he intended "to continue absolutely unbroken" the policies of McKinley. But Roosevelt was as different from McKinley as the twentieth century was from the nineteenth. An activist and a moralist, imbued with the progressive spirit, Roosevelt would turn the White House into a "bully pulpit," advocating conservation and antitrust reforms and championing the nation's emergence as a world power. In the process, Roosevelt would work to shift the nation's center of power from Wall Street to Washington.

After serving nearly two full terms as president, Roosevelt left office at the height of his powers. Any man would have found it difficult to follow in his footsteps, but his handpicked successor, William Howard Taft, proved hopelessly ill suited to the task. Taft's presidency

Theodore Roosevelt
Aptly described by a contemporary observer as "a steam engine in trousers," Theodore Roosevelt, at forty-two, was the youngest president ever to occupy the White House. He brought to the office energy, intellect, and activism in equal measure. Roosevelt boasted that he used the presidency as a "bully pulpit" — a forum from which he advocated reforms ranging from trust-busting to conservation. Library of Congress.

was marked by a progressive stalemate, a bitter break with Roosevelt, and a schism in the Republican Party.

The Square Deal

At age forty-two, Theodore Roosevelt became the youngest man ever to move into the White House. A patrician by birth and an activist by temperament, Roosevelt brought to the job enormous talent and energy. By the time he graduated from Harvard, he was already an accomplished naturalist, an enthusiastic historian, and a naval strategist. He could have chosen from any of those promising careers; instead, he chose politics, not a bad choice for a man who relished competition and craved power.

Roosevelt was shrewd enough to realize that the path to power did not lie in the good government leagues formed by his well-bred friends. "If it is the muckers that govern," he wrote, "then I want to see if I cannot hold my own with them." So he apprenticed himself early on to the local Republican ward boss Thomas C. Platt, who held court in a grimy, smoke-filled club above a Manhattan saloon. Roosevelt's rise in politics was swift and sure. He went from the New York assembly at the age of twenty-three to the presidency in less than twenty years, with time out as a cowboy in the Dakotas, police commissioner of New York City, assistant secretary of the navy, colonel of the Rough Riders, and governor of New York. Elected governor in 1898 as a moderate reformer, Roosevelt soon clashed with Platt, who finagled to get him "kicked upstairs" as a candidate for the vice presidency in 1900. As vice president, the party bosses reasoned, Roosevelt could do little harm. But one bullet proved the error of their logic.

As president, Roosevelt would harness his explosive energy to strengthen the power of the federal government, putting business on notice that it could no longer count on a laissez-faire government to give it free rein. In Roosevelt's eyes, self-interested capitalists like John D. Rockefeller, whose Standard Oil trust monopolized the refinery business, constituted "the most dangerous members of the criminal class — the criminals of great wealth." The "absolutely vital question" facing the country, Roosevelt wrote to a friend in 1901, was "whether or not the government has the power to control the trusts." The Sherman Antitrust Act of 1890 had been badly weakened by a conservative Supreme Court and by attorneys general more willing to use it against labor unions than against monopolies. To determine whether the law had any teeth left, Roosevelt, in one of his first acts as president, ordered his attorney general to begin a secret antitrust investigation of the Northern Securities Company.

> **"Wall Street is paralyzed at the thought that a President of the United States would sink so low as to try to enforce the law."**
> — A newspaper editor

He picked a good target. Northern Securities had resulted from one of the most controversial mergers of the era. Two railroad magnates had fought a ruinous rate war that precipitated a panic on Wall Street, bankrupting thousands of small investors. To bring peace to the warring factions, financier J. P. Morgan stepped in and created the Northern Securities Company in 1901, linking three competing railroads under one management. This new behemoth monopolized railroad traffic in the Northwest. Small investors still smarting from their losses, farmers worried about freight rates, and the public in general saw in Northern Securities the symbol of corporate highhandedness.

In February 1902, just five months after Roosevelt took office, Wall Street rocked with the news that the government had filed an antitrust suit against Northern Securities. As one newspaper editor sarcastically observed, "Wall Street is paralyzed at the thought that a President of the United States would sink so low as to try to enforce the law." An indignant J. P. Morgan demanded to know why he had not been consulted. "If we have done anything wrong," he told the attorney general, "send your man to my man and they can fix it up." Roosevelt, amused, later noted that Morgan "could not help regarding me as a big rival operator." Roosevelt's thunderbolt put Wall Street on notice that the new president expected to be treated as an equal and was willing to use government as a weapon to curb business excesses. Perhaps sensing the new mood, the Supreme Court, in a significant turnaround, upheld the Sherman Act and called for the dissolution of Northern Securities in 1904.

"Hurrah for Teddy the Trustbuster," cheered the papers. Roosevelt went on to use the Sherman Act against forty-three trusts, including such giants as American Tobacco, Du Pont, and Standard Oil. Always the moralist, he insisted on a "rule of reason." He would punish "bad" trusts (those that broke the law) and leave "good" ones alone. In practice, he preferred regulation to antitrust suits. In 1903, he pressured Congress to pass the Elkins Act, outlawing railroad rebates. And he created the new cabinet-level Department of Commerce and Labor with the subsidiary Bureau of Corporations to act as a corporate watchdog.

Observing Roosevelt in action, journalist Joseph Pulitzer remarked, "He has subjugated Wall Street." Pulitzer exaggerated, but Roosevelt had masterfully asserted the moral and political authority of the executive, underscoring, in his words, the "duty of the President to act upon the theory that he is the steward of the people." In his handling of the anthracite coal strike in 1902, Roosevelt again demonstrated his willingness to assert the authority of the presidency, this time to mediate between labor and management.

In May, 147,000 coal miners in Pennsylvania went on strike. The United Mine Workers (UMW) demanded a reduction in the workday from twelve to ten hours, an equitable system of weighing each miner's output, and a 10 percent wage increase, along with recognition of the union. When asked about the appalling conditions in the mines that led to the strike, George Baer, the mine operators' spokesman, scoffed, "The miners don't suffer, why they can't even speak English." Buttressed by social Darwinism, Baer observed that "God in his infinite wisdom" had placed "the rights and interests of the laboring man" in the hands of the capitalists, not "the labor agitators."

The strike dragged on through the summer and into the fall. Hoarding and profiteering drove the price of coal from $2.50 to $6.00 a

Breaker Boys
Child labor in America's mines and mills was common at the turn of the twentieth century, despite state laws that tried to restrict it. Here, "breaker boys," some as young as seven years old, pick over coal in a Pennsylvania mine. Their unsmiling faces bear witness to the difficulty and danger of their work. A committee investigating child labor found more than ten thousand children illegally employed in the Pennsylvania coalfields. Brown Brothers.

ton. As winter approached, coal shortages touched off near riots in the nation's big cities. At this juncture, Roosevelt stepped in to mediate, inviting representatives from both sides to meet in Washington in October. His unprecedented intervention served notice that government counted itself an independent force in business and labor disputes. At the same time, it gave unionism a boost by granting the UMW a place at the table.

At the meeting, Baer and the mine owners refused to talk with the union representative — a move that angered the attorney general and insulted the president. The meeting ended in an impasse. Beside himself with rage over the "woodenheaded obstinacy and stupidity" of management, Roosevelt threatened to seize the mines and run them with federal troops. It was a powerful bluff, one that called into question not only the supremacy of private property but also the rule of law. But the specter of federal troops being used to operate the mines quickly brought management around. In the end, the miners won a reduction in hours and a wage increase, but the owners succeeded in preventing formal recognition of the UMW.

Taken together, Roosevelt's actions in the Northern Securities case and the anthracite coal strike marked a dramatic departure from the presidential passivity of the Gilded Age. Roosevelt's actions demonstrated conclusively that government intended to act as a countervailing force to the power of the big corporations. Pleased with his role in the anthracite strike, Roosevelt announced that all he had tried to do was give labor and capital a square deal.

The phrase **Square Deal** became Roosevelt's campaign slogan in the 1904 election. But to win the presidency in his own right, Roosevelt needed to wrest control of the Republican Party from kingmaker and party boss Mark Hanna. Roosevelt adroitly used patronage to win supporters and weaken Hanna's power. Hanna died of typhoid fever in 1904, leaving Roosevelt the undisputed leader of the party.

In the presidential election of 1904, Roosevelt easily defeated the Democrats, who abandoned their former candidate, William Jennings Bryan, to support Judge Alton B. Parker, a "safe" choice they hoped would lure business votes away from Roosevelt. In the months before the election, the president prudently toned down his criticism of

The Birth of Photojournalism

Photography changed the way Americans viewed their world and strongly influenced American memory. By the 1840s, Americans had embraced photography, importing the technology of Frenchman Louis Daguerre to make portraits called daguerreotypes. During the Civil War, Mathew Brady carried his darkroom on wheels into the battlefields and took pictures that brought the bloody war into focus. By the 1890s, Americans could purchase a Kodak camera that George Eastman marketed with the slogan "You push the button, we do the rest." As the poet Oliver Wendell Holmes observed, the camera became not just "the mirror of reality" but "the mirror with a memory." How do you think photography affected American memory?

Yet for Jacob Riis, the progressive reformer who wished to document the grim horrors of tenement life, photography was useless because it required daylight or careful studio lighting. Riis, who covered the police beat for the *New York Tribune*, never thought of buying a camera. He could only crudely sketch the dim hovels, the criminal nightlife, and the windowless tenement rooms of New

Five Cents a Spot

York. Then came the breakthrough: "One morning scanning my newspaper at my breakfast table, I put it down with an outcry. . . . There it was, the thing I had been looking for all these years. . . . A way had been

big business. Wealthy Republicans like J. P. Morgan may have grumbled privately, branding Roosevelt a class traitor, but they remained loyal to the party. Roosevelt swept into office with the largest popular majority — 57.9 percent — any candidate had polled up to that time.

Roosevelt the Reformer

"Tomorrow I shall come into my office in my own right," Roosevelt is said to have remarked on the eve of his election. "Then watch out for me!" Roosevelt's stunning victory gave him a mandate for reform. He would need all the popularity and political savvy he could muster, however, to guide his reform measures through

Congress. The Senate remained controlled by a staunchly conservative Republican "old guard," with many senators on the payrolls of the corporations Roosevelt sought to curb. Roosevelt's pet project remained railroad regulation. The Elkins Act prohibiting rebates had not worked. No one could stop big shippers like Standard Oil from wringing concessions from the railroads. Roosevelt determined that the only solution lay in giving the Interstate Commerce Commission (ICC) real power to set rates and prevent discriminatory practices. But the right to determine the price of goods or services was an age-old prerogative of private enterprise, and one that business had no intention of yielding to government.

Five Cents a Spot

flash. By looking at a line drawing side by side with the corresponding photograph, we can compare the impact of the two mediums. Look at Riis's line drawing of a "Five Cents a Spot" lodgers' tenement that appeared in *How the Other Half Lives*, and compare it with the photograph on which it was based. Riis had followed a policeman who was raiding the tenement to evict the lodgers. In his book, he describes the room as "not thirteen feet either way," in which "slept twelve men and women, two or three in bunks in a sort of alcove, the rest on the floor." Note how the flash catches the sleepy faces and tired bodies, the crowding, dirt, and disorder. What details visible in the photograph are lost in the drawing? Which portrayal has a greater impact on the viewer?

Riis's pioneering photojournalism shocked the nation and led not only to tenement reform but also to the development of city playgrounds, neighborhood parks, and child labor laws. Would you agree that his photographs are "a mirror of reality," or did Riis interpret and frame the "reality" he photographed?

SOURCE: *Five Cents a Spot*, drawing and photo: Library of Congress.

discovered to take pictures by flashlight." Armed with new magnesium cartridge flash pistols, Riis set out to shine light in the dark corners of New York. "Our party carried terror wherever it went," Riis recalled. "The spectacle of strange men invading a house in the midnight hours armed with [flash] pistols which they shot off recklessly was hardly reassuring." But the results were a huge step forward for photojournalism.

Riis's book *How the Other Half Lives* (1890) made photographic history. Along with Riis's text and engravings of his drawings, it contained reproductions of seventeen photographs taken with his camera and

To ensure passage of the **Hepburn Act**, which would increase the power of the ICC, Roosevelt worked skillfully behind the scenes. In its final form, the Hepburn Act, passed in May 1906, gave the ICC the power to set rates subject to court review. Committed progressives like La Follette judged the law a defeat for reform. Die-hard conservatives branded it a "piece of populism." Both sides exaggerated. The law left the courts too much power and failed to provide adequate means for the ICC to determine rates, but its passage proved a landmark in federal control of private industry. For the first time, a government commission had the power to investigate private business records and to set rates.

Always an apt reader of the public temper, Roosevelt witnessed a growing appetite for reform. Revelations of corporate and political wrongdoing and social injustice filled the papers and boosted the sales of popular magazines. Roosevelt, who wielded publicity like a weapon in his pursuit of reform, counted many of the new investigative journalists, including Jacob Riis, among his friends. (See "Visualizing History," above.) But he warned them against going too far, citing the allegorical character in *Pilgrim's Progress* who was so busy raking muck that he took no notice of higher things. Roosevelt's criticism gave the American vocabulary a new word, *muckraker,* which journalists soon appropriated as a title of honor.

Muckraking, as Roosevelt well knew, provided enormous help in securing progressive legislation. In the spring of 1906, publicity generated by the muckrakers about poisons in patent medicines goaded the Senate, with Roosevelt's backing, into passing a pure food and drug bill. Opponents in the House of Representatives hoped to keep the legislation locked up in committee. There it would have died, were it not for the publication of Upton Sinclair's novel *The Jungle* (1906), with its sensational account of filthy conditions in meatpacking plants.

The Jungle

Upton Sinclair, a lifelong socialist, wrote *The Jungle* to expose the evils of capitalism. But readers were more horrified by his descriptions of the unsanitary conditions in the meatpacking industry, where the novel's hapless hero sees rats, filth, and diseased animals processed into meat products. After reading the book, President Theodore Roosevelt could no longer stomach sausage for breakfast. The president immediately ordered a study of conditions in the meatpacking industry. The public outcry surrounding *The Jungle* contributed to the enactment of pure food and drug legislation and a federal meat inspection law. Sinclair ruefully remarked, "I aimed at the public's heart, but I hit them in the stomach." Picture Research Consultants, Inc.

A massive public outcry led to the passage of the **Pure Food and Drug Act** and the Meat Inspection Act in 1906.

In the waning years of his administration, Roosevelt allied with the more progressive elements of the Republican Party. In speech after speech, he attacked "malefactors of great wealth." Styling himself a "radical," he claimed credit for leading the "ultra conservative" party of McKinley to a position of "progressive conservatism and conservative radicalism."

When an economic panic developed in the fall of 1907, business interests quickly blamed the president. The panic of 1907 proved severe but short. Once again, J. P. Morgan stepped in to avert disaster, this time switching funds from one bank to another to prop up weak institutions. For his services, he claimed the Tennessee Coal and Iron Company, an independent steel business that had long been coveted by the U.S. Steel Corporation. Morgan dispatched his lieutenants to Washington, where they told Roosevelt that the sale of the company would aid the economy "but little benefit" U.S. Steel. Willing to take the word of a gentleman, Roosevelt tacitly agreed not to institute antitrust proceedings against U.S. Steel over the acquisition. Roosevelt later learned that Morgan had been less than candid. U.S. Steel acquired Tennessee Coal and Iron for a price well below market value, doing away with a competitor and undercutting the economy of the Southeast. Roosevelt's promise not to institute antitrust proceedings against U.S. Steel would give rise to the charge that he acted as a tool of the Morgan interests.

The charge of collusion between business and government underscored the extent to which corporate leaders like Morgan found federal regulation preferable to unbridled competition or harsher state measures. During the Progressive Era, enlightened business leaders cooperated with government in the hope of avoiding antitrust prosecution. Convinced that regulation and not trust-busting offered the best way to deal with big business, Roosevelt never acknowledged that his regulatory policies fostered an alliance between business and government that today is called corporate liberalism.

Roosevelt and Conservation

In the area of conservation, Roosevelt proved indisputably ahead of his time. When he took office, some 43 million acres of forestland remained as government reserves. He more than quadrupled that number to 194 million acres. To conserve natural resources, he fought western cattle barons, lumber kings, mining interests, and powerful leaders in Congress, including Speaker of the House Joseph Cannon, who vowed to spend "not one cent for scenery."

As the first president to have lived and worked in the West, Roosevelt came to the White House convinced of the need for better management of the nation's rivers and forests and the preservation of wildlife and wilderness. During his presidency, he placed the nation's conservation policy in the hands of scientifically trained experts like his chief forester, Gifford Pinchot. Pinchot preached conservation — the efficient use of natural resources. Willing to permit grazing, lumbering, and the development of hydroelectric power, conservationists fought private interests only when they felt business acted irresponsibly

or threatened to monopolize water and electric power. Preservationists like John Muir, founder of the Sierra Club, believed that the wilderness needed to be protected. Roosevelt, who hiked Yosemite with Muir, understood the need for both preservation and conservation. (See "Historical Question," page 692.)

Roosevelt's multifaceted personality encompassed many contradictions. A fervent Darwinian naturalist and an (overly) enthusiastic game hunter, a conservationist who built big dams and a preservationist who saved the redwoods, Roosevelt aimed to have it both ways. And he did.

One of Roosevelt's first acts as president was to establish a pelican refuge in Florida. An avid bird-watcher since his youth, he added 50 more bird reservations from Florida to Alaska

MAP ACTIVITY

Map 21.1   National Parks and Forests

The national park system in the West began with Yellowstone in 1872. Grand Canyon, Yosemite, Kings Canyon, and Sequoia followed in the 1890s. During his presidency, Theodore Roosevelt added six parks — Crater Lake, Wind Cave, Petrified Forest, Lassen Volcanic, Mesa Verde, and Zion.

READING THE MAP: Collectively, do national parks or national forests encompass more land? According to the map, how many national parks were created before 1910? How many were created after 1910?

CONNECTIONS: How do conservation and preservation differ? Why did Roosevelt believe that saving land in the West was important? What principles guided the national land use policy of the Roosevelt administration?

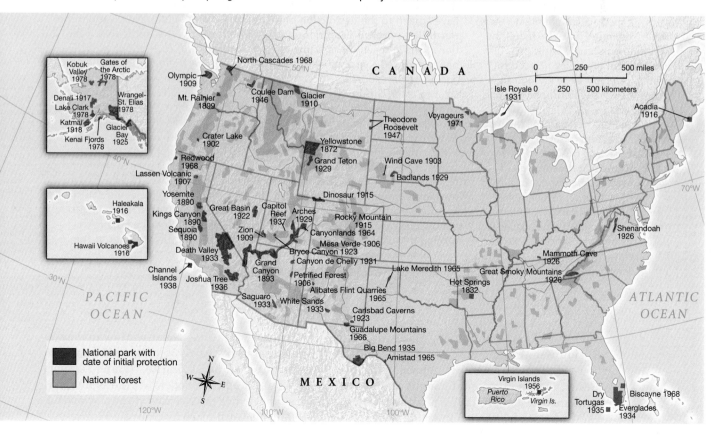

Progressives and Conservation: Should Hetch Hetchy Be Dammed or Saved?

In 1890, President Benjamin Harrison signed into law an act setting aside two million acres in California's Yosemite Valley and designating Yosemite a national park. For naturalist John Muir, the founder of the Sierra Club, the act marked a victory in his crusade to guarantee that "incomparable Yosemite" would be preserved for posterity. But Muir's fight was not yet over.

The growing city of San Francisco needed water and power, and Mayor James Phelan soon sought to obtain water rights in Hetch Hetchy, a spectacular mountain valley within Yosemite's borders. There, the Tuolumne River could easily be dammed and the valley flooded to create a reservoir large enough to ensure the city's water supply for one hundred years.

When Muir heard of the plan, he sprang into action to save Hetch Hetchy. "That any one would try to destroy such a place seems incredible," he wrote, describing the valley as "one of Nature's rarest and most precious mountain temples." All of Yosemite National Park, he argued, should remain sacrosanct. In 1903, the secretary of the interior concurred, denying San Francisco

supervisors commercial use of Hetch Hetchy on the grounds that it lay within the national park.

But the San Francisco earthquake and resulting fire in 1906 created a groundswell of sympathy for the devastated city. In this climate, San Francisco renewed its efforts to obtain Hetch Hetchy and in 1907 succeeded in gaining authorization to proceed with plans to dam the river and flood the valley.

Given President Theodore Roosevelt's commitment to conservation, how could his administration have agreed to the destruction of the Hetch Hetchy valley? Historians traditionally have styled the struggle as one that pitted conservationists against preservationists. Roosevelt's chief forester, Gifford Pinchot, represented the forces of conservation, or managed use. To him, the battle was not over preservation but over public versus private control of water and power. Roosevelt somewhat reluctantly agreed, although he softened the blow by designating a redwood sanctuary north of San Francisco a national monument in 1907 and naming it Muir Woods.

California progressives, who swept into office with the election of

Hiram Johnson as governor in 1910, argued that if Congress did not grant the city of San Francisco the right to control Hetch Hetchy, the powerful Pacific Gas and Electric Company (PG&E) would monopolize the city's light and power industry. These progressives dismissed Muir and his followers as "nature fakers" and judged them little more than dupes in the machinations of PG&E.

For their part, Muir and the preservationists, although they fought for the integrity of the national parks, did not champion the preservation of wilderness for its own sake. The urban professional men and women who joined the Sierra Club saw nature as a retreat and restorative for city dwellers. The club hosted an annual camping trip to popularize Yosemite and spoke in glowing terms of plans to build new roads and hotels that would make the "healing power of Nature" accessible to "thousands of tired, nerve-shaken, over-civilized people." As historian Robert Righter has pointed out, the battle over Hetch Hetchy represented not so much conservation versus preservation, or managed use versus wilderness, as it did the victory of water and power over tourism and recreation.

Nevertheless, the engineers and irrigation men who dammed Hetch Hetchy demonstrated a breathtaking arrogance. Speaking for them, Franklin Lane, interior secretary under Woodrow Wilson, proclaimed, "The mountains are our enemy. We must pierce them and make them serve. The sinful rivers we must curb." Lane and the conservationists won the day. In 1913, Congress passed the Raker Act authorizing the building of the O'Shaughnessy Dam, completed a decade later. To build the dam, the

during his presidency. The passage of the Antiquities Act in 1906 gave the president unchecked power to protect archaeological, scientific, and environmentally significant federal lands instead of "dilly dallying" with a "tortoise-paced Congress." Roosevelt wielded his power

with relish, creating 18 national monuments, 6 national parks, and 150 national forests. He prided himself on saving the Grand Canyon from miners and developers. At the same time, he supported the Newlands Reclamation Act (1902), much criticized by today's ecologists, as

Hetch Hetchy valley was first denuded of its trees and then flooded under two hundred feet of water. Muir did not live to see the destruction of Hetch Hetchy. He died in 1914, cursing the "dark damn-dam-damnation." But his fight to save Hetch Hetchy galvanized the preservation movement and led to the passage of the National Park Service Act in 1916 creating a federal agency to protect the nation's parks.

The last chapter in the battle over Hetch Hetchy may yet be written. In 1987, President Ronald Reagan's secretary of the interior, Donald Hodel, shocked San Francisco by suggesting the removal of the O'Shaughnessy Dam and the restoration of the Hetch Hetchy valley. Although it is unlikely that the dam will be demolished (it supplies San Francisco not only with water but also with revenue from electric power), advocates for the restoration of the Hetch Hetchy valley continue to rally to the cause. As Ken Browner of the Sierra Club wrote, "Waiting in Yosemite National Park, under water, is a potential masterpiece of restoration" and a chance "to correct the biggest environmental mistake ever committed against the National Park System."

Thinking about Beliefs and Attitudes

1. What does the damming of Hetch Hetchy tell us about the Roosevelt administration's conservation policies in the West?

2. Given Roosevelt's conservation policies overall, are critics right in accusing him of failing to preserve the wilderness?

Roosevelt and Muir in Yosemite
This 1903 photograph shows President Theodore Roosevelt on a camping trip in Yosemite National Park with John Muir. Roosevelt and Muir later clashed over the flooding of the Hetch Hetchy valley in Yosemite. Roosevelt and his chief forester, Gifford Pinchot, favored giving San Francisco the right to dam the valley to supply water and power. Muir bitterly noted that Pinchot had never bothered to visit the valley he condemned to a watery grave. Theodore Roosevelt Collection, Harvard College Library.

a measure to irrigate the West by building large dams and reservoirs in the "conquest" of the desert ecosystem and the promotion of population growth.

In 1907, Congress attempted to put the brakes on Roosevelt's conservation program by passing a law limiting his power to create forest reserves in six western states. In the days leading up to the law's enactment, Roosevelt feverishly created twenty-one new reserves and enlarged eleven more, saving 16 million acres from development. Once again, Roosevelt had outwitted his adversaries.

"Opponents of the forest service turned hand-springs in their wrath," he wrote, "but the threats . . . were really only a tribute to the efficiency of our action." Worried that private utilities were gobbling up waterpower sites and creating a monopoly of hydroelectric power, he connived with Pinchot to withdraw 2,565 power sites from private use by designating them "ranger stations." Firm in his commitment to wild America, Roosevelt proved willing to stretch the law when it served his ends. His legacy is more than 234 million acres of American wilderness saved for posterity (Map 21.1).

The Big Stick

Roosevelt's activism extended to his foreign policy, where he worked to buttress the nation's newly won place among world leaders. A fierce proponent of America's interests abroad, he believed that Congress was inept in foreign affairs, and he relied on executive power to pursue a vigorous foreign policy, sometimes stretching the powers of the presidency beyond legal limits. In his relations with the European powers, he relied on military strength and diplomacy, a combination he aptly described with the aphorism "Speak softly but carry a big stick." In the Caribbean, Roosevelt jealously guarded the U.S. sphere of influence defined in the Monroe Doctrine. His proprietary attitude toward the Western Hemisphere became evident in the case of the Panama Canal. Roosevelt had long been a supporter of a canal linking the Caribbean and the Pacific. By enabling ships to move quickly from the Atlantic to the Pacific, a canal would trim 8,000 miles from a coast-to-coast voyage and effectively double the U.S. Navy's power.

VISUAL ACTIVITY

"The World's Constable"

In this political cartoon from 1905, President Theodore Roosevelt, dressed as a constable, wields the club of "The New Diplomacy" in one hand with "Arbitration" tucked under his arm. The Roosevelt Corollary to the Monroe Doctrine made the United States the Western Hemisphere's policeman, a role Roosevelt relished. The Granger Collection, NYC.

READING THE IMAGE: How does this political cartoon visually represent Roosevelt's foreign policy? Does it appear to be supportive or critical of his policies? How does it treat the other peoples of the world?

CONNECTIONS: What aspects of Roosevelt's foreign policy ideas and actions are depicted in the cartoon?

THE WORLD'S CONSTABLE.

Having decided on a route across the Panamanian isthmus (a narrow strip of land connecting North and South America), then part of Colombia, Roosevelt in 1902 offered the Colombian government a one-time sum of $10 million and an annual rent of $250,000. When the government in Bogotá refused to accept the offer, Roosevelt became incensed at what he called the "homicidal corruptionists" in Colombia for trying to "blackmail" the United States. At the prompting of a group of New York investors, the Panamanians staged an uprising in 1903, and with unseemly haste the U.S. government recognized the new government within twenty-four hours. The Panamanians promptly accepted the $10 million, and the building got under way. The canal would take eleven years and $375 million to complete; it opened in 1914 (Map 21.2).

In the wake of the Panama affair, a confrontation with Germany over Venezuela, and yet another default on a European debt, this time in the Dominican Republic, Roosevelt announced in 1904 what became known as the **Roosevelt Corollary** to the Monroe Doctrine. Couched in the moralistic rhetoric typical of Roosevelt, the corollary declared that the United States would not intervene in Latin America as long as nations there conducted their affairs with "decency." But the United States would step in if any Latin American nation proved guilty of "brutal wrongdoing." The Roosevelt Corollary in effect made the United States the policeman of the Western Hemisphere and served notice to the European powers to keep out.

In Asia, Roosevelt inherited the Open Door policy initiated by Secretary of State John Hay in 1899, designed to ensure U.S. commercial entry into China. As Britain, France, Russia, Japan, and Germany raced to secure Chinese trade and territory, Roosevelt was tempted to use force to enter the fray and gain economic or possibly territorial concessions. As a result of victory in the Spanish-American War, the United States already enjoyed a foothold in the Philippines. Realizing that Americans would not support an aggressive Asian policy, Roosevelt sensibly held back.

In his relations with Europe, Roosevelt sought to establish the United States, fresh from its victory over Spain, as a rising force in world affairs. When tensions flared between France and Germany in Morocco in 1905, Roosevelt mediated at a conference in Algeciras, Spain, where he worked to maintain a balance of power that helped neutralize German ambitions. His skillful mediation gained him a reputation as an astute player on the world stage and demonstrated the nation's new presence in world affairs.

The Roosevelt Corollary in Action

MAP ACTIVITY

Map 21.2 The Panama Canal, 1914
The Panama Canal, completed in 1914, bisects the isthmus in a series of massive locks and dams. As Theodore Roosevelt had planned, the canal greatly strengthened the U.S. Navy by allowing ships to move from the Atlantic to the Pacific in a matter of days.

READING THE MAP: How long was the trip from New York to San Francisco before the Panama Canal was built? After it was built?

CONNECTIONS: How did Roosevelt's desire for a canal lead to independence for Panama? How did the canal benefit the U.S. Navy?

Roosevelt earned the Nobel Peace Prize in 1906 for his role in negotiating an end to the Russo-Japanese War, which had broken out when the Japanese invaded Chinese Manchuria, threatening Russia's sphere of influence in the area. Once again, Roosevelt sought to maintain a balance of power, in this case working to curb Japanese expansionism. Roosevelt admired the Japanese, judging them "the most dashing fighters in the world," but he did not want Japan to become too strong in Asia.

When good relations with Japan were jeopardized by discriminatory legislation in California calling for segregated public schools for Asians, Roosevelt smoothed over the incident and negotiated the "Gentlemen's Agreement" in 1907, which allowed the Japanese to save face by voluntarily restricting immigration to the United States. To demonstrate America's naval power and to counter Japan's growing bellicosity, Roosevelt dispatched the Great White Fleet, sixteen of the navy's most up-to-date battleships, on a "goodwill mission" around the world. U.S. relations with Japan improved, and in the 1908 Root-Takahira agreement the two nations pledged to maintain the Open Door and support the status quo in the Pacific. Roosevelt's show of American force constituted a classic example of his dictum "Speak softly but carry a big stick."

The Troubled Presidency of William Howard Taft

Roosevelt had promised on the eve of his election in 1904 that he would not seek another term. So he retired from the presidency in 1909 at age fifty and removed himself from the political scene by going on safari in Africa. He turned the White House over to **William Howard Taft**, a lawyer who had served as governor-general of the Philippines. In the presidential election of 1908, Taft soundly defeated the perennial Democratic candidate, William Jennings Bryan, in the electoral college. But Taft's popular majority amounted to only half of Roosevelt's record win in 1904.

A genial man with a talent for law, Taft had no experience in elective office, no feel for politics, and no nerve for controversy. His ambitious wife coveted the office and urged him to seek it. He would have been better off listening to his mother, who warned, "Roosevelt is a good fighter and enjoys it, but the malice of politics would make you miserable." Her words proved prophetic.

Once in office, Taft proved a perfect tool in the hands of Republicans who yearned for a return to the days of a less active executive. A lawyer by training and instinct, Taft believed that it was up to the courts, not the president, to arbitrate social issues. Roosevelt had carried presidential power to a new level, often flouting the separation of powers and showing thinly veiled contempt for Congress and the courts. A legalist, Taft found it difficult to condone Roosevelt's actions. Wary of the progressive insurgents in Congress, Taft relied increasingly on conservatives in the Republican Party. As a progressive senator lamented, "Taft is a ponderous and amiable man completely surrounded by men who know exactly what they want."

Taft's troubles began on the eve of his inaugural, when he called a special session of Congress to deal with the tariff, which had grown inordinately high under Republican rule. Roosevelt had been too politically astute to tackle the troublesome tariff issue, even though he knew that rates needed to be lowered. Taft blundered into the fray. The House of Representatives passed a modest downward revision, but the conservative Senate struck down the tax and added more than eight hundred crippling amendments to the tariff. The Payne-Aldrich bill that emerged actually raised the tariff, benefiting big business and the trusts at the expense of consumers. As if paralyzed, Taft neither fought for changes nor vetoed the measure. On a tour of the Midwest in 1909, he was greeted with jeers when he claimed, "I think the Payne bill is the best bill that the Republican Party ever passed." In the eyes of a growing number of Americans, Taft's praise of the tariff made him either a fool or a liar.

Taft's legalism soon got him into hot water in the area of conservation. He undid Roosevelt's work to preserve hydroelectric power sites when he learned that they had been improperly designated as ranger stations. And when Gifford Pinchot publicly denounced Taft's secretary of the interior as a tool of western land-grabbers, Taft fired Pinchot, touching off a storm of controversy that damaged Taft and alienated Roosevelt.

When Roosevelt returned to the United States in June 1910, he received a hero's welcome and attracted a stream of visitors and reporters seeking his advice and opinions. Hurt, Taft kept his distance. By late summer, Roosevelt had taken sides with the progressive insurgents in his party. "Taft is utterly hopeless as a leader," Roosevelt confided to his son as he set out on a speaking tour of the West. Reading the mood of the country, Roosevelt began to sound more and more like a candidate.

With the Republican Party divided, the Democrats swept the congressional elections of

William Howard Taft

William Howard Taft had little aptitude for politics. When Theodore Roosevelt tapped him as his successor in 1908, Taft had never held an elected office. A legalist by training and temperament, Taft moved congenially in the conservative circles of the Republican Party. His actions dismayed progressives and eventually led Roosevelt to challenge him for the presidency in 1912. The break with Roosevelt saddened and embittered Taft. One symptom of his unhappiness was his weight. Already a hefty 320 pounds when he was elected, Taft ballooned to more than 355 pounds by the time he left office. Library of Congress.

1910. Branding the Payne-Aldrich tariff "the mother of trusts," they captured a majority in the House of Representatives and won several key governorships. The revitalized Democratic Party could look to new leaders, among them the progressive governor of New Jersey, Woodrow Wilson.

The new Democratic majority in the House, working with progressive Republicans in the Senate, achieved a number of key reforms, including legislation to regulate mine and railroad safety, to create the Children's Bureau in the Department of Labor, and to establish an eight-hour day for federal workers. Two significant constitutional amendments — the Sixteenth Amendment, which provided for a modest graduated income tax, and the Seventeenth Amendment, which called for the direct election of senators (formerly chosen by state legislatures) — went to the states, where they would win ratification in 1913. While Congress rode the high tide of progressive reform, Taft sat on the sidelines.

In foreign policy, Taft continued Roosevelt's policy of extending U.S. influence abroad, but here, too, Taft had a difficult time following in Roosevelt's footsteps. His policy of **dollar diplomacy** championed commercial goals rather than the strategic aims Roosevelt had pursued. Taft naively assumed he could substitute "dollars for bullets." In the Caribbean, he provoked anti-American feeling by attempting to force commercial treaties on Nicaragua and Honduras and by dispatching U.S. Marines to Nicaragua and the Dominican Republic in 1912 pursuant to the Roosevelt Corollary. In Asia, he openly avowed his intent to promote "active intervention to secure for . . . our capitalists opportunity for profitable investment." Lacking Roosevelt's understanding of power politics, Taft never recognized that an aggressive commercial policy could not exist without the willingness to use military might to back it up.

Taft faced the limits of dollar diplomacy when revolution broke out in Mexico in 1911. Under pressure to protect American investments, which amounted to more than $4 billion, he mobilized troops along the border. In the end, however, with no popular support for a war with Mexico, he had to fall back on diplomatic pressure to salvage American interests.

Taft hoped to encourage world peace through the use of a world court and arbitration. He unsuccessfully sponsored a series of arbitration treaties that Roosevelt, who prized national honor more than international law, vehemently opposed as weak and cowardly. By 1910, Roosevelt had become a vocal critic of Taft's foreign policy, which he dismissed as "maudlin folly." The final breach between Taft and Roosevelt came in 1911, when Taft's attorney general filed an antitrust suit against U.S. Steel. In its brief against the corporation, the government cited Roosevelt's agreement with the Morgan interests in the 1907 acquisition

Taft's "Dollar Diplomacy"

BAHAMAS (Br.)
Gulf of Mexico
CUBA
HAITI
MEXICO   Jamaica (Br.)
BRITISH HONDURAS
DOMINICAN REPUBLIC
HONDURAS
Caribbean Sea
NICARAGUA
GUAT.
COSTA RICA   PANAMA
VEN.

◼ U.S. intervention   COLOMBIA

of Tennessee Coal and Iron. The incident greatly embarrassed Roosevelt. Thoroughly enraged, he lambasted Taft's "archaic" antitrust policy and hinted that he might be persuaded to run for president again.

> **REVIEW**   In what ways did Roosevelt's domestic policies respond to progressive demands?

▶ Woodrow Wilson and Progressivism at High Tide

Progressives' disillusionment with Taft resulted in a split in the Republican Party and the creation of a new Progressive Party led by Theodore Roosevelt. In the election of 1912, four candidates, including Socialist Eugene V. Debs, styled themselves "progressives." Democrat **Woodrow Wilson**, with a minority of the popular vote, won the election. Born in Virginia and raised in Georgia, he became the first southerner to be elected president since 1844 and only the second Democrat to occupy the White House since Reconstruction. A believer in states' rights, Wilson nevertheless promised legislation to break the hold of the trusts.

> **"We shall not falter, we stand at Armageddon and do battle for the Lord."**
> — THEODORE ROOSEVELT, speaking at the Bull Moose Party convention

This lean, ascetic scholar was, as one biographer conceded, a man whose "political convictions were never as fixed as his ambition." Although he owed his governorship to the Democratic machine, he quickly turned his back on the bosses and, with his eye on the presidency, put New Jersey in the vanguard of progressivism. He brought to the White House a gift for oratory, a stern will, and a set of fixed beliefs. Wilson proved rarely able to compromise. His tendency to turn differences of opinion into personal hatreds would impair his leadership and damage his presidency. Fortunately for Wilson, he came to power with a Democratic Congress eager to do his bidding.

Progressive Insurgency and the Election of 1912

Convinced that Taft was "hopelessly inept," Roosevelt announced his candidacy for the Republican nomination with the colorful phrase "My hat is in the ring." But for all his popularity, Roosevelt no longer controlled the party machinery. Taft, with uncharacteristic strength, refused to step aside. As he bitterly told a journalist, "Even a rat in a corner will fight." Roosevelt took advantage of newly passed primary election laws and ran in thirteen states, winning 278 delegates to Taft's 48. But at the Chicago convention, Taft's bosses refused to seat the Roosevelt delegates. Fistfights broke out on the convention floor as Taft won nomination on the first ballot. Crying robbery, Roosevelt's supporters bolted the party.

Seven weeks later, in the same Chicago auditorium, the hastily organized Progressive Party met to nominate Roosevelt. Amid a thunder of applause, Jane Addams seconded Roosevelt's nomination. Full of reforming zeal, the delegates chose Roosevelt and Hiram Johnson to head the new party and approved the most ambitious platform since that of the Populists. Planks called for woman suffrage, presidential primaries, conservation of natural resources, an end to child labor, workers' compensation, a minimum wage that would include women workers, social security, and a federal income tax.

Roosevelt arrived in Chicago to accept the nomination and announced that he felt "as fit as a bull moose," giving the new party a nickname and a mascot. But for all the excitement and the cheering, the new Progressive Party was doomed, and the candidate knew it. The people may have supported the party, but the politicians, even progressives such as La Follette, stayed within the Republican fold. "I am under no illusion about it," Roosevelt confessed to a friend. "It is a forlorn hope." But he had gone too far to turn back. He led the Bull Moose Party into the fray, exhorting his followers in ringing biblical tones, "We shall not falter, we stand at Armageddon and do battle for the Lord."

The Democrats, delighted at the split in the Republican ranks, smelled victory. Their convention turned into a bitter fight for the nomination. After forty-six ballots, Woodrow Wilson became the party's nominee. Wilson's career in politics was nothing short of meteoric. He was elected governor of New Jersey in 1910, and after only eighteen months in office the former professor of political science and president of Princeton University found himself running for president of the United States.

Voters in 1912 could choose among four candidates who claimed to be progressives. Taft, Roosevelt, and Wilson each embraced the label, and even the Socialist candidate, Eugene V. Debs, styled himself a progressive. That the term *progressive* could stretch to cover these diverse candidates underscored major disagreements in

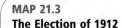

1912 Election Cartoon
In this 1912 political cartoon, an elephant — the mascot of the Republican Party (the Grand Old Party, or GOP) — and a donkey — representing the Democratic Party — react in alarm as a bull moose charges into the fray. The bull moose, with its spectacles and gleaming teeth, caricatures Theodore Roosevelt, the new Progressive Party's presidential candidate. Granger Collection.

progressive thinking about the relationship between business and government. Taft, in spite of his trust-busting, was generally viewed as the candidate of the old guard. The real contest for the presidency was between Roosevelt and Wilson and the two political philosophies summed up in their respective campaign slogans: "**The New Nationalism**" and "**The New Freedom**."

The New Nationalism expressed Roosevelt's belief in federal planning and regulation. He accepted the inevitability of big business but demanded that government act as "a steward of the people" to regulate the giant corporations. Wilson, schooled in the Democratic principles of limited government and states' rights, set a markedly different course with his New Freedom. Wilson promised to use antitrust legislation to get rid of big corporations and to give small businesses and farmers better opportunities in the marketplace.

The energy and enthusiasm of the Bull Moosers made the race seem closer than it was. In the end, the Republican vote split, while the Democrats remained united. No candidate claimed a majority in the race. Wilson captured a bare 42 percent of the popular vote. Roosevelt and his Bull Moose Party won 27 percent, an unprecedented tally for a new party. Taft came in third with 23 percent. The Socialist Party, led by Debs, captured 6 percent. In the electoral college, however, Wilson won a decisive 435 votes, with 88 going to Roosevelt and only 8 to Taft (Map 21.3). The Republican Party moved in a conservative direction, while the Progressive Party essentially collapsed after Roosevelt's defeat. It had always been, in the words of one astute observer, "a house divided against itself and already mortgaged."

Wilson's Reforms: Tariff, Banking, and the Trusts

Although he endorsed states' rights and opposed big government in his campaign, Wilson was prepared to work on the base built by Roosevelt to strengthen presidential power, exerting leadership to achieve banking reform and working through his party in Congress to accomplish the

MAP 21.3
The Election of 1912

Candidate	Electoral Vote	Popular Vote	Percent of Popular Vote
Woodrow Wilson (Democrat)	435	6,293,454	41.9
Theodore Roosevelt (Progressive)	88	4,119,538	27.4
William H. Taft (Republican)	8	3,484,980	23.2
Eugene V. Debs (Socialist)	0	900,672	6.1

Wilson Ribbon

With the Republicans divided in 1912, the Democrats turned to Woodrow Wilson to lead the party, nominating him on the forty-sixth ballot. In those days, prospective candidates generally did not attend the nominating convention. The ribbon in the photograph belonged to a member of the Democratic National Committee, who traveled to Wilson's summer home in Sea Girt, New Jersey, on August 7, 1912, to inform Wilson officially of his nomination. Democrats hoping for a wild celebration at Wilson's inauguration had their hopes dashed when Wilson, a Presbyterian teetotaler, called instead for a day of prayer. Collection of Janice L. and David J. Frent.

Democratic agenda. Before he was finished, Wilson presided over progressivism at high tide and lent his support not only to the platform of the Democratic Party but also to many of the Progressive Party's social reforms.

In March 1913, Wilson showed off his oratorical ability by becoming the first president since John Adams to go to Capitol Hill and speak directly to Congress. With the Democratic Party firmly in control, he called for tariff reform. "The object of the tariff," Wilson told Congress, "must be effective competition." The Democratic House of Representatives hastily passed the Underwood tariff, which lowered rates by 15 percent. To compensate for lost revenue, the House approved a moderate federal income tax. In the Senate, lobbyists for industries quietly went to work to get the tariff raised, but Wilson rallied public opinion by attacking the "industrious and insidious lobby." In the harsh glare of publicity, the Senate passed the Underwood tariff, which earned praise as "the most honest tariff since the Civil War."

Wilson next turned his attention to banking. The panic of 1907 dramatically testified to the failure of the banking system. That year, Roosevelt, like President Grover Cleveland before him, had to turn to J. P. Morgan to avoid economic catastrophe. But by the time Wilson came to office, Morgan's legendary power had come under close scrutiny. In 1913, a Senate committee investigated the "money trust," calling J. P. Morgan himself to testify. The committee uncovered an alarming concentration of banking power. J. P. Morgan and Company and its affiliates held 341 directorships in 112 corporations, controlling assets of more than $22 billion ($500 billion in today's dollars). The sensational findings created a mandate for banking reform.

The **Federal Reserve Act** of 1913 marked the most significant piece of domestic legislation of Wilson's presidency. It established a national banking system composed of twelve regional banks, privately controlled but regulated and supervised by the Federal Reserve Board, appointed by the president. It gave the United States its first efficient banking and currency system and, at the same time, provided for a greater degree of government control over banking. The new system made currency more elastic and credit adequate for the needs of business and agriculture. It did not, however, attempt to take control of the boom and bust cycles in the U.S. economy, which would produce the Great Depression of the 1930s (as discussed in chapters 23 and 24).

Wilson, flush with success, tackled the trust issue next. When Congress reconvened in January 1914, he supported the introduction and passage of the Clayton Antitrust Act to outlaw "unfair competition" — practices such as price discrimination and interlocking directorates (directors from one corporation sitting on the board of another). By spelling out unfair practices, Wilson hoped to guide business activity back to healthy competition without resorting to regulation. In the midst of the successful fight for the Clayton Act, Wilson changed course and threw his support behind the creation of the **Federal Trade Commission** (FTC), precisely the kind of federal regulatory agency that Roosevelt had advocated in his New Nationalism platform. The FTC, created in 1914, had not only wide investigatory powers but also the authority to prosecute corporations for "unfair trade practices" and to enforce its judgments by issuing "cease and desist" orders. Despite his campaign promises, Wilson's antitrust program worked to regulate rather than to break up big business.

By the fall of 1914, Wilson had exhausted the stock of ideas that made up the New Freedom. He alarmed progressives by declaring that the progressive movement had fulfilled its mission and that the country needed "a time of healing." Disgruntled progressives also disapproved of Wilson's conservative appointments. Having fought provisions in the Federal Reserve Act that would give bankers control, Wilson promptly named a banker as the first chief of the Federal Reserve Board. Appointments to the new FTC also went to conservative businessmen. The progressive penchant for expertise helps explain Wilson's choices. Believing that experts in the field could best understand the complex issues at stake, Wilson appointed bankers to oversee the banks and businessmen to regulate business.

Wilson, Reluctant Progressive

As Wilson repeatedly obstructed or obstinately refused to endorse further progressive reforms, progressives watched in dismay. He failed to support labor's demand for an end to court injunctions against labor unions. He twice threatened to veto legislation providing farm credits for nonperishable crops. He refused to support child labor legislation or woman suffrage. Wilson used the rhetoric of the New Freedom to justify his actions, claiming that his administration would condone "special privileges to none." But, in fact, his stance often reflected the interests of his small-business constituency.

In the face of Wilson's obstinacy, reform might have ended in 1913 had not politics intruded. In the congressional elections of 1914, the Republican Party, no longer split by Roosevelt's Bull Moose faction, won substantial gains. Democratic strategists, with their eyes on the 1916 presidential race, recognized that Wilson needed to pick up support in the Midwest and the West by capturing votes from former Bull Moose progressives. Wilson responded belatedly by lending his support to reform in the months leading up to the election of 1916. In a sharp about-face, he cultivated union labor, farmers, and social reformers. To please labor, he appointed progressive Louis Brandeis to the Supreme Court. To woo farmers, he threw his support behind legislation to obtain rural credits. And he won praise from labor by supporting workers' compensation and the Keating-Owen child labor law (1916), which outlawed the regular employment of children younger than sixteen. When a railroad strike threatened in the months before the election, Wilson practically ordered Congress to establish an eight-hour day on the railroads. He had moved a long way from his position in 1912 to embrace many of the social reforms championed by Theodore Roosevelt. As Wilson boasted, the Democrats had "opened their hearts to the demands of social justice" and had "come very near to car-

Progressive Poster Condemning Child Labor
This poster attacks child labor, borrowing the convention of the business flowchart to portray graphically how industries employing children were "making human junk." Progressives' concern for the plight of poor children won them the label "child savers." Although activists worked hard to pass the Keating-Owen Act prohibiting child labor in 1916, the Supreme Court declared the law unconstitutional two years later on the grounds that Congress had no right to regulate manufacturing within states. In its appeal to end child labor, what does this poster emphasize more — concern for children or concern for society? Library of Congress.

rying out the platform of the Progressive Party." Wilson's shift toward reform, along with his claim that he had kept the United States out of the war in Europe (as discussed in chapter 22), helped him win reelection in 1916.

REVIEW   How and why did Wilson's reform program evolve during his first term?

▶ The Limits of Progressive Reform

While progressivism called for a more active role for the liberal state, at heart it was a movement that sought reforms designed to preserve American institutions and stem the tide of more radical change. Its basic conservatism can be seen by comparing it with the more radical movements of socialism, radical labor, and birth control — and by looking at the groups progressive reform left behind, including women and African Americans.

Radical Alternatives

The year 1900 marked the birth of the Social Democratic Party in America, later called simply the **Socialist Party**. Like the progressives, the socialists were middle-class and native-born. They had broken with the older, more militant Socialist Labor Party precisely because of its dogmatic approach and immigrant constituency. The new group of socialists proved eager to appeal to a broad mass of disaffected Americans.

The Socialist Party chose as its presidential standard-bearer Eugene V. Debs, whose experience in the Pullman strike of 1894 (see chapter 20) convinced him that "there is no hope for the toiling masses of my countrymen, except by the pathways mapped out by Socialism." Debs would run for president five times, in every election (except 1916) from 1900 to 1920. The socialism Debs advocated preached cooperation over competition and urged men and women to liberate themselves from "the barbarism of private ownership and wage slavery." In the 1912 election, Debs indicted both old parties as "Tweedledee and Tweedledum," each dedicated to the preservation of capitalism and the continuation of the wage system. Only through socialism, he argued, could democracy exist. Styling the Socialist Party the "revolutionary party of the working class," he urged voters to rally to his standard. Debs's best showing came in 1912, when his 6 percent of the popular vote totaled more than 900,000 votes.

Farther to the left than the socialists stood the **Industrial Workers of the World** (IWW), nicknamed the Wobblies. In 1905, Debs, along with Western Federation of Miners leader William Dudley "Big Bill" Haywood, created the IWW, "one big union" dedicated to organizing the most destitute segment of the workforce, the unskilled workers disdained by Samuel Gompers's AFL: western miners, migrant farmwork-

ers, lumbermen, and immigrant textile workers. Haywood, a craggy-faced miner with one eye (he had lost the other in a childhood accident), was a charismatic leader and a proletarian intellectual. Seeing workers on the lowest rung of the social ladder as the victims of violent repression, the IWW advocated direct action, sabotage, and the general strike — tactics designed to trigger a workers' uprising. The IWW never had more than 10,000 members at any one time, although possibly as many as 100,000 workers belonged to the union at one time or another in the early twentieth century. Nevertheless, the IWW's influence on the country extended far beyond its numbers (as discussed in chapter 22).

In contrast to political radicals like Debs and Haywood, **Margaret Sanger** promoted birth control as a movement for social change. Sanger, a nurse who had worked among the poor on New York's Lower East Side, coined the term *birth control* in 1915 and launched a movement with broad social implications. Sanger and her followers saw birth control not only as a sexual and medical reform but also as a means to alter social and political power relationships and to alleviate human misery.

The desire for family limitation was widespread, and in this sense birth control was nothing new. The birthrate in the United States had been falling consistently throughout the nineteenth century. The average number of children per family dropped from 7.0 in 1800 to 3.6 by 1900. But the open advocacy of *contraception*, the use of artificial means to prevent pregnancy, struck many people as both new and shocking. And it was illegal. Anthony Comstock, New York City's commissioner of vice, promoted laws in the 1870s making it a felony not only to sell contraceptive devices like condoms and cervical caps but also to publish information on how to prevent pregnancy.

When Margaret Sanger used her militant feminist newspaper, the *Woman Rebel*, to promote birth control, the Post Office confiscated Sanger's publication and brought charges of obscenity against her. Facing arrest, she fled to Europe, only to return in 1916 as something of a national celebrity. In her absence, birth control had become linked with free speech and had been taken up as a liberal cause. Under public pressure, the government dropped the charges against Sanger, who undertook a nationwide tour to publicize the birth control cause.

Sanger then turned to direct action, opening the nation's first birth control clinic in the Brownsville section of Brooklyn in October 1916. Located in the heart of a Jewish and Italian immigrant

WE WANT DEBS

Margaret Sanger's Brownsville Birth Control Clinic
Margaret Sanger opened the first birth control clinic in the United States in the Brownsville section of Brooklyn in 1916. During the nine days it operated before police shut it down, more than four hundred women visited the clinic. Here, they are shown waiting patiently in line with their baby carriages. Sanger published her fliers in English, Yiddish, and Italian. Her clinic, located in the heart of an immigrant neighborhood, proved that immigrant women — including Italian Catholics and Russian Jews — wanted information about birth control as much as their middle- and upper-class Protestant counterparts did. Sophia Smith Collection, Smith College.

neighborhood, the clinic attracted 464 clients. On the tenth day, police shut down the clinic and threw Sanger in jail. By then, she had become a national figure, and the cause she championed had gained legitimacy, if not legality. After World War I, the birth control movement would become much less radical as Sanger turned to medical doctors for support and mouthed popular racist genetic theories. But in its infancy, the movement Sanger led was part of a radical vision for reforming the world that made common cause with the socialists and the IWW in challenging the limits of progressive reform.

Progressivism for White Men Only

The day before President Woodrow Wilson's inauguration in March 1913, the largest mass march to that date in the nation's history took place as more than five thousand demonstrators took to the streets in Washington to demand the vote for women. A rowdy crowd on hand to celebrate the Democrats' triumph attacked the marchers. Men spat at the suffragists and threw lighted cigarettes and matches at their clothing. "If my wife were

where you are," a burly cop told one suffragist, "I'd break her head." But for all the marching, Wilson pointedly ignored woman suffrage in his inaugural address the next day.

The march served as a reminder that the political gains of progressivism were not spread equally throughout the population. As the twentieth century dawned, women still could not vote in most states, although they had won major victories in the West. Increasingly, however, woman suffrage had become an international movement. In Great Britain, Emmeline Pankhurst and her daughters Cristabel and Sylvia promoted a new, militant suffragism. They seized the spotlight in a series of marches, mass meetings, and acts of civil disobedience that sometimes escalated into riots, violence, and arson.

Alice Paul, a Quaker social worker who had visited England and participated in suffrage activism there, returned to the United States in 1910 in time to plan the mass march on the eve of Wilson's inauguration and to lobby for a federal amendment to give women the vote. Paul's

> **"If my wife were where you are, I'd break her head."**
> —A Washington cop to a suffragist marcher

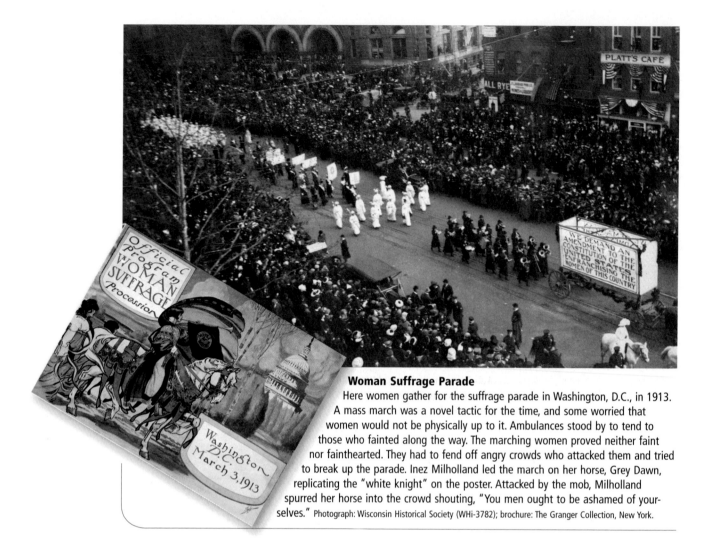

Woman Suffrage Parade
Here women gather for the suffrage parade in Washington, D.C., in 1913. A mass march was a novel tactic for the time, and some worried that women would not be physically up to it. Ambulances stood by to tend to those who fainted along the way. The marching women proved neither faint nor fainthearted. They had to fend off angry crowds who attacked them and tried to break up the parade. Inez Milholland led the march on her horse, Grey Dawn, replicating the "white knight" on the poster. Attacked by the mob, Milholland spurred her horse into the crowd shouting, "You men ought to be ashamed of yourselves." Photograph: Wisconsin Historical Society (WHi-3782); brochure: The Granger Collection, New York.

dramatic tactics alienated many in the National American Woman Suffrage Association. In 1916, Paul founded the militant National Woman's Party, which became the radical voice of the suffrage movement, advocating direct action such as mass marches and civil disobedience.

Women weren't the only group left out in progressive reform. Progressivism, as it was practiced in the West and South, was tainted with racism and sought to limit the rights of African and Asian Americans. Anti-Asian bigotry in the West led to a renewal of the Chinese Exclusion Act in 1902. At first, California governor Hiram Johnson stood against the strong anti-Asian prejudice of his state. But in 1913, he caved in to popular pressure and signed the Alien Land Law, which barred Japanese immigrants from purchasing land in California. The law was largely symbolic — ineffectual in practice because Japanese children born in the United States were U.S. citizens and property could be purchased in their names.

South of the Mason-Dixon line, the progressives' racism targeted African Americans.

Progressives preached the disfranchisement of black voters as a "reform." During the bitter electoral fights that had pitted Populists against Democrats in the 1890s, the party of white supremacy held its power by votes purchased or coerced from African Americans. Southern progressives proposed to "reform" the electoral system by eliminating black voters. Beginning in 1890 with Mississippi, southern states curtailed the African American vote through devices such as poll taxes (fees required for voting) and literacy tests. The racist intent of southern voting legislation became especially clear after 1900 when states resorted to the grandfather clause, a legal provision that allowed men who failed a literacy test to vote if their grandfathers had cast a ballot. Grandfathering thus permitted illiterate southern white men to vote while excluding illiterate blacks.

The Progressive Era also witnessed the rise of Jim Crow laws to segregate public facilities. The new railroads precipitated segregation in the South where it had rarely existed before, at least on paper. Soon, separate railcars, separate waiting rooms, separate bathrooms, and separate dining facilities for blacks sprang up across the South. In courtrooms in Mississippi, blacks were required to swear on a separate Bible.

In the face of this growing repression, **Booker T. Washington**, the preeminent black leader of the day, urged caution and restraint. A former slave, Washington had opened the Tuskegee Institute in Alabama in 1881 to teach vocational skills to African Americans. He emphasized education and economic progress for his race and urged African Americans to put aside issues of political and social equality. In an 1895 speech in Atlanta that came to be known as the **Atlanta Compromise**, he stated, "In all things that are purely social we can be as separate as the fingers, yet one as the hand in all things essential to mutual progress." Washington's accommodationist policy appealed to whites and elevated "the wizard of Tuskegee" to the role of national spokesman for African Americans.

The year after Washington proclaimed the Atlanta Compromise, the Supreme Court upheld the legality of racial segregation, affirming in *Plessy v. Ferguson* (1896) the constitutionality of the doctrine of "separate but equal." Blacks could be segregated in separate schools, restrooms, and other facilities as long as the facilities were "equal" to those provided for whites. Of course, facilities for blacks rarely proved equal. In the North, where racism of a different sort led to a clamor for legislation to restrict immigration, support for African American equality found few advocates. And with anti-Asian bigotry strong in the West, the doctrine of "white supremacy" found increasing support in all sections of the country.

When Theodore Roosevelt invited Booker T. Washington to dine at the White House in 1901, a storm of racist criticism erupted. One southern editor fumed that the White House "had been painted black." But Roosevelt summoned Washington to talk politics and patronage, not African American rights. Roosevelt's unquestioned racial prejudice became clear in the Brownsville incident in 1906, when he dishonorably discharged an entire battalion of 167 black soldiers because he suspected (although there was no proof) that they were shielding the murderer of a white saloon-keeper killed in a shoot-out in the Texas town.

Woodrow Wilson brought to the White House southern attitudes toward race and racial segregation. He instituted segregation in the federal workforce, especially the Post Office, and approved segregated drinking fountains and restrooms in the nation's capital. When critics attacked the policy, Wilson insisted that segregation was "in the interest of the Negro."

In 1906, a major race riot in Atlanta called into question Booker T. Washington's strategy of uplift and accommodation. For three days in September, the streets of Atlanta ran red with blood as angry white mobs chased and cornered any blacks they happened upon, pulling passengers from streetcars and invading black

DINNER GIVEN AT THE WHITE HOUSE BY PRESIDENT ROOSEVELT TO BOOKER T. WASHINGTON, OCTOBER 17th, 1901

Booker T. Washington and Theodore Roosevelt Dine at the White House
When Theodore Roosevelt invited Booker T. Washington to the White House in 1901, he stirred up a hornet's nest of controversy that continued into the election of 1904. This Republican campaign piece gives the meeting a positive slant, showing Roosevelt and a light-skinned Washington sitting under a portrait of Abraham Lincoln, a symbol of the party's historic commitment to African Americans. Democrats portrayed the meeting in a very different light; their campaign buttons pictured Washington with darker skin and implied that Roosevelt favored "race mingling" and had "painted the White House black." Collection of Janice L. and David J. Frent.

neighborhoods to kill and loot. An estimated 250 African Americans died in the riots — members of Atlanta's black middle class along with the poor and derelict. Professor William Crogman of Clark College noted the central irony of the riot: "Here we have worked and prayed and tried to make good men and women of our colored population," he observed, "and at our very doorstep the whites kill these good men." In Dark Town, a working-class neighborhood, blacks fought back to defend their homes, shooting into the white mob and driving off the attackers. In the aftermath of the riot, the city's leaders, black and white, managed to quash any nascent black unity by falling back on the old strategy of allying "the best white people and the best colored people." Yet the riot caused many African Americans to question Washington's strategy of gradualism and accommodation.

Foremost among Washington's critics stood **W. E. B. Du Bois**, a Harvard graduate who urged African Americans to fight for civil rights and racial justice. In *The Souls of Black Folk* (1903),

Du Bois attacked the "Tuskegee Machine," comparing Washington to a political boss who used his influence to silence his critics and reward his followers. Du Bois founded the Niagara movement in 1905, calling for universal male suffrage, civil rights, and leadership composed of a black intellectual elite. The Atlanta riot only bolstered his resolve. In 1909, the Niagara movement helped found the **National Association for the Advancement of Colored People** (NAACP), a coalition of blacks and whites that sought legal and political rights for African Americans through the courts. In the decades that followed, the NAACP came to represent the future for African Americans, while Booker T. Washington, who died in 1915, represented the past.

REVIEW   How did race, class, and gender shape the limits of progressive reform?

▶ Conclusion: The Transformation of the Liberal State

Progressivism was never a radical movement. Its goal remained to reform the existing system — by government intervention if necessary — but without uprooting any of the traditional American political, economic, or social institutions. As Theodore Roosevelt, the bellwether of the movement, insisted, "The only true conservative is the man who resolutely sets his face toward the future." Roosevelt was such a man, and progressivism was such a movement. But although progressivism was never radical, neither was it the laissez-faire liberalism of the previous century. Progressives' willingness to use the power of government to regulate business and achieve a measure of social justice redefined liberalism in the twentieth century, tying it to the expanded power of the state.

Progressivism contained many paradoxes. A diverse coalition of individuals and interests, the progressive movement began at the grass roots but left as its legacy a stronger presidency and unprecedented federal involvement in the economy and social welfare. A movement that believed in social justice, progressivism often promoted social control. And while progressives called for greater democracy, they fostered elitism with their worship of experts and efficiency and often failed to champion equality for women and minorities.

Whatever its inconsistencies and limitations, progressivism took action to deal with the problems posed by urban industrialism. Progressivism

W. E. B. Du Bois

W. E. B. Du Bois grew up in Great Barrington, Massachusetts, and in 1895 he became the first African American to earn a doctorate from Harvard. Throughout his life, he urged African Americans not only to focus on their own education and economic prospects but also to work politically for racial equality. In *The Souls of Black Folk* (1903), he wrote that he wished "to make it possible for a man to be both a Negro and an American, without being cursed and spit upon by his fellows, without having the doors of Opportunity closed roughly in his face." Special Collections Department, W. E. B. Du Bois Library, University of Massachusetts Amherst.

saw grassroots activists address social problems on the local and state levels and search for national solutions. By increasing the power of the presidency and expanding the power of the state, progressives worked to bring about greater social justice and to achieve a better balance between government and business. Jane Addams and Theodore Roosevelt could lay equal claim to the movement that redefined liberalism and launched the liberal state of the twentieth century. War on a global scale would provide progressivism with yet another challenge even before it had completed its ambitious agenda.

▶ Selected Bibliography

General

Maureen A. Flanagan, *America Reformed: Progressives and Progressivisms, 1890s–1920s* (2007).

Jackson Lears, *Rebirth of a Nation: The Making of Modern America, 1877–1920* (2009).

Michael McGerr, *A Fierce Discontent: The Rise and Fall of the Progressive Movement in America* (2005).

Eric Ruchway, *Blessed among Nations: How the World Made America* (2006).

Grassroots Progressivism

Victoria Bissell Brown, *The Education of Jane Addams* (2004).

Robert Kanigel, *The One Best Way: Frederick Winslow Taylor* (1997).

Louise W. Knight, *Citizen: Jane Addams and the Struggle for Democracy* (2005).

Seth Koven and Sonya Michel, eds., *Mothers of a New World: Maternalist Politics and the Origins of the Welfare State* (1993).

Robyn Muncy, *Creating a Female Dominion in American Reform* (1991).

Kathryn Kish Sklar, *Florence Kelley and the Nation's Work: The Rise of Women's Political Culture, 1830–1900* (1995).

Landon R. Y. Storre, *Civilizing Capitalism: The National Consumers' League, Women's Activism, and Labor Standards in the New Deal Era* (2000).

Nancy C. Unger, *Fighting Bob La Follette: The Righteous Reformer* (2000).

David Von Drehle, *Triangle: The Fire That Changed America* (2003).

Progressive Politics and Diplomacy

Douglas Brinkley, *The Wilderness Warrior: Theodore Roosevelt and the Crusade for America* (2009).

John Milton Cooper, *Woodrow Wilson: A Biography* (2009).

Alan Dawley, *Changing the World: American Progressives in War and Revolution* (2003).

Lewis L. Gould, *Four Hats in the Ring: The 1912 Election and the Birth of Modern American Politics* (2008); *William Howard Taft: Presidency* (2009).

Kristin Hoganson, *Consumers' Imperium: The Global Production of American Domesticity, 1865–1920* (2007).

Matthew Frye Jacobson, *Barbarian Virtues: The United States Encounters Foreign Peoples at Home and Abroad, 1876–1917* (2000).

Robert Johnston, *The Radical Middle Class: Populist Democracy and the Question of Capitalism in Progressive Era Portland, Oregon* (2003).

Walter LaFeber, *The American Search for Opportunity, 1865–1913* (1994).

Kevin Matson, *Creating a Democratic Public: The Struggle for Urban Participatory Democracy during the Progressive Era* (1998).

Robert W. Righter, *The Battle over Hetch Hetchy: America's Most Controversial Dam and the Birth of Modern Environmentalism* (2005).

Daniel T. Rodgers, *Atlantic Crossings: Social Politics in a Progressive Age* (1998).

Radicals, Race Relations, and Woman Suffrage

Mary Jo Buhle, *Women and American Socialism, 1870–1920* (1981).

Ellen Chesler, *Woman of Valor: Margaret Sanger and the Birth Control Movement in America* (1993).

Melvyn Dubofsky, *"Big Bill" Haywood* (1987).

Gary Gerstle, *American Crucible: Race and Nation in the Twentieth Century* (2002).

Glenda Elizabeth Gilmore, *Gender and Jim Crow: Women and the Politics of White Supremacy in North Carolina, 1896–1920* (1996).

David Fort Godshalk, *Veiled Visions: The 1906 Atlanta Race Riot and the Reshaping of American Race Relations* (2005).

Evelyn Higginbotham, *Righteous Discontent: The Women's Movement in the Black Baptist Church, 1880–1920* (1993).

David Levering Lewis, *W. E. B. Du Bois: Biography of a Race, 1868–1919* (1993).

Rebecca J. Mead, *How the Vote Was Won: Woman Suffrage in the Western United States, 1868–1914* (2004).

Nick Salvatore, *Eugene V. Debs: Citizen and Socialist* (1982).

▶ **FOR MORE BOOKS ABOUT TOPICS IN THIS CHAPTER,** see the Online Bibliography at **bedfordstmartins.com/roark.**

▶ **FOR ADDITIONAL PRIMARY SOURCES FROM THIS PERIOD,** see Michael Johnson, ed., *Reading the American Past*, Fifth Edition.

▶ **FOR WEB SITES, IMAGES, AND DOCUMENTS RELATED TO TOPICS AND PLACES IN THIS CHAPTER,** visit Make History at **bedfordstmartins.com/roark.**

Reviewing Chapter 21

KEY TERMS

Explain each term's significance.

Grassroots Progressivism
    progressivism (p. 677)
    settlement house (p. 677)
    Jane Addams (p. 677)
    social gospel (p. 678)
    social purity movement (p. 679)
    Women's Trade Union League
      (WTUL) (p. 680)
    Muller v. Oregon (p. 682)
    National Consumers' League (NCL) (p. 682)
    municipal housekeeping (p. 683)

Progressivism: Theory and Practice
    reform Darwinism (p. 683)
    scientific management (p. 683)
    Thomas Loftin Johnson (p. 684)
    Robert M. La Follette (p. 684)
    Hiram Johnson (p. 684)

Progressivism Finds a President: Theodore Roosevelt
    Square Deal (p. 687)
    Hepburn Act (p. 689)
    muckraking (p. 690)
    Pure Food and Drug Act (p. 690)
    Roosevelt Corollary (p. 695)
    William Howard Taft (p. 696)
    dollar diplomacy (p. 697)

Woodrow Wilson and Progressivism at High Tide
    Woodrow Wilson (p. 698)
    The New Nationalism (p. 699)
    The New Freedom (p. 699)
    Federal Reserve Act (p. 700)
    Federal Trade Commission (FTC) (p. 700)

The Limits of Progressive Reform
    Socialist Party (p. 702)
    Industrial Workers of the World
      (IWW) (p. 702)
    Margaret Sanger (p. 702)
    Alice Paul (p. 703)
    Booker T. Washington (p. 705)
    Atlanta Compromise (p. 705)
    Plessy v. Ferguson (p. 705)
    W. E. B. Du Bois (p. 706)
    National Association for the
      Advancement of Colored People
      (NAACP) (p. 706)

REVIEW QUESTIONS

Use key terms and dates to support your answer.

1. What types of people were drawn to the progressive movement, and what motivated them? (pp. 677–683)

2. How did progressives justify their demand for more activist government? (pp. 683–685)

3. In what ways did Roosevelt's domestic policies respond to progressive demands? (pp. 685–698)

4. How and why did Wilson's reform program evolve during his first term? (pp. 698–701)

5. How did race, class, and gender shape the limits of progressive reform? (pp. 702–706)

MAKING CONNECTIONS

Draw on key terms, the timeline, and review questions.

1. Diverse approaches to reform came under the umbrella of progressivism. Discuss the work of three progressive reformers working at the grassroots or local government level. What do your examples reveal about progressivism? What characteristics connected their reform efforts? What separated them?

2. Theodore Roosevelt's foreign policy was summed up in the dictum "Speak softly but carry a big stick." Using two examples, describe how this policy worked. By contrast, why did Taft's policy of dollar diplomacy fail?

3. Opponents on the campaign stump, Theodore Roosevelt and Woodrow Wilson shared a commitment to domestic reform. Compare their legislative programs, including the evolution of their policies over time and their ability to respond to shifting political circumstances. What do their policies reveal about their understandings of the roles of the executive and the federal government?

4. What contemporary movements lay beyond the limits of progressive reform? Why did progressive reform coincide with the restriction of minority rights? In your answer, discuss how radical movements provide insights into the character of progressivism itself.

LINKING TO THE PAST

Link events in this chapter to earlier events.

1. In what ways did Populism and progressivism differ? In what ways were they similar? (See chapter 20.)

2. During the Gilded Age, industrial capitalism concentrated power in the hands of corporations. How did Theodore Roosevelt respond to this problem? How did his approach differ from that of the Gilded Age presidents? Was his strategy effective? (See chapter 18.)

▶ FOR PRACTICE QUIZZES AND OTHER STUDY TOOLS, visit the Online Study Guide at bedfordstmartins.com/roark.

TIMELINE 1889–1916

1889	• Jane Addams opens Hull House.
1895	• Booker T. Washington enunciates Atlanta Compromise.
1896	• *Plessy v. Ferguson.*
1900	• Socialist Party founded.
1901	• William McKinley assassinated; Theodore Roosevelt becomes president.
1902	• Antitrust lawsuit filed against Northern Securities Company. • Roosevelt mediates anthracite coal strike.
1903	• Women's Trade Union League (WTUL) founded. • United States begins construction of Panama Canal. • Elkins Act.
1904	• Roosevelt Corollary to Monroe Doctrine.
1905	• Industrial Workers of the World (IWW) founded. • W. E. B. Du Bois founds Niagara movement.
1906	• Pure Food and Drug Act and Meat Inspection Act. • Atlanta race riot. • Hepburn Act.
1907	• Panic on Wall Street. • Roosevelt signs "Gentlemen's Agreement" with Japan restricting immigration.
1908	• *Muller v. Oregon.* • Republican William Howard Taft elected president.
1909	• Garment workers' strike in New York City. • National Association for the Advancement of Colored People (NAACP) formed.
1910	• Hiram Johnson elected governor of California.
1911	• Triangle fire in New York City. • Taft launches antitrust suit against U.S. Steel.
1912	• Roosevelt runs for president on Progressive Party ticket. • Democrat Woodrow Wilson elected president.
1913	• Suffragists march in Washington, D.C. • Federal Reserve Act.
1914	• Federal Trade Commission (FTC) created. • Clayton Antitrust Act.
1916	• Alice Paul launches National Woman's Party. • Margaret Sanger opens first U.S. birth control clinic. • Keating-Owen child labor law.

GAS MASK

Before World War I, the use of poison gas was considered uncivilized, but on April 22, 1915, the Germans used poison gas for the first time in battle. The Allies condemned the German innovation as diabolic but quickly developed poison gas of their own. Despite the crude appearance of this gas mask, filter respirators (using charcoal or antidote chemicals) proved highly effective. Fewer than 1500 American soldiers died from gas, but many of those who were gassed and survived were disabled and likely to die young. The soldiers trudging along this muddy road in France in 1918 kept their masks handy.

Mask: Collection of Colonel Stuart S. Corning Jr./Picture Research Consultants & Archives; background: Library of Congress.

22

World War I: The Progressive Crusade at Home and Abroad
1914–1920

GEORGE "BROWNIE" BROWNE WAS ONE OF 2 MILLION SOLDIERS WHO crossed the Atlantic during World War I to serve in the American Expeditionary Force (AEF) in France. The twenty-three-year-old civil engineer from Waterbury, Connecticut, volunteered in July 1917, three months after the United States entered the war, serving with the 117th Engineers Regiment, 42nd Division. Two-thirds of the "doughboys" (American soldiers in Europe) saw action during the war, and few white troops saw more than Brownie did.

When Brownie and the 42nd arrived at the front in northeastern France, veteran French troops provided advanced instruction in the techniques of trench warfare. They taught Brownie's regiment of engineers how to build and maintain trenches, barbed-wire entanglements, and artillery and machine-gun positions. Although his sector of the front was deemed "quiet," Brownie came under German artillery, machine-gun, and rifle fire each day. Still, in February 1918, he wrote Martha Johnson, his girlfriend back home, "the longer I'm here the more spirit I have to 'stick it out' for the good of humanity and the U.S. which is the same thing."

Training ended abruptly in the spring of 1918 when the Germans launched a massive offensive, and the 42nd entered the trenches in the Champagne region. The German bombardment made the night "as light as daytime, and the ground . . . was a mass of flames and whistling steel from the bursting shells." Wave after wave of German soldiers rushed forward. One doughboy from the 42nd remembered, "The destruction was terrible and the advancing waves were torn and split apart. The great gaps [in the line of soldiers] were filled, only to be again torn and shattered by the direct artillery fire." Another said, "Dead bodies were all around me. Americans, French, Hun [Germans] in all phases and positions of death." A third declared that soon "the odor was something fierce. We had to put on our gas masks to keep from getting sick." In Champagne, the engineers became infantry. After helping to stop the German advance during eight days of combat, the 42nd suffered nearly 6,500 dead, wounded, and missing, 20 percent of the division.

Brownie came through the campaign unscathed, but he had not had a bath in four weeks, was covered with "cooties" (body lice), and was bone tired. After only ten days' rest, however, his unit joined in the first major American offensive, an attack against German defenses at Saint-Mihiel. To maintain secrecy, the 42nd marched sixty miles in six rainy nights. Widespread misery and confusion prompted one doughboy to remark, "Now I know why they call us the A.E.F. It means 'Ass End First.'" At 1:00 a.m. on September 12, 3,000 American artillery launched more than a million rounds against German positions. This time the engineers preceded the advancing infantry, cutting through or blasting any barbed wire that remained. The battle cost the 42nd another 1,200 casualties, but Brownie was not among them.

At the end of September, the 42nd shifted to the Meuse-Argonne region, where it participated in the most brutal American fighting of the war. And it was there that Brownie's war ended. While the engineers were clearing paths through the barbed wire for the infantry, the Germans fired thousands of poison gas shells. The gas, "so thick you could cut it with a knife," felled Brownie. When the war ended on November 11, 1918, he was recovering from his respiratory wounds at a camp behind the lines. Discharged from the army in February 1919, Brownie returned home, where he and Martha married. Like the rest of the country, they were eager to get on with their lives.

President Woodrow Wilson had never expected to lead the United States into the Great War, as the Europeans called it. When war erupted in 1914, he declared America's absolute neutrality. But trade and principle entangled the United States in Europe's troubles and gradually drew the nation into the conflict. Wilson claimed that America's participation would serve grand purposes and uplift both the United States and the entire world.

At home, the war helped progressives finally achieve their goals of national prohibition and woman suffrage, but it also promoted a vicious attack on Americans' civil liberties. While George Browne and the other doughboys were helping to win the war in Europe, hyperpatriotism meant intolerance, repression, and vigilante violence at home. In 1919, Wilson sailed for Europe to secure a just peace. Unable to dictate terms to the victors, Wilson accepted disappointing compromises. Upon his return to the United States, he met a crushing defeat that marked the end of Wilsonian internationalism. Crackdowns on dissenters, immigrants, racial and ethnic minorities, and unions signaled the end of the Progressive Era at home.

George "Brownie" Browne
Mobilizing an army was easy compared with preparing men for battle. Training at Fort Slocum, New York, Brownie complained about the Army's red tape, bad food, shortage of equipment, inexperienced officers, lack of sleep, and physical exhaustion. Writing to his girlfriend just before evening taps in August 1917, Brownie said, "Believe me I *am* tired." Despite the hardships, however, Brownie enjoyed the camaraderie of the camp and was, as this photograph reveals, a happy soldier. When his unit arrived at Saint-Nazaire in October 1917, Brownie was proud to be one of the first doughboys to set foot in France. Courtesy of Janet W. Hansen.

▶ Woodrow Wilson and the World

Shortly after winning election to the presidency in 1912, **Woodrow Wilson** confided to a friend: "It would be an irony of fate if my administration had to deal with foreign affairs." Indeed, Wilson had focused his life and career on domestic concerns, seldom venturing far from home and traveling abroad only on brief vacations. As president of Princeton University and then governor of New Jersey, he had remained rooted in local affairs. In his campaign for the presidency, Wilson spoke passionately about domestic reform but hardly mentioned foreign affairs.

Wilson, however, could not avoid the world and the rising tide of militarism, nationalism, and violence that beat against American shores. Economic interests compelled the nation outward. Moreover, Wilson was drawn abroad by his own progressive political principles. He believed that the United States had a moral duty to champion national self-determination, peaceful free trade, and political democracy. "We have no selfish ends to serve," he proclaimed. "We desire no conquest, no dominion. . . . We are but one of the champions of the rights of mankind." Yet as president, Wilson revealed that he was as ready as any American president to apply military solutions to problems of foreign policy.

Taming the Americas

When he took office, Wilson sought to distinguish his foreign policy from that of his Republican predecessors. To Wilson, Theodore Roosevelt's "big stick" and William Howard Taft's "dollar diplomacy" appeared crude flexing of military and economic muscle. To signal a new direction, Wilson appointed **William Jennings Bryan** as secretary of state. A pacifist on religious grounds, Bryan immediately

MAP 22.1

U.S. Involvement in Latin America and the Caribbean, 1895–1941

Victory against Spain in 1898 made Puerto Rico an American possession and Cuba a protectorate. The United States later gained control of the Panama Canal Zone. The nation was quick to protect expanding economic interests with military force by propping up friendly, though not necessarily democratic, governments.

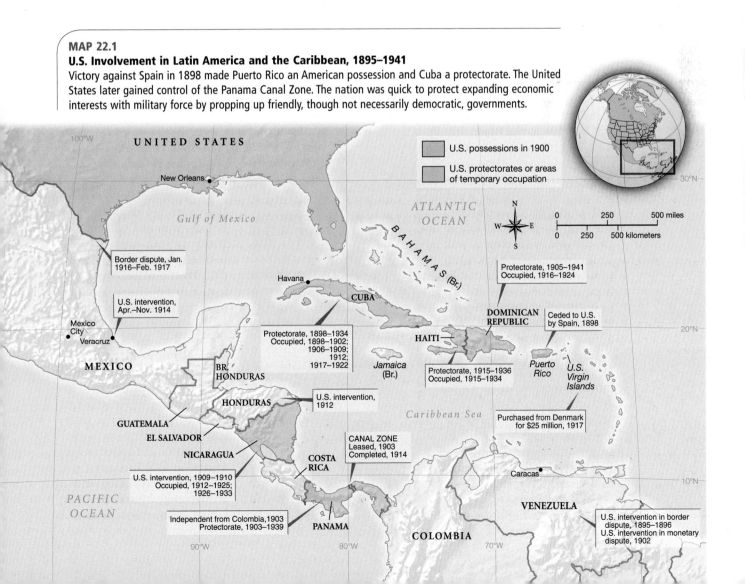

Francisco "Pancho" Villa
The dashing Mexican revolutionary Pancho Villa gallops along a column of his soldiers in 1914. After Villa's raid into New Mexico in 1916 to punish Americans for aiding his revolutionary rivals, General John J. Pershing dove across the border, pursued Villa for three hundred miles into Mexico, and then returned home almost a year later empty-handed. Brown Brothers.

turned his attention to making agreements with thirty nations for the peaceful settlement of disputes.

But Wilson and Bryan, like Roosevelt and Taft, also believed that the Monroe Doctrine gave the United States special rights and responsibilities in the Western Hemisphere. Issued in 1823 to warn Europeans not to attempt to colonize the Americas again, the doctrine had become a cloak for U.S. domination. Thus, when it appeared that unrest might undermine American interests in Nicaragua, Haiti, and the Dominican Republic, Wilson authorized U.S. military intervention, paving the way for U.S. banks and corporations to assert financial control. All the while, Wilson believed that U.S. actions were promoting order and democracy. "I am going to teach the South American Republics to elect good men!" he declared (Map 22.1).

Wilson's most serious involvement in Latin America

U.S. Intervention in Mexico, 1916–1917

ARIZ.   N. MEX.
Culberson's Ranch
Columbus March 9
El Paso
TEXAS
Ascensión
Colonia Dublán
Carrizal June 21
Casas Grandes
Galeana
Namiquipa
MEXICO
Guerrero March 29
Bachiniva
Chihuahua
Tomochic April 21
San Francisco de Borja
Raids and clashes
U.S. main force
U.S. cavalry
Parral April 12

came in Mexico, where revolution broke out in 1910. When General Victoriano Huerta seized power by violent means three years later, most European nations promptly recognized Mexico's new government, but Wilson refused, declaring that he would not support a "government of butchers." In April 1914, Wilson sent 800 Marines to seize the port of Veracruz to prevent the unloading of a large shipment of arms for Huerta, who was by then involved in a civil war of his own. Huerta fled to Spain, and the United States welcomed a more compliant government.

Wilson could not tame Mexico that easily, however. A rebellion erupted among desperately poor farmers who believed that the new government of Venustiano Carranza, aided by U.S. business interests, had betrayed the revolution's promise to help the common people. In January 1916, the rebel army, commanded by **Francisco "Pancho" Villa**, seized a train carrying gold to

Texas from an American-owned mine in Mexico and killed the 17 American engineers aboard. In March, a band of some 400 to 500 of Villa's men crossed the border for a predawn raid on Columbus, New Mexico. They stayed for less than two hours, but they burned much of the town and killed 18 Americans. Wilson promptly dispatched 12,000 troops, led by Major General John J. Pershing. The wily Villa avoided capture, and in January 1917 Wilson recalled Pershing so that the general might prepare the army for the possibility of fighting in the Great War.

The European Crisis

Before 1914, Europe had enjoyed decades of peace, but just beneath the surface lay the potentially destructive forces of nationalism and imperialism. The consolidation of the German and Italian states into unified nations and the similar ambition of Russia to create a Pan-Slavic union initiated new rivalries throughout Europe. As the conviction spread that colonial possessions were a mark of national greatness, competition expanded onto the world stage. Most ominously, Germany under Kaiser **Wilhelm II** meant to challenge Great Britain's world supremacy by creating industrial muscle at home, an empire abroad, and a mighty navy. The German challenge threatened the balance of power and thus the peace.

European nations sought to avoid an explosion by developing a complex web of military and diplomatic alliances. By 1914, Germany, Austria-Hungary, and Italy (the **Triple Alliance**) stood opposed to Great Britain, France, and Russia (the **Triple Entente**, also known as "the Allies"). But in their effort to prevent war through a balance of power, Europeans had actually magnified the possibility of large-scale conflict by creating trip wires along the boundaries of two heavily armed power blocs (Map 22.2). Treaties, some of them secret, obligated members of the alliances to come to the aid of another member if attacked.

The fatal sequence began on June 28, 1914, in the Bosnian city of Sarajevo, when a Bosnian Serb terrorist assassinated **Archduke Franz Ferdinand**, heir to the Austro-Hungarian throne. On July 18, Austria-Hungary declared war on Serbia, holding it accountable for the killing. The elaborate alliance system meant that the war could not remain local. Russia announced that it would back the Serbs. Compelled by treaty to support Austria-Hungary, Germany on August 3 attacked Russia and France. In response, Great Britain, upholding its pact with France, declared war on Germany on August 4. Within weeks, Europe was engulfed in war. The conflict became a world war when Japan, seeing an opportunity to rid itself of European competition in China, joined the cause against Germany. The evenly matched alliances would fight a disastrous war lasting more than four years, at a cost of 8.5 million soldiers' lives — an entire generation of young men. A war that started with a solitary murder proved impossible to stop. Indeed, Britain's foreign secretary, Edward Grey, announced sadly: "The lamps are going out all over Europe. We shall not see them lit again in our lifetime."

The Ordeal of American Neutrality

Woodrow Wilson promptly announced that the war was purely a European matter. Because it engaged no vital American interest and involved no significant principle, he said, the United States would remain neutral and continue normal relations with the warring nations. America had traditionally insisted that "free ships made free goods" — that neutral nations were entitled to trade safely with all nations at war. But more was involved than lofty principle. In the year before Europe went to war, the U.S. economy had slipped into a recession that wartime disruption of European trade could drastically worsen.

Although Wilson proclaimed neutrality, his sympathies, like those of many Americans, lay with Great Britain and France. Americans gratefully remembered crucial French assistance in the American Revolution and shared with the British a language, a culture, and a commitment to liberty. Germany, by contrast, was a monarchy with strong militaristic traditions. The British portrayed the German ruler, Kaiser Wilhelm II, as personally responsible for the war's atrocities, and before long American newspapers were labeling him "the Mad Dog of Europe" and "the Beast of Berlin." Still, Wilson insisted on neutrality, in part because he feared the conflict's effects on the United States as a nation of immigrants, millions of whom had only recently come from countries now at war. As he told the German ambassador, "We definitely have to be neutral, since otherwise our mixed populations would wage war on each other."

Britain's powerful fleet controlled the seas and quickly set up an economic blockade of Germany. The United States

MAP 22.2

European Alliances after the Outbreak of World War I

With Germany and Austria-Hungary wedged between their Entente rivals and all parties fully armed, Europe was poised for war when Archduke Franz Ferdinand of Austria-Hungary was assassinated in Sarajevo in June 1914.

vigorously protested, but Britain refused to give up its naval advantage. The blockade actually had little economic impact on the United States. Between 1914 and the spring of 1917, while trade with Germany evaporated, war-related exports to Britain — food, clothing, steel, and munitions — escalated by some 400 percent, enough to pull the American economy out of its prewar slump. Although the British blockade violated American neutrality, the Wilson administration gradually acquiesced, thus beginning the fateful process of alienation from Germany.

Germany retaliated with a submarine blockade of British ports. This terrifying new form of combat by *Unterseebooten*,

Sinking of the *Lusitania*, 1915

or **U-boats**, threatened traditional rules of war. Unlike surface warships that could harmlessly stop freighters and prevent them from entering a war zone, submarines relied on sinking their quarry. And once they sank a ship, the tiny U-boats could not possibly pick up survivors. Britain portrayed the submarine as an outlaw weapon that violated notions of "civilized" warfare. Nevertheless, in February 1915, Germany announced that it intended to sink on sight enemy ships en route to the British Isles. On May 7, 1915, a German U-boat torpedoed the British passenger liner *Lusitania*, killing 1,198 passengers, 128 of them U.S. citizens.

American newspapers featured drawings of drowning women and children, and some demanded war. Calmer voices pointed out that Germany had warned prospective passengers and that the *Lusitania* carried millions of rounds of ammunition and so was a legitimate target. Secretary of State Bryan resisted the hysteria and declared that a ship carrying war materiel "should not rely on passengers to protect her from attack — it would be like putting women and children in front of an army." He counseled Wilson to warn American citizens that they traveled on ships of belligerent countries at their own risk.

Wilson sought a middle course that would retain his commitment to peace and neutrality without condoning German attacks on passenger ships. On May 10, 1915, he rejected American intervention, declaring that "there is such a thing as a man being too proud to fight." But Wilson also rejected Bryan's position. Any further destruction of ships, Wilson announced, would be regarded as "deliberately unfriendly" and might lead the United States

to break off diplomatic relations with Germany. Wilson essentially demanded that Germany abandon unrestricted submarine warfare. Bryan resigned, predicting that the president had placed the United States on a collision course with Germany. Wilson's replacement for Bryan, **Robert Lansing**, was far from neutral. He believed that Germany's antidemocratic character and goal of "world dominance" meant that it "must not be permitted to win this war or even to break even."

> ## "There is such a thing as a man being too proud to fight."
> —WOODROW WILSON

After Germany apologized for the civilian deaths on the *Lusitania*, tensions subsided. But in 1916, to ensure continued U.S. neutrality, Germany went further, promising no more submarine attacks without warning and without provisions for the safety of civilians. Wilson's supporters celebrated the success of his middle-of-the-road strategy that steered a course between belligerence and pacifism.

Wilson's diplomacy proved helpful in his bid for reelection in 1916. In the contest against Republican Charles Evans Hughes, the Democratic Party ran Wilson under the slogan "He kept us out of war." Wilson felt uneasy with the claim, recognizing that any "little German lieutenant can push us into the war at any time by some calculated outrage." But the Democrats' case for Wilson's neutrality appealed to enough of those in favor of peace to eke out a majority. Wilson won, but only by the razor-thin margins of 600,000 popular and 23 electoral votes.

The United States Enters the War

Step-by-step, the United States backed away from "absolute neutrality" and more forthrightly sided with the Allies (the Triple Entente). The consequence of protesting the German blockade of Great Britain but accepting the British blockade of Germany was that by 1916 the United States was supplying the Allies with 40 percent of their war materiel. When France and Britain ran short of money to pay for U.S. goods and asked for loans, Wilson argued that "loans by American bankers to any foreign government which is at war are inconsistent with the true spirit of neutrality." But rather than jeopardize America's wartime prosperity, Wilson relaxed his objections, and billions of dollars in loans kept American goods flowing to Britain and France.

In January 1917, Germany decided that it could no longer afford to allow neutral shipping

"Enlist"
This poster depicting a young mother and her baby sinking beneath the cold waters of the Atlantic Ocean brought home the terrible cost of Germany's sinking of the British passenger liner *Lusitania* in 1915. When a German propagandist in the United States sought to defend the sinking, the American response was so ferocious that the German ambassador was forced to send him back to Germany. Burned into American memory, the sinking of the *Lusitania* remained a compelling reason to enlist in the armed forces after the United States entered the war in 1917. Library of Congress.

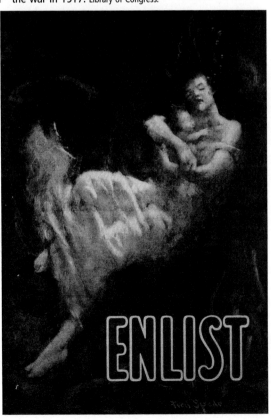

to reach Great Britain while Britain's blockade gradually starved Germany. It announced that its navy would resume unrestricted submarine warfare and sink without warning any ship, enemy or neutral, found in the waters off Great Britain. Germany understood that the decision would probably bring the United States into the war but gambled that the submarines would strangle the British economy and allow German armies to win a military victory in France before American troops arrived in Europe.

Resisting demands for war, Wilson continued to hope for a negotiated peace and only broke off diplomatic relations with Germany. Then on February 25, 1917, British authorities informed Wilson of a secret telegram sent by the German foreign secretary, Arthur Zimmermann, to the German minister in Mexico. It promised that in the event of war between Germany and the United States, Germany would see that Mexico regained its "lost provinces" of Texas, New Mexico, and Arizona if Mexico would declare war against the United States. Wilson angrily responded to the **Zimmermann telegram** by asking Congress to approve a policy of "armed neutrality" that would allow merchant ships to fight back against any attackers. Germany's overture to Mexico convinced Wilson that the war was, indeed, a defense of democracy against German aggression.

In March, German submarines sank five American vessels off Britain, killing 66 Americans. On April 2, the president asked Congress to issue a declaration of war. He accused Germany of "warfare against all mankind." Still, he called for a "war without hate" and insisted that the destruction of Germany was not the goal of the United States. Rather, America fought to "vindicate the principles of peace and justice." He promised a world made "safe for democracy." On April 6, 1917, by majorities of 373 to 50 in the House and 82 to 6 in the Senate, Congress voted to declare war. Among those voting no was Representative Jeannette Rankin of Montana, the first woman elected to Congress.

Wilson feared what war would do at home. He said despairingly, "Once lead this people into war, and they'll forget there ever was such a thing as tolerance. To fight you must be brutal and ruthless, and the spirit of ruthless brutality will infect Congress, the courts, the policeman on the beat, the man in the street."

REVIEW Why did President Wilson fail to maintain U.S. neutrality during World War I?

▶ "Over There"

American soldiers sailed for France with songwriter George M. Cohan's rousing "Over There" ringing in their ears:

> Over there, over there
> Send the word, send the word over there,
> That the Yanks are coming, the Yanks are coming
> The drums rum-tumming ev'rywhere.

America's military venture in Europe was by far the largest the nation had ever undertaken on foreign soil. Filled with a sense of democratic mission and trained to be morally upright as well as fiercely effective, some doughboys, such as George Browne, found the adventure exhilarating and maintained their idealism to the end. The majority, however, saw little that was gallant in rats, lice, and poison gas and — despite the progressives' hopes — little to elevate the human soul in a landscape of utter destruction and death. Most were dedicated simply to defeating the "Huns" and returning home.

The Call to Arms

When America entered the war, Britain and France were nearly exhausted after almost three years of conflict. Millions of soldiers had perished; food and morale were dangerously low. Another Allied power, Russia, was in turmoil. In March 1917, a revolution had forced Czar Nicholas II to abdicate, and eight months later, in a separate peace with Germany, the **Bolshevik** revolutionary government withdrew Russia from the war. Peace with Russia allowed Germany to withdraw hundreds of thousands of its soldiers from the eastern front and to deploy them against the Allies on the western front in France.

On May 18, 1917, to meet the demand for fighting men, Wilson signed a sweeping **Selective Service Act**, authorizing a draft of all young men into the armed forces. Conscription helped transform a tiny volunteer armed force of 80,000 men into a vast army and navy. Although almost 350,000 inductees either failed to report or claimed conscientious objector status, draft boards eventually inducted 2.8 million men into the armed services, in addition to the 2 million, including George Browne, who volunteered.

Among the 4.8 million men under arms, 370,000 were black Americans. Although African Americans remained understandably skeptical about President Wilson's war for democracy, most followed W. E. B. Du Bois's advice to "close ranks" and to temporarily "forget our special

"Men Wanted for the United States Army"
The exuberant soldiers swarming over this truck were so thrilled with their task of recruiting new men that they managed to display the flag backward. Their urgency reflects the fact that when America declared war on Germany in April 1917, its army numbered only 127,000, roughly the size of Chile's army. Unwilling to trust voluntary enlistments, Wilson called for a draft, and within months nearly 10 million American men had registered for the draft. When the war ended, 2 million men had volunteered for military service, and 2.8 million had been drafted. The navy was as desperate for men as the army. This heroic poster helped attract thousands of volunteers. Photo: Brown Brothers; Poster: Image by © Swim Ink 2, LLC/Corbis.

FOLLOW THE FLAG

ENLIST IN THE NAVY
U.S. NAVY RECRUITING STATION
34 East 23rd Street, New York

grievances" until the nation had won the war. During training, black recruits suffered the same prejudices that they encountered in civilian life. Rigidly segregated, they faced crude abuse and miserable conditions, and they were usually assigned to labor battalions, where they shouldered shovels more often than rifles.

Training camps sought to transform raw white recruits into fighting men. Progressives in the government were also determined that the camps turn out soldiers with the highest moral and civic values. Secretary of War Newton D. Baker created the Commission on Training Camp Activities, staffed by YMCA workers and veterans of the settlement house and playground movements.

Military training included games, singing, and college extension courses. The army asked soldiers to stop thinking about sex, explaining that a "man who is thinking below the belt is not efficient." The Military Draft Act of 1917 prohibited prostitution and alcohol near training camps.

Wilson's choice to command the **American Expeditionary Force (AEF)** on the battlefields of France, Major General **John "Black Jack" Pershing**, was as morally upright as he was militarily uncompromising. "The standards for the American Army will be those of West Point," the ramrod-straight Pershing announced early in the war. "The upright bearing, attention to detail, uncomplaining obedience to instruction required of the cadet will be required of every officer and soldier of our armies in France." Described by one observer as "lean, clean, keen," he gave progressives perfect confidence.

The War in France

At the front, the AEF discovered a desperate situation. The war had degenerated into a stalemate of armies defensively dug into hundreds of miles of trenches that stretched across France.

> **"Why, then, fight the Germans, only for the benefit of the Wall Street robbers?"**
> — A German leaflet given to African American troops

Huddling in the mud among the corpses and rats, soldiers were separated from the enemy by only a few hundred yards of "no-man's-land." When ordered "over the top," troops raced desperately toward the enemy's trenches, only to be entangled in barbed wire, enveloped in poison gas, and mowed down by machine guns. In three days of fighting at the battle of the Somme in 1916, French and British forces lost 600,000 dead and wounded and the Germans 500,000. The deadliest battle of the war allowed the Allies to advance their trenches only a few meaningless miles across devastated land.

Still, U.S. troops saw almost no combat in 1917. The major exception was the 92nd Division of black troops. When Pershing received an urgent call for troops from the French, he sent the 92nd to the front because he did not want to lose command over the white troops he valued more. In the 191 days they spent in battle — longer than any other American outfit — the 369th Regiment of the 92nd Division won more medals than any other American combat unit. Black soldiers recognized the irony of having to serve with the French to gain respect. Pershing told the French that their failure to draw the color line risked "spoiling the Negroes." German propagandists raised some painful questions. In a leaflet that aviators dropped among black troops, the Germans reminded them of their second-class citizenship and asked, "Why, then, fight the Germans, only for the benefit of the Wall Street robbers and to protect the millions they have loaned to the British, French, and Italians?"

White troops continued to train and used their free time to explore places that most of them otherwise could never have hoped to see. True to the crusader image, American officials allowed only morally uplifting tourism. Paris's temptations were off limits, and French premier

Doughboys in France
Stretched out in the mud in the middle of what used to be a forest, men in the 23rd Infantry of the 2nd Division fire a 37 mm gun at German positions. The black tree trunks offer dramatic testimony to the devastating power of the massive artillery bombardments. We can only imagine the cost to soldiers who were dug in here when the artillery opened up. One doughboy described a German bombardment like this: "The intensity of it simply enters your heart and brain, and tears every nerve to pieces." National Archives.

Georges Clemenceau's offer to supply U.S. troops with licensed prostitutes was declined with the half-serious remark that if Wilson found out, he would stop the war.

Sightseeing and training ended abruptly in March 1918. When the Brest-Litovsk treaty signed that month by Germany and the Bolsheviks officially took Russia out of the war, the Germans launched a massive offensive aimed at French ports on the Atlantic. After 6,000 cannons unleashed the heaviest barrage in history, a million German soldiers smashed a hole in the Allied lines at a cost of 250,000 casualties on each side. Pershing, who believed the right moment for U.S. action had finally come, visited Ferdinand Foch, head of the French army, to ask for the "great honor" of becoming "engaged

in the greatest battle in history." Foch agreed to Pershing's terms of a separate American command and in May assigned the Americans to the central sector.

In May and June, at Cantigny and then at Château-Thierry, the eager but green Americans checked the German advance with a series of dashing assaults (Map 22.3). Then they headed toward the forest stronghold of Belleau Wood, moving against streams of retreating Allied soldiers who cried defeat: "La guerre est finie!" (The war is over!) A French officer commanded the Americans to retreat with them, but the American commander replied sharply, "Retreat, hell. We just got here." After charging through a wheat field against withering machine-gun fire, the Marines plunged into hand-to-hand

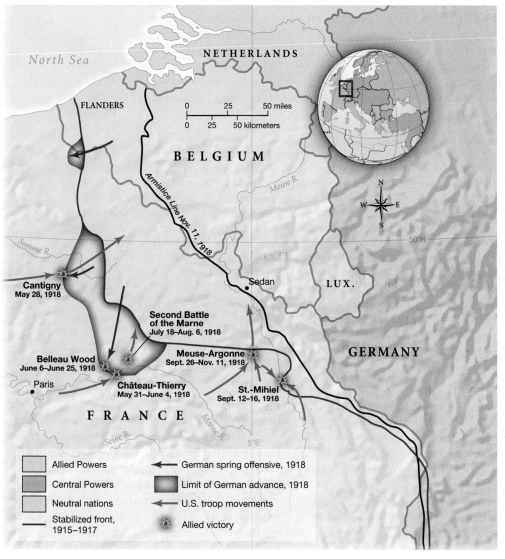

MAP ACTIVITY

Map 22.3 The American Expeditionary Force, 1918
In the last year of the war, the AEF joined the French army on the western front to respond to the final German offensive and pursue the retreating enemy until surrender.

READING THE MAP: Across which rivers did the Germans advance in 1918? Where did the armistice line of November 11, 1918, lie in relation to the stabilized front of 1915–1917? Through which countries did the armistice line run?
CONNECTIONS: What events paved the way for the AEF to join the combat effort in 1918? What characteristic(s) differentiated American troops from other Allied forces and helped them achieve victory?

VISUAL ACTIVITY

Life in the Trenches

One U.S. soldier in a rat-infested trench tensely looks out for danger, while three others sit or lie in exhausted sleep. They offer a glimpse of the reality of the Great War, minus the noise, stench, and danger. This trench is dry for the moment, but with the rains came mud so deep that wounded men drowned in it. By the time American doughboys arrived in Europe, hostile troops had faced each other for more than three years, burrowed into a double line of trenches that were protected by barbed wire, machine-gun nests, and mortars and backed by heavy artillery. Trenches with millions of combatants stretched from French ports on the English Channel all the way to Switzerland. Nothing could make living in such holes anything better than miserable, but a decent shave with a Gillette safety razor and a friendly game of checkers offered doughboys temporary relief. Inevitably, however, the whistles would blow, sending the young men "over the top" and rushing toward enemy lines. Photo: Imperial War Museum; shaving kit and checkers set: Collection of Colonel Stuart S. Corning Jr./Picture Research Consultants, Inc.

READING THE IMAGE: What do these images suggest about the reality of life for American soldiers during World War I? CONNECTIONS: How does the photograph of the trench contrast with the larger tactical approach to war employed by the American Expeditionary Force in France?

combat. Victory came hard, but a German report praised the enemy's spirit, noting that "the Americans' nerves are not yet worn out." Indeed, it was German morale that was on the verge of cracking.

In the summer of 1918, the Allies launched a massive counteroffensive that would end the war. A quarter of a million U.S. troops joined in the rout of German forces along the Marne River. In September, more than a million Americans

took part in the assault that threw the Germans back from positions along the Meuse River. In four brutal days during the Meuse-Argonne offensive, the AEF sustained 45,000 casualties. Pershing had predicted that German defenses would crack in thirty-six hours; six weeks later, the Germans gave way. In November, a revolt against the German government sent Kaiser Wilhelm II fleeing to Holland. On November 11, 1918, a delegation from the newly established

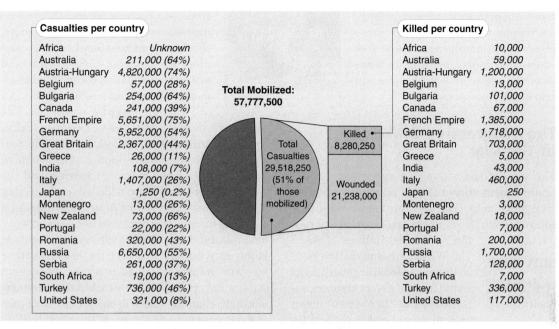

Casualties per country	
Africa	Unknown
Australia	211,000 (64%)
Austria-Hungary	4,820,000 (74%)
Belgium	57,000 (28%)
Bulgaria	254,000 (64%)
Canada	241,000 (39%)
French Empire	5,651,000 (75%)
Germany	5,952,000 (54%)
Great Britain	2,367,000 (44%)
Greece	26,000 (11%)
India	108,000 (7%)
Italy	1,407,000 (26%)
Japan	1,250 (0.2%)
Montenegro	13,000 (26%)
New Zealand	73,000 (66%)
Portugal	22,000 (22%)
Romania	320,000 (43%)
Russia	6,650,000 (55%)
Serbia	261,000 (37%)
South Africa	19,000 (13%)
Turkey	736,000 (46%)
United States	321,000 (8%)

Total Mobilized: 57,777,500

Total Casualties 29,518,250 (51% of those mobilized)

Killed 8,280,250

Wounded 21,238,000

Killed per country	
Africa	10,000
Australia	59,000
Austria-Hungary	1,200,000
Belgium	13,000
Bulgaria	101,000
Canada	67,000
French Empire	1,385,000
Germany	1,718,000
Great Britain	703,000
Greece	5,000
India	43,000
Italy	460,000
Japan	250
Montenegro	3,000
New Zealand	18,000
Portugal	7,000
Romania	200,000
Russia	1,700,000
Serbia	128,000
South Africa	7,000
Turkey	336,000
United States	117,000

FIGURE 22.1   GLOBAL COMPARISON: Casualties of the First World War
There is no agreement about the number of casualties in World War I. Record keeping in many countries was only rudimentary. Moreover, the destructive nature of the war meant that countless soldiers were wholly obliterated or instantly buried. The chart above provides estimates of casualties (the combined number of wounded and killed soldiers) per country. The percentage listed with each casualty figure represents the portion of soldiers mobilized who were killed. However approximate, these figures make clear that the conflict that raged from 1914 to 1918 was a truly catastrophic world war. Although soldiers came from almost every part of the globe, the human devastation was not evenly distributed. Which country suffered the most casualties? Which country suffered the greatest percentage of casualties? What do you think was the principal reason that the United States suffered a smaller percentage of casualties than most other nations?

German republic met with the French high command to sign an armistice that brought the fighting to an end.

The adventure of the AEF was brief, bloody, and victorious. When Germany had resumed unrestricted U-boat warfare in 1917, it had been gambling that it could defeat Britain and France before the Americans could raise and train an army and ship it to France. The German military had miscalculated badly. Of the 2 million American troops in Europe, 1.4 million saw some action. By the end, 112,000 AEF soldiers perished from wounds and disease, while another 230,000 Americans, including George Browne, suffered casualties but survived. Only the Civil War, which lasted much longer, had been more costly in American lives. European nations, however, suffered much greater losses: 2.2 million Germans, 1.9 million Russians, 1.4 million French, and 900,000 Britons (Figure 22.1). Where they had fought, the landscape was as blasted and barren as the moon.

REVIEW How did the American Expeditionary Force contribute to the defeat of Germany?

▶ The Crusade for Democracy at Home

Many progressives hoped that the war would improve the quality of American life as well as free Europe from tyranny and militarism. Mobilization helped propel the crusades for woman suffrage and prohibition to success. Progressives enthusiastically channeled industrial and agricultural production into the war effort. Labor shortages caused by workers entering the military provided new opportunities for women in the booming wartime economy. With labor at a premium, unionized workers gained higher pay and shorter hours. To instill loyalty in Americans whose ancestry was rooted in the belligerent nations, Wilson launched a campaign to foster patriotism. The campaign included the creation of a government agency to promote official propaganda, indoctrination in the schools, and parades, rallies, and films. But fanning patriotism led to suppressing dissent. When the government launched a harsh assault on civil liberties, mobs gained license to attack those whom they considered disloyal. As Wilson feared, the progressive ideals of rational progress and free expression took a beating at home when the nation undertook its foreign crusade for democracy.

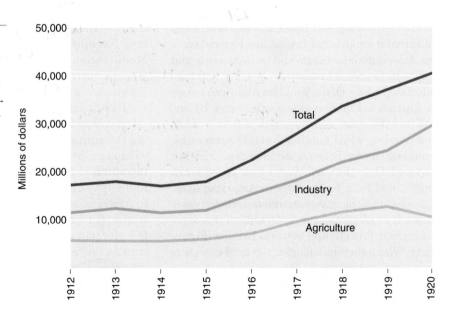

The Progressive Stake in the War

The idea of the war as an agent of national improvement stirred the old zeal of the progressive movement. The influential philosopher-educator John Dewey urged Americans to embrace the "social possibilities of war." The Wilson administration realized that the federal government would have to assert greater control to mobilize the nation's human and physical resources. The nation's capital soon bristled with agencies charged with managing the war effort. Bernard Baruch headed the War Industries Board, created to stimulate and direct industrial production. A wealthy Wall Street stockbroker and a reform Democrat, Baruch brought industrial management and labor together into a team that produced everything from boots to bullets and made U.S. troops the best-equipped soldiers in the world.

Herbert Hoover, a self-made millionaire engineer, headed the Food Administration. He led remarkably successful "Hooverizing" campaigns for "meatless" Mondays and "wheatless"

> **"Shall the many have food or the few drink?"**
> —Prohibitionist slogan

Wednesdays and other ways of conserving resources. Guaranteed high prices, the American heartland not only supplied the needs of U.S. citizens and armed forces but also became the breadbasket of America's allies.

Wartime agencies multiplied: The Railroad Administration directed railroad traffic, the Fuel Administration coordinated the coal industry and other fuel suppliers, the Shipping Board organized the merchant marine, and the National War Labor Policies Board resolved labor disputes. Their successes gave progressives reason to believe that the war promoted harmony between business and labor. Some progressives, however, stubbornly refused to accept the argument that war and reform marched together. Wisconsin senator Robert La Follette attacked the war unrelentingly, claiming that Wilson's promises of peace and democracy were a case of "the blind leading the blind" at home and abroad.

Industrial leaders found that wartime agencies enforced efficiency, which helped corporate profits triple. Some working people also had cause to celebrate. Mobilization meant high prices for farmers and plentiful jobs at high wages in the new war industries (Figure 22.2). Because increased industrial production required peaceful labor relations, the National War Labor Policies Board enacted the eight-hour day, a living minimum wage, and collective bargaining rights in some industries. Wages rose sharply during the war (as did prices), and the American Federation

FIGURE 22.2
Industrial Wages, 1912–1920
With help from unions and progressive reformers, wageworkers gradually improved their economic condition. The entry of millions of young men into the armed forces during World War I caused labor shortages and led to a rapid surge in industrial wages.

Agriculture: cash receipts.
Industry: includes mining, electric power, manufacturing, construction, and communications.

of Labor (AFL) saw its membership soar from 2.7 million to more than 5 million.

The war also provided a huge boost to the stalled moral crusade to ban alcohol. By 1917, prohibitionists had convinced nineteen states to go dry. Liquor's opponents now argued that banning alcohol would make the cause of democracy powerful and pure. At the same time, shutting down the distilleries would save millions of bushels of grain that could feed the United States and its allies. "Shall the many have food or the few drink?" the drys asked. Prohibitionists added a patriotic twist by arguing that closing breweries with German names such as Schlitz, Pabst, and Anheuser-Busch would deal a blow to the German cause. In December 1917, Congress passed the **Eighteenth Amendment**, which banned the manufacture, transportation, and sale of alcohol. After swift ratification by the states, the amendment went into effect on January 1, 1920.

Women, War, and the Battle for Suffrage

Women had made real strides during the Progressive Era, and war presented new opportunities. More than 25,000 women served in France. About half were nurses. The others drove ambulances; ran canteens for the Salvation Army, Red Cross, and YMCA; worked with French civilians in devastated areas; and acted as telephone operators and war correspondents. (See "Seeking the American Promise," page 726.) Like men who joined the war effort, they believed that they were taking part in a great national venture. "I am more than willing to live as a soldier and know of the hardships I would have to undergo," one canteen worker declared when applying to go overseas, "but I want to help my country. . . . I want . . . to do the *real* work." And like men, women struggled against disillusionment in France. One woman explained: "Over in America, we thought we knew something about the war . . . but when you get here the difference is [like the one between] studying the laws of electricity and being struck by lightning."

At home, long-standing barriers against hiring women fell when millions of workingmen became soldiers and few new immigrant workers crossed the Atlantic. Tens of thousands of women found work in defense plants as welders, metalworkers, and heavy machine operators — jobs traditionally reserved for men — and with the railroads. A black woman, a domestic before the war, celebrated her job as a laborer in a railroad

yard: "We are making more money at this than any work we can get, and we do not have to work as hard as at housework which requires us to be on duty from six o'clock in the morning until nine or ten at night, with might[y] little time off and at very poor wages." Other women found white-collar work. Between 1910 and 1920, the number of women clerks doubled. Before the war ended, more than a million women had found work in war industries.

The most dramatic advance for women came in the political arena. Since the Seneca Falls convention of 1848, where women voiced their first formal demand for the ballot, the struggle for woman suffrage had inched forward. Adopting a state-by-state approach, suffragists had achieved some success, but before 1910 only four sparsely populated western states had adopted woman suffrage (Map 22.4). Elsewhere, voting rights for women met strong hostility and defeat. After 1910, suffrage leaders added a federal campaign to amend the Constitution, targeting Congress and the president, to the traditional state-by-state strategy for suffrage.

MAP ACTIVITY

Map 22.4 Women's Voting Rights before the Nineteenth Amendment
The long campaign for women's voting rights reversed the pioneer epic that moved from east to west. From its first successes in the new democratic West, suffrage rolled eastward toward the entrenched, male-dominated public life of the Northeast and South.

READING THE MAP: What was the first state to grant woman suffrage? How many states extended full voting rights to women before 1914? How many extended these rights during World War I (1914–1918)?
CONNECTIONS: Suffragists redirected their focus during the war. What strategies did they use then?

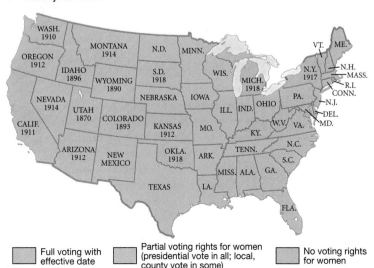

Seeking to Serve: An American Woman in Wartime France

When World War I broke out in Europe in 1914, nineteen-year-old Nora Saltonstall was vacationing in Maine with other wellborn young people. A daughter of privilege, she belonged to one of Massachusetts's most distinguished families. But she was no silly, idle debutante. The Saltonstalls instilled in their children a strong sense of the obligation to serve. Within months, she was rolling bandages for the Red Cross in Boston and raising money for the relief of Belgian refugees. By the time the United States entered the war in April 1917, her two Harvard-educated brothers had already volunteered for military service. In October 1917, she volunteered for Red Cross work in France.

After an eleven-day voyage across the submarine-infested Atlantic, Saltonstall arrived in Bordeaux without any idea what she would be doing. She was assigned to long hours of dull work in Paris finding housing for refugees, and like many other American women in France, she contracted "frontline fever," an obsession with getting as far forward in the war zone as she could. She longed for what she called a "man's size job,"

something that would test her mettle and contribute to victory.

By January 1918, Saltonstall had found "real work," which would be "a direct help, even if it is the tiniest drop in the bucket." She joined a group of female Red Cross volunteers attached to a mobile surgical hospital that followed closely behind the French armies. Lacking training as a nurse, she became the unit's driver, responsible for chauffeuring personnel, transporting the wounded, and hauling supplies as the unit moved from place to place. Soon she was driving on muddy, shell-pocked roads in the dark without lights. She also became a mechanic, with the responsibility for maintaining and repairing the vehicles. "I usually cover myself with grease and oil every morning, tinker about a bit and do more harm than good," she wrote home shortly after arriving. But before long, she announced proudly, "I fixed the steering shaft on the Ford all by myself." Her life, she told her mother, consisted of "choked carburetors, broken springs, long hours on the road, food snatched when you can get it, and sleep." Her work brought changes. "I have developed a most

enormous muscle in my right arm, and I am really rather ashamed of it because it literally stands out." She joked, "I'll have to try to direct it into a tennis stroke after the war."

But Saltonstall's sense of humor was tested by the death and destruction she confronted every day. The "stream of wounded men and refugees still makes me ache," she said. "I never hated the war so much before. I have seen enough wounds to hate them, and I don't see how people who have been in it for 3½ years can bear up at all, just one long unending hashing up of people." She lived, she said, in an "insane asylum."

At the same time, she never felt more alive. She believed that she was "learning more . . . than I could learn in years of regular living at home." Saltonstall loved being in the thick of things and "at last feeling as if I were doing something necessary here." She felt proud: "Because we are here, work is being done better and lives saved which might otherwise have been lost. . . . I love my job." She never expressed regrets about coming to France: "If I had not come over I would have felt not to have belonged to this generation and would have felt all my life as if there were something lacking to me on a level with all the up and coming crowd of my own age." Of this she was certain: "After the war there is going to be a difference between those who were in France and those not."

In November 1918, after nearly a year at the front, she scribbled in

The radical wing of the suffragists, led by the indomitable Alice Paul, picketed the White House, where the marchers unfurled banners that proclaimed "America Is Not a Democracy. Twenty Million Women Are Denied the Right to Vote." They chained themselves to fences and went to jail, where many engaged in hunger strikes. "They seem bent on making their cause as obnoxious as possible," Woodrow Wilson declared. His wife, Edith, detested the idea of "masculinized" voting women.

But membership in the mainstream organization, the National American Woman Suffrage Association (NAWSA), led by Carrie Chapman Catt, soared to some two million. The NAWSA even accepted African American women into its ranks, though not on an equal basis. Seeing the handwriting on the wall, the Republican and Progressive parties endorsed woman suffrage in 1916.

In 1918, Wilson gave his support to suffrage, calling the amendment "vital to the winning of the war." He conceded that it

her diary: "Great excitement, guns stopped firing at midnight. Peace in the air." She celebrated the armistice with the others, but she also realized that her great adventure was almost over. She contemplated her return to the ordinariness of her civilian life: "I wonder when I get to Boston whether I will ever have the courage to motor 80 miles to a party, arrive at midnight, dance until 5 A.M. and then after a wonderful lunch and supper, motor back the next evening." Demobilization left her with a "very flat feeling." In December, the French government decorated Nora and her unit with the Croix de Guerre for their courageous service, and in March 1919 she sailed for home. Nora Saltonstall never got to confront her concerns about reentering American life, however. Just months after returning, on a camping trip in the West, she contracted typhoid fever and died.

Nora Saltonstall

Born into Boston's elite, Nora Saltonstall, seen here at the wheel of the yawl *Comanche* off the coast of Maine, grew into a self-assured, adventurous young woman. Although no rebel (she wasn't a suffragist, for example), she was certain that she had something to offer to America's war effort. Unlike most Americans who arrived in Paris during the war, she was no stranger to Europe. While her brothers studied at Harvard, she had spent a year studying art and history while touring the continent. Photo no. 33.3192, Saltonstall-Brooks-Lewis Papers, Massachusetts Historical Society, Boston.

Questions for Consideration

1. How did Nora Saltonstall's gender shape her wartime service? How was her experience different from or similar to that of George "Brownie" Browne?

2. Considering domestic developments during and just after the war (discussed later in this chapter), do you think that Saltonstall's worries about life in America after the war were justified? Why or why not?

would be wrong not to reward the wartime "partnership of suffering and sacrifice" with a "partnership of privilege and right." By linking their cause to the wartime emphasis on national unity, the advocates of woman suffrage finally triumphed. In 1919, Congress passed the **Nineteenth Amendment**, granting women the vote, and by August 1920 the required two-thirds of the states had ratified it. (See "Documenting the American Promise," page 728.) But rather than being the end of the long road to women's full equality, as some suffragists contended, woman suffrage proved to be only the beginning.

Rally around the Flag — or Else

When Congress committed the nation to war, most peace advocates rallied around the flag. The Carnegie Endowment for International Peace adopted new stationery with the heading "Peace through Victory" and issued a resolution saying that "the most effectual means of promoting peace is to prosecute the war against the Imperial German Government."

DOCUMENTING THE AMERICAN PROMISE

The Final Push for Woman Suffrage

By the early twentieth century, the women's movement had mobilized millions, who increasingly concentrated on the passage of an amendment to the U.S. Constitution to ensure women's voting rights. Nothing came easily to the suffragists, but in 1920 their passion and courage were rewarded by the ratification of the Nineteenth Amendment.

DOCUMENT 1
Passing the Baton

Elizabeth Cady Stanton and Susan B. Anthony were best friends and close colleagues in the woman suffrage movement. In this October 1902 letter to Stanton, Anthony acknowledges that neither of them would live to see victory, but she nevertheless remains confident that the campaign will succeed. Stanton died days after receiving this letter, and Anthony died four years later.

My dear Mrs. Stanton . . .

It is fifty-one years since first we met and we have been busy through every one of them, stirring up the world to recognize the rights of women. The older we grow, the more keenly we feel the humiliation of disfranchisement and the more vividly we realize its disadvantages in every department of life and most of all in the labor market.

We little dreamed when we began this contest, optimistic with the hope and buoyancy of youth, that half a century later we would be compelled to leave the finish of the battle to another generation of women. But our hearts are filled with joy to know that they enter upon this task equipped with a college education, with business experience, with the fully admitted right to speak in public — all of which were denied to women fifty years ago. They have practically but one point to gain — the suffrage; we had all. These strong, courageous, capable young women will take our place and complete our work. There is an army of them, where we were but a handful. Ancient prejudice has become so softened, public sentiment so liberalized and women have so thoroughly demonstrated their ability as to leave not a shadow of doubt that they will carry our cause to victory. . . .

Ever lovingly yours, Susan B. Anthony

SOURCE: From *The Elizabeth Cady Stanton–Susan B. Anthony Reader: Correspondence, Writings, Speeches*, 298–99, edited by Ellen Carol DuBois. By permission of Northeastern University Press, 1992.

DOCUMENT 2
Politicking for Suffrage

While radical suffragists chained themselves to the White House fence and went on hunger strikes, other women followed more traditional political channels — methodically gathering petitions, lobbying legislators, building alliances, and rounding up votes. Mary Garrett Hay, vice president of the National American Woman Suffrage Association (NAWSA), reports her efforts with New York state legislators.

New York City, N.Y.
March 13th, 1919

Mrs. Maud Wood Park
1626 Rhode Island Avenue
Washington, D.C.

Dear Mrs. Park,

. . . I kept in very close touch on the telephone and telegraph wire with New York Congressmen and they reported to me, really twice a day what was going on, as far as Speaker, Floor Leader and Suffrage Committee was concerned. I can do more in the House than in the Senate, and I have asked Mr. Hays on the long distance telephone to try and see that things are perfectly straight for our Cause there.

Things will be all right, I believe, but I have made up my mind not to trust either Democrats or Republicans, until the Suffrage Amendment is passed; however, I do not say this to the men[,] only to you, and I shall keep my eyes and ears open and busy, and on the job all I can.

SOURCE: *Women and Social Movements in the United States, 1600–2000*, "How Did Suffragists Lobby to Obtain Congressional Approval of a Woman Suffrage Amendment to the U.S. Constitution, 1917–1920?" Document #10. Courtesy of the Schlesinger Library, Radcliffe Institute, Harvard University (Cambridge, MA).

DOCUMENT 3
The President Intervenes

Although some people urged suffragists to muffle their demands during the war so that the nation could concentrate on victory, Carrie Chapman Catt, president of the NAWSA since 1915, pressed on, recognizing that the war offered a special opportunity. Catt prodded President Woodrow Wilson quietly but persistently, and on September 30, 1918, Wilson finally intervened directly, urging the Senate to pass the Nineteenth Amendment. His argument on behalf of democracy mirrored precisely that of radical suffragists who were protesting in front of the White House.

[The Senate's] adoption is, in my judgment, clearly necessary to the successful prosecution of the war and the successful realization of the objects for which the war is being fought.

. . . If we be indeed democrats and wish to lead the world to democracy, we can ask other peoples to accept in proof of our sincerity and our ability to lead them whither they wish to be led, nothing less persuasive and convincing than our actions.

. . . They are looking to the great, powerful, famous democracy of the West to lead them to a new day for which they have so long waited; and they think, in their logical simplicity, that democracy means that women shall play their part in affairs alongside men and upon an equal footing with them.

. . . We have made partners of the women in this war. Shall we admit them only to a partnership of suffering and sacrifice and toil and not to a partnership of privilege and right?

This war could not have been fought, either by the other nations engaged or by America, if it had not been for the services of the women — services rendered in every sphere. . . .

. . . I tell you plainly that this measure which I urge upon you is vital to the winning of the war and to the energies alike of preparation and of battle.

. . . And not to winning the war only. It is vital to the right solution of the great problems which we must settle, and settle immediately, when the war is over. We shall need in our vision of affairs, as we have never needed them before, the sympathy and insight and clear moral instinct of the women of the world. . . . We shall need their moral sense to preserve what is right and fine and worthy in our system of life as well as to discover just what it is that ought to be purified and reformed. Without their counsellings we shall be only half wise.

SOURCE: "Appeal of President Wilson to the Senate of the United States to Submit the Federal Amendment for Woman Suffrage Delivered in Person Sept. 20, 1918," in *History of Woman Suffrage*, Vol. 5: 1900–1920, 760–63.

DOCUMENT 4
Reflections on Victory

Carrie Chapman Catt celebrates the passage of the Nineteenth Amendment in this letter to her staff at the NAWSA on Thanksgiving Day 1920. She reflects on the long road to victory and considers the satisfactions of the journey.

I have kept Thanksgiving sacred to reflections upon the long trail behind us, and the triumph which was its inevitable conclusion. John Adams said long after the Revolution that only about one third of the people were for it, a third being against it, and the remaining third utterly indifferent. Perhaps this proportion applies to all movements. At least a third of the women were for our cause at the end. . . . As I look back over the years . . . I realize that the greatest thing in the long campaign for us was not its crowning victory, but the discipline it gave us all. . . . It was a great crusade, the world has seen none more wonderful. . . . My admiration, love and reverence go out to that band which fought and won a revolution . . . with congratulations that we were permitted to establish a new and good thing in the world.

SOURCE: Carrie Chapman Catt to NAWSA Office Staff, Thanksgiving Day 1920, in Elizabeth Frost and Kathryn Cullen-DuPont, *Women's Suffrage in America: An Eyewitness History* (1992), 335–36.

Questions for Analysis and Debate

1. Why was Susan B. Anthony confident that woman suffrage would soon become a reality?
2. Why were some legislators in New York and elsewhere willing to work closely with suffragists such as Mary Garrett Hay?
3. What, according to Woodrow Wilson, would America's rejection of the Nineteenth Amendment have jeopardized?
4. What do you suppose Carrie Chapman Catt meant when she said that the greatest gain for women in the suffrage campaign was "discipline"?

D. W. Griffith's *Hearts of the World*
Hollywood joined in the government's efforts to stir up rage against the "brutal Huns," as Germans were often called. In a film made for the British and French governments by America's leading filmmaker, D. W. Griffith, a hulking German is about to whip a defenseless farm woman (played by Lillian Gish, one of the nation's favorite actors). When the film premiered in Washington, D.C., in 1918, First Lady Edith Wilson wrote to Griffith, pleading with him to cut or soften the violent whipping scene. Edith Wilson was one of the few people in the nation's capital who sought to moderate the hate campaign. Library of Congress.

Only a handful of reformers resisted the tide of patriotism. A group of professional women, led by settlement house leader Jane Addams and economics professor Emily Greene Balch, denounced what Addams described as "the pathetic belief in the regenerative results of war." The Women's Peace Party, which emerged in 1915, and its foreign affiliates in the Women's International League for Peace and Freedom led the struggle to persuade governments to negotiate peace and spare dissenters from harsh punishment. After America entered the conflict, advocates for peace were routinely labeled cowards and traitors, their efforts crushed by the steamroller of conformity.

To suppress criticism of the war, Wilson stirred up patriotic fervor. In 1917, the president created the **Committee on Public Information** under the direction of George Creel, a journalist, who became the nation's cheerleader for war. He sent "Four-Minute Men," a squad of 75,000 volunteers, around the country to give brief pep talks that celebrated successes on the battlefields and in the factories. Posters, pamphlets, and cartoons depicted brave American soldiers and sailors defending freedom and democracy against the evil "Huns."

America rallied around Creel's campaign. The film industry cranked out melodramas about battle-line and home-front heroes and taught audiences to hiss at the German kaiser. A musical, *The Kaiser: The Beast of Berlin*, opened on Broadway in 1918. Faculties of colleges and universities generated war propaganda in the guise of scholarship. When Professor James McKeen Cattell of Columbia University urged that America seek peace with Germany short of victory, university president Nicholas Murray Butler fired him on the grounds that "what had been folly is now treason."

A firestorm of anti-German passion erupted. Across the nation, "100% American" campaigns enlisted ordinary people to sniff out disloyalty. German, the most widely taught foreign language in 1914, practically disappeared from the nation's schools. Targeting German-born Americans, the *Saturday Evening Post* declared that it was time to rid the country of "the scum of the melting pot." Rabid anti-German action reached its extreme with the lynching of Robert Prager, a baker in Collinsville, Illinois. In the eyes of the mob, it was enough that Prager was German-born and had socialist leanings, even though he had not opposed American participation in the war. Persuaded by the defense lawyer who praised what he called a "patriotic murder," the jury at the trial of the killers took only twenty-five minutes to acquit.

As hysteria increased, the campaign reached absurd levels. In Montana, a school board barred a history text that had good things to say about medieval Germany. Menus across the nation changed German toast to French toast and sauerkraut to liberty cabbage. In Milwaukee, vigilantes mounted a machine gun outside the Pabst Theater to prevent the staging of Schiller's *Wilhelm Tell*, a powerful protest against tyranny. One vigilant citizen claimed to see a periscope in the Great Lakes, and the fiancée of one of the war's leading critics, caught dancing on the dunes of Cape Cod, was held on suspicion of signaling to German submarines.

The Wilson administration's zeal in suppressing dissent contrasted sharply with its war aims of defending democracy. In the name of self-defense, the Espionage Act (June 1917), the Trading with the Enemy Act (October 1917), and the Sedition Act (May 1918) gave the government sweeping powers to punish any opinion or activity it considered "disloyal, profane, scurrilous, or abusive." When Postmaster General Albert Burleson blocked mailing privileges for dissenting publications, dozens of journals were forced to close down. Of the 1,500 individuals eventually charged with sedition, all but a dozen had merely spoken words the government found objectionable. One of them was Eugene V. Debs, the leader of the Socialist Party, who was convicted under the Espionage Act for speeches condemning the war as a capitalist plot and sent to the Atlanta penitentiary.

The president hoped that national commitment to the war would silence partisan politics, but his Republican rivals used the war as a weapon against the Democrats. The trick was to oppose Wilson's conduct of the war but not the war itself. Republicans outshouted Wilson on the nation's need to mobilize for war but then complained that Wilson's War Industries Board was a tyrannical agency that crushed free enterprise. Such attacks appealed to widely diverse business, labor, and patriotic groups. As the war progressed, Republicans gathered power against the Democrats, who had narrowly reelected Wilson in 1916.

In 1918, Republicans gained a narrow majority in both the House and the Senate. The end of Democratic control of Congress not only halted further domestic reform but also meant that the United States would advance toward military victory in Europe with political power divided between a Democratic president and a Republican Congress likely to challenge Wilson's plans for international cooperation.

REVIEW   How did progressive ideals fare during wartime?

▶ A Compromised Peace

Wilson decided to reaffirm his noble war ideals by announcing his peace aims before the end of hostilities. He hoped the victorious Allies would adopt his plan for international democracy, but he was sorely disappointed. The leaders of Britain, France, and Italy (which had joined the Allies in 1915 in hopes of postwar gains) understood that Wilson's principles jeopardized their own postwar plans for the acquisition of enemy territory, new colonial empires, and reparations. Wilson also faced strong opposition at home from those who feared that his enthusiasm for international cooperation would undermine American sovereignty.

Wilson's Fourteen Points

On January 8, 1918, President Wilson revealed to Congress his **Fourteen Points**, his blueprint for a new democratic world order. The first five points affirmed basic liberal ideals: an end to secret treaties; freedom of the seas; removal of economic barriers to free trade; reduction of weapons of war; and recognition of the rights of colonized peoples. The next eight points supported the right to self-determination of European peoples who had been dominated by Germany or its allies. Wilson's fourteenth point called for a "general association of nations" — a **League of Nations** — to provide "mutual guarantees of political independence and territorial integrity to great and small states alike." A League of Nations reflected Wilson's lifelong dream of a "parliament of man." Only such an organization of "peace-loving nations," he believed, could justify the war and secure a lasting peace.

Citizens of the United States and of every Allied country greeted the Fourteen Points enthusiastically. Wilson felt confident that he could prevail against undemocratic and selfish forces at the peace table. During the final year of the war, he pressured the Allies to accept the Fourteen Points as the basis of the postwar settlement.

The Paris Peace Conference

From January 18 to June 28, 1919, the eyes of the world focused on Paris. There, powerful men wrestled with difficult problems. Although no other American president had ever gone to Europe while in office, Wilson, inspired by his mission, decided to head the U.S. delegation. He said he owed it to the American soldiers. "It is now my duty," he announced, "to play my full part in making good what they gave their life's blood to obtain." A dubious British diplomat retorted that Wilson was drawn to Paris "as a debutante is

> "God himself was content with ten commandments."
> — French premier GEORGES CLEMENCEAU, disparaging Wilson's Fourteen Points

entranced by the prospect of her first ball." The decision to leave the country at a time when his political opponents challenged his leadership was risky enough, but his stubborn refusal to include prominent Republicans in the delegation proved foolhardy and eventually cost him his dream of a new world order with the United States at its center.

After four terrible years of war, the common people of Europe almost worshipped Wilson, believing that he would create a safer, more decent world. When the peace conference convened at Louis XIV's magnificent palace at Versailles, however, Wilson encountered a different reception. Representing the Allies were the decidedly unidealistic David Lloyd George, prime minister of Britain; Georges Clemenceau,

premier of France; and Vittorio Orlando, former prime minister of Italy. To the Allied leaders, Wilson appeared a naive and impractical moralist. His desire to gather former enemies within a new international democratic order showed how little he understood hard European realities. Clemenceau claimed that Wilson "believed you could do everything by formulas" and "empty theory." Disparaging the Fourteen Points, he added, "God himself was content with ten commandments."

The Allies wanted to fasten blame for the war on Germany, totally disarm it, and make it pay so dearly that it would never threaten its neighbors again. The French demanded retribution in the form of territory containing Germany's richest mineral resources. The British made it

Leaders of the Paris Peace Conference

The three leaders in charge of putting the world back together after the Great War — from left to right, British prime minister David Lloyd George, French premier Georges Clemenceau, and U.S. president Woodrow Wilson — amiably and confidently stride toward the peace conference at the Versailles palace. Clemenceau is caught offering animated instruction to Wilson, whom he considered naively idealistic. Indeed, in an unguarded moment, Clemenceau expressed his contempt for the entire United States as a country that was unique in having passed directly from barbarism to decadence without an intervening period of civilization. Gamma Liaison/ Getty Images.

clear that they were not about to give up the powerful weapon of naval blockade for the vague principle of freedom of the seas.

The Allies forced Wilson to make drastic compromises. In return for France's moderating its territorial claims, he agreed to support Article 231 of the peace treaty, assigning war guilt to Germany. Though saved from permanently losing Rhineland territory to the French, Germany was outraged at being singled out as the instigator of the war and being saddled with more than $33 billion in damages. Many Germans felt that their nation had been betrayed. After agreeing to an armistice in the belief that peace terms would be based in Wilson's generous Fourteen Points, they faced hardship and humiliation instead.

Wilson had better success in establishing the principle of self-determination. But from the beginning, Secretary of State Robert Lansing knew that the president's concept of self-determination was "simply loaded with dynamite." Lansing won-

dered, "What unit has he in mind? Does he mean a race, a territorial area, or a community?" Even Wilson was vague about what self-determination actually meant. "When I gave utterance to those words," he admitted, "I said them without the knowledge that nationalities existed, which are coming to us day after day." Lansing suspected that the notion "will raise hopes which can never be realized. It will, I fear, cost thousands of lives. In the end it is bound to be discredited, to be called the dream of an idealist who failed to realize the danger until it was too late."

Yet partly on the basis of self-determination, the conference redrew the map of Europe and parts of the rest of the world. Portions of Austria-Hungary were ceded to Italy, Poland, and Romania, and the remainder was reassembled into Austria, Hungary, Czechoslovakia, and Yugoslavia — independent republics whose boundaries were drawn with attention to concentrations of major ethnic groups. More arbitrarily, the Ottoman empire was carved

MAP 22.5
Europe after World War I
The post–World War I settlement redrew boundaries to create new nations based on ethnic groupings. Within defeated Germany and Russia, this outcome left bitter peoples who resolved to recover the territory taken from them.

up into small mandates (including Palestine) run by local leaders but under the control of France and Great Britain. The conference reserved the mandate system for those regions it deemed insufficiently "civilized" to have full independence. Thus, the reconstructed nations — each beset with ethnic and nationalist rivalries — faced the challenge of making a new democratic government work (Map 22.5). Many of today's bitterest disputes — in the Balkans and Iraq, between Greece and Turkey, between Arabs and Jews — have roots in the decisions made in Paris in 1919.

Wilson hoped that self-determination would also dictate the fate of Germany's colonies in Asia and Africa. But the Allies, who had taken over the colonies during the war, allowed the League of Nations only a mandate to administer them. Technically, the mandate system rejected imperialism, but in reality it allowed the Allies to maintain control. Thus, while denying Germany its colonies, the Allies retained and added to their own far-flung territories.

The cause of democratic equality suffered another setback when the peace conference rejected Japan's call for a statement of racial equality in the treaty. Wilson's belief in the superiority of whites, as well as his apprehension about how white Americans would respond to such a declaration, led him to oppose the clause. To soothe hurt feelings, Wilson agreed to grant Japan a mandate over the Shantung Peninsula in northern China, which had formerly been controlled by Germany. The gesture mollified Japan's moderate leaders, but the military faction preparing to take over the country used bitterness toward racist Western colonialism to build support for expanding Japanese power throughout Asia.

Closest to Wilson's heart was finding a new way to manage international relations. In Wilson's view, war had discredited the old strategy of balance of power. Instead, he proposed a League of Nations that would provide collective security. The league would establish rules of international conduct and resolve conflicts between nations through rational and peaceful means. When the Allies agreed to the league, Wilson was overjoyed. He believed that the league would rectify the errors his colleagues had forced on him in Paris. The league would solidify and extend the noble work he had begun.

To some Europeans and Americans, the **Versailles treaty** came as a bitter disappointment. Wilson's admirers were shocked that the president dealt in compromise like any other politician. But without Wilson's presence, the treaty that was signed on June 28, 1919, surely would have been

more vindictive. Wilson returned home in July 1919 consoled that, despite his frustrations, he had gained what he most wanted — a League of Nations. In Wilson's judgment, "We have completed in the least time possible the greatest work that four men have ever done."

The Fight for the Treaty

The tumultuous reception Wilson received when he arrived home persuaded him, probably correctly, that the American people supported the treaty. When the president submitted the treaty to the Senate in July 1919, he warned that failure to ratify it would "break the heart of the world." By then, however, criticism of the treaty was mounting, especially from Americans convinced that their countries of ethnic origin had not been given fair treatment. Irish Americans, Italian Americans, and German Americans launched especially sharp attacks. Others worried that the president's concessions at Versailles had jeopardized the treaty's capacity to provide a generous plan for rebuilding Europe and to guarantee world peace.

Some of the most potent critics were found in the Senate. Bolstered by a slight Republican majority in Congress, a group of Republican "irreconcilables," which included such powerful isolationist senators as Hiram Johnson of California and William Borah of Idaho, condemned the treaty for entangling the United States in world affairs. A larger group of Republicans did not object to American participation in world politics but feared that membership in the League of Nations would jeopardize the nation's ability to act independently. No Republican, in any case, was eager to hand Wilson and the Democrats a foreign policy victory with the 1920 presidential election little more than a year away.

At the center of Republican opposition was Wilson's archenemy, Senator **Henry Cabot Lodge** of Massachusetts. Lodge's hostility was in part personal. "I never thought I could hate a man as much as I hate Wilson," he once admitted. But Lodge also raised cogent objections to the treaty and the league. Lodge was no isolationist, but he thought that much of the Fourteen Points was a "general bleat about virtue being better than vice." Lodge expected the United States' economic and military power to propel the nation into a major role in world affairs. But he insisted that membership in the League of Nations, which would require collective action to maintain peace, threatened the nation's independence in foreign relations.

Wilson decided to take his case directly to the people. On September 3, 1919, still exhausted from the peace conference and against the objections of his doctors, he set out by train on the most ambitious speaking tour ever undertaken by a president. On September 25 in Pueblo, Colorado, Wilson collapsed and had to return to Washington. There, he suffered a massive stroke that partially paralyzed him. From his bedroom, Wilson sent messages instructing Democrats in the Senate to hold firm against any and all reservations. Wilson commanded enough loyalty to ensure a vote against the Lodge reservations. But when the treaty without reservations came before the Senate in March 1920, the combined opposition of the Republican irreconcilables and reservationists left Wilson six votes short of the two-thirds majority needed for passage. Wilson told his doctor, "The Devil is a busy man."

The nations of Europe organized the League of Nations at Geneva, Switzerland. Although Woodrow Wilson received the Nobel Peace Prize in 1920 for his central role in creating the league, the United States never became a member. In refusing to accept relatively minor compromises with Senate moderates, Wilson lost his treaty and American membership in the league. Whether American membership could have prevented the world war that would begin in Europe in 1939 is highly unlikely, but the United States' failure to join certainly weakened the league from the start. Woodrow Wilson and Henry Cabot Lodge both died in 1924, never seeing international order or security, never knowing the whirlwind of resentment and violence that would eventually follow the Great War's failure to make the world safe for democracy.

REVIEW Why did the Senate fail to ratify the Versailles treaty?

▶ Democracy at Risk

The defeat of Wilson's plan for international democracy proved the crowning blow to progressives who had hoped that the war could boost reform at home. When the war ended, Americans wanted to demobilize swiftly. In the process, servicemen, defense workers, and farmers lost their war-related jobs. The volatile combination — of unemployed veterans returning home, a stalled economy, and leftover wartime patriotism looking for a new cause—threatened to explode. Wartime anti-German passion was quickly followed by

"Refusing to Give the Lady a Seat"
Woodrow Wilson promised that the League of Nations would usher in an age of international peace. When stiff opposition to American membership in the league developed in the United States, friends of the league mounted a counterattack. This cartoon skewers the three leading Republican opponents of the league — Senators William Borah of Idaho, Henry Cabot Lodge of Massachusetts, and Hiram Johnson of California — who stubbornly refuse to budge an inch for the angel of peace. Clever cartoons could not save the league, however. Only shrewd diplomacy could do that, and Wilson was not able to deliver. Picture Research Consultants & Archives.

Lodge used his position as chairman of the Senate Foreign Relations Committee to air every sort of complaint. Out of the committee hearings came several amendments, or "reservations," that sought to limit the consequences of American membership in the league. For example, several reservations required approval of both the House and the Senate before the United States could participate in league-sponsored economic sanctions or military action.

It gradually became clear that ratification of the treaty depended on acceptance of the Lodge reservations. Democratic senators, who overwhelmingly supported the treaty, urged Wilson to accept Lodge's terms, arguing that they left the essentials of the treaty intact. Wilson, however, insisted that the reservations cut "the very heart out of the treaty." He expressed personal hatred as well. "*Lodge* reservations?" he thundered. "Never! I'll never consent to adopt any policy with which that impossible name is so prominently identified."

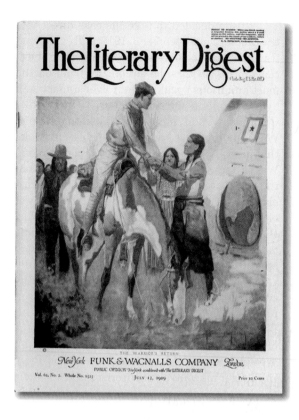

"The Warrior's Return"
About 16,000 Native Americans served in the U.S. armed forces during World War I. This magazine cover offers a romanticized reconstruction of one homecoming. The young soldier, still in uniform and presumably fresh from France, rides his pony to the tepee of his parents, who proudly welcome their brave warrior. The tepee is decorated with a star, a national symbol that families with sons in the military displayed on their homes. The painting sought to demonstrate that even Americans on the margins of national life were sufficiently assimilated and loyal to join the national sacrifice to defeat the enemy. Picture Research Consultants & Archives.

antiradicalism, a fevered campaign that ensnared unionists, socialists, dissenters, and African Americans and Mexicans who had committed no offense but to seek to escape rural poverty. The 1920 election marked the end of Wilson's two terms in the White House and his crusades.

Economic Hardship and Labor Upheaval

Americans greeted peace with a demand that the United States return to a peacetime economy. The government abruptly abandoned its wartime economic controls and canceled war contracts worth millions of dollars. In a matter of months, 3 million soldiers mustered out of the military and flooded the job market just as war production ceased. Unemployment soared. At the same time, consumers went on a postwar spending spree that drove inflation skyward. In 1919, prices rose 75 percent over prewar levels, and in 1920 prices rose another 28 percent.

Most of the gains workers had made during the war evaporated. Freed from government controls, business turned against the eight-hour day and attacked labor unions. With inflation eating up their paychecks, workers fought back. The year 1919 witnessed nearly 3,600 strikes involving 4 million workers. The

most spectacular strike occurred in February 1919 in Seattle, where shipyard workers had been put out of work by demobilization. When a coalition of the radical Industrial Workers of the World (IWW, called Wobblies) and the moderate American Federation of Labor called a general strike, the largest work stoppage in American history shut down the city. Newspapers claimed that the walkout was "a Bolshevik effort to start a revolution." The suppression of the **Seattle general strike** by city officials cost the AFL many of its wartime gains and contributed to the destruction of the IWW soon afterward.

A strike by Boston policemen in the fall of 1919 underscored postwar hostility toward labor militancy. Although the police had received no raise since before the war and were paid less than pick-and-shovel laborers, they won little sympathy. Once the officers stopped walking their beats, looters sacked the city. Massachusetts governor Calvin Coolidge called in the National Guard to restore order and broke the **Boston police strike**. The public, yearning for peace and security in the wake of war, welcomed Coolidge's anti-union assurance that "there is no right to strike against the public safety by anybody, anywhere, any time." Labor strife climaxed in the grim **steel strike of 1919**. Faced with the industry's plan to revert to seven-day

Returning Veterans and Work
After the triumphal parades ended, attention turned to the question of what the heroes would do at home. The Department of Labor poster tries to convey a strong image of purposefulness and prosperity by portraying a soldier in front of a booming industrial landscape. But the U.S. Employment Service had little to offer veterans beyond posters, and unions were unprepared to cope with the massive numbers of former soldiers who needed retraining. As workplace conditions deteriorated, the largest number of strikes in the nation's history broke out in 1919. Veterans: © Bettmann/Corbis; poster: Library of Congress.

weeks, twelve-hour days, and weekly wages of about $20, Samuel Gompers, head of the AFL, called for a strike. In September, 350,000 workers in fifteen states walked out. The steel industry hired 30,000 strikebreakers (many of them African Americans) and convinced the public that the strikers were radicals bent on subverting democracy and capitalism. In January 1920, after 18 striking workers were killed, the strike collapsed. That devastating defeat initiated a sharp decline in the fortunes of the labor movement, a trend that would continue for almost twenty years.

The Red Scare

Suppression of labor strikes was one response to the widespread fear of internal subversion that swept the

nation in 1919. The **Red scare** ("Red" referred to the color of the Bolshevik flag) far outstripped even the assault on civil liberties during the war. It had homegrown causes: the postwar recession, labor unrest, terrorist acts, and the difficulties of reintegrating millions of returning veterans. But unsettling events abroad also added to Americans' anxieties.

Two epidemics swept the globe in 1918. One was Spanish influenza, which brought on a lethal accumulation of fluid in the lungs. A nurse near the front lines in France observed that victims "run a high temperature, so high that we can't believe it's true. . . . It is accompanied by vomiting and dysentery. When they die, as about half of them do, they turn a ghastly dark gray and are taken out at once and cremated." Before the flu virus had run its course, 40 million people had died world-wide, including some 700,000 Americans.

The other epidemic was Russian bolshevism, which seemed to most Americans at the time equally contagious and deadly. Bolshevism became even more menacing in March 1919, when the new Soviet leaders created the Comintern, a world-wide association of Communists intent on fomenting revolution in capitalist countries. (See "Beyond America's Borders," page 740.) A Communist revolution in the United States was extremely unlikely, but edgy Americans, faced with a flurry of terrorist acts, believed otherwise. Dozens of prominent individuals had received bombs through the mail. On September 16, 1920, a wagon filled with dynamite and iron exploded on Wall Street, killing 38 and maiming 143 others. Authorities never caught the terrorists, and the successful attack on America's financial capital fed the nation's fear, anger, and uncertainty.

Even before the Wall Street bombing, the government had initiated a hunt for domestic revolutionaries. Led by Attorney General **A. Mitchell Palmer**, the campaign targeted men and women who harbored ideas that Palmer believed could lead to violence, even though the individuals may not have done anything illegal. In January 1920, Palmer ordered a series of raids that netted 6,000 alleged subversives. Finding no revolutionary conspiracies, Palmer nevertheless ordered 500 noncitizen suspects deported. His action came in the wake of a cam-

paign against the most notorious radical alien, Russian-born **Emma Goldman**. Before the war, Goldman's passionate support of labor strikes, women's rights, and birth control had made her a symbol of radicalism. Finally, after a stay in prison for denouncing military conscription, she was ordered deported by J. Edgar Hoover, the eager director of the Justice Department's Radical Division. In December 1919, as Goldman and 250 others boarded a ship for exile in Russia, she turned defiantly to thumb her nose at a jeering crowd.

The effort to rid the country of alien radicals was matched by efforts to crush troublesome citizens. Law enforcement officials and vigilante groups joined hands against so-called Reds. In November 1919 in the rugged lumber town of Centralia, Washington, a menacing crowd gathered in front of the IWW hall. Nervous Wobblies inside opened fire, killing three people. Three IWW members were arrested and later convicted of murder, but another, ex-soldier Wesley Everett, was carried off by the mob, which castrated him, hung him from a bridge, and then riddled his body with bullets. His death was officially ruled a suicide.

Public institutions joined the attack on civil liberties. Local libraries removed dissenting books. Schools fired unorthodox teachers. Police shut down radical newspapers. State legislatures refused to seat elected representatives who professed socialist ideas. And in 1919, Congress

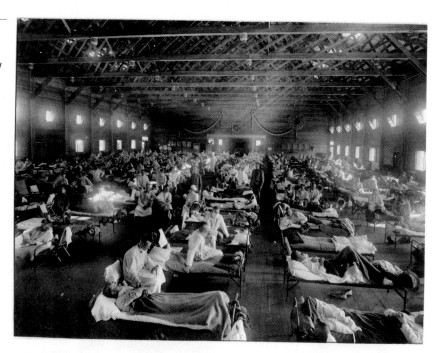

Emergency Hospital
Despite its name, the Spanish flu was first observed in the spring of 1918 in Kansas. Army camps, with their close troop quarters, proved perfect incubators. This emergency hospital at Camp Funston, Kansas, is filled with soldiers who were among the flu's early victims. Crowded troopships quickly spread the virus to Europe. Civilians were not immune. In October 1918 in Philadelphia, more than 4500 people died in a single week. Contracting the Spanish flu was not a death sentence, but it disproportionately killed young adults. National Museum of Health & Medicine, Armed Forces Institute of Pathology.

Rooting out Reds
On January 2, 1920, Attorney General A. Mitchell Palmer ordered hundreds of federal agents to thirty-three American cities to smash the alleged Bolshevik conspiracy. Led by J. Edgar Hoover, the agents arrested more than six thousand individuals on charges of plotting to overthrow the government. The agents who carried out Palmer's Red-hunting were not particularly careful about protecting the property of those they targeted. This photograph of the Industrial Workers of the World (IWW) headquarters in New York City shows the results of one raid. Labadie Collection, University of Michigan.

removed its lone socialist representative, Victor Berger, on the pretext that he was a threat to national safety.

That same year, the Supreme Court provided a formula for restricting free speech. In upholding the conviction of socialist Charles Schenck for publishing a pamphlet urging resistance to the draft during wartime (***Schenck v. United States***), the Court established a "clear and present danger" test. Such utterances as Schenck's during a time of national peril, Justice Oliver Wendell Holmes wrote, were equivalent to shouting "Fire!" in a crowded theater. But Schenck's pamphlet had little power to provoke a public firmly opposed to its message.

In 1920, the assault on civil liberties provoked the creation of the **American Civil Liberties Union (ACLU)**, which was dedicated to defending the individual rights that the Constitution guaranteed. One of the ACLU's founders, Roger Baldwin, declared, "So long as we have enough people in this country willing to fight for their rights, we'll be called a democracy." The ACLU championed the targets of Attorney General Palmer's campaign — politically radical immigrants, trade unionists, socialists and Communists, and antiwar activists who still languished in jail.

But in the end, the Red scare collapsed because of its excesses. In particular, the antiradical campaign lost credibility after Palmer warned in the spring of 1920 that radicals were planning to

celebrate the Bolshevik Revolution with a nation-wide wave of violence on May 1, international workers' day. Officials called out state militias, mobilized bomb squads, and even placed machine-gun nests at major city intersections. When May 1 came and went without a single disturbance, the public mood turned from fear to scorn.

The Great Migrations of African Americans and Mexicans

Before the Red scare lost steam, the government raised alarms about the loyalty of African Americans. A Justice Department investigation concluded that Reds were fomenting racial unrest among blacks. Although the report was wrong about Bolshevik influence, it was correct in noticing a new stirring among African Americans, an assertiveness born of participation in the war effort and the massive migration out of the South.

In 1900, nine of every ten blacks still lived in the South, where poverty, disfranchisement, segregation, and violence dominated their lives. A majority of black men continued to toil in agriculture as dirt-poor tenants or sharecroppers or worked for wages of 60 cents a day. Black women worked in the homes of whites as domestics for $2 a week. Whites remained committed to keeping blacks down. "If we own a good farm or horse, or cow, or bird-dog, or yoke of oxen," a

Bolshevism

In March 1917, revolutionaries overthrew the Russian czar, whose conservative autocracy was the target of peasants and urban workers seeking a more democratic government. But Marxist radicals, who called themselves Bolsheviks, were not satisfied with the regime change. In November, the Bolsheviks seized control of Russia and made their leader, Vladimir Ilyich Lenin, ruler. Lenin scoffed at the idea that the Allies were fighting for democracy and insisted that greedy capitalists were waging war for international dominance. In March 1918, he shocked Woodrow Wilson and the Allies by signing a separate peace with Germany and withdrawing Russia from the war. Still locked in the desperate struggle with Germany, the Allies cried betrayal.

The Bolshevik regime dedicated itself to ending capitalism in Russia (known as the Soviet Union after 1922) and to instituting what it called a "dictatorship of the proletariat." In theory, workers — agricultural and industrial — would control the economy and exercise political power. But very quickly a gap opened between the workers and party leaders, who instituted a top-down apparatus that institutionalized the bloody repression of their opponents.

Prodded by British leader Winston Churchill, who declared that "the Bolshevik infant should be strangled in its cradle," Britain and France urged the United States to join them in sending troops to Russia in support of Russian democrats opposing the new revolutionary regime. Several prominent Americans spoke out against American intervention. Senator William Borah of Idaho declared: "The Russian people have the same right to establish a Socialist state as we have to establish a republic." But Wilson concluded that the Bolsheviks were a dictatorial party that had come to power through a violent coup that denied Russians political choice, and in September 1918 he ordered 14,000 U.S. troops to join British and French forces in Russia. U.S., British, and French troops fought to overthrow Lenin and annul the Bolshevik Revolution, but the Bolsheviks (by now calling themselves Communists) prevailed. U.S. troops withdrew from Russia in June 1919, after the loss of more than 200 American lives.

The Bolshevik regime also committed itself to overthrowing capitalist and imperialist regimes around the world. Clearly, Lenin's imagined future was at odds with Wilson's proposed liberal new world order. Wilson withheld U.S. diplomatic recognition of the Soviet Union (a policy that persisted until 1934) and joined the Allies in an economic boycott to bring down the Bolshevik government. Unbowed, Lenin promised that his party would "incite rebellion among all the peoples now oppressed," and revolutionary agitation became central to Soviet foreign policy. Just after the armistice, Communist revolutions erupted in Bavaria and Hungary. Though short-lived, the Communist regimes there sent shock waves throughout the West. In 1919, moreover, a Russian official bragged that monies being sent to Europe to foment Bolshevik rebellion were "nothing compared to the funds transmitted to New York for the purpose of spreading bolshevism in the United States." American attention shifted from revolutionaries in Europe to revolutionaries at home. The Red scare was on.

Attorney General A. Mitchell Palmer perceived a "blaze of Revolution sweeping over every American institution of law and order . . . licking the altars of churches . . . crawling into the sacred corners of American homes." In 1919, the U.S. government launched an all-out attack on the Communist ("Red") menace. In the same year, disgruntled socialists founded the American Communist Party, but it attracted only a handful of members, who spent most of their time arguing the fine points of doctrine, not manufacturing bombs. However, the few radicals who did resort to bombs prompted near panic

black sharecropper in Mississippi observed in 1913, "we are harassed until we are bound to sell, give away, or run away, before we can have any peace in our lives."

The First World War provided African Americans with the opportunity to escape the South's cotton fields and kitchens. War channeled almost 5 million American workers into military service and caused the number of European immigrants to fall from more than a million in 1914 to 31,000 in 1918. Deprived of their traditional sources of laborers just as production

demands were increasing, northern industrialists turned to black labor. Young black men, who made up the bulk of the early migrants, found work in steel mills, shipyards, munitions plants, railroad yards, automobile factories, and mines. From 1915 to 1920, a half million blacks (approximately 10 percent of the South's black population) boarded trains bound for Philadelphia, Detroit, Cleveland, Chicago, St. Louis, and other industrial cities.

Thousands of migrants wrote home to tell family and friends about their experiences in the

in some quarters. Even mild dissenters faced bullying and threats. Workers seeking better wages and conditions, women and African Americans demanding equal rights, and anyone else pushing for change found the government hurling the epithet "Red" at them. Before the hysteria subsided, the nation witnessed beatings, jailings, and deportations.

The Bolshevik Revolution had endless consequences. In the Soviet Union, it initiated a brutal reign of terror that lasted for more than seven decades. In international politics, it set up a polarity that lasted nearly as long. In a very real sense, the Cold War, which set the United States and the Soviet Union at each other's throats after World War II, began in 1917. America's abortive military intervention against the Bolshevik regime and the Bolsheviks' call for worldwide revolution convulsed relations from the very beginning. In the United States, the rabid antiradicalism of the Red scare threatened traditional American values. Commitment to the protection of dissent succumbed to irrational anticommunism. Even mild reform became tarred with the brush of bolshevism. Although the Red scare quickly withered, the habit of crushing dissent in the name of security would live on. Years later, in the 1950s, when Americans' anxiety mounted and their confidence waned once again, witch-hunts against radicalism reemerged to undermine American democracy.

Vladimir Ilyich Lenin
After the Bolshevik success in Russia in 1917, Lenin became the face of the Communist revolution. His call for workers everywhere to rise against the ruling classes and end capitalism and imperialism sent chills down spines throughout much of Western Europe and the United States. Rather than viewing Lenin as a bloodthirsty monster, however, this dramatic portrait presents him as the courageous hero of the people's revolution. Lenin admitted that in the United States revolution would "probably not come soon," but that gave Americans little comfort. AP/Wide World Photos.

America in a Global Context

1. Why did U.S.-Bolshevik relations get off to such a rocky start? Were harsh relations the result of certain policy decisions or inherent in the clashing value systems?

2. In the United States, is there an inevitable tension between national security and free expression? Why or why not?

North. One man announced proudly that he had recently been promoted to "first assistant to the head carpenter." He added, "I should have been here twenty years ago. I just begin to feel like a man. . . . My children are going to the same school with the whites and I don't have to [h]umble to no one. I have registered — will vote the next election and there ain't any 'yes sir' — it's all yes and no and Sam and Bill."

But the North was not the promised land. Black men stood on the lowest rungs of the labor ladder. Jobs of any kind proved scarce for black women, and most worked as domestic servants as they did in the South. The existing black middle class sometimes shunned the less educated, less sophisticated rural southerners crowding into northern cities. Many whites, fearful of losing jobs and status, lashed out against the new migrants. Savage race riots ripped through two dozen northern cities. The worst occurred in July 1917 when a mob of whites invaded a section of East St. Louis, Illinois, crowded with blacks who had been recruited to help break a strike. The mob murdered at least

If You are a Stranger in the City

If you want a job   If you want a place to live
If you are having trouble with your employer
If you want information or advice of any kind
CALL UPON

The CHICAGO LEAGUE ON URBAN
CONDITIONS AMONG NEGROES
3719 South State Street
Telephone Douglas 9098   T. ARNOLD HILL, Executive Secretary

No charges—no fees. We want to help YOU

SELF-HELP

1. Do not loaf. Get a job at once.
2. Do not live in crowded rooms. Others can be obtained.
3. Do not carry on loud conversations in street cars and public places.
4. Do not keep your children out of school.
5. Do not send for your family until you get a job.
6. Do not think you can hold your job unless you are industrious, sober, efficient and prompt.

Cleanliness and fresh air are necessary for good health. In case of sickness send immediately for a good physician. Become an active member in some church as soon as you reach the city.

Issued by

African Americans Migrate North
Wearing their Sunday best and carrying the rest of what they owned in two suitcases, this southern family waits to board a northern-bound train in 1912. In Chicago, the League on Urban Conditions among Negroes, which eventually became the Urban League, sought to ease the transition of southern blacks to life in the North by distributing cards such as the one shown here (front and back). Other cards advised hard work, sobriety, cleanliness, finding a church, getting children into school, and speaking softly in public places. Photo: Photographs and Prints Division, Schomburg Center for Research in Black Culture, New York Public Library, Astor, Lenox, and Tilden Foundations; card: Arthur and Graham Aldis papers (Aldis neg-1A & 1B), Special Collections, The University Library, University of Illinois at Chicago.

39 people and left most of the black district in flames. In 1918, the nation witnessed 96 lynchings of blacks, some of them decorated war veterans still in uniform.

Still, most black migrants stayed in the North and encouraged friends and family to follow. By 1940, more than one million blacks had left the South, profoundly changing their own lives and the course of the nation's history. Black enclaves such as Harlem in New York and the South Side of Chicago, "cities within cities," emerged in the North. These assertive communities provided a foundation for black protest and political organization in the years ahead.

At nearly the same moment that black Americans streamed into northern cities, another migration was under way in the American Southwest. Between 1910 and 1920, the Mexican-born population in the United States soared from 222,000 to 478,000. Mexican immigration resulted from developments on both sides of the border. In Mexico, dictator Porfirio Díaz initiated land policies that decimated poor farmers. When the Mexicans revolted against Díaz in 1910, initiating a ten-year civil war, the trickle of migration became a flood. North of the border, the Chinese Exclusion Act of 1882 and later the disruption of World War I cut off the supply of cheap foreign labor and caused western employers in the expanding rail, mining, construction, and agricultural industries to look south to Mexico for workers.

As a result of Americans' racial stereotyping of Mexicans — a U.S. government economist

Mexican Women Arriving in El Paso, 1911
These Mexican women, carrying bundles and wearing traditional shawls, try to get their bearings upon arriving in El Paso, Texas — the Ellis Island for Mexican immigrants. Perhaps they are looking for a family member who preceded them, or perhaps they are alone and calculating their next step. In any case, they were part of the first modern wave of Mexican immigration to the United States. Women like them found work in the cotton and sugar beet fields, canneries, and restaurants of the Southwest, as well as at home taking in sewing, laundry, and boarders. Whatever their work, their journey across the border was life changing. Courtesy of the Rio Grande Historical Collections, New Mexico State University, Las Cruces, NM.

three-fourths of laborers in the cotton fields and in construction there.

Like immigrants from Europe and black migrants from the South, Mexicans in the American Southwest dreamed of a better life. And like the others, they found both opportunity and disappointment. Wages were better than in Mexico, but life in the fields, mines, and factories was hard, and living conditions — in boxcars, labor camps, or urban barrios — often were dismal. Signs warning "No Mexicans Allowed" increased rather than declined. Mexican women nurtured families, but many also worked picking cotton or as domestics. Among Mexican Americans, some of whom had lived in the Southwest for a century or more, *los recién llegados* (the recent arrivals) encountered mixed reactions. One Mexican American expressed this ambivalence: "We are all Mexicans anyway because the gueros [Anglos] treat us all alike." But he also called for immigration quotas because the recent arrivals drove down wages and incited white prejudice that affected all ethnic Mexicans.

Despite friction, large-scale immigration into the Southwest meant a resurgence of the Mexican cultural presence, which became the basis for greater solidarity and political action for the ethnic Mexican population. In 1929 in Texas, Mexican Americans formed the League of United Latin American Citizens.

Postwar Politics and the Election of 1920

A thousand miles away in Washington, D.C., President Woodrow Wilson, bedridden and paralyzed, stubbornly ignored the mountain of domestic troubles — labor strikes, the Red Scare, race riots, immigration backlash — and insisted that the 1920 election would be a "solemn referendum" on the League of Nations. Dutifully, the Democratic nominees for president, James M. Cox of Ohio, and for vice president, Franklin Delano Roosevelt of New York, campaigned on Wilson's international ideals. The Republican Party chose the handsome, gregarious Warren Gamaliel Harding, senator from Ohio. Harding's rise in Ohio politics was a tribute to his amiability, not his mastery of the issues.

Harding found the winning formula when he declared that "America's present need is not heroics, but healing; not nostrums [questionable remedies] but normalcy." But what was "normalcy"? Harding explained: "By 'normalcy' I don't mean the old order but a regular steady order of things. I mean normal procedure, the

described them as "docile, patient, usually orderly in camp, fairly intelligent under competent supervision, obedient and cheap" — Mexicans were considered excellent prospects for manual labor but not for citizenship. Employers tried to dampen racial fears by stressing that the immigrants were only temporary residents, not a lasting threat. In 1917, when anti-immigration advocates convinced Congress to do something about foreigners coming into the United States, the restrictive legislation bowed to southwestern industry and exempted Mexicans. By 1920, ethnic Mexicans made up about three-fourths of California's farm laborers. They were also crucial to the Texas economy, accounting for

Candidate	Electoral Vote	Popular Vote	Percent of Popular Vote
Warren G. Harding (Republican)	404	16,143,407	60.5
James M. Cox (Democrat)	127	9,130,328	34.2
Eugene V. Debs (Socialist)	0	919,799	3.4

MAP 22.6

The Election of 1920

natural way, without excess." Eager to put wartime crusades and postwar strife behind them, voters responded by giving Harding the largest presidential victory ever: 60.5 percent of the popular vote and 404 out of 531 electoral votes (Map 22.6). Once in office, Harding and his wife, Florence, threw open the White House gates, which had been closed since the declaration of war in 1917. Their welcome brought throngs of visitors and lifted the national pall, signaling a new, more easygoing era.

> **REVIEW** How did the Red scare contribute to the erosion of civil liberties after the war?

▶ Conclusion: Troubled Crusade

America's experience in World War I was exceptional. For much of the world, the Great War produced great destruction, endless blackened fields, thousands of ruined factories, and millions of casualties. But in the United States, war and prosperity marched hand in hand. America emerged from the war with the strongest economy in the world and a position of international preeminence.

Still, the nation paid a heavy price both at home and abroad. American soldiers like George Browne encountered unprecedented horrors — submarines, poison gas, machine guns — and

more than 100,000 died. On Memorial Day 1919, at the Argonne Cemetery, where 14,200 Americans lie, General John J. Pershing said, "It is . . . for us to uphold the conception of duty, honor and country for which they fought and for which they died. It is for the living to carry forward their purpose and make fruitful their sacrifice." Rather than redeeming their sacrifice as Pershing intoned and Wilson promised, however, the peace that followed the armistice tarnished it. The flawed treaty forced a humiliating peace on Germany and contributed to the rise of Adolf Hitler and a second world war even more catastrophic than the first.

At home, rather than permanently improving working conditions, advancing public health, and spreading educational opportunity, as progressives had hoped, the war threatened to undermine the achievements of the previous two decades. Moreover, rather than promoting democracy in the United States, the war bred fear, intolerance, and repression that led to a crackdown on dissent and a demand for conformity. Reformers could count only woman suffrage as a permanent victory and prohibition as, ultimately, a temporary one.

Woodrow Wilson had promised more than anyone could deliver. Progressive hopes of extending democracy and liberal reform nationally and internationally were dashed. In 1920, a bruised and disillusioned society stumbled into a new decade. The era coming to an end had called on Americans to crusade and sacrifice. The new era promised peace, prosperity, and a good time.

▶ Selected Bibliography

General Works

John Milton Cooper, *Woodrow Wilson: A Biography* (2009).

Thomas Fleming, *The Illusion of Victory: America in World War I* (2003).

Robert H. Zieger, *America's Great War: World War I and the American Experience* (2000).

"Over There"

Gerald Astor, *The Right to Fight: A History of African Americans in the Military* (1998).

Peter Boyle, *American-Soviet Relations: From the Russian Revolution to the Fall of Communism* (1993).

Edward M. Coffman, *The War to End All Wars: The American Military Experience in World War I* (1968).

Byron Farwell, *Over There: The United States in the Great War, 1917–1918* (1999).

Lloyd C. Gardner, *Safe for Democracy: The Anglo-American Response to Revolution, 1913–1923* (1987).

Judith S. Graham, ed., *"Out Here at the Front": The World War I Letters of Nora Saltonstall* (2004).

Jennifer D. Keene, *Doughboys, the Great War, and the Remaking of America* (2001).

Thomas Knock, *To End All Wars: Woodrow Wilson and the Quest for a New World Order* (1992).

Edward G. Lengel, *To Conquer Hell: The Meuse-Argonne, 1918* (2008).

Margaret Olwen Macmillan, *Paris 1919: Six Months That Changed the World* (2002).

Gary Mead, *The Doughboys: America and the First World War* (2000).

Emily S. Rosenberg, *Financial Missionaries to the World: The Politics and Culture of Dollar Diplomacy, 1890–1930* (1999).

Gene Smith, *Until the Last Trumpet Sounds: The Life of General of the Armies John J. Pershing* (1998).

David L. Snead, ed., *An American Soldier in World War I: George Browne* (2006).

David F. Trask, *The AEF and Coalition Warmaking, 1917–1918* (1993).

Susan Zeiger, *In Uncle Sam's Service: Women with the AEF, 1917–1919* (1999).

The Home Front

Jean Baker, *Sisters: The Lives of America's Suffragists* (2005).

Nancy Cott, *The Grounding of American Feminism* (1987).

Leslie Midkiff DeBauche, *Reel Patriotism: The Movies and World War I* (1997).

Marc A. Eisner, *From Warfare State to Welfare State: World War I, Compensatory State Building, and the Limits of the Modern Order* (2000).

Ernest Freeberg, *Democracy's Prisoner: Eugene V. Debs, the Great War, and the Right to Dissent* (2008).

Elizabeth Frost and Kathryn Cullen-DuPont, eds., *Women's Suffrage in America: An Eyewitness History* (1992).

Maurine Weiner Greenwald, *Women, War, and Work: The Impact of World War I on Women Workers in the United States* (1980).

James N. Gregory, *Southern Diaspora: How the Great Migrations of Black and White Southerners Transformed America* (2005).

James R. Grossman, *Land of Hope: Chicago, Black Southerners, and the Great Migration* (1989).

David Kennedy, *Over Here: The First World War and American Society* (1980).

David Levering Lewis, *W. E. B. Du Bois: Biography of a Race, 1868–1919* (1993).

Robert K. Murray, *Red Scare: A Study in National Hysteria, 1919–1920* (1955).

Tammy M. Proctor, *Civilians in a World at War, 1914–1918* (2010).

George J. Sanchez, *Becoming Mexican American: Ethnicity, Culture, and Identity in Chicano Los Angeles, 1900–1945* (1993).

William H. Thomas Jr., *Unsafe for Democracy: World War I and the U.S. Justice Department's Covert Campaign to Suppress Dissent* (2008).

Joe William Trotter Jr., ed., *The Great Migration in Historical Perspective* (1991).

▶ **FOR MORE BOOKS ABOUT TOPICS IN THIS CHAPTER,** see the Online Bibliography at **bedfordstmartins.com/roark.**

▶ **FOR ADDITIONAL PRIMARY SOURCES FROM THIS PERIOD,** see Michael Johnson, ed., *Reading the American Past,* Fifth Edition.

▶ **FOR WEB SITES, IMAGES, AND DOCUMENTS RELATED TO TOPICS AND PLACES IN THIS CHAPTER,** visit Make History at **bedfordstmartins.com/roark.**

Reviewing Chapter 22

REVIEW QUESTIONS

Use key terms and dates to support your answer.

1. Why did President Wilson fail to maintain U.S. neutrality during World War I? (pp. 713–718)

2. How did the American Expeditionary Force contribute to the defeat of Germany? (pp. 718–723)

3. How did progressive ideals fare during wartime? (pp. 723–731)

4. Why did the Senate fail to ratify the Versailles treaty? (pp. 731–735)

5. How did the Red scare contribute to the erosion of civil liberties after the war? (pp. 735–743)

MAKING CONNECTIONS

Draw on key terms, the timeline, and review questions.

1. Why did the United States at first resist intervening in World War I? Why did it later retreat from this policy and send troops? In your answer, discuss whether these decisions revised or reinforced earlier U.S. foreign policy.

2. Some reformers were optimistic that World War I would advance progressive ideals at home. Discuss specific wartime domestic developments that displayed progressivism's influence. How did the war contribute to these developments? Did they endure in peacetime? Why or why not?

3. A conservative reaction in American politics followed peace, most vividly in the labor upheaval and Red scare that swept the nation. What factors drove these developments? How did they shape the postwar political spectrum?

4. During World War I, the nation witnessed important demographic changes. What drove African American and Mexican migration north? How did the war facilitate these changes? In your answer, explain the significance of these developments to the migrants and the nation.

LINKING TO THE PAST

Link events in this chapter to earlier events.

1. How did America's experience in World War I compare with its experience during the Spanish-American War, its previous war abroad? Discuss the decision to go to war in each case, the military aspects, and the outcome. (See chapter 20.)

2. How did the experience of America's workers during World War I compare with their experience in the previous three decades? Consider the composition of the workforce, wages, conditions, and labor's efforts to organize. (See chapters 20 and 21.)

▶ FOR PRACTICE QUIZZES AND OTHER STUDY TOOLS, visit the Online Study Guide at bedfordstmartins.com/roark.

TIMELINE 1914–1920

1914
- **April** U.S. Marines occupy Veracruz, Mexico.
- **June 28** Assassination of Archduke Franz Ferdinand.
- **July 18** Austria-Hungary declares war on Serbia.
- **August 3** Germany attacks Russia and France.
- **August 4** Great Britain declares war on Germany.

1915
- *Lusitania* sunk.
- Women's Peace Party formed.
- Italy joins Allies.

1916
- Pancho Villa attacks Americans in Mexico and New Mexico.
- Wilson reelected.

1917
- Zimmermann telegram intercepted.
- **April 6** United States declares war on Germany.
- Committee on Public Information created.
- Selective Service Act.
- Espionage Act and Trading with the Enemy Act.
- East St. Louis, Illinois, race riot.

1918
- **January 8** President Wilson gives Fourteen Points speech.
- **March** Russia arranges separate peace with Germany.
- **May** Sedition Act.
- **May–June** U.S. Marines see first major combat at Cantigny and Château-Thierry.
- **November 11** Armistice signed ending World War I.

1919
- **January** Paris peace conference begins.
- **June** Treaty of Versailles signed.
- **September** Wilson undertakes speaking tour.
- Wave of labor strikes.

1920
- American Civil Liberties Union founded.
- **January** Prohibition begins.
- **January** Palmer raids.
- **March** Senate votes against ratification of Treaty of Versailles.
- **August** Nineteenth Amendment ratified.
- **November** Republican Warren G. Harding elected president.

MODEL T FORD

Nothing symbolized the 1920s more than the automobile. When Henry Ford introduced the Model T in 1908, Americans thought of automobiles as toys of the rich, far too costly for average people. But by the 1920s, millions of Americans owned Fords, and their lives were never the same. One of novelist Booth Tarkington's characters expressed some reservations about automobiles: "With all their speed forward, they may be a step backward in civilization." But most Americans loved their automobiles and sped away into the future. Behind this Model T, workers install the wheels on a Ford chassis on a moving assembly line.

Car: National Museum of American History, Smithsonian Institution, Behring Center; background: From the Collections of The Henry Ford.

23

From New Era to Great Depression
1920–1932

AMERICANS IN THE 1920S CHEERED HENRY FORD AS AN AUTHENTIC American hero. When the decade began, he had already produced six million automobiles; by 1927, the figure reached fifteen million. In 1920, one car rolled off the Ford assembly line every minute; in 1925, one appeared every ten seconds. In 1920, a Ford car cost $845; in 1928, the price was less than $300, within range of most of the country's skilled workingmen. Henry Ford put America on wheels, and in the eyes of most Americans he was an honest man who made an honest car: basic, inexpensive, and reliable. He became the greatest example of free enterprise's promise and achievement. But like the age in which he lived, Henry Ford was many-sided, more complex and more contradictory than this simple image suggests.

Born in 1863 on a farm in Dearborn, Michigan, Ford hated the drudgery of farmwork and loved tinkering with machines. At sixteen, he fled rural life for Detroit, where he became a journeyman machinist and experimented with internal combustion engines. In 1893, he put together one of the first successful gasoline-driven carriages in the United States. His ambition, he said, was to "make something in quantity." The product he chose reflected American restlessness, the desire to be on the move. "Everybody wants to be someplace he ain't," Ford declared. "As soon as he gets there he wants to go right back." In 1903, with $28,000 from a few backers, Ford gathered twelve workers in a 250-by-50-foot shed and created the Ford Motor Company.

Ford's early cars were custom-made one at a time. By 1914, his cars were being built along a continuously moving assembly line: Workers bolted on parts brought to them by cranes and conveyor belts. Ford made only one kind of car, the Model T, which became synonymous with mass production. A boxlike black vehicle, it was cheap, easy to drive, and simple to repair. The Model T dominated the market. Throughout the rapid expansion of the automotive industry, the Ford Motor Company remained the

Henry Ford, 1921

A dapper Henry Ford inspects a new Model T in Buffalo, New York, in 1921, while curious onlookers inspect him. Henry Ford was a man of genius whose compelling vision of modern mass production led the way in the 1920s, but he was also cranky, pinched, and mean-spirited. He hated Jews and Catholics, bankers and doctors, and liquor and tobacco, and his millions allowed him to act on his prejudices. Still, his name became synonymous with American success. From the Collections of The Henry Ford.

industry leader, peaking in 1925, when it outsold all its rivals combined (Map 23.1).

Nobody entertained grander or more contradictory visions of the new America he had helped to create than Henry Ford himself. When he began his rise, progressive critics condemned the industrial giants of the nineteenth century as "robber barons" who lived in luxury while reducing their workers to wage slaves. Ford, however, identified with the common folk and saw himself as the benefactor of Americans yearning to be free and mobile.

Ford's automobile plants made him a billionaire, but their highly regimented assembly lines reduced Ford workers to near robots. On the cutting edge of modern technology, Ford nevertheless remained nostalgic about rural values. He sought to revive the past in Greenfield Village, a museum outside Detroit, where he relocated buildings from a bygone era, including his parents' farmhouse. His museum contrasted sharply with the roaring Ford plant farther along the Detroit River at River Rouge. The African American and immigrant workers who worked at the plant found no place in Greenfield Village. Yet all would be well, Ford insisted, if Americans remained true to their agrarian past and somehow managed to be modern and scientific at the same time.

Tension between traditional values and modern conditions lay at the heart of the conflicted 1920s. For the first time, more Americans lived in urban than in rural areas, yet Americans remained nostalgic about farms and small towns. Although the nation generally prospered, the new wealth widened the gap between rich and poor. While millions admired urban America's sophisticated new style and consumer products, others condemned postwar society for its vulgar materialism. A great outpouring of artistic talent led, ironically, to incessant critiques of America's artistic barrenness. The Ku Klux Klan and other champions of an idealized older America resorted to violence as well as words when they chastised the era's "new woman," "New Negro," and surging immigrant populations.

The public, disillusioned with the outcome of World War I, turned away from the Christian moralism and idealism of the Progressive Era. In the 1920s, Ford and businessmen like him replaced political reformers such as Theodore Roosevelt and Woodrow Wilson as the models of progress. The U.S. Chamber of Commerce crowed, "The American businessman is the most influential person in the nation." Social justice gave way to individual advancement. At the center of it all, President Calvin Coolidge spoke in praise of those in power when he declared, "The business of America is business." The fortunes of the era rose, then crashed, according to the values and practices of the business community.

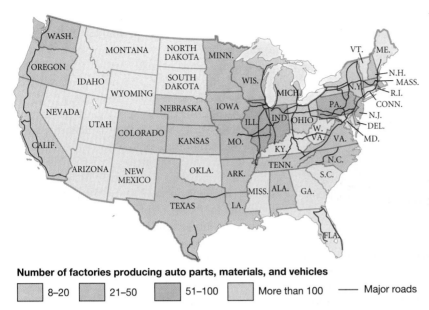

Number of factories producing auto parts, materials, and vehicles

| | 8–20 | | 21–50 | | 51–100 | | More than 100 | —— Major roads |

MAP ACTIVITY

Map 23.1 Auto Manufacturing

By the mid-1920s, the massive coal and steel industries of the Midwest had made that region the center of the new automobile industry. A major road-building program by the federal government carried the thousands of new cars produced each day to every corner of the country.

READING THE MAP: How many states had factories involved with the manufacture of automobiles? In what regions was auto manufacturing concentrated?

CONNECTIONS: On what related industries did auto manufacturing depend? How did the integration of the automobile into everyday life affect American society?

▶ The New Era

The 1920s were a time of contradiction and ambivalence. Once Woodrow Wilson left the White House, the energy flowed away from government activism and civic reform and toward private economic endeavor. The rise of a free-wheeling economy and a heightened sense of individualism caused Secretary of Commerce Herbert Hoover to declare that America had entered a "New Era," one of many labels used to describe the complex 1920s. Some terms focus on the decade's high-spirited energy and cultural changes: Roaring Twenties, Jazz Age, Flaming Youth, Age of the Flapper. Others echo the rising importance of money—Dollar Decade, Golden Twenties, Prosperity Decade—or reflect the sinister side of gangster profiteering—Lawless Decade. Still others emphasize the lonely confusion of the Lost Generation and the stress and anxiety of the Aspirin Age.

America in the twenties was many things, but there was no getting around the truth of Calvin Coolidge's insight: The business of America *was* business. Politicians and diplomats proclaimed business the heart of American civilization. Average men and women bought into the idea that business and its wonderful products were what made America great, as they snatched up the flood of new consumer items American factories sent forth.

A Business Government

Republicans controlled the White House from 1921 to 1933. The first of the three Republican presidents was **Warren Gamaliel Harding**, the Ohio senator who in his 1920 campaign called for a "return to normalcy," by which he meant the end of public crusades and a return to private pursuits. Harding promised a government run by the best minds, and he appointed a few men of real stature to his cabinet. Herbert Hoover, the energetic and ambitious former head of the wartime Food Administration, became secretary of commerce. However, wealth also counted: Andrew Mellon, one of the richest men in America, became secretary of the treasury. And friendship counted, too. Harding handed out jobs to members of his old "Ohio gang," whose only qualification was their friendship. This curious combination of merit and cronyism made for a disjointed administration in which a few men debated national needs, while other men looked for ways to advance their own interests.

When Harding was elected in 1920 in a landslide over Democratic opponent James Cox (see chapter 22, Map 22.6), the unemployment rate hit 20 percent, the highest ever up to that point. Farmers fared the worst; their bankruptcy rate increased tenfold. Harding pushed measures to regain national prosperity — high tariffs to protect American businesses (the Fordney-McCumber tariff in 1922 raised duties

Warren G. Harding and Babe Ruth
President Warren G. Harding shakes hands with New York Yankee home run king George Herman "Babe" Ruth Jr. during an April 4, 1923, visit to Yankee Stadium. The 1920s were the Golden Age of Sports, and Ruth was the best-paid and most highly acclaimed athlete of the decade. In 1920, a man died of excitement when Ruth slugged a ball into the bleachers. Even when he struck out, "the Babe" usually attracted more attention than any politician—even the president of the United States. © Bettmann/Corbis.

In the early morning of August 2, Vice President **Calvin Coolidge** was awakened at his family's farmhouse in Vermont with the news that Harding had died of a heart attack. By the flickering light of an oil lamp, Coolidge's father, a justice of the peace, swore his son in as president.

This rustic drama calmed a nation confronting the death of a president and continuing scandal in Washington. Coolidge was a modest man of integrity who had once expressed his belief that "the man who builds a factory builds a temple, the man who works there worships there." Reverence for free enterprise meant that Coolidge continued and extended Harding's policies of promoting business and limiting government. With Coolidge's approval, Secretary of the Treasury Andrew Mellon reduced the government's control over the economy and cut taxes for corporations and wealthy individuals. New rules for the Federal Trade Commission severely limited its power to regulate business. Secretary of Commerce Herbert Hoover limited government authority by encouraging trade associations that would keep business honest and efficient through voluntary cooperation.

Coolidge found a staunch ally in the Supreme Court. For many years, the Court had opposed federal regulation of hours, wages, and working conditions on the grounds that such legislation was the proper concern of the states. With Coolidge, the Court also found ways to curtail a state's ability to regulate business. It ruled against closed shops — businesses where only union members could be employed — while confirming the right of owners to form exclusive trade associations. In 1923, the Court declared unconstitutional the District of Columbia's minimum-wage law for women, asserting that the law interfered with the freedom of employer and employee to make labor contracts. The Court and the president attacked government intrusion in the free market, even when the prohibition of government regulation threatened the welfare of workers.

The election of 1924 confirmed the defeat of the progressive principle that the state should take a leading role in ensuring the general welfare. To oppose Coolidge, the Democrats nominated John W. Davis, a corporate lawyer whose conservative views differed little from Republican principles. Only the Progressive Party and its presidential nominee, Senator Robert La Follette of Wisconsin, offered a genuine alternative. When La Follette championed labor unions, regulation of business, and protection of civil liberties, Republicans coined the

to unprecedented levels), price supports for agriculture, and the dismantling of wartime government control over industry in favor of unregulated private business. "Never before, here or anywhere else," the U.S. Chamber of Commerce said proudly, "has a government been so completely fused with business."

Harding's policies to boost American enterprise made him very popular, but ultimately his small-town congeniality and trusting ways did him in. Some of his friends in the Ohio gang were up to their necks in lawbreaking. Three of Harding's appointees would go to jail. Interior Secretary Albert Fall was convicted of accepting bribes of more than $400,000 for leasing oil reserves on public land in Teapot Dome, Wyoming, and "**Teapot Dome**" became a synonym for political corruption.

Baffled about how to deal with "my Goddamned friends," Harding in the summer of 1923 took a trip to Alaska to escape his troubles. But the president found no rest, and his health declined.

> **"Never before, here or anywhere else, has a government been so completely fused with business."**
> — U.S. Chamber of Commerce

slogan "Coolidge or Chaos." Turning their backs on what they considered labor radicalism and reckless reform, voters chose Coolidge in a landslide. Coolidge was right when he declared, "This is a business country, and it wants a business government." What was true of the government's relationship to business at home was also true abroad.

Promoting Prosperity and Peace Abroad

After orchestrating the Senate's successful effort to block U.S. membership in the League of Nations, Henry Cabot Lodge boasted, "We have torn Wilsonism up by the roots." But repudiation of Wilsonian internationalism and rejection of collective security through the League of Nations did not mean that the United States retreated into isolationism. The United States emerged from World War I with its economy intact and enjoyed a decade of stunning growth. Economic involvement in the world and the continuing chaos in Europe made withdrawal impossible. New York replaced London as the center of world finance, and the United States became the world's chief creditor.

One of the Republicans' most ambitious foreign policy initiatives was the Washington Disarmament Conference, which convened to establish a global balance of naval power. Secretary of State Charles Evans Hughes shaped the **Five-Power Naval Treaty of 1922** committing Britain, France, Japan, Italy, and the United States to a proportional reduction of naval forces. The treaty led to the scrapping of more than two million tons of warships, by far the world's greatest success in disarmament. Americans celebrated President Harding for safeguarding the peace while remaining outside the League of Nations. By fostering international peace, he also helped make the world a safer place for American trade.

A second major effort on behalf of world peace came in 1928, when Secretary of State Frank Kellogg joined French foreign minister Aristide Briand to produce the **Kellogg-Briand pact**. Nearly fifty nations signed the solemn pledge to renounce war and settle international disputes peacefully. Most Americans considered the nation's signature an affirmation of its commitment to peace rather than to Wilson's foolish notion of a progressive, uplifting war.

But Republican administrations preferred private-sector diplomacy to state action. With the blessing of the White House, a team of American

Charles Evans Hughes and Disarmament
As Secretary of State, Charles Evans Hughes, the distinguished man in the white beard in the middle of this 1921 photograph, brought the world's major powers to Washington for naval disarmament talks. The gathering resulted in the United States's greatest diplomatic achievement of the 1920s. A former presidential candidate and Supreme Court justice, Hughes lent respectability and high-mindedness to his office, although few Americans cared about foreign affairs. The handwritten page is from the treaty that President Coolidge signed in 1923. Photo: Library of Congress; treaty: ©Bettmann/Corbis.

financiers led by Chicago banker Charles Dawes swung into action when Germany suspended its war reparation payments in 1923. Impoverished, Germany was staggering under the massive bill of $33 billion presented by the victorious Allies in the Versailles treaty. When Germany failed to meet its annual payment, France occupied Germany's industrial Ruhr Valley, creating the worst international crisis since the war. In 1924, American corporate leaders produced the **Dawes Plan**, which halved Germany's annual reparation payments, initiated fresh American loans to Germany, and caused the French to retreat from the Ruhr. Although the United States failed to join the league, it continued to exercise significant economic and diplomatic influence abroad. These Republican successes overseas helped fuel prosperity at home.

Automobiles, Mass Production, and Assembly-Line Progress

The automobile industry emerged as the largest single manufacturing industry in the nation. Aided by the federal government's decision to spend more on roads than on anything else, cars, trucks, and buses surged past railroads as the primary haulers of passengers and freight. **Henry Ford** shrewdly located his company in Detroit, knowing that key materials for his automobiles were manufactured in nearby states (see Map 23.1). Keystone of the American economy, the automobile industry not only employed hundreds of thousands of workers directly but also brought whole industries into being — filling stations, garages, fast-food restaurants, and "guest cottages" (motels). The need for tires, glass, steel, highways, oil, and refined gasoline for automobiles provided millions of related jobs. By 1929, one American in four found employment directly or indirectly in the automobile industry. "Give us our daily bread" was no longer addressed to the Almighty, one commentator quipped, but to Detroit.

Automobiles altered the face of America. Cars changed where people lived, what work they did, how they spent their leisure, even how they thought. Hundreds of small towns decayed because the automobile enabled rural people to bypass them in favor of more distant cities and towns. Urban streetcars began to disappear as workers moved to the suburbs and commuted to work along crowded highways. In Los Angeles, which boasted of the nation's most extensive system of electronic trolleys, almost a thousand miles of track suffered a slow death at the hands of the automobile. Nothing shaped modern America more than the automobile, and efficient mass production made the automobile revolution possible.

Mass production by the assembly-line technique had become standard in almost every factory, from automobiles to meatpacking to cigarettes. To improve efficiency, corporations reduced assembly-line work to the simplest, most repetitive tasks. They also established specialized divisions — purchasing, production, marketing, and employee relations — each with its own team of professionally trained managers. Changes on the assembly line and in man-

agement, along with technological advances, significantly boosted overall efficiency. Between 1922 and 1929, productivity in manufacturing increased 32 percent. Average wages, however, increased only 8 percent. As assembly lines became standard, workers lost many of the skills in which they had once taken pride, but corporations reaped great profits from these changes.

Industries also developed programs for workers that came to be called **welfare capitalism**. Some businesses improved safety and sanitation inside factories and instituted paid vacations and pension plans. Welfare capitalism encouraged loyalty to the company and discouraged traditional labor unions. Not wanting to relive the chaotic strikes of 1919, industrialists sought to eliminate reasons for workers to join unions. One labor organizer in the steel industry bemoaned the success of welfare capitalism. "So many workmen here had been lulled to sleep by the company union, the welfare plans, the social organizations fostered by the employer," he declared, "that they had come to look upon the employer as their protector, and had believed vigorous trade union organization unnecessary for their welfare."

Consumer Culture

Mass production fueled corporate profits and national economic prosperity. During the 1920s, per capita income increased by a third, the cost of living stayed the same, and unemployment remained low. But the rewards of the economic boom were not evenly distributed. Americans who labored with their hands inched ahead, while white-collar workers enjoyed significantly more spending money and more leisure time to spend it. Mass production of a broad range of new products — automobiles, radios, refrigerators, electric irons, washing machines — produced a consumer goods revolution.

In this new era of abundance, more people than ever conceived of the American dream in terms of the things they could acquire. In *Middletown* (1929), a study of the inhabitants of Muncie, Indiana, sociologists Robert and Helen Lynd revealed how the business boom and business values of the 1920s affected average Americans. Muncie was,

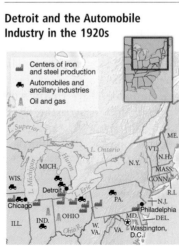

Detroit and the Automobile Industry in the 1920s

- Centers of iron and steel production
- Automobiles and ancillary industries
- Oil and gas

THE PROMISE OF TECHNOLOGY

Household Appliances

By the end of the 1920s, most urban homes in America had electricity, and middle-class urban families began acquiring household appliances that transformed women's daily lives. Before electricity, most chores were day-long ordeals. Washing machines saved housewives long hours spent hauling and heating water and hand-washing clothes. Ironing had been one of the most dreaded chores, especially in the summer when the kitchen stove had to be kept hot for heavy irons that needed frequent reheating. Electric irons eased the burden enormously. Vacuum cleaners saved the labor of hauling rugs out of the house to be beaten. Although household appliances relieved women of backbreaking labor, housework did not take less time. With the appearance of appliances, standards of cleanliness rose, and so did the frequency of many household chores. Nevertheless, an advertisement from a leading women's magazine insisted that "the wise woman delegates to electricity all that electricity can do." Ads like this promoted new technologies and reminded prospective buyers that this beautiful Eden washing machine could be theirs through an "easy-payment plan." How did housekeeping change with the introduction of electrical appliances? Picture Research Consultants & Archives.

above all, "a culture in which everything hinges on money." Moreover, faced with technological and organizational change beyond their comprehension, many citizens had lost confidence in their ability to play an effective role in civic affairs. More and more they became passive consumers, deferring to the supposed expertise of leaders in politics and economics.

The pied piper of these disturbing changes was the rapidly expanding business of advertising, which stimulated the desire for new products and hammered away at the traditional values of thrift and saving. Newspapers, magazines, radios, and billboards told Americans what they had to have in order to be popular, secure, and successful. Advertising linked material goods to the fulfillment of every spiritual and emotional need. Americans increasingly defined and measured their social status, and indeed their personal worth, on the yardstick of material possessions. Happiness itself rode on owning a car and choos-

ing the right cigarettes and toothpaste. (See "Visualizing History," page 758.)

By the 1920s, the United States had achieved the physical capacity to satisfy Americans' material wants (Figure 23.1). The economic problem shifted from production to consumption: Who would buy the goods flying off American assembly lines? One solution was to expand America's markets in foreign countries, and government and business joined in that effort. Another solution to the problem of consumption was to expand the market at home.

Henry Ford realized early on that "mass production requires mass consumption." He understood that automobile workers not only produced cars but would also buy them if they made enough money. "One's own employees ought to be one's own best customers," Ford said. In 1914, he raised wages in his factories to $5 a day, more than twice the going rate. High wages made for workers who were more loyal and more

VISUAL ACTIVITY

Colorado Filling Station and Gas Pump

Gulf Oil Company gave away the first free road map in 1914. By 1929, when Conoco (Continental Oil Company) produced this lavish map with Colorado's spectacular mountains looming in the background, nearly every oil company was supplying road maps as part of its campaign to attract the booming tourist trade. This appealing drive-through station is a far cry from the first retail outlets for gas — blacksmith shops and hardware stores, the same places individuals bought kerosene to burn in their lamps. Because motorists did not trust what they could not see, companies in the 1910s introduced glass-cylinder, gravity-flow gas pumps.
Courtesy, Colorado Historical Society.

READING THE IMAGE: What does this road map and accompanying image of a gravity-flow gasoline pump tell us about American consumer culture on the eve of the Great Depression?
CONNECTIONS: Does the road map accurately reflect the economic direction of the U.S. economy in 1929?

exploitable, and high wages returned as profits when workers bought Fords.

Not all industrialists were as farseeing as Ford. Because the wages of many workers barely edged upward, many people's incomes were too puny to satisfy the growing desire for consumer goods. Business supplied the solution: Americans could realize their dreams through credit. Installment buying — a little money down, a payment each month — allowed people to purchase expensive items they could not otherwise afford or to purchase items before saving the

necessary money. As one newspaper announced, "The first responsibility of an American to his country is no longer that of a citizen, but of a consumer." During the 1920s, America's motto became spend, not save. Old values — "Use it up, wear it out, make it do or do without" — seemed about as pertinent as a horse and buggy. American culture had shifted.

REVIEW   How did the spread of the automobile transform the United States?

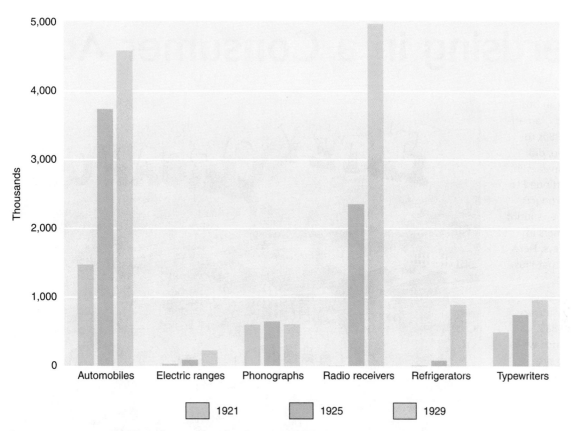

FIGURE 23.1   Production of Consumer Goods, 1921–1929
Transportation, communications, and entertainment changed the lives of consumers in the 1920s. Laborsaving devices for the home were popular, but the vastly greater sales of automobiles and radios showed that consumerism was powerful in moving people's attention beyond their homes.

▶ The Roaring Twenties

By the beginning of the decade, psychoanalyst **Sigmund Freud** had become a household name. Most Americans knew little of the complexity of his pioneering work in the psychology of the unconscious, but people realized that Freud offered a way of looking at the world that was radically different. In the twenties, much to Freud's disgust, the American media turned his ideas about the sexual origins of behavior on its head. If it is wrong to deny that we are sexual beings, some reasoned, then the key to health and fulfillment must lie in following impulse freely. Those who doubted this reasoning were simply "repressed." The new ethic of personal freedom excited many Americans to seek pleasure without guilt in a whirl of activity that earned the decade the name "Roaring Twenties." Prohibition made lawbreakers of millions of

otherwise decent folk. Flappers and "new women" challenged traditional gender boundaries. Other Americans enjoyed the Roaring Twenties through the words and images of vastly expanded mass communication. Motion pictures, radio, and magazines marketed celebrities. In the freedom of America's big cities, particularly New York, a burst of creativity produced the "New Negro," who confounded and disturbed white Americans. The "Lost Generation" of writers, profoundly disillusioned with mainstream America's cultural direction, fled the country.

Prohibition

Republicans generally sought to curb the powers of government, but the twenties witnessed a great exception to this rule when the federal government implemented one of the last reforms of the Progressive Era: the Eighteenth Amendment, which banned the manufacture and sale of alcohol

Advertising in a Consumer Age

Just as American business changed dramatically from the 1880s to the 1920s, so, too, did advertising. Businesses in the New Era continued to promote their products, of course, but they sought to attract customers in very different ways. Here are two images that illustrate the changes.

Look at the Estey Organ Company advertisement from 1885. Can you tell at a glance what product is being promoted? First and foremost, the ad features the company's huge industrial complex — two red brick kilns with smoke belching from their chimneys, surrounded by lumberyards and milling, woodworking, metalworking, and varnishing shops. If the prospective customer somehow failed to get the message, the advertisement announces that Estey's plant is "The Most Extensive

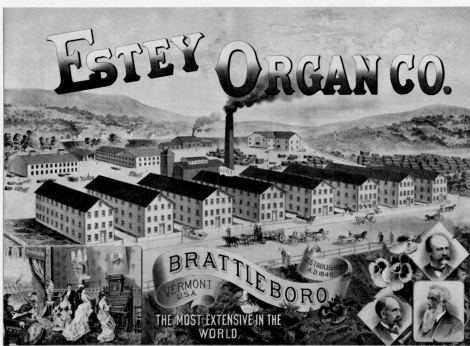

Estey Organ Company

in the World." Indeed, Estey was the world's largest organ manufacturer, selling 1,800 organs a year around the globe. Why do you think the size of the factory was featured so prominently in the ad? How might

customers in 1885 have responded to such an ad?

The men who presided over Estey's impressive manufacturing operation — founder Jason Estey; his son, Julius; and his son-in-law, Levi

and took effect in January 1920 (see chapter 22). Drying up the rivers of liquor that Americans consumed, supporters of **prohibition** claimed, would eliminate crime, boost production, and lift the nation's morality. Instead, prohibition initiated a fourteen-year orgy of lawbreaking unparalleled in the nation's history.

Charged with enforcing prohibition, the Treasury Department faced a staggering task. Although it smashed more than 172,000 illegal stills in 1925 alone, there were never enough Treasury agents. Moreover, loopholes in the law almost guaranteed failure. Sacramental wine was permitted, allowing fake clergy to party with bogus congregations. Farmers were allowed to ferment their

own "fruit juices." Doctors and dentists could prescribe liquor for medicinal purposes. America's wettest city was probably Detroit, known widely as "the city on a still." Detroit was home to more than 20,000 illegal drinking establishments, making the alcohol business the city's second-largest industry, behind automobile manufacturing.

In 1929, a Treasury agent in Indiana reported intense local resistance to enforcement of prohibition. "Conditions in most important cities very bad," he declared. "Lax and corrupt public officials great handicap . . . prevalence of drinking among minor boys and the . . . middle or better classes of adults." The "speakeasy," an illegal nightclub, became a common feature of the urban

UPHOLD 18TH AMENDMENT

REPEAL 18TH AMENDMENT

Fuller — appear in the lower right corner. What is the purpose of including the company founder and managers in the advertisement? In the other corner, the ad imagines an Estey organ in the parlor of a well-to-do family that gathers to hear one of its accomplished daughters play. How might this image influence potential customers?

Based on this advertisement, what did the Estey Organ Company believe was its most important selling factor? What other factors were important?

By the 1920s, companies employed advertising specialists who created ads that would appeal to the consumer's anxieties and personal needs and would even stimulate needs that didn't yet exist. As a result, advertisements changed dramatically.

In this 1929 advertisement for Lucky Strike cigarettes, the factory and its owners are nowhere to be found. Instead, it offers a woman in a bathing suit. What does she have to do with cigarettes? Millions of Americans smoked billions of cigarettes in the 1920s. In countless tobacco advertisements, smoking promised instant maturity, sophistication, and worldliness. What is this ad's promise to smokers? To whom is it appealing?

Look at the various elements of the ad — the headline, the pictures, the quoted slogans, the text, and the footnote. What health claims are made? Does the ad's small print undermine the main message?

Before the 1920s, advertising often focused on production. Even small businesses presented themselves as powerful and efficient producers of consumer goods such as organs, furniture, and stoves. In the consumer society of the 1920s, companies sought to teach Americans to judge themselves and others by what they bought, rather than by what they produced. How might an ad for Lucky Strike have looked if it had been done in 1885? What might an Estey Organ Company ad have looked like in the 1920s?

Lucky Strike

landscape. Speakeasies' dance floors led to the sexual integration of the formerly all-male drinking culture, changing American social life forever. One liquor dealer, trading on common knowledge that whiskey still flowed in the White House, distributed cards advertising himself as the "President's Bootlegger."

Eventually, serious criminals took over the liquor trade. Alphonse "Big Al" Capone became the era's most notorious gang lord by establishing in Chicago a bootlegging empire that the government estimated brought in $95 million a year, when a chicken dinner cost 5 cents. During the first four years of prohibition, Chicago witnessed more than two hundred gang-related killings as rival mobs struggled for control of the lucrative liquor trade. The most notorious event

came on St. Valentine's Day 1929, when Capone's Italian-dominated mob machine-gunned seven members of a rival Irish gang. Federal authorities finally sent Capone to prison for income tax evasion. Capone never denied being a bootlegger. "I violate the Prohibition law — sure," he told a reporter. "Who doesn't? The only difference is, I take more chances than the man who drinks a cocktail before dinner."

While prohibition did cut down on drinking and alcohol-related illnesses, Americans overwhelmingly favored the repeal of the Eighteenth Amendment.

> "I violate the Prohibition law — sure. Who doesn't? The only difference is, I take more chances than the man who drinks a cocktail before dinner."
> —AL CAPONE

Confiscated Liquor
Revenue agents, some holding rifles, proudly display the bootleg liquor they have confiscated during a raid in Washington, D.C., in 1922. The carefully staged scene and the photographer on the roof indicate that the agents were eager to publicize their success. Successes like this were common during prohibition, but the criminalization of liquor could not permanently defeat "Satan in a bottle." The Granger Collection, NYC.

When the Nineteenth Amendment, ratified in 1920, granted women the vote, feminists felt liberated and expected women to reshape the political landscape. A Kansas woman declared, "I went to bed last night a *slave*[;] I awoke this morning a *free woman*." Women began pressuring Congress to pass laws that especially concerned women, including measures to protect women in factories and grant federal aid to schools. Black women lobbied particularly for federal courts to assume jurisdiction over the crime of lynching. But women's only significant national legislative success came in 1921 when Congress enacted the Sheppard-Towner Act, which extended federal assistance to states seeking to reduce high infant mortality rates. Rather than the beginning of women's political success, the act marked the high tide of women's influence in the 1920s.

A number of factors helped thwart women's political influence. Male domination of both political parties, the rarity of female candidates, and lack of experience in voting, especially among recent immigrants, kept many women away from the polls. In some places, male-run election machines actually disfranchised women, despite the Nineteenth Amendment. In the South, poll taxes, literacy tests, and outright terrorism continued to decimate the vote of African Americans, men and women alike.

Most important, rather than forming a solid voting bloc, feminists divided. Some argued for women's right to special protection; others demanded equal protection. The radical National Woman's Party fought for an **Equal Rights Amendment** that stated flatly: "Men and women shall have equal rights throughout the United States." The more moderate League of Women Voters feared that the amendment's wording threatened state laws that provided women special protection, such as preventing them from working on certain machines. Put before Congress in 1923, the Equal Rights Amendment went down to defeat, and radical women were forced to work for the causes of birth control, legal equality for minorities, and the end of child labor through other means.

Economically, more women worked for pay —approximately one in four by 1930—but they clustered in "women's jobs." The proportion of women working in manufacturing fell, while the number of women working as secretaries, stenographers, and typists skyrocketed. Women almost monopolized the occupations of librarian,

In 1931, a panel of distinguished experts reported that prohibition, which supporters had defended as "a great social and economic experiment," had failed. The social and political costs of prohibition outweighed the benefits. Prohibition fueled criminal activity, corrupted the police, demoralized the judiciary, and caused ordinary citizens to disrespect the law. In 1933, the nation ended prohibition with the Twenty-first Amendment, making the Eighteenth Amendment the only constitutional amendment to be repealed.

The New Woman

Of all the changes in American life in the 1920s, none sparked more heated debate than the alternatives offered to the traditional roles of women. Increasing numbers of women worked and went to college, defying older gender hierarchies and norms. Even mainstream magazines such as the *Saturday Evening Post* began publishing stories about young, college-educated women who drank gin cocktails, smoked cigarettes, and wore skimpy dresses and dangly necklaces. Before the Great War, the **new woman** dwelt in New York City's bohemian Greenwich Village, but afterward the mass media brought her into middle-class America's living rooms.

nurse, elementary school teacher, and telephone operator. Women also represented 40 percent of salesclerks by 1930. More female white-collar workers meant that fewer women were interested in protective legislation for women; new women wanted salaries and opportunities equal to men's.

Increased earnings gave working women more buying power in the new consumer culture. A stereotype soon emerged of the **flapper**, so called because of the short-lived fad of wearing unbuckled galoshes. The flapper had short "bobbed" hair and wore lipstick and rouge. She spent freely on the latest styles — dresses with short skirts and drop waists, no sleeves, and no petticoats — and she danced all night to wild jazz.

The new woman both reflected and propelled the modern birth control movement. Margaret Sanger, the crusading pioneer for contraception during the Progressive Era (see chapter 21), restated her principal conviction in 1920: "No woman can call herself free until she can choose consciously whether she will or will not be a mother." By shifting strategy in the twenties, Sanger courted the conservative American Medical Association; linked birth control with the eugenics movement, which advocated limiting reproduction among "undesirable" groups; and thus made contraception a respectable subject for discussion.

Flapper style and values spread from coast to coast through films, novels, magazines, and advertisements. New women challenged American convictions about separate spheres for women and men, the double standard of sexual conduct, and Victorian ideas of proper female appearance and behavior. (See "Historical Question," page 762.) Although only a minority of American women became flappers, all women, even those who remained at home, felt the great changes of the era.

The New Negro

The 1920s witnessed the emergence not only of the "new woman" but also of the "New Negro." Both new identities riled conservatives and reactionaries. African Americans who challenged the caste system that confined dark-skinned Americans to the lowest levels of society confronted whites who insisted that race relations would not change. Cheers for black soldiers quickly faded after their return from World War I, and African Americans soon faced grim days of economic hardship and race riots (see chapter 22).

The prominent African American intellectual W. E. B. Du Bois and the National Association for the Advancement of Colored People (NAACP) aggressively pursued the passage of a federal antilynching law to counter mob violence against blacks in the South. Many poor blacks, however, disillusioned with mainstream politics, turned for new leadership to a Jamaican-born visionary named **Marcus Garvey**. Garvey urged African Americans to rediscover the heritage of Africa, take pride in their own achievements, and maintain racial purity by avoiding miscegenation. In 1917, Garvey launched the Universal Negro Improvement Association (UNIA) to help African Americans gain economic and political independence entirely outside white society. In 1919, the UNIA created its own shipping company, the Black Star Line, to support the "Back to Africa" movement among black Americans. But the business was an economic failure, and in 1927 the federal government pinned charges of illegal practices on Garvey and deported him to Jamaica. Nevertheless, the issues Garvey raised

"The Girls' Rebellion"
The August 1924 cover of *Redbook*, a popular women's magazine, portrays the kind of postadolescent girl who was making respectable families frantic. Flappers scandalized their middle-class parents by flouting the old moral code. This young woman sports the "badges of flapperhood," including what one critic called an "intoxication of rouge." The cover promises a story inside about girls gone wild. Fictionalized, emotion-packed stories such as this brought the new woman into every woman's home.
Picture Research Consultants & Archives.

Was There a Sexual Revolution in the 1920s?

"Cigarette in hand, shimmying to the music of the masses, the New Woman and the New Morality have made their theatric debut upon the modern scene," lamented one commentator in 1926. A moral chasm, the *Atlantic* magazine declared, had opened between the generations. The old and young in America "were as far apart in point of view, codes, and standards as if they belonged to different races." Charlotte Perkins Gilman represented many older feminists who were disappointed with the outcome of recent advances for women: "It is sickening to see so many of the newly freed abusing that freedom in a mere imitation of masculine weakness and vice." Older Americans wholeheartedly agreed that the younger generation was in full-fledged revolt against traditional standards of morality and that America was in danger of going to hell in a handbasket.

Critics had, it seemed, plenty of evidence. Between newspapers, movies, and magazines, even the small towns of America were "literally saturated with sex," one observer complained. Flappers and college coeds claimed the privileges of men, smoking cigarettes, drinking from hip flasks, and staying out all night. When eight hundred college women met to discuss life on campus and what "nice girls" should do, they concluded, "Learn temperance in petting, not abstinence." Anxious observers counseled intervention. The

Ohio legislature debated whether to prohibit any "female over fourteen years of age" from wearing a "skirt which does not reach to that part of the foot known as the instep." The *Ladies' Home Journal* urged "legal prohibition" of jazz dancing.

But were the concerned observers correct? Was there really a sexual revolution in the 1920s? The principal movers of the new morality were youths, and without a doubt young, middle-class men and women felt freer than ever to express openly their feelings about sex. But we must separate the new candor from actual sexual behavior. Although solid evidence is difficult to come by, correspondence, diaries, and other personal documents; physicians' records; divorce proceedings; advice literature; and a few early sex surveys provide important clues.

A good place to begin the investigation is where youth congregated: college campuses. Campus life included a self-conscious ethos of experimentation and innovation, but as students demolished old rules, they also created new ones. One major innovation was "dating" — that is, going out unsupervised rather than receiving callers at home or meeting at church socials. Dating was encouraged by the automobile, that "house of prostitution on wheels," as one juvenile judge in Indiana labeled it. Dating led to a second innovation: "petting," or any sexual activity short

of intercourse. One examination of coed behavior at the end of the 1920s found that 92 percent of women admitted engaging in petting.

Like dating, petting represented a significant change in female behavior. But it was not a total rejection of traditional morality because it took place within the search for the ideal marriage partner. There was also a modest increase in premarital sexual intercourse, made possible by the widespread acceptance of contraceptives. But sexual intercourse usually took place between partners who assumed they would marry. The new woman of the 1920s, though freer sexually, continued to focus on romance, marriage, and family.

Did the new sexual behavior mark a drastic change from the past? Evidence of sexual habits before World War I is even more difficult to come by than for the 1920s, but it appears that changes in attitudes and behaviors had been under way for decades. Nineteenth-century Victorian notions of sexless women who felt little or no passion had been eroding since at least the 1890s. A small survey of the sexual practices of middle-class women in the 1890s conducted by Dr. Clelia Duel Mosher, a physician at Stanford University, found that women were enthusiastic about sex and often found satisfaction. The primary ideologues of the sexual revolution, Havelock Ellis, who celebrated female passion, and Sigmund Freud, who stressed the centrality of sex in human endeavor, reached large American audiences before World War I.

Changes in sexual morality, therefore, were evolutionary rather than revolutionary. Still, liberal attitudes and behaviors had their greatest impact in the 1920s. American culture was being remade, and young people, especially women,

about racial pride, black identity, and the search for equality persisted, and his legacy remains at the center of black nationalist thought.

Still, most African Americans maintained hope in the American promise. In New York City, hope and talent came together. Poor blacks

from the South, as well as sophisticated immigrants from the West Indies, poured into Harlem in uptown Manhattan. New York City's black population jumped 115 percent (from 152,000 to 327,000) in the 1920s, while its white population increased only 20 percent. Similar

Heroes and Heroines
Two kinds of women look up adoringly at two kinds of 1920s heroes. A wholesome image is seen on the left in a 1927 cover of *People's Popular Monthly* magazine. The healthy outdoor girl, smartly turned out in her raccoon coat and pennant, flatters a naive college football hero. On the right, the pale, sensitive Vilma Banky kneels imploringly before the hypnotic gaze of the movies' greatest heartthrob, Rudolph Valentino. Magazine: Picture Research Consultants & Archives; Poster: Billy Rose Theatre Collection, The New York Public Library at Lincoln Center.

were at the cutting edge. Now equal at the polling booth, women were also growing more economically independent. Changes in women's political and economic lives were reflected in their sexual attitudes and behaviors. In place of the idea that women were naturally pure, the new morality proclaimed the equality of desire. Only the boldest women rejected a "double standard" (the notion that the sexual behavior of women should be more circumscribed than that of men), but many jettisoned notions of female submission, obedience, and endless childbearing. Charges that the giddy flapper and her partner were bringing down American civilization were overblown, but young women certainly were changing the culture.

Thinking about Evidence

1. Is there any evidence for the contention that changes in sexual behavior in the 1920s were more evolutionary than revolutionary?

2. How did changes in women's political and economic lives affect their sexual behaviors?

demographic changes occurred on a smaller scale throughout the North. Overcrowding and unsanitary housing accompanied this black population explosion, but so too did a new self-consciousness and self-confidence that fed into artistic accomplishment.

In Harlem, an extraordinary mix of black artists, sculptors, novelists, musicians, and poets deliberately set out to create a distinctive African American culture that drew on their identities as Americans and Africans. As scholar Alain Locke put it in 1925, they introduced to the world

Duke Ellington at the Cotton Club
Duke Ellington, at the piano, presides over the floor show at the Cotton Club in Harlem, where black performers played for white audiences. The chorus girls—who were all supposed to be "tall, tan, and terrific"—dance in the "jungle style" that whites expected. During the years from 1927 to 1931 that his orchestra was the house band at the Cotton Club, Ellington recorded more than one hundred of his compositions, establishing him as America's greatest jazz composer and bandleader. The Frank Driggs Collection.

the "**New Negro**," who rose from the ashes of slavery and segregation to proclaim African Americans' creative genius.

The emergence of the New Negro came to be known as the **Harlem Renaissance**. Building on the independence and pride displayed by black soldiers during the war, black artists sought to defeat the fresh onslaught of racial discrimination and violence with poems, paintings, and plays. "We younger Negro artists . . . intend to express our individual dark-skinned selves without fear or shame," poet Langston Hughes said of the Harlem Renaissance. "If white people are pleased, we are glad. If they are not, it doesn't matter. We know we are beautiful. And ugly, too."

The Harlem Renaissance produced dazzling talent. Black writer James Weldon Johnson, who in 1903 had written the Negro national anthem, "Lift Every Voice," wrote *God's Trombones* (1927), in which he expressed the wisdom and beauty of black folktales from the South. The poetry of Langston Hughes, Claude McKay, and Countee Cullen celebrated the vitality of life in Harlem. Zora Neale Hurston's novel *Their Eyes Were Watching God* (1937) explored the complex passions of black people in a southern community. Black painters, led by Aaron Douglas, linked African art, which had recently inspired European modernist artists, to the concept of the New Negro.

Despite such vibrancy, Harlem for most whites remained a separate black ghetto known only for its lively nightlife. Fashionable whites crowded into Harlem's segregated nightclubs, the most famous of which was the Cotton Club, where they believed they could hear "real" jazz, a relatively new musical form, in its "natural" surroundings. The vigor of the Harlem Renaissance left a powerful legacy for black Americans, but the creative burst did little in the short run to dissolve the prejudice of white society. (See "Seeking the American Promise," page 766.)

Entertainment for the Masses

By the late 1920s, jazz had captured the nation, and jazz giants such as Louis Armstrong, Jelly Roll Morton, Duke Ellington, and Bessie Smith performed for huge audiences. Jazz was only one of the entertainment choices of Americans in the 1920s. Popular culture, like consumer goods, was mass-produced and mass-consumed. The proliferation of movies, radios, music, and sports meant that Americans found plenty to do, and in doing the same things, they helped create a national culture.

Nothing offered escapist delights like the movies. Hollywood, California, discovered the successful formula of combining opulence, sex, and adventure. By 1929, the movies were drawing more than 80 million people in a single week, as many as lived in the entire country. Admission was cheap, and blacks as well as whites attended, although they entered theaters through different entrances and sat separately. Rudolph Valentino, described as "catnip to women," and Clara Bow, the "It Girl" (everyone knew what *it* was), became household names. Most loved of all was the comic Charlie Chaplin, whose famous character, the wistful Little Tramp, showed an endearing inability to cope with the rules and complexities of modern life.

Americans also found heroes in sports. Baseball, professionalized since 1869 and segregated into white and black leagues, solidified its place as the national pastime in the 1920s. It remained essentially a game played by and for the working class. In George Herman "Babe" Ruth, baseball had the most cherished free spirit of the time. "The Sultan of Swat" mixed his record-setting home runs with rowdy escapades, demonstrating to fans that sports offered a way to break out of the ordinariness of everyday life. By "his sheer exuberance," one sportswriter declared, Ruth "has lightened the cares of the world."

The public also fell in love with a young boxer from the grim mining districts of Colorado. As a teenager, Jack Dempsey had made his living hanging around saloons betting he could beat anyone in the house. When he took the heavyweight crown just after World War I, he was revered as the people's champ, an American equalizer who was a stand-in for the average American who felt increasingly confined by bureaucracy and machine-made culture. In Philadelphia in 1926, a crowd of 125,000 fans saw challenger Gene Tunney pummel and defeat the people's champ.

Football, essentially a college sport, held greater sway with the upper classes. The most famous coach, Knute Rockne of Notre Dame, celebrated football for its life lessons of hard work and teamwork. Let the professors make learning as interesting and significant as football, Rockne advised, and the problem of getting young people to learn would disappear. But in keeping with the times, football moved toward a more commercial spectacle. Harold "Red" Grange, "the Galloping Ghost," led the way by going from stardom at the University of Illinois to the Chicago Bears in the new professional football league.

The decade's hero worship reached its zenith in the celebration of **Charles Lindbergh**, a young pilot who set out on May 20, 1927, from Long Island in his single-engine plane, *The Spirit of St. Louis*, to become the first person to fly nonstop across the Atlantic. Newspapers tagged Lindbergh "the Lone Eagle" — the perfect hero for an age

that celebrated individual accomplishment. "Charles Lindbergh," one journalist proclaimed, "is the stuff out of which have been made the pioneers that opened up the wilderness. His are the qualities which we, as a people, must nourish." Lindbergh realized, however, that technical and organizational complexity was fast reducing chances for solitary achievement. Consequently, he titled his book about the flight *We* (1927) to include the machine that had made it all possible.

Another machine — the radio — became important to mass culture. The nation's first licensed radio station, KDKA in Pittsburgh, began broadcasting in 1920, and soon American airwaves buzzed with news, sermons, soap operas, sports, comedy, and music. For the first time, Americans on the West Coast laughed at the latest jokes from New York, and citizens everywhere listened to the voices of political candidates without leaving home. Because they could now reach prospective customers in their own homes, advertisers bankrolled radio's rapid growth. Between 1922 and 1929, the number of radio stations in the United States increased from 30 to 606. In just seven years, homes with radios jumped from 60,000 to a staggering 10.25 million.

Radio added to the spread of popular music, especially jazz. Jazz — with its energy and freedom — provided the sound track for a new, distinct social class of youths. As the traditional bonds of community, religion, and family loosened, the young felt less pressure to imitate their elders and more freedom to develop their own culture. An increasing number of college students helped the "rah-rah" style of college life become a fad promoted in movies, songs, and advertisements. The collegiate set was the vanguard of the decade's "flaming youth."

The Lost Generation

Some writers and artists felt alienated from America's mass-culture society, which they found shallow, anti-intellectual, and materialistic. Adoration of silly movie stars disgusted them. Moreover, they believed that business culture blighted American life. To their minds, Henry Ford made a poor hero. Young, white, and mostly college educated, these expatriates, as they came to be called, felt embittered by the war and renounced the progressives who had promoted it as a crusade. For them, Europe — not Hollywood or Harlem — seemed the place to seek their renaissance.

The American-born writer Gertrude Stein, long established in Paris, remarked famously as the young exiles gathered around her, "They are

The Quest for Home Ownership in Segregated Detroit

Owning a place of one's own has always been important in America. In the nineteenth century, with the rise of industry and cities, the goal of a family farm gave way to the goal of a single-family house. Home ownership has been widely realized today, with roughly two-thirds of Americans (with the assistance of mortgage companies) owning their own homes.

In the 1920s, decent housing was in short supply in Detroit, America's great boomtown, as thousands poured in to work in Henry Ford's automobile factories. Arriving before World War I, blue-collar German, Irish, and Polish immigrants found homes in working-class neighborhoods scattered around the city center. The great migration out of the South sent Detroit's black population soaring, and the newcomers frightened white property owners who believed that blacks would drive down property values, cause neighborhood decay, and fill their streets with criminals.

The property owners resolved to keep their neighborhoods all-white by channeling blacks into Black Bottom, the downtown ghetto. Although the U.S. Supreme Court had struck down a law mandating segregated housing in 1917, inventive white homeowners created other means to draw racial boundaries. Real estate agents refused to show blacks houses in white neighborhoods. Banks turned down blacks for mortgages. Whites signed restrictive covenants, promising not to sell their homes to blacks. If a black family managed to slip through their defenses, whites resorted to violence.

Dr. Ossian Sweet, a black physician, arrived in Detroit in 1921. He set up his medical practice in Black Bottom and prospered. He soon had the down payment for a home, but he refused to settle his wife and baby daughter in the congested, rat-infested ghetto. In 1925, Sweet bought a substantial bungalow at 2905 Garland Avenue, several blocks inside a working-class white neighborhood. His brother said later, "He wasn't looking for trouble. He just wanted to bring up his little girl in good surroundings." Sweet understood the danger; whites had recently run other black professionals out of their Detroit neighborhoods. "Well, we have decided we are not going to run," Sweet told a friend. "We're not going to look for any trouble, but we're going to be prepared to protect ourselves if trouble arises." When Gladys and Ossian Sweet moved into their home on September 8, 1925, nine friends and family members accompanied them. The moving van that brought their furniture also carried a shotgun, two rifles, six pistols, and four hundred rounds of ammunition.

Hundreds of white men quickly filled the streets, greatly outnumbering the few police who hoped to keep the peace. Shouting that they would send the "niggers" back where they belonged, the mob began throwing rocks, breaking windows, and advancing. Suddenly, gunfire erupted from the second story of the Sweet house, and two white men were shot; one was killed. The police kept the mob away long enough for a paddy wagon to haul the eleven blacks to the police station, where they were all indicted for murder.

Asked why he wanted to move to a white neighborhood, where there was likely to be trouble, Sweet said, "Because I bought the house, and it was my house, and I felt I had a right to live in it." The NAACP, which saw the case as an opportunity to strike a legal blow in favor of self-defense against racial violence, hired Clarence Darrow to defend the accused. Darrow was the most celebrated defense lawyer in the country and fresh from the Scopes trial in Tennessee (see page 770). Darrow told the jury that the facts were simple: "When they defended their home, they were arrested and charged with murder." He reminded the all-white jury that "every man's home is his castle, which even the king may not enter. Every man has a right to kill to defend himself or his family, or others, either in defense of the home, or in defense of themselves." A split jury caused the judge to declare a mistrial. A second trial

the lost generation." Most of the expatriates, however, believed to the contrary that they had finally found themselves. The **Lost Generation** helped launch the most creative period in American art and literature in the twentieth century. The novelist whose spare, clean style best exemplified the expatriate efforts to make art mirror basic reality was Ernest Hemingway. Hemingway's experience in the Great War convinced him that the world in which he was raised, with its Christian moralism and belief in progress, was bankrupt. Admirers found the terse language and hard lessons of his novel *The Sun Also Rises* (1926) to be perfect expressions of a world stripped of illusions.

Many writers who remained in America were exiles in spirit. Before the war, intellectuals had eagerly joined progressive reform movements.

Dr. Ossian Sweet and His House
Dr. Ossian Sweet's substantial two-story brick home is listed on the National Register of Historic Places. In September 1925, Sweet tried to move his family into the then all-white Detroit suburb where the house is located. Residents reacted violently, determined to uphold "the present high standards of the neighborhood." The Detroit News.

ended in not guilty verdicts for all the defendants.

Over the next several decades, housing discrimination became entrenched throughout the nation. Blacks succeeded in breaking out of the inner cities and moving into the suburbs, where today more than one-third of African Americans live, but breaching city boundaries did not mean leaving residential segregation behind. Of all the nation's segregated cities, none was more segregated than Detroit. As late as 1963, Martin Luther King Jr. declared: "I have a dream this afternoon that one day right here in Detroit Negroes will be able to buy a house or rent a house anywhere their money will carry them." As for Sweet, he moved back into his home on Garland Avenue in 1928, but without his wife and daughter, both of whom had died. He stayed in the bungalow for more than twenty-five years, and when he left, the neighborhood around him was still largely white.

Questions for Consideration

1. Why did whites in Dr. Sweet's neighborhood oppose his living there?

2. Why didn't the Supreme Court's 1917 decision and Dr. Sweet's acquittal end residential segregation in Detroit and other American cities?

Afterward, they were more likely critics of American cultural vulgarity. Novelist Sinclair Lewis in *Main Street* (1920) and *Babbitt* (1922) satirized his native Midwest as a cultural wasteland. Humorists such as James Thurber created outlandish characters to poke fun at American stupidity and inhibitions. And southern writers, led by William Faulkner, explored the South's grim class and race heritage. Worries about alienation surfaced as well. Although F. Scott Fitzgerald gained fame as the chronicler of flaming youth, he spoke sadly in *This Side of Paradise* (1920) of a disillusioned generation "grown up to find all Gods dead, all wars fought, all faiths in man shaken."

REVIEW   How did the new freedoms of the 1920s challenge older conceptions of gender and race?

▶ Resistance to Change

Large areas of the country did not share in the wealth of the 1920s. By the end of the decade, 40 percent of the nation's farmers were landless, and 90 percent of rural homes lacked indoor plumbing, gas, or electricity. Rural America's wariness and distrust of urban America turned to despair in the 1920s when the census reported that the majority of the population had shifted to the city (Map 23.2). Urban domination over the nation's political and cultural life and sharply rising economic disparity drove rural Americans in often ugly, reactionary directions.

Cities seemed to stand for everything rural areas stood against. Rural America imagined itself as solidly Anglo-Saxon (despite the presence of millions of African Americans in the South and Mexican Americans, Native Americans, and Asian Americans in the West), and the cities seemed to be filled with undesirable immigrants. Rural America was the home of old-time Protestant religion, and the cities teemed with Catholics, Jews, liberal Protestants, and atheists. Rural America championed old-fashioned moral standards — abstinence and self-denial — while the cities spawned every imaginable vice. In the 1920s, frustrated rural people sought to recapture their country by helping to push through prohibition, dam the flow of immigrants, revive the Ku Klux Klan, defend the Bible as literal truth, and defeat an urban Roman Catholic for president.

MAP ACTIVITY

Map 23.2   The Shift from Rural to Urban Population, 1920–1930

The movement of whites and Hispanics toward urban and agricultural opportunity made Florida, the West, and the Southwest the regions of fastest population growth. By contrast, large numbers of blacks left the rural South to find a better life in the North. Because almost all migrating blacks went from the countryside to cities in distant parts of the nation, while white and Hispanic migrants tended to move shorter distances toward familiar places, the population shift brought more drastic overall change to blacks than to whites and Hispanics.

READING THE MAP: Which states had the strongest growth? To which cities did southern blacks predominantly migrate?

CONNECTIONS: What conditions in the countryside made the migration to urban areas appealing to many rural Americans? In what social and cultural ways did rural America view itself as different from urban America?

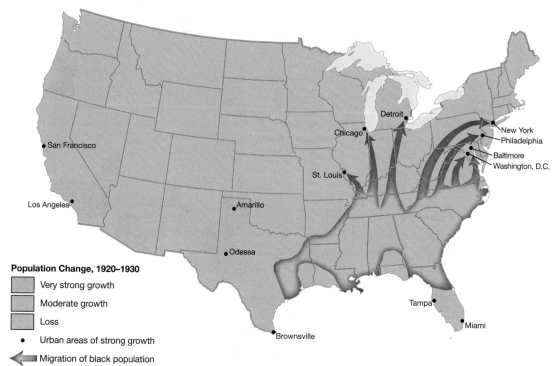

Population Change, 1920–1930

☐ Very strong growth
☐ Moderate growth
☐ Loss
● Urban areas of strong growth
◀ Migration of black population

Rejecting the Undesirables

Before the war, when about a million immigrants arrived each year, some Americans warned that unassimilable foreigners were smothering the nation. War against Germany and its allies expanded nativist and antiradical sentiment. After the war, large-scale immigration resumed (another 800,000 immigrants arrived in 1921) at a moment when industrialists no longer needed new factory laborers. Returning veterans, as well as African American and Mexican migration, had relieved labor shortages. Moreover, union leaders feared that millions of poor immigrants would undercut their efforts to organize American workers. Rural America's God-fearing Protestants were particularly alarmed that most of the immigrants were Catholic or Jewish. In 1921, Congress responded by severely restricting immigration.

In 1924, Congress very nearly slammed the door shut. The **Johnson-Reed Act** limited the number of immigrants to no more than 161,000 a year and gave each European nation a quota based on 2 percent of the number of people from that country in America in 1890. The act revealed the fear and bigotry that fueled anti-immigration legislation. While it cut immigration by more than 80 percent, it squeezed some nationalities far more than others. Backers of Johnson-Reed openly declared that America had become the "garbage can and the dumping ground of the world," and they manipulated quotas to ensure entry only to "good" immigrants. By basing quotas on the 1890 census, in which western Europeans predominated, the law effectively reversed the trend toward immigration from southern and eastern Europe, which by 1914 had amounted to 75 percent of the yearly total. For example, the Johnson-Reed Act allowed Great Britain 62,458 entries, but Russia could send only 1,992.

The 1924 law reaffirmed the 1880s legislation barring Chinese immigrants and added Japanese and other Asians to the list of the excluded. But it left open immigration from the Western Hemisphere. Farmers in the Southwest demanded continued access to cheap agricultural labor, and during the 1920s some 500,000 Mexicans crossed the border. In addition,

Congress in 1924 passed the Indian Citizenship Act, which extended suffrage and citizenship to all American Indians. Indian veterans of World World I had already been made citizens, but now Congress deemed every Indian worthy of participating in American democracy.

Rural Americans, who had most likely never laid eyes on a Polish packinghouse worker, a Slovak coal miner, an Armenian sewing machine operator, or a Chinese laundry worker, strongly supported the Johnson-Reed Act, as did industrialists and labor leaders. The immigration restriction laws of the 1920s provided the framework for immigration policy until the 1960s. These laws marked the end of an era — the denial of the Statue of Liberty's open-arms welcome to Europe's "huddled masses yearning to breathe free."

Antiforeign hysteria climaxed in the trial of two anarchist immigrants from Italy, **Nicola Sacco and Bartolomeo Vanzetti.** Arrested in 1920 for robbery and murder in South Braintree, Massachusetts, the men were sentenced to death by a judge who openly referred to them as "anarchist bastards." In response to doubts about the

Sacco and Vanzetti
After the guilty verdicts were announced, American artist Ben Shahn produced a series of paintings to preserve the memory of Nicola Sacco and Bartolomeo Vanzetti, who many immigrants, liberals, and civil libertarians believed were falsely accused and unfairly convicted. Even today, the 1927 executions symbolize for some the shortcomings of American justice. Digital Image © Museum of Modern Art/Licensed by Scala/Art Resource, NY.

fairness of the verdict, a blue-ribbon review committee found the trial judge guilty of a "grave breach of official decorum" but refused to recommend a motion for retrial. Massachusetts's execution of Sacco and Vanzetti on August 23, 1927, provoked international outrage. Fifty thousand American mourners followed the caskets in the rain, convinced that the men had died because they were immigrants and radicals, not because they were murderers.

The Rebirth of the Ku Klux Klan

The nation's sour antiforeign mood struck a responsive chord in members of the **Ku Klux Klan**. The Klan first appeared in the South during Reconstruction to thwart black freedom and expired with the reestablishment of white supremacy (see chapter 16). In 1915, the Klan was reborn at Stone Mountain, Georgia, but when the new Klan extended its targets beyond black Americans, it quickly spread beyond the South. Under a banner proclaiming "100 percent Americanism," the Klan promised to defend family, morality, and traditional American values against the threats posed by blacks, immigrants, radicals, feminists, Catholics, and Jews.

Building on the frustrations of rural America, the Klan attracted three million to four million members — women as well as men. By the mid-1920s, the Klan had spread throughout the nation, almost controlling Indiana and influencing politics in Illinois, California, Oregon, Texas, Louisiana, Oklahoma, and Kansas. In 1926, Klan imperial wizard Hiram Wesley Evans described the assault of modernity: "One by one all our traditional moral standards went by the boards or were so disregarded that they ceased to be binding," he explained. "The sacredness of our Sabbath, of our homes, of chastity, and finally even of our right to teach our own children in schools [represented] fundamental facts and truth torn away from us." The Klan's uniforms and rituals offered a certain counterfeit dignity to old-stock, Protestant, white Americans who felt passed over, and the hoods allowed members to beat and intimidate their victims with little fear of consequences.

WKKK Badge
Some half a million women were members of the Women of the Ku Klux Klan (WKKK). Young girls could join the female youth auxiliary, the Tri-K for Girls. Klanswomen fit perfectly within the KKK because the organization proclaimed itself the defender of the traditional virtues of pure womanhood and decent homes. This badge from Harrisburg, Pennsylvania, advertises the local WKKK's support for a home for "orphan and dependent children." Klanswomen also joined in boycotts of businesses owned by Jews and others whom they did not consider "100% American." Collection of Janice L. and David J. Frent.

Eventually, social changes, along with lawless excess, crippled the Klan. Immigration restrictions eased the worry about invading foreigners, and sensational wrongdoing by Klan leaders cost it the support of traditional moralists. Grand Dragon David Stephenson of Indiana, for example, went to jail for the kidnapping and rape of a woman who subsequently committed suicide. Yet the social grievances, economic problems, and religious anxieties of the countryside and small towns remained, ready to be ignited.

The Scopes Trial

In 1925 in a Tennessee courtroom, old-time religion and the new spirit of science went head-to-head. The confrontation occurred after several southern states passed legislation against the teaching of Charles Darwin's theory of evolution in the public schools. Fundamentalist Protestants insisted that the Bible's creation story be taught as the literal truth. Scientists and civil liberties organizations clamored for a challenge to the law, and John Scopes, a young biology teacher in Dayton, Tennessee, offered to test his state's ban on teaching evolution. When Scopes came to trial, Clarence Darrow, a brilliant defense lawyer from Chicago, volunteered to defend him. Darrow, an avowed agnostic, took on the prosecution's fundamentalist William Jennings Bryan. Bryan, a three-time Democratic nominee for president and a symbol of rural America, was eager to defeat the proposition that humans had evolved from apes.

The **Scopes trial** quickly degenerated into a media circus. The first trial to be covered live on radio, it attracted a nationwide audience. Most of the reporters from big-city newspapers were hostile to Bryan, none more so than the cynical H. L. Mencken, who painted Bryan as a sort of Darwinian missing link ("a sweating anthropoid" and a "gaping primate"). When, under relentless questioning by Darrow, Bryan declared on the witness stand that he did indeed believe that the world had been created in six days and that Jonah had lived in the belly of a whale, his humiliation in the eyes of most urban observers was complete. Nevertheless, the Tennessee court upheld the law and punished Scopes with a $100 fine. Although fundamentalism won the battle, it lost the war. Mencken had the last word in a merciless obituary for Bryan, who died just a week after the trial ended. Portraying the "monkey trial" as a battle between the country and the city, Mencken flayed Bryan as a "charlatan, a mountebank, a zany without shame or dignity," motivated solely by "hatred of the city men who had laughed at him for so long."

As Mencken's acid prose indicated, Bryan's humiliation was not purely a victory of reason and science. It also revealed the disdain urban people felt for country people and the values they clung to. The Ku Klux Klan revival and the Scopes trial dramatized and inflamed divisions between city and country, intellectuals and the uneducated, the privileged and the poor, the scoffers and the faithful.

Al Smith and the Election of 1928

The presidential election of 1928 brought many of the developments of the 1920s — prohibition, immigration, religion, and the clash of rural and urban values — into sharp focus. Republicans emphasized the economic success of their party's pro-business government and turned to Herbert Hoover, the energetic secretary of commerce and leading public symbol of 1920s prosperity. But because both parties generally agreed that the American economy was basically sound, the campaign turned on social issues that divided Americans.

The Democrats nominated four-time governor of New York **Alfred E. Smith**. Smith adopted "The Sidewalks of New York" as a campaign theme song and seemed to represent all that rural Americans feared and resented. A child of immigrants, Smith got his start in politics with the help of Tammany Hall, New York City's Irish-dominated political machine and to many

the epitome of big-city corruption. He denounced immigration quotas, signed New York State's anti-Klan bill, and opposed prohibition, believing that it was a nativist attack on immigrant customs. When Smith supposedly asked reporters in 1922, "Wouldn't you like to have your foot on the rail and blow the foam off some suds?" prohibition forces dubbed him "Alcohol Al."

Smith's greatest vulnerability in the heartland, however, was his religion. He was the first Catholic to run for president. A Methodist bishop in Virginia denounced Roman Catholicism as "the Mother of ignorance, superstition, intolerance and sin" and begged Protestants not to vote for a candidate who represented "the kind of dirty people that you find today on the sidewalks of New York." The magazine *Baptist and Commoner* argued that Smith's election would mean "granting the Pope the right to dictate to this government what it should do."

> **"The Mother of ignorance, superstition, intolerance, and sin."**
> — A Methodist bishop, speaking of Roman Catholicism

Hoover, who neatly combined the images of morality, efficiency, service, and prosperity, won the election by a landslide (Map 23.3). He received nearly 58 percent of the vote and gained 444 electoral votes to Smith's 87. The Republicans' most notable success came in the previously solid Democratic South, where Smith's religion, views

MAP 23.3
The Election of 1928

Candidate	Electoral Vote	Popular Vote	Percent of Popular Vote
Herbert Hoover (Republican)	444	21,391,381	57.4
Alfred E. Smith (Democrat)	87	15,016,443	40.3
Norman Thomas (Socialist)	0	881,951	2.3

on prohibition, and big-city persona allowed them to take four states. The only bright spot for Democrats was the nation's cities, which voted Democratic, indicating the rising strength of ethnic minorities, including Smith's fellow Catholics.

REVIEW Why did the relationship between urban and rural America deteriorate in the 1920s?

▶ The Great Crash

At his inauguration in 1929, Herbert Hoover told the American people, "Given a chance to go forward with the policies of the last eight years, we shall soon with the help of God be in sight of the day when poverty will be banished from this nation." Those words came back to haunt Hoover, for within eight months the Roaring Twenties came to a crashing halt. The prosperity Hoover touted collapsed with the stock market, and the nation ended nearly three decades of barely interrupted economic growth. Like much of the world, the United States fell into the most serious economic depression of all time. Hoover and his reputation were among the first casualties, along with the reverence for business that had been the hallmark of the New Era.

Herbert Hoover: The Great Engineer

When **Herbert Hoover** became president in 1929, he seemed the perfect choice to lead a prosperous business nation. He personified America's rags-to-riches ideal, having risen from poor Iowa orphan to one of the world's most celebrated mining engineers by the time he was thirty. His success in managing efforts to feed civilian victims of the fighting during World War I won him acclaim as "the Great Humanitarian" and led Woodrow Wilson to name him head of the Food Administration once the United States entered the war. Hoover's reputation soared even higher as secretary of commerce in the Harding and Coolidge administrations.

> "We want to see a nation built of home owners and farm owners. . . . We want them all secure."
> — President HERBERT HOOVER

Hoover belonged to the progressive wing of the Republican Party, and as early as 1909 he declared, "The time when the employer could ride roughshod over his labor[ers] is disappearing with the doctrine of 'laissez-faire' on which it is founded." He urged a limited business-government partnership that would manage the sweeping changes Americans experienced. When Hoover entered the White House, he brought a reform agenda: "We want to see a nation built of home owners and farm owners. We want to see their savings protected. We want to see them in steady jobs. We want to see more and more of them insured against death and accident, unemployment and old age. We want them all secure."

But Hoover also had ideological and political liabilities. Principles that appeared strengths in the prosperous 1920s — individual self-reliance, industrial self-management, and a limited federal government — became straitjackets when economic catastrophe struck. Moreover, Hoover had never held an elected public office, had a poor political touch, and was too thin-skinned to be an effective politician. Even so, most Americans considered him "a sort of superman" able to solve any problem. Prophetically, he confided to a friend his fear that "if some unprecedented calamity should come upon the nation . . . I would be sacrificed to the unreasoning disappointment of a people who expected too much." The distorted national economy set the stage for the calamity Hoover so feared.

The Distorted Economy

In the spring of 1929, the United States enjoyed a fragile prosperity. Although America had become the world's leading economy, it had done little to help rebuild Europe's shattered economy after World War I. Instead, the Republican administrations demanded that Allied nations repay their war loans, creating a tangled web of debts and reparations that sapped Europe's economic vitality. Moreover, to boost American business, the United States enacted tariffs that prevented other nations from selling their goods to Americans. Fewer sales meant that foreign nations had less money to buy American goods, which were pouring out in record abundance. American banks propped up the nation's export trade by extending credit to foreign customers, and fresh debt piled onto existing debt in an absurd pyramid.

American prosperity was real enough, but the domestic economy was also in trouble. Wealth was badly distributed. Farmers continued to suffer from low prices and chronic indebtedness; the average income of families working the land

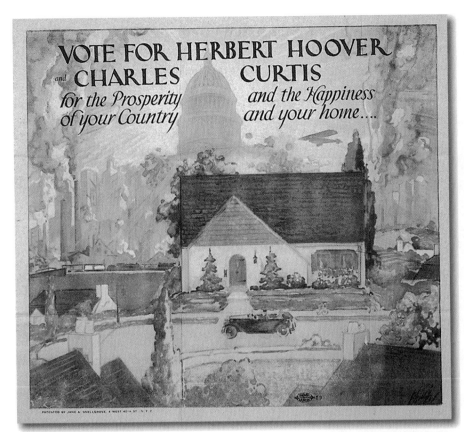

Hoover Campaign Poster
This poster effectively illustrates Herbert Hoover's 1928 campaign message: Republican administrations in the 1920s had produced middle-class prosperity, complete with a house in the suburbs and the latest automobile. To remind voters that Hoover as secretary of commerce had promoted industry that made the suburban dream possible, the poster portrays smoking chimneys at a discreet distance. The poster gives no hint that this positive message would give way to outright religious bigotry in the campaign against Democrat (and Catholic) Al Smith. Collection of Janice L. and David J. Frent.

amounted to only $240 per year. The wages of industrial workers, though rising during the decade, failed to keep up with productivity and corporate profits. Overall, nearly two-thirds of all American families lived on less than the $2,000 per year that economists estimated would "supply only basic necessities." Statistics captured the grim reality. The wealthiest 1 percent of the population received 15 percent of the nation's income — the same amount received by the poorest 42 percent. The Coolidge administration worsened the deepening inequality by cutting taxes on the wealthy.

By 1929, the inequality of wealth produced a serious problem in consumption. The rich spent lavishly, but they could absorb only a tiny fraction of the nation's output. Ordinary folk, on whom the system ultimately depended, were unable to take up the slack. For a time, the new device of installment buying — buying on credit — kept consumer demand up. By the end of the decade, four out of five cars and two out of three radios were bought on credit.

Signs of economic trouble began to appear at mid-decade. New construction slowed down. Automobile sales faltered. Companies began cutting back production and laying off workers. Between 1921 and 1928, as investment and loan opportunities faded, five thousand banks failed, wiping out the life savings of hundreds of thousands of people. Still, the boom seemed to roar on, muffling the sounds of economic distress just beneath the surface.

The Crash of 1929

Even as the international and domestic economies faltered, Americans remained remarkably upbeat. Hoping for even bigger slices of the economic pie, Americans speculated wildly in the stock market on Wall Street. Between 1924 and 1929, the values of stocks listed on the New York Stock Exchange increased by more than 400 percent. In September 1929, General Electric traded at $396 a share, three times the price of a year earlier. Buying stocks on margin — that is, putting up only part of the money at the time of purchase — accelerated. Many people got rich this way, but those who bought on credit could finance their loans only if their stocks increased in value. Speculators could not imagine that the market might fall and that they would be forced

Stock Market Crash
Edward Laning, a mural painter who lost his personal fortune in the stock market crash, gained a measure of revenge in this melodramatic version of the panic on the Stock Exchange floor. Stock Exchange president Richard Whitney stands illuminated and unperturbed in the center as prices and brokers collapse around him. A few years later, however, Whitney went to prison for stealing from other people's accounts to cover his own losses. Laning went on to fame for his murals at Ellis Island and the New York Public Library. Collection of John P. Axelrod/Picture Research Consultants & Archives.

ing confidence. They injected $100 million of their assets to bolster the market and issued brave declarations of faith. But more panic selling came on **Black Tuesday**, October 29, the day the market suffered a greater fall than ever before. In the next six months, the stock market lost six-sevenths of its total value.

It was once thought that the crash alone caused the Great Depression. It did not. In 1929, the national and international economies were already riddled with severe problems. But the dramatic losses in the stock market crash and the fear of risking what was left acted as a great brake on economic activity. The collapse on Wall Street shattered the New Era's confidence that America would enjoy perpetually expanding prosperity.

Hoover and the Limits of Individualism

At first, Americans expressed relief that Herbert Hoover resided in the White House when the bubble broke. Unlike some conservatives who believed that the government should do nothing during economic downturns, Hoover believed that "we should use the powers of government to cushion the situation." Not surprisingly for a man who had been such an active secretary of commerce, Hoover acted quickly to arrest the decline.

In November 1929, to keep the stock market collapse from ravaging the entire economy, Hoover called a White House conference of business and labor leaders and urged them to join in a voluntary plan for recovery: Businesses would maintain production and keep their workers on the job; labor would accept existing wages, hours, and conditions. Within a few months, however, the bargain fell apart. As demand for their products declined, industrialists cut production, sliced wages, and laid off workers. Poorly paid or unemployed workers could not buy much, and their decreased spending led to further cuts in production and further loss of jobs. Thus began the terrible spiral of economic decline.

To deal with the problems of rural America, Hoover got Congress to pass the Agricultural Marketing Act in 1929. The act created the **Farm Board**, which used its budget of $500 million to buy up agricultural surpluses and thus, it was hoped, raise prices. But prices declined. To help end the decline, Hoover joined conservatives in urging protective tariffs on agricultural goods, and the **Hawley-Smoot tariff** of 1930 established the highest rates in history. The same year, Congress also authorized $420 million for public

to meet their margin loans with cash they did not have. A Yale economist assured doubters that stock prices had reached "a permanently high plateau."

Finally, in the autumn of 1929, the market hesitated. Investors nervously began to sell their overvalued stocks. The dip quickly became a panic on October 24, the day that came to be known as Black Thursday. Brokers jammed the stock exchange desperately trying to unload shares. The giants of finance gathered in the offices of J. P. Morgan Jr., son of the nineteenth-century Wall Street lion, to plot ways of restor-

works projects to give the unemployed jobs and create more purchasing power. In three years, the Hoover administration nearly doubled federal public works expenditures.

But with each year of Hoover's term, the economy weakened. Tariffs did not end the suffering of farmers because foreign nations retaliated with increased tariffs of their own that crippled American farmers' ability to sell abroad. In 1932, Hoover hoped to help hard-pressed industry with the **Reconstruction Finance Corporation (RFC)**, a federal agency empowered to lend government funds to endangered banks and corporations. The theory was **trickle-down economics**: Pump money into the economy at the top, and in the long run the people at the bottom would benefit. Or as one wag put it, "Feed the sparrows by feeding the horses." In the end, very little of what critics of the RFC called a "millionaires' dole" trickled down to the poor.

And the poor multiplied. Hundreds of thousands of workers lost their jobs each month. By 1932, an astounding one-quarter of the American workforce — some thirteen million people — were unemployed. There was no direct federal assistance, and state services and private charities were swamped. The depression that began in 1929 devastated much of the world, but no other industrialized nation provided such feeble support to the jobless. Cries grew louder for the federal government to give hurting people relief.

Hoover was no do-nothing president, but there were limits to his activism. He intended a limited role for the federal government in fighting the economic disaster. He compared direct federal aid to the needy to the "dole" in Britain, which he thought destroyed the moral fiber of the chronically unemployed. "Prosperity cannot be restored by raids upon the public Treasury," he declared. Besides, he said, the poor could rely on the charitable spirit of their neighbors to protect them "from hunger and cold." In 1931, he allowed the Red Cross to distribute government-owned agricultural surpluses to the hungry. In 1932, he relaxed his principles further to offer small federal loans, not gifts, to the states to help them in their relief efforts. But Hoover's circumscribed notions of legitimate government action proved vastly inadequate to address the problems of restarting the economy and ending human suffering.

REVIEW Why did the American economy collapse in 1929?

▶ Life in the Depression

In 1930, suffering on a massive scale set in. Despair settled over the land. Men and women hollow-eyed with hunger grew increasingly bewildered and angry in the face of cruel contradictions. They saw agricultural surpluses pile up in the countryside and knew that their children were going to bed hungry. They saw factories standing idle and knew that they and millions of others were willing to work. The gap between the American people and leaders who failed to resolve these contradictions widened as the depression deepened. By 1932, America's economic problems had created a dangerous social and political crisis.

The Human Toll

Statistics only hint at the human tragedy of the Great Depression. When Herbert Hoover took office in 1929, the American economy stood at its peak. When he left in 1933, it had reached its twentieth-century low (Figure 23.2). In 1929, national income was $88 billion. By 1933, it had declined to $40 billion. In 1929, unemployment was 3.1 percent, or 1.5 million workers. By 1933, unemployment stood at 25 percent, almost 13 million workers. In Cleveland, Ohio, 50 percent of the workforce was jobless, and in Toledo, 80 percent. The nation's steel industry operated at only 12 percent of capacity. By 1932, more than 9,000 banks had shut their doors, wiping out some 9 million savings accounts.

Jobless, homeless victims wandered in search of work, and the tramp, or hobo, became one of the most visible figures of the decade. Riding the rails or hitchhiking, a million vagabonds moved southward and westward looking for seasonal agricultural work. Other unemployed men and women, sick or less hopeful, huddled in doorways, overcome, one man remembered, by "helpless despair and submission." Scavengers haunted alleys behind restaurants in search of food. One writer told of an elderly woman who always took off her glasses to avoid seeing the maggots crawling over the garbage she ate. The Children's Bureau announced that one in five schoolchildren did not get enough to eat. "I don't want to steal," a Pennsylvania man wrote to the governor in 1931,

"I don't want to steal, but I won't let my wife and boy cry for something to eat. . . . How long is this going to keep up? I cannot stand it any longer."
—A Pennsylvania man in 1931

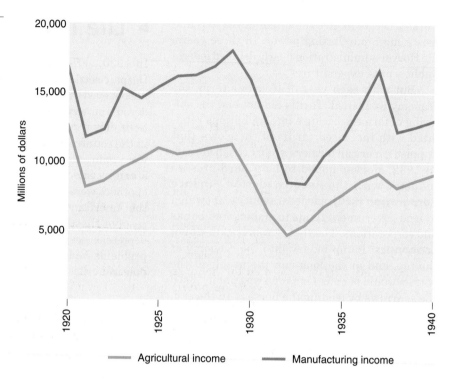

FIGURE 23.2 Manufacturing and Agricultural Income, 1920–1940
After economic collapse, recovery in the 1930s began under New Deal auspices. The sharp declines in 1937–1938, when federal spending was reduced, indicated that New Deal stimuli were still needed to restore manufacturing and agricultural income.

Agricultural income ——— Manufacturing income

"but I won't let my wife and boy cry for something to eat. . . . How long is this going to keep up? I cannot stand it any longer."

Rural poverty was most acute. Tenant farmers and sharecroppers, mainly in the South, came to symbolize how poverty crushed the human spirit. Eight and a half million people, three million of them black, crowded into cabins without plumbing, electricity, or running water. They subsisted—just barely—on salt pork, cornmeal, molasses, beans, peas, and whatever they could hunt or fish. All the diseases of dietary and vitamin deficiencies wracked them. When economist John Maynard Keynes was asked whether anything like this degradation had existed before, he replied, "Yes, it was called the Dark Ages and it lasted four hundred years."

There was no federal assistance to meet this human catastrophe. Instead, Hoover relied on a patchwork of strapped charities and destitute

An Unemployed Youth
Joblessness was frightening and humiliating. Brought up to believe that if you worked hard, you got ahead, the unemployed had difficulty seeing failure to find work as anything other than personal failure. Many slipped into despair and depression. We can only imagine this young man's story. Utterly alone, sitting on a bench that might be his bed, his hat on the ground and his head in his hands, he looks emotionally battered and perhaps defeated. Whether he found work, joined the throngs of beggars and panhandlers on the streets, or cast his lot with the army of hoboes who rode the rails looking for something better is unknown. Library of Congress.

state and local agencies. For a family of four without any income, the best the city of Philadelphia could do was provide $5.50 per week. That was not enough to live on but was still comparatively generous. New York City provided only $2.39 per week. Detroit, devastated by the auto industry's failure, allotted 60 cents a week before the city ran out of money altogether, joining a hundred other cities in 1932 that appropriated no money at all for the indigent.

The deepening crisis roused old fears and caused some Americans to look for scapegoats. Among the most thoroughly scapegoated were Mexican Americans. During the 1920s, cheap agricultural labor from Mexico flowed legally across the U.S. border, welcomed by the large farmers. In the 1930s, however, the public denounced the newcomers as dangerous aliens who took jobs from Americans. Government officials, most prominently those in Los Angeles County, targeted Mexican residents for deportation regardless of citizenship status. As many as half a million Mexicans and Mexican Americans were deported or fled to Mexico.

The depression deeply affected the American family. Young people postponed marriage; between 1929 and 1932, marriages declined by 31 percent. When they did marry, they produced few children. For the first time in American history, the birthrate was on the verge of dropping below the death rate. Moreover, white women, who generally worked in low-paying service areas, did not lose their jobs as often as men who worked in steel, automobile, and other heavy industries. Idle husbands suffered a loss of self-esteem. "Before the depression," one unemployed man reported, "I wore the pants in this family, and rightly so." Jobless, he lost "self-respect" and also "the respect of my children, and I am afraid that I am losing my wife." Another unemployed father said, "A man is not a man without work." Employers discriminated against married women workers, but necessity continued to drive women into the marketplace. As a result, by 1940 some 25 percent more women were employed for wages than in 1930.

Denial and Escape

President Hoover had no idea of how to reach out to the suffering nation. To express his optimism about economic recovery, he maintained formal dress and manners in the White House and continued to keep a retinue of valets and waiters to attend him. All he did was to repeat that economic recovery was on its way. Contradicting the president's optimism were makeshift shantytowns, called "**Hoovervilles**," that sprang up on the edges of America's cities. Newspapers used as cover by those sleeping on the streets were "Hoover blankets." An empty pocket turned inside out was a "Hoover flag," and jackrabbits caught for food were "Hoover hogs." Bitter jokes circulated about the increasingly unpopular president. One told of Hoover asking for a nickel to telephone a friend. Flipping him a dime, an aide said, "Here, call them both."

Deportation to Mexico
A crowd gathered at the train depot in Miami, Arizona, to say good-bye to friends and family who were being pushed to leave depression-wracked America. Scenes like this one were repeated throughout the Southwest. In 1931, Los Angeles County chartered trains to carry Mexicans and Mexican Americans out of the country, arguing that the $15,000 expense "would be recovered within six weeks in saving on charity." But contrary to popular belief, immigrants did not put undue pressure on social services. Moreover, some of the deportees were American citizens who had never been south of the border. Arizona State University Library.

While Hoover practiced denial, other Americans sought refuge from reality at the movies. Throughout the depression, between 60 million and 75 million people (nearly two-thirds of the nation) scraped together enough change to fill the movie palaces every week. Box office hits such as *Forty-second Street* and *Gold Diggers of 1933* capitalized on the hope that prosperity lay just around the corner. But a few filmmakers grappled with realities rather than escape them. *The Public Enemy* (1931) taught hard lessons about gangsters' ill-gotten gains. Indeed, under the new production code of 1930, designed to protect public morals, all movies had to find some way to show that crime did not pay.

Despite Hollywood's efforts to keep Americans on the right side of the law, crime increased. Out in the countryside, the plight of people who had lost their farms to bank foreclosures led to the romantic idea that bank robbers were only getting back what banks had stolen from the poor. Woody Guthrie, the populist folksinger from Oklahoma, captured the public's tolerance for outlaws in his tribute to a murderous bank robber with a choirboy face, "The Ballad of Pretty Boy Floyd":

> Yes, as through this world I ramble,
> I see lots of funny men,
> Some will rob you with a six-gun,
> Some will rob you with a pen.
> But as through your life you'll travel,
> Wherever you may roam,
> You won't never see an outlaw drive
> A family from their home.

Working-Class Militancy

It was the nation's working class that bore the brunt of the economic collapse. In Chicago, workingwomen received less than twenty-five cents an hour. Sawmill workers in the West got a nickel. By 1931, William Green, head of the American Federation of Labor (AFL), had turned militant. "I warn the people who are exploiting the workers," he shouted, "that they can drive them only so far before they will turn on them and destroy them. They are taking no account of the history of nations in which governments have been overturned. Revolutions grow out of the depths of hunger."

The American people were slow to anger, but on March 7, 1932, several thousand unemployed autoworkers massed at the gates of Henry Ford's River Rouge factory in Dearborn, Michigan, to demand work. Pelted with rocks, Ford's private security forces responded with gunfire, killing four demonstrators. Forty thousand outraged citizens turned out for the unemployed men's funerals.

Farmers mounted uprisings of their own. When Congress refused to guarantee farm prices that would at least equal the cost of production, several thousand farmers created the National Farmers' Holiday Association in 1932, so named because its members planned to take a "holiday" from shipping crops to market. When some farmers persisted, militants barricaded roads and dumped thousands of gallons of milk in ditches. Farm militants also resorted to what they called "penny sales." When banks foreclosed and put farms up for auction, neighbors warned others not to bid, bought the foreclosed property for a few pennies, and returned it to the bankrupt owners. Under this kind of pressure, some states suspended debts or reduced mortgages. In California in 1933, when landowners cut their laborers' already substandard wages, more than 50,000 farmworkers, most of them Mexicans, went on strike. Militancy won farmers little in the way of long-term solutions, but one individual observed that "the biggest and finest crop of revolutions you ever saw is sprouting all over the country right now."

Even those who had proved their patriotism by serving in World War I rose up in protest against the government. In June and July 1932, tens of thousands of unemployed veterans traveled to Washington, D.C., to petition Congress for the immediate payment of the pension (known as a "bonus") that Congress had promised them in 1924. The throng included, according to a Washington reporter, "truck drivers and blacksmiths, steel workers and coal miners, stenographers and common laborers," in all "a fair cross section" of the nation. President Hoover feared that the veterans would spark a riot and ordered the U.S. Army to evict the **Bonus Marchers** from their camp on the outskirts of the city. Tanks decimated the squatters' encampments while five hundred soldiers wielding bayonets and tear gas sent the ragtag protesters fleeing. The mayhem, which was captured on newsreels, appalled the nation and further undermined public support for the beleaguered Hoover. "So all the misery and suffering had finally come to this," reported one journalist, "soldiers

"Scottsboro Boys"
Nine black youths, ranging in age from thirteen to twenty-one, stand in front of rifle-bearing National Guard troops called up by Alabama governor B. M. Miller, who feared a mob lynching after two white women accused the nine of rape in March 1931. In less than two weeks, an all-white jury heard flimsy evidence, convicted the nine of rape, and sentenced them to death. Although none was executed, all nine spent years in jail. Eventually, the state dropped the charges against the youngest four and granted paroles to the others. The last "Scottsboro Boy" left jail in 1950.

marching with their guns against American citizens."

Such scenes during the Great Depression — the massive failure of capitalism — brought socialism back to life in the United States and catapulted the Communist Party to its greatest size and influence in American history. Some 100,000 Americans — workers, intellectuals, college students — joined the Communist Party in the belief that only an overthrow of the capitalist system could save the victims of the depression. In 1931, the party, through its National Miners Union, moved into Harlan County, Kentucky, to support a strike by brutalized coal miners. The mine owners unleashed thugs against the strikers and eventually beat the miners down. But the Communist Party gained a reputation as the most dedicated and fearless champion of the union cause.

The left also led the fight against racism. While both major parties refused to challenge segregation in the South, the Socialist Party, led by Norman Thomas, attacked the system

Harlan County Coal Strike, 1931

of sharecropping that left many African Americans in near servitude. The Communist Party also took action. When nine young black men in Scottsboro, Alabama (the **Scottsboro Boys**), were arrested on trumped-up rape charges in 1931, a team of lawyers sent by the party saved the defendants from the electric chair.

Radicals on the left often sparked action, but protests by moderate workers and farmers occurred on a far greater scale. Breadlines, soup kitchens, foreclosures, unemployment, government violence, and cold despair drove patriotic men and women to question American capitalism. "I am as conservative as any man could be," a Wisconsin farmer explained, "but any economic system that has in its power to set me and my wife in the streets, at my age — what can I see but red?"

REVIEW   How did the depression reshape American politics?

▶ Conclusion: Dazzle and Despair

In the aftermath of World War I, America turned its back on progressive crusades and embraced conservative Republican politics, the growing influence of corporate leaders, and business values. Changes in the nation's economy — Henry Ford's automobile revolution, advertising, mass production — propelled fundamental change throughout society. Living standards rose, economic opportunity increased, and Americans threw themselves into private pleasures — gobbling up the latest household goods and fashions, attending baseball and football games and boxing matches, gathering around the radio, and going to the movies. As big cities came to dominate American life, the culture of youth and flappers became the leading edge of what one observer called a "revolution in manners and morals." At home in Harlem and abroad in Paris, American literature, art, and music flourished.

For many Americans, however, none of the glamour and vitality had much meaning. Instead of seeking thrills at speakeasies, plunging into speculation on Wall Street, or escaping abroad, the vast majority struggled to earn a decent living. Blue-collar America did not participate fully in white-collar prosperity. Rural America was almost entirely left out of the Roaring Twenties. Country folk, deeply suspicious and profoundly discontented, championed prohibition, revived the Klan, attacked immigration, and defended old-time Protestant religion.

Just as the dazzle of the Roaring Twenties hid deep divisions in society, extravagant prosperity masked structural flaws in the economy. The crash of 1929 and the depression that followed starkly revealed the economy's crises of international trade and consumption. Hard times swept high living off the front pages of the nation's newspapers. Different images emerged: hoboes hopping freight trains, strikers confronting police, malnourished sharecroppers staring blankly into the distance, empty apartment buildings alongside cardboard shantytowns, and mountains of food rotting in the sun while guards with shotguns chased away the hungry.

The depression hurt everyone, but the poor were hurt most. As farmers and workers sank into aching hardship, businessmen rallied around Herbert Hoover to proclaim that private enterprise would get the country moving again. But things fell apart, and Hoover faced increasingly radical opposition. Membership in the Socialist and Communist parties surged, and more and more Americans contemplated desperate measures. By 1932, the depression had nearly brought the nation to its knees. America faced its greatest crisis since the Civil War, and citizens demanded new leaders who would save them from the "Hoover Depression."

▶ Selected Bibliography

General Works

David M. Kennedy, *Freedom from Fear: The American People in Depression and War, 1929–1945* (1999).

William E. Leuchtenburg, *The Perils of Prosperity, 1914–1932* (1958).

Michael Parrish, *Anxious Decades: America in Prosperity and Depression, 1920–1941* (1992).

Politics and Economy

Kristi Anderson, *After Suffrage: Women in Partisan and Electoral Politics before the New Deal* (1996).

Douglas Brinkley, *Wheels for the World: Henry Ford, His Company, and a Century of Progress, 1903–2003* (2003).

Kendrick A. Clements, *Hoover, Conservation, and Consumerism: Engineering the Good Life* (2000).

Warren I. Cohen, *Empire without Tears: America's Foreign Relations, 1921–1933* (1987).

Steve Fraser, *Every Man a Speculator: A History of Wall Street* (2005).

Colin Gordon, *New Deals: Business, Labor, and Politics in America, 1920–1935* (1994).

David Greenberg, *Calvin Coolidge* (2006).

Owen Gutfreund, *Twentieth-Century Sprawl: Highways and the Reshaping of the American Landscape* (2004).

Jill Jonnes, *Empires of Light: Edison, Tesla, and Westinghouse, and the Race to Electrify the World* (2003).

William E. Leuchtenburg, *Herbert Hoover: 31st President, 1929–1933* (2009).

Martha L. Olney, *Buy Now, Pay Later: Advertising, Credit, and Consumer Durables in the 1920s* (1991).

Lorrai Schuyler, *Weight of Their Votes: Southern Women and Political Leverage in the 1920s* (2006).

Steven Watts, *People's Tycoon: Henry Ford and the American Century* (2005).

Society and Culture

Douglas Carl Abrams, *Selling the Old-Time Religion: American Fundamentalists and Mass Culture, 1920–1940* (2001).

Francisco E. Balderrama and Raymond Rodriguez, *Decade of Betrayal: Mexican Repatriation in the 1930s* (1995).

Kevin Boyle, *Arc of Justice: A Saga of Race, Civil Rights, and Murder in the Jazz Age* (2004).

Liz Conor, *Spectacular Modern Woman: Feminine Visibility in the 1920s* (2004).

Ruth Schwartz Cowan, *More Work for Mother: The Ironies of Household Technology from the Open Hearth to the Microwave* (1983).

Roger Daniels, *Guarding the Golden Door: American Immigration Policy and Immigrants since 1882* (2004).

Paula S. Fass, *The Damned and the Beautiful: American Youth in the 1920s* (1977).

David J. Goldberg, *Discontented America: The United States in the 1920s* (1999).

David M. Kennedy, *Birth Control in America: The Career of Margaret Sanger* (1970).

David E. Kyvig, *Daily Life in the United States, 1920–1940* (2002).

Edward J. Larson, *Summer of the Gods: The Scopes Trial and America's Continuing Debate over Science and Religion* (1997).

David Levering Lewis, *W. E. B. Du Bois: The Fight for Equality and the American Century, 1919–1963* (2000).

Nancy MacLean, *Behind the Mask of Chivalry: The Making of the Second Ku Klux Klan* (1994).

David E. Nye, *Electrifying America: Social Meanings of a New Technology, 1880–1940* (1990).

Daniel Okrent, *Last Call: The Rise and Fall of Prohibition* (2010).

David M. Reimers, *Unwelcome Strangers: American Identity and the Turn against Immigration* (1998).

Susan Smulyan, *Selling Radio: The Commercialization of American Broadcasting, 1920–1934* (1994).

Judith Stein, *The World of Marcus Garvey* (1986).

Andrew Wiese, *Places of Their Own: African American Suburbanization in the Twentieth Century* (2004).

▶ **FOR MORE BOOKS ABOUT TOPICS IN THIS CHAPTER,** see the Online Bibliography at **bedfordstmartins.com/roark.**

▶ **FOR ADDITIONAL PRIMARY SOURCES FROM THIS PERIOD,** see Michael Johnson, ed., *Reading the American Past,* Fifth Edition.

▶ **FOR WEB SITES, IMAGES, AND DOCUMENTS RELATED TO TOPICS AND PLACES IN THIS CHAPTER,** visit Make History at **bedfordstmartins.com/roark.**

Reviewing Chapter 23

KEY TERMS

Explain each term's significance.

The New Era

Warren Gamaliel Harding (p. 751)
Teapot Dome (p. 752)
Calvin Coolidge (p. 752)
Five-Power Naval Treaty of 1922
  (p. 753)
Kellogg-Briand pact (p. 753)
Dawes Plan (p. 753)
Henry Ford (p. 754)
welfare capitalism (p. 754)

The Roaring Twenties

Sigmund Freud (p. 757)
prohibition (p. 758)
new woman (p. 760)
Equal Rights Amendment (p. 760)
flapper (p. 761)
Marcus Garvey (p. 761)
New Negro (p. 764)
Harlem Renaissance (p. 764)
Charles Lindbergh (p. 765)
Lost Generation (p. 766)

Resistance to Change

Johnson-Reed Act (p. 769)
Nicola Sacco and Bartolomeo Vanzetti
  (p. 769)
Ku Klux Klan (p. 770)
Scopes trial (p. 770)
Alfred E. Smith (p. 771)

The Great Crash

Herbert Hoover (p. 772)
Black Tuesday (p. 774)
Farm Board (p. 774)
Hawley-Smoot tariff (p. 774)
Reconstruction Finance Corporation
  (RFC) (p. 775)
trickle-down economics (p. 775)

Life in the Depression

Hoovervilles (p. 777)
Bonus Marchers (p. 778)
Scottsboro Boys (p. 779)

REVIEW QUESTIONS

Use key terms and dates to support your answer.

1. How did the spread of the automobile transform the United States? (pp. 751–756)

2. How did the new freedoms of the 1920s challenge older conceptions of gender and race? (pp. 757–767)

3. Why did the relationship between urban and rural America deteriorate in the 1920s? (pp. 768–772)

4. Why did the American economy collapse in 1929? (pp. 772–775)

5. How did the depression reshape American politics? (pp. 775–779)

MAKING CONNECTIONS

Draw on key terms, the timeline, and review questions.

1. In the 1920s, Americans' wariness of the concentration of power in the hands of industrial capitalists gave way to unrestrained confidence in American business. What drove this shift in popular opinion? How did it influence Republicans' approach to governance and the development of the American economy in the 1920s?

2. Americans' encounters with the wealth and increased personal freedom characteristic of the 1920s varied greatly. Discuss the impact such variation had on Americans' responses to new circumstances. Why did some embrace the era's changes, while others resisted them? Ground your answer in a discussion of specific political, legal, or cultural conflicts.

3. How did shifting government policy contribute to both the boom of the 1920s and the bust of 1929? In your answer, consider the part domestic and international policy played in these developments, including taxation, tariffs, and international banking.

4. The Great Depression plunged the nation into a profound crisis with staggering personal and national costs. How did Americans attempt to lessen the impact of these circumstances? In your answer, discuss and compare the responses of individual Americans and the federal government.

LINKING TO THE PAST

Link events in this chapter to earlier events.

1. How did America's experience in World War I — both at home and abroad — help shape the 1920s? (See chapter 22.)

2. How did attitudes toward government in the Progressive Era differ from those in the 1920s? (See chapter 21.)

▶ FOR PRACTICE QUIZZES AND OTHER STUDY TOOLS, visit the Online Study Guide at bedfordstmartins.com/roark.

TIMELINE 1920–1932

1920
- Eighteenth Amendment goes into effect.
- Nineteenth Amendment ratified.
- Republican Warren G. Harding elected president.

1921
- Sheppard-Towner Act.
- Congress restricts immigration.

1922
- Fordney-McCumber tariff.
- Five-Power Naval Treaty.

1923
- Equal Rights Amendment defeated in Congress.
- Harding dies; Vice President Calvin Coolidge becomes president.

1924
- Dawes Plan.
- Coolidge elected president.
- Johnson-Reed Act.
- Indian Citizenship Act.

1925
- Scopes trial.

1927
- Charles Lindbergh flies nonstop across the Atlantic.
- Nicola Sacco and Bartolomeo Vanzetti executed.

1928
- Kellogg-Briand pact.
- Republican Herbert Hoover elected president.

1929
- St. Valentine's Day murders.
- Agricultural Marketing Act.
- Publication of *Middletown*.
- Stock market collapses.

1930
- Congress authorizes $420 million for public works projects.
- Hawley-Smoot tariff.

1931
- Scottsboro Boys arrested.
- Harlan County, Kentucky, coal strike.

1932
- River Rouge factory demonstration.
- Reconstruction Finance Corporation established.
- National Farmers' Holiday Association formed.

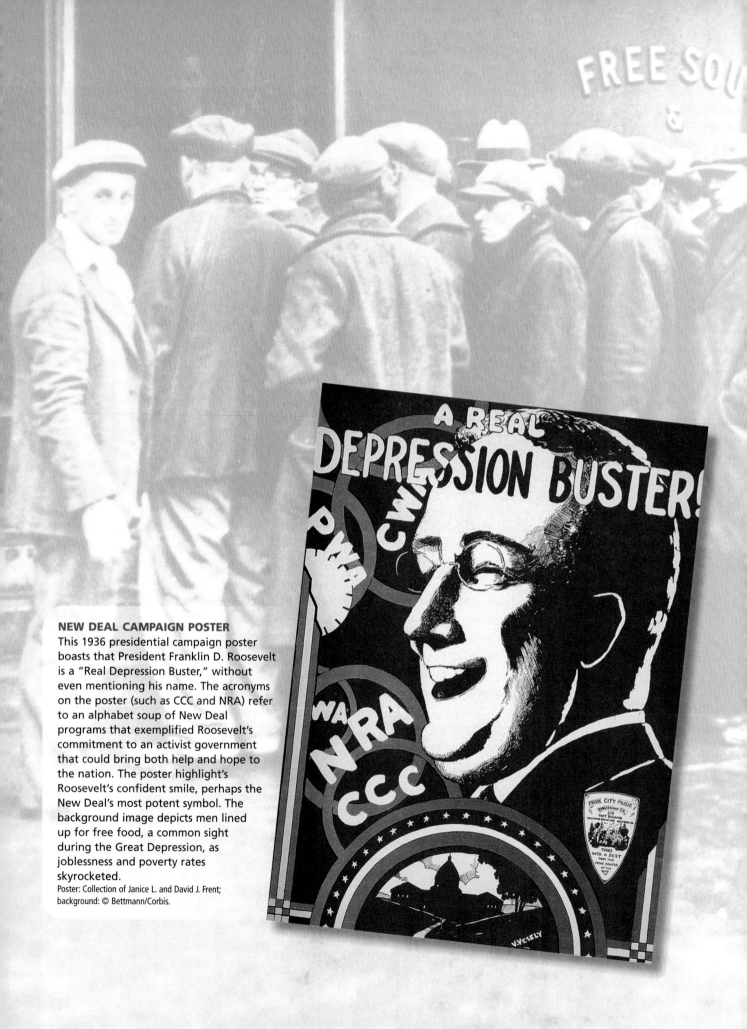

NEW DEAL CAMPAIGN POSTER
This 1936 presidential campaign poster boasts that President Franklin D. Roosevelt is a "Real Depression Buster," without even mentioning his name. The acronyms on the poster (such as CCC and NRA) refer to an alphabet soup of New Deal programs that exemplified Roosevelt's commitment to an activist government that could bring both help and hope to the nation. The poster highlight's Roosevelt's confident smile, perhaps the New Deal's most potent symbol. The background image depicts men lined up for free food, a common sight during the Great Depression, as joblessness and poverty rates skyrocketed.

24

The New Deal Experiment
1932–1939

IN EARLY MARCH 1936, FLORENCE OWENS PILED HER SEVEN CHILDREN, ages one to fourteen, into an old Hudson. Owens and her family had been picking beets in the Imperial Valley of southern California, near the Mexican border, but the harvest was over now. Owens headed north toward Watsonville, where she hoped to find work picking lettuce. About halfway there, near the small town of Nipomo, her car broke down. She coasted into a labor camp of more than two thousand migrant workers who were hungry, out of work, and stuck, lacking the money to look for work elsewhere. They had been attracted by growers' advertisements of work in the pea fields, only to find the crop ruined by a heavy frost. Owens set up a lean-to shelter and prepared food for her family while two of her sons worked on the car. They ate half-frozen peas from the field and small birds the children killed. Owens recalled later, "I started to cook dinner for my kids, and all the little kids around the camp came in. 'Can I have a bite? Can I have a bite?' And they was hungry, them people was."

Florence Owens was born in 1903 in Oklahoma, or what was then Indian Territory. Both of Florence's parents were Cherokee. When she was a baby, her father abandoned her mother, who soon remarried a Choctaw man, and the young family moved to a small farm near Tahlequah, Oklahoma, where Florence grew up. When she was seventeen, Florence married Cleo Owens, a farmer who, after a few years, moved his growing family to California, where he worked in sawmills. Cleo died of tuberculosis in 1931, leaving Florence a widow with six young children.

Florence began to work as a farm laborer in California's Central Valley to support herself and her children. She picked cotton, earning about $2 a day. "I'd leave home before daylight and come in after dark," she explained. "We just existed! Anyway, we survived, let's put it that way." To survive, she worked nights as a waitress, making "50-cents a day and the leftovers." Sometimes, she remembered, "I'd carry home two water buckets full" of leftovers to feed her children.

Like tens of thousands of other migrant laborers, Owens followed the crops, planting, cultivating, and harvesting as jobs opened up in the fields along the West Coast from California to Oregon and Washington. Joining Owens and other migrants — many of whom were Mexicans and Filipinos — were Okie refugees from the Dust Bowl, the large swath of Great Plains states that suffered drought, failed crops, and foreclosed mortgages during the 1930s. As one Okie told a government official in California about the Dust Bowl, "Back there we like to starve to death"; working as a migrant laborer, tough as it was, he said, "beats starvin to death."

Soon after Florence Owens fed her children at the pea pickers' camp, a car pulled up, and a woman with a camera got out and began to take photographs of Owens. The woman was Dorothea Lange, a photographer employed by a New Deal agency to document conditions among farmworkers in California. Lange snapped six photos of Owens, moving closer each time until, with the last shot, she filled the frame with Owens and three of her children. After about ten minutes, Lange climbed back in her car and headed to Berkeley. Owens and her family, their car now repaired, drove off to the lettuce fields of Watsonville.

Within days, Lange's last photograph of Owens was published in San Francisco, and news of the near-famine conditions in the pea pickers' camp reached Washington, D.C. Federal officials rushed twenty thousand pounds of food to the camp, but Owens and her children were long gone when it arrived. The photograph of Owens, however, subsequently known as *Migrant Mother*, became an icon of the desperation among Americans that President Franklin Roosevelt's New Deal sought to alleviate. *Migrant Mother* became Dorothea Lange's most famous photograph, but Florence Owens continued to work in the fields, "ragged, hungry, and broke," as a San Francisco newspaper noted. One of Owens's daughters recalled, "That photo never gave mother or us kids any relief."

Unlike Owens, her children, and other migrant workers, many Americans received government help from Roosevelt's New Deal initiatives to provide relief for the needy, to speed economic recovery, and to reform basic economic and governmental institutions. Roosevelt's New Deal elicited bitter opposition from critics on the right and the left and failed to satisfy fully its own goals of relief, recovery, and reform. But within the Democratic Party, the New Deal energized a powerful political coalition that helped millions of Americans withstand the privations of the Great Depression. In the process, the federal government became a major presence in the daily lives of most American citizens.

Florence Owens and Children

This classic photograph of migrant farm laborer Florence Owens and her children, known as *Migrant Mother*, was taken in 1936 in the labor camp of a pea field in California by New Deal photographer Dorothea Lange. The photo depicts the privations common among working people during the depression, but it also evokes a mother's leadership, dignity, and affection, qualities that helped shelter her family from poverty and joblessness. The photo suggests the depression's cruel assault on most Americans' first safety net — their families — a reality that the New Deal sought to remedy with its proposals for relief, recovery, and reform. Library of Congress.

▶ Franklin D. Roosevelt: A Patrician in Government

Unlike the millions of impoverished Americans, Franklin Roosevelt came from a wealthy and privileged background that contributed to his optimism, self-confidence, and vitality. He constantly drew on these personal qualities in his political career to bridge the economic, social, and cultural chasm that separated him from the struggles of ordinary people like Florence Owens. During the twelve years he served as president (1933–1945), many elites came to hate him as a traitor to his class, while millions more Americans, especially the hardworking poor and dispossessed, revered him because he cared about them and their problems.

The Making of a Politician

Born in 1882, **Franklin Delano Roosevelt** grew up on his father's leafy estate at Hyde Park on the Hudson River, north of New York City. Roosevelt was steeped at home and school in high-minded doctrines of public service and Christian duty to help the poor and weak. He prepared for a career in politics, hoping to follow in the political footsteps of his fifth cousin, Theodore Roosevelt. In 1905, Franklin married his distant cousin, Eleanor Roosevelt. Theodore Roosevelt — the current president of the United States — gave the bride away, an indication of Franklin's gilt-edged connections.

Unlike his cousin Teddy, Franklin Roosevelt sought his political fortune in the Democratic Party. He served in Woodrow Wilson's administration as assistant secretary of the navy, fueling a lifelong interest in maritime matters. In 1920, he catapulted to the second spot on the national Democratic ticket as the vice presidential candidate of presidential nominee James M. Cox. Although Cox lost the election (see chapter 22), Roosevelt's energetic campaigning convinced Democratic leaders that he had a bright future in national politics.

In the summer of 1921, at the age of thirty-nine, Roosevelt caught polio, which paralyzed both his legs. For the rest of his life, he wore heavy steel braces, and he could walk a few steps only by leaning on another person. Tireless physical therapy helped him regain his vitality and intense desire for

Roosevelt's Common Touch
Understanding the political importance of appearing both neighborly and physically robust, Franklin Roosevelt set up a friendly chat outside the polls during his bid for reelection as New York's governor in 1930. In this photograph with working-class voter Ruben Appel, Roosevelt's upright position was a feat of stagecraft. His legs rendered useless by polio, Roosevelt could remain standing only by propping himself up on his cane. Rare photos like this and a taboo against showing Roosevelt in his wheelchair kept the public from thinking of Roosevelt as a "cripple" and unfit for office; many did not even realize he was disabled. Franklin D. Roosevelt Library.

high political office. But he recaptured his political momentum mostly from a sitting position, although he carefully avoided being photographed in the wheelchair he used routinely.

Fascism: Adolf Hitler and National Socialism

The Great Depression paralyzed economies around the globe and seemed to demonstrate that capitalism had failed. Individual working people and even businesses could do little to restore prosperity. Only governments had the power to kick-start the economy. Many people believed that democracies such as the United States were too weak and divided to take the necessary steps.

President Franklin Roosevelt optimistically declared that the "democratic faith" of Americans in 1933 was "too sturdy" to turn to "alien ideologies like communism and fascism." But authoritarian, anti-democratic Communist and fascist parties battled to seize control of national governments across Europe. In Germany, Adolf Hitler and his fascist National Socialist Party, also known as the Nazis, came to power in 1933 and improved the economy while crushing democracy.

Hitler rose to power as the leader of a political coalition (composed of Nazis, other conservative parties, and the army) that sought to bring order to Germany in the years following World War I. Hitler stoked discontent by proclaiming his fantasy that an international conspiracy of Communists and financiers — mostly Jews — caused Germany's defeat and was responsible for its postwar woes. During the 1920s, economic distress and political turmoil increased support for Hitler's National Socialist Party among disgruntled veterans, farmers, residents of small towns, shopkeepers, artisans, and other members of the middle and lower-middle classes. The Nazis became the most popular political party by 1932, but they still commanded only one-third of the vote when Hitler became head of the German government in January 1933.

Within a few months, Hitler seized dictatorial power. The Nazis outlawed all political opposition, murdering hundreds and imprisoning more than 100,000 Communists, socialists, union members, and others in the summer of 1933, creating a one-party government. To stifle any lingering dissent, the Nazis seized control of every institution in German society, from local governments to choirs and hiking clubs. They created an elaborate system of spies who punished anyone suspected of questioning Nazi rule. Hitler boasted that "every person should know for all time that if he raises his hand to strike at the [Nazi] State, certain death will be his lot." The Nazi Gestapo (secret police) routinely carried out Hitler's threat, making lawless, life-threatening terror a reality throughout German society.

Hitler's obsessive anti-Semitism made Jews a special target of the Nazi police state. The Nazis organized boycotts of Jewish businesses, destroyed and confiscated Jews' property, purged Jews from civilian and military employment, and passed laws prohibiting marriages between Jews and non-Jews. In reality, Jews accounted for only about 1 percent of the German population, and most of them were fully acculturated members of German society. Hitler claimed, however, that Jews and other "enemies of the people" — such as Gypsies, homosexuals, the chronically ill, and the mentally or physically disabled — polluted the purity of the German race. Hitler and the Nazis relished the persecution of Jews, profited from robbing Jews of their property, and constantly warned about the grave threat Jews posed to Germany — a claim that was completely false.

Hitler's fascist dictatorship had one overriding goal: to rearm Germany and expand German territory until it encompassed all of Europe and much of the Soviet Union. Hitler grandiosely planned a campaign of conquest that would result in the Nazis' thousand-year dominion over the world. He announced in 1933 that "the re-armament of the German people . . . must always and everywhere stand in the foreground." In consultation

After his polio attack, Roosevelt frequented a polio therapy facility at Warm Springs, Georgia. There, he combined the health benefits of the soothing waters with political overtures to southern Democrats, which helped make him a rare political creature: a New Yorker from the Democratic Party's urban and immigrant wing with whom whites from the Democratic Party's entrenched southern wing felt comfortable.

By 1928, Roosevelt had recovered sufficiently to campaign to become governor of New York, and he squeaked out a victory. As governor of the nation's most populous state, Roosevelt showcased his leadership and his suitability for a presidential campaign of his own. His activist policies as governor became a dress rehearsal for his presidency.

As the Great Depression spread hard times throughout the nation, Governor Roosevelt believed that government should intervene to protect citizens from economic hardships rather than wait for the law of supply and demand to improve the economy. According to the

with military leaders, the Nazis mobilized German industries to build tanks, ships, aircraft, and weapons as rapidly as possible, all in violation of the terms of the Versailles treaty.

Unlike the Communists in the Soviet Union, fascists in Nazi Germany worked with privately owned industrial firms, which welcomed military production that brought them increased investment, productivity, and profits. The rearmament campaign reduced unemployment from more than 11 million in 1933 to less than 1 million by 1937. Likewise, although the peace treaty limited the size of the German military to 100,000 men, the Nazis had nearly 2.5 million men in uniform by 1939. They financed this massive militarization by forcing civilians to consume less and work more and by extortion and robbery of private wealth.

The Nazis barraged Germany with propaganda designed to promote a cult of Hitler worship. The führer (leader) was portrayed as having almost superhuman powers. The famous Nazi film director Leni Riefenstahl echoed this Hitler cult when she wrote to the führer, "You exceed anything human imagination has the power to conceive, achieving deeds without parallel in the history of mankind." Hitler welcomed such flattery, which masked the underlying terror, lawlessness, and corruption of his fascist dictatorship. The Nazis reduced unemployment and brought a measure of

Germans Salute a Nazi Parade
This photograph depicts the enthusiasm of German men, women, and children who raise their hands in the Nazi salute as fascist officials parade through the streets of Nuremberg in 1938. Although Hitler's police state never won the allegiance of all Germans, most welcomed the economic prosperity and political order imposed by Hitler, and they willingly cooperated with the Nazis' reign of terror, persecution, and rearmament. United States Holocaust Memorial Museum.

prosperity to many Germans during the 1930s by outlawing democracy, suppressing dissent, imprisoning and murdering tens of thousands of people, and preparing for a war that would leave Germany a smoldering ruin twelve years after Hitler seized power.

America in a Global Context

1. How did Hitler's Nazism compare with Roosevelt's New Deal?

2. To what degree was Roosevelt correct about the "democratic faith" of Americans compared, for example, with that of Germans?

laissez-faire views of many conservatives — especially Republicans, but also numerous Democrats — the depression simply represented market forces separating strong survivors from weak losers. Unlike Roosevelt, conservatives believed that government help for the needy sapped individual initiative and impeded the self-correcting forces of the market by rewarding people for losing the economic struggle to survive. Roosevelt lacked a full-fledged counterargument to these conservative claims, but he sympathized with the plight of poor people.

"To these unfortunate citizens," he proclaimed, "aid must be extended by governments, not as a matter of charity but as a matter of social duty. . . . [No one should go] unfed, unclothed, or unsheltered."

The highlight of Roosevelt's efforts to relieve the economic woes of New Yorkers was the Temporary Emergency Relief Administration, created in 1931. It provided an unprecedented $20 million in aid for the poor, earning him the gratitude of needy New Yorkers and the attention of national politicians.

To his supporters, Roosevelt seemed to be a leader determined to attack the economic crisis without deviating from democracy—unlike the fascist parties gaining strength in Europe—or from capitalism—unlike the Communists in power in the Soviet Union. (See "Beyond America's Borders," page 788.) Roosevelt's ideas about precisely how to revive the economy were vague. A prominent journalist described Roosevelt in 1931 as "a kind of amiable boy scout . . . a pleasant man who, without any important qualifications for the office, would very much like to be president." Such sneering comments did not sway his many supporters who appreciated his energy and activism. His conviction that government should do something to help Americans climb out of the economic abyss propelled him into the front ranks of the national Democratic Party.

The Election of 1932

Democrats knew that Herbert Hoover's unpopularity gave them a historic opportunity to recapture the White House in 1932. Since Abraham Lincoln's election, Republicans had occupied the White House three-fourths of the time, a trend Democrats hoped to reverse. Democrats, however, had to overcome warring factions that divided the party by region, religion, culture, and commitment to the status quo. Southern Democrats chaired powerful committees in Congress thanks to their continual reelection in a one-party South devoted to white supremacy. This southern, native-born, white, rural, Protestant, conservative wing of the Democratic Party found little common ground with the northern, immigrant, urban, disproportionately Catholic, liberal wing. Rural and native-born drys (supporters of prohibition) clashed with urban and foreign-born wets (opponents of prohibition). Eastern-establishment Democratic dignitaries shared few goals with angry farmers and factory workers. Still, this unruly coalition managed to agree on Franklin Roosevelt as its presidential candidate.

In his acceptance speech, Roosevelt vowed to help "the forgotten man at the bottom of the pyramid" with "bold, persistent experimentation." Highlighting his differences with Hoover and the Republicans, he pledged "a new deal for the American people." Few details about what Roosevelt meant by "a new deal" emerged in the presidential campaign. He declared that "the people

Candidate	Electoral Vote	Popular Vote	Percent of Popular Vote
Franklin D. Roosevelt (Democrat)	472	22,821,857	57.4
Herbert C. Hoover (Republican)	59	15,761,841	39.7
Norman Thomas (Socialist)	0	881,951	2.2
William Z. Foster (Communist)	0	102,991	0.3

MAP 24.1
The Election of 1932

of America want more than anything else . . . two things: work . . . with all the moral and spiritual values that go with work . . . and a reasonable measure of security . . . for themselves and for their wives and children." Although Roosevelt never explained exactly how the federal government could provide either work or security, voters decided that whatever his new deal might be, it was better than reelecting Hoover.

Roosevelt won the 1932 presidential election in a historic landslide. He received 57 percent of the nation's votes, the first time a Democrat had won a majority of the popular vote since 1852 (Map 24.1). He amassed 472 electoral votes to Hoover's 59, carrying state after state that had voted Republican for years (Map 24.2). Roosevelt's coattails swept Democrats into control of Congress by large margins. The popular mandate for change was loud and clear.

Roosevelt's victory represented the emergence of what came to be known as the **New Deal coalition**. Attracting support from farmers, factory workers, immigrants, city folk, African Americans, women, and progressive intellectuals, Roosevelt launched a realignment of the nation's political loyalties. The New Deal coalition dominated American politics throughout Roosevelt's presidency and remained powerful long after his death in 1945.

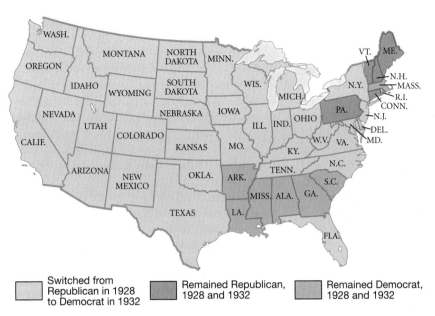

MAP ACTIVITY

Map 24.2 Electoral Shift, 1928–1932
The Democratic victory in 1932 signaled the rise of a New Deal coalition within which women and minorities, many of them new voters, made the Democrats the majority party for the first time in the twentieth century.

READING THE MAP: How many states voted Democratic in 1928? How many states voted Republican in 1932? How many states shifted from Republican to Democratic between 1928 and 1932?

CONNECTIONS: What factions within the Democratic Party opposed Franklin Roosevelt's candidacy in 1932, and why did they do so? To what do you attribute his landslide victory?

Switched from Republican in 1928 to Democrat in 1932

Remained Republican, 1928 and 1932

Remained Democrat, 1928 and 1932

United less by ideology or support for specific policies, voters in the New Deal coalition instead expressed faith in Roosevelt's promise of a government that would, somehow, change things for the better. Nobody, including Roosevelt, knew exactly what the New Deal would change or whether the changes would revive the nation's ailing economy and improve Americans' lives. But Roosevelt and many others knew that the future of American capitalism and democracy was at stake.

REVIEW Why did Franklin D. Roosevelt win the 1932 presidential election by such a large margin?

▶ Launching the New Deal

At noon on March 4, 1933, Americans gathered around their radios to hear the inaugural address of the newly elected president. Roosevelt began by asserting his "firm belief that the only thing we have to fear is fear itself — nameless, unreasoning, unjustified terror which paralyzes needed efforts to convert retreat into advance." He promised "direct, vigorous action," and the first months of his administration, termed "the Hundred Days," fulfilled that promise in a whirlwind of government initiatives that launched the New Deal.

Roosevelt and his advisers had three interrelated objectives: to provide relief to the destitute, especially the one out of four Americans who were unemployed; to foster the economic recovery of farms and businesses, thereby creating jobs and reducing the need for relief; and to reform the government and economy in ways that would reduce the risk of devastating consequences in future economic slumps. The New Deal never fully achieved these goals of relief, recovery, and reform. But by aiming for them, Roosevelt's experimental programs enormously expanded government's role in the nation's economy and society.

The New Dealers

To design and implement the New Deal, Roosevelt needed ideas and people. He convened a "Brains Trust" of economists and other leaders to offer suggestions and advice about the problems facing the nation. Among the most important reformers to join the Roosevelt administration were two veterans of Roosevelt's New York governorship: **Harry Hopkins** and **Frances Perkins**. Hopkins, a social worker, administered New Deal relief efforts and served as one of the president's loyal confidants. Perkins, who had extensive experience trying to improve working conditions in shops and factories, served as secretary of labor, making her the first woman cabinet member in American history.

"One of my great pleasures was meeting Mrs. Roosevelt. . . . [S]he was so free of prejudice . . . and she was always willing to take a stand, and there were stands to take about blacks and women."
—A North Carolina women's rights activist

No New Dealers were more important than the president and his wife, Eleanor. The gregarious president radiated charm and good cheer, giving the New Deal's bureaucratic regulations a benevolent human face. **Eleanor Roosevelt** became the New Deal's unofficial ambassador. She served, she said, as "the eyes and ears of the New Deal," traveling throughout the nation meeting Americans of all colors and creeds in church basements, town halls, and front parlors. A North Carolina women's rights activist recalled, "One of my great pleasures was meeting Mrs. Roosevelt. . . . [S]he was so free of prejudice . . . and she was always willing to take a stand, and there were stands to take about blacks and women."

As Roosevelt's programs swung into action, the millions of beneficiaries of the New Deal became grassroots New Dealers who expressed their appreciation by voting Democratic on election day. In this way, the New Deal created a

durable political coalition of Democrats that reelected Roosevelt in 1936, 1940, and 1944.

As Roosevelt and his advisers developed plans to meet the economic emergency, their watchwords were *action*, *experiment*, and *improvise*. Without a sharply defined template for how to provide relief, recovery, and reform, they moved from ideas to policies as quickly as possible, hoping to identify ways to help people and to boost the economy. Four guiding ideas shaped their policies.

First, Roosevelt and his advisers sought capitalist solutions to the economic crisis. They believed that the depression had resulted from basic imbalances in the nation's capitalist economy — imbalances they wanted to correct. They had no desire to eliminate private property or impose socialist programs, such as public ownership of productive resources. Instead, they hoped to save the capitalist economy by remedying its flaws.

Second, Roosevelt's Brains Trust persuaded him that the greatest flaw of America's capitalist economy was **underconsumption**, the root cause of the current economic paralysis. Underconsumption, New Dealers argued, resulted from the gigantic productive success of capitalism. Factories and farms produced more than they could sell to consumers, causing factories to lay off workers and farmers to lose money on bumper crops. Workers without wages and farmers without profits shrank consumption and choked the economy. Somehow, the balance between consumption and production needed to be restored.

Third, New Dealers believed that the immense size and economic power of American corporations needed to be counterbalanced by government and by organization among workers and small producers. Unlike progressive trust-busters, New Dealers did not seek to splinter big businesses. Huge businesses had developed for good economic reasons and were here to stay. Roosevelt and his advisers hoped to counterbalance big economic institutions with government programs focused on protecting individuals and the public interest.

Fourth, New Dealers felt that government must somehow moderate the imbalance of wealth created by American capitalism. Wealth concentrated in a few hands reduced consumption by most

Eleanor Roosevelt Serving Unemployed Women
Eleanor Roosevelt used her First Lady status to highlight New Dealers' sympathy for the poor, the unemployed, and neglected working people. Shown here in December 1932, Roosevelt serves soup to jobless women and their children. The carefully posed scene contrasts Roosevelt's broad smile with the somewhat awed concern on the faces of the two women facing her and with the casual, workaday indifference of the kitchen workers in the background. The photo depicts both the value of personal, face-to-face relief efforts and the impossibility of such limited, private gestures to help the millions of Americans in need. © Bettmann/Corbis.

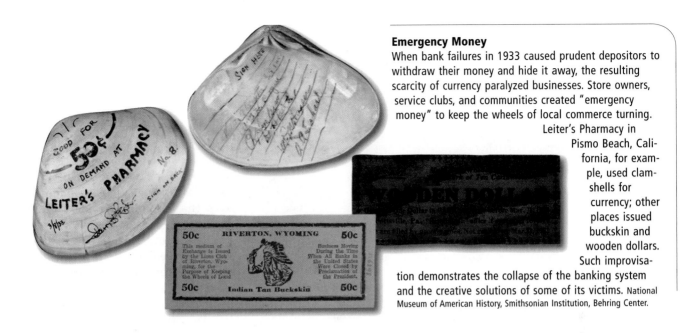

Emergency Money
When bank failures in 1933 caused prudent depositors to withdraw their money and hide it away, the resulting scarcity of currency paralyzed businesses. Store owners, service clubs, and communities created "emergency money" to keep the wheels of local commerce turning. Leiter's Pharmacy in Pismo Beach, California, for example, used clamshells for currency; other places issued buckskin and wooden dollars. Such improvisation demonstrates the collapse of the banking system and the creative solutions of some of its victims. National Museum of American History, Smithsonian Institution, Behring Center.

Americans and thereby contributed to the current economic gridlock. In the long run, government needed to find a way to permit ordinary working people to share more fully in the fruits of the economy. In the short term, New Dealers sought to lend a helping hand to poor people who suffered from the maldistribution of wealth.

Banking and Finance Reform

Roosevelt wasted no time making good on his inaugural pledge for "action now." As he took the oath of office on March 4, the nation's bank-ing system was on the brink of collapse. Roosevelt immediately declared a four-day "bank holiday" to devise a plan to shore up banks and restore depositors' confidence. Working round the clock, New Dealers drafted the Emergency Banking Act, which gave the secretary of the treasury the power to decide which banks could be safely reopened and to release funds from the Reconstruction Finance Corporation to bolster banks' assets. To secure the confidence of depositors, Congress passed the Glass-Steagall Banking Act, setting up the **Federal Deposit Insurance Corporation (FDIC)**, which guaranteed bank

Fireside Chat
President Roosevelt explained New Deal programs to ordinary Americans in his frequent radio broadcasts. People throughout the nation, like the man shown here, listened to Roosevelt's fireside chats in the quiet of their homes. The chats reassured many Americans that Washington cared about their suffering and was trying to relieve it. One New Yorker wrote the president that he felt Roosevelt had "walked into my home, sat down, and in plain and forceful language explained to me how he was tackling the job I and my fellow citizens gave him." Franklin D. Roosevelt Library.

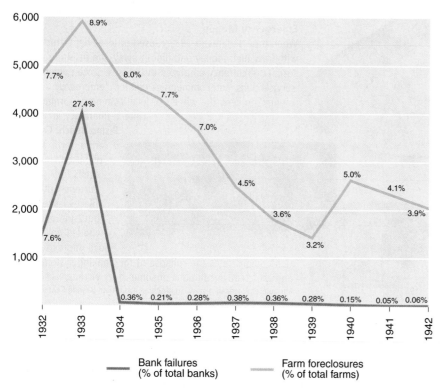

FIGURE 24.1   Bank Failures and Farm Foreclosures, 1932–1942
New Deal legislation to stabilize the economy had its most immediate and striking effect in preventing banks, along with their depositors, from going under and farmers from losing their land.

customers that the federal government would reimburse them for deposits if their banks failed. In addition, the act required the separation of commercial banks (which accept deposits and make loans to individuals and small businesses) and investment banks (which make speculative investments with their funds), in an effort to insulate the finances of Main Street America from the risky speculations of Wall Street wheeler-dealers.

On Sunday night, March 12, while the banks were still closed, Roosevelt broadcast the first of a series of **fireside chats**. Speaking in a friendly, informal manner, he explained the new banking legislation that, he said, made it "safer to keep your money in a reopened bank than under the mattress." With such plain talk, Roosevelt translated complex matters into common sense. This and subsequent fireside chats forged a direct connection — via radio waves — between Roosevelt and millions of Americans, a connection felt by a man from Paris, Texas, who wrote to Roosevelt, "You are the one & only President that ever helped a Working Class

of People. . . . Please help us some way I Pray to God for relief."

The banking legislation and fire-side chat worked. Within a few days, most of the nation's major banks reopened, and they remained solvent as reassured depositors switched funds from their mattresses to their bank accounts (Figure 24.1). Some radical critics of the New Deal believed that Roosevelt should have nationalized the banks and made them a cornerstone of economic planning by the federal government. Instead, these first New Deal measures propped up the private banking system with federal funds and subjected banks to federal regulation and oversight.

In his inaugural address, Roosevelt criticized financiers for their greed and incompetence. To prevent the fraud, corruption, and insider trading that had tainted Wall Street and contributed to the crash of 1929, Roosevelt pressed Congress to regulate the stock market. Legislation in 1934 created the **Securities and Exchange Commission (SEC)** to oversee financial markets by licensing investment dealers, monitoring all stock transactions, and requiring corporate officers to make full disclosures about their companies. To head the SEC, Roosevelt named an abrasive and ambitious Wall Street financier, Joseph P. Kennedy, who had a somewhat shady reputation for stock manipulation. When critics complained about his selection, Roosevelt replied, "Set a thief to catch a thief." Under Kennedy's leadership, the SEC helped a cleaned-up and regulated Wall Street to recover slowly, although the stock market stayed well below its frothy heights during the 1920s.

Relief and Conservation Programs

Patching the nation's financial structure provided little relief for the hungry and unemployed. A poor man from Nebraska asked Eleanor Roosevelt "if the folk who was borned here in America . . . are this Forgotten Man, the President had in mind, [and] if we are this Forgotten Man then we are still Forgotten." Since its founding, the federal government had never assumed responsibility for needy people, except in moments of natural disaster or emergencies such as the Civil War. Instead, churches, private charities, county and municipal governments, and occasionally states assumed the burden of poor relief, usually with meager payments. The depression necessitated unprecedented federal relief efforts, according to Harry Hopkins and other New Dealers. As one New Yorker who still had a job wrote the government, "We work, ten hours a day for six days. In the grime and dirt of a nation [for] . . . low pay [making us] . . . slaves — slaves of the depression!"

Hopkins galvanized support for the **Federal Emergency Relief Administration (FERA)**, established in May 1933, which supported four million to five million households with $20 or $30 a month. FERA also created jobs for the unemployed on thousands of public works projects, organized by Hopkins into the Civil Works Administration (CWA), which put paychecks worth more than $800 million into the hands of previously jobless workers. Earning wages between 40 and 60 cents an hour, laborers renovated schools, dug sewers, and rebuilt roads and bridges. FERA extended the scope of relief to include health and education, funding literacy classes and providing vaccinations for millions.

The most popular work relief program was the **Civilian Conservation Corps (CCC)**, established in March 1933. It offered unemployed young men a chance to earn wages while working to conserve natural resources, a long-standing interest of Roosevelt. Women were excluded from working in the CCC until Eleanor Roosevelt demanded that a token number of young women be hired. One of the young men who enlisted in the CCC, Blackie Gold, had been out of work and had to "beg for coal, [and] buy bread that's two, three days old" to support his large family. After he joined the CCC, Gold earned $30 a month and was required to send all but $5 of it home to his family. By the end of the program in 1942, the three million CCC workers had checked soil erosion, tamed rivers, and planted more than two billion trees. CCC workers left a legacy of vast new recreation areas, along with roads that made those areas accessible to millions of Americans. Just as important, the CCC, CWA, and other work relief efforts replaced the

Civil Conservation Corps (CCC)
During the New Deal, the Civilian Conservation Corps provided work and wages for about two-and-a-half million young men to improve parks, build roads, plant trees, and engage in other conservation projects, as symbolized by the evergreen tree emblazoned on the CCC insignia patch. The CCC workers shown here carrying cross-cut saws for clearing trees from roads and trails in Yosemite National Park marched in quasi-military order. The U.S. Army administered the CCC, but offered no military training. Instead, CCC workers earned wages of about $30 a month, all but $5 of which went to their parents. Photograph: National Archives Pacific Region; patch: ©Bettmann/Corbis.

stigma of welfare with the dignity of jobs. As one woman said about her husband's work relief job, "We aren't on relief anymore. My husband is working for the Government."

The New Deal also sought to harness natural resources for hydroelectric power. Continuing a project begun under Hoover, the New Deal completed the colossal Hoover Dam across the Colorado River in Nevada, providing not only electricity but also flood control and irrigation water for Arizona and southern California. Building the dam also provided badly needed jobs and wages for thousands of unemployed workers.

The New Deal's most ambitious and controversial natural resources development project was the **Tennessee Valley Authority (TVA)**, created in May 1933 to build dams along the Tennessee River to supply impoverished rural communities with cheap electricity (Map 24.3). The TVA planned model towns for power station workers and new homes for the farmers who would benefit from electricity and flood control. The most ambitious example of New Deal enthusiasm for planning,

MAP ACTIVITY

Map 24.3 The Tennessee Valley Authority

The New Deal created the Tennessee Valley Authority to modernize a vast impoverished region with hydroelectric power dams and, at the same time, to reclaim eroded land and preserve old folkways.

READING THE MAP: How many states were affected by the TVA? How many miles of rivers (approximately) were affected?

CONNECTIONS: What kinds of benefits — economic as well as social and cultural — did TVA programs bring to the region? How might the lives of a poor farming family in Alabama or Tennessee have changed after the mid-1930s owing to these programs?

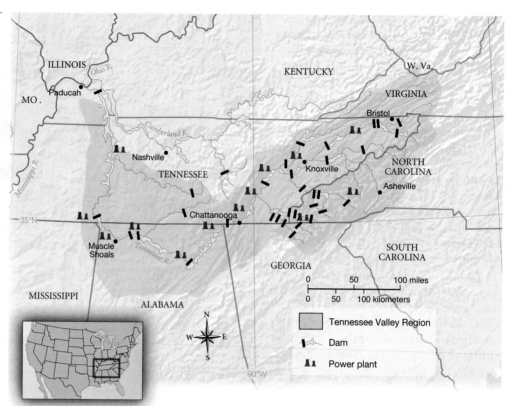

the TVA set out to demonstrate that a partnership between the federal government and local residents could overcome the barriers of state governments and private enterprises to make efficient use of abundant natural resources and break the ancient cycle of poverty. The TVA never fully realized these utopian ends, but it improved the lives of millions in the region with electric power, flood protection, soil reclamation, and jobs.

New sources of hydroelectric power helped the New Deal bring the wonders of electricity to country folk, fulfilling an old progressive dream. When Roosevelt became president, 90 percent of rural Americans lacked electricity. Private electric companies refused to build transmission lines into the sparsely settled countryside when they had a profitable market in more accessible and densely populated urban areas. Beginning in 1935, the **Rural Electrification Administration (REA)** made low-cost loans available to local cooperatives for power plants and transmission lines to serve rural communities. Within ten years, the REA delivered electricity to nine out of ten farms, giving rural Americans access for the first time to modern conveniences that urban people had enjoyed for decades.

Agricultural Initiatives

Farmers had been mired in a depression since the end of World War I. New Dealers diagnosed the farmers' plight as a classic case of overproduction and underconsumption. Following age-old practices, farmers tried to compensate for low crop prices by growing more crops, hoping to boost their earnings by selling larger quantities. Instead, producing more crops pushed prices lower still. Farm income sank from a disastrously low $6 billion in 1929 to a catastrophically low $2 billion in 1932. Income among farm families plunged to $167 a year, barely one-tenth of the national average.

New Dealers sought to cut agricultural production, thereby raising crop prices and farmers' income. With more money in their pockets, farm families — who made up one-third of all Americans — would then buy more goods and lift consumption in the entire economy. To reduce production, the **Agricultural Adjustment Act (AAA)** authorized the "domestic allotment plan," which paid farmers *not* to grow crops. Individual farmers who agreed not to plant crops on a portion of their fields (their "allotment") would receive a government payment compensating them for the crops they did not plant. Since crops were already in the ground by the time the act was passed in May 1933, drastic measures were necessary to reduce production immediately. While millions of Americans like Florence Owens and her children went to bed hungry, farmers slaughtered countless cattle, hogs, sheep, and other livestock and destroyed untold acres of crops to qualify for their allotment payments.

With the formation of the Commodity Credit Corporation, the federal government allowed farmers to hold their harvested crops off the market and wait for a higher price. In the meantime, the government stored the crop and gave farmers a "commodity loan" based on a favorable price. In effect, commodity loans addressed the problem of underconsumption by making the federal government a major consumer of agricultural goods and reducing farmers' vulnerability to low prices. New Dealers also sponsored the Farm Credit Act (FCA) to provide long-term credit on mortgaged farm property, allowing debt-ridden farmers to avoid foreclosures that were driving thousands off their land (see Figure 24.1).

Crop allotments, commodity loans, and mortgage credit made farmers major beneficiaries of the New Deal. Crop prices rose impressively, farm income jumped 50 percent by 1936, and FCA loans financed 40 percent of farm mortgage debt by the end of the decade. These gains were distributed fairly equally among farmers in the corn, hog, and wheat region of the Midwest. In the South's cotton belt, however, landlords controlled the distribution of New Deal agricultural benefits and shamelessly rewarded themselves while denying benefits to many sharecroppers and tenant farmers — blacks and whites — by taking the land they worked out of production and assigning it to the allotment program. When that happened, tenants and sharecroppers got booted off the land they worked, and their privation worsened. As the president of the Oklahoma Tenant Farmers' Union explained, large farmers who got "Triple-A" payments often used the money to buy tractors and then "forced their tenants and [share]croppers off the land," causing these "Americans to be starved and dispossessed of their homes in our land of plenty."

Industrial Recovery

Unlike farmers, industrialists cut production with the onset of the depression. Between 1929 and 1933, industrial production fell more than 40 percent in an effort to balance low demand with

Rural Electrification and Running Water
New Deal programs brought housing and electricity to rural families like those in this east-central Tennessee village. The Tennessee Valley Authority provided the houses shown here as well as the electric power they received. The New Deal's Rural Electrification Administration built the necessary infrastructure to bring running water to villages like these, where the pump operated by the children in the foreground was the only source of water. The REA used posters like this one to increase awareness of the benefits of running water. What difference do you think electricity and running water made in the daily lives of the people in this village? Pump: FDR Library; poster: Digital Image ©The Museum of Modern Art/Licensed by SCALA/Art Resource, NY.

low supply and thereby maintain prices. But falling industrial production meant that millions of working people lost their jobs. Unlike farmers, most working people lived in towns and cities and needed jobs to eat. Mass unemployment also reduced consumer demand for industrial products, contributing to a downward spiral in both production and jobs, with no end in sight. Industries responded by reducing wages for employees who still had jobs, further reducing demand — a trend made worse by competition among industrial producers. New Dealers struggled to find a way to break this cycle of unemployment and underconsumption — a way consistent with corporate profits and capitalism.

The New Deal's National Industrial Recovery Act opted for a government-sponsored form of industrial self-government through the **National Recovery Administration (NRA)**, established in June 1933. The NRA encouraged industrialists in every part of the economy to agree on rules,

Textile Workers Strike for Better Wages and Working Conditions

"The 'Stretch-out System' is the cause of the whole trouble," a textile worker declared in 1930, echoing the sentiments of thousands of other mill workers. The "stretch-out" was the term coined by mill workers for the cost-cutting efficiencies implemented by mill owners that led to layoffs and poor working conditions for textile workers during the 1920s and 1930s. Textile manufacturers drastically increased the workload of their employees to cut labor costs and raise productivity. A mill worker who tended thirty looms in 1920 was responsible for ninety or more looms by 1929 — if she or he still had a job. Layoffs of mill hands in the midst of the Great Depression contributed to further deterioration in wages and working conditions. So many people were desperate for work, no matter what the wage, that manufacturers were able to cut wages in half. The result, as one textile worker wrote Roosevelt, was that "the ones who are Still at Work are Being Treated as Bad or Worse tha[n] the Slaves were in Slavery times."

Like so many other textile workers who faced the tough choice of working with the stretch-out or not working, Icy Norman was relieved to find work in 1929 at Burlington Mills in Piedmont Heights, North Carolina, where the supervisor happened to be a friend of her deceased father's. He hired Norman to wind thread onto bobbins for weaving. At first, she earned only 15 cents a day, but as she became more skilled, her wages rose to $10 a week, a little over 15 cents an hour. "After I got used to being in there," Norman recalled, "I really loved my work. . . . I got pleasure out of it and it made me happy to do my job." Still, as one mill worker wrote to Roosevelt, "every textile worker in the South would walk out of the mill today if they were not afraid of starvation."

In September 1934, hundreds of thousands of textile workers throughout the nation overcame their fears and walked out of the mills in the largest strike in American history. Strikers shut down mills from Maine to Alabama. More than half of all textile workers nationwide and about two-thirds of mill hands in the southern heartland of the textile industry walked out, including Icy Norman. Loosely organized by the Textile Workers' Union, the strikers demanded better working conditions and wages through enforcement of the textile code established by the New Deal's National Recovery Administration (NRA).

Like other NRA codes, the textile code was written and administered by the leading textile manufacturers. It provided for a maximum forty-hour workweek, a minimum weekly wage of $12 for southern mill hands, and the right of workers to organize unions. Textile workers celebrated the passage of the NRA in June 1933. "It seemed too good to be true," one textile worker observed. Mill hands told a New Dealer, "We trust in the Supreme Being and Franklin Roosevelt. . . . [We] know that the President will see that [we] have work and proper wages; and that the stretchout will be abandoned."

But their faith was misplaced, and the code was widely ignored. When workers complained that mill owners continued the stretch-out, cutting wages and firing any mill hands they suspected of union sympathies, their grievances were heard by the textile manufacturers who headed the NRA code authority. In the year before the strike, the textile code authority received nearly 4,000 complaints, investigated 96, and resolved just 1 in favor of a worker. Boiling with frustration over the failure of the textile code, more than 400,000 mill hands went on strike. Seeking to realize what they viewed as the unfulfilled promises of the New Deal's NRA, they aimed to organize a union to bargain with mill owners to improve wages and working conditions.

The strike lasted three weeks and led to numerous violent confrontations with police and National Guardsmen. It ended because of the

known as codes, to define fair working conditions, to set prices, and to minimize competition. The idea behind codes was to stabilize existing industries and maintain their workforces while avoiding what both industrialists and New Dealers termed "destructive competition," which forced employers to cut wages and jobs. Industry after industry wrote elaborate codes addressing detailed features of production, pricing, and competition. In exchange for the relaxation of federal antitrust regulations that prohibited such business agreements, the participating businesses promised to recognize the right of working people to organize and engage in collective bargaining. To encourage consumers to patronize businesses participating in NRA codes, the New Deal mounted a

Striking Mill Workers Jeer Strikebreakers
Textile workers on strike against the Cannon Textile Mills in North Carolina in September 1934 shouted taunts and curses at "scabs," the derogatory term for employees who refused to honor the strikers' picket line. Notice the contrast between the clothing of the strikers and that of the strikebreakers. What might explain this contrast? Although thousands of women like Icy Norman joined the strike, there are no women among the strikers shown here. What might account for the absence of women mill hands in this picket line? © Bettmann/Corbis.

combination of the mill owners' intransigence, the Textile Workers' Union's lack of resources, the mill workers' increasingly desperate financial situation, and Roosevelt's focus on the need for industrial peace to achieve economic recovery.

The mill hands achieved virtually nothing as a result of the strike. Mill owners continued to flout the textile codes, the stretch-out continued without interruption, and working conditions did not improve. Angry mill owners fired and blacklisted strike leaders, succeeding in their efforts to crush workers' organizations.

Icy Norman went back to work after the strike ended, and since she was not a union activist, she managed to keep her job until she retired in 1976, after forty-seven years at Burlington Mills. For her efforts, the company rewarded her with a free visit to a local hairdresser, a tour of the Burlington executive suite, and a farewell handshake.

Questions for Consideration

1. How did the stretch-out contribute to unemployment for textile workers?

2. Why was textile workers' faith in Roosevelt and NRA codes misplaced?

3. Why do you think unions failed to organize textile workers when they succeeded in organizing autoworkers, for example?

public relations campaign that displayed the NRA's Blue Eagle in shop windows and on billboards throughout the nation.

New Dealers hoped that NRA codes would yield businesses with a social conscience, ensuring fair treatment of workers and consumers and promotion of the general economic welfare. Instead, NRA codes tended to strengthen conventional business practices. Large corporations wrote codes that served primarily their own interests rather than the needs of workers or the welfare of the national economy. (See "Seeking the American Promise," page 798.) The failure of codes to cover domestic workers or agricultural laborers like Florence Owens led one woman to complain to Roosevelt that the NRA "never mentioned the

Major Legislation of the New Deal's First Hundred Days

	Name of Act	Basic Provisions
March 9, 1933	Emergency Banking Act	Provides for reopening stable banks and authorizing the Reconstruction Finance Corporation to supply funds.
March 31, 1933	Civilian Conservation Corps Act	Provides jobs for unemployed young men.
May 12, 1933	Agricultural Adjustment Act	Provides funds to pay farmers for not growing crops.
May 12, 1933	Federal Emergency Relief Act	Provides relief funds for the destitute.
May 18, 1933	Tennessee Valley Authority Act	Creates the TVA to bring electric power and conservation to the area.
June 16, 1933	National Industrial Recovery Act	Specifies cooperation among business, government, and labor in setting fair prices and working conditions.
June 16, 1933	Glass-Steagall Banking Act	Creates the Federal Deposit Insurance Corporation (FDIC) to insure bank deposits.

robbery of the Housewives" by the privations caused by the depression.

Many business leaders criticized NRA codes as heavy-handed government regulation of private enterprise. Some even claimed that the NRA was a homegrown version of Benito Mussolini's fascism, then taking shape in Italy. In reality, however, compliance with NRA codes was voluntary, and government enforcement efforts were weak to nonexistent. The NRA did little to reduce unemployment, raise consumption, or relieve the depression. In effect, it represented a peace offering to business leaders by Roosevelt and his advisers, conveying the message that the New Deal did not intend to wage war against profits or private enterprise. The peace offering failed, however. Most corporate leaders became active and often bitter opponents of Roosevelt and the New Deal.

REVIEW   How did the New Dealers try to steer the nation toward recovery from the Great Depression?

▶ Challenges to the New Deal

The first New Deal initiatives engendered fierce criticism and political opposition. From the right, Republicans and business people charged that New Deal programs were too radical, undermining private property, economic stability, and democracy. Critics on the left faulted the New Deal for its failure to allay the human suffering caused by the depression and for its timidity in attacking corporate power and greed.

Resistance to Business Reform

New Deal programs rescued capitalism, but business leaders lambasted Roosevelt, even though their economic prospects improved more than those of most other Americans during the depression. Republicans and business leaders denounced New Deal efforts to regulate or reform what they considered their private enterprises. Although concentrated corporate power avoided reform, business leaders still conducted stridently anti–New Deal campaigns that expressed their resentment and fear of regulations, taxes, and unions. One opponent called the president "Stalin Delano Roosevelt" and insisted that the New Deal was really a "Raw Deal."

By 1935, two major business organizations, the National Association of Manufacturers and the Chamber of Commerce, had become openly anti–New Deal. Their critiques were amplified by the American Liberty League, founded in 1934, which blamed the New Deal for betraying basic constitutional guarantees of freedom and individualism. To them, the AAA was a "trend toward fascist control of agriculture," relief programs marked "the end of democracy," and the NRA was a plunge into the "quicksand of visionary experimentation." Although the Liberty League's membership never exceeded 125,000, its well-financed publicity campaign widened the rift between Roosevelt and business people.

Economists who favored rational planning in the public interest and labor leaders who sought to influence wages and working conditions by organizing unions attacked the New Deal from the left. In their view, the NRA stifled enterprise by permitting monopolistic practices. They pointed out that industrial trade associations twisted NRA codes to suit their aims, thwarted competition, and engaged in price gouging. Labor leaders especially resented the NRA's willingness to allow businesses to form company-controlled unions while blocking workers from organizing genuine grassroots unions to bargain for themselves.

The Supreme Court stepped into this cross fire of criticisms in May 1935 and declared that the NRA unconstitutionally conferred powers reserved to Congress on an administrative agency staffed by government appointees. The NRA codes soon lost the little authority they had. The failure of the NRA demonstrated the depth of many Americans' resistance to economic planning and the stubborn refusal of business leaders to yield to government regulations or reforms.

Casualties in the Countryside

The AAA weathered critical battering by champions of the old order better than the NRA. Allotment checks for keeping land fallow and crop prices high created loyalty among farmers with enough acreage to participate. As a white farmer in North Carolina declared, "I stand for the New Deal and Roosevelt . . . , the AAA . . . and crop control." Agricultural processors and distributors, however, criticized the AAA. They objected that the program reduced the volume of crop production — the only source of their profits — while they paid a tax on processed crops that funded the very program that disadvantaged them. In 1936, the Supreme Court agreed with their contention that they were victims of an illegal attempt to tax one group (processors and distributors) to enrich another (farmers).

Evicted Sharecroppers
An unintended consequence of the New Deal's Agricultural Adjustment Administration's plan to maintain farm prices by reducing acreage in production was the eviction of tenant farmers when the land they worked was left idle. These African American sharecroppers were part of a squatters camp that stretched for 150 miles along the western floodplain of the Mississippi River in southeastern Missouri in January 1939. They protested AAA policies that caused cotton farmers to evict them from their homes. Homeless and jobless, camping out with all their earthly belongings, these families were among the many rural laborers whose lives were made worse by New Deal agricultural policies. © Bettmann/Corbis.

Down but not out, the AAA rebounded from the Supreme Court ruling by eliminating the offending tax and funding allotment payments from general government revenues.

Protests stirred, however, among those who did not qualify for allotments. The Southern Farm Tenants Union argued passionately that the AAA enriched large farmers while it impoverished small farmers who rented rather than owned their land. One black sharecropper explained why only $75 a year from New Deal agricultural subsidies trickled down to her: "De landlord is landlord, de politicians is landlord, de judge is landlord, de shurf [sheriff] is landlord, ever'body is landlord, en we [sharecroppers] ain' got nothin'!" Such testimony showed that the AAA, like the NRA, tended to help most those who least needed help. Roosevelt's political dependence on southern Democrats caused him to avoid confronting such economic and racial inequities in the South's entrenched order.

Displaced tenants often joined the army of migrant workers like Florence Owens who straggled across rural America during the 1930s, some to flee Great Plains dust storms. Many migrants came from Mexico to work Texas cotton, Michigan beans, Idaho sugar beets, and California crops of all kinds. But since the number of people willing to take agricultural jobs usually exceeded the number of jobs available, wages fell and native-born white migrants fought to reserve even these low-wage jobs for themselves. Hundreds of thousands of "Okies" streamed out of the **Dust Bowl** of Oklahoma, Kansas, Texas, and Colorado, where chronic drought and harmful agricultural practices blasted crops and hopes. Parched, poor, and windblown, Okies — like the Joad family immortalized in John Steinbeck's novel *The Grapes of Wrath* (1939) — migrated to the lush fields and orchards of California, congregating in labor camps and hoping to find work and a future. But migrant laborers seldom found steady or secure work. As one Okie said, "When they need us they call us migrants, and when we've picked their crop, we're bums and we got to get out."

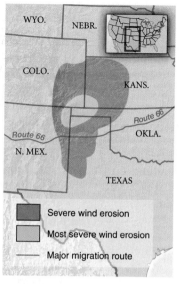

The Dust Bowl

Severe wind erosion

Most severe wind erosion

Major migration route

Politics on the Fringes

Politically, the New Deal's staunchest opponents were in the Republican Party — organized, well heeled, mainstream, and determined to challenge Roosevelt at every turn. But the New Deal also faced challenges from the political fringes, fueled by the hardship of the depression and the hope for a cure-all.

Socialists and Communists accused the New Deal of being the handmaiden of business elites and of rescuing capitalism from its self-inflicted crisis. Socialist author **Upton Sinclair** ran for governor of California in 1934 on a plan he called "End Poverty in California." Sinclair demanded that the state take ownership of idle factories and unused land and give them to cooperatives of working people, a first step toward what he envisioned as a "Cooperative Commonwealth" that would put the needs of people above profits. Sinclair lost the election, ending the most serious socialist electoral challenge to the New Deal.

Some intellectuals and artists sought to advance the cause of more radical change by joining left-wing organizations, including the American Communist Party. At its high point in the 1930s, the party had about thirty thousand members, the large majority of them immigrants, especially Scandinavians in the upper Midwest and eastern European Jews in major eastern and midwestern cities. Individual Communists worked to organize labor unions, protect the civil rights of black people, and help the destitute, but the party preached the overthrow of "bourgeois democracy" and the destruction of capitalism in favor of Soviet-style communism. Party spokesmen termed the NRA a "fascist slave program" and likened Roosevelt and the New Deal to Hitler and the Nazis. Such talk attracted few followers among the nation's millions of poor and unemployed. They wanted jobs and economic security within American capitalism and democracy, not violent revolution to establish a dictatorship of the Communist Party.

Okie Family
This tenant farmer worked land near Eagleton, Oklahoma, but became sick with pneumonia and lost his farm. The county he had lived in for fifteen years refused to give him Works Progress Administration benefits because he briefly left the county after recovering from his illness. Accompanied by his five children, he carted all his possessions in a toy wagon along a highway while looking for work. Such poor, jobless migrants were common along America's roads during the 1930s. Library of Congress.

More powerful radical challenges to the New Deal sprouted from homegrown roots. Many Americans felt overlooked by New Deal programs that concentrated on finance, agriculture, and industry but did little to produce jobs or aid the poor. The merciless reality of the depression also continued to erode the security of people who still had jobs but worried constantly that they, too, might be pushed into the legions of the unemployed and penniless.

A Catholic priest in Detroit named **Charles Coughlin** spoke to and for many worried Americans in his weekly radio broadcasts, which reached a nationwide audience of 40 million. Father Coughlin expressed outrage at the suffering and inequities that he blamed on Com-munists, bankers, and "predatory capitalists" who, he claimed, appealing to widespread anti-Semitic sentiments, were mostly Jews. In 1932, Coughlin applauded Roosevelt's election and declared, "The New Deal is Christ's deal." But Coughlin became frustrated by Roosevelt's refusal to grant him influence, turned against the New Deal, and in 1935 founded the National Union for Social Justice, or Union Party, to challenge Roosevelt in the 1936 presidential election.

Dr. **Francis Townsend**, of Long Beach, California, also criticized the timidity of the New Deal. Angry that many of his retired patients lived in misery, Townsend proposed in 1934 the creation of the Old Age Revolving Pension, which would pay every American over age sixty a pension of $200 a month. To receive the pension, senior citizens had to agree to spend the entire amount within thirty days, thereby stimulating the economy.

> ## "Every man a king, but no one wears a crown."
> —Campaign slogan of Louisiana governor HUEY LONG

Townsend organized pension clubs with more than two million paying members and petitioned the federal government to enact his scheme. When the major political parties rebuffed his impractical plan, Townsend merged his forces with Coughlin's Union Party in time for the 1936 election.

A more formidable challenge to the New Deal came from the powerful southern wing of the Democratic Party. **Huey Long**, son of a backcountry Louisiana farmer, was elected governor of the state in 1928 with his slogan "Every man a king, but no one wears a crown." Unlike nearly all other southern white politicians who harped on white supremacy, Long championed the poor over the rich, country people over city folk, and the humble over elites. As governor, "the Kingfish" — as he liked to call himself — delivered on his promises to provide jobs and build roads, schools, and hospitals, but he also behaved ruthlessly to achieve his goals. Journalists routinely referred to him as the "dictator of Louisiana." Swaggering and bullying to get his way, Long delighted his supporters, who elected him to the U.S. Senate in 1932. Senator Long introduced a sweeping "soak the rich" tax bill that would outlaw personal incomes of more than $1 million and inheritances of more than $5 million. When the Senate rejected his proposal, Long decided to run for president, mobilizing more than five million Americans behind his "Share Our Wealth" plan. Like Townsend's scheme, Long's program promised far more than it could deliver. The Share Our Wealth campaign died when Long was assassinated in 1935, but his constituency and the wide appeal of a more equitable distribution of wealth persisted.

The challenges to the New Deal from both Republicans and more radical groups stirred Democrats to solidify their winning coalition. In the midterm congressional elections of 1934 — normally a time when a president loses support — voters gave New Dealers a landslide victory. Democrats increased their majority in the House of Representatives and gained a two-thirds majority in the Senate.

> **REVIEW**   Why did groups at both ends of the political spectrum criticize the New Deal?

Huey Long

Huey Long's ability to adapt his captivating stump-speech style to the radio made him the one rival politician who gave Roosevelt serious concern in the mid-1930s. Long is shown here in 1932 campaigning in Arkansas in support of Hattie Carraway's bid for election to the U.S. Senate. Stigmatized as both a woman and a populist reformer, Carraway seemed a sure loser until Long crossed the border from Louisiana on her behalf. In two weeks of speaking and pressing the flesh, Long brushed aside criticism that he was an interloper and boosted Carraway to victory as part of his crusade to share the wealth. Corbis.

▶ Toward a Welfare State

The popular mandate for the New Deal revealed by the congressional elections persuaded Roosevelt to press ahead with bold new efforts to achieve relief, recovery, and reform. Despite the initiatives of the Hundred Days, the depression still strangled the economy. Rumbles of discontent from Father Coughlin, Huey Long, and their supporters showed that New Deal programs had fallen far short of their goals. In 1935, Roosevelt capitalized on his congressional majorities to enact major new programs that signaled the emergence of an American welfare state.

Taken together, these New Deal efforts stretched a safety net under the lives of ordinary Americans. Although many citizens remained unprotected, New Deal programs helped millions with jobs, relief, and government support. Knitting together the safety net was the idea that when individual Americans suffered because of forces beyond their control, the federal government bore responsibility to support and protect them. The safety net of welfare programs tied the political loyalty of working people to the New Deal and the Democratic Party. As a North Carolina mill worker said, "Mr. Roosevelt is the only man we ever had in the White House who would understand that my boss is a sonofabitch."

Relief for the Unemployed

First and foremost, Americans still needed jobs. Since the private economy left eight million people jobless by 1935, Roosevelt and his advisers launched a massive work relief program. Roosevelt believed that direct government handouts crippled recipients with "spiritual and moral disintegration . . . destructive to the human spirit." Jobs, by contrast, bolstered individuals' "self-respect, . . . self-confidence, . . . courage, and determination." With a congressional appropriation of nearly $5 billion — more than all government revenues in 1934 — the New Deal created the **Works Progress Administration (WPA)** to

VISUAL ACTIVITY

City Activities Mural

During the 1930s, artists — many of them employed by New Deal agencies — painted thousands of murals depicting the variety and vigor of American life. These murals often appeared in public buildings. The mural shown here, by Missouri-born artist Thomas Hart Benton, illustrates urban life, emphasizing the intoxicating and seductive pleasures of the flesh and the spirit to be found in American cities. © AXA Financial, Inc. Thomas Hart Benton, City Activities with Subway, from America Today, 1930. Distemper and egg tempera on gessoed linen with oil glaze 92 x 134$^1/_2$". Collection of AXA Financial, Inc., through its subsidiary, The Equitable Life Assurance Society of the U.S.

READING THE IMAGE: What features of urban experience does Benton emphasize in this mural? What ideas and attitudes, if any, link the people shown here?

CONNECTIONS: To what extent does the mural highlight activities distinct to U.S. cities, compared with urban life in Europe, Africa, or Asia?

give unemployed Americans government-funded jobs on public works projects. The WPA put millions of jobless citizens to work on roads, bridges, parks, public buildings, and more. In addition, Congress passed — over Roosevelt's veto — the bonus long sought by the Bonus Marchers (see chapter 23), giving veterans an average of $580 and further stimulating the economy.

By 1936, WPA funds provided jobs for 7 percent of the nation's labor force. In effect, the WPA made the federal government the employer of last resort, creating useful jobs when the capitalist economy failed to do so. In hiring, WPA officials tended to discriminate in favor of white men and against women and racial minorities. But by the time the WPA ended in 1943 — because mobilization for World War II created full employment — it had made major contributions to both relief and recovery. Overall, WPA jobs put thirteen million men and women to work and gave them paychecks worth $10 billion.

About three out of four WPA jobs involved construction and renovation of the nation's physical infrastructure. WPA workers built 572,000 miles of roads, 78,000 bridges, 67,000 miles of city streets, 40,000 public buildings, 8,000 parks, 350 airports, and much else. In addition, the WPA gave jobs to thousands of artists, musicians, actors, journalists, poets, and novelists. The WPA also organized sewing rooms for jobless women, giving them work and wages and allowing them to produce more than 100 million pieces of clothing that were donated to the needy. The WPA reached the most isolated corners of the nation, funding librarians and nurses on horseback to deliver books and health care to remote cabins in Appalachia. Throughout the nation, WPA projects displayed tangible evidence of the New Deal's commitment to public welfare.

Grand Coulee Dam
The New Deal's Works Progress Administration helped pay for these and other workers to construct the giant Grand Coulee Dam on the Columbia River in eastern Washington state. Like other WPA projects, the Grand Coulee Dam gave employment to thousands of Americans and harnessed natural resources for what officials considered the public good. Once completed in 1942, the dam provided electricity for major war industries in Oregon and Washington, including uranium processing for the wartime Manhattan Project that resulted in the atomic bomb. Library of Congress.

Empowering Labor

During the Great Depression, factory workers who managed to keep their jobs worried constantly about being laid off while their wages and working hours were cut. When workers tried to organize labor unions to protect themselves, municipal and state governments usually sided with employers. Since the Gilded Age, state and federal governments had been far more effective at busting unions than at busting trusts. The New Deal dramatically reversed the federal government's stance toward unions. With legislation and political support, the New Deal encouraged an unprecedented wave of union organizing among the nation's working people. When the head of the United Mine Workers, John L. Lewis, told coal miners that "the President wants you to join a union," he exaggerated only a little. New Dealers believed that unions would counterbalance the organized might of big corporations by defending working people, maintaining wages, and replacing the bloody violence that often accompanied strikes with economic peace and commercial stability.

Violent battles on the nation's streets and docks showed the determination of militant labor leaders to organize unions that would protect jobs as well as wages. In 1934, striking workers in Toledo, Minneapolis, San Francisco, and elsewhere were beaten and shot by police and the National Guard. In Congress, labor leaders lobbied for the National Labor Relations Act, a bill sponsored by Senator Robert Wagner of New York that authorized the federal government to intervene in labor disputes and supervise the organization of labor unions. Justly considered a "Magna Carta for labor," the **Wagner Act**, as it came to be called, guaranteed industrial workers the right to organize unions, putting the might of federal law behind the appeals of labor leaders. The Wagner Act created the National Labor Relations Board to sponsor and oversee elections for union representation. If the majority of workers at a company voted for a union, the union became the sole bargaining agent for the entire workplace, and the employer was required to negotiate with the elected union leaders. Roosevelt signed the Wagner Act in July 1935, for the first time providing federal support for labor organization — the most important New Deal reform of the industrial order.

The achievements that flowed from the Wagner Act and renewed labor militancy were impressive. When Roosevelt became president

Women's Emergency Brigade Supports Sit-Down Strikers
During the depression, General Motors cut employment and wages in half, leading to a wave of strikes. In February 1937, the wives of strikers occupying a plant in Flint, Michigan, organized the Women's Emergency Brigade, shown here. Not shown are the thousands of armed police and National Guardsmen surrounding the plant. Strikers and their supporters smashed the windows of the plant to vent tear gas deployed by security agents. The marching women carried clubs to deflect the blows of the General Motors cops. The American flag asserted the patriotism of the strikers and their supporters, whom General Motors and other strike opponents labeled "outside agitators, radicals, and Communists." © Bettmann/Corbis.

in 1933, union membership — composed almost entirely of skilled workers in trade unions affiliated with the American Federation of Labor (AFL) — stood at three million, down by half since the end of World War I. With the support of the Wagner Act, union membership expanded almost fivefold, to fourteen million, by the time of Roosevelt's death in 1945. By then, 30 percent of the workforce was unionized, the highest union representation in American history.

Most of the new union members were factory workers and unskilled laborers, many of them immigrants, women, and African Americans. For decades, established AFL unions had no desire to organize factory and unskilled workers, who struggled along without unions. In 1935, under the aggressive leadership of the mine workers' John L. Lewis and the head of the Amalgamated Clothing Workers, Sidney Hillman, a coalition of unskilled workers formed the **Committee for Industrial Organization** (CIO; later the Congress of Industrial Organizations). The CIO, helped by the Wagner Act, mobilized organizing drives in major industries. The exceptional courage and organizing skill of labor militants earned the CIO the leadership role in the campaign to organize the bitterly anti-union automobile and steel industries.

The bloody struggle by the CIO-affiliated United Auto Workers (UAW) to organize workers at General Motors climaxed in January 1937. Striking workers occupied the main assembly plant in Flint, Michigan, in a **sit-down strike** that slashed the plant's production of 15,000 cars a week to a mere 150. Stymied, General Motors eventually surrendered and agreed to make the UAW the sole bargaining agent for all the company's workers and to refrain from interfering with union activity. Having subdued the auto industry's leading producer, the UAW expanded its campaign until, after much violence, the entire industry was unionized when the Ford Motor Company capitulated in 1941.

The CIO hoped to ride organizing success in auto plants to victory in the steel mills. But after unionizing the industry giant U.S. Steel, the CIO ran up against ruthless opposition from smaller steel firms. Following a police attack that killed ten

> "It is our plain duty to provide for that security upon which welfare depends . . . and undertake the great task of furthering the security of the citizen and his family through social insurance."
>
> —President FRANKLIN ROOSEVELT to Congress

strikers at Republic Steel outside Chicago in May 1937, the battered steelworkers halted their organizing campaign. In steel and other major industries, such as the stridently anti-union southern textile mills, organizing efforts stalled until after 1941, when military mobilization created labor shortages that gave workers greater bargaining power.

Social Security and Tax Reform

The single most important feature of the New Deal's emerging welfare state was **Social Security**. An ambitious, far-reaching, and permanent reform, Social Security was designed to provide a modest income to relieve the poverty of elderly people. Only about 15 percent of older Americans had private pension plans, and during the depression corporations and banks often failed to pay the meager pensions they had promised. Corporations routinely fired or demoted employees to avoid or reduce pension payments. Prompted by the popular but impractical panaceas of Dr. Townsend, Father Coughlin, and Huey Long, Roosevelt became the first president to advocate protection for the elderly. He told Congress that "it is our plain duty to provide for that security upon which welfare depends . . . and undertake the great task of furthering the security of the citizen and his family through social insurance."

The political struggle for Social Security highlighted class differences among Americans. Support for the measure came from a coalition of advocacy groups for the elderly and the poor, traditional progressives, leftists, social workers, and labor unions. Arrayed against them were economic conservatives, including the American Liberty League, the National Association of Manufacturers, the Chamber of Commerce, and the American Medical Association. Enact the Social Security system, these conservatives and their representatives in the Republican Party warned, and the government will ruin private property, destroy initiative, and reduce proud individuals to spineless loafers.

The large New Deal majority in Congress passed the Social Security Act in August 1935. The act provided that contributions from workers and their employers would fund pensions for the elderly, giving contributing workers a personal stake in the system and making it politically invulnerable. When eligible workers reached retirement age, they were not subject to a means test to prove that they were needy. Instead, they had earned benefits based on their contributions

Social Security Card

The Social Security Act required each working American who participated in the system to register with the government and obtain a unique number — the "SSN" familiar to every citizen today — inscribed on an identity card, making benefits portable from one job and one state to another. For the first time in the nation's history, millions of ordinary citizens were numbered, registered, and identified by a federal government bureaucracy. Picture Research Consultants & Archives.

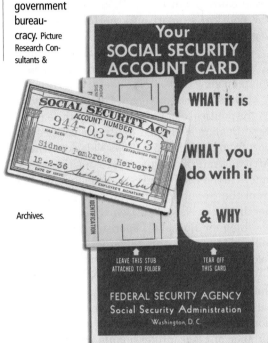

and years of work. Social Security also created unemployment insurance that provided modest benefits for workers who lost their jobs.

Not all workers benefited from the Social Security Act. It excluded domestic and agricultural workers like Florence Owens, thereby making ineligible about half of all African Americans and more than half of all employed women — about five million people in all. In addition, the law excluded workers employed by religious and nonprofit organizations, such as schools and hospitals, rendering ineligible even more working women and minorities.

In a bow to traditional beliefs about local governments' responsibility for public assistance, Social Security issued multimillion-dollar grants to the states to help support dependent children, public health services, and the blind. After the Supreme Court in 1937 upheld Social Security, the program was expanded to include benefits for dependent survivors of deceased recipients. Although the first Social Security check (for

$41.30) was not issued until 1940, the system gave millions of working people the assurance that when they became too old to work, they would receive a modest income from the federal government. This safety net protected many ordinary working people from fears of a penniless and insecure old age.

Fervent opposition to Social Security struck New Dealers as evidence that the rich had learned little from the depression. Roosevelt had long felt contempt for the moneyed elite who ignored the suffering of the poor. He looked for a way to redistribute wealth that would weaken conservative opposition, advance the cause of social equity, and defuse political challenges from Huey Long and Father Coughlin. In June 1935, as the Social Security Act was being debated, Roosevelt delivered a message to Congress outlining comprehensive tax reform. Charging that large fortunes put "great and undesirable concentration of control in [the hands of] relatively few individuals," Roosevelt urged a graduated tax on corporations, an inheritance tax, and an increase in maximum personal income taxes. Congress endorsed Roosevelt's basic principle by taxing those with higher incomes at a somewhat higher rate.

Neglected Americans and the New Deal

The patchwork of New Deal reforms erected a two-tier welfare state. In the top tier, organized workers in major industries were the greatest beneficiaries of New Deal initiatives. In the bottom tier, millions of neglected Americans — women, children, and old folks, along with the unorganized, unskilled, uneducated, and unemployed — often fell through the New Deal safety net. Many working people remained more or less untouched by New Deal benefits. The average unemployment rate for the 1930s stayed high — 17 percent. Workers in industries that resisted unions received little help from the Wagner Act or the WPA. Tens of thousands of women in southern textile mills, for example, commonly received wages of less than ten cents an hour and were fired if they protested. Domestic workers — almost all of them women — and agricultural workers — many of them African, Hispanic, or Asian Americans — were neither unionized nor eligible for Social Security.

The New Deal neglected few citizens more than African Americans. About half of black Americans in cities were jobless, more than double the unemployment rate among whites.

In the rural South, where the vast majority of African Americans lived, conditions were worse, given the New Deal agricultural policies such as the AAA that favored landowners, who often pushed blacks off the land they farmed. Only 11 of more than 10,000 WPA supervisors in the South were black, even though African Americans accounted for a third of the region's population. Disfranchisement by intimidation and legal subterfuge prevented southern blacks from protesting their plight at the ballot box. Protesters

Mary McLeod Bethune
At the urging of Eleanor Roosevelt, Mary McLeod Bethune, a southern educational and civil rights leader, became director of the National Youth Administration's Division of Negro Affairs. The first black woman to head a federal agency, Bethune used her position to promote social change. Here, Bethune takes her mission to the streets to protest the discriminatory hiring practices of the Peoples Drug Store chain in the nation's capital. Moorland-Spingarn Research Center, Howard University.

risked vicious retaliation from local whites. After years of decline, lynching increased during the 1930s. In 1935, a riot in Harlem focused on white-owned businesses, dramatizing blacks' resentment and despair. Bitter critics charged that the New Deal's NRA stood for "Negro Run Around" or "Negroes Ruined Again."

Roosevelt responded to such criticisms with great caution, since New Deal reforms required the political support of powerful conservative, segregationist, southern white Democrats who would be alienated by programs that aided blacks. A white Georgia relief worker expressed the common view that "any Nigger who gets over $8 a week is a spoiled Nigger, that's all." Stymied by the political clout of entrenched white racism, New Dealers still tried to attract political support from black leaders. Roosevelt's overtures to African Americans prompted northern black voters in the 1934 congressional elections to shift from the Republican to the Democratic Party, helping elect New Deal Democrats.

Eleanor Roosevelt sponsored the appointment of **Mary McLeod Bethune** — the energetic cofounder of the National Council of Negro Women — as head of the Division of Negro Affairs in the National Youth Administration. The highest-ranking black official in Roosevelt's administration, Bethune used her position to guide a small number of black professionals and civil rights activists to posts within New Deal agencies. Nicknamed the "Black Cabinet," these men and women composed the first sizable representation of African Americans in white-collar posts in the federal government, and they ultimately helped about one in four African Americans get access to New Deal relief programs.

Despite these gains, by 1940 African Americans still suffered severe handicaps. Most of the thirteen million black workers toiled at low-paying menial jobs, unprotected by the New Deal safety net. Making a mockery of the "separate but equal" doctrine, segregated black schools had less money and worse facilities than white schools, and only 1 percent of black students earned college degrees. In southern states, there were no black police officers or judges and hardly any black lawyers. Vigilante violence against blacks went unpunished. For these problems of black Americans, the New Deal offered few remedies.

Hispanic Americans fared no better. About a million Mexican Americans lived in the United States in the 1930s, most of them first- or second-generation immigrants who worked crops throughout the West. During the depression,

Mexican Migrant Farmworkers
These Mexican immigrants are harvesting sugar beets in 1937 in northwestern Minnesota. Between 1910 and 1940, when refugees from the Mexican revolution poured across the American border, the Hispanic-American Alliance and other such organizations sought to protect Mexican Americans' rights against nativist fears and hostility. Alliance banners such as this one flew in opposition to the deportation of Mexican aliens, the disproportionately high use of the death penalty against convicted Mexicans, and a 1926 attempt to bar Mexican Americans from city jobs in Los Angeles. The alliance steadfastly emphasized Mexican Americans' desire to receive permanent legal status in the United States. Photo: Library of Congress; Banner: Collection of the Oakland Museum of California, Gift of the Arizona Historical Society.

field workers saw their low wages plunge lower still to about a dime an hour. Ten thousand Mexican American pecan shellers in San Antonio, Texas, earned only a nickel an hour. To preserve scarce jobs for U.S. citizens, the federal government choked off immigration from Mexico, while state and local officials prohibited the employment of aliens on work relief projects and deported tens of thousands of Mexican Americans, many with their American-born children. Local white administrators of many New Deal programs throughout the West discriminated against Hispanics and other people of color. A New Deal study concluded that "the Mexican is . . . segregated from the rest of the community as effectively as the Negro . . . [by] poverty and low wages."

Asian Americans had similar experiences. Asian immigrants were still excluded from U.S. citizenship and in many states were not permitted to own land. By 1930, more than half of Japanese Americans had been born in the United States, but they were still liable to discrimination. One young Asian American expressed the frustration felt by many others: "I am a fruit-stand worker. I would much rather it were doctor or lawyer . . . but my aspirations [were] frustrated long ago by circumstances. . . . I am only what I am, a professional carrot washer."

Native Americans also suffered neglect from New Deal agencies. As a group, they remained the poorest of the poor. Since the Dawes Act of 1887 (see chapter 17), the federal government had encouraged Native Americans to assimilate — to

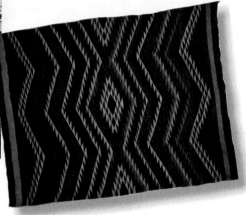

John Collier Meets with Navajo Representatives
Commissioner of Indian Affairs John Collier receives a Navajo delegation protesting restrictions in the Indian Reorganization Act (IRA) of 1934. The Navajos dyed and wove the wool of their sheep into beautiful designs like those shown here. The importance of their weavings caused them to protest the IRA's limits on the number of sheep they could raise. Collier had designed the act to revive Native American society by granting tribes an independent land base and many self-governing powers. However, his attempt to make the reservations economically viable through conservation measures, including restrictions on grass-devouring sheep, roused resistance by Indians who chose traditional ways of using resources. Photo: Wide World Photos, Inc.; rug: Morning Star Gallery/Photo by Addison Doty.

abandon their Indian identities and adopt the cultural norms of the majority society. Under the leadership of the New Deal's commissioner of Indian affairs, John Collier, the New Deal's **Indian Reorganization Act (IRA)** of 1934 largely reversed that policy. Collier claimed that "the most interesting and important fact about Indians" was that they "do not expect much, often they expect nothing at all; yet they are able to be happy." Given such views, the IRA provided little economic aid to Native Americans, but it did restore their right to own land communally and to have greater control over their own affairs, including a vote on whether they should live under the IRA, as more than two-thirds opted to do. The IRA brought little immediate benefit to Native Americans and remained a divisive issue for decades, but it provided an important foundation for Indians' economic, cultural, and political resurgence a generation later.

Voicing common experiences among Americans neglected by the New Deal, singer and songwriter Woody Guthrie traveled the nation for eight years during the 1930s and heard other rambling men tell him "the story of their life": "how the home went to pieces, how . . . the crops got to where they wouldn't bring nothing, work in factories would kill a dog . . . and — always, always [you] have to fight and argue and cuss and swear . . . to try to get a nickel more out of the rich bosses."

REVIEW   What features of a welfare state did the New Deal create and why?

▶ The New Deal from Victory to Deadlock

To accelerate the sputtering economic recovery, Roosevelt shifted the emphasis of the New Deal in the mid-1930s. Instead of seeking cooperation from conservative business leaders, he decided to rely on the growing New Deal coalition to enact reforms over the strident opposition of the Supreme Court, Republicans, and corporate interests.

Added to New Deal strength in farm states and big cities were some new allies on the left. Throughout Roosevelt's first term, socialists and Communists denounced the slow pace of change and accused the New Deal of failing to serve the interests of the workers who produced the nation's wealth. But in 1935, the Soviet Union, worried about the threat of fascism in Europe, instructed Communists throughout the world to join hands with non-Communist progressives in a "Popular Front" to advance the fortunes of the working class. With varying degrees of enthusiasm, many radicals switched from opposing the New Deal to supporting its relief programs and encouragement of labor unions.

Roosevelt's conservative opponents reacted to the massing of New Deal force by intensifying their opposition to the welfare state. To Roosevelt, the situation seemed part of a historic drama that dated to the nation's origins, pitting a Hamiltonian faction of wealth and privilege against the heirs of Jefferson, who like Roosevelt, favored a more equitable distribution of wealth and opportunity.

The Election of 1936

Roosevelt believed that the presidential election of 1936 would test his leadership and progressive ideals. The depression still had a stranglehold on the economy. Nearly eight million Americans remained jobless, and millions more were stuck in poverty. Conservative leaders believed that the New Deal's failure to lift the nation out of the depression indicated that Americans were ready for a change. Left-wing critics insisted that the New Deal had missed the opportunity to displace capitalism with a socialist economy and that voters would embrace candidates who recommended more radical remedies.

Republicans turned to the Kansas heartland to select Governor Alfred (Alf) Landon as their presidential nominee. A moderate who had supported some New Deal measures, Landon stressed mainstream Republican proposals to achieve a balanced federal budget and to ease the perils of illness and old age with old-fashioned neighborliness instead of faceless government bureaucracies such as Social Security.

Roosevelt believed that the growing coalition of New Deal supporters would help him liberate the nation from a long era of privilege and wealth for a few and "economic slavery" for the rest. Roosevelt assailed his "old enemies . . . business and financial monopoly, speculation, reckless

banking, [and] class antagonism," and proclaimed, "Never before in all our history have these forces been so united against one candidate. . . . They are unanimous in their hate for me — and I welcome their hatred."

Roosevelt triumphed spectacularly. He won 60.8 percent of the popular vote, making it the widest margin of victory in a presidential election to date. Third parties — including the Socialist and Communist parties — fell pitifully short of the support they expected and never again mounted a significant challenge to the New Deal. Congressional results were equally lopsided, with Democrats outnumbering Republicans more than three to one in both houses. In his inaugural address, Roosevelt pledged to use his mandate to help all citizens achieve a decent standard of living. He announced, "I see one third of a nation ill-housed, ill-clad, [and] ill-nourished," and he promised to devote his second term to alleviating their hardship.

New Deal "Needle-Book"
In the 1936 presidential campaign, Democrats distributed this sewing-needle book to celebrate New Deal achievements during Roosevelt's first term. The illustrations on the cover emphasize the return of harmony in agriculture, of booming factories providing plenty of jobs, and above all of "happiness restored" at a prosperous home. Notice that the working people in factories are faceless but the white-collar worker and the family are individualized sympathetically. The needle-book signifies Democrats' attempt to mobilize women to vote in gratitude for the happiness supplied by Roosevelt and the New Deal. Like most campaign materials, the needle-book's claims of New Deal success were greatly exaggerated. Collection of Janice L. and David J. Frent.

Court Packing

In the afterglow of his reelection triumph, Roosevelt pondered how to remove the remaining obstacles to New Deal reforms. He decided to target the Supreme Court. Laden with conservative justices appointed by Republican presidents, the Court had invalidated eleven New Deal measures as unconstitutional interferences with free enterprise. Now, Social Security, the Wagner Act, the Securities and Exchange Commission, and other New Deal innovations were about to be considered by the justices.

To ensure that the Supreme Court's "horse and buggy" notions did not dismantle the New Deal, Roosevelt proposed a **court-packing plan** that added one new justice for each existing judge who had served for ten years and was over the age of seventy. In effect, the proposed law would give Roosevelt the power to pack the Court with up to six New Dealers who could outvote the elderly, conservative, Republican justices.

But the president had not reckoned with Americans' deeply rooted deference to the independent authority of the Supreme Court. More than two-thirds of Americans believed that the Court should be free from political interference. Even New Deal supporters were disturbed by the court-packing scheme. The suggestion that individuals over age seventy had diminished mental capacity offended many elderly members of Congress, and the Senate defeated the bill in 1937.

> **"[The New Deal is the] repudiation of Democracy [and] the Republican Party alone [is] the guardian of . . . the charter of freedom."**
>
> —Former President
> HERBERT HOOVER

Although Roosevelt's court-packing plan failed, Supreme Court justices got the message. After the furor abated, Chief Justice Charles Evans Hughes and fellow moderate Owen Roberts changed their views enough to keep the Court from invalidating the Wagner Act and Social Security. Then the most conservative of the elderly justices — the "four horsemen of reaction," one New Dealer called them — retired. Roosevelt eventually named eight justices to the Court — more than any other president — ultimately giving New Deal laws safe passage through the Court.

Reaction and Recession

Emboldened by their defeat of the court-packing plan, Republicans and southern Democrats rallied around their common conservatism to obstruct additional reforms. Former president Herbert Hoover proclaimed that the New Deal was the "repudiation of Democracy" and that "the Republican Party alone [was] the guardian of . . . the charter of freedom." Democrats' arguments over whether the New Deal needed to be expanded — and if so, how — undermined the consensus among reformers and sparked antagonism between Congress and the White House. The ominous rise of belligerent regimes in Germany, Italy, Japan, and elsewhere slowed reform as some Americans began to worry more about defending the nation than changing it.

Roosevelt himself favored slowing the pace of the New Deal. He believed that existing New Deal measures had steadily boosted the economy and largely eliminated the depression crisis. In fact, the gross national product in 1937 briefly equaled the 1929 level before dropping lower for the rest of the decade. Unemployment declined to 14 percent in 1937 but quickly spiked upward and stayed higher until 1940. Roosevelt's unwarranted optimism about the economic recovery persuaded him that additional deficit spending by the federal government was no longer necessary.

Roosevelt's optimism failed to consider the stubborn realities of unemployment and poverty, and the reduction in deficit spending reversed the improving economy. Even at the high-water mark of recovery in the summer of 1937, seven million people lacked jobs. In the next few months, national income and production slipped so steeply that almost two-thirds of the economic gains since 1933 were lost by June 1938. Farm prices dropped 20 percent, and unemployment rose by more than two million.

This economic reversal hurt the New Deal politically. Conservatives argued that this recession proved that New Deal measures produced only an illusion of progress. The way to weather the recession was to tax and spend less and wait for the natural laws of supply and demand to restore prosperity. Many New Dealers insisted instead that the continuing depression demanded that Roosevelt revive federal spending and redouble efforts to stimulate the economy. In 1938, Congress heeded such pleas and enacted a massive new program of federal spending.

The recession scare of 1937–1938 taught the president the lesson that economic growth had to be carefully nurtured. The English economist John Maynard Keynes, in a theory that became known as **Keynesian economics**, argued in his influential work *The General Theory of Employment, Interest, and Money* (1936) that

Distributing Surplus Food to the Needy
When bountiful harvests produced surplus crops that would depress prices if they were sent to market, the New Deal arranged to distribute some of them to needy Americans. Here, farmworkers in east-central Arizona near the New Mexico border line up to receive a ration of potatoes authorized by the New Deal agent checking the box of index cards. Surplus commodity distribution represented New Dealers' attempt to provide relief for the hungry with crops that otherwise would rot or need to be destroyed in order to limit supply and thereby maintain agricultural prices. Library of Congress.

only government intervention could pump enough money into the economy to restore prosperity. Roosevelt never had the inclination or time to master Keynesian theory. But in a commonsense way, he understood that escape from the depression required a plan for large-scale spending to alleviate distress and stimulate economic growth (Figure 24.2).

The Last of the New Deal Reforms

From the moment he was sworn in, Roosevelt sought to expand the powers of the presidency. He believed that the president needed more authority to meet emergencies such as the depression and to administer the sprawling federal bureaucracy. In September 1938, Congress passed the Administrative Reorganization Act, which gave Roosevelt (and future presidents) new influ-

ence over the bureaucracy. Combined with a Democratic majority in Congress, a now-friendly Supreme Court, and the revival of deficit spending, the newly empowered White House seemed to be in a good position to move ahead with a revitalized New Deal.

Resistance to further reform was also on the rise, however. Conservatives argued that the New Deal had pressed government centralization too far. Even the New Deal's friends became weary of one emergency program after another while economic woes continued to shadow New Deal achievements. By the midpoint of Roosevelt's second term, restive members of Congress balked at new initiatives. Clearly, the New Deal was losing momentum, but enough support remained for one last burst of reform.

Agriculture still had strong claims on New Deal attention in the face of drought, declining crop prices, and impoverished sharecroppers and

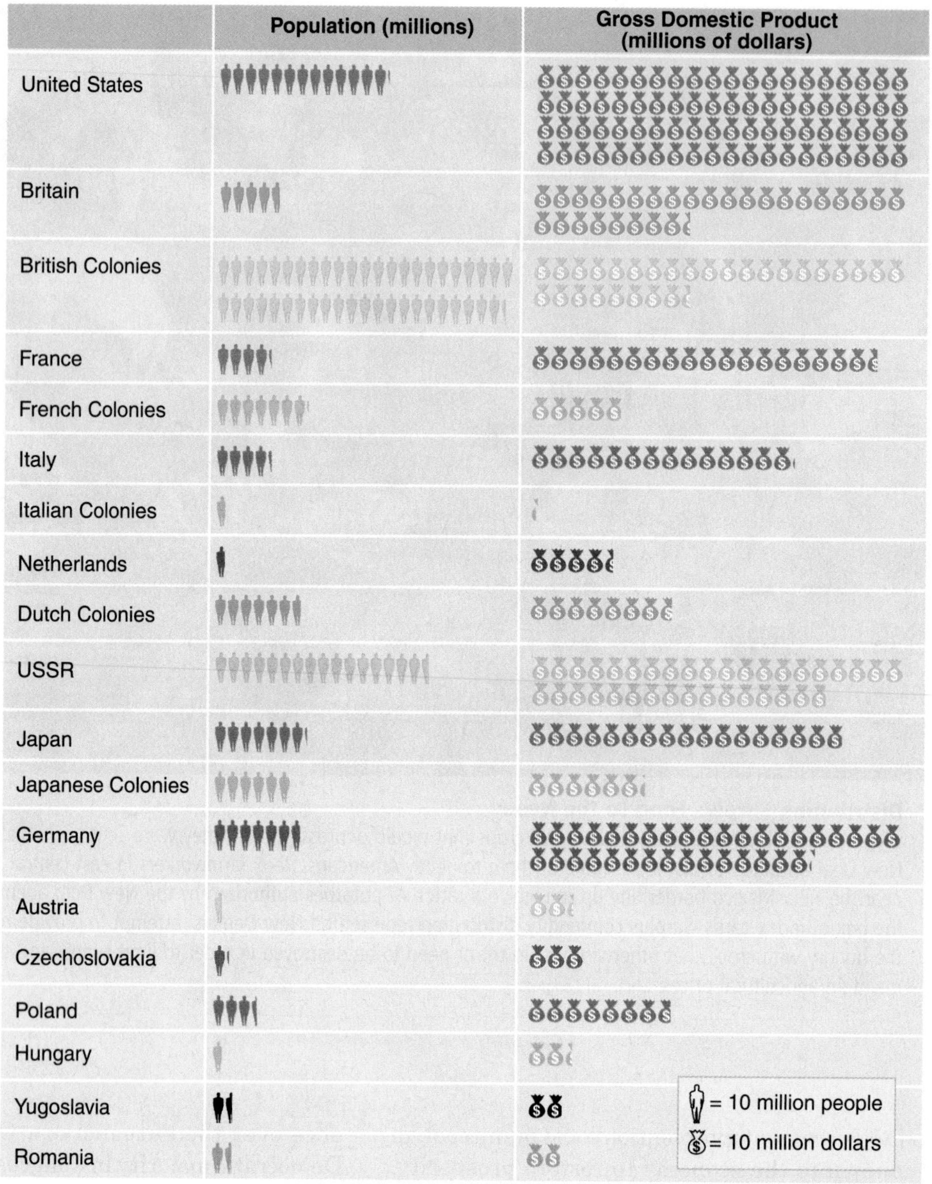

FIGURE 24.2 GLOBAL COMPARISON: National Populations and Economies, ca. 1938

Throughout the Great Depression, the United States remained more productive than any other nation in the world. Despite the lingering effects of the depression, by 1938 the United States produced more than twice as much as Germany and the Soviet Union, nearly three times as much as Britain, more than four times as much as France and Japan, and more than five times as much as Italy. From the viewpoint of Germany, if the European nations listed here could be brought under German control, its economy would be greater than that of the United States and would become the mightiest in the world. Economically, how important were colonies to the major powers? In general, what do these data suggest about the relationship between population and gross domestic product?

tenants. In 1937, the Agriculture Department created the Farm Security Administration (FSA) to provide housing and loans to help tenant farmers become independent. A black tenant farmer in North Carolina who received an FSA loan told a New Deal interviewer, "I wake up in the night sometimes and think I must be half-dead and gone to heaven." But relatively few tenants received loans, because the FSA was starved for funds and ran up against major farm organizations intent on serving their own interests. For those who owned farms, the New Deal offered renewed prosperity with a second Agricultural Adjustment Act (AAA) in 1938. To

moderate price swings by regulating supply, the plan combined production quotas on five staple crops — cotton, tobacco, wheat, corn, and rice — with storage loans through its Commodity Credit Corporation. The most prosperous farmers benefited most, but the act's Federal Surplus Commodities Corporation added an element of charity by issuing food stamps so that the poor could obtain surplus food. The AAA of 1938 brought stability to American agriculture and ample food to most — but not all — tables.

Advocates for the urban poor also made modest gains after decades of neglect. New York senator Robert Wagner convinced Congress to pass the **National Housing Act** in 1937. By 1941, some 160,000 residences had been made available to poor people at affordable rents. The program did not come close to meeting the need for affordable housing, but for the first time the federal government took an active role in providing decent urban housing.

The last major piece of New Deal labor legislation, the **Fair Labor Standards Act** of June 1938, reiterated the New Deal pledge to provide workers with a decent standard of living. After lengthy haggling and compromise that revealed the waning strength of the New Deal, Congress finally agreed to intervene in the long-sacrosanct realm of worker contracts. The new law set wage and hours standards and at long last curbed the use of child labor. The minimum-wage level was modest — twenty-five cents an hour for a maximum of forty-four hours a week. To critics of the minimum wage law who said it was "government interference," one New Dealer responded, "It was. It interfered with the fellow running that pecan shelling plant . . . [and] told him he couldn't pay that little widow seven cents an hour." To attract enough conservative votes, the act exempted merchant seamen, fishermen, domestic help, and farm laborers — relegating most women and African Americans to lower wages. Enforcement of the minimum-wage standards was weak and haphazard. Nevertheless, the Fair Labor Standards Act slowly advanced Roosevelt's inaugural promise to improve the living standards of the poorest Americans.

The final New Deal reform effort failed to make much headway against the hidebound system of racial injustice. Although Roosevelt denounced lynching as murder, he would not jeopardize his vital base of southern political support by demanding antilynching legislation, and Congress voted down attempts to make lynching a federal crime. Laws to eliminate the poll tax — used to deny blacks the opportunity to vote — encountered the same overwhelming resistance. The New Deal refused to confront racial injustice with the same vigor it brought to bear on economic hardship.

By the end of 1938, the New Deal had lost steam and encountered stiff opposition. In the congressional elections of 1938, Republicans made gains that gave them more congressional influence than they had enjoyed since 1932. New Dealers could claim unprecedented achievements since 1933, but nobody needed reminding that those achievements had not ended the depression. In his annual message to Congress in January 1939, Roosevelt signaled a halt to New Deal reforms by speaking about preserving the progress already achieved rather than extending it. Roosevelt pointed to the ominous threats posed by fascist aggressors in Germany and Japan, and he proposed defense expenditures that surpassed New Deal appropriations for relief and economic recovery.

REVIEW   Why did political support for New Deal reforms decline?

▶ Conclusion: Achievements and Limitations of the New Deal

The New Deal reflected Roosevelt's confidence, optimism, and energetic pragmatism. A growing majority of Americans agreed with Roosevelt that the federal government should help those in need, thereby strengthening the political coalition that propelled the New Deal. Through programs that sought relief, recovery, and reform, the New Deal vastly expanded the size and influence of the federal government and changed the way many Americans viewed Washington. New Dealers achieved significant victories, such as Social Security, labor's right to organize, and guarantees that farm prices would be maintained through controls on production and marketing. New Deal measures marked the emergence of a welfare state, but the New Deal's limited, two-tier character left many needy Americans like Florence Owens and her children with little aid.

Full-scale relief, recovery, and reform eluded New Deal programs. Even though millions of Americans benefited from New Deal initiatives, both relief and recovery were limited and temporary. In 1940, the depression still plagued the economy. Perhaps the most impressive achievement of the New Deal was what did not happen. Although authoritarian governments and anticapitalist policies were common outside the United States during the 1930s, they were shunned by the New Deal. The greatest economic crisis the nation had ever faced did not cause Americans to abandon democracy, as happened in Germany, where Adolf Hitler seized dictatorial power. Nor did the nation turn to radical alternatives such as socialism or communism.

Republicans and other conservatives claimed that the New Deal amounted to a form of socialism that threatened democracy and capitalism. But rather than attack capitalism, Franklin Roosevelt sought to save it. And he succeeded. That success also marked the limits of the New Deal's achievements. Franklin Roosevelt believed that a shift of authority toward the federal government would allow capitalist enterprises to be balanced by the nation's democratic tradition. The New Deal stopped far short of challenging capitalism either by undermining private property or by imposing strict national planning.

New Dealers repeatedly described their programs as a kind of warfare against the depression of the 1930s. In the next decade, the Roosevelt administration had to turn from the economic crisis at home to participate in a worldwide conflagration to defeat the enemies of democracy abroad.

Nonetheless, many New Deal reforms continued for decades to structure the basic institutions of banking, the stock market, union organizations, agricultural markets, Social Security, minimum-wage standards, and more. Opponents of these measures and of the basic New Deal notion of an activist government remained powerful, especially in the Republican Party. They claimed that government was the problem, not the solution — a slogan that Republicans championed during and after the 1980s and that led, with the cooperation of some Democrats, to the dismantling of a number of New Deal programs, including the regulation of banking. The deregulation of financial institutions was in large part responsible for the economic collapse that began in 2008.

▶ Selected Bibliography

General Works

Gary Dean Best, *The Retreat from Liberalism: Collectivists versus Progressives in the New Deal Years* (2002).

William H. Chafe, ed., *The Achievement of American Liberalism: The New Deal and Its Legacies* (2003).

Morris Dickstein, *Dancing in the Dark: A Cultural History of the Great Depression* (2010).

Ronald Edsforth, *The New Deal: America's Response to the Great Depression* (2000).

David M. Kennedy, *Freedom from Fear: The American People in Depression and War, 1929–1945* (1999).

Alan Lawson, *A Commonwealth of Hope: The New Deal Response to Crisis* (2006).

William Edward Leuchtenburg, *Franklin D. Roosevelt and the New Deal, 1932–1940* (2009).

Eric Rauchway, *The Great Depression and the New Deal: A Very Short Introduction* (2008).

Amity Shlaes, *The Forgotten Man: A New History of the Great Depression* (2008).

New Deal Politics

Roger Biles, *The South and the New Deal* (2006).

Blanche Wiesen Cook, *Eleanor Roosevelt*, 2 vols. (1992, 1999).

Kirstin Downey, *The Woman behind the New Deal: The Life and Legacy of Frances Perkins* (2010).

Alonzo L. Hamby, *For the Survival of Democracy: Franklin Roosevelt and the World Crisis of the 1930s* (2004).

Joseph E. Lowndes, *From the New Deal to the New Right: Race and the Southern Origins of Modern Conservatism* (2009).

Marian C. McKenna, *Franklin Roosevelt and the Great Constitutional War: The Court-Packing Crisis of 1937* (2002).

Kim Phillips-Fein, *Invisible Hands: The Businessmen's Crusade against the New Deal* (2010).

Theodore Rosenof, *Economics in the Long Run: New Deal Theorists and Their Legacies, 1933–1993* (1997).

Robert Shogan, *Backlash: The Killing of the New Deal* (2006).

Mary Triece, *On the Picket Line: Strategies of Working-Class Women during the Depression* (2007).

Clyde P. Weed, *The Nemesis of Reform: The Republican Party during the New Deal* (1994).

New Deal Policies

Lizbeth Cohen, *Making a New Deal: Industrial Workers in Chicago, 1919–1939* (1990).

Kathleen G. Donohue, *Freedom from Want: American Liberalism and the Idea of the Consumer* (2004).

Jan Goggans, *California on the Breadlines: Dorothea Lange, Paul Taylor, and the Making of a New Deal Narrative* (2010).

Linda Gordon, *Dorothea Lange: A Life beyond Limits* (2009).

Michael R. Grey, *New Deal Medicine: The Rural Health Programs of the Farm Security Administration* (1999).

Janet Irons, *Testing the New Deal: The General Textile Strike of 1934 in the American South* (2000).

Jennifer Klein, *For All These Rights: Business, Labor, and the Shaping of America's Public-Private Welfare State* (2003).

Lawrence Levine et al., *The Fireside Conversations: America Responds to FDR during the Great Depression* (2010).

Julie Novkov, *Constituting Workers, Protecting Women: Gender, Law, and Labor in the Progressive Era and New Deal Years* (2001).

Sarah Phillips, *This Land, This Nation: Conservation, Rural America, and the New Deal* (2007).

Patrick D. Reagan, *Designing a New America: The Origins of New Deal Planning, 1890–1936* (1999).

John A. Salmond, *The General Textile Strike of 1934: From Maine to Alabama* (2002).

Jason Scott Smith, *Building New Deal Liberalism: The Political Economy of Public Works, 1933–1956* (2005).

Landon R. Y. Stors, *Civilizing Capitalism: The National Consumers' League, Women's Activism, and Labor Standards in the New Deal Era* (2000).

David A. Taylor, *Soul of a People: The WPA Writers' Project Uncovers Depression America* (2010).

▶ FOR MORE BOOKS ABOUT TOPICS IN THIS CHAPTER, see the Online Bibliography at **bedfordstmartins.com/roark.**

▶ FOR ADDITIONAL PRIMARY SOURCES FROM THIS PERIOD, see Michael Johnson, ed., *Reading the American Past*, Fifth Edition.

▶ FOR WEB SITES, IMAGES, AND DOCUMENTS RELATED TO TOPICS AND PLACES IN THIS CHAPTER, visit Make History at **bedfordstmartins.com/roark.**

Reviewing Chapter 24

KEY TERMS

Explain each term's significance.

Franklin D. Roosevelt: A Patrician in Government

    Franklin Delano Roosevelt (p. 787)

    New Deal coalition (p. 790)

Launching the New Deal

    Harry Hopkins (p. 791)

    Frances Perkins (p. 791)

    Eleanor Roosevelt (p. 792)

    underconsumption (p. 792)

    Federal Deposit Insurance Corporation
      (FDIC) (p. 793)

    fireside chats (p. 794)

    Securities and Exchange Commission
      (SEC) (p. 794)

    Federal Emergency Relief Administration
      (FERA) (p. 795)

    Civilian Conservation Corps (CCC) (p. 795)

    Tennessee Valley Authority (TVA) (p. 795)

    Rural Electrification Administration
      (REA) (p. 796)

    Agricultural Adjustment Act (AAA)
      (p. 796)

    National Recovery Administration
      (NRA) (p. 797)

Challenges to the New Deal

    Dust Bowl (p. 802)

    Upton Sinclair (p. 802)

    Charles Coughlin (p. 803)

    Francis Townsend (p. 803)

    Huey Long (p. 804)

Toward a Welfare State

    Works Progress Administration
      (WPA) (p. 805)

    Wagner Act (p. 807)

    Committee for Industrial Organization
      (CIO) (p. 808)

    sit-down strike (p. 808)

    Social Security (p. 808)

    Mary McLeod Bethune (p. 810)

    Indian Reorganization Act (IRA) (p. 812)

The New Deal from Victory to Deadlock

    court-packing plan (p. 814)

    Keynesian economics (p. 814)

    National Housing Act (p. 817)

    Fair Labor Standards Act (p. 817)

REVIEW QUESTIONS

Use key terms and dates to support your answer.

1. Why did Franklin D. Roosevelt win the 1932 presidential election by such a large margin? (pp. 787–791)

2. How did the New Dealers try to steer the nation toward recovery from the Great Depression? (pp. 791–800)

3. Why did groups at both ends of the political spectrum criticize the New Deal? (pp. 800–804)

4. What features of a welfare state did the New Deal create and why? (pp. 804–812)

5. Why did political support for New Deal reforms decline? (pp. 812–817)

MAKING CONNECTIONS

Draw on key terms, the timeline, and review questions.

1. Franklin Roosevelt's landslide victory in 1932 changed the political landscape. How did Roosevelt build an effective interregional political coalition for the Democratic Party? How did the challenges of balancing interests within the coalition shape the policies of the New Deal? In your answer, discuss the character of the coalition and specific reforms.

2. New Dealers experimented with varied solutions to the economic disorder of the 1930s. Compare reform efforts targeting rural and industrial America. Were they effective? Why or why not? What do they reveal about how the Roosevelt administration understood the underlying causes of the Great Depression?

3. Although the New Deal enjoyed astonishing popularity, some Americans were consistently critical of Roosevelt's reforms. Why? In your answer, discuss three opponents of the New Deal, being attentive to changes over time in their opinions. Were they able to influence the New Deal? If so, how?

4. Although the New Deal extended help to many Americans, all did not benefit equally from the era's reforms. Who remained outside the reach of New Deal assistance? Why? In your answer, consider how politics shaped the limits of reform, both in constituents' ability to demand assistance and in the federal government's response to their demands.

LINKING TO THE PAST

Link events in this chapter to earlier events.

1. To what degree did the New Deal reflect a continuation of the progressive movement of the late nineteenth and early twentieth centuries? In what ways was the New Deal a departure from progressive ideals? In general, how new was the New Deal? (See chapters 21 and 22.)

2. How did the New Deal coalition compare to the long-standing political coalition that had elected Republicans to the presidency since 1920? What accounted for the differences and similarities? (See chapter 23.)

▶ FOR PRACTICE QUIZZES AND OTHER STUDY TOOLS, visit the Online Study Guide at bedfordstmartins.com/roark.

TIMELINE 1933–1938

1933
- Democrat Franklin D. Roosevelt becomes president.
- **March–June** Legislation of the Hundred Days establishes the New Deal.
- Roosevelt closes the nation's banks for a four-day "bank holiday."
- Federal Emergency Relief Administration (FERA) established.

1934
- Securities and Exchange Commission (SEC) created.
- Upton Sinclair loses bid for governorship of California.
- American Liberty League founded.
- Dr. Francis Townsend devises Old Age Revolving Pension scheme.
- Indian Reorganization Act.

1935
- Legislation creates Works Progress Administration (WPA).
- Wagner Act.
- Committee for Industrial Organization (CIO) founded.
- Social Security Act.
- Father Charles Coughlin begins National Union for Social Justice.

1936
- John Maynard Keynes publishes *The General Theory of Employment, Interest, and Money*.
- Franklin Roosevelt elected to a second term by a landslide.

1937
- United Auto Workers stages successful sit-down strike at General Motors plant in Flint, Michigan.
- Roosevelt's court-packing legislation defeated in the Senate.
- Economic recession slows recovery from depression.

1938
- Second Agricultural Adjustment Act and Fair Labor Standards Act.
- Congress rejects administration's antilynching bill.
- Administrative Reorganization Act.

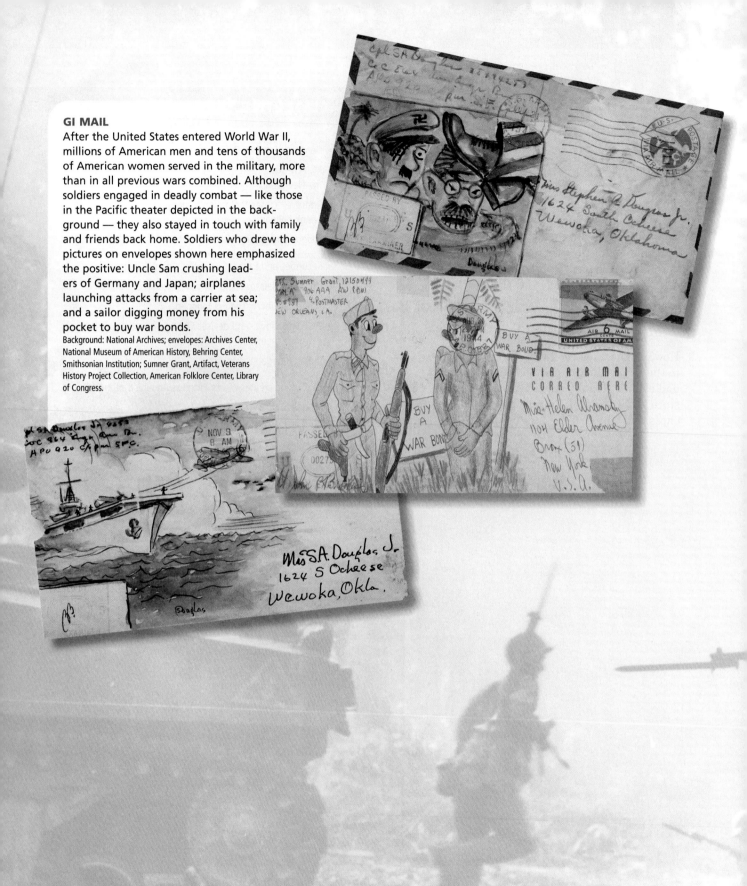

GI MAIL

After the United States entered World War II,
millions of American men and tens of thousands
of American women served in the military, more
than in all previous wars combined. Although
soldiers engaged in deadly combat — like those
in the Pacific theater depicted in the background — they also stayed in touch with family
and friends back home. Soldiers who drew the
pictures on envelopes shown here emphasized
the positive: Uncle Sam crushing leaders of Germany and Japan; airplanes
launching attacks from a carrier at sea;
and a sailor digging money from his
pocket to buy war bonds.

Background: National Archives; envelopes: Archives Center,
National Museum of American History, Behring Center,
Smithsonian Institution; Sumner Grant, Artifact, Veterans
History Project Collection, American Folklore Center, Library
of Congress.

25

The United States and the Second World War
1939–1945

ON A SUN-DRENCHED FLORIDA AFTERNOON IN JANUARY 1927, twelve-year-old Paul Tibbets cinched on a leather helmet and clambered into the front seat of the open cockpit of a biplane for his first airplane ride. While the pilot sitting behind him brought the plane in low over the Hialeah racetrack in Miami, Tibbets pitched Baby Ruth candy bars tethered to small paper parachutes to racing fans in the grandstands below. After two more candy-bar drops over the racetrack, the pilot raced to the beach, and Tibbets tossed out the remaining candy bars and watched the bathers scramble for chocolate from heaven. After this stunt, sales of Baby Ruths soared, and Tibbets was hooked on flying.

In 1937, Tibbets joined the Army Air Corps and became a military pilot. Shortly after the Japanese attack on Pearl Harbor in December 1941, Tibbets led a squadron of airplanes flying antisubmarine patrol against German U-boats lurking along the East Coast. When the heavily armored B-17 Flying Fortress bombers began to come off American assembly lines early in 1942, he took a squadron of the new planes from the United States to England. On August 17, 1942, he led the first American daytime bombing raid on German-occupied Europe, releasing 1,100 pounds of bombs from his B-17, nicknamed *Butcher Shop*, on railroad yards in northern France, the first of some 700,000 tons of explosives dropped by American bombers during the air war in Europe.

After numerous raids over Europe, Tibbets was reassigned to the North African campaign, where his duties included ferrying the American commander, General Dwight D. Eisenhower, into the battle zone. After eight months of combat missions, Tibbets returned to the United States and was ordered to test the new B-29 Super Fortress being built in Wichita, Kansas. The B-29 was much bigger than the B-17 and could fly higher and faster, making it ideal for the campaign against Japan. Tibbets's mastery of the B-29 caused him to be singled out in September 1944 to command a top-secret unit training for a special mission.

The mission was to be ready to drop on Japan a bomb so powerful that it might end the war. No such bomb yet existed, but American scientists

823

Colonel Paul Tibbets
Before taking off to drop the world's first atomic bomb on Hiroshima, Tibbets posed on the tarmac next to his customized B-29 Super Fortress bomber, named *Enola Gay* in honor of his mother. A crew of eleven handpicked airmen accompanied Tibbets on the top-secret mission. After the war, President Harry S. Truman invited Tibbets to the White House and told him, "Don't you ever lose any sleep over the fact that you planned and carried out that mission. It was my decision. You had no choice." © Bettmann/Corbis.

and engineers were working around the clock to build one. Tibbets kept this secret from his men but took them and his B-29s to Utah to develop a way to drop such a powerful weapon without getting blown up by it. In May 1945, Tibbets and his men went to Tinian Island in the Pacific, where they trained for their secret mission by flying raids over Japanese cities and dropping ordinary bombs. The atomic bomb arrived on Tinian on July 26, just ten days after a successful test explosion in the New Mexico desert. Nicknamed "Little Boy," the bomb packed the equivalent of 40 million pounds of TNT, or 200,000 of the 200-pound bombs Tibbets and other American airmen had dropped on Europe.

At 2:30 a.m. on August 6, 1945, Tibbets, his crew, and their atomic payload took off in the B-29 bomber *Enola Gay*, named for Tibbets's mother, and headed for Japan. Less than seven hours later, over the city of Hiroshima, Tibbets and his men released Little Boy from the *Enola Gay's* bomb bay. The plane bucked upward after dropping the 4.5-ton explosive, while Tibbets struggled to maintain control as the shock wave from the explosion blasted past and a purple cloud mushroomed nearly ten miles into the air. Three days later, airmen from Tibbets's command dropped a second atomic bomb on Nagasaki, and within five days Japan surrendered.

Paul Tibbets's experiences traced an arc followed by millions of Americans during World War II, from the innocence of bombarding Miami with candy bars to the deadly nuclear firestorms that rained down on Japan. Like Tibbets, Americans joined their allies to fight the Axis powers in Europe and Asia. Like his *Enola Gay* crewmen — who hailed from New York, Texas, California, New Jersey, New Mexico, Maryland, North Carolina, Pennsylvania, Michigan, and Nevada — Americans from all regions united to defeat the fascist aggressors. American industries mobilized to produce advanced bombers — like the ones Tibbets piloted — along with enough other military equipment to supply the American armed forces and their allies. At enormous cost in human life and suffering, the war resulted in employment and prosperity to most Americans at home, ending the depression, providing new opportunities for women, and ushering the nation into the postwar world as a triumphant economic and — on the wings of Tibbets's *Enola Gay* — atomic superpower.

► Peacetime Dilemmas

The First World War left a dangerous and ultimately deadly legacy. The victors — especially Britain, France, and the United States — sought to avoid future wars at almost any cost. The defeated nation, Germany, aspired to reassert its power and avenge its losses by means of renewed warfare. Italy and Japan felt humiliated by the Versailles peace settlement and saw war as a legitimate way to increase their global power. Japan invaded the northern Chinese province of Manchuria in 1931 with ambitions to expand throughout Asia. Italy, led by the fascist **Benito Mussolini** since 1922, hungered for an empire in Africa. In Germany, National Socialist **Adolf Hitler** rose to power in 1933 in a quest to dominate Europe and the world. (See chapter 24, "Beyond America's Borders," page 788.) These aggressive, militaristic, antidemocratic regimes seemed a smaller threat to most people in the United States during the 1930s than did the economic crisis at home. Shielded from external threats by the Atlantic and Pacific oceans, Americans hoped to avoid entanglement in foreign woes and to concentrate on climbing out of the nation's economic abyss.

Roosevelt and Reluctant Isolation

Like most Americans during the 1930s, Franklin Roosevelt believed that the nation's highest priority was to attack the domestic causes and consequences of the depression. But unlike most Americans, Roosevelt had long advocated an active role for the United States in international affairs. After World War I, Roosevelt embraced Woodrow Wilson's vision that the United States should take the lead in making the world "safe for democracy," and he continued to advocate American membership in the League of Nations during the isolationist 1920s.

The depression forced Roosevelt to retreat from his previous internationalism. He came to believe that energetic involvement in foreign affairs diverted resources and political support from domestic recovery. Once in office, Roosevelt sought to combine domestic economic recovery with a low-profile foreign policy that encouraged free trade and disarmament.

Roosevelt's pursuit of international amity was constrained by economic circumstances and American popular opinion. After an opinion poll demonstrated popular support for recognizing the Soviet Union — an international pariah since the Bolshevik Revolution in 1917 — Roosevelt established formal diplomatic relations in 1933. But when the League of Nations condemned Japanese and German aggression, Roosevelt did not support the league's attempts to keep the peace because he feared jeopardizing isolationists' support for New Deal measures in Congress. America watched from the sidelines when Japan withdrew from the league and ignored the limitations on its navy imposed after World War I. The United States also looked the other way when Hitler rearmed Germany and recalled its representative to the league in 1933, declaring that the international organization sought to thwart Germany's national ambitions. Roosevelt worried that German and Japanese violations of league sanctions and the Versailles settlement threatened world peace. But he re-assured Americans that the nation would not "use its armed forces for the settlement of any [international] dispute anywhere."

> **"[The nation will not] use its armed forces for the settlement of any [international] dispute anywhere."**
> — President FRANKLIN ROOSEVELT in 1933

The Good Neighbor Policy

In his 1933 inaugural address, Franklin Roosevelt announced that the United States would pursue "the policy of the good neighbor" in international relations. A few weeks later, he emphasized that this policy applied specifically to Latin America, where U.S. military forces had often intervened in local affairs (see Map 22.1, page 713). In December 1933, Secretary of State Cordell Hull formalized the good neighbor pledge that no nation had the right to intervene in the internal or external affairs of another.

The **good neighbor policy** did not indicate a U.S. retreat from empire in Latin America. Instead, it declared that the United States would not depend on military force to exercise its influence in the region. When Mexico nationalized American oil holdings and revolution boiled over in Nicaragua, Guatemala, and Cuba during the 1930s, Roosevelt refrained from sending troops to defend the interests of American corporations. In 1934, Roosevelt even withdrew American Marines from Haiti, which they had occupied since 1916. While nonintervention honored the principle of national self-determination, it also permitted the rise of dictators, such as Anastasio Somoza in Nicaragua and Fulgencio Batista in Cuba, who exploited and terrorized their nations

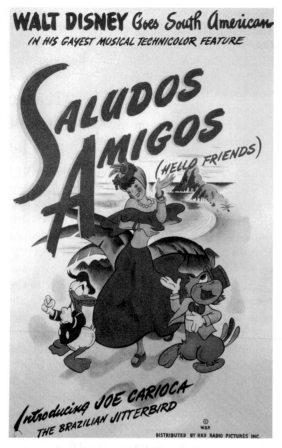

Promoting the Good Neighbor Policy

To encourage continuing friendly relations with Latin America during World War II, the Roosevelt administration urged Walt Disney to make the 1942 film *Saludos Amigos* — starring Donald Duck, Goofy, and "the Brazilian Jitterbird," Joe Carioca — largely for distribution south of the border. The good neighbor policy helped prevent Latin American nations from developing meaningful military alliances with the Axis powers during World War II. © Disney Enterprises, Inc.

The Price of Noninvolvement

In Europe, fascist governments in Italy and Germany threatened military aggression. Italian dictator Benito Mussolini proclaimed, "War is to the man what maternity is to the woman. . . . Peace [is] . . . depressing and a negation of all the fundamental virtues of man." Hitler rebuilt Germany's military strength, openly defying the terms of the Versailles peace treaty. Britain and France only made verbal protests. Emboldened, Hitler plotted to avenge defeat in World War I by recapturing territories with German inhabitants, all the while accusing Jews of polluting the purity of the Aryan master race. The virulent anti-Semitism of Hitler and his Nazi Party unified non-Jewish Germans and attracted sympathizers among many other Europeans, even in France and Britain, thereby weakening support for those who opposed Hitler or defended Jews.

In Japan, a stridently militaristic government planned to follow the invasion of Manchuria in 1931 with conquests extending throughout Southeast Asia. The Manchurian invasion bogged down in a long and vicious war when Chinese Nationalists rallied around their leader, **Jiang Jieshi (Chiang Kai-shek)**, to fight against the Japanese. Preparations for new Japanese conquests continued, however. In 1936, Japan openly violated naval limitation treaties it had agreed to and began to build a battle-ready fleet to achieve naval superiority in the Pacific.

In the United States, the hostilities in Asia and Europe reinforced isolationist sentiments. Popular disillusionment with the failure of Woodrow Wilson's idealistic goals caused many Americans to question the nation's participation in World War I. In 1933, Gerald Nye, a Republican from North Dakota, chaired a Senate committee that investigated why the United States had gone to war in 1917. The Nye committee concluded that greedy "merchants of death" — American weapons makers, bankers, and financiers — dragged the nation into the war to line their own pockets. The Nye committee persuaded many Americans that war profiteers might once again push the nation into a world war. International tensions and the Nye committee report prompted Congress to pass a series of **neutrality acts** between 1935 and 1937 designed to avoid entanglement in foreign wars. The neutrality acts prohibited making loans and selling arms to nations at war.

with private support from U.S. businesses and the hands-off policy of Roosevelt's administration.

Military nonintervention also did not prevent the United States from exerting its economic influence in Latin America. In 1934, Congress passed the Reciprocal Trade Agreements Act, which gave the president the power to reduce tariffs on goods imported into the United States from nations that agreed to lower their own tariffs on U.S. exports. By 1940, twenty-two nations had agreed to reciprocal tariff reductions, helping to double U.S. exports to Latin America and contributing to the New Deal's goal of boosting the domestic economy through free trade. Although the economic power of the United States continued to overshadow that of its neighbors, the nonintervention policy planted seeds of friendship and hemispheric solidarity.

By 1937, the growing conflicts overseas caused some Americans to call for a total embargo on all trade with warring countries. Roosevelt and Congress worried that such an embargo would hurt the nation's economy by reducing production and boosting unemployment. The Neutrality Act of 1937 attempted to reconcile the nation's desire for both peace and foreign trade with a "cash-and-carry" policy that required warring nations to pay cash for nonmilitary goods and to transport them in their own ships. This policy supported foreign trade and thereby benefited the nation's economy, but it also helped foreign aggressors by supplying them with goods and thereby undermining peace.

The desire for peace in France, Britain, and the United States led Germany, Italy, and Japan to launch offensives on the assumption that the Western democracies lacked the will to oppose them. In March 1936, Nazi troops marched into the industry-rich Rhineland on Germany's western border, in blatant violation of the Treaty of Versailles. One month later, Italian armies completed their conquest of Ethiopia, projecting fascist power into Africa. In December 1937, Japanese invaders captured Nanjing (Nanking) and celebrated their triumph in the "Rape of Nanking," a deadly rampage of murder, rape, and plunder that killed 200,000 Chinese civilians.

In Spain, a bitter civil war broke out in July 1936 when the Nationalists, fascist rebels led by General Francisco Franco, attacked the democratically elected Republican government. Both Germany and Italy reinforced Franco with soldiers, weapons, and aircraft, while the Soviet Union provided much less aid to the Republican Loyalists. The **Spanish civil war** seemed to many observers a dress rehearsal for a coming worldwide conflict, but it did not cause European democracies or the U.S. government to help the Loyalists, despite sympathy for their cause. More than 3,000 individual Americans enlisted in the Russian-sponsored Abraham Lincoln Brigade to fight on the Republican side. But, abandoned by the Western nations, the Republican Loyalists and their allies were defeated in 1939, and Franco built a fascist bulwark in southwestern Europe.

Hostilities in Europe, Africa, and Asia alarmed Roosevelt and some Americans. The president sought to persuade most Americans to moderate

Spanish Civil War, 1936–1939

their isolationism and find a way to support the victims of fascist aggression. Speaking in Chicago in October 1937, Roosevelt declared that the "epidemic of world lawlessness is spreading" and warned that "mere isolation or neutrality" offered no remedy. Instead, he proposed that the United States "quarantine" aggressor nations and stop the spread of war's contagion.

Roosevelt's speech ignited a storm of protest from isolationists. Critics accused the president of seeking to replace "Americanism" with "internationalism." Disappointed by the strength of isolationism and the absence of congressional support for his quarantine policy, Roosevelt remarked, "It's a terrible thing to look over your shoulder when you are trying to lead and find no one there." The popularity of isolationist sentiment convinced Roosevelt that he needed to maneuver carefully if the United States were to help prevent fascist aggressors from conquering Europe and Asia, leaving the United States an isolated and imperiled island of democracy.

REVIEW Why did isolationism during the 1930s concern Roosevelt?

▶ The Onset of War

Between 1939 and 1941, fascist victories overseas eventually eroded American isolationism. Continuing German and Japanese aggression caused more and more Americans to believe that it was time for the nation to take a stand. At first, taking a stand was limited to providing material support to the enemies of Germany and Japan, principally Britain, China, and the Soviet Union. But Japan's surprise attack on Pearl Harbor eliminated that restraint, and the nation began to mobilize for an all-out assault on foreign foes.

Nazi Aggression and War in Europe

Under the spell of isolationism, Americans passively watched Hitler's relentless campaign to dominate Europe. In 1938, Hitler bullied Austria into accepting incorporation — *Anschluss* — into the Third Reich, the Nazis' name for Germany. Next, Hitler turned his attention to the German-speaking Sudetenland, granted to Czechoslovakia by the World War I peace settlement. Hoping to avoid war, British prime minister Neville Chamberlain went to Munich, Germany, in September 1938 and offered Hitler terms of **appeasement** that would give the Sudetenland

to Germany if Hitler agreed to leave the rest of Czechoslovakia alone. Hitler accepted Chamberlain's offer and promised that he would make no more territorial claims in Europe. But he never intended to honor his promise. In March 1939, the German army boldly marched into Czechoslovakia and conquered it without firing a shot (Map 25.1).

MAP 25.1

Axis Aggression through 1941

For different reasons, Hitler and Mussolini launched a series of surprise military strikes before 1942. Mussolini sought to re-create the Roman empire in the Mediterranean. Hitler struck to reclaim German territories occupied by France after World War I and to annex Austria. When the German dictator began his campaign to rule "inferior" peoples beyond Germany's border by attacking Poland, World War II broke out.

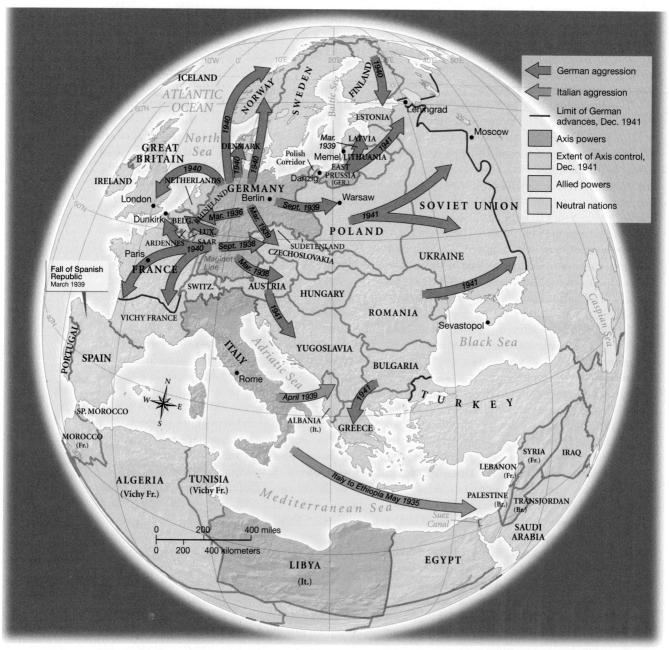

Nazi Invasion of Poland
Adolf Hitler relished the early success of the German army's *blitzkrieg* against Poland in 1939. This photo shows Hitler reviewing a victory parade of his soldiers in Warsaw. Nazi insignia hanging from every lamp post declare the German conquest of Poland. After the conquest, Germans systematically murdered hundreds of thousands of Polish civilians and confined even more to slave labor camps. Notably, the photo shows no Poles celebrating Hitler's victory. PHoto by Hugo Jaeger/Timepix/Time Life Pictures/Getty Images.

In April 1939, Hitler demanded that Poland return the German territory it had been awarded after World War I. Recognizing that appeasement had failed, Britain and France assured Poland that they would go to war with Germany if Hitler launched an attack across the Polish border. In turn, Hitler negotiated with his bitter enemy, Soviet premier **Joseph Stalin**, offering him concessions in order to prevent the Soviet Union from joining Britain and France in opposing a German attack on Poland. Despite the enduring hatred between fascist Germany and the Communist Soviet Union, the two powers signed the Nazi-Soviet treaty of nonaggression in August 1939, exposing Poland to an onslaught by both the German Wehrmacht (army) and the Soviet Red Army.

At dawn on September 1, 1939, Hitler unleashed his *blitzkrieg* (literally, "lightning war") on Poland. "Act brutally!" Hitler exhorted his generals. "Send [every] man, woman, and child of Polish descent and language to their deaths, pitilessly and remorselessly." The attack triggered Soviet attacks on eastern Poland and declarations of war from France and Britain two days later, igniting a conflagration that raced around the globe. In September 1939, Germany seemed invincible, causing many people to fear that all of Europe would soon share Poland's fate.

After the Nazis overran Poland, Hitler paused for a few months before launching a westward blitzkrieg. In April 1940, German forces smashed through Denmark and Norway. In May, Germany invaded the Netherlands, Belgium, Luxembourg, and France. The French believed that their Maginot Line, a concrete fortification built after World War I, would halt the German attack (see Map 25.1). But the Maginot Line proved little more than a detour for Hitler's mechanized divisions, which wheeled around it and raced south toward Paris.

The speed of the German attack trapped more than 300,000 British and French soldiers, who retreated to the port of Dunkirk, where an improvised armada of British vessels hurriedly ferried them to safety across the English Channel. By mid-June 1940, France had surrendered the largest army in the world, signed an armistice that gave Germany control of the entire French coastline and nearly two-thirds of the countryside, and installed a collaborationist government at Vichy in southern France. With an empire that stretched across Europe from Poland to France, Hitler seemed poised to attack Britain.

The new British prime minister, **Winston Churchill**, vowed that Britain, unlike France, would never surrender to Hitler. "We shall fight on the seas and oceans [and] . . . in the air," he proclaimed, "whatever the cost may be, we shall fight on the beaches, . . . and in the fields and in the streets." Churchill's defiance stiffened British resolve for a defense against Hitler's attack, which began in mid-June 1940 when wave after wave of German bombers targeted

British military installations and cities, killing tens of thousands of civilians. The undermanned and outgunned Royal Air Force fought as doggedly as Churchill had predicted and finally won the **Battle of Britain** by November, clearing German bombers from British skies and handing Hitler his first defeat. Churchill praised the valiant British pilots, declaring that "never . . . was so much owed by so many to so few." Advance knowledge of German plans aided British pilots. The British made use of the new technology of radar and also learned to decipher Germany's top-secret military codes. Battered and exhausted by German attacks, Britain needed American help to continue to fight, as Churchill repeatedly wrote Roosevelt in private.

From Neutrality to the Arsenal of Democracy

When Hitler attacked Poland, Roosevelt issued an official proclamation of American neutrality. Most Americans condemned German aggression and favored Britain and France, but isolationism remained powerful. Roosevelt feared that if Congress did not repeal the arms embargo mandated by the Neutrality Act of 1937, France and Britain would soon succumb to the Nazi onslaught. After heated debate, Congress voted in November 1939 to revise the neutrality legislation and allow belligerent nations to buy

arms, as well as nonmilitary supplies, on a cash-and-carry basis.

In practice, the revised neutrality law permitted Britain and France to purchase American war materiel and carry it across the Atlantic in their own ships, thereby shielding American vessels from attack by German submarines lurking in the Atlantic. Roosevelt wrote a friend, "What worries me is that public opinion . . . is patting itself on the back every morning and thanking God for the Atlantic Ocean (and the Pacific Ocean)" and underestimating "the serious implications" of the European war "for our own future." Roosevelt searched for a way to aid Britain short of entering a formal alliance or declaring war against Germany. Churchill pleaded for American destroyers, aircraft, and munitions, but he had no money to buy them under the prevailing cash-and-carry neutrality law. By late summer in 1940, as the Battle of Britain raged, Roosevelt concocted a scheme to deliver fifty old destroyers to Britain in exchange for American access to British bases in the Western Hemisphere. Claiming the constitutional power to strengthen America's defenses by swapping destroyers for bases, Roosevelt took the first steps toward building a firm Anglo-American alliance against Hitler.

While German Luftwaffe (air force) pilots bombed Britain, Roosevelt decided to run for an unprecedented third term as president in

Battle of Britain Survivors
During the Battle of Britain, German bombers targeted civilians in British cities. Luftwaffe pilots destroyed the Liverpool home (in the background) of Sarah Manson, the sixty-eight-year-old woman shown here with her daughter and grandchildren. Thousands of other British families suffered similar fates before the Royal Air Force managed to sweep the Luftwaffe from the skies over Britain. Subsequently, the British Bomber Command conducted saturation bombing raids against German cities, causing hundreds of thousands of civilian casualties. During World War II, more civilians were killed in military engagements than in any previous war.
© Bettmann/Corbis.

Enigma Machine
German commanders used the Enigma machine throughout World War II to send top-secret military messages. British agents broke the Enigma code in late August 1941 and began deciphering German messages, dubbing the decoded intelligence "Ultra." Since the Germans made several Enigma code changes during the war, temporary Ultra blackouts occurred until the new codes could be decrypted. Still, Allied military planners used Ultra to sink submarines, anticipate German movement, and send disinformation to the German command. After World War II, Allied intelligence agencies gave thousands of Enigma machines to other nations, permitting the United States and Britain to eavesdrop on unwitting recipients of these "gifts." Museum of World War II, Natick, MA, museum of worldwarii.com.

1940. He hoped to woo voters away from their complacent isolationism to back the nation's international interests as well as New Deal reforms. But the presidential election, which Roosevelt won handily, provided no clear mandate for American involvement in the European war. The Republican candidate, Wendell Willkie, a former Democrat who generally favored New Deal measures and Roosevelt's foreign policy, attacked Roosevelt as a warmonger. Willkie's accusations caused the president to promise voters, "Your boys are not going to be sent into any foreign wars," a pledge counterbalanced by his repeated warnings about the threats to America posed by Nazi aggression.

Once reelected, Roosevelt maneuvered to support Britain in every way short of war. In a fireside chat shortly after Christmas 1940, he proclaimed that it was incumbent on the United States to become "the great arsenal of democracy" and send "every ounce and every ton of munitions and supplies that we can possibly spare to help the defenders who are in the front lines."

In January 1941, Roosevelt proposed the **Lend-Lease Act**, which allowed the British to obtain arms from the United States without paying cash but with the promise to reimburse the United States when the war ended. The purpose of Lend-Lease, Roosevelt proclaimed, was to defend democracy and human rights throughout the world, specifically the Four Freedoms: "freedom of speech and expression . . . freedom of every person to worship God in his own way . . .

freedom from want . . . [and] freedom from fear." The Lend-Lease Act passed in March 1941 and started a flow of support to Britain that totaled more than $50 billion during the war, far more than all federal expenditures combined since Roosevelt had become president in 1933.

Stymied in his plans for an invasion of England, Hitler turned his massive army eastward and on June 22, 1941, sprang a surprise attack on the Soviet Union, his ally in the 1939 Nazi-Soviet nonaggression pact. Neither Roosevelt nor Churchill had any love for Joseph Stalin or communism, but they both welcomed the Soviet Union to the anti-Nazi cause. Both Western leaders understood that Hitler's attack on Russia would provide relief for the hard-pressed British. Roosevelt quickly persuaded Congress to extend Lend-Lease to the Soviet Union, beginning the shipment of millions of tons of trucks, jeeps, and other equipment that, in all, supplied about 10 percent of Russian war materiel.

> **"We must be the great arsenal of democracy."**
> — President FRANKLIN ROOSEVELT in late 1940

As Hitler's Wehrmacht raced across the Russian plains and Nazi U-boats tried to choke off supplies to Britain and the Soviet Union, Roosevelt met with Churchill aboard a ship near Newfoundland to cement the Anglo-American alliance. In August 1941, the two leaders issued the **Atlantic Charter**, pledging the two nations to freedom of the seas and free trade as well as the right of national self-determination.

Japan Attacks America

Although the likelihood of war with Germany preoccupied Roosevelt, Hitler exercised a measure of restraint in directly provoking America. Japanese ambitions in Asia clashed more openly with American interests and commitments, especially in China and the Philippines. And unlike Hitler, the Japanese high command planned to attack the United States if necessary to pursue Japan's aspirations to rule an Asian empire it termed the Greater East Asia Co-Prosperity Sphere. Appealing to widespread Asian bitterness toward such white colonial powers as the British in India and Burma, the French in Indochina (now Vietnam), and the Dutch in the East Indies (now Indonesia), the Japanese campaigned to preserve "Asia for the Asians." Japan's invasion of China — which had lasted for ten years by 1941 — proved that its true goal was Asia for the Japanese (Map 25.2). Japan coveted the raw materials available from China and

MAP 25.2

Japanese Aggression through 1941

Beginning with the invasion of Manchuria in 1931, Japan sought to extend its imperialist control over most of East Asia. Japanese aggression was driven by the need for raw materials for the country's expanding industries and by the military government's devotion to martial honor.

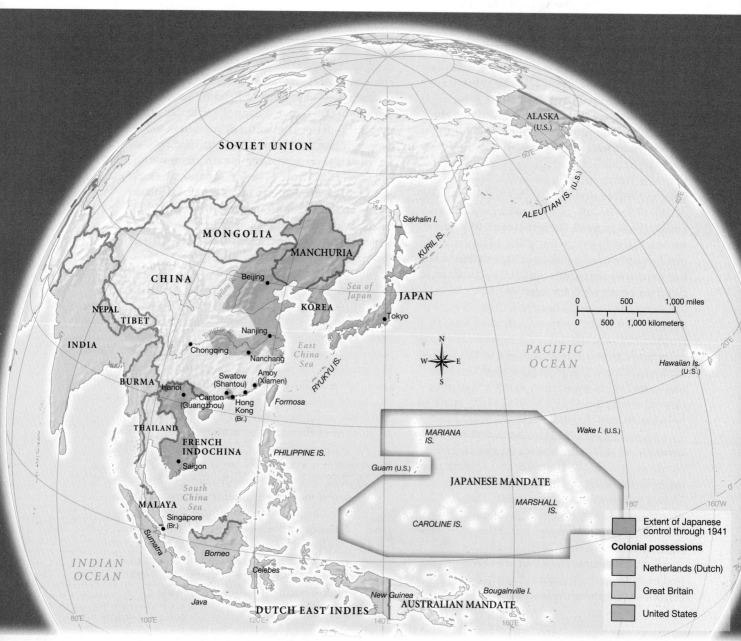

Southeast Asia and ignored American demands to stop its campaign of aggression.

In 1940, Japan signaled a new phase of its imperial designs by entering a defensive alliance with Germany and Italy — the Tripartite Pact. To thwart Japanese plans to invade the Dutch East Indies, in July 1941 Roosevelt announced a trade embargo that denied Japan access to oil, scrap iron, and other goods essential for its war machines. Roosevelt hoped the embargo would strengthen factions within Japan that opposed the militarists and sought to restore relations with the United States.

Instead, the American embargo played into the hands of Japanese militarists headed by General Hideki Tojo, who seized control of the government in October 1941 and persuaded other leaders, including Emperor Hirohito, that swift destruction of American naval bases in the Pacific would leave Japan free to follow its

destiny. On December 7, 1941, 183 attack aircraft lifted off six Japanese carriers and attacked the U.S. Pacific Fleet at **Pearl Harbor** on the Hawai'ian island of Oahu. The devastating surprise attack sank or disabled eighteen ships, including all of the fleet's battleships; killed more than 2,400 Americans; and wounded more than 1,000, almost crippling U.S. war-making capacity in the Pacific. Luckily for the United States, Japanese pilots failed to destroy the vital machine shops and oil storage facilities at Pearl Harbor, and none of the nation's aircraft carriers happened to be in port at the time of the attack.

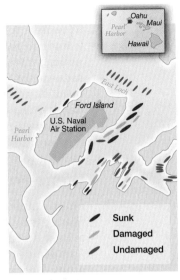

Bombing of Pearl Harbor, December 7, 1941

The Japanese scored a stunning tactical victory at Pearl Harbor, but in the long run the attack proved a colossal blunder. The victory made many Japanese commanders overconfident about their military prowess. Worse for the Japanese, Americans instantly united in their desire to fight and avenge the attack, which Roosevelt termed "dastardly and unprovoked." The president vowed that "this form of treachery shall never endanger us again." On December 8, Congress endorsed the president's call for a declaration of war. Neither Hitler nor Mussolini knew about the Japanese attack in advance, but they both declared war against America on December 11, bringing the United States into all-out war with the Axis powers in both Europe and Asia.

REVIEW   How did Roosevelt attempt to balance American isolationism with the increasingly ominous international scene of the late 1930s?

▶ Mobilizing for War

The time had come, Roosevelt announced, for the prescriptions of "Dr. New Deal" to be replaced by the stronger medicines of "Dr. Win-the-War." Military and civilian leaders rushed to secure the nation against possible attacks, causing Americans of Japanese descent to be stigmatized and sent to internment camps. Roosevelt and his advisers lost no time enlisting millions of Americans in the armed forces to bring the

Pearl Harbor Attack
This Japanese postcard celebrates the successful surprise attack on Pearl Harbor on December 7, 1941, highlighting the airborne supremacy of the Japanese, the weak defenses of the United States, and the smoking destruction caused by Japanese carrier-based aircraft. Photo: Museum of World War II, Natick, MA, www.museumofworldwarii.com.

isolationist-era military to fighting strength for a two-front war. The war emergency also required economic mobilization unparalleled in the nation's history. As Dr. Win-the-War, Roosevelt set aside the New Deal goal of reform and plunged headlong into transforming the American economy into the world's greatest military machine, thereby achieving full employment and economic recovery, goals that had eluded the New Deal.

Home-Front Security

Shortly after declaring war against the United States, Hitler dispatched German submarines to hunt American ships along the Atlantic coast from Maine to Florida, where Paul Tibbets and other American pilots tried to destroy them. The U-boats had devastating success for about eight months, sinking hundreds of U.S. ships and threatening to disrupt the Lend-Lease lifeline to Britain and the Soviet Union. But by mid-1942, the U.S. Navy had chased German submarines away from the East Coast and into the mid-Atlantic, reducing the direct threat to the nation.

> **"A Jap's a Jap. . . . It makes no difference whether he is an American citizen or not."**
> —A U.S. official in the West

Within the continental United States, Americans remained sheltered from the chaos and destruction the war was bringing to hundreds of millions in Europe and Asia. Nevertheless, the government worried constantly about espionage and internal subversion. The campaign for patriotic vigilance focused on German and Japanese foes, but Americans of Japanese descent became targets of official and popular persecution because of Pearl Harbor and long-standing racial prejudice against people of Asian descent.

About 320,000 people of Japanese descent lived in U.S. territory in 1941, two-thirds of them in Hawai'i, where they largely escaped such wartime persecution because they were essential and valued members of society. On the mainland, however, Japanese Americans were a tiny minority — even along the West Coast, where most of them worked on farms and in small businesses — subject to frenzied wartime suspicions and persecution. Although an official military survey concluded that Japanese Americans posed no danger, popular hostility fueled a campaign to round up all mainland Japanese Americans — two-thirds of them U.S. citizens. "A Jap's a Jap. . . . It makes no difference whether he is an American citizen or not," one official declared.

On February 19, 1942, Roosevelt issued Executive Order 9066, which authorized sending all Americans of Japanese descent to ten makeshift **internment camps** — euphemistically termed "relocation centers" — located in remote areas of the West (Map 25.3). Allowed little time to secure or sell their property, Japanese Americans lost homes and businesses worth about $400 million and lived out the war penned in by barbed wire and armed guards. (See "Documenting the American Promise," page 836.) Although several thousand Japanese Americans served with distinction in the U.S. armed forces and no case of subversion by a Japanese American was ever uncovered, the

Japanese Internment Camp at Manzanar, California

Japanese American families line up to enter the mess hall at the Manzanar, California, internment camp in May 1943. The camp was located on the barren, windswept eastern slope of the Sierra Nevada. The artist, Kango Takamura, immigrated to the United States in 1921. Like other internees, he was utterly loyal to the United States, and he tried to make the best of a bad situation. He recalled that the people at Manzanar "had plenty of food . . . not gourmet stuff, but good enough for health." After the war, Takamura returned to his work in Los Angeles movie studios. Gift of Kango Takamura, Department of Special Collections, Charles E. Young Research Library, UCLA.

GI did on his way to the European front, "Why fight for America when you have not been treated as an American?" Only black Americans were trained in segregated camps, confined in segregated barracks, and assigned to segregated units. Most black Americans were consigned to manual labor, and relatively few served in combat until late in 1944, when the need for military manpower in Europe intensified. Then, as General George Patton told black soldiers in a tank unit in Normandy, "I don't care what color you are, so long as you go up there and kill those Kraut sonsabitches."

Homosexuals also served in the armed forces, although in much smaller numbers than black Americans. Allowed to serve as long as their sexual preferences remained covert, gay Americans, like other minorities, sought to demonstrate their worth under fire. "I was superpatriotic," a gay combat veteran

MAP 25.3
Western Relocation Authority Centers
Responding to prejudice and fear of sabotage, President Roosevelt authorized the roundup and relocation of all Americans of Japanese descent in 1942. Taken from their homes in the cities and fertile farmland of the far West, more than 120,000 Japanese Americans were confined in desolate camps scattered as far east as the Mississippi River.

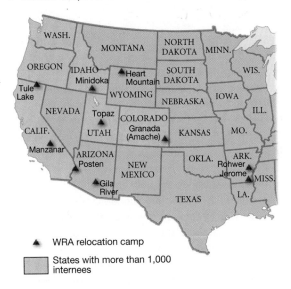

▲ WRA relocation camp

☐ States with more than 1,000 internees

Supreme Court, in its 1944 *Korematsu* decision, upheld Executive Order 9066's blatant violation of constitutional rights as justified by "military necessity."

Building a Citizen Army

In 1940, Roosevelt encouraged Congress to pass the **Selective Service Act** to register men of military age who would be subject to a draft if the need arose. More than 6,000 local draft boards registered more than 30 million men and, when war came, rapidly inducted them into military service. In all, more than 16 million men and women served in uniform during the war, two-thirds of them draftees, mostly young men. Women were barred from combat duty, but they worked at nearly every noncombatant task, eroding traditional barriers to women's military service.

The Selective Service Act prohibited discrimination "on account of race or color," and almost a million African American men and women donned uniforms, as did half a million Mexican Americans, 25,000 Native Americans, and 13,000 Chinese Americans. The racial insults and discrimination suffered by all people of color made some soldiers ask, as a Mexican American

African American Pilot
This poster urging Americans to buy war bonds featured Robert Deiz, one of nearly 1,000 African American pilots who trained for military service at Tuskegee University in Alabama. The Tuskegee airmen served with distinction in the European theater. Although the American military — like much else in American society — was racially segregated, the poster illustrates the patriotic appeal for all Americans to contribute to the war effort. The poster also hints that war against Nazi racism somewhat discredited white supremacy at home. National Archives.

Japanese Internment

Determined that the bombing of Pearl Harbor would not be followed by more sneak attacks, military and political leaders on the West Coast targeted persons of Japanese descent — aliens and citizens alike — as potential saboteurs.

DOCUMENT 1
Final Recommendations of the Commanding General, Western Defense Command and Fourth Army, Submitted to the Secretary of War

Early in 1942, General John DeWitt, commander of the Western Defense Command, persuaded President Franklin Roosevelt to issue an executive order authorizing the removal of Japanese living in the United States.

Subsequently, 110,000 Japanese Americans were confined to relocation camps for the duration of the war. DeWitt's recommendation expressed concern for military security by appealing to racist conceptions long used to curb Asian immigration. Japanese Americans and their supporters fought the internment order in the courts as a violation of fundamental constitutional rights, an argument rejected during the war by the U.S. Supreme Court. Long after the war ended, the U.S. government officially apologized for Japanese American internment and issued modest monetary payments to survivors.

February 14, 1942
Memorandum for the Secretary of War

Subject: Evacuation of Japanese and Other Subversive Persons from the Pacific Coast.

1. In presenting a recommendation for the evacuation of Japanese and other subversive persons from the Pacific Coast, the following facts have been considered:
   a. Mission of the Western Defense Command and Fourth Army.
   1) Defense of the Pacific Coast of the Western Defense Command, as extended, against attacks by sea, land, or air;
   2) Local protection of establishment and communications vital to the National Defense for which adequate defense cannot be provided by local civilian authorities.
   b. Brief Estimate of the Situation.
   1) . . . The following are possible and probable enemy activities: . . .
   (a) Naval attack on shipping on coastal waters;

(b) Naval attack on coastal cities and vital installations;
(c) Air raids on vital installations, particularly within two hundred miles of the coast;
(d) Sabotage of vital installations throughout the Western Defense Command. . . .

Hostile Naval and air raids will be assisted by enemy agents signaling from the coastline and the vicinity thereof; and by supplying and otherwise assisting enemy vessels and by sabotage. . . .

In the war in which we are now engaged racial affinities are not severed by migration. The Japanese race is an enemy race and while many second and third generation Japanese born on United States soil, possessed of United States citizenship, have become "Americanized," the racial strains are undiluted. To conclude otherwise is to expect that children born of white parents on Japanese soil sever all racial affinity and become loyal Japanese subjects, ready to fight and, if necessary, to die for Japan in a war against the nation of their parents. . . .

It, therefore, follows that along the vital Pacific Coast over 112,000 potential enemies, of Japanese extraction, are at large today. There are indications that these are organized and ready for concerted action at a favorable opportunity. The very fact that no sabotage has taken place to date is a disturbing and confirming indication that such action will be taken.

SOURCE: *Final Recommendations*, report by General John Lesesne DeWitt to the United States Secretary of War, February 14, 1942.

DOCUMENT 2
An Oral History of Life in the Japanese American Detention Camps

Imprisoned in bleak surroundings far from home, Japanese American internees sometimes succumbed to despair and bitterness. Looking back after forty years, Kazue Yamane recalled her confinement as a disturbing and baffling experience.

In April 1942, my husband and I and our two children left for camp, and my mother-in-law and father-in-law came about a month later. I wasn't afraid, but I kept asking in my mind, how could they? This is impossible. Even today I still think it was a nightmarish thing. I cannot reconcile myself to the fact that I had to go, that I was interned, that I was segregated, that I was taken away, even though it goes back forty years. . . .

I was separated from my husband; he went to the Santa Fe, New Mexico, camp. All our letters were censored; all our letters were cut in parts and all that. So we were not too sure what messages was getting through and not getting through, but I do know that I informed him many times of his mother's condition. He should have been allowed to come back to see her, because I thought she wouldn't live too long, but they never did allow him to come back, even for her funeral. They did not allow that. I learned that a lot of the messages didn't get to him; they were crossed out. I now have those letters with me.

In 1944 I was left with his parents and our kids. But I had no time to think of what was going to happen because my child was always sick and I had been quite sick. . . .

My son knew what was going on, and he too had many times asked me why . . . you know, why? why? Of course, I had no explanation why this was happening to us.

SOURCE: Excerpt from *And Justice for All*, by John Tateishi. Copyright © 1999 by John Tateishi. Reprinted by permission of the University of Washington Press.

DOCUMENT 3
The Kikuchi Diary

Charles Kikuchi, a student at the University of California at Berkeley, sought in his prison camp diary to make sense of the internment and to judge where it would lead.

December 7, 1941
Berkeley, California
Pearl Harbor. We are at war! Jesus Christ, the Japs bombed Hawai'i and the entire fleet has been sunk. I just can't believe it. I don't know what in the hell is going to happen to us, but we will all be called into the Army right away.

. . . The next five years will determine the future of the Nisei [Japanese American citizens]. They are now at the crossroads. Will they be able to take it or will they go under? If we are ever going to prove our Americanism, this is the time. The Anti-Jap feeling is bound to rise to hysterical heights, and it is most likely that the Nisei will be included as Japs. I wanted to go to San Francisco tonight, but Pierre says I am crazy. He says it's best we stick on campus. In any event, we can't remain on the fence, and a positive approach must be taken if we are to have a place in fulfilling the Promise of America. I think the U.S. is in danger of going Fascist too, or maybe Socialist. . . .

I don't know what to think or do. Everybody is in a daze.

April 30, 1942, Berkeley
Today is the day that we are going to get kicked out of Berkeley. It certainly is degrading. . . .

I'm supposed to see my family at Tanforan as Jack told me to give the same family number. I wonder how it is going to be living with them as I haven't done this for years and years? I should have gone over to San Francisco and evacuated with them, but I had a last final to take. I understand that we are going to live in the horse stalls. I hope that the Army has the courtesy to remove the manure first. . . .

July 14, 1942
Marie, Ann, Mitch, Jimmy, Jack, and myself got into a long discussion about how much democracy meant to us as individuals. Mitch says that he would even go in the army and die for it, in spite of the fact that he knew he would be kept down. Marie said that although democracy was not perfect, it was the only system that offered any hope for a future, if we could fulfill its destinies. Jack was a little more skeptical. He even suggested that we [could] be in such grave danger that we would then realize that we were losing something. Where this point was he could not say. I said that this was what happened in France and they lost all. Jimmy suggested that the colored races of the world had reason to feel despair and mistrust the white man because of the past experiences. . . .

In reviewing the four months here, the chief value I got out of this forced evacuation was the strengthening of the family bonds. I never knew my family before this and this was the first chance that I have had to really get acquainted.

SOURCE: Excerpts (pp. 43, 51, 183, 252) from *The Kikuchi Diary: Chronicle from an American Concentration Camp*, edited by John Modell. Copyright © 1973 by the Board of Trustees of the University of Illinois. Used with the permission of the University of Illinois Press and the author.

Questions for Analysis and Debate

1. What explains General DeWitt's insistence on evacuating the Japanese after he received the report of military investigators that no acts of sabotage had occurred?

2. How do the Kikuchi diary and the oral histories of life in the camps describe the meaning of internment for the detainees?

3. Despite the internment of their families and friends in concentration camps, the Japanese American army unit in Italy earned a larger number of citations for combat heroism than any comparable army group. What hints in the documents here might help explain this combat record?

4. How did the internment camp experience influence the detainees' attitudes about their identity as Americans of Japanese descent?

Airplane Production Milestone
The Douglas Aircraft Corporation, like many other manufacturers, employed both women and men to make military equipment. Douglas built thousands of military aircraft in its facilities in California and Oklahoma. Here, hundreds of male and female workers celebrate the completion of the 3,000th C-47 Skytrain, a workhorse transport plane that carried soldiers and equipment throughout the world during the war. In all, more than 10,000 were built, and they continued in military and civilian use for decades after World War II. © Bettmann/Corbis.

recalled. Another gay GI remarked, "Who in the hell is going to worry about [homosexuality]" in the midst of the life-or-death realities of war?

Conversion to a War Economy

In 1940, the American economy remained mired in the depression. Nearly one worker in seven was still without a job, factories operated far below their productive capacity, and the total federal budget was under $10 billion. Shortly after the attack on Pearl Harbor, Roosevelt announced the goal of converting the economy to produce "overwhelming . . . , crushing superiority of equipment in any theater of the world war." Factories were converted from making passenger cars to assembling tanks and airplanes, and production soared to record levels. By the end of the war, jobs exceeded workers, plants operated at full capacity, and the federal budget topped $100 billion.

To organize and oversee this tidal wave of military production, Roosevelt called upon business leaders to come to Washington and, for the token payment of a dollar a year, head new government agencies such as the **War Production Board**, which, among other things, set production priorities and pushed for maximum output. Contracts flowed to large corporations, often on a basis that guaranteed their profits. During the first half of 1942, the government issued contracts worth more than the entire gross national product in 1941.

Booming wartime employment swelled union membership. To speed production, the government asked unions to pledge not to strike. Despite the relentless pace of work, union members kept their no-strike pledge, with the important exception of members of the United Mine Workers, who walked out of the coal mines in 1943, demanding a pay hike and earning the enmity of many Americans.

Overall, conversion to war production achieved Roosevelt's ambitious goal of "crushing superiority" in military goods. At a total cost of $304 billion during the war, the nation produced an avalanche of military equipment, more than double the combined production of Germany, Japan, and Italy (Figure 25.1). This outpouring of military goods supplied not only U.S. forces but also America's allies, giving tangible meaning to Roosevelt's pledge to make America the "arsenal of democracy."

REVIEW How did the Roosevelt administration mobilize the human and industrial resources necessary to fight a two-front war?

▶ Fighting Back

The United States confronted a daunting military challenge in December 1941. The attack on Pearl Harbor destroyed much of its Pacific Fleet, crippling the nation's ability to defend against Japan's offensive throughout the southern Pacific. In the Atlantic, Hitler's U-boats sank American ships, while German armies occupied most of western Europe and relentlessly advanced eastward into the Soviet Union. Roosevelt and his military advisers believed that defeating Germany took top priority. To achieve that victory required preventing Hitler from defeating America's allies, Britain and the Soviet Union. If they fell, Hitler would command all the resources of Europe in a probable assault on the United States. To fight back effectively against Germany and Japan, the United States had to coordinate military and political strategy with its allies and muster all its human and economic assets. But in 1941, nobody knew whether that would be enough.

Turning the Tide in the Pacific

In the Pacific theater, Japan's leading military strategist, Admiral Isoroku Yamamoto, believed that if his forces did not quickly conquer and secure the territories they targeted, Japan would eventually lose the war as a result of America's far greater resources. Swiftly, the Japanese assaulted American airfields in the Philippines and captured U.S. outposts on Guam and Wake Island. After capturing Singapore and Burma, Japan sought to complete its domination of the southern Pacific with an attack on the American stronghold in the Philippines.

The Japanese unleashed a withering assault against the Philippines in January 1942 (see Map 25.5, page 853). American defenders surrendered to the Japanese in May. The Japanese victors sent captured American and Filipino soldiers on the infamous Bataan Death March to a concentration camp, causing thousands to die. By the summer of 1942, the Japanese war machine had conquered the Dutch East Indies and was poised to strike Australia and New Zealand.

In the spring of 1942, U.S. forces launched a major two-pronged counteroffensive that military officials hoped would reverse the Japanese advance. Forces led by General **Douglas MacArthur**, commander of the U.S. armed forces in the Pacific theater, moved north from Australia and eventually attacked the Japanese in the Philippines. Far more decisively, Admiral **Chester W. Nimitz** sailed his battle fleet west from Hawai'i to retake Japanese-held islands in the southern and mid-Pacific. On May 7–8, 1942, in the Coral Sea just north of Australia, the American fleet and carrier-based warplanes defeated a Japanese armada that was sailing around the coast of New Guinea.

Nimitz then learned from an intelligence intercept that the Japanese were massing an invasion force aimed at Midway Island, an outpost guarding the Hawai'ian Islands. Nimitz maneuvered his carriers and cruisers into the Central Pacific to surprise the Japanese. In a furious battle that raged on June 3–6, American

The Road to War: The United States and World War II

1931	Japan invades Manchuria.
1933	Franklin D. Roosevelt becomes U.S. president. Adolf Hitler becomes German chancellor.
1935–1937	Congress passes series of neutrality acts to protect United States from involvement in world conflicts.
1936	**March.** Nazi troops invade Rhineland, violating Treaty of Versailles.
	July. Civil war breaks out in Spain.
	Mussolini's fascist Italian regime conquers Ethiopia.
	November. Roosevelt reelected president.
1937	**December.** Japanese troops capture Nanjing, China.
1938	Hitler annexes Austria.
	September 29. Hitler accepts offer of "appeasement" in Munich from British prime minister Neville Chamberlain.
1939	**March.** Hitler invades Czechoslovakia.
	August. Hitler and Stalin sign Nazi-Soviet nonaggression pact.
	September 1. Germany invades Poland, beginning World War II. United States and Britain conclude cash-and-carry agreement for arms sales.
1940	**Spring.** German blitzkrieg smashes through Denmark, Norway, Belgium, Luxembourg, Netherlands, and northern France.
	Japan signs Tripartite Pact with Germany and Italy.
	May–June. German armies flank Maginot Line. British and French evacuated from Dunkirk. France surrenders to Germany.
	Summer/Fall. Germany conducts bombing campaign against England.
	November. Roosevelt wins third term as president. Royal Air Force wins Battle of Britain.
1941	**March.** Congress approves Lend-Lease Act, making arms available to Britain.
	June 22. Hitler invades Soviet Union.
	August. Roosevelt and Churchill issue Atlantic Charter.
	October. Militarists led by Hideki Tojo take over Japan.
	December 7. Japanese bomb Pearl Harbor. United States declares war on Japan.
	December 11. Germany and Italy declare war on United States.

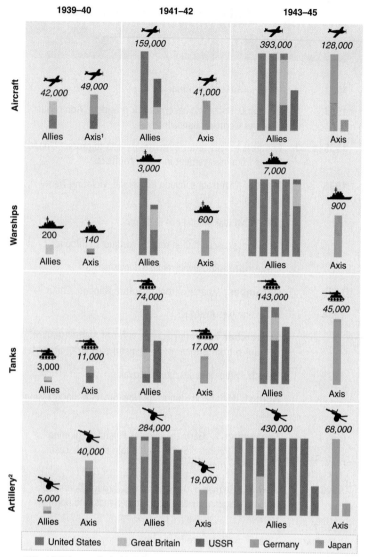

Japanese Pilot's Flag
Japanese pilots often carried small flags covered with admonitions to fight hard and well. This flag belonged to a pilot named Imano, whose relatives sent him aloft with an inscription that read, "Let your divine plane soar in the sky. We who are left behind pray only for your certain success in sinking an enemy ship." Notably, the inscription emphasized harming Japan's enemies rather than returning home safely. © U.S. Naval Academy Museum/photo by Richard D. Bond Jr.

¹ The USSR was allied with Germany 1939–40.
² No reliable data exist for Japan.

FIGURE 25.1   GLOBAL COMPARISON: Weapons Production by the Axis and Allied Powers during World War II
This chart demonstrates the massive contribution of the United States to Allied weapons production during World War II. In the air and on the sea, U.S. weapons predominated, after 1940 accounting for more aircraft and many more warships than those of Britain and the Soviet Union combined. Together, the three Allied powers produced about three times as many aircraft and five to eight times as many warships as the two Axis powers. On the ground, the Soviet Union led the other Allies in the production of tanks and artillery, an outgrowth of the colossal battles on the eastern front. What do these data suggest about the significance of America's entry into the war in December 1941? What do they suggest about the kind of warfare emphasized by each of the belligerents? What does the chronology of weapons production suggest about the course of the war?

ships and planes delivered a devastating blow to the Japanese navy.

The **Battle of Midway** reversed the balance of naval power in the Pacific and put the Japanese

at a disadvantage for the rest of the war. Japan managed to build only six more large aircraft carriers during the war, while the United States launched dozens, proving the wisdom of Yamamoto's prediction. But the Japanese still occupied and defended the many places they had conquered.

The Campaign in Europe

After Pearl Harbor, Hitler's eastern-front armies marched ever deeper into the Soviet Union while his western-front forces prepared to invade Britain. As in World War I, the Germans attempted to starve the British into submission by destroying their seaborne lifeline. In 1941 and 1942, they sank Allied ships faster than new ones could be built. Overall, the U-boat campaign sank 4,700 merchant vessels and nearly 200 warships and killed 40,000 Allied seamen.

Until mid-1943, the outcome of the war in the Atlantic remained in doubt. Then, newly invented radar detectors and production of suf-

Flamethrower in Combat in the Solomon Islands
American soldiers used flamethrowers in both the Pacific and European theaters. They were especially effective against enemy soldiers dug into bunkers that were difficult to penetrate by rifle or machine-gun fire. The Marine shown here, fighting in the Solomon Islands in 1943, carried on his back canisters of jellied gasoline and compressed air that were combined and projected through the gunlike machine. The dangerous, deadly weapon ignited the mixture and spouted an intensely hot flame. Carrying a flamethrower made one a high-priority target for enemy sharpshooters, and a stray piece of hot shrapnel could cause the weapon to explode on impact. National Museum of American History, Smithsonian Institution, Behring Center, National Archives.

ficient destroyer escorts for merchant vessels allowed the Allies to prey upon the lurking U-boats. After suffering a 75 percent casualty rate among U-boat crews, Hitler withdrew German submarines from the North Atlantic in late May 1943, allowing thousands of American supply ships to cross the Atlantic unimpeded. Winning the battle of the Atlantic allowed the United States to continue to supply its British and Soviet allies for the duration of the war and to reduce the imminent threat of a German invasion of Britain.

The most important strategic questions confronting the United States and its allies were when and where to open a second front against the Nazis. Stalin demanded that America and Britain mount an immediate and massive assault across the English Channel into western France to force Hitler to divert his armies from the eastern front and relieve the pressure on the Soviet Union. Churchill and Roosevelt instead delayed opening a second front, allowing the Germans and the Soviets to slug it out. This drawn-out conflict weakened both the Nazis and the Communists and made an eventual Allied attack on western France more likely to succeed. Churchill and Roosevelt promised Stalin that they would open a second front, but they decided to strike first in North Africa, a region of long-standing British influence that could help secure Allied control of the Mediterranean.

In October and November 1942, British forces at El-Alamein in Egypt halted German general Erwin Rommel's drive to capture the Suez Canal, Britain's lifeline to the oil of the Middle East and to British colonies in India and South Asia (see Map 25.4, page 850). In November, an American army under General **Dwight D. Eisenhower** landed far to the west, in French Morocco. Propelled by American tank units commanded by General **George Patton**, the Allied armies defeated the Germans in North Africa in May 1943. The North African campaign killed and captured 350,000 Axis soldiers, pushed the Germans out of Africa, made the Mediterranean safe for Allied shipping, and opened the door for an Allied invasion of Italy.

In January 1943, while the North African campaign was still under way, Roosevelt and Churchill met in Casablanca and announced that they would accept nothing less than the "unconditional surrender" of the Axis powers, ruling out peace negotiations. They concluded that while continuing to amass forces for the cross-Channel invasion of France, they should capitalize on their success in North Africa and strike against Italy, consigning the Soviet Union to bear the brunt of the Nazi war machine for another year.

On July 10, 1943, combined American and British amphibious forces landed 160,000 troops in Sicily. The badly equipped Italian defenders quickly withdrew to the mainland. Soon afterward, Mussolini was deposed in Italy, ending the reign of Italian fascism. Quickly, the Allies invaded the mainland, and the Italian government surrendered unconditionally. The Germans responded by rushing reinforcements to Italy and seizing control of Rome, turning the Allies' Italian campaign

Relief Column, Tunisia, North Africa

This eyewitness painting depicts a column of American soldiers moving toward the front lines to relieve exhausted and wounded comrades in Tunisia in 1943. The artist, Peter Sanfilippo, a twenty-three-year-old private from Brooklyn, New York, wrote that the "arrival of a relief column of fresh soldiers . . . reassures a battered man's faith in his fellow comrades. The unnerved and wounded are resurrected in spirit to thrive, and thus persevere into a new day." Painting watercolors allowed Sanfilippo to "maintain a mental toughness that would defy the savagery of war's violence." Peter Sanfilippo/Veterans History Project, Library of Congress, Institute on World War II and the Human Experience, Florida State University, Tallahassee, FL.

into a series of battles to liberate Italy from German occupation.

German troops dug into strong fortifications and fought to defend every inch of Italy's rugged terrain. Only after a long, deadly, and frustrating campaign up the Italian peninsula did the Allies finally liberate Rome in June 1944. Allied forces continued to push into northern Italy against stubborn German defenses for the remainder of the war, making the Italian campaign the war's deadliest for American infantrymen. One soldier wrote that his buddies "died like butchered swine."

Stalin denounced the Allies' Italian campaign because it left "the Soviet Army, which is fighting not only for its country, but also for its Allies, to do the job alone, almost single-handed." The Italian campaign exacted a high cost from the Americans and British, bringing the Nazis no closer to surrender and consuming men and materiel that might have been reserved for a second front in France.

> **REVIEW** How did the United States seek to counter the Japanese in the Pacific and the Germans in Europe?

▶ The Wartime Home Front

The war effort mobilized Americans as never before. Factories churned out ever more bombs, bullets, tanks, ships, and airplanes, which workers rushed to assemble, leaving their farms and small towns and congregating in cities. Women took jobs with wrenches and welding torches, boosting the nation's workforce and fraying traditional notions that a woman's place was in the home rather than on the assembly line. Despite rationing and shortages, unprecedented government expenditures for war production brought prosperity to many Americans after years of depression-era poverty. Although Americans in uniform risked their lives on battlefields in Europe and Asia, Americans on the U.S. mainland enjoyed complete immunity from foreign attack — in sharp contrast to their Soviet and British allies. The wartime ideology of human rights provided justification for the many sacrifices Americans were required to make in support of the military effort. It also established a standard of basic human equality that became a potent weapon in the campaign for equal rights at home and in condemning the atrocities of the Holocaust perpetrated by the Nazis.

Women and Families, Guns and Butter

Millions of American women gladly took their places on assembly lines in defense industries. At the start of the war, about a quarter of adult women worked outside the home, most as teachers, nurses, social workers, and domestic servants. Few women worked in factories, except for textile mills and sewing industries, because employers and male workers often discriminated against them. But wartime mobilization of the economy and the siphoning of millions of men into the armed forces left factories begging for women workers.

> **"If you've sewed on buttons, or made buttonholes, on a [sewing] machine, you can learn to do spot welding on airplane parts."**
> —Proclaimed on a billboard

Government advertisements urged women to take industrial jobs by assuring them that their household chores had prepared them for work on the "Victory Line." One billboard proclaimed, "If you've sewed on buttons, or made buttonholes, on a [sewing] machine, you can learn to do spot welding on airplane parts." Millions of women responded. Advertisers often referred to a woman who worked in a war industry as "**Rosie the Riveter**," a wartime term that became popular. By the end of the war, women working outside the home numbered 18 million, 50 percent more than in 1939. Contributing to the war effort also paid off in wages. A Kentucky woman remembered her job at a munitions plant, where she earned "the fabulous sum of $32 a week. To us it was an absolute miracle." Although men were paid an average of $54 for comparable wartime work, women accepted the pay differential and welcomed their chance to earn wages and help win the war at the same time.

The majority of married women remained at home, occupied with domestic chores and child care. But they, too, supported the war effort, planting Victory Gardens to provide homegrown vegetables, saving tin cans and newspapers for recycling into war materiel, and hoarding pennies and nickels to buy war bonds. Many families scrimped to cope with the 30 percent inflation during the war, but families supported by men and women

Riveting Rosies
American women flocked to war industries, and manufacturers welcomed them in jobs previously restricted to men. Here Dora Miles and Dorothy Johnson rivet an airplane frame in a plant in Long Beach, California. The tool in Miles's hands drove a rivet into the metal and another tool (not shown) held by Johnson smashed the end of the rivet snug against the airframe, securing it. War industries employed an unprecedented number of African American women and men who often worked alongside whites, as shown here. Workers wore identification badges, like the one here from a shipyard in Baltimore, Maryland. Photo: Library of Congress; badge: World War II, National Homefront National Historical Park.

in manufacturing industries enjoyed wages that grew twice as fast as inflation.

The war influenced how all families spent their earnings. Buying a new washing machine or car was out of the question, since factories that formerly built them now made military goods. Many other consumer goods — such as tires, gasoline, shoes, and meat — were rationed at home to meet military needs overseas. But most Americans had more money in their pockets than ever before, and they readily found things to buy, including movie tickets, cosmetics, and music recordings.

The wartime prosperity and abundance enjoyed by most Americans contrasted with the experiences of their hard-pressed allies. Personal consumption fell by 22 percent in Britain, and food output plummeted to just one-third of prewar levels in the Soviet Union, creating widespread hunger and even starvation. Few went hungry in the United States. New Deal restraints on agricultural production were lifted, and farm output grew by 25 percent each year during the war, providing a cornucopia of food to be exported to the Allies.

The Double V Campaign

Fighting against Nazi Germany and its ideology of Aryan racial supremacy, Americans were confronted with the extensive racial prejudice in their own country. The *Pittsburgh Courier*, a leading black newspaper, asserted that the wartime emergency called for a **Double V campaign** seeking "victory over our enemies at home and victory over our enemies on the battlefields abroad." It was time, the *Courier* proclaimed, "to persuade, embarrass, compel and shame our government and our nation . . . into a more enlightened attitude."

In 1941, black organizations demanded that the federal government require companies receiving defense contracts to integrate their workforces. **A. Philip Randolph**, head of the Brotherhood of

Home Front Patriotism
To support the war effort, Americans on the home front were encouraged to be frugal—save tin cans and newspapers; grow vegetables in Victory Gardens; and preserve surplus food by canning it, using the aluminum pressure cooker to sterilize food, then storing it in jars for later use. In order to funnel supplies to the military, the federal government rationed food, gasoline, and many other items consumers might otherwise have purchased. The poster's slogan (obscured by the pressure cooker) announces, "I'm as patriotic as can be — And ration points [that restricted food purchases] won't worry me." Poster: Courtesy of Northwestern University Library; canning implements: Atlanta History Museum. Photograph by Rod Smith.

Sleeping Car Porters, promised that 100,000 African American marchers would descend on Washington if the president did not eliminate discrimination in defense industries. Roosevelt decided to risk offending his white allies in the South and in unions and issued Executive Order 8802 in mid-1941. It authorized the **Committee on Fair Employment Practices** to investigate and prevent racial discrimination in employment. Civil rights champions hailed the act, and Randolph triumphantly called off the march.

Progress came slowly, however. In 1940, nine out of ten black Americans lived below the federal poverty line, and those who worked earned an average of just 39 percent of whites' wages. In search of better jobs and living conditions, 5.5 million black Americans migrated from the South to centers of industrial production in the North and West, making a majority of African Americans city dwellers for the first time in U.S. history. Many discovered that unskilled jobs were available but that unions and employers often barred blacks from skilled trades. At least eighteen major unions explicitly prohibited black members. Severe labor shortages and government fair employment standards opened assembly-line jobs in defense plants to African Americans, causing black unemployment to drop by 80 percent during the war. But more jobs did not mean equal pay for blacks. The average income of black families rose during the war, but by the end of the conflict it still stood at only half of what white families earned.

Blacks' migration to defense jobs intensified racial antagonisms, which boiled over in the hot summer of 1943, when 242 race riots erupted in 47 cities. In the "zoot suit riots" in Los Angeles, hundreds of white servicemen, claiming they were punishing draft dodgers, chased and beat young Mexican American men who dressed in distinctive broad-shouldered, peg-legged zoot suits. The worst mayhem occurred in Detroit, where a long-simmering conflict between whites and blacks over racially segregated housing ignited into a race war. Whites with clubs smashed through black neighborhoods, and blacks retaliated by destroying and looting white-owned businesses. In two days of violence, twenty-five blacks and nine whites were killed, and scores more were injured.

Racial violence created the impetus for the Double V campaign, officially supported by the National Association for the Advancement of Colored People (NAACP), which asserted black Americans' demands for the rights and privileges enjoyed by all other Americans — demands reinforced by the Allies' wartime ideology of freedom and democracy. While the NAACP focused on court challenges to segregation, a new organization founded in 1942, the Congress of Racial Equality, organized picketing and sit-ins against racially segregated restaurants and theaters. The Double V campaign greatly expanded membership in the NAACP but achieved only limited success against racial discrimination during the war.

Nazi Anti-Semitism and the Atomic Bomb

During the 1930s, Jewish physicists fled Adolf Hitler's fanatical anti-Semitic persecutions and came to the United States, where they played a leading role in the research and development of the atomic bomb. In this way, Nazi anti-Semitism contributed to making the United States the first atomic power.

One of Germany's greatest scientists, Albert Einstein, won the Nobel Prize for physics in 1921. Among other things, Einstein's work demonstrated that the nuclei of atoms of physical matter stored almost inconceivable quantities of energy. A fellow scientist praised Einstein's discoveries as "the greatest achievements in the history of human thought." But Einstein was a Jew, and his ideas were ridiculed by German anti-Semites. A German physicist who had won the Nobel Prize in 1905 attacked Einstein for his "Jewish nonsense," which was "hostile to the German spirit." Einstein wrote to a friend, "Anti-Semitism is strong here [in Berlin] and political reaction is violent." Einstein's associates warned him that the anti-Semites had targeted him for assassination.

In his manifesto, *Mein Kampf*, Hitler proclaimed that Jews were "a foreign people," "inferior beings," the "personification of the devil," "a race of dialectical liars," "parasites," and "eternal bloodsuckers," who had the "clear aim of ruining the . . . white race." Hitler's rantings attracted a huge audience in Germany, and his personal Nazi army, which numbered 400,000 by 1933, terrorized and murdered anyone who got in the way.

In January 1933, just weeks before Franklin Roosevelt's inauguration as president of the United States, Hitler became chancellor of Germany on a tidal wave of popular support for his Nazi Party. Within months, he abolished freedom of speech and assembly, outlawed all political opposition, and exercised absolute dictatorial power. On April 7, Hitler announced the Law for the Restoration of the Professional Civil Service, which stipulated that "civil servants of non-Aryan descent must retire." A non-Aryan was defined as any person "descended from non-Aryan, especially Jewish, parents or grandparents." The law meant that

scientists of Jewish descent who worked for state institutions, including universities, no longer had jobs. About 1,600 intellectuals in Germany immediately lost their livelihood and their future in Hitler's Reich. Among them were about a quarter of the physicists in Germany, including Einstein and ten other Nobel Prize winners. The Nazis' anti-Semitism laws forced many leading scientists to leave Germany. Between 1933 and 1941, Einstein and about 100 other Jewish physicists joined hundreds of Jewish intellectuals in an exodus from Nazi Germany to the safety of the United States.

The refugee physicists scrambled to find positions at American universities and research institutes that would allow them to continue their studies. The accelerating pace of research in physics during the 1930s raised the possibility that a way might exist to release the phenomenal energy bottled up in atomic nuclei, perhaps even to create a superbomb. Einstein and other scientists considered that possibility remote. But many worried that if scientists loyal to Germany discovered a way to harness nuclear energy, Hitler would have the power to spread Nazi terror throughout the world. The refugee physicists asked Einstein to write a letter to President Roosevelt explaining the military and political threats posed by the latest research in nuclear physics.

Wartime Politics and the 1944 Election

Americans rallied around the war effort in unprecedented unity. Despite the consensus on war aims, the strains and stresses of the nation's massive wartime mobilization made it difficult for Roosevelt to maintain his political coalition. Whites often resented blacks who migrated to northern cities, took jobs, and made themselves at home. Many Americans complained about government price controls and the rationing of scarce goods while the war dragged on. Republicans seized the opportunity to roll back New Deal reforms. A conservative coalition of

Republicans and southern Democrats succeeded in abolishing several New Deal agencies in 1942 and 1943, including the Works Progress Administration and the Civilian Conservation Corps.

In June 1944, Congress recognized the sacrifices made by millions of veterans, unanimously passing the landmark **GI Bill of Rights**, which gave GIs government funds for education, housing, and health care and provided loans to help them start businesses and buy homes. The GI Bill put the financial resources of the federal government behind the abstract goals of freedom and democracy for which veterans were fighting, and it empowered millions

In early October 1939, as Hitler's blitzkrieg swept through Poland, Roosevelt received Einstein's letter and immediately grasped the central point, exclaiming, "What you are after is to see that the Nazis don't blow us up." Roosevelt quickly convened a small group of distinguished American scientists, who convinced the president to mount an all-out effort to learn whether an atomic bomb could be built and, if so, to build it. Only weeks before the Japanese attack on Pearl Harbor, Roosevelt decided to launch the Manhattan Project, the top-secret atomic bomb program.

Leading scientists from the United States and Britain responded to the government's appeal: "No matter what you do with the rest of your life, nothing will be as important to the future of the World as your work on this Project right now." Many of the most creative, productive, and irreplaceable scientists involved in the Manhattan Project were physicists who had fled Nazi Germany. Their efforts had brought the possibility of an atomic bomb to Roosevelt's attention. Having personally experienced Nazi anti-Semitism, they understood what was at stake — a world in which either Hitler had the atomic bomb or his enemies did.

In the end, Hitler's scientists failed to develop an atomic bomb, and Germany surrendered before the American bomb was ready to go. But

Einstein Becomes a U.S. Citizen
Nazi anti-Semitism caused Albert Einstein to renounce his German citizenship, immigrate to the United States, and — in the 1940 naturalization ceremony recorded in this photo — officially become an American citizen. He is joined here by his secretary, Helen Dukas (right), and his stepdaughter, Margot Einstein (left). Courtesy, American Institute of Physics Emilio Segré Visual Archives/Brown Brothers.

the Manhattan Project succeeded, as Paul Tibbets proved over Hiroshima, Japan, on August 6, 1945. After the war, Leo Szilard, a leader among the refugee physicists, remarked, "If Congress knew the true history of the atomic energy project . . . it would create a special medal to be given to meddling foreigners for distinguished services."

America in a Global Context

1. How did German anti-Semitism contribute to the United States' willingness to build and employ the atomic bomb?

2. In what ways were the United States' development and use of the atomic bomb "important to the future of the World"?

of GIs to better themselves and their families after the war.

After twelve turbulent years in the White House, Roosevelt was exhausted and gravely ill with heart disease, but he was determined to remain president until the war ended. His poor health made the selection of a vice presidential candidate unusually important. Convinced that many Americans had soured on liberal reform, Roosevelt chose Senator **Harry S. Truman** of Missouri as his running mate. A reliable party man from a southern border state, Truman satisfied urban Democratic leaders while not worrying white southerners who were nervous about challenges to racial segregation.

The Republicans, confident of a strong conservative upsurge in the nation, nominated as their presidential candidate the governor of New York, Thomas E. Dewey, who had made his reputation as a tough crime fighter. In the 1944 presidential campaign, Roosevelt's failing health alarmed many observers, but his frailty was outweighed by Americans' unwillingness to change presidents in the midst of the war and by Dewey's failure to persuade most voters that the New Deal was a creeping socialist menace. Voters gave Roosevelt a 53.5 percent majority, his narrowest presidential victory, ensuring his continued leadership as Dr. Win-the-War.

The Holocaust, 1933–1945

SWEDEN
DENMARK
LITH.
EAST PRUSSIA
GERMANY
POLAND
CZECHOSLOVAKIA
SWITZ. AUSTRIA HUNGARY
ITALY   YUGO.

Principal German
◆ concentration and
extermination camp

Reaction to the Holocaust

Since the 1930s, the Nazis had persecuted Jews in Germany and every German-occupied territory, causing many Jews to seek asylum beyond Hitler's reach. (See "Beyond America's Borders," page 846.) Roosevelt sympathized with the refugees' pleas for help, but he did not want to jeopardize his foreign policy or offend American voters. After Hitler's Anschluss in 1938, thousands of Austrian Jews sought to immigrate to the United States, but 82 percent of Americans opposed admitting them, and they were turned away. Roosevelt tried to persuade countries in Latin America and Africa to accept Jewish refugees, but only the Dominican Republic agreed to do so, eventually providing refuge for about 800 people.

In 1942, numerous reports reached the United States that Hitler was sending Jews, Gypsies, religious and political dissenters, homosexuals, and others to concentration camps, where old people, children, and others deemed too weak to work were systematically slaughtered and cremated, while the able-bodied were put to work at slave labor until they died of starvation and abuse. Despite such reports, U.S. officials refused to grant asylum to Jewish refugees. Most Americans, including top officials, believed that reports of the killing camps were exaggerated. Only 152,000 of Europe's millions of Jews managed to gain refuge in the United States prior to America's entry into the war. Afterward, the number of refugees admitted dropped steadily, to just 2,400 by 1944.

Desperate to stem the killing, the World Jewish Congress appealed to the Allies to bomb the death camps and the railroad tracks leading to them in order to hamper the killing and block further shipments of victims. Intent on achieving military victory as soon as possible, the Allies repeatedly turned down such bombing requests, arguing that the air forces could not spare resources from their military missions.

The nightmare of the **Holocaust** was all too real. When Russian troops arrived at Auschwitz in Poland in January 1945, they found emaciated prisoners, skeletal corpses, gas chambers, pits filled with human ashes, and loot the Nazis had stripped from the dead, including hair, gold fillings, and false teeth. At last, the truth about the Holocaust began to be known beyond the Germans who had perpetrated and tolerated these atrocities and the men, women, and children who had succumbed to the genocide. By then, it was too late for the 11 million civilian victims — mostly Jews — of the Nazis' crimes against humanity.

REVIEW   How did the war influence American society?

Mass Execution of Jewish Women and Children
On October 14, 1942, Jewish women and children from the village of Mizocz in present-day Ukraine were herded into a ravine, forced to undress and lie facedown, and then shot at point-blank range by German police. This rare photograph, taken by one of the authorities at the scene, shows German officers killing the women who survived the initial gunfire. Throughout the war, Germans routinely murdered defenseless people they considered subhuman. To centralize such executions, the Nazis built death camps, where they systematically slaughtered millions of Jews and other "undesirables." Taken together, such atrocities amounted to genocide, which became known as the Holocaust. United States Holocaust Memorial Museum.

▶ Toward Unconditional Surrender

By February 1943, Soviet defenders had finally defeated the massive German offensive against **Stalingrad**, turning the tide of the war in Europe. After gargantuan sacrifices in fighting that had lasted for eighteen months and killed more than 95 percent of the Russian soldiers and noncommissioned officers engaged at Stalingrad, the Red Army forced Hitler's Wehrmacht to turn back toward the west. Stalin continued to urge Britain and the United States to open a second front in France, but that offensive was postponed for more than a year after the victory at Stalingrad. In the Pacific, the Allies had halted the expansion of the Japanese empire but now had the deadly task of dislodging Japanese defenders from the far-flung outposts they still occupied. Allied military planners devised a strategy to annihilate Axis resistance by taking advantage of America's industrial superiority.

From Bombing Raids to Berlin

While the Allied campaigns in North Africa and Italy were under way, British and American pilots flew bombing missions from England to German-occupied territories and to Germany itself as an airborne substitute for the delayed second front on the ground. During night raids, British bombers targeted general areas, hoping to hit civilians, create terror, and undermine morale. Beginning with Paul Tibbets's flight in August 1942, American pilots flew heavily armored B-17s from English airfields in daytime raids on industrial targets vital for the German war machine.

German air defenses took a fearsome toll on Allied pilots and aircraft. In 1943, two-thirds of American airmen did not survive to complete their twenty-five-mission tours of duty. In all, 85,000 American airmen were killed in the skies over Europe. Many others were shot down and held as prisoners of war. In February 1944, the arrival of America's durable and deadly P-51 Mustang fighter gave Allied bombers superior protection. The Mustangs slowly began to sweep the Luftwaffe from the skies, allowing bombers to penetrate deep into Germany and pound civilian and military targets around the clock.

In November 1943, Churchill, Roosevelt, and Stalin met in Teheran to discuss wartime strategy and the second front. Roosevelt conceded to Stalin that the Soviet Union would exercise de facto control of the eastern European countries that the Red Army occupied as it rolled back the still-potent German Wehrmacht. Stalin agreed to enter the war against Japan once Germany finally surrendered, in effect promising to open a second front in the Pacific theater. Roosevelt and Churchill promised that they would at last launch a massive second-front assault in northern France, code-named Overlord, scheduled for May 1944.

General Eisenhower was assigned overall command of Allied forces and stockpiled mountains of military supplies in England. German defenders, directed by General Erwin Rommel, fortified the cliffs and mined the beaches of northwestern France. But the huge deployment of Hitler's armies in the east, which were trying to halt the Red Army's westward offensive, left too few German troops to stop the millions of Allied soldiers waiting to attack. More decisive, years of Allied air raids had decimated the German Luftwaffe, which could send aloft only 300 fighter planes against 12,000 Allied aircraft.

> **"[We] were exhausted and we were exultant. We had survived D Day!"**
> —Naval officer TRACY SUGARMAN

After frustrating delays caused by stormy weather, Eisenhower launched the largest amphibious assault in world history on **D Day**, June 6, 1944 (Map 25.4). Rough seas and deadly fire from German machine guns slowed the assault, but Allied soldiers finally succeeded in securing the beachhead. As naval officer Tracy Sugarman recalled, "What I thought were piles of cordwood [on the beach] I later learned were the bodies of 2,500 men killed by withering fire from the Nazi gun emplacements." An officer told his men, "The only people on this beach are the dead and those that are going to die — now let's get the hell out of here." And they did, finally surmounting the cliffs that loomed over the beach and destroying the German defenses. Sugarman reported that he and the other GIs who made the landing "were exhausted and we were exultant. We had survived D Day!"

Within a week, a flood of soldiers, tanks, and other military equipment swamped the Normandy beaches and propelled Allied forces toward Germany. On August 25, the Allies liberated Paris from four years of Nazi occupation. As the giant pincers of the Allied and Soviet armies closed on Germany in December 1944, Hitler ordered a counterattack to capture the Allies' essential supply port at Antwerp, Belgium. In the Battle of the Bulge (December 16, 1944, to January 31,

Map legend:
- Axis powers, including annexed territory
- Extent of Axis control, early Nov. 1942
- Allied powers
- Neutral nations
- Allied forces
- Major battle (Allied victory)

Map labels:
ICELAND, ATLANTIC OCEAN, NORWAY, SWEDEN, FINLAND, Murmansk, Archangel, Moscow, Leningrad Besieged Sept. 1942–Jan. 1943, Sept. 1944, Baltic Sea, DENMARK, North Sea, GREAT BRITAIN, IRELAND, London, Berlin Captured May 2, 1945, Danzig, Warsaw, SOVIET UNION, July 1944, NETH., BELG., Apr. 1945, GERMANY, Mar. 1944, Aug. 1943, Normandy D Day June 6, 1944, LUX., Battle of the Bulge Dec. 16, 1944–Jan. 31, 1945, POLAND, UKRAINE, Stalingrad Aug. 21, 1942–Jan. 31, 1943, Aug. 1944, Paris Liberated Aug. 25, 1944, FRANCE, SLOVAKIA, AUSTRIA, HUNGARY, SWITZ., VICHY FRANCE, CROATIA, ROMANIA, Black Sea, PORTUGAL, SPAIN, Aug. 1944, Corsica, Adriatic Sea, ITALY, SERBIA, BULGARIA, TURKEY, Rome Liberated June 4, 1944, MONTENEGRO, Casablanca, Sardinia, Tunis Occupied May 12, 1943, ALBANIA (It.), GREECE, Nov. 1942, SP. MOROCCO, Jul 1943, Sicily, Rhodes (It.), Cyprus (Br.), LEBANON (Fr.), SYRIA, IRAQ, MOROCCO, FRENCH NORTH AFRICA (Vichy France) Joined Allies Nov. 1942, TUNISIA, Crete (Gr.), Mediterranean Sea, PALESTINE (Br.), TRANSJORDAN, Kasserine Pass Feb. 14–26, 1943, ALGERIA, El-Alamein Oct. 23–Nov. 5, 1942, Alexandria, Suez Canal, SAUDI ARABIA, LIBYA (It.), Nov. 1942, EGYPT

Scale: 0 200 400 miles / 0 200 400 kilometers

MAP ACTIVITY

Map 25.4   The European Theater of World War II, 1942–1945

The Russian reversal of the German offensive at Stalingrad and Leningrad, combined with Allied landings in North Africa and Normandy, trapped Germany in a closing vise of Allied armies on all sides.

READING THE MAP: By November 1942, which nations or parts of nations in the European theater were under Axis control? Which had been absorbed by the Axis powers before the war? Which nations remained neutral? Which ones were affiliated with the Allies?

CONNECTIONS: What were the three fronts in the European theater? When did the Allies initiate actions on each front, and why did Churchill, Stalin, and Roosevelt disagree on the timing of the opening of these fronts?

1945), as the Allies termed it, German forces drove fifty-five miles into Allied lines before being stopped at Bastogne. More than 70,000 Allied soldiers were killed, including more Americans than in any other battle of the war. The Nazis lost more than 100,000 men and hundreds of tanks, fatally depleting Hitler's reserves.

In February 1945, while Allied armies relentlessly pushed German forces backward, Churchill, Stalin, and Roosevelt met secretly at the **Yalta Conference** (named for the Russian resort town where it was held) to discuss their plans for the postwar world. Seriously ill and noticeably frail, Roosevelt managed to secure Stalin's promise to permit votes of self-determination in the eastern European countries occupied by the Red Army. The Allies pledged to support Jiang Jieshi (Chiang Kai-shek) as the leader of China. The Soviet Union obtained a role in the postwar governments of Korea and Manchuria in exchange for entering the war against Japan after the defeat of Germany.

The "Big Three" also agreed on the creation of a new international peacekeeping organization, the **United Nations (UN)**. All nations would have a place in the UN General Assembly, but the Security Council would wield decisive power, and its permanent representatives from the Allied powers — China, France, Great Britain, the Soviet Union, and the United States — would possess a veto over UN actions. The Senate ratified the United Nations Charter in July 1945 by a vote of 89 to 2, reflecting the triumph of internationalism during the nation's mobilization for war.

While Allied armies sped toward Berlin, Allied warplanes dropped more bombs after D Day than in all the previous European bombing raids combined. By April 11, Allied armies

D-Day Invasion

"Taxi to Hell—and Back" is what Robert Sargent called his photograph of the D-Day invasion of Normandy on June 6, 1944. Amid a dense fleet of landing craft, men lucky enough to have made it through rough seas and enemy fire struggle onto the beach to open a second front in Europe. Most of the soldiers in this first wave were cut down by enemy fire from the cliffs beyond the beach. Library of Congress.

sweeping in from the west reached the banks of the Elbe River, the agreed-upon rendezvous with the Red Army, and paused while the Soviets smashed into Berlin. In three weeks of vicious house-to-house fighting, the Red Army captured Berlin on May 2. Hitler committed suicide on April 30, and the provisional German government surrendered unconditionally on May 7. The war in Europe was finally over, with the sacrifice of 135,576 American soldiers, nearly 250,000 British troops, and 9 million Russian combatants. (See "Historical Question," page 854.)

Roosevelt did not live to witness the end of the war. On April 12, while resting in Warm Springs, Georgia, he suffered a fatal stroke. Americans grieved for the man who had led them through years of depression and world war, and they worried about his untested successor, Vice President Harry Truman.

The Defeat of Japan

After the punishing defeats in the Coral Sea and at Midway, Japan had to fend off Allied naval and air attacks. In 1943, British and American forces, along with Indian and Chinese allies, launched an offensive against Japanese outposts in southern Asia, pushing through Burma and into China, where Jiang's armies continued to

resist conquest. In the Pacific, Americans and their allies attacked Japanese strongholds by sea, air, and land, moving island by island toward the Japanese homeland (Map 25.5).

The island-hopping campaign began in August 1942, when American Marines landed on Guadalcanal in the southern Pacific. For the next six months, a savage battle raged for control of the strategic area. Finally, during the night of February 8, 1943, Japanese forces withdrew. The terrible losses on both sides indicated to the Marines how costly it would be to defeat Japan. After the battle, Joseph Steinbacher, a twenty-one-year-old from Alabama, sailed from San Francisco to New Guinea, where, he recalled, "all the cannon fodder waited to be assigned" to replace the killed and wounded.

In mid-1943, Allied forces launched offensives in New Guinea and the Solomon Islands that gradually secured the South Pacific. In the Central Pacific, amphibious forces conquered the Gilbert and Marshall islands, which served as forward bases for air assaults on the Japanese home islands. As the Allies attacked island after island, Japanese soldiers were ordered to refuse to surrender no matter how hopeless their plight. The fierce Japanese resistance spurred remorseless Allied bombing attacks on Japanese-occupied islands, followed by amphibious landings by Marines and grinding,

Yalta Conference
In February 1945, U.S. president Franklin Roosevelt (middle) and British prime minister Winston Churchill (left) met with Russian leader Joseph Stalin (right) at the Black Sea resort of Yalta to plan the postwar reconstruction of Europe. Roosevelt, near the end of his life, and Churchill, soon to suffer a reelection defeat, look weary next to the resolute "Man of Steel." Controversy would later arise over whether a stronger stand by the American and British leaders could have prevented the Soviet Union from imposing Communist rule on eastern Europe. U.S. Army.

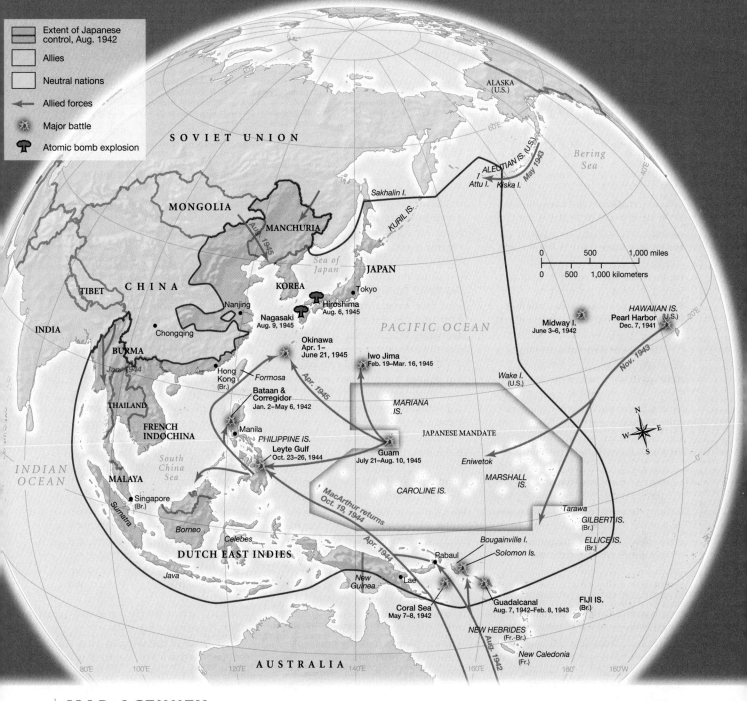

Legend:
- Extent of Japanese control, Aug. 1942
- Allies
- Neutral nations
- → Allied forces
- ✳ Major battle
- ☁ Atomic bomb explosion

MAP ACTIVITY

Map 25.5 The Pacific Theater of World War II, 1941–1945

To drive the Japanese from their far-flung empire, the Allies launched two combined naval and military offensives — one to recapture the Philippines and then attack Japanese forces in China, the other to hop from island to island in the Central Pacific toward the Japanese mainland.

READING THE MAP: What was the extent of Japanese control up until August 1942? Which nations in the Pacific theater sided with the Allies? Which nations remained neutral?

CONNECTIONS: Describe the economic and military motivations behind Japanese domination of the region. How and when did they achieve this dominance? Judging from this map, what strategic and geographic concerns might have prompted Truman and his advisers to consider using the atomic bomb against Japan?

inch-by-inch combat to root Japanese fighters out of bunkers and caves.

While the island-hopping campaign kept pressure on Japanese forces, the Allies invaded the Philippines in the fall of 1944. In the four-day **Battle of Leyte Gulf**, one of the greatest naval battles in world history, the American fleet crushed the Japanese armada, clearing the

Why Did the Allies Win World War II?

An indispensable factor in Allied victory in World War II was the alliance among the major powers: the United States, Great Britain, and the Soviet Union. Fighting alone, none of the Allies could have prevailed against Nazi Germany. Together, they were able to defeat what had been the strongest military power in the world.

The major Axis nations — Germany and Japan — did almost nothing to help each other. In the Pacific, Japan fought alone against the United States and its other allies, especially Australia and China. Britain and the Soviet Union contributed relatively little to Allied efforts in the Pacific.

In Europe, Germany enjoyed the support of Hungary, Romania, Bulgaria, and Italy, but none of these nations had the resources and industrial might to field a fully modern army. The Germans conscripted tens of thousands of men from the territories they occupied as their armies swept east, but such coerced recruits made poorly motivated soldiers.

In contrast, the Allies had a single galvanizing purpose: to defeat Hitler. The United States devoted only about 15 percent of its war effort to defeat Japan; the remaining 85 percent was directed against Germany. Little else united the Allies. Political and ideological differences between the capitalist democracies and a Communist dictatorship produced suspicion and mistrust. Nonetheless, the Allies collaborated to force the unconditional surrender of Germany. Three militarily

significant consequences of the wartime alliance stand out as decisive ingredients of Allied victory: American material support for Britain and the Soviet Union; American and British bombing campaigns and the D Day invasion of Europe; and the Red Army's success in stopping the eastward advance of the German army at Stalingrad, then relentlessly driving it back to Berlin.

The flood of military supplies that poured out of American factories during the war made Allied victory possible. In total, the United States produced two-thirds of all Allied military equipment. In addition to shipping hundreds of millions of tons of supplies to Britain and stockpiling equipment for the D Day invasion, the United States sent more than half a million military vehicles to the Soviet Union, accounting for the bulk of the Red Army's motorized transportation. By 1944, American refineries supplied 90 percent of the Allies' high-octane gasoline, prompting Stalin to raise a toast at the Teheran conference "to the American auto industry and the American oil industry," which met the needs of "this . . . war of engines and octanes." American food shipments provided the equivalent of one meal a day for each Russian soldier. The American canned meat Spam was distributed so widely that Soviet troops called it "The Second Front," a sarcastic reference to the Americans' delay in opening a second front in western Europe.

The British and American bombing campaign against German targets in western Europe served as a crucial second-front surrogate until D Day, and it eventually allowed Allied pilots to rule the skies. The bombing campaign reduced the production of tanks, airplanes, and trucks by more than a third and diverted two-thirds of Germany's aircraft and three-quarters of its antiaircraft weapons from supporting the infantry on the eastern front to protecting German cities from Allied air attacks. In addition, improvements in Allied fighter planes allowed British and American pilots to decimate the Luftwaffe. Although the German civilian population and Allied air crews suffered huge casualties as a result of the air campaign, it decisively aided the Soviets' battle against the Germans on the eastern front.

But neither the bombing campaign nor the mountains of American supplies would have won the war if the Soviet Union had not stopped the seemingly unstoppable advance of the German Wehrmacht in the east. Within six months of Hitler's surprise attack on the Soviet Union in June 1941, Stalin's army had lost 4 million soldiers and nearly all its tanks and airplanes, and German armies threatened Moscow. U.S. military officials expected Stalin to capitulate within two or three months. Instead, the Red Army regrouped and managed to halt the Germans' eastward advance by early 1943.

Reversal of the German assault required colossal sacrifices by the people of the Soviet Union. As the German army swept east during 1941, Russians frantically dismantled more than 1,500 industrial plants about to be captured by the Nazis, shipped them east of the Ural Mountains, and reassembled them there. They also built new plants and soon began producing thousands of

way for Allied victory in the Philippines. While the Philippine campaign was under way, American forces captured two crucial islands — Iwo Jima and Okinawa — from which they planned to launch an attack on the Japanese homeland. To defend Okinawa, Japanese leaders ordered thousands of suicide pilots, known as *kamikaze*, to

crash their bomb-laden planes into Allied ships. But instead of destroying the American fleet, they demolished the last vestige of the Japanese air force. By June 1945, the Japanese were nearly defenseless on the sea and in the air. Still, their leaders prepared to fight to the death for their homeland.

МЫ ЗЛОМУ ВРАГУ ВСЕ ОТРЕЖЕМ ПУТИ, ИЗ ПЕТЛИ, ИЗ ЭТОЙ ЕМУ НЕ УЙТИ!

VISUAL ACTIVITY

The Allied War Effort

The Russian poster shown here illustrates the combined efforts of the Allies, declaring, "We won't let the evil enemy escape the noose. He will not evade it." Museum of World War II, Natick, MA, www.museumofworldwarii.com.

READING THE IMAGE: What does the depiction of Hitler on the Russian poster suggest about his leadership and character?
CONNECTIONS: What does the poster suggest about the importance of the alliance among the major Allied powers?

new tanks, aircraft, and artillery to rearm the Soviet military. Through sheer hard work, the productivity of Soviet war industries more than doubled during the war. Meanwhile, food production plummeted, allowing the average Russian only one-fourth the amount of food available to the average German. Soviet casualties dwarfed the losses of the other Allies. For every American killed during the war, forty-five Soviets died. No contribution to Allied victory was more important than the monumental success of the Soviet Union on the eastern front.

Thinking about Cause and Effect

1. Specifically, how did the Allies help one another defeat the Axis powers?

2. Why was the eastern front so important to the Allied victory?

Joseph Steinbacher and other GIs who had suffered "horrendous" casualties in the Philippines were now told by their commanding officer, "Men, in a few short months we are going to invade [Japan]. . . . We will be going in on the first wave and are expecting ninety percent casualties the first day. . . . For the few of us left alive the war will be over." Steinbacher later recalled his mental attitude at that moment: "I know that I am now a walking dead man and will not have a snowball's chance in hell of making it through the last great battle to conquer the home islands of Japan."

Marine Attack on Saipan

Marines fought Japanese soldiers on Saipan in close-quarter combat in 1944, as in many subsequent island campaigns in the Pacific theater. Here, Marines have overtaken a Japanese position and are fighting in the midst of enemy soldiers they have just killed. Japanese soldiers were commanded to fight to their deaths rather than surrender, even after their ultimate defeat was certain — a command they mostly obeyed. Such determined, suicidal resistance drastically increased American casualties and delayed American progress in the Pacific island-hopping campaign. National Archives.

Atomic Warfare

In mid-July 1945, as Allied forces prepared for the final assault on Japan, American scientists tested a secret weapon at an isolated desert site near Los Alamos, New Mexico. In 1942, Roosevelt had authorized the top-secret **Manhattan Project** to find a way to convert nuclear energy into a superbomb before the Germans added such a weapon to their arsenal. More than 100,000 Americans, led by scientists, engineers, and military officers at Los Alamos, worked frantically to win the race for an atomic bomb. Germany surrendered two and a half months before the test on July 16, 1945, when scientists first witnessed an atomic explosion that sent a mushroom cloud of debris eight miles into the atmosphere. After watching the successful test of the bomb, J. Robert Oppenheimer, the head scientist at Los Alamos, remarked soberly, "Lots of boys not grown up yet will owe their life to it."

President Truman heard about the successful bomb test when he was in Potsdam, Germany, negotiating with Stalin about postwar issues. Truman realized that the atomic bomb could hasten the end of the war with Japan, perhaps before the Russians could attack the Japanese, as Stalin had pledged at Yalta. Within a few months after the defeat of Germany, Truman also recognized that the bomb gave the United States a devastating atomic monopoly that could be used to counter Soviet ambitions and advance American interests in the postwar world.

Truman saw no reason not to use the atomic bomb against Japan if doing so would save American lives. Despite numerous defeats, Japan still had more than 6 million reserves at home for a last-ditch defense against the anticipated Allied assault, which U.S. military advisers estimated would kill at least 250,000 Americans. But first he issued an ultimatum: Japan must surrender unconditionally or face utter ruin. When the Japanese failed to respond by the deadline, Truman ordered that an atomic bomb be dropped on a Japanese city not already heavily damaged by American raids. The bomb that Colonel Paul Tibbets and his crew released over **Hiroshima** on August 6 leveled the city and incinerated about 100,000 people. Three days later, after the Japanese government still refused to surrender, the second atomic bomb killed nearly as many civilians at **Nagasaki**. Robert Oppenheimer celebrated the bombings with other Los Alamos scientists responsible for creating the weapons by declaring that "his only regret was that we hadn't developed the bomb in time to have used it against the Germans."

With American assurance that the emperor could retain his throne after the Allies took over, Japan surrendered on August 14. On a troop ship departing from Europe for what would have been the final assault on Japan, an American soldier spoke for millions of others when he heard the wonderful news that the killing was over: "We are going to grow to adulthood after all."

While all Americans welcomed peace, Robert Oppenheimer and others worried about the consequences of unleashing atomic power. Shortly after the war, Oppenheimer warned: "We have made a thing, a most terrible weapon that has altered abruptly and profoundly the nature of the world . . . a thing that by all the standards of the world we grew up in is an evil thing." Almost every American, including Oppenheimer, believed that the "evil thing" had brought peace in 1945, but nobody knew what it would bring in the future, although everybody knew it would inevitably shape the world to come, as in fact it did.

REVIEW Why did Truman elect to use the atomic bomb against Japan?

► Conclusion: Allied Victory and America's Emergence as a Superpower

Shortly after Pearl Harbor, Hitler pronounced America "a decayed country . . . half Judaized, and the other half Negrified"; a country "where everything is built on the dollar" and bound to

Major Campaigns and Battles of World War II, 1939–1945

September 1, 1939	Germany attacks Poland.
September 3, 1939	Britain and France declare war on Germany.
April 1940	Germany attacks Denmark and Norway.
May 1940	Germany invades Netherlands, Belgium, Luxembourg, and France.
June 1940	Italy joins Germany in war against Allies.
June–November 1940	Battle of Britain.
June 22, 1941	Germany invades Soviet Union.
December 7, 1941	Japan attacks Pearl Harbor.
December 8, 1941	U.S. Congress declares war on Japan.
December 11, 1941	Germany and Italy declare war on United States.
January 2–May 6, 1942	Battles of Bataan and Corregidor.
May 7–8, 1942	Battle of the Coral Sea.
June 3–6, 1942	Battle of Midway.
August 1942–February 1943	Battle of Guadalcanal.
August 21, 1942–January 31, 1943	Battle of Stalingrad.
October 23–November 5, 1942	British halt Germans at Battle of El-Alamein.
November 1942–May 1943	Allies mount North African campaign.
July 10, 1943	Allies begin Italian invasion through Sicily.
June 4, 1944	Allies liberate Rome from German occupation.
June 6, 1944	D Day — Allied forces invade Normandy.
August 25, 1944	Allies liberate Paris.
September 12, 1944	Allies enter Germany.
October 23–26, 1944	Battle of Leyte Gulf.
December 16, 1944–January 31, 1945	Battle of the Bulge.
February 19–March 16, 1945	Battle of Iwo Jima.
April 1–June 21, 1945	Battle of Okinawa.
May 2, 1945	Soviet forces capture Berlin.
August 6, 1945	United States drops atomic bomb on Hiroshima.
August 9, 1945	United States drops atomic bomb on Nagasaki.

Hiroshima
This photo shows part of Hiroshima shortly after the atomic bomb dropped from the *Enola Gay*, leveling the densely populated city. The watch shown here was recovered from the incinerated rubble; it stopped at 8:16, when the bomb exploded. The destructive force unleashed by the atomic bomb included not only the heat and blast of the explosion itself but also the deadly radiation that maimed and killed Japanese civilians for years afterward. National Archives.

fall apart. American mobilization for World War II disproved Hitler's arrogant prophecy, as Paul Tibbets's historic flight dramatized. At a cost of 405,399 American lives, the nation united with its allies to crush the Axis aggressors into unconditional surrender. Almost all Americans believed they had won a "good war" against totalitarian evil. The Allies saved Asia and Europe from enslavement and finally halted the Nazis' genocidal campaign against Jews and many others whom the Nazis considered inferior. To secure human rights and protect the world against future wars, the Roosevelt administration took the lead in creating the United Nations.

Wartime production lifted the nation out of the Great Depression. The gross national product soared to four times what it had been when Roosevelt became president in 1933. Jobs in defense industries eliminated chronic unemployment, provided wages for millions of women workers and African American migrants from southern farms, and boosted Americans' prosperity. Ahead stretched the challenge of maintaining that prosperity while reintegrating millions of uniformed men and women.

By the end of the war, the United States had emerged as a global superpower. Wartime mobilization made the American economy the strongest in the world, buttressed by the military clout of the nation's nuclear monopoly. Although the war left much of the world a rubble-strewn wasteland, the American mainland had enjoyed immunity from attack. The Japanese occupation of China had left 50 million people without homes and millions more dead, maimed, and orphaned. The German offensive against the Soviet Union had killed more than 20 million Russian soldiers and civilians. Germany and Japan lay in ruins, their economies and societies as shattered as their military forces. But in the gruesome balance sheet of war, the Axis powers had inflicted far more grief, misery, and destruction on the global victims of their aggression than they had suffered in return.

As the dominant Western nation in the postwar world, the United States asserted its leadership in the reconstruction of Europe while occupying Japan and overseeing its economic and political recovery. America soon confronted new challenges in the tense aftermath of the war, as the Soviets seized political control of eastern Europe, a Communist revolution swept China, and national liberation movements emerged in the colonial empires of Britain and France. The forces unleashed by World War II would shape the United States and the rest of the world for decades to come. Before the ashes of World War II had cooled, America's wartime alliance with the Soviet Union fractured, igniting a Cold War between the superpowers. To resist global communism, the United States became, in effect, the policeman of the free world, repudiating the pre–World War II legacy of isolationism.

▶ Selected Bibliography

General Works

Max Arthur, ed., *Forgotten Voices of the Second World War: A New History of World War Two in the Words of the Men and Women Who Were There* (2004).
Michael Beschloss, *The Conquerors: Roosevelt, Truman, and the Destruction of Hitler's Germany, 1941–1945* (2002).
Richard Evans, *The Third Reich at War* (2010).
Thomas Fleming, *The New Dealers' War: Franklin D. Roosevelt and the War within World War II* (2001).
Martin Folly, *The U.S. and World War II: The Awakening Giant* (2002).
Peter Fritzsche, *Life and Death in the Third Reich* (2009).
David M. Kennedy, *Freedom from Fear: The American People in Depression and War, 1929–1945* (1999).
Mark Mazower, *Hitler's Empire: How the Nazis Ruled Europe* (2008).
Timothy Snyder, *Bloodlands: Europe between Hitler and Stalin* (2010).
Paul W. Tibbets Jr., *The Tibbets Story* (1978).
John Toland, *The Rising Sun: The Decline and Fall of the Japanese Empire, 1936–1945* (2001).
Adam Tooze, *The Wages of Destruction: The Making and Breaking of the Nazi Economy* (2006).

Foreign Policy

Tokomo Akami, *Internationalizing the Pacific: The U.S., Japan, and the Institute of Pacific Relations in War and Peace, 1919–1945* (2002).
Elizabeth Borgwardt, *A New Deal for the World: America's Vision for Human Rights* (2005).
Tsuyoshi Hasegawa, *Racing the Enemy: Stalin, Truman, and the Surrender of Japan* (2005).
J. Robert Moskin, *Mr. Truman's War: The Final Victories of World War II and the Birth of the Postwar World* (2002).

David Reynolds, *From Munich to Pearl Harbor: Roosevelt's America and the Origins of the Second World War* (2001).
Gaddis Smith, *American Diplomacy during the Second World War, 1941–1945* (1985).

Mobilization and the Home Front

Gerald Astor, *The Right to Fight: A History of African Americans in the Military* (1998).
Jeffrey F. Burton et al., *Confinement and Ethnicity: An Overview of World War II Japanese American Relocation Sites* (2002).
Stephanie A. Carpenter, *On the Farm Front: The Women's Land Army in World War II* (2003).
Mark Jonathan Harris, Franklin D. Mitchell, and Steve J. Schechter, *The Home Front: America during World War II* (1985).
Susan Hartmann, *The Home Front and Beyond: American Women in the 1940s* (1982).
John W. Jeffries, *Wartime America: The World War II Home Front* (1996).
Christopher Moore, *Fighting for America: Black Soldiers — The Unsung Heroes of World War II* (2005).
Wendy Ng, *Japanese American Internment during World War II* (2002).

Military Events

Rick Atkinson, *The Day of Battle: The War in Sicily and Italy, 1943–1944* (2008).
Antony Beevor, *D-Day: The Battle for Normandy* (2009).
John Dower, *War without Mercy: Race and Power in the Pacific War* (1986).
Max Hastings, *Overlord: D-Day and the Battle for Normandy* (2006).
Gerald F. Linderman, *The World within War: America's Combat Experience in World War II* (1997).
Peter Novick, *The Holocaust in American Life* (1999).
Richard Overy, *Why the Allies Won* (1996).
Peter Schrijvers, *The GI War against Japan: American Soldiers in Asia and the Pacific during World War II* (2002).
Thomas W. Zeiler, *Unconditional Defeat: Japan, America, and the End of World War II* (2004).

▶ FOR MORE BOOKS ABOUT TOPICS IN THIS CHAPTER, see the Online Bibliography at **bedfordstmartins.com/roark**.

▶ FOR ADDITIONAL PRIMARY SOURCES FROM THIS PERIOD, see Michael Johnson, ed., *Reading the American Past*, Fifth Edition.

▶ FOR WEB SITES, IMAGES, AND DOCUMENTS RELATED TO TOPICS AND PLACES IN THIS CHAPTER, visit Make History at **bedfordstmartins.com/roark**.

Reviewing Chapter 25

KEY TERMS

Explain each term's significance.

Peacetime Dilemmas
Benito Mussolini (p. 825)
Adolf Hitler (p. 825)
good neighbor policy (p. 825)
Jiang Jieshi (Chiang Kai-shek) (p. 826)
neutrality acts (p. 826)
Spanish civil war (p. 827)

The Onset of War
appeasement (p. 828)
Joseph Stalin (p. 829)
Winston Churchill (p. 829)
Battle of Britain (p. 830)
Lend-Lease Act (p. 831)
Atlantic Charter (p. 831)
Pearl Harbor (p. 833)

Mobilizing for War
internment camps (p. 834)
Selective Service Act (p. 835)
War Production Board (p. 838)

Fighting Back
Douglas MacArthur (p. 839)
Chester W. Nimitz (p. 839)
Battle of Midway (p. 840)
Dwight D. Eisenhower (p. 842)
George Patton (p. 842)

The Wartime Home Front
Rosie the Riveter (p. 843)
Double V campaign (p. 844)
A. Philip Randolph (p. 844)
Committee on Fair Employment
  Practices (p. 845)
GI Bill of Rights (p. 846)
Harry S. Truman (p. 847)
Holocaust (p. 848)

Toward Unconditional Surrender
Stalingrad (p. 849)
D Day (p. 849)
Yalta Conference (p. 851)
United Nations (UN) (p. 851)
Battle of Leyte Gulf (p. 853)
Manhattan Project (p. 856)
Hiroshima (p. 857)
Nagasaki (p. 857)

REVIEW QUESTIONS

Use key terms and dates to support your answer.

1. Why did isolationism during the 1930s concern Roosevelt? (pp. 825–827)

2. How did Roosevelt attempt to balance American isolationism with the increasingly ominous international scene of the late 1930s? (pp. 827–833)

3. How did the Roosevelt administration mobilize the human and industrial resources necessary to fight a two-front war? (pp. 833–838)

4. How did the United States seek to counter the Japanese in the Pacific and the Germans in Europe? (pp. 838–843)

5. How did the war influence American society? (pp. 843–848)

6. Why did Truman elect to use the atomic bomb against Japan? (pp. 849–857)

MAKING CONNECTIONS

Draw on key terms, the timeline, and review questions.

1. Did isolationism bolster or undermine national security and national economic interests? Discuss Roosevelt's evolving answer to this question as revealed in his administration's policies toward Europe. In your answer, consider how other constraints (such as politics, history, and ethics) affected administration policies.

2. World War II brought new prosperity to many Americans. Who benefited most from the wartime economy? What financial limitations did various members of society face, and why?

3. Japan's attack on Pearl Harbor plunged the United States into war with the Axis powers. How did the United States recover from this attack to play a decisive role in the Allies' victory? Discuss three American military or diplomatic actions and their contribution to the defeat of the Axis powers.

4. As the United States battled racist regimes abroad, the realities of discrimination at home came sharply into focus. How did minorities' contributions to the war effort as soldiers and laborers draw attention to these problems? What were the political implications of these developments? In your answer, consider both grassroots political action and federal policy.

LINKING TO THE PAST

Link events in this chapter to earlier events.

1. How did America's involvement in World War II differ from its participation in World War I? Consider diplomacy, allies and enemies, wartime military and economic policies, and social and cultural changes. (See chapter 22.)

2. Why did World War II succeed in creating the full economic recovery that remained elusive during the New Deal? Consider specifically the scope and limits of New Deal economic reforms and how they changed, if at all, during World War II. (See chapter 24.)

▶ FOR PRACTICE QUIZZES AND OTHER STUDY TOOLS, visit the Online Study Guide at bedfordstmartins.com/roark.

TIMELINE 1935–1945

1935–1937	• Congress passes neutrality acts.
1936	• Nazi Germany occupies Rhineland.
	• Italian armies conquer Ethiopia.
	• Spanish civil war begins.
1937	• Japanese troops capture Nanjing.
	• Roosevelt introduces his quarantine policy.
1938	• Hitler annexes Austria.
1939	• German troops occupy Czechoslovakia.
	• Nazi-Soviet nonaggression pact.
	• **September 1.** Germany's attack on Poland begins World War II.
1940	• Germany invades Denmark, Norway, France, Belgium, Luxembourg, and the Netherlands.
	• British and French evacuate from Dunkirk.
	• Vichy government installed in France.
	• Battle of Britain.
	• Tripartite Pact signed by Japan, Germany, and Italy.
1941	• Lend-Lease Act.
	• **June.** Germany invades Soviet Union.
	• **August.** Atlantic Charter issued.
	• **December 7.** Japanese attack Pearl Harbor.
1942	• Roosevelt authorizes internment of Japanese Americans.
	• Japan captures Philippines.
	• Congress of Racial Equality founded.
	• Battles of Coral Sea and Midway.
	• Roosevelt authorizes Manhattan Project.
	• **November.** U.S. forces invade North Africa.
1943	• Allied leaders demand unconditional surrender of Axis powers.
	• Race riots in 47 cities.
	• U.S. and British forces invade Sicily.
1944	• **June 6.** D Day.
1945	• **February.** Yalta Conference.
	• **April 12.** Roosevelt dies; Vice President Harry Truman becomes president.
	• **May 7.** Germany surrenders.
	• **July.** United States joins United Nations.
	• **August 6, 9.** United States drops atomic bombs on Hiroshima and Nagasaki.
	• **August 14.** Japan surrenders, ending World War II.

IS THIS TOMORROW

AMERICA UNDER COMMUNISM!

COLD WAR COMIC BOOK

In August 1945, Americans all over the world celebrated the end of World War II, as did these servicemen and -women stationed in London, shown in the background photo. Very quickly, however, a new threat emerged. Fear of communism dominated much of postwar American life and politics, even invading popular culture. Four million copies of this comic book, published by a religious organization in 1947, painted a terrifying picture of what would happen to Americans if the Soviets took over the country. Such takeover stories appeared in movies, cartoons, and magazines as well as in other comic books.

Comic book: Collection of Charles H. Christensen; background: National Archives.

26

Cold War Politics in the Truman Years
1945–1953

HEADS TURNED WHEN CONGRESSWOMAN HELEN GAHAGAN DOUGLAS walked through the U.S. Capitol. When she served there from 1945 to 1951, she had no more than 10 female colleagues in the 435-member House of Representatives. Not only did she stand out as a woman in a thoroughly male institution, but she also drew attention as a strikingly attractive former Broadway star and opera singer. She served in Congress when the fate of the New Deal was up for grabs and the nation charted a dramatic new course in foreign policy.

Born in 1900, Helen Gahagan grew up in Brooklyn, New York. Drawn to the theater as a child, she defied her father and left Barnard College for the stage after her sophomore year. She quickly won fame on Broadway, starring in show after show until she fell in love with one of her leading men, Melvyn Douglas. They married in 1931, and she followed him to Hollywood, where he hoped to advance his movie career. During the 1930s, she bore two children and continued to appear onstage, but her career was on the wane.

Helen Gahagan Douglas admired Franklin D. Roosevelt's leadership during the depression, and both she and her husband were drawn into Hollywood's liberal political circles. The Douglases were shaken by the anti-Semitism and militarism that they witnessed on a visit to Germany in 1937, and they subsequently joined the Anti-Nazi League in California. But it was the plight of poor migrant farmworkers moving to California from Oklahoma and other states that pushed Helen Douglas into politics. Visiting migrant camps, she saw "faces stamped with poverty and despair," a "human calamity" that prompted her to head the John Steinbeck Committee to Aid Migratory Workers.

Douglas's work on behalf of migrant farmworkers connected her to the White House. She testified before Congress and became a friend of Eleanor Roosevelt and a campaigner for the president in 1940. In California, she rose fast in party politics, becoming vice chair of the state Democratic Party and head of the Women's Division. In 1944, she won election to Congress, representing not the posh Hollywood district where she lived, but the multiracial population of the Fourteenth Congressional District in downtown Los Angeles, which cemented her dedication to progressive politics.

Like many liberals devoted to Roosevelt, Douglas was devastated by his death and unsure of his successor, Harry S. Truman. "Who was Harry Truman anyway?" she asked. A compromise choice for the vice presidency, this "accidental president" lacked the charisma and political skills with which Roosevelt had transformed foreign and domestic policy, won four presidential elections, and forged a Democratic Party coalition that dominated national politics. Truman faced a resurgent Republican Party, which had gained strength in Congress, as well as revolts from within his own party. Besides confronting domestic problems that the New Deal had not solved — how to avoid another depression without the war to fuel the economy — Truman faced new international challenges that threatened to undermine the nation's security.

By 1947, a new term described the intense rivalry that had emerged between the United States and the Soviet Union: Cold War. Truman and his advisers became convinced that the Soviet Union posed a major threat to the United States, and they gradually shaped a policy to contain Soviet power wherever it threatened to spread. As a member of the House Foreign Affairs Committee, Douglas urged cooperation with the Soviet Union, and she initially opposed aid to Greece and Turkey, the first step in the new containment policy. Yet thereafter, Douglas was Truman's loyal ally, supporting the Marshall Plan, the creation of the North Atlantic Treaty Organization, and the war in Korea. The containment policy achieved its goals in Europe, but communism spread in Asia, and at home a wave of anti-Communist hysteria — a second Red scare — harmed many Americans and stifled dissent and debate.

Douglas's earlier links with leftist groups and her advocacy of civil rights, women's rights, and social welfare programs made her and other liberals easy targets for conservative politicians seeking to capitalize on anti-Communist fervor. When she ran for the U.S. Senate in 1950, she faced Republican Richard M. Nixon, who had gained national attention as a member of the House Un-American Activities Committee, which sought to expose Communists in government. Nixon's campaign labeled Douglas as "pink right down to her underwear" and telephoned thousands of homes with the anonymous message, "I think you should know Helen Douglas is a Communist." Nixon won a decisive victory but throughout his life carried the appellation Douglas gave him, "Tricky Dick." Douglas's political career ended in defeat, just as much of Truman's domestic agenda fell victim to the Red scare.

Helen Gahagan Douglas at the Democratic National Convention
Long accustomed as an actress to appearing before an audience, the congresswoman from California was a popular campaigner for the Democrats and a featured speaker at Democratic National Conventions. Her appeal, shown in this photo from the 1948 convention, sparked interest in her for higher office. *The Washington Post* called it the "first genuine boom in history for a woman for vice-president," but she made it clear that she was not in the running. © Bettmann/Corbis.

▶ From the Grand Alliance to Containment

With Japan's surrender in August 1945, Americans besieged the government for the return of their loved ones. Baby booties arrived at the White House with a note, "Please send my daddy home." Americans wanted to dismantle the large military establishment and expected the Allies, led by the United States and working within the United Nations, to cooperate in the management of international peace. Postwar realities quickly dashed these hopes. New threats arose as the wartime alliance forged by the United States, Great Britain, and the Soviet Union crumbled, and the United States began to focus on strategies for containing the spread of Soviet power around the globe.

The Cold War Begins

"The guys who came out of World War II were idealistic," reported Harold Russell, a young paratrooper who had lost both hands in a training accident. "We felt the day had come when the wars were all over." Public opinion polls echoed the veterans' confidence in the promise of peace. But these hopes were quickly dashed. Once the Allies had overcome a common enemy, the prewar mistrust and antagonism between the Soviet Union and the West resurfaced over their very different visions of the postwar world.

The Western Allies' delay in opening a second front in Western Europe aroused Soviet suspicions during the war. The Soviet Union made supreme wartime sacrifices, losing more than twenty million citizens and vast portions of its agricultural and industrial capacity. Soviet leader **Joseph Stalin** wanted to make Germany pay for Soviet economic reconstruction and to expand Soviet influence in the world. Above all, he wanted friendly governments on the Soviet Union's borders in Eastern Europe, especially in Poland, through which German troops had marched to attack Russia twice in the past twenty-five years. A ruthless dictator, Stalin also wanted to maintain his own power.

In contrast to the Soviet devastation, enemy fire had never touched the mainland of the United States, and its 405,000 dead amounted to just 2 percent of the Soviet loss. With a vastly expanded economy and a monopoly on atomic weapons, the United States was the most powerful nation on the planet. That sheer power, along with U.S. economic interests, policymakers' views about how the recent war might have been avoided, and a belief in the superiority of American institutions and intentions, all affected how American leaders approached the Soviet Union.

Fearing a return of the depression, U.S. officials believed that a healthy economy depended on opportunities abroad. American companies needed access to raw materials, markets for their goods, and security for their investments overseas. These needs could be met best in countries with similar economic and political systems, not in those where government controls interfered with the free flow of products and dollars. As President **Harry S. Truman** put it in 1947, "The American system can survive in America only if it becomes a world system." Yet leaders and citizens alike regarded their foreign policy not as a self-interested campaign to guarantee economic interests, but as the means to preserve national security and bring freedom, democracy, and capitalism to the rest of the world. Laura Briggs, a woman from Jerome, Idaho, spoke for many Americans who believed "it was our destiny to prove that we were the children of God and that our way was right for the world."

> "The American system can survive in America only if it becomes a world system."
> — President HARRY S. TRUMAN

Recent history also shaped postwar foreign policy. Americans believed that World War II might have been avoided had Britain and France resisted rather than appeased Hitler's initial aggression. Navy Secretary James V. Forrestal argued against trying to "buy [the Soviets'] understanding and sympathy. We tried that once with Hitler." This "appeasement" analogy would be invoked repeatedly when the United States faced challenges to the international status quo.

The man with ultimate responsibility for U.S. policy was a keen student of history but came to the White House with little international experience. Harry S. Truman anticipated Soviet-American cooperation, as long as the Soviet Union conformed to U.S. plans for the postwar world and restrained its expansionist impulses. Proud of his ability to make quick decisions, Truman determined to be firm with the Soviets, knowing well that America's nuclear monopoly gave him the upper hand.

Soviet and American interests clashed first in Eastern Europe. Stalin insisted that the Allies' wartime agreements gave him a free hand in the countries defeated or liberated by the Red Army, just as the United States was unilaterally

Joseph Stalin: From Ally to Enemy
These two portrayals indicate how quickly the World War II alliance disintegrated into the Cold War. The photograph on the left, from a 1944 issue of the popular magazine *Look*, shows Stalin with two adoring schoolchildren. Only four years later, in 1948, *Look* published Stalin's life story, framing his photo with communism's emblem, the hammer and sickle. The 1944 piece called Stalin a "man of indomitable will and extraordinary mental capacity [and a] lover of literature." The 1948 article depicted him as a "small man with drooping shoulders [who] tyrannizes one-fifth of the world." What do these two items suggest about the role of the press in American society? The Michael Barson Collection/Past Perfect.

reconstructing governments in Italy and Japan. The Soviet dictator used harsh methods to install Communist governments in neighboring Poland and Bulgaria. Elsewhere, the Soviets initially tolerated non-Communist governments in Hungary and Czechoslovakia. In the spring of 1946, Stalin responded to pressure from the West and removed troops from Iran on the Soviet Union's southwest border, allowing U.S. access to the rich oil fields there.

Stalin considered U.S. officials hypocritical in demanding democratic elections in Eastern Europe while supporting dictatorships friendly to U.S. interests in Latin America. The United States clung to its sphere of influence while opposing Soviet efforts to create its own. But the Western Allies were unwilling to match tough words with military force against the largest army in the world. They issued sharp protests but failed to prevent the Soviet Union from establishing satellite countries throughout Eastern Europe.

In 1946, the wartime Allies contended over Germany's future. Both sides wanted to demilitarize Germany, but U.S. policymakers sought rapid industrial revival there to foster European economic recovery and thus America's own long-term prosperity. By contrast, the Soviet Union wanted Germany weak both militarily and economically, and Stalin demanded heavy reparations from Germany to help rebuild the devastated Soviet economy. Unable to settle their differences, the Allies divided Germany. The Soviet Union installed a puppet Communist government in the eastern section, and Britain, France, and the United States began to unify their occupation zones, a process that eventually established the Federal Republic of Germany — West Germany — in 1949 (Map 26.1).

The war of words escalated early in 1946. Boasting of the superiority of the Soviet system, Stalin told a Moscow audience in February that capitalism inevitably produced war. One month later, Truman accompanied Winston Churchill to Westminster College in Fulton, Missouri, where the former prime minister denounced Soviet interference in Eastern and central Europe. "From Stettin in the Baltic to Trieste in the Adriatic, an **iron curtain** has descended across the Continent," Churchill said. (See "Documenting the American Promise," page 868.) Stalin saw Churchill's proposal for joint British-

MAP ACTIVITY

Map 26.1   The Division of Europe after World War II

The "iron curtain," a term coined by Winston Churchill to refer to the Soviet grip on Eastern and central Europe, divided the continent for nearly fifty years. Communist governments controlled the countries along the Soviet Union's western border. The only exception was Finland, which remained neutral.

READING THE MAP: Is the division of Europe between NATO, Communist, and neutral countries about equal? Why would the location of Berlin pose a problem for the Western allies?

CONNECTIONS: When was NATO founded, and what was its purpose? How did the postwar division of Europe compare with the wartime alliances?

American action to combat Soviet aggression as "a call to war against the USSR."

In February 1946, **George F. Kennan**, a career diplomat and expert on Russia, wrote a comprehensive rationale for hard-line foreign policy. Downplaying the influence of Communist ideology in Soviet policy, he instead stressed the Soviets' insecurity and Stalin's need to maintain authority at home. These factors, he believed, prompted Stalin to exaggerate threats from abroad and motivated the Soviet government to try to "fill every nook and cranny available to it in the basin of world power." Kennan believed that the Soviet Union would retreat from its expansionist efforts if the United States would respond with "unalterable counterforce." He predicted that this approach, which came to be called **containment**, would eventually end in "either the breakup or the gradual mellowing of Soviet power." Kennan later expressed dismay when his ideas were used to justify what he considered indiscriminate American interventions wherever

The Emerging Cold War

Although antagonism between the Soviet Union and the West stretched back to the Russian Revolution of 1917, the United States, the Soviet Union, Britain, and other powers had cooperated to win World War II. Early in 1946, however, Soviet and Western leaders publicly expressed distrust and attributed hostile motivations to each other. Within the United States, disagreement arose about how to deal with the Soviet Union.

DOCUMENT 1
Joseph Stalin Addresses a Rally in Moscow, February 9, 1946

In early 1946, Premier Joseph Stalin called on the Soviet people to support his program for economic development. Although Stalin did not address Cold War issues, leaders in the West viewed his comments about communism and capitalism and his boasts about the strength of the Red Army as a threat to peace.

The [Second World War] arose as the inevitable result of the development of the world economic and political forces on the basis of monopoly capitalism. . . .

. . . The uneven development of the capitalist countries leads in time to sharp disturbances in their relations, and the group of countries which consider themselves inadequately provided with raw materials and export markets try usually to change this situation and to change the position in their favor by means of armed force. As a result of these factors, the capitalist world is split into two hostile camps and war follows. . . . The Soviet social system has proved to be more capable of life and more stable than a non-Soviet social system. . . .

. . . The Red Army heroically withstood all the adversities of the war, routed completely the armies of our enemies and emerged victoriously from the war. This is recognized by everybody — friend and foe.

[Stalin talks about his new Five-Year Plan.] Apart from the fact that in the very near future the rationing system will be abolished, special attention will be focused on expanding the production of goods for mass consumption, on raising the standard of life of the working people by consistent and systematic reduction of the costs of all goods, and on wide-scale construction of all kinds of scientific research institutes to enable science to develop its forces. I have no doubt that if we render the necessary assistance to our scientists they will be able not only to overtake but also in the very near future to surpass the achievements of science outside the boundaries of our country.

SOURCE: Excerpts from Joseph Stalin, *Vital Speeches of the Day*, February 9, 1946.

DOCUMENT 2
Winston Churchill Delivers His "Iron Curtain" Speech at Westminster College in Fulton, Missouri, March 5, 1946

With Truman sitting on the podium, Winston Churchill, former prime minister of Great Britain, assessed Soviet actions in harsh terms. In response, Stalin equated Churchill with Hitler, as a "firebrand of war."

The United States stands at this time at the pinnacle of world power. It is a solemn moment for the American democracy. With primacy in power is also joined an awe-inspiring accountability to the future. [Churchill then speaks of the need to support the United Nations.]

It would nevertheless be wrong and imprudent to intrust the secret knowledge or experience of the atomic bomb, which the United States, Great Britain and Canada now share, to the world organization [the United Nations], while it is still in its infancy. It would be criminal madness to cast it adrift in this still agitated and ununited world. . . .

. . . I have a strong admiration and regard for the valiant Russian people and for my war-time comrade, Marshal Stalin. . . . We understand the Russians need to be secure on her western frontiers from all renewal of German aggression. . . . It is my duty, however, to place before you certain facts. . . .

From Stettin in the Baltic to Trieste in the Adriatic, an iron curtain has descended across the Continent. Behind that line lie all the capitals of the ancient states of central and eastern Europe. Warsaw, Berlin, Prague, Vienna,

Budapest, Belgrade, Bucharest and Sofia, all these famous cities and the populations around them lie in the Soviet sphere and all are subject in one form or another, not only to Soviet influence but to a very high and increasing measure of control from Moscow. . . . The Communist parties, which were very small in all these eastern states of Europe, have been raised to preeminence and power far beyond their numbers and are seeking everywhere to obtain totalitarian control. Police governments are prevailing in nearly every case. . . .

. . . In a great number of countries, far from the Russian frontiers and throughout the world, Communist fifth columns are established and work in complete unity and absolute obedience to the directions they receive from the Communist center.

I do not believe that Soviet Russia desires war. What they desire is the fruits of war and the indefinite expansion of their power and doctrines. . . . Our difficulties and dangers will not be removed by . . . mere waiting to see what happens; nor will they be relieved by a policy of appeasement. . . . I am convinced that there is nothing [the Russians] admire so much as strength, and there is nothing for which they have less respect than for military weakness.

SOURCE: Excerpts from Winston Churchill, *Vital Speeches of the Day*, March 5, 1946.

DOCUMENT 3
Henry A. Wallace Addresses an Election Rally at Madison Square Garden, New York, September 12, 1946

Throughout 1946, Henry A. Wallace, Truman's secretary of commerce and predecessor as vice president, urged the president to take a more conciliatory approach toward the Soviet Union, a position reflected in a speech Wallace gave to a rally of leftist and liberal groups in New York City. Truman believed that Wallace's words undermined his foreign policy and demanded Wallace's resignation.

We cannot rest in the assurance that we invented the atom bomb — and therefore that this agent of destruction will work best for us. He who trusts in the atom bomb will sooner or later perish by the atom bomb — or something worse. . . .

To achieve lasting peace, we must study in detail just how the Russian character was formed — by invasions of Tartars, Mongols, Germans, Poles, Swedes, and French; by the czarist rule based on ignorance, fear and force; by the intervention of the British, French and Americans in Russian affairs from 1919 to 1921; by the geography of the huge Russian land mass situated strategically between Europe and Asia; and by the vitality derived from the rich Russian soil and the strenuous Russian climate. Add to all this the tremendous emotional power which Marxism and Leninism gives to the Russian leaders — and then we can realize that we are reckoning with a force which cannot be handled successfully by a "Get tough with Russia" policy. "Getting tough" never bought anything real and lasting — whether for schoolyard bullies or businessmen or world powers. The tougher we get, the tougher the Russians will get. . . .

. . . We want cooperation. And I believe that we can get cooperation once Russia understands that our primary objective is neither saving the British Empire nor purchasing oil in the Near East with the lives of American soldiers. . . .

On our part we should recognize that we have no more business in the political affairs of Eastern Europe than Russia has in the political affairs of Latin America, Western Europe and the United States. . . . We have to recognize that the Balkans are closer to Russia than to us — and that Russia cannot permit either England or the United States to dominate the politics of that area. . . .

. . . Under friendly peaceful competition the Russian world and the American world will gradually become more alike. The Russians will be forced to grant more and more of the personal freedoms; and we shall become more and more absorbed with the problems of social-economic justice.

SOURCE: Excerpts from Henry A. Wallace, *Vital Speeches of the Day*, September 12, 1946. Reprinted with permission.

Questions for Analysis and Debate

1. What lessons did these three leaders draw from World War II? What did they see as the most critical steps to preventing another war?

2. What differences did these men see between the political and economic systems of the Soviet Union and those of the United States and Western Europe? How do their predictions about these systems differ?

3. What motives did these three men ascribe to Soviet actions? How do Churchill's and Wallace's proposals for the Western response to the Soviet Union differ?

4. Which leader do you think was most optimistic about the prospects for good relationships between Russia and the West? Which was most correct? Why?

communism seemed likely to arise. Nonetheless, his analysis marked a critical turning point in the development of the **Cold War**, providing a compelling rationale for wielding U.S. power throughout the world.

Not all public figures accepted the toughening line. In September 1946, Secretary of Commerce Henry A. Wallace urged greater understanding of the Soviets' concerns about their nation's security, insisting that "we have no more business in the political affairs of Eastern Europe than Russia has in the political affairs of Latin America." (See "Documenting the American Promise," page 868.) State Department officials were furious at this challenge to the hardening of U.S. policy, and Truman fired Wallace.

The Truman Doctrine and the Marshall Plan

In 1947, the United States began to implement the doctrine of containment that would guide foreign policy for the next four decades. It was not an easy transition; Americans approved taking a hard line against the Soviet Union, but they wanted to keep their soldiers and tax dollars at home. In addition to selling containment to the public, Truman had to gain the support of a Republican-controlled Congress, which included a forceful bloc opposed to a strong U.S. presence in Europe.

Crises in two Mediterranean countries triggered the implementation of containment. In February 1947, Britain informed the United States that its crippled economy could no longer sustain military assistance either to Greece, where the autocratic government faced a leftist uprising, or to Turkey, which was trying to resist Soviet pressures. Truman promptly sought congressional authority to send the two countries military and economic missions, along with $400 million in aid. Meeting with congressional leaders, Undersecretary of State Dean Acheson predicted that if Greece and Turkey fell, communism would soon consume three-fourths of the world. After a stunned silence, Michigan senator Arthur Vandenberg, the Republican foreign policy leader and a recent convert from isolationism, warned that to get approval, Truman would have to "scare hell out of the country."

Truman did just that. Outlining what would later be called the "domino theory," he warned that if Greece fell to the rebels, "confusion and disorder might well spread throughout the entire Middle East" and then create instability in Europe.

Failure to act, he said, "may endanger the peace of the world — and shall surely endanger the welfare of the nation." According to what came to be called the **Truman Doctrine**, the United States would not only resist Soviet military power but also "support free peoples who are resisting attempted subjugation by armed minorities or by outside pressures." The president failed to convince Helen Gahagan Douglas and some of her colleagues in Congress, who wanted the United States to work through the United Nations before acting unilaterally and who opposed propping up the authoritarian Greek government. But the administration won the day, setting a precedent for forty years of Cold War interventions that would aid any kind of government if the only alternative appeared to be communism. Said one World War II veteran in response to the Truman Doctrine, "I told my wife to dust off my uniform."

A much larger assistance program for Europe followed aid to Greece and Turkey. In May 1947, Acheson described a war-ravaged Western Europe, with "factories destroyed, fields impoverished, transportation systems wrecked, populations scattered and on the borderline of starvation." American citizens were sending generous amounts of private aid, but most Europeans were surviving on diets of 1,500 calories a day. Acheson insisted that Europe needed large-scale assistance to keep desperate citizens from turning to socialism or communism.

When British Foreign Secretary Ernest Bevin heard Secretary of State George C. Marshall propose the European Recovery Program, Bevin compared it to "a lifeline to a sinking man." Congress approved the measure, which came to be called the **Marshall Plan**, in March 1948, and over the next five years the United States spent $13 billion ($117 billion in 2010 dollars) to restore the economies of sixteen Western European nations. Marshall invited all European nations and the Soviet Union to cooperate in a request for aid, but as administration officials expected, the Soviets objected to the American terms of free trade and financial disclosure and ordered their Eastern European satellites likewise to reject the offer.

Humanitarian impulses as well as the goal of keeping Western Europe free of communism drove the adoption of this enormous aid program, one of the outstanding achievements of U.S. postwar foreign policy. But the Marshall Plan also helped boost the U.S. economy because the participating European nations spent most of

Marshall Plan Bread for Greek Children
Greece was one of sixteen European nations that participated in the European Recovery Program. In this photograph taken in 1949, Greek children receive loaves of bread made from the first shipment of Marshall Plan flour from the United States. © Bettmann/Corbis.

the dollars to buy American products and Europe's economic recovery created new markets and opportunities for American investment. In addition, by insisting that the recipient nations work together, the Marshall Plan marked the first step toward the European Union.

While Congress had been debating the Marshall Plan, in February 1948 the Soviets staged a brutal coup and installed a Communist regime in Czechoslovakia, the last democracy left in Eastern Europe. Next, Stalin threatened Western access to Berlin. That former capital of Germany lay within Soviet-controlled East Germany, but all four Allies jointly occupied Berlin, dividing it into separate administrative units. As the Western Allies moved to organize West Germany as a separate nation, the Soviets retaliated by blocking roads and rail lines between West Germany and the Western-held sections of Berlin, cutting off food, fuel, and other essentials to two million inhabitants.

Berlin Divided, 1948

French sector
Soviet sector
British sector
Brandenburg Gate
West Berlin
East Berlin
American sector
Potsdam
EAST GERMANY

"We stay in Berlin, period," Truman vowed. To avoid a confrontation with Soviet troops, for nearly a year U.S. and British pilots airlifted 2.3 million tons of goods to sustain the West Berliners. Stalin hesitated to shoot down these cargo planes, and in 1949 he lifted the blockade. The city was then divided into East Berlin, under Soviet control, and West Berlin, which became part of West Germany.

For many Americans, the **Berlin airlift** confirmed the wisdom of containment: When challenged, the Russians backed down, as George Kennan had predicted.

Building a National Security State

During the Truman years, advocates of the new containment policy fashioned a six-pronged defense strategy: (1) development of atomic weapons, (2) strengthening of traditional military power, (3) military alliances with other nations,

The Berlin Airlift

After the Soviet Union blockaded land routes into West Berlin in June 1948, the Western allies used airplanes to deliver food, fuel, and other necessities to Germans living there. At the peak of the airlift, U.S. or British planes landed every three minutes twenty-four hours a day. These children may have been watching for Air Force pilot Gail S. Halvorsen, who, after meeting hungry schoolchildren, began to drop candy and gum as his plane approached the landing strip. The vulnerability of Germans like these helped to ease hostile feelings that Americans and other Europeans felt toward their former enemies. Photo: Charles Fenno Jacobs/Hulton Archive/Getty Images; candy bar: Haraz N. Ghanbari.

(4) military and economic aid to friendly nations, (5) an espionage network and secret means to subvert Communist expansion, and (6) a propaganda offensive to win popular admiration for the United States around the world.

In September 1949, the United States lost its nuclear monopoly when the Soviet Union detonated its own atomic bomb. To keep the United States ahead, in January 1950 Truman approved the development of a **hydrogen bomb**, equivalent to five hundred atomic bombs. He rejected the counterarguments of several scientists who had worked on the atomic bomb and of George Kennan, who warned of an endless arms race. The "super bomb" was ready by 1954, but the U.S. advantage was brief. In November 1955, the Soviets exploded their own hydrogen bomb.

From the 1950s through the 1980s, deterrence formed the basis of American nuclear strategy. To deter the Soviet Union from attacking, the United States strove to maintain a nuclear force more powerful than the Soviets'. Because the Russians pursued a similar policy, the superpowers became locked in an ever-escalating nuclear weapons race. Albert Einstein, whose mathematical discoveries had laid the founda-

tions for nuclear weapons, commented grimly on the enormous destructive force the superpowers now possessed. The war that came after World War III, he warned, would "be fought with sticks and stones."

Implementing the second component of its containment strategy, the United States beefed up its conventional military power to deter Soviet threats that might not warrant nuclear retaliation. The National Security Act of 1947 streamlined defense planning by uniting the military branches under a single secretary of defense and creating the National Security Council (NSC) to advise the president. During the Berlin crisis in 1948, Congress hiked military appropriations and enacted a peacetime draft. In addition, Congress granted permanent status to the women's military branches, though it limited their numbers and rank and banned them from combat. General Dwight D. Eisenhower had recognized the contributions women could make in such traditionally female jobs as office work and nursing, and he assured Congress that "after an enlistment or two women will ordinarily — and thank God — they will get married." With 1.5 million men and women in uniform in 1950, the military strength of the United States had

Cold War Spying
"Intelligence," the gathering of information about the capabilities and intentions of the enemy, is as old as human warfare, but it took on new importance with the onset of the Cold War. Created in 1947, the Central Intelligence Agency (CIA) became an important Cold War tool. While much of the intelligence work took place in Washington, where analysts combed through Communist newspapers, official reports, and speeches, secret agents operating behind the iron curtain gathered information with bugs and devices such as these cameras hidden in cigarette packs. Spying soon gained a prominent place in popular culture, most notably in more than a dozen movies featuring James Bond, British agent 007. Jack Naylor Collection/Picture Research Consultants & Archives.

quadrupled since the 1930s, and defense expenditures claimed one-third of the federal budget.

Collective security, the third prong of containment strategy, marked a sharp reversal of the nation's traditional foreign policy. In 1949, the United States joined Canada and Western European nations in its first peacetime military alliance, the **North Atlantic Treaty Organization (NATO)**, designed to counter a Soviet threat to Western Europe (see Map 26.1). For the first time in its history, the United States pledged to go to war if one of its allies was attacked.

The fourth element of defense strategy involved foreign assistance programs to strengthen friendly countries, such as aid to Greece and Turkey and the Marshall Plan. In addition, in 1949 Congress approved $1 billion of military aid to its NATO allies, and the government began economic assistance to nations in other parts of the world.

The fifth ingredient of containment improved the government's espionage capacities and ability to thwart communism through covert activities. The National Security Act of 1947 created the **Central Intelligence Agency (CIA)** not only to gather information but also to perform any activities "related to intelligence affecting the national security" that the NSC might authorize. Such functions included propaganda, sabotage, economic warfare, and support for "anti-communist elements in threatened countries of the free world." In 1948, secret CIA operations helped defeat Italy's Communist Party. Subsequently, CIA agents would intervene even more actively, helping to topple legitimate foreign governments and violating the rights of U.S. citizens.

Finally, the U.S. government sought, through cultural exchanges and propaganda, to win "hearts and minds" throughout the world. The government expanded the Voice of America, created during World War II to broadcast U.S. propaganda abroad. In addition, the State Department sent books, exhibits, jazz musicians, and other performers to foreign countries as "cultural ambassadors."

By 1950, the United States had abandoned age-old tenets of foreign policy. Isolationism and neutrality had given way to a peacetime military alliance and efforts to control events far beyond U.S. borders. Short of war, the United States could not stop the descent of the iron curtain, but it aggressively and successfully promoted economic recovery and a military shield for the rest of Europe.

Superpower Rivalry around the Globe

Efforts to implement containment moved beyond Europe. In Africa, Asia, and the Middle East, World War II accelerated a tide of national liberation movements against war-weakened imperial powers. By 1960, forty countries, with more than a quarter of the world's people, had won

Louis Armstrong in Düsseldorf
As one of its Cold War weapons, the United States sent representatives of American culture abroad. Jazz was especially popular around the world, and the State Department sponsored tours by black jazz artists in part to counter the image of the United States as a racist nation. Louis Armstrong, the great trumpet player, singer, and jazz innovator, is shown here captivating a German crowd in 1952. Later, when Armstrong became disillusioned with President Eisenhower's failure to act vigorously on civil rights, he canceled a tour of the Soviet Union, explaining, "The people over there ask me what's wrong with my country, what am I supposed to say?" AP Photo.

mination gave way to American leaders' concern about the nature of the new governments supplanting the old empires. Policymakers wanted to preserve opportunities for American trade, and U.S. corporations coveted the vast oil reserves in the Middle East. The United States viewed its own Revolution as the best model for independence movements and expected newly emerging nations to create institutions in the American democratic and capitalist image.

Yet leaders of many liberation movements, impressed with Russia's rapid economic growth, adopted socialist or Communist ideas. Although few of these movements had formal ties with the Soviet Union, American leaders saw them as a threatening extension of Soviet power. Seeking to hold communism at bay by fostering economic development and political stability, the Truman administration initiated the Point IV Program in 1949, providing technical aid to developing nations.

Civil war raged in China, where the Communists, led by **Mao Zedong** (Mao Tse-tung), fought the official Nationalist government under Jiang Jieshi (Chiang Kai-shek) as it sought to recover from the Japanese occupation. While the Communists gained support among the peasants for their land reforms and valiant stand against the Japanese, Jiang's corrupt and incompetent government alienated much of the population. Failing to promote negotiations between Jiang and Mao, the United States provided almost $3 billion in aid to the Nationalists during the civil war. Yet, recognizing the ineptness of Jiang's government, Truman and his advisers refused to divert further resources from Europe to China.

In October 1949, Mao established the People's Republic of China (PRC), and the Nationalists fled to the island of Taiwan. Fearing a U.S.-supported invasion to recapture China for the Nationalists, Mao signed a mutual defense treaty with the Soviet Union in which each nation pledged to defend the other in case of attack. The United States refused to recognize the PRC, blocked its admission to the United Nations, and supported the Nationalist government in Taiwan. Only a massive U.S. military commitment could have stopped the Chinese Communists, yet some Republicans charged that Truman and "pro-Communists

their independence. These nations, along with Latin America, came to be referred to collectively as the third world, a term denoting countries outside the Western (first world) and Soviet (second world) orbits that had not yet developed industrial economies.

Like Woodrow Wilson during World War I, Roosevelt and Truman promoted the ideal of self-determination. The United States granted independence to the Philippines in 1946, applauded the British withdrawal from India, and encouraged France to give up its control of Indochina. At the same time, both the United States and the Soviet Union cultivated governments in emerging nations that were friendly to their own interests. As the Cold War intensified, however, the ideal of self-deter-

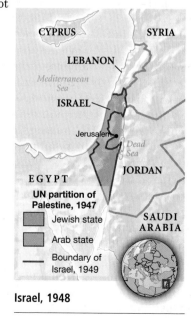

CYPRUS SYRIA
LEBANON
Mediterranean Sea
ISRAEL
Jerusalem
Dead Sea
JORDAN
EGYPT
UN partition of Palestine, 1947
☐ Jewish state
☐ Arab state
— Boundary of Israel, 1949
SAUDI ARABIA

Israel, 1948

Mao Zedong on the Way to Victory
During World War II, Mao Zedong, leader of China's Communist Party, mobilized peasants around his revolution by implementing land reform where the Communists had control and by fighting valiantly against the Japanese. By the end of 1944, when this photo of Mao addressing his followers was taken, the Communists had a military force of more than half a million and control of more than eighty million Chinese. © Bettmann/Corbis.

in the State Department" had "lost" China. China became a political albatross for the Democrats, who resolved never again to be vulnerable to charges of being soft on communism.

With China in turmoil, the administration reconsidered its plans for postwar Japan. U.S. policy shifted to helping Japan rapidly reindustrialize and secure access to natural resources and markets in Asia. In a short time, the Japanese economy was flourishing, and the official military occupation ended when the two nations signed a peace treaty and a mutual security pact in September 1951. Like West Germany, Japan now sat squarely within the American orbit, ready to serve as an economic hub in a vital area.

The one place where Cold War considerations did not control American policy was Palestine. In 1943, then-senator Harry Truman spoke passionately about Nazi Germany's annihilation of the Jews, asserting, "This is not a Jewish problem, it is an American problem — and we must . . . face it squarely and honorably." As president, he made good on his words. Jews had been migrating to Palestine, their biblical homeland, since the nineteenth century, resulting in tension and hostilities with the Palestinian Arabs. After World War II, as hundreds of thousands of European Jews sought refuge and the creation of a national homeland in Palestine, fighting escalated into brutal terrorism on both sides.

Truman's foreign policy experts sought American-Arab friendship as a barrier against Soviet influence in the Middle East and as a means to secure access to Arabian oil. Uncharacteristically defying his advisers, the president responded instead to pleas from Jewish organizations, his moral commitment to Holocaust survivors, and his interest in the American Jewish vote for the 1948 election. When Jews in Palestine declared the state of Israel in May 1948, Truman quickly recognized the new country and made its defense the cornerstone of U.S. policy in the Middle East.

REVIEW Why did relations between the United States and the Soviet Union deteriorate after World War II?

▶ Truman and the Fair Deal at Home

Referring to the Civil War general who coined the phrase "War is hell," Truman said in December 1945, "Sherman was wrong. I'm telling you I find peace is hell." Challenged by crises abroad, Truman also faced shortages, strikes, inflation, and other problems as the economy shifted to peacetime production. At the same time, he tried to expand New Deal reform with his own **Fair Deal** agenda of initiatives in civil rights, housing, education, and health care — efforts hindered by the wave of anti-Communist hysteria sweeping the country. In sharp contrast to his success with Congress in foreign policy, Truman achieved but a modest slice of his domestic agenda.

Reconverting to a Peacetime Economy

Despite scarcities and deprivations during World War II, most Americans had enjoyed a higher standard of living than ever before. Economic

Women's Role in Peacetime

Like many manufacturers forced to convert to war production during World War II, Proctor Electric Company, which had switched from making appliances to producing bomb fuses, cartridges, and airplane wing flaps, hoped to profit after the war from pent-up consumer demand. Even before the company had fully reconverted its plants, ads tempted consumers with products soon to come and asked them to be patient until Proctor could meet their needs, as this 1946 ad indicates. Why do you think a woman was featured in this ad? What message about women's employment during and after the war is conveyed here? Picture Research Consultants & Archives.

experts as well as ordinary citizens worried about sustaining that standard and providing jobs for millions of returning soldiers. Truman wasted no time unveiling his plan, asking Congress to enact a twenty-one-point program of social and economic reforms. He wanted to maintain the government's power to regulate the economy while it adjusted to peacetime production, and he sought government programs to provide basic essentials such as housing and health care to those in need, programs that had been on the drawing board during the New Deal. "Not even President Roosevelt ever asked for as much at one sitting," exploded Republican leader Joseph W. Martin Jr.

Congress approved one of Truman's key proposals — full-employment legislation — but even that was watered down. The Employment Act of 1946 invested the federal government with the responsibility "to promote maximum employ-

ment, production, and purchasing power," thereby formalizing what had been implicit in Roosevelt's antidepression measures — government's responsibility for maintaining a healthy economy. The law created the Council of Economic Advisors to assist the president, but it authorized no new powers to translate the government's obligation into effective action.

Inflation, not unemployment, turned out to be the most severe problem in the early postwar years. Consumers had $30 billion in wartime savings to spend, but shortages of meat, automobiles, housing, and other items persisted. Until industry could convert fully to civilian production and make more goods available, consumer demand would continue to drive up prices. With a basket of groceries on her arm to dramatize rising costs, Helen Gahagan Douglas urged Congress to support Truman's efforts to maintain price and rent controls. Those efforts fell, however, to pressures from business groups and others determined to trim government powers.

Labor relations were another thorn in Truman's side. Organized labor survived the war stronger than ever, its 14.5 million members making up 35 percent of the civilian workforce. Yet union members feared the erosion of wartime gains and launched an intense struggle to preserve them. Turning to the weapon they had set aside during the war, 5 million workers went out on strike in 1946, affecting nearly every major industry. Workers saw corporate executives profiting at their expense. Shortly before voting to strike, a former Marine and his coworkers calculated that a lavish party given by a company executive had cost more than they would earn in a whole year at the steel mill. "That sort of stuff made us realize, hell we had to bite the bullet. . . . The bosses sure didn't give a damn for us." Although most Americans approved of unions in principle, they became fed up with strikes, blamed unions for shortages and rising prices, and called for government restrictions on organized labor. When the wave of strikes subsided, workers had won wage increases of about 20 percent, but the loss of overtime pay along with rising prices left their purchasing power only slightly higher than in 1942.

Women workers fared even worse. Polls indicated that as many as 68 to 85 percent wanted to keep their wartime jobs, but most who remained in the workforce had to settle for relatively low-paying jobs in light industry or the service sector (Figure 26.1). Displaced from her shipyard work, Marie Schreiber took a cashier's job, lamenting, "You were back to women's wages, you know . . . practically in half." (See "Historical Question," page 878.) With the backing of women's organizations and union women, Congresswoman Douglas sponsored bills to require equal pay for equal work, to provide child care for employed mothers, and to create a government commission to study the status of women. But at a time when women were viewed primarily as wives and mothers and a strong current of opinion resisted further expansion of federal powers, these initiatives got nowhere.

By 1947, the economy had stabilized, avoiding the postwar depression that so many had feared. Wartime profits enabled businesses to expand. Consumers could now spend their wartime savings on houses, cars, and appliances that had lain beyond their reach during the depression and war. Defense spending and foreign aid that enabled war-stricken countries to purchase American products also stimulated the economy. A soaring birthrate further sustained consumer demand.

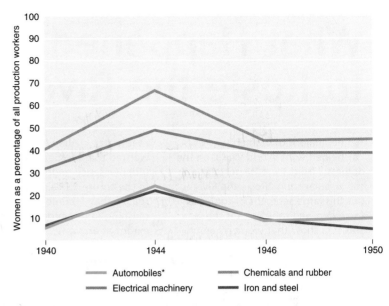

*During World War II, this industry did not produce cars, but rather military transportation such as jeeps, tanks, aircraft, etc.

FIGURE 26.1 Women Workers in Selected Industries, 1940–1950
Women demolished the idea that some jobs were "men's work" during World War II, but they failed to maintain their gains in the manufacturing sector after the war.

Veterans Go to College
So many World War II veterans wanted to use their GI benefits for higher education that colleges were overwhelmed. Many institutions had to turn away students, and they frequently limited the enrollments of women so that they could accommodate veterans. At the University of Iowa, where this photo was taken, veterans like these men comprised 60 percent of the student body. Veterans' organizations helped former GIs gain access to benefits with pamphlets like the one shown here. Photo: Margaret Bourke-White/Time Life Pictures /Getty Images; brochure: Minnesota Historical Society.

Although prosperity was far from universal, the United States entered into a remarkable economic boom that lasted through the 1960s (as discussed in chapter 27).

Another economic boost came from the only large welfare measure passed after the New Deal. The **Servicemen's Readjustment Act (GI Bill)**, enacted in 1944, offered 16 million veterans job training and education; unemployment compensation while they looked for jobs; and low-interest loans to purchase homes, farms, and small businesses. By 1948, some

What Happened to Rosie the Riveter?

The millions of women who helped fight World War II on the domestic front were immortalized in the popular song "Rosie the Riveter," but this large segment of the workforce declined rapidly after the war. Statistics show that women's employment fell by more than two million between 1945 and 1947. Gross statistics, however, do not reveal which women left the labor force and why, and they obscure the experiences of women who continued to work but in different jobs.

Undoubtedly, public officials and business and labor leaders expected women who had taken up men's work during the war to return to domestic life. With the shadow of depression-era unemployment still hovering, women were bombarded with the message that they should quit their jobs "for the sake of their homes as well as the labor situation." The company newspaper at Kaiser shipyards in the Pacific Northwest proclaimed in May 1945, "The Kitchen — Women's Big Post-War Goal." A General Electric ad predicted that women would welcome a return to "their old housekeeping routine" because GE intended to transform housework with new appliances. Some experts connected married women's employment to their husbands' ability to

readjust to civilian life. A psychiatrist warned that women's economic independence might "raise problems in the future," urging women to realize that "reunion means relinquishing [independence] — to some extent at any rate."

Many women gave up their wartime jobs eagerly. Skyrocketing marriage and birth rates reveal the attraction of domesticity to people compelled to postpone marriage and childbearing by depression and war. The accumulation of wartime savings along with veterans' benefits enabled most families to rely on a single wage earner. Moreover, the double burdens placed on married women and mothers who took wartime jobs provided another reason for women's voluntary withdrawal from the workforce.

Yet surveys reported that 75 percent of women in wartime jobs wanted — and usually needed — to keep working. As two women employed at a Ford plant put it, "Women didn't stop eating when the war stopped." Those who struggled to remain in the workforce experienced the most wrenching changes. The vast majority managed to find jobs; in fact, women's workforce participation began growing again in 1947 and equaled the wartime peak by 1950. But women lost

the traditionally male, higher-paying jobs in heavy industries such as steel and automobile production and were pushed back into the lower-paying light manufacturing and service industries that had customarily welcomed them.

Statistics tell part of the story of this displacement. Women virtually disappeared from shipbuilding, and their share of jobs in the auto industry fell from 25 percent in 1944 to 10 percent in 1950. In light manufacturing, such as the electrical goods industry, where women had claimed one-third of the prewar jobs, women maintained their numbers but were bumped down to lower-paying work. During the war, women had narrowed the wage gap between men and women, but in 1950 employed women earned only 53 percent of what men did.

How women felt about their displacement can be pieced together to some extent from what they said to reporters and oral history interviewers and what they wrote to government agencies and labor unions. "Women do not expect or want to hold jobs at the expense of returning soldiers," resolved the Women's Trade Union League. Tina Hill, a black worker laid off from North American Aircraft in Los Angeles, remembered, "I was just glad that the war was over . . . [and] my husband had a job." Nonetheless, after doing domestic work, she leaped at the chance when North American called her back: "Was I a happy soul!"

1.3 million veterans had bought houses with government loans. Helping 2.2 million ex-soldiers attend college, the subsidies sparked a boom in higher education. A drugstore clerk before his military service, Don Condren was able to get an engineering degree and buy his first house. "I think the GI Bill gave the whole country an upward boost economically," he said.

Condren overlooked the disparate ways in which the GI Bill operated. As wives and daughters of veterans, women did benefit indirectly from the GI subsidies. Yet because women had

filled just a small proportion of military slots during the war, most women did not qualify for the employment and educational preferences available to some 15 million men. As a result, while women's enrollments increased after the war, their share of college degrees plunged below the prewar level.

Like key New Deal programs such as unemployment insurance and aid to mothers with dependent children, GI programs were administered at the state and local levels, which especially in the South routinely discriminated

When management violated women's seniority rights by hiring nonveterans, some women protested bitterly. According to one automobile worker, "We have women laid off with seniority . . . and every day they hire in new men off the street. They hire men, they say, to do the heavy work. . . . During the war they didn't care what kind of work we did." When Ford laid off women with as much as twenty-seven years' seniority, 150 women picketed with signs that read, "The Hand That Rocks the Cradle Can Build Tractors, Too."

Protests from a minority of women workers could not save the jobs that the "Rosies" had held during the war. Despite women's often exemplary performance, most employers — and most Americans — still saw women and men as different species fit for different roles and deserving of different rewards. Labor unions paid lip service to representing all their members, but few gave high priority to protecting women's seniority rights. In the absence of any federal laws against sex discrimination or a feminist movement that could have given visibility and credibility to their claims for equal treatment, most Rosie the Riveters resigned themselves to "women's work."

Sisters under the apron—Yesterday's war worker becomes today's housewife.

What's Become of Rosie the Riveter?

Women's Postwar Future
This photograph headed a *New York Times Magazine* article in June 1946. The article discussed the needs of women workers, stressing their right to work and to receive equal pay, but it also assumed that women would all but vanish from heavy manufacturing. Ellen Kaiper Collection, Oakland.

Thinking about Evidence

1. What can statistics tell us about women's work after World War II? What can we learn about women's postwar employment experiences by examining individual women's statements, letters, and interviews?

2. What are the limitations of the types of sources mentioned in this feature? How does combining different types of sources help to overcome those limitations? What other kinds of sources might be useful?

3. Based on the evidence in this feature, for what reasons did women leave the labor force? For what reasons did they remain in it?

against African Americans. Southern universities remained segregated, and the small historically black colleges could not accommodate all who wanted to attend. Black veterans who sought jobs for which the military had trained them were shuttled into menial labor. One decorated veteran said that the GI Bill "draws no color line," yet "my color bars me from most decent jobs, and if, instead of accepting menial work, I collect my $20 a week readjustment allowance, I am classified as a 'lazy nigger.'" Thousands of black veterans did benefit from the GI Bill, but it did not help all ex-soldiers equally.

Blacks and Mexican Americans Push for Their Civil Rights

"I spent four years in the army to free a bunch of Frenchmen and Dutchmen," an African American corporal declared, "and I'm hanged if I'm going to let the Alabama version of the Germans kick me around when I get home." Black veterans as well as civilians resolved that the return to peace would not be a return to the racial injustices of prewar America. Their political clout had grown with the migration of two million African Americans to northern and western cities, where they could vote and participate in ongoing struggles to end discrimination in housing and education. Pursuing civil rights through the courts and Congress, the National Association for the Advancement of Colored People (NAACP) counted half a million members.

In the postwar years, individual African Americans broke through the color barrier, achieving several "firsts." Jackie Robinson integrated major league baseball, playing for the Brooklyn Dodgers and braving abuse from fans and players to win the Rookie of the Year Award in 1947. In 1950, Ralph J. Bunche received the Nobel Peace Prize for his United Nations work, and Gwendolyn Brooks won the Pulitzer Prize for poetry. Charlie "Bird" Parker, Ella Fitzgerald, and a host of other black musicians were hugely popular across racial lines.

Still, for most African Americans little had changed, especially in the South, where most blacks still lived and where violence greeted their attempts to assert their rights. Armed white men turned back Medgar Evers (who would become a key civil rights leader in the 1960s) and four other veterans trying to vote in Mississippi. A mob lynched Isaac Nixon for voting in Georgia, and an all-white jury acquitted the men accused of his murder. In the South, political leaders and local vigilantes routinely intimidated potential black voters with threats of violence and warnings that they could lose their livelihoods.

The Cold War heightened American leaders' sensitivity to racial issues, as the superpowers vied for the allegiance of newly independent nations with nonwhite populations. Soviet propaganda repeatedly highlighted racial injustice in the United States. Republican senator Henry Cabot Lodge called race relations "our Achilles' heel before the world," while Secretary of State Dean Acheson noted that systematic segregation and discrimination endangered "our moral leadership of the free and democratic nations of the world."

"My very stomach turned over when I learned that Negro soldiers just back from overseas were being dumped out of army trucks in Mississippi and beaten," wrote Truman. Despite his need for southern white votes, Truman spoke more boldly

Segregation
The segregation visible on this bus was a feature of life in the South from the late nineteenth century until the 1960s. State and local laws mandated separation from the cradle to the grave. African Americans could not use white hospitals, cemeteries, schools, libraries, swimming pools, restrooms, or drinking fountains. They were relegated to balconies in movie theaters and kept apart from whites in all public meetings. Segregated buses would become the target of the first large-scale civil rights protest, in Montgomery, Alabama, in 1955–1956.
Stan Wayman/Time Life Pictures/Getty Images.

on civil rights than any previous president had, thus appealing more to northern black and liberal voters. In 1946, he created the President's Committee on Civil Rights, and in February 1948 he asked Congress to enact the committee's recommendations. The first president to address the NAACP, Truman asserted that all Americans should have equal rights to housing, education, employment, and the ballot.

As with much of his domestic program, the president failed to act aggressively on his bold words. Congress rejected Truman's proposals for national civil rights legislation, although some northern and western states did pass laws against discrimination in employment and public accommodations. Running for reelection in 1948, Truman issued an executive order to desegregate the armed services, but it lay unimplemented until the Korean War, when the cost of segregation to military efficiency became apparent. Army officers gradually integrated their ranks, and by 1953, 95 percent of all African Americans served in mixed units. Despite the gap between Truman's words and what his administration actually accomplished, desegregation of the military and the administration's support of civil rights cases in the Supreme Court contributed to far-reaching changes, while his Committee on Civil Rights set an agenda for years to come.

Although discussion of race and civil rights usually focused on African Americans, Mexican Americans endured similar injustices. In 1929, they had formed the League of United Latin-

American Citizens (LULAC) to combat discrimination and segregation in the Southwest. Like black soldiers after World War II, Mexican American veterans believed, as one of them insisted, that "we had earned our credentials as American citizens. We had paid our dues." Problems with getting their veterans' benefits spurred the formation of a new organization in 1948 in Corpus Christi, Texas — the **American GI Forum**. Dr. **Héctor Peréz García**, president of the local LULAC chapter and a combat surgeon who had received the Bronze Star, led the GI Forum, which became a key national organization for battling discrimination against Latinos and electing sympathetic officials.

"Education is our freedom," read the GI Forum's motto, yet Mexican American children were routinely segregated in public schools. In 1945, with the help of LULAC, parents filed a class action suit in southern California, challenging several school districts that barred their children from white schools. In the resulting decision, *Mendez v. Westminster* (1947), a federal court for the first time struck down school segregation. NAACP lawyer Thurgood Marshall filed a supporting brief in the case, which foreshadowed the landmark *Brown* decision in 1954 (as discussed in chapter 27). Efforts to gain equal education, along with challenges to discrimination in employment and campaigns for political representation, demonstrated a growing mobilization of Mexican Americans in the Southwest.

Dr. Héctor P. García
Héctor García, shown here with patients, came from Mexico to the United States as a small boy and, like all of his five siblings, became a doctor. While leading the G.I. Forum and advocating for Mexican-American rights, García treated all who needed his medical care regardless of whether they could pay for it. An associate referred to García, who also became active in politics, as "a man who in the space of one week delivers 20 babies, 20 speeches, and 20 thousand votes." He was appointed as an alternate U.S. Ambassador to the United Nations and served on the U.S. Commission on Civil Rights. Héctor P. García Papers, Special Collections & Archives, Texas A&M. University, Corpus Christi, Bell Library.

The Fair Deal Flounders

Republicans capitalized on public frustrations with strikes and shortages in the 1946 congressional election, accusing the administration of "confusion, corruption, and communism." Helen Gahagan Douglas hung on to her seat, but the Republicans captured control of Congress for the first time in fourteen years. Many had campaigned against New Deal "bureaucracy" and "radicalism" in 1946, and in the Eightieth Congress they suc- ceeded in weakening some reform programs and enacting tax cuts favoring higher-income groups.

Organized labor took the most severe blow when Congress passed the **Taft-Hartley Act** over Truman's veto in 1947. Called a "slave labor" law by unions, the measure reduced the power of organized labor and made it more difficult to organize workers. For example, states could now pass "right-to-work" laws, which banned the practice of requiring all workers to join a union once a majority had voted for it. Many states,

VISUAL ACTIVITY

Harry Truman rallies a crowd from his campaign train in Bridgeport, Pennsylvania, in October 1948. This was the last presidential election in which pollsters predicted the wrong winner. They stopped taking polls in mid-October, after which many voters apparently changed their minds. One commentator praised the American citizenry, who "couldn't be ticketed by the polls, knew its own mind, and had picked the rather unlikely but courageous figure of Truman to carry on its banner." Truman's support for civil rights cost him four southern states but helped him win votes from liberals and blacks. Photo: Truman Library; campaign button: Collection of Janice L. and David J. Frent.

READING THE IMAGE: This photo was taken one month before the election. Why might his opponent's campaign have dismissed the importance of these large crowds in support of Truman?

CONNECTIONS: President Truman was under attack by the Republicans and could not enact the Fair Deal. Almost everyone thought he would lose the election. Why do you think the American people responded so well to his campaign? In what ways have presidential campaigns changed since Harry Truman's time?

especially in the South and West, rushed to enact such laws, encouraging industries to relocate there. Taft-Hartley maintained the New Deal principle of government protection for collective bargaining, but it put the government more squarely between labor and management.

In the 1948 elections, Truman faced not only a resurgent Republican Party headed by New York governor Thomas E. Dewey but also two revolts within his own party. On the left, Henry A. Wallace, whose foreign policy views had cost him his cabinet seat, led the new Progressive Party. On the right, South Carolina governor J. Strom Thurmond headed the States' Rights Party — the Dixiecrats — formed by southern Democrats who had walked out of the 1948 Democratic Party convention when it passed a liberal civil rights plank.

Almost alone in believing he could win, Truman crisscrossed the country by train, answering supporters' cries of "Give 'em hell, Harry." So bleak were Truman's prospects that on election night the *Chicago Daily Tribune* printed its next day's issue with the headline "Dewey Defeats Truman." But even though the Dixiecrats won four southern states, Truman took 303 electoral votes to Dewey's 189, and his party regained control of Congress (Map 26.2). His unexpected victory attested to the broad support for his foreign policy and the enduring popularity of New Deal reform.

While the major New Deal programs survived Republican attacks, Truman failed to enact his Fair Deal agenda. Congress made modest improvements in Social Security and raised the minimum wage, but it passed only one significant reform measure. Enacted with significant Republican support, the **Housing Act of 1949** authorized 810,000 units of government-constructed housing over the next six years and represented a landmark commitment by the government to address the housing needs of the poor. Yet it fell far short of actual need — just 61,000 units had been built when Truman left office — and slum clearance frequently displaced the poor without providing decent alternatives.

With southern Democrats posing a primary obstacle, Congress rejected Truman's proposals for civil rights, a powerful medical lobby blocked plans for a universal health care program based on the Social Security model, and conflicts over race and religion thwarted federal aid to education. Truman's efforts to revise immigration policy were mixed. The McCarran-Walter Act of 1952 ended the outright ban on immigration and citizenship for Japanese and other Asians, but it also authorized the government to bar suspected Communists and homosexuals and maintained the discriminatory quota system established in the 1920s. The president denounced that provision as "unworthy of our traditions and our ideals," but Congress overrode his veto.

Truman's concentration on foreign policy rather than domestic proposals contributed to the failure of his Fair Deal. Moreover, by late 1950, the Korean War embroiled the president in controversy and depleted his power as a legislative leader (see pages 887–892). Truman's failure to make good on his domestic proposals and expand the framework of the welfare state begun by Roosevelt set the United States apart from most European nations. By the 1950s, most other industrial democracies had in place comprehensive health, housing, and employment security programs to underwrite the material well-being of their populations.

The Domestic Chill: McCarthyism

Truman's domestic program also suffered from a wave of anticommunism that weakened liberal and leftist forces. "Red-baiting" (attempts to discredit individuals or ideas by associating them with communism) and official retaliation against leftist critics of the government had flourished during the Red scare at the end of World War I (see chapter 22). A second Red

MAP 26.2
The Election of 1948

Candidate	Electoral Vote	Popular Vote	Percent of Popular Vote
Harry S. Truman (Democrat)	303	24,105,695	49.5
Thomas E. Dewey (Republican)	189	21,969,170	45.1
J. Strom Thurmond (States' Rights)	39	1,169,021	2.4
Henry A. Wallace (Progressive)	0	1,156,103	2.4

An Immigrant Scientist Encounters the Anti-Communist Crusade

Qian Xuesen (Tsien Hsue-shen) was born to a privileged family in Hangzhou, China, in 1911. Qian's father, an education official, encouraged academic excellence in his son from the start, giving him a name that means "study to be wise." After spending most of his youth in Beijing (Peking), Qian attended Jiaotong University in Shanghai, graduating at the top of his class from China's best engineering school. Deciding that aviation was the wave of the future and aware of how far behind his country lagged in this area, Qian looked abroad to further his education. In 1935, with his country torn by Japanese aggression and internal opposition to the Nationalist government, he accepted an American-sponsored scholarship and quickly earned a master's degree in aeronautical engineering from the Massachusetts Institute of Technology (MIT). One year later, he began doctoral work at the California Institute of Technology (Caltech) in Pasadena.

At Caltech, Qian joined a group of scientists working on questions about flight and contributed to the development of theoretical aerodynamics and jet propulsion, which eventually provided a foundation for America's space program. School officials were so impressed with Qian's work that they helped him get a visa extension, and in 1942 the government gave him security clearance so that he could work on the military's secret projects. Qian served on the air force's Scientific Advisory Board, and after World War II he went on a U.S. mission to interview Nazi scientists in Germany. He spent a year on the faculty at MIT and then traveled home to China amid the turmoil of a civil war between the Communists, led by Mao Zedong (Mao Tse-tung), and the Nationalist government of Jiang Jieshi (Chiang Kai-shek). While in China, Qian spent time with his father, gave motivational speeches to large audiences of students, and married a woman he had known in childhood, an opera singer named Jiang Ying (Tsiang Ying), who was the daughter of one of Jiang Jieshi's generals.

In 1949, when he returned to Caltech to direct the Jet Propulsion Center, teach, continue his research, and entertain a close circle of colleagues with classical music and elaborate dinners, Qian seemed to have everything necessary to lead a rich life and pursue his lifelong passion for science. He applied for U.S. citizenship. One year later, after the Communists had taken control of China, the U.S. government revoked Qian's security clearance. The FBI interrogated him about his associations with a group he had socialized with in the 1930s, which the FBI said was a cell of the Communist Party. Qian denied any participation in Communist activities, but the proud, angry, and humiliated scientist concluded that, given the "cloud of suspicion . . . the only gentlemanly thing left to do is to depart." The promise of a brilliant career shattered, he resisted the entreaties of Caltech officials who begged him to remain; instead, he readied a shipment of his belongings to send on to China. The government seized the shipment and accused Qian of taking secret documents. Although the claim was later refuted, the Immigration and Naturalization Service arrested him. He was released after two weeks, but for the next five years the government refused to let him go, and he and his family were kept under constant surveillance. Although Caltech administrators worked furiously to clear his name, some of his associates began to avoid him, fearing that they, too, would be caught up in the hunt for Communists. Finally, in 1955, he was deported as part of a prisoner of war exchange following the Korean War.

Qian disembarked in China with his wife and two children to a hero's reception and a career that scare followed World War II, born of partisan political maneuvering, the collapse of the Soviet-American alliance, setbacks in U.S. foreign policy, and disclosures of Soviet espionage in the United States, Canada, and Great Britain.

Republicans who had attacked the New Deal as a plot of radicals now jumped on such Cold War events as the Soviet takeover of Eastern Europe and the Communist triumph in China to accuse Democrats of fostering internal subversion. Wisconsin senator **Joseph R. McCarthy** avowed that "the Communists within our borders have been more responsible for the success of Communism abroad than Soviet Russia." McCarthy's charges — such as the allegation that retired general George C. Marshall belonged to a Communist conspiracy — were reckless and

would eventually earn him the title of "father of Chinese rocketry." Denied the full use of his talents by the United States, he organized and led China's rocketry program, developing its ballistic missiles and satellites. He became a trusted Communist Party official and loyal supporter of the government, as did anyone who hoped to have a successful career in China. Though the extremely private Qian said little about his experiences in the United States, he refused to return in 1979 to accept Caltech's Distinguished Alumni Award. Qian had lost faith in the U.S. government, but former colleagues who visited him reported that he maintained affection for the American people, and both his son and his daughter studied at American universities. Qian died in China in 2009 at the age of ninety-eight.

Questions linger about Qian's associations and intentions in the United States. A 1999 congressional report maintained that he had been a spy, but his supporters claimed that the report lacked evidence. Every one of his Caltech colleagues vouched for his integrity, and some went to great lengths to defend him against government charges. Dan A. Kimball, who was secretary of the navy in the early 1950s, later said that Qian's deportation "was the stupidest thing this country ever did. He was no more a Communist than I was — and we forced him to go." The Red scare dashed Qian's belief that America promised an opportunity for any talented individual to live a free and prosperous life. It also delivered a brilliant scientist to the nation's enemy.

Qian Xuesen

Qian Xuesen, the Chinese-American rocket scientist, teaches a class at the California Institute of Technology in 1955, shortly before he was deported back to China. Students who worked with him in the 1940s were "awe-struck" by his brilliance. He generously mentored those whose mental powers matched his, but was impatient, unbending, and harsh toward those he deemed intellectually incapable. "Students were scared stiff of him," remembered one. By the 1950s, however, students found Qian to be kinder and more supportive, perhaps because of his own ordeal with the FBI. © Bettmann/Corbis.

Questions for Consideration

1. What particular aspects of American life and institutions attracted Qian to the United States in the first place, and what made him want to stay in the country?

2. How did the timing of events in Qian's case correlate with domestic and international developments related to the Cold War and McCarthyism?

often ludicrous, but the press covered him avidly, and McCarthyism became a term synonymous with the anti-Communist crusade.

Revelations of Soviet espionage gave some credibility to fears of internal communism. For example, a number of ex-Communists, including Whittaker Chambers and Elizabeth Bentley, testified that they and others had provided secret documents to the Soviets. Chambers asserted that Alger Hiss, a former New Dealer who had served in the wartime State Department, had belonged to a secret Communist cell. Although Hiss denied the charges and prominent Democrats defended him, in 1950 a jury convicted him of lying to congressional investigators about his connections with Chambers, and he spent four years in prison. Most alarming of all, in 1950 a British physicist working on the atomic bomb project confessed that he was a spy and implicated several Americans, including Ethel and Julius Rosenberg. The Rosenbergs pleaded not guilty but were convicted of conspiracy to commit espionage and electrocuted in 1953, the only Americans to be executed for treason during the Red scare.

Records opened in the 1990s showed that the Soviet Union did receive secret documents from Americans that probably hastened its development of nuclear weapons by a year or two. Yet the vast majority of individuals hunted down in the Red scare had done nothing more than at one time joining the Communist Party, associating with Communists, or supporting radical causes. And most of those activities had taken place long before the Cold War had made the Soviet Union an enemy. Investigators often cared little for such distinctions, however.

The hunt for subversives was conducted by both Congress and the executive branch. Stung by charges of communism in the 1946 midterm elections, Truman issued Executive Order 9835 in March 1947, establishing loyalty review boards to investigate every federal employee. "A nightmare from which there [was] no awakening" was how State Department employee Esther Brunauer described it when she and her husband, a chemist in the navy, both lost their jobs because he had joined a Communist youth organization in the 1920s and associated with suspected radicals. Government investigators routinely violated the Bill of Rights by allowing anonymous informers to make charges and by placing the burden of proof on the accused. More than two thousand civil service employees lost their jobs, and another ten thousand resigned as **Truman's loyalty program** continued into the mid-1950s. Hundreds of homosexuals resigned or were fired over charges of "sexual perversion," which anti-Communist crusaders said could subject them to blackmail. Years later, Truman admitted that the loyalty program had been a mistake.

Congressional committees, such as the **House Un-American Activities Committee (HUAC)**, also investigated individuals' past and present political associations. When those under scrutiny refused to name names, investigators charged that silence was tantamount to confession, and these "unfriendly witnesses" lost their jobs and suffered public ostracism. In 1947, HUAC inves-

> "[If you called for] a square deal for the underdog, will they call you a Commie? . . . Are they going to scare us into silence?"
>
> — Singer FRANK SINATRA

Senator Joseph R. McCarthy
The Wisconsin senator made his reputation on anticommunism, seizing that issue when he needed to have a platform for his 1950 reelection campaign. McCarthy had loved politics since his high school days in Appleton, Wisconsin, and he easily distorted the truth to promote his political ambitions. The 1946 campaign poster in this photograph highlights his service in World War II, which he presented as involving dangerous combat missions as a tail gunner. In fact, he spent his time as an intelligence officer debriefing combat pilots. His only missions were flights over islands no longer controlled by the Japanese.
© Bettmann/Corbis.

tigated radical activity in Hollywood. Singer Frank Sinatra protested, wondering if someone called for "a square deal for the underdog, will they call you a Commie? . . . Are they going to scare us into silence?" Some actors and directors cooperated, but ten refused, citing their First Amendment rights. The "Hollywood Ten" served jail sentences for contempt of Congress — a punishment that Helen Gahagan Douglas fought — and then found themselves blacklisted in the movie industry.

The Truman administration went after the Communist Party directly, prosecuting its leaders under the Smith Act of 1940, which made it a crime to "advocate the overthrow and destruction of the Government of the United States by force and violence." Although civil libertarians argued that the guilty verdicts violated First Amendment rights of freedom of speech, press, and association, the Supreme Court ruled in

The Red Scare in Popular Culture
In 1949, producer Howard Hughes provided fodder for the Red scare with his movie *I Married a Communist*. Featuring an all-star cast, the movie tells the story of a dockworker who rose to become a shipping executive and then was used by the Communists, who threatened to expose his left-wing associations in the 1930s. The Michael Barson Collection/Past Perfect.

1951 (*Dennis v. United States*) that the Communist threat overrode constitutional guarantees.

The domestic Cold War spread beyond the nation's capital. State and local governments investigated citizens, demanded loyalty oaths, fired employees suspected of disloyalty, banned books from public libraries, and more. College professors and public school teachers lost their jobs in New York, California, and elsewhere. (See "Seeking the American Promise," page 884.) Because the Communist Party had helped organize unions and championed racial justice, labor and civil rights activists fell prey to McCarthyism as well. African American activist Jack O'Dell remembered that segregationists pinned the tag of Communist on "anybody who supported the right of blacks to have civil rights."

McCarthyism caused untold harm to thousands of innocent individuals. Anti-Communist crusaders humiliated and discredited law-abiding citizens, hounded them from their jobs, and in some cases even sent them to prison. Throughout the nearly ten years of the second Red scare, fundamental constitutional rights of freedom of speech and association were violated, the expression of dissenting ideas was stifled, and unpopular causes were removed from public contemplation.

REVIEW Why did Truman have limited success in implementing his domestic agenda?

▶ The Cold War Becomes Hot: Korea

The Cold War erupted into a shooting war in June 1950 when troops from Communist North Korea invaded South Korea. For the first time, Americans went into battle to implement containment. Confirming the global reach of the Truman Doctrine, U.S. involvement in Korea also marked the militarization of American foreign policy. The United States, in concert with the United Nations, ultimately held the line in Korea, but at a great cost in lives, dollars, and domestic unity.

Korea and the Military Implementation of Containment

The war grew out of the artificial division of Korea after World War II. Having expelled the Japanese, who had controlled Korea since 1904, the United States and the Soviet Union created two occupation zones separated by the thirty-eighth parallel (Map 26.3). With Moscow and Washington unable to agree on a unification plan, the United Nations sponsored elections in South Korea in July 1948. The American-favored candidate, Syngman Rhee, was elected president, and the United States withdrew most of its troops. In the fall of 1948, the Soviets established the People's Republic of North Korea under Kim Il-sung and also withdrew. Although doubting that Rhee's repressive government could sustain popular support, U.S. officials appreciated his staunch anticommunism and provided small amounts of economic and military aid to South Korea.

Insurgencies of workers and peasants against factory owners, landlords, and the Rhee government claimed 100,000 lives between 1946 and

MAP ACTIVITY

Map 26.3 The Korean War, 1950–1953
Although each side had plunged deep into enemy territory, the war ended in 1953 with the dividing line between North and South Korea nearly where it had been before the fighting began.

READING THE MAP: How far south did the North Korean forces progress at the height of their invasion? How far north did the UN forces get? What countries border Korea?
CONNECTIONS: What dangers did the forays of MacArthur's forces to within forty miles of the Korean-Chinese border pose? Why did Truman forbid MacArthur to approach that border? What political considerations on the home front influenced Truman's policy and military strategy regarding Korea?

mid-1950, and skirmishes between North and South Korean troops at the thirty-eighth parallel began in 1948. Then, in June 1950, 90,000 North Koreans swept into South Korea. Truman's advisers assumed that the Soviet Union or China had instigated the attack, but later revelations pinned the initiative on Kim Il-sung, who won only reluctant acquiescence from China and

Russia. Truman wasted little time deciding to intervene, viewing Korea as "the Greece of the Far East." With the Soviet Union boycotting the UN Security Council to protest the council's refusal to seat a representative from the People's Republic of China, the United States obtained UN sponsorship of a collective effort to repel the attack. Authorized to appoint a commander for the UN force, Truman named General **Douglas MacArthur**, World War II hero and head of the postwar occupation of Japan.

Sixteen nations, including many NATO allies, sent troops to Korea, but the United States furnished most of the personnel and weapons, deploying almost 1.8 million troops and dictating military strategy. By dispatching troops without asking Congress for a declaration of war, Truman violated the spirit if not the letter of the Constitution and contributed to the expansion of executive power that would characterize the Cold War. Congress did appropriate funds to fight the **Korean War**, but the absence of a congressional declaration of war enabled the president's political opponents to call it "Truman's war" when the military situation worsened.

The first American soldiers rushed to Korea unprepared and ill equipped. One regimental commander grumbled that troops had "spent a lot of time listening to lectures on the differences between communism and Americanism and not enough time crawling on their bellies on maneuvers [or learning] how to clear a machine gun when it jams." U.S. forces suffered severe defeats in the first three months of the war. The North Koreans took the capital of Seoul and drove deep into South Korea, forcing UN troops to retreat to Pusan. Then, in September 1950, General MacArthur launched a bold counteroffensive at Inchon, 180 miles behind North Korean lines. The attack succeeded, and by October UN and South Korean forces had retaken Seoul and pushed the North Koreans back to the thirty-eighth parallel. These victories posed the momentous decision of whether to invade North Korea and seek to unify the country.

From Containment to Rollback to Containment

"Troops could not be expected . . . to march up to a surveyor's line and stop," remarked Secretary of State Dean Acheson, reflecting popular and official support for transforming the military objective from containment to elimination of the enemy and unification of Korea. Thus, for the only time during the Cold War, the United States

POWs in Korea
These demoralized U.S. soldiers reflect the grim situation for U.S. forces during the early months of the Korean War. Their North Korean captors forced them to march through Seoul in July 1950 carrying a banner proclaiming the righteousness of the Communist cause and attacking U.S. intervention. AP Images.

tried to roll back communism by force. With UN approval, on September 27, 1950, Truman authorized MacArthur to cross the thirty-eighth parallel. Concerned about possible intervention by China or the Soviet Union, the president directed him to keep UN troops away from the Korean-Chinese border. Disregarding the order, MacArthur sent UN forces to within forty miles of China, whereupon 300,000 Chinese soldiers crossed the Yalu River into Korea. With Chinese help, the North Koreans recaptured Seoul.

After three months of grueling battle, UN forces fought their way back to the thirty-eighth parallel. At that point, Truman decided to seek a negotiated settlement. MacArthur was furious when the goal of the war reverted to containment, which to him represented defeat. In comments to the press and letters to sympathetic members of Congress, the general challenged both the president's authority to conduct foreign policy and the principle of civilian control of the military. Fed up with MacArthur's insubordination, Truman relieved him of command in April 1951. Many Americans, however, sided with MacArthur. "Quite an explosion. . . . Letters of abuse by the dozens," Truman recorded in his diary. The adulation for MacArthur reflected Americans' frustration with containment. Why should Americans die simply to preserve the status quo? Why not destroy the enemy once and for all? In siding with MacArthur, Americans assumed that the United States was all-powerful and that stalemate in Korea resulted from the government's ineptitude or willingness to shelter subversives.

When Congress investigated MacArthur's dismissal, all of the top military leaders supported

> **"Troops could not be expected . . . to march up to a surveyor's line and stop."**
> — Secretary of State DEAN ACHESON

The 1952 Republican Ticket
At the Republican convention in 1952, presidential nominee Dwight D. Eisenhower stands with his wife, Mamie (right); his running mate, Richard Nixon; and Nixon's wife, Patricia (left), at the start of their campaign. The campaign poster refers to scandals involving Truman associates and his failure to end the Korean War. Photo: © Bettmann/Corbis; Poster: Collection of Janice L. and David J. Frent.

the president. According to the chairman of the Joint Chiefs of Staff, MacArthur wanted to wage "the wrong war, at the wrong place, at the wrong time, with the wrong enemy." Yet Truman never recovered from the political fallout. Nor was he able to end the war. Negotiations began in July 1951, but peace talks dragged on for two more years while twelve thousand more U.S. soldiers died.

Korea, Communism, and the 1952 Election

Popular discontent with President Truman's war boosted Republican candidates in the 1952 election. The Republicans' presidential nominee, General **Dwight D. Eisenhower**, had emerged from World War II with immense popularity. Reared in modest circumstances in Abilene, Kansas, Eisenhower attended West Point and

rose steadily through the army ranks. As supreme commander in Europe, he won widespread acclaim for leading the Allied armies to victory over Germany. After the war, he served as army chief of staff, and in 1950 Truman appointed Eisenhower the first supreme commander of NATO forces.

Both Republicans and Democrats had courted Eisenhower for the presidency in 1948. Although Eisenhower believed that professional soldiers should stay out of politics, he found compelling reasons to run in 1952. He largely agreed with Democratic foreign policy, but he deplored the Democrats' propensity to solve domestic problems with costly new federal programs. He equally disliked the foreign policy views of the leading Republican presidential contender, Senator Robert A. Taft, an opponent of NATO, who sought to cut defense spending and limit the nation's involvement abroad. Eisenhower decided to run both to stop Taft and the conservative wing of the

Republican Party and to turn the Democrats out of the White House.

Eisenhower defeated Taft for the nomination, but the old guard prevailed on the party platform. It excoriated containment as "negative, futile, and immoral" and charged the Truman administration with shielding "traitors to the Nation in high places." By choosing thirty-nine-year-old Senator **Richard M. Nixon** for his running mate, Eisenhower helped to appease the right wing of the party and ensured that anticommunism would be a major theme of the campaign.

Richard Milhous Nixon grew up in southern California, worked his way through college and law school, served in the navy, and briefly practiced law. In 1946, he helped the Republicans recapture Congress by defeating a liberal incumbent for a seat in the House of Representatives. Nixon quickly made a name for himself as a member of HUAC (see page 886) and a key anti-Communist, moving to the Senate with his victory over Helen Gahagan Douglas in 1950.

With his public approval ratings plummeting, Truman decided not to run for reelection. The Democrats nominated Adlai E. Stevenson, the popular governor of Illinois, who was acceptable to both liberals and southerners. Stevenson could not escape the domestic fallout from the Korean War, however; nor could he match the widespread appeal of Eisenhower. The Republican campaign stumbled just once, over the last item of its "Korea, Communism, and Corruption" policy. When the press reported that Nixon had accepted money from a private political fund supported by wealthy Californians, Democrats jumped to the attack, even though such gifts were common and legal. While Eisenhower deliberated about whether to dump Nixon from the ticket, Nixon saved himself by making an emotional nationwide appeal on the new medium of television. He disclosed his finances and documented his modest standard of living. Conceding that the family pet, Checkers, might be considered an illegal gift, Nixon refused to break his daughters' hearts by returning the cocker spaniel. The overwhelmingly positive response to the "Checkers speech" kept Nixon on the ticket.

Shortly before the election, Eisenhower announced dramatically, "I shall go to Korea," and voters registered their confidence in his ability to end the war. Cutting sharply into traditional Democratic territory, Eisenhower won several southern states and garnered 55 percent of the popular vote overall. His coattails carried a narrow Republican majority to Congress.

An Armistice and the War's Costs

Eisenhower made good on his pledge to end the Korean War. In July 1953, the two sides reached an armistice that left Korea divided, again roughly at the thirty-eighth parallel, with North and South separated by a two-and-a-half-mile-wide demilitarized zone (see Map 26.3). The war took the lives of 36,000 Americans and wounded more than 100,000. Nick Tosques, one of thousands of U.S. soldiers taken as prisoners of war, spent more than two years in a POW camp. "They interrogated us every day," he recalled. "Pretty soon I was telling them anything, just to keep from getting hit." South Korea lost more than 1 million people to war-related causes, and more than 1.8 million North Koreans and Chinese were killed or wounded.

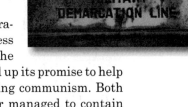

The Truman administration judged the war a success for containment, since the United States had backed up its promise to help nations that were resisting communism. Both Truman and Eisenhower managed to contain what amounted to a world war — involving twenty nations altogether — within a single country and to avoid the use of nuclear weapons.

The Korean War had an enormous effect on defense policy and spending. In April 1950, two months before the war began, the National Security Council completed a top-secret report, known as **NSC 68**, on the United States' military strength. It warned that the survival of the nation required a massive military buildup and a tripling of the defense budget. Truman took no immediate action on these recommendations, but the Korean War brought about nearly all of the military expansion called for in NSC 68, vastly increasing U.S. capacity to act as a global power. Military spending shot up from $14 billion in 1950 to $50 billion in 1953 and remained above $40 billion thereafter. By 1952, defense spending claimed nearly 70 percent of the federal budget, and the size of the armed forces had tripled.

To General Matthew Ridgway, MacArthur's successor as commander of the UN forces, Korea taught the lesson that U.S. forces should never again fight a land war in Asia. Eisenhower concurred. Nevertheless, the Korean War induced the Truman administration to expand its role in Asia by increasing aid to the French, who were fighting to hang on to their colonial empire in Indochina. As U.S. Marines retreated from a battle against Chinese soldiers in 1950, they sang, prophetically, "We're Harry's police force on call, / So put back your pack on, / The next step is Saigon, / Cheer up, me lads, bless 'em all."

> **REVIEW**   How did the Korean War shape American foreign policy in the 1950s?

▶ Conclusion: The Cold War's Costs and Consequences

Arguing that the United Nations rather than unilateral American intervention should be the means of resolving foreign crises, Helen Gahagan Douglas opposed the implementation of containment with aid to Greece and Turkey in 1947, and she initially resisted designating the Soviet Union as an enemy. By 1948, however, Douglas had gotten behind Truman's decision to fight communism throughout the world, which marked the most momentous foreign policy initiative in the nation's history.

More than any development in the postwar world, the Cold War defined American politics and society for decades to come. It transformed the federal government, shifting its priorities from domestic to external affairs, greatly expanding its budget, and substantially increasing the power of the president. Military spending helped transform the nation itself, as defense contracts encouraged economic and population booms in the West and Southwest. The nuclear arms race put the people of the world at risk, consumed resources that might have been used to improve living standards, and skewed the economy toward dependence on military projects.

In sharp contrast to foreign policy, the domestic policies of the postwar years reflected continuity with the past. Most of the New Deal reforms remained in place despite Republicans' promises to turn back the clock. Helen Gahagan Douglas had come to Congress hoping to expand the New Deal, to help find "a way by which all people can live out their lives in dignity and decency." She avidly supported Truman's proposals for new programs in education, health, and civil rights, but a majority of her colleagues did not. Consequently, the poor and minorities suffered even while a majority of Americans enjoyed a higher standard of living in an economy boosted by Cold War spending and the reconstruction of Western Europe and Japan.

Another high cost of the early Cold War years was the anti-Communist hysteria that swept the nation, denying Douglas a Senate seat and more generally stifling debate and narrowing the range of ideas acceptable for political discussion. Partisan politics and Truman's warnings about the Communist menace fueled McCarthyism, but the obsession with subversion also fed on popular frustrations over the failure of containment to produce clear-cut victories. Convulsing the nation in bitter disunity, McCarthyism reflected a loss of confidence in American power. The Korean War, which ended in stalemate rather than the defeat of communism, exacerbated feelings of frustration. It would be a major challenge of the Eisenhower administration to restore national unity and confidence.

▶ Selected Bibliography

General Works

Rodolfo Acuña, *Occupied America: A History of Chicanos* (5th ed., 2004).

Carol Anderson, *Eyes off the Prize: The United Nations and the African American Struggle for Human Rights, 1944–1955* (2003).

Peter L. Hahn, *Caught in the Middle East: U.S. Policy toward the Arab-Israeli Conflict, 1945–1961* (2004).

Alonzo L. Hamby, *Man of the People: A Life of Harry S. Truman* (1995).

Ira Katznelson, *When Affirmative Action Was White: An Untold History of Racial Inequality in Twentieth-Century America* (2005).

James T. Patterson, *Grand Expectations: The United States, 1945–1974* (1996).

Brenda Gayle Plummer, *Rising Wind: Black Americans and U.S. Foreign Affairs, 1935–1960* (1996).

Ingrid Winther Scobie, *Center Stage: Helen Gahagan Douglas: A Life* (1992).

Domestic Politics and Policies

Glenn C. Altschuler and Stuart M. Blumin, *The GI Bill: A New Deal for Veterans* (2009).

Jonathan Bell, *The Liberal State on Trial: The Cold War and American Politics in the Truman Years* (2004).

Kevin Boyle, *The UAW and the Heyday of American Liberalism, 1945–1968* (1995).

Griffin Fariello, *Red Scare: Memories of the American Inquisition* (1995).

Kari Frederickson, *The Dixiecrat Revolt and the End of the Solid South, 1932–1968* (2001).

Ignacio M. García, *Hector P. García: In Relentless Pursuit of Justice* (2002).

David K. Johnson, *The Lavender Scare: The Cold War Persecution of Gays and Lesbians in the Federal Government* (2004).

Suzanne Mettler, *Soldiers to Citizens: The G.I. Bill and the Making of the Greatest Generation* (2005).

Richard Gid Powers, *Not without Honor: The History of American Anticommunism* (1995).

Henry A. J. Ramos, *The American GI Forum: In Pursuit of the Dream, 1948–1983* (1998).

Ellen W. Schrecker, *Many Are the Crimes: McCarthyism in America* (1998).

The Cold War

Greg Behrman, *The Most Noble Adventure: The Marshall Plan and the Time When America Helped Save Europe* (2007).

Robert L. Beisner, *Dean Acheson: A Life in the Cold War* (2006).

Campbell Craig and Fredric Logevall, *America's Cold War: The Politics of Insecurity* (2009).

Carolyn Eisenberg, *Drawing the Line: The American Decision to Divide Germany, 1944–1949* (1996).

John L. Gaddis, *The Cold War: A New History* (2005).

Lawrence S. Kaplan, *1948: The Birth of the Transatlantic Alliance* (2007).

Melvyn Leffler, *For the Soul of Mankind: The United States, the Soviet Union, and the Cold War* (2007).

Arnold A. Offner, *Another Such Victory: President Truman and the Cold War, 1945–1953* (2002).

Richard Rhodes, *Dark Sun: The Making of the Hydrogen Bomb* (1995).

Katherine A. S. Sibley, *Red Spies in America: Stolen Secrets and the Dawn of the Cold War* (2004).

Julian E. Zelizer, *Arsenal of Democracy: The Politics of National Security—From World War II to the War on Terrorism* (2010).

Asia and the Korean War

Gordon H. Chang, *Friends and Enemies: The United States, China, and the Soviet Union, 1948–1972* (1990).

Bruce Cumings, *The Korean War* (2010).

Allen R. Millett, *The War for Korea, 1945–1950: A House Burning* (2005).

Michael Schaller, *Altered States: The United States and Japan since the Occupation* (1997).

William Stueck, *Rethinking the Korean War: A New Diplomatic and Strategic History* (2002).

Stanley Weintraub, *MacArthur's War: Korea and the Undoing of an American Hero* (2000).

▶ **For more books about topics in this chapter,** see the Online Bibliography at **bedfordstmartins.com/roark.**

▶ **For additional primary sources from this period,** see Michael Johnson, ed., *Reading the American Past*, Fifth Edition.

▶ **For Web sites, images, and documents related to topics and places in this chapter,** visit Make History at **bedfordstmartins.com/roark.**

Reviewing Chapter 26

KEY TERMS

Explain each term's significance.

From the Grand Alliance to Containment

Joseph Stalin (p. 865)

Harry S. Truman (p. 865)

iron curtain (p. 866)

George F. Kennan (p. 867)

containment (p. 867)

Cold War (p. 870)

Truman Doctrine (p. 870)

Marshall Plan (p. 870)

Berlin airlift (p. 871)

hydrogen bomb (p. 872)

North Atlantic Treaty Organization (NATO) (p. 873)

Central Intelligence Agency (CIA) (p. 873)

Mao Zedong (p. 874)

Truman and the Fair Deal at Home

Fair Deal (p. 875)

Servicemen's Readjustment Act (GI Bill) (p. 877)

American GI Forum (p. 881)

Héctor Peréz García (p. 881)

Mendez v. Westminster (p. 881)

Taft-Hartley Act (p. 882)

Housing Act of 1949 (p. 883)

Joseph R. McCarthy (p. 884)

Truman's loyalty program (p. 886)

House Un-American Activities Committee (HUAC) (p. 886)

The Cold War Becomes Hot: Korea

Douglas MacArthur (p. 888)

Korean War (p. 888)

Dwight D. Eisenhower (p. 890)

Richard M. Nixon (p. 891)

NSC 68 (p. 891)

REVIEW QUESTIONS

Use key terms and dates to support your answer.

1. Why did relations between the United States and the Soviet Union deteriorate after World War II? (pp. 865–875)

2. Why did Truman have limited success in implementing his domestic agenda? (pp. 875–887)

3. How did the Korean War shape American foreign policy in the 1950s? (pp. 887–892)

MAKING CONNECTIONS

Draw on key terms, the timeline, and review questions.

1. What was the containment policy, and how successful was it up to 1953? In your answer, discuss both the supporters and the critics of the policy.

2. How did returning American servicemen change postwar domestic life in the areas of education and civil rights? In your answer, discuss how wartime experiences influenced their demands.

3. Why did anti-Communist hysteria sweep the country in the early 1950s? How did it shape domestic politics? In your answer, be sure to consider the influence of developments abroad and at home.

LINKING TO THE PAST

Link events in this chapter to earlier events.

1. What events and decisions during World War II contributed to the rise of the Cold War in the late 1940s? (See chapter 25.)

2. What did the anti-Communist hysteria of the late 1940s and the 1950s have in common with the Red scare that followed World War I, and how did these two phenomena differ? (See chapter 22.)

▶ FOR PRACTICE QUIZZES AND OTHER STUDY TOOLS, visit the Online Study Guide at bedfordstmartins.com/roark.

TIMELINE 1945–1953

1945
- Roosevelt dies; Vice President Harry S. Truman becomes president.

1946
- Postwar labor unrest.
- President's Committee on Civil Rights created.
- George F. Kennan drafts a containment policy.
- United States grants independence to Philippines.
- Employment Act.
- Republicans gain control of Congress.

1947
- National Security Act: National Security Council (NSC) and Central Intelligence Agency (CIA) created.
- Truman asks for aid to Greece and Turkey and announces Truman Doctrine.
- Truman establishes loyalty program.
- *Mendez v. Westminster* invalidates segregation of Mexican Americans in California schools.

1948
- Congress approves Marshall Plan.
- Women become permanent part of armed services.
- Truman orders desegregation of armed services.
- American GI Forum founded.
- United States recognizes state of Israel.
- Truman elected president.

1948–1949
- Berlin crisis and airlift.

1949
- Communists take over mainland China; Nationalists retreat to Taiwan.
- North Atlantic Treaty Organization (NATO) formed.
- Soviet Union explodes atomic bomb.

1950
- Senator Joseph McCarthy begins to accuse U.S. government of harboring Communists.
- Truman approves development of hydrogen bomb.
- United States sends troops to South Korea.

1951
- Truman relieves General Douglas MacArthur of command in Korea.
- United States ends occupation of Japan and signs peace treaty and mutual security pact.

1952
- Republican Dwight D. Eisenhower elected president.

1953
- Armistice halts Korean War.

895

1956 CADILLAC CONVERTIBLE

The automobile reflected both corporate and family prosperity in the 1950s. By 1960, three of every four households had a car, and the automotive industry generated one of every six jobs. This Cadillac was the top-of-the-line product manufactured by General Motors, the biggest and richest corporation in the world. Even the cheaper models purchased by average Americans featured the gas-guzzling size and space-age design of this Cadillac. The background photo shows a piece of the massive interstate highway system begun in 1956 and suburban housing developments in Los Angeles, both of which fueled Americans' mobility and devotion to consumption.

Car: Ron Kimball/Kimball Stock; background: Picture Research Consultants & Archives.

27

The Politics and Culture of Abundance

1952–1960

TRAILED BY REPORTERS, U.S. VICE PRESIDENT RICHARD M. NIXON LED Soviet premier Nikita Khrushchev through the American National Exhibition in Moscow in July 1959. The display of American consumer goods followed an exhibition of Soviet products in New York, part of a cultural exchange between the two superpowers that reflected a slight thaw in the Cold War after Khrushchev replaced Stalin. In Moscow, both Khrushchev and Nixon seized on the propaganda potential of the moment. As they made their way through the display, their verbal sparring turned into a slugfest of words and gestures that reporters dubbed the kitchen debate.

Showing off a new color television set, Nixon said the Soviet Union "may be ahead of us . . . in the thrust of your rockets for . . . outer space," but he insisted to Khrushchev that the United States outstripped the Soviets in consumer goods. Nixon linked capitalism with democracy, asserting that the array of products represented "what freedom means to us . . . our right to choose." Moreover, "any steelworker could buy this house," Nixon boasted, as they walked through a model of a six-room ranch-style home. Khrushchev retorted that in the Soviet Union "you are entitled to housing," whereas in the United States the homeless slept on pavements.

While the two men inspected household appliances, Nixon declared, "These are designed to make things easier for our women." Khrushchev responded that his country did not have "the capitalist attitude toward women" and appreciated women's contributions to the economy, not their domesticity. The Soviet leader found many of the items on display interesting, but he said, "they are not needed in life. . . . They are merely gadgets." In reply, Nixon insisted, "Isn't it far better to be talking about washing machines than machines of war?" Khrushchev agreed, yet Cold War tensions surfaced when he later blustered, "We too are giants. You want to threaten — we will answer threats with threats."

The Eisenhower administration (1953–1961) in fact had begun with threats to the Soviet Union. During the 1952 campaign, Republicans had vowed to roll back communism and liberate "enslaved" peoples under Soviet rule. In practice, however, President Dwight D. Eisenhower settled for a containment policy much like that of his predecessor, Harry S. Truman, though Eisenhower relied more on nuclear weapons and on secret actions

The Kitchen Debate
Soviet premier Nikita Khrushchev (left) and Vice President Richard M. Nixon (center) debate the relative merits of their nations' economies at the American National Exhibition held in Moscow in 1959. "You are a lawyer for capitalism and I am a lawyer for communism," Khrushchev told Nixon as each tried to outdo the other. Howard Sochurek/TimePix/Getty.

by the Central Intelligence Agency (CIA) against left-leaning governments. Yet as Nixon's visit to Moscow demonstrated, Eisenhower seized on political changes in the Soviet Union to reduce tensions in Soviet-American relations.

Continuity with the Truman administration also characterized domestic policy. Although Eisenhower favored corporations with tax cuts and opposed strong federal efforts in health care, education, and race relations, he did not propose to roll back New Deal programs. He even extended the reach of the federal government with a massive highway program, and he remained immensely popular through his two terms in office.

Although poverty clung stubbornly to some 20 percent of the population, the Moscow display testified to the unheard-of material gains savored by most Americans in the postwar era. Cold War weapons production spurred the economy, whose vitality stimulated suburban development, contributed to the burgeoning population and enterprise in the West and Southwest (the Sun Belt), and enabled millions of Americans to buy a host of new products.

As new homes, television sets, and household appliances transformed living patterns, Americans took part in a consumer culture that celebrated marriage, family, and traditional gender roles, even as more and more married women took jobs outside the home. Also challenging dominant norms were an emerging youth culture and dissenting writers known as the Beats.

The Cold War and the economic boom helped African Americans mount the most dramatic challenge of the 1950s, a struggle against the system of segregation and disfranchisement that had replaced slavery. Large numbers of African Americans took direct action against the institutions of injustice, developing the organizations, leadership, and strategies to mount a civil rights movement of unprecedented size and influence.

▶ Eisenhower and the Politics of the "Middle Way"

Moderation was the guiding principle of Eisenhower's domestic agenda and leadership style. In 1953, he pledged a "middle way between untrammeled freedom of the individual and the demands for the welfare of the whole Nation," promising that his administration would "avoid government by bureaucracy as carefully as it avoids neglect of the helpless." On the one hand, Eisenhower generally resisted expanding the federal government's power, he acted reluctantly when the Supreme Court ordered schools to desegregate, and his administration terminated the federal trusteeship of dozens of Indian tribes.

On the other hand, as a moderate Republican, Eisenhower supported the continuation, and in some cases the expansion, of New Deal programs. He signed key legislation establishing a national highway system and enlarged the federal bureaucracy with a new Department of Health, Education, and Welfare. Nicknamed "Ike," the confident war hero remained popular, but he was not able to lift the Republican Party to national dominance.

allowing federal executives to dismiss thousands of employees on grounds of loyalty, security, or "suitability." Reflecting his inclination to avoid controversial issues, Eisenhower refused to denounce Senator Joseph McCarthy publicly. In 1954, McCarthy began to destroy himself when he went after the army. As he hurled reckless charges of communism against military personnel during weeks of televised hearings, public opinion turned against him. When the army's lawyer demanded of McCarthy, "Have you left no sense of decency?" those in the hearing room applauded. A Senate vote to condemn McCarthy in December 1954 marked the end of his influence, but not the end of searching out radicals.

Eisenhower sometimes echoed the conservative Republicans' conviction that government was best left to the states and economic decisions to private business. "If all Americans want is security, they can go to prison," he commented about social welfare in 1949. Yet the welfare state grew somewhat during his administration, and Eisenhower signed laws bringing ten million

> "Should any political party attempt to abolish social security and eliminate labor laws and farm programs, you would not hear of that party again."
> —President DWIGHT D. EISENHOWER

Modern Republicanism

In contrast to the old guard conservatives in his party who criticized containment and wanted to repeal much of the New Deal, **Dwight D. Eisenhower** preached "modern Republicanism." This meant resisting additional federal intervention in economic and social life, but it did not mean turning the clock back to the 1920s. "Should any political party attempt to abolish social security and eliminate labor laws and farm programs," he wrote to his brother in 1954, "you would not hear of that party again in our political history." Democratic control of Congress after the elections of 1954 further contributed to Eisenhower's moderate approach, which overall maintained the course charted by Roosevelt and Truman.

The new president attempted to distance himself from the anti-Communist fervor that had plagued the Truman administration, even as he intensified Truman's loyalty program,

Polio Vaccine Distribution in the South
In 1954, American children lined up to be inoculated with the new vaccine to prevent polio. But as this scene from Blytheville, Arkansas, shows, children waiting to receive the vaccine stood in strictly segregated lines. Charles Bell, *Memphis Commercial Appeal*.

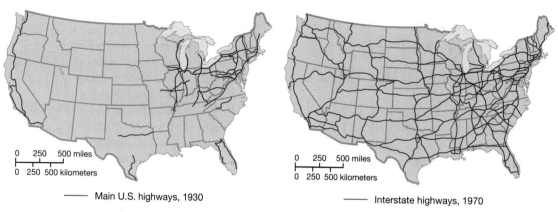

— Main U.S. highways, 1930   — Interstate highways, 1970

MAP ACTIVITY

Map 27.1 The Interstate Highway System, 1930 and 1970

Built with federal funds authorized in the Interstate Highway and Defense System Act of 1956, superhighways soon crisscrossed the nation. Trucking, construction, gasoline, and travel were among the industries that prospered, but railroads suffered from the subsidized competition.

READING THE MAP: What regions of the United States had main highways in 1930? What regions did not? How had the situation changed by 1970?

CONNECTIONS: What impact did the growth of the interstate highway system have on migration patterns in the United States? What benefits did the new interstate highways bring to Americans and at what costs?

more workers into Social Security, increasing the minimum wage, and continuing the federal government's modest role in financing public housing. He created a new Department of Health, Education, and Welfare, appointing as its head former Women's Army Corps commander Oveta Culp Hobby, the second woman to hold a cabinet post. And when the spread of polio neared epidemic proportions and terrified parents, Eisenhower obtained funds from Congress to distribute a vaccine, even though conservatives wanted to leave that responsibility to the states.

Eisenhower's greatest domestic initiative was the **Interstate Highway and Defense System Act of 1956** (Map 27.1), which involved the federal government in activities previously left to the states and localities. Promoted as essential to national defense and an impetus to economic growth, the act authorized the construction of a national highway system, with the federal government paying most of the costs through increased fuel and vehicle taxes. The new highways accelerated the mobility of Americans and the movement of goods and spurred suburban expansion, shopping malls, and growth in the fast-food and motel industries. The trucking, construction, and automobile industries had lobbied hard for the law and benefited substantially from it. Eventually, the monumental highway project exacted unforeseen costs in the form of

air pollution, energy consumption, declining railroads and mass transportation, and decay of central cities.

In other areas, Eisenhower restrained federal activity in favor of state governments and private enterprise. His large tax cuts directed most benefits to business and the wealthy, he resisted federal aid to primary and secondary education, and he avoided strong White House leadership on behalf of civil rights. Eisenhower opposed national health insurance, preferring the growing practice of private insurance through employment. Moreover, whereas Democrats sought to keep nuclear power in government hands, Eisenhower signed legislation authorizing the private manufacture and sale of nuclear energy. The first commercial nuclear power plant in the United States opened in 1958 in Shippingport, Pennsylvania, northwest of Pittsburgh.

Termination and Relocation of Native Americans

Eisenhower's efforts to limit the federal government were consistent with a new direction in Indian policy, which reversed the emphasis on strengthening tribal governments and preserving Indian culture that had been established in the 1930s (see chapter 24). After World War II, when some 25,000 Indians had left their homes for military service and another 40,000 for work in defense industries, policymakers began to favor assimilating Native Americans and ending their special relationships with the government.

To some officials, who reflected the Cold War emphasis on conformity to dominant American values, the communal practices of Indians resembled socialism and stifled individual initiative. Eisenhower's commissioner of Indian affairs, Glenn Emmons, did not believe that tribal lands could produce income sufficient to lift Indians from poverty, but he also revealed the ethnocentrism of policymakers when he insisted that Indians wanted to "work and live like Americans." Moreover, government treaties with Indian nations protected Indian rights to water, land, minerals, and other resources that were increasingly attractive to state governments and private entrepreneurs.

By 1960, the government had implemented a three-part program of compensation, termination, and relocation. In 1946, Congress established the Indian Claims Commission to discharge outstanding claims by Native Americans for land taken by the government. When it closed in 1978, the commission had settled 285 cases, with compensation exceeding $800 million. Yet the awards were based on land values at the time the land was taken and did not include interest.

The second policy, termination, also originated in the Truman administration, during which Commissioner Dillon S. Myer asserted that his Bureau of Indian Affairs should do "nothing for Indians which Indians can do for themselves." Beginning in 1953, Eisenhower signed bills transferring jurisdiction over tribal land to state and local governments and ending the trusteeship relationship between Indians and the federal government. The loss of federal hospitals, schools, and other special arrangements devastated Indian tribes. As had happened after passage of the Dawes Act in 1887 (see chapter 17), some corporate interests and individuals took advantage of the opportunity to purchase Indian land cheaply. For many Indians, termination was "like the strike of doom." The government abandoned termination in the 1960s after some 13,000 Indians and more than one million acres of their land had been affected. Several tribes, including the Menominee and the Klamath, fought successfully to reverse termination and to secure restoration of their tribal status.

The **Indian Relocation Program**, the third piece of Native American policy, began in 1948 and involved more than 100,000 Native Americans by 1973. The government encouraged Indians to move to cities, where relocation centers were supposed to help with housing, job training, and

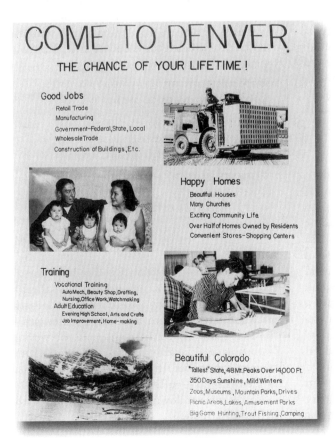

medical care. Even though government officials made it difficult to return home by sending Indians far away from their reservations, about one-third returned to the reservation.

Most who stayed in cities faced racism, lack of adequately paying jobs for which they had skills, poor housing, and the loss of their traditional culture. "I wish we had never left home," said one woman whose husband was out of work and drinking heavily. "It's dirty and noisy, and people all around, crowded. . . . It seems like I never see the sky or trees." Moreover, Native Americans who relocated to cities found them to be on the decline, as urban wealth began to shift to the suburbs throughout the 1950s and 1960s. Like African Americans who migrated to cities in great numbers in the 1950s, Indians found declining opportunities for economic progress (see page 912).

Reflecting long-standing disagreements among Indians themselves, some who overcame these obstacles applauded the program. But most urban Indians remained in or near poverty, and even many who had welcomed relocation began to worry that "we would lose our identity as Indian people, lose our culture and our [way] of living." Within two decades, a national pan-Indian movement emerged to resist assimilation and to demand much more for Indians (as discussed in chapter 28). The new militancy and connections across tribal lines that arose were a by-product of the urbanization of Native Americans.

Major Indian Relocations, 1950–1970

with Congress over the budget and vetoed bills to expand housing, urban development, and public works projects. The president and Congress did reach agreement in two key areas: enacting the first, though largely symbolic, civil rights legislation in a century and extending the federal government's role in education, largely in the interest of national security (as discussed on pages 906–908 and 915).

In the end, the first Republican administration after the New Deal left the size and functions of the federal government intact, though it tipped policy somewhat more in favor of corporate interests. Unparalleled prosperity graced the Eisenhower years, and inflation was kept low. The economy weathered two recessions without testing the president's aversion to substantial federal intervention. Eisenhower celebrated what he called the "wide diffusion of wealth and incomes" across the United States. Yet neglected amid the remarkable abundance were some forty million Americans who lived below the poverty level. Rural deprivation was particularly pronounced, as was poverty among African Americans and other minorities, who failed to benefit from the massive defense spending that fueled the economy as a whole.

REVIEW How did Eisenhower's domestic policies reflect his moderate political vision?

The 1956 Election and the Second Term

Not all citizens were living the American dream, but with the nation at peace and the economy booming, Eisenhower easily defeated Adlai Stevenson in 1956, doubling his victory margin of 1952. Yet Democrats kept control of Congress, and in the midterm elections two years later, they all but wiped out the Republican Party, gaining a 64–34 majority in the Senate and a 282–135 advantage in the House. Although Ike captured voters' hearts, a majority of Americans remained wedded to the programs and policies of the Democrats.

Eisenhower faced more serious leadership challenges in his second term. When the economy plunged into a recession in late 1957, he fought

▶ Liberation Rhetoric and the Practice of Containment

At his 1953 inauguration, Eisenhower warned that "forces of good and evil are massed and armed and opposed as rarely before in history." Like Truman, he saw communism as a threat to the nation's security and economic interests and wanted to maintain the United States' position as the most powerful country in the world. Eisenhower's foreign policy differed from Truman's, however, in three areas: its rhetoric, its means, and — after Stalin's death in 1953 — its movement toward accommodation with the Soviet Union.

Republican rhetoric, voiced most prominently by Secretary of State John Foster Dulles, deplored containment as "negative, futile, and immoral" because it accepted the existing Soviet sphere of control. Yet despite promises to roll back Soviet power, the Eisenhower administration continued the containment policy. The United States intervened at the margins of Communist power — in Asia, the Middle East, and Latin America — but not at its core in Europe. Eisenhower assigned nuclear weapons and CIA secret operations larger roles in defense strategy, and he took steps to ease tensions between the two superpowers.

The "New Look" in Foreign Policy

To meet his goals of balancing the budget and cutting taxes, Eisenhower was determined to control military expenditures. Moreover, he feared that massive defense spending would threaten the nation's economic strength. As he declared in 1953, "Every gun that is made, every warship launched, every rocket fired signifies, in the final sense, a theft from those who hunger and are not fed, those who are cold and not clothed."

Reflecting Americans' confidence in technology and their opposition to a large peacetime army, Eisenhower's defense strategy concentrated U.S. military strength in nuclear weapons and the planes and missiles to deliver them. Instead of maintaining large ground forces of its own, the United States would give friendly nations American weapons and back them up with an ominous nuclear arsenal, providing, according to the secretary of defense, "more bang for the buck." This was Eisenhower's "New Look" in foreign policy. Secretary of State Dulles believed that America's willingness to "go to the brink" of war with its intimidating nuclear weapons — a strategy called brinksmanship — would block any Soviet efforts to expand.

Throughout the 1950s, the United States far outpaced the Soviet Union in nuclear warheads and delivery missiles, yet its superiority did not ensure security. Nuclear weapons could not stop a Soviet nuclear attack. In response to one, however, they could inflict enormous destruction. This certainty of "massive retaliation" was meant to deter the Soviets from launching an attack. Because the Soviet Union could respond similarly to an American first strike, this nuclear standoff became known as **mutually assured destruction, or MAD**. Leaders of both nations pursued an ever-escalating arms race.

Missiles in the Nuclear Arms Race
After World War II, both the United States and the Soviet Union dug for information about rocketry from German installations and German scientists and engineers, who were leaders in the development of missiles. By the 1950s, both nations were arming missiles with nuclear weapons. In 1957, the United States began building intercontinental ballistic missiles (ICBMs) that could hit the Soviet Union from a launching site in the American Midwest. Shown here are missiles being manufactured by Boeing, a leading corporation in the aerospace industry, housed in Seattle, Washington. Photo by B. Anthony Stewart/ National Geographic/Getty Images.

Nuclear weapons could not roll back the iron curtain. When a revolt against the Soviet-controlled government began in Hungary in 1956, Dulles's liberation rhetoric proved to be empty. As Soviet tanks arrived to crush the revolt, a radio plea from freedom fighters cried, "SOS! They just brought us a rumor that the American troops will be here within one or two hours." But help did not come. Eisenhower was unwilling to risk U.S. soldiers and possible nuclear war, and Soviet troops soon suppressed the insurrection, killing or wounding thousands of Hungarians.

Applying Containment to Vietnam

A major challenge to the containment policy came in Southeast Asia. During World War II, Ho Chi Minh, a Vietnamese nationalist who also embraced communism, had founded a coalition called the Vietminh to fight both the occupying Japanese forces and the French colonial rulers. In 1945, the Vietminh declared Vietnam's independence from France, and when France fought to maintain its colony, the area plunged into war. After the Communists won control of China, the Truman administration quietly began to provide aid to the French and recognized their puppet government in the southern part of Vietnam (see chapter 29, Map 29.2). American principles of national self-determination took a backseat to the battle against communism.

Eisenhower viewed communism in Vietnam much as Truman had regarded it in Greece and Turkey, a view that became known as the **domino theory**. "You have a row of dominoes," Eisenhower explained, and "you knock over the first one, and what will happen to the last one is the certainty that it will go over very quickly." A Communist victory in Southeast Asia, he warned, could trigger the fall of Japan, Taiwan, and the Philippines. By 1954, the United States was contributing 75 percent of the cost of France's war, but Eisenhower resisted a larger role. When the French asked for troops and airplanes from the United States to avert almost certain defeat at Dien Bien Phu, Eisenhower, conscious of U.S. losses in the Korean War (see chapter 26), said no.

Dien Bien Phu fell in May 1954 and with it the French colony of Vietnam. Two months later in Geneva, France signed a truce. The **Geneva accords** temporarily partitioned Vietnam at the seventeenth parallel, separating the Vietminh in the north from the puppet government established by the French in the south. Within two years, the Vietnamese people were to vote in elections for a unified government. Some officials warned against U.S. involvement in Vietnam. Defense Secretary Charles Wilson saw "nothing but grief in store for us if we remained in that area." Eisenhower and Dulles nonetheless moved to prop up the dominoes with a new alliance. In September 1954, the United States joined with Britain, France, Australia, New Zealand, Thailand, Pakistan, and the Philippines in the Southeast Asia Treaty Organization, committed to the defense of Cambodia, Laos, and South Vietnam. Shortly thereafter, Eisenhower began to send weapons and military advisers to South Vietnam and put the CIA to work infiltrating and destabilizing North Vietnam. Fearing a Communist victory in the elections mandated by the Geneva accords, the United States supported South Vietnamese prime minister Ngo Dinh Diem's refusal to hold the vote.

Geneva Accords, 1954

Between 1955 and 1961, the United States provided $800 million to the South Vietnamese army (the Army of the Republic of Vietnam, or ARVN). Yet the ARVN proved grossly unprepared for the guerrilla warfare that began in the late 1950s. With military assistance from Ho Chi Minh's government in Hanoi, Vietminh rebels in the south stepped up their guerrilla attacks on the Diem government. The insurgents gained support from the largely Buddhist peasants, who were outraged by the repressive regime of the Catholic, Westernized Diem. Unwilling to abandon containment, Eisenhower left his successor with the deteriorating situation and a firm commitment to defend South Vietnam against communism.

Interventions in Latin America and the Middle East

While supporting friendly governments in Asia, the Eisenhower administration worked secretly to topple unfriendly ones in Latin America and the Middle East. Officials saw internal civil wars in terms of the Cold War conflict between the superpowers and tended to view nationalist uprisings as Communist threats to democracy. They acted against governments that not only seemed too leftist but also threatened U.S. economic interests. The Eisenhower administration took this course of action out of sight of Congress and the public, making the CIA an important arm of foreign policy.

The government of Guatemala, under the popularly elected reformist president Jacobo Arbenz, was not Soviet controlled, but it accepted support from the local Communist Party (see chapter 29, Map 29.1). In 1953, Arbenz moved to help landless, poverty-stricken peasants by nationalizing uncultivated land owned by the United Fruit Company, a U.S. corporation whose annual profits were twice the size of the Guatemalan government's budget. United Fruit refused Arbenz's offer to compensate the company at the value of the land it had declared for tax purposes. Then, in response to the nationalization program, the CIA organized and supported an opposition army that overthrew the elected government and installed a military dictatorship in 1954. United Fruit kept its land, and Guatemala descended into a series of destructive civil wars that lasted through the 1990s.

In 1959, the desire for political and economic autonomy erupted into the **Cuban revolution**, led by **Fidel Castro**. At the time, a CIA agent promised "to take care of Castro just like we took care of Arbenz." American companies had long controlled major Cuban resources, and decisions made in Washington directly influenced the lives of the Cuban people. The 1959 uprising drove out the U.S.-supported dictator Fulgencio Batista and led the CIA to warn Eisenhower that "Communists and other extreme radicals appear to have penetrated the Castro movement." When the United States denied Castro's requests for loans, he turned to the Soviet Union. And when U.S. companies refused Castro's offer to purchase them at their assessed value, he began to nationalize their property. Many anti-Castro Cubans fled to the United States and reported his atrocities, including the execution of hundreds of Batista's supporters. (See "Seeking the American Promise," page 906.) Before leaving office, Eisenhower broke off diplomatic relations with Cuba and authorized the CIA to train Cuban exiles for an invasion.

In the Middle East, the CIA intervened to oust an elected government, support an unpopular dictatorship, and maintain Western access to Iranian oil (see chapter 30, Map 30.3). In 1951, the Iranian parliament, led by **Mohammed Mossadegh**, the nationalist prime minister, nationalized the country's oil fields and refineries. Most of the oil operations had been held by a British company for decades, and Iran received less than 20 percent of the profits from its own resources. The British strongly objected to the takeover and eventually sought help from the United States.

Advisers convinced Eisenhower that Mossadegh, whom *Time* magazine had called "the Iranian George Washington," left Iran vulnerable to communism, and the president wanted to keep oil-rich areas "under the control of people who are friendly." With his authorization, CIA agents instigated a coup by bribing army officers and financing demonstrations against the government. In August 1953, Iranian army officers captured the prime minister and reestablished the authority of the shah of Iran, Mohammad Reza Pahlavi, known for favoring Western interests and the Iranian wealthy classes. Iran renegotiated its oil concessions, giving U.S. companies a 40 percent share. Resentment over this use of force would poison U.S.-Iranian relations into the twenty-first century.

Elsewhere in the Middle East, the Eisenhower administration continued Truman's support of

The CIA Helps Restore the Shah of Iran
In 1952, *Time* magazine called Iranian premier Mohammed Mossadegh "the Iranian George Washington," for his passionate commitment to nationalism and democracy. But Secretary of State John Foster Dulles believed that restoring the power of Shah Reza Pahlevi would produce a more stable U.S. ally and persuaded President Eisenhower to approve a CIA-supported coup. Here an Iranian army officer rallies supporters of the shah outside the home of Mossadegh, who was eventually forced out. The shah had dozens of Mossadegh's supporters executed, and the elderly Mossadegh spent three years in prison and the rest of his life under house arrest. AP Images.

Israel but also sought to foster friendships with Arab nations to secure access to oil and build a bulwark against communism. Yet U.S. officials demanded that smaller nations take the American side in the Cold War, even when those nations preferred to remain nonaligned, with the opportunity for assistance from both Western and Communist nations. In 1955, as part of the U.S. effort to win Arab allies, Secretary of State Dulles began talks with Egypt about American support to build the Aswan Dam on the Nile River. The following year, Egypt's leader, **Gamal Abdel Nasser**, sought arms from Communist Czechoslovakia, formed a military alliance with other Arab nations, and recognized the People's Republic of China. Unwilling to tolerate such independence, Dulles called off the deal for the dam.

On July 26, 1956, Nasser responded by seizing the Suez Canal, then owned by Britain

The Suez Crisis, 1956

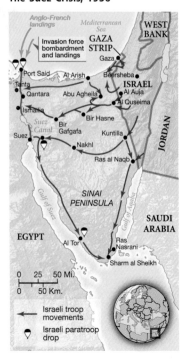

Operation Pedro Pan: Young Political Refugees Take Flight

Six-year-old María was awakened before dawn one summer day in Cuba in 1962. Her parents drove her to the Havana airport, with one suitcase and her favorite doll. A paper pinned to her gingham dress gave her name and the phone number of family friends in Miami who were to meet her. She traveled with a six-year-old boy whose father in Miami had obtained the visa waivers the children would need to enter the United States. María, excited but anxious, had never been away from her parents before; she would not see them for four months.

On a different flight that summer, ten-year-old Carlos flew to Miami with his older brother, leaving behind a father they would never see again. Because of their age difference, the boys were separated on arrival and sent to different refugee camps in rural Florida. A family acquaintance — a Cuban lawyer working as a janitor in Miami — helped them gain temporary placement with foster families just ten blocks apart. A few months later, they were transferred to a juvenile delinquent facility that provided only one meal a day. Finally, a Cuban uncle arrived and took them with him to a small midwestern town where no one spoke Spanish. After three years of traumatic separation, their mother fled Cuba and joined them.

María and Carlos were just two of more than fourteen thousand unaccompanied children, ages six to eighteen, who left Cuba as part of a special U.S. government–facilitated program called Operation Pedro Pan, which functioned from December 1960 to October 1962. With little money, no knowledge of English, and often no friends or relatives to receive them, the children faced daunting loneliness and possibly neglect. What drove the parents of these children to take such an extraordinary step?

The U.S. government had already made unusual accommodation for the large exodus of adults fleeing Cuba after Fidel Castro came to power in 1959. Assuming that the refugees would return to Cuba as soon as Castro's government fell, the United States relaxed immigration restrictions for Cubans, allowed refugees to work, and authorized millions of dollars in relief and resettlement funds for people "subjected to the captivity of Communist despotism." The U.S. government felt an obligation to shelter Cubans who had worked in the government or military of deposed dictator Fulgencio Batista, a close U.S. ally. Many other Cubans who fled to the United States after the revolution had worked for U.S.-owned businesses. Still others were wealthy merchants and professionals — doctors, lawyers, university professors. By the fall of 1962, 248,000 Cubans had chosen to flee communism, furnishing the United States with a powerful symbolic statement of Cold War politics.

An even more potent symbol was Operation Pedro Pan, with its implication that Castro's Cuba had to be truly terrible for parents to part with their children, even though they expected to see their children soon. Cuban parents who opposed Castro feared not for their children's lives, but for their minds. Public schools in Cuba reportedly taught an escalating rhetoric of revolution, while private schools were shut down. Compulsory military service

and France but scheduled to revert to Egypt within seven years. In response to the seizure, Israel, whose forces had been skirmishing with Egyptian troops along their common border since 1948, attacked Egypt, with military help from Britain and France. Eisenhower opposed the intervention, recognizing that the Egyptians had claimed their own territory and that Nasser "embodie[d] the emotional demands of the people . . . for independence." He put economic pressure on Britain and France while calling on the United Nations to arrange a truce. The French and British soon pulled back, forcing Israel to retreat.

Despite staying out of the **Suez crisis**, Eisenhower made it clear that the United States would actively combat communism in the Middle East. In March 1957, Congress passed a joint resolution approving aid to any Middle Eastern nation "requesting assistance against armed aggression from any country controlled by international communism." The president invoked this **Eisenhower Doctrine** to send aid to Jordan in 1957 and troops to Lebanon in 1958 to counter anti-Western pressures on those governments.

The Nuclear Arms Race

While Eisenhower moved against perceived Communist inroads abroad, he also sought to reduce superpower tensions. After Stalin's death

for boys and summer programs relocating teenagers to jobs teaching literacy in the rural countryside threatened parental rights to determine their children's activities. Relatively prosperous Cuban families did not benefit from Castro's reforms, which focused on improving health and education for the impoverished masses. Their fears of socialized child rearing were reinforced by a program of disinformation allegedly broadcast from a CIA radio station, which warned parents that "the Revolutionary Government will take [your children] away from you when they turn five and will keep them until they are eighteen." Rumors of Communist indoctrination ran rampant.

Fear of communism gripped the United States in the 1950s, and the Pedro Pan exodus both demonstrated and heightened that fear. The belief that Communists brainwashed children and turned them against their parents led some Cuban parents to try to save their children by sending them to a country that celebrated freedom. And, as with the adult refugees who had fled Cuba for the United States, parents of the Pedro Pan children believed that the trip would be temporary, until the fall of Castro's regime. But some of the children themselves, now grown, have questioned whether coming to America was worth the trauma they endured

Leaving Havana
A family camera captures María de los Angeles Torres (far left) at the airport in Havana, before her flight to Miami in July 1961. AP Images.

and have speculated that Cold War politics might have shaped the operation more than humanitarian concerns. María de los Angeles Torres and Carlos Eire, two among the thousands, grew up to become university professors in the United States. Like the majority of Pedro Pan children, they are now glad they came here, but they also wonder about the choices their families made.

Questions for Consideration

1. What were the parents of the boys and girls in Operation Pedro Pan trying to save their children from?

2. What did the United States stand to gain from harboring Cuban exiles, especially children?

in 1953, a more moderate leadership under **Nikita Khrushchev** emerged. Like Eisenhower, who remarked privately that the arms race would lead "at worst to atomic warfare, at best to robbing every people and nation on earth of the fruits of their own toil," Khrushchev wanted to reduce defense spending and the threat of nuclear devastation. Eisenhower and Khrushchev met in Geneva in 1955 at the first summit conference since the end of World War II. Although the meeting produced no new agreements, it symbolized what Eisenhower called "a new spirit of conciliation and cooperation."

In August 1957, the Soviets test-fired their first intercontinental ballistic missile (ICBM) and two months later beat the United States

into space by launching *Sputnik*, the first artificial satellite to circle the earth. The United States launched a successful satellite of its own in January 1958, but *Sputnik* raised fears that the United States lagged behind the Soviets not only in missile development and space exploration but also in science and education. In response, Eisenhower established the National Aeronautics and Space Administration (NASA), approving a huge budget increase for space research and development. Also in 1958, Congress passed the National Defense Education Act, providing support for instruction at all levels in math, foreign languages, and science and technology. Eisenhower assured the public that the United States possessed nuclear superiority.

The Age of Nuclear Anxiety
As schools routinely held drills to prepare for possible Soviet attacks, children directly experienced the anxiety and insecurity of the 1950s nuclear arms race. This pamphlet about how to protect oneself from an atomic attack was published by the federal government and distributed to the general public. How effective do you think the strategy pictured here would be in a nuclear attack? Why would the government publish a pamphlet indicating that civilians could protect themselves? Photo: Archive Photos/Getty Images; Pamphlet: Lynn Historical Society

In fact, during his presidency, the stockpile of nuclear weapons more than quadrupled; the United States had installed ICBMs at home and in Britain and was prepared to deploy more in Italy and Turkey. The first Polaris submarine carrying nuclear missiles was launched in November 1960. Yet these weapons could not guarantee security because both superpowers possessed sufficient nuclear capacity to devastate each other. Most Americans did not follow Civil Defense Administration recommendations to construct home bomb shelters, but they did realize how precarious nuclear weapons had made their lives.

In the midst of the arms race, the superpowers continued to talk. In 1959, Khrushchev visited the United States, and Nixon went to the Soviet Union, where he engaged in the famous kitchen debate. By 1960, the two sides were close to a ban on nuclear testing. But just before a planned summit in Paris, a Soviet missile shot down an American U-2 spy plane over Soviet territory. The State Department first denied that U.S. planes had been violating Soviet airspace, but the Soviets produced the pilot and the photos taken on his flight. Eisenhower and Khrushchev met briefly in Paris, but the U-2 incident dashed all prospects for a nuclear arms agreement.

As Eisenhower left office, he warned about the growing influence of the **military-industrial complex** in American government and life. Eisenhower had struggled against persistent pressures from defense contractors who, in tandem with the military, sought more dollars for newer, more powerful weapons systems. In his farewell address, he warned that the "conjunction of an immense military establishment and a large arms industry . . . exercised a total influence . . . in every city, every state house, every office of the federal government." The Cold War had created a warfare state.

REVIEW   Where and how did Eisenhower practice containment?

▶ New Work and Living Patterns in an Economy of Abundance

Stimulated in part by Cold War spending, economic productivity increased enormously in the 1950s. A multitude of new items came on the market, and consumption became the order of the day. Millions of Americans enjoyed new homes in the suburbs, and higher education enrollments skyrocketed. Although every section of the nation enjoyed the new abundance, the West and Southwest — the **Sun Belt** — especially boomed in production, commerce, and population.

Work itself was changing. Fewer people labored on farms, service sector employment overtook manufacturing jobs, and women's employment grew. These economic shifts disadvantaged some Americans, and they did little to help the forty million who lived in poverty. Most Americans, however, enjoyed a higher standard of living, prompting economist John Kenneth Galbraith to call the United States "the affluent society."

Technology Transforms Agriculture and Industry

Between 1940 and 1960, agricultural output mushroomed even while the number of farmworkers declined by almost one-third. Farmers achieved nearly miraculous productivity through greater crop specialization, intensive use of fertilizers, and, above all, mechanization. A single mechanical cotton picker, for example, replaced fifty people and cut the cost of harvesting a bale of cotton from $40 to $5.

The decline of family farms and the growth of large commercial farming, or agribusiness, were both causes and consequences of mechanization. Benefiting handsomely from federal price supports begun in the New Deal, larger farmers could afford technological improvements, whereas smaller producers lacked capital to invest in the machinery necessary to compete. Consequently, average farm size more than doubled between 1940 and 1964, and the number of farms fell by more than 40 percent.

Many small farmers who hung on constituted a core of rural poverty often overlooked in the

Technology Transforms Agriculture
The years from 1945 to 1970 saw a second agricultural revolution in the United States. In 1954, tractors outnumbered mules and horses on farms for the first time. In 1940, one farmer could feed 10.7 people. By 1960, one farmer could supply 25.8 people, and in 1970 that ratio was 1 to 75.8. Threshing machines sweeping across a midwestern wheat field in 1960 exemplify the onslaught of agribusiness. The advertisement shows how one person could plant several rows of corn by barely lifting a finger. Threshing machine: © Bettmann/Corbis; Advertisement: International Harvester Company.

Poverty in an Era of Abundance
The Whiteheads, a coal-mining family in Kentucky, represented the hidden side of the affluent 1950s. Mrs. John Whitehead lived with her husband, their six children, and their six grandchildren in this three-room house. It had neither running water nor electricity, and the only access to the house was over a mountain trail. National Archives.

celebration of affluence. Southern landowners replaced sharecroppers and tenants with machines, forcing them off the land. Hundreds of thousands of African Americans joined an exodus to cities, where racial discrimination and a lack of jobs for which they could qualify mired many in urban poverty. A Mississippi mother whose family had worked on a plantation since slavery reported that most of her relatives headed for Chicago when they realized that "it was going to be machines now that harvest the crops." Worrying that "it might be worse up there" for her children, she agonized, "I'm afraid to leave and I'm afraid to stay."

Industrial production was also transformed by new technologies. Between 1945 and 1960, for example, the number of labor-hours needed to manufacture a car fell by 50 percent. Technology transformed industries such as electronics, chemicals, and air transportation and promoted the growth of television, plastics, computers, and other newer industries. American businesses enjoyed access to cheap oil, ample markets abroad, and little foreign competition. Moreover, even with Eisenhower's conservative fiscal policies, government spending reached $80 billion annually and created new jobs.

Labor unions enjoyed their greatest success during the 1950s, and real earnings for production workers shot up 40 percent. The merger in 1955 of the American Federation of Labor (AFL) and the Congress of Industrial Organizations (CIO) improved labor's bargaining position. As one worker put it, "We saw continual improvement in wages, fringe benefits like holidays, vacation, medical plans . . . all sorts of things that provided more security for people." In most industrial nations, government programs underwrote their citizens' security, but the United States developed a mixed system in which company-funded programs won by unions through collective bargaining played a much larger role in providing for retirement, health care, and the like. This system, often called a private welfare state, resulted in wide disparities among workers, severely disadvantaging those not represented by unions and those with irregular employment.

While the absolute number of organized workers continued to grow, union membership peaked at 27.1 percent of the labor force in 1957. Technological advances eliminated jobs in heavy industry, reducing the number of workers in the steel, copper, and aluminum industries by 17 percent. "You are going to have trouble collecting union dues from all of these machines," commented a Ford manager to union leader Walter Reuther. Moreover, the economy as a whole was shifting from production to service as more workers distributed goods, performed services, provided education, and carried out government work. Unions made some headway in these fields, especially among government employees, but most service industries resisted unionization.

The growing clerical and service occupations swelled the demand for female workers. By the end of the 1950s, 35 percent of all women over age sixteen worked outside the home, and women held nearly one-third of all jobs. The vast majority of them worked in offices, light manufacturing, domestic service, teaching, and nursing; because these occupations were occupied primarily by women, wages were relatively low. In 1960, the average female full-time worker earned just 60 percent of the average male worker's wages. At the bottom of the employment ladder, black women took home only 42 percent of what white men earned.

Burgeoning Suburbs and Declining Cities

Although suburbs had existed since the nineteenth century, nothing symbolized the affluent society more than their tremendous expansion in the 1950s. Eleven million new homes went up in the suburbs, and by 1960 one in four Americans lived there. As Nixon boasted to Khrushchev during the **kitchen debate** (see pages 897–98), the suburbs were accessible to families with modest incomes. Builder William

J. Levitt adapted the factory assembly-line process to home building, planning nearly identical units so that individual construction workers could move from house to house and perform the same single operation in each one. In 1949, families could purchase mass-produced houses in his 17,000-home development, called Levittown, on Long Island, New York, for just under $8,000 each. Developments similar to Levittown, as well as more luxurious ones, quickly went up throughout the country. The government underwrote home ownership by guaranteeing low-interest mortgages through the Federal Housing Administration and the Veterans Administration and by making interest on mortgages tax deductible. Thousands of miles of government-funded interstate highway running through urban areas indirectly subsidized suburban development.

The growing suburbs helped polarize society, especially along racial lines. Each Levittown homeowner signed a contract pledging not to rent or sell to a non-Caucasian. The Supreme Court declared such covenants unenforceable in 1948, but suburban America remained dramatically segregated. Social critic Lewis Mumford blasted the suburbs as "a multitude of uniform, unidentifiable houses in a treeless communal wasteland, inhabited by people of the same class, the same income, the same age group." By the 1960s, suburbs also came under attack for bulldozing the natural environment, creating

> "A multitude of uniform, unidentifiable houses in a treeless communal wasteland."
> —Social critic LEWIS MUMFORD, describing the suburbs

The New Suburbs
A family surveys Levittown as it appeared in 1956. Levitt & Sons provided each family with a nineteen-page brochure explaining all the features of their new home. The brochure included several pages of "those special restrictions" about when and where to hang laundry, the location and size of shrubbery, and how often to mow the lawn. Fences were prohibited, to preserve a "maximum of openness and park-like appearance." State Museum of PA, PA Historical and Museum Commission.

HOMEOWNERS GUIDE.
SOME INFORMATION FOR RESIDENTS OF LEVITTOWN TO HELP THEM ENJOY THEIR NEW HOMES

An African American Suburb
The pioneer of mass-produced suburban housing, William J. Levitt, reflected the racism that kept blacks out of suburbia when he said, "We can solve a housing problem, or we can try and solve a racial problem, but we cannot combine the two." These African Americans developed their own suburb, a planned community for middle-class blacks in Richmond, California, which welcomed the first families in 1950. Richmond Public Library.

groundwater contamination, and disrupting wildlife patterns.

Although some African Americans joined the suburban migration, most moved to cities in search of economic opportunity, increasing their numbers in most cities by 50 percent during the 1950s. These migrants, however, came to cities that were already in decline, losing not only population but also commerce and industry to the suburbs or to southern and western states. Shoppers gradually chose new suburban malls over downtown department stores. Many of the new jobs lay beyond the reach of the recent black arrivals to the inner cities.

The Rise of the Sun Belt

No regions experienced the postwar economic and population booms more intensely than the West and Southwest (Map 27.2). Architect Frank Lloyd Wright quipped, "Everything loose will land in Los Angeles." California overtook New York as the most populous state. Sports franchises followed fans: In 1958, the Brooklyn Dodgers moved to Los Angeles, joined by the Minneapolis Lakers three years later.

A pleasant natural environment drew new residents to the West and Southwest, but no magnet proved stronger than the promise of economic opportunity. As railroads had fueled western growth in the nineteenth century, so the automobile and airplane spurred the post-

World War II surge. The technology of air-conditioning facilitated industrial development and by 1960 cooled nearly eight million homes in the so-called Sun Belt, which stretched from Florida to California.

So important was the defense industry to the South and West that the area was later referred to as the "Gun Belt." The aerospace industry boomed in Seattle–Tacoma, Los Angeles, and Dallas–Fort Worth, and military bases helped underwrite prosperity in cities such as San Diego and San Antonio. Although defense dollars benefited other regions, the Sun Belt captured the lion's share of Cold War spending. By the 1960s, nearly one of every three California workers held a defense-related job.

The surging populations and industries soon threatened the environment. Providing sufficient water and power to cities and to agribusiness meant building dams and reservoirs on free-flowing rivers. Native Americans lost fishing sites on the Columbia River, and dams on the Upper Missouri displaced nine hundred Indian families. Sprawling urban and suburban settlement without efficient public transportation contributed to blankets of smog over Los Angeles and other cities.

The high-technology basis of postwar economic development drew well-educated, highly skilled workers to the West, but the economic promise also attracted the poor. "We see opportunity all around us here. . . . We smell freedom

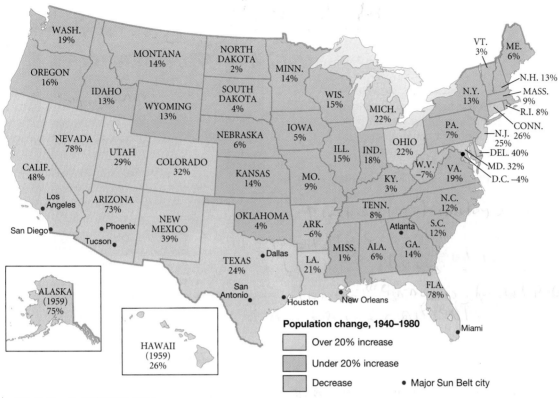

MAP ACTIVITY

Map 27.2   The Rise of the Sun Belt, 1940–1980

The growth of defense industries, a non-unionized labor force, and the spread of air-conditioning all helped spur economic development and population growth in the West and South, which made the Sun Belt the fastest-growing region of the country between 1940 and 1980.

READING THE MAP: Which states experienced population growth of more than 20 percent? Which states experienced the largest population growth?

CONNECTIONS: What stimulated the population boom in the Southwest? What role did the Cold War play in this expansion? What developments made the Southwest diverse in the composition of its population?

here, and maybe soon we can taste it," commented a black mother in California. Between 1945 and 1960, more than one-third of the African Americans who left the South moved west.

The Mexican American population also grew, especially in California and Texas. To supply California's vast agribusiness industry, the government continued the *bracero* program begun during World War II, under which Mexican laborers were permitted to enter the United States to work for a limited period. Until the program ended in 1964, more than 100,000 Mexicans entered the United States each year to labor in the fields — and many of them stayed, legally or illegally. But permanent Mexican immigration was not as welcome as Mexicans' low-wage labor. In 1954, the government launched a series of raids called "Operation Wetback," resulting in

the deportation of more than three million Mexicans. Even Mexicans with legal status felt unwelcome and vulnerable to incidents of mistaken identity.

At the same time, Mexican American citizens gained a victory in their ongoing struggle for civil rights in *Hernandez v. Texas*. When a Texas jury convicted Pete Hernandez of murder, lawyers from the American GI Forum and the League of United Latin-American Citizens (see chapter 26) appealed on the grounds that persons of Mexican origin had been routinely excluded from jury service. In 1954, the Supreme Court decided its first Mexican American civil rights case of the post–World War II era, ruling unanimously that Mexican Americans constituted a distinct group and that their systematic exclusion from juries violated the Fourteenth Amendment guarantee

THE PROMISE OF TECHNOLOGY

Air-Conditioning

In 1902, Willis Haviland Carrier, a twenty-six-year-old American engineer, designed the first system to control temperature and humidity and installed it in a Brooklyn printing plant. Room air conditioners began to appear in the 1930s and spread rapidly in the 1950s. Fewer than one million homes had room air conditioners in 1950, but nearly eight million did in 1960, and more than half of all homes had some form of air-conditioning by 1975, as its status changed from a luxury to a necessity. By cooling homes, businesses, factories, and hotels, air-conditioning made possible the industrial and popula-tion explosion in the Sun Belt. While this ad promised consumers clean as well as cool air inside the house, it failed to note that air-conditioning consumed large amounts of energy and contributed to air pollution out-side the house. What have been some of the effects of air-conditioning on social life and people's interactions with their neighbors? Hotpoint/General Electric Company.

of equal protection. Legal scholar Ian Haney-López called the *Hernandez* ruling "huge for the Mexican American community. They now had the highest court in the land saying it's unconstitutional to treat Mexicans as if they're an inferior race."

Free of the discrimination faced by minori-ties, white Americans enjoyed the fullest pros-perity in the West. In April 1950, when California developers opened Lakewood, a large housing

development in Los Angeles County, thirty thou-sand people lined up to buy houses at prices ranging from $71,000 to $89,000 in 2010 dollars. Many of the new homeowners were veterans, blue-collar, and lower-level white-collar workers whose defense-based jobs at aerospace corpora-tions enabled them to fulfill the American dream of the 1950s. A huge shopping mall, Lakewood Center, offered myriad products of the consumer

Rounding Up Undocumented Migrants

Not all Mexican Americans who wanted to work in the United States were accommodated by the *bracero* program. In 1953, Los Angeles police arrested these men, who did not have legal documents and were hiding in a freight train. Some Americans used the crude term "wetback" to refer to illegal Mexican immigrants because many of them swam across the Rio Grande, which forms part of the border between the United States and Mexico. © Bettmann/Corbis.

culture, and the workers' children lived within commuting distance of community colleges and six state universities.

The Democratization of Higher Education

California's university system exemplified a spectacular transformation of higher education. Between 1940 and 1960, college enrollments in the United States more than doubled. More than 40 percent of young Americans attended college by the mid-1960s, up from 15 percent in the 1940s. Prosperity enabled more families to keep their children in school longer, and the federal government subsidized the education of more than two million veterans. The Cold War also sent millions of federal dollars to universities for defense-related research. And state governments vastly expanded the number of public colleges and universities, while municipalities began to build two-year community colleges.

All Americans did not benefit equally from the democratization of higher education. Although their college enrollments surged from 37,000 in 1941 to 90,000 in 1961, African Americans constituted only about 5 percent of all college students. Black men and women attended college in nearly equal numbers, but for a time the educational gap between white men and women grew, even while the number of women attending college increased. In 1940, women had earned 40 percent of undergraduate degrees, but as veterans flocked to college campuses, women's proportion fell to 25 percent in 1950 and rebounded to only 33 percent by 1960. The large veteran enrollments moved colleges to relax rules that had forbidden students to marry. Unlike men, however, women tended to drop out of college after marriage and to take jobs so their husbands could stay in school. Reflecting gender norms of the 1950s, most college women agreed that "it is natural for a woman to be satisfied with her husband's success and not crave personal achievement."

> **REVIEW** How did technology contribute to changes in the economy, suburbanization, and the growth of the Sun Belt?

▶ The Culture of Abundance

Prosperity in the 1950s intensified the transformation of the nation into a consumer society, changing the way Americans lived and converting the traditional work ethic into an ethic of consumption. People married at earlier ages, the

birthrate soared, and dominant values celebrated family life and traditional gender roles. Religious observance expanded even as Americans sought satisfaction in material possessions. Television entered the homes of most Americans, both reflecting and helping to promote a consumer culture. Undercurrents of rebellion, especially among young people, and women's increasing employment defied some of the dominant norms but did not greatly disrupt the complacency of the 1950s.

Consumption Rules the Day

Journalist Robert Samuelson remembered that in the 1950s "you were a daily witness to the marvels of affluence . . . a seemingly endless array of new gadgets and machines." Scorned by Khrushchev during the kitchen debate as unnecessary contrivances, consumer items flooded American society. Although the purchase and display of consumer goods was not new (see chapter 23), by the 1950s consumption had become a reigning value, vital for economic prosperity and essential to individuals' identity and status. In place of the traditional emphasis on work and savings, the consumer culture encouraged satisfaction and happiness through the purchase and use of new products.

> "You were a daily witness to the marvels of affluence . . . a seemingly endless array of new gadgets and machines."
> —Journalist ROBERT SAMUELSON, speaking of life in the 1950s

The consumer culture rested on a firm material base. Between 1950 and 1960, both the gross national product (the value of all goods and services produced) and median family income grew by 25 percent in constant dollars (Figure 27.1). Economists claimed that 60 percent of Americans enjoyed middle-class incomes in 1960. Referring to the popular ranch-style houses in the new suburbs, *House Beautiful* magazine boasted, "Our houses are all on one level, like our class structure." Though ignoring the one in five Americans who still lived in poverty, the statement did reflect the increasing ability of people to consume products that made class differences less visible. By 1960, four out of every five families owned a television set, nearly all had a refrigerator, and most owned at least one car. The number of shopping centers quadrupled between 1957 and 1963.

Several forces spurred this unparalleled abundance. A population surge — from 152 million in 1950 to 180 million in 1960 — expanded the demand for products and boosted industries ranging from housing to baby goods. Consumer borrowing also fueled the economic boom, as people increasingly made purchases on installment plans and began to use credit cards. In what *Life* magazine referred to as a "revolution in consumer purchasing,"

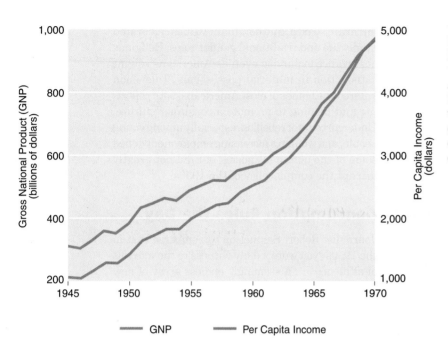

FIGURE 27.1   The Postwar Economic Boom: GNP and Per Capita Income, 1945–1970
American dominance of the worldwide market, innovative technologies that led to new industries such as computers and plastics, population growth, and increases in worker productivity all contributed to the enormous economic growth of the United States after World War II.

Americans now enjoyed their possessions while they paid for them instead of saving their money for future purchases.

Although the sheer need to support themselves and their families explained most women's employment, a desire to secure some of the new abundance sent growing numbers of women to work. In fact, married women's employment rose more than that of any other group in the 1950s. As one woman remarked, "My Joe can't put five kids through college . . . and the washer had to be replaced, and Ann was ashamed to bring friends home because the living room furniture was such a mess, so I went to work." The standards for family happiness imposed by the consumer culture increasingly required a second income.

The Revival of Domesticity and Religion

Despite married women's growing employment, a dominant ideology celebrated traditional family life and conventional gender roles. Both popular culture and public figures defined the ideal family as a male breadwinner, a full-time homemaker, and three or four children. The emphasis on home and family life reflected in part the desire for security amid anxieties about the Cold War and the nuclear menace. Writer and feminist **Betty Friedan** gave a name to the idealization of women's domestic roles in her 1963 book *The Feminine Mystique*. Friedan criticized scholars, advertisers, and public officials for promulgating a set of ideas based on the assumption that biological differences dictated different roles for men and women. According to this feminine mystique, women should find fulfillment in devotion to their homes, families, and serving others. Not many women directly challenged these ideas, but Edith Stern, a college-educated writer, maintained that "many arguments about the joys of housewifery have been advanced, largely by those who have never had to work at it."

Although the glorification of domesticity clashed with women's increasing employment, many Americans' lives did embody the family ideal. Postwar prosperity enabled people to marry earlier and to have more children. The American birthrate soared between 1945 and 1960, peaking in 1957 with 4.3 million births and producing the **baby boom** generation (Figure 27.2 and appendix II, page A-33). Experts encouraged mothers to devote even more attention to child rearing, while they also urged fathers to cultivate family "togetherness" by spending more time with their children.

The 1950s also witnessed a surge of interest in religion. From 1940 to 1960, membership in churches and synagogues rose from 50 to 63 percent of all Americans. Polls reported that 95 percent of the population believed in God. Evangelism took on new life, most notably in the nationwide crusades of Baptist minister **Billy Graham**. Congress linked religion more closely to the state by adding "under God" to the pledge of allegiance and by requiring that "In God We Trust" be printed on all currency.

Religion helped to calm anxieties in the nuclear age, while ministers such as Graham made the Cold War a holy war, labeling communism "a great sinister anti-Christian movement masterminded by

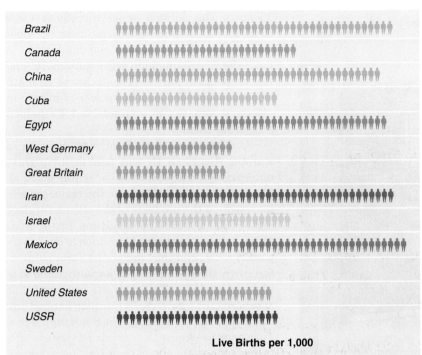

	Live Births per 1,000
Brazil	
Canada	
China	
Cuba	
Egypt	
West Germany	
Great Britain	
Iran	
Israel	
Mexico	
Sweden	
United States	
USSR	

FIGURE 27.2 GLOBAL COMPARISON: The Baby Boom in International Perspective The United States was not alone in welcoming bumper crops of babies in the 1950s. High fertility continued in nonindustrialized countries, while in Europe, as in the United States, birthrates rebounded from low levels during the Great Depression and World War II. Which countries had birthrates comparable to those of the United States? What might explain why countries such as Brazil, China, Iran, and Mexico had birthrates so much higher than those in the United States? What might explain why birthrates in Europe were lower than those in the United States?

Satan." Some critics questioned the depth of the religious revival, attributing the growth in church membership to a desire for conformity and a need for social outlets. One commentator, for example, noted that 53 percent of Americans could not name any book of the Christian Bible's New Testament.

Television Transforms Culture and Politics

Just as family life and religion offered a respite from Cold War anxieties, so too did the new medium of television. By 1960, close to 90 percent of American homes boasted a television set, and the average viewer spent more than five hours each day in front of the screen. Audiences were especially attracted to situation comedies, which projected the family ideal and the feminine mystique into millions of homes. On TV, married women did not have paying jobs, and they deferred to their husbands, though they often got the upper hand through subtle manipulation. In the most popular television show of the early 1950s, *I Love Lucy*, the husband-and-wife team of Lucille Ball and Desi Arnaz played the couple Lucy and Ricky Ricardo. Ricky would not let Lucy get a

Evangelist Billy Graham Preaches in New York City

Billy Graham, a young Baptist minister from North Carolina, electrified mass audiences, exhorting them to find salvation in Jesus Christ and to uphold Christian moral standards. Americans flocked to his crusades, even as he implicitly condemned their avid participation in consumerism as "materialistic, worldly, secular, greedy, and covetous." Here he addresses a crowd of 500,000 in Madison Square Garden during a crusade in New York City over the summer of 1957. One hundred thousand people heard Graham preach in Yankee Stadium, and millions watched the revivals on television. Martin Luther King Jr. joined Graham at one of the New York rallies. Photo: Gjon Mili/Time Life Pictures/Getty Images; brochure: Archives of the Billy Graham Center, Wheaton, Illinois.

The Made-for-TV Family
The Adventures of Ozzie and Harriet ran on television from 1952 to 1966. Like other family sitcoms, it idealized white family life, in which no one got divorced, no one took drugs or seriously misbehaved, fathers held white-collar jobs, and mothers did not work outside the home. Following the 1950s norm, Ozzie sought to fulfill his role as head of the household, but the impeccably dressed Harriet more often appeared as the wise and sensible one who rescued Ozzie and the teenage boys, David and Ricky, from their misadventures. In what ways do today's sitcoms differ from those of the 1950s? Picture Research Consultants & Archives.

TV spots. The ability to appeal directly to voters in their living rooms put a premium on personal attractiveness and encouraged candidates to build their own campaign organizations, relying less on political parties. The declining strength of parties and the growing power of money in elections were not new trends, but TV helped accelerate them.

Unlike government-financed television in Europe, American TV was paid for by private enterprise. What NBC called a "selling machine in every living room" became the major vehicle for hawking the products of the affluent society and creating a consumer culture. In the mid-1950s, advertisers spent $10 billion to push their goods on TV, and they did not hesitate to interfere with shows that might jeopardize the sale of their products. The cigarette company that sponsored the *Camel News Caravan* banned any news film clips showing "No Smoking" signs. Television programs also tantalized viewers with things to buy. On *Queen for a Day*, for example, the women with the most pitiful personal stories won fur coats, vacuum cleaners, and other merchandise.

In 1961, Newton Minow, chairman of the Federal Communications Commission, called television a "vast wasteland." While acknowledging some of TV's great achievements, particularly documentaries and drama, Minow depicted it as "a procession of game shows, . . . formula comedies about totally unbelievable families, blood and thunder, mayhem, violence, sadism, murder . . . and cartoons." But viewers kept tuning in. In little more than a decade, television came to dominate Americans' leisure time, influence their consumption patterns, and shape their perceptions of the nation's leadership.

Countercurrents

Pockets of dissent underlay the complacency of the 1950s. Some intellectuals took exception to the materialism and conformity of the era. In *The Lonely Crowd* (1950), sociologist David Riesman lamented a shift from the "inner-directed" to the "other-directed" individual, as Americans replaced independent thinking with an eagerness to adapt to external standards of behavior and belief. Sharing that distaste for the importance of "belonging," William H. Whyte Jr., in his popular book *The Organization Man* (1956), blamed the modern corporation for making employees tailor themselves to the group. Vance Packard's 1959 best seller, *The Status Seekers*, decried "the vigorous merchandising of goods as status-symbols" and argued that "class lines . . . appear to be hardening."

job, and many plots depicted her zany attempts to get around him.

Television also began to affect politics. Eisenhower's 1952 presidential campaign used TV ads for the first time, although he was not happy that "an old soldier should come to this." By 1960, television played a key role in election campaigns. Reflecting on his narrow victory in 1960, president-elect John F. Kennedy remarked, "We wouldn't have had a prayer without that gadget."

Television transformed politics in other ways. Money played a much larger role in elections because candidates needed to pay for expensive

Implicit in much of the critique of consumer culture was concern about the loss of traditional masculinity. Consumption itself was associated with women and their presumed greater susceptibility to manipulation. Men, required to conform to get ahead, moved farther away from the nineteenth-century masculine ideals of individualism and aggressiveness. Moreover, the increase in married women's employment compromised the male ideal of breadwinner.

Into this gender confusion came *Playboy*, which began publication in 1953 and quickly gained a circulation of one million. The new magazine idealized masculine independence in the form of bachelorhood and assaulted the reigning middle-class norms of domesticity and respectability. By associating the sophisticated bachelor with good wine, music, furnishings, and the like, the magazine made consumption more masculine while promoting sexual freedom, at least for men.

In fact, new research on Americans' sexual behavior disclosed that it often departed from the postwar family ideal. Two books published by **Alfred Kinsey** and other researchers at Indiana University — *Sexual Behavior in the Human Male* (1948) and *Sexual Behavior in the Human Female* (1953)

— uncovered a surprising range of sexual conduct. In a large survey, Kinsey found that 85 percent of the men and 50 percent of the women had had sex before marriage, half of the husbands and a quarter of the wives had engaged in adultery, and one-third of the men and one-seventh of the women reported homosexual experiences. Although Kinsey's sampling procedures later cast doubt on his ability to generalize across the population, the books became best sellers. They also drew a firestorm of outrage, especially because Kinsey insisted on the natural variability of human sexuality and refused to make moral judgments.

Less direct challenges to mainstream standards appeared in the everyday behavior of young Americans. "Roll over Beethoven and tell Tchaikovsky the news!" belted out Chuck Berry in his 1956 hit record celebrating **rock and roll**, a new form of music that combined country sounds and black rhythm and blues. White teenagers lionized Elvis Presley, who shocked their parents with his tight pants, hip-rolling gestures, and sensuous rock-and-roll music. "Before there was Elvis . . . I started going crazy for 'race music,'" recalled a white man of his

Elvis Presley
Elvis Presley began recording in 1954, and within two years — by the age of 21 — he was a national star, appearing frequently on television and scoring his first number one single hit, "Heartbreak Hotel." He drew adoring teenage crowds wherever he performed, including this appearance in his hometown of Tupelo, Mississippi, in 1956. His fans' parents were not so enthralled, complaining about his "grunt and groin antics" and "unnecessary bump and grind routine." Those trademark moves were captured on this button, which, when moved slightly, created an illusion of Elvis's gyrations.
Photograph: Elvis Presley Enterprises, Inc.; button: Elvis Presley Enterprises, Inc.

Jackson Pollock
The leading artist of the post–World War II revolution in painting, Jackson Pollock often worked with the canvas on the floor, dripping paint onto it with sticks, turkey basters, and hard brushes, prompting *Time* magazine to dub him, "Jack the Dripper." He struggled with alcohol and died in 1956, at the age of forty-four, crashing his car while drunk and speeding near his Long Island home. He is shown here in 1949 with his painting, *Number 9*. Photo by Arnold Newman/Getty Images.

teenage years. "That got me into trouble with my parents and the schools." His recollection underscored African Americans' contributions to rock and roll, as well as the rebellion expressed by white youths' attraction to black music.

The most blatant revolt against conventionality came from the self-proclaimed **Beat generation**, a small group of primarily male literary figures based in New York City and San Francisco. Rejecting nearly everything in mainstream culture — patriotism, consumerism, technology, conventional family life, discipline — the Beats celebrated spontaneity and absolute personal freedom, including drug consumption and free-wheeling sex. In his landmark poem *Howl* (1956), Allen Ginsberg denounced the social forces that "frightened me out of my natural ecstasy!" Jack Kerouac, who gave the Beat generation its name, published the best-selling novel *On the Road* (1957), whose energetic, stream-of-consciousness, bebop-style prose narrated the impetuous cross-country travels of two young men. "The only people for me," he wrote, "are the mad ones . . . the ones who never yawn or say a commonplace thing, but burn, burn, burn like fabulous yellow roman candles exploding like spiders across the stars." The Beats' lifestyles shocked "square" Americans, but they would provide a model for a much larger movement of youthful dissidents in the 1960s.

Bold new styles in the visual arts also showed the 1950s to be more than a decade of bland conventionality. In New York City, an artistic revolution known as "action painting" or "abstract expressionism" flowered, rejecting the idea that painting should represent recognizable forms. Jackson Pollock and other abstract expressionists, emphasizing spontaneity, poured, dripped, and threw paint on canvases or substituted sticks

and other implements for brushes. The new form of painting so captivated and redirected the Western art world that New York replaced Paris as its center.

> **REVIEW** Why did American consumption expand so dramatically in the 1950s, and what aspects of society and culture did it influence?

▶ The Emergence of a Civil Rights Movement

Building on the civil rights initiatives begun during World War II, African Americans posed the most dramatic challenge to the status quo of the 1950s as they sought to overcome the political, economic, and social barriers that had replaced the literal bonds of slavery. Every southern state mandated rigid segregation in public settings ranging from hospitals and schools to drinking fountains and restrooms. Voting laws and practices in the South disfranchised the vast majority of African Americans; employment discrimination kept them at the bottom of the economic ladder throughout the country; and schools, restaurants, and other public spaces were often as segregated, though not usually by law, in the North as they were in the South.

Although black protest was as old as American racism, in the 1950s grassroots movements arose that attracted national attention and the support of white liberals. Pressed by civil rights groups, the Supreme Court delivered significant institutional reforms, but the most important changes of all occurred among blacks themselves. Ordinary African Americans in substantial numbers sought their own liberation, building a movement that would transform race relations in the United States.

African Americans Challenge the Supreme Court and the President

Several factors spurred black protest in the 1950s. Between 1940 and 1960, more than three million African Americans moved from the South into areas where they had a political voice. Black leaders made sure that foreign policy officials realized how racist practices at home tarnished the U.S. image abroad and handicapped the United States in its competition with the Soviet Union. The very system of segregation meant that African Americans controlled certain organizational resources, such as churches, colleges, and newspapers, where leadership skills could be honed, networks developed, and information spread.

The legal strategy of the major civil rights organization, the National Association for the Advancement of Colored People (NAACP), reached its crowning achievement with the Supreme Court decision in **Brown v. Board of Education** in 1954.

Brown consolidated five separate suits that reflected the growing determination of black Americans to fight for their rights. Oliver Brown, a World War II veteran in Topeka, Kansas, filed suit because his daughter had to pass by a white school just seven blocks from their home to attend a black school more than a mile away. In Virginia, sixteen-year-old Barbara Johns initiated a student strike over wretched conditions in her black high school, leading to another of the suits joined in *Brown*.

The NAACP's lead lawyer, future Supreme Court justice Thurgood Marshall, urged the Court to overturn the "separate but equal" precedent established in *Plessy v. Ferguson* in 1896 (see chapter 21). A unanimous Court, headed by Chief Justice Earl Warren, declared, "Separate educational facilities are inherently unequal" and thus violated the Fourteenth Amendment.

Ultimate responsibility for enforcement of the decision lay with President Eisenhower, but he refused to endorse *Brown*. He also kept silent in 1955 when whites murdered Emmett Till, a fourteen-

School Integration in Little Rock, Arkansas

The nine African American teenagers who integrated Central High School in Little Rock, Arkansas, endured nearly three weeks of threats and hateful taunts before they even got through the doors. Here Elizabeth Eckford tries to ignore angry students and adults as she approaches the entrance to the school, only to be blocked by Arkansas National Guardsmen. Even after President Eisenhower intervened to enable the "Little Rock Nine" to attend school, they were called names, tripped, spat upon, and otherwise harassed by some white students. Francis Miller/TimePix/Getty.

The *Brown* Decision

Brown v. Board of Education of Topeka was the principal Supreme Court decision in the transformation of African Americans' legal and political status during the 1950s and 1960s. Responding to lawsuits argued by NAACP lawyers, *Brown* was the culmination of a series of Supreme Court rulings between 1938 and 1950 that chipped away at an earlier Court's decision in *Plessy v. Ferguson* (1896) permitting "separate but equal" public facilities.

DOCUMENT 1
Brown v. Board of Education of Topeka, May 1954

In 1954, Chief Justice Earl Warren delivered the unanimous opinion of the Supreme Court in Brown v. Board of Education of Topeka, *declaring racial segregation in public education unconstitutional and explaining why.*

In these days, it is doubtful that any child may reasonably be expected to succeed in life if he is denied the opportunity of an education. Such an opportunity, if the state has undertaken to provide it, is a right that must be made available to all on equal terms. . . .

We come then to the question presented: Does segregation of children in public schools solely on the basis of race, even though the physical facilities and other "tangible" factors may be equal, deprive the children of the minority group of equal educational opportunities?

We believe that it does. . . . In *McLaurin* [a 1950 case], the Court, in requiring that a Negro admitted to a white graduate school be treated like all other students, again resorted to intangible considerations: ". . . his ability to study, to engage in discussions and exchange views with other students, and, in general, to learn his profession." Such considerations apply with added force to children in grade and high schools. To separate them from others of similar age and qualifications solely because of their race generates a feeling of inferiority as to their status in the community that may affect their hearts and minds in a way unlikely ever to be undone.

We conclude that in the field of public education the doctrine of "separate but equal" has no place. Separate educational facilities are inherently unequal

SOURCE: *Brown*, 347 U.S. 483 (1954).

DOCUMENT 2
Southern Manifesto on Integration, March 1956

The Brown *decision outraged many southern whites. In 1956, more than one hundred members of Congress signed a manifesto pledging resistance to the ruling.*

We regard the decision of the Supreme Court in the school cases as a clear abuse of judicial power. It climaxes a trend in the Federal judiciary undertaking to legislate . . . and to encroach upon the reserved rights of the states and the people.

The original Constitution does not mention education. Neither does the Fourteenth Amendment nor any amendment. . . . The Supreme Court of the United States, with no legal basis for such action, undertook to exercise their naked judicial power and substituted their personal political and social ideas for the established law of the land.

This unwarranted exercise of power by the court, contrary to the Constitution, is creating chaos and confusion in the states principally affected. It is destroying the amicable relations between the white and negro races that have been created through ninety years of patient effort by the good people of both races. It has planted hatred and suspicion where there has been heretofore friendship and understanding. . . .

We pledge ourselves to use all lawful means to bring about a reversal of this decision which is contrary to the Constitution and to prevent the use of force in its implementation.

SOURCE: "Southern Manifesto on Integration" (1956).

In the face of white hostility, black children carried the burden of implementing the Brown *decision. The following accounts by black students reflect varied experiences, but even those who entered white schools fairly easily faced obstacles to their full participation in school activities. Nonetheless, they cherished the new opportunities, favoring integration for reasons different from those given by the Supreme Court.*

DOCUMENT 3
A High School Boy in Oak Ridge, Tennessee, 1957

I like it a whole lot better than the colored school. You have a chance to learn more and you have more sports.

I play forward or guard on the basketball team, only I don't get to participate in all games. Some teams don't mind my playing. Some teams object not because of the fellows on the team, but because of the people in their community. Mostly it's the fans or the board of education that decides against me. . . . The same situation occurs in baseball. I'm catcher, but the first game I didn't get to participate in. A farm club of the major league wrote the coach that they were interested in seeing me play so maybe I'll get to play the next time.

SOURCE: Dorothy Sterling, *Tender Warriors* (New York: Hill and Wang, 1958), 83. Copyright © 1958 by Hill and Wang. Reprinted with permission.

DOCUMENT 4
A High School Girl in Louisville, Kentucky, 1957

I'm accepted now as an individual rather than as a person belonging to the Negro race. People say to me, "I'm glad I met you because if I met someone else I might not have liked them." I don't think it's fair, this individual acceptance. I feel like I was some ambassador from some foreign country.

I couldn't go out for any extracurricular activities. Cheerleading, band, drum majorettes, the people who are members of these organizations, they go to camps in the summer which are segregated. Well, what can you do? It just leaves me out. It's not the school, it's the community.

SOURCE: Dorothy Sterling, *Tender Warriors* (New York: Hill and Wang, 1958), 83. Copyright © 1958 by Hill and Wang. Reprinted with permission.

DOCUMENT 5
A High School Girl in the Deep South, May 1966

The first day a news reporter rode the bus with us. All around us were state troopers. In front of them were federal marshals. When we got to town there were lines of people and cars all along the road. A man without a badge or anything got on the bus and started beating up the newspaper reporter. . . . He was crying and bleeding. When we got to the school the students were all around looking through the windows. The mayor said we couldn't come there because the school was already filled to capacity [and] if six of us came in it would be a fire hazard. He told us to turn around and go back. We turned around and the students started yelling and clapping. When we went back [after obtaining a court order] there were no students there at all. There were only two

teachers left so they had to bring a couple of teachers from other places. [The white students did not return, so the six black students finished the year by themselves.] The shocking thing was during the graduation ceremonies. All six of the students got together to make a speech. After we finished, I looked around and saw three teachers crying. The principal had tears in his eyes and he got up to make a little speech about us. He said at first he didn't think he would enjoy being around us. You could see in his face that he was really touched. We said something like we really enjoyed school together and that we were glad they stuck it out and all that kind of stuff.

SOURCE: *In Their Own Words: A Student Appraisal of What Happened after School Desegregation* (Washington, D.C.: Department of Health, Education, and Welfare, Office of Education, 1966), 17–18.

DOCUMENT 6
A High School Girl in the Deep South, May 1966

I chose to go because I felt that I could get a better education here. I knew that the [black] school that I was then attending wasn't giving me exactly what I should have had. As far as the Science Department was concerned, it just didn't have the chemicals we needed and I just decided to change. When I went over the students there weren't very friendly and when I graduated they still weren't. They didn't want us there and they made that plain, but we went there anyway and we stuck it out. The lessons there were harder, lots harder, but I studied and I managed to pass all my subjects.

SOURCE: *In Their Own Words: A Student Appraisal of What Happened after School Desegregation* (Washington, D.C.: Department of Health, Education, and Welfare, Office of Education, 1966), 44.

Questions for Analysis and Debate

1. What reasons did the Supreme Court give in favor of desegregation? What reasons did black students give for wanting to attend integrated schools? How do these reasons differ?

2. What arguments did the southern legislators make against the Supreme Court decision?

3. What obstacles remained for African American students to confront once they had been admitted to integrated schools?

4. What conditions do you feel would be worth enduring to obtain a better education?

year-old black boy who had allegedly whistled at a white woman in Mississippi. Reflecting his own prejudice, his preference for limited federal intervention in the states, and a leadership style that favored consensus and gradual progress, Eisenhower kept his distance from civil rights issues. Such inaction fortified southern resistance to school desegregation and contributed to the gravest constitutional crisis since the Civil War.

The crisis came in Little Rock, Arkansas, in September 1957, when Governor Orval Faubus sent Arkansas National Guard troops to block the enrollment of nine black students in Little Rock's Central High School. Later, he allowed them to enter but withdrew the National Guard, leaving the students to face an angry white mob. "During those years when we desperately needed approval from our peers," Melba Patillo Beals remembered, "we were victims of the most harsh rejection imaginable." As television cameras transmitted the ugly scene, Eisenhower was forced to send regular army troops to Little Rock, the first federal military intervention in the South since Reconstruction. Paratroopers escorted the "**Little Rock Nine**" into the school, but forty-four teachers who had supported them lost their jobs. Despite Eisenhower's explanation that he had acted to preserve the law, not to promote integration, southern leaders were outraged. Other southern cities avoided integration by closing public schools and using tax dollars to support private ones. Seven years after *Brown*, only 6.4 percent of southern black students attended integrated schools. (See "Documenting the American Promise," page 922.)

School segregation outside the South was not usually sanctioned by law, but northern school districts separated black and white students through manipulation of neighborhood boundaries and through other devices. Even before *Brown*, black parents in dozens of northern cities challenged the assignment of their children to inferior "colored" schools. While their boycotts reaped some successes, the structure of residential segregation, often supported by official action, made school segregation a severe disadvantage for African Americans in the North as well as in the South.

Although Eisenhower rejected an aggressive approach to racial issues, he did order the integration of public facilities in Washington, D.C., and on military bases, and he supported the first federal civil rights legislation since Reconstruction. Yet southern members of Congress made sure that the Civil Rights Acts of 1957 and 1960 were little more than symbolic. Baseball star Jackie Robinson spoke for many African Americans when he wired Eisenhower in 1957, "We disagree that half a loaf is better than none. Have waited this long for a bill with meaning—can wait a little longer." Eisenhower

appointed the first black professional to the White House staff, E. Frederick Morrow, but Morrow confided in his diary, "I feel ridiculous . . . trying to defend the administration's record on civil rights."

Montgomery and Mass Protest

What set the civil rights movement of the 1950s and 1960s apart from earlier acts of black protest was its widespread presence in the South, the large number of people involved, their willingness to confront white institutions directly, and the use of nonviolent protest and civil disobedience to bring about change. The Congress of Racial Equality and other groups had experimented with these tactics in the 1940s, organizing, for example, to integrate movie theaters in Cincinnati, restaurants in Chicago, swimming pools in New Jersey, and a public playground in Washington, D.C. In the South, African Americans boycotted the segregated bus system in Baton Rouge, Louisiana, in 1953, but the first sustained protest to claim national attention began in Montgomery, Alabama, on December 1, 1955.

That day, police arrested **Rosa Parks** for violating a local segregation ordinance. Riding a crowded bus home from her job as a seamstress in a department store, she refused to give up her seat so that a white man could sit down. "People always say that I didn't give up my seat because I was tired, but that isn't true," Parks recalled. "I was not tired physically. . . . I was not old. . . . I was forty-two. No, the only tired I was, was tired of giving in." The bus driver called the police, who promptly arrested her.

Parks had long been active in the local NAACP, headed by E. D. Nixon. They had already talked about challenging bus segregation. So had the Women's Political Council (WPC), composed of black professional women and led by Jo Ann Robinson, an English professor at Alabama State, who had once been humiliated by a bus driver when she accidentally sat in the white section. Such local individuals and organizations, long committed to improving conditions for African Americans, laid critical foundations for the black freedom struggle throughout the South.

When word came that Parks would fight her arrest, WPC leaders mobilized teachers and students to distribute fliers calling for blacks to stay off the buses. E. D. Nixon called a mass meeting at the Holt Street Baptist Church, where those assembled founded the Montgomery Improvement Association (MIA) to organize a bus boycott. The MIA arranged volunteer car pools and marshaled more than 90 percent of the black community to sustain the yearlong **Montgomery bus boycott**.

Civil Rights Activism in the North
While civil rights activism in the South gained national attention in the 1950s and 1960s, black protest had a long history in the North. Especially after the birth of the NAACP in 1909, African Americans and their allies mobilized against job discrimination and against segregation in the schools, housing, and public accommodations. In this photo, demonstrators march outside the Stork Club in New York City in 1951, protesting its refusal to serve the world famous dancer, singer, and actress Josephine Baker. Photo by FPG/Hulton Archive/Getty Images.

Elected to head the MIA was twenty-six-year-old **Martin Luther King Jr.**, a young Baptist pastor with a doctorate in theology from Boston University. As a seminary student in 1950, he had been denied service in a New Jersey restaurant and refused to leave until the owner chased him and his friends out with a gun. A captivating speaker, King addressed mass meetings at churches throughout the bus boycott, inspiring blacks' courage and commitment by linking racial justice to Christianity. He promised, "If you will protest courageously and yet with dignity and Christian love . . . historians will have to pause and say, 'There lived a great people — a black people — who injected a new meaning and dignity into the veins of civilization.'"

Montgomery blacks summoned their courage and determination in abundance. An older woman insisted, "I'm not walking for myself, I'm walking for my children and my grandchildren." Boycotters walked miles or carpooled to get to work, contributed their meager financial resources, and stood up with dignity to intimidation and police

harassment. Jo Ann Robinson, a cautious driver, got seventeen tickets in the space of two months. Authorities arrested several leaders, and whites firebombed King's house. Yet the movement persisted until November 1956, when the Supreme Court declared unconstitutional Alabama's laws requiring bus segregation. African Americans had demonstrated that they could sustain a lengthy protest and would not be intimidated.

King's face on the cover of *Time* magazine in February 1957 marked his rapid rise to national and international fame. In January, black clergy from across the South had chosen King to head the **Southern Christian Leadership Conference (SCLC)**, newly established to coordinate local protests against segregation and disfranchisement. The prominence of King and other ministers obscured the substantial

> "People always say that I didn't give up my seat because I was tired, but that isn't true. I was not tired physically. . . . I was tired of giving in."
> —Civil rights activist
> **ROSA PARKS**

Martin Luther King, Jr.
The twenty-six-year-old Martin Luther King, Jr. had been in Montgomery, Alabama, for less than two years when he was selected in 1955 to lead the city-wide bus boycott, which had been started by more-seasoned community leaders. Here he is shown greeting members of his Dexter Avenue Baptist Church congregation near the Montgomery State Capitol. King's philosophy of nonviolent resistance to injustice derived in part from his study of the principles of the Indian nationalist leader Mahatma Gandhi, and in 1964, he became the youngest person to be awarded the Nobel Peace Prize. Dan Weiner, Courtesy Sandra Weiner.

► Conclusion: Peace and Prosperity Mask Unmet Challenges

At the American National Exhibition in Moscow in 1959, the consumer goods that Nixon proudly displayed to Khrushchev and the Cold War competition that crackled through their dialogue reflected two dominant themes of the 1950s: the prosperity of the U.S. economy and the superpowers' success in keeping their antagonism within the bounds of peace. The tremendous economic growth of the 1950s, which raised the standard of living for most Americans, resulted in part from the Cold War: One of every ten American jobs depended directly on defense spending.

Affluence changed the very landscape of the United States. Suburban housing developments sprang up, interstate highways began to cut up cities and connect the country, farms declined in number but grew in size, and population and industry moved south and west. Daily habits and even the values of ordinary people shifted as the economy became more service oriented and the appearance of a host of new products intensified the growth of a consumer culture that had begun decades earlier.

The prosperity, however, masked a number of developments and problems that Americans would face head-on in later years: rising resistance to racial injustice, a 20 percent poverty rate, married women's movement into the labor force, and the emergence of a self-conscious youth generation. Although the federal government's defense spending and housing, highway, and education subsidies helped to sustain the economic boom, in general Eisenhower tried to curb domestic programs and let private enterprise have its way. His administration maintained the welfare state inherited from the New Deal but resisted the expansion of federal programs.

In global affairs, Eisenhower exercised restraint on large issues, recognizing the limits of U.S. power. In the name of deterrence, he promoted the development of more destructive atomic weapons, but he withstood pressures for even larger defense budgets. Nonetheless, Eisenhower shared Truman's fundamental assumption that the United States must fight communism everywhere, and when movements in Iran, Guatemala, Cuba, and Vietnam seemed too radical, too friendly to communism, or too inimical to American economic interests, he tried to undermine them, often with secret operations and severe consequences for native populations.

numbers and critical importance of black women in the movement. In fact, the SCLC owed much of its success to Ella Baker, a seasoned activist who came from New York to manage its office in Atlanta. King's prominence and the media's focus on the South also hid the national scope of racial injustice and the struggles for racial equality in the North that both encouraged and benefited from the black freedom struggle in the South.

REVIEW   What were the goals and strategies of civil rights activists in the 1950s?

Although Eisenhower presided over eight years of peace and prosperity, his foreign policy inspired anti-Americanism, established dangerous precedents for the expansion of executive power, and forged commitments and interventions that future generations would deem unwise. As Eisenhower's successors took on the struggle against communism and grappled with the domestic challenges of race, poverty, and urban decay that he had avoided, the tranquility and consensus of the 1950s would give way to the turbulence and conflict of the 1960s.

▶ Selected Bibliography

Eisenhower's Administration

Steven Z. Freiberger, *Dawn over Suez: The Rise of American Power in the Middle East, 1953–1957* (1992).

David Halberstam, *The Fifties* (1993).

George C. Herring, *America's Longest War: The United States and Vietnam, 1950–1975* (2nd rev. ed., 1986).

Stephen Kinzer, *All the Shah's Men: An American Coup and the Roots of Middle East Terror* (2003).

David A. Nichols, *A Matter of Justice: Eisenhower and the Beginning of the Civil Rights Revolution* (2007).

Chester J. Pach Jr. and Elmo Richardson, *The Presidency of Dwight D. Eisenhower* (rev. ed., 1991).

Stephen G. Rabe, *Eisenhower and Latin America: The Foreign Policy of Anticommunism* (1988).

Economic and Social Developments

Lizabeth Cohen, *A Consumers' Republic: The Politics of Mass Consumption in Postwar America* (2003).

Gail Cooper, *Air-Conditioning America: Engineers and the Controlled Environment, 1900–1960* (1998).

Kenneth T. Jackson, *Crabgrass Frontier: The Suburbanization of the United States* (1985).

Tom Lewis, *Divided Highways: Building the Interstate Highways, Transforming American Life* (1999).

David Oshinsky, *Polio: An American Story* (2005).

Adam Rome, *The Bulldozer in the Countryside: Suburban Sprawl and the Rise of American Environmentalism* (2001).

Bruce J. Schulman, *From Cotton Belt to Sunbelt: Federal Policy, Economic Development, and the Transformation of the South, 1938–1980* (1994).

Gender, the Family, and Culture

Glenn C. Altschuler, *All Shook Up: How Rock 'n' Roll Changed America* (2004).

Erik Barnouw, *Tube of Plenty: The Evolution of American Television* (rev. ed., 1982).

Stephanie Coontz, *The Way We Never Were: American Families and the Nostalgia Trip* (1992).

Robert Ellwood, *The Fifties Spiritual Marketplace: American Religion in a Decade of Conflict* (1997).

Elizabeth Fraterrigo, *"Playboy" and the Making of the Good Life in Modern America* (2009).

James Gilbert, *Men in the Middle: Searching for Masculinity in the 1950s* (2005).

James Howard Jones, *Alfred C. Kinsey: A Public/Private Life* (1998).

Elaine Tyler May, *Homeward Bound: American Families in the Cold War Era* (1988).

Joanne Meyerowitz, ed., *Not June Cleaver: Women and Gender in Postwar America, 1945–1960* (1994).

Alan Petigny, *The Permissive Society: America, 1941–1965* (2009).

Lynn Spigel, *Make Room for TV: Television and the Family Ideal in Postwar America* (1992).

Steven Watson, *The Birth of the Beat Generation: Visionaries, Rebels, and Hipsters, 1944–1960* (1995).

Minorities and Civil Rights

Melba Patillo Beals, *Warriors Don't Cry: A Searing Memoir of the Battle to Integrate Little Rock's Central High* (1994).

Taylor Branch, *Parting the Waters: America in the King Years, 1954–1963* (1988).

Mary L. Dudziak, *Cold War Civil Rights: Race and the Image of American Democracy* (2000).

Donald L. Fixico, *Termination and Relocation: Federal Indian Policy, 1945–1960* (1986).

David J. Garrow, ed., *The Montgomery Boycott and the Women Who Started It: The Memoir of Jo Ann Gibson Robinson* (1987).

James T. Patterson, Brown v. Board of Education: *A Civil Rights Milestone and Its Troubled Legacy* (2001).

Barbara Ransby, *Ella Baker and the Black Freedom Movement* (2003).

Thomas J. Sugrue, *Sweet Land of Liberty: The Forgotten Struggle for Civil Rights in the North* (2008).

Juan Williams, *Thurgood Marshall: American Revolutionary* (1998).

▶ FOR MORE BOOKS ABOUT TOPICS IN THIS CHAPTER, see the Online Bibliography at **bedfordstmartins.com/roark.**

▶ FOR ADDITIONAL PRIMARY SOURCES FROM THIS PERIOD, see Michael Johnson, ed., *Reading the American Past,* Fifth Edition.

▶ FOR WEB SITES, IMAGES, AND DOCUMENTS RELATED TO TOPICS AND PLACES IN THIS CHAPTER, visit Make History at **bedfordstmartins.com/roark.**

Reviewing Chapter 27

KEY TERMS

Explain each term's significance.

Eisenhower and the Politics of the "Middle Way"
    Dwight D. Eisenhower (p. 899)
    Interstate Highway and Defense System
       Act of 1956 (p. 900)
    Indian Relocation Program (p. 901)

Liberation Rhetoric and the Practice of Containment
    mutually assured destruction (MAD)
      (p. 903)
    domino theory (p. 904)
    Geneva accords (p. 904)
    Cuban revolution (p. 905)
    Fidel Castro (p. 905)
    Mohammed Mossadegh (p. 905)
    Gamal Abdel Nasser (p. 905)
    Suez crisis (p. 906)
    Eisenhower Doctrine (p. 906)
    Nikita Khrushchev (p. 907)
    Sputnik (p. 907)
    military-industrial complex (p. 908)

New Work and Living Patterns in an Economy of Abundance
    Sun Belt (p. 909)
    kitchen debate (p. 911)
    Hernandez v. Texas (p. 913)

The Culture of Abundance
    Betty Friedan (p. 916)
    baby boom (p. 916)
    Billy Graham (p. 916)
    Alfred Kinsey (p. 919)
    rock and roll (p. 919)
    Beat generation (p. 920)

The Emergence of a Civil Rights Movement
    Brown v. Board of Education (p. 921)
    Little Rock Nine (p. 924)
    Rosa Parks (p. 924)
    Montgomery bus boycott (p. 924)
    Martin Luther King Jr. (p. 925)
    Southern Christian Leadership Conference
      (SCLC) (p. 925)

REVIEW QUESTIONS

Use key terms and dates to support your answer.

1. How did Eisenhower's domestic policies reflect his moderate political vision? (pp. 899–902)

2. Where and how did Eisenhower practice containment? (pp. 902–908)

3. How did technology contribute to changes in the economy, suburbanization, and the growth of the Sun Belt? (pp. 909–915)

4. Why did American consumption expand so dramatically in the 1950s, and what aspects of society and culture did it influence? (pp. 915–920)

5. What were the goals and strategies of civil rights activists in the 1950s? (pp. 920–926)

MAKING CONNECTIONS

Draw on key terms, the timeline, and review questions.

1. Eisenhower was the first Republican president since the New Deal had transformed the role of the federal government. How did his "modern Republicanism" address Roosevelt's legacy? How did the shape and character of government change or not change during Eisenhower's administration?

2. The 1950s brought significant changes to the everyday lives of many Americans. Discuss the economic and demographic changes that contributed to the growth of suburbs and the Sun Belt. In your answer, consider both Americans who participated in these trends and those who did not.

3. What actual developments in American society in the 1950s were at odds with prevailing norms and values?

4. During the 1950s, actions by the federal government and the courts had a significant impact on African Americans, Native Americans, and Mexican Americans. Discuss how new policies and court actions came about and how laws affected these groups for better and for worse.

LINKING TO THE PAST

1. How did the policies of termination and relocation differ from the New Deal's policy toward Indians? (See chapter 24.)

2. What developments stemming from World War II influenced U.S. foreign policy in such areas as Vietnam and Latin America? (See chapter 25.)

▶ FOR PRACTICE QUIZZES AND OTHER STUDY TOOLS, visit the Online Study Guide at bedfordstmartins.com/roark.

TIMELINE 1952–1960

1952	• Republican Dwight D. Eisenhower elected president.
1953	• Termination of special status of Native Americans and relocation of thousands off reservations. • CIA engineers coup against government of Iran.
1954	• CIA stages coup against government of Guatemala. • France signs Geneva accords, withdrawing from Vietnam. • United States begins aid to South Vietnam. • Government launches Operation Wetback. • *Hernandez v. Texas.* • *Brown v. Board of Education.* • Senate condemns Senator Joseph McCarthy.
1955	• Eisenhower and Khrushchev meet in Geneva.
1955–1956	• Montgomery, Alabama, bus boycott.
1956	• Interstate Highway and Defense System Act. • Eisenhower reelected by landslide to second term. • *Howl* published.
1957	• Southern Christian Leadership Conference (SCLC) founded. • Soviets launch *Sputnik.* • Labor union membership peaks at 27.1 percent of labor force. • Civil Rights Act of 1957. • *On the Road* published.
1958	• National Aeronautics and Space Administration (NASA) established. • National Defense Education Act.
1959	• Kitchen debate between Nixon and Khrushchev.
1960	• Soviets shoot down U.S. U-2 spy plane. • One-quarter of Americans live in suburbs. • Thirty-five percent of women work outside the home.

PROTEST BANNER

Banners flew in streets across the nation during the 1960s as millions of Americans made visible their positions on issues ranging from racial justice to the Vietnam War to women's equality. This pennant represents the earliest protest movement, the black freedom struggle, which invigorated a host of other movements and contributed to reforms that transformed the role of the federal government in securing individual rights. The background image captures the 1963 March on Washington for Jobs and Justice at which Martin Luther King, Jr. gave his famous "I Have a Dream" speech.

Banner: Collection of Mark Hooper; background: © Bettmann/Corbis.

28

Reform, Rebellion, and Reaction
1960–1974

ON AUGUST 31, 1962, FANNIE LOU HAMER BOARDED A BUS CARRYING eighteen African Americans from Ruleville, Mississippi, to the county seat in Indianola, where they intended to register to vote. Blacks accounted for more than 60 percent of Sunflower County's population but only 1.2 percent of registered voters. Before civil rights activists arrived in Ruleville to start a voter registration drive, Hamer recalled, "I didn't know that a Negro could register and vote." Her forty-five years of poverty, exploitation, and political disfranchisement typified the lives of most blacks in the rural South. The daughter of sharecroppers, Hamer began work in the cotton fields at age six, attending school in a one-room shack from December to March and only until she was twelve. After marrying Perry Hamer, she moved onto a plantation, where she worked in the fields, did domestic work for the owner, and recorded the cotton that sharecroppers harvested.

At the Indianola County courthouse, Hamer and her companions had to pass through a hostile, white, gun-carrying crowd. Using a common practice to deny blacks the vote, the registrar tested Hamer on an obscure section of the state constitution. She failed the test but resolved to try again. When the plantation owner ordered Hamer to withdraw her registration application or get off his land, she left the plantation. Ten days later, bullets flew into the home of friends who had taken her in. Refusing to be intimidated, she registered to vote on her third attempt, attended a civil rights leadership training conference, and began to mobilize others to vote. In 1963, she and other activists were arrested in Winona, Mississippi, and brutally beaten. Hamer went from jail to the hospital, where her sister could not recognize her battered face.

Fannie Lou Hamer's courage and determination made her a prominent figure in the black freedom struggle. Such activists shook the nation's conscience, provided a protest model for other groups, and pushed the government to enact not only civil rights legislation but also a host of other liberal policies. Although the federal government often tried to curb civil rights protest, the two Democratic presidents of the 1960s favored using government to ameliorate social and economic problems. After John F. Kennedy was assassinated in November 1963, Lyndon B. Johnson launched the Great Society — a multitude of efforts to promote racial justice, education, medical care, urban development, environmental and economic health, and more. Those who struggled for racial justice lost property and sometimes their lives, but by the end of the decade American law had caught up with the American ideal of equality.

Yet strong civil rights legislation and pathbreaking Supreme Court decisions could not alone mitigate the deplorable economic conditions of African Americans nationwide, on which Hamer and others increasingly focused after 1965. Nor were liberal politicians reliable supporters, as Hamer found out in 1964 when President Johnson and his allies rebuffed black Mississippi Democrats' efforts to be represented at the Democratic National Convention. "We followed all the laws," she said, only to find that "the white man is not going to give up his power to us. . . . We have to take [it] for ourselves." By 1966, a minority of African American activists were demanding black power; the movement soon splintered, and white support sharply declined. The war in Vietnam stifled liberal reform, while a growing conservative movement, protesting that the Great Society went too far, condemned the challenge to American traditions and institutions mounted by blacks, students, and others.

Though disillusioned and often frustrated, Fannie Lou Hamer remained an activist until her death in 1977, participating in new social movements stimulated by the black freedom struggle. In 1969, she supported students at Mississippi Valley State College who demanded black studies courses and a voice in campus decisions. In 1972, she attended the first conference of the National Women's Political Caucus, established to achieve greater representation for women in government. The caucus was part of a diverse feminist movement that transformed women's legal status as well as everyday relationships between women and men.

Feminists and other groups, including ethnic minorities, environmentalists, and gays and lesbians, carried the tide of reform into the 1970s. They pushed Richard M. Nixon's Republican administration to sustain the liberalism of the 1960s, with its emphasis on a strong government role in regulating the economy, guaranteeing the welfare and rights of all individuals, and improving the quality of life. Despite its conservative rhetoric, the Nixon administration implemented school desegregation and affirmative action and adopted pathbreaking measures in environmental regulation, equality for women, and justice for Native Americans. The years between 1960 and 1974 witnessed the greatest efforts to reconcile America's promise with reality since the New Deal.

Mississippi Freedom Democratic Party Rally
Fannie Lou Hamer (left foreground) and other activists sing at a rally outside the Democratic National Convention hall in 1964, supporting the Mississippi Freedom Democratic Party (MFDP) in its challenge to the all-white delegation sent by the regular state Democratic Party. Next to Hamer is Eleanor Holmes Norton, a civil rights lawyer, and Ella Baker (far right), who helped organize the Southern Christian Leadership Conference and later managed MFDP headquarters in Washington, D.C. In the rear is SNCC leader, Stokely Carmichael (in the straw hat). © George Ballis/Take Stock/The Image Works.

▶ Liberalism at High Tide

At the Democratic National Convention in 1960, John F. Kennedy announced "a New Frontier" that would confront "unsolved problems of peace and war, unconquered pockets of ignorance and prejudice, unanswered questions of poverty and surplus." Four years later, Lyndon B. Johnson invoked the ideal of a "Great Society, [which] rests on abundance and liberty for all [and] demands an end to poverty and racial injustice." Acting under the liberal faith that government should use its power to solve social and economic problems, end injustice, and promote the welfare of all citizens, the Democratic administrations of the 1960s won legislation on civil rights, poverty, education, medical care, housing, consumer safeguards, and environmental protection. These measures, along with path-breaking Supreme Court decisions, advanced the unfulfilled agendas of the New Deal and Fair Deal, responded to demands for rights from African Americans and other groups, and addressed problems arising from rapid economic growth.

The Unrealized Promise of Kennedy's New Frontier

John F. Kennedy grew up in privilege, the child of an Irish Catholic businessman who served as ambassador to Great Britain and nourished political ambitions for his sons. Helped by a distinguished World War II navy record, Kennedy won election to the House of Representatives in 1946 and the Senate in 1952. With a powerful political machine, his family's fortune, and a dynamic personal appeal, Kennedy won the Democratic presidential nomination in 1960. He stunned many Democrats by choosing as his running mate Lyndon B. Johnson of Texas, a rival for the presidential nomination whom liberals disparaged as a typical southern conservative.

Kennedy defeated his Republican opponent, Vice President Richard M. Nixon, in an excruciatingly close election (Map 28.1). African American voters contributed to his victory, helping to offset the 52 percent of the white vote cast for Nixon and contributing to Kennedy's 118,550-vote margin overall. Lyndon Johnson helped carry most of the South, and a rise in unemployment in 1960 also favored the Democrats. Finally, Kennedy benefited from the nation's

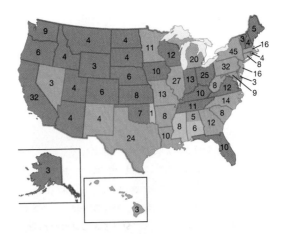

Candidate	Electoral Vote	Popular Vote	Percent of Popular Vote
John F. Kennedy (Democrat)	303	34,227,096	49.9
Richard M. Nixon (Republican)	219	34,108,546	49.6
Harry F. Byrd (Independent)	15	501,643	0.7

MAP 28.1 The Election of 1960

first televised presidential debates, at which he appeared cool and confident beside a nervous and pale Nixon.

The Kennedy administration projected energy, idealism, and glamour, although Kennedy was in most ways a cautious, pragmatic politician. The first president to hold televised press conferences, Kennedy charmed the audience with his grace and wit. Journalists kept from the public Kennedy's serious health problems and extramarital affairs, instead projecting warm images of a vigorous president with his chic and cultured wife, Jacqueline.

At his inauguration, the forty-three-year-old Kennedy called on Americans to serve the common good. "Ask not what your country can do for you," he implored, "ask what you can do for your country." Although Kennedy's idealism inspired many, he failed to redeem campaign promises to expand the welfare state with federal education and health care programs. Moreover, he resisted leadership on behalf of racial justice until civil rights activists gave him no choice and he issued a dramatic call for a comprehensive civil rights bill, marking a turning point in his domestic agenda.

Moved by the desperate conditions he observed while campaigning in Appalachia, Kennedy pushed poverty onto the national agenda. In 1962, he read Michael Harrington's

The Kennedy Appeal
The youth and glamour of the Kennedy administration are apparent in this photo of the president and his wife hosting a White House dinner for French Minister of Culture André Malraux in May 1962. Jacqueline Kennedy had a keen interest in history and the arts, and she designed White House social events to elevate Washington's cultural life by featuring artists, writers, scholars, and musicians. Well aware of the First Lady's appeal to the public, the president once asked their driver to "turn on the lights so they can see Jackie." John F. Kennedy Library.

The Other America, which described the poverty that left more than one in five Americans "maimed in body and spirit, existing at levels beneath those necessary for human decency." By 1962, Kennedy had won support for a $2 billion urban renewal program that offered incentives to businesses to locate in economically depressed areas and a training program for the unemployed. In the summer of 1963, he asked aides to plan a full-scale attack on poverty. Kennedy had promised to make economic growth a key objective. "A rising tide lifts all boats" expressed his belief that economic growth could eradicate poverty. To that end, he asked Congress to pass an enor-

mous tax cut in 1963, arguing that reducing taxes would infuse money into the economy and thus increase demand, boost production, and reduce unemployment. Passed in February 1964, the law contributed to an economic boom, as unemployment dropped to 4.1 percent and the gross national product shot up by 7 to 9 percent annually between 1964 and 1966. Some liberal critics of the tax cut, however, pointed out that it favored the well-off and that economic growth alone would not eliminate poverty. They argued instead for increased spending on social programs.

Kennedy's antipoverty, civil rights, and economic initiatives had not reached fruition when an assassin's bullets struck him down on November 22, 1963. Within minutes of the shooting — which occurred as Kennedy's motorcade passed through Dallas, Texas — radio and television broadcast the unfolding horror to the nation. Millions watched as *Air Force One* returned to Washington bearing the president's coffin, his widow in a bloodstained suit, and the new president, Lyndon Baines Johnson.

Stunned Americans struggled to understand what had happened. Soon after the assassination, police arrested Lee Harvey Oswald and concluded that he had fired the shots from a nearby building. Two days later, while officers were transferring Oswald from one jail to another, a local nightclub operator, Jack Ruby, killed him. Suspicions arose that Ruby murdered Oswald to cover up a conspiracy by ultraconservatives who hated Kennedy, or by Communists who supported Castro's Cuba (as discussed in chapter 29). To get at the truth, President Johnson appointed a commission headed by Chief Justice Earl Warren, which concluded that both Oswald and Ruby had acted alone. Although some contested the lone-killer explanation, most scholars agreed that no conspiracy had existed.

Debate continued over how to assess Kennedy's domestic record. It had been unremarkable in his first two years, but his proposals on taxes, civil rights, and poverty in 1963 suggested an important shift. Whether Kennedy could have persuaded Congress to enact them remained in question. In the words of journalist James Reston, "What was killed was not only the president but the promise. . . . He never reached his meridian: We saw him only as a rising sun."

Johnson Fulfills the Kennedy Promise

Lyndon B. Johnson assumed the presidency with a wealth of political experience. A self-made man from Texas's Hill Country, he had won election in 1937 to the House of Representatives and in 1948 to the Senate, where, after 1955, he served skillfully as Senate majority leader. Although his Texas base required caution on civil rights and issues affecting oil and other big businesses, Johnson's presidential aspirations led him to take more liberal stands. His own modest upbringing in an impoverished area, his admiration for Franklin Roosevelt, and his fierce ambition to outdo the New Deal president all spurred his commitment to reform in order to build what he called a **Great Society**. Equally compelling were external pressures generated by the black freedom struggle and the host of movements it helped inspire.

Johnson's coarse wit and vanity repulsed those who preferred the sophisticated Kennedy style. Lacking his predecessor's charm and eloquence, Johnson excelled behind the scenes, where he could entice, maneuver, or threaten legislators to support his objectives. His persuasive power, known as the "Johnson treatment," became legendary. In his ability to achieve consensus around his goals, Johnson had few peers in American history.

Johnson entreated Congress to act so that "John Fitzgerald Kennedy did not live or die in vain." He signed Kennedy's tax cut bill in February 1964. More remarkable was passage of the **Civil Rights Act of 1964**, which Kennedy had proposed in response to black protest. The strongest such measure since Reconstruction, the law required every ounce of Johnson's political skill to pry sufficient votes from Republicans to balance the "nays" of southern Democrats. Senate Republican leader Everett Dirksen's aide reported that Johnson "never left him alone for thirty minutes."

Antipoverty legislation followed fast on the heels of the Civil Rights Act. Just two months after Johnson announced "an unconditional war on poverty" in his January 1964 State of the Union message, the administration rushed a draft bill to Congress, which responded with equal haste in August. The Economic Opportunity Act of 1964 authorized ten new programs, allocating $800 million — about 1 percent of the federal budget — for the first year. Many provisions targeted children and youths, including Head Start for preschoolers, work-study grants for college students, and the Job Corps for unemployed young people. The Volunteers in Service to America (VISTA) program paid modest wages to volunteers working with the disadvantaged, and a legal services program provided lawyers for the poor.

The most novel and controversial part of the law, the Community Action Program (CAP), required "maximum feasible participation" of the poor themselves in antipoverty projects. Poor people began to organize community action programs to take control of their neighborhoods and to make welfare agencies, school boards, police departments, and housing authorities more accountable to the people they served. When mayors complained that activists were challenging local governments and "fostering class struggle," Johnson backed off from pushing genuine representation for the poor. Nonetheless, CAP gave people usually excluded from government an opportunity to act on their own behalf and develop leadership skills. To a Mississippi sharecropper, the local CAP literacy program "meant more to me than I can express," providing him basic skills and self-respect.

Policymaking for a Great Society

As the 1964 election approached, Johnson projected stability and security in the midst of a booming economy. Few voters wanted to risk the dramatic change promised by his Republican opponent, Arizona senator Barry M. Goldwater, who attacked the welfare state and suggested using nuclear weapons if necessary to crush communism in Vietnam.

The "Johnson Treatment"
Abe Fortas, a distinguished lawyer who had argued a major criminal rights case, *Gideon v. Wainwright* (1963), before the Supreme Court, was a close friend of and adviser to President Johnson. This photograph of the president and Fortas taken in July 1965 illustrates how Johnson used his body as well as his voice to bend people to his will. Yoichi R. Okamoto/LBJ Library Collection.

Although Goldwater captured five southern states, Johnson achieved a record-breaking landslide of 61 percent of the popular vote, and Democrats won resounding majorities in the House (295–140) and Senate (68–32). Still, Goldwater's campaign aroused considerable grassroots support, and a movement on the right grew alongside the more visible left-wing and liberal movements (as discussed in chapter 30).

"I want to see a whole bunch of coonskins on the wall," Johnson told his aides, using a hunting analogy to stress his ambitious legislative goals for what he called the "Great Society." The large Democratic majorities in Congress, his own political skills, and pressure from the black freedom struggle enabled Johnson to succeed mightily. He persuaded Congress to act on discrimination, poverty, education, medical care, housing, consumer and environmental protection, and more. Reporters called the legislation of the Eighty-ninth Congress (1965–1966) "a political miracle."

The **Economic Opportunity Act of 1964** was the opening shot in the **War on Poverty**. Congress doubled the program's funding in 1965, enacted new economic development measures for depressed regions, and authorized more than $1 billion to improve the nation's slums. Direct aid included a new food stamp program, giving poor people greater choice in obtaining food, and rent supplements that provided alternatives to public housing projects for some poor families. Moreover, a movement of welfare mothers, the National Welfare Rights Organization, assisted by antipoverty lawyers, pushed administrators of Aid to Families with Dependent Children (AFDC) to ease restrictions on welfare recipients. The number of families receiving assistance jumped from less than one million in 1960 to three million by 1972, benefiting 90 percent of those eligible.

Central to Johnson's War on Poverty were efforts to equip the poor with the skills necessary to find jobs. A former schoolteacher, Johnson saw federal support for public education as a natural extension of the New Deal; it had been on the Democratic Party agenda for two decades. His Elementary and Secondary Education Act of 1965 marked a turning point by involving the federal government in K–12

education. The measure sent federal dollars to local school districts based on the number of poor children they enrolled, and it provided equipment and supplies to private and parochial schools serving the poor. That same year, Congress passed the Higher Education Act, vastly expanding federal assistance to colleges and universities for buildings, programs, scholarships, and loans.

The federal government's responsibility for health care marked an even more significant watershed. Faced with a powerful medical lobby that opposed national health insurance as "socialized medicine," Johnson pared down Truman's proposal for government-sponsored universal care. Instead, he focused on the elderly, who constituted a large portion of the nation's poor. Congress responded with the **Medicare** program, providing the elderly with universal compulsory medical insurance financed largely through Social Security taxes. A separate program, **Medicaid**, authorized federal grants to supplement state-paid medical care for poor people. By the twenty-first century, these two programs covered 87 million Americans, nearly 30 percent of the population.

Whereas programs such as Medicare fulfilled New Deal and Fair Deal promises, the Great Society's civil rights legislation represented a break with tradition and an expansion of liberalism. Racial minorities were neglected or discriminated against in many New Deal programs, and Truman's civil rights proposals bore few results. By contrast, the Civil Rights Act of 1964 made discrimination in employment, education, and public accommodations illegal. The **Voting Rights Act of 1965** banned literacy tests like the one that had stymied Fannie Lou Hamer and authorized federal intervention to ensure access to the voting booth.

Another form of bias fell with the **Immigration and Nationality Act of 1965**, which abolished the

A Tribute to Johnson for Medicare
George Niedermeyer, who lived in Hollywood, Florida, and received a Social Security pension, painted pieces of wood and glued them together to create this thank-you to President Johnson for establishing Medicare. Niedermeyer entrusted his congressional representative, Claude Pepper, known for his support of the interests of the elderly, to deliver the four-foot-tall tribute to Johnson in 1967. LBJ Library, photo by Henry Groskinsky.

fifty-year-old quota system based on national origins that discriminated against immigrants from areas outside northern and western Europe (see chapter 23). The law maintained caps on the total number of immigrants and for the first time limited those from the Western Hemisphere; preference was now given to immediate relatives of U.S. citizens and to those with desirable skills. Massachusetts senator Edward Kennedy predicted that "our cities will not be flooded with a million citizens annually," but the measure's unanticipated consequences did nearly that, triggering a surge of immigration near the end of the century (as discussed in chapter 31).

Great Society benefits reached well beyond victims of discrimination and the poor. Medicare, for example, covered the elderly, regardless of income. A groundswell of consumer activism fueled by Ralph Nader's exposé of the auto industry, *Unsafe at Any Speed* (1965), won legislation making cars safer and raising standards for the food, drug, and cosmetics industries.

Johnson himself insisted that the Great Society meet "not just the needs of the body but the desire for beauty and hunger for community." In 1965, he sent Congress the first presidential message on the environment, obtaining measures to control water and air pollution and to preserve the natural beauty of the American landscape. First Lady "Lady Bird" Johnson made beautification of the environment her primary public project. In addition, the National Arts and Humanities Act of 1965 funded artists, musicians, writers, and scholars and brought their work to public audiences.

The flood of reform legislation dwindled after 1966, when Democratic majorities in Congress diminished and a backlash against government programs arose. Some Americans expressed their opposition with buttons reading "I fight poverty — I work." The Vietnam War dealt the largest blow to Johnson's ambitions, diverting his attention, spawning an antiwar movement that crippled his leadership, and devouring tax dollars that might have been used for reform (as discussed in chapter 29).

Against these odds, in 1968 Johnson pried out of Congress one more civil rights law, which banned discrimination in housing and jury service (see page 944). He also signed the National Housing Act of 1968, which authorized an enormous increase in low-income housing — 1.7 million units over three years — and, by leaving construction and ownership in private hands, a new way of providing it.

Assessing the Great Society

Measured by statistics, the reduction in poverty in the 1960s was considerable. The number of poor Americans fell from more than 20 percent of the population in 1959 to around 13 percent in 1968. Those who in Johnson's words "live on the outskirts of hope" gained more control of their circumstances and a sense of their right to a fairer share of America's bounty. To Rosemary Bray, what turned her family of longtime welfare recipients into taxpaying workers "was the promise of the civil rights movement and the war on poverty." A Mexican American who learned to be a sheet metal worker through a jobs program reported, "[My children] will finish high school and maybe go to college. . . . I see my family and I know the chains are broken."

> ## "[My children] will finish high school and maybe go to college. . . . I see my family and I know the chains are broken."
>
> —A Mexican American who trained in a jobs program

Certain groups fared better than others. Many of the aged and many male-headed families rose out of poverty, while impoverishment among female-headed families actually increased. Whites escaped poverty at a faster rate than racial and ethnic minorities. Great Society programs contributed to a burgeoning black middle class, and the proportion of African Americans who were poor fell by 10 percentage points between 1966 and 1974. Still, one out of three remained poverty-stricken (Figure 28.1).

Conservative critics charged that Great Society programs discouraged initiative and sustained a "cycle of poverty" across generations by giving the poor "handouts." Liberal critics claimed that focusing on training and education wrongly placed the cause of poverty on the poor themselves rather than on an economic system that could not provide enough adequately paying jobs. Most government training programs prepared graduates for low-skilled labor and could not guarantee employment. In contrast to the New Deal, the Great Society avoided structural reform of the economy and spurned public works projects as a means of providing jobs for the disadvantaged.

Who reaped the greatest advantages from Great Society programs? Programs such as Medicare and those addressing consumer safety and environmental reform benefited Americans across the board. Funds for economically depressed areas built highways, benefiting the construction industry. Real estate developers, investors, and moderate-income families benefited most from

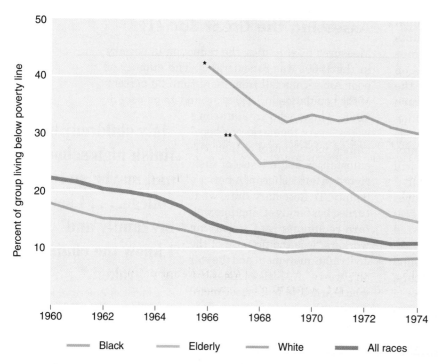

*Statistics on blacks for years 1960–1965 not available.
**Statistics on the elderly for years 1960–1966 not available.

FIGURE 28.1   Poverty in the United States, 1960–1974
The short-term effects of economic growth and the Great Society's attack on poverty are seen here. Which groups experienced the sharpest decline in poverty, and what might account for the differences?

the National Housing Act of 1968. Urban renewal often relied on slum clearance programs, which displaced the poor and caused blacks to refer to it as "Negro removal." Physicians' fees and hospital costs soared after the enactment of Medicare and Medicaid, resulting in advantages for both health care providers and the elderly and poor.

Some critics argued that ending poverty required a redistribution of income — raising taxes and using those funds to create jobs, overhaul welfare systems, and rebuild slums. Great Society programs did invest more heavily in the public sector, but they were funded from economic growth rather than from new taxes on the rich or middle class. There was no significant redistribution of income, despite large increases in subsidies for food stamps, housing, medical care, and AFDC. Economic prosperity allowed spending for the poor to rise and improved the lives of millions, but that spending never approached the amounts necessary to claim victory in the War on Poverty. Between 1965 and 1968, the Office of Economic Opportunity spent an average of $40 to $65 each year for each poor person in the country.

The Judicial Revolution

A key element of liberalism's ascendancy emerged in the Supreme Court under Chief Justice Earl Warren (1953–1969). In contrast to the federal courts of the Progressive Era and New Deal, which blocked reform, the **Warren Court** often moved out in front of Congress and public opinion. Expanding the Constitution's promise of equality and individual rights, the Court's decisions supported an activist government to prevent injustice and provided new protections to disadvantaged groups and accused criminals.

Following the pathbreaking *Brown v. Board of Education* school desegregation decision of 1954 (see chapter 27), the Court struck down southern states' educational plans to avoid integration and defended civil rights activists' rights to freedom of assembly and speech. In addition, a unanimous Court in *Loving v. Virginia* (1967) struck down state laws banning interracial marriage. The justices' declaration that marriage was one of the "basic civil rights of man" would later be repeated by gay men and lesbians seeking the right to marry.

Chief Justice Warren considered *Baker v. Carr* (1963) his most important decision. The case grew out of a complaint that Tennessee electoral districts were drawn so inequitably that sparsely populated rural districts had far more representatives than densely populated urban areas. Using the Fourteenth Amendment guarantee of "equal protection of the laws," *Baker* established the principle of "one person, one vote" for both state legislatures and the House of Representatives. As states redrew electoral districts, legislatures became more responsive to metropolitan interests.

The Warren Court also reformed the criminal justice system, overturning a series of convictions on the grounds that the accused had been deprived of "life, liberty, or property, without due process of law," guaranteed in the Fourteenth Amendment. In decisions that dramatically altered law enforcement practices and the treatment of individuals accused of crimes, the Court declared that states, as well as the federal government, were subject to the Bill of Rights. *Gideon v. Wainwright* (1963) ruled that when an accused criminal could not afford to hire a lawyer, the

Reforms of the Great Society, 1964–1968

1964

Twenty-fourth Amendment	Abolishes poll tax as prerequisite for voting.
Tax Reduction Act	Provides $10 billion in tax cuts in 1964 and 1965.
Civil Rights Act	Bans discrimination in public accommodations, public education, and employment and extends protections to American Indians on reservations.
Economic Opportunity Act	Creates programs for the disadvantaged, including Head Start, VISTA, the Job Corps, and CAP.

1965

Elementary and Secondary Education Act	Provides $1.3 billion in aid to elementary and secondary schools.
Medical Care Act	Provides health insurance (Medicare) for all citizens age sixty-five and over and extends federal health benefits to welfare recipients (Medicaid).
Voting Rights Act	Bans literacy tests and other voting restrictions and authorizes the federal government to act directly to enable African Americans to both register and vote.
Executive Order 11246	Bans discrimination on the basis of race, religion, and national origin by employers awarded government contracts and requires them to "take affirmative action to ensure equal opportunity."
Department of Housing and Urban Development	Created to provide programs to improve housing and neighborhoods in urban areas.
National Arts and Humanities Act	Creates National Endowment for the Arts (NEA) and Humanities (NEH) to support the work of artists, musicians, writers, and scholars.
Water Quality Act	Requires states to set and enforce water quality standards.
Immigration and Nationality Act	Abolishes fifty-year-old discriminatory quotas based on national origins and sets equal limits for all countries.
Air Quality Act	Imposes air pollution standards for motor vehicles.
Higher Education Act	Expands federal assistance to colleges and universities.

1966

National Traffic and Motor Vehicle Safety Act	Establishes federal safety standards.
Department of Transportation	Created to administer transportation programs and policies.
Model Cities Act	Authorizes more than $1 billion to ameliorate the nation's slums.

1967

Executive Order 11375	Extends an earlier executive order banning discrimination and requiring affirmative action by federal contractors to cover women.

1968

Civil Rights Act of 1968	Bans discrimination in housing and jury service.
National Housing Act	Subsidizes the private construction of 1.7 million units of low-income housing.

state had to provide one. In 1966, *Miranda v. Arizona* required police officers to inform suspects of their rights upon arrest. The Court also overturned convictions based on evidence obtained by unlawful arrest, by electronic surveillance, or without a search warrant. Critics accused the justices of "handcuffing the police" and letting criminals go free; liberals argued that these rulings promoted equal treatment in the criminal justice system.

The Court's decisions on religion provoked even greater outrage. *Abington School District v. Schempp* (1963) ruled that requiring Bible reading and prayer in the schools violated the First Amendment principle of separation of church and state. Later judgments banned official prayer in public schools even if students were not required to participate. These decisions left students free to pray on their own, but an infuriated Alabama legislator complained, "They put Negroes in the schools and now they've driven God out." The Court's supporters, however, declared that the religion cases protected the rights of non-Christians and atheists.

Critics of the Court, part of a larger backlash mounting against Great Society liberalism, worked to pass laws or constitutional amendments that would upset despised decisions, and billboards demanded, "Impeach Earl Warren." Nonetheless, the Court's major decisions withstood the test of time.

REVIEW How did the Kennedy and Johnson administrations exemplify a liberal vision of the federal government?

▶ The Second Reconstruction

"We were just people, ordinary people, and we did it."

—Selma voting-rights activist
SHEYANN WEBB

As much as Supreme Court decisions, the black freedom struggle distinguished the liberalism of the 1960s from that of the New Deal. Before the Great Society reforms — and, in fact, contributing to them — African Americans had mobilized a movement that struck down legal separation and discrimination in the South. Whereas the first Reconstruction reflected the power of northern Republicans in the aftermath of the Civil War, the second Reconstruction depended heavily on the courage and determination of black people themselves. Sheyann Webb, one of the thousands of marchers in the 1965 Selma, Alabama, campaign for voting rights, recalled, "We were just people, ordinary people, and we did it."

Civil rights activism that focused on the South and on voting and other legal rights won widespread acceptance. But when African Americans stepped up protest against racial injustice in the rest of the country and challenged the economic deprivation that equal rights left untouched, a strong backlash developed, and Martin Luther King's vision faced challenges from other black activists.

The Flowering of the Black Freedom Struggle

The Montgomery bus boycott of 1955–1956 gave racial issues national visibility and produced a leader in **Martin Luther King Jr.** In the 1960s, protest expanded dramatically, mobilizing blacks into direct confrontation with the people and institutions that segregated and discriminated against them: retail establishments, public parks and libraries, buses and depots, voting registrars, and police forces.

Massive direct action in the South began in February 1960, when four African American college students in Greensboro, North Carolina, requested service at the whites-only Woolworth's lunch counter. Within days, hundreds of young people joined them, and others launched sit-ins in thirty-one southern cities.

From Southern Christian Leadership Conference headquarters, Ella Baker telephoned her young contacts at black colleges: "What are you going to do? It's time to move." Baker organized a meeting of student activists in April 1960 and supported their decision to form a new organization, the **Student Nonviolent Coordinating Committee (SNCC)**, pronounced "snick." Embracing civil disobedience and the nonviolence principles of Martin Luther King Jr., activists would confront their oppressors and stand up for their rights, but they would not respond if attacked. In the words of SNCC leader James Lawson, "Nonviolence nurtures the atmosphere in which reconciliation and justice become actual possibilities." SNCC, however, rejected the top-down leadership of King and the established civil rights organizations, adopting a decentralized structure that fostered decision making and the development of leadership at the grassroots level.

The activists' optimism and commitment to nonviolence soon underwent severe tests. Although some cities quietly met student demands, more typically activists encountered violence. Hostile whites poured food over demonstrators, burned them with cigarettes, called them "niggers," and pelted them with rocks. Local police attacked protesters with dogs, clubs, fire hoses, and tear gas; they arrested more than 3,600 demonstrators in the year following the Greensboro sit-in.

Another wave of protest occurred in May 1961, when the Congress of Racial Equality

VISUAL ACTIVITY

Lunch Counter Sit-in

John Salter Jr., a professor at Tougaloo College, and students Joan Trumpauer and Anne Moody take part in a 1963 sit-in at the Woolworth's lunch counter in Jackson, Mississippi. Shortly before this photograph was taken, whites had thrown two students to the floor, and police had arrested one student. Salter was spattered with mustard and ketchup. In 1968, Moody published *Coming of Age in Mississippi*, a popular book about her experiences in the black freedom struggle. State Historical Society of Wisconsin.

READING THE IMAGE: What does the photograph tell you about black civil rights activity of the early 1960s?
CONNECTIONS: How would you describe the changes in race relations between African Americans and whites in the United States in the first half of the 1960s?

(CORE) organized Freedom Rides to integrate interstate transportation in the South. When a group of six whites and seven blacks reached Alabama, whites bombed their bus and beat them with baseball bats so fiercely that an observer "couldn't see their faces through the blood." CORE rebuffed President Kennedy's pleas to call off the rides. But after a huge mob attacked the riders in Montgomery, Alabama, Attorney General Robert Kennedy dispatched federal marshals to restore order. Although violence against the riders abated, Freedom Riders arriving in Jackson, Mississippi, were promptly arrested, and several hundred spent weeks in jail. All told, more than four hundred blacks and whites participated in the Freedom Rides, which typified the black freedom struggle: administration efforts to stop the protests, officials' reluctance to intervene to protect demonstrators, and the steely courage of civil rights activists in the face of violence.

Encouraged by Kennedy administration officials who preferred voter registration to civil disobedience, SNCC and other groups began the Voter Education Project in the summer of 1961. They, too, met violence. Whites bombed black churches, threw tenant farmers out of their homes, and beat and jailed activists such as **Fannie Lou Hamer** (see pages 931–932). In June 1963, a white man gunned down Mississippi NAACP leader Medgar Evers in front of his house in Jackson. Similar violence met King's 1963

Civil Rights Freedom Rides, May 1961

campaign in Birmingham, Alabama, to integrate public facilities and open jobs to blacks. The police attacked demonstrators with dogs, cattle prods, and fire hoses — brutalities that television broadcast around the world.

The largest demonstration drew 250,000 blacks and whites to the nation's capital in August 1963 in the **March on Washington for Jobs and Freedom**, inspired by the strategy of A. Philip Randolph in 1941 (see chapter 25). Its chief architect was Bayard Rustin, a radical Christian and pacifist, who had helped Martin Luther King develop the principles and practice of nonviolence. Speaking from the Lincoln Memorial, King put his indelible stamp on the day, drawing on all the passion and skills that made him the greatest orator of his day. "I have a dream," he repeated again and again, imagining the day "when all of God's children . . . will be able to join hands and sing . . . 'Free at last, free at last; thank God Almighty, we are free at last.'"

The euphoria of the March on Washington faded as activists returned to face continued violence in the South. In 1964, the **Mississippi Freedom Summer Project** mobilized more than a thousand northern black and white college students to conduct voter registration drives. Resistance was fierce, intensified by the sight of white activist women working alongside black men. By the end of the summer, only twelve hundred new voters had been allowed to register. Southern whites had killed several activists, beaten eighty, arrested more than a thousand, and burned thirty-five black churches. Hidden resistance came from the federal government itself, as the FBI spied on King and other leaders and expanded its activities to "expose, disrupt, misdirect, discredit, or otherwise neutralize" black protest.

Still, the movement persisted. In March 1965, Alabama state troopers used such violent force to turn back a voting rights march from Selma to the state capitol in Montgomery that the incident earned the name "Bloody Sunday" and compelled President Johnson to call up the Alabama National Guard to protect the marchers. Battered and hospitalized on Bloody Sunday, John Lewis, chairman of SNCC (and later a congressman from Georgia), managed to make the final stretch of the **Selma march** to the capitol. Calling the Voting Rights Act, which passed that October, "every bit as momentous as the Emancipation Proclamation," he said, "we all felt we'd had a part in it."

The Response in Washington

Civil rights leaders would have to wear sneakers, Lyndon Johnson said, if they were going to keep up with him. But both Kennedy and Johnson, reluctant to alienate southern voters and their congressional representatives, tended to move only when events gave them little choice. Kennedy sent federal marshals to protect the Freedom Riders, dispatched troops to enable air force veteran James H. Meredith to enroll in the all-white University of Mississippi in 1962, and called up the Alabama National Guard during the Birmingham demonstrations. But, aware of the political costs of deploying federal force, he told activists pleading for more protection that law enforcement was a local matter.

The Children's Crusade
A month into the civil rights campaign in Birmingham, Alabama, in May 1963, children and teenagers poured out of the Sixteenth Street Baptist Church to demonstrate in the downtown business section. As shown here, police stopped the children and led them into jail. After the jails filled with more than one thousand young people, police turned on the next stream of demonstrators with high-pressure water hoses and dogs, bringing national attention and sympathy to the protesters, who ultimately forced Birmingham leaders to accede to many of their demands. AP Photo/Bill Hudson.

The Selma March for Voting Rights
In 1963, the Student Nonviolent Coordinating Committee began a campaign for voting rights in Selma, Alabama, where white officials had registered only 335 of the 15,000 eligible African Americans. In March 1965, demonstrators began a fifty-four-mile march from Selma to Montgomery, the state capital, to insist that blacks be registered. In this photograph, young African Americans march with nuns, priests, and other supporters. During the march, Juanita Williams wore out her shoes (shown here), which are now displayed at the National Museum of History in Washington, D.C. What do you think motivated the marchers to carry the American flag? Photo: Steve Shapiro/TimePix/Getty; Shoes: Smithsonian Institution, Washington, D.C.

In June 1963, Kennedy finally made good on his promise to seek strong antidiscrimination legislation. Pointing to the injustice suffered by blacks, Kennedy asked white Americans, "Who among us would then be content with the counsels of patience and delay?" Johnson took up Kennedy's commitment with passion, as scenes of violence against peaceful demonstrators appalled television viewers across the nation. The resulting public support, the "Johnson treatment," and the president's appeal to memories of the martyred Kennedy all produced the most important civil rights law since Reconstruction.

The Civil Rights Act of 1964 guaranteed access for all Americans to public accommodations, public education, employment, and voting. It sounded the death knell for the South's system of segregation, outlawed job discrimination that was rampant throughout the nation, and extended constitutional protections to Indians on reservations. Title VII of the measure, banning discrimination in employment, not only attacked racial discrimination but also outlawed discrimination against women. Because Title VII applied to every aspect of employment, including wages, hiring, and promotion, it represented a giant step toward equal employment opportunity for white women as well as for racial minorities.

Responding to black voter registration drives in the South, Johnson demanded legislation to remove "every remaining obstacle to the right and the opportunity to vote." In August 1965, he signed the Voting Rights Act, empowering the federal government to intervene directly to enable African Americans to register and vote, thereby launching a major transformation in southern politics. Black voting rates shot up dramatically (Map 28.2). In turn, the number of African Americans holding political office in the South increased from a handful in 1964 to more than a thousand by 1972. Such gains translated into tangible benefits as black officials upgraded public facilities, police protection, and other basic services for their constituents. When Unita Blackwell became the first black female mayor in Mississippi, a resident of her town recalled, "She brought in the water tower. . . . Sewage, too. There wasn't nothing but those little outdoor houses."

Johnson also declared the need to realize "not just equality as a right and theory, but equality as fact and result." To this end, he issued an executive order in 1965 to require employers holding government contracts (affecting about one-third of the labor force) to take affirmative action to ensure equal opportunity. Extended to cover women

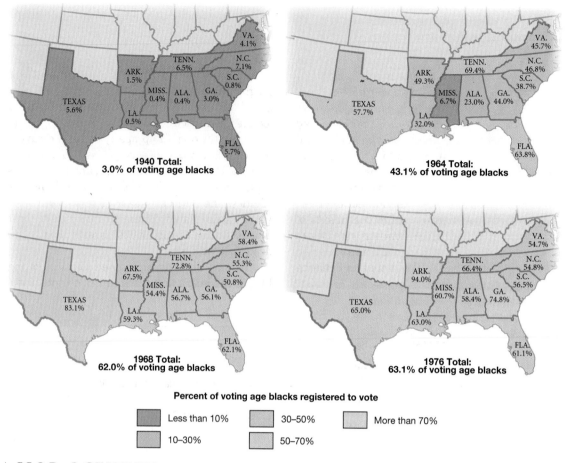

1940 Total:
3.0% of voting age blacks

1964 Total:
43.1% of voting age blacks

1968 Total:
62.0% of voting age blacks

1976 Total:
63.1% of voting age blacks

Percent of voting age blacks registered to vote

Less than 10%   30–50%   More than 70%

10–30%   50–70%

MAP ACTIVITY

Map 28.2   The Rise of the African American Vote, 1940–1976

Voting rates of southern blacks increased gradually in the 1940s and 1950s but shot up dramatically in the deep South after the Voting Rights Act of 1965 provided for federal agents to enforce African Americans' right to vote.

READING THE MAP: When did the biggest change in African American voter registration occur in the South? In 1968, which states had the highest and which had the lowest voter registration rates?

CONNECTIONS: What role did African American voters play in the 1960 election? What were the targets of three major voting drives in the 1960s?

in 1967, the affirmative action program was called "reverse discrimination" by people who incorrectly thought that it required quotas and the hiring of unqualified candidates. In fact, it required employers to counter the effects of centuries of oppression by acting forcefully to align their labor force with the available pool of qualified candidates. Most corporations came to see affirmative action as a good employment practice.

In 1968, Johnson maneuvered one final bill through Congress. While those in other regions often applauded the gains made by the black freedom struggle in the South, they were just as likely to resist claims for racial justice in their own locations. In 1963, for example, California voters rejected a law passed by the legislature banning discrimination in housing; a majority of voters were more concerned with their right to do as they pleased with their property than with the rights of minorities to be free of discrimination. And when Martin Luther King Jr. launched a campaign against de facto segregation in Chicago in 1966, thousands of whites jeered and threw stones at demonstrators. Johnson's efforts to get a federal open-housing law succeeded only in the wake of King's assassination in 1968. The **Civil Rights Act of 1968** banned racial discrimination in housing and jury selection and authorized federal intervention when states failed to protect civil rights workers from violence.

Black Power and Urban Rebellions

By 1966, black protest was visible throughout the nation, demanding not just legal equality but also economic justice and no longer holding non-violence as a basic principle. These developments were not entirely new. African Americans had waged campaigns for decent jobs, housing, and education outside the South since the 1930s. Moreover, some African Americans had always armed themselves in self-defense, and even in the early 1960s many activists doubted that their passive suffering would change the hearts of racists. Still, the black freedom struggle began to appear more threatening to the white majority.

The new emphases resulted from a combination of heightened activism and unrealized promise.

Legal equality could not quickly improve the material conditions of blacks, and black rage at oppressive conditions erupted in waves of urban uprisings from 1965 to 1968 (Map 28.3). In a situation where virtually all-white police forces patrolled black neighborhoods, incidents between police and local blacks typically sparked rioting and resulted in looting, destruction of property, injuries, and deaths. The worst looting and property damage occurred in the Watts district of Los Angeles in August 1965, Newark and Detroit in July 1967, and the nation's capital in April 1968, but violence visited hundreds of cities. The Detroit riots ended in 43 deaths (30 at the hands of law enforcement officers, with most of the victims black), 7,000 arrests, and 1,300 destroyed buildings.

Rioting and looting seemed to many young blacks the only means available to protest the

MAP ACTIVITY

Map 28.3 Urban Uprisings, 1965–1968

When a white police officer in the Watts district of Los Angeles struck a twenty-one-year-old African American, whom he had just pulled over for driving drunk, one onlooker shouted, "We've got no rights at all — it's just like Selma." The altercation escalated into a five-day uprising, during which young blacks set fires, looted, and attacked police and firefighters. When National Guardsmen and police finally quelled the riot, 34 people were dead, 900 blacks had been injured and 4,000 arrested, hundreds of families had lost their homes, and scores of businesses had been wiped out. Similar violence, though usually not on such a large scale, erupted in dozens of cities across the nation during the next three summers, as this map indicates.

READING THE MAP: In what regions and cities of the United States were the 1960s uprisings concentrated? What years saw the greatest unrest?

CONNECTIONS: What were some of the causes of racial unrest in America's cities during this period? Whom did whites generally hold responsible for the violence and why?

Uprisings in urban ghettos
● 1965–1966   ■ 1967–1968

poverty, lack of opportunity, and official insensitivity they experienced daily. "Since the riot, we're not niggers anymore. We're black men," reported a New Jersey activist. In Los Angeles, an observer said to a reporter, "I don't understand all this talk about 'looting.' They rob us every day. They rob us on the rent, on the food, on the job. They rob our kids on education." Most whites, however, saw the riots as criminal activity, plain and simple, blaming them on radicals who were challenging the principles of King.

Malcolm X was one of those who resisted an emphasis on integration and passive resistance. In 1952, he joined the Nation of Islam, whose adherents called themselves Black Muslims and drew on the long tradition of black nationalism. Calling for black pride and autonomy, separation from the "corrupt [white] society," and self-defense against white violence, Malcolm X attracted a large following, especially in urban ghettos.

At a June 1966 rally in Greenwood, Mississippi, SNCC chairman **Stokely Carmichael** gave the ideas espoused by Malcolm X a new name when he shouted, "We want black power." Those words quickly became the rallying cry in SNCC and CORE, and the **black power movement** riveted national attention in the late 1960s. Carmichael called integration "a subterfuge for the maintenance of white supremacy" and rejected assimilation because it implied white superiority. African Americans were encouraged to develop independent businesses and control their own schools, communities, and political organizations. The phrase "Black is beautiful" emphasized pride in African American culture and connections to dark-skinned people around the world, who were claiming their independence from colonial domination. According to black power advocates, nonviolence brought only more beatings and killings. After police killed an unarmed black teenager in San Francisco in 1966, Huey Newton and Bobby Seale organized the Black Panther Party for Self-Defense to combat police brutality.

The press paid inordinate attention to black radicals, and the civil rights movement encountered a severe white backlash. Although the urban riots of the mid-1960s erupted spontaneously, triggered by specific incidents of alleged police mistreatment, horrified whites blamed black power militants. By 1966, 85 percent of the white population — up from 34 percent two years earlier — thought that African Americans were pressing for too much too quickly.

Agreeing with black power advocates about the need for "a radical reconstruction of society," Martin Luther King Jr. expanded the scope of the struggle. In 1965, he mounted a drive for better jobs, schools, and housing in Chicago. Yet he clung to nonviolence and integration as the means to this end. In April 1968, the thirty-nine-year-old leader went to Memphis to support striking municipal sanitation workers. There, on April 4, he was murdered by an escaped white convict.

Although black power organizations captured the headlines, they failed to gain the massive support from African Americans that King and other leaders had attracted. Nor could they alleviate the poverty and racism entrenched in the urban North and West. Black radicals were harassed by the FBI and jailed; some encounters left both black militants and police dead. Yet black power's emphasis on racial pride and its critique of American institutions resonated loudly and helped shape the protest activities of other groups.

REVIEW How and why did the civil rights movement change in the mid-1960s?

Malcolm X in Egypt

Malcolm X stands in front of the pyramids in Egypt during a trip to Africa and the Middle East in 1964. Partly as a result of meeting Muslims of all colors, as well as other whites who were committed to ending racism, he no longer equated whites with the devil. "The white man is not inherently evil," he concluded, "but America's racist society influences him to act evilly." John Launois/Black Star/Stockphoto.com.

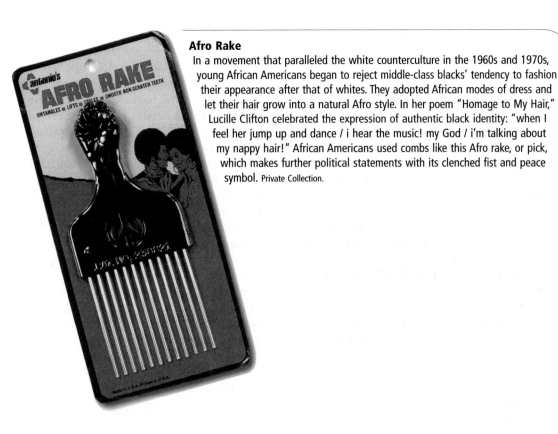

Afro Rake
In a movement that paralleled the white counterculture in the 1960s and 1970s, young African Americans began to reject middle-class blacks' tendency to fashion their appearance after that of whites. They adopted African modes of dress and let their hair grow into a natural Afro style. In her poem "Homage to My Hair," Lucille Clifton celebrated the expression of authentic black identity: "when I feel her jump up and dance / i hear the music! my God / i'm talking about my nappy hair!" African Americans used combs like this Afro rake, or pick, which makes further political statements with its clenched fist and peace symbol. Private Collection.

▶ A Multitude of Movements

The civil rights movement's undeniable moral claims helped make protest more respectable, while its successes encouraged other groups with grievances. Native Americans, Latinos, college students, women, gay men and lesbians, and others drew on the black freedom struggle for inspiration and models of activism. Many of these groups engaged in direct-action protests, expressed their own cultural nationalism, and challenged dominant institutions and values. Like participants in the black freedom struggle, they met strong resistance, and their accomplishments fell far below their aims. Still, their grievances gained attention in the political arena, and they expanded justice and opportunity for many of their constituents.

Native American Protest

The cry "red power" reflected the influence of black radicalism on young Native Americans, whose activism took on fresh militancy and goals in the 1960s. The termination and relocation programs of the 1940s and 1950s, contrary to their intent, stirred a sense of Indian identity across tribal lines and a determination to preserve traditional culture. Native Americans demonstrated and occupied land and public buildings, claiming rights to natural resources and territory they had owned collectively before European settlement.

In 1969, Native American militants captured world attention when several dozen seized Alcatraz Island, an abandoned federal prison in San Francisco Bay, claiming their right of "first discovery" of this land. They held the island for nineteen months, using the occupation to publicize injustices against Indians, promote pan-Indian cooperation, and celebrate traditional cultures. One of the organizers, Dr. LaNada Boyer, the first Native American to attend the University of California, Berkeley, said of Alcatraz, "We were able to reestablish our identity as Indian people, as a culture, as political entities."

In Minneapolis in 1968, two Chippewa Indians, Dennis Banks and George Mitchell, founded the **American Indian Movement (AIM)** to attack problems in cities, where about 300,000 Indians lived. AIM sought to protect Indians from police harassment, secure antipoverty funds, and establish "survival schools" to teach Indian history and values. The movement's appeal quickly

> **"We were able to reestablish our identity as Indian people, as a culture, as political entities."**
> —Dr. LANADA BOYER, on the Alcatraz occupation

AIM leaders helped organize the "Trail of Broken Treaties" caravan to the nation's capital in 1972, when activists occupied the Bureau of Indian Affairs to express their outrage at the bureau's policies and bureaucratic interference in Indians' lives. In 1973, a much longer siege occurred on the Lakota Sioux reservation in South Dakota. Conflicts there between AIM militants and older tribal leaders led AIM to take over for seventy-two days the village of Wounded Knee, where U.S. troops had massacred more than one hundred Sioux Indians in 1890 (see chapter 17).

Although these dramatic occupations failed to achieve their specific goals, Indians won the end of relocation and termination policies, greater tribal sovereignty and control over community services, protection of Indian religious practices, and a measure of respect and pride. A number of laws and court decisions restored rights to ancestral lands and compensated tribes for land seized in violation of treaties.

Latino Struggles for Justice

The fastest-growing minority group in the 1960s was Latino, or Hispanic American, an extraordinarily varied population encompassing people of Mexican, Puerto Rican, Caribbean, and other Latin American origins. (The term *Latino* stresses their common bonds as a minority group in the United States. The older, less political term *Hispanic* also includes people with origins in Spain.) People of Puerto Rican and Caribbean descent flocked to East Coast cities, but more than half of the nation's Latino population — including some six million Mexican Americans — lived in the Southwest. In addition, thousands illegally crossed the border between Mexico and the United States yearly in search of economic opportunity. Political organization of Mexican Americans dated back to the League of United Latin-American Citizens (LULAC), founded in 1929, which fought segregation and discrimination through litigation (see chapter 26). In the 1960s, however, young Mexican Americans increasingly rejected traditional politics in favor of direct action. One symbol of this generational challenge was young activists' adoption of the term *Chicano* (from *mejicano*, the Spanish word for "Mexican").

Chicano protest drew national attention to California, where **Cesar Chavez** and **Dolores Huerta** organized a movement to improve the wretched conditions of migrant agricultural workers. As a child moving from farm to farm with his family, living in soggy tents and exploited by

Native Americans Occupy Alcatraz Island
Alcatraz Island, in San Francisco Bay, housed the first U.S. military post on the West Coast and from 1936 to 1963 a federal penitentiary. In November 1969, claiming original possession of the island, Indian students and others from the Bay Area began what would become a nineteen-month-long occupation. Some one hundred Native Americans occupied the island, calling themselves "Indians of All Tribes" to reflect their diversity. They demanded the deed to the island and the creation there of an Indian university, museum, and cultural center. Although failing to achieve their goals, they brought attention to the Native American cause and spurred further activism. Photo by Ralph Crane/Time Life Pictures/Getty Images.

spread and filled many Indians with a new sense of purpose. AIM members did not have "that hangdog reservation look I was used to," Lakota activist and author Mary Crow Dog wrote, and their visit to her South Dakota reservation "loosened a sort of earthquake inside me."

labor contractors, Chavez changed schools frequently and encountered indifference and discrimination. One teacher, he recalled, "hung a sign on me that said, 'I am a clown, I speak Spanish.'" After serving in World War II, Chavez began to organize voter registration drives among Mexican Americans.

In contrast to Chavez, Dolores Huerta grew up in an integrated urban neighborhood where she avoided the farmworkers' grinding poverty but witnessed subtle forms of discrimination. Once, a high school teacher challenged her authorship of an essay because it was so well written. Believing that a labor union was the key to prog-

Cesar Chavez and Dolores Huerta
Under posters showing Senator Robert Kennedy and Mahatma Gandhi, Chavez and Huerta confer in 1968 during the United Farm Workers' five-year struggle with grape growers for better wages and working conditions and union recognition. Chavez, like Martin Luther King, had studied the ideas of Gandhi, who used civil disobedience and nonviolence to gain independence for India. People across the country supported the UFW's grape boycott, including Robert Kennedy. Huerta left her teaching job to organize workers, saying, "I thought I could do more by organizing farm workers than by trying to teach their hungry children." Arthur Schatz/TimePix/Getty Images.

ress, she and Chavez founded the United Farm Workers (UFW) in 1962. Although Chavez headed the union until his death in 1993, Huerta was indispensable to its vitality.

To gain leverage for striking workers, the UFW mounted a nationwide boycott of California grapes, which drew support from millions of Americans and helped win a wage increase for the workers in 1970. Although the UFW struggled and lost membership during the 1970s, it helped politicize Mexican Americans and improve farmworkers' lives.

Other Chicanos mobilized to force the Equal Employment Opportunity Commission (EEOC), the enforcement agency of Title VII of the Civil Rights Act of 1964, to act against job discrimination against Mexican Americans. LULAC, the American GI Forum (see chapter 26), and other groups picketed government offices. President Johnson responded in 1967 by appointing Vicente T. Ximenes as the first Mexican American EEOC commissioner and by creating a special committee on Mexican American affairs.

Claiming "brown power," Chicanos organized to end discrimination in education, gain political power, and combat police brutality. In Denver, Rodolfo "Corky" Gonzales set up "freedom schools" where Chicano children studied the Spanish language and Mexican American history. The nationalist strains of Chicano protest were evident in La Raza Unida (the United Race), a political party founded in 1970 in Texas and based on cultural pride and brotherhood. Along with blacks and Native Americans, Chicanos continued to be disproportionately represented among the poor, but they gradually won more political offices, more effective enforcement of antidiscrimination legislation, and greater respect for their culture.

Student Rebellion, the New Left, and the Counterculture

Although materially and legally more secure than their African American, Indian, and Latino counterparts, white youths also expressed dissent, supporting the black freedom struggle and launching student protests, the antiwar movement, and the new feminist movement. Challenging establishment institutions and traditional values, young activists helped change higher education, the family, the national government, and other key institutions. They were part of a larger international phenomenon, as student movements arose in Mexico, Germany, Turkey, Czechoslovakia, Japan, and other nations around the globe. (See chapter 29, "Beyond America's Borders," page 984.)

Student Protest

The waves of student protest that rolled across college campuses in the 1960s were all the more surprising because observers had found the "silent generation" of the 1950s so complacent and conformist. Although the majority of college students did not participate in the rebellions, a sizable number of students at all kinds of colleges and universities challenged traditional authority, criticized established institutions, and demanded a voice in the decisions that affected their lives.

DOCUMENT 1
Edward Schwartz on Student Power, October 1967

Student activist Edward Schwartz wrote this statement to represent the views of the National Student Association, the largest college student organization in the 1960s. Ironically, this association, which contributed to the student upheaval of the sixties, had been founded a decade earlier, with secret funding from the CIA, as a liberal group to counter communism.

The educational premise behind demands for student power reflects the notion that people learn through living, through the process of integrating their thoughts with their actions, through testing their values against those of a community, through a capacity to act. College presidents who invoke legal authority to prove educational theory assume that growth is the ability to accept what the past has created. Student power is a medium through which people integrate their own experience with a slice of the past which seems appropriate, with their efforts to intensify the relationships between the community within the university.

Let this principle apply — he who must obey the rule should make it.

Students should make the rules governing dormitory hours, boy-girl visitation, student unions, student fees, clubs, newspapers, and the like. Faculty and administrators should advise — attempt to persuade, even. Yet the student should bear the burden of choice.

Students and faculty should co-decide curricular policy.

Students, faculty, and administration should co-decide admissions policy, overall college policy affecting the community, even areas like university investment. . . . Student power should not be argued on legal grounds. It is not a legal principle. It is an educational principle.

Student power is threatening to those who wield power now, but this is understandable. A student should threaten his administrators outside of class, just as bright students threaten professors inside of class.

Student power ultimately challenges everyone in the university — the students who must decide; the faculty and administrators who must rethink their own view of community relations in order to persuade.

People who say that student power means anarchy imply really that students are rabble who have no ability to form community and to adhere to decisions made by community. Student power is not the negation of rules — it is the creation of a new process for the enactment of rules. Student power is not the elimination of authority, it is the development of a democratic standard of authority.

SOURCE: Excerpt from "He Who Must Obey the Rule Should Make It," from *The University Crisis Reader*, vol. 1, *The Liberal University under Attack* by Immanuel Wallerstein and Paul Starr, eds., pp. 482–84. Copyright © 1971 by Random House, Inc. Reprinted with permission.

DOCUMENT 2
SDS Explanation of the Columbia Strike, September 1968

One of the longest and most violent student protests occurred in New York City at Columbia University in April and May 1968, when white and black students occupied five buildings for a week. A subsequent student strike closed the university for the rest of the academic year. One of the key issues arose from the university's expansion through buying up land in neighboring Harlem and evicting black tenants. The members of the Columbia chapter of Students for a Democratic Society (SDS), one of various factions among the protesters, rationalized their actions in the following statement.

When we seized five buildings at Columbia University, we engaged the force of wealth, privilege, property — and the force of state violence that always accompanies them — with little more than our own ideals, our fears, and a vague sense of outrage at the injustices of our society. Martin Luther King had just been shot, his name demeaned by

Columbia officials who refused to grant a decent wage to Puerto Rican workers, and who had recently grabbed part of Harlem for a student gym. . . .

For years Columbia Trustees had evicted tenants from their homes, taken land through city deals, and fired workers for trying to form a union. For years they had trained officers for Vietnam who, as ROTC literature indicates, killed Vietnamese peasants in their own country. In secret work for the IDA [Institute for Defense Analysis] and the CIA, in chemical-biological war research for the Department of War, the Trustees implicated their own University in genocide. They had consistently . . . lied to their own constituents and published CIA books under the guise of independent scholarship. . . . We lived in an institution that channeled us, marked us, ranked us, failed us, used us, and treated masses of humanity with class contempt. . . .

Columbia, standing at the top of a hill, looked down on Harlem. . . . People who survived in Harlem had been evicted by the Trustees from Morningside or still paid rent to Columbia. . . . We walked to our classrooms across land that had been privatized; we studied in buildings that had once been homes in a city that is underhoused; and we listened to the apologies for Cold War and capital in our classes.

Columbia professors often claim that the University is a neutral institution. . . . Many professors pursue all sides of a question as an end in itself. They find a certain refuge in the difficulty of defining good and evil. The result is a clogging of their moral sense, their capacity for collective justice. . . . What liberals call neutrality is really one of the ways by which the faculty protects its special status in society.

A University could not, even if it wanted, choose to be really value-free. It can choose good values; it can choose bad values; or it can remain ignorant of the values on which it acts. . . . A social institution should at least articulate its own perspective, so that its own values may be consciously applied or modified. It is a typical fallacy of American teaching, that to remain silent on crucial issues is to be objective with your own constituents. Actually a "neutral" institution is far more manipulative than a University committed to avowed goals and tasks.

SOURCE: Excerpt from "The Columbia Statement," Columbia SDS, from *The University Crisis Reader*, vol. 1, *The Liberal University under Attack* by Immanuel Wallerstein and Paul Starr, eds., pp. 23–47. Copyright © 1971 by Random House, Inc. Reprinted with permission.

DOCUMENT 3
Counterthrust on Student Power, Spring 1967

While the majority of students simply avoided involvement in campus rebellions, some students actively criticized the protesters. The largest conservative student organization was Young Americans for Freedom, which more than doubled in size during the 1960s. The following selection, from a leaflet titled "Student Power Is a Farce," reflected the views of Counterthrust, a conservative group at Wayne State University in Michigan.

Our University is being treated to the insanity of Left-Wing students demanding the run of the University. . . . Wayne students are told by the Left that "student power" merely means more democracy on campus. This is an outright lie! Student power is a Left-Wing catchword symbolizing campus militancy and radicalism. In actuality, the Left-Wing, spearheaded by the SDS [Students for a Democratic Society], want to radically alter the university community. . . .

The Leftists charge a sinister plot by private enterprise to train students for jobs at taxpayers' expense. Evidently it never occurred to the SDS that private enterprise is also the biggest single taxpayer for schools. But, of course, that would require a little thought on the part of the SDS which they have already demonstrated they are incapable of. . . .

The byword of student power-union advocates is Radicalism. . . . Fraternities and student Governments will have no place in student power-unions since both are considered allies of the status quo and thus useless. . . . As responsible Wayne students, we cannot allow our University to be used by Leftists for their narrow purposes. We were invited to this campus by the Michigan Taxpayer to receive an education. Let us honor that invitation.

SOURCE: "Student Power Is a Farce," Counterthrust, from *The University Crisis Reader*, vol. 1, *The Liberal University under Attack* by Immanuel Wallerstein and Paul Starr, eds., pp. 487–88. Copyright © 1971 by Random House, Inc. Reprinted with permission.

Questions for Analysis and Debate

1. How do the statements by Edward Schwartz and the Columbia SDS chapter differ in terms of the issues they address?

2. What did Counterthrust see as the biggest problem with student protesters?

3. Do you agree or disagree with the Columbia SDS chapter's assertion that it is impossible for a university to be neutral or value-free? Explain your position.

4. To what extent do your own campus policies and practices suggest that student protest during the 1960s and 1970s made a difference?

5. What changes that the protesters demanded have not been implemented at your college or university? Should they be?

Anti-Establishment Clothing

Youthful hippies embraced distinctive and colorful clothing to help define their identities as rebels in the new counterculture taking shape in the late 1960s. The well-worn artifacts shown here typify the self-expression of young people who scorned the older generation's button-down shirts, business suits, teased bouffant hair, sheath dresses, and all that they stood for.

Hippie first emerged as a new word in 1965, derived from *hip* and *hipster*, slang words from the realm of jazz and beatniks. But the teenagers and young adults morphing into hippies came disproportionately from the middle-class suburbs that at the time symbolized the success of the American dream. Hippies rejected the classic aspirations of steady work, home ownership, and consumer goods. In the summer of 1967, some 100,000 of them converged on the Haight-Ashbury district of San Francisco, lured by the call of the "Summer of Love." Those who stayed beyond the summer lived in voluntary poverty, relying on panhandling, crash pads, soup kitchens, and free clinics to support their freedom from middle-class values. Hippie enclaves sprouted in low-rent districts of coastal cities and in rural communes.

Clothing provided an obvious way for hippies to express their disdain for the "Establishment." What other attitudes can you decode in this

Bell-bottom Jeans

pair of bell-bottom jeans? Is it is a men's or a women's garment? Consider the degree of sewing expertise required to repurpose straight-leg pants into the bell-bottom flare. Who among the hippies was trained to do that work? Think about the typical stress points in pants. Are the patches here functional or decorative?

The fringed jacket illustrates two common themes: the Native American/cowboy-style fringe, and the red-white-blue motif. How might mainstream patriots have regarded this jacket? Was it intentionally inflammatory, or might the wearer be expressing an alternative form of patriotism? Most states had decades-old laws forbidding the desecration of the U.S. flag. Would this jacket have put its wearer at risk for arrest? In Massachusetts, a young man sporting a 4-by-6-inch flag on the left rear of his jeans was jailed for treating the flag "contemptuously," but in 1974 the U.S. Supreme Court overturned his conviction on grounds that the law's contempt provision was unconstitutionally vague.

What was rebellious about the denim shorts and halter top? Can you think of any time or place when such immodest dress would have

The central organization of white student protest was **Students for a Democratic Society (SDS)**, formed in 1960. In 1962, the organizers wrote in their statement of purpose, "We are people of this generation, bred in at least modest comfort, housed now in universities, looking uncomfortably at the world we inherit." The idealistic students criticized the complacency of their elders, the remoteness of decision makers from those affected by their actions, and the powerlessness and alienation generated by a bureaucratic society. SDS aimed to mobilize a "New Left" around the goals of civil rights, peace, and universal economic

security. Other forms of student activism soon followed.

The first large-scale white student protest arose at the University of California, Berkeley, in 1964, when university officials banned students from setting up tables to recruit support for various causes. Led by whites returning from civil rights work in the South, the students claimed the right to freedom of expression and political action. Members of the "free speech" movement occupied the administration building, and more than seven hundred students were arrested before the California Board of Regents overturned the new restrictions.

Fringed Jacket

Halter and Shorts

been acceptable? Can you guess how high school dress codes responded to these innovations? How the fashion industry responded? (Hint: Hot pants and miniskirts soon hit the fashion runways.)

Authentic hippie clothing remains rare; most of it probably fell apart and was junked by the mid-1970s, with occasional garments showing up in thrift stores or vintage clothing shops. By the 1980s, patterned bell-bottoms and daring short shorts looked as old-fashioned as a flapper dress from the 1920s. Nevertheless, the impact of counterculture clothing on mainstream dress was profound, leading within a few years to a much greater informality in everyday attire, even among the Establishment.

SOURCE: Jacket: Collection of Mark Hooper / Nancy Gewirz / Antique Textile Research; jeans: Nancy Gewirz / Antique Textile Research; halter and shorts: Picture Research Consultants & Archives.

Hundreds of student rallies and building occupations followed on campuses across the country, especially after 1965, when opposition to the Vietnam War mounted and students protested against universities' ties with the military (as discussed in chapter 29). Students also changed the collegiate environment. Women at the University of Chicago, for example, charged in 1969 that all universities "discriminate against women, impede their full intellectual development, deny them places on the faculty, exploit talented women and mistreat women students." At Howard University, African American students called for a "Black Awareness Research Institute," demanding that academic departments "place more emphasis on how these disciplines may be used to effect the liberation of black people." Across the country, students won curricular reforms such as black studies and women's studies programs, more financial aid for minority and poor students, independence from paternalistic rules, and a larger voice in campus decision making. (See "Documenting the American Promise," page 950.)

Student protest bewildered and angered older Americans, even more so when it blended into a cultural revolution against nearly every conventional standard of behavior. Drawing on the ideas of the Beats of the 1950s (see chapter 27), the "hippies," as they were called, rejected mainstream values such as materialism, order, and sexual control. Seeking personal rather than political change, they advocated "Do your own thing" and drew attention with their long hair, wildly colorful clothing, and use of marijuana, LSD, and other illegal drugs. Across the country, thousands of radicals established communes in cities or on farms, where they renounced private property and shared everything, often including sexual partners. (See "Visualizing History," page 952.)

Rock and folk music defined both the counterculture and the political left. English groups such as the Beatles and the Rolling Stones and homegrown performers such as Bob Dylan, Janis Joplin, and the Grateful Dead took American youth by storm. Music during the 1960s often carried insurgent political and social messages

that reflected radical youth culture. "Eve of Destruction," a top hit of 1965, reminded young men at a time when the voting age was twenty-one, "You're old enough to kill but not for votin'." The Woodstock Music Festival epitomized the centrality of music to the youth rebellion. Woodstock featured the greatest rock and folk musicians of the era and drew 400,000 young people to a farm in Bethel, New York, in 1969.

Hippies faded away in the 1970s, but many elements of the counterculture — rock music, jeans, and long hair, as well as new social attitudes — filtered into the mainstream. More tolerant approaches to sexual behaviors spawned what came to be called the "sexual revolution," with help from the birth control pill, which became available in the 1960s. Self-fulfillment became a dominant concern of many Americans, and questioning of authority became more widespread.

Rock Music
Rock music provided the sound track for the youth rebellion of the 1960s. Heavily influenced by the blues as she grew up in east Texas, Janis Joplin developed a style that captivated audiences with her raw emotions and passionate delivery, paving the way for women to break into the male-dominated rock culture. Here she appears (second from left) in 1968 with the psychedelic rock band, Big Brother and the Holding Company, at Fillmore East, a famous New York City rock venue known for its fabulous light shows. Still wildly popular, Joplin died from a drug overdose in 1970. © Elliot Landy / The Image Works.

Gay Men and Lesbians Organize

More permissive sexual norms did not stretch easily to include tolerance of homosexuality. Gay men and lesbians escaped discrimination and ridicule only by concealing their very identities. Those who couldn't or wouldn't found themselves fired from jobs, arrested for their sexual activities, deprived of their children, or accused of being "perverted." While most kept their sexuality hidden, in the 1950s some gays and lesbians began to organize.

Gay Rights Protests

In the 1960s, inspired by the black freedom struggle, homosexual rights groups began to demonstrate at the White House and at government offices. This photograph, published on the cover of the *Ladder*, a magazine launched by the lesbian rights group Daughters of Bilitis in October 1956, shows a protest in front of the Civil Service Commission. Although the demonstrators agreed to look "conservative and conventional," one *Washington Post* reporter remembered, "I thought they must be totally reckless or weird." Courtesy of Department of Special Collections, Stanford University Libraries.

THE LADDER
Adults Only
Oct. 1965
a LESBIAN review

QUARTER MILLION
HOMOSEXUAL
FEDERAL EMPLOYEES
PROTEST
CIVIL SERVICE
POLICY

HOMOPHILE
GROUPS PICKET
IN NATION'S CAPITAL

Some of the first gay activism challenged the government's aggressive efforts to keep homosexuals out of the civil service. In October 1965, a picket line formed outside the White House with signs calling discrimination against homosexuals "as immoral as discrimination against Negroes and Jews." Not until ten years later, however, did the Civil Service Commission formally end its antigay policy.

The spark that ignited a larger movement was struck in 1969 when police raided a gay bar, the Stonewall Inn, in New York City's Greenwich Village, and gay men and lesbians fought back. "Suddenly, they were not submissive anymore," a police officer remarked. Energized by the defiance shown at the **Stonewall riots**, gay men and lesbians organized a host of new groups, such as the Gay Liberation Front. A more reformist organization, the National Gay and Lesbian Task Force, was founded in 1973 to ensure that gay issues received sustained national attention.

The gay rights movement struggled much longer and harder to win recognition than did other social movements. In 1972, Ann Arbor, Michigan, passed the first antidiscrimination ordinance, and two years later Elaine Noble's election to the Massachusetts legislature marked the first time an openly gay candidate won state office. In 1973, gay activists persuaded the American Psychiatric Association to withdraw its designation of homosexuality as a mental disease. It would take decades for these initial gains to improve conditions for most homosexuals, but by the mid-1970s gay men and lesbians had established a movement through which they could claim equal rights and express pride in their identities.

REVIEW How did the black freedom struggle influence other reform movements of the 1960s and 1970s?

▶ The New Wave of Feminism

On August 26, 1970, fifty years after women won the right to vote, tens of thousands of women across the country — from radical women in jeans to conservatively dressed suburbanites, peace activists, and politicians — took to the streets. They carried signs reading "Sisterhood Is Powerful" and "Don't Cook Dinner — Starve a Rat Today." Some of the banners opposed the

1644, a38

THE PROMISE OF TECHNOLOGY

The Pill

Longtime birth control advocate Margaret Sanger (see chapter 21) believed that the Pill was "the key to liberty" for women. In the early 1950s, she enlisted Katharine Dexter McCormick to bankroll research on oral contraception, which was conducted principally by biologists Gregory Pincus and Min-Chueh Chang and physician John Rock. They found that the hormones estrogen and progestin prevented ovulation, and in 1960 the Food and Drug Administration approved the first birth control pill, which soon became the leading form of contraception for American women. Condoms and diaphragms had been available for decades, but they required action at the time of sexual relations and were subject to failure. Surgical procedures for both men and women were also options for the prevention of pregnancy, but they were largely irreversible. After early Pill users raised concerns about its safety, manufacturers reduced the amounts of estrogen and progestin to decrease side effects and the risk for stroke, cancer, and other illnesses. This 1965 ad shows doctors how the

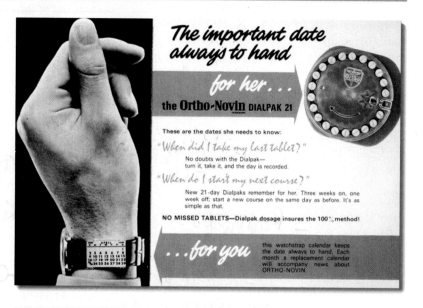

Ortho-Novin Dialpak will help women remember to take the daily tablet. What assumptions does this ad make about women and about physicians? From a woman's perspective, what are the advantages and disadvantages of the Pill compared to other contraceptive methods?
National Museum of American History, Smithsonian Institution, Behring Center.

war in Vietnam, others demanded racial justice, but women's own liberation stood at the forefront.

Becoming visible by the late 1960s, the women's movement reached its high tide in the 1970s and persisted into the twenty-first century. By that time, despite a powerful countermovement, women had experienced tremendous transformations in their legal status, public opportunities, and personal and sexual relationships, and popular expectations about appropriate gender roles had shifted dramatically.

A Multifaceted Movement Emerges

Beginning in the 1940s, large demographic changes laid the preconditions for a resurgence of feminism. As more and more women took jobs, the importance of their paid work to the economy and their families belied the idea of women as dependent, domestic beings and awakened many women workers, especially labor union women, to the inferior conditions of their employment. The democratization of higher education brought more women to college campuses, where their aspirations exceeded the confines of domesticity and of routine, subordinate jobs.

Policy initiatives in the early 1960s reflected both these larger transformations and the efforts of women's rights activists. In 1961, Assistant Secretary of Labor Esther Peterson persuaded President Kennedy to create the President's Commission on the Status of Women (PCSW). In 1963, the commission reported widespread discrimination against women and recommended remedies, although it did not challenge women's domestic roles. Counterparts of the PCSW sprang up in every state, filled with women eager for action. One of the commission's concerns was addressed even before it issued its report, when Congress passed the Equal Pay Act of 1963, making it illegal to pay women less than men for the same work.

Like other movements, the rise of feminism owed much to the black freedom struggle. Women gained protection from employment discrimination through Title VII of the Civil Rights Act of 1964 and the extension of affirmative action to women by piggybacking onto civil rights measures. They soon grew impatient when the government failed to take these new policies seriously.

Women's Strike for Equality
On the fiftieth anniversary of the Nineteenth Amendment granting woman suffrage, Betty Friedan and others organized a nationwide Women's Strike for Equality. While the numbers who participated were relatively small, in New York City more than ten thousand women marched down Fifth Avenue, in defiance of police who tried to keep them on the sidewalks. The three central demands of the protest were equal opportunity in employment and education, child care, and abortion rights. During what were still the early days of second-wave feminism, ABC News showed a U.S. senator calling the demonstrators "a small band of bra-less bubble heads." Getty John Olson/Time & Life Pictures/Getty Images.

Outraged by the government's slowness in enforcing Title VII, Betty Friedan, civil rights activist Pauli Murray, several union women, and others founded the **National Organization for Women (NOW)** in 1966.

Simultaneously, a more radical feminism grew among civil rights and New Left activists. In 1965, two white women, Mary King and Casey Hayden, wrote that their work in SNCC had awakened them to sex discrimination. Although most black women did not consider themselves to be marginalized in the movement, King and Hayden presented their ideas to white male radicals in the New Left, who responded with indifference or ridicule. By contrast, their message invigorated other white women who shared their frustration with subordinate roles. Many women walked out of New Left organizations and created an independent women's liberation movement composed of small groups across the nation.

Women's liberation began to gain public attention, especially when dozens of women picketed the Miss America beauty pageant in 1968, protesting against being forced "to compete for male approval [and] enslaved by ludicrous 'beauty' standards." Women began to speak publicly about personal experiences that had always been shrouded in secrecy, such as rape and abortion. Throughout the country, women joined consciousness-raising groups, where they discovered that what they had considered "personal" problems reflected an entrenched system of discrimination against and devaluation of women.

Radical feminists, who called their movement "women's liberation," differed from feminists in NOW and other more mainstream groups in several ways. NOW focused on equal treatment for women in the public sphere; women's liberation emphasized ending women's subordination in family and other personal relationships. Groups such as NOW wanted to integrate

Transnational Feminisms

Organizations of women across national borders originated in the nineteenth century, but global connections among women increased dramatically in 1945 with the creation of the United Nations. Its charter affirmed "the equal rights of men and women," and in 1947 it established the Commission on the Status of Women, creating a forum for women from around the globe to meet and be heard. The UN helped launch a global feminist movement of unparalleled size and diversity when it declared 1975 International Women's Year and sponsored a conference in Mexico City. Six thousand women came to Mexico City on their own; official delegates from 125 nations approved the World Plan of Action for Women and prompted the UN to declare 1976 to 1985 the UN Decade for Women.

In response to the call for action in individual countries, the U.S. government funded the National Women's Conference in Houston, Texas, in 1977. More than two thousand state delegates attended, representing a cross section of American womanhood. They adopted the National Plan of Action, not only supporting ratification of the ERA and reproductive freedom but also addressing the needs of specific groups of women, including the elderly, lesbians, racial minorities, women with disabilities, rural women, and homemakers. For the first time, the U.S. women's movement had a comprehensive national agenda setting goals for decades to come.

The three themes of the UN Decade for Women — equality, development, and peace — reflected an effort to address the enormously diverse needs of women throughout the world. Feminists from Western nations who focused on equal rights met criticism from women who represented impoverished third world countries and insisted that "to talk feminism to a woman who has no water, no food, and no home is to talk nonsense." Ever larger UN-sponsored meetings followed Mexico City — Copenhagen in 1980, Nairobi in 1985, and Beijing in 1995, where twenty thousand women gathered. These global exchanges taught American feminists that to participate in a truly international movement, they would have to revise their Western-centered perspective on women's needs and understand that women's issues must include economic development and anticolonialism.

American feminists also learned that theirs was not always the most advanced nation when it came to women's welfare and status. Employed women in most industrialized countries had access to paid maternity leave and public child care. By 2010, women had headed governments in more than thirty countries, including India, Israel, Britain, and Germany. Many nations, such as Argentina, Egypt, and members of the European Union, had some form of affirmative action to increase the numbers of women in government. And whereas American women held just 17 percent of the seats in Congress, women constituted more than 35 percent of national legislatures in such countries as Sweden, South Africa, Costa Rica, and Belgium.

Despite enormous differences among women around the world, internationally minded feminists continued to seek common ground. As women into existing institutions; radical groups insisted that women's liberation required a total transformation of economic, political, and social institutions. Differences between these two strands of feminism blurred in the 1970s, as NOW and other mainstream groups embraced many of the issues raised by radicals.

Although NOW elected a black president, Aileen Hernandez, in 1970, the new feminism's leadership and constituency were predominantly white and middle-class. Women of color criticized white feminists for their inadequate attention to the disproportionate poverty experienced by minority women and to the additional layers of discrimination based on race or ethnicity. One black woman said, "My mother took care of rich white kids. I didn't think they were oppressed." To black women, who were much more frequently compelled to work in the lowest-paying jobs for their families' survival, employment did not necessarily look like liberation.

In addition to struggling with vast differences among women, feminism also contended with the refusal of the mass media to take women's grievances seriously. When the House of Representatives passed an equal rights amendment to the U.S. Constitution in 1970, the *New*

> "My mother took care of rich white kids. I didn't think they were oppressed."
> —A black woman, speaking about feminism

International Women's Year Tribune
Along with the official UN conference in Mexico City in 1975, nongovernmental organizations associated with the UN sponsored a tribune, where six thousand women gathered. Participants expressed the conflicting priorities of Western women and women from developing countries, and they argued over whether issues such as apartheid in South Africa and self-government for Palestinians were women's issues. Despite their disagreements, most women left Mexico City enlightened and energized. © Bettye Lane

Gertrude Mongella, secretary general of the Beijing conference, insisted in 1995, "A revolution has begun and there is no going back. . . . This revolution is too just, too important, and too long overdue."

America in a Global Context

1. What were the three themes of the UN Decade for Women? How were these three themes related to women's status and well-being?

2. In what ways were women in the United States ahead of women in other countries? In what ways were they behind? What might account for the differences?

York Times criticized it in an editorial titled "The Henpecked House." After Gloria Steinem founded *Ms: The New Magazine for Women* in 1972, feminists had their own mass-circulation periodical controlled by women and featuring articles on a broad range of feminist issues.

Ms. reported on a movement that was exceedingly multifaceted. Most African American women worked through their own groups, such as the older National Council of Negro Women and the National Black Feminist Organization, founded in 1973. Similarly, in the early 1970s, Native American women and Mexican American women founded national organizations, and Asian American women formed local movements.

Labor union women, who had long struggled for workplace gender justice, organized the National Coalition of Labor Union Women in 1974. Lesbians established collectives throughout the country, as well as their own caucuses in organizations such as NOW. Welfare mothers formed the National Welfare Rights Organization, and religious women mobilized in the National Council of Churches of Christ to "place the question of women's liberation in the main stream of the church's concern." Other new groups focused on single issues such as health, abortion rights, education, and violence against women. In addition, U.S. feminists interacted with women abroad, joining a movement that crossed national boundaries. (See "Beyond America's Borders," page 958.)

Common threads underlay the great diversity of organizations, issues, and activities. Above all, feminism represented the belief that women were barred from, unequally treated in, or poorly served by the male-dominated public arena, encompassing politics, medicine, law, education, culture, and religion. Many feminists also sought equality in the private sphere, challenging traditional norms that identified women primarily as wives and mothers or sex objects, subservient to men.

Feminist Gains Spark a Countermovement

Although more an effect than a cause of women's rising employment, feminism lifted female aspirations and helped lower barriers to posts monopolized by men. Between 1970 and 2000, women's share of law degrees shot up from 5 percent to nearly 50 percent, and their proportion of medical degrees from less than 10 percent to more than 35 percent. Women gained political offices very slowly; yet by 2010, they constituted about 17 percent of Congress and more than 20 percent of all state executives and legislators.

Feminists encountered frustrations along with achievements. Despite some inroads into male-dominated occupations, women still tended to concentrate in low-paying, traditionally female jobs, and their earnings lagged below men's well into the twenty-first century. Employed women continued to bear primary responsibility for their homes and families, thereby working a "double day."

Although public opinion polls registered support for most feminist goals, by the mid-1970s feminism faced a powerful countermovement, organized around opposition to a central goal of the women's movement: an **Equal Rights Amendment (ERA)** that would outlaw differential treatment of men and women under all state and federal laws. After Congress passed the ERA in 1972, Phyllis Schlafly, a conservative activist in the Republican Party, mobilized thousands of women at the grassroots level who feared that the ERA would devalue their own God-given roles as wives and mothers. These women, marching on state capitols, persuaded some

male legislators to block ratification. When the time limit ran out in 1982, only thirty-five states had ratified the amendment, three short of the necessary three-fourths majority. (See chapter 30, "Historical Question," page 1026.)

Powerful opposition likewise arose to feminists' quest for the right to abortion. "Without the full capacity to limit her own reproduction," abortion rights activist Lucinda Cisler insisted, "a woman's other 'freedoms' are tantalizing mockeries that cannot be exercised." In 1973, the Supreme Court issued the landmark *Roe v. Wade* decision, ruling that the Constitution protects the right to abortion, which states cannot prohibit in the early stages of pregnancy. This decision galvanized many Americans who believed that human life begins with conception and equated abortion with murder. Like ERA opponents, with whom they often overlapped, activists in the right-to-life movement mobilized thousands of women who believed that abortion disparaged motherhood and that feminism threatened their traditional roles. Beginning in 1977, abortion foes successfully pressured Congress to restrict the right to abortion by prohibiting coverage under Medicaid and other government-financed health programs, and the Supreme Court allowed states to impose additional obstacles.

Despite resistance, feminists won other lasting gains. **Title IX** of the Education Amendments Act of 1972 banned sex discrimination in all aspects of education, such as admissions, athletics, and hiring. Congress also outlawed sex discrimination in credit in 1974, opened U.S. military academies to women in 1976, and prohibited discrimination against pregnant workers in 1978. Moreover, the Supreme Court struck down laws that treated men and women differently in Social Security, welfare and military benefits, and workers' compensation.

At the state and local levels, women saw reforms in areas that radical feminists had first introduced. They won laws forcing police departments and the legal system to treat rape victims more justly and humanely. Activists also pushed domestic violence onto the public agenda, obtaining government financing for shelters for battered women as well as laws ensuring both greater protection for victims of domestic violence and more effective prosecution of abusers.

REVIEW What were the key goals of feminist reformers, and why did a countermovement arise to resist them?

▶ Liberal Reform in the Nixon Administration

Opposition to civil rights measures, Great Society reforms, and protest groups — along with frustrations surrounding the war in Vietnam (as discussed in chapter 29) — delivered the White House to Republican **Richard M. Nixon** in 1968. Nixon attacked the Great Society for "pouring billions of dollars into programs that have failed," and he promised to represent the "forgotten Americans, the non-shouters, the non-demonstrators." Yet despite Nixon's desire to capitalize on the backlash against civil rights and the Great Society, his administration either promoted or accepted substantially greater federal assistance to the poor, new protections for minorities and women, major environmental regulations, and financial policies deviating sharply from traditional Republican economics.

Extending the Welfare State and Regulating the Economy

A number of factors shaped the liberal policies of the Nixon administration. Not only did the Democrats continue to control Congress, but Nixon also saw political advantages in accepting some liberal programs. Nor could he entirely ignore grassroots movements, and several of his advisers were sympathetic to particular concerns, such as environmentalism and Native American rights. Serious economic problems also compelled new approaches, and although Nixon's real passion lay in foreign policy, he knew that his domestic record would in part determine whether he enjoyed history's approving gaze.

Under Nixon, government assistance programs grew. Congress resisted his attempts to eliminate the Office of Economic Opportunity. Key programs such as Medicaid, Head Start, and Legal Services remained intact. Social Security benefits increased and were now required to rise with the cost of living; subsidies for low-income housing tripled; a new billion-dollar program provided Pell grants for low-income students to attend college; and the food stamp program expanded to benefit 12.5 million recipients. Noting the disparity between what Nixon said and what he did, his speechwriter, the archconservative Pat Buchanan, grumbled, "Vigorously did we inveigh against the Great Society, enthusiastically did we fund it."

> "Vigorously did we inveigh against the Great Society, enthusiastically did we fund it."
> —Archconservative PAT BUCHANAN, speaking of the Nixon administration

Nixon also acted contrary to his antigovernment rhetoric when economic crises and energy shortages induced him to increase the federal government's power in the marketplace. By 1970, both inflation and unemployment had surpassed 6 percent, an unprecedented combination dubbed "stagflation." Domestic troubles were compounded by the decline of American dominance in the international economy. With the productive capacity of Japan and Western Europe fully recovered from World War II, foreign cars, electronic equipment, and other products now competed favorably

Nixon's 1968 Campaign
Seeking the presidency in 1968, Richard Nixon tried to appeal to a broad spectrum of voters. Prominent Republicans of all stripes appear in this campaign poster, including the liberal Nelson Rockefeller and the conservative Barry Goldwater. While Nixon's slogan "Champion of Forgotten America" spoke to white Americans alienated by Great Society programs for minorities and the poor, the poster's inclusion of black Republican senator Edward Brooke and basketball player Wilt Chamberlain of the Los Angeles Lakers gave a nod to African Americans. Nixon also appealed to youths by supporting the vote for eighteen-year-olds and promising to end the draft. Collection of Janice L. and David J. Frent.

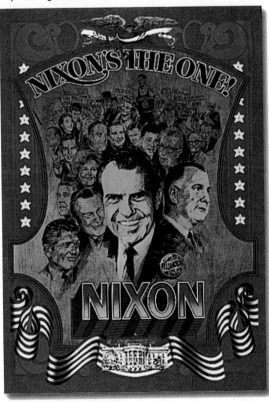

with American goods. In 1971, for the first time in decades, the United States imported more than it exported. Because the amount of dollars in foreign hands exceeded U.S. gold reserves, the nation could no longer back up its currency with gold.

In 1971, Nixon abandoned the convertibility of dollars into gold and devalued the dollar to increase exports. To protect domestic manufacturers, he imposed a 10 percent surcharge on most imports, and he froze wages and prices, thus enabling the government to stimulate the economy without fueling inflation. In the short run, these policies worked, and Nixon was resoundingly reelected in 1972. Yet by 1974, unemployment had crept back up and inflation soared, leaving to Nixon's successor the most severe economic crisis since the 1930s.

Skyrocketing energy prices intensified stagflation. Throughout the post–World War II economic boom, the nation's abundant oil deposits and access to cheap Middle Eastern oil had encouraged the building of large cars and skyscrapers with no concern for fuel efficiency. By the 1970s, the United States was consuming one-third of the world's fuel resources.

In the fall of 1973, the United States faced its first energy crisis. Arab nations, furious at the administration's support of Israel during the Yom Kippur War (as discussed in chapter 29), cut off oil shipments to the United States. Long lines formed at gas stations, where prices had nearly doubled, and many homes were cold. In response, Nixon authorized temporary emergency measures allocating petroleum and establishing a national 55-mile-per-hour speed limit to save gasoline. The energy crisis eased, but the nation had yet to come to grips with its seemingly unquenchable demand for fuel and dependence on foreign oil.

Responding to Environmental Concerns

The oil crisis dovetailed with a rising environmental movement, which was pushing the government to conserve energy and protect nature and human beings from the hazards of rapid economic growth. Like the conservation movement born in the Progressive Era (see chapter 21), the new environmentalists sought to preserve natural areas for recreational and aesthetic purposes and to conserve natural resources for future use. Especially in the West, the post–World War II explosion of economic growth and mushrooming population, with the resulting demands for electricity and water, made such efforts seem even more critical. Environmental groups began mobilizing in the 1950s to stop the construction of dams that would disrupt national parks and wilderness areas.

The new environmentalists, however, went beyond conservationism to attack the ravaging effects of industrial development and technological advances on human life and health. To the leaders of a new organization, Friends of the Earth, unlimited economic growth was "no longer healthy, but a cancer."

Earth Day in the Nation's Capital
Building on the success of teach-ins about the Vietnam War, Democratic senator Gaylord Nelson of Wisconsin came up with the idea of Earth Day "to shake up the political establishment and force this issue [environmentalism] onto the national agenda." As a result, on April 22, 1970, some twenty million people participated in grassroots demonstrations all over the country. This banner displayed on the Mall in Washington, D.C., focused on clean air. Other activists dramatized oil spills, toxic dumps, pesticides, polluted rivers and lakes, the loss of wilderness, and the extinction of wildlife. Dennis Brack/Black Star/Stockphoto.com.

Biologist Rachel Carson drew national attention in 1962 with her best seller *Silent Spring*, which described the harmful effects of toxic chemicals such as the pesticide DDT. The Sierra Club and other older conservation organizations expanded their agendas, and a host of new groups arose. Millions of Americans expressed environmental concerns on the first observation of Earth Day in April 1970.

Responding to these concerns, Nixon built on the efforts begun in the Johnson administration. He called "clean air, clean water, open spaces . . . the birthright of every American" and urged Congress to "end the plunder of America's natural heritage." In 1970, he created the **Environmental Protection Agency (EPA)** to conduct research, enforce environmental laws, and reduce human health and environmental risks from pollutants. He also signed the Occupational Safety and Health Act, protecting workers against job-related accidents and disease, and the Clean Air Act of 1970, setting national standards for air quality and restricting factory and automobile emissions of carbon dioxide and other pollutants. Environmentalists claimed that Nixon failed to do enough, pointing particularly to his veto — for budgetary reasons — of the Clean Water Act of 1972, which Congress overrode. Yet his environmental initiatives surpassed those of previous administrations.

Expanding Social Justice

Nixon's 1968 campaign had exploited hostility to black protest and new civil rights policies to appeal to southern Democrats and white workers, but his administration had to answer to the courts and to Congress. In 1968, fourteen years after the *Brown* decision, school desegregation had barely touched the South. Like Eisenhower, Nixon was reluctant to use federal power to compel integration, but the Supreme Court overruled the administration's efforts to delay court-ordered desegregation and compelled it to enforce the law. By the time Nixon left office, fewer than one in ten southern black children attended totally segregated schools.

Nixon also began to implement affirmative action among federal contractors and unions and awarded more government contracts and loans to minority businesses. Congress took the initiative in other areas. In 1970, it extended the Voting Rights Act of 1965, and in 1972 it strengthened the Civil Rights Act of 1964 by enlarging the powers of the Equal Employment Opportunity Commission. In 1971, Congress also responded to the massive youth movement with the Twenty-sixth Amendment to the Constitution, which reduced the voting age to eighteen.

Women as well as minority groups benefited from the implementation of affirmative action and the strengthened EEOC, but several measures of the Nixon administration also specifically attacked sex discrimination. The president privately expressed patronizing attitudes about women. "Thank God we don't have any in the Cabinet," he told aides. Yet again, he confronted a growing movement that included Republican feminists. Nixon vetoed a comprehensive child care bill and publicly opposed abortion, but he signed the pathbreaking Title IX, guaranteeing equality in all aspects of education, and allowed his Labor Department to push affirmative action.

President Nixon gave more public support for justice to Native Americans than to any other protest group. While not bowing to radical demands, the administration dealt cautiously with extreme protests, such as the occupation of the Bureau of Indian Affairs in Washington, D.C. Nixon signed measures recognizing claims of Alaskan and New Mexican Indians and set in motion legislation restoring tribal lands and granting Indians more control over their schools and other service institutions.

> **REVIEW** Why and how did Republican president Richard Nixon expand the liberal reforms of previous administrations?

▶ Conclusion: Achievements and Limitations of Liberalism

Senate majority leader Mike Mansfield was not alone in concluding that Lyndon Johnson "has done more than FDR ever did, or ever thought of doing." Building on initiatives from John F. Kennedy's New Frontier, the Great Society expanded the New Deal's focus on economic security, refashioning liberalism to embrace individual rights and to extend material well-being to groups left out of or discriminated against in New Deal programs. Yet opposition to Johnson's leadership grew so strong that by 1968 his liberal vision lay in ruins. "How," he asked, "was it possible that all these people could be so ungrateful to me after I have given them so much?"

Fannie Lou Hamer could have responded by pointing out how slowly the government acted when efforts to win African Americans' rights met with violence. In addition, Hamer's failed attempts to use Johnson's antipoverty programs to help poor blacks in Mississippi resulted in part from internal problems, but those failures also reflected some of the more general shortcomings of the War on Poverty. Hastily planned and inadequately funded, antipoverty programs focused more on remediating individual shortcomings than on reforms that would ensure adequately paying jobs for all. Because Johnson launched an all-out war in Vietnam and refused to ask for sacrifices from prosperous Americans, the Great Society never commanded the resources necessary for victory over poverty.

Furthermore, black aspirations exceeded white Americans' commitment to genuine equality. When the civil rights movement attacked racial barriers long entrenched throughout the nation and sought equality in fact as well as in law, it faced a powerful backlash. By the end of the 1960s, the revolution in the legal status of African Americans was complete, but the black freedom struggle had lost momentum, and African Americans remained, with Native Americans and Chicanos, at the bottom of the economic ladder.

Johnson's critics overlooked the Great Society's more successful and lasting elements. Medicare and Medicaid continue to provide access to health care for the elderly and the poor. Federal aid for education and housing became permanent elements of national policy. Moreover, Richard Nixon's otherwise conservative administration implemented school desegregation in the South and affirmative action, initiated substantial environmental reforms, and secured new rights for Native Americans and women. Women especially benefited from the decline of discrimination, and significant numbers of African Americans and other minority groups began to enter the middle class.

Yet the perceived shortcomings of government programs contributed to social turmoil and fueled the resurgence of conservative politics. Young radicals launched direct confrontations with the government and universities, calling for both domestic reform and an end to the war in Vietnam. The combination of racial conflict and youth activism escalated into widespread political discord and social disorder. The Vietnam War polarized American society as much as did racial issues or the behavior of young people, and it devoured resources that might have been used for social reform even as it undermined faith in presidential leadership.

▶ Selected Bibliography

The Black Freedom Struggle

Raymond Arsenault, *Freedom Riders: 1961 and the Struggle for Racial Justice* (2006).
Taylor Branch, *America in the King Years*, 3 vols. (1988, 1998, 2006).
Michael Eric Dyson, *Making Malcolm: The Myth and Meaning of Malcolm X* (1995).
Wesley C. Hogan, *Many Minds, One Heart: SNCC's Dream for a New America* (2009).
Chana Kai Lee, *For Freedom's Sake: The Life of Fannie Lou Hamer* (1999).
Jeffrey O. G. Ogbar, *Black Power: Radical Politics and African American Identity* (2005).
Charles Payne, *I've Got the Light of Freedom: The Organizing Tradition and the Mississippi Freedom Struggle* (1995).
Barbara Ransby, *Ella Baker and the Black Freedom Movement: A Radical Democratic Vision* (2003).
Stephen Tuck, *We Ain't What We Ought to Be: The Black Freedom Struggle from Emancipation to Obama* (2010).
Timothy Tyson, *Radio Free Dixie: Robert F. Williams and the Roots of Black Power* (1999).
Bruce Watson, *Freedom Summer: The Savage Season That Made Mississippi Burn and Made America a Democracy* (2010).

Politics, Policies, and Court Decisions

Robert Dallek, *An Unfinished Life: John F. Kennedy, 1917–1963* (2003).
Maurice Isserman and Michael Kazin, *America Divided: The Civil War of the 1960s* (2000).
Michael B. Katz, *The Undeserving Poor: From the War on Poverty to the War on Welfare* (1989).
Nancy MacLean, *Freedom Is Not Enough: The Opening of the American Workplace* (2006).
Gerald Posner, *Case Closed: Lee Harvey Oswald and the Assassination of JFK* (1993).
Lucas A. Powe Jr., *The Warren Court and American Politics* (2000).
John D. Skrentny, *The Minority Rights Revolution* (2002).
Irwin Unger, *The Best of Intentions: The Triumph and Failure of the Great Society* (1996).

Tom Wicker, *One of Us: Richard Nixon and the American Dream* (1991).

Randall B. Woods, *LBJ: Architect of American Ambition* (2006).

Protest Movements

Terry H. Anderson, *The Movement and the Sixties* (1995).

David Barber, *A Hard Rain Fell: SDS and Why It Failed* (2010).

Daniel M. Cobb, *Native Activism in Cold War America: The Struggle for Sovereignty* (2008).

John D'Emilio, William B. Turner, and Urvashi Vaid, *Creating Change: Sexuality, Public Policy, and Civil Rights* (2000).

Troy R. Johnson, *The American Indian Occupation of Alcatraz Island: Red Power and Self-Determination* (2008).

F. Arturo Rosales, *Chicano! The History of the Mexican American Civil Rights Movement* (1997).

Randy Shaw, *Beyond the Fields: Cesar Chavez, the UFW, and the Struggle for Justice in the Twenty-first Century* (2008).

William Wei, *The Asian American Movement* (1993).

Cultural Change, Sexual Revolution, and Feminism

David Allyn, *Make Love, Not War: The Sexual Revolution, an Unfettered History* (2000).

Glenn C. Altschuler, *All Shook Up: How Rock 'n' Roll Changed America* (2004).

Sara Evans, *Tidal Wave: How Women Changed America at Century's End* (2003).

David Garrow, *Liberty and Sexuality: The Right to Privacy and the Making of* Roe v. Wade (1994).

Carol Giardina, *Freedom for Women: Forging the Women's Liberation Movement, 1953–1970* (2010).

Elaine Tyler May, *America and the Pill: A History of Promise, Peril, and Liberation* (2010).

Benita Roth, *Separate Roads to Feminism: Black, Chicana, and White Feminist Movements in America's Second Wave* (2004).

▶ **FOR MORE BOOKS ABOUT TOPICS IN THIS CHAPTER,** see the Online Bibliography at bedfordstmartins.com/roark.

▶ **FOR ADDITIONAL PRIMARY SOURCES FROM THIS PERIOD,** see Michael Johnson, ed., *Reading the American Past*, Fifth Edition.

▶ **FOR WEB SITES, IMAGES, AND DOCUMENTS RELATED TO TOPICS AND PLACES IN THIS CHAPTER,** visit Make History at bedfordstmartins.com/roark.

Reviewing Chapter 28

KEY TERMS

Explain each term's significance.

Liberalism at High Tide
- John F. Kennedy (p. 933)
- Lyndon B. Johnson (p. 934)
- Great Society (p. 935)
- Civil Rights Act of 1964 (p. 935)
- War on Poverty (p. 936)
- Medicare (p. 936)
- Medicaid (p. 936)
- Voting Rights Act of 1965 (p. 936)
- Immigration and Nationality Act of 1965 (p. 936)
- Warren Court (p. 938)

The Second Reconstruction
- Martin Luther King Jr. (p. 940)
- Student Nonviolent Coordinating Committee (SNCC) (p. 940)
- Fannie Lou Hamer (p. 941)
- March on Washington for Jobs and Freedom (p. 942)
- Mississippi Freedom Summer Project (p. 942)
- Selma march (p. 942)
- Civil Rights Act of 1968 (p. 944)
- Malcolm X (p. 946)
- Stokely Carmichael (p. 946)
- black power movement (p. 946)

A Multitude of Movements
- American Indian Movement (AIM) (p. 947)
- Cesar Chavez (p. 948)
- Dolores Huerta (p. 948)
- Students for a Democratic Society (SDS) (p. 952)
- Stonewall riots (p. 955)

The New Wave of Feminism
- National Organization for Women (NOW) (p. 957)
- Equal Rights Amendment (ERA) (p. 960)
- *Roe v. Wade* (p. 960)
- Title IX (p. 960)

Liberal Reform in the Nixon Administration
- Richard M. Nixon (p. 961)
- Environmental Protection Agency (EPA) (p. 963)

REVIEW QUESTIONS

Use key terms and dates to support your answer.

1. How did the Kennedy and Johnson administrations exemplify a liberal vision of the federal government? (pp. 933–940)

2. How and why did the civil rights movement change in the mid-1960s? (pp. 940–946)

3. How did the black freedom struggle influence other reform movements of the 1960s and 1970s? (pp. 947–955)

4. What were the key goals of feminist reformers, and why did a countermovement arise to resist them? (pp. 955–960)

5. Why and how did Republican president Richard Nixon expand the liberal reforms of previous administrations? (pp. 961–963)

MAKING CONNECTIONS

Draw on key terms, the timeline, and review questions.

1. In what ways did Lyndon Johnson's Great Society build on the initiatives of John F. Kennedy? Why were Johnson's reforms so much more far-reaching?

2. During the 1960s, African Americans made substantial gains in asserting their freedoms and rights. What specific gains did the civil rights movement achieve? Were there limits to its success? What part did government play in this process?

3. Women participated in various ways in the feminism that emerged in the 1960s. How can we explain the rise of this movement? What assumptions and goals were held in common in this diverse movement?

4. Most of the reform movements of the 1960s sought equality as one of their key priorities, but significant differences existed among Americans in general about what equality meant. Should equality be limited to equal treatment under the law, or should it extend to economic welfare, education, sexual relations, and other aspects of life? Examining two reform movements, discuss how different ideas of equality contributed to the accomplishments and disappointments of each movement.

Link events in this chapter to earlier events.

1. Both Franklin Roosevelt's New Deal and Lyndon Johnson's Great Society attacked poverty. How was Johnson's approach different from Roosevelt's? Which was more successful, and what contributed to the relative successes and failures of each approach? (See chapter 24.)

2. What changes that had been taking place in the United States since 1940 laid a foundation for the rise of a feminist movement in the 1960s? (See chapters 25 and 26.)

▶ FOR PRACTICE QUIZZES AND OTHER STUDY TOOLS, visit the Online Study Guide at bedfordstmartins.com/roark.

TIMELINE 1960–1973

1960	• Democrat John F. Kennedy elected president. • Student Nonviolent Coordinating Committee (SNCC) established. • Students for a Democratic Society (SDS) founded.
1961	• Congress of Racial Equality (CORE) sponsors Freedom Rides.
1962	• United Farm Workers (UFW) founded.
1963	• President's Commission on the Status of Women issues report. • Equal Pay Act. • *Baker v. Carr.* • *Abington School District v. Schempp.* • March on Washington for Jobs and Freedom. • President Kennedy assassinated; Lyndon B. Johnson becomes president.
1964	• Civil Rights Act. • Mississippi Freedom Summer Project. • Economic Opportunity Act. • Major tax cuts enacted.
1965	• Voting Rights Act.
1965–1966	• Congress passes most of Johnson's Great Society domestic programs.
1965–1968	• Riots in major cities.
1966	• Black Panther Party for Self-Defense founded. • *Miranda v. Arizona.* • National Organization for Women (NOW) founded.
1967	• *Loving v. Virginia.*
1968	• Martin Luther King Jr. assassinated. • American Indian Movement (AIM) founded. • Republican Richard M. Nixon elected president.
1969	• Stonewall riots.
1970	• First Earth Day celebrated. • Environmental Protection Agency (EPA) established. • Clean Air Act.
1971	• Constitutional amendment lowers voting age to eighteen.
1972	• Title IX of Education Amendments Act. • Congress passes Equal Rights Amendment; sends it to states for ratification. • American Indians' "Trail of Broken Treaties" caravan to Washington, D.C.
1973	• *Roe v. Wade.*

FATIGUE HAT
This fatigue hat belonged to a soldier who served two tours of duty in Vietnam. The button reflects some veterans' response to the many Americans who just wanted to forget the war that had torn the country apart and that it had failed to win. Because their war was so different from other American wars, Vietnam veterans often returned home to hostility or indifference. Gradually attitudes about those who fought shifted, symbolized by the erection of the Vietnam Veterans Memorial, shown in the background. After the memorial was dedicated in 1982, millions of Americans visited it each year.
Hat: Nancy Gewitz/Antique Textile Resource/Picture Research Consultants & Archives; background: Library of Congress.

29

Vietnam and the End of the Cold War Consensus
1961–1975

LIEUTENANT FREDERICK DOWNS GREW UP ON A FARM IN INDIANA, played football in high school, and finished three years of college before enlisting in the army at the age of twenty-two. Leaving a ten-month-old daughter behind, he graduated from officer candidate school at Fort Benning, Georgia, and arrived in Vietnam in September 1967, prepared to lead an infantry platoon. He and his fellow soldiers went to Vietnam, "cocky and sure of our destiny, gung ho, invincible."

That confidence was tempered by the conditions he found in Vietnam. Unlike most of America's previous wars, there was no fixed battle front; helicopters ferried fighting units all over South Vietnam, as U.S. and South Vietnamese troops attempted to defeat the South Vietnamese rebels and their North Vietnamese allies. In a civil conflict characterized by guerrilla warfare, Downs led his men out on search-and-destroy missions in areas where they struggled to distinguish civilians from combatants and burned down villages just because they might be used by the enemy. He had faith that his country could win the war, but he found its ally, the South Vietnamese army, to be lazy and ineffective. "Maybe the people in Nam are worth saving, but their army isn't worth shit," he wrote in his memoir. Downs won several medals for bravery, but his one-year stint in Vietnam was cut short when a land mine blew off his left arm and wedged shrapnel into his legs and back.

Downs's service in Vietnam came at the height of a U.S. engagement that began with the Cold War commitments made in the 1940s and 1950s by Presidents Harry S. Truman and Dwight D. Eisenhower. John F. Kennedy wholeheartedly took on those commitments, promising more flexible and vigorous efforts to thwart communism. The most memorable words of his 1961 inaugural address declared that the United States would "pay any price, bear any burden, meet any hardship, support any friend, oppose any foe to assure the survival and the success of liberty."

Lieutenant Frederick Downs, Jr., in 1967
Frederick Downs—shown here before he lost his arm in Vietnam—returned from the war with a shoulder full of medals and spent the rest of his life helping other soldiers. After earning a masters degree in business administration, he worked for the Veterans Administration and eventually became director of its prosthetics and sensory aids program. In the 1980s, Downs visited Vietnam several times. As he got to know the former enemy as individuals, he lost the hatred he had once harbored, feeling "only sorrow at the ways of man." Collection of Frederick Downs.

Vietnam became the foremost test of John F. Kennedy's anticommunism. He sent increasing amounts of American arms and personnel to sustain the South Vietnamese government, but it was Lyndon B. Johnson who dramatically escalated that commitment in 1965 and turned a civil war among the Vietnamese into America's war. At peak strength in 1968, 543,000 U.S. military personnel served in Vietnam; all told, some 2.6 million saw duty there. Yet this massive intervention not only failed to defeat North Vietnam but also created intense discord at home, "poisoning the soul of America," as Downs put it. It cost President Johnson another term in office and contributed to the downfall of his Republican successor, Richard M. Nixon. Some Americans supported the government's goal in Vietnam and decried only its failure to pursue it effectively. Others believed that preserving a non-Communist South Vietnam was neither in the best interests of the United States nor within its capacity or moral right to achieve. Back home in college after months of surgery, Downs encountered a man who asked about the hook descending from his sleeve. When he said that he had lost his arm in Vietnam, the man shot back, "Serves you right."

This internal conflict was just one of the war's great costs. Like Downs, more than 150,000 soldiers suffered severe wounds, and more than 58,000 lost their lives. Martin Luther King Jr. mourned "the promises of the Great Society . . . shot down on the battlefield of Vietnam." In addition to derailing domestic reform, the war depleted the federal budget, disrupted the economy, kindled internal conflict, and led to the violation of protesters' rights, leaving a lasting mark on the nation.

Even while fighting communism in Vietnam and, on a much smaller scale, in other third world countries, American leaders moved to ease Cold War tensions with the major Communist powers. After a dramatic standoff with the Soviet Union during the Cuban missile crisis, the United States began to cooperate with its Cold War enemy to limit the spread of nuclear weapons. In addition, Nixon's historic visit to China in 1972 marked the abandonment of the policy of isolating China and paved the way for normal diplomatic relations by the end of the 1970s.

▶ New Frontiers in Foreign Policy

John F. Kennedy moved quickly to pursue containment more aggressively and with more flexible means. In contrast to the Eisenhower administration's emphasis on nuclear weapons, Kennedy expanded not only the nation's nuclear capacity but also its ability to fight conventional battles and to engage in guerrilla warfare. To ensure U.S. superiority over the Soviet Union in every domain, Kennedy accelerated the nation's space exploration program and increased attention to the third world. When the Soviets tried to establish a nuclear outpost in the Western Hemisphere in Cuba in 1962, he took the United States to the brink of war. Less dramatically

but no less resolutely, Kennedy sent increasing amounts of American arms and personnel to save the South Vietnamese government from Communist insurgents.

Meeting the "Hour of Maximum Danger"

Underlying Kennedy's foreign policy was an assumption that the United States had "gone soft — physically, mentally, spiritually soft," as he put it in 1960. Calling the Eisenhower era "years of drift and impotency," he associated that administration with femininity when he mocked Nixon's celebration of American consumer goods in the kitchen debate with **Nikita Khrushchev**. "I would rather take my television black and white and have the largest rockets in the world,"

MAP ACTIVITY

Map 29.1   U.S. Involvement in Latin America and the Caribbean, 1954–1994
During the Cold War, the United States frequently intervened in Central American and Caribbean countries to suppress Communist or leftist movements.

READING THE MAP: How many and which Latin American countries did the United States invade directly? What was the extent of indirect U.S. involvement in other upheavals in the region?
CONNECTIONS: What role, if any, did geographic proximity play in U.S. policy toward the region? What was the significance of the Cuban missile crisis for U.S. foreign policy?

Kennedy declared. Criticizing the Eisenhower administration for relying too heavily on nuclear weapons, Kennedy built up conventional ground forces to provide a flexible response to Communist expansion. He also charged that limits on defense spending had caused the United States to fall behind even in nuclear capability. In January 1961, Kennedy warned that the nation faced a grave peril: "Each day the crises multiply. . . . Each day we draw nearer the hour of maximum danger."

Kennedy exaggerated the threat to national security; the United States remained ahead of the Soviets in nuclear capacity. Yet several developments in 1961 heightened the sense of crisis and provided a rationalization for his military buildup. Shortly before Kennedy's inauguration, Khrushchev publicly encouraged "wars of national liberation," thereby aligning the Soviet Union with independence movements in the third world that were often anti-Western. His statement reflected in part the Soviet competition with China for the allegiance of emerging nations, but U.S. officials saw in his words a threat to the status quo of containment.

Cuba, just ninety miles off the Florida coast, posed the most immediate threat to the United States. The revolution led by **Fidel Castro** had already moved Cuba into the Soviet orbit, and Eisenhower's Central Intelligence Agency (CIA) had been planning an invasion of the island by Cuban exiles living in Florida. Kennedy ordered the invasion to proceed even though his military advisers gave it only a fair chance of success.

> "I would rather take my television black and white and have the largest rockets in the world."
>
> — President
> JOHN F. KENNEDY

On April 17, 1961, about 1,400 anti-Castro exiles trained and armed by the CIA landed at the **Bay of Pigs** on the south shore of Cuba (Map 29.1). Contrary to U.S. expectations, no popular uprising materialized to support the anti-Castro brigade. Kennedy refused to provide direct military support, and the invaders quickly fell to Castro's forces. The disaster humiliated Kennedy and the United States, posing a stark contrast to the president's inaugural promise of a new, more effective foreign policy. The attempted invasion evoked memories of Yankee imperialism among Latin Americans and aligned Cuba even more closely with the Soviet Union.

Days before the Bay of Pigs invasion, the Soviet Union delivered a psychological blow when a Soviet astronaut became the first human being to orbit the earth. In May 1961, Kennedy called for a huge new commitment to the space program, with the goal of sending a man to the moon by 1970. Congress authorized the **Apollo program** and boosted appropriations for space exploration. John H. Glenn orbited the earth in 1962, and the United States beat the Soviets to the moon, landing two astronauts there in 1969.

Early in his presidency, Kennedy determined to show American toughness to Khrushchev. But when the two met in June 1961 in Vienna, Austria, Khrushchev was belligerent and shook the president's confidence. The stunned Kennedy reported privately, "He just beat [the] hell out of me. . . . If he thinks I'm inexperienced and have no guts . . . we won't get anywhere with him." Khrushchev demanded an agreement recognizing the existence of two Germanys and made veiled threats about America's occupation rights in and access to West Berlin.

Khrushchev was concerned about the massive exodus of East Germans into West Berlin,

John Glenn Orbits the Earth
In February 1962, 40-year-old Marine Lieutenant John Glenn, who had flown combat missions in World War II and Korea, became the first American to circle the earth in space. The Soviets had already sent their own cosmonaut into orbit ten months earlier, but by the end of the 1960s the U.S. took over leadership in the space race. Glenn, shown here with his spacecraft before the flight, became a national hero and subsequently served as U.S. Senator from Ohio. © Bettmann/Corbis.

a major embarrassment for the Communists. To stop this flow, in August 1961 East Germany shocked the world by erecting a wall between East and West Berlin. With the **Berlin Wall** stemming the tide of migration and Kennedy insisting that West Berlin was "the great testing place of Western courage and will," Khrushchev backed off from his threats. But not until 1972 did the superpowers recognize East and West Germany as separate nations and guarantee Western access to West Berlin.

Kennedy used the Berlin crisis to add $3.2 billion to the defense budget. He increased draft calls and mobilized the reserves and National Guard, adding 300,000 troops to the military. This buildup of conventional forces provided for a "flexible response," offering "a wider choice than humiliation or all-out nuclear action." Still, Kennedy also pushed for the development of new nuclear weapons and delivery systems, more than doubling the nation's nuclear force within three years.

Peace Corps Volunteers Build a School in Gabon
Young men and women who joined the Peace Corps helped increase food production, build public works, and curb diseases in developing countries, but the majority worked on educational projects. In this photo taken in 1964, volunteers work side-by-side with a local resident to build a school in the west central African nation of Gabon, which had won its independence from France in 1960. James P. Blair/National Geographic/Getty Images.

New Approaches to the Third World

Complementing Kennedy's hard-line policy toward the Soviet Union were fresh approaches to the nationalist movements that had multiplied since the end of World War II. In 1960 alone, seventeen African nations gained their independence. Much more than his predecessors, Kennedy publicly supported third world aspirations, believing that the United States could win the hearts and minds of people in developing nations by helping to fulfill hopes for autonomy and democracy.

To that end, Kennedy created the Alliance for Progress in 1961, pledging $20 billion in Latin American aid over the next decade. Like the Marshall Plan (see chapter 26), the Alliance for Progress was designed to thwart communism and hold nations within the American sphere by fostering economic development. Yet by 1969, the United States had provided only half of the promised $20 billion, much of which went to military projects or corrupt ruling elites.

Kennedy launched his most dramatic third world initiative in 1961 with an idea borrowed from Senator Hubert H. Humphrey: the **Peace Corps.** The program recruited young people to work in developing countries, attracting many who had been moved by Kennedy's appeal for idealism and sacrifice in his inaugural address. One volunteer's service eased his guilt at having been "born between clean sheets when others were issued into the dust with a birthright of hunger." After studying a country's language and culture, Peace Corps volunteers went to work directly with its people, opening schools, providing basic health care, and assisting with agriculture and small economic enterprises. By the mid-1970s, more than 60,000 volunteers had served in Latin America, Africa, and Asia. Peace Corps projects were generally welcomed, but they did not address the receiving countries' larger economic and political structures.

Kennedy also used direct military means to bring political stability to the third world. He rapidly expanded the elite

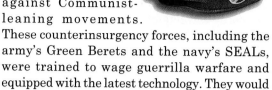

special forces corps established under Eisenhower to aid groups fighting against Communist-leaning movements. These counterinsurgency forces, including the army's Green Berets and the navy's SEALs, were trained to wage guerrilla warfare and equipped with the latest technology. They would get their first test in Vietnam.

The Arms Race and the Nuclear Brink

The final piece of Kennedy's defense strategy was to strengthen American nuclear dominance. He upped the number of nuclear weapons based in Europe from 2,500 to 7,200 and multiplied fivefold the supply of intercontinental ballistic missiles (ICBMs). Concerned that this buildup would enable the United States to launch a first strike and wipe out Soviet missile sites before they could respond, the Soviet Union stepped up its own ICBM program. Thus began the most intense arms race in history.

The superpowers came perilously close to using their weapons during the **Cuban missile crisis** in 1962. Khrushchev decided to install nuclear missiles in Cuba to protect Castro's regime from further U.S. attempts at intervention and to balance the U.S. missiles aimed at the Soviet Union from Britain, Italy, and Turkey. The thirteen-day crisis began on October 16, when the CIA showed Kennedy aerial photographs of missile launching sites under construction. Considering this an intolerable threat to the United States, the president decided to react. On October 22, he announced to a television audience that the military was on full alert and that the navy would turn back any Soviet vessel suspected of carrying offensive missiles to Cuba. Kennedy warned that any attack launched from Cuba would trigger a full nuclear assault against the Soviet Union.

Projecting the appearance of toughness was paramount to President Kennedy. Conceding that the missiles did not "alter the strategic balance in fact," one of his aides insisted that "that balance would have been

Cuban Missile Crisis, 1962

substantially altered in appearance; and in matters of national will and world leadership such appearances contribute to reality." Kennedy also worried that "Communism and Castroism are going to be spread [in Latin America] as governments frightened by this new evidence of power [fall]."

But if Kennedy risked nuclear war for appearances, both he and Khrushchev also exercised caution. Kennedy refused advice from the military to bomb the missile sites. On October 24, Russian ships carrying nuclear warheads toward Cuba suddenly turned back. When one ship crossed the blockade line, Kennedy ordered the navy to follow the ship rather than attempt to stop it.

While Americans experienced the Cold War's most dangerous days, Kennedy and Khrushchev negotiated an agreement. The Soviets removed the missiles and pledged not to introduce new

offensive weapons into Cuba. The United States promised not to invade the island. Secretly, Kennedy also agreed to remove U.S. missiles from Turkey. The Cuban crisis contributed to Khrushchev's fall from power two years later, while Kennedy emerged triumphant. "I cut his balls off," Kennedy rejoiced in private. The image of an inexperienced president fumbling the Bay of Pigs invasion gave way to that of a strong leader bearing the United States through its "hour of maximum danger."

Having proved his toughness, Kennedy worked with Khrushchev to prevent future confrontations by installing a special "hot line" to speed top-level communication. In a major speech at American University in June 1963, Kennedy called for a reexamination of Cold War assumptions, asking Americans "not to see conflict as inevitable." Acknowledging the superpowers' differences, Kennedy stressed

Preparing for the Worst during the Cuban Missile Crisis
Waiting out the tense days after President Kennedy issued the ultimatum to the Soviet Union to halt shipments of missile materials to Cuba, many Americans prepared for the worst possible outcome. Owners of Chalet Suzanne, a hotel in Lake Wales, Florida—less than 500 miles from Cuba—canned several thousand cases of well water, labeled "NASK" for Nuclear Attack Survival Kit. The background is a U.S. Navy reconnaissance photo taken on October 23, 1962, showing details of the missile site in Cuba. Can of water: Courtesy Chalet Suzanne Foods, Inc., Lake Wales, Florida. Photo by David Woods; reconnaissance photo: © Bettmann/Corbis.

U.S. Involvement in Vietnam

1954   French colonial presence ends with Vietnamese victory at Dien Bien Phu.

Geneva accords establish temporary division of North and South Vietnam at seventeenth parallel and provide for free elections.

United States joins with European, East Asian, and other nations to form Southeast Asia Treaty Organization.

Eisenhower administration begins to send weapons and military advisers to South Vietnam to bolster Diem government.

1955–1961   United States sends $800 million in aid to South Vietnamese army (ARVN) to support its struggle with South Vietnamese rebels and their North Vietnamese allies.

1961–1963   Under Kennedy administration, military aid to South Vietnam doubles, and number of military advisers reaches 9,000.

1963   South Vietnamese military overthrows Diem's government.

1964   President Johnson uses Gulf of Tonkin incident to escalate war.

1965   Johnson administration initiates Operation Rolling Thunder, intensifying bombing of North Vietnam.

1965–1967   Number of U.S. troops in Vietnam increases, reaching 543,000 in 1968, but U.S. and ARVN forces make only limited progress against the guerrilla forces, resulting in a stalemate.

1968   Tet Offensive causes widespread destruction and heavy casualties.

Johnson announces reduction in bombing of North Vietnam, plans for peace talks, and his decision not to run for another presidential term.

1969   Nixon administration initiates secret bombing of Cambodia, increases bombing of North Vietnam while reducing U.S. troops in the South, and pursues peace talks.

1970   Nixon orders joint U.S.-ARVN invasion of Cambodia.

1970–1971   U.S. troops in Vietnam decrease from 334,600 to 140,000.

1972   With peace talks stalled in December, Nixon administration orders the war's most devastating bombing of North Vietnam.

1973   On January 27, United States, North Vietnam, and South Vietnam sign formal accord in Paris marking end of U.S. involvement.

1975   North Vietnam launches new offensive in South Vietnam, defeating ARVN. Vietcong troops occupy Saigon, renaming it Ho Chi Minh City.

reducing the threat of radioactive fallout from nuclear testing and raising hopes for further superpower accord.

A Growing War in Vietnam

In his American University speech, Kennedy criticized the idea of "a Pax Americana enforced on the world by American weapons of war," but in 1961 he began to increase the flow of those weapons into South Vietnam. Kennedy's strong anticommunism and attachment to a vigorous foreign policy prepared him to expand the commitment in Vietnam that he had inherited from Eisenhower. Convinced that China and the Soviet Union were behind the efforts of North Vietnamese leader **Ho Chi Minh** to unify Vietnam under communism, Kennedy's key military adviser, General Maxwell Taylor, argued that holding firm in Vietnam would show the Soviets and Chinese that wars of national liberation were "costly, dangerous, and doomed to failure."

By the time Kennedy took office, more than $1 billion in aid and seven hundred U.S. military advisers had failed to stabilize South Vietnam. Two major obstacles stood in the way. First, the South Vietnamese insurgents — whom Americans called Vietcong, short for *Vietnam Cong-san* ("Vietnamese Communists") — were an indigenous force whose initiative came from within, not from the Soviet Union or China. Because the Saigon government refused to hold elections, the rebels saw no choice but to take up arms. Increasingly, Ho Chi Minh's Communist government in North Vietnam supplied them with weapons and soldiers.

Second, the South Vietnamese government refused to satisfy the demands of the insurgents, but the **Army of the Republic of Vietnam (ARVN)** could not defeat them militarily. Ngo Dinh Diem, South Vietnam's premier from 1954 to 1963, chose self-serving military leaders for their personal loyalty rather than for their effectiveness. Many South Vietnamese, the majority of whom were Buddhists, saw the Catholic Diem as a corrupt and brutal tool of the West. Even Secretary of State Dean Rusk called him "an oriental despot."

The growing intervention by North Vietnam made matters worse. In 1960, the Hanoi government established the **National Liberation Front (NLF)**, composed of South Vietnamese rebels but directed by the northern army. In addition, Hanoi constructed a network of infiltration

what they had in common: "We all breathe the same air. We all cherish our children's future and we are all mortal." In August 1963, the United States, the Soviet Union, and Great Britain signed a limited nuclear test ban treaty,

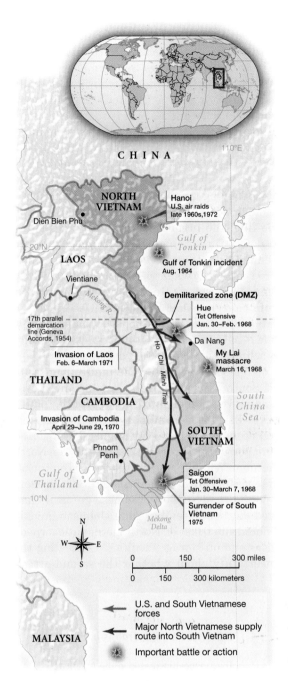

CHINA

NORTH VIETNAM

Dien Bien Phu

Hanoi
U.S. air raids
late 1960s, 1972

Gulf of Tonkin

LAOS

Vientiane

Gulf of Tonkin incident
Aug. 1964

Demilitarized zone (DMZ)

Hue
Tet Offensive
Jan. 30–Feb. 1968

17th parallel
demarcation
line (Geneva
Accords, 1954)

Da Nang

Invasion of Laos
Feb. 6–March 1971

My Lai
massacre
March 16, 1968

THAILAND

CAMBODIA

South China Sea

Invasion of Cambodia
April 29–June 29, 1970

SOUTH VIETNAM

Phnom Penh

Gulf of Thailand

Saigon
Tet Offensive
Jan. 30–March 7, 1968

Surrender of South Vietnam
1975

Mekong Delta

0   150   300 miles
0   150   300 kilometers

→ U.S. and South Vietnamese forces

→ Major North Vietnamese supply route into South Vietnam

✳ Important battle or action

MALAYSIA

MAP ACTIVITY

Map 29.2 The Vietnam War, 1964–1975

The United States sent 2.6 million soldiers to Vietnam and spent more than $150 billion on the longest war in American history, but it was unable to prevent the unification of Vietnam under a Communist government.

READING THE MAP: What accords divided Vietnam into two nations? When were these accords signed, and where was the line of division drawn? Through what countries did the Ho Chi Minh Trail go?

CONNECTIONS: What was the Gulf of Tonkin incident, and how did the United States respond? What was the Tet Offensive, and how did it affect the war?

routes, called the Ho Chi Minh Trail, in neighboring Laos and Cambodia, through which it sent people and supplies to help liberate the South (Map 29.2). Violence escalated between 1960 and 1963, bringing the Saigon government close to collapse.

Kennedy responded to the deteriorating situation with measured steps. Some advisers called for using any force necessary to save South Vietnam from communism. Others questioned whether such a victory was either necessary or possible. Taking the middle ground, Kennedy gradually escalated the U.S. commitment. By the spring of 1963, military aid had doubled, and the 9,000 Americans serving in Vietnam as military advisers occasionally participated in actual combat. The South Vietnamese government promised reform but never made good on its promises.

Reflecting racist attitudes of American superiority over nonwhite populations, officials assumed that U.S. technology and sheer power could win in Vietnam. Yet advanced weapons were ill suited to the guerrilla warfare practiced by the enemy, whose surprise attacks were designed to weaken support for the South Vietnamese government. In addition, U.S. weapons and strategy harmed the very people they were intended to save. Thousands of peasants were uprooted and resettled in "strategic hamlets," supposedly secure from the Communists. Those left in the countryside fell victim to bombs — containing the highly flammable substance napalm — dropped by the South Vietnamese air force to quell the Vietcong. In January 1962, U.S. planes began to spray herbicides such as **Agent Orange** to destroy the Vietcong's jungle hideouts and food supply.

With tacit permission from Washington, South Vietnamese military leaders executed a coup against Diem and his brother, who headed the secret police, in November 1963. Kennedy expressed shock when the two were murdered but indicated no change in policy. In a speech to be given on the day he was assassinated, Kennedy referred specifically to Southeast Asia and warned, "We dare not weary of the task." At his death, 16,700 Americans were stationed in Vietnam, and 100 had died there.

REVIEW Why did Kennedy believe that engagement in Vietnam was crucial to his foreign policy?

▶ Lyndon Johnson's War against Communism

The Cold War assumptions that had shaped Kennedy's foreign policy underlay his successor's approach to Southeast Asia and Latin America. Retaining Kennedy's key advisers — Secretary of State Rusk, Secretary of Defense Robert McNamara, and National Security Adviser McGeorge Bundy — **Lyndon B. Johnson** continued the massive buildup of nuclear weapons and conventional and counterinsurgency forces. In 1965, Johnson made the fateful decisions to order U.S. troops into combat in Vietnam and to initiate sustained bombing of the North. That same year, Johnson sent U.S. Marines to the Dominican Republic to crush a leftist rebellion.

> "I don't think it's worth fighting for and I don't think we can get out."
> — President **LYNDON B. JOHNSON,** speaking of Vietnam

An All-Out Commitment in Vietnam

The president who wanted to make his mark on domestic policy was compelled to deal with the commitments his predecessors had made in Vietnam. Some advisers, politicians, and international leaders raised questions about the wisdom of a greater commitment there, viewing the situation as a civil war rather than Communist aggression. Most U.S. allies did not consider Vietnam crucial to containing communism and were not prepared to share the military burden in more than token ways. Senate majority leader Mike Mansfield wondered whether Vietnam could be won with a "limited expenditure of American lives and resources somewhere commensurate with our national interests." Johnson expressed his own doubt privately: "I don't think it's worth fighting for and I don't think we can get out."

Believing that the nation's reputation as a staunch defender against communism was on the line, the president expanded the United States' military involvement. Moreover, like Kennedy, he remembered how Truman had suffered politically when the Communists took over China. Johnson wanted to prevent Republicans from charging that Democrats were weak on national security, and he believed that conceding defeat in Vietnam would undermine his ability to achieve his Great Society.

Johnson understood the ineffectiveness of his South Vietnamese allies and agonized over sending young men into combat. Yet he continued to dispatch more military advisers, weapons, and economic aid and, in August 1964, seized an opportunity to increase the pressure on North Vietnam. While spying in the Gulf of Tonkin, off the coast of North Vietnam, two U.S. destroyers reported that North Vietnamese gunboats had fired on them (see Map 29.2). Johnson quickly ordered air strikes on North Vietnamese torpedo bases and oil storage facilities. Concealing the uncertainty about whether the second attack

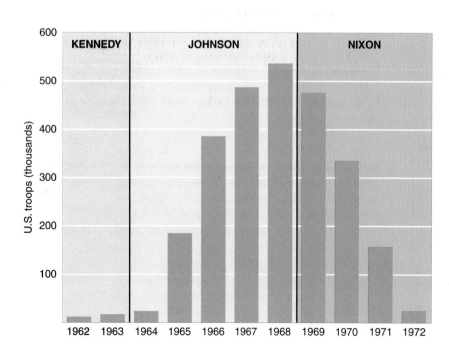

FIGURE 29.1   U.S. Troops in Vietnam, 1962–1972
The steepest increases in the American military presence in Vietnam came with Johnson's escalation of the war in 1965 and 1966. Although Nixon reduced troop levels significantly in 1971 and 1972, the United States continued massive bombing attacks.

had even occurred and the provocative U.S. operations along the North Vietnamese coast, he won from Congress the **Gulf of Tonkin Resolution**, authorizing him to take "all necessary measures to repel any armed attacks against the forces of the United States and to prevent further aggression."

The president's tough stance only two months before the 1964 election helped counter the charges made by his opponent, Arizona senator Barry Goldwater, that he was "soft on communism." Yet Johnson also presented himself as the peace candidate, assuring Americans that "we are not going to send American boys nine or ten thousand miles away from home to do what Asian boys ought to be doing for themselves."

Johnson might have used the political capital from his overwhelming reelection victory to disengage from Vietnam. Instead he widened the war, rejecting peace overtures from North Vietnam, because it insisted on American withdrawal and a coalition government in South Vietnam as steps toward ultimate unification of the country. In February 1965, Johnson authorized **Operation Rolling Thunder**, a strategy of gradually intensified bombing of North Vietnam. Less than a month later, Johnson ordered the first U.S. combat troops to South Vietnam, and in July he shifted U.S. troops from defensive to offensive operations, dispatching 50,000 more soldiers (Figure 29.1). Although the administration downplayed the import of these decisions, they marked a critical turning point. Now it was genuinely America's war.

Preventing Another Castro in Latin America

Closer to home, Johnson faced persistent problems in Latin America. Thirteen times during the 1960s, military coups toppled Latin American governments, and local insurgencies grew apace. The administration's response varied from case to case but centered on the determination to prevent any more Castro-type revolutions.

In 1964, riots erupted in the Panama Canal Zone, which the United States had seized and made a U.S. territory early in the century (see chapter 21). Instigated by Panamanians who viewed the United States as a colonial power, the riots left four U.S. soldiers and more than twenty Panamanians dead. Johnson sent troops to quell the disturbance, but he also initiated negotiations that eventually returned the canal to Panamanian authority in 2000.

U.S. Troops in the Dominican Republic
These U.S. paratroopers were among the 20,000 troops sent to the Dominican Republic in April and May 1965. The American invasion helped restore peace but kept the popularly elected government of Juan Bosch from regaining office. Dominicans expressed their outrage in anti-American slogans that greeted troops throughout the capital, Santo Domingo. Bosch himself said, "This was a democratic revolution smashed by the leading democracy in the world." © Bettmann/Corbis.

Elsewhere, Johnson's Latin American policy generated new cries of "Yankee imperialism." In 1961, voters in the Dominican Republic ousted a longtime dictator and elected a constitutional government headed by reformist Juan Bosch, who was overthrown by a military coup two years later. In 1965, when Bosch supporters launched an uprising against the military government, Johnson sent more than 20,000 soldiers to quell what he perceived to be a leftist revolt and to take control of the island. A truce was arranged,

THE PROMISE OF TECHNOLOGY

The Military Helicopter

The U.S. military employed helicopters for medical evacuations in Korea, but not until smaller, lighter gas-turbine engines replaced piston engines did helicopters play a central role in war. Particular conditions in Vietnam — the guerrilla tactics of the enemy, the conduct of fighting all over South Vietnam rather than across a fixed battlefront, and the mountains and dense jungles with limited landing areas — put a premium on the helicopter's mobility and maneuverability. Choppers carried infantry units all over South Vietnam, transported artillery and ammunition, performed reconnaissance, picked up downed pilots, and evacuated the dead and wounded. Mounted with machine guns and grenade launchers, helicopters also served as attack vehicles. Here men of the First Squadron, Ninth Cavalry, First Cavalry Division leap from a Bell UH-1 Iro-

quois ("Huey") helicopter near Chu Lai, South Vietnam, in 1967 as they begin a reconnaissance mission. © Bettmann/ Corbis.

and in 1966 Dominicans voted in a constitutional government under a moderate rightist.

This first outright show of Yankee force in Latin America in four decades damaged the administration at home and abroad. Although Johnson had justified intervention as necessary to prevent "another Cuba," no Communists were found among the rebels, and U.S. intervention kept the reform-oriented Boschists from returning to power. Moreover, the president had not consulted the Dominicans or the Organization of American States (OAS), to which the United States had promised it would respect national sovereignty in Latin America.

The Americanized War

The military success in the Dominican Republic no doubt encouraged the president to press on in Vietnam. From 1965 to early 1968, the United States gradually escalated the war. While increasing numbers of U.S. troops fought the National Liberation Front in South Vietnam, Operation Rolling Thunder sought to break the will and capacity of the North Vietnamese to support the insurgents. Johnson carefully calibrated the attacks, boasting, "They can't even bomb an outhouse without my approval."

Some military officials chafed at the restrictions placed on the air war, but Johnson remembered what had happened in Korea and that "China is there on the [North Vietnamese] border with 700 million men." The administration banned strikes near that border and on sites where Chinese or Soviet advisers might be present, determined to avoid provoking intervention by either China or the Soviet Union, both of which now possessed nuclear weapons. To contain both domestic and international criticism of the war, Johnson also prohibited bombing targets where high civilian casualties might result.

Despite restrictions, U.S. pilots dropped 643,000 tons of bombs on North Vietnam and more than twice that amount in the South, a total surpassing all the explosives the United States dropped in World War II. Yet the bombing was no match for the determination and ingenuity of the North Vietnamese. Their sheer effort compensated for the destruction of transportation lines, industry sites, and power plants. For example, when bombs struck a rail line, civilians rushed in with bicycles to unload a train's cargo, carry it beyond the break, and load it onto a second train. In South Vietnam, the massive U.S. bombing campaign destroyed villages and fields, alienating the very population that the Americans had come to save.

On the ground, General William Westmoreland's strategy of attrition was designed to seek out and kill the Vietcong and North Vietnamese regular army. With no fixed battle front, officials calculated progress not in territory seized but in "body counts" and "kill ratios" — the number of enemies killed relative to the cost in American and ARVN lives. According to Lieutenant Frederick Downs, "To win a battle, we had to kill them. For them to win, all they had to do was survive." He realized that "we would fight and bleed to take ground," and the enemy would withdraw "after they had exacted their toll"; but then U.S. forces would leave, and the Vietcong could come back whenever they liked. The Americans, Downs said, "never owned anything except the ground they stood on."

Those Who Served

Teenagers fought the Vietnam War, in contrast to World War II, in which the average soldier was twenty-six years old. All the men in Lieutenant Downs's platoon were between the ages of eighteen and twenty-one, and the average age for all soldiers was nineteen. Until a constitutional amendment dropped the voting age from twenty-one to eighteen in 1971, most could not even vote for the officials who sent them to war. Men of all classes had fought in World War II, but in Vietnam the poor and working class constituted about 80 percent of the troops. More privileged youths avoided the draft by using college deferments or family connections to get into the National Guard. Sent from Plainville, Kansas, to Vietnam in 1965, Mike Clodfelter could not recall "a single middle-class son of the town's businessmen, lawyers, doctors, or ranchers from my high school graduating class who experienced the Armageddon of our generation."

Much more than World War II, Vietnam was a men's war. Because the United States did not undergo full mobilization for Vietnam, officials did not seek women's sacrifices for the war effort. Still, between 7,500 and 10,000 women served in Vietnam, the vast majority of them nurses. Some women were exposed to enemy fire, and eight lost their lives. Many more struggled with their helplessness in the face of the dead and maimed bodies they tended. "When you finally saved a life," said Peggy DuVall, "you wondered what kind of life you had saved."

Early in the war, African Americans constituted 31 percent of combat troops, often choosing

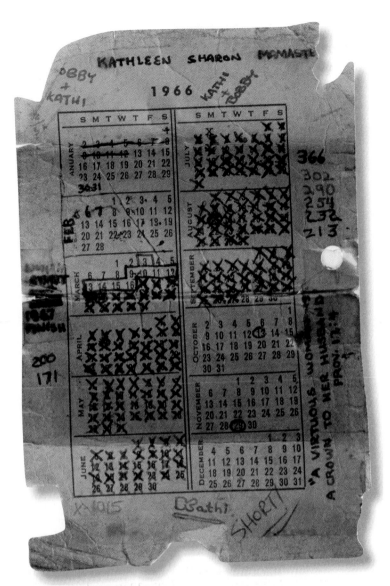

Counting the Days in Vietnam
Unlike previous wars, most soldiers served tours of duty in Vietnam lasting just one year. The soldier who carried this calendar expressed an obsession with time "in country" that many of his comrades shared. Soldiers considered themselves "short" when they had fewer than 100 days left. Bobby McMaster was thinking of either his wife or of the woman he would marry when, and if, he returned home. What might his inscription of the Bible verse suggest about his feelings about the woman he left behind? © Bettmann/Corbis.

the military over the meager opportunities in the civilian economy. Special forces ranger Arthur E. Woodley Jr. recalled, "I was just what my country needed. A black patriot. . . . The only way I could possibly make it out of the ghetto was to be the best soldier I possibly could." Death rates among black soldiers were disproportionately high until 1966, when the military adjusted personnel assignments to achieve a better racial balance.

The young troops faced extremely difficult conditions. Frederick Downs's platoon fought in

Chemical Weapons

In 1964, the U.S. military began to use the tear gas CS (o-chlorobenzylidenemalononitrile) in grenades in Vietnam, discharging more than two million pounds of CS a year by 1969. Here, a Marine has just thrown a CS grenade into a tunnel to flush out the enemy and make the tunnel unusable for several months. Military planes also dispersed CS to rid large areas of enemy forces. CS is incapacitating but usually not lethal; nonetheless, its use evoked criticism both at home and abroad, including condemnation by the UN. Marine: James H. Pickerell/Stock Connection; Gas: Ordinance Museum/Aberdeen Proving Grounds.

thick jungles filled with leeches, in rain and oppressive heat, always vulnerable to sniper bullets and land mines. He remembered that "the terror of an explosion never failed to send a shiver through our guts." Soldiers in previous wars had served "for the duration," but in Vietnam a soldier served a one-year tour of duty. A commander called it "the worst personnel policy in history," because men had less incentive to fight near the end of their tours, wanting merely to stay alive and whole.

The U.S. military inflicted great losses on the enemy, yet the war remained a stalemate. Dispatched to an area thick with Vietcong sympathizers, Downs wondered how to win the people's hearts and minds: "How could we compete with countrymen who could speak to them, live with them, were related to them?" He remained convinced that his country was doing the right thing yet recognized that "all Vietnamese had a common desire — to see us go home."

The South Vietnamese government was an enormous obstacle to victory, even though in 1965 it settled into a period of stability when it was headed by two military leaders. Graft and corruption continued to flourish in the government. In the intensified fighting and with the inability to distinguish friend from foe, ARVN and American troops killed and wounded thousands of South Vietnamese civilians and destroyed their villages. By 1968, nearly 30 percent of the population had become refugees. The failure to stabilize South Vietnam even as the U.S. military presence expanded enormously created grave challenges for the administration at home.

REVIEW   Why did massive amounts of airpower and ground troops fail to bring U.S. victory in Vietnam?

▶ A Nation Polarized

Soon President Johnson was fighting a war on two fronts. Domestic opposition to the war swelled after 1965 as daily television broadcasts made it the first "living-room war." In March 1968, torn between his domestic critics and the military's clamor for more troops, Johnson announced a halt to the bombing, a new effort at negotiations, and his decision not to pursue reelection. Throughout 1968, demonstrations, violence, and assassinations convulsed the increasingly polarized nation. Vietnam took center stage in the election, and voters narrowly favored the Republican candidate, former vice president Richard Nixon, who promised to achieve "peace with honor."

The Widening War at Home

Johnson's authorization of Operation Rolling Thunder expanded the previously quiet doubts and criticism into a mass movement against the war. In April 1965, Students for a Democratic Society (SDS) recruited 20,000 people for the first major demonstration against the war in Washington, D.C. SDS chapters sprang up on more than three hundred college campuses. Thousands of students protested against Reserve Officers Training Corps (ROTC) programs, CIA recruiters, military research projects, and manufacturers of war materiel. Martin Luther King Jr. deployed his moral authority, rebuking the U.S. government in 1967 as "the greatest purveyor of violence in the world today."

Mothers against the War
Founded in 1961 to work for nuclear disarmament, Women Strike for Peace (WSP) began to "alert the public to the dangers and horrors of the war in Vietnam" in 1963. Identifying themselves as "concerned housewives" and mothers, members mobilized around the slogan "Not Our Sons, Not Your Sons, Not Their Sons." In February 1967, WSP held the first antiwar protest at the Pentagon. More than 2,000 women, some shown here, banged their shoes on Pentagon doors, which were locked as they approached. What characteristics of the war did these women focus on? How were their objections to the war similar to and different from those of other protesters? © Bettmann/Corbis.

Environmentalists attacked the use of chemical weapons, such as the deadly Agent Orange.

Antiwar sentiment entered society's mainstream. The *New York Times* began questioning the war in 1965, and by 1968 media critics included the *Wall Street Journal, Life* magazine, and popular TV anchorman Walter Cronkite. Clergy, business people, scientists, and physicians formed their own groups to pressure Johnson to stop the bombing and start negotiations. Prominent Democratic senators, including J. William Fulbright, George McGovern, and Mike Mansfield, urged Johnson to substitute negotiation for force.

Opposition to the war took diverse forms: letters to officials, teach-ins on college campuses,

mass marches, student strikes, withholding of federal taxes, draft card and flag burnings, and attempts to stop trains carrying troops. Although the peace movement never claimed a majority of the population, it focused media attention on the war and severely limited the administration's options. The twenty-year-old consensus around Cold War foreign policy had broken down.

Many would not fight in the war. The World Boxing Association stripped Muhammad Ali of his world heavyweight title when he refused to serve in what he called a "white man's war." More than 170,000 men who opposed the war on moral or religious grounds gained conscientious objector status and performed nonmilitary duties at home or in Vietnam. About 60,000 fled the country to escape the draft, and more than 200,000 were accused of failing to register or of committing other draft offenses.

Opponents of the war held diverse views. Those who saw the conflict in moral terms wanted total withdrawal, insisting that their country had no right to interfere in a civil war and stressing the suffering of the Vietnamese people. A larger segment of antiwar sentiment reflected practical considerations — the belief that the war could not be won at a bearable cost. Those activists wanted Johnson to stop bombing North Vietnam and seek negotiations.

Working-class people were no more antiwar than other groups, but they recognized the class dimensions of the war and the antiwar movement. A firefighter whose son had died in Vietnam said bitterly, "It's people like us who give up our sons for the country. The businesspeople, they run the country and make money from it. The college types . . . go to Washington and tell the government what to do. . . . But their sons don't end up in the swamps over there, in Vietnam." The antiwar movement outraged millions of Americans who supported the war. Some members of the generation who had fought against Hitler could not understand younger men's refusal to support their government. They expressed their anger at war protesters with bumper stickers that read "America: Love It or Leave It."

By 1967, the administration realized that "discontent with the war is now wide and deep." President Johnson used various means to silence critics. He equated opposition to the war with communism and assistance to the enemy. To avoid focusing attention on the war's costs, he eschewed measures to control inflation and delayed asking for a tax increase to pay for the

1968: A Year of Protest

To many people living through it, 1968 looked like the start of a worldwide political revolution. A surge of protests against the U.S. war in Vietnam and demands for greater democracy and economic justice jumped over borders and challenged authorities in many countries around the world. Although local grievances ignited many of the protests in 1968, a common feature of them all was the central role played by university students. The protests of 1968 unfolded rapidly, giving rise to excitement and apprehension. From February to December, demonstrations erupted in North and South America, Europe, and Asia. Many demonstrators expressed transnational solidarity by carrying the flag of Vietnam's National Liberation Front or placards bearing the image of Ernesto "Che" Guevara, a Latin American radical killed by the Bolivian military in 1967. And yet there was in fact little international coordination of events or any shared plan for remaking the world.

One of the first large-scale protests occurred in February at West Berlin's Free University, where some 10,000 participants from ten countries at the "Vietnam Congress" called for "an international manifestation of solidarity" with the people of Vietnam. Protests continued throughout the spring, prompting the West German government to pass emergency laws to stifle disorder. In February and March, demonstrations flared up in Madrid, Warsaw, Rome, São Paulo, and London, met by police with clubs. As with the protesters, police also took their cues from worldwide events, reacting more forcefully to demonstrations in light of commotions in other countries. Charges of police brutality, disseminated in television and newspaper reports, fed the cycle of protest further.

In April and May, violence erupted in the United States. Martin Luther King Jr.'s assassination on April 4 ignited riots in many U.S. cities. Less than a month later, students at Columbia University in New York City seized buildings and shut down the campus, leading to a bloody showdown between police and protesters.

In May, rebellion paralyzed France. It began with students' complaints about services at a university north of Paris and spread to the Sorbonne in the capital city. Police teargassed a small rally, only to face tens of thousands of students streaming into Paris over the next few days. Violence escalated as protesters barricaded streets. Independent radio stations broadcast live interviews with demonstrators, and soon a million people were in the streets. Workers joined the rebellion, shutting down factories across France. Students proclaimed that "exceptional domestic and international conditions" had brought powerless students and workers together around the world. By late May, France was in deep crisis.

Prague, the capital of Communist Czechoslovakia, also stirred in May. A liberal president, Alexander Dubček, pushed for reforms against heavy-handed Soviet control, giving rise to hopes for greater freedom. Students demonstrated, and thousands signed manifestos. But this "Prague Spring" was cut short in August when Soviet tanks rumbled into the country and Dubček was arrested. Throughout Europe, students marched on Soviet embassies to protest the crackdown. At the same moment in the United States, Chicago police battled young protesters near the Democratic National Convention.

In July, Mexican police attacked marchers carrying posters of Fidel Castro and Che Guevara. When thousands rallied against the violence, police fired into the crowd, killing several students. Violent clashes continued into August and September, as activists protested the Olympic Games, scheduled to open in Mexico City in October. Insisting that the money spent on the Olympics should have been used to alleviate the country's widespread poverty, protesters chanted, "We don't want Olympic Games; we want revolution." The upcoming Olympics created pressure for the authorities to clear the city of dissidents. When some 10,000 students assembled for a rally on October 2, jeeps with machine guns arrived. At

war. Not until June 1968 did Congress pass a 10 percent income tax surcharge. Great Society programs suffered, and the surcharge failed to check inflation.

The administration deceived the public by making optimistic statements and concealing officials' ever-graver doubts about the possibility of success in Vietnam. Johnson ordered the CIA to spy on peace advocates, and without the president's specific authorization, the FBI infiltrated the peace movement, disrupted its work, and spread false information about activists. Even the resort to illegal measures failed to subdue the opposition.

The Tet Offensive and Johnson's Move toward Peace

The year 1968 was marked by violent confrontations around the world. Protests against governments erupted from Mexico City to Paris to Tokyo, usually led by students in collaboration with

Students Protest in Mexico City
After riot police reacted violently to skirmishes between students from rival schools in Mexico City in July 1968, students began to demonstrate against the repressive measures of the government and political interference in their universities. These students, marching on August 13, 1968, were part of a movement that two weeks later swelled to a demonstration of a half million and was then dispersed by soldiers and tanks. One of their signs promises to defend their demands until "total victory." Marcel·lí Perelló.

least 100 to 200 protesters were killed, and another several hundred were wounded. The Olympic Games went on as scheduled ten days later.

In the wake of the massacre, protesters staged demonstrations and attacks on Mexican embassies in Latin America and Europe. By December, more episodes of violence against protesters occurred in Spain, Pakistan, and Northern Ireland. In the United States, violence diminished generally, but not in urban ghettos.

By year's end, a kind of stunned exhaustion set in. The Soviets had shut down the Prague Spring, the student-led protests in France and Germany had reached a stalemate, and Republican Richard Nixon had won the U.S. presidential election with promises to maintain law and order at home and to end the war in Vietnam. The year of global protest ended with despair and fear on all sides. Student protest did not disappear, but the excitement of worldwide revolutionary solidarity was blunted by

the very real threat of fatal consequences faced by protesters.

America in a Global Context

1. What did the global protests of 1968 have in common?

2. How did protest in the United States differ from that in other countries, both in the composition of the protesters and in the reaction from authorities?

---

workers. (See "Beyond America's Borders," page 984.) American society also became increasingly polarized. On one side, the so-called hawks charged that the United States was fighting with one hand tied behind its back and called for intensification of the war. The doves wanted de-escalation or withdrawal. As U.S. troop strength neared half a million and military deaths approached 20,000 by the end of 1967, most people were torn between weariness with the war and a desire to fulfill the U.S. commitment.

As one woman said, "I want to get out but I don't want to give up."

Grave doubts penetrated the administration itself in 1967. Secretary of Defense **Robert McNamara**, a principal architect of U.S. involvement, now believed that the North Vietnamese "won't quit no matter how much bombing we do." He feared for the image of the United States, "the world's greatest superpower, killing or seriously injuring 1,000 noncombatants a week, while trying to pound a tiny, backward nation into submission

The Battle for Hue
During the Tet Offensive in early 1968, North Vietnamese troops captured the city of Hue, the ancient capital of Vietnam, rich with the country's history and culture. It took nearly a month of brutal house-to-house fighting for U.S. and ARVN troops to retake the city, eighty percent of which had by then been destroyed. The great cost in lives, housing, and cultural treasure contributed to the mounting disaffection of Americans for the war, even though the Tet Offensive was ultimately a military victory for the U.S. and South Vietnam. Here U.S. Marines are pinned down near the center of Hue. © Bettmann/Corbis.

on an issue whose merits are hotly disputed." McNamara did not publicly oppose the war, but in early 1968 he left the administration.

A critical turning point came with the **Tet Offensive**. On January 30, 1968, the North Vietnamese and Vietcong launched attacks on key cities, every major American base in South Vietnam, and the U.S. Embassy in Saigon. This was the biggest surprise of the war, and not simply because both sides had customarily observed a truce during Tet, the Vietnamese New Year holiday. The offensive displayed the Communists' vitality and refusal to be intimidated by the presence of half a million American soldiers. Militarily, the enemy suffered a defeat, losing ten times as many soldiers as ARVN and U.S. forces. Psychologically, however, Tet was devastating to the United States.

> **"What the hell is going on? I thought we were winning the war."**
> — TV anchorman **WALTER CRONKITE**

The Tet Offensive underscored the credibility gap between official statements and the war's actual progress. TV anchorman Walter Cronkite wondered, "What the hell is going on? I thought we were winning the war." The attacks created a million more South Vietnamese refugees as well as widespread destruction. Explaining how he had defended a village, a U.S. Army official said, "We had to destroy the town to save it." The statement epitomized for more and more Americans the brutality and senselessness of the war. Public approval of Johnson's handling of it dropped to 26 percent.

In the aftermath of Tet, Johnson conferred with advisers in the Defense Department and an unofficial group of foreign policy experts who had been key architects of Cold War policies for two decades. Dean Acheson, Truman's secretary of state, summarized their conclusion: "We can no longer do the job we set out to do in the time we have left and we must begin to take steps to disengage."

African American Antiwar Protest
The first expression of African American opposition to the war in Vietnam occurred in Mississippi in July 1965 when a group of civil rights workers called for draft resistance. Blacks should not fight for freedom in Vietnam "until all the Negro People are free in Mississippi," the activists said, and they should not risk their lives "and kill other Colored People in Santo Domingo and Viet Nam." This protester on the West Coast expresses similar sentiments in April 1967. Joe Flowers/Black Star/Stockphoto.com.

On March 31, 1968, Lyndon Johnson announced in a televised speech that the United States would sharply curtail its bombing of North Vietnam and that he was prepared to begin peace talks. He added the stunning declaration that he would not run for reelection. The gradual escalation of the war was over, and military strategy shifted from "Americanization" to "Vietnamization" of the war. But this was not a shift in policy. The goal remained a non-Communist South Vietnam; the United States would simply rely more heavily on the South Vietnamese to achieve it.

Negotiations began in Paris in May 1968. The United States would not agree to recognition of the Hanoi government's National Liberation Front, to a coalition government, or to American withdrawal. The North Vietnamese would agree to nothing less. Although the talks continued, so did the fighting.

Meanwhile, violence escalated at home. Protests occurred on two hundred college campuses in the spring of 1968, and as many as one million students participated in nationwide strikes. In the bloodiest action, students occupied buildings at Columbia University in New York City, making demands connected to the university's war-related research and to its treatment of African Americans. (See chapter 28, "Documenting the American Promise," page 950.) When negotiations failed, university officials called in the city police, who cleared the buildings, injuring scores of demonstrators and arresting hundreds. An ensuing student strike prematurely ended the academic year.

The Tumultuous Election of 1968

Disorder and violence also entered the election process. In June, two months after the murder of Martin Luther King Jr. and the riots that followed, another assassination shook the nation. Antiwar candidate Senator Robert F. Kennedy, campaigning in California for the Democratic Party's presidential nomination, was shot by a Palestinian Arab refugee who was outraged by Kennedy's support for Israel.

In August, protesters battled the police in Chicago, where the Democratic Party had convened to nominate its presidential ticket. Several thousand demonstrators came to the city, some to support the peace candidate Senator Eugene McCarthy, others to cause disruption. The Youth International Party (Yippies), a splinter group of SDS, urged protesters to demonstrate their hatred of the establishment by provoking the police and creating chaos. On August 25, when demonstrators jeered at orders to disperse, police attacked them with tear gas and clubs. Street battles continued for three days, culminating in a police riot on the night of August 28. Taunted by the crowd, the police used Mace and nightsticks, clubbing not only those who had come to provoke violence but also reporters, peaceful demonstrators, and convention delegates.

Although the bloodshed in Chicago horrified those who saw it on television, it had little effect on the convention's outcome. An assassin had ended Robert Kennedy's promising campaign in June, and Vice President **Hubert H. Humphrey**

Protest in Chicago
The worst violence surrounding the 1968 Democratic National Convention in Chicago came on August 28 when protesters assembled in Grant Park and marched to the convention site. Near the Hilton Hotel, where most of the delegates stayed, some 3,000 protesters came up against a line of police. The police attacked not only the demonstrators but also reporters, hotel guests, and bystanders with nightsticks and Mace, driving a crowd through the plate-glass window of the hotel and injuring hundreds. AP Photo/Michael Boyer.

trounced the remaining antiwar candidate, McCarthy, by nearly three to one for the Democratic nomination.

In contrast to the turmoil around the Democratic convention, the Republican convention met peacefully and nominated former vice president Richard Nixon on the first ballot. For

MAP 29.3
The Election of 1968

Candidate	Electoral Vote	Popular Vote	Percent of Popular Vote
Richard M. Nixon (Republican)	301	31,770,237	43.4
Hubert H. Humphrey (Democrat)	191	31,270,533	42.7
George C. Wallace (American Independent)	46	9,906,141	13.5

3 — Washington, D.C.

Note: North Carolina split its vote, with one elector voting for Wallace.

his running mate, Nixon chose Maryland governor Spiro T. Agnew, hoping to gather southern support. A strong third candidate entered the electoral scene when the American Independent Party nominated former Alabama governor and staunch segregationist **George C. Wallace**. Wallace appealed to Americans' dissatisfaction with the reforms and rebellions of the 1960s and their outrage at the assaults on traditional values. Nixon guardedly played on resentments that fueled the Wallace campaign, calling for "law and order" and attacking liberal Supreme Court decisions, busing for school desegregation, and protesters.

Nixon and Humphrey differed little on the central issue of Vietnam. Nixon promised "an honorable end" to the war but did not indicate how he would do it. Humphrey had strong reservations about U.S. policy in Vietnam, yet as vice president he was tied to Johnson's policies. With nearly 13 percent of the total popular vote, the American Independent Party produced the strongest third-party finish since 1924. Nixon edged out Humphrey by just half a million popular votes but garnered 301 electoral college votes to Humphrey's 191 and Wallace's 46 (Map 29.3). The Democrats maintained control of Congress.

The 1968 election revealed deep cracks in the coalition that had kept the Democrats in power for most of the previous thirty years. Johnson's liberal policies on race shattered a century of Democratic Party dominance in the South, which delivered all its electoral votes to Wallace and

Nixon. Elsewhere, large numbers of blue-collar workers broke with labor's traditional support for the Democratic Party to vote for Wallace or Nixon, as did other groups that associated the Democrats with racial turmoil, poverty programs, changing sexual mores, and failure to turn the tide in Vietnam. These resentments would soon be mobilized into a resurging right in American politics (as discussed in chapter 30).

REVIEW How did the Vietnam War shape the election of 1968?

▶ Nixon, Détente, and the Search for Peace in Vietnam

Richard M. Nixon took office with ambitious foreign policy goals, hoping to make his mark on history by applying his broad understanding of international relations to a changing world. Diverging from Republican orthodoxy, he made dramatic overtures to the Soviet Union and China. Yet anticommunism remained central to U.S. policy. In Latin America, Africa, and the Middle East, Nixon backed repressive regimes when the alternatives suggested victories for the left. Relying even more than his predecessor on public deception, secrecy, and silencing opponents, Nixon aggressively pursued the war in Vietnam. He expanded the conflict into Cambodia and Laos and ferociously bombed North Vietnam. Yet in the end, he was forced to settle for peace without victory.

Moving toward Détente with the Soviet Union and China

In Nixon's view, the "rigid and bipolar world of the 1940s and 1950s" was giving way to "the fluidity of a new era of multilateral diplomacy." America's European allies were seeking to ease East-West tensions. Moreover, Nixon and his national security adviser **Henry A. Kissinger** recognized the increasing conflict between the Soviet Union and China and believed they could exploit the situation. This Soviet-Chinese hostility, according to Nixon, "served our purpose best if we maintained closer relations with each side than they did with each other." In addition, these two nations might be used to help the United States extricate itself from Vietnam.

Following two years of secret negotiations, in February 1972 Nixon became the nation's first president to set foot on Chinese soil — an astonishing act by a man whose career had rested on fervent anticommunism. In fact, his anti-Communist credentials enabled him to conduct this shift in U.S.-Chinese relations with no significant domestic repercussions. Although his visit was largely symbolic, cultural and scientific exchanges followed, and American manufacturers began to find markets in China — small steps in the process of globalization that would take giant strides in the 1990s (as discussed in chapter 31). China had been

> "[Soviet-Chinese hostility] served our purpose best if we maintained closer relations with each side than they did with each other."
>
> — President RICHARD M. NIXON

Nixon in China
"This was the week that changed the world," proclaimed President Nixon in February 1972, emphasizing the stunning turnaround in relations with America's former enemy, the People's Republic of China. Nixon's trip was meticulously planned to dramatize the event on television and, aside from criticism from some conservatives, won overwhelming support from Americans. The Great Wall of China forms the setting for this photograph of Nixon and his wife, Pat. Nixon Presidential Materials Project, National Archives and Record Administration.

admitted to the United Nations in 1971, and in 1979 the United States and China would establish formal diplomatic relations.

As Nixon and Kissinger had hoped, the warming of U.S.-Chinese relations furthered their strategy of **détente**, their term for easing conflict with the Soviet Union. Détente did not mean abandoning containment but instead meant focusing on issues of common concern, such as arms control and trade. Containment would be achieved not only by military threat but also by ensuring that the Soviets and Chinese had stakes in a stable international order. Nixon's goal was "a stronger healthy United States, Europe, Soviet Union, China, Japan, each balancing the other."

Arms control, trade, and stability in Europe were three areas where the United States and the Soviet Union had common interests. In May 1972, Nixon visited Moscow, signing several agreements on trade and cooperation in science and space. Most significantly, Soviet and U.S. leaders concluded arms limitation treaties that had grown out of the **Strategic Arms Limitation Talks (SALT)** begun in 1969, agreeing to limit antiballistic missiles (ABMs) to two each. Giving up pursuit of a defense against nuclear weapons was a crucial move, because it prevented either nation from building so secure an ABM defense against a nuclear attack that it would risk a first strike.

Although the policy of détente made little progress after 1974, U.S., Soviet, and European leaders signed a historic agreement in 1975 in Helsinki, Finland, that formally recognized the post–World War II boundaries in Europe. The **Helsinki accords** were controversial because they acknowledged Soviet domination over Eastern Europe — a condition that had triggered the Cold War thirty years earlier. Yet they also contained a clause committing the signing countries to recognize "the universal significance of human rights and fundamental freedoms." Dissidents in the Soviet Union and its Eastern European satellites used this official promise of rights to challenge the Soviet dictatorship and help force its overthrow fifteen years later.

Shoring Up U.S. Interests around the World

Nixon promised in 1973 that "the time has passed when America will make every other nation's conflict our own . . . or presume to tell the people of other nations how to manage their own affairs." Yet in Vietnam and elsewhere, Nixon and Kissinger continued to view left-wing movements as threats to U.S. interests and actively resisted social revolutions that might lead to communism.

Consequently, the Nixon administration helped to overthrow **Salvador Allende**, a self-proclaimed Marxist who was elected president of Chile in 1970. Since 1964, the CIA and U.S. corporations concerned about nationalization of their Chilean properties had assisted Allende's opponents. After Allende became president, Nixon ordered the CIA director to destabilize his government by making the Chilean economy "scream." In 1973, the CIA helped the Chilean military engineer a coup, killing Allende and establishing a brutal dictatorship under General Augusto Pinochet. Representative government did not return until 1990.

In other parts of the world, too, the Nixon administration stood by repressive regimes. In southern Africa, it eased pressures on white minority governments that tyrannized blacks. In the Middle East, the United States sent massive arms shipments to support the shah of Iran's harsh regime because Iran had enormous petroleum reserves and seemed a stable anti-Communist ally. Unnoticed by most Americans, the administration cemented a relationship that turned many Iranians against the United States and would ignite a new crisis when the shah was overthrown in 1979 (as discussed in chapter 30).

Like his predecessors, Nixon pursued a delicate balance between defending Israel's security and seeking the goodwill of Arab nations strategically and economically important to the United States. Conflict between Israel and the Arab nations had escalated into the **Six-Day War** in 1967, when Israel attacked Egypt after that nation had massed troops on the Israeli border and cut off sea passage to

Chile

0   250 500 mi.

0   500 km.

Israel's southern port. Although Syria and Jordan joined the war on Egypt's side, Israel won a stunning victory, seizing territory that amounted to twice its original size. Israeli forces took control of the Sinai Peninsula and the Gaza Strip from Egypt, the Golan Heights from Syria, and the West Bank, where hundreds of thousands of Palestinians lived, from Jordan.

That decisive victory did not quell Middle Eastern turmoil. In October 1973, on the Jewish holiday Yom Kippur, Egypt and Syria surprised Israel with a full-scale attack. When the Nixon administration sided with Israel in the **Yom Kippur War**, Arab nations retaliated with an oil embargo that created severe shortages in the United States. After Israel repulsed the attack, Kissinger attempted to mediate between Israel and the Arab nations, but with very limited success. The Arab countries refused to recognize Israel's right to exist, Israel began to settle its citizens in the West Bank and other territories occupied during the Six-Day War, and no solution could be found for the Palestinian refugees who had been displaced by the creation of Israel in the late 1940s (see chapter 26). The simmering conflict contributed to anti-American sentiment among Arabs who viewed the United States as Israel's supporter.

Vietnam Becomes Nixon's War

"I'm not going to end up like LBJ, holed up in the White House afraid to show my face on the street," the new president asserted. "I'm going to stop that war. Fast." Nixon gradually withdrew U.S. ground troops, but he was no more willing than Eisenhower, Kennedy, or Johnson to be the president who allowed South Vietnam to fall to the Communists. That goal was tied to the larger objective of maintaining American credibility. Regardless of the wisdom of the initial intervention, Kissinger asserted, "the commitment of 500,000 Americans has settled the importance of Vietnam. For what is involved now is confidence in American promises."

From 1969 to 1972, Nixon and Kissinger pursued a four-pronged approach. First, they tried

Israeli Territorial Gains in the Six-Day War, 1967

to strengthen the South Vietnamese military and government. Second, to disarm the antiwar movement at home, Nixon gradually replaced U.S. forces with South Vietnamese soldiers and American technology and bombs. Third, the United States negotiated with both North Vietnam and the Soviet Union. Fourth, the military applied intensive bombing to persuade Hanoi to accept American terms at the bargaining table.

As part of the Vietnamization of the war, ARVN forces grew to more than a million, and the South Vietnamese air force became the fourth largest in the world. The United States also promoted land reform, village elections, and the building of schools, hospitals, and transportation facilities. Meanwhile, U.S. forces withdrew, decreasing from 543,000 in 1968 to 140,000 by the end of 1971, a move that critics called merely "changing the color of the corpses." Even with the reduction of U.S. forces, however, more than 20,000 Americans perished in Vietnam between 1969 and 1973.

In the spring of 1969, Nixon began a ferocious air war in Cambodia, carefully hiding it from Congress and the public for more than a year. Seeking to knock out North Vietnamese sanctuaries in Cambodia, Americans dropped more than 100,000 tons of bombs but succeeded only in sending the North Vietnamese to other hiding places. Echoing Johnson, Kissinger believed that a "fourth-rate power like North Vietnam" had to have a "breaking point," but the massive bombing failed to find it.

To support a new, pro-Western Cambodian government installed through a military coup in 1970 and "to show the enemy that we were still serious about our commitment in Vietnam," Nixon ordered a joint U.S.-ARVN invasion of Cambodia in April 1970. That

U.S. Invasion of Cambodia, 1970

VISUAL ACTIVITY

Pro-War Demonstrators

Advocates as well as opponents of the war in Vietnam took to the streets, as these New Yorkers did in support of the U.S. invasion of Cambodia in May 1970. Construction workers — called "hard hats" — and other union members marched with American flags and posters championing President Nixon's policies and blasting New York mayor John Lindsay for his antiwar position. Following the demonstration, sympathetic union leaders presented Nixon with an honorary hard hat. Paul Fusco/Magnum Photos, Inc.

READING THE IMAGE: What do the hard hats in the photograph symbolize in terms of identity and politics?

CONNECTIONS: What, if anything, was the relationship between President Nixon being presented with a hard hat after a pro-war demonstration and the unraveling of the Democratic Party coalition?

order made Vietnam "Nixon's war" and provoked outrage at home. Nixon made a belligerent speech defending his move and emphasizing the importance of U.S. credibility: "If when the chips are down, the world's most powerful nation acts like a pitiful helpless giant, the forces of totalitarianism and anarchy will threaten free nations" everywhere.

Upon reading a draft of the speech, a cabinet member predicted, "This will make the students puke." They did more than that. In response, more than 100,000 people protested in Washington, D.C., and students boycotted classes on hundreds of campuses. At **Kent State University** in Ohio, National Guard troops were dispatched after protesting students burned an old ROTC building. Then, at a rally there on May 4, when some students threw rocks at the

troops, they fired at the students, killing four and wounding ten others. "They're starting to treat their own children like they treat us," commented a black woman in Harlem. In a confrontation at **Jackson State College** in Mississippi on May 14, police shot into a dormitory, killing two black students. And in August, police in Los Angeles used tear gas and clubs against Chicano antiwar protesters.

Congressional reaction to the invasion of Cambodia revealed increasing concern about abuses of presidential power. In the name of national security, presidents since Franklin Roosevelt had conducted foreign policy without the consent or sometimes even the knowledge of Congress — for example, Eisenhower in Iran and Johnson in the Dominican Republic. But in their determination to win the war in Vietnam, Johnson and Nixon had taken extreme measures to deceive the public and silence their critics. The bombing and invasion of Cambodia infuriated enough legislators that the Senate voted to terminate the Gulf of Tonkin Resolution, which had given the president virtually a blank check in Vietnam, and to cut off funds for the Cambodian operation. The House refused to go along, but by the end of June 1970 Nixon had pulled all U.S. troops out of Cambodia.

The Cambodian invasion failed to break the will of North Vietnam, but it set in motion a terrible tragedy for the Cambodian people. The North Vietnamese moved farther into Cambodia and strengthened the Khmer Rouge, Communist insurgents attempting to overthrow the U.S.-supported government of Lon Nol. A brutal civil war raged until 1975, when the Khmer Rouge triumphed and imposed a savage rule, slaughtering millions of Cambodians and giving the name "killing fields" to the land of a historically peaceful people.

In 1971, Vietnam veterans became a visible part of the peace movement, the first men in U.S. history to protest a war in which they had fought. They held a public investigation of "war crimes" in Vietnam, rallied in front of the Capitol, and cast away their war medals. In May 1971, veterans numbered among the 40,000 protesters who engaged in civil disobedience in an effort to shut down Washington. Officials made more than 12,000 arrests, which courts later ruled violations of protesters' rights.

After the spring of 1971, there were fewer massive antiwar demonstrations, but protest continued. Public attention focused on the court-martial of Lieutenant William Calley, which began in November 1970. During the trial,

Americans learned that in March 1968 Calley's company had systematically killed every inhabitant of the hamlet of **My Lai**, even though the soldiers had encountered no enemy forces and the four hundred villagers were nearly all old men, women, and children. The military covered up the atrocity for more than a year before a journalist exposed it. Eventually, twelve officers and enlisted men were charged with murder or assault, but only Calley was convicted.

Administration policy suffered another blow in June 1971 when the *New York Times* published the **Pentagon Papers**, secret government documents consisting mostly of an internal study of the war begun in 1967. Nixon sent government lawyers to court to stop further publication, in part out of fear that other information would be leaked. The Supreme Court, however, ruled that the attempt to stop publication was a "flagrant, indefensible" violation of the First Amendment. Subsequent circulation of the *Pentagon Papers*, which revealed considerable pessimism among officials even as they made rosy promises, heightened disillusionment with the war by casting doubts on the government's credibility. More than 60 percent of Americans polled in 1971 considered it a mistake to have sent American troops to Vietnam; 58 percent believed the war to be immoral.

Military morale sank in the last years of the war. Having been exposed to the antiwar movement at home, many of the remaining soldiers had less faith in the war than their predecessors had had. Racial tensions among soldiers mounted, many soldiers sought escape in illegal drugs, and enlisted men committed hundreds of "fraggings," attacks on officers. In a 1971 report, "The Collapse of the Armed Forces," a retired Marine Corps colonel described the lack of discipline: "Our army that now remains in Vietnam [is] near mutinous."

The Peace Accords

Nixon and Kissinger continued to believe that intensive firepower could bring the North Vietnamese to their knees. In March 1972, responding to a strong North Vietnamese offensive, the United States resumed sustained bombing of the North, mined Haiphong and other harbors for the first time, and announced a naval blockade. With peace talks stalled, in December Nixon ordered the most devastating bombing of North Vietnam yet, producing worldwide condemnation. The intense bombing, which Kissinger

Students Killed at Kent State
On May 4, 1970, John Filo, a photojournalism student at Kent State University in Ohio, took his camera to a student demonstration against President Nixon's decision to invade Cambodia. He observed some protesters throwing rocks at National Guardsmen, who in turn sprayed tear gas. Suddenly, some guardsmen opened fire, killing four students and wounding ten. Filo took this photograph of Mary Ann Vecchio sobbing over the dead body of Jeffrey Miller. He sent his photographs to the Associated Press, which published this photo around the world. Filo won a Pulitzer Prize for this picture. John Filo.

called "jugular diplomacy," was costly to both sides, but it brought renewed negotiations. On January 27, 1973, representatives of the United States, North Vietnam, South Vietnam, and the Vietcong (now called the People's Revolutionary Government) signed a formal peace accord in Paris. The agreement required removal of all U.S. troops and military advisers from South Vietnam but allowed North Vietnamese forces to remain. Both sides agreed to return prisoners of war. Nixon called the agreement "peace with honor," but in fact it allowed only a face-saving withdrawal for the United States.

Fighting resumed immediately among the Vietnamese. Nixon's efforts to support the South

From the Fall of Saigon to the House of Representatives

Three days before the end of April 1975, eight-year-old Anh Quang Cao was rushed to the crowded airfield near Saigon, South Vietnam, along with his brother and sister. His mother entrusted the children to their aunt, who accompanied them on a flight out of Vietnam. Anh's father had been an officer in the South Vietnamese army, which put the entire family at extreme risk as the People's Army of Vietnam approached from the north for its final assault on Saigon. Anh's mother could send only three of her children; five more remained with their parents.

South Vietnam's capital was in an uproar, with tens of thousands of inhabitants seeking escape. Anyone who had worked for or cooperated with the Americans feared bloody reprisals at the hands of the North Vietnamese. Two days after Anh's plane departed, rockets and artillery fire heavily damaged the airport. Thereafter helicopters took over, shuttling thousands out of Saigon; thousands more made for the docks to get passage on any seaworthy vessel. Both the helicopters and the boats were trying to reach the many ships of the U.S. Seventh Fleet, anchored just beyond Vietnamese territorial waters.

The ships and planes headed for a U.S. military base on Guam, 2,600 miles away, where large camps had been rapidly constructed. Anh found himself among some 64,000 other refugees in a huge tent city pitched on freshly bulldozed land. Among them, the boy located an uncle. Three times a day, the refugees lined up for eggs and bacon, hamburgers, mashed potatoes, fruit cocktail, and other classics of the American diet. The new food was part of a U.S. program dubbed "Operation New Life," rolled out in May to deal with the refugees, who by summer's end numbered 130,000.

After three weeks on Guam, Anh and his uncle joined an airlift of five hundred flights taking refugees to four military bases in the United States. The two were sent to Fort Chaffee, an army reserve base in northwest Arkansas. There they received a limited program of English-language instruction and awaited resettlement.

The U.S. plan for the initial wave of refugees was to disperse them in small numbers to communities in all fifty states. Charitable groups were encouraged to sponsor refugees with minimal government assistance — just $500 per person. Anh and his uncle were sponsored by a Lutheran church in Goshen, Indiana, where the boy entered first grade and his uncle worked in a fast-food restaurant. Anh learned to love snow, and he took an Americanized name: Joseph Cao. After four years in Goshen, Cao and his uncle moved to Texas.

By 1978, a second and larger exodus began leaving Vietnam by boat. Some 20,000 "boat people" per month paid extortionate fees and endured great hardship in crossing the South China Sea. Bad weather and inadequate food and water were less dreaded than horrific attacks by pirates, who robbed, raped, and murdered the expatriates on approximately one-third of the boats. As many as 100,000 people perished, but some half a million came to the United States, aided by the Refugee Act of 1980, which accepted the international definition of a refugee as a person unable to return to his or her country because of a "well-founded fear of persecution." Among late arrivals in this migration stream were Cao's family, his father severely traumatized by nearly seven years of imprisonment and torture in a Communist "reeducation" camp.

An able student, Cao completed high school and earned degrees in physics at Baylor University, in philosophy at Fordham University, and in law at Loyola University. Along the way, he

---

Vietnamese government, and indeed his ability to govern at all, were increasingly eroded by what came to be known as the Watergate scandal (as discussed in chapter 30). Nixon had been forced to give up his office by 1975, when North Vietnam launched a new offensive. On April 30, it occupied Saigon and renamed it Ho Chi Minh City to honor the Communist leader. The Americans hastily evacuated, along with 150,000 of their South Vietnamese allies. (See "Seeking the American Promise," above.)

Confusion, humiliation, and tragedy marked the rushed departure. The United States lacked sufficient transportation capabilities and time to evacuate all the South Vietnamese who had supported the South Vietnamese government and were desperate to leave. Former lieutenant Philip Caputo, who had returned to South Vietnam as a journalist, reported that his departing helicopter "took some ground fire from South Vietnamese soldiers who probably felt that the Americans had betrayed them."

continued to practice Catholicism, the religion of his childhood in Saigon, and he spent six years in a Jesuit seminary, doing missionary work among the poor. He became an immigration lawyer, serving the Vietnamese community in New Orleans. After Hurricane Katrina destroyed his house, he developed political ambitions and ran as an independent for the Louisiana state legislature.

Cao failed in that bid, but Republican Party leaders in Louisiana tapped him to run for Congress in 2008 in a heavily Democratic district. Cao agreed to run as a Republican, citing the debt he felt to John McCain, that year's Republican presidential candidate, who had spent five and a half years in a Hanoi POW camp. In a close election, Cao defeated the incumbent (who was embroiled in corruption charges) and thus became the first Vietnamese American to be elected to the House of Representatives.

In office, Cao proved to be an unconventional Republican, one who called out Wall Street bankers in hearings and cast the lone Republican vote for the first version of the health care reform bill in late 2009. His 2010 campaign for reelection was an uphill battle, and he lost decisively to a Democrat. Cao has returned to his law practice and his young family in New Orleans. In a *New York Times* interview before the election, he credited his philosophical studies for teaching him that "life is absurd but one cannot succumb to the absurdity of it," a fitting adage for his remarkable life story.

Congressman Cao
Vietnamese-American Ahn "Joseph" Cao speaks to constituents at a town hall meeting in Westwego, Louisiana in August 2009. AP Photo/Bill Haber.

Questions for Consideration

1. What were some of the fortunate circumstances in Cao's turbulent life?

2. How was Cao similar to and different from other immigrants in the United States?

During the four years it took Nixon to end the war, he had expanded the conflict into Cambodia and Laos and launched massive bombing campaigns. Although increasing numbers of legislators criticized the war, Congress never denied the president the funds to fight it. Only after the peace accords did the legislative branch try to reassert its constitutional authority in the making of war. The War Powers Act of 1973 required the president to secure congressional approval for any substantial, long-term deployment of troops abroad. The new law, however, did little to dispel the distrust of and disillusionment with the government that resulted from Americans' realization that their leaders had not told the truth about Vietnam.

The Legacy of Defeat

The disorder that had accompanied antiwar protests and bitter divisions among Americans were other legacies of the war. Vietnam diverted

Evacuating South Vietnam

As Communist troops rolled south toward Saigon in the spring of 1975, desperate South Vietnamese attempted to flee along with the departing Americans. These South Vietnamese, carrying little or nothing, attempt to scale the wall of the U.S. Embassy to reach evacuation helicopters. Thousands of Vietnamese who wanted to be evacuated were left behind. Even though space for evacuees was desperately limited, South Vietnamese president Nguyen Van Thieu fled to Taiwan on a U.S. plane, taking with him fifteen tons of baggage. AP Images

of 1975, the rest of Southeast Asia did not. When China and Vietnam reverted to their historically hostile relationship, the myth of a monolithic Communist power overrunning Asia evaporated.

The long pursuit of victory in Vietnam complicated the United States' relations with other nations, as even its staunchest ally, Britain, doubted the wisdom of the war. The spectacle of terrifying American power used against a small Asian country alienated many in the third world and compromised efforts to win the hearts and minds of people in developing nations.

The cruelest legacy of Vietnam fell on those who had served. "The general public just wanted to ignore us," remembered Frederick Downs, while opponents of the war "wanted to argue with us until we felt guilty about what we had done over there." The failure of the United States to win the war, its unpopularity at home, and its character as a guerrilla war denied veterans the traditional soldiers' homecoming. Veterans themselves expressed different reactions to the defeat. Many believed in the war's purposes and felt betrayed by the government for not letting them win it. Other veterans blamed the government for sacrificing the nation's youth in an immoral, unnecessary, or useless war, expressing their sense of the war's futility by referring to their dead comrades as having been "wasted." Some veterans belonging to minority groups had more reason to doubt the nobility of their purpose. A Native American soldier assigned to resettle Vietnamese civilians found it to be "just like when they moved us to the rez [reservation]. We shouldn't have done that."

Because the Vietnam War was a civil war involving guerrilla tactics, combat was especially brutal (Table 29.1). The terrors of conventional warfare were multiplied, and so were the motivations to commit atrocities. The 1968 massacre at My Lai was only the most widely publicized war crime. To demonstrate the immorality of the war, peace advocates stressed the atrocities, contributing to a distorted image of the Vietnam veteran as dehumanized and violent. "Antiwar types considered us to be psychopathic killers," Downs maintained.

Most veterans came home to public neglect. Government benefits were less generous to Vietnam veterans than they had been to those of the previous two wars. While two-thirds of Vietnam veterans said that they would serve again, and while most veterans readjusted well to civilian life, some suffered long after the

money from domestic programs and sounded the death knell for Johnson's Great Society. It created federal budget deficits and triggered inflation that contributed to ongoing economic crises throughout the 1970s (as discussed in chapter 30).

Four presidents had declared that the survival of South Vietnam was essential for U.S. containment policy, but their dire predictions that a Communist victory in South Vietnam would set the dominoes cascading did not materialize. Although Vietnam, Laos, and Cambodia all fell within the Communist camp in the spring

TABLE 29.1	VIETNAM WAR CASUALTIES
United States	
Battle deaths	47,434
Other deaths	10,786
Wounded	153,303
South Vietnam	
Killed in action	110,357
Military wounded	499,026
Civilians killed	415,000
Civilians wounded	913,000
Communist Regulars and Guerrillas	
Killed in action	66,000

Source: U.S. Department of Defense

war ended. The Veterans Administration estimated that nearly one-sixth of the veterans suffered from post-traumatic stress disorder, with its symptoms of recurring nightmares, feelings of guilt and shame, violence, drug and alcohol abuse, and suicidal tendencies. Thirty years after performing army intelligence work in Saigon, Doris Allen "still hit the floor sometimes when [she heard] loud bangs." Many of those who had served in Vietnam began to

produce children with deformities and fell ill themselves with cancer, severe skin disorders, and other ailments. Veterans claimed a link between those illnesses and Agent Orange, which had exposed many to the deadly poison dioxin in Vietnam. Not until 1991 did Congress provide assistance to veterans with diseases linked to the poison.

By then, the climate had changed. The war began to enter the realm of popular culture, with novels, TV shows, and hit movies depicting a broad range of military experience — from soldiers reduced to brutality, to men and women serving with courage and integrity. The incorporation of the Vietnam War into the collective experience was symbolized most dramatically in the Vietnam Veterans Memorial unveiled in Washington, D.C., in November 1982. Designed by Yale architecture student Maya Lin, the black, V-shaped wall inscribed with the names of 58,200 men and women lost in the war became one of the most popular sites in the nation's capital. In an article describing the memorial's dedication, a Vietnam combat veteran spoke to and for his former comrades: "Welcome home. The war is over."

REVIEW   What strategies did Nixon implement to bring American involvement in Vietnam to a close?

The Three Servicemen Statue
This statue was added as an integral part of the Vietnam Veterans Memorial in 1984, after some veterans and politicians protested that the stark, black wall was not an appropriate tribute to the fallen soldiers. Frederick Hart, the sculptor who had placed third in the original competition, created this more traditional memorial. He said, "The contrast between the innocence of their youth and the weapons of war underscores the poignancy of their sacrifice."
© Bettmann/Corbis.

▶ Conclusion: An Unwinnable War

Lieutenant Frederick Downs fought in America's longest war. The United States spent more than $150 billion (more than $800 billion in 2011 dollars) and sent 2.6 million young men and women to Vietnam. Of those, 58,200 never returned, and 150,000, like Downs, suffered serious injury. The war shattered consensus at home, increased presidential power at the expense of congressional authority and public accountability, weakened the economy, and contributed to the downfall of two presidents.

Even as Nixon and Kissinger took steps to ease Cold War tensions with the major Communist powers — the Soviet Union and China — they also acted vigorously throughout the third world to install or prop up anti-Communist governments. They embraced their predecessors' commitment to South Vietnam as a necessary Cold War engagement: To do otherwise would threaten American credibility and make the United States appear weak. Defeat in Vietnam did not make the United States the "pitiful helpless giant" predicted by Nixon, but it did mark a relative decline of U.S. power and the impossibility of containment on a global scale.

One of the constraints on U.S. power was the tenacity of revolutionary movements determined to achieve national independence. Overestimating the effectiveness of American technological superiority, U.S. officials badly underestimated the sacrifices that the enemy was willing to make and failed to realize how easily the United States could be perceived as a colonial intruder. Simply put, Americans were not well prepared for a guerrilla war. "It's a hell of a thing," Downs discovered, "to try to fight a war with all these goddamn civilians around."

A second constraint on Eisenhower, Kennedy, Johnson, and Nixon was their resolve to avoid a major confrontation with the Soviet Union or China. For Johnson, who conducted the largest escalation of the war, caution was critical so as not to provoke direct intervention by the Communist superpowers. After China exploded its first atomic bomb in 1964, the potential heightened for the Vietnam conflict to escalate into worldwide disaster.

Third, in Vietnam the United States sought to prop up an extremely weak ally engaged in a civil war. The South Vietnamese government failed to win the support of its people, and the

intense devastation the war brought to civilians only made things worse. Short of taking over the South Vietnamese government and military, the United States could do little to strengthen South Vietnam's ability to resist communism.

Finally, domestic opposition to the war, which by 1968 had spread to mainstream America, constrained the options of Johnson and Nixon. As the war dragged on, with increasing American casualties and growing evidence of the damage being inflicted on innocent Vietnamese, more and more civilians wearied of the conflict. Even some who had fought in the war joined the peace movement, sending their military ribbons and bitter letters of protest to the White House. In 1973, Nixon and Kissinger bowed to the resolution of the enemy and the limitations of U.S. power. As the war wound down, passions surrounding it contributed to a rising conservative movement that would substantially alter the post–World War II political order.

▶ Selected Bibliography

Foreign Policy under Kennedy, Johnson, and Nixon

H. W. Brands, *The Wages of Globalism: Lyndon Johnson and the Limits of American Power* (1995).
Robert Dallek, *Nixon and Kissinger: Partners in Power* (2007).
Michael Dobbs, *One Minute to Midnight: Kennedy, Khrushchev, and Castro on the Brink of Nuclear War* (2008).
Lawrence Freedman, *Kennedy's Wars: Berlin, Cuba, Laos, and Vietnam* (2000).
Michael Grow, *U.S. Presidents and Latin American Interventions: Pursuing Regime Change in the Cold War* (2008).
Elizabeth Cobbs Hoffman, *All You Need Is Love: The Peace Corps and the Spirit of the 1960s* (1998).
Howard Jones, *The Bay of Pigs* (2008).
Margaret Macmillan, *Nixon and Mao: The Week That Changed the World* (2007).
Walter A. McDougall, *The Heavens and the Earth: A Political History of the Space Age* (1985).
Keith L. Nelson, *The Making of Détente: Soviet-American Relations in the Shadow of Vietnam* (1995).
Stephen G. Rabe, *The Most Dangerous Area in the World: John F. Kennedy Confronts Communist Revolution in Latin America* (1999).

Jeremi Suri, *Power and Protest: Global Revolution and the Rise of Détente* (2003).

The War in Vietnam

Arnold R. Isaacs, *Vietnam Shadows: The War, Its Ghosts, and Its Legacy* (1997).

David Kaiser, *American Tragedy: Kennedy, Johnson, and the Origins of the Vietnam War* (2000).

Jeffrey P. Kimball, *Nixon's Vietnam War* (1998).

A. J. Langguth, *Our Vietnam/Nuoc Viet Ta: A History of the War, 1954–1975* (2000).

Fredrik Logevall, *Choosing War: The Lost Chance for Peace and the Escalation of the War in Vietnam* (1999).

David F. Schmitz, *The Tet Offensive: Politics, War, and Public Opinion* (2005).

Marilyn B. Young, *The Vietnam Wars, 1945–1990* (1991).

Those Who Served

Christian G. Appy, *Working-Class War: American Combat Soldiers in Vietnam* (1993).

Philip Caputo, *A Rumor of War* (1977).

David Donovan, *Once a Warrior King: Memories of an Officer in Vietnam* (1985).

Frederick Downs, *The Killing Zone: My Life in the Vietnam War (1978); Aftermath: A Soldier's Return from Vietnam (1984); No Longer Enemies, Not Yet Friends: An American Soldier Returns to Vietnam* (1991).

Kathryn Marshall, *In the Combat Zone: Vivid Personal Recollections of the Vietnam War from the Women Who Served There* (1987).

Harry Maurer, *Strange Ground: Americans in Vietnam, 1945–1975, an Oral History* (1998).

Al Santoli, *Everything We Had: An Oral History of the Vietnam War* (1981).

James E. Westheider, *Fighting on Two Fronts: African Americans and the Vietnam War* (1997).

Politics and the Antiwar Movement

Dan T. Carter, *The Politics of Race: George Wallace, the Origins of the New Conservatism, and the Transformation of American Politics* (1995).

Charles DeBenedetti, with Charles Chatfield, *An American Ordeal: The Antiwar Movement in the Vietnam Era* (1990).

Michael S. Foley, *Confronting the War Machine: Draft Resistance during the Vietnam War* (2003).

Andrew E. Hunt, *The Turning: A History of Vietnam Veterans against the War* (1999).

Rhodri Jeffreys-Jones, *Peace Now! American Society and the Ending of the Vietnam War* (1999).

David Rudenstine, *The Day the Presses Stopped: A History of the Pentagon Papers Case* (1996).

Amy Swerdlow, *Women Strike for Peace: Traditional Motherhood and Radical Politics in the 1960s* (1993).

▶ FOR MORE BOOKS ABOUT TOPICS IN THIS CHAPTER, see the Online Bibliography at bedfordstmartins.com/roark.

▶ FOR ADDITIONAL PRIMARY SOURCES FROM THIS PERIOD, see Michael Johnson, ed., *Reading the American Past*, Fifth Edition.

▶ FOR WEB SITES, IMAGES, AND DOCUMENTS RELATED TO TOPICS AND PLACES IN THIS CHAPTER, visit Make History at bedfordstmartins.com/roark.

Reviewing Chapter 29

REVIEW QUESTIONS

Use key terms and dates to support your answer.

1. Why did Kennedy believe that engagement in Vietnam was crucial to his foreign policy? (pp. 971–977)

2. Why did massive amounts of airpower and ground troops fail to bring U.S. victory in Vietnam? (pp. 978–982)

3. How did the Vietnam War shape the election of 1968? (pp. 982–989)

4. What strategies did Nixon implement to bring American involvement in Vietnam to a close? (pp. 989–997)

MAKING CONNECTIONS

Draw on key terms, the timeline, and review questions.

1. Cuba featured prominently in the most dramatic foreign policy actions of the Kennedy administration. Citing specific events, discuss why Cuba was an area of great concern to the administration. How did Cuba figure into Kennedy's Cold War policies? Were his actions regarding Cuba effective?

2. Explain the Gulf of Tonkin incident and its significance to American foreign policy. How did President Lyndon Johnson respond to the incident? What considerations, domestic and international, contributed to his course of action?

3. The United States' engagement in Vietnam divided the nation. Discuss the range of American responses to the war. How did they change over time? How did the war shape domestic politics in the 1960s and early 1970s?

4. What was détente, and how did it affect the United States' Cold War foreign policy? What were its achievements and limitations? In your answer, discuss how Nixon's approach to communism built on and departed from the approaches of the previous two administrations.

LINKING TO THE PAST

Link events in this chapter to earlier events.

1. What commitments were made in the Truman and Eisenhower administrations that resulted in the United States' full-scale involvement in Vietnam? (See chapters 26 and 27.)

2. Compare public sentiment during America's involvement in World War II to that during its involvement in Vietnam. What policies, events, attitudes, and technological advancements contributed to the differences? (See chapter 25.)

▶ **FOR PRACTICE QUIZZES AND OTHER STUDY TOOLS,** visit the Online Study Guide at bedfordstmartins.com/roark.

TIMELINE 1961–1975

1961
- Bay of Pigs invasion.
- Berlin Wall erected.
- Kennedy administration increases military aid to South Vietnam.
- Alliance for Progress established.
- Peace Corps created.

1962
- Cuban missile crisis.

1963
- Limited nuclear test ban treaty signed.
- President Kennedy assassinated; Lyndon B. Johnson becomes president.

1964
- Anti-American rioting brings U.S. troops to Panama Canal Zone.
- Gulf of Tonkin Resolution.

1965
- First major demonstration against Vietnam War.
- Operation Rolling Thunder begins.
- Johnson orders first combat troops to Vietnam.
- U.S. troops invade Dominican Republic.

1967
- Arab-Israeli Six-Day War.

1968
- Demonstrations against Vietnam War increase.
- Tet Offensive.
- Johnson decides not to seek second term.
- Police and protesters clash near Democratic convention in Chicago.
- Republican Richard Nixon elected president.

1969
- American astronauts land on moon.

1970
- Nixon orders invasion of Cambodia.
- Students killed during protests at Kent State and Jackson State.

1971
- *New York Times* publishes *Pentagon Papers*.

1972
- Nixon becomes first U.S. president to visit China.
- Nixon visits Moscow to sign arms limitation treaties with Soviets.

1973
- Paris Peace Accords.
- War Powers Act.
- CIA-backed military coup in Chile.
- Arab oil embargo following Yom Kippur War.

1975
- North Vietnam takes over South Vietnam, ending the war.
- Helsinki accords.

MAKING AMERICA "REAGAN COUNTRY"

This delegate badge from the 1980 Republican National Convention displayed themes that would characterize Ronald Reagan's presidential campaigns and politics in the 1980s. Images of the flag, the Statue of Liberty, and the space program invoked patriotic sentiments, and Reagan's image as a cowboy spoke to the rugged individualism of the West, where he had made his home. The West housed key elements in the surge of conservatism that ensured Reagan's victory in 1980, shaped his administration's antigovernment, anti-Communist agenda, and helped reverse the liberal direction that national politics had taken in the 1960s. In the background conventional delegates cheer for their nominee.
Badge: National Museum of American History, Smithsonian Institution, Behring Center; background: Ronald Reagan Presidential Library.

30

America Moves to the Right
1969–1989

PHYLLIS SCHLAFLY CALLED IT "ONE OF THE MOST EXCITING DAYS OF my life" when she heard conservative Republican Barry Goldwater address the National Federation of Republican Women in 1963. Like Goldwater, Schlafly opposed the moderate stance of the Eisenhower administration and current Republican leadership. Both Schlafly and Goldwater wanted the United States to do more than just contain communism — they wanted to eliminate that threat entirely. They also wanted to cut back the federal government, especially its role in providing social welfare and enforcing civil rights. Goldwater's loss to Lyndon Johnson in 1964 did not diminish Schlafly's conservative commitment. She assailed the policy innovations and turmoil of the 1960s, adding new issues to the conservative agenda and cultivating a grassroots movement that would redefine the Republican Party and American politics into the twenty-first century.

Phyllis Stewart was born in St. Louis in 1924, attended Catholic schools, and worked her way through Washington University testing ammunition at a World War II defense plant. She earned a master's degree in government from Radcliffe College in 1945 and went to work at the American Enterprise Institute, where she imbibed the think tank's conservatism. Returning to the Midwest, she married Fred Schlafly, an Alton, Illinois, attorney whose anticommunism and antigovernment passions equaled hers. The mother of six children, Schlafly claimed, "I don't think there's anything as much fun as taking care of a baby," and she asserted that she would "rather scrub bathroom floors" than write political articles.

Yet while insisting that caring for home and family was women's most important career, Schlafly spent much of her time on the road — writing, speaking, leading Republican women's organizations, and testifying before legislative committees. She ran twice for Congress but lost in her heavily Democratic district in Illinois. Her book, *A Choice Not an Echo*, pushed Barry Goldwater for president and sold more than three million copies. In 1967, she began publishing *The Phyllis Schlafly Report*, a monthly newsletter about current political issues. Throughout the 1950s and 1960s, Schlafly called for stronger efforts to combat communism at home and abroad, a more powerful military, and a less active government in domestic affairs — all traditional conservative goals.

In the 1970s, Schlafly began to address new issues, including feminism and the Equal Rights Amendment, abortion, gay rights, busing for racial integration, and religion in the schools. Her positions resonated with many Americans who were fed up with the expansion of government, the Supreme Court decisions, the protest movements, the challenges to authority, and the loosening of moral standards that seemed to define the 1960s. And the votes of those Americans began to reshape politics — in Richard Nixon's victories in 1968 and 1972; in the presidency of Jimmy Carter, whose policies stood to the right of his Democratic predecessors; and in the conservative Ronald Reagan's capture of the Republican Party, the presidency, and the political agenda in 1980.

Although Richard Nixon did not embrace the entire conservative agenda, he sought to make the Republicans the dominant party by appealing to disaffected blue-collar and southern white Democrats. The Watergate revelations forced Nixon to resign the presidency in 1974, and his Republican successor, Gerald Ford, occupied the Oval Office for little more than two years, but the shift of the political spectrum to the right continued even when Democrat Jimmy Carter captured the White House in 1976.

Antigovernment sentiment grew out of the deceptions of the Johnson administration, Nixon's abuse of presidential powers, and the inability of Presidents Ford and Carter to resolve domestic and foreign crises. As Americans saw their incomes shrink from an unprecedented combination of unemployment and inflation — called stagflation — their confidence in government and willingness to pay taxes eroded.

In 1980, Phyllis Schlafly's earlier call for "a choice not an echo" was realized when Ronald Reagan won the presidency. Cutting taxes and government regulations, attacking social programs, expanding the nation's military capacity, and pressuring the Soviet Union and communism in the third world, Reagan addressed the hopes of traditional conservatives. Like Schlafly, he also championed the concerns of Christian conservatives, who opposed abortion and sexual permissiveness and supported a larger role for religion in public life.

Reagan's goals encountered resistance from feminists, civil rights groups, environmentalists, and others who fought to keep what they had won in the 1960s and 1970s. Although Reagan failed to enact the entire conservative agenda, enormously increased the national debt, and engaged in illegal activities to thwart communism in Latin America, his popularity helped send his vice president, George H. W. Bush, to the White House at the end of his second term. And Reagan's determined optimism and spirited leadership contributed to a revival in national pride and confidence.

The Phyllis Schlafly Report

Phyllis Schlafly began her newsletter in 1967 with articles attacking federal social programs and calling for stronger measures and weapons to fight communism. When Congress passed the Equal Rights Amendment in 1972, the *Report* added antifeminism and other concerns of the New Right to its agenda, including opposition to abortion rights, to sex education in the schools, and to protections for gays and lesbians. Schlafly had more than 35,000 newsletter subscribers in the mid-1970s; she also had many adversaries. Feminist leader Betty Friedan told Schlafly, "I consider you a traitor to your sex. I consider you an Aunt Tom." Courtesy of Phyllis Schlafly.

▶ Nixon, Conservatism, and Constitutional Crisis

As we saw in chapter 28, Nixon acquiesced in continuing most Great Society programs and even approved pathbreaking environmental and minority and women's rights measures. Yet his public rhetoric and some of his actions signaled the country's rightward move. Whereas Kennedy had appealed to Americans to contribute to the common good, Nixon invited Americans to "let each of us ask — not just what will government do for me, but what can I do for myself?" His words invoked individualism and reliance on private enterprise rather than on government. These preferences would grow stronger in the nation during the 1970s and beyond, as a new strand of conservatism joined the older movement that focused on anticommunism, a strong national defense, and a limited federal role in domestic affairs. New conservatives, whom **Phyllis Schlafly** helped mobilize, wanted to restore what they considered traditional moral values by increasing the presence of Christianity in public life.

Nixon won a resounding victory in the 1972 election. Two years later, however, his abuse of power and efforts to cover up crimes committed by subordinates, revealed in the so-called Watergate scandal, forced the first presidential resignation in history. His handpicked successor, Gerald Ford, faced the aftermath of Watergate and severe economic problems, which returned the White House to the Democrats in 1976. Nonetheless, the rising conservative tide challenged the Democratic administration that followed.

Emergence of a Grassroots Movement

Hidden beneath Lyndon Johnson's landslide victory over Arizona senator Barry Goldwater in 1964 lay a rising conservative movement. Defining his purpose as "enlarging freedom at home and safeguarding it from the forces of tyranny abroad," Goldwater echoed the ideas of conservative intellectuals who argued that government intrusions into economic life hindered prosperity, stifled personal responsibility, and interfered with individuals' rights to determine their own values. Conservatives assailed big government in domestic affairs but demanded a strong military to eradicate "Godless communism."

Behind Goldwater's nomination was a growing grassroots movement. Vigorous especially in the South and West, it included middle-class suburban women and men, members of the rabidly anti-Communist John Birch Society, and college students in the new Young Americans for Freedom (YAF). They did not give up when Goldwater lost the election. In California, newly energized conservatives helped Ronald Reagan defeat the incumbent liberal governor, Edmund Brown, in 1966. Linking Brown with the Watts riot and student disruptions at the University of California at Berkeley (see chapter 28), Reagan exploited popular fears about rising taxes, student rebellion, and black demands for justice.

Grassroots conservatism was not limited to the West and South, but a number of Sun Belt characteristics made it especially strong in places such as Orange County, California; Dallas, Texas; and Scottsdale, Arizona. Such predominantly white areas contained relatively homogeneous, skilled, and economically comfortable populations, as well as military bases and defense production facilities. The West harbored a long-standing tradition of Protestant morality, individualism, and opposition to interference by a remote federal government. That tradition continued with the growing conservative movement, even though it was hardly consistent with the Sun Belt's economic dependence on defense spending and on huge federal projects providing water and power for the burgeoning population and its economy.

The South, which also benefited from military bases and the space program, shared the West's antipathy toward the federal government. Hostility to racial change, however, was much more central to the South's conservatism. After signing the Civil Rights Act of 1964, President Lyndon Johnson remarked privately, "I think we just delivered the South to the Republican Party." Indeed, Barry Goldwater carried five southern states in 1964.

Grassroots movements proliferated around what conservatives believed marked the "moral decline" of their nation. For example, in 1962 Mel and Norma Gabler succeeded in getting the Texas board of education to drop books that they found not in conformity with "the Christian-Judeo morals, values, and standards as given to us by God through . . . the Bible." Sex education roused the ire of Eleanor

> "Nothing [in the sex education curriculum] depicted my values. . . . It wasn't so much the information. It was the shift in values."
>
> —ELEANOR HOWE, a parent from Anaheim, California

A Mother Campaigns for a Say in Her Children's Education

Although historians usually trace the rise of conservatism through national politics, the most intense political battles of the 1970s and 1980s were often fought at the local level. None were more impassioned than those mounted by parents over what their children should be taught in the public schools. The introduction of sex education and new textbooks in the Kanawha County, West Virginia, school district prompted Alice Moore to challenge instruction she deemed harmful to her children and to organize a movement to gain parents' control over their children's education.

The diverse school district of Kanawha County encompassed the state capital of Charleston as well as surrounding towns and rural areas containing chemical plants, coal mines, and small hamlets. Alice Moore, a native of Mississippi, and her husband, a fundamentalist minister, lived in a small town on the outskirts of Charleston, where their four children attended local schools. When she heard that sex education was coming to Kanawha County, she rallied like-minded citizens and won a seat on the five-person school board in 1970. She failed to terminate the sex education program, which she found a "humanistic, atheistic attack on God," but managed to dilute the curriculum.

The district's adoption of a new English language arts curriculum in 1974 provoked even greater controversy. The program, similar to those sweeping school districts across the country, sought to teach children about the larger world, incorporated writings by African Americans and other minority groups, and encouraged students to think critically and independently.

Objecting to both the philosophy and the content of the new curriculum, Alice Moore began to mobilize opposition, calling on fundamentalist ministers and holding meetings in churches. In June 1974, at a meeting before an impassioned crowd of more than a thousand, she persuaded the school board to eliminate 8 of the curriculum's 325 books but failed to prevent adoption of the curriculum by a vote of three to two. Opponents then redoubled their efforts, and the textbook war was on, echoing concerns that were energizing the Christian Right across the country.

Protesters condemned what they considered disrespect for authority, American patriotism, and the free enterprise system in the new materials. One of Moore's allies, a conservative chemical company owner, vilified the curriculum as "liberal, socialist, even communist-inspired." Textbook

opponents also challenged the authority of distant "experts" to decide what was best for their children.

Furthermore, Moore and her supporters objected to the curriculum's multicultural materials, designed to illustrate the diversity of American society. Antitextbook forces disliked the nonstandard English that appeared in some of the literature, as well as what they considered the "trashy" aspects of urban ghetto life. "Why the hell do we have to indoctrinate our children out here in semi-rural communities with the problems of the inner city?" a protester asked.

The new sexual permissiveness emerging in the 1960s also aroused antitextbook forces. The sexual realism in some of the materials inflamed fundamentalist protesters above all because it defied their belief in the system of right and wrong laid out in the Bible, which they interpreted literally. To Moore, morality was not a relative issue: "God's law is absolute."

Such deeply held beliefs inspired opponents to keep their children home when school opened in September, achieving an absentee rate of around 20 percent. Defying their union leadership, thousands of miners went out on a sympathy strike while protesters set up picket lines and staged demonstrations. Three schools were bombed, district headquarters were dynamited, and guns were fired on both sides. Antitextbook supporters streamed into Charleston, including representatives from the Heritage Foundation, the John Birch Society, and the Ku Klux Klan. The violence gradually subsided, but protests went on through April 1975.

The school board ended up keeping most of the new curriculum, but

Howe in Anaheim, California, who felt that "nothing [in the sex education curriculum] depicted my values. . . . It wasn't so much the information. It was the shift in values." (See "Seeking the American Promise," above.) The Supreme Court's liberal decisions on issues such as school prayer, obscenity, and abortion also galvanized conservatives to restore "traditional values" to the nation.

In the 1970s, grassroots protests against taxes grew alongside concerns about morality. As Americans struggled with inflation and unemployment, many found themselves paying higher taxes, especially higher property taxes as the value of their homes increased. In 1978, Californians revolted in a popular referendum, reducing property taxes by more than one-half

parents were allowed to designate those books they did not want their children to read, and many teachers avoided hassles by not using any of the new books. The board also set new guidelines for choosing textbooks, which included banning materials that contained profanity, that looked favorably on different forms of government, or that "intrude[d] into the privacy of students' homes by asking personal questions about the inner feelings or behavior of themselves or their parents."

Conflicts over public school curricula, involving such topics as evolution, continued to strike communities throughout the nation into the twenty-first century, although none equaled the war in Kanawha County. Some conservative parents retreated from the public schools entirely. By 2007, parents were homeschooling 1.5 million children, and the number of private Christian schools soared, accommodating parents who, in Moore's words, "can't put their children in public schools and allow them to have their beliefs torn away." Those who believed that students should be exposed to a diversity of ideas in order to form their own beliefs were in the majority, but Christian conservatives such as Moore continued to fight for control over what their children were taught.

Questions for Consideration

1. What specific features of the new English arts curriculum did Alice Moore and her supporters object to?

2. What values of the New Right were reflected in the antitextbook campaign?

RE-ELECT
ALICE MOORE
FOR
BOARD of EDUCATION

Dear Friends,

The schools belong to the people who pay for them, not Washington Bureaucrats, not School Administrators, not National Education Organizations.

Nationally, education is costing us more than **61 billion dollars** a year, more than is spent on education by all the rest of the world combined. This is a **1000 percent increase** in 20 years while enrollment has barely doubled. Yet, almost **one third** of our high school graduates cannot pass college placement exams and this number **increases** annually.

Are your children getting the education you want for them? I am convinced most parents expect the schools, for which we pay and for which we provide the children, to:

- Offer the best academic education possible with emphasis on basic skills.

- Respect family privacy and our right as parents to rear our children according to **our own moral, ethical and religious beliefs** without interference.

- Provide a disciplined and morally up-lifting educational climate for the safety and peace of mind for both students and teachers. **Stop coddling the class trouble-makers at the expense of serious minded students.**

- Operate the schools as efficiently as private enterprise.

As a board member, I have tried to represent the **public interest,** not an Educational Bureaucracy. This is the kind of education I want for my five children. If this is what you want, please give me your vote and contact your friends on my behalf.

Sincerely yours,

(Mrs.) Alice Moore

The **final** board vote is at the May 11 primary. Democrats, Republicans and Independents can vote for me, for this non-partisan position.

Alice Moore Campaigns for the School Board
Alice Moore's campaign for reelection to the Kanawha County Board of Education in 1976 emphasized moral issues and fiercely attacked "Washington Bureaucrats" and government expenditures. Moore had run her first campaign for the board with the slogan "We need a mother on the board of education." She bore her fifth child while serving on the board, but one of the policies she championed prohibited pregnant girls from attending high school because she considered them "disruptive." Moore left Charleston in 1980 when her husband moved to a new church in Ohio. WV Division of Culture & History.

---

and limiting the state legislature's ability to raise taxes. Howard Jarvis, leader of the antitax movement, insisted, "You will have to take control of the government again, or else it is going to control you." What a newspaper called a "primal scream by the People against Big Government" spread to similar antitax crusades in other states.

Nixon Courts the Right

In his 1968 presidential campaign, Richard Nixon exploited hostility to black protest and new civil rights policies, wooing white southerners and a considerable number of northern voters away from the Democratic Party. As president, he used this "southern strategy" to make further

The Tax Revolt
Neighbors gather on the lawn of Los Angeles homeowner Mark Slade to rally for Proposition 13, an initiative campaign launched by conservative activist Howard Jarvis in 1978. Many homeowners rallied to Jarvis's antitax movement because rising land values and new assessments had increased their property taxes sharply, as their signs indicate. After Californians passed Proposition 13 by a large majority, tax revolts spread across the nation. Some thirty-seven states cut property taxes, and twenty-eight reduced income taxes. The tax issue helped the Republican Party end nearly half a century of Democratic dominance. Tony Korody/Getty Images.

"We've had all we can take of judicial interference with local schools," Phyllis Schlafly railed in 1972.

Children had been riding buses to school for decades, but busing for racial integration provoked fury. Violence erupted in Boston in 1974 when a district judge found that school officials had maintained what amounted to a dual system based on race and ordered busing "if necessary to achieve a unitary school system." When black students began to attend the formerly all-white South Boston High School, white students boycotted classes, and angry whites threw rocks at black students getting off buses. The whites most affected by busing came from working-class families who remained in cities abandoned by the more affluent and whose children often rode buses to predominantly black, overcrowded schools with deficient facilities. Clarence McDonough decried the liberal officials who bused his "kid half way around Boston so that a bunch of politicians can end up their careers with a clear conscience." African Americans themselves were conflicted about sending their children on long rides to schools where white teachers might not welcome or respect them.

White parents eventually became more accepting of integration, especially after the creation of magnet schools and other new mechanisms for desegregation offered more choice. Nonetheless, integration propelled white flight to the suburbs. By 1987, the number of white students in Boston public schools was just one-third of what it had been in 1974. Nixon failed to persuade Congress to end court-ordered busing, but after he had appointed four new justices, the Supreme Court imposed strict limits on the use of that tool to achieve racial balance.

Nixon's judicial appointments also reflected the southern strategy. He criticized the Supreme Court under Chief Justice Earl Warren for being "unprecedentedly politically active . . . using their interpretation of the law to remake American society according to their own social, political, and ideological precepts." When Warren resigned in 1969, Nixon replaced him with **Warren E. Burger**, a federal appeals court judge who was a strict constructionist — someone inclined to interpret the Constitution narrowly and to limit government intervention on behalf of individual rights. The Burger Court proved

inroads into traditional Democratic strongholds in the 1972 election.

The Nixon administration reluctantly enforced court orders to achieve high degrees of integration in southern schools, but it resisted efforts to deal with segregation outside the South. In northern and western cities, where segregation resulted from discrimination in housing and in the drawing of school district boundaries, half of all African American children attended nearly all-black schools. After courts began to order the transfer of students between schools in white and black neighborhoods to achieve desegregation, busing became "political dynamite," according to a Gallup poll.

Integration of Public Schools, 1968

Percent of black students statewide attending schools more than 50% white

60% or more	30–40%
50–60%	20–30%
40–50%	20% or less

School Busing
Controversy over busing as a means to integrate public schools erupted in Boston when the 1974–1975 school year started. Opposition was especially high in white ethnic neighborhoods such as South Boston. Residents there resented liberal judges from the suburbs assigning them the burden of integration. Clashes between blacks and whites in South Boston, such as this one in February 1975 outside Boston's Hyde Park High School, prompted authorities to dispatch police to protect black students.
AP Photo.

more sympathetic than the Warren Court to the president's agenda, restricting somewhat the protections of individual rights established by the previous Court, but continuing to uphold many of the liberal programs of the 1960s. For example, the Court limited the range of affirmative action in *Regents of the University of California v. Bakke* (1978), but it allowed universities to consider race as one factor in admission decisions if they avoided strict quotas.

Nixon's southern strategy and other repercussions of the civil rights revolution of the 1960s ended the Democratic hold on the "solid South." In 1964, South Carolina senator Strom Thurmond, leader of the Dixiecrat challenge to Truman in 1948 (see chapter 26), changed his party affiliation to Republican. North Carolina senator Jesse Helms followed suit in 1971, and politicians throughout the South began to realize that the future for Democratic candidates had darkened there. By 2005, Republicans held the majority of southern seats in Congress and governorships in seven southern states.

In addition to exploiting racial fears, Nixon aligned himself with those anxious about women's changing roles and new demands. In 1971, he vetoed a bill providing federal funds for day care centers with a message that combined the old and new conservatism. Parents should purchase

child care services "in the private, open market," he insisted, not rely on government. He appealed to social conservatives by warning about the measure's "family-weakening implications." In response to the movement to liberalize abortion laws, Nixon sided with "defenders of the right to life of the unborn." He did not comment publicly on *Roe v. Wade* (1973), which legalized abortion, but his earlier stance against abortion anticipated the Republican Party's eventual embrace of this as a key issue.

The Election of 1972

Nixon's ability to attract Democrats and appeal to concerns about Vietnam, race, law and order, and traditional morality heightened his prospects for reelection in 1972. Although the war in Vietnam continued, antiwar protests diminished with the decrease in American ground forces and casualties. Nixon's economic initiatives had temporarily checked inflation and unemployment (see chapter 28), and his attacks on busing and antiwar protesters had won increasing support from the right.

A large field of contenders vied for the Democratic nomination, including New York congresswoman **Shirley Chisholm**, the first African American to make a serious bid for the presidency. South Dakota senator George S. McGovern came to the Democratic convention as the clear leader, and the new makeup of the convention delegates made his position even stronger. After the bitter 1968 convention in Chicago (see chapter 29), the Democrats reformed their rules, requiring delegations to represent the proportions of minorities, women, and young people in their states. These newcomers displaced many regular Democrats — officeholders, labor leaders, and representatives of older ethnic groups. One labor leader grumbled that "the Democratic party was taken over by the kooks," referring to the considerable numbers of young people and women who were to the left of party regulars. Though easily nominated, McGovern struggled against Nixon from the outset. Republicans portrayed him as a left-wing extremist, and his support for busing, a generous welfare program, and immediate withdrawal from Vietnam alienated conservative Democrats.

Nixon achieved a landslide victory, winning 60.7 percent of the popular vote and every state except Massachusetts. Although the Democrats maintained control of Congress, Nixon won majorities among traditional Democrats — southerners, Catholics, urbanites, and blue-collar workers. The president, however, had little time to savor his triumph, as revelations began to emerge about crimes committed to ensure the victory.

Watergate

During the early-morning hours of June 17, 1972, five men working for Nixon's reelection campaign crept into Democratic Party headquarters in the Watergate complex in Washington, D.C. Intending to repair a bugging device installed in an earlier break-in, they were discovered and arrested. Nixon and his aides then tried to cover up the intruders' connection to administration officials, setting in motion the most serious constitutional crisis since the Civil War. Reporters dubbed the scandal **Watergate**.

Over the next two years, Americans learned that Nixon and his associates had engaged in other abuses, such as accepting illegal contributions and unlawfully attempting to silence critics of the administration. Nixon was not the first president to lie to the public or to misuse power. Every president since Franklin D. Roosevelt had enlarged the powers of his office in the name of national security. This expansion of executive powers, often called the "imperial presidency," weakened the traditional checks and balances on the executive branch and opened the door to abuses. No president, however, had dared go as far as Nixon, who saw opposition to his policies as a personal attack and was willing to violate the Constitution to stop it.

Upon the arrest of the Watergate burglars, Nixon publicly denied any connection to them, while plotting secretly to have the CIA keep the FBI from investigating the crime. In April 1973, after investigations by a grand jury and the Senate suggested that White House aides had been involved in the cover-up effort, Nixon accepted official responsibility for Watergate but denied any knowledge of the break-in or cover-up. He also announced the resignations of three White House aides and the attorney general. In May, he authorized the appointment of an independent special prosecutor, Archibald Cox, to conduct an investigation.

The Gap in the Watergate Tapes
Franklin Roosevelt installed the first recording apparatus in the White House in 1940, but Nixon was the first president to use a voice-activated system, taping about 2,800 hours of conversations. When Nixon turned over the tapes during the Watergate investigation, an eighteen-and-a-half-minute gap appeared in a conversation between Nixon and his chief of staff, H. R. Haldeman, just three days after the Watergate break-in. Nixon's secretary, Rose Mary Woods, said that her foot must have slipped on the controls while she was transcribing the tape, using the transcription machine pictured here. Others suspected that Nixon had tampered with the evidence. Nixon Presidential Materials Project, National Archives and Records Administration.

Meanwhile, sensational revelations exploded in testimony before the Senate investigating committee, headed by Democrat Samuel J. Ervin of North Carolina. White House counsel John Dean described projects to harass "enemies" through tax audits and other illegal means and implicated the president in efforts to cover up the Watergate break-in. Another White House aide struck the most damaging blow when he disclosed that all conversations in the Oval Office were taped. Both Cox and the Ervin committee immediately asked for the tapes related to Watergate. When Nixon refused, citing executive privilege and separation of powers, Cox and Ervin won a unanimous decision from the Supreme Court ordering him to release the tapes.

Additional disclosures exposed Nixon's misuse of federal funds and tax evasion. In August 1973, Vice President Spiro Agnew resigned after an investigation revealed that he had taken bribes while governor of Maryland. Although Nixon's choice of House minority leader Gerald Ford of Michigan to succeed Agnew won widespread approval, Agnew's resignation further tarnished the administration, and Nixon's popular support plummeted to 27 percent.

In February 1974, the House of Representatives voted to begin an impeachment investigation. Upon reading passages from the White House tapes, House Republican leader Hugh Scott of Pennsylvania abandoned his support of the president, calling the transcripts a "deplorable, shabby, disgusting, and immoral performance by all." The transcripts revealed Nixon's orders

to aides in March 1973: "I don't give a shit what happens. I want you all to stonewall it, let them plead the Fifth Amendment, cover up or anything else, if it'll save it — save the plan."

In July 1974, the House Judiciary Committee voted to impeach the president on three counts: obstruction of justice, abuse of power, and contempt of Congress. Seven or eight Republicans on the committee sided with the majority, and it seemed certain that the House would follow suit. Georgia state legislator and civil rights activist Julian Bond commented, "The prisons of Georgia are full of people who stole $5 or $10, and this man tried to steal the Constitution."

To avoid impeachment, Nixon announced his resignation to a national television audience on August 8, 1974. Acknowledging some incorrect judgments, he insisted that he had always tried to do what was best for the nation. The next morning, Nixon ended a rambling, emotional farewell to his staff with some advice: "Always give your best, never get discouraged, never get petty; always remember, others may hate you, but those who hate you don't win unless you hate them, and then you destroy yourself." Had he practiced that advice, he might have saved his presidency.

The Ford Presidency and the 1976 Election

Gerald R. Ford, who had represented Michigan in the House of Representatives since 1948, had built a reputation as a middle-of-the-road party

Nixon Resigns
The first president in U.S. history to resign his office, Nixon refused to admit guilt, even though tapes of his conversations indicated that he had obstructed justice, abused his power, and lied. In the decades after his resignation, he gradually rehabilitated his reputation and became an elder statesman and foreign policy adviser. All the living presidents attended his funeral in 1994. Here, he and his wife, Pat, are escorted by his successor, Gerald Ford, and his wife, Betty, as they leave the White House. © Bettmann/Corbis.

loyalist known for his integrity, humility, and dedication to public office. "I'm a Ford, not a Lincoln," he acknowledged. Most of official Washington and the American public looked favorably on his succession as president.

Upon taking office, Ford announced, "Our long national nightmare is over." But he shocked many Americans one month later by granting Nixon a pardon "for all offenses against the United States which he . . . has committed or may have committed or taken part in" during his presidency. Prompted by Ford's concern for Nixon's physical and mental health and by his hope to get the country beyond Watergate, this sweeping pardon saved Nixon from nearly certain indictment and trial, and it provoked a tremendous outcry from Congress and the public. Democrats made impressive gains in the November congressional elections, while Ford's action gave Nixon a new political life. Having gained a pardon without having to admit that he had violated the law, Nixon rebuilt his image over the next two decades into that of an elder statesman. Thirty of his associates ultimately pleaded guilty to or were convicted of crimes related to Watergate.

Congress's efforts to guard against the types of abuses revealed in the Watergate investigations had only limited effects. The **Federal Election Campaign Act of 1974** established public financing of presidential campaigns and imposed some restrictions on contributions to help prevent the selling of political favors. Yet politicians found other ways of raising money—for example, through political action committees (PACs), to which individuals could contribute more than they could to candidates. Moreover, in the 1976 case *Buckley v. Valeo*, the Supreme Court struck down limitations on campaign spending as violations of freedom of speech. Ever-larger campaign donations flowed to candidates from interest groups, corporations, labor unions, and wealthy individuals.

Special congressional investigating committees discovered a host of illegal FBI and CIA activities stretching back to the 1950s, including harassment of political dissenters and plots to assassinate Fidel Castro and other foreign leaders. In response to these revelations, President Ford established new controls on covert operations, and Congress created permanent committees to oversee the intelligence agencies. Yet these measures did little to diminish the public's cynicism about their government.

Disillusionment grew as the Ford administration struggled with serious economic problems: a low growth rate, high unemployment, a foreign trade deficit, and soaring energy prices. Ford

carried these burdens into the election campaign of 1976, while contending with a major challenge from the Republican right. Blasting Nixon's and Ford's foreign policy of détente for causing the "loss of U.S. military supremacy," California governor Reagan came close to capturing the nomination.

The Democrats nominated **James Earl "Jimmy" Carter Jr.**, former governor of Georgia. A graduate of the U.S. Naval Academy, Carter spent seven years as a nuclear engineer in the navy before returning to Plains, Georgia, to run the family peanut farming business. Carter prided himself on his knowledge of policy issues, but people responded most to his promise of honesty and decency in government. He stressed his faith as a "born-again Christian" and his distance from the government in Washington. Although he selected liberal senator **Walter F. Mondale** of Minnesota as his running mate, Carter's nomination nonetheless marked a rightward turn in the party.

Carter had considerable appeal as a candidate who carried his own bags, lived modestly, and taught a Bible class at his Baptist church. He also benefited from Ford's failure to solve the country's economic problems, which helped him win the traditional Democratic coalition of blacks, organized labor, and ethnic groups and even

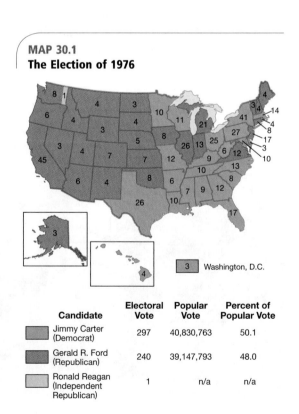

MAP 30.1
The Election of 1976

Candidate	Electoral Vote	Popular Vote	Percent of Popular Vote
Jimmy Carter (Democrat)	297	40,830,763	50.1
Gerald R. Ford (Republican)	240	39,147,793	48.0
Ronald Reagan (Independent Republican)	1	n/a	n/a

recapture some of the white southerners who had voted for Nixon in 1972. Still, Carter received just 50 percent of the popular vote to Ford's 48 percent (Map 30.1), although Democrats retained substantial margins in Congress.

REVIEW How did Nixon's policies reflect the increasing influence of conservatives on the Republican Party?

▶ The "Outsider" Presidency of Jimmy Carter

Carter promised a government that was "competent" as well as "decent, open, fair, and compassionate." He also warned Americans "that even our great Nation has its recognized limits, and that we can neither answer all questions nor solve all problems." Carter's humility and personal integrity helped revive trust in the presidency, but he faltered in the face of domestic and foreign crises.

Energy shortages and stagflation worsened, exposing Carter's deficiencies in working with Congress and rallying the public to his objectives. His administration achieved notable advances in environmental and energy policies, and he oversaw foreign policy successes concerning the Panama Canal, China, and the Middle East. Yet near the end of his term, Soviet-American relations deteriorated, new crises emerged in the Middle East, and the economy plummeted, all costing him a second term.

Retreat from Liberalism

Jimmy Carter vowed "to help the poor and aged, to improve education, and to provide jobs," but at the same time "not to waste money." When these goals conflicted, reform took second place to budget balancing. Carter's approach pleased increasing numbers of Americans unhappy about their tax dollars being used to benefit the disadvantaged while stagflation eroded their own standard of living. But his fiscal stringency frustrated liberal Democrats pushing for major welfare reform and a national health insurance program. Carter himself said, "In many cases I feel more at home with the conservative Democratic and Republican members of Congress than I do with the others."

Carter did fulfill liberals' desire to make government more inclusive. He appointed Andrew Young, former congressman and assistant to Martin Luther King Jr., as the first African American ambassador to the United Nations; and he named four women, including the first two black women, as cabinet heads. Moreover, Carter began to transform the federal judiciary. He appointed forty women to federal judgeships, five times as many as had

> "In many cases I feel more at home with the conservative Democratic and Republican members of Congress than I do with the others."
>
> —President
> JIMMY CARTER

Jimmy Carter Honors Martin Luther King Jr.
On January 14, 1979, the day before the anniversary of King's birthday, President Carter and his wife, Rosalyn, worshipped at Ebenezer Baptist Church in Atlanta, Georgia, where both King and his father had been pastors. Carter had been pushing to establish King's birthday as a national holiday, but Congress did not enact such a law until 1983. Here the Carters sing with Martin Luther King Sr.; Andrew Young, a minister who had worked with King, served in the U.S. House of Representatives, and was currently Carter's Ambassador to the United Nations; and Coretta Scott King. Jimmy Carter Presidential Library.

all his predecessors combined. He also increased the numbers of African American and Latino and Latina judges and named the first Latino ambassador to Mexico.

In contrast to his appointments, a number of factors hindered Carter's ability to transform his goals into policy. His outsider status helped him win the election but left him without strong ties to party leaders in Congress. Democrats complained of inadequate consultation and Carter's tendency to flood them with comprehensive proposals without devising a strategy to get them enacted. In addition, Carter refused to offer simple solutions to the American people, who were impatient for quick action against the forces that were squeezing their pocketbooks.

Even if he had possessed Lyndon Johnson's political skills, Carter might not have done much better. The economic problems he inherited — unemployment, inflation, and sluggish economic growth — confounded economic doctrine. Usually, rising prices accompanied a humming economy with a strong demand for labor. Now, however, stagflation burdened the economy with both steep inflation and high unemployment.

Carter first targeted unemployment. Although liberals complained that his programs did not do enough, Carter signed bills pumping $14 billion into the economy through public works and public service jobs programs and cutting taxes by $34 billion. Unemployment receded, but then inflation surged. Working people, wrote one journalist, "winced and ached" as their paychecks bought less and less, "hollowing their hopes and dreams, their plans for a house or their children's college education." To curb inflation, Carter curtailed federal spending, and the Federal Reserve Board tightened the money supply. Not only did these measures fail to halt inflation, which surpassed 13 percent in 1980, but they also contributed to rising unemployment, reversing the gains made in Carter's first two years.

Carter's commitment to holding down the federal budget frustrated Democrats pushing for comprehensive welfare reform, national health insurance, and a substantial jobs program that would make government the employer of last resort. His refusal to propose a comprehensive national health insurance plan, long a key Democratic Party objective, led to a bitter split with Massachusetts senator Ted Kennedy, who fought Carter for the 1980 presidential nomination. Carter did sign legislation to ensure solvency in the Social Security system, but the measure increased both employer and employee contributions, thereby increasing the tax burden on lower- and middle-income Americans.

By contrast, corporations and wealthy individuals gained from new legislation, such as a sharp cut in the capital gains tax. When the Chrysler Corporation approached bankruptcy in 1979, Congress provided $1.5 billion in loan guarantees to bail out the tenth-largest corporation in the country. Congress also acted on Carter's proposals to deregulate airlines in 1978 and the banking, trucking, and railroad industries in 1980. Carter's successor, Ronald Reagan, would move much further, implementing conservatives' attachment to a free market and unfettered private enterprise.

VISUAL ACTIVITY

The Fuel Shortage

This billboard was sponsored by the Outdoor Advertising Association of America in 1980, while Iran held Americans hostage in Teheran (see page 1018) and gasoline shortages and rising gas prices vexed motorists all over the country. The shortages and high prices were sparked by the Iranian revolution, which brought to power Ayatollah Ruholla Khomeini, pictured on the billboard. The ad appeals to drivers to observe the fuel-saving 55-mile-per-hour national speed limit imposed in 1974 during the first oil crisis. John W. Hartman Center/Duke University Special Collections Library.

READING THE IMAGE: What assumptions does the billboard make about Americans' reactions to the Iran hostage crisis? What reasons does the ad give for drivers to respect the speed limit? What reasons are not mentioned? CONNECTIONS: What impact did the hostage and oil crises have on American politics?

Energy and Environmental Reform

Complicating the government's efforts to deal with stagflation was the nation's enormous consumption of energy and its dependence on foreign nations to fill one-third of its energy demands. Consequently, Carter proposed a comprehensive program to conserve energy, and he elevated its importance by establishing the Department of Energy. Beset with competing demands among energy producers and consumers, Congress picked Carter's program apart. The **National Energy Act of 1978** penalized manufacturers of gas-guzzling automobiles and provided other incentives for conservation and development of alternative fuels, such as wind and solar power, but the act fell far short of a long-term, comprehensive program, and Carter's successor dismantled much of the regulation that did succeed.

In 1979, a new upheaval in the Middle East, the Iranian revolution, created the most severe energy crisis yet. In midsummer, shortages caused 60 percent of gasoline stations to close down; frustrated drivers waited in long lines and paid unprecedentedly high prices for gas. "We are struggling with a profound transition from a time of abundance to a time of growing scarcity in energy," Carter told the nation, asking for additional measures to address the shortages. Congress reduced controls on the oil and gas industry to stimulate American production and imposed a windfall profits tax on producers to redistribute some of the profits they would reap from deregulation.

Congress rejected a key Carter proposal to conserve oil by taxing it at the wellhead and thus ultimately increasing its cost to consumers. European nations were just as dependent on foreign oil as was the United States, but they more successfully controlled consumption. They levied high taxes on gasoline, which impelled people to rely more on public transportation and manufacturers to produce more energy-efficient cars. In the automobile-dependent United States, however, with inadequate public transit, people accustomed to driving long distances, and an aversion to taxes, politicians dismissed that approach. By the end of the century, the United States, with 6 percent of the world's population, would consume more than 25 percent of global oil production (Figure 30.1 and Map 30.2).

One alternative fuel, nuclear energy, aroused opposition from a vigorous environmental movement. Activists warned of radiation leakage, potential accidents, and the hazards of radioactive wastes from nuclear power plants, which provided about 10 percent of the nation's electricity in the 1970s. In 1976, hundreds of members of the Clamshell Alliance went to jail for attempting

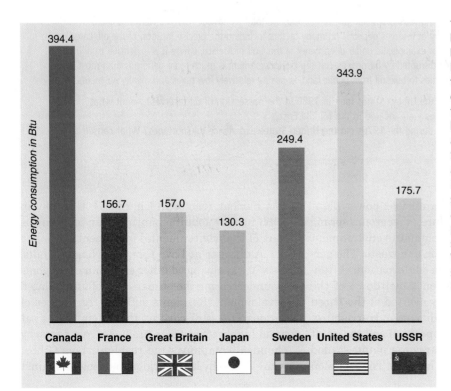

FIGURE 30.1   GLOBAL COMPARISON: Energy Consumption per Capita, 1980
Relative to most other industrialized nations, the United States consumed energy voraciously, with a per capita rate of consumption in 1980 that was more than twice as high as that of Britain, France, and Japan and nearly twice as high as that of the Soviet Union. A number of factors influence a nation's energy consumption (shown here in British thermal units, or Btu), including standard of living, climate, size of landmass and dispersal of population, availability and price of energy, and government policies such as support for public transportation. What country had a per capita rate of consumption even higher than that of the United States?

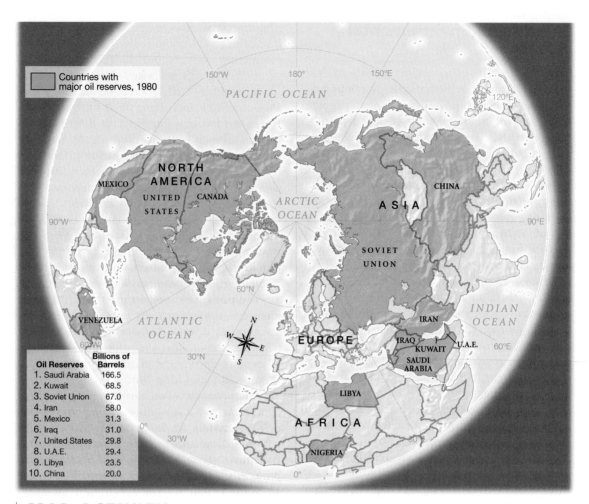

Countries with major oil reserves, 1980

Oil Reserves	Billions of Barrels
1. Saudi Arabia	166.5
2. Kuwait	68.5
3. Soviet Union	67.0
4. Iran	58.0
5. Mexico	31.3
6. Iraq	31.0
7. United States	29.8
8. U.A.E.	29.4
9. Libya	23.5
10. China	20.0

MAP ACTIVITY

Map 30.2 Worldwide Oil Reserves, 1980

Data produced by geologists and engineers enable experts to estimate the size of "proved oil reserves," quantities that are recoverable with existing technology and prices. In 1980, the total worldwide reserves were estimated at 645 billion barrels. The recovery of reserves depends on many factors, including the precise location of the oil. Large portions of the U.S. reserves, for example, lie under deep water in the Gulf of Mexico, where it is expensive to drill and where operations can be disrupted by hurricanes. But the U.S. government is much more generous than most nations in allowing oil companies to take oil from public land, imposing relatively low taxes and royalty payments.

READING THE MAP: Where did the United States rank in 1980 in the possession of oil reserves? About what portion of the total oil reserves were located in the Middle East?

CONNECTIONS: At what points during the 1970s did the United States experience oil shortages? What caused these shortages?

to block construction of a nuclear power plant in Seabrook, New Hampshire; other groups sprang up across the country to demand an environment safe from nuclear radiation and waste. The perils of nuclear energy claimed international attention in March 1979, when a meltdown of the reactor core was narrowly averted at the **Three Mile Island** nuclear facility near Harrisburg, Pennsylvania. Popular opposition and the great expense of building nuclear power plants stalled further development of the industry. The explosion of a nuclear reactor in Chernobyl, Ukraine, in 1986 further solidified antinuclear concerns as part of the environmental movement.

A disaster at Love Canal in Niagara Falls, New York, advanced other environmental goals by underscoring the human costs of unregulated development. Residents suffering high rates of serious illness discovered that their homes sat amid highly toxic waste products from a nearby chemical company. One resident, Lois Gibbs, who eventually led a national movement against toxic wastes, explained how women were galvanized to become environmentalists: "I never thought of myself as an activist. I was a housewife, a mother, but all of a sudden it was my family, my children, and my neighbors." Finally responding to the residents' claims in 1978, the state of New York agreed to help families relocate, and the Carter administration sponsored legislation in 1980 that created the so-called Superfund, $1.6 billion for cleanup of hazardous wastes left by the chemical industry around the country.

Carter's environmental legislation did not stop there. He signed bills to improve clean air and water programs; to expand the Arctic National Wildlife Refuge (ANWR) preserve in Alaska; and to control strip-mining, which left destructive scars on the land. During the 1979 gasoline crisis, Carter attempted to balance the development of domestic fuel sources with environmental concerns, winning legislation to conserve energy and to provide incentives for the development of solar energy and environmentally friendly alternative fuels.

Promoting Human Rights Abroad

"We're ashamed of what our government is as we deal with other nations around the world," Jimmy Carter charged. Asserting that his predecessors' foreign policy violated the nation's principles of freedom and dignity, he promised to reverse the cynical support of dictators, secret diplomacy, interference in the internal affairs of other countries, and excessive reliance on military solutions.

Human rights formed the cornerstone of his approach. The Carter administration applied economic pressure on governments that denied their citizens basic rights, refusing aid or trading privileges to nations such as Chile and El Salvador, as well as to the white minority governments of Rhodesia and South Africa, which brutally violated the rights of their black majorities. Yet in other instances, Carter sacrificed human rights ideals to strategic and security considerations. He invoked no sanctions against repressive governments in Iran, South Korea, and the Philippines, for example, and he established formal diplomatic relations with the People's Republic of China in 1979, even though its government blatantly withheld democratic rights.

Carter's human rights principles faced another test when a popular movement overthrew an oppressive dictatorship in Nicaragua. U.S. officials were uneasy about the leftist Sandinistas who led the rebellion and had ties to Cuba. Once they assumed power in 1979, however, Carter recognized the new government and sent economic aid, signaling that the way a government treated its citizens was as important as how anti-Communist and friendly to American interests it was.

Applying moral principles to relations with Panama, Carter sped up negotiations over control of the Panama Canal and in 1977 signed a treaty providing for Panama's takeover of the canal in 2000. Supporters viewed the treaty as recompense for the barefaced use of U.S. power to obtain the canal in 1903. Opponents insisted on retaining the vital waterway. "We bought it, we paid for it, it's ours," claimed Ronald Reagan during the presidential primaries of 1976. It took a massive effort by the administration to get Senate ratification of the **Panama Canal treaty**, which passed by just one vote.

Seeking to promote peace in the Middle East, Carter seized on the courage of Egyptian president Anwar Sadat, the first Arab leader to risk his political career by talking directly with Israeli officials. In 1979, Carter invited Sadat and Israeli prime minister Menachem Begin to the presidential retreat at Camp David, Maryland, where he applied his tenacious diplomacy for thirteen days. These talks led to the **Camp David accords**, whereby Egypt became the first Arab state to recognize Israel, and Israel agreed to gradual withdrawal from the Sinai Peninsula, which it had seized in the 1967 Six-Day War (Map 30.3). Although the issues of Palestinian self-determination in other Israeli-occupied territories (the West Bank and Gaza) and the plight of Palestinian refugees remained unresolved, Carter had nurtured the first meaningful steps toward peace in the Middle East.

The Cold War Intensifies

Consistent with his human rights approach, Carter preferred to pursue national security through nonmilitary means and initially sought accommodation with the nation's Cold War enemies. In June 1979, Carter and Soviet premier Leonid Brezhnev signed a second strategic arms reduction treaty, setting limits on strategic missiles. Earlier that year, Carter had also followed up on another Nixon initiative, formally recognizing the People's Republic of China.

Yet that same year, Carter decided to pursue a military buildup when the Soviet Union invaded neighboring Afghanistan (see Map 30.3). Afghanistan's recently installed Communist government was threatened by Muslim opposition, which even before the invasion had received secret support from the CIA. Announcing that

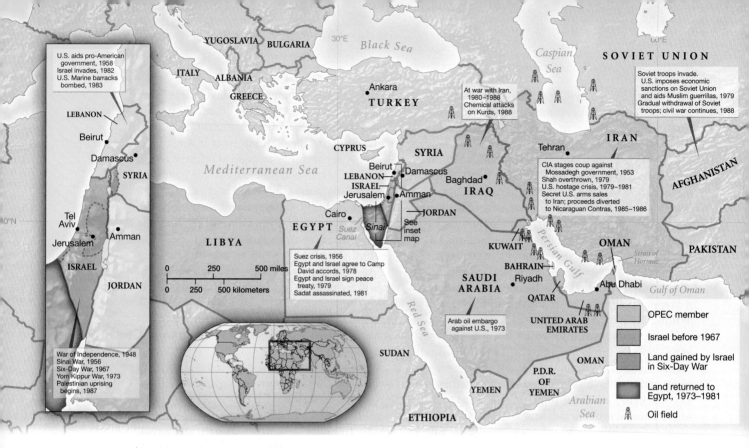

U.S. aids pro-American government, 1958
Israel invades, 1982
U.S. Marine barracks bombed, 1983

War of Independence, 1948
Sinai War, 1956
Six-Day War, 1967
Yom Kippur War, 1973
Palestinian uprising begins, 1987

At war with Iran, 1980–1988
Chemical attacks on Kurds, 1988

Soviet troops invade. U.S. imposes economic sanctions on Soviet Union and aids Muslim guerrillas, 1979
Gradual withdrawal of Soviet troops; civil war continues, 1988

CIA stages coup against Mossadegh government, 1953
Shah overthrown, 1979
U.S. hostage crisis, 1979–1981
Secret U.S. arms sales to Iran; proceeds diverted to Nicaraguan Contras, 1985–1986

Suez crisis, 1956
Egypt and Israel agree to Camp David accords, 1978
Egypt and Israel sign peace treaty, 1979
Sadat assassinated, 1981

Arab oil embargo against U.S., 1973

OPEC member
Israel before 1967
Land gained by Israel in Six-Day War
Land returned to Egypt, 1973–1981
Oil field

MAP ACTIVITY

Map 30.3   The Middle East, 1948–1989

Determination to preserve access to the rich oil reserves of the Middle East and commitment to the security of Israel were the fundamental — and often conflicting — principles of U.S. foreign policy in that region.

READING THE MAP: Where did the United States become involved diplomatically or militarily in the Middle East between 1948 and 1989?

CONNECTIONS: What role did U.S. foreign policy regarding the Middle East and events in Israel play in provoking the 1973 Arab oil embargo against the United States? What precipitated the taking of U.S. hostages in Iran in 1979? Was U.S. intervention in the country a factor? If so, why?

the Soviet action "could pose the greatest threat to peace since the Second World War," Carter imposed economic sanctions on the Soviet Union, barred U.S. participation in the 1980 Summer Olympic Games in Moscow, and obtained legislation requiring all nineteen-year-old men to register for the draft.

Claiming that Soviet actions jeopardized oil supplies from the Middle East, the president announced the "Carter Doctrine," threatening the use of any means necessary to prevent an outside force from gaining control of the Persian Gulf. His human rights policy fell by the wayside as the United States stepped up aid to the military dictatorship in Afghanistan's neighbor, Pakistan, and the CIA funneled secret aid through Pakistan to the Afghan rebels. Finally, Carter called for hefty increases in defense spending.

Events in Iran also encouraged this hard-line approach. All the U.S. arms and aid had not enabled the shah to crush Iranian dissidents who still

resented the CIA's role in the overthrow of the Mossadegh government in 1953 (see chapter 27). Dissidents condemned the shah's savage attempts to silence opposition and detested his adoption of Western culture and values. These grievances erupted into a revolution in 1979 that forced the shah out of Iran and brought to power Shiite Islamic fundamentalists led by Ayatollah Ruholla Khomeini, whom the shah had exiled in 1964.

Carter's decision to allow the shah into the United States for medical treatment enraged Iranians, who believed that the United States would restore the shah to power as it had done in 1953. Anti-American demonstrations escalated in the capital city of Teheran. On November 4, 1979, a crowd broke into the U.S. Embassy and seized sixty-six U.S. diplomats, CIA officers, citizens, and military attachés. Refusing the captors' demands that the shah be returned to Iran for trial, Carter froze Iranian assets in U.S. banks and placed an embargo on Iranian oil. In

American Hostages in Iran
For more than a year — from November 4, 1979, to January 20, 1981 — Americans regularly saw TV images of the hostages taken by Iranian militants when they occupied the U.S. Embassy in Teheran. Early in the crisis, Ayatollah Khomeini ordered the release of thirteen of the sixty-six hostages, all of them women or African Americans, because he believed they were not spies and had already endured "the oppression of American society." Here the thirteen are presented to the press shortly before their release. © Sygma/Corbis.

April 1980, he sent a small military operation into Iran, but the rescue mission failed.

The disastrous rescue attempt and scenes of blindfolded U.S. citizens paraded before TV cameras fed Americans' feelings of impotence, simmering since the defeat in Vietnam. These frustrations in turn increased support for a more militaristic foreign policy. Opposition to Soviet-American détente, combined with the Soviet invasion of Afghanistan, nullified the thaw in superpower relations that had begun in the 1960s. The **Iran hostage crisis** dominated the news during the 1980 presidential campaign and contributed to Carter's defeat. Iran freed the hostages the day he left office, but relations with the United States remained tense.

REVIEW How and where did Carter implement his commitment to human rights, and where and why did human rights give way to other priorities?

► Ronald Reagan and the Conservative Ascendancy

The election of Ronald Reagan in 1980 marked the most important turning point in politics since Franklin D. Roosevelt won the presidency in 1932. Eisenhower and Nixon were middle-of-the-road Republicans, but Reagan's victory established conservatism's dominance in the Republican Party. Since the 1930s, the Democrats had defined the major issues. In the 1980s, the Republicans assumed that initiative, while Democrats searched for voter support by moving toward the right. The United States was not alone in this political shift. Conservatives rose to power in Britain with Prime Minister Margaret Thatcher, and they led governments in Germany, Canada, and Sweden, while socialist and social democratic governments elsewhere trimmed their welfare states.

Ronald Reagan Addresses Religious Conservatives
Reagan's victory in the 1980 election helped to reshape the Republican party by attracting millions of evangelical Christians who had favored Jimmy Carter in 1976. In his March 1983 address to the National Association of
Evangelicals, he took a hard line on anticommunism, calling the Soviet Union an "evil empire." He also echoed
the sentiments of religious conservatives with strong words about abortion and prayer in the schools and
rejoiced that "America is in the midst of a spiritual awakening and a moral renewal." Ronald Reagan Presidential Library.

On the domestic front, the Reagan administration embraced the conservative Christian
values of the New Right, but it left its most important mark on the economy: victory over inflation,
deregulation of industry, enormous tax cuts, and
a staggering federal budget deficit. Economic
expansion, which took off after 1983, helped the
middle class and brought great wealth to some,
but the percentage of poor Americans increased,
and income inequality grew. Although the Reagan
era did not see a policy revolution comparable
to that of the New Deal, it dealt a sharp blow to
the liberalism that had informed American politics since the 1930s.

Appealing to the New Right and Beyond

Sixty-nine-year-old **Ronald Reagan** was the oldest candidate ever nominated for the presidency.
Born in Tampico, Illinois, Reagan attended a
small religious college and worked as a sportscaster
before becoming a movie actor. He initially shared

the politics of his staunchly Democratic father
but moved to the right in the 1940s and 1950s
and campaigned for Goldwater in 1964.

Reagan's political career took off when he
was elected governor of California in 1966. He
ran as a conservative, but in office he displayed
considerable flexibility, approving a major tax
increase, a strong water pollution bill, and a
liberal abortion law. Displaying similar agility
in the 1980 presidential campaign, he softened
earlier attacks on programs such as Social Security
and chose the moderate George H. W. Bush as
his running mate.

Nonetheless, some Republicans balked at
his nomination and at the party platform, which
reflected the concerns of the party's right wing.
For example, after Phyllis Schlafly persuaded
the party to reverse its forty-year support for the
Equal Rights Amendment, moderate and liberal
Republican women protested outside the convention hall. (See "Historical Question," page 1026.)
Some Republicans found a more acceptable presidential candidate in Illinois representative

John B. Anderson, who deserted his party to run as an independent.

Reagan's campaign capitalized on the economic recession and the international challenges symbolized by the Americans held hostage in Iran. Repeatedly, Reagan asked voters, "Are you better off now than you were four years ago?" He promised to "take government off the backs of the people" and to restore Americans' morale and other nations' respect. Fifty-one percent of voters responded favorably to Reagan's upbeat message, while Carter won 41 percent, and 7 percent went to Anderson. Republicans won control of the Senate for the first time since the 1950s.

While the economy and the Iran hostage crisis sealed Reagan's victory, he also benefited from the burgeoning grassroots conservative movements. An extraordinarily adept politician, Reagan appealed to a wide spectrum of groups and sentiments: free market advocates, militant anti-Communists, fundamentalist Christians, white southerners, and white working-class Democrats — the so-called Reagan Democrats disenchanted with the Great Society and suffering from the stagflation of the 1970s.

Reagan's support from religious conservatives, predominantly Protestants, constituted a relatively new phenomenon in politics known as the **New Right** or **New Christian Right**. During the 1970s, evangelical and fundamentalist Christianity claimed thousands of new adherents. Evangelical ministers such as Pat Robertson preached to huge television audiences, attacking feminism, abortion, and homosexuality and calling for the restoration of old-fashioned "family values." They wanted prayer back in the schools and sex education out of them. A considerable number of Catholics, such as Phyllis Schlafly, shared the fundamentalists' goal of a return to "Christian values."

Conservatives created political organizations such as the Moral Majority, founded by the Reverend Jerry Falwell in 1979, to fight "left-wing, social welfare bills, . . . pornography, homosexuality, [and] the advocacy of immorality in school textbooks." Dr. James Dobson, a clinical psychologist with a popular Christian talk show, founded the Family Research Council in 1983 to lobby Congress for measures to curb abortion, divorce, homosexuality, and single motherhood. The instruments of more traditional conservatives, who stressed limited government at home and militant anticommunism abroad, likewise flourished. Decades-old institutions like the *National Review* and the American Enterprise Institute were joined by new institutions such as the Heritage Foundation, a think tank that formulated and promoted conservative ideas. The monthly *Phyllis Schlafly Report* merged the sentiments of the old and new right.

Reagan embraced the full spectrum of conservatism, but he actually delivered more to the traditional right. He spoke for the New Right on such issues as abortion and school prayer, but he did not push hard for so-called moral or social policies. Instead, his major achievements fulfilled goals of the older right — strengthening the nation's anti-Communist posture and reducing taxes and government restraints on free enterprise. "In the present crisis," Reagan declared, "government is not the solution to our problem, government is the problem."

Reagan's admirers stretched far beyond conservatives. The extraordinarily popular president was liked even by Americans who opposed his policies and even when he made glaring mistakes. Reagan's optimism, confidence, and easygoing humor formed a large part of his appeal. Ignoring the darker moments of the American past, he presented a version of history that Americans could feel good about. Listeners understood his declaration that it was "morning in America" as a promise that the best was yet to come. Reagan also gained public sympathy after being shot by a would-be assassin in March 1981. Just before surgery to remove the bullet, Reagan joked to physicians, "I hope you're Republicans." His tremendous popularity helped him withstand serious charges of executive branch misconduct in his second term.

Unleashing Free Enterprise

Reagan's first domestic objective was a massive tax cut. Although tax cuts in the face of a large budget deficit contradicted traditional Republican economic doctrine, Reagan relied on a new theory called **supply-side economics**, which held that cutting taxes would actually increase revenue by enabling businesses to expand and encouraging individuals to work harder because they could keep more of their earnings. Business expansion would increase the production of goods and services — the supply — which in turn would boost demand. Reagan promised that the economy would grow so much that the government would recoup the lost taxes, but instead it incurred a galloping deficit.

In the summer of 1981, Congress passed the **Economic Recovery Tax Act**, the largest tax reduction in U.S. history. Rates were cut from 14 percent to 11 percent for the lowest-income individuals and from 70 percent to 50 percent for the wealthiest. The law gave corporations tax breaks and reduced levies on capital gains, gifts, and inheritances. A second measure, the Tax Reform Act of 1986, went even further, lowering the maximum rate on individual income to 28 percent and on business income to 35 percent. Although the 1986 law narrowed loopholes used primarily by the wealthy, affluent Americans saved far more on their tax bills than did average taxpayers, and the distribution of wealth tipped further in favor of the rich. Moreover, the total federal tax burden barely declined, from 19.4 percent of national income in 1981 to 19.3 percent in 1989.

> **"Hack, chop, crunch!"**
> —*Time* magazine, on Reagan's efforts to free private enterprise from government restraints

"Hack, chop, crunch!" were *Time* magazine's words for Reagan's efforts to free private enterprise from government restraints. Carter had confined deregulation to particular industries, such as air transportation and banking, while increasing health, safety, and environmental regulations. The Reagan administration, by contrast, pursued across-the-board deregulation. It declined to enforce the Sherman Antitrust Act (see chapter 18), which limited monopolies, against an unprecedented number of business mergers and takeovers. Reagan also loosened regulations protecting employee health and safety, and he weakened labor unions. When members of the Professional Air Traffic Controllers Organization—one of the few unions to support him in 1980—struck in 1981, Reagan pointed to the illegality of the strike, gave workers two days to go back to work, and then fired thousands who didn't. Although federal workers had struck before without being penalized, Reagan demonstrated decisiveness and toughness, destroying the union and intimidating organized labor.

Ronald Reagan loved the outdoors and his remote ranch in southern California, where altogether he spent nearly one-eighth of his two-term presidency. Yet he blamed environmental laws for the nation's sluggish economic growth and targeted them for deregulation. His first secretary of the interior, James Watt, declared, "We will mine more, drill more, cut more timber," and released federal lands to private exploitation. Meanwhile, the head of the Environmental Protection Agency relaxed enforcement of air and water pollution standards. Of environmentalists, Reagan wisecracked, "I don't think they'll be happy until the White House looks like a bird's nest," but their numbers grew in opposition

to his policies. Popular support for environmental protection forced several officials to resign and blocked full realization of Reagan's deregulatory goals.

Deregulation of the banking industry, begun under Carter with bipartisan support, created a crisis in the savings and loan industry. Some of the newly deregulated savings and loan institutions (S&Ls) extended enormous loans to real estate developers and invested in other high-yield but risky ventures. S&L owners reaped lavish profits, and their depositors enjoyed high interest rates. But when real estate values began to plunge, hundreds of S&Ls went bankrupt. After Congress voted to bail out the S&L industry in 1989, American taxpayers bore the burden of the largest financial scandal in U.S. history, estimated at more than $100 billion.

Deregulation did little to reduce the size of government or the federal deficit. The administration cut funds for food stamps, job training, student aid, and other social welfare programs, and hundreds of thousands of people lost benefits. Yet increases in defense spending far exceeded the budget cuts, and the deficit climbed from $74 billion in 1981 to a high of $220 billion in 1986. Under Reagan, the nation's debt tripled to $2.3 trillion, and interest on the debt consumed one-seventh of all federal expenditures. Despite Reagan's antigovernment rhetoric, the number of federal employees increased from 2.9 million to 3.1 million during his presidency.

It took the severest recession since the 1930s to squeeze inflation out of the U.S. economy. Unemployment approached 11 percent late in 1982, and record numbers of banks and businesses closed. The threat of unemployment further undermined organized labor, forcing unions to make concessions that management insisted were necessary for industry's survival. In 1983, the economy recovered and entered a period of unprecedented growth.

That economic upswing and Reagan's own popularity posed a formidable challenge to the Democrats in the 1984 election. They nominated Carter's vice president, Walter F. Mondale, to head the ticket, but even his precedent-breaking move in choosing a woman as his running mate—New York representative Geraldine A. Ferraro—did not save the Democrats from a humiliating defeat. Reagan charged his opponents with concentrating on America's failures, while he emphasized success and possibility. Democrats, he claimed, "see an America where every day is April 15th [the deadline for income tax returns] . . . we see an America where every day is the Fourth of July."

Voters responded to the president's sunny vision and the economic comeback, giving him a landslide victory with 59 percent of the popular vote and every state but Minnesota. Stung by Republican charges that the Democratic Party was captive to "special interests" such as labor, women, and minorities, some Democratic leaders, including the young Arkansas governor, Bill Clinton, urged the party to shift more toward the right.

Winners and Losers in a Flourishing Economy

After the economy took off in 1983, some Americans won great fortunes. Popular culture celebrated making money and displaying wealth. Books by business wizards topped best seller lists, the press described lavish million-dollar parties, and a new television show, *Lifestyles of the Rich and Famous*, drew large audiences. College students listed making money as their primary ambition.

Participating conspicuously in the new affluence were members of the baby boom generation, known popularly as "yuppies," short for "young urban professionals." These mostly white, well-educated young men and women lived in urban condominiums and consumed lavishly — fancy cars, health clubs, expensive vacations, and electronic gadgets. Though definitely a minority, they established consumption standards that many tried to emulate. And, in fact, millions of Americans enjoyed larger houses that they filled with such new products as VCRs, microwave ovens, and personal computers.

Many of the newly wealthy got rich from moving assets around rather than from producing goods. Notable exceptions included Steven Jobs, who invented the Apple computer in his garage; Bill Gates, who transformed the software industry; and Liz Claiborne, who created a billion-dollar fashion enterprise. But many others made money by manipulating debt and restructuring corporations through mergers and takeovers. "To say these guys are entrepreneurs is like saying Jesse James was an entrepreneur," said Texas businessman Ross Perot, who defined entrepreneurship as making things rather than making money. Most financial wizards operated within the law, but greed sometimes led to criminal convictions.

Older industries faced increasing international pressures. Americans bought more Volkswagens and Hondas and fewer Fords and Chevrolets, as German and Japanese corporations overtook U.S. manufacturing in steel, automobiles, and electronics. International competition forced the collapse of some older companies. Others moved factories and jobs abroad to be closer to foreign markets or to benefit from the low wages in countries such as Mexico and Korea. Service industries expanded and created new jobs at home, but this work paid substantially lower wages than did manufacturing jobs. When David Ramos was laid off in 1982 from his $12.75-an-hour job in a steel plant, his wages fell to $5 an hour as a security guard, forcing his family to rely on food stamps. The number of full-time workers earning wages below the poverty level ($12,195 for a family of four in 1990) rose from 12 percent to 18 percent of all workers in the 1980s.

The weakening of organized labor combined with the decline in manufacturing to erode the

The S&L Crisis
These workers are removing the company's name from the Denver-based Silverado Banking, Savings and Loan Association, which collapsed in 1988, along with many other so-called "thrifts" that had speculated in risky loans for commercial real estate development. Neil Bush, son of President George H.W. Bush and one of Silverado's directors, was found by federal investigators to have had engaged in conflicts of interest, but he was not indicted on criminal charges. The Silverado failure cost the government more than a billion dollars. In 1989 Congress enacted strict regulations over the savings and loan industry. ©Bettmann/Corbis.

Homelessness
The increased presence of homeless people in cities across the nation challenged the view of the 1980s as a decade of prosperity. Hundreds of homeless people could be found on the sidewalks of the nation's capital every night. In November 1987, during the first snowfall of the season, a homeless man sleeps in Washington, D.C.'s Lafayette Square, across from the White House. What might the location of this homeless man suggest to viewers of the photograph? © Bettmann/Corbis.

position of blue-collar workers. Chicago steelworker Ike Mazo, who contemplated the $6-an-hour jobs available to him, fumed, "It's an attack on the living standards of workers." Increasingly, a second income was needed to stave off economic decline. By 1990, nearly 60 percent of married women with young children worked outside the home. Yet even with two incomes, families struggled. Speaking of her children, Mazo's wife confessed, "I worry about their future every day. Will we be able to put them through college?" The average $10,000 gap between men's and women's annual earnings made things even harder for the nearly 20 percent of families headed by women.

In keeping with conservative philosophy, Reagan adhered to trickle-down economics, insisting that a booming economy would benefit everyone. Average personal income did rise during his tenure, but the trend toward greater economic inequality that had begun in the 1970s intensified in the 1980s, encouraged in part by his tax policies. Between 1979 and 1987, personal income shot up sharply for the wealthiest 20 percent of Americans, while it fell by 9.8 percent for the

poorest. During Reagan's presidency, the percentage of Americans living in poverty increased from 11.7 to 13.5, the highest poverty rate in the industrialized world. Social Security and Medicare helped to stave off destitution among the elderly. Less fortunate were other groups that the economic boom had bypassed: racial minorities, female-headed families, and children. One child in five lived in poverty.

Even as the economy boomed, affluent urbanites walked past men and women sleeping in subway stations and on park benches. Experts debated the number of homeless Americans — estimates ranged from 350,000 upward — but no one doubted that homelessness had increased. Those without shelter included the victims of long-term unemployment, the erosion of welfare benefits, and slum clearance, as well as Vietnam veterans and individuals suffering from mental illness, drug addiction, and alcoholism.

REVIEW   Why did economic inequality increase during the Reagan administration?

▶ Continuing Struggles over Rights

The rise of conservatism put liberal social movements on the defensive, as the Reagan administration moved away from the national commitment to equal opportunity undertaken in the 1960s and the president's federal court appointments reflected that shift. Feminists and minority groups fought to keep protections they had recently won, and they achieved some limited gains. The gay and lesbian rights movement actually grew in numbers, edging attitudes toward greater tolerance and winning important protections in some states and cities.

Battles in the Courts and Congress

Ronald Reagan agreed with conservatives that the nation had moved too far in guaranteeing rights to minority groups. Crying "reverse discrimination," conservatives maintained that affirmative action unfairly hurt whites. Brian Weber, a Kaiser Aluminum production worker, filed a lawsuit when some African Americans with less seniority were admitted to a training program to which he had applied. Ignoring the discrimination that had prevented blacks from accruing seniority, he insisted that he should not "be made to pay for what someone did 150 years ago." Weber and other critics of affirmative action called for "color-blind" policies, ignoring statistics showing that minorities and white women still lagged far behind white men in opportunities and income.

Intense mobilization by civil rights groups, educational leaders, labor, and even corporate America prevented the administration from abandoning affirmative action, and the Supreme Court upheld important antidiscrimination policies, including the one that Weber challenged. Moreover, against Reagan's wishes, Congress voted to extend the Voting Rights Act with veto-proof majorities. The administration did, however, put the brakes on civil rights enforcement by appointing conservatives to the Justice Department, the Civil Rights Commission, and other agencies and by slashing their budgets.

Congress stepped in to defend antidiscrimination programs after the Justice Department persuaded the Supreme Court to severely weaken Title IX of the Education Amendments Act of 1972, a key law promoting equal opportunity in education. *Grove City v. Bell* (1984) allowed the Justice Department to abandon dozens of civil rights cases against schools and colleges, which in turn galvanized a coalition of civil rights organizations and groups representing women, the aged, and the disabled, along with their allies. In 1988, Congress passed the Civil Rights Restoration Act over Reagan's veto, reversing the administration's victory in *Grove City* and banning government funding of any organization that practiced discrimination on the basis of race, color, national origin, sex, disability, or age.

The *Grove City* decision reflected a rightward movement in the federal judiciary, upon which liberals had counted as a powerful ally. With the opportunity to appoint half of the 761 federal court judges and three new Supreme Court justices, President Reagan encouraged this trend by carefully selecting conservative candidates. He endured only one setback, when in 1987 the Senate denied confirmation of arch-conservative Robert Bork. Thus, Reagan's appointments turned the tide back toward strict construction — the literal interpretation of the Constitution that narrowly adheres to the words of its authors, thereby limiting judicial power to protect individual rights. The full impact of these appointments became clear after Reagan left office, as the Court allowed states to impose restrictions that weakened access to abortion for poor and uneducated women, reduced protections against employment discrimination, and whittled down legal safeguards against the death penalty.

Feminism on the Defensive

A signal achievement of the New Right was taking control of the Republican Party's position on women's rights. For the first time in its history, the Republican Party took an explicitly anti-feminist tone, opposing both the **Equal Rights Amendment (ERA)** and a woman's right to abortion, key goals of women's rights activists. When the time limit for ratification of the ERA ran out in 1982, Phyllis Schlafly celebrated victory on the issue that had first galvanized her antifeminist campaign, while amendment supporters looked for the silver lining. Sonia Johnson, who was excommunicated by the Mormon Church for her feminism in 1979, exag-

Ratified the ERA

Did not ratify the ERA

Ratified and then voted to rescind ratification

The Fight for the Equal Rights Amendment

Why Did the ERA Fail?

The proposed Equal Rights Amendment to the U.S. Constitution guaranteed simply that "Equality of rights under the law shall not be denied or abridged by the United States or by any State on account of sex." Two more short sections gave Congress enforcement powers and provided that the ERA would take effect two years after ratification. By the 1970s, it had become the symbol of the women's movement, and the controversy it sparked revealed profound differences in beliefs and values among the American public.

The National Woman's Party, a militant suffrage organization that had helped win the vote for women in 1920, first proposed an equal rights amendment to the Constitution in 1923. The proposal won little support, however, before the resurgence of feminism in the late 1960s, when the National Organization for Women and other major women's groups made the ERA a key objective.

Both houses of Congress passed the ERA in March 1972 by overwhelming margins, 354 to 23 in the House and 84 to 8 in the Senate. Within three hours, Hawaii rushed to become the first state to ratify, and twenty-three states quickly followed. Public opinion heavily favored ratification, peaking at

74 percent in favor in 1974 and never falling below 52 percent, while opposition never topped 31 percent. Yet even after Congress extended the ratification period until 1982, the ERA fell three short of the three-fourths of the states required by the Constitution (see the map on page 1025). Why did a measure with so much congressional and popular support fail?

The ERA encountered well-organized and passionate opposition linked to the growing conservative forces in the 1970s. Conservatives' opposition to the ERA reflected in part their distaste for big government, but even more it signaled the New Right's determination to preserve traditional gender roles and "family values." What feminists saw as a simple measure to ensure equal rights for all citizens, ERA opponents saw as a threat to women's God-given and natural right to be protected and supported by men. They raised fears by suggesting extravagant ways in which courts might interpret the amendment. Senator Samuel J. Ervin Jr. claimed that the ERA would eliminate laws against rape, require coed housing for prisoners, and deprive women of alimony and child support. Others claimed it would legalize homosexual marriage and send women into combat.

Anti-ERA arguments drew on conservative Christian beliefs. Evangelical minister and politician Jerry Falwell declared the ERA "a definite violation of holy Scripture [and its] mandate that 'the husband is the head of the wife.'" Anti-ERA rhetoric also appealed to some women's understandings of their own self-interest. Many ERA opponents were full-time housewives who had no stake in equal treatment in the marketplace and who feared that the amendment would eliminate the duty of men to support their families.

Phyllis Schlafly and other conservative leaders skillfully mobilized women who saw their traditional roles threatened. In October 1972, she established a national movement called STOP (Stop Taking Our Privileges) ERA, whose members deluged legislators with letters and lobbied them personally in state capitols. In Illinois, they gave lawmakers apple pies with notes that read, "My heart and my hand went into this dough / For the sake of the family please vote 'no.'" Opponents also brought baby girls to the legislature wearing signs that pleaded, "Please don't draft me."

ERA opponents had an easier task than supporters, because the framers of the Constitution had stacked the odds against revision. All opponents had to do was to convince a minority of legislators in a minority of states to preserve the status quo. In addition, unlike their suffragist predecessors, ERA forces

> "The struggle over [ERA] ratification has provided the greatest political training ground for women in the history of the world."
> —Feminist SONIA JOHNSON

gerated only somewhat when she called the ratification struggle "the greatest political training ground for women in the history of the world." (See chapter 28 and "Historical Question," above.)

Cast on the defensive, feminists focused more on women's economic and family problems, where they found some common ground with the Reagan administration. The Child Support Enforcement Amendments Act

helped single and divorced mothers collect court-ordered child support payments from absent fathers. The Retirement Equity Act of 1984 benefited divorced and older women by strengthening their claims to their husbands' pensions and enabling women to qualify more easily for private retirement pensions.

The Reagan administration had its own concerns about women, specifically about the gender gap in voting — women's tendency to support liberal and Democratic candidates in larger numbers than men did. Reagan eventually appointed three women to cabinet posts

had concentrated on winning Congress and were not prepared for the state campaigns.

The very gains feminists made in the 1960s and 1970s also worked against ratification. Congress had banned sex discrimination in employment, education, and other areas, and the Supreme Court had struck down several discriminatory laws, thus making it harder for ERA advocates to demonstrate the urgency of constitutional revision.

The ERA failed because a handful of men in a handful of state legislatures voted against it. The shift of only a few votes in states such as Illinois and North Carolina would have meant ratification. Schlafly's forces played a key role in the defeat, because men could vote "no" and take cover behind the many women who opposed it. And those women proved willing to commit time, energy, and money to block ratification because conservative leaders convinced them that the ERA threatened their very way of life.

Feminists did not leave the ERA battle empty-handed, however. Thousands of women were mobilized across the political spectrum, participating in the public arena for the first time. Fourteen states passed their own equal rights amendments after 1970. And feminists continued to fight legislative and judicial battles for the expansion of women's rights, struggles that continue to bear fruit in the twenty-first century.

Phyllis Schlafly Derails the ERA in Illinois
Illinois was one of the most hotly contested states in the battle over ratification of the Equal Rights Amendment. Here Schlafly rallies ERA opponents in the state capitol in 1975. Schlafly's STOP ERA movement succeeded in Illinois, her home state and the only northern state that failed to ratify. Despite time-consuming and energetic political activities that involved traveling and speaking across the country, Schlafly insisted on calling herself a housewife.
© Bettmann/Corbis.

Thinking about Beliefs and Attitudes

1. In what ways did the New Right see the Equal Rights Amendment as a threat to traditional values?

2. How did attitudes about the ERA differ from those about woman suffrage in the period leading up to ratification of the Nineteenth Amendment? (See chapter 22.)

and, in 1981, selected the first woman, **Sandra Day O'Connor**, a moderate conservative, for the Supreme Court, despite the Christian Right's objection to her support of abortion. But these actions accompanied a general decline in the number of women and minorities in high-level government positions. And with higher poverty rates than men, women suffered most from Reagan's cuts in social programs.

A powerful antiabortion movement won Supreme Court decisions that placed restrictions on women's ability to obtain abortions, but feminists fought successfully to retain the basic principles of *Roe v. Wade.* Moreover, they won a key decision from the Supreme Court ruling that sexual harassment in the workplace constituted sex discrimination. Feminists also made some gains at the state level in such areas as pay equity, rape, and domestic violence.

The Gay and Lesbian Rights Movement

In contrast to feminism and other social movements, gay and lesbian rights activism grew during the 1980s, galvanized in part by the

The Abortion Debate

After the Supreme Court upheld women's right to abortion in *Roe v. Wade* in 1973, several state legislatures instituted restrictions on that right that fell within the parameters outlined by the Court. In 1989, the Court upheld a Missouri law that prohibited public employees from performing abortions not necessary to save the life of the woman, banned the use of public buildings for providing abortions, and required physicians to perform viability tests on the fetus in pregnancies beyond the twentieth week. Here, activists on both sides of the issue rally before the Supreme Court on the day of its decision. AP Images/Ron Edmonds.

discovery in 1981 of a devastating disease, **acquired immune deficiency syndrome (AIDS)**. Because initially the disease disproportionately affected male homosexuals in the United States, activists mobilized to promote public funding for AIDS education, prevention, and treatment. Such efforts, along with the death from AIDS of a friend, movie star Rock Hudson, spurred President Reagan during his second term to attack the epidemic, which he had previously refused to address.

The gay and lesbian rights movement helped closeted homosexuals experience the relief of "coming out," and their visibility increased awareness, if not always acceptance, of homosexuality among the larger population. Beginning with the election of Elaine Noble to the Massachusetts legislature in 1974, several openly gay politicians won offices ranging from mayor to member of Congress, and the Democrats began to include gay rights in their party platforms. Activists organized gay rights marches throughout the

Gay Pride Parades

Since June 1970, when gays and lesbians marched in New York City on the first anniversary of Stonewall (see chapter 28), annual gay pride parades have taken place throughout the United States. According to history professor Robert Dawidoff, the parades are not about "flaunting private things in public," as some people charged, but a way for gay men and lesbians to express "pride . . . in having survived the thousand petty harassments and reminders of a special status we neither seek nor merit." Friends and families of homosexuals participate in the parades, as this sign from a parade in Los Angeles indicates. © Bettmann/Corbis.

country, turning out half a million people in New York City in 1987.

Popular attitudes about homosexuality moved toward greater tolerance but remained complex, leading to uneven changes in policies. (See "Documenting the American Promise," page 1028.) Dozens of cities banned job discrimination against homosexuals, and beginning with Wisconsin in 1982, eleven states made sexual orientation a protected category under civil rights laws. Local governments and large corporations began to offer health insurance and other benefits to same-sex domestic partners.

Yet a strong countermovement challenged the drive for recognition of gay rights. The Christian Right targeted gays and lesbians as symbols of national immorality and succeeded in overturning some homosexual rights measures, which already lagged far behind antidiscrimination guarantees for minorities and women. Many states removed antisodomy laws from the books, but in 1986 the Supreme Court upheld the constitutionality of such laws. Until the Court reversed that opinion in 2003, more than a dozen states retained statutes that left homosexuals vulnerable to criminal charges for private consensual behavior.

REVIEW What gains and setbacks did minorities, feminists, and gays and lesbians experience during the Reagan years?

► Ronald Reagan Confronts an "Evil Empire"

Campaigning for president in the wake of the Soviet invasion of Afghanistan and the Iran hostage crisis, Reagan accused Carter of weakening the military and losing the confidence of the nation's allies and the respect of its enemies. As president, he accelerated Carter's arms buildup and harshly censured the Soviet Union, calling it "an evil empire." Yet despite the new aggressiveness — or, as some argued, because of it — Reagan presided over the most impressive thaw in superpower conflict since the Cold War had begun.

On the periphery of the Cold War, however, Reagan practiced militant anticommunism, assisting antileftist movements in Asia, Africa, and Central America and dispatching troops to the Middle East and the Caribbean. When Congress blocked Reagan's efforts to help overthrow the leftist government in Nicaragua, administration officials resorted to secret and illegal means to achieve their agenda.

Militarization and Interventions Abroad

Reagan expanded the military with new bombers and missiles, an enhanced nuclear force in Europe, a larger navy, and a rapid-deployment force. Despite the growing budget deficit, Congress approved most of these programs, and military expenditures shot up by one-third in the first half of the 1980s. Throughout Reagan's presidency, defense spending averaged $216 billion a year, up from $158 billion in the Carter years and higher even than in the Vietnam era.

Reagan startled many of his own advisers in March 1983 by announcing plans for research on the **Strategic Defense Initiative (SDI)**. Immediately dubbed "Star Wars" by critics who doubted its feasibility, the project would deploy lasers in space to destroy enemy missiles before they could reach their targets. Reagan conceded that SDI could appear to be "an aggressive policy" that would allow the United States to strike first and not fear retaliation. The Soviets reacted angrily because SDI violated the 1972 Antiballistic Missile Treaty and because they would have to make huge investments to develop their own Star Wars technology. Nonetheless, Reagan persisted, and subsequent administrations continued to spend billions on SDI research without producing a working system.

Reagan justified the military buildup and SDI as a means to negotiate with the Soviets from a position of strength, but he provoked an outburst of pleas to halt the arms race. In 1982, a rally demanding a freeze on additional nuclear weapons drew 700,000 people in New York City. That same year the National Conference of Catholic Bishops issued a strong call for nuclear disarmament. Hundreds of thousands demonstrated across Europe, stimulated by fears of new U.S. missiles scheduled for deployment there in 1983.

The U.S. military buildup was impotent before the growing threat of terrorism by nonstate organizations that sought political objectives by attacking civilian populations. Terrorism had a long history throughout the world, but in the 1970s and 1980s Americans saw it escalate in the Middle East, used by Palestinians after the Israeli occupation of the West Bank and by other

Protecting Gay and Lesbian Rights

Since the 1970s, the gay and lesbian rights movement has worked for passage of laws and ordinances to protect homosexuals from discrimination. In 1982, Wisconsin became the first state to ban discrimination on the basis of sexual orientation, following the lead of several cities throughout the United States that passed gay rights ordinances in the 1970s. By 2010, twenty-one states and the District of Columbia outlawed employment discrimination against gays, and dozens of cities did so. These measures ignited controversy, but whether homosexuals should have the right to marry aroused even more contention.

DOCUMENT 1
Ordinance of the City of Minneapolis, 1974

In 1974, the city council of Minneapolis amended its civil rights ordinance to cover discrimination based on sexual preference. The law provided a rationale for banning discrimination and, unlike some laws focusing exclusively on employment, encompassed a broad range of activities.

It is determined that discriminatory practices based on race, color, creed, religion, national origin, sex, or affectional or sexual preference, with respect to employment, labor union membership, housing accommodations, property rights, education, public accommodations, and public services, or any of them, tend to create and intensify conditions of poverty, ill health, unrest, civil disobedience, lawlessness, and vice and adversely affect the public health, safety, order, convenience, and general welfare; such discriminatory practices threaten the rights, privileges, and opportunities of all inhabitants of the city and such rights, privileges, and opportunities are hereby to be declared civil rights, and the adoption of this Chapter is deemed to be an exercise of the policy power of the City to protect such rights.

SOURCE: Excerpt from *The Rights of Gay People: The Basic ACLU Guide to a Gay Person's Rights*, edited by Norman Dorsen and Aryeh Neier, p. 251.

DOCUMENT 2
Letter to the Editor of the *New York Times* from Paul Moore, November 23, 1981

Paul Moore, Episcopal bishop of New York, made a religious argument for gay rights in his letter to the editor of the New York Times.

I quote our diocesan resolution: "Whereas this Convention, without making any judgment on the morality of homosexuality, agrees that homosexuals are entitled to full civil rights. Now therefore be it resolved this Convention supports laws guaranteeing homosexuals all civil rights guaranteed to other citizens." The Bible stands for justice and compassion for all of God's children. To deny civil rights to anyone for something he or she cannot help is against the clear commandment of justice and love, which is the message of the word of God. As a New Yorker I find it incredible that this great city, populated by more gay persons than any other city in the world, still denies them basic human rights. They make an enormous contribution to the commercial, artistic, and religious life of our city.

SOURCE: Paul Moore, reprinted with permission.

DOCUMENT 3
Vatican Congregation for the Doctrine of the Faith, August 6, 1992

The following statement from the Roman Catholic Church reflects the views of many religious groups that take positions against gay rights.

"Sexual orientation" does not constitute a quality comparable to race, ethnic background, etc., in respect to nondiscrimination. Unlike these, homosexual orientation is an objective disorder and evokes moral concern.

There are areas in which it is not unjust discrimination to take sexual orientation into account, for example, in the placement of children for adoption or foster care, in employment of teachers or athletic coaches, and in military recruitment.

SOURCE: Vatican Congregation for the Doctrine of the Faith, *Origins*, August 6, 1992. Reprinted with permission.

---

groups hostile to Western policies. The terrorist organization Hezbollah, composed of Shiite Muslims and backed by Iran and Syria, arose in Lebanon in 1982 after Israeli forces invaded that country to stop the Palestine Liberation Organization from using sanctuaries in Lebanon to launch attacks on Israel.

Reagan's effort to stabilize Lebanon by sending 2,000 Marines to join an international peacekeeping mission failed. In April 1983, a suicide

DOCUMENT 4
Testimony of Charles Cochrane Jr. before the House Subcommittee on Employment Opportunities of the Committee on Education and Labor, January 27, 1982

Although the U.S. Congress has never enacted legislation banning discrimination on the basis of sexual orientation, it has considered a number of bills for that purpose. Charles Cochrane Jr., an army veteran and police sergeant, testified on behalf of such a bill in 1982.

I am very proud of being a New York City policeman. And I am equally proud of being gay. I have always been gay.

I have been out of the closet for 4 years. November 6 was my anniversary. It took me 34 years to muster enough courage to declare myself openly.

We gays are loathed by some, pitied by others, and misunderstood by most. We are not cruel, wicked, cursed, sick, or possessed by demons. We are artists, business people, police officers, and clergymen. We are scientists, truck drivers, politicians; we work in every field. We are loving human beings who are in some ways different. . . .

During the early years of my association with the New York City Police Department a great deal of energy did go into guarding and concealing my innermost feelings. I believed that I would be subjected to ridicule and harassment were my colleagues to learn of my sexual orientation. Happily, when I actually began to integrate the various aspects of my total self, those who knew me did not reject me.

Then what need is there for such legislation as H.R. 1454? The crying need of others, still trapped in their closets, who must be protected, who must be reassured that honesty about themselves and their lives will not cost them their homes or their jobs. . . .

The bill before you will not act as a proselytizing agent in matters of sexual orientation or preference. It will not include affirmative action provisions. Passage of this bill will protect the inherent human rights of all people of the United States, while in no way diminishing the rights of those who do not see the need for such legislation. Finally, it will signify, quite clearly, recognition and compassion for a group which is often maligned without justification.

SOURCE: U.S. House Subcommittee on Employment Opportunities of the Committee on Education and Labor, Hearing on H.R. 1454, 97th Cong., 2nd sess., 1982, 54–56.

DOCUMENT 5
Carl F. Horowitz, "Homosexuality's Legal Revolution," May 1991

Carl Horowitz, a policy analyst at the Heritage Foundation, a conservative think tank, expresses some of the arguments of those opposed to government protection of homosexual rights.

Homosexual activists have all but completed their campaign to persuade the nation's educational establishment that homosexuality is normal "alternative" behavior, and thus any adverse reaction to it is akin to a phobia, such as fear of heights, or an ethnic prejudice, such as anti-Semitism.

The movement now stands on the verge of fully realizing its use of law to . . . intimidate heterosexuals uncomfortable about coming into contact with it. . . . The movement seeks to win sinecures through the state, and over any objections by "homophobic" opposition. With a cloud of a heavy fine or even a jail sentence hanging over a mortgage lender, a rental agent, or a job interviewer who might be discomforted by them, homosexuals under these laws can win employment, credit, housing, and other economic entitlements. Heterosexuals would have no right to discriminate against homosexuals, but apparently, not vice versa. . . .

These laws will create market bottlenecks. Heterosexuals and even "closeted" homosexuals will be at a competitive disadvantage for jobs and housing. . . .

The new legalism will increase heterosexual anger — and even violence — toward homosexuals.

SOURCE: Carl F. Horowitz, "Homosexuality's Legal Revolution," *Freeman*, May 1991.

Questions for Analysis and Debate

1. Which of these documents discuss how heterosexuals would be affected by laws protecting gay and lesbian rights? What effects did they anticipate?

2. Which of these documents suggest that the civil rights movement influenced the authors' views on homosexual rights?

3. What do you think is the strongest argument for government protection of homosexual rights? What do you think is the strongest argument against government protection?

---

attack on the U.S. Embassy in Beirut killed 63 people, and in October a Hezbollah fighter drove a bomb-filled truck into a U.S. barracks there, killing 241 Marines (see Map 30.3). The attack prompted the withdrawal of U.S. troops, and Lebanon remained in chaos, while incidents of murder, kidnapping, and hijacking by various Middle Eastern extremist groups continued.

Following a Cold War pattern begun under Eisenhower, the Reagan administration sought

Attack on the Marine Barracks in Beirut
On October 23, 1983, members of Islamic Jihad, an anti-Israel, anti-Western terrorist group sponsored by Iran, demonstrated their hostility toward the U.S. troops stationed in Lebanon by exploding a car bomb outside the U.S. Marine compound near the Beirut airport and killing 241 Americans. In the aftermath of the attack, army colonel Colin Powell, assistant to the secretary of defense, approved the decision to withdraw from Lebanon, believing that "America [was] sticking its hand into a thousand-year-old hornet's nest" in the Middle East. Shown here are military personnel searching for and removing bodies of their dead comrades.
© Bettmann/Corbis.

to contain leftist movements across the globe. In October 1983, 5,000 U.S. troops invaded Grenada, a small island nation in the Caribbean where Marxists had staged a successful coup. In Asia, the United States moved more quietly, aiding the Afghan rebels' war against Afghanistan's Soviet-backed government. In the African nation of Angola, the United States armed rebel forces against the government supported by both the Soviet Union and Cuba. Reagan also sided with the South African government, which was brutally suppressing black protest against apartheid, forcing Congress to override his veto in order to impose economic sanctions against South Africa.

Administration officials were most fearful of left-wing movements in Central America, which Reagan claimed could "destabilize the entire region from the Panama Canal to Mexico." When a leftist uprising occurred in El Salvador in 1981, the United States sent money and military advisers to prop up the authoritarian government even though it had committed murderous human rights violations. In neighboring Nicaragua, the administration secretly aided the Contras (literally, "opposers"), an armed coalition seeking to unseat the left-wing Sandinistas, who had toppled a long-standing dictatorship.

The Iran-Contra Scandal

The Reagan administration's commitment to the Contras highlighted the issue of presidential versus congressional authority in using force abroad. Fearing another Vietnam, many Americans opposed aligning the United States with reactionary forces not supported by the majority of Nicaraguans. Congress repeatedly instructed the president to stop aiding the Contras, but the administration continued to secretly provide them with weapons and training and helped wreck the Nicaraguan economy. With support for his government undermined, Nicaragua's president, Daniel Ortega, agreed to a political settlement, and when he was defeated by a coalition of all the opposition groups, he stepped aside.

Secret aid to the Contras was part of a larger project that came to be known as the **Iran-Contra**

El Salvador and Nicaragua

scandal. It began in 1985 when officials of the National Security Council and CIA secretly arranged to sell arms to Iran, then in the midst of an eight-year war with neighboring Iraq, even while the United States openly supplied Iraq with funds and weapons. The purpose was to get Iran to pressure Hezbollah to release seven American hostages being held in Lebanon (see Map 30.3). Funds from the arms sales were then channeled through Swiss bank accounts to aid the Nicaraguan Contras. Over the objections of his secretary of state and secretary of defense, Reagan approved the arms sales, but the three subsequently denied knowing that the proceeds were diverted to the Contras.

When news of the affair surfaced in November 1986, the Reagan administration faced serious charges. The president's aides had defied Congress's express ban on military aid for the Contras. Investigations by an independent prosecutor appointed by Reagan led to a trial in which seven individuals pleaded guilty or were convicted of lying to Congress and destroying evidence. One felony conviction was later overturned on a technicality, and President George H. W. Bush pardoned the other six officials in December 1992. The independent prosecutor's final report found no evidence that Reagan had broken the law, but it concluded that he had known about the diversion of funds to the Contras and had "knowingly participated or at least acquiesced" in covering up the scandal — the most serious case of executive branch disregard for the law since Watergate.

A Thaw in Soviet-American Relations

A momentous reduction in Cold War tensions soon overshadowed the Iran-Contra scandal. The new Soviet-American accord depended in part on Reagan's flexibility, his profound desire to end the possibility of nuclear war, and his fortitude in standing up to conservatives and the national security establishment. It also depended on an innovative Soviet head of state who recognized that his country's domestic problems demanded an easing of Cold War antagonism. **Mikhail Gorbachev** assumed power in 1985 determined to revitalize an inefficient Soviet economy incapable of delivering basic consumer goods. As Reagan remarked privately, Gorbachev

Nuclear Freeze Campaign
Sixteen-year-old Justin Martino made this mask to wear in a 1985 march on the Pentagon in support of disarmament and world peace. Martino wanted to express his belief that "the arms race has no end except the end of life," and he later donated the mask to the Smithsonian Museum of American History. Worldwide demonstrations for nuclear disarmament achieved limited success when the United States and Soviet Union signed arms limitation agreements in 1987. Smithsonian Institution, Washington, D.C.

knew that "his economy is a basket case." Hoping to stimulate production and streamline distribution, Gorbachev introduced some elements of free enterprise and proclaimed a new era of *glasnost* (greater freedom of expression), eventually allowing contested elections and challenges to Communist rule.

Concerns about immense defense budgets moved both Reagan and Gorbachev to the negotiating table. Enormous military expenditures stood between the Soviet premier and his goal of economic revival. With growing popular support for arms reductions, along with a push from his wife, Nancy, Reagan made disarmament a major goal in his last years in office and readily responded when Gorbachev took the initiative. A positive personal chemistry developed between them, and they met four times between 1985 and 1988. Although Reagan's insistence on proceeding with SDI nearly killed the talks, by December 1987 the superpowers had completed an **intermediate-range nuclear forces (INF) agreement**. The treaty marked a major turning point in U.S.-Soviet relations. It eliminated all short- and medium-range missiles from Europe and provided for on-site inspection for the first time. This was also the first time that either nation had agreed to eliminate weapons already in place.

In 1988, Gorbachev further reduced tensions by announcing a gradual withdrawal from Afghanistan, which had become the Soviet equivalent of America's Vietnam. In addition, the Soviet Union, the United States, and Cuba agreed on a political settlement of the civil war in the African nation of Angola. In the Middle East,

The Fireside Summit
This photograph captures the warmth that developed between President Ronald Reagan and Soviet leader Mikhail Gorbachev at their first meeting at Geneva in November 1985. Although the meeting did not produce any key agreements, the two men spent much more time in private meetings than had been scheduled. They began to appreciate each other's concerns and to build trust, launching a relationship that would lead to nuclear arms reductions and the end of the Cold War. Ronald Reagan Presidential Library.

both superpowers supported a cease-fire and peace talks in the eight-year war between Iran and Iraq. Within three years, the Cold War that had defined the world for nearly half a century would be history.

> **REVIEW** How did anticommunism shape Reagan's foreign policy?

▶ Conclusion: Reversing the Course of Government

"Ours was the first revolution in the history of mankind that truly reversed the course of government," boasted Ronald Reagan in his farewell address in 1989. The word *revolution* exaggerated the change, but his administration did mark the slowdown or reversal of expanding federal budgets for domestic programs and regulations that had taken off in the 1930s. Although he did not deliver on the social or moral issues dear to the heart of the New Right, Reagan represented the "choice not an echo" that Phyllis Schlafly had called for in 1964, as he used his skills as "the Great Communicator" to cultivate antigovernment sentiment and undo the liberal assumptions of the New Deal.

Antigovernment sentiment grew along with the backlash against the reforms of the 1960s and the conduct of the Vietnam War. Watergate and other lawbreaking by Nixon administration

officials further disillusioned Americans. Presidents Ford and Carter restored morality to the White House, but neither could solve the gravest economic problems since the Great Depression — slow economic growth, stagflation, and an increasing trade deficit. Even the Democrat Carter gave higher priority to fiscal austerity than to social reform, and he began the government's retreat from regulation of key industries.

A new conservative movement helped Reagan win the presidency and flourished during his administration. Reagan's tax cuts, combined with hefty increases in defense spending, created a federal deficit crisis that justified cuts in social welfare spending, made new federal initiatives unthinkable, and burdened the country for years to come. These policies also contributed to a widening income gap between the rich and poor, weighing heavily especially on minorities, female-headed families, and children. Many Americans continued to support specific federal programs — especially those, such as Social Security and Medicare, that reached beyond the poor — but public sentiment about the government in general had taken a U-turn from the Roosevelt era. Instead of seeing the government as a helpful and problem-solving institution, many believed that not only was it ineffective at solving national problems, but it also often made things worse. As Reagan appointed new justices, the Supreme Court retreated from liberalism, curbing the government's authority to protect individual rights and regulate the economy.

With the economic recovery that set in after 1982 and his optimistic rhetoric, Reagan lifted the confidence of Americans about their nation and its promise — confidence that had eroded with the economic and foreign policy blows of the 1970s. He began his presidency voicing harsh rhetoric against the Soviet Union and intensifying the military buildup begun by Carter; he left office having helped move the two superpowers to the highest level of cooperation since the Cold War began. Although that accord was not welcomed by strong anti-Communist conservatives like Phyllis Schlafly, it signaled developments that would transform American-Soviet relations — and the world — in the next decade.

▶ Selected Bibliography

General Works

Edward D. Berkowitz, *Something Happened: A Political and Cultural Overview of the Seventies* (2006).
Steven F. Hayward, *The Age of Reagan: The Conservative Counterrevolution, 1980–1989* (2009).
Burton I. Kaufman and Scott Kaufman, *The Presidency of James Earl Carter, Jr.* (2006).
Robert Mason, *Richard Nixon and the Quest for a New Majority* (2004).
Keith W. Olson, *Watergate: The Presidential Scandal That Shook America* (2003).
James T. Patterson, *Restless Giant: The United States from Watergate to Bush v. Gore* (2005).
Gil Troy, *Morning in America: How Ronald Reagan Invented the 1980s* (2005).
Sean Wilentz, *The Age of Reagan: A History, 1974–2008* (2008).

Foreign Policy

David Farber, *Taken Hostage: The Iran Hostage Crisis and America's First Encounter with Radical Islam* (2004).
Beth A. Fischer, *The Reagan Reversal: Foreign Policy and the End of the Cold War* (1997).
Frances FitzGerald, *Way Out There in the Blue: Reagan, Star Wars, and the End of the Cold War* (2000).
Scott Kaufman, *Plans Unraveled: The Foreign Policy of the Carter Administration* (2008).
William M. LeoGrande, *Our Own Backyard: The United States in Central America, 1977–1992* (1998).
Douglas Little, *American Orientalism: The United States and the Middle East since 1945* (2002).
James Mann, *The Rebellion of Ronald Reagan: A History of the End of the Cold War* (2009).

The Economy, Energy, and the Environment

W. Carl Biven, *Jimmy Carter's Economy: Policy in an Age of Limits* (2003).
Elizabeth D. Blum, *Love Canal Revisited: Race, Class, and Gender in Environmental Activism* (2008).

Jefferson Cowie, *Stayin' Alive: The 1970s and the Last Days of the Working Class* (2010).
Samuel P. Hays, *A History of Environmental Politics since 1945* (2000).
Christopher Jencks, *The Homeless* (1994).
Hal K. Rothman, *The Greening of a Nation? Environmentalism in the United States since 1945* (1998).
Robert J. Samuelson, *The American Dream in the Age of Entitlement, 1945–1995* (1996).
John W. Sloan, *The Reagan Effect: Economics and Presidential Leadership* (1999).
Judith Stein, *Pivotal Decade: How the United States Traded Factories for Finance in the Seventies* (2010).

Social Movements and Contests over Rights

Terry H. Anderson, *The Pursuit of Fairness: A History of Affirmative Action* (2004).
John A. Andrew, *The Other Side of the Sixties: Young Americans for Freedom and the Rise of Conservative Politics* (1997).
Elizabeth A. Armstrong, *Forging Gay Identities: Organizing Sexuality in San Francisco, 1950–1994* (2003).
Donald T. Critchlow, *The Conservative Ascendancy: How the GOP Right Made Political History* (2007).
Donald T. Critchlow, *Phyllis Schlafly and Grassroots Conservatism: A Woman's Crusade* (2005).
Godfrey Hodgson, *The World Turned Right Side Up: A History of the Conservative Ascendancy in America* (1996).
Laura Kalman, *Right Star Rising: A New Politics, 1974–1980* (2010).
J. Anthony Lukas, *Common Ground: A Turbulent Decade in the Lives of Three American Families* (1986).
William Martin, *With God on Our Side: The Rise of the Religious Right in America* (1996).
Donald G. Mathews and Jane Sherron De Hart, *Sex, Gender, and the Politics of the ERA* (1990).
Lisa McGirr, *Suburban Warriors: The Origins of the New American Right* (2001).
James F. Simon, *The Center Holds: The Power Struggle inside the Rehnquist Court* (1995).

▶ **FOR MORE BOOKS ABOUT TOPICS IN THIS CHAPTER,** see the Online Bibliography at **bedfordstmartins.com/roark.**

▶ **FOR ADDITIONAL PRIMARY SOURCES FROM THIS PERIOD,** see Michael Johnson, ed., *Reading the American Past*, Fifth Edition.

▶ **FOR WEB SITES, IMAGES, AND DOCUMENTS RELATED TO TOPICS AND PLACES IN THIS CHAPTER,** visit Make History at **bedfordstmartins.com/roark.**

Reviewing Chapter 30

KEY TERMS

Explain each term's significance.

Nixon, Conservatism, and Constitutional Crisis
- Phyllis Schlafly (p. 1005)
- Warren E. Burger (p. 1008)
- Shirley Chisholm (p. 1009)
- Watergate (p. 1010)
- Gerald R. Ford (p. 1011)
- Federal Election Campaign Act of 1974 (p. 1012)
- James Earl "Jimmy" Carter Jr. (p. 1012)
- Walter F. Mondale (p. 1012)

The "Outsider" Presidency of Jimmy Carter
- National Energy Act of 1978 (p. 1015)
- Three Mile Island (p. 1016)
- Panama Canal treaty (p. 1017)
- Camp David accords (p. 1017)
- Iran hostage crisis (p. 1019)

Ronald Reagan and the Conservative Ascendancy
- Ronald Reagan (p. 1020)
- New (Christian) Right (p. 1021)
- supply-side economics (p. 1021)
- Economic Recovery Tax Act (p. 1021)

Continuing Struggles over Rights
- Equal Rights Amendment (ERA) (p. 1025)
- Sandra Day O'Connor (p. 1027)
- acquired immune deficiency syndrome (AIDS) (p. 1028)

Ronald Reagan Confronts an "Evil Empire"
- Strategic Defense Initiative (SDI) (p. 1029)
- Iran-Contra scandal (p. 1032)
- Mikhail Gorbachev (p. 1033)
- *glasnost* (p. 1033)
- intermediate-range nuclear forces (INF) agreement (p. 1033)

REVIEW QUESTIONS

Use key terms and dates to support your answer.

1. How did Nixon's policies reflect the increasing influence of conservatives on the Republican Party? (pp. 1005–1013)

2. How and where did Carter implement his commitment to human rights, and where and why did human rights give way to other priorities? (pp. 1013–1019)

3. Why did economic inequality increase during the Reagan administration? (pp. 1019–1025)

4. What gains and setbacks did minorities, feminists, and gays and lesbians experience during the Reagan years? (pp. 1026–1029)

5. How did anticommunism shape Reagan's foreign policy? (pp. 1029–1034)

MAKING CONNECTIONS

Draw on key terms, the timeline, and review questions.

1. What was Watergate's legacy for American politics in the following decade? In your answer, explain what led to Nixon's resignation. How did Congress try to prevent such abuses of power in the future?

2. Both the Republican and Democratic parties changed significantly in the 1970s and 1980s. Describe these changes, and discuss how they shaped contemporary American politics. In your answer, be sure to cite specific political developments.

3. Recent experiences in Vietnam hung over the foreign policy decisions of Presidents Carter and Reagan. How did each president try to reconcile the lessons of that conflict and the ongoing Cold War? In your answer, be sure to discuss the impact of the Vietnam War on specific policies in the 1970s and 1980s.

4. American regional politics shifted in significant ways during the 1970s and 1980s. Why was grassroots conservatism particularly strong in the Sun Belt? What was its relationship to the civil rights and equal opportunity developments of the 1960s? What was its relationship to economic development?

LINKING TO THE PAST

Link events in this chapter to earlier events.

1. How were the conservatives of the 1980s similar to and different from the conservatives who opposed the New Deal in the 1930s? (See chapter 24.)

2. Presidents Jimmy Carter and Woodrow Wilson both claimed human rights as a central principle of their foreign policy. Which one do you think pursued human rights more consistently? Which one was more successful in spreading human rights? Explain your answers. (See chapter 22.)

▶ FOR PRACTICE QUIZZES AND OTHER STUDY
TOOLS, visit the Online Study Guide at
bedfordstmartins.com/roark.

TIMELINE 1966–1988

1966	• Republican Ronald Reagan elected governor of California.
1968	• Republican Richard Nixon elected president.
1969	• Warren E. Burger appointed chief justice of U.S. Supreme Court.
1971	• Nixon vetoes comprehensive child care bill.
1972	• Nixon campaign aides arrested at Watergate complex.
	• Nixon reelected president.
1974	• Nixon resigns; Gerald Ford becomes president.
	• Ford pardons Nixon of any crimes he may have committed while president.
1976	• Democrat Jimmy Carter elected president.
1977	• United States signs Panama Canal treaty.
1978	• *Regents of University of California v. Bakke.*
	• Congress deregulates airlines.
1979	• Camp David accords signed.
	• Carter establishes formal diplomatic relations with China.
	• Soviet Union invades Afghanistan.
	• Hostage crisis in Iran begins.
	• Moral Majority founded.
1980	• Congress deregulates banking, trucking, and railroad industries.
	• Congress passes Superfund legislation.
	• Republican Ronald Reagan elected president.
1981	• Researchers discover AIDS virus.
	• Economic Recovery Tax Act.
1982	• Large demonstrations against nuclear weapons.
1983	• Terrorist bomb kills 241 U.S. Marines in Beirut, Lebanon.
	• Reagan announces plans for Strategic Defense Initiative ("Star Wars").
	• Family Research Council founded.
	• Reagan reelected president.
1986	• Iran-Contra scandal.
1987	• INF agreement signed.
1988	• Civil Rights Restoration Act.

1037

CONTAINER BOX

Containerized shipping revolutionized the maritime industry and contributed to the intensifying globalization that occurred near the end of the twentieth century. The use of truck-size boxes to move goods without loading and unloading individual items began in the 1950s and became the norm by the 1980s. The container box's efficiency and cost-effectiveness stimulated industrial development around the world and gave Americans access to an unheralded array of cheap consumer goods. After the terrorist attacks against the United States on September 11, 2001, some Americans worried that weapons of mass destruction might be concealed within container boxes. In the background, container ships unload at Port Elizabeth, New Jersey.

Container box: Shutterstock Images LLC; background: © Bettmann/ Corbis.

31

The Promises and Challenges of Globalization

Since 1989

IN HIS MOSCOW HOTEL ROOM ON APRIL 22, 1988, RONALD REAGAN'S national security adviser, Colin L. Powell, contemplated the plans that Premier Mikhail Gorbachev had just announced, which would dramatically alter the Soviet Union's government and economy. "Lying there in bed," Powell recalled, "I realized that one phase of my life had ended, and another was about to begin. Up until now, as a soldier, my mission had been to confront, contain, and, if necessary, combat communism. Now I had to think about a world without a Cold War." For the next sixteen years, Powell labored to redefine his country's role in a world transformed.

Colin Powell was born in Harlem in 1937 and grew up in the Bronx, the son of Jamaican immigrants. His father headed the shipping department in a garment factory, where his mother worked as a seamstress. After attending public schools, Powell enrolled in City College of New York. There he joined the army's Reserve Officers Training Corps (ROTC) program, the defining experience of his college years. "The discipline, the structure, the camaraderie, the sense of belonging," he said, "were what I craved." When he graduated in 1958, Powell began a lifelong career in military and public service, rising to the highest rank of four-star general. He chose to stay in the army primarily because "I loved what I was doing." But he also recognized that "for a black, no other avenue in American society offered so much opportunity." Powell's two tours of duty in Vietnam taught him that "you do not squander courage and lives without clear purpose, without the country's backing, and without full commitment." In his subsequent positions as national security adviser to Ronald Reagan, chairman of the Joint Chiefs of Staff in the George H. W. Bush and Bill Clinton administrations, and secretary of state under George W. Bush, Powell endeavored to keep his country out of "halfhearted warfare for half-baked reasons that the American people could not understand or support."

Powell's sense that Gorbachev's reforms would ring down the curtain on the Cold War became a reality more quickly than anyone anticipated. Eastern Europe broke free from Communist control in 1989, and the Soviet Union disintegrated in 1991. Throughout the 1990s, as the lone superpower, the United States deployed both military and diplomatic power during episodes of instability in Latin America, the Middle East, eastern Europe, and

1039

Asia, almost always in concert with the major nations of Europe and Asia. In 1991, in its first full-fledged war since Vietnam, the United States led a United Nations–authorized force of twenty-eight nations to repel Iraq's invasion of Kuwait.

During a temporary retirement from public service in the 1990s, Powell remarked that "neither of the two major parties fits me comfortably." Many Americans seemed to agree: They turned Republican George H. W. Bush out of office in 1992 but elected Republican Congresses during Democrat Bill Clinton's administration. When Republican George W. Bush (son of George H. W. Bush) entered the White House in 2001, he faced a nearly evenly divided Congress. Between 1989 and 2000, domestic policies reflected a slight retreat from the conservatism of the Reagan years. The first Bush administration approved tighter environmental protections and new rights for people with disabilities, and President Clinton signed measures strengthening gun control and aiding low-wage earners. But the pendulum swung back to the right in the second Bush presidency.

All three presidents shared a commitment to hastening the globalization processes that were linking nations together in an increasingly connected economy. As capital, products, information, and people crossed national boundaries in greater numbers and at greater speed, a surge of immigration rivaled the stream of a century earlier that had brought Powell's parents to the United States. Powell cheered globalization, predicting that the world would become "defined by trade relations, by the flow of information, capital, technology, and goods, rather than by armies glaring at each other across borders."

He was not so naive as to anticipate a world "without war or conflict," recognizing challenges such as nuclear proliferation, nationalist passions in areas of former Soviet dominance and the Middle East, civil wars in Africa, and Islamic extremism. But he shared other Americans' shock when in September 2001 deadly terrorist attacks in New York City and Washington, D.C., exposed American vulnerability to new and horrifying threats and sent U.S. soldiers into Afghanistan to overthrow the government that harbored the attackers. The administration's response to terrorism overwhelmed Secretary of State Powell's commitments to internationalism, multilateralism, and military restraint. In 2003, George W. Bush began a second war against Iraq, implementing a distinct shift to a foreign policy based on preemptive attacks against presumed threats and going it alone if necessary. The unpopularity of that war and a severe financial crisis helped the Democrats regain power and elect Barack Obama as the first African American president.

Secretary of State Colin Powell

Colin Powell's loyalty and discretion helped him rise through the ranks of the army and serve in four presidential administrations. The U.S. invasion of Iraq in March 2003 ran counter to Powell's commitment to acting through the international community and sacrificing American lives only when a vital interest was at stake and an exit plan had been established. Nonetheless, he stayed in his job until 2005 and defended administration policy. In this photo taken at the White House in February 2003, Powell listens to Secretary of Defense Donald Rumsfeld. National Security Adviser Condoleezza Rice stands behind them. Charles Ommanney/Contact Press Images for *Newsweek*.

▶ Domestic Stalemate and Global Upheaval: The Presidency of George H. W. Bush

Announcing his bid for the presidency in 1988, Vice President **George H. W. Bush** declared, "We don't need radical new directions." Generally satisfied with the agenda set by Ronald Reagan and facing a Democratic-controlled Congress, Bush proposed few domestic initiatives. His dispatch of troops to oust the corrupt dictator of Panama, Manuel Noriega, represented a much longer continuity, following a century of U.S. intervention in Latin America.

Yet as the most dramatic changes since the 1940s swept through the world, Bush confronted situations that did not fit the simpler free world versus communism framework that had guided foreign policy since World War II. Most Americans approved of Bush's handling of two challenges to U.S. foreign policy: the disintegration of the Soviet Union and its hold over Eastern Europe, and Iraq's invasion of neighboring Kuwait. But voters' concern over a sluggish economy limited Bush to one term in the White House.

Gridlock in Government

The son of a wealthy New England senator, George Herbert Walker Bush fought in World War II, earned a Yale degree, and then settled in Texas to make his own way in the oil industry and politics. He served in Congress during the 1960s and headed the CIA during the Nixon and Ford years. When Ronald Reagan achieved a commanding lead in the 1980 presidential primaries, Bush adjusted his more moderate policy positions to fit Reagan's conservative agenda and accepted second place on the Republican ticket. At the end of Reagan's second term, Republicans rewarded him with the presidential nomination.

Several candidates competed for the Democratic nomination in 1988. The Reverend Jesse Jackson — whose Rainbow Coalition campaign centered on the needs of minorities, women, the working class, and the poor — made an impressive bid, winning several primaries and seven million votes. But a more centrist candidate, Massachusetts governor Michael Dukakis, won the nomination. On election day, half the eligible voters stayed home, indicating their disgust with the negative campaigning or their satisfaction with the Republican record on peace and prosperity. Divided government would remain, however, as Bush won 54 percent of the vote but the Democrats gained seats in Congress.

Although President Bush saw himself primarily as guardian and beneficiary of the Reagan legacy, he promised "a kinder, gentler nation" and was more inclined than Reagan to approve government activity in the private sphere. An oil spill from an Exxon tanker that ruined eight hundred miles of Alaska shoreline in 1989 heightened environmental awareness and helped Bush convince Congress to approve the **Clean Air Act of 1990**, the strongest, most comprehensive environmental law in history.

"Let the shameful wall of exclusion finally come tumbling down," proclaimed Bush when he signed another regulatory measure in 1990, the **Americans with Disabilities Act**. Benefiting some forty million Americans, this measure banned discrimination in employment, transportation, public accommodation, communications, and governmental activities, requiring that private businesses and public facilities be accessible to people with disabilities. Cynthia Jones, publisher of a magazine on disability politics, noticed a breeze stirring over the White House lawn at the signing of the bill. She said, "It was kind of like a new breath of air was sweeping across America. . . . People knew they had rights. That was wonderful." (See "Seeking the American Promise," page 1042.)

> **"It was kind of like a new breath of air was sweeping across America. . . . People knew they had rights."**
> — Disability rights activist **CYNTHIA JONES**

Yet Bush also needed to satisfy conservatives whose strength in the Republican Party continued to rise. His most famous campaign pledge had been "Read my lips: No new taxes," and he opposed most proposals requiring additional federal funds. Bush vetoed thirty-six bills, including those lifting abortion restrictions, extending unemployment benefits, raising taxes, and mandating family and medical leave for workers. Press reports increasingly used the words *stalemate, gridlock,* and *divided government.*

Continuing a trend begun during the Reagan years, states tried to compensate for this paralysis, becoming more innovative than Washington. States passed bills to block corporate takeovers, establish parental leave policies, improve food labeling, and protect the environment. In the 1980s, a few states began to pass

Suing for Access: Disability and the Courts

When the Americans with Disabilities Act (ADA) passed in 1990, Beverly Jones expressed her elation: "For me, the passage of the ADA was like opening a door that had been closed to me for so long." The measure promised to protect people with disabilities from discrimination by private employers, public agencies, and state and local governments. This civil rights act providing equal access and opportunity followed in a long tradition of Americans fighting for their rights, struggles not only to enact laws but also to see them enforced.

Jones, a single mother with two children, joined the ranks of the 2.2 million Americans who use a wheelchair after she was in an automobile accident in 1984 that resulted in paraplegia. Determined not to "allow what I wanted in life to be denied because of . . . physical limitations," she trained as a court reporter and went to work to support her family. But Jones discovered that despite the requirements of the ADA, in Tennessee seven out of ten courthouses were not wheelchair accessible. "I was often forced to ask complete strangers to carry me up the stairs," Jones recalled, and she found the experiences "humiliating and frightening."

Jones pleaded in vain with local, state, and federal officials to obtain compliance with the law. "The door that I thought had been opened was still closed and my freedom to live my dream was turning into a nightmare," she said. Finally, in 1998, after having to ask a judge to carry her to a restroom, she decided to appeal to the courts.

Jones filed a lawsuit against the state of Tennessee, joining five other plaintiffs who alleged that the state was in violation of Title II of the ADA, which prohibits governmental entities from denying public services, programs, and activities to individuals because of a disability. Another plaintiff, George Lane, had injured his hip and pelvis in a car accident. Cited for reckless driving, he went to the courthouse in a wheelchair but had to crawl up the stairs. When the court adjourned for lunch, he crawled back down. That afternoon, he refused to crawl upstairs again and was jailed for failing to appear in court. Lane said that he would never forget the humiliation of having to drag his body up the thirty tile steps of the Polk County Courthouse. Lane, Jones, and the four other plaintiffs sought legal redress and damages of $250,000 each.

Tennessee immediately countersued, challenging the constitutionality of the ADA's requirement that states make public facilities accessible to people with disabilities. Finally, in 2004, the case of *Tennessee v. Lane* reached the Supreme Court, where conservative justices espoused a "new federalism" that challenged the right of Congress to tell the states what to do. Citing sovereign immunity (protection from lawsuits), granted to states by the Eleventh Amendment to the Constitution, courts began to question the right of Congress to make federal laws binding on the states. In 2001, in a dramatic example of the trend to limit Congress's power, the Supreme Court held that Congress lacked a constitutional basis for permitting states

measures guaranteeing gay and lesbian rights. In the 1990s, dozens of cities passed ordinances requiring businesses receiving tax abatements or other city benefits to pay wages well above the federal minimum wage. And in 1999, California passed a gun control bill with much tougher restrictions on assault weapons than reformers had been able to get through Congress.

The huge federal budget deficit inherited from the Reagan administration impelled the president in 1990 to abandon his "no new taxes" pledge, outraging conservatives. The new law, which Bush depended on Democrats to pass, authorized modest tax increases for high-income Americans and higher taxes on gasoline, cigarettes, alcohol, and luxury items. Yet it had little effect on the massive tax reductions of the early 1980s, leaving intact a key element of Reagan's legacy. Neither the new revenues nor controls on spending curbed the deficit, which was boosted by rising costs for Social Security, Medicare, and Medicaid and spending on war and natural disasters.

Bush also continued Reagan's efforts to create a more conservative Supreme Court. His first nominee, federal appeals court judge David Souter, was a moderate. But in 1991, when the only African American on the Court, Justice Thurgood Marshall, retired, Bush set off a national controversy. He nominated Clarence Thomas, a conservative black appeals court judge who had

to be sued under Title I of the ADA, which applies to state employment.

In *Tennessee v. Lane*, the state cited this decision, claiming sovereign immunity and challenging the constitutionality of the ADA. Carol Westlake, executive director of the Tennessee Disability Coalition, pointed out that Tennessee's claim of states' rights was the same argument used to deny civil rights to African Americans in the 1950s and 1960s. In January 2004, as the Supreme Court heard arguments in the case, activists demonstrated outside the Court, chanting, "Justice for all; we won't crawl."

At stake was not only the right of people with disabilities to sue a state when denied access to public facilities but also the right of Congress to make federal laws binding on the states. In May 2004, in a five-to-four decision, the Supreme Court ruled that states failing to make their courthouses accessible to people with disabilities could be sued for damages under federal disability law. But it confined its ruling to the specific context presented in the case: access to courts. By the narrowest possible margin, with the crucial fifth vote cast by Justice Sandra Day O'Connor, the Court focused on one narrow application of the ADA and upheld it in the face of Tennessee's claim of constitutional immunity.

"My case is over," Jones acknowledged. "We have accomplished what

Beverly Jones

Beverly Jones is shown here in her wheelchair next to one of the Tennessee courthouse stairways that made her job as a court reporter so difficult. "As a single mom supporting myself and two kids," she said, "I could not afford to quit my job or strictly limit my work to accessible courthouses." In 1998, Jones filed suit under the Americans with Disabilities Act. Six years later, in 2004, the Supreme Court upheld her right to enforce the protections the ADA granted to those with disabilities. AP Photo/John Russell.

we wanted to be achieved." Nonetheless, the narrow grounds on which the Court decided her case meant that people with disabilities would continue to seek judicial acknowledgment of their rights to opportunity and access.

Questions for Consideration

1. What arguments did Tennessee use in its effort to defeat Jones's lawsuit?

2. In what ways was the struggle for disability rights similar to and different from minority rights movements?

---

opposed affirmative action as head of the Equal Employment Opportunity Commission (EEOC) under Reagan. Charging that Thomas would not protect minority rights, civil rights groups and other liberal organizations fought the nomination. Then Anita Hill, a black law professor, accused Thomas of sexually harassing her while she was his employee at the EEOC.

Thomas angrily denied the charges, claiming that he was the victim of a "high-tech lynching for uppity blacks." Hill's testimony failed to sway the Senate, which voted narrowly to confirm Thomas. The hearings angered many women, who noted that only two women sat in the Senate and denounced the male senators for failing to

take sexual harassment seriously. Feminists complained that men "still don't get it" and redirected their anger to electoral politics, making 1992 a banner year for female candidates. Thomas's confirmation solidified the Supreme Court's shift to the right.

Going to War in Central America and the Persian Gulf

President Bush won greater support for his actions abroad than for his domestic policy, and he twice sent U.S. soldiers into battle. In Central America, the United States had tolerated and, in fact, paid Panamanian dictator Manuel Noriega for helping

Bush and Taxes
When George H. W. Bush ran as the Republican candidate for president in 1988, he addressed an issue central to conservative politics. "Read my lips," he said. "No new taxes." Yet the federal budget deficit he inherited from Ronald Reagan grew even larger, compelling Bush to agree to a fiscal package of both budget cuts and tax increases. Many Republicans were outraged, and Bush had to depend on Democrats' votes in Congress to pass the measure. Editorial cartoonists had a field day with the controversy. Here, conservative cartoonist Scott Stantis likened Bush to Pinocchio, whose nose grew when he lied. Scott Stantis/Copley News Service.

the Contras in Nicaragua and providing the CIA with information about Communist activities in the region. But in 1989, after Noriega was indicted for drug trafficking by an American grand jury and after his troops killed an American Marine, President Bush ordered 25,000 military personnel into Panama. In **Operation Just Cause**, U.S. forces quickly overcame Noriega's troops, sustaining 23 deaths, while hundreds of Panamanians, including many civilians, died. Chairman of the Joint Chiefs of Staff Colin Powell noted that "our euphoria over our victory in Just Cause was not universal." Both the United Nations and the Organization of American States censured the unilateral action by the United States.

By contrast, Bush's second military engagement rested solidly on international approval. Considering Iran to be America's major enemy in the Middle East, U.S. officials had quietly assisted the Iraqi dictator **Saddam Hussein** in the Iran-Iraq war, which began in 1980 and ended inconclusively in 1988. In August 1990, Hussein sent troops into the small, oil-rich country of Kuwait to the south (Map 31.1), and within days the invasion neared the Saudi Arabian border, threatening the world's largest oil reserves. President Bush quickly ordered a massive mobilization of American forces and assembled an international coalition to stand up to Iraq. He invoked principles of national self-determination and international law, but long-standing interests in Middle Eastern oil also drove the U.S. response. As the largest importer of oil, the United States

consumed one-fourth of the world's supply, 20 percent of which came from Iraq and Kuwait.

Reflecting the easing of Cold War tensions, the Soviet Union voted for a UN resolution declaring an embargo on Iraqi oil and authorizing the use of force if Iraq did not withdraw from Kuwait by January 15, 1991. By then, the United States had deployed more than 400,000 soldiers to Saudi Arabia, joined by 265,000 troops from some two dozen other nations, including several Arab states. "The community of nations has resolutely gathered to condemn and repel lawless aggression," Bush announced. "With few exceptions, the world now stands as one."

With Iraqi forces still in Kuwait, in January 1991 Bush asked Congress to approve war. Considerable sentiment favored waiting to see if the embargo and other means would force Hussein to back down, a position quietly urged within the administration by Colin Powell. Linking the crisis to the failure of U.S. energy conservation, Democratic senator Edward M. Kennedy insisted, "Not a single American life should be sacrificed in a war for the price of oil." Congress debated for three days and then authorized war by a margin of five votes in the Senate and sixty-seven in the House, with most Democrats in opposition. On January 17, 1991, the U.S.-led coalition launched Operation Desert Storm, a forty-day bombing campaign against Iraqi military targets, power plants, oil refineries, and transportation networks. Having severely crippled Iraq by air, the coalition then stormed into Kuwait

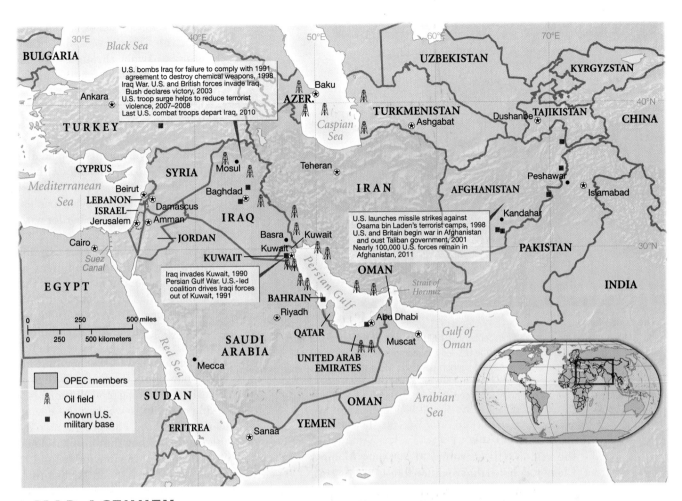

U.S. bombs Iraq for failure to comply with 1991 agreement to destroy chemical weapons, 1998
Iraq War. U.S. and British forces invade Iraq. Bush declares victory, 2003
U.S. troop surge helps to reduce terrorist violence, 2007–2008
Last U.S. combat troops depart Iraq, 2010

U.S. launches missile strikes against Osama bin Laden's terrorist camps, 1998
U.S. and Britain begin war in Afghanistan and oust Taliban government, 2001
Nearly 100,000 U.S. forces remain in Afghanistan, 2011

Iraq invades Kuwait, 1990
Persian Gulf War. U.S.-led coalition drives Iraqi forces out of Kuwait, 1991

OPEC members
Oil field
Known U.S. military base

MAP ACTIVITY

Map 31.1 Events in the Middle East, 1989–2011

During the Persian Gulf War of 1991, Egypt, Syria, and other Middle Eastern nations joined the coalition against Iraq, and the twenty-two-member Arab League supported the war as a means to liberate Kuwait. After September 11, 2001, the Arab League approved of U.S. military operations in Afghanistan because the attacks "were an attack on the common values of the world, not just on the United States." Yet, except for the countries where the United States had military bases — Bahrain, Kuwait, Qatar, and Saudi Arabia — no Arab country supported the American invasion and occupation of Iraq in 2003. Arab hostility toward the United States also reflected the deterioration of Israeli-Palestinian relations after 1999, as Arabs charged that the United States allowed Israel to deny Palestinians land and liberty.

READING THE MAP: In what countries are the sources of oil located? In what countries does the United States have military bases?

CONNECTIONS: What conditions prompted the U.S. military interventions in Iraq and Afghanistan in 1991, 2001, and 2003? What were the U.S. goals in each of these interventions? To what extent were those goals realized?

with massive ground forces, forcing Iraqi troops to withdraw (see Map 31.1).

"By God, we've kicked the Vietnam syndrome once and for all," President Bush exulted on March 1. Most Americans found no moral ambiguity in the **Persian Gulf War** and took pride in the display of military prowess. In contrast to the loss of 58,000 American lives in Vietnam, 270 U.S. service members perished in Desert Storm.

The United States stood at the apex of global leadership, steering a coalition in which Arab nations fought beside their former colonial rulers.

Some Americans criticized the Bush administration for ending the war without deposing Hussein. But Bush pointed to the UN mandate that limited the mission to driving Iraqi forces out of Kuwait and to Middle Eastern leaders' concern that an invasion of Iraq would destabilize

The Gulf War
This soldier arriving in Saudi Arabia in September 1990 was part of the massive military buildup in the Persian Gulf area before the U.S.-led coalition drove Iraqi forces out of Kuwait. For the first time, women served in combat-support positions. More than 33,000 women were stationed throughout the area; eleven died, and two were held as prisoners. Among their duties were piloting planes and helicopters, directing artillery, and fighting fires. © Bettmann/Corbis.

the region. His secretary of defense, Richard Cheney, doubted that coalition forces could secure a stable government to replace Hussein and considered the price of a long occupation too high. Administration officials counted on economic sanctions and Hussein's pledges not to rearm or develop weapons of mass destruction, secured by a system of UN inspections, to contain the dictator.

Yet Middle Eastern stability remained elusive. Israel, which had endured Iraqi missile attacks, was more secure, but the Israeli-Palestinian conflict remained intractable. Despite military losses, Saddam Hussein remained in power and turned his war machine on Iraqi Kurds and Shiite Muslims whom the United States had encouraged to rebel. Hussein also found ways to conceal arms from UN weapons inspectors before he threw them out in 1998. Finally, the decision to keep U.S. troops based in Saudi Arabia, the holy land of Islam, fueled the hatred and determination of Muslim extremists like Osama bin Laden and served as a recruiting tool.

The Cold War Ends

Soviet support in the Persian Gulf War marked a momentous change in relations between the United States and the Soviet Union. The progres-

sive forces that Gorbachev had encouraged in the Communist world (see chapter 30) swept through Eastern Europe in 1989, when popular uprisings in Hungary, Poland, East Germany, and elsewhere demanded an end to state repression and inefficient economic bureaucracies. Communist governments toppled like dominoes (Map 31.2), virtually without bloodshed, because Gorbachev refused to prop them up with Soviet armies. East Germany opened its border with West Germany, and in November 1989 ecstatic Germans danced on the Berlin Wall and swung sledgehammers to demolish that dominant symbol of the Cold War, which had separated East and West since 1961. An amazed East Berliner crossed the line exclaiming, "They just let us go. I can't believe it."

Bush assured Gorbachev that he would not "climb the Berlin Wall and make high-sounding pronouncements," taking care not to weaken the Soviet leader at home. The president persuaded Gorbachev that unification of East and West Germany was inevitable, and it sped to completion in 1990. Soon former iron curtain countries such as Hungary and Poland lined up to join NATO. Although U.S. military forces remained in Europe as part of NATO, Europe no longer depended on the United States for its security. Its economic clout also grew as Western Europe formed a common economic market in 1992. The destiny of Europe, to which the United States and the Soviet Union had held the key for forty-five years, now lay in European hands.

Inspired by the liberation of Eastern Europe, republics within the Soviet Union soon sought their own independence. In December 1991, Boris Yeltsin, president of the Russian Republic, announced that Russia and eleven other republics had formed a new entity, the Commonwealth of Independent States, and other former Soviet states declared their independence. With nothing left to govern, Gorbachev resigned. The Soviet Union had dissolved, and with it the Cold War conflict that had defined U.S. foreign policy for decades.

Colin Powell joked that he was "running out of villains. I'm down to Castro and Kim Il Sung," the North Korean dictator who, along with China's leaders, resisted the liberalizing tides sweeping the world. In 1989, Chinese

VISUAL ACTIVITY

Fall of the Berlin Wall

After 1961, the Berlin Wall stood as the prime symbol of the Cold War and the iron grip of communism over Eastern Europe and the Soviet Union. More than four hundred Eastern Europeans were killed trying to flee to the West. After Communist authorities opened the wall on November 9, 1989, permitting free travel between East and West Germany, Berliners from both sides gathered at the wall to celebrate. Eric Bouvet/Gamma Press Images.

READING THE IMAGE: What does the image tell you about the revolutions in Eastern Europe in 1989?
CONNECTIONS: What were the major factors that made possible the dismantling of the Berlin Wall, the major symbol of the Cold War in Europe?

soldiers killed hundreds of pro-democracy demonstrators in Tiananmen Square in Beijing, and the Communist government arrested some ten thousand reformers. North Korea remained a Communist dictatorship, committed to developing nuclear weapons. "The post–Cold War world is decidedly not post-nuclear," declared one U.S. official. In 1990, the United States and the Soviet Union signed the Strategic Arms Reduction Talks (START) treaty, which cut about 30 percent of each superpower's nuclear arsenal. And in 1996, the UN General Assembly overwhelmingly approved a total nuclear test ban treaty. Yet India and Pakistan, hostile neighbors, refused to sign the treaty, and both exploded atomic devices in 1998, increasing the nuclear risk in South Asia. Moreover, the Republican-controlled Senate defeated U.S. ratification of the test ban treaty in October 1999, halting a decade of progress on nuclear weapons control. The potential for rogue nations and terrorist groups to develop nuclear weapons posed an ongoing threat to international peace and security.

The 1992 Election

In March 1991, Bush's chances for reelection in 1992 looked golden. The Gulf War victory catapulted his approval rating to 88 percent, causing the most prominent Democrats to opt out of the presidential race. But that did not deter **William Jefferson "Bill" Clinton**, who at age forty-five had served as governor of Arkansas for twelve years. Like Carter in 1976, Clinton and his running mate, Tennessee senator Albert Gore Jr., presented themselves as "New Democrats" and sought to rid the party of its liberal image.

Clinton promised to work for the "forgotten middle class," who "do the work, pay the taxes, raise the kids, and play by the rules." Disavowing the "tax and spend" label that Republicans pinned on his party, he promised a tax cut for the middle class, pledged to reinvigorate government and the economy, and vowed "to put an end to welfare as we know it." Bush was vulnerable to voters' concerns about the ailing economy, as unemployment reached 7 percent, and to the

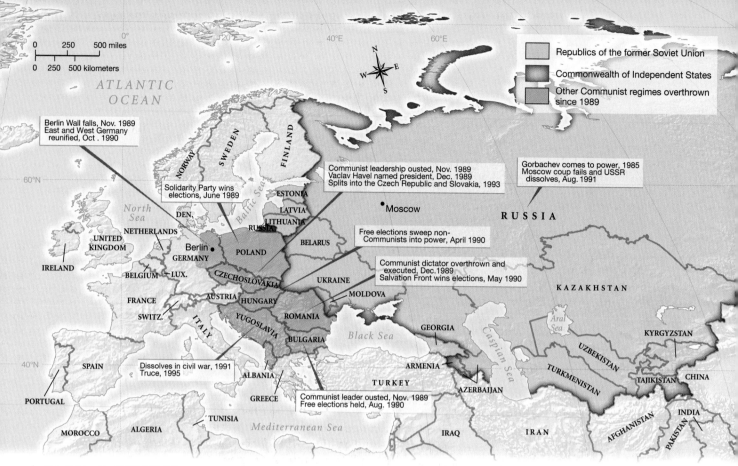

MAP ACTIVITY

Map 31.2 Events in Eastern Europe, 1989–2002

The overthrow of Communist governments throughout Eastern Europe and the splintering of the Soviet Union into more than a dozen separate nations were the most momentous changes in world history since World War II.

READING THE MAP: Which country was the first to overthrow its Communist government? Which was the last? In which nations did elections usher in a change in government?

CONNECTIONS: What problems did Mikhail Gorbachev try to solve, and how did he try to solve them? What policy launched by Ronald Reagan contributed to Soviet dilemmas? (See chapter 30.) Did it create any problems in the United States?

Clinton campaign's emphasis on bread-and-butter issues. The popularity of a third candidate, self-made Texas billionaire H. Ross Perot, revealed Americans' frustrations with government and the major parties. Railing against the huge federal budget deficit, Perot mobilized a sizable grassroots movement and established the deficit as a key campaign issue.

Fifty-five percent of those eligible voted, just barely reversing the thirty-year decline in voter turnout. Clinton won 43 percent of the popular vote, Bush 38 percent, and Perot 19 percent — the strongest third-party finish in eighty years. By casting nearly two-thirds of their votes against Bush, voters suggested a mandate for change but not the direction that change should take.

REVIEW How did George H. W. Bush respond to threats to U.S. interests as the Cold War came to an end?

▶ The Clinton Administration's Search for the Middle Ground

Bill Clinton's assertion that "the era of big government is over" reflected the Democratic Party's move to the right that had begun with Jimmy Carter in the 1970s. Clinton did not completely abandon liberal principles. He extended benefits for the working poor; delivered incremental reforms to feminists, environmentalists, and other groups; and spoke out in favor of affirmative action and gay rights. Yet his administration attended more to the concerns of middle-class Americans than to the needs of the disadvantaged.

Clinton's eight-year presidency witnessed the longest economic boom in history and ended

Clinton and Gore on Tour
The gregarious Bill Clinton excelled at political campaigning, and the youth of the first baby boomer candidates appealed to many. During the 1992 presidential campaign, Clinton and his wife, Hillary — accompanied by running mate Al Gore and his wife, Tipper — went out on several bus tours as a way of demonstrating the Democrats' connection to ordinary people. Not far from this campaign stop in Sylvester, Georgia, the bus caravan passed by a handmade sign that read "Bubbas for Clinton/Gore." © Ira Wyman/Sygma/Corbis.

with a budget surplus. Although various factors generated the prosperity, many Americans identified Clinton with the buoyant economy, elected him to a second term, and continued to support him even when his reckless sexual behavior resulted in impeachment. The Senate failed to convict the president, but the scandal crippled Clinton's leadership in his last years in office.

Clinton's Reforms

Clinton wanted to restore confidence in government as a force for good while not alienating antigovernment voters. The huge budget deficit that he inherited — $4.4 trillion in 1993 — further precluded substantial federal initiatives. Moreover, Perot's challenges denied Clinton a majority of the popular vote in both 1992 and 1996, and the Republicans controlled Congress for all but his first two years in office. Throughout most of his presidency, Clinton was burdened by investigations into past financial activities and private indiscretions. While the president had an extraordinary knack for making voters feel that he liked and understood them, he struggled to translate that appeal into gains for his agenda.

Despite these obstacles, Clinton achieved a number of incremental reforms. He used his executive authority to ease restrictions on abortion and signed several bills that Republicans had previously blocked. In 1993, Congress enacted gun control legislation and the Family and Medical Leave Act, which entitled workers in larger companies to unpaid leave for childbirth, adoption, and family medical emergencies. The Violence against Women Act of 1994 authorized $1.6 billion and new remedies for combating sexual assault and domestic violence. Clinton won stricter air pollution controls and greater protection for national forests and parks. Other liberal measures included a minimum-wage increase, the largest expansion of aid for college students since the GI Bill (see chapter 25), and the creation of AmeriCorps, which enabled students to pay for their education with community service.

Most significantly, Clinton pushed through a substantial increase in the **Earned Income Tax Credit (EITC)** for low-wage earners, a program begun in 1975. The EITC gave tax cuts to people who worked full-time at meager wages or, if they paid no taxes, a subsidy to lift their family income above the poverty line. By 2003, some fifteen million low-income families were benefiting from the EITC, almost half of them minorities. One expert called it "the largest antipoverty program since the Great Society."

> **"The largest antipoverty program since the Great Society."**
> — A policy expert, commenting on the Earned Income Tax Credit

Shortly before Clinton took office, the economy had begun to rebound, and the boom that followed helped boost his popularity through the 1990s. Economic expansion, along with spending cuts, tax increases, and declining unemployment, produced a budget surplus in 1998, the first since 1969. Despite a substantial tax cut in 1997 that reduced levies on estates and capital gains and provided tax credits for families with children and for higher education, the surplus grew. The seemingly inexorable growth of government debt had turned around.

Clinton's Appointments
Not only did President Clinton appoint more women to high government posts than any previous president, but he also broke new ground by appointing them to offices traditionally considered to be male territory. During his presidency, Janet Reno served as attorney general, Laura Tyson as chair of the President's Council of Economic Advisers, Sheila Widnall as secretary of the air force, and Madeleine Albright first as ambassador to the United Nations and then as secretary of state. Here, Albright (left) and Reno (second from right) applaud Clinton's 1999 State of the Union address with other cabinet members. AP Images/Doug Mills.

Clinton failed, however, to provide universal health insurance and to curb skyrocketing medical costs. Under the direction of First Lady Hillary Rodham Clinton and with very little congressional consultation, the administration proposed a complicated plan that drew criticism from both sides. Liberals wanted a single-payer plan similar to Medicare, while conservatives charged that the proposal would increase taxes and government interference in medical decisions. Congress enacted smaller reforms enabling workers who changed jobs to retain health insurance and underwriting health care for five million uninsured children, but affordable health care for all remained elusive.

Pledging to change the face of government to one that "looked like America," Clinton built on the gradual progress women and minorities had made since the 1960s. For example, African Americans and women had become mayors in major cities from New York to San Francisco. Virginia had elected the first black governor since Reconstruction, and Florida the first Latino. In the executive branch, Clinton appointed the most diverse group of department heads ever assembled, including six women,

three African Americans, and two Latinos. Secretary of Commerce Norman Y. Mineta became the first Asian American to hold a cabinet post. Janet Reno became the first female attorney general and Madeleine K. Albright the first female secretary of state. Clinton's judicial appointments had a similar cast, and in 1993 he named the second woman to the Supreme Court, Ruth Bader Ginsburg, whose arguments before she became an appeals court judge had won key women's rights rulings from the Supreme Court.

Accommodating the Right

Although much of Clinton's agenda fell within the liberal tradition, the continuing strength of conservatism and his own determination to move his party to the center led him to make compromises with the right. The 1994 midterm elections swept away the Democratic majorities in Congress. Led by Representative Newt Gingrich of Georgia, Republicans claimed the 1994 election as a mandate for their "contract with America," a conservative platform to end "government that is too big, too intrusive, and too easy with the public's money" and to elect "a Congress that respects the values and shares the faith of the American family." Opposition from Democrats and moderate Republicans blocked passage of most of the contract's pledges, but Gingrich succeeded in moving the debate to the right.

The most extreme antigovernment sentiment developed far from Washington in the form of grassroots armed militias. They celebrated white Christian supremacy and reflected conservatives' hostility to such diverse institutions as taxes and the United Nations. Claiming the need to defend themselves from government tyranny, they stockpiled weapons. The militia movement grew in reaction to the passage of new gun control legislation and after government agents stormed the headquarters of an armed religious cult in Waco, Texas, in April 1993, killing more than 80. On the second anniversary of that event, a bomb leveled a federal building in Oklahoma City, taking 169 lives in the worst terrorist attack in the nation's history up to that point.

Clinton bowed to conservative views on gay and lesbian rights, backing away from a campaign promise to lift the ban on gays in the military. Although many other nations, including France and Israel, welcomed homosexual soldiers, U.S. military leaders and key legislators objected to the proposal, and Clinton reverted to a **"don't ask, don't tell" policy** in 1993. Officials were forbidden to ask military personnel about their sexuality, but soldiers who said they were gay or who engaged in homosexual behavior could be dismissed. Eventually, more than ten thousand homosexuals were discharged, including army Arabic linguist Cathleen Glover, who lamented, "The army preaches integrity, but asks you to lie to everyone around you." In 1996, Clinton signed the Defense of Marriage Act, prohibiting the federal government from recognizing state-licensed marriages between same-sex couples.

Nonetheless, gays and lesbians continued to make strides as attitudes about homosexuality became more tolerant. By 2006, more than half of the country's five hundred largest companies provided health benefits to same-sex domestic partners and included sexual orientation in their nondiscrimination policies. More than twenty-five states banned discrimination in public employment, and many of those laws extended to private employment, housing, and education. By 2010, gay marriage was legal in Massachusetts, Connecticut, Vermont, Iowa, Maine, New Hampshire, and the District of Columbia; moreover, several states recognized civil unions and domestic partnerships, extending to same-sex couples rights available to married

Domestic Terrorism
The most devastating product of anti-government extremism in the 1990s was the explosion of the Alfred P. Murrah Federal Building in Oklahoma City. On the morning of April 23, 1995, Timothy McVeigh, wearing a T-shirt with the words shouted by John Wilkes Booth when he assassinated Abraham Lincoln—*Sic Semper Tyrranis* ("thus ever to tyrants")—drove a bomb-rigged truck to the federal building, where it exploded at 9 A.M. The building housed a day care center, and nineteen infants and toddlers were killed. McVeigh was executed in 2001, and his co-conspirator, Terry Nichols, was sentenced to life imprisonment without parole. Zuma Press.

couples such matters as inheritance, taxation, and medical decisions.

Clinton's efforts to cast himself as a centrist were apparent in his handling of the New Deal program Aid to Families with Dependent Children (AFDC), which most people called welfare. Public sentiment about poverty had shifted since the 1960s. Instead of blaming poverty on the lack of adequate jobs or other external circumstances, more people blamed the poor themselves and believed that welfare programs trapped the poor in cycles of dependency. Many questioned why they should subsidize poor mothers now that so many women had joined the labor force. Nearly everyone considered work to be better than welfare, but supporters of AFDC doubted that the economy could provide sufficient jobs at decent wages.

After vetoing two welfare reform bills, Clinton forced through a less punitive measure, which he signed as the 1996 election approached. The **Personal Responsibility and Work Opportunity Reconciliation Act** abolished AFDC and with it the nation's fifty-year pledge to provide a minimum level of subsistence for all children. The law provided grants to the states to assist the poor, but it limited welfare payments to two years, regardless of whether the recipient could find a job, and it set a lifetime limit of aid at five years. Reflecting growing controversy over immigration, it also barred legal immigrants from obtaining food stamps and other benefits and allowed states to stop Medicaid for legal immigrants. New York senator Daniel Patrick Moynihan called it "the most brutal act of social policy since Reconstruction."

In its first decade, the law produced neither the horrors predicted by its critics nor the successes promised by its advocates. As intended, it did force single mothers to seek employment,

cutting welfare rolls from 12.5 million to 4.5 million between 1996 and 2006. Yet not all former welfare recipients became self-supporting. Forty percent of former welfare mothers were not working regularly after being cut from the rolls, and those who did find jobs earned on average only about $12,000 a year. More than one-third of children living in female-headed families still lived in poverty.

Clinton's signature on the new law denied Republicans a partisan issue in the 1996 presidential campaign. The president ran as a moderate who would save the country from extremist Republicans, while the Republican Party also moved to the center, nominating Kansan Robert Dole, a World War II hero and former Senate majority leader. Clinton won 49 percent of the votes; 41 percent went to Dole and 9 percent to third-party candidate Ross Perot. Although Clinton won reelection with room to spare, voters sent a Republican majority back to Congress.

In 1999, Clinton and Congress bowed to calls from the financial industry for deregulation by repealing key aspects of the Glass-Steagall Act, passed during the New Deal to avoid another Great Depression. This Financial Services Modernization Act ended the separation between banking, securities, and insurance services, allowing financial institutions to engage in all three, practices that leading economists would link to the severe financial meltdown of 2008.

The End of Welfare
When Congress ended Aid to Families with Dependent Children, the welfare system established during the New Deal, and replaced it with Temporary Assistance for Needy Families, LuAnne St. Clair wondered how she and her five children would fare when her welfare payments ended. American Indian mothers had to overcome, with other welfare recipients, the problems of acquiring job training and child care so they could find employment. But Indian women also faced the lack of sufficient jobs on reservations, to which they had strong family, cultural, and religious ties. AP/Wide World.

Impeaching the President

Clinton's magnetic and articulate style, his ability to capture the middle ground of the electorate, and the nation's economic resurgence enabled the self-proclaimed "comeback kid" to survive scandals and an impeachment trial in 1999. Early in his presidency, charges related to firings of White House staff, political use of FBI records, and "Whitewater" — the nickname for real estate investments that the Clintons had made in Arkansas — led to an official investigation by an independent prosecutor. The president also faced a sexual harassment lawsuit filed in 1994 by a state employee. A federal court threw out that case in 1998, but another sexual scandal more seriously threatened Clinton's presidency.

In January 1998, Kenneth Starr, independent prosecutor for Whitewater, began to investigate the charge that Clinton had had sexual relations with a twenty-one-year-old White House intern and then lied about it to a federal grand jury. At first, Clinton vehemently denied the charge, but subsequently he bowed to the mounting evidence against him. Starr prepared a case for the House of Representatives, which in December 1998 voted to impeach the president on two counts: perjury and obstruction of justice. Clinton became the second president (after Andrew Johnson, in 1868) to be impeached by the House and tried by the Senate.

The Senate trial took place in early 1999. Most Americans condemned the president's behavior but approved of the job he was doing and opposed his removal from office. Some saw Starr as a fanatic invading individuals' privacy. One man said, "Let him get a divorce from his wife. Don't take him out of office and disrupt the country." Those favoring removal insisted that the president must set a high moral standard for the nation and that lying to a grand jury, even over a private matter, was a serious offense. A number of senators did not believe that Clinton's actions constituted the high crimes and misdemeanors required by the Constitution for conviction. With a two-thirds majority needed for that result, the Senate voted 45 to 55 on the perjury count and 50 to 50 on the obstruction of justice count. A majority, including some Republicans, seemed to agree with a Clinton supporter that the president's behavior, though "indefensible, outrageous, unforgivable, shameless," did not warrant his removal from office.

The investigation that triggered events leading up to impeachment ended in 2000 when the independent prosecutor reported insufficient evidence of illegalities related to the Whitewater land deals. Although more than 60 percent of Americans gave Clinton high marks on his job performance throughout the scandal, it distracted him from domestic and international problems and precluded the possibility of significant policy advances in his last years in office.

The Booming Economy of the 1990s

Clinton's ability to weather the impeachment crisis owed much to the prosperous economy, which in 1991 began its longest period of expansion in U.S. history. During the 1990s, the gross domestic product grew by more than one-third, thirteen million new jobs were created, inflation remained in check, unemployment reached 4 percent — its lowest point in twenty-five years — and the stock market soared.

The president took credit for the thriving economy, and his policies did contribute to the boom. He made deficit reduction a priority, and in exchange the Federal Reserve Board and bond market traders lowered interest rates, encouraging economic expansion by making money easier to borrow. Businesses also prospered because they had lowered their costs through restructuring and laying off workers. Economic problems in Europe and Asia helped American firms become more competitive in the international market. And the computer revolution and the application of information technology boosted productivity.

People at all income levels benefited from the economic boom, but the gaps between the rich and the poor and between the wealthy and the middle class, which had been growing since the 1970s, endured (Figure 31.1). This persistence of inequality was linked in part to the growing use of information technology, which increased demand for highly skilled workers, while the movement of manufacturing jobs abroad diminished opportunities and wages for the less skilled. In addition, deregulation and the continuing decline of unions hurt lower-skilled workers, tax cuts had favored the better-off, and the national minimum wage failed to keep up with inflation.

Although more minorities than ever attained middle-class status, in general people of color remained lowest on the economic ladder, reflecting Colin Powell's observation that "race still casts a shadow over our society." For instance, in 1999 the median income for white households surpassed $45,000, but it stood at only $29,423

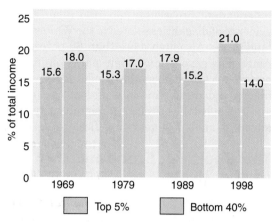

FIGURE 31.1   THE GROWTH OF INEQUALITY: Changes in Family Income, 1969–1998
For most of the post–World War II period, income increased for all groups on the economic ladder. But after 1979, the income of the poorest families actually declined, while the income of the richest 20 percent of the population grew substantially. Adapted from the *New York Times*, 1989.

and $33,676 for African American and Latino households, respectively. In 2000, poverty afflicted about 22 percent of blacks, 21 percent of Latinos, and 10 percent of Asian Americans, in contrast to 7.5 percent of whites.

REVIEW   What policies of the Clinton administration moved the Democratic Party to the right?

▶ The United States in a Globalizing World

America's economic success in the 1990s was linked to its dominance in the world economy. From that position, President Clinton tried to shape the tremendous transformations occurring in a process called **globalization** — the growing integration and interdependence of national citizens and economies. Building on the initiatives of Reagan and Bush, Clinton lowered a number of trade barriers, despite stiff opposition from critics who emphasized the economic deprivation and environmental devastation that often resulted. Debates likewise arose over the large numbers of immigrants entering the United States.

Clinton agreed with Bush that the United States must retain its economic and military dominance over all other nations. The president took military action in Somalia, Haiti, the Middle East, and eastern Europe, and he pushed hard to ease the conflict between Israel and the Palestinians. Yet no new global strategy emerged to replace the containment of communism as the decisive factor in the exercise of American power abroad. And safeguarding American interests from terrorist attacks around the world proved much more difficult than combating communism.

Defining America's Place in a New World Order

In 1991, President George H. W. Bush declared a "new world order" emerging from the ashes of the Cold War. As the sole superpower, the United States was determined to let no nation challenge its military superiority or global leadership (Figure 31.2). Yet policymakers struggled to define guiding principles for deciding when and how to use the nation's military and diplomatic power in a post–Cold War world. Combating Saddam Hussein's naked aggression seemed the obvious course of action in 1991, but dealing with other areas of instability proved more difficult.

Africa, where civil wars and extreme human suffering rarely evoked a strong American response, was a case in point. In 1992, guided largely by humanitarian concern, President Bush had attached U.S. forces to a UN operation in the small northern African country of Somalia, where famine and civil war raged. In 1993, President Clinton allowed that humanitarian mission to turn into "nation building" — an effort to establish a stable government — and eighteen U.S. soldiers were killed. After Americans saw film of Somalis dragging a soldier's corpse through the streets, the outcry at home suggested that most citizens were unwilling to sacrifice lives when no vital interest seemed threatened. Indeed, both the United States and the United Nations stood by in 1994 when more than half a million people were massacred in a brutal civil war in the central African nation of Rwanda.

As always, the United States was more inclined to use force nearer its borders, but in the case of Haiti it gained international support for intervention. In 1994, after a military coup overthrew Jean-Bertrand Aristide, Haiti's democratically elected president, Clinton persuaded the United Nations to impose economic sanctions on Haiti and to authorize military intervention. Hours before U.S. forces were to invade, Haitian military leaders promised to step down. U.S. forces peacefully landed, and Aristide was restored to power. Initially a huge success, U.S. policy continued to be tested as Haiti faced grave economic challenges and political instability.

In eastern Europe, the collapse of communism ignited a severe crisis, triggering U.S.-NATO intervention in Yugoslavia. During the Cold War, the Communist government of Yugoslavia, a federation of six republics, had held ethnic tensions in check, and many Muslims, Croats, and Serbs had grown accustomed to living and working together. After the Communists were swept out in 1989, ruthless leaders exploited ethnic differences to bolster their power, and Yugoslavia splintered into separate states and fell into civil war.

The Serbs' aggression under President Slobodan Milosevic against Bosnian Muslims in particular horrified much of the world, but European and U.S. leaders hesitated to use military force. As reports of rape, torture, and mass killings in Bosnia increased, American leaders worried about the image of the world's strongest nation being unwilling to stop the violence. Finally, in 1995, Clinton ordered U.S. fliers to join NATO forces in intensive bombing of Serbian military concentrations. That effort and successful offensives by the Croatian and Bosnian armies forced Milosevic to the bargaining table. After representatives from Serbia, Croatia, and Bosnia hammered

FIGURE 31.2 GLOBAL COMPARISON: Countries with the Highest Military Expenditures, 2005
During the Cold War, the military budgets of the United States and the Soviet Union were relatively even. For example, in 1983 U.S. military expenditures stood at $217 billion, compared to $213 billion for the Soviet Union. Even before the Iraq War, which began in 2003, the U.S. military budget constituted 47 percent of total world military expenditures. That proportion rose to 48 percent in 2005, with the United States spending nearly ten times as much as its nearest competitor. The U.S. defense budget reflects the determination of Democratic and Republican administrations alike to maintain dominance in the world, even while the capacities of its traditional enemies have been greatly diminished.

out a peace treaty, Clinton then agreed to send twenty thousand American troops to Bosnia as part of a NATO peacekeeping mission.

In 1998, new fighting broke out in the southern Serbian province of Kosovo, where ethnic Albanians, who constituted 90 percent of the population, demanded independence. The Serbian army brutally retaliated, driving out one-third of Kosovo's 1.8 million Albanian Muslims. In 1999, NATO launched a U.S.-led bombing attack on Serbian military and government targets that, after three months, forced Milosevic to agree to a peace settlement. Serbians voted Milosevic out of office in October 2000, and he died in 2006 while on trial for genocide by a UN war crimes tribunal.

Elsewhere, Clinton remained willing to deploy U.S. power when he could send missiles rather

Breakup of Yugoslavia

than soldiers, and he was prepared to act without international support or UN sanction.
In August 1998, bombs exploded
at the U.S. embassies in Kenya
and Tanzania, killing 12
Americans and more than 250
Africans. Clinton retaliated with
missile attacks on terrorist
training camps in Afghanistan
and facilities in Sudan controlled
by **Osama bin Laden**, a Saudi-
born millionaire who financed
the Islamic-extremist terrorist
network linked to the embassy
attacks. Clinton also launched
air strikes against Iraq in 1993
when a plot to assassinate former president Bush was uncovered, in 1996 after Saddam
Hussein attacked the Kurds in
northern Iraq, and repeatedly
between 1998 and 2000 after
Hussein expelled UN weapons
inspectors. Whereas Bush had acted in the Gulf
War with the support of an international force
that included Arab states, Clinton acted unilaterally and in the face of Arab opposition.

Israel and PLO sign accords, 1993
Israel and Jordan sign peace treaty, 1994
Progress of Israeli-Palestinian negotiations
halts and violence escalates, 2000
Israel withdraws from Gaza, 2005
Israel at war with Hezbollah in Lebanon, 2006
Israel invades Gaza, 2008

Events in Israel since 1989

Ethnic Strife in Kosovo
These ethnic Albanians seeking to escape the Serbian province of Kosovo into Macedonia were among hundreds of thousands of victims of the ethnic violence that devastated Yugoslavia after the cold war ended. In 1999, in response to the brutality of the Serbian army against the Albanians, the United States first led a NATO bombing campaign against Serbian strongholds and then contributed troops to a NATO peacekeeping unit in Kosovo after the bombing had forced the Serbian army to withdraw. Reuters.

To defuse the Israeli-Palestinian conflict, a major source of Arab hostility toward the West, Clinton used diplomatic rather than military power. In 1993, largely because of the efforts of the Norwegian government, Yasir Arafat, head of the Palestine Liberation Organization (PLO), and Yitzhak Rabin, Israeli prime minister, recognized the existence of each other's states for the first time and agreed to Israeli withdrawal from the Gaza Strip and Jericho, allowing for Palestinian self-government there. In July 1994, Clinton presided over another turning point as Rabin and King Hussein of Jordan signed a declaration of peace. Yet difficult issues remained to be settled: control of Jerusalem; the fate of Palestinian refugees; and the presence of more than 200,000 Israeli settlers in the West Bank, the land seized by Israel in 1967, where 3 million Palestinians were determined to establish their own state. Clinton's last effort to broker negotiations between the PLO and Israel failed in 2000, and continuing violence between Israelis and Palestinians strengthened anti-American sentiment among Arabs, who saw the United States as Israel's ally.

Debates over Globalization

The Clinton administration moved energetically on the economic side to speed up the growth of a "global marketplace." The process of globalization had begun in the fifteenth century, when Europeans began to penetrate other parts of the world. Between the U.S. Civil War and World War I, products, capital, and labor crossed national boundaries in ever-larger numbers. In that era, globalization was based on imperialism; Western nations took direct control of foreign territories, extracted their natural resources, and restricted manufacturing. By contrast, late-twentieth-century globalization advanced among sovereign nations and involved the industrialization of less developed areas, such as Korea and China. Other distinguishing marks of the more recent globalization were its scope and intensity: New communications technologies such as the Internet and cell phones connected nations, corporations, and individuals at much greater speed and much less cost than ever before.

Building on efforts by Presidents Reagan and Bush, Clinton sought to speed up globalization, seeking new measures to ease restrictions on international commerce. In November 1993, he won congressional approval of the **North American Free Trade Agreement (NAFTA)**, which eliminated all tariffs and trade barriers among the United States, Canada, and Mexico. Organized labor and others fearing loss of jobs and industries to Mexico lobbied vigorously against NAFTA, and a majority of Democrats opposed it, but Republican support ensured approval. In 1994, the Senate ratified the General Agreement on Tariffs and Trade, establishing the **World Trade Organization (WTO)** to enforce substantial tariff reductions and elimination of import quotas among some 135 member nations. And in 2005, Clinton's successor, George W. Bush, lowered more trade barriers with the passage of the Central American–Dominican Republic Free Trade Agreement.

The free trade issue was intensely contested. Much of corporate America welcomed the elimination of trade barriers. "Ideally, you'd have every plant you own on a barge," remarked Jack Welch, CEO of General Electric. Critics linked globalization to the loss of manufacturing jobs, the erosion of the social safety net provided for workers since the 1930s, and the growing gap between rich and poor. (See "Beyond America's Borders," page 1058.) Demanding "fair trade" rather than simply free trade, critics wanted trade treaties to require decent wage and labor standards. Environmentalists insisted that countries seeking increased commerce with the United States agree to eliminate or reduce pollution and prevent the destruction of endangered species.

> **"Ideally, you'd have every plant you own on a barge."**
> — General Electric CEO JACK WELCH, on the outsourcing of jobs

Globalization controversies often centered on relationships between the United States, which dominated the world's industrial core, and the developing nations on the periphery, whose cheap labor and lax environmental standards caught the eye of investors. United Students against Sweatshops, for example, attacked the international conglomerate Nike, which paid Chinese workers $1.50 to produce a pair of shoes selling for more than $100 in the United States. Yet leaders of developing nations actively sought

THE PROMISE OF TECHNOLOGY

The Internet

Like many new technologies, the Internet developed through government funding. In 1958, in response to the Soviet launch of *Sputnik*, President Eisenhower created the Advanced Research Projects Agency (ARPA), one of whose projects led to ARPANET, a system that routed digitized messages between computers to provide security for military secrets and to enable communications during an enemy attack. The technology spread quickly beyond the military; by 2000, even the poorest countries had some access to what came to be called the Internet, and a majority of Americans regularly went online at home or at work. Even more people—some 2 billion throughout the world—had cell phones by 2006, and Internet-enabled "smart phones" were abundant by 2011. Using online social networks such as Facebook and Twitter, people around the world can connect virtually to exchange opinions, coordinate events, and participate in politics. During the revolutions that swept through North Africa and the Middle East in 2011, activists used digital

networks to communicate with one another, organize protests, and broadcast their stories and images. What forms of technology do you see among these Egyptian protesters? What are some pros and cons of using these technologies for political activism? ©Bettmann/Corbis.

Jobs in a Globalizing Era

In November 2001, Paul Sufronko, a supervisor at Rocky Shoes and Boots in Nelsonville, Ohio, handed out final paychecks to the company's last sixty-seven employees in the United States, ending a process of outsourcing jobs that had begun in the 1980s. Before his own job ended, Sufronko traveled to Rocky plants in Puerto Rico and the Dominican Republic to train local workers to replace him. Asked about his job loss, the thirty-six-year-old said, "I had other plans. Things just didn't work out."

Other Americans did not take the loss of their jobs to foreign workers so philosophically. An autoworker believed that "corporations are looking for a disposable workforce. . . . No commitment to community; no commitment to country."

In 1960, American workers made 96 percent of all shoes bought in the United States; by 2000, nearly all shoes came from abroad. The globalizing process was not a new experience for Julio Lopez, a temporary beneficiary of Rocky's outsourcing of labor. After Lopez lost his job of twenty-three years when his employer moved its operations overseas, he found work at Rocky's Puerto Rico plant at a rate of $5.15 an hour, less than half of what Nelsonville workers had earned. Lopez hoped that the factory would stay in Puerto Rico for eight more years. "Then I will be sixty-two, and I can retire." His hopes were not unusual. Lillian Chaparro, the plant manager, spoke about the perpetual motion of jobs: "It's like a chain, you know? The jobs leave the U.S. They come here. Then they go to the Dominican, to China. That's why I push people — we have to be able to compete."

The athletic shoe manufacturer Nike was one of the first companies to exploit the advantages of production abroad, turning to Japan in the 1960s. When labor costs there began to rise, Nike shifted production to South Korea. When Korean workers demanded better wages and working conditions, Nike moved production to China and other Asian countries. Local contractors in Indonesia paid workers as little as fifteen cents an hour as they churned out seventy million pairs of shoes in 1996.

Charles Seitz, who lost his job at Eastman Kodak when the company moved some operations to China and Mexico, was not entirely wrong when he said, "There's nothing made here anymore." The proportion of American workers who held manufacturing jobs fell from one-third in the 1950s to 10 percent by the twenty-first century. Of course, not all the job losses resulted from outsourcing. At Kodak, for example, a machine replaced fourteen workers who previously had mixed film-making ingredients. In the 1980s and 1990s, American corporations sought increased productivity so that they could downsize their workforces and reduce costs. Moreover, some companies built plants abroad to be close to burgeoning markets there. Buick, for example, was China's most popular brand in the early twenty-first century. Because so many companies, like Nike, contracted out production to foreign companies rather than employing foreign workers directly, the number of U.S. jobs lost to foreign workers is difficult to calculate.

The outsourcing of work did not end with manufacturing jobs. By 2003, corporations were relying on workers abroad, especially in India, for a wide range of service and professional work. For example, 1,700 engineers and scientists conducted research for General Electric in Bangalore, India. Technology experts in Bangalore provided telephone help for Dell computer users, and American schoolchildren received online tutoring from teachers in Cochin, India. A research firm executive pointed to the power

foreign investment, insisting that wages deemed pitiful by Americans offered their impoverished people a much better living than they could otherwise obtain. At the same time, developing countries often pointed to American hypocrisy in advocating free trade in industry while heavily subsidizing the U.S. agricultural sector. "When countries like America, Britain and France subsidize their farmers," complained a grower in Uganda, "we get hurt."

Whereas globalization's cheerleaders argued that everyone would benefit in the long run, critics focused on the short-term victims. American businessman George Soros conceded that international trade and investments generated wealth, "but they cannot take care of other social needs, such as the preservation of peace, alleviation of poverty, protection of the environment, labor conditions, or human rights." The critics enjoyed a few successes. In 2000, President Clinton signed an executive order requiring an environmental impact review before the signing of any trade agreement. Beyond the United States, officials from the World Bank and the International Monetary Fund, along with representatives from wealthy economies,

of technology to overcome distance and noted, "You can get cracker-jack Java programmers in India right out of college for $5,000 a year versus $60,000."

The flight of jobs has not been entirely one-way. Seeking to move production closer to its market, in 1983 Japan's second-largest automaker, Nissan, opened a plant in Smyrna, Tennessee, which would become the largest auto plant in the United States. The plant was non-union, and wages were lower than those of Michigan autoworkers. Yet Daren Shanks, who came from a Tennessee farming town, felt that his job on the engine line gave him "the opportunity to do stuff for my kids that I'd never have had the opportunity to do." In all, by 2007 nearly 5 percent of all American workers, and more than 10 percent of those in manufacturing, received their paychecks from foreign companies operating in the United States.

The majority of jobs, however, moved in the opposite direction. In 2003, the blue jeans company founded in 1853 by Levi Strauss closed its last plants in the United States, contracting out its work to suppliers in fifty other countries from Latin America to Asia. Marivel Gutierez, a side-seam operator in the San Antonio plant, acknowledged that workers in Mexico and elsewhere would benefit, suggesting the globalization of the American dream. "But what hap-

Making Nikes in Vietnam

In 1995 Nike began to contract with Vietnamese factories to produce footwear. The average monthly wage in South Korea, where Nike had been contracting out its production, was nearly $800, but stood at just $45 in Vietnam. In the United States, the Oregon-based company faced protests and boycotts over working conditions in Vietnamese plants, but Nike wages surpassed those available to most Vietnamese. These workers putting the finishing touches on shoes in a plant just outside of Ho Chi Minh City (formerly Saigon) were among some 130,000 Vietnamese producing Nike products in 2005. AP Images.

pens to our American dream?" Workers like Gutierez stood as stark reminders that as the benefits of the free flow of economic enterprise across national borders reached many, globalization left multitudes of victims in its wake.

America in a Global Context

1. Why did manufacturing jobs move from the United States to other countries in the 1980s and beyond?

2. What impact did the outsourcing of jobs have on workers in the United States and elsewhere?

promised in 2000 to provide poor nations more debt relief and a greater voice in decisions about loans and grants. According to World Bank president James D. Wolfensohn, "Our challenge is to make globalization an instrument of opportunity and inclusion — not fear."

The Internationalization of the United States

Globalization was typically associated with the expansion of American enterprise and culture to other countries, yet the United States

experienced the dynamic forces of globalization within its own borders. Already in the 1980s, Japanese, European, and Middle Eastern investors had purchased American stocks and bonds, real estate, and corporations such as Firestone and 20th Century Fox. Local communities welcomed foreign capital, and states competed to recruit foreign automobile plants. American non-union workers began to produce Hondas in Marysville, Ohio, and BMWs in Spartanburg, South Carolina. By 2002, the paychecks of nearly four million American workers came from foreign-owned companies.

Globalization was transforming not just the economy but American society as well, as the United States experienced a tremendous surge of immigration, part of a worldwide trend that counted some 214 million immigrants across the globe in 2010. By 2006, the United States' 35.7 million immigrants constituted 12.4 percent of the population. The 20 million who arrived between 1980 and 2005 surpassed the previous peak immigration of the first two decades of the twentieth century and exhibited a striking difference in country of origin. Eighty-five percent of the earlier immigrants had come from Europe; by the 1980s, the vast majority came from Asia and Latin America. Consequently, immigration changed the racial and ethnic composition of the nation. By 2004, Asian Americans numbered 13 million, while 41 million Latinos constituted — at 14 percent — the largest minority group in the nation.

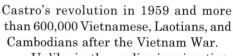

The promise of economic opportunity, as always, lured immigrants to America, and the Immigration and Nationality Act of 1965 enabled them to come. Although the law set an annual limit of 270,000 immigrants, it allowed close relatives of U.S. citizens to enter above the ceiling, thus creating family migration chains. In addition, the Cold War dispersal of U.S. military and other personnel around the world enabled foreigners to learn about the nation and form relationships with citizens. Moreover, during the Cold War, U.S. immigration policy was generous to refugees from communism, welcoming more than 800,000 Cubans after Castro's revolution in 1959 and more than 600,000 Vietnamese, Laotians, and Cambodians after the Vietnam War.

Unlike in the earlier immigration, women comprised more than half of all newcomers to the United States in the 1990s. But it was the racial composition of the new immigration that heightened the century-old wariness of native-born Americans toward newcomers. Pressure for more restrictive policies stemmed from beliefs that immigrants took jobs from the native-born, suppressed wages by accepting low pay, strained the capability of social services, or eroded the dominant culture and language. Americans expressed particular hostility toward immigrants who were in the country illegally — an estimated 12 million in 2008 — even though the economy depended on their cheap labor. The Immigration Reform and Control Act of 1986 did little to stem the tide. It penalized employers who hired undocumented aliens but also granted amnesty to some 2 million illegal immigrants who had been in the country before 1982.

The new immigration was once again making America an international, interracial society. The largest numbers of immigrants flocked to California, New York, Texas, Florida, New Jersey, and Illinois, but new immigrants dispersed throughout the country. Taquerias, sushi bars, and Vietnamese restaurants appeared in southeastern and midwestern towns; cable TV companies added Spanish-language stations; and the international sport of soccer soared in popularity. Mixed marriages displayed the growing

Immigrant Labor
Large commercial farms depended on Latino workers, who constituted more than 45 percent of agricultural labor in 2002. A majority of these workers were citizens, and not all were immigrants, but growers insisted that they could not supply Americans with fresh produce without the labor of immigrants, legal and illegal. The dependence of agriculture and service industries on immigrant labor helped block movements for greater immigration restrictions. The workers here are harvesting strawberries near Carlsbad, California. In 2002, the median weekly pay for migrant farmworkers was $300. Sandy Huffaker/ Getty Images.

fusion of cultures, recognized in 2000 on Census Bureau forms, where Americans could check more than one racial category. Only half-joking, the famous golfer Tiger Woods called himself a "Cablinasian" to reflect his mixed heritage of Caucasian, black, American Indian, and Asian.

Like their predecessors, the majority of post-1965 immigrants were unskilled and poor. They took the lowest-paying jobs, constituting, for example, nearly half of all farmworkers and housekeepers and performing other work that employers insisted native-born Americans would not do. Yet a significant number of immigrants were highly skilled workers, sought after by burgeoning high-tech industries. By 2006, nearly one-third of all software developers were foreign-born, as were 28 percent of all physicians.

REVIEW Who criticized free trade agreements and why?

▶ **President George W. Bush: Conservatism at Home and Radical Initiatives Abroad**

The election of **George W. Bush** in 2000 marked the second time that a son of a former president gained the White House. But the younger Bush pushed an agenda that was closer to Ronald Reagan's than to that of George H. W. Bush. He signed key legislation to improve public school education and to subsidize prescription drugs for elderly citizens. But he also persuaded Congress to pass enormous tax cuts favoring the wealthy, reduced environmental protections, and tipped the balance on the Supreme Court with two conservative appointments. The tax cuts, along with spending on new international and domestic crises, turned the substantial budget surplus that Bush had inherited into the largest deficit in the nation's history, and a financial crisis near the end of his presidency sent the economy into a recession.

As Islamist terrorism replaced communism as the primary threat to U.S. security, the Bush administration launched a war in Afghanistan in 2001 and expanded the federal government's powers to investigate and detain individuals. In distinct contrast to his father's multilateral and cautious approach to foreign policy, George W.

Bush adopted a policy of unilateralism and preemption by going to war against Iraq in 2003. He won reelection in 2004, but stability in Iraq and Afghanistan, despite huge costs, remained elusive, and Bush confronted serious foreign and domestic crises in his second term. Democrats capitalized on widespread dissatisfaction with his administration to gain control of Congress in 2006.

The Disputed Election of 2000

Clinton's presidency ended with a flourishing economy, and public opinion polls indicated that a majority of Americans agreed with the Democrats on most issues. Yet his vice president, Albert Gore, failed to succeed him in 2000. To many voters, Gore seemed stiff and pompous and too willing to change his positions for political advantage. He was further burdened with the taint of Clinton administration scandals.

George W. Bush won the Republican nomination after a series of richly funded, hard-fought primaries. The oldest son of former president George H. W. Bush, he had earned degrees from Yale and Harvard, worked in the oil industry, and served as governor of Texas since 1994. Inexperienced in national and international affairs, Bush chose for his running mate a seasoned official, Richard B. Cheney, who had served in the Nixon, Ford, and first Bush administrations.

Many observers predicted that the amazingly strong economy would give Gore the edge, and he did surpass Bush by more than half a million votes. Once the polls closed, however, it became clear that Florida's 25 electoral college votes would decide the presidency. Bush's tiny margin in Florida prompted an automatic recount of the votes, which eventually gave him an edge of 537 votes in that state.

Meanwhile, the Democrats asked for hand-counting of Florida ballots in several heavily Democratic counties where machine errors and confusing ballots may have left thousands of Gore votes unrecorded. The Republicans, in turn, went to court to try to stop the hand-counts. The outcome of the 2000 election hung in the balance for weeks as cases went all the way to the Supreme Court. Finally, a bitterly divided Court ruled five to four against further recounts, and Gore conceded the presidency to Bush on December 13, 2000. For the first time since 1888, a president who failed to win the popular vote took office (Map 31.3). Despite the lack of a popular mandate, the Bush administration set out to make dramatic policy changes.

The Disputed Election
While attorneys representing George W. Bush and Al Gore pursued lawsuits over the counting of ballots in Florida, partisan supporters took to the streets. Here, backers of both sides rally outside the Supreme Court on December 11, 2000, the day before the Court issued its five-to-four ruling that ended the recounting of ballots and thus secured the presidency for Bush. Critics charged that the five justices in the majority had ruled from partisanship rather than objectivity, pointing out that if those justices had followed their custom of favoring state over federal authority, they would have allowed Florida to continue the recounts. AP Photo.

The Domestic Policies of a "Compassionate Conservative"

Bush's appointments, like Clinton's, brought significant diversity to the executive branch. He chose African Americans Colin Powell as secretary of state and Condoleezza Rice first as national security adviser and subsequently as secretary of state when Powell resigned in January 2005. Five of

Bush's top-level appointees were women, including Secretary of Labor Elaine L. Chao, the first Asian American woman to serve in the cabinet.

Bush had promised to govern as a "compassionate conservative." A devout born-again Christian, he immediately established the White House Office of Faith-Based and Community Initiatives to encourage religious groups to participate in government programs aimed at prison inmates, the unemployed, and others. The religious right praised the initiatives, but others charged that they violated the constitutional separation of church and state, and federal courts ruled in several dozen cases that faith ministries were using government funds to indoctrinate the people they served.

Bush's fiscal policies were more compassionate toward the rich than toward average Americans. In 2001, he signed a bill reducing taxes over the next ten years by $1.35 trillion. A 2003 tax law slashed another $320 billion. The laws heavily favored the rich by reducing income taxes, phasing out estate taxes, and cutting tax rates on capital gains and dividends. They also provided benefits for married couples and families with children and offered tax deductions for college expenses.

The administration insisted that the tax cuts would promote economic growth and jolt the economy out of the recession that had begun in 2000. The economy did recover, but opponents stressed inequities in the tax cuts and pointed to a mushrooming federal deficit — the highest in U.S. history — that surpassed $400 billion in 2004, although Republicans had traditionally railed against budget deficits. In 2009, the deficit surpassed $1

MAP 31.3   The Election of 2000

Candidate	Electoral Vote	Popular Vote	Percent of Popular Vote
George W. Bush (Republican)	271	50,456,062	47.8
Al Gore (Democrat)	267	50,996,862	48.4
Ralph Nader (Green Party)	0	2,858,843	2.7
Patrick J. Buchanan (Reform Party)	0	438,760	0.4

trillion as the government struggled to combat a recession. By then, the national debt had risen to $9.6 trillion, making the United States increasingly dependent on China and other foreign investors, who held more than half of the debt.

Bush used regulatory powers that did not require congressional approval to weaken environmental protection as part of his larger goals of reducing government regulation, promoting economic growth, and increasing energy production. The administration opened millions of wilderness acres to mining, oil, and timber industries and relaxed environmental requirements under the Clean Air and Clean Water Acts. To worldwide dismay, the administration withdrew from the **Kyoto Protocol** on global warming, signed in 1997 by 178 nations to reduce greenhouse gas emissions.

While environmentalists pushed for measures to limit American energy consumption, the administration called for more rapid development of energy resources. During his second term, as gasoline prices reached all-time highs in 2005, Bush signed the Energy Policy Act, a compromise bill providing $14 billion in subsidies to producers of oil, coal, nuclear power, and alternative sources of energy. But when gas prices shot up even higher in 2008 and Bush sought to lift restrictions on offshore drilling for oil, Congress blocked the president's efforts, and it continued to thwart his calls to allow drilling for oil in the Arctic National Wildlife Refuge.

Bush had the opportunity to replace two Supreme Court justices, and conservatives hailed his choices. In 2005, John Roberts, who had served in the Reagan and George H. W. Bush administrations, was named chief justice. Bush then replaced the moderate Sandra Day O'Connor with Samuel A. Alito, a staunch conservative who won confirmation by a narrow margin. While the Court stood up to the administration in rulings on the rights of accused terrorists, it tilted right on cases concerning abortion, gun control, sex discrimination in employment, campaign financing, and regulation of business.

In contrast to the partisan conflict over judicial appointments and tax and environmental policy, Bush won bipartisan support for the **No Child Left Behind Act** of 2002, marking the greatest change in federal education policy since the 1960s and substantially extending the role of the federal government in public education. Promising to end, in Bush's words, "the story of children being just shuffled through the system," the law required every school to meet annual testing standards, penalized failing schools, and allowed parents to transfer their children out of such schools. It authorized an increase in federal aid, but not enough for Senator Paul Wellstone of

Minnesota, one of the few critics of the measure, who asked, "How can you reach the goal of leaving no child behind on a tin cup budget?" In addition to struggling to finance the new standards, school officials began to criticize the one-size-fits-all approach and pointed to family and community impoverishment as sources of student deficiencies.

The Bush administration's second major effort to co-opt Democratic Party issues constituted what the president hailed as "the greatest advance in health care coverage for America's seniors" since the start of Medicare in 1965. In 2003, Bush signed a bill authorizing prescription drug benefits for the elderly and at the same time expanding the role of private insurers in the Medicare system. Most Democrats opposed the legislation, charging that it left big gaps in coverage, subsidized private insurers with federal funds to compete with Medicare, banned imports of low-priced drugs, and prohibited the government from negotiating with drug companies to reduce prices. Legislators of both parties worried about the cost of the new drug benefit. More than 80 percent of the elderly who signed up for the benefit were at least "somewhat satisfied" with the program, but medical costs overall continued to soar, and the number of uninsured Americans surpassed forty million in 2008.

One domestic undertaking of the Bush administration found little approval anywhere: its handling of **Hurricane Katrina**, which in August 2005 devastated the coasts of Alabama, Louisiana, and Mississippi and ultimately resulted in some fifteen hundred deaths. The catastrophe that ensued when New Orleans's levees broke, flooding 80 percent of the city, shook a deeply rooted assumption held by Americans: that government owed its citizens protection from natural disasters. Federal, state, and local officials failed the citizens of New Orleans in two ways: They had not built the levees to withstand such a deluge, and they failed to rescue citizens when the levees broke and flooded their homes.

New Orleans residents who were too old, too poor, or too sick to flee the flooding spent anguished days waiting on rooftops for help; wading in filthy, toxic water; and enduring the heat, disorder, and lack of basic necessities at the convention center and Superdome, where they had been told to go for safety and protection. "How can we save the world if we can't save our own people?" wondered one Louisianan. Thousands of volunteers rushed to help, and millions more opened their pocketbooks to aid the victims. Yet the immense private generosity and the superb

> "How can you reach the goal of leaving no child behind on a tin cup budget?"
> — Minnesota senator PAUL WELLSTONE, on the No Child Left Behind Act

Hurricane Katrina
Residents of the poverty-stricken Lower Ninth Ward of New Orleans plead for help after floods submerged 80 percent of the city in the wake of Hurricane Katrina in August 2005. The boat was useless to these people because it had lost its motor. Some residents waited as long as five days to be rescued. A historian of the disaster wrote, "Americans were not used to seeing their country in ruins, their people in want." AP Photo/David J. Phillip.

response of a few groups, such as the U.S. Coast Guard and the Louisiana Department of Wildlife and Fisheries, could not make up for the feeling that the nation had failed some of its citizens when they needed it most. Since so many of Katrina's hardest-hit victims were poor and black, the disaster also highlighted the severe injustices and deprivations remaining in American society.

The Globalization of Terrorism

The response to Hurricane Katrina contrasted sharply with the Bush administration's decisive

reaction to the horror that had unfolded four years earlier on the morning of **September 11, 2001**. In the most deadly attack ever launched on American soil, nineteen terrorists hijacked four planes and flew two of them into the twin towers of New York City's World Trade Center and one into the Pentagon in Washington, D.C.; the fourth crashed in a field in Pennsylvania. The attacks took nearly 2,800 lives, including U.S. citizens and people from ninety countries. The nation, indeed the world, was stunned.

The hijackers belonged to Osama bin Laden's **Al Qaeda** international terrorist network, and some of them had been living in the United States for several years. Organized from bin Laden's sanctuaries in Afghanistan, where the radical Muslim Taliban government had taken control, the attacks reflected Islamic extremists' rage at the spread of Western goods, culture, and values into the Muslim world, as well as their opposition to the 1991 Persian Gulf War against Iraq and the stationing of American troops in Saudi Arabia. Bin Laden sought to rid the Middle East of Western influence and install puritanical Muslim control.

The 9/11 terrorists and others who came after them ranged from poor to middle-class; some lived in Middle Eastern homelands governed by undemocratic and corrupt governments, others in Western cities where they felt alienated and despised. All saw the West, especially the United States, as the evil source of their humiliation and the supporter of Israel's oppression of Palestinian Muslims. In the wake of the September 11 attacks, President Bush's public approval rating skyrocketed as he sought a global alliance against terrorism and won at least verbal support from most governments.

On October 11, the United States and Britain began bombing Afghanistan, and American special forces aided the Northern Alliance, the Taliban government's main opposition. By December, the Taliban government was destroyed, but bin Laden eluded capture, continuing to direct Al Qaeda forces throughout the world, until U.S. special forces killed him in Pakistan in 2011. Afghans elected a new national government, but the Taliban remained strong in large parts of the county, and economic stability and physical security remained out of reach.

At home, the balance between liberty and security tilted. Throughout the country, anti-immigrant sentiment revived, and anyone appearing to be Middle Eastern or practicing Islam was likely to arouse suspicion. Even though President Bush reminded Americans that "the enemy of America is not our many Muslim friends," authorities arrested more than a thousand Arabs and Muslims, and a

9/11

The magnitude of the destruction and loss of lives in the 9/11 attacks made Americans feel more vulnerable than they had since the Cold War ended. The attacks also affected people around the world who streamed to U.S. embassies or expressed their shock and sympathy in other ways. The surge of patriotism that overtook Americans is demonstrated in this button, which also recognizes the heroism of the first responders. It was made from a photograph taken just hours after the attack, when three firefighters raised an American flag on the ruins. What historic photograph does the image on the button recall? Photograph: Steve Ludlum/The New York Times/Redux; button: Collection of Janice L. and David J. Frent.

Justice Department study later reported that many people with no connection to terrorism spent months in jail, denied their rights. "I think America overreacted . . . by singling out Arab-named men like myself," said Shanaz Mohammed, who was jailed for eight months for an immigration violation.

In October 2001, Congress passed the **USA Patriot Act** by huge majorities. The law gave the government new powers to monitor suspected terrorists and their associates, including the ability to access personal information, while allowing more exchange of information between criminal investigators and those investigating foreign threats. It soon provoked calls for revision from both conservatives and liberals. Kathleen MacKenzie, a councilwoman in Ann Arbor, Michigan, explained why the council opposed the Patriot Act: "As concerned as we were about national safety, we felt that giving up [rights] was too high a price to pay." A security official countered, "If you don't violate someone's human rights some of the time, you probably aren't doing your job."

Insisting that presidential powers were virtually limitless in times of national crisis, Bush

Afghanistan

stretched his authority as commander in chief until he met resistance from the courts and Congress. In 2001, the administration established special military commissions to try prisoners captured in Afghanistan and taken to the U.S. military base at Guantánamo, Cuba. But in 2006, responding to a suit filed by one of the approximately five hundred detainees who had languished there for years, the Supreme Court ruled five to three that Congress had not authorized such tribunals and that they violated international law. That year, congressional leaders became openly critical of the administration for wiretapping phone conversations of U.S. residents without obtaining the warrants required by law.

The government also sought to protect Americans from future terrorist attacks through the greatest reorganization of the executive branch since 1948. In November 2002, Congress authorized the new **Department of Homeland Security**, combining 170,000 federal employees from twenty-two agencies that had responsibilities for various aspects of domestic security. Chief among the department's duties were intelligence analysis; immigration and border security; chemical, biological, and nuclear countermeasures; and emergency preparedness and response.

Unilateralism, Preemption, and the Iraq War

The Bush administration sought collective action against the Taliban, but on most other international issues it adopted a go-it-alone approach. In addition to withdrawing from the Kyoto Protocol on global warming and violating international rules about the treatment of military prisoners, it scrapped the 1972 Antiballistic Missile Treaty in order to develop the space-based Strategic Defense Initiative first proposed by Ronald Reagan. Bush also withdrew the nation from the UN's International Criminal Court, and he rejected an agreement to enforce bans on the development and possession of biological weapons — an agreement signed by all of America's European allies.

Nowhere was the new policy of unilateralism more striking than in a new war against Iraq, a war endorsed by Vice President Dick Cheney and Secretary of Defense Donald H. Rumsfeld, but not by Secretary of State Colin Powell. Addressing West Point graduates in June 2002, President Bush proclaimed a new policy for American security based not on containment but on preemption: "Traditional concepts of deterrence will not work against a terrorist enemy whose avowed tactics are wanton destruction and the targeting of innocents; whose so-called soldiers seek martyrdom in death and whose most potent protection is statelessness." Because nuclear, chemical, and biological weapons enabled "even weak states and small groups [to] attain a catastrophic power to strike great nations," the United States had to "be ready for preemptive action." The president's claim that the United States had the right to start a war was at odds with international law and with many Americans' understanding of their nation's ideals. It distressed most of America's great-power allies.

The Bush administration moved deliberately to apply the doctrine of preemption to Iraq, whose dictator, Saddam Hussein, appeared to be in violation of UN resolutions from the 1991 Gulf War requiring Iraq to destroy and stop further development of nuclear, chemical, and biological weapons. In November 2002, the United States persuaded the UN Security Council to pass a resolution requiring Iraq to disarm or face "serious consequences." When Iraq failed to comply fully with new UN inspections, the Bush administration decided on war. Making claims (subsequently refuted) that Hussein had links to Al Qaeda and harbored terrorists and that Iraq possessed weapons of mass destruction, the president insisted that the threat was immediate and great enough to justify preemptive action. In opposition were the Arab world and most major nations — including France, Germany, China, and Russia — which preferred to give the UN inspectors more time. Nevertheless, the United States and Britain invaded Iraq on March 19, 2003, supported by some thirty nations (see Map 31.1). Coalition forces won an easy and decisive victory, and Bush declared the end of the **Iraq War** on May 1. Saddam Hussein remained at large until December 2003.

Chaos followed the quick victory over Hussein. Damage from U.S. bombing and widespread looting resulting from the failure of U.S. troops to secure order and provide basic necessities left Iraqis wondering how much they had gained. "With Saddam there was tyranny, but at least you had a salary to put food on your family's table," said a young father from Hussein's hometown of Tikrit. A Baghdad hospital worker complained,

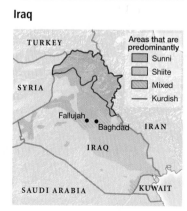

Iraq

"They can take our oil, but at least they should let us have electricity and water." Five years after the invasion, Iraqis had less electricity than they had had before the war, and a majority lacked access to clean water. Continuing violence had caused 2 million to flee their country and displaced 1.9 million within Iraq.

The administration had not planned adequately for the occupation and sent far fewer forces to Iraq than it had deployed in 1991 in response to Iraq's invasion of Kuwait. The 140,000 American forces in Iraq came under attack almost daily from remnants of the former Hussein regime, religious extremists, and hundreds of foreign terrorists now entering the chaotic country. Seeking to divide Iraqis and undermine the occupation, terrorists launched deadly assaults on such targets as the UN mission in Baghdad, as well as on major mosques and Iraqi citizens, resulting in the death of tens of thousands.

The war became an issue in the presidential campaign of 2004, which registered the highest voter turnout since 1968. Massachusetts senator John Kerry, the Democratic nominee, criticized Bush's unilateralist foreign policy and the administration's conduct of the war. A slim majority of voters, however, indicated their belief that Bush would better protect American security from terrorist threats than Kerry. The president eked out a 286 to 252 victory in the electoral college, winning 50.7 percent of the popular vote to Kerry's 48.3 percent and carrying Republican majorities into Congress.

In June 2004, the United States transferred sovereignty to an interim Iraqi government, and in January 2005 Iraqis elected a national assembly. The daunting challenge facing the national assembly was to organize a government satisfactory to Iraq's three major groups — Sunnis, Shiites, and Kurds. Violence escalated against government officials, Iraqi civilians, and occupation forces. A nineteen-year-old Iraqi confined to his house by his parents, who feared he could be killed or lured into terrorist activities, said, "If I'm killed, it doesn't even matter because I'm dead right now." By 2006, when U.S. military deaths approached 3,000 and Iraqi civilian casualties reached tens of thousands, public opinion polls in the United States found that a majority of Americans believed that the Iraq War was a mistake.

The president's father, George H. W. Bush, had refused to invade Iraq at the end of the 1991 Gulf War. He explained that Colin Powell, Dick Cheney, and other advisers agreed that "unilaterally exceeding the United Nations' mandate would have destroyed the precedent of international

Transferring Authority to Iraqis
In March 2007, as part of the troop surge in Iraq, U.S. forces set up three joint security stations in Ghazaliya, one of the most dangerous areas around Baghdad. By 2009, the counterinsurgency strategy had produced significant results. Attacks throughout Iraq fell sharply, while U.S. military deaths dropped from 904 in 2007 to 314 in 2008. The improved security fed Iraqis' determination to regain control of their country. In January 2009, U.S. forces transferred control of Joint Security Station III in Ghazaliya to the Iraqi army. Here, U.S. Army Specialist Anthony Perez and an Iraqi soldier raise the Iraqi flag above the station. AP Images/Karim Kadim.

response to aggression that we hoped to establish." The first Bush administration resisted making the nation "an occupying power in a bitterly hostile land," refusing to incur the "incalculable human and political costs" that such an invasion would produce.

By 2006, his son's very different approach was subject to criticism that crossed party lines and included leading military figures. Critics acknowledged that the U.S. military had felled a brutal dictator, but coalition forces were not large enough or adequately prepared for the turmoil that followed the invasion. Nor did they find the weapons of mass destruction or links to Osama bin Laden that administration officials had insisted made the war necessary. Rather, in the chaos induced by the invasion, more than a thousand terrorists entered Iraq — the place, according to one expert, "for fundamentalists to go . . . to stick it to the West."

The war and occupation exacted a steep price not only in dollars but also in American and Iraqi lives, U.S. relations with the other great powers, and the nation's reputation in the world, especially among Arab nations. Revelations of prisoner abuse in the Abu Ghraib prison in Iraq and in the Guantánamo detention camp housing captives from the Afghan war further tarnished the United States' image. Anti-Americanism around the world rose to its highest point in history. The budget deficit swelled, and resources were diverted to Iraq from other national security challenges, including the stabilization of Afghanistan, the elimination of bin Laden and Al Qaeda, and the threats posed by North Korea's and Iran's pursuit of nuclear weapons.

Voters registered their dissatisfaction in 2006, turning control of both houses of Congress over to the Democrats for the first time since 1994. President Bush replaced Secretary of Defense Donald Rumsfeld, and the administration displayed more willingness to work with other nations in dealing with Iraq, Iran, and North Korea. Yet Bush clung to the goal of bringing democracy to the Middle East, even as the situation in Iraq deteriorated. Despite opposition from Democrats in Congress, who wanted a timetable for withdrawal from Iraq, in 2007 the administration began a troop surge that increased U.S. forces there to 160,000. The surge, along with actions by Iraqi leaders, contributed to a significant reduction in terrorist violence, and the administration began planning for the eventual withdrawal of U.S. forces by the end of 2011.

REVIEW   Why did the United States invade Iraq in March 2003?

▶ The Obama Presidency: Reform and Backlash

Despite the improving situation in Iraq, President Bush's approval ratings sank below 30 percent, posing severe difficulties for the Republican Party in the 2008 elections. The Republicans

nominated John McCain, a Vietnam War hero and longtime senator from Arizona, who chose as his running mate Alaska governor Sarah Palin, the second woman to run for vice president on a major party ticket. Even more historic changes occurred in the Democratic Party when, for the first time, an African American and a woman were the top two contenders. (See "Visualizing History," page 1070.) In hard-fought battles that continued until the last primaries in June, **Barack Obama** edged out New York senator and former First Lady **Hillary Rodham Clinton**, for the presidential nomination.

Born to a white mother and a Kenyan father and raised in Hawai'i and Indonesia, Obama was the first African American to head the *Harvard Law Review*. He settled in Chicago, served in the Illinois Senate, and won election to the U.S. Senate in 2004. At the age of forty-seven, Obama won the Democratic nomination with a combination of a brilliant campaign strategy based on grassroots and Internet organizing and the ability to speak to deep-seated longings for a new kind of politics and racial reconciliation. He won 53 percent of the popular vote and defeated McCain 365 to 173 in the electoral college, while Democrats increased their majorities in the House and Senate (Map 31.4).

Obama hoped to work across party lines, nodding to both conservatives and liberals when he defined "individual responsibility and mutual responsibility" as "the essence of the American promise." The first African American president

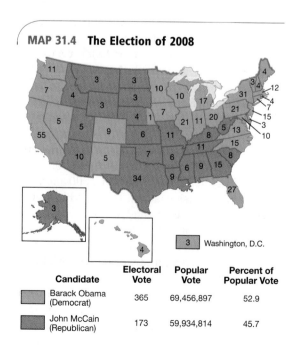

MAP 31.4   The Election of 2008

Candidate	Electoral Vote	Popular Vote	Percent of Popular Vote
Barack Obama (Democrat)	365	69,456,897	52.9
John McCain (Republican)	173	59,934,814	45.7

3 Washington, D.C.

pledged to pursue a series of reforms in health care, education, the environment, and immigration policy, but he confronted the worst economic crisis since the 1980s. A recession struck in 2008, fueled by a breakdown in financial institutions that had accumulated trillions of dollars of bad debt, largely from the making of loans for over-priced houses to people who lacked the capacity to repay them. As the recession spread to other parts of the world, home mortgage foreclosures skyrocketed, major companies went bankrupt, and unemployment rose to 9.8 percent in late 2010, the highest rate in more than twenty-five years. The financial crisis was so severe that Congress passed the Bush administration's $700 billion Troubled Assets Relief Program in 2008 to inject credit into the economy and shore up banks and other businesses. Obama followed with the **American Recovery and Reinvestment Act of 2009**, $787 billion worth of spending and tax cuts to stimulate the economy and relieve unemployment. Finally, in an effort to prevent the conditions that triggered the financial crisis, he persuaded Congress to expand governmental regulation with the **Wall Street Reform and Consumer Protection Act** in 2010.

Obama's judicial appointments increased the number of women on the Supreme Court to three and included the first ever Latina justice. The president implemented reforms in education, and he signed laws strengthening women's right to equal pay and protecting credit-card holders. His most substantial domestic achievement was passage of a health care reform bill over unanimous Republican opposition. The **Patient Protection and Affordable Care Act** of 2010 extended health insurance to thirty million Americans. It provided subsidies and compelled larger businesses to offer coverage, imposed new regulations on insurance companies to protect their customers, and contained provisions to limit health care costs. Although liberals failed to get a public option to allow government-managed programs to compete with private insurance plans, the law represented the largest expansion of government since the Great Society. One journalist remarked that its passage made Obama "a figure in history for reasons far beyond the color of his skin."

In foreign affairs, Obama reached out to Muslim nations, recommitted the United States to multilateralism, and worked to contain the proliferation of nuclear weapons. He continued the Bush administration's plan to withdraw from Iraq. When the last combat troops departed in 2010, 50,000 U.S. military personnel remained

to train and assist Iraqi security forces while leaders struggled to build a stable government that could win the confidence of the three major factions. On Afghanistan, even though corruption permeated its government and a majority of Americans opposed that war, Obama accepted the advice of military leaders that more troops were needed to contain the Taliban insurgents and secure the government. He dispatched an additional 50,000 military personnel to Afghanistan with the promise that the United States could begin to draw down its commitment in mid-2011.

Voters were much more concerned with domestic issues when they issued a sharp rebuke

> "Individual responsibility and mutual responsibility [are] the essence of the American promise."
> — President BARACK OBAMA

The Inauguration of Barack Obama

President Barack Obama and his wife, Michelle, walk down Pennsylvania Avenue after his inauguration at the Capitol on January 20, 2009. In his inaugural address, Obama spoke of "this winter of our hardship," referring to economic crisis, wars in Iraq and Afghanistan, and other challenges facing the nation. While the most people ever to attend an inauguration absorbed his sober message, they also radiated feelings of sheer joy and hope. AP Images/Doug Mills/Pool.

Caricaturing the Candidates: Clinton and Obama in 2008

In the Democratic presidential primaries of 2008, political cartoonists faced an unusual challenge. For the first time, a woman and an African American squared off as major rivals. Cartoonists had a free hand at portraying the unpopular outgoing president, George W. Bush — often pictured as a simian or monkeylike creature of dim intelligence. But how could they portray a woman and a black man without raising charges of sexism or racism?

Hillary Clinton, of course, had a history in political cartoons as First Lady and then as senator from New York. Her caricatures at the hands of the press had already drawn fire from her supporters for being as personal as they were political. After viewing the cartoons shown here, do you agree that her caricatures are sexist?

Political cartoonists drawing Barack Obama faced the challenge of avoiding obvious racial stereotypes. Fortunately for them, in his 2004 Democratic convention keynote address, Obama had already described himself as "a skinny kid with big ears and a funny name," and cartoonists capitalized on that image. Do you think the cartoons here avoid racism in their portrayal of Obama?

In the first cartoon, from February 2008, Hillary Clinton is in

"The Clinton Machine."

the driver's seat of "The Clinton Machine," which is about to crush Barack Obama. Who is shown as powering the steamroller? How does the portrayal of Obama compare with that of Clinton in this cartoon? What does this cartoon imply about Clinton's chances for capturing the Democratic nomination?

The second cartoon shows Clinton melting, in the style of the Wicked Witch of the West from *The Wizard of Oz.* A smiling Obama,

dressed as Dorothy, holds a pail of water labeled "High Tone Rhetoric," which is apparently responsible for Clinton's demise. The cartoon, inked by the well-known political cartoonist Steve Benson, ran in late February after Obama had won a series of primary contests. What anti-Clinton messages are included in this cartoon? Is Obama depicted as a powerful victor?

In the third cartoon, Clinton appears as "The Incredible Sulk,"

to Obama in the 2010 midterm elections, turning over the House to the Republicans and cutting into the Democratic majority in the Senate. Nearly 10 percent of American workers were unemployed, the federal deficit that Obama had inherited from the Bush administration soared to $1.4 trillion, and a vocal minority of older and mostly white voters expressed their fury at what they considered an overreaching government by joining grassroots movements that took the name the Tea Party revolt. As one Tea Party

supporter put it, "The government is taking over everything — I want my freedom back." The intensely polarized political environment would complicate Obama's efforts to reduce unemployment and cut into the enormous federal debt and would imperil his agenda of reform in environmental and immigration policy.

REVIEW What obstacles stood in the way of Obama's reform agenda?

"I'm Melting."

of Clinton and Obama vary in these three cartoons? For each candidate, would you say there is a progression of change, or do their depictions generally remain static?

Although cartoonists tended to portray Clinton and Obama as bitter enemies throughout the primaries, the two politicians began an effective partnership when president-elect Obama selected Clinton for the position of secretary of state in November 2008.

SOURCE: "The Clinton Machine," Pat Bagley, *The Salt Lake Tribune*, Cagle Cartoons; "I'm Melting," by permission of Steve Benson and Creators Sydicate, Inc.; "The Incredible Sulk," HOLBERT ©2008 Jerry Holbert. Used by permission of UNIVERSAL UCLICK for UFS. All rights reserved.

a monster who threatens a nervous Obama as he contemplates choosing a running mate. The cartoon ran in June 2008, in the lead-up to the Democratic National Convention in Denver. Why do you think the artist styled Clinton as a cartoon character who morphs into a monster when provoked? Why do you think the artist portrayed Obama as cowering before his former rival?

The political cartoons reproduced here are a tiny sample of the larger world of political commentary. Yet they convey many of the beliefs and attitudes held by the American public as the 2008 primary elections played out. How do the portrayals

"The Incredible Sulk."

▶ Conclusion: Defining the Government's Role at Home and Abroad

More than two hundred years after the birth of the United States, Colin Powell referred to the unfinished nature of the American promise when he declared that the question of America's role in the world "isn't answered yet." In fact, the end of the Cold War, the rise of international terrorism, and the George W. Bush administration's doctrines of preemption and unilateralism sparked new debates over the long-standing question of how the United States should act beyond its borders.

Nor had Americans set to rest questions about the role of government at home. In a population so greatly derived from people fleeing oppressive governments, Americans had debated for more than two centuries what responsibilities the government should shoulder and what was best left to private enterprise, families, churches, and other voluntary institutions. Far more than most industrialized democracies, the United States had relied on private rather than public obligation, individual rather than collective solutions. In the twentieth century, Americans had significantly enlarged the federal government's powers and responsibilities, but the years since the 1960s had seen a decline of trust in government's ability to improve people's lives, even as a poverty rate of 20 percent among children and a growing gap between rich and poor survived the economic boom of the 1990s.

The shifting of control of the government back and forth between Republicans and Democrats from 1989 to 2010 revealed a dynamic debate over government's role in domestic affairs. The protections enacted for people with disabilities during the first Bush administration and Bill Clinton's incremental reforms both built on a deep-rooted tradition that sought to realize the American promise of justice and human well-being. Those who mobilized against the ravages of globalization worked internationally for what populists, progressives, New Deal reformers, and many activists of the 1960s had sought for the domestic population: protection of individual rights, curbs on capitalism, assistance for victims of rapid economic change, and fiscal policies that placed greater responsibility on those best able to pay for the collective good. Even the second Bush administration, which sought to limit government's reach, supported the No Child Left Behind Act and the Medicare prescription drug program, and it departed from traditional conservative policy in the gigantic program to bail out failing businesses when the financial crisis hit the economy in 2008. The bitter controversy surrounding Obama's health care reform replayed America's long-standing debate about the government's appropriate role.

The United States became ever more deeply embedded in the global economy as products, information, and people crossed borders with amazing speed and frequency. Although the end of the Cold War brought about unanticipated cooperation between the United States and its former enemies, globalization also contributed to international instability and the threat of deadly terrorism to a nation unaccustomed to foreign attacks within its own borders. In response to those dangers, the second Bush administration departed from the multilateral approach to foreign policy that had been built up by Republican

and Democratic administrations alike since World War II. Toward the end of his second term, however, Bush worked to improve international relationships, and Obama promised a new approach in American relations with the world.

► Selected Bibliography

Domestic Politics, Policies, and Economic Change

Jonathan Alter, *The Promise: President Obama, Year One* (2010).

David Blumenthal and James A. Morone, *The Heart of Power: Health and Politics in the Oval Office* (2009).

Douglas Brinkley, *The Great Deluge: Hurricane Katrina, New Orleans, and the Mississippi Gulf Coast* (2006).

Alfred D. Chandler Jr., *Inventing the Electronic Century: The Epic Story of the Consumer Electronics and Computer Science Industries* (2001).

Robert Draper, *"Dead Certain": The Presidency of George W. Bush* (2007).

John F. Harris, *The Survivor: Bill Clinton in the White House* (2005).

Bruce D. Meyer and Douglas Holtz-Eakin, *Making Work Pay: The Earned Income Tax Credit and Its Impact on America's Families* (2002).

Richard A. Posner, *A Failure of Capitalism: The Crisis of '08 and the Descent into Depression* (2009).

Jack N. Rakove, ed., *The Unfinished Election of 2000* (2001).

Richard K. Scotch, *From Good Will to Civil Rights: Transforming Federal Disability Policy* (rev. ed., 2001).

David K. Shipler, *The Working Poor: Invisible in America* (2004).

Julian E. Zelizer, ed., *The Presidency of George W. Bush: A First Historical Assessment* (2010).

Kate Zernike, *Boiling Mad: Inside Tea Party America* (2010).

Globalization and Immigration

Frank D. Bean and Gillian Stevens, *America's Newcomers and the Dynamics of Diversity* (2003).

Jeremy Brecher, Tim Costello, and Brendan Smith, *Globalization from Below* (2000).

Thomas L. Friedman, *The World Is Flat* (2005).

Otis L. Graham, *Unguarded Gates: A History of America's Immigration Crisis* (2004).

John R. MacArthur, *The Selling of "Free Trade": NAFTA, Washington, and the Subversion of American Democracy* (2000).

David M. Reimers, *Other Immigrants: The Global Origins of the American People* (2005).

Joseph E. Stiglitz, *Globalization and Its Discontents* (2002).

Foreign Policy after the Cold War

Andrew J. Bacevich, *American Empire: The Realities and Consequences of U.S. Diplomacy* (2002).

Ivo H. Daalder and James M. Lindsay, *America Unbound: The Bush Revolution in Foreign Policy* (2003).

Karen DeYoung, *Soldier: The Life of Colin Powell* (2006).

David Halberstam, *War in a Time of Peace: Bush, Clinton, and the Generals* (2001).

Paul Kennedy, *The Parliament of Man: The Past, Present, and Future of the United Nations* (2006).

James Mann, *Rise of the Vulcans: The History of Bush's War Cabinet* (2004).

Terrorism and the Afghan and Iraq Wars

Seth G. Jones, *In the Graveyard of Empires: America's War in Afghanistan* (2009).

Gilles Kepel, *Jihad: The Trail of Political Islam* (2002).

Daniel Levitas, *The Terrorist Next Door: The Militia Movement and the Radical Right* (2002).

National Commission on Terrorist Attacks, *The 9/11 Commission Report: Final Report of the National Commission on Terrorist Attacks upon the United States* (2004).

George Packer, *The Assassins' Gate: America in Iraq* (2005).

Gary Rosen, ed., *The Right War? The Conservative Debate on Iraq* (2005).

Anthony Shadid, *Night Draws Near: Iraq's People in the Shadow of America's War* (2005).

Ron Suskind, *The One Percent Doctrine: Deep Inside America's Pursuit of Its Enemies since 9/11* (2006).

Lawrence Wright, *The Looming Tower: Al-Qaeda and the Road to 9/11* (2006).

▶ **FOR MORE BOOKS ABOUT TOPICS IN THIS CHAPTER,** see the Online Bibliography at bedfordstmartins.com/roark.

▶ **FOR ADDITIONAL PRIMARY SOURCES FROM THIS PERIOD,** see Michael Johnson, ed., *Reading the American Past*, Fifth Edition.

▶ **FOR WEB SITES, IMAGES, AND DOCUMENTS RELATED TO TOPICS AND PLACES IN THIS CHAPTER,** visit Make History at bedfordstmartins.com/roark.

Reviewing Chapter 31

KEY TERMS

Explain each term's significance.

Domestic Stalemate and Global Upheaval: The Presidency of George H. W. Bush

George H. W. Bush (p. 1041)
Clean Air Act of 1990 (p. 1041)
Americans with Disabilities Act (p. 1041)
Operation Just Cause (p. 1044)
Saddam Hussein (p. 1044)
Persian Gulf War (p. 1045)
William Jefferson "Bill" Clinton (p. 1047)

The Clinton Administration's Search for the Middle Ground

Earned Income Tax Credit (EITC) (p. 1049)
"don't ask, don't tell" policy (p. 1051)
Personal Responsibility and Work Opportunity Reconciliation Act (p. 1052)

The United States in a Globalizing World

globalization (p. 1054)
Osama bin Laden (p. 1056)
North American Free Trade Agreement (NAFTA) (p. 1057)
World Trade Organization (WTO) (p. 1057)

President George W. Bush: Conservatism at Home and Radical Initiatives Abroad

George W. Bush (p. 1061)
Kyoto Protocol (p. 1063)
No Child Left Behind Act (p. 1063)
Hurricane Katrina (p. 1063)
September 11, 2001 (p. 1064)
Al Qaeda (p. 1064)
USA Patriot Act (p. 1065)
Department of Homeland Security (p. 1066)
Iraq War (p. 1066)

The Obama Presidency: Reform and Backlash

Barack Obama (p. 1068)
Hillary Rodham Clinton (p. 1068)
American Recovery and Reinvestment Act of 2009 (p. 1069)
Wall Street Reform and Consumer Protection Act (p. 1069)
Patient Protection and Affordable Care Act (p. 1069)

REVIEW QUESTIONS

Use key terms and dates to support your answer.

1. How did George H. W. Bush respond to threats to U.S. interests as the Cold War came to an end? (pp. 1041–1048)

2. What policies of the Clinton administration moved the Democratic Party to the right? (pp. 1048–1054)

3. Who criticized free trade agreements and why? (pp. 1054–1061)

4. Why did the United States invade Iraq in March 2003? (pp. 1061–1068)

5. What obstacles stood in the way of Obama's reform agenda? (pp. 1068–1071)

MAKING CONNECTIONS

Draw on key terms, the timeline, and review questions.

1. How did George H. W. Bush continue the policies of his predecessor, Ronald Reagan? How did he depart from them?

2. President Bill Clinton called himself a "New Democrat." How did his policies and goals differ from those of Democrats in the past?

3. In the late twentieth century, economic globalization transformed the United States. Explain what globalization is, and describe how it affected the U.S. economy and population in the 1990s.

4. The terrorist attacks of September 11, 2001, were unprecedented. What gave rise to the attacks? How did the nation respond?

LINKING TO THE PAST

Link events in this chapter to earlier events.

1. How did George W. Bush's doctrine of preemption differ from the doctrine of containment? (See chapter 26.)

2. What features did the immigration after 1980 have in common with the immigration between 1880 and 1920? What was different? (See chapter 19.)

► **For practice quizzes and other study tools,** see the Online Study Guide at bedfordstmartins.com/roark.

TIMELINE 1988–2011

1988	• Republican George H. W. Bush elected president.
1989	• Communism collapses in Eastern Europe. • United States invades Panama.
1990	• Americans with Disabilities Act.
1991	• Persian Gulf War.
1992	• Democrat William Jefferson "Bill" Clinton elected president.
1993	• Israel and PLO sign peace accords. • North American Free Trade Agreement (NAFTA).
1994	• United States sends troops to Haiti. • General Agreement on Tariffs and Trade establishes World Trade Organization (WTO).
1995	• Bombing of federal building in Oklahoma City. • United States, with NATO, bombs Serbia.
1996	• Personal Responsibility and Work Opportunity Reconciliation Act. • President Clinton reelected.
1998	• United States bombs terrorist sites in Afghanistan and Sudan.
1998–2000	• United States bombs Iraq
1999	• Senate trial fails to approve impeachment of Clinton.
2000	• Republican George W. Bush elected president.
2001	• September 11. Terrorists attack World Trade Center and Pentagon. • U.S.-led coalition attacks Afghanistan, driving out Taliban government. • USA Patriot Act. • $1.35 trillion tax cut.
2002	• No Child Left Behind Act. • Department of Homeland Security established.
2003	• United States attacks Iraq. • Prescription drug coverage added to Medicare.
2004	• George W. Bush reelected president.
2005	• Hurricane Katrina.
2007	• Bush begins troop surge in Iraq.
2008	• Worst financial crisis since the Great Depression. • Troubled Asset Relief Program. • Democrat Barack Obama elected president.
2009	• American Recovery and Reinvestment Act.
2010	• Patient Protection and Affordable Care Act. • Wall Street Reform and Consumer Protection Act. • United States ends combat operations in Iraq, increases troops in Afghanistan.
2011	• U.S. forces kill Osama bin Laden in Pakistan

Appendix Directory

THE DECLARATION OF INDEPENDENCE

In Congress, July 4, 1776,

THE UNANIMOUS DECLARATION OF THE THIRTEEN UNITED STATES OF AMERICA

When in the course of human events, it becomes necessary for one people to dissolve the political bands which have connected them with another, and to assume, among the powers of the earth, the separate and equal station to which the laws of nature and of nature's God entitle them, a decent respect to the opinions of mankind requires that they should declare the causes which impel them to the separation.

We hold these truths to be self-evident, that all men are created equal; that they are endowed by their Creator with certain unalienable rights; that among these, are life, liberty, and the pursuit of happiness. That, to secure these rights, governments are instituted among men, deriving their just powers from the consent of the governed; that, whenever any form of government becomes destructive of these ends, it is the right of the people to alter or to abolish it, and to institute a new government, laying its foundation on such principles, and organizing its powers in such form, as to them shall seem most likely to effect their safety and happiness. Prudence, indeed, will dictate that governments long established, should not be changed for light and transient causes; and, accordingly, all experience hath shown, that mankind are more disposed to suffer, while evils are sufferable, than to right themselves by abolishing the forms to which they are accustomed. But, when a long train of abuses and usurpations, pursuing invariably the same object, evinces a design to reduce them under absolute despotism, it is their right, it is their duty, to throw off such government and to provide new guards for their future security. Such has been the patient sufferance of these colonies, and such is now the necessity which constrains them to alter their former systems of government. The history of the present King of Great Britain is a history of repeated injuries and usurpations, all having, in direct object, the establishment of an absolute tyranny over these States. To prove this, let facts be submitted to a candid world: He has refused his assent to laws the most wholesome and necessary for the public good.

He has forbidden his governors to pass laws of immediate and pressing importance, unless suspended in their operation till his assent should be obtained; and, when so suspended, he has utterly neglected to attend to them.

He has refused to pass other laws for the accommodation of large districts of people, unless those people would relinquish the right of representation in the legislature; a right inestimable to them, and formidable to tyrants only.

He has called together legislative bodies at places unusual, uncomfortable, and distant from the depository of their public records, for the sole purpose of fatiguing them into compliance with his measures.

He has dissolved representative houses repeatedly for opposing, with manly firmness, his invasions on the rights of the people.

He has refused, for a long time after such dissolutions, to cause others to be elected; whereby the legislative powers, incapable of annihilation, have returned to the people at large for their exercise; the state remaining in the mean-time exposed to all the danger of invasion from without, and convulsions within.

He has endeavoured to prevent the population of these States; for that purpose, obstructing the laws for naturalization of foreigners, refusing to pass others to encourage their migration hither, and raising the conditions of new appropriations of lands.

He has obstructed the administration of justice, by refusing his assent to laws for establishing judiciary powers.

He has made judges dependent on his will alone, for the tenure of their offices, and the amount and payment of their salaries.

He has erected a multitude of new offices, and sent hither swarms of officers to harass our people, and eat out their substance.

He has kept among us, in times of peace, standing armies, without the consent of our legislature.

He has affected to render the military independent of, and superior to, the civil power.

He has combined, with others, to subject us to a jurisdiction foreign to our Constitution, and unacknowledged by our laws; giving his assent to their acts of pretended legislation:

For quartering large bodies of armed troops among us:

For protecting them by a mock trial, from punishment, for any murders which they should commit on the inhabitants of these States:

For cutting off our trade with all parts of the world:

For imposing taxes on us without our consent:

For depriving us, in many cases, of the benefit of trial by jury:

For transporting us beyond seas to be tried for pretended offences:

For abolishing the free system of English laws in a neighboring province, establishing therein an arbitrary government, and enlarging its boundaries, so as to render it at once an example and fit instrument for introducing the same absolute rule into these colonies:

For taking away our charters, abolishing our most valuable laws, and altering, fundamentally, the powers of our governments:

For suspending our own legislatures, and declaring themselves invested with power to legislate for us in all cases whatsoever.

He has abdicated government here, by declaring us out of his protection, and waging war against us.

He has plundered our seas, ravaged our coasts, burnt our towns, and destroyed the lives of our people.

He is, at this time, transporting large armies of foreign mercenaries to complete the works of death, desolation, and tyranny, already begun, with circumstances of cruelty and perfidy scarcely paralleled in the most barbarous ages, and totally unworthy the head of a civilized nation.

He has constrained our fellow citizens, taken captive on the high seas, to bear arms against their country, to become the executioners of their friends, and brethren, or to fall themselves by their hands.

He has excited domestic insurrections amongst us, and has endeavored to bring on the inhabitants of our frontiers, the merciless Indian savages, whose known rule of warfare is an undistinguished destruction of all ages, sexes, and conditions.

In every stage of these oppressions, we have petitioned for redress; in the most humble terms; our repeated petitions have been answered only by repeated injury. A prince, whose character is thus marked by every act which may define a tyrant, is unfit to be the ruler of a free people.

Nor have we been wanting in attention to our British brethren. We have warned them, from time to time, of attempts made by their legislature to extend an unwarrantable jurisdiction over us. We have reminded them of the circumstances of our emigration and settlement here. We have appealed to their native justice and magnanimity, and we have conjured them, by the ties of our common kindred, to disavow these usurpations, which would inevitably interrupt our connections and correspondence. They, too, have been deaf to the voice of justice and consanguinity. We must, therefore, acquiesce in the necessity which denounces our separation, and hold them as we hold the rest of mankind, enemies in war, in peace, friends.

We, therefore, the representatives of the United States of America, in general Congress assembled, appealing to the Supreme Judge of the world for the rectitude of our intentions, do, in the name, and by authority of the good people of these colonies, solemnly publish and declare, that these united colonies are, and of right ought to be, free and independent states: that they are absolved from all allegiance to the British Crown, and that all political connection between them and the state of Great Britain is, and ought to be, totally dissolved; and that, as free and independent states, they have full power to levy war, conclude peace, contract alliances, establish commerce, and to do all other acts and things which independent states may of right do. And, for the support of this declaration, with a firm reliance on the protection of Divine Providence, we mutually pledge to each other our lives, our fortunes, and our sacred honor.

The foregoing Declaration was, by order of Congress, engrossed, and signed by the following members:

JOHN HANCOCK

New Hampshire
Josiah Bartlett
William Whipple
Matthew Thornton

Massachusetts Bay
Samuel Adams
John Adams
Robert Treat Paine
Elbridge Gerry

Rhode Island
Stephen Hopkins
William Ellery

Connecticut
Roger Sherman
Samuel Huntington
William Williams
Oliver Wolcott

New York
William Floyd
Phillip Livingston
Francis Lewis
Lewis Morris

New Jersey
Richard Stockton
John Witherspoon
Francis Hopkinson
John Hart
Abraham Clark

Pennsylvania
Robert Morris
Benjamin Rush
Benjamin Franklin
John Morton
George Clymer

James Smith
George Taylor
James Wilson
George Ross
Caesar Rodney
George Read
Thomas M'Kean

Maryland
Samuel Chase
William Paca
Thomas Stone
Charles Carroll,
   of Carrollton

North Carolina
William Hooper
Joseph Hewes
John Penn

South Carolina
Edward Rutledge
Thomas Heyward, Jr.
Thomas Lynch, Jr.
Arthur Middleton

Virginia
George Wythe
Richard Henry Lee
Thomas Jefferson
Benjamin Harrison
Thomas Nelson, Jr.
Francis Lightfoot Lee
Carter Braxton

Georgia
Button Gwinnett
Lyman Hall
George Walton

Resolved, That copies of the Declaration be sent to the several assemblies, conventions, and committees, or councils of safety, and to the several commanding officers of the continental troops; that it be proclaimed in each of the United States, at the head of the army.

THE ARTICLES OF CONFEDERATION AND PERPETUAL UNION

Agreed to in Congress, November 15, 1777.
Ratified March 1781.

BETWEEN THE STATES OF NEW HAMPSHIRE, MASSACHUSETTS BAY, RHODE ISLAND AND PROVIDENCE PLANTATIONS, CONNECTICUT, NEW YORK, NEW JERSEY, PENNSYLVANIA, DELAWARE, MARYLAND, VIRGINIA, NORTH CAROLINA, SOUTH CAROLINA, GEORGIA.*

Article 1

The stile of this confederacy shall be "The United States of America."

Article 2

Each State retains its sovereignty, freedom and independence, and every power, jurisdiction, and right, which is not by this confederation expressly delegated to the United States, in Congress assembled.

Article 3

The said states hereby severally enter into a firm league of friendship with each other for their common defence, the security of their liberties and their mutual and general welfare; binding themselves to assist each other against all force offered to, or attacks made upon them, or any of them, on account of religion, sovereignty, trade, or any other pretence whatever.

Article 4

The better to secure and perpetuate mutual friendship and intercourse among the people of the different states in this union, the free inhabitants of each of these states, paupers, vagabonds, and fugitives from justice excepted, shall be entitled to all privileges and immunities of free citizens in the several states; and the people of each State shall have free ingress and regress to and from any other State, and shall enjoy therein all the privileges of trade and commerce, subject to the same duties, impositions, and restrictions, as the inhabitants thereof respectively; provided, that such restrictions shall not extend so far as to prevent the removal of property, imported into any State, to any other State of which the owner is an inhabitant; provided also, that no imposition, duties, or restriction, shall be laid by any State on the property of the United States, or either of them. If any person guilty of, or charged with treason, felony, or other high misdemeanor in any State, shall flee from justice and be found in any of the United States, he shall, upon demand of the governor or executive power of the State from which he fled, be delivered up and removed to the State having jurisdiction of his offence. Full faith and credit shall be given in each of these states to the records, acts, and judicial proceedings of the courts and magistrates of every other State.

Article 5

For the more convenient management of the general interests of the United States, delegates shall be annually appointed, in such manner as the legislature of each State shall direct, to meet in Congress, on the 1st Monday in November in every year, with a power reserved to each State to recall its delegates, or any of them, at any time within the year, and to send others in their stead for the remainder of the year.

No State shall be represented in Congress by less than two, nor by more than seven members; and no person shall be capable of being a delegate for more than three years in any term of six years; nor shall any person, being a delegate, be capable of holding any office under the United States, for which he, or any other for his benefit, receives any salary, fees, or emolument of any kind.

Each State shall maintain its own delegates in a meeting of the states, and while they act as members of the committee of the states.

In determining questions in the United States, in Congress assembled, each State shall have one vote.

Freedom of speech and debate in Congress shall not be impeached or questioned in any court or place out of Congress: and the members of Congress shall be protected in their persons from arrests and imprisonments, during the time of their going to and from, and attendance on Congress, except for treason, felony, or breach of the peace.

---

*This copy of the final draft of the Articles of Confederation is taken from the Journals, 9:907–925, November 15, 1777.

Article 6

No State, without the consent of the United States, in Congress assembled, shall send any embassy to, or receive any embassy from, or enter into any conference, agreement, alliance, or treaty with any king, prince, or state; nor shall any person, holding any office of profit or trust under the United States, or any of them, accept of any present, emolument, office or title, of any kind whatever, from any king, prince, or foreign state; nor shall the United States, in Congress assembled, or any of them, grant any title of nobility.

No two or more states shall enter into any treaty, confederation, or alliance, whatever, between them, without the consent of the United States, in Congress assembled, specifying accurately the purposes for which the same is to be entered into, and how long it shall continue.

No state shall lay any imposts or duties which may interfere with any stipulations in treaties entered into by the United States, in Congress assembled, with any king, prince, or state, in pursuance of any treaties already proposed by Congress to the courts of France and Spain.

No vessels of war shall be kept up in time of peace by any State, except such number only as shall be deemed necessary by the United States, in Congress assembled, for the defence of such State or its trade; nor shall any body of forces be kept up by any State, in time of peace, except such number only as, in the judgment of the United States, in Congress assembled, shall be deemed requisite to garrison the forts necessary for the defence of such State; but every State shall always keep up a well regulated and disciplined militia, sufficiently armed and accoutred, and shall provide, and constantly have ready for use, in public stores, a due number of field pieces and tents, and a proper quantity of arms, ammunition and camp equipage.

No State shall engage in any war without the consent of the United States, in Congress assembled, unless such State be actually invaded by enemies, or shall have received certain advice of a resolution being formed by some nation of Indians to invade such State, and the danger is so imminent as not to admit of a delay till the United States, in Congress assembled, can be consulted; nor shall any State grant commissions to any ships or vessels of war, nor letters of marque or reprisal, except it be after a declaration of war by the United States, in Congress assembled, and then only against the kingdom or state, and the subjects thereof, against which war has been so declared, and under such regulations as shall be established by the United States, in Congress assembled, unless such State be infested by pirates, in which case vessels of war may be fitted out for that occasion, and kept so long as the danger shall continue, or until the United States, in Congress assembled, shall determine otherwise.

Article 7

When land forces are raised by any State for the common defence, all officers of or under the rank of colonel, shall be appointed by the legislature of each State respectively, by whom such forces shall be raised, or in such manner as such State shall direct; and all vacancies shall be filled up by the State which first made the appointment.

Article 8

All charges of war and all other expences, that shall be incurred for the common defence or general welfare, and allowed by the United States, in Congress assembled, shall be defrayed out of a common treasury, which shall be supplied by the several states, in proportion to the value of all land within each State, granted to or surveyed for any person, as such land and the buildings and improvements thereon shall be estimated according to such mode as the United States, in Congress assembled, shall, from time to time, direct and appoint.

The taxes for paying that proportion shall be laid and levied by the authority and direction of the legislatures of the several states, within the time agreed upon by the United States, in Congress assembled.

Article 9

The United States, in Congress assembled, shall have the sole and exclusive right and power of determining on peace and war, except in the cases mentioned in the 6th article; of sending and receiving ambassadors; entering into treaties and alliances, provided that no treaty of commerce shall be made, whereby the legislative power of the respective states shall be restrained from imposing such imposts and duties on foreigners as their own people are subjected to, or from prohibiting the exportation or importation of any species of goods or commodities whatsoever; of establishing rules for deciding, in all cases, what captures on land or water shall be legal, and in what manner prizes, taken by land or naval forces in the service of the United States, shall be divided or appropriated; of granting letters of marque and reprisal in times of peace; appointing courts for the trial of piracies and felonies committed on the high seas, and establishing courts for receiving and determining, finally, appeals in all cases of captures; provided, that no member of Congress shall be appointed a judge of any of the said courts.

The United States, in Congress assembled, shall also be the last resort on appeal in all disputes and differences now subsisting, or that hereafter may arise between two or more states concerning boundary, jurisdiction or any other cause whatever; which authority shall always be exercised in the manner following: whenever the legislative or executive authority, or lawful agent of any State, in controversy with another, shall present a petition to Congress, stating the matter in question, and praying for a hearing, notice thereof shall be given, by order of Congress, to the legislative or executive authority of the other State in controversy, and a day assigned for the appearance of the parties by their lawful agents, who shall then be directed to appoint, by joint consent, commissioners or judges to constitute a court for hearing and determining the matter in question; but, if they cannot agree, Congress shall name three persons out of each of the United States, and from the list of such persons each party shall alternately strike out one, the petitioners beginning, until the number shall be reduced to thirteen; and from that number not less than seven, nor more than nine names, as Congress shall direct, shall, in the presence of Congress, be drawn out by lot; and the persons whose names shall be so drawn, or any five of them, shall be commissioners or judges to hear and finally determine the controversy, so always as a major part of the judges who shall hear the cause shall agree in the determination; and if either party shall neglect to attend at the day appointed, without shewing reasons which Congress shall judge sufficient, or, being present, shall refuse to strike, the Congress shall proceed to nominate three persons out of each State, and the secretary of Congress shall strike in behalf of such party absent or refusing; and the judgment and sentence of the court to be appointed, in the manner before prescribed, shall be final and conclusive; and if any of the parties shall refuse to submit to the authority of such court, or to appear or defend their claim or cause, the court shall nevertheless proceed to pronounce sentence or judgment, which shall, in like manner, be final and decisive, the judgment or sentence and other proceedings begin, in either case, transmitted to Congress, and lodged among the acts of Congress for the security of the parties concerned: provided, that every commissioner, before he sits in judgment, shall take an oath, to be administered by one of the judges of the supreme or superior court of the State where the cause shall be tried, "well and truly to hear and determine the matter in question, according to the best of his judgment, without favour, affection, or hope of reward:" provided, also, that no State shall be deprived of territory for the benefit of the United States.

All controversies concerning the private right of soil, claimed under different grants of two or more states, whose jurisdictions, as they may respect such lands and the states which passed such grants, are adjusted, the said grants, or either of them, being at the same time claimed to have originated antecedent to such settlement of jurisdiction, shall, on the petition of either party to the Congress of the United States, be finally determined, as near as may be, in the same manner as is before prescribed for deciding disputes respecting territorial jurisdiction between different states.

The United States, in Congress assembled, shall also have the sole and exclusive right and power of regulating the alloy and value of coin struck by their own authority, or by that of the respective states; fixing the standard of weights and measures throughout the United States; regulating the trade and managing all affairs with the Indians not members of any of the states; provided that the legislative right of any State within its own limits be not infringed or violated; establishing and regulating post offices from one State to another throughout all the United States, and exacting such postage on the papers passing through the same as may be requisite to defray the expences of the said office; appointing all officers of the land forces in the service of the United States, excepting regimental officers; appointing all the officers of the naval forces, and commissioning all officers whatever in the service of the United States; making rules for the government and regulation of the said land and naval forces, and directing their operations.

The United States, in Congress assembled, shall have authority to appoint a committee to sit in the recess of Congress, to be denominated "a Committee of the States," and to consist of one delegate from each State, and to appoint such other committees and civil officers as may be necessary for managing the general affairs of the United States, under their direction; to appoint one of their number to preside; provided that no person be allowed to serve in the office of president more than one year in any term of three years; to ascertain the necessary sums of money to be raised for the service of the United States, and to appropriate and apply the same for defraying the public expences; to borrow money or emit bills on the credit of the United States, transmitting, every half year, to the respective states, an account of the sums of money so borrowed or emitted; to build and equip a navy; to agree upon the number of land forces, and to make requisitions from each State for its quota, in proportion to the number of white inhabitants in such State; which requisitions shall be binding; and thereupon, the legislature of each State shall appoint the regimental officers, raise the men, and cloathe, arm, and equip them in a soldier-like manner, at the expence of the United States; and the officers and men so cloathed, armed, and equipped, shall march to the place appointed and within the time agreed on by the United States, in Congress assembled; but if the United States, in Congress assembled, shall, on consideration of circumstances, judge proper that any State should not raise men, or should raise a smaller number than its quota, and that any other State should raise a greater number of men than the quota thereof, such extra number shall be raised, officered, cloathed, armed, and equipped in the same manner as the quota of such State, unless the legislature of such State shall judge that such extra number cannot be safely spared out of the same, in which case they shall raise, officer, cloathe, arm, and equip as many of such extra number as they judge can be safely spared. And the officers and men so cloathed, armed, and equipped, shall march to the place appointed and within the time agreed on by the United States, in Congress assembled.

The United States, in Congress assembled, shall never engage in a war, nor grant letters of marque and reprisal in time of peace, nor enter into any treaties or alliances, nor coin money, nor regulate the value thereof, nor ascertain the sums and expences necessary for the defence and welfare of the United States, or any of them: nor emit bills, nor borrow money on the credit of the United States, nor appropriate money, nor agree upon the number of vessels of war to be built or purchased, or the number of land or sea forces to be raised, nor appoint a commander in chief of the army or navy, unless nine states assent to the same; nor shall a question on any other point, except for adjourning from day to day, be determined, unless by the votes of a majority of the United States, in Congress assembled.

The Congress of the United States shall have power to adjourn to any time within the year, and to any place within the United States, so that no period of adjournment be for a longer duration than the space of six months, and shall publish the journal of their proceedings monthly, except such parts thereof, relating to treaties, alliances or military operations, as, in their judgment, require secrecy; and the yeas and nays of the delegates of each State on any question shall be entered on the journal, when it is desired by any delegate; and the delegates of a State, or any of them, at his, or their request, shall be furnished with a transcript of the said journal, except such parts as are above excepted, to lay before the legislatures of the several states.

Article 10

The committee of the states, or any nine of them, shall be authorized to execute, in the recess of Congress, such of the powers of Congress as the United States, in Congress assembled, by the consent of nine states, shall, from time to time, think expedient to vest them with; provided, that no power be delegated to the said committee, for the exercise of which, by the articles of confederation, the voice of nine states, in the Congress of the United States assembled, is requisite.

Article 11

Canada acceding to this confederation, and joining in the measures of the United States, shall be admitted into and entitled to all the advantages of this union; but no other colony shall be admitted into the same, unless such admission be agreed to by nine states.

Article 12

All bills of credit emitted, monies borrowed and debts contracted by, or under the authority of Congress before the assembling of the United States, in pursuance of the present confederation, shall be deemed and considered as a charge against the United States, for payment and satisfaction whereof the said United States and the public faith are hereby solemnly pledged.

Article 13

Every State shall abide by the determinations of the United States, in Congress assembled, on all questions which, by this confederation, are submitted to them. And the articles of this confederation shall be inviolably observed by every State, and the union shall be perpetual; nor shall any alteration at any time hereafter be made in any of them, unless such alteration be agreed to in a Congress of the United States, and be afterwards confirmed by the legislatures of every State.

These articles shall be proposed to the legislatures of all the United States, to be considered, and if approved of by them, they are advised to authorize their delegates to ratify the same in the Congress of the United States; which being done, the same shall become conclusive.

THE CONSTITUTION OF THE UNITED STATES*

Agreed to by Philadelphia Convention, September 17, 1787. Implemented March 4, 1789.

Preamble

We the people of the United States, in order to form a more perfect union, establish justice, insure domestic tranquility, provide for the common defense, promote the general welfare, and secure the blessings of liberty to ourselves and our posterity, do ordain and establish this Constitution for the United States of America.

---

*Passages no longer in effect are in italic type.

Article I

Section 1 All legislative powers herein granted shall be vested in a Congress of the United States, which shall consist of a Senate and a House of Representatives.

Section 2 The House of Representatives shall be composed of members chosen every second year by the people of the several States, and the electors in each State shall have the qualifications requisite for electors of the most numerous branch of the State Legislature.

No person shall be a Representative who shall not have attained to the age of twenty-five years, and been seven years a citizen of the United States, and who shall not, when elected, be an inhabitant of that State in which he shall be chosen.

Representatives and direct taxes shall be apportioned among the several States which may be included within this Union, according to their respective numbers, *which shall be determined by adding to the whole number of free persons, including those bound to service for a term of years and excluding Indians not taxed, three-fifths of all other persons.* The actual enumeration shall be made within three years after the first meeting of the Congress of the United States, and within every subsequent term of ten years, in such manner as they shall by law direct. The number of Representatives shall not exceed one for every thirty thousand, but each State shall have at least one Representative; *and until such enumeration shall be made, the State of New Hampshire shall be entitled to choose three, Massachusetts eight, Rhode Island and Providence Plantations one, Connecticut five, New York six, New Jersey four, Pennsylvania eight, Delaware one, Maryland six, Virginia ten, North Carolina five, South Carolina five, and Georgia three.*

When vacancies happen in the representation from any State, the Executive authority thereof shall issue writs of election to fill such vacancies.

The House of Representatives shall choose their Speaker and other officers; and shall have the sole power of impeachment.

Section 3 The Senate of the United States shall be composed of two Senators from each State, *chosen by the legislature thereof,* for six years; and each Senator shall have one vote.

Immediately after they shall be assembled in consequence of the first election, they shall be divided as equally as may be into three classes. The seats of the Senators of the first class shall be vacated at the expiration of the second year, of the second class at the expiration of the fourth year, and of the third class at the expiration of the sixth year, so that one-third may be chosen every second year; *and if vacancies happen by resignation or otherwise, during the recess of the legislature of any State, the Executive thereof may make temporary appointments until the next meeting of the legislature, which shall then fill such vacancies.*

No person shall be a Senator who shall not have attained to the age of thirty years, and been nine years a citizen of the United States, and who shall not, when elected, be an inhabitant of that State for which he shall be chosen.

The Vice-President of the United States shall be President of the Senate, but shall have no vote, unless they be equally divided.

The Senate shall choose their other officers, and also a President pro tempore, in the absence of the Vice-President, or when he shall exercise the office of President of the United States.

The Senate shall have the sole power to try all impeachments. When sitting for that purpose, they shall be on oath or affirmation. When the President of the United States is tried, the Chief Justice shall preside: and no person shall be convicted without the concurrence of two-thirds of the members present.

Judgment in cases of impeachment shall not extend further than to removal from the office, and disqualification to hold and enjoy any office of honor, trust or profit under the United States: but the party convicted shall nevertheless be liable and subject to indictment, trial, judgment and punishment, according to law.

Section 4 The times, places and manner of holding elections for Senators and Representatives shall be prescribed in each State by the legislature thereof; but the Congress may at any time by law make or alter such regulations, except as to the places of choosing Senators.

The Congress shall assemble at least once in every year, and such meeting *shall be on the first Monday in December, unless they shall by law appoint a different day.*

Section 5 Each house shall be the judge of the elections, returns and qualifications of its own members, and a majority of each shall constitute a quorum to do business; but a smaller number may adjourn from day to day, and may be authorized to compel the attendance of absent members, in such manner, and under such penalties, as each house may provide.

Each house may determine the rules of its proceedings, punish its members for disorderly behavior, and with the concurrence of two-thirds, expel a member.

Each house shall keep a journal of its proceedings, and from time to time publish the same, excepting such parts as may in their judgment require secrecy; and the yeas and nays of the members of either house on any question shall, at the desire of one-fifth of those present, be entered on the journal.

Neither house, during the session of Congress, shall, without the consent of the other, adjourn for more than three days, nor to any other place than that in which the two houses shall be sitting.

Section 6 The Senators and Representatives shall receive a compensation for their services, to be ascertained by law and paid out of the treasury of the United States. They shall in all cases except treason, felony and breach of the peace, be privileged from arrest during their attendance at the session of their respective houses, and in going to and returning from the same; and for any speech or debate in either house, they shall not be questioned in any other place.

No Senator or Representative shall, during the time for which he was elected, be appointed to any civil office under the authority of the United States, which shall have been created, or the emoluments whereof shall have been increased, during such time; and no person holding any office under the United States shall be a member of either house during his continuance in office.

Section 7 All bills for raising revenue shall originate in the House of Representatives; but the Senate may propose or concur with amendments as on other bills.

Every bill which shall have passed the House of Representatives and the Senate, shall, before it become a law, be presented to the President of the United States; if he approve he shall sign it, but if not he shall return it with objections to that house in which it shall have originated, who shall enter the objections at large on their journal, and proceed to reconsider it. If after such reconsideration two-thirds of that house shall agree to pass the bill, it shall be sent, together with the objections, to the other house, by which it shall likewise be reconsidered, and, if approved by two-thirds of that house, it shall become a law. But in all such cases the votes of both houses shall be determined by yeas and nays, and the names of the persons voting for and against the bill shall be entered on the journal of each house respectively. If any bill shall not be returned by the President within ten days (Sundays excepted) after it shall have been presented to him, the same shall be a law, in like manner as if he had signed it, unless the Congress by their adjournment prevent its return, in which case it shall not be a law.

Every order, resolution, or vote to which the concurrence of the Senate and House of Representatives may be necessary (except on a question of adjournment) shall be presented to the President of the United States; and before the same shall take effect, shall be approved by him, or being disapproved by him, shall be repassed by two-thirds of the Senate and House of Representatives, according to the rules and limitations prescribed in the case of a bill.

Section 8 The Congress shall have power

To lay and collect taxes, duties, imposts, and excises, to pay the debts and provide for the common defense and general welfare of the United States; but all duties, imposts and excises shall be uniform throughout the United States;

To borrow money on the credit of the United States;

To regulate commerce with foreign nations, and among the several States, and with the Indian tribes;

To establish an uniform rule of naturalization, and uniform laws on the subject of bankruptcies throughout the United States;

To coin money, regulate the value thereof, and of foreign coin, and fix the standard of weights and measures;

To provide for the punishment of counterfeiting the securities and current coin of the United States;

To establish post offices and post roads;

To promote the progress of science and useful arts by securing for limited times to authors and inventors the exclusive right to their respective writings and discoveries;

To constitute tribunals inferior to the Supreme Court;

To define and punish piracies and felonies committed on the high seas and offences against the law of nations;

To declare war, grant letters of marque and reprisal, and make rules concerning captures on land and water;

To raise and support armies, but no appropriation of money to that use shall be for a longer term than two years;

To provide and maintain a navy;

To make rules for the government and regulation of the land and naval forces;

To provide for calling forth the militia to execute the laws of the Union, suppress insurrections and repel invasions;

To provide for organizing, arming, and disciplining the militia, and for governing such part of them as may be employed in the service of the United States, reserving to the States respectively the appointment of the officers, and the authority of training the militia according to the discipline prescribed by Congress;

To exercise exclusive legislation in all cases whatsoever, over such district (not exceeding ten miles square) as may, by cession of particular States, and the acceptance of Congress, become the seat of the government of the United States, and to exercise like authority over all places purchased by the consent of the legislature of the State, in which the same shall be, for erection of forts, magazines, arsenals, dockyards, and other needful buildings;—and

To make all laws which shall be necessary and proper for carrying into execution the foregoing powers, and all other powers vested by this Constitution in the government of the United States, or in any department or officer thereof.

Section 9 *The migration or importation of such persons as any of the States now existing shall think proper to admit shall not be prohibited by the Congress prior to the year one thousand eight hundred and eight; but a tax or duty may be imposed on such importation, not exceeding ten dollars for each person.*

The privilege of the writ of habeas corpus shall not be suspended, unless when in cases of rebellion or invasion the public safety may require it.

No bill of attainder or ex post facto law shall be passed.

No capitation, or other direct, tax shall be laid, unless in proportion to the census or enumeration herein before directed to be taken.

No tax or duty shall be laid on articles exported from any State.

No preference shall be given by any regulation of commerce or revenue to the ports of one State over those of another; nor shall vessels bound to, or from, one State be obliged to enter, clear, or pay duties in another.

No money shall be drawn from the treasury, but in consequence of appropriations made by law; and a regular statement and account of the receipts and expenditures of all public money shall be published from time to time.

No title of nobility shall be granted by the United States: and no person holding any office of profit or trust under them, shall, without the consent of the Congress, accept of any present, emolument, office, or title, of any kind whatever, from any king, prince, or foreign state.

Section 10 No State shall enter into any treaty, alliance, or confederation; grant letters of marque and reprisal; coin money; emit bills of credit; make anything but gold and silver coin a tender in payment of debts; pass any bill of attainder, ex post facto law, or law impairing the obligation of contracts, or grant any title of nobility.

No State shall, without the consent of Congress, lay any imposts or duties on imports or exports, except what may be absolutely necessary for executing its inspection laws: and the net produce of all duties and imposts, laid by any State on imports or exports, shall be for the use of the treasury of the United States; and all such laws shall be subject to the revision and control of the Congress.

No State shall, without the consent of Congress, lay any duty of tonnage, keep troops, or ships of war in time of peace, enter into any agreement or compact with another State, or with a foreign power, or engage in war, unless actually invaded, or in such imminent danger as will not admit of delay.

Article II

Section 1 The executive power shall be vested in a President of the United States of America. He shall hold his office during the term of four years, and, together with the Vice-President, chosen for the same term, be elected as follows:

Each State shall appoint, in such manner as the legislature thereof may direct, a number of electors, equal to the whole number of Senators and Representatives to which the State may be entitled in the Congress; but no Senator or Representative, or person holding an office of trust or profit under the United States, shall be appointed an elector.

The electors shall meet in their respective States, and vote by ballot for two persons, of whom one at least shall not be an inhabitant of the same State with themselves. And they shall make a list of all the persons voted for, and of the number of votes for each; which list they shall sign and certify, and transmit sealed to the seat of government of the United States, directed to the President of the Senate. The President of the Senate shall, in the presence of the Senate and House of Representatives, open all the certificates, and the votes shall then be counted. The person having the greatest number of votes shall be the President, if such number be a majority of the whole number of electors appointed; and if there be more than one who have such majority, and have an equal number of votes, then the House of Representatives shall immediately choose by ballot one of them for President; and if no person have a majority, then from the five highest on the list said house shall in like manner choose the President. But in choosing the President the votes shall be taken by States, the representation from each State having one vote; a quorum for this purpose shall consist of a member or members from two-thirds of the States, and a majority of all the States shall be necessary to a choice. In every case, after the choice of the President, the person having the greatest number of votes of the electors shall be the Vice-President. But if there should remain two or more who have equal votes, the Senate shall choose from them by ballot the Vice-President.

The Congress may determine the time of choosing the electors, and the day on which they shall give their votes; which day shall be the same throughout the United States.

No person except a natural-born citizen, *or a citizen of the United States at the time of the adoption of this Constitution*, shall be eligible to the office of President; neither shall any person be eligible to that office who shall not have attained to the age of thirty-five years, and been fourteen years a resident within the United States.

In cases of the removal of the President from office or of his death, resignation, or inability to discharge the powers and duties of the said office, the same shall devolve on the Vice-President, and the Congress may by law provide for the case of removal, death, resignation, or inability, both of the President and Vice-President, declaring what officer shall then act as President, and such officer shall act accordingly, until the disability be removed, or a President shall be elected.

The President shall, at stated times, receive for his services a compensation, which shall neither be increased nor diminished during the period for which he shall have been elected, and he shall not receive within that period any other emolument from the United States, or any of them.

Before he enter on the execution of his office, he shall take the following oath or affirmation:—"I do solemnly swear (or affirm) that I will faithfully execute the office of the President of the United States, and will to the best of my ability preserve, protect and defend the Constitution of the United States."

Section 2 The President shall be commander in chief of the army and navy of the United States, and of the militia of the several States, when called into the actual service of the United States; he may require the opinion, in writing, of the principal officer in each of the executive departments, upon any subject relating to the duties of their respective offices, and he shall have power to grant reprieves and pardons for offenses against the United States, except in cases of impeachment.

He shall have power, by and with the advice and consent of the Senate, to make treaties, provided two-thirds of the Senators present concur; and he shall nominate, and by and with the advice and consent of the Senate, shall appoint ambassadors, other public ministers and consuls, judges of the Supreme Court, and all other officers of the United States, whose appointments are not herein otherwise provided for, and which shall be established by law: but Congress may by law vest the appointment of such inferior officers, as they think proper, in the President alone, in the courts of law, or in the heads of departments.

The President shall have power to fill up all vacancies that may happen during the recess of the Senate, by granting commissions which shall expire at the end of their next session.

Section 3 He shall from time to time give to the Congress information of the state of the Union, and recommend to their consideration such measures as he shall judge necessary and expedient; he may, on extraordinary occasions, convene both houses, or either of them, and in case of disagreement between them, with respect to the time of adjournment, he may adjourn them to such time as he shall think proper; he shall receive ambassadors and other public ministers; he shall take care that the laws be faithfully executed, and shall commission all the officers of the United States.

Section 4 The President, Vice-President and all civil officers of the United States shall be removed from office on impeachment for, and on conviction of, treason, bribery, or other high crimes and misdemeanors.

Article III

Section 1 The judicial power of the United States shall be vested in one Supreme Court, and in such inferior courts as the Congress may from time to time ordain and establish. The judges, both of the Supreme and inferior courts, shall hold their offices during good behavior, and shall, at stated times, receive for their services a compensation which shall not be diminished during their continuance in office.

Section 2 The judicial power shall extend to all cases, in law and equity, arising under this Constitution, the laws of the United States, and treaties made, or which shall be made, under their authority;—to all cases affecting ambassadors, other public ministers and consuls;—to all cases of admiralty and maritime jurisdiction;—to controversies to which the United States shall be a party;—to controversies between two or more States;—*between a State and citizens of another State*;—between citizens of different States;— between citizens of the same State claiming lands under grants of different States, and between a State, or the citizens thereof, and foreign states, citizens or subjects.

In all cases affecting ambassadors, other public ministers and consuls, and those in which a State shall be party, the Supreme Court shall have original jurisdiction. In all the other cases before mentioned, the Supreme Court shall have appellate jurisdiction, both as to law and fact, with such exceptions, and under such regulations, as the Congress shall make.

The trial of all crimes, except in cases of impeachment, shall be by jury; and such trial shall be held in the State where said crimes shall have been committed; but when not committed within any State, the trial shall be at such place or places as the Congress may by Law have directed.

Section 3 Treason against the United States shall consist only in levying war against them, or in adhering to their enemies, giving them aid and comfort. No person shall be convicted of treason unless on the testimony of two witnesses to the same overt act, or on confession in open court.

The Congress shall have power to declare the punishment of treason, but no attainder of treason shall work corruption of blood, or forfeiture except during the life of the person attainted.

Article IV

Section 1 Full faith and credit shall be given in each State to the public acts, records, and judicial proceedings of every other State. And the Congress may by general laws prescribe the manner in which such acts, records, and proceedings shall be proved, and the effect thereof.

Section 2 The citizens of each State shall be entitled to all privileges and immunities of citizens in the several States.

A person charged in any State with treason, felony, or other crime, who shall flee from justice, and be found in another State, shall on demand of the executive authority of the State from which he fled, be delivered up, to be removed to the State having jurisdiction of the crime.

No Person held to service or labor in one State, under the laws thereof, escaping into another, shall, in consequence of any law or regulation therein, be discharged from such service or labor, but shall be delivered up on claim of the party to whom such service or labor may be due.

Section 3 New States may be admitted by the Congress into this Union; but no new State shall be formed or erected within the jurisdiction of any other State; nor any State be formed by the junction of two or more States, or parts of States, without the consent of the legislatures of the States concerned as well as of the Congress.

The Congress shall have power to dispose of and make all needful rules and regulations respecting the territory or other property belonging to the United States; and nothing in this Constitution shall be so construed as to prejudice any claims of the United States, or of any particular State.

Section 4 The United States shall guarantee to every State in this Union a republican form of government, and shall protect each of them against invasion; and on application of the legislature, or of the executive (when the legislature cannot be convened), against domestic violence.

Article V

The Congress, whenever two-thirds of both houses shall deem it necessary, shall propose amendments to this Constitution, or, on the application of the legislatures of two-thirds of the several States, shall call a convention for proposing amendments, which, in either case, shall be valid to all intents and purposes, as part of this Constitution, when ratified by the legislatures of three-fourths of the several States, or by conventions in three-fourths thereof, as the one or the other mode of ratification may be proposed by the Congress; provided *that no amendments which may be made prior to the year one thousand eight hundred and eight shall in any manner affect the first and fourth clauses in the ninth section of the first article*; and that no State, without its consent, shall be deprived of its equal suffrage in the Senate.

Article VI

All debts contracted and engagements entered into, before the adoption of this Constitution, shall be as valid against the United States under this Constitution, as under the Confederation.

This Constitution, and the laws of the United States which shall be made in pursuance thereof; and all treaties made, or which shall be made, under the authority of the United States, shall be the supreme law of the land; and the judges in every State shall be bound thereby, anything in the Constitution or laws of any State to the contrary notwithstanding.

The Senators and Representatives before mentioned, and the members of the several State legislatures, and all executive and judicial officers, both of the United States and of the several States, shall be bound by oath or affirmation to support this Constitution; but no religious test shall ever be required as a qualification to any office or public trust under the United States.

Article VII

The ratification of the conventions of nine States shall be sufficient for the establishment of this Constitution between the States so ratifying the same.

Done in convention by the unanimous consent of the States present, the seventeenth day of September in the year of our Lord one thousand seven hundred and eighty-seven and of the Independence of the United States of America the twelfth. In witness whereof we have hereunto subscribed our names.

GEORGE WASHINGTON
PRESIDENT AND DEPUTY FROM VIRGINIA

New Hampshire
John Langdon
Nicholas Gilman

Massachusetts
Nathaniel Gorham
Rufus King

Connecticut
William Samuel
   Johnson
Roger Sherman

New York
Alexander Hamilton

New Jersey
William Livingston
David Brearley
William Paterson
Jonathan Dayton

Pennsylvania
Benjamin Franklin
Thomas Mifflin
Robert Morris
George Clymer
Thomas FitzSimons
Jared Ingersoll
James Wilson
Gouverneur Morris

Delaware
George Read
Gunning Bedford, Jr.
John Dickinson
Richard Bassett
Jacob Broom

Maryland
James McHenry
Daniel of St. Thomas
   Jenifer
Daniel Carroll

Virginia
John Blair
James Madison, Jr.

North Carolina
William Blount
Richard Dobbs Spaight
Hugh Williamson

South Carolina
John Rutledge
Charles Cotesworth
   Pinckney
Charles Pinckney
Pierce Butler

Georgia
William Few
Abraham Baldwin

AMENDMENTS TO THE CONSTITUTION WITH ANNOTATIONS (including the six unratified amendments)

▶ *IN THEIR EFFORT TO GAIN Antifederalists' support for the Constitution, Federalists frequently pointed to the inclusion of Article 5, which provides an orderly method of amending the Constitution. In contrast, the Articles of Confederation, which were universally recognized as seriously flawed, offered no means of amendment. For their part, Antifederalists argued that the amendment process was so "intricate" that one might as easily roll "sixes an hundred times in succession" as change the Constitution.*

The system for amendment laid out in the Constitution requires that two-thirds of both houses of Congress agree to a proposed amendment, which must then be ratified by three-quarters of the legislatures of the states. Alternatively, an amendment may be proposed by a convention called by the legislatures of two-thirds of the states. Since 1789, members of Congress have proposed thousands of amendments. Besides the seventeen amendments added since 1789, only the six "unratified" ones included here were approved by two-thirds of both houses and sent to the states for ratification.

Among the many amendments that never made it out of Congress have been proposals to declare dueling, divorce, and interracial marriage unconstitutional as well as proposals to establish a national university, to acknowledge the sovereignty of Jesus Christ, and to prohibit any person from possessing wealth in excess of $10 million.*

Among the issues facing Americans today that might lead to constitutional amendment are efforts to balance the federal budget, to limit the number of terms elected officials may serve, to limit access to or prohibit abortion, to establish English as the official language of the United States, and to prohibit flag burning. None of these proposed amendments has yet garnered enough support in Congress to be sent to the states for ratification.

Although the first ten amendments to the Constitution are commonly known as the Bill of Rights, only Amendments 1–8 actually provide guarantees of individual rights. Amendments 9 and 10 deal with the structure of power within the constitutional system. The Bill of Rights was promised to appease Antifederalists who refused to ratify the Constitution without guarantees of individual liberties and limitations to federal power. After studying more than two hundred amendments recommended by the ratifying conventions of the states, Federalist James Madison presented a list of seventeen to Congress, which used Madison's list as the founda-

tion for the twelve amendments that were sent to the states for ratification. Ten of the twelve were adopted in 1791. The first on the list of twelve, known as the Reapportionment Amendment, was never adopted (see page A-15). The second proposed amendment was adopted in 1992 as Amendment 27 (see page A-24).

Amendment I

Congress shall make no law respecting an establishment of religion, or prohibiting the free exercise thereof; or abridging the freedom of speech, or of the press; or the right of the people peaceably to assemble, and to petition the government for a redress of grievances.

♦ ♦ ♦

▶ *The First Amendment is a potent symbol for many Americans. Most are well aware of their rights to free speech, freedom of the press, and freedom of religion and their rights to assemble and to petition, even if they cannot cite the exact words of this amendment.*

The First Amendment guarantee of freedom of religion has two clauses: the "free exercise clause," which allows individuals to practice or not practice any religion, and the "establishment clause," which prevents the federal government from discriminating against or favoring any particular religion. This clause was designed to create what Thomas Jefferson referred to as "a wall of separation between church and state." In the 1960s, the Supreme Court ruled that the First Amendment prohibits prayer (see Engel v. Vitale, online) and Bible reading in public schools.

Although the rights to free speech and freedom of the press are established in the First Amendment, it was not until the twentieth century that the Supreme Court began to explore the full meaning of these guarantees. In 1919, the Court ruled in Schenck v. United States (online) that the government could suppress free expression only where it could cite a "clear and present danger." In a decision that continues to raise controversies, the Court ruled in 1990, in Texas v. Johnson, that flag burning is a form of symbolic speech protected by the First Amendment.

Amendment II

A well-regulated militia being necessary to the security of a free State, the right of the people to keep and bear arms shall not be infringed.

♦ ♦ ♦

---

*Richard B. Bernstein, *Amending America* (New York: Times Books, 1993), 177–81.

▶ *Fear of a standing army under the control of a hostile government made the Second Amendment an important part of the Bill of Rights. Advocates of gun ownership claim that the amendment prevents the government from regulating firearms. Proponents of gun control argue that the amendment is designed only to protect the right of the states to maintain militia units.*

In 1939, the Supreme Court ruled in United States v. Miller *that the Second Amendment did not protect the right of an individual to own a sawed-off shotgun, which it argued was not ordinary militia equipment. Since then, the Supreme Court has refused to hear Second Amendment cases, while lower courts have upheld firearms regulations. Several justices currently on the bench seem to favor a narrow interpretation of the Second Amendment, which would allow gun control legislation. The controversy over the impact of the Second Amendment on gun owners and gun control legislation will certainly continue.*

Amendment III

No soldier shall, in time of peace, be quartered in any house without the consent of the owner, nor in time of war, but in a manner to be prescribed by law.

◆ ◆ ◆

▶ *The Third Amendment was extremely important to the framers of the Constitution, but today it is nearly forgotten. American colonists were especially outraged that they were forced to quarter British troops in the years before and during the American Revolution. The philosophy of the Third Amendment has been viewed by some justices and scholars as the foundation of the modern constitutional right to privacy. One example of this can be found in Justice William O. Douglas's opinion in* Griswold v. Connecticut *(online).*

Amendment IV

The right of the people to be secure in their persons, houses, papers, and effects, against unreasonable searches and seizures, shall not be violated, and no warrants shall issue but upon probable cause, supported by oath or affirmation, and particularly describing the place to be searched, and the persons or things to be seized.

◆ ◆ ◆

▶ *In the years before the Revolution, the houses, barns, stores, and warehouses of American colonists were ransacked by British authorities under "writs of assistance" or general warrants. The British, thus empowered, searched for seditious material or smuggled goods that could then be used as evidence against colonists who were charged with a crime only after the items were found. The first part of the Fourth Amendment protects citizens from "unreasonable" searches and seizures.*

The Supreme Court has interpreted this protection as well as the words search *and* seizure *in different ways at different times. At one time, the Court did not recognize electronic eavesdropping as a form of search and seizure, though it does today. At times, an "unreasonable" search has been almost any search carried out without a warrant, but in the two decades before 1969, the Court sometimes sanctioned warrantless searches that it considered reasonable based on "the total atmosphere of the case."*

The second part of the Fourth Amendment defines the procedure for issuing a search warrant and states the requirement of "probable cause," which is generally viewed as evidence indicating that a suspect has committed an offense.

The Fourth Amendment has been controversial because the Court has sometimes excluded evidence that has been seized in violation of constitutional standards. The justification is that excluding such evidence deters violations of the amendment, but doing so may allow a guilty person to escape punishment.

Amendment V

No person shall be held to answer for a capital, or otherwise infamous crime, unless on a presentment or indictment of a grand jury, except in cases arising in the land or naval forces, or in the militia, when in actual service in time of war or public danger; nor shall any person be subject for the same offence to be twice put in jeopardy of life or limb; nor shall be compelled in any criminal case to be a witness against himself, nor be deprived of life, liberty, or property, without due process of law; nor shall private property be taken for public use without just compensation.

◆ ◆ ◆

▶ *The Fifth Amendment protects people against government authority in the prosecution of criminal offenses. It prohibits the state, first, from charging a person with a serious crime without a grand jury hearing to decide whether there is sufficient evidence to support the charge and, second, from charging a person with the same crime twice. The best-known aspect of the Fifth Amendment is that it prevents a person from being "compelled . . . to be a witness against himself." The last clause, the "takings clause," limits the power of the government to seize property.*

Although invoking the Fifth Amendment is popularly viewed as a confession of guilt, a person may be innocent yet still fear prosecution. For example, during the Red-baiting era of the late 1940s and 1950s, many people who had participated in legal activities that were associated with the Communist Party claimed the Fifth Amendment privilege rather than testify before the House Un-American Activities Committee because the mood of the times cast those activities in a negative light. Since "taking the Fifth" was viewed as an admission of guilt, those people often lost their jobs or became unemployable. (See chapter 26.) Nonetheless, the right to protect oneself against self-incrimination plays an important role in guarding against the collective power of the state.

Amendment VI

In all criminal prosecutions, the accused shall enjoy the right to a speedy and public trial, by an impartial jury of the State and district wherein the crime shall have been committed, which district shall have been previously ascertained by law, and to be informed of the nature and cause of the accusation; to be confronted with the witnesses against him; to have compulsory process for obtaining witnesses in his favor, and to have the assistance of counsel for his defence.

♦ ♦ ♦

▶ *The original Constitution put few limits on the government's power to investigate, prosecute, and punish crime. This process was of great concern to the early Americans, however, and of the twenty-eight rights specified in the first eight amendments, fifteen have to do with it. Seven rights are specified in the Sixth Amendment. These include the right to a speedy trial, a public trial, a jury trial, a notice of accusation, confrontation by opposing witnesses, testimony by favorable witnesses, and the assistance of counsel.*

Although this amendment originally guaranteed these rights only in cases involving the federal government, the adoption of the Fourteenth Amendment began a process of applying the protections of the Bill of Rights to the states through court cases such as Gideon v. Wainwright (online).

Amendment VII

In suits at common law, where the value in controversy shall exceed twenty dollars, the right of trial by jury shall be preserved, and no fact tried by a jury shall be otherwise reexamined in any court of the United States, than according to the rules of the common law.

♦ ♦ ♦

▶ *This amendment guarantees people the same right to a trial by jury as was guaranteed by English common law in 1791. Under common law, in civil trials (those involving money damages) the role of the judge was to settle questions of law and that of the jury was to settle questions of fact. The amendment does not specify the size of the jury or its role in a trial, however. The Supreme Court has generally held that those issues be determined by English common law of 1791, which stated that a jury consists of twelve people, that a trial must be conducted before a judge who instructs the jury on the law and advises it on facts, and that a verdict must be unanimous.*

Amendment VIII

Excessive bail shall not be required, nor excessive fines imposed, nor cruel and unusual punishments inflicted.

♦ ♦ ♦

▶ *The language used to guarantee the three rights in this amendment was inspired by the English Bill of Rights of 1689. The Supreme Court has not had a lot to say about "excessive fines." In recent years it has agreed that, despite the provision against "excessive bail," persons who are believed to be dangerous to others can be held without bail even before they have been convicted.*

Although opponents of the death penalty have not succeeded in using the Eighth Amendment to achieve the end of capital punishment, the clause regarding "cruel and unusual punishments" has been used to prohibit capital punishment in certain cases (see Furman v. Georgia, online) and to require improved conditions in prisons.

Amendment IX

The enumeration in the Constitution, of certain rights, shall not be construed to deny or disparage others retained by the people.

♦ ♦ ♦

▶ *Some Federalists feared that inclusion of the Bill of Rights in the Constitution would allow later generations of interpreters to claim that the people had surrendered any rights not specifically enumerated there. To guard against this, Madison added language that became the Ninth Amendment. Interest in this heretofore largely ignored amendment revived in 1965 when it was used in a concurring opinion in Griswold v. Connecticut (online). While Justice William O. Douglas called on the Third Amendment to support the right to privacy in deciding that case, Justice Arthur Goldberg, in the concurring opinion, argued that the right to privacy regarding contraception was an unenumerated right that was protected by the Ninth Amendment.*

In 1980, the Court ruled that the right of the press to attend a public trial was protected by the Ninth Amendment. While some scholars argue that modern judges cannot identify the unenumerated rights that the framers were trying to protect, others argue that the Ninth Amendment should be read as providing a constitutional "presumption of liberty" that allows people to act in any way that does not violate the rights of others.

Amendment X

The powers not delegated to the United States by the Constitution, nor prohibited by it to the States, are reserved to the States respectively, or to the people.

♦♦♦

▶ *The Antifederalists were especially eager to see a "reserved powers clause" explicitly guaranteeing the states control over their internal affairs. Not surprisingly, the Tenth Amendment has been a frequent battleground in the struggle over states' rights and federal supremacy. Prior to the Civil War, the Democratic Republican Party and Jacksonian Democrats invoked the Tenth Amendment to prohibit the federal government from making decisions about whether people in individual states could own slaves. The Tenth Amendment was virtually suspended during Reconstruction following the Civil War. In 1883, however, the Supreme Court declared the Civil Rights Act of 1875 unconstitutional on the grounds that it violated the Tenth Amendment. Business interests also called on the amendment to block efforts at federal regulation.*

The Court was inconsistent over the next several decades as it attempted to resolve the tension between the restrictions of the Tenth Amendment and the powers the Constitution granted to Congress to regulate interstate commerce and levy taxes. The Court upheld the Pure Food and Drug Act (1906), the Meat Inspection Acts (1906 and 1907), and the White Slave Traffic Act (1910), all of which affected the states, but struck down an act prohibiting interstate shipment of goods produced through child labor. Between 1934 and 1935, a number of New Deal programs created by Franklin D. Roosevelt were declared unconstitutional on the grounds that they violated the Tenth Amendment. (See chapter 24.) As Roosevelt appointees changed the composition of the Court, the Tenth Amendment was declared to have no substantive meaning. Generally, the amendment is held to protect the rights of states to regulate internal matters such as local government, education, commerce, labor, and business, as well as matters involving families such as marriage, divorce, and inheritance within the state.

Unratified Amendment

Reapportionment Amendment (proposed by Congress September 25, 1789, along with the Bill of Rights)

After the first enumeration required by the first article of the Constitution, there shall be one Representative for every thirty thousand, until the number shall amount to one hundred, after which the proportion shall be so regulated by Congress, that there shall be not less than one hundred Representatives, nor less than one Representative for every forty thousand persons, until the number of Representatives shall amount to two hundred; after which the proportion shall be so regulated by Congress, that there shall not be less than two hundred Representatives, nor more than one Representative for every fifty thousand persons.

♦♦♦

▶ *If the Reapportionment Amendment had passed and remained in effect, the House of Representatives today would have more than 5,000 members rather than 435.*

Amendment XI
[Adopted 1798]

The judicial power of the United States shall not be construed to extend to any suit in law or equity, commenced or prosecuted against one of the United States by citizens of another State, or by citizens or subjects of any foreign state.

♦♦♦

▶ *In 1793, the Supreme Court ruled in favor of Alexander Chisholm, executor of the estate of a deceased South Carolina merchant. Chisholm was suing the state of Georgia because the merchant had never been paid for provisions he had supplied during the Revolution. Many regarded this Court decision as an error that violated the intent of the Constitution.*

Antifederalists had long feared a federal court system with the power to overrule a state court.

When the Constitution was being drafted, Federalists had assured worried Antifederalists that section 2 of Article 3, which allows federal courts to hear cases "between a State and citizens of another State," did not mean that the federal courts were authorized to hear suits against a state by citizens of another state or a foreign country. Antifederalists and many other Americans feared a powerful federal court system because they worried that it would become like the British courts of this period, which were accountable only to the monarch. Furthermore, Chisholm v. Georgia prompted a series of suits against state governments by creditors and suppliers who had made loans during the war.

In addition, state legislators and Congress feared that the shaky economies of the new states, as well as the country as a whole, would be destroyed, especially if loyalists who had fled to other countries sought reimbursement for land and property that had been seized. The day after the Supreme Court announced its decision, a resolution proposing the Eleventh Amendment, which overturned the decision in Chisholm v. Georgia, *was introduced in the U.S. Senate.*

Amendment XII
[Adopted 1804]

The electors shall meet in their respective States, and vote by ballot for President and Vice-President, one of whom, at least, shall not be an inhabitant of the same State with themselves; they shall name in their ballots the person voted for as President, and in distinct ballots the person voted for as Vice-President, and they shall make distinct lists of all persons voted for as President, and of all persons voted for as Vice-President, and of the number of votes for each, which lists they shall sign and certify, and transmit sealed to the seat of government of the United States, directed to the President of the Senate;—the President of the Senate shall, in the presence of the Senate and House of Representatives, open all the certificates and the votes shall then be counted;—the person having the greatest number of votes for President shall be the President, if such number be a majority of the whole number of electors appointed; and if no person have such majority, then from the persons having the highest numbers not exceeding three on the list of those voted for as President, the House of Representatives shall choose immediately, by ballot, the President. But in choosing the President, the votes shall be taken by States, the representation from each State having one vote; a quorum for this purpose shall consist of a member or members from two-thirds of the States, and a majority of all the States shall be necessary to a choice. And if the House of Representatives shall not choose a President whenever the right of choice shall devolve upon them, before the fourth day of March next following, then the Vice-President shall act as President, as in the case of the death or other constitutional disability of the President.

The person having the greatest number of votes as Vice-President shall be the Vice-President, if such number be a majority of the whole number of electors appointed; and if no person have a majority, then from the two highest numbers on the list the Senate shall choose the Vice-President; a quorum for the purpose shall consist of two-thirds of the whole number of Senators, and a majority of the whole number shall be necessary to a choice. But no person constitutionally ineligible to the office of President shall be eligible to that of Vice-President of the United States.

◆ ◆ ◆

▶ *The framers of the Constitution disliked political parties and assumed that none would ever form. Under the original system, electors chosen by the states would each vote for two candidates. The candidate who won the most votes would become president, while the person who won the second-highest number of votes would become vice president. Rivalries between Federalists and Antifederalists led to the formation of political parties, however, even before George Washington had left office. Though Washington was elected unanimously in 1789 and 1792, the elections of 1796 and 1800 were procedural disasters because of party maneuvering (see chapters 9 and 10). In 1796, Federalist John Adams was chosen as president, and his great rival, the Antifederalist Thomas Jefferson (whose party was called the Republican Party), became his vice president. In 1800, all the electors cast their two votes as one of two party blocs. Jefferson and his fellow Republican nominee, Aaron Burr, were tied with 73 votes each. The contest went to the House of*

Representatives, which finally elected Jefferson after 36 ballots. The Twelfth Amendment prevents these problems by requiring electors to vote separately for the president and vice president.

Unratified Amendment

Titles of Nobility Amendment (proposed by Congress May 1, 1810)

If any citizen of the United States shall accept, claim, receive or retain any title of nobility or honor or shall, without the consent of Congress, accept and retain any present, pension, office or emolument of any kind whatever, from any emperor, king, prince or foreign power, such person shall cease to be a citizen of the United States, and shall be incapable of holding any office of trust or profit under them or either of them.

◆ ◆ ◆

▶ *This amendment would have extended Article 1, section 9, clause 8 of the Constitution, which prevents the awarding of titles by the United States and the acceptance of such awards from foreign powers without congressional consent. Historians speculate that general nervousness about the power of the emperor Napoleon, who was at that time extending France's empire throughout Europe, may have prompted the proposal. Though it fell one vote short of ratification, Congress and the American people thought the proposal had been ratified, and it was included in many nineteenth-century editions of the Constitution.*

The Civil War and Reconstruction Amendments (Thirteenth, Fourteenth, and Fifteenth Amendments)

▶ *In the four months between the election of Abraham Lincoln and his inauguration, more than 200 proposed constitutional amendments were presented to Congress as part of a desperate attempt to hold the rapidly dissolving Union together. Most of these were efforts to appease the southern states by protecting the right to own slaves or by disfranchising African Americans through constitutional amendment. None were able to win the votes required from Congress to send them to the states. The relatively innocuous Corwin Amendment seemed to be the only hope for preserving the Union by amending the Constitution.*

The northern victors in the Civil War tried to restructure the Constitution just as the war had restructured the nation. Yet they were often divided in their goals. Some wanted to end slavery; others hoped for social and economic equality regardless of race; others hoped that extending the power of the ballot box to former slaves would help create a new political order. The debates over the Thirteenth, Fourteenth, and Fifteenth Amendments were bitter. Few of those who fought for these changes were satisfied with the amendments themselves; fewer still were satisfied with their interpretation. Although the amendments put an end to the legal status of slavery, it took nearly a hundred years after the amendments' passage before most of the descendants of former slaves could begin to experience the economic, social, and political equality the amendments had been intended to provide.

Unratified Amendment
Corwin Amendment (proposed by Congress March 2, 1861)

No amendment shall be made to the Constitution which will authorize or give to Congress the power to abolish or interfere, within any State, with the domestic institutions thereof, including that of persons held to labor or service by the laws of said State.

◆ ◆ ◆

▶ *Following the election of Abraham Lincoln, Congress scrambled to try to prevent the secession of the slaveholding states. House member Thomas Corwin of Ohio proposed the "unamendable" amendment in the hope that by protecting slavery where it existed, Congress would keep the southern states in the Union. Lincoln indicated his support for the proposed amendment in his first inaugural address. Only Ohio and Maryland ratified the Corwin Amendment before it was forgotten.*

Amendment XIII
[Adopted 1865]

Section 1 Neither slavery nor involuntary servitude, except as a punishment for crime whereof the party shall have been duly convicted, shall exist within the United States, or any place subject to their jurisdiction.

Section 2 Congress shall have power to enforce this article by appropriate legislation.

◆ ◆ ◆

▶ *Although President Lincoln had abolished slavery in the Confederacy with the Emancipation Proclamation of 1863, abolitionists wanted to rid the entire country of slavery. The Thirteenth Amendment did this in a clear and straightforward manner. In February 1865, when the proposal was approved by the House, the gallery of the House was newly opened to black Americans who had a chance at last to see their government at work. Passage of the proposal was greeted by wild cheers from the gallery as well as tears on the House floor, where congressional representatives openly embraced one another.*

The problem of ratification remained, however. The Union position was that the Confederate states were part of the country of thirty-six states. Therefore, twenty-seven states were needed to ratify the amendment. When Kentucky and Delaware rejected it, backers realized that without approval

from at least four former Confederate states, the amendment would fail. Lincoln's successor, President Andrew Johnson, made ratification of the Thirteenth Amendment a condition for southern states to rejoin the Union. Under those terms, all the former Confederate states except Mississippi accepted the Thirteenth Amendment, and by the end of 1865 the amendment had become part of the Constitution and slavery had been prohibited in the United States.

Amendment XIV
[Adopted 1868]

Section 1 All persons born or naturalized in the United States, and subject to the jurisdiction thereof, are citizens of the United States and of the State wherein they reside. No State shall make or enforce any law which shall abridge the privileges or immunities of citizens of the United States; nor shall any State deprive any person of life, liberty, or property, without due process of law; nor deny to any person within its jurisdiction the equal protection of the laws.

Section 2 Representatives shall be appointed among the several States according to their respective numbers, counting the whole number of persons in each State, excluding Indians not taxed. But when the right to vote at any election for the choice of Electors for President and Vice-President of the United States, Representatives in Congress, the executive and judicial officers of a State, or the members of the legislature thereof, is denied to any of the male inhabitants of such State, being twenty-one years of age and citizens of the United States, or in any way abridged, except for participation in rebellion, or other crime, the basis of representation therein shall be reduced in the proportion which the number of such male citizens shall bear to the whole number of male citizens twenty-one years of age in such State.

Section 3 No person shall be a Senator or Representative in Congress, or Elector of President and Vice-President, or hold any office, civil or military, under the United States, or under any State, who, having previously taken an oath, as a member of Congress, or as an officer of the United States, or as a member of any State legislature, or as an executive or judicial officer of any State, to support the Constitution of the United States, shall have engaged in insurrection or rebellion against the same, or given aid or comfort to the enemies thereof. Congress may, by a vote of two-thirds of each house, remove such disability.

Section 4 The validity of the public debt of the United States, authorized by law, including debts incurred for payment of pensions and bounties for services in suppressing insurrection or rebellion, shall not be questioned. But neither the United States nor any State shall assume or pay any debt or obligation incurred in aid of insurrection or rebellion against the United States, or any claim for the loss or emancipation of any slave; but all such debts, obligations, and claims shall be held illegal and void.

Section 5 The Congress shall have power to enforce, by appropriate legislation, the provisions of this article.

♦ ♦ ♦

▶ *Without Lincoln's leadership in the reconstruction of the nation following the Civil War, it soon became clear that the Thirteenth Amendment needed additional constitutional support. Less than a year after Lincoln's assassination, Andrew Johnson was ready to bring the former Confederate states back into the Union with few changes in their governments or politics. Anxious Republicans drafted the Fourteenth Amendment to prevent that from happening. The most important provisions of this complex amendment made all native-born or naturalized persons American citizens and prohibited states from abridging the "privileges or immunities" of citizens; depriving them of "life, liberty, or property, without due process of law"; and denying them "equal protection of the laws." In essence, it made all ex-slaves citizens and protected the rights of all citizens against violation by their own state governments.*

As occurred in the case of the Thirteenth Amendment, former Confederate states were forced to ratify the amendment as a condition of representation in the House and the Senate. The intentions of the Fourteenth Amendment, and how those intentions should be enforced, have been the most debated point of constitutional history. The terms due process and equal protection have been especially troublesome. Was the amendment designed to outlaw racial segregation? Or was the goal simply to prevent the leaders of the rebellious South from gaining political power?

The framers of the Fourteenth Amendment hoped Article 2 would produce black voters who would increase the power of the Republican Party. The federal government, however, never used its power to punish states for denying blacks their right to vote. Although the Fourteenth Amendment had an immediate impact in giving black Americans citizenship, it did nothing to protect blacks from the vengeance of whites once Reconstruction ended. In the late nineteenth and early twentieth centuries, section 1 of the Fourteenth Amendment was often used to protect business interests and strike down laws protecting workers on the grounds that the rights of "persons," that is, corporations, were protected by "due process." More recently, the Fourteenth Amendment has been used to justify school desegregation and affirmative action programs, as well as to dismantle such programs.

Amendment XV
[Adopted 1870]

Section 1 The right of citizens of the United States to vote shall not be denied or abridged by the United States or by any State on account of race, color, or previous condition of servitude.

Section 2 The Congress shall have power to enforce this article by appropriate legislation.

♦ ♦ ♦

▶ *The Fifteenth Amendment was the last major piece of Reconstruction legislation. While earlier Reconstruction acts had already required black suffrage in the South, the Fifteenth Amendment extended black voting rights to the entire nation. Some Republicans felt morally obligated to do away with the double standard between North and South since many northern states had stubbornly refused to enfranchise blacks. Others believed that the freedman's ballot required the extra protection of a constitutional amendment to shield it from white counterattack. But partisan advantage also played an important role in the amendment's passage, since Republicans hoped that by giving the ballot to northern blacks, they could lessen their political vulnerability.*

Many women's rights advocates had fought for the amendment. They had felt betrayed by the inclusion of the word "male" in section 2 of the Fourteenth Amendment and were further angered when the proposed Fifteenth Amendment failed to prohibit denial of the right to vote on the grounds of sex as well as "race, color, or previous condition of servitude." In this amendment, for the first time, the federal government claimed the power to regulate the franchise, or vote. It was also the first time the Constitution placed limits on the power of the states to regulate access to the franchise. Although ratified in 1870, the amendment was not enforced until the twentieth century.

The Progressive Amendments (Sixteenth–Nineteenth Amendments)

▶ *No amendments were added to the Constitution between the Civil War and the Progressive Era. America was changing, however, in fundamental ways. The rapid industrialization of the United States after the Civil War led to many social and economic problems. Hundreds of amendments were proposed, but none received enough support in Congress to be sent to the states. Some scholars believe that regional differences and rivalries were so strong during this period that it was almost impossible to gain a consensus on a constitutional amendment. During the Progressive Era, however, the Constitution was amended four times in seven years.*

Amendment XVI
[Adopted 1913]

The Congress shall have power to lay and collect taxes on incomes, from whatever source derived, without apportionment among the several States, and without regard to any census or enumeration.

◆ ◆ ◆

▶ *Until passage of the Sixteenth Amendment, most of the money used to run the federal government came from customs duties and taxes on specific items, such as liquor. During the Civil War, the federal government taxed incomes as an emergency measure. Pressure to enact an income tax came from those who were concerned about the growing gap between rich and poor in the United States. The Populist Party began campaigning for a graduated income tax in 1892, and support continued to grow. By 1909, thirty-three proposed income tax amendments had been presented in Congress, but lobbying by corporate and other special interests had defeated them all. In June 1909, the growing pressure for an income tax, which had been endorsed by Presidents Roosevelt and Taft, finally pushed an amendment through the Senate. The required thirty-six states had ratified the amendment by February 1913.*

Amendment XVII
[Adopted 1913]

Section 1 The Senate of the United States shall be composed of two Senators from each State, elected by the people thereof, for six years; and each Senator shall have one vote. The electors in each State shall have the qualifications requisite for electors of [voters for] the most numerous branch of the State legislatures.

Section 2 When vacancies happen in the representation of any State in the Senate, the executive authority of such State shall issue writs of election to fill such vacancies: Provided, that the Legislature of any State may empower the executive thereof to make temporary appointments until the people fill the vacancies by election as the Legislature may direct.

Section 3 This amendment shall not be so construed as to affect the election or term of any Senator chosen before it becomes valid as part of the Constitution.

◆ ◆ ◆

▶ *The framers of the Constitution saw the members of the House as the representatives of the people and the members of the Senate as the representatives of the states. Originally senators were to be chosen by the state legislators. According to reform advocates, however, the growth of private industry and transportation conglomerates during the Gilded Age had created a network of corruption*

in which wealth and power were exchanged for influence and votes in the Senate. Senator Nelson Aldrich, who represented Rhode Island in the late nineteenth and early twentieth centuries, for example, was known as "the senator from Standard Oil" because of his open support of special business interests.

Efforts to amend the Constitution to allow direct election of senators had begun in 1826, but since any proposal had to be approved by the Senate, reform seemed impossible. Progressives tried to gain influence in the Senate by instituting party caucuses and primary elections, which gave citizens the chance to express their choice of a senator who could then be officially elected by the state legislature. By 1910, fourteen of the country's thirty senators received popular votes through a state primary before the state legislature made its selection. Despairing of getting a proposal through the Senate, supporters of a direct election amendment had begun in 1893 to seek a convention of representatives from two-thirds of the states to propose an amendment that could then be ratified. By 1905, thirty-one of forty-five states had endorsed such an amendment. Finally, in 1911, despite extraordinary opposition, a proposed amendment passed the Senate; by 1913, it had been ratified.

Amendment XVIII
[Adopted 1919; repealed 1933 by Amendment XXI]

Section 1 After one year from the ratification of this article the manufacture, sale, or transportation of intoxicating liquors within, the importation thereof into, or the exportation thereof from the United States and all territory subject to the jurisdiction thereof, for beverage purposes, is hereby prohibited.

Section 2 The Congress and the several States shall have concurrent power to enforce this article by appropriate legislation.

Section 3 This article shall be inoperative unless it shall have been ratified as an amendment to the Constitution by the legislatures of the several States, as provided by the Constitution, within seven years from the date of the submission thereof to the States by the Congress.

◆ ◆ ◆

▶ *The Prohibition Party, formed in 1869, began calling for a constitutional amendment to outlaw alcoholic beverages in 1872. A prohibition amendment was first proposed in the Senate in 1876 and was revived eighteen times before 1913. Between 1913 and 1919, another thirty-nine attempts were made to prohibit liquor in the United States through a constitutional amendment. Prohibition became a key element of the progressive agenda as reformers linked alcohol and drunkenness to numerous* social problems, including the corruption of immigrant voters. While opponents of such an amendment argued that it was undemocratic, supporters claimed that their efforts had widespread public support. The admission of twelve "dry" western states to the Union in the early twentieth century and the spirit of sacrifice during World War I laid the groundwork for passage and ratification of the Eighteenth Amendment in 1919. Opponents added a time limit to the amendment in the hope that they could thus block ratification, but this effort failed. (See also Amendment XXI.)

Amendment XIX
[Adopted 1920]

Section 1 The right of citizens of the United States to vote shall not be denied or abridged by the United States or by any State on account of sex.

Section 2 Congress shall have the power to enforce this article by appropriate legislation.

◆ ◆ ◆

▶ *Advocates of women's rights tried and failed to link woman suffrage to the Fourteenth and Fifteenth Amendments. Nonetheless, the effort for woman suffrage continued. Between 1878 and 1912, at least one and sometimes as many as four proposed amendments were introduced in Congress each year to grant women the right to vote. While over time women won very limited voting rights in some states, at both the state and federal levels opposition to an amendment for woman suffrage remained very strong. President Woodrow Wilson and other officials felt that the federal government should not interfere with the power of the states in this matter. Others worried that granting suffrage to women would encourage ethnic minorities to exercise their own right to vote. And many were concerned that giving women the vote would result in their abandoning traditional gender roles. In 1919, following a protracted and often bitter campaign of protest in which women went on hunger strikes and chained themselves to fences, an amendment was introduced with the backing of President Wilson. It narrowly passed the Senate (after efforts to limit the suffrage to white women failed) and was adopted in 1920 after Tennessee became the thirty-sixth state to ratify it.*

Unratified Amendment
Child Labor Amendment (proposed by Congress June 2, 1924)

Section 1 The Congress shall have power to limit, regulate, and prohibit the labor of persons under eighteen years of age.

Section 2 The power of the several States is unimpaired by this article except that the operation of State laws shall be suspended to the extent necessary to give effect to legislation enacted by Congress.

◆ ◆ ◆

▶ *Throughout the late nineteenth and early twentieth centuries, alarm over the condition of child workers grew. Opponents of child labor argued that children worked in dangerous and unhealthy conditions, that they took jobs from adult workers, that they depressed wages in certain industries, and that states that allowed child labor had an economic advantage over those that did not. Defenders of child labor claimed that children provided needed income in many families, that working at a young age developed character, and that the effort to prohibit the practice constituted an invasion of family privacy.*

    In 1916, Congress passed a law that made it illegal to sell goods made by children through interstate commerce. The Supreme Court, however, ruled that the law violated the limits on the power of Congress to regulate interstate commerce. Congress then tried to penalize industries that used child labor by taxing such goods. This measure was also thrown out by the courts. In response, reformers set out to amend the Constitution. The proposed amendment was ratified by twenty-eight states, but by 1925, thirteen states had rejected it. Passage of the Fair Labor Standards Act in 1938, which was upheld by the Supreme Court in 1941, made the amendment irrelevant.

Amendment XX
[Adopted 1933]

Section 1 The terms of the President and Vice-President shall end at noon on the 20th day of January, and the terms of Senators and Representatives at noon on the 3rd day of January, of the years in which such terms would have ended if this article had not been ratified; and the terms of their successors shall then begin.

Section 2 The Congress shall assemble at least once in every year, and such meeting shall begin at noon on the 3rd day of January, unless they shall by law appoint a different day.

Section 3 If, at the time fixed for the beginning of the term of the President, the President-elect shall have died, the Vice-President-elect shall become President. If a President shall not have been chosen before the time fixed for the beginning of his term, or if the President-elect shall have failed to qualify, then the Vice-President-elect shall act as President until a President shall have qualified; and the Congress may by law provide for the case wherein neither a President-elect nor a Vice-President-elect shall have qualified, declaring who shall then act as President, or the manner in which one who is to act shall be selected, and such person shall act accordingly until a President or Vice-President shall have qualified.

Section 4 The Congress may by law provide for the case of the death of any of the persons from whom the House of Representatives may choose a President whenever the right of choice shall have devolved upon them, and for the case of the death of any of the persons from whom the Senate may choose a Vice-President whenever the right of choice shall have devolved upon them.

Section 5 Sections 1 and 2 shall take effect on the 15th day of October following the ratification of this article.

Section 6 This article shall be inoperative unless it shall have been ratified as an amendment to the Constitution by the Legislatures of three-fourths of the several States within seven years from the date of its submission.

◆ ◆ ◆

▶ *Until 1933, presidents took office on March 4. Since elections are held in early November and electoral votes are counted in mid-December, this meant that more than three months passed between the time a new president was elected and when he took office. Moving the inauguration to January shortened the transition period and allowed Congress to begin its term closer to the time of the president's inauguration. Although this seems like a minor change, an amendment was required because the Constitution specifies terms of office. This amendment also deals with questions of succession in the event that a president- or vice president-elect dies before assuming office. Section 3 also clarifies a method for resolving a deadlock in the electoral college.*

Amendment XXI
[Adopted 1933]

Section 1 The eighteenth article of amendment to the Constitution of the United States is hereby repealed.

Section 2 The transportation or importation into any State, Territory, or Possession of the United States for delivery or use therein of intoxicating liquors, in violation of the laws thereof, is hereby prohibited.

Section 3 This article shall be inoperative unless it shall have been ratified as an amendment to the Constitution by conventions in the several States, as provided in the Constitution, within seven years from the date of the submission thereof to the States by the Congress.

◆ ◆ ◆

▶ *Widespread violation of the Volstead Act, the law enacted to enforce prohibition, made the United States a nation of lawbreakers. Prohibition*

caused more problems than it solved by encouraging crime, bribery, and corruption. Further, a coalition of liquor and beer manufacturers, personal liberty advocates, and constitutional scholars joined forces to challenge the amendment. By 1929, thirty proposed repeal amendments had been introduced in Congress, and the Democratic Party made repeal part of its platform in the 1932 presidential campaign. The Twenty-first Amendment was proposed in February 1933 and ratified less than a year later. The failure of the effort to enforce prohibition through a constitutional amendment has often been cited by opponents to subsequent efforts to shape public virtue and private morality.

Amendment XXII
[Adopted 1951]

Section 1 No person shall be elected to the office of the President more than twice, and no person who has held the office of President, or acted as President, for more than two years of a term to which some other person was elected President shall be elected to the office of President more than once. But this article shall not apply to any person holding the office of President when this Article was proposed by the Congress, and shall not prevent any person who may be holding the office of President, or acting as President, during the term within which this Article becomes operative from holding the office of President or acting as President during the remainder of such term.

Section 2 This article shall be inoperative unless it shall have been ratified as an amendment to the Constitution by the legislatures of three-fourths of the several States within seven years from the date of its submission to the States by the Congress.

◆ ◆ ◆

▶ *George Washington's refusal to seek a third term of office set a precedent that stood until 1912, when former president Theodore Roosevelt sought, without success, another term as an independent candidate. Democrat Franklin Roosevelt was the only president to seek and win a fourth term, though he did so amid great controversy. Roosevelt died in April 1945, a few months after the beginning of his fourth term. In 1946, Republicans won control of the House and the Senate, and early in 1947 a proposal for an amendment to limit future presidents to two four-year terms was offered to the states for ratification. Democratic critics of the Twenty-second Amendment charged that it was a partisan posthumous jab at Roosevelt.*

Since the Twenty-second Amendment was adopted, however, the only presidents who might have been able to seek a third term, had it not existed, were Republicans Dwight Eisenhower, Ronald Reagan, and George W. Bush, and Democrat Bill Clinton. Since 1826, Congress has entertained 160 proposed amendments to limit the president to one six-year term. Such amendments have been backed by fifteen presidents, including Gerald Ford and Jimmy Carter.

Amendment XXIII
[Adopted 1961]

Section 1 The District constituting the seat of Government of the United States shall appoint in such manner as the Congress may direct: A number of electors of President and Vice-President equal to the whole number of Senators and Representatives in Congress to which the District would be entitled if it were a State, but in no event more than the least populous State; they shall be in addition to those appointed by the States, but they shall be considered for the purposes of the election of President and Vice-President, to be electors appointed by a State; and they shall meet in the District and perform such duties as provided by the twelfth article of amendment.

Section 2 The Congress shall have the power to enforce this article by appropriate legislation.

♦ ♦ ♦

▶ *When Washington, D.C., was established as a federal district, no one expected that a significant number of people would make it their permanent and primary residence. A proposal to allow citizens of the district to vote in presidential elections was approved by Congress in June 1960 and was ratified on March 29, 1961.*

Amendment XXIV
[Adopted 1964]

Section 1 The right of citizens of the United States to vote in any primary or other election for President or Vice-President, for electors for President or Vice-President, or for Senator or Representative in Congress, shall not be denied or abridged by the United States or any State by reason of failure to pay any poll tax or other tax.

Section 2 The Congress shall have the power to enforce this article by appropriate legislation.

♦ ♦ ♦

▶ *In the colonial and Revolutionary eras, financial independence was seen as necessary to political independence, and the poll tax was used as a requirement for voting. By the twentieth century, however, the poll tax was used mostly to bar poor people, especially southern blacks, from voting. While conservatives complained that the amendment interfered with states' rights, liberals thought that the amendment did not go far enough because it barred the poll tax only in national elections and not in state or local elections. The amendment was ratified in 1964,*

however, and two years later, the Supreme Court ruled that poll taxes in state and local elections also violated the equal protection clause of the Fourteenth Amendment.

Amendment XXV
[Adopted 1967]

Section 1 In case of the removal of the President from office or of his death or resignation, the Vice-President shall become President.

Section 2 Whenever there is a vacancy in the office of the Vice-President, the President shall nominate a Vice-President who shall take office upon confirmation by a majority vote of both Houses of Congress.

Section 3 Whenever the President transmits to the President pro tempore of the Senate and the Speaker of the House of Representatives his written declaration that he is unable to discharge the powers and duties of his office, and until he transmits to them a written declaration to the contrary, such powers and duties shall be discharged by the Vice-President as Acting President.

Section 4 Whenever the Vice-President and a majority of either the principal officers of the executive departments or of such other body as Congress may by law provide, transmit to the President pro tempore of the Senate and the Speaker of the House of Representatives their written declaration that the President is unable to discharge the powers and duties of his office, the Vice-President shall immediately assume the powers and duties of the office as Acting President.

Thereafter, when the President transmits to the President pro tempore of the Senate and the Speaker of the House of Representatives his written declaration that no inability exists, he shall resume the powers and duties of his office unless the Vice-President and a majority of either the principal officers of the executive department[s] or of such other body as Congress may by law provide, transmit within four days to the President pro tempore of the Senate and the Speaker of the House of Representatives their written declaration that the President is unable to discharge the powers and duties of his office. Thereupon Congress shall decide the issue, assembling within forty-eight hours for that purpose if not in session. If the Congress, within twenty-one days after receipt of the latter written declaration, or, if Congress is not in session, within twenty-one days after Congress is required to assemble, determines by two-thirds vote of both Houses that the President is unable to discharge the powers and duties of his office, the Vice-President shall continue to discharge the same as Acting President; otherwise, the President shall resume the powers and duties of his office.

♦ ♦ ♦

▶ *The framers of the Constitution established the office of vice president because someone was needed to preside over the Senate. The first president to die in office was William Henry Harrison, in 1841. Vice President John Tyler had himself sworn in as president, setting a precedent that was followed when seven later presidents died in office. The assassination of President James A. Garfield in 1881 posed a new problem, however. After he was shot, the president was incapacitated for two months before he died; he was unable to lead the country, while his vice president, Chester A. Arthur, was unable to assume leadership. Efforts to resolve questions of succession in the event of a presidential disability thus began with the death of Garfield.*

In 1963, the assassination of President John F. Kennedy galvanized Congress to action. Vice President Lyndon Johnson was a chain smoker with a history of heart trouble. According to the 1947 Presidential Succession Act, the two men who stood in line to succeed him were the seventy-two-year-old Speaker of the House and the eighty-six-year-old president of the Senate. There were serious concerns that any of these men might become incapacitated while serving as chief executive. The first time the Twenty-fifth Amendment was used, however, was not in the case of presidential death or illness, but during the Watergate crisis. When Vice President Spiro T. Agnew was forced to resign following allegations of bribery and tax violations, President Richard M. Nixon appointed House Minority Leader Gerald R. Ford vice president. Ford became president following Nixon's resignation eight months later and named Nelson A. Rockefeller as his vice president. Thus, for more than two years, the two highest offices in the country were held by people who had not been elected to them.

Amendment XXVI
[Adopted 1971]

Section 1 The right of citizens of the United States, who are eighteen years of age or older, to vote shall not be denied or abridged by the United States or by any State on account of age.

Section 2 The Congress shall have power to enforce this article by appropriate legislation.

◆ ◆ ◆

▶ *Efforts to lower the voting age from twenty-one to eighteen began during World War II. Recognizing that those who were old enough to fight a war should have some say in the government policies that involved them in the war, Presidents Eisenhower, Johnson, and Nixon endorsed the idea. In 1970, the combined pressure of the antiwar movement and the demographic pressure*

of the baby boom generation led to a Voting Rights Act lowering the voting age in federal, state, and local elections.

In Oregon v. Mitchell (1970), the state of Oregon challenged the right of Congress to determine the age at which people could vote in state or local elections. The Supreme Court agreed with Oregon. Since the Voting Rights Act was ruled unconstitutional, the Constitution had to be amended to allow passage of a law that would lower the voting age. The amendment was ratified in a little more than three months, making it the most rapidly ratified amendment in U.S. history.

Unratified Amendment
Equal Rights Amendment (proposed by Congress March 22, 1972; seven-year deadline for ratification extended to June 30, 1982)

Section 1 Equality of rights under the law shall not be denied or abridged by the United States or by any State on account of sex.

Section 2 The Congress shall have the power to enforce, by appropriate legislation, the provisions of this article.

Section 3 This amendment shall take effect two years after the date of ratification.

◆ ◆ ◆

▶ *In 1923, soon after women had won the right to vote, Alice Paul, a leading activist in the woman suffrage movement, proposed an amendment requiring equal treatment of men and women. Opponents of the proposal argued that such an amendment would invalidate laws that protected women and would make women subject to the military draft. After the 1964 Civil Rights Act was adopted, protective workplace legislation was removed anyway.*

The renewal of the women's movement, as a byproduct of the civil rights and antiwar movements, led to a revival of the Equal Rights Amendment (ERA) in Congress. Disagreements over language held up congressional passage of the proposed amendment, but on March 22, 1972, the Senate approved the ERA by a vote of 84 to 8, and it was sent to the states. Six states ratified the amendment within two days, and by the middle of 1973 the amendment seemed well on its way to adoption, with thirty of the needed thirty-eight states having ratified it. In the mid-1970s, however, a powerful "Stop ERA" campaign developed. The campaign portrayed the ERA as a threat to "family values" and traditional relationships between men and women. Although thirty-five states ultimately ratified the ERA, five of those state legislatures voted to rescind ratification, and the amendment was never adopted.

Unratified Amendment

D.C. Statehood Amendment (proposed by Congress August 22, 1978)

Section 1 For purposes of representation in the Congress, election of the President and Vice-President, and article V of this Constitution, the District constituting the seat of government of the United States shall be treated as though it were a State.

Section 2 The exercise of the rights and powers conferred under this article shall be by the people of the District constituting the seat of government, and as shall be provided by Congress.

Section 3 The twenty-third article of amendment to the Constitution of the United States is hereby repealed.

Section 4 This article shall be inoperative, unless it shall have been ratified as an amendment to the Constitution by the legislatures of three-fourths of the several states within seven years from the date of its submission.

◆ ◆ ◆

▶ *The 1961 ratification of the Twenty-third Amendment, giving residents of the District of Columbia the right to vote for a president and vice president, inspired an effort to give residents of the district full voting rights. In 1966, President Lyndon Johnson appointed a mayor and city council; in 1971, D.C. residents were allowed to name a non-voting delegate to the House; and in 1981, residents were allowed to elect the mayor and city council. Congress retained the right to overrule laws that might affect commuters, the height of federal buildings, and selection of judges and prosecutors. The district's nonvoting delegate to Congress, Walter Fauntroy, lobbied fiercely for a congressional amendment granting statehood to the district. In 1978, a proposed amendment was approved and sent to the states. A number of states quickly ratified the amendment, but, like the ERA, the D.C. Statehood Amendment ran into trouble.*

Opponents argued that section 2 created a separate category of "nominal" statehood. They argued that the federal district should be eliminated and that the territory should be reabsorbed into the state of Maryland. Although these theoretical arguments were strong, some scholars believe that racist attitudes toward the predominantly black population of the city were also a factor leading to the defeat of the amendment.

Amendment XXVII
[Adopted 1992]

No law, varying the compensation for the services of the Senators and Representatives, shall take effect, until an election of Representatives shall have intervened.

◆ ◆ ◆

▶ *While the Twenty-sixth Amendment was the most rapidly ratified amendment in U.S. history, the Twenty-seventh Amendment had the longest journey to ratification. First proposed by James Madison in 1789 as part of the package that included the Bill of Rights, this amendment had been ratified by only six states by 1791. In 1873, however, it was ratified by Ohio to protest a massive retroactive salary increase by the federal government. Unlike later proposed amendments, this one came with no time limit on ratification.*

In the early 1980s, Gregory D. Watson, a University of Texas economics major, discovered the "lost" amendment and began a single-handed campaign to get state legislators to introduce it for ratification. In 1983, it was accepted by Maine. In 1984, it passed the Colorado legislature. Ratifications trickled in slowly until May 1992, when Michigan and New Jersey became the thirty-eighth and thirty-ninth states, respectively, to ratify. This amendment prevents members of Congress from raising their own salaries without giving voters a chance to vote them out of office before they can benefit from the raises.

THE CONSTITUTION OF THE CONFEDERATE STATES OF AMERICA

▶ *In framing the Constitution of the Confederate States, the authors adopted, with numerous small but significant changes and additions, the language of the Constitution of the United States, and followed the same order of arrangement of articles and sections. The revisions that they made to the original Constitution are shown here. The parts stricken out are enclosed in brackets, and the new matter added in framing the Confederate Constitution is printed in italics.*

Adopted March 11, 1861

WE, the People of the [United States] *Confederated States, each State acting in its sovereign and independent character*, in order to form a [more perfect

Union] *permanent Federal government*, establish Justice, insure domestic Tranquillity [provide for the common defense, promote the general Welfare], and secure the Blessings of Liberty to ourselves and our Posterity, *invoking the favor and guidance of Almighty God*, do ordain and establish this Constitution for the [United] Confederate States of America.

Article I

Section I All legislative Powers herein [granted] *delegated*, shall be vested in a Congress of the [United] *Confederate* States, which shall consist of a Senate and House of Representatives.

Section II The House of Representatives shall be composed of Members chosen every second Year by the People of the several States, and the Electors in each State shall *be citizens of the Confederate States, and* have the Qualifications requisite for Electors of the most numerous Branch of the State Legislature; *but no person of foreign birth, and not a citizen of the Confederate States, shall be allowed to vote for any officer, civil or political, State or federal.*

No Person shall be a Representative who shall not have attained to the Age of twenty-five Years, and [been seven Years a Citizen of the United] *be a citizen of the Confederate States*, and who shall not, when elected, be an Inhabitant of that State in which he shall be chosen.

Representatives and direct Taxes shall be apportioned among the several States which may be included within this [Union] *Confederacy*, according to their respective Numbers, which shall be determined by adding to the whole Number of free Persons, including those bound to Service for a Term of Years, and excluding Indians not taxed, three-fifths of all [other Persons] *slaves*. The actual Enumeration shall be made within three Years after the first Meeting of the Congress of the [United] *Confederate States*, and within every subsequent Term of ten Years, in such Manner as they shall by Law direct. The Number of Representatives shall not exceed one for every [thirty] *fifty* Thousand, but each State shall have at Least one Representative; and until such enumeration shall be made, the State of [New Hampshire shall be entitled to choose three, Massachusetts eight, Rhode Island and Providence Plantations one, Connecticut five, New York six, New Jersey four, Pennsylvania eight, Delaware one, Maryland six, Virginia ten, North Carolina five, South Carolina five, and Georgia three] *South Carolina shall be entitled to choose six, the State of Georgia ten, the State of Alabama nine, the State of Florida two, the State of Mississippi seven, the State of Louisiana six, and the State of Texas six.*

When vacancies happen in the Representation from any State, the Executive Authority thereof shall issue Writs of Election to fill such Vacancies.

The House of Representatives shall choose their Speaker and other Officers; and shall have the sole Power of Impeachment; *except that any judicial or other federal officer resident and acting solely within the limits of any State, may be impeached by a vote of two-thirds of both branches of the Legislature thereof.*

Section III The Senate of the [United] *Confederate* States shall be composed of two Senators from each State, chosen by the Legislature thereof, for six Years, *at the regular session next immediately preceding the commencement of the term of service*; and each Senator shall have one Vote.

Immediately after they shall be assembled in Consequence of the first Election, they shall be divided as equally as may be into three Classes. The Seats of the Senators of the first Class shall be vacated at the Expiration of the second Year, of the second Class at the Expiration of the fourth Year, and of the third Class at the Expiration of the sixth Year, so that one-third may be chosen every second Year; and if Vacancies happen by Resignation, or otherwise, during the Recess of the Legislature of any State, the Executive thereof may make temporary Appointments until the next Meeting of the Legislature, which shall then fill such Vacancies.

No Person shall be a Senator who shall not have attained to the Age of thirty Years, and [been nine Years a Citizen of the United] *be a citizen of the Confederate* States, and who shall not, when elected, be an Inhabitant of that State for which he shall be chosen.

The Vice President of the [United] *Confederate* States shall be President of the Senate, but shall have no Vote, unless they be equally divided.

The Senate shall choose their other Officers, and also a President pro tempore, in the Absence of the Vice President, or when he shall exercise the Office of President of the United States.

The Senate shall have the sole Power to try all Impeachments. When sitting for that Purpose, they shall be on Oath or Affirmation. When the President of the [United] *Confederate* States is tried, the Chief Justice shall preside: And no Person shall be convicted without the Concurrence of two-thirds of the Members present.

Judgment in Cases of Impeachment shall not extend further than to removal from Office, and Disqualification to hold and enjoy any Office of honour, Trust or Profit under the [United] *Confederate* States; but the Party convicted shall nevertheless be liable and subject to Indictment, Trial, Judgment and Punishment, according to Law.

Section IV The Times, Places and Manner of holding Elections for Senators and Representatives, shall be prescribed in each State by the Legislature thereof, *subject to the provisions of this Constitution*; but the Congress may at any time by Law make or alter such Regulations, except as to the *times and* places of choosing Senators.

The Congress shall assemble at least once in every Year, and such Meeting shall be on the first Monday in December, unless they shall by Law appoint a different Day.

Section V Each House shall be the Judge of the Elections, Returns and Qualifications of its own Members, and a Majority of each shall constitute a Quorum to do Business; but a smaller Number may adjourn from day to day, and may be authorized to compel the Attendance of absent Members, in such Manner, and under such Penalties as each House may provide.

Each House may determine the Rules of its Proceedings, punish its Members for disorderly Behaviour, and, with the Concurrence of two-thirds *of the whole number* expel a Member.

Each House shall keep a Journal of its Proceedings, and from time to time publish the same, excepting such Parts as may in their Judgment require Secrecy; and the Yeas and Nays of the Members of either House on any question shall, at the Desire of one-fifth of those Present, be entered on the Journal.

Neither House, during the Session of Congress, shall, without the Consent of the other, adjourn for more than three days, nor to any other Place than that in which the two Houses shall be sitting.

Section VI The Senators and Representatives shall receive a Compensation for their Services, to be ascertained by Law, and paid out of the Treasury of the [United] *Confederate* States. They shall in all Cases, except Treason [Felony] and Breach of the Peace, be privileged from Arrest during their Attendance at the Session of their respective Houses, and in going to and returning from the same; and for any Speech or Debate in either House, they shall not be questioned in any other Place.

No Senator or Representative shall, during the Time for which he was elected, be appointed to any civil Office under the Authority of the [United] *Confederate* States, which shall have been created, or the Emoluments whereof shall have been increased during such time; and no Person holding any Office under the [United] *Confederate* States, shall be a Member of either House during his Continuance in Office. *But Congress may, by law, grant to the principal officers in each of the executive departments a seat upon the floor of either House, with the privilege of discussing any measures appertaining to his department.*

Section VII All Bills for raising Revenue shall originate in the House of Representatives; but the Senate may propose or concur with Amendments as on other Bills.

Every Bill which shall have passed [the House of Representatives and the Senate] *both Houses*, shall, before it become a Law, be presented to the President of the [United] *Confederate* States; If he approve he shall sign it, but if not he shall return it, with his Objections to that House in which it shall have originated, who shall enter the Objections at large on their Journal, and proceed to reconsider it. If after such Reconsideration two-thirds of that House shall agree to pass the Bill, it shall be sent, together with the Objections, to the other House, by which it shall likewise be reconsidered, and if approved by two-thirds of that House, it shall become a Law. But in all *such* Cases the Votes of both Houses shall be determined by Yeas and Nays, and the Names of the Persons voting for and against the Bill shall be entered on the Journal of each House respectively. If any Bill shall not be returned by the President within ten Days (Sundays excepted) after it shall have been presented to him, the Same shall be a law, in like Manner as if he had signed it, unless the Congress by their Adjournment prevent its return, in which Case it shall not be a Law. *The President may approve any appropriation and disapprove any other appropriation in the same bill. In such case he shall, in signing the bill, designate the appropriation disapproved, and shall return a copy of such appropriation, with his objections, to the House in which the bill shall have originated; and the same proceedings shall then be had as in case of other bills disapproved by the President.*

Every Order, Resolution, or Vote to which the Concurrence of [the Senate and House of Representatives] *both Houses* may be necessary (except on a question of Adjournment), shall be presented to the President of the [United] *Confederate* States; and before the Same shall take Effect, shall be approved by him, or being disapproved by him, [shall] *may* be repassed by two-thirds of [the Senate and House of Representatives] *both Houses*, according to the Rules and Limitations prescribed in the Case of a Bill.

Section VIII The Congress shall have Power.

To lay and collect Taxes, Duties, Imposts and *Excises, for revenue necessary* to pay the Debts [and], provide for the common Defense [and general Welfare of the United States; but], *and carry on the government of the Confederate States; but no bounties shall be granted from the treasury, nor shall any duties, or taxes, or importation from foreign nations be laid to promote or foster any branch of industry; and* all Duties, Imposts and Excises shall be uniform throughout the [United] Confederate States;

To borrow Money on the credit of the [United] Confederate States;

To regulate Commerce with foreign Nations, and among the several States, and with the Indian Tribes; *but neither this, nor any other clause contained in this Constitution, shall ever be construed to delegate the power to Congress to appropriate money for any internal improvement intended to facilitate commerce; except for the purpose of furnishing lights, beacons, and buoys, and other aids to navigation upon the coasts, and the improvement of harbors, and the removing of obstructions in river navigation; in all such cases such duties shall be laid on the navigation facilitated thereby, as may be necessary to pay the costs and expenses thereof;*

To establish an uniform Rule of Naturalization, and uniform Laws on the subject of Bankruptcies throughout the [United] *Confederate* States; *but no law of Congress shall discharge any debt contracted before the passage of the same;*

To coin Money, regulate the Value thereof, and of foreign Coin, and fix the Standard of Weights and Measures;

To provide for the Punishment of counterfeiting the Securities and current Coin of the [United] *Confederate* States;

To establish Post Offices and post [Roads] *routes; but the expenses of the Postoffice Department, after the first day of March, in the year of our Lord eighteen hundred and sixty-three, shall be paid out of its own revenues*;

To promote the progress of Science and useful Arts, by securing for limited Times to Authors and Inventors the exclusive Right to their respective Writings and Discoveries;

To constitute Tribunals inferior to the supreme Court;

To define and punish Piracies and Felonies committed on the high Seas, and Offences against the Law of Nations;

To declare War, grant Letters of Marque and Reprisal, and make Rules concerning Captures on Land and Water;

To raise and support Armies, but no Appropriation of Money to that Use shall be for a longer Term than two Years;

To provide and maintain a Navy;

To make Rules for the Government and Regulation of the land and naval Forces;

To provide for calling forth the Militia to execute the Laws of the [Union] *Confederate States*, suppress Insurrections and repel Invasions;

To provide for organizing, arming, and disciplining the Militia and for governing such Part of them as may be employed in the Service of the [United] *Confederate* States, reserving to the States respectively, the Appointment of the Officers, and the Authority of training the Militia according to the Discipline prescribed by Congress;

To exercise exclusive Legislation in all Cases whatsoever, over such District (not exceeding ten Miles square) as may, by Cession of particular States, and the Acceptance of Congress, become the Seat of the Government of the [United] *Confederate* States, and to exercise like Authority over all Places purchased by the Consent of the Legislature of the State in which the Same shall be, for the Erection of Forts, Magazines, Arsenals, Dock Yards, and other needful Buildings;—And

To make all Laws which shall be necessary and proper for carrying into Execution the foregoing Powers, and all other Powers vested by this Constitution in the Government of the [United] *Confederate* States or in any Department or Officer thereof.

Section IX [The Migration or Importation of such Persons as any of the States now existing shall think proper to admit, shall not be prohibited by the Congress prior to the Year one thousand eight hundred and eight, but a Tax or Duty may be imposed on such Importation, not exceeding ten dollars for each Person.] *The importation of negroes of the African race from any foreign country other than the slaveholding States or territories of the United States of America, is hereby forbidden; and Congress is required to pass such laws as shall effectually prevent the same. Congress shall also have power to prohibit the introduction of slaves from any State not a member of, or territory not belonging to, this Confederacy.*

The Privilege of the Writ of Habeas Corpus shall not be suspended, unless when in Cases of Rebellion or Invasion the public Safety may require it. No Bill of Attainder or ex post facto Law, *or law denying or impairing the right of property in negro slaves,* shall be passed.

No Capitation, or other direct, Tax shall be laid, unless in Proportion to the Census or Enumeration herein before directed to be taken.

No Tax or Duty shall be laid on Articles exported from any State, *except by a vote of two-thirds of both Houses.*

No Preference shall be given by any Regulation of Commerce or Revenue to the Ports of one State over those of another; nor shall Vessels bound to, or from, one State, be obliged to enter, clear, or pay Duties in another.

No Money shall be drawn from the Treasury, but in Consequence of Appropriations made by Law; and a regular Statement and Account of the Receipts and Expenditures of all public Money shall be published from time to time.

Congress shall appropriate no money from the Treasury except by a vote of two-thirds of both Houses, taken by yeas and nays, unless it be asked and estimated for by some one of the heads of departments and submitted to Congress by the President; or for the purpose of paying its own expenses and contingencies; or for the payment of claims against the Confederate States, the justice of which shall have been officially declared by a tribunal for the investigation of claims against the Government, which it is hereby made the duty of Congress to establish.

All bills appropriating money shall specify in Federal currency the exact amount of each appropriation and the purposes for which it is made; and Congress shall grant no extra compensation to any public contractor, officer, agent or servant, after such contract shall have been made or such service rendered.

No Title of Nobility shall be granted by the [United] *Confederate States*; and no Person holding any Office of Profit or Trust under them, shall, without the Consent of the Congress, accept of any present, Emolument, Office, or Title, of any kind whatever, from any King, Prince or foreign State.

[Here the framers of the Confederate Constitution insert the U.S. Bill of Rights.] Congress shall make no law respecting an establishment of religion, or prohibiting the free exercise thereof; or abridging the freedom of speech, or of the press; or the right of the people peaceably to assemble, and to petition the Government for a redress of grievances.

A well-regulated Militia, being necessary to the security of a free State, the right of the people to keep and bear Arms shall not be infringed.

No Soldier shall, in time of peace, be quartered in any house, without the consent of the Owner, nor in time of war, but in a manner to be prescribed by law.

The right of the people to be secure in their persons, houses, papers, and effects, against unreasonable searches and seizures, shall not be violated, and no Warrants shall issue, but upon probable cause, supported by Oath or affirmation, and particularly describing the place to be searched, and the persons or things to be seized.

No person shall be held to answer for a capital, or otherwise infamous crime, unless on a presentment or indictment of a Grand Jury, except in cases arising in the land or naval forces, or in the Militia, when in actual service in time of War or public danger; nor shall any person be subject for the same offence to be twice put in jeopardy of life or limb; nor shall be compelled in any Criminal Case to be a witness against himself, nor be deprived of life, liberty or property without due process of law; nor shall private property be taken for public use, without just compensation.

In all criminal prosecutions, the accused shall enjoy the right to a speedy and public trial, by an impartial jury of the State and district wherein the crime shall have been committed, which district shall have been previously ascertained by law, and to be informed of the nature and cause of the accusation; to be confronted with the witnesses against him; to have Compulsory process for obtaining Witnesses in his favour, and to have the Assistance of Counsel for his defence.

In Suits at common law, where the value in controversy shall exceed twenty dollars, the right of trial by jury shall be preserved, and no fact tried by a jury shall be otherwise reexamined in any Court of the [United] *Confederate* States, than according to the rules of the common law.

Excessive bail shall not be required, nor excessive fines imposed, nor cruel and unusual punishments inflicted.

Every law or resolution having the force of law, shall relate to but one subject, and that shall be expressed in the title.

Section X No State shall enter into any Treaty, Alliance, or Confederation; grant Letters of Marque and Reprisal; coin Money; [emit Bills of Credit;] make any Thing but gold and silver Coin a Tender in Payment of Debts; pass any Bill of Attainder, or ex post facto Law, or Law impairing the Obligation of Contracts, or grant any Title of Nobility.

No State shall, without the consent of the Congress, lay any Imposts or Duties on Imports or Exports, except what may be absolutely necessary for executing its inspection Laws: and the net Produce of all Duties and Imposts, laid by any State on Imports or Exports, shall be for the Use of the Treasury of the [United] *Confederate* States; and all such Laws shall be subject to the Revision and Control of the Congress.

No State shall, without the Consent of Congress, lay any Duty of Tonnage, *except on seagoing vessels, for the improvement of its rivers and harbors navigated*

by the said vessels; but such duties shall not conflict with any treaties of the Confederate States with foreign nations; and any surplus of revenue thus derived shall, after making such improvement, be paid into the common treasury; nor shall any State keep Troops, or Ships of War in time of Peace, enter into any Agreement or Compact with another State, or with a foreign Power, or engage in War, unless actually invaded, or in such imminent Danger as will not admit of Delay. *But when any river divides or flows through two or more States, they may enter into compacts with each other to improve the navigation thereof.*

Article II

Section I [The executive Power shall be vested in a President of the United States of America. He shall hold his Office during the Term of four Years, and, together with the Vice President, chosen for the same Term, be elected, as follows:] *The executive power shall be vested in a President of the Confederate States of America. He and the Vice President shall hold their offices for the term of six years; but the President shall not be reeligible.*

The President and Vice President shall be elected as follows: Each State shall appoint in such Manner as the Legislature thereof may direct, a Number of Electors, equal to the whole Number of Senators and Representatives to which the State may be entitled in the Congress; but no Senator or Representative, or Person holding an Office of Trust or Profit under the [United] *Confederate* States, shall be appointed an Elector.

The Electors shall meet in their respective States, and vote by ballot for President and Vice President, one of whom, at least, shall not be an inhabitant of the same State with themselves; they shall name in their ballots the person voted for as President, and in distinct ballots the person voted for as Vice President, and they shall make distinct lists of all persons voted for as President, and of all persons voted for as Vice President, and of the number of votes for each, which lists they shall sign and certify, and transmit sealed to the seat of the government of the [United] *Confederate* States, directed to the President of the Senate;— The President of the Senate shall, in the presence of the Senate and House of Representatives, open all the certificates and the votes shall then be counted;—The person having the greatest number of votes for President shall be the President, if such number be a majority of the whole number of Electors appointed; and if no person have such majority, then from the persons having the highest numbers not exceeding three on the list of those voted for as President, the House of Representatives shall choose immediately, by ballot, the President. But in choosing the President, the votes shall be taken by States, the representation from each State having one vote; a quorum for this purpose shall consist of a member or members from two-thirds of the States, and a majority of all the States shall be necessary to a choice. And if the House of Representatives shall not choose a President whenever the right of choice shall devolve upon them, before the fourth day of March next following, then the Vice President shall act as President, as in the case of the death or other constitutional disability of the President. The person having the greatest number of votes as Vice President shall be the Vice President, if such number be a majority of the whole number of Electors appointed, and if no person have a majority, then from the two highest numbers on the list the Senate shall choose the Vice President; a quorum for the purpose shall consist of two-thirds of the whole number of Senators, and a majority of the whole number shall be necessary to a choice. But no person constitutionally ineligible to the office of President shall be eligible to that of Vice President of the [United] *Confederate* States.

The Congress may determine the Time of choosing the Electors, and the Day on which they shall give their Votes; which Day shall be the same throughout the [United] *Confederate* States.

No Person except a natural-born Citizen [or a Citizen of the United States] *of the Confederate States, or a citizen thereof,* at the time of the Adoption of this Constitution, *or a citizen thereof born in the United States prior to the 20th of December, 1860,* shall be eligible to the Office of President; neither shall any Person be eligible to that Office who shall not have attained to the Age of thirty-five Years, and been fourteen Years a Resident within the [United States] *limits of the Confederate States, as they may exist at the time of his election.*

In Cases of the Removal of the President from Office, or of his Death, Resignation, or Inability to discharge the Powers and Duties of the said Office, the same shall devolve on the Vice President, and the Congress may by Law provide for the Case of Removal, Death, Resignation, or Inability, both of the President and Vice President, declaring what Officer shall then act as President, and such Officer shall act accordingly, until the Disability be removed, or a President shall be elected.

The President shall, at stated Times, receive for his Services, a Compensation, which shall neither be increased nor diminished during the Period for which he shall have been elected, and he shall not receive within that Period any other Emolument from the [United] *Confederate* States or any of them.

Before he enters on the Execution of his Office, he shall take the following Oath or Affirmation—"I do solemnly swear (or affirm) that I will faithfully execute the Office of President of the [United] *Confederate* States, and will to the best of my Ability, preserve, protect and defend the Constitution [of the United States] *thereof.*"

Section II The President shall be Commander in Chief of the Army and Navy of the [United] *Confederate* States, and of the Militia of the several States, when called into the actual Service of the [United] *Confederate* States; he may require the Opinion, in writing, of the principal Officer in each of the executive Departments, upon any Subject relating to the Duties of their respective Offices, and he shall have Power to grant Reprieves and Pardons for Offenses against the [United] *Confederate* States, except in Cases of Impeachment.

He shall have Power, by and with the Advice and Consent of the Senate, to make Treaties, provided two-thirds of the Senators present concur; and he shall nominate, and by and with the Advice and Consent of the Senate, shall appoint Ambassadors, other public Ministers and Consuls, Judges of the supreme Court, and all other Officers of the [United] *Confederate* States, whose Appointments are not herein otherwise provided for, and which shall be established by Law: but the Congress may by Law vest the Appointment of such inferior Officers, as they think proper, in the President alone, in the Courts of Law, or in the Heads of Departments. *The principal officer in each of the executive departments, and all persons connected with the diplomatic service, may be removed from office at the pleasure of the President. All other civil officers of the executive department may be removed at any time by the President, or other appointing power, when their services are unnecessary, or for dishonesty, incapacity, inefficiency, misconduct, or neglect of duty; and when so removed, the removal shall be reported to the Senate, together with the reasons therefor.*

The President shall have Power to fill [up] all Vacancies that may happen during the Recess of the Senate, by granting Commissions which shall expire at the End of their next Session.

Section III [He] *The President* shall from time to time give to the Congress Information of the State of the [Union] *Confederacy*, and recommend to their Consideration such Measures as he shall judge necessary and expedient; he may, on extraordinary Occasions, convene both Houses, or either of them, and in Case of Disagreement between them, with Respect to the Time of Adjournment, he may adjourn them to such Time as he shall think proper; he shall receive Ambassadors and other public Ministers; he shall take Care that the Laws be faithfully executed, and shall Commission all the officers of the [United] *Confederate* States.

Section IV The President, Vice President and all civil Officers of the [United] *Confederate* States, shall be removed from Office or Impeachment for, and Conviction of, Treason, Bribery, or other high Crimes and Misdemeanors.

Article III

Section I The judicial Power of the [United] *Confederate* States shall be vested in one [supreme] *Superior* Court, and in such inferior Courts as the Congress may from time to time ordain and establish. The Judges, both of the supreme and inferior Courts, shall hold their Offices during good Behavior, and shall, at stated Times, receive for their Services a Compensation, which shall not be diminished during their Continuance in Office.

Section II The judicial Power shall extend to all cases [in Law and Equity, arising under this Constitution], *arising under this Constitution, in law and equity*, the Laws of the [United] *Confederate* States, and Treaties made, or which shall be made, under their Authority;—to all Cases affecting Ambassadors, other public Ministers, and Consuls;—to all Cases of admiralty and maritime Jurisdiction;—to Controversies to which the [United] *Confederate* States shall be a Party;—to Controversies between two or more States;—between a State and Citizens of another State *where the State is plaintiff*;—*between* Citizens *claiming lands under grants* of different States,—[between Citizens of the same State claiming Lands under Grants of different States,] and between a State, or the Citizens thereof, and foreign States, Citizens or Subjects; *but no State shall be sued by a citizen or subject of any foreign State.*

In all Cases affecting Ambassadors, other public Ministers and Consuls, and those in which a State shall be Party, the supreme Court shall have original Jurisdiction. In all the other Cases before mentioned, the supreme Court shall have appellate Jurisdiction, both as to Law and Fact, with such Exceptions, and under such Regulations as the Congress shall make.

The Trial of all Crimes, except in Cases of Impeachment, shall be by Jury; and such Trial shall be held in the State where the said Crime[s] shall have been committed; but when not committed within any State, the Trial shall be at such Place or Places as the Congress may by Law have directed.

Section III Treason against the [United] *Confederate* States shall consist only in levying War against them, or in adhering to their Enemies, giving them Aid and Comfort. No Person shall be convicted of Treason unless on the Testimony of two Witnesses to the same overt Act, or on Confession in open Court.

The Congress shall have Power to declare the Punishment of Treason, but no Attainder of Treason shall work Corruption of Blood, or Forfeiture except during the Life of the Person attainted.

Article IV

Section I Full Faith and Credit shall be given in each State to the public Acts, Records, and judicial Proceedings of every other State. And the Congress may by general Laws prescribe the Manner in which such Acts, Records and Proceedings shall be proved, and the Effect thereof.

Section II The Citizens of each State shall be entitled to all Privileges and Immunities of Citizens in the several States, *and shall have the right of transit and sojourn in any State of this Confederacy, with their slaves and other property; and the right of property in such slaves shall not be impaired.*

A Person charged in any State with Treason, Felony, or other Crime, who shall flee from Justice, and be found in another State, shall on Demand of the executive Authority of the State from which he fled, be delivered up, to be removed to the State having Jurisdiction of the Crime.

No *slave* or Person held to Service or Labor in [one State] *any State or Territory of the Confederate States* under the Laws thereof, escaping *or unlawfully carried* into another, shall, in Consequence of any Law or Regulation therein, be discharged from such Service or Labor, but shall be delivered up on Claim of the Party to whom such *slave belongs, or to whom such* Service or Labor may be due.

Section III [New States may be admitted by the Congress into this Union;] *Other States may be admitted into this Confederacy by a vote of two-thirds of the whole House of Representatives and two-thirds of the Senate, the Senate voting by States*; but no new State shall be formed or erected within the Jurisdiction of any other State; nor any State be formed by the Junction of two or more States, or Parts of States, without the Consent of the Legislatures of the States concerned as well as of the Congress.

The Congress shall have Power to dispose of and make all needful Rules and Regulations [respecting the Territory or other Property belonging to the United States; and nothing in this Constitution shall be so construed as to Prejudice any Claims of the United States, or of any particular State] *concerning the property of the Confederate States, including the lands thereof.*

The Confederate States may acquire new territory, and Congress shall have power to legislate and provide governments for the inhabitants of all territory belonging to the Confederate States lying without the limits of the several States, and may permit them, at such times and in such manner as it may by law provide, to form States to be admitted into the Confederacy. In all such territory the institution of negro slavery as it now exists in the Confederate States shall be recognized and protected by Congress and by the territorial government, and the inhabitants of the several Confederate States and territories shall have the right to take to such territory any slaves lawfully held by them in any of the States or Territories of the Confederate States.

Section IV The [United] *Confederate* States shall guarantee to every State [in this Union] *that now is, or hereafter may become, a member of this Confederacy*, a Republican Form of Government, and shall protect each of them against Invasion; and on Application of the Legislature, or of the Executive (when the Legislature [cannot be convened] *is not in session*) against domestic Violence.

Article V

[The Congress, whenever two-thirds of both Houses shall deem it necessary, shall propose Amendments to this Constitution, or on the Application of the Legislatures of two-thirds of the several States, shall call a Convention for proposing Amendments, which, in either Case, shall be valid to all Intents and Purposes, as Part of this Constitution, when ratified by the Legislatures of three-fourths of the several States, or by Conventions in three-fourths thereof, as the one or the other Mode of Ratification may be proposed by the Congress; Provided that no Amendment which may be made prior to the Year one thousand eight hundred and eight shall in any Manner affect the first and fourth Clauses in the Ninth Section of the first Article; and that no State, without its Consent, shall be deprived of its equal Suffrage in the Senate.] *Upon the demand of any three States, legally assembled in their several Conventions, the Congress shall summon a Convention of all the States, to take into consideration such amendments to the Constitution as the said States shall concur in suggesting at the time when the said demand is made; and should any of the proposed amendments to the Constitution be agreed on by the said Convention—voting by States—and the same be ratified by the Legislatures of two-thirds of the several States, or by Conventions in two-thirds thereof—as the one or the other mode of ratification may be proposed by the general Convention—they shall henceforward form a part of this Constitution. But no State shall, without its consent, be deprived of its equal representation in the Senate.*

Article VI

The Government established by this Constitution is the successor of the Provisional Government of the Confederate States of America, and all laws passed by the latter shall continue in force until the same shall be repealed or modified; and all the officers appointed by the same shall remain in office until their successors are appointed and qualified or the offices abolished.

All Debts contracted and Engagements entered into, before the Adoption of this Constitution, shall be as valid against the [United] *Confederate* States under this Constitution, as under the [Confederation] *Provisional Government.*

This Constitution and the Laws of the [United] *Confederate* States [which shall be] made in Pursuance thereof; and all Treaties made, or which shall be made, under the authority of the [United] *Confederate* States,

shall be the supreme Law of the Land; and the Judges in every State shall be bound thereby, any Thing in the Constitution or Laws of any State to the Contrary notwithstanding.

The Senators and Representatives before mentioned, and the Members of the several State Legislatures, and all executive and judicial Officers, both of the [United] *Confederate* States and of the several States, shall be bound by Oath or Affirmation, to support this Constitution; but no religious Test shall ever be required as a Qualification to any Office or public Trust under the [United] *Confederate* States.

The enumeration in the Constitution, of certain rights, shall not be construed to deny or disparage others retained by the people *of the several States.*

The powers not delegated to the [United] *Confederate* States by the Constitution, nor prohibited by it to the States, are reserved to the States respectively, or to the people.

Article VII

The Ratification of the Conventions of [nine] *five* States shall be sufficient for the Establishment of this Constitution between the States so ratifying the same.

When five States shall have ratified this Constitution, in the manner before specified, the Congress under the Provisional Constitution shall prescribe the time for holding the election of President and Vice President; and for the meeting of the electoral college; and for counting the votes and inaugurating the President. They shall also prescribe the time for holding the first election of members of Congress under this Constitution, and the time for assembling the same. Until the assembling of such Congress, the Congress under the Provisional Constitution shall continue to exercise the legislative powers granted them, not extending beyond the time limited by the Constitution of the Provisional Government.

[Done in Convention by the Unanimous Consent of the States present, the Seventeenth Day of September in the Year of our Lord one thousand seven hundred and eighty-seven and of the Independence of the United States of America the Twelfth.] *Adopted unanimously March 11, 1861.*

APPENDIX II. Facts and Figures: Government, Economy, and Demographics

U.S. Politics and Government

PRESIDENTIAL ELECTIONS

Year	Candidates	Parties	Popular Vote	Percentage of Popular Vote	Electoral Vote	Percentage of Voter Participation
1789	**GEORGE WASHINGTON (Va.)***				69	
	John Adams				34	
	Others				35	
1792	**GEORGE WASHINGTON (Va.)**				132	
	John Adams				77	
	George Clinton				50	
	Others				5	
1796	**JOHN ADAMS (Mass.)**	Federalist			71	
	Thomas Jefferson	Democratic-Republican			68	
	Thomas Pinckney	Federalist			59	
	Aaron Burr	Dem.-Rep.			30	
	Others				48	
1800	**THOMAS JEFFERSON (Va.)**	Dem.-Rep.			73	
	Aaron Burr	Dem.-Rep.			73	
	John Adams	Federalist			65	
	C. C. Pinckney	Federalist			64	
	John Jay	Federalist			1	
1804	**THOMAS JEFFERSON (Va.)**	Dem.-Rep.			162	
	C. C. Pinckney	Federalist			14	
1808	**JAMES MADISON (Va.)**	Dem.-Rep.			122	
	C. C. Pinckney	Federalist			47	
	George Clinton	Dem.-Rep.			6	
1812	**JAMES MADISON (Va.)**	Dem.-Rep.			128	
	De Witt Clinton	Federalist			89	
1816	**JAMES MONROE (Va.)**	Dem.-Rep.			183	
	Rufus King	Federalist			34	
1820	**JAMES MONROE (Va.)**	Dem.-Rep.			231	
	John Quincy Adams	Dem.-Rep.			1	
1824	**JOHN Q. ADAMS (Mass.)**	Dem.-Rep.	108,740	30.5	84	26.9
	Andrew Jackson	Dem.-Rep.	153,544	43.1	99	
	William H. Crawford	Dem.-Rep.	46,618	13.1	41	
	Henry Clay	Dem.-Rep.	47,136	13.2	37	
1828	**ANDREW JACKSON (Tenn.)**	Democratic	647,286	56.0	178	57.6
	John Quincy Adams	National Republican	508,064	44.0	83	
1832	**ANDREW JACKSON (Tenn.)**	Democratic	687,502	55.0	219	55.4
	Henry Clay	National Republican	530,189	42.4	49	
	John Floyd	Independent			11	
	William Wirt	Anti-Mason	33,108	2.6	7	

*State of residence when elected president.

Year	Candidates	Parties	Popular Vote	Percentage of Popular Vote	Electoral Vote	Percentage of Voter Participation
1836	**MARTIN VAN BUREN (N.Y.)**	Democratic	765,483	50.9	170	57.8
	W. H. Harrison	Whig			73	
	Hugh L. White	Whig	739,795	49.1	26	
	Daniel Webster	Whig			14	
	W. P. Mangum	Independent			11	
1840	**WILLIAM H. HARRISON (Ohio)**	Whig	1,274,624	53.1	234	78.0
	Martin Van Buren	Democratic	1,127,781	46.9	60	
	J. G. Birney	Liberty	7,069		—	
1844	**JAMES K. POLK (Tenn.)**	Democratic	1,338,464	49.6	170	78.9
	Henry Clay	Whig	1,300,097	48.1	105	
	J. G. Birney	Liberty	62,300	2.3	—	
1848	**ZACHARY TAYLOR (La.)**	Whig	1,360,099	47.4	163	72.7
	Lewis Cass	Democratic	1,220,544	42.5	127	
	Martin Van Buren	Free-Soil	291,263	10.1	—	
1852	**FRANKLIN PIERCE (N.H.)**	Democratic	1,601,117	50.9	254	69.6
	Winfield Scott	Whig	1,385,453	44.1	42	
	John P. Hale	Free-Soil	155,825	5.0	—	
1856	**JAMES BUCHANAN (Pa.)**	Democratic	1,832,995	45.3	174	78.9
	John C. Frémont	Republican	1,339,932	33.1	114	
	Millard Fillmore	American	871,731	21.6	8	
1860	**ABRAHAM LINCOLN (Ill.)**	Republican	1,866,452	39.8	180	81.2
	Stephen A. Douglas	Democratic	1,375,157	29.4	12	
	John C. Breckinridge	Democratic	847,953	18.1	72	
	John Bell	Union	590,631	12.6	39	
1864	**ABRAHAM LINCOLN (Ill.)**	Republican	2,213,665	55.1	212	73.8
	George B. McClellan	Democratic	1,805,237	44.9	21	
1868	**ULYSSES S. GRANT (Ill.)**	Republican	3,012,833	52.7	214	78.1
	Horatio Seymour	Democratic	2,703,249	47.3	80	
1872	**ULYSSES S. GRANT (Ill.)**	Republican	3,597,132	55.6	286	71.3
	Horace Greeley	Democratic; Liberal Republican	2,834,125	43.9	66	
1876	**RUTHERFORD B. HAYES (Ohio)**	Republican	4,036,298	48.0	185	81.8
	Samuel J. Tilden	Democratic	4,288,590	51.0	184	
1880	**JAMES A. GARFIELD (Ohio)**	Republican	4,454,416	48.5	214	79.4
	Winfield S. Hancock	Democratic	4,444,952	48.1	155	
1884	**GROVER CLEVELAND (N.Y.)**	Democratic	4,874,986	48.5	219	77.5
	James G. Blaine	Republican	4,851,981	48.3	182	
1888	**BENJAMIN HARRISON (Ind.)**	Republican	5,439,853	47.9	233	79.3
	Grover Cleveland	Democratic	5,540,309	48.6	168	
1892	**GROVER CLEVELAND (N.Y.)**	Democratic	5,555,426	46.1	277	74.7
	Benjamin Harrison	Republican	5,182,690	43.0	145	
	James B. Weaver	People's	1,029,846	8.5	22	
1896	**WILLIAM McKINLEY (Ohio)**	Republican	7,104,779	51.1	271	79.3
	William J. Bryan	Democratic-People's	6,502,925	47.7	176	
1900	**WILLIAM McKINLEY (Ohio)**	Republican	7,207,923	51.7	292	73.2
	William J. Bryan	Dem.-Populist	6,358,133	45.5	155	
1904	**THEODORE ROOSEVELT (N.Y.)**	Republican	7,623,486	57.9	336	65.2
	Alton B. Parker	Democratic	5,077,911	37.6	140	
	Eugene V. Debs	Socialist	402,283	3.0	—	
1908	**WILLIAM H. TAFT (Ohio)**	Republican	7,678,908	51.6	321	65.4
	William J. Bryan	Democratic	6,409,104	43.1	162	
	Eugene V. Debs	Socialist	420,793	2.8	—	

Year	Candidates	Parties	Popular Vote	Percentage of Popular Vote	Electoral Vote	Percentage of Voter Participation
1912	**WOODROW WILSON (N.J.)**	Democratic	6,293,454	41.9	435	58.8
	Theodore Roosevelt	Progressive	4,119,538	27.4	88	
	William H. Taft	Republican	3,484,980	23.2	8	
	Eugene V. Debs	Socialist	900,672	6.1	—	
1916	**WOODROW WILSON (N.J.)**	Democratic	9,129,606	49.4	277	61.6
	Charles E. Hughes	Republican	8,538,221	46.2	254	
	A. L. Benson	Socialist	585,113	3.2	—	
1920	**WARREN G. HARDING (Ohio)**	Republican	16,143,407	60.5	404	49.2
	James M. Cox	Democratic	9,130,328	34.2	127	
	Eugene V. Debs	Socialist	919,799	3.4	—	
1924	**CALVIN COOLIDGE (Mass.)**	Republican	15,725,016	54.0	382	48.9
	John W. Davis	Democratic	8,386,503	28.8	136	
	Robert M. La Follette	Progressive	4,822,856	16.6	13	
1928	**HERBERT HOOVER (Calif.)**	Republican	21,391,381	57.4	444	56.9
	Alfred E. Smith	Democratic	15,016,443	40.3	87	
	Norman Thomas	Socialist	881,951	2.3	—	
	William Z. Foster	Communist	102,991	0.3	—	
1932	**FRANKLIN D. ROOSEVELT (N.Y.)**	Democratic	22,821,857	57.4	472	56.9
	Herbert Hoover	Republican	15,761,841	39.7	59	
	Norman Thomas	Socialist	881,951	2.2	—	
1936	**FRANKLIN D. ROOSEVELT (N.Y.)**	Democratic	27,751,597	60.8	523	61.0
	Alfred M. Landon	Republican	16,679,583	36.5	8	
	William Lemke	Union	882,479	1.9	—	
1940	**FRANKLIN D. ROOSEVELT (N.Y.)**	Democratic	27,244,160	54.8	449	62.5
	Wendell Willkie	Republican	22,305,198	44.8	82	
1944	**FRANKLIN D. ROOSEVELT (N.Y.)**	Democratic	25,602,504	53.5	432	55.9
	Thomas E. Dewey	Republican	22,006,285	46.0	99	
1948	**HARRY S. TRUMAN (Mo.)**	Democratic	24,105,695	49.5	303	53.0
	Thomas E. Dewey	Republican	21,969,170	45.1	189	
	J. Strom Thurmond	States'-Rights Democratic	1,169,021	2.4	38	
	Henry A. Wallace	Progressive	1,156,103	2.4	—	
1952	**DWIGHT D. EISENHOWER (N.Y.)**	Republican	33,936,252	55.1	442	63.3
	Adlai Stevenson	Democratic	27,314,992	44.4	89	
1956	**DWIGHT D. EISENHOWER (N.Y.)**	Republican	35,575,420	57.6	457	60.6
	Adlai Stevenson	Democratic	26,033,066	42.1	73	
	Other	—	—		1	
1960	**JOHN F. KENNEDY (Mass.)**	Democratic	34,227,096	49.9	303	62.8
	Richard M. Nixon	Republican	34,108,546	49.6	219	
	Other	—	—		15	
1964	**LYNDON B. JOHNSON (Texas)**	Democratic	43,126,506	61.1	486	61.7
	Barry M. Goldwater	Republican	27,176,799	38.5	52	
1968	**RICHARD M. NIXON (N.Y.)**	Republican	31,770,237	43.4	301	60.9
	Hubert H. Humphrey	Democratic	31,270,533	42.7	191	
	George Wallace	American Indep.	9,906,141	13.5	46	
1972	**RICHARD M. NIXON (N.Y.)**	Republican	47,169,911	60.7	520	55.2
	George S. McGovern	Democratic	29,170,383	37.5	17	
	Other	—	—		1	
1976	**JIMMY CARTER (Ga.)**	Democratic	40,830,763	50.0	297	53.5
	Gerald R. Ford	Republican	39,147,793	48.0	240	
	Other	—	1,575,459	2.1	—	
1980	**RONALD REAGAN (Calif.)**	Republican	43,901,812	51.0	489	54.0
	Jimmy Carter	Democratic	35,483,820	41.0	49	
	John B. Anderson	Independent	5,719,722	7.0	—	
	Ed Clark	Libertarian	921,188	1.1	—	

Year	Candidates	Parties	Popular Vote	Percentage of Popular Vote	Electoral Vote	Percentage of Voter Participation
1984	RONALD REAGAN (Calif.)	Republican	54,455,075	59.0	525	53.1
	Walter Mondale	Democratic	37,577,185	41.0	13	
1988	GEORGE H. W. BUSH (Texas)	Republican	47,946,422	54.0	426	50.2
	Michael S. Dukakis	Democratic	41,016,429	46.0	112	
1992	WILLIAM J. CLINTON (Ark.)	Democratic	44,908,254	43.0	370	55.9
	George H. W. Bush	Republican	39,102,282	38.0	168	
	H. Ross Perot	Independent	19,721,433	19.0	—	
1996	WILLIAM J. CLINTON (Ark.)	Democratic	47,401,185	49.2	379	49.0
	Robert Dole	Republican	39,197,469	40.7	159	
	H. Ross Perot	Independent	8,085,294	8.4	—	
2000	GEORGE W. BUSH (Texas)	Republican	50,456,062	47.8	271	51.2
	Al Gore	Democratic	50,996,862	48.4	267	
	Ralph Nader	Green Party	2,858,843	2.7	—	
	Patrick J. Buchanan	—	438,760	0.4	—	
2004	GEORGE W. BUSH (Texas)	Republican	61,872,711	50.7	286	60.3
	John F. Kerry	Democratic	58,894,584	48.3	252	
	Other	—	1,582,185	1.3	—	
2008	BARACK OBAMA (Illinois)	Democratic	69,456,897	52.9	365	56.8
	John McCain	Republican	59,934,314	45.7	173	

PRESIDENTS, VICE PRESIDENTS, AND SECRETARIES OF STATE

The Washington Administration (1789–1797)
Vice President	John Adams	1789–1797
Secretary of State	Thomas Jefferson	1789–1793
	Edmund Randolph	1794–1795
	Timothy Pickering	1795–1797

The John Adams Administration (1797–1801)
Vice President	Thomas Jefferson	1797–1801
Secretary of State	Timothy Pickering	1797–1800
	John Marshall	1800–1801

The Jefferson Administration (1801–1809)
Vice President	Aaron Burr	1801–1805
	George Clinton	1805–1809
Secretary of State	James Madison	1801–1809

The Madison Administration (1809–1817)
Vice President	George Clinton	1809–1813
	Elbridge Gerry	1813–1817
Secretary of State	Robert Smith	1809–1811
	James Monroe	1811–1817

The Monroe Administration (1817–1825)
Vice President	Daniel Tompkins	1817–1825
Secretary of State	John Quincy Adams	1817–1825

The John Quincy Adams Administration (1825–1829)
Vice President	John C. Calhoun	1825–1829
Secretary of State	Henry Clay	1825–1829

The Jackson Administration (1829–1837)
Vice President	John C. Calhoun	1829–1833
	Martin Van Buren	1833–1837
Secretary of State	Martin Van Buren	1829–1831
	Edward Livingston	1831–1833
	Louis McLane	1833–1834
	John Forsyth	1834–1837

The Van Buren Administration (1837–1841)
Vice President	Richard M. Johnson	1837–1841
Secretary of State	John Forsyth	1837–1841

The William Harrison Administration (1841)
Vice President	John Tyler	1841
Secretary of State	Daniel Webster	1841

The Tyler Administration (1841–1845)
Vice President	None	
Secretary of State	Daniel Webster	1841–1843
	Hugh S. Legaré	1843
	Abel P. Upshur	1843–1844
	John C. Calhoun	1844–1845

The Polk Administration (1845–1849)
Vice President	George M. Dallas	1845–1849
Secretary of State	James Buchanan	1845–1849

The Taylor Administration (1849–1850)
Vice President	Millard Fillmore	1849–1850
Secretary of State	John M. Clayton	1849–1850

The Fillmore Administration (1850–1853)

Vice President	None	
Secretary of State	Daniel Webster	1850–1852
	Edward Everett	1852–1853

The Pierce Administration (1853–1857)

Vice President	William R. King	1853–1857
Secretary of State	William L. Marcy	1853–1857

The Buchanan Administration (1857–1861)

Vice President	John C. Breckinridge	1857–1861
Secretary of State	Lewis Cass	1857–1860
	Jeremiah S. Black	1860–1861

The Lincoln Administration (1861–1865)

Vice President	Hannibal Hamlin	1861–1865
	Andrew Johnson	1865
Secretary of State	William H. Seward	1861–1865

The Andrew Johnson Administration (1865–1869)

Vice President	None	
Secretary of State	William H. Seward	1865–1869

The Grant Administration (1869–1877)

Vice President	Schuyler Colfax	1869–1873
	Henry Wilson	1873–1877
Secretary of State	Elihu B. Washburne	1869
	Hamilton Fish	1869–1877

The Hayes Administration (1877–1881)

Vice President	William A. Wheeler	1877–1881
Secretary of State	William M. Evarts	1877–1881

The Garfield Administration (1881)

Vice President	Chester A. Arthur	1881
Secretary of State	James G. Blaine	1881

The Arthur Administration (1881–1885)

Vice President	None	
Secretary of State	F. T. Frelinghuysen	1881–1885

The Cleveland Administration (1885–1889)

Vice President	Thomas A. Hendricks	1885–1889
Secretary of State	Thomas F. Bayard	1885–1889

The Benjamin Harrison Administration (1889–1893)

Vice President	Levi P. Morton	1889–1893
Secretary of State	James G. Blaine	1889–1892
	John W. Foster	1892–1893

The Cleveland Administration (1893–1897)

Vice President	Adlai E. Stevenson	1893–1897
Secretary of State	Walter Q. Gresham	1893–1895
	Richard Olney	1895–1897

The McKinley Administration (1897–1901)

Vice President	Garret A. Hobart	1897–1901
	Theodore Roosevelt	1901
Secretary of State	John Sherman	1897–1898
	William R. Day	1898
	John Hay	1898–1901

The Theodore Roosevelt Administration (1901–1909)

Vice President	Charles Fairbanks	1905–1909
Secretary of State	John Hay	1901–1905
	Elihu Root	1905–1909
	Robert Bacon	1909

The Taft Administration (1909–1913)

Vice President	James S. Sherman	1909–1913
Secretary of State	Philander C. Knox	1909–1913

The Wilson Administration (1913–1921)

Vice President	Thomas R. Marshall	1913–1921
Secretary of State	William J. Bryan	1913–1915
	Robert Lansing	1915–1920
	Bainbridge Colby	1920–1921

The Harding Administration (1921–1923)

Vice President	Calvin Coolidge	1921–1923
Secretary of State	Charles E. Hughes	1921–1923

The Coolidge Administration (1923–1929)

Vice President	Charles G. Dawes	1925–1929
Secretary of State	Charles E. Hughes	1923–1925
	Frank B. Kellogg	1925–1929

The Hoover Administration (1929–1933)

Vice President	Charles Curtis	1929–1933
Secretary of State	Henry L. Stimson	1929–1933

The Franklin D. Roosevelt Administration (1933–1945)

Vice President	John Nance Garner	1933–1941
	Henry A. Wallace	1941–1945
	Harry S. Truman	1945
Secretary of State	Cordell Hull	1933–1944
	Edward R. Stettinius Jr.	1944–1945

The Truman Administration (1945–1953)

Vice President	Alben W. Barkley	1949–1953
Secretary of State	Edward R. Stettinius Jr.	1945
	James F. Byrnes	1945–1947
	George C. Marshall	1947–1949
	Dean G. Acheson	1949–1953

The Eisenhower Administration (1953–1961)

Vice President	Richard M. Nixon	1953–1961
Secretary of State	John Foster Dulles	1953–1959
	Christian A. Herter	1959–1961

The Kennedy Administration (1961–1963)

Vice President	Lyndon B. Johnson	1961–1963
Secretary of State	Dean Rusk	1961–1963

The Lyndon Johnson Administration (1963–1969)

Vice President	Hubert H. Humphrey	1965–1969
Secretary of State	Dean Rusk	1963–1969

The Nixon Administration (1969–1974)

Vice President	Spiro T. Agnew	1969–1973
	Gerald R. Ford	1973–1974
Secretary of State	William P. Rogers	1969–1973
	Henry A. Kissinger	1973–1974

The Ford Administration (1974–1977)

Vice President	Nelson A. Rockefeller	1974–1977
Secretary of State	Henry A. Kissinger	1974–1977

The Carter Administration (1977–1981)

Vice President	Walter F. Mondale	1977–1981
Secretary of State	Cyrus R. Vance	1977–1980
	Edmund Muskie	1980–1981

The Reagan Administration (1981–1989)

Vice President	George H. W. Bush	1981–1989
Secretary of State	Alexander M. Haig	1981–1982
	George P. Shultz	1982–1989

The George H. W. Bush Administration (1989–1993)

Vice President	J. Danforth Quayle	1989–1993
Secretary of State	James A. Baker III	1989–1992
	Lawrence S. Eagleburger	1992–1993

The Clinton Administration (1993–2001)

Vice President	Albert Gore	1993–2001
Secretary of State	Warren M. Christopher	1993–1997
	Madeleine K. Albright	1997–2001

The George W. Bush Administration (2001–2009)

Vice President	Richard Cheney	2001–2009
Secretary of State	Colin Powell	2001–2005
	Condoleezza Rice	2005–2009

The Barack Obama Administration (2009–)

Vice President	Joseph Biden	2009–
Secretary of State	Hillary Clinton	2009–

ADMISSION OF STATES TO THE UNION

State	Date of Admission	State	Date of Admission
Delaware	December 7, 1787	Rhode Island	May 29, 1790
Pennsylvania	December 12, 1787	Vermont	March 4, 1791
New Jersey	December 18, 1787	Kentucky	June 1, 1792
Georgia	January 2, 1788	Tennessee	June 1, 1796
Connecticut	January 9, 1788	Ohio	March 1, 1803
Massachusetts	February 6, 1788	Louisiana	April 30, 1812
Maryland	April 28, 1788	Indiana	December 11, 1816
South Carolina	May 23, 1788	Mississippi	December 10, 1817
New Hampshire	June 21, 1788	Illinois	December 3, 1818
Virginia	June 25, 1788	Alabama	December 14, 1819
New York	July 26, 1788	Maine	March 15, 1820
North Carolina	November 21, 1789	Missouri	August 10, 1821

ADMISSION OF STATES TO THE UNION

State	Date of Admission	State	Date of Admission
Arkansas	June 15, 1836	Colorado	August 1, 1876
Michigan	January 16, 1837	North Dakota	November 2, 1889
Florida	March 3, 1845	South Dakota	November 2, 1889
Texas	December 29, 1845	Montana	November 8, 1889
Iowa	December 28, 1846	Washington	November 11, 1889
Wisconsin	May 29, 1848	Idaho	July 3, 1890
California	September 9, 1850	Wyoming	July 10, 1890
Minnesota	May 11, 1858	Utah	January 4, 1896
Oregon	February 14, 1859	Oklahoma	November 16, 1907
Kansas	January 29, 1861	New Mexico	January 6, 1912
West Virginia	June 19, 1863	Arizona	February 14, 1912
Nevada	October 31, 1864	Alaska	January 3, 1959
Nebraska	March 1, 1867	Hawaii	August 21, 1959

SUPREME COURT JUSTICES

Name	Service	Appointed by	Name	Service	Appointed by
John Jay*	1789–1795	Washington	Philip P. Barbour	1836–1841	Jackson
James Wilson	1789–1798	Washington	John Catron	1837–1865	Van Buren
John Blair	1789–1796	Washington	John McKinley	1837–1852	Van Buren
John Rutledge	1790–1791	Washington	Peter V. Daniel	1841–1860	Van Buren
William Cushing	1790–1810	Washington	Samuel Nelson	1845–1872	Tyler
James Iredell	1790–1799	Washington	Levi Woodbury	1845–1851	Polk
Thomas Johnson	1791–1793	Washington	Robert C. Grier	1846–1870	Polk
William Paterson	1793–1806	Washington	Benjamin R. Curtis	1851–1857	Fillmore
John Rutledge†	1795	Washington	John A. Campbell	1853–1861	Pierce
Samuel Chase	1796–1811	Washington	Nathan Clifford	1858–1881	Buchanan
Oliver Ellsworth	1796–1799	Washington	Noah H. Swayne	1862–1881	Lincoln
Bushrod Washington	1798–1829	J. Adams	Samuel F. Miller	1862–1890	Lincoln
Alfred Moore	1799–1804	J. Adams	David Davis	1862–1877	Lincoln
John Marshall	1801–1835	J. Adams	Stephen J. Field	1863–1897	Lincoln
William Johnson	1804–1834	Jefferson	**Salmon P. Chase**	1864–1873	Lincoln
Henry B. Livingston	1806–1823	Jefferson	William Strong	1870–1880	Grant
Thomas Todd	1807–1826	Jefferson	Joseph P. Bradley	1870–1892	Grant
Gabriel Duval	1811–1836	Madison	Ward Hunt	1873–1882	Grant
Joseph Story	1811–1845	Madison	**Morrison R. Waite**	1874–1888	Grant
Smith Thompson	1823–1843	Monroe	John M. Harlan	1877–1911	Hayes
Robert Trimble	1826–1828	J. Q. Adams	William B. Woods	1880–1887	Hayes
John McLean	1829–1861	Jackson	Stanley Matthews	1881–1889	Garfield
Henry Baldwin	1830–1844	Jackson	Horace Gray	1882–1902	Arthur
James M. Wayne	1835–1867	Jackson	Samuel Blatchford	1882–1893	Arthur
Roger B. Taney	1836–1864	Jackson	Lucius Q. C. Lamar	1888–1893	Cleveland
			Melville W. Fuller	1888–1910	Cleveland
			David J. Brewer	1889–1910	B. Harrison
			Henry B. Brown	1890–1906	B. Harrison
			George Shiras	1892–1903	B. Harrison
			Howell E. Jackson	1893–1895	B. Harrison

*Chief Justices appear in bold type.
†Acting Chief Justice; Senate refused to confirm appointment.

Name	Service	Appointed by	Name	Service	Appointed by
Edward D. White	1894–1910	Cleveland	Frederick M. Vinson	1946–1953	Truman
Rufus W. Peckham	1896–1909	Cleveland	Tom C. Clark	1949–1967	Truman
Joseph McKenna	1898–1925	McKinley	Sherman Minton	1949–1956	Truman
Oliver W. Holmes	1902–1932	T. Roosevelt	Earl Warren	1953–1969	Eisenhower
William R. Day	1903–1922	T. Roosevelt	John Marshall Harlan	1955–1971	Eisenhower
William H. Moody	1906–1910	T. Roosevelt	William J. Brennan Jr.	1956–1990	Eisenhower
Horace H. Lurton	1910–1914	Taft	Charles E. Whittaker	1957–1962	Eisenhower
Charles E. Hughes	1910–1916	Taft	Potter Stewart	1958–1981	Eisenhower
Willis Van Devanter	1910–1937	Taft	Byron R. White	1962–1993	Kennedy
Edward D. White	1910–1921	Taft	Arthur J. Goldberg	1962–1965	Kennedy
Joseph R. Lamar	1911–1916	Taft	Abe Fortas	1965–1969	L. Johnson
Mahlon Pitney	1912–1922	Taft	Thurgood Marshall	1967–1991	L. Johnson
James C. McReynolds	1914–1941	Wilson	Warren E. Burger	1969–1986	Nixon
Louis D. Brandeis	1916–1939	Wilson	Harry A. Blackmun	1970–1994	Nixon
John H. Clarke	1916–1922	Wilson	Lewis F. Powell Jr.	1972–1988	Nixon
William H. Taft	1921–1930	Harding	William H. Rehnquist	1972–1986	Nixon
George Sutherland	1922–1938	Harding	John Paul Stevens	1975–	Ford
Pierce Butler	1923–1939	Harding	Sandra Day O'Connor	1981–2006	Reagan
Edward T. Sanford	1923–1930	Harding	William H. Rehnquist	1986–2005	Reagan
Harlan F. Stone	1925–1941	Coolidge			
Charles E. Hughes	1930–1941	Hoover	Antonin Scalia	1986–	Reagan
Owen J. Roberts	1930–1945	Hoover	Anthony M. Kennedy	1988–	Reagan
Benjamin N. Cardozo	1932–1938	Hoover	David H. Souter	1990–2009	G. H. W. Bush
Hugo L. Black	1937–1971	F. Roosevelt			
Stanley F. Reed	1938–1957	F. Roosevelt	Clarence Thomas	1991–	G. H. W. Bush
Felix Frankfurter	1939–1962	F. Roosevelt			
William O. Douglas	1939–1975	F. Roosevelt	Ruth Bader Ginsburg	1993–	Clinton
Frank Murphy	1940–1949	F. Roosevelt	Stephen Breyer	1994–	Clinton
Harlan F. Stone	1941–1946	F. Roosevelt	John G. Roberts Jr.	2005–	G. W. Bush
James F. Byrnes	1941–1942	F. Roosevelt	Samuel Anthony Alito Jr.	2006–	G. W. Bush
Robert H. Jackson	1941–1954	F. Roosevelt			
Wiley B. Rutledge	1943–1949	F. Roosevelt	Sonia Sotomayor	2009–	Obama
Harold H. Burton	1945–1958	Truman	Elena Kagan	2010–	Obama

SIGNIFICANT SUPREME COURT CASES

Marbury v. Madison (1803)

This case established the right of the Supreme Court to review the constitutionality of laws. The decision involved judicial appointments made during the last hours of the administration of President John Adams. Some commissions, including that of William Marbury, had not yet been delivered when President Thomas Jefferson took office. Infuriated by the last-minute nature of Adams's Federalist appointments, Jefferson refused to send the undelivered commissions out, and Marbury decided to sue. The Supreme Court, presided over by John Marshall, a Federalist who had assisted Adams in the judicial appointments, ruled that although Marbury's commission was valid and the new president should have delivered it, the Court could not compel him to do so. The Court based its reasoning on a finding that the grounds of Marbury's suit, resting in the Judiciary Act of 1789, were in conflict with the Constitution.

For the first time, the Court had overturned a national law on the grounds that it was unconstitutional. John Marshall had quietly established the concept of judicial review: The Supreme Court had given itself the authority to nullify acts of the other branches of the federal government. Although the Constitution provides for judicial review, the Court had not exercised this power before and did not use it again until 1857. It seems likely that if the Court had waited until 1857 to use this power, it would have been difficult to establish.

McCulloch v. Maryland (1819)

In 1816, Congress authorized the creation of a national bank. To protect its own banks from competition with a branch of the national bank in Baltimore, the state legislature of Maryland placed a tax of 2 percent on all notes issued by any bank operating in Maryland that was not chartered by the state. McCulloch, cashier of the Baltimore branch of the Bank of the United States, was convicted for refusing to pay the tax. Under the leadership of Chief Justice John Marshall, the Court ruled that the federal government had the power to establish a bank, even though that specific authority was not mentioned in the Constitution.

Marshall maintained that the authority could be reasonably implied from Article 1, section 8, which gives Congress the power to make all laws that are necessary and proper to execute the enumerated powers. Marshall also held that Maryland could not tax the national bank because in a conflict between federal and state laws, the federal law must take precedence. Thus he established the principles of implied powers and federal supremacy, both of which set a precedent for subsequent expansion of federal power at the expense of the states.

Scott v. Sandford (1857)

Dred Scott was a slave who sued for his own and his family's freedom on the grounds that, with his master, he had traveled to and lived in free territory that did not allow slavery. When his case reached the Supreme Court, the justices saw an opportunity to settle once and for all the vexing question of slavery in the territories. The Court's decision in this case proved that it enjoyed no special immunity from the sectional and partisan passions of the time. Five of the nine justices were from the South and seven were Democrats.

Chief Justice Roger B. Taney hated Republicans and detested racial equality; his decision reflects those prejudices. He wrote an opinion not only declaring that Scott was still a slave but also claiming that the Constitution denied citizenship or rights to blacks, that Congress had no right to exclude slavery from the territories, and that the Missouri Compromise was unconstitutional. While southern Democrats gloated over this seven-to-two decision, sectional tensions were further inflamed, and the young Republican Party's claim that a hostile "slave power" was conspiring to destroy northern liberties was given further credence. The decision brought the nation closer to civil war and is generally regarded as the worst decision ever rendered by the Supreme Court.

Butchers' Benevolent Association of New Orleans v. Crescent City Livestock Landing and Slaughterhouse Co. (1873)

The *Slaughterhouse* cases, as the cases docketed under the *Butchers'* title were known, were the first legal test of the Fourteenth Amendment. To cut down on cases of cholera believed to be caused by contaminated water, the state of Louisiana prohibited the slaughter of livestock in New Orleans except in one slaughterhouse, effectively giving that slaughterhouse a monopoly. Other New Orleans butchers claimed that the state had deprived them of their occupation without due process of law, thus violating the Fourteenth Amendment.

In a five-to-four decision, the Court upheld the Louisiana law, declaring that the Fourteenth Amendment protected only the rights of federal citizenship, like voting in federal elections and interstate travel. The federal government thus was not obliged to protect basic civil rights from violation by state governments. This decision would have significant implications for African Americans and their struggle for civil rights in the twentieth century.

United States v. E. C. Knight Co. (1895)

Also known as the *Sugar Trust* case, this was among the first cases to reveal the weakness of the Sherman Antitrust Act in the hands of a pro-business Supreme Court. In 1895, American Sugar Refining Company purchased four other sugar producers, including the E. C. Knight Company, and thus took control of more than 98 percent of the sugar refining in the United States. In an effort to limit monopoly, the government brought suit against all five of the companies for violating the Sherman Antitrust Act, which outlawed trusts and other business combinations in restraint of trade. The Court dismissed the suit, however, arguing that the law applied only to commerce and not to manufacturing, defining the latter as a local concern and not part of the interstate commerce that the government could regulate.

Plessy v. Ferguson (1896)

African American Homer Plessy challenged a Louisiana law that required segregation on trains passing through the state. After ensuring that the railroad and the conductor knew that he was of mixed race (Plessy appeared to be white but under the racial code of Louisiana was classified as "colored" because he was one-eighth black), he refused to move to the "colored only" section of the coach. The Court ruled against Plessy by a vote of seven to one, declaring that "separate but equal" facilities were permissible according to section 1 of the Fourteenth Amendment, which calls upon the states to provide "equal protection of the laws" to anyone within their jurisdiction. Although the case was viewed as relatively insignificant at the time, it cast a long shadow over several decades.

Initially, the decision was viewed as a victory for segregationists, but in the 1930s and 1940s civil rights advocates referred to the doctrine of "separate but equal" in their efforts to end segregation. They argued that segregated institutions and accommodations were often not equal to those available to whites, and finally succeeded in overturning *Plessy* in *Brown v. Board of Education* in 1954 (see below).

Lochner v. New York (1905)

In this case, the Court ruled against a New York state law that prohibited employees from working in bakeries more than ten hours a day or sixty hours a week. The purpose of the law was to protect the health of workers, but the Court ruled that it was unconstitutional because it violated "freedom of contract" implicitly protected by the due process clause of the Fourteenth Amendment. Most of the justices believed strongly in a laissez-faire economic system that favored survival of the fittest. They felt that government protection of workers interfered with this system. In a dissenting opinion, Justice Oliver Wendell Holmes accused the majority of distorting the Constitution and of deciding the case on "an economic theory which a large part of the country does not entertain."

Muller v. Oregon (1908)

In 1905, Curt Muller, owner of a Portland, Oregon, laundry, demanded that one of his employees, Mrs. Elmer Gotcher, work more than the ten hours allowed as a maximum workday for women under Oregon law. Muller argued that the law violated his "freedom of contract" as established in prior Supreme Court decisions.

Progressive lawyer Louis D. Brandeis defended the Oregon law by arguing that a state could be justified in abridging freedom of contract when the health, safety, and welfare of workers was at issue. His innovative strategy drew on ninety-five pages of excerpts from factory and medical reports to substantiate his argument that there was a direct connection between long hours and the health of women and thus the health of the nation. In a unanimous decision, the Court upheld the Oregon law, but later generations of women fighting for equality would question the strategy of arguing that women's reproductive role entitled them to special treatment.

Schenck v. United States (1919)

During World War I, Charles Schenck and other members of the Socialist Party printed and mailed out flyers urging young men who were subject to the draft to oppose the war in Europe. In upholding the conviction of Schenck for publishing a pamphlet urging draft resistance, Justice Oliver Wendell Holmes established the "clear and present danger" test for freedom of speech. Such utterances as Schenck's during a time of national peril, Holmes wrote, could be considered the equivalent of shouting "Fire!" in a crowded theater. Congress had the right to protect the public against such an incitement to panic, the Court ruled in a unanimous decision. But the analogy was a false one. Schenck's pamphlet had little power to provoke a public firmly opposed to its message. Although Holmes later modified his position to state that the danger must relate to an immediate evil and a specific action, the "clear and present danger" test laid the groundwork for those who later sought to limit First Amendment freedoms.

Schechter Poultry Corp. v. United States (1935)

During the Great Depression, the National Industrial Recovery Act (NIRA), which was passed under President Franklin D. Roosevelt, established fair competition codes that were designed to help businesses. The Schechter brothers of New York City, who sold chickens, were convicted of violating the codes. The Supreme Court ruled that the NIRA unconstitutionally conferred legislative power on an administrative agency and overstepped the limits of federal power to regulate interstate commerce. The decision was a significant blow to the New Deal recovery program, demonstrating both historic American resistance to economic planning and the refusal of the business community to yield its autonomy unless it was forced to do so.

Brown v. Board of Education (1954)

In 1950, the families of eight Topeka, Kansas, children sued the Topeka Board of Education. The children were blacks who lived within walking distance of a whites-only school. The segregated school system required them to take a time-consuming, inconvenient, and dangerous route to get to a black school, and their parents argued that there was no reason their children should not be allowed to attend the nearest school. By the time the case reached the Supreme Court, it had been joined with similar cases regarding segregated schools in other states and the District of Columbia. A team of lawyers from the National Association for the Advancement of Colored People (NAACP), led by Thurgood Marshall (who would later be appointed to the Supreme Court), urged the Court to overturn the fifty-eight-year-old precedent established in *Plessy v. Ferguson*, which had enshrined "separate but equal" as the law of the land. A unanimous Court, led by Chief Justice Earl Warren, declared that "separate educational facilities are inherently unequal" and thus violate the Fourteenth Amendment. In 1955, the Court called for desegregation "with all deliberate speed" but established no deadline.

Roth v. United States (1957)

In 1957, New Yorker Samuel Roth was convicted of sending obscene materials through the mail in a case that ultimately reached the Supreme Court. With a six-to-three vote, the Court reaffirmed the historical view that obscenity is not protected by the First Amendment. Yet it broke new ground by declaring that a work could be judged obscene only if, "taken as a whole," it appealed to the "prurient interest" of "the average person."

Prior to this case, work could be judged obscene if portions were thought able to "deprave and corrupt" the most susceptible part of an audience (such as children). Thus, serious works of literature such as Theodore Dreiser's *An American Tragedy*, which was banned in Boston when first published, had received no protection. Although this decision continued to pose problems of definition, it did help to protect most works that attempt to convey ideas, even if those ideas have to do with sex, from the threat of obscenity laws.

Engel v. Vitale (1962)

In 1959, five parents with ten children in the New Hyde Park, New York, school system sued the school board. The parents argued that the so-called Regents' Prayer that public school students in New York recited at the start of every school day violated the doctrine of separation of church and state outlined in the First Amendment. In 1962, the Supreme Court voted six to one in favor of banning the Regents' Prayer.

The decision threw the religious community into an uproar. Many religious leaders expressed dismay and even shock; others welcomed the decision. Several efforts to introduce an amendment allowing school prayer have failed. Subsequent Supreme Court decisions have banned reading of the Bible in public schools. The Court has also declared mandatory flag saluting to be an infringement of religious and personal freedoms.

Gideon v. Wainwright (1963)

When Clarence Earl Gideon was tried for breaking into a poolroom, the state of Florida rejected his demand for a court-appointed lawyer as guaranteed by the Sixth Amendment. In 1963, the Court upheld his demand in a unanimous decision that established the obligation of states to provide attorneys for indigent defendants in felony cases. Prior to this decision, the right to an attorney had applied only to federal cases, not state cases. In its ruling in *Gideon v. Wainwright*, the Supreme Court applied the Sixth through the Fourteenth Amendments to the states. In 1972, the Supreme Court extended the right to legal representation to all cases, not just felony cases, in its decision in *Argersinger v. Hamlin*.

Griswold v. Connecticut (1965)

With a vote of seven to two, the Supreme Court reversed an "uncommonly silly law" (in the words of Justice Potter Stewart) that made it a crime for anyone in the state of Connecticut to use any drug, article, or instrument to prevent conception. *Griswold* became a landmark case because here, for the first time, the Court explicitly invested with full constitutional status "fundamental personal rights," such as the right to privacy, that were not expressly enumerated in the Bill of Rights. The majority opinion in the case held that the law infringed on the constitutionally protected right to privacy of married persons.

Although the Court had previously recognized fundamental rights not expressly enumerated in the Bill of Rights (such as the right to procreate in *Skinner v. Oklahoma* in 1942), *Griswold* was the first time the Court had justified, at length, the practice of investing such unenumerated rights with full constitutional status. Writing for the majority, Justice William O. Douglas explained that the First, Third, Fourth, Fifth, and Ninth Amendments imply "zones of privacy" that are the foundation for the general right to privacy affirmed in this case.

Miranda v. Arizona (1966)

In 1966, the Supreme Court, by a vote of five to four, upheld the case of Ernesto Miranda, who appealed a murder conviction on the grounds that police had gotten him to confess without giving him access to an attorney. The *Miranda* case was the culmination of the Court's efforts to find a meaningful way of determining whether police had used due process in extracting confessions from people accused of crimes. The *Miranda* decision upholds the Fifth Amendment protection against self-incrimination outside the courtroom and requires that suspects be given what came to be known as the "Miranda warning," which advises them of their right to remain silent and warns them that anything they say might be used against them in a court of law. Suspects must also be told that they have a right to counsel.

New York Times Co. v. United States (1971)

With a six-to-three vote, the Court upheld the right of the *New York Times* and the *Washington Post* to print materials from the so-called *Pentagon Papers*, a secret government study of U.S. policy in Vietnam, leaked by dissident Pentagon official Daniel Ellsberg. Since the papers revealed deception and secrecy in the conduct of the Vietnam War, the Nixon administration had quickly obtained a court injunction against their further publication, claiming that suppression was in the interests of national security. The Supreme Court's decision overturning the injunction strengthened the First Amendment protection of freedom of the press.

Furman v. Georgia (1972)

In this case, the Supreme Court ruled five to four that the death penalty for murder or rape violated the cruel and unusual punishment clause of the Eighth Amendment because the manner in which the death penalty was meted out was irregular, "arbitrary," and "cruel." In response, most states enacted new statutes that allow the death penalty to be imposed only after a postconviction hearing at which evidence must be presented to show that "aggravating" or "mitigating" circumstances were factors in the crime. If the post-conviction hearing hands down a death sentence, the case is automatically reviewed by an appellate court.

In 1976, the Court ruled in *Gregg v. Georgia* that these statutes were not unconstitutional. In 1977, the Court ruled in *Coker v. Georgia* that the death penalty for rape was "disproportionate and excessive," thus allowing the death penalty only in murder cases. Between 1977 and 1991, some 150 people were executed in the United States. Public opinion polls indicate that about 70 percent of Americans favor the death penalty for murder. Capital punishment continues to generate controversy, however, as opponents argue that there is no evidence that the death penalty deters crime and that its use reflects racial and economic bias.

Roe v. Wade (1973)

In 1973, the Court found, by a vote of seven to two, that state laws restricting access to abortion violated a woman's right to privacy guaranteed by the due process clause of the Fourteenth Amendment. The decision was based on the cases of two women living in Texas and Georgia, both states with stringent antiabortion laws. Upholding the individual rights of both women and physicians, the Court ruled that the Constitution protects the right to abortion and that states cannot prohibit abortions in the early stages of pregnancy.

The decision stimulated great debate among legal scholars as well as the public. Critics argued that since abortion was never addressed in the Constitution, the Court could not claim that legislation violated fundamental values of the Constitution. They also argued that since abortion was a medical procedure with an acknowledged impact on a fetus, it was inappropriate to invoke the kind of "privacy" argument that was used in *Griswold v. Connecticut* (see page A-43), which was about contraception. Defenders suggested that the case should be argued as a case of gender discrimination, which did violate the equal protection clause of the Fourteenth Amendment. Others said that the right to privacy in sexual matters was indeed a fundamental right.

Regents of the University of California v. Bakke (1978)

When Allan Bakke, a white man, was not accepted by the University of California Medical School at Davis, he filed a lawsuit alleging that the admissions program, which set up different standards for test scores and grades for members of certain minority groups, violated the Civil Rights Act of 1964, which outlawed racial or ethnic preferences in programs supported by federal funds. Bakke further argued that the university's practice of setting aside spaces for minority applicants denied him equal protection as guaranteed by the Fourteenth Amendment. In a five-to-four decision, the Court ordered that Bakke be admitted to the medical school, yet it sanctioned

affirmative action programs to attack the results of past discrimination as long as strict quotas or racial classifications were not involved.

Webster v. Reproductive Health Services (1989)

By a vote of five to four, the Court upheld several restrictions on the availability of abortions as imposed by Missouri state law. It upheld restrictions on the use of state property, including public hospitals, for abortions. It also upheld a provision requiring physicians to perform tests to determine the viability of a fetus that a doctor judged to be twenty weeks of age or older. Although the justices did not go so far as to overturn the decision in *Roe v. Wade* (see at left), the ruling galvanized interest groups on both sides of the abortion issue. Opponents of abortion pressured state legislatures to place greater restrictions on abortions; those who favored availability of abortion tried to mobilize public action by presenting the decision as a major threat to the right to choose abortion.

Cipollone v. Liggett (1992)

In a seven-to-two decision, the Court ruled in favor of the family of Rose Cipollone, a woman who died of lung cancer after smoking for forty-two years. The Court rejected arguments that health warnings on cigarette packages protected tobacco manufacturers from personal injury suits filed by smokers who contract cancer and other serious illnesses.

Miller v. Johnson (1995)

In a five-to-four decision, the Supreme Court ruled that voting districts created to increase the voting power of racial minorities were unconstitutional. The decision threatens dozens of congressional, state, and local voting districts that were drawn to give minorities more representation as had been required by the Justice Department under the Voting Rights Act. If states are required to redraw voting districts, the number of black members of Congress could be sharply reduced.

Romer v. Evans (1996)

In a six-to-three decision, the Court struck down a Colorado amendment that forbade local governments from banning discrimination against homosexuals. Writing for the majority, Justice Anthony Kennedy said that forbidding communities from taking action to protect the rights of homosexuals and not of other groups unlawfully deprived gays and lesbians of opportunities that were available to others. Kennedy based the decision on the guarantee of equal protection under the law as provided by the Fourteenth Amendment.

Bush v. Palm Beach County Canvassing Board (2000)

In a bitterly argued five-to-four decision, the Court reversed the Florida Supreme Court's previous order for a hand recount of contested presidential election ballots in several counties of that battleground state, effectively securing the presidency for Texas Republican governor George W. Bush. The ruling ended a protracted legal dispute between presidential candidates Bush and Vice President Al Gore while inflaming public opinion: For the first time since 1888, a president who failed to win the popular vote took office. Critics charged that the Supreme Court had applied partisanship rather than objectivity to the case, pointing out that the decision went against this Court's customary interpretation of the Constitution to favor state over federal authority.

Lawrence v. Texas (2003)

In the 1986 case *Bowers v. Hardwick*, the Supreme Court upheld the constitutionality of a Georgia law that outlawed sodomy, ruling that sexual privacy was not protected by the Constitution. This decision came into question, however, when *Lawrence v. Texas* arrived at the Supreme Court in 2002, challenging the constitutionality of a Texas anti-sodomy statute. In this case, the Court voted six to three to strike down the statute, asserting that the 1986 decision was based on an interpretation of constitutional liberties that was too narrow. This decision thus overruled *Bowers v. Hardwick*, with the majority holding that the Texas law violated the Fourteenth Amendment's declaration that no state shall "deprive any person of life, liberty, or property, without due process of law." The decision in *Lawrence v. Texas* was hailed as a legal victory for the gay and lesbian community. It was landmark in its implication that laws cannot be made on the basis of morality, without proof of harm.

Hamdan v. Rumsfeld (2005)

In 2001, Salim Ahmed Hamdan, driver for al-Qaeda leader Osama bin Laden, was arrested in Afghanistan as a suspected terrorist. He was charged with conspiracy to commit terrorist offenses after being held in the U.S. military base in Guantanamo Bay, Cuba, for two years. It was decided that Hamdan would be tried by a military commission under an order from President George W. Bush that commissions be established for express non-citizens, including those with connections to al-Qaeda. Hamdan, however, claimed that trial by military commission was unlawful under the Geneva Conventions and Uniform Code of Military Justice (UCMJ).

In the case's first round through the courts, the U.S. District Court of the District of Columbia ruled in Hamdan's favor. Upon appeal, the decision was reversed, the new court ruling that the military commission was indeed lawful, and that the Geneva Conventions could not be enforced by the U.S. judicial systems. The Supreme Court issued a writ of certiorari in 2005 and ultimately upheld Hamdan's case by a vote of five to three, stating that the military commission was unlawful under both the Geneva Conventions and the UCMJ. This decision put a halt to all Guantanamo Bay tribunals, and was praised by human rights activists and lawyers.

Citizens United v. Federal Election Commission (2010)

In 2010, the Supreme Court overruled a ban on political spending by corporations in a vote of five to four. The case went to court after Citizens United, a conservative nonprofit organization, tried to air its critical documentary on Hillary Clinton, *Hillary: The Movie*, during the 2008 presidential campaign. *Citizens United v. Federal Election Commission* quickly became a matter of free speech and raised the sensitive question of whether corporations should be viewed as individuals under the First Amendment.

The Court's decision overturned two precedents and divided the nation in an already heated time in the political sphere. Advocates for the ruling felt that the previous ban would have given the Supreme Court power to prohibit other political outlets, such as newspapers and television programs. Dissenters, including President Barack Obama, believed that the vote created an opening for wealthy corporations to take advantage of the democratic system. In reversing years of policy, the ruling left all to speculate on its possible impact not only on the 2008 election, but also on American politics as a whole.

THE AMERICAN ECONOMY

THESE SIX "SNAPSHOTS" OF THE U.S. ECONOMY show significant changes over the past century and a half. In 1849, the agricultural sector was by far the largest contributor to the economy. By the turn of the century, with advances in technology and an abundance of cheap labor and raw materials, the country had experienced remarkable industrial expansion, and the manufacturing industries dominated. By 1950, the service sector had increased significantly, fueled by the consumerism of the 1920s and the post–World War II years, and the economy was becoming more diversified. Note that by 1990, the government's share in the economy had grown to more than 10 percent and activity in both the trade and manufacturing sectors had declined, partly as a result of competition from Western Europe and Asia. Manufacturing continued to decline, and by 2008 the service and finance, real estate, and insurance sectors had all grown steadily to eclipse it.

Main Sectors of the U.S. Economy: 1849, 1899, 1950, 1990, 2001, 2008

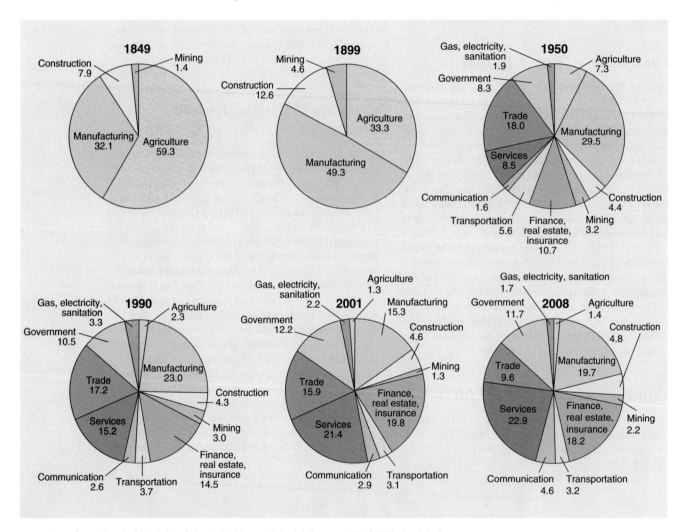

SOURCE: Data from *Historical Statistics of the United States, Colonial Times to 1970* (1975); *Statistical Abstract of the United States, 2010;* U.S. Bureau of Economic Analysis, *Industry Accounts Data, 2010.*

FEDERAL SPENDING AND THE ECONOMY, 1790–2009

Year	Gross Domestic Product (in billions)	Foreign Trade (in billions)		Federal Federal Budget (in billions)	Surplus/Deficit (in billions)	Federal Debt (in billions)
		Exports	Imports			
1790	4.03	0.43	0.50	0.09	0.0032	1.64
1800	7.40	1.10	1.41	0.17	0.0010	1.29
1810	10.6	1.02	1.29	0.12	0.0187	0.81
1820	14.4	1.44	1.52	0.37	−0.0078	1.87
1830	22.2	1.62	1.55	0.33	0.2120	1.07
1840	31.5	2.66	2.16	0.48	−0.0977	0.08
1850	49.6	2.95	3.45	0.78	0.0788	1.24
1860	82.1	7.56	6.84	1.19	−0.1340	1.23
1870	112	6.54	6.70	4.50	1.47	34.8
1880	192	15.8	14.1	4.96	1.22	38.9
1890	319	19.3	17.5	6.73	1.80	23.3
1900	423	30.8	19.1	10.7	0.95	26.7
1910	534	30.6	26.2	11.1	−0.29	17.6
1920	688	67.4	45.0	49.8	2.27	189
1930	893	39.3	34.3	33.7	7.22	159
1940	1,167	46.4	85.6	104	−41.50	495
1950	2,006	94.3	82.1	294	−14.30	257
1960	2,831	145	125	629	2.10	291
1970	4,270	270	246	983	−14.30	381
1980	5,839	470	513	1,369	−171	909
1990	8,034	545	686	1,832	−323	3,206
2000	11,226	1,071	1,449	2,041	270	5,269
2009	12,703	1,571	1,946	3,186	−1,280	11,876

NOTE: All Figures are in 2005 dollars.

SOURCE: *Historical Statistics of the U.S., 1789–1945* (1949), *Statistical Abstract of the U.S., 1965* (1965), *Statistical Abstract of the U.S., 1990* (1990), *Statistical Abstract of the U.S., 2011* (2011), and Louis Johnston and Samuel H. Williamson, "What Was the U.S. GDP Then?" MeasuringWorth, 2011, www.measuringworth.org/usgdp.

A DEMOGRAPHIC PROFILE OF THE UNITED STATES AND ITS PEOPLE

Population

FROM AN ESTIMATED 4,600 white inhabitants in 1630, the country's population grew to a total of more than 308 million in 2010. It is important to note that the U.S. census, first conducted in 1790 and the source of these figures, counted blacks, both free and slave, but did not include American Indians until 1860. The years 1790 to 1900 saw the most rapid population growth, with an average increase of 25 to 35 percent per decade. In addition to "natural" growth—birthrate exceeding death rate—immigration was also a factor in that rise, especially between 1840 and 1860, 1880 and 1890, and 1900 and 1910 (see table on page A-51). The twentieth century witnessed slower growth, partly a result of 1920s immigration restrictions and a decline in the birthrate, especially during the depression era and the 1960s and 1970s. The U.S. population is expected to pass 340 million by the year 2020.

POPULATION GROWTH, 1630–2010

Year	Population	Percent Increase	Year	Population	Percent Increase
1630	4,600	—	1830	12,866,020	33.5
1640	26,600	473.3	1840	17,069,453	32.7
1650	50,400	89.1	1850	23,191,876	35.9
1660	75,100	49.0	1860	31,443,321	35.6
1670	111,900	49.1	1870	39,818,449	26.6
1680	151,500	35.4	1880	50,155,783	26.0
1690	210,400	38.9	1890	62,947,714	25.5
1700	250,900	19.3	1900	75,994,575	20.7
1710	331,700	32.2	1910	91,972,266	21.0
1720	466,200	40.5	1920	105,710,620	14.9
1730	629,400	35.0	1930	122,775,046	16.1
1740	905,600	43.9	1940	131,669,275	7.2
1750	1,170,800	30.0	1950	150,697,361	14.5
1760	1,593,600	36.1	1960	179,323,175	19.0
1770	2,148,100	34.8	1970	203,302,031	13.4
1780	2,780,400	29.4	1980	226,542,199	11.4
1790	3,929,214	41.3	1990	248,718,302	9.8
1800	5,308,483	35.1	2000	281,422,509	13.1
1810	7,239,881	36.4	2010	308,745,538	9.7
1820	9,638,453	33.1			

SOURCE: *Historical Statistics of the U.S.* (1960), *Historical Statistics of the U.S., Colonial Times to 1970* (1975), *Statistical Abstract of the U.S., 1996* (1996), *Statistical Abstract of the U.S., 2003* (2003), and United States Census (2010).

Birthrate, 1820–2007

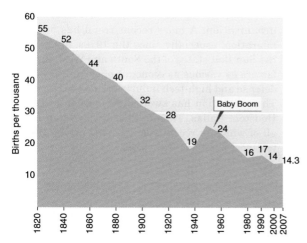

SOURCE: Data from *Historical Statistics of the U.S., Colonial Times to 1970* (1975) and *Statistical Abstract of the U.S., 2007* (2007).

Death Rate, 1900–2007

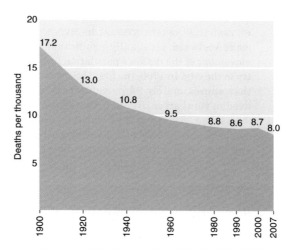

SOURCE: Data from *Historical Statistics of the U.S., Colonial Times to 1970* (1975) and *Statistical Abstract of the U.S., 2007* (2007).

Life Expectancy, 1900–2007

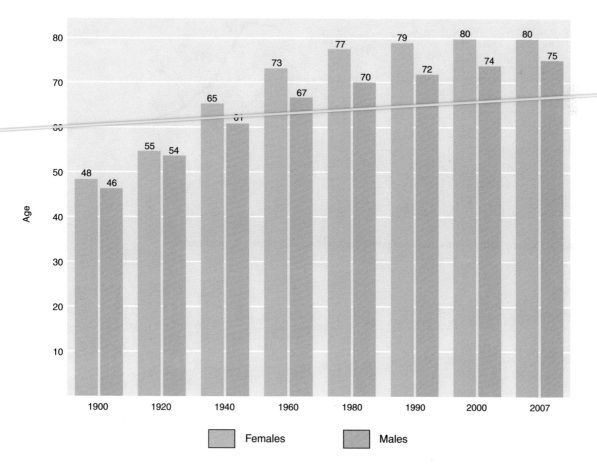

SOURCE: Data from *Historical Statistics of the U.S., Colonial Times to 1970* (1975) and *Statistical Abstract of the U.S., 2007* (2007).

MIGRATION AND IMMIGRATION

WE TEND TO ASSOCIATE INTERNAL MIGRATION with movement westward, yet equally significant has been the movement of the nation's population from the country to the city. In 1790, the first U.S. census recorded that approximately 95 percent of the population lived in rural areas. By 1990, that figure had fallen to less than 25 percent. The decline of the agricultural way of life, late-nineteenth-century industrialization, and immigration have all contributed to increased urbanization. A more recent trend has been the migration, especially since the 1970s, of people to the Sun Belt states of the South and West, lured by factors as various as economic opportunities in the defense and high-tech industries and good weather. This migration has swelled the size of cities like Houston, Dallas, Tucson, Phoenix, and San Diego, all of which in recent years ranked among the top ten most populous U.S. cities.

Rural and Urban Population, 1750–2000

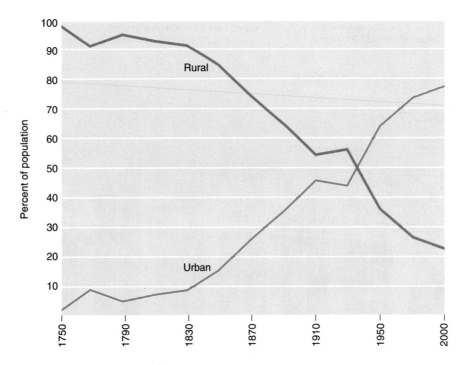

SOURCE: *Statistical Abstract of the U.S., 1991* (1991), *Statistical Abstract of the U.S., 2002* (2002).

THE QUANTITY AND CHARACTER OF IMMIGRATION to the United States has varied greatly over time. During the first major influx, between 1840 and 1860, newcomers hailed primarily from northern and western Europe. From 1880 to 1915, when rates soared even more dramatically, the profile changed, with 80 percent of the "new immigration" coming from central, eastern, and southern Europe. Following World War I, strict quotas reduced the flow considerably. Note also the significant falloff during the years of the Great Depression and World War II. The sources of immigration during the last half century have changed significantly, with the majority of people coming from Latin America, the Caribbean, and Asia. The latest surge during the 1980s and 1990s brought more immigrants to the United States than in any decade except 1901–1910.

RATES OF IMMIGRATION, 1821–2009

Year	Number	Rate per Thousand of Total Resident Population
1821–1830	151,824	1.6
1831–1840	599,125	4.6
1841–1850	1,713,521	10.0
1851–1860	2,598,214	11.2
1861–1870	2,314,824	7.4
1871–1880	2,812,191	7.1
1881–1890	5,246,613	10.5
1891–1900	3,687,546	5.8
1901–1910	8,795,386	11.6
1911–1920	5,735,811	6.2
1921–1930	4,107,209	3.9
1931–1940	528,431	0.4
1941–1950	1,035,039	0.7
1951–1960	2,515,479	1.6
1961–1970	3,321,677	1.8
1971–1980	4,493,300	2.2
1981–1990	7,338,100	3.0
1991	1,827,167	7.2
1992	973,977	3.8
1993	904,292	3.5
1994	804,416	3.1
1995	720,461	2.7
1996	915,900	3.4
1997	798,378	2.9
1998	654,451	2.4
1999	646,568	2.3
2000	849,807	3.0
2001	1,064,318	3.7
2002	1,063,732	3.7
2003	704,000	2.4
2004	958,000	3.3
2005	1,122,000	3.8
2006	1,266,129	4.2
2007	1,052,415	3.5
2008	1,107,126	3.6
2009	1,130,818	3.7

SOURCE: *Historical Statistics of the U.S., Colonial Times to 1970* (1975), *2002 Yearbook of Immigration Statistics* (2002), and *Statistical Abstract of the U.S., 1996, 1999, 2003, 2005,* and *2011* (1996, 1999, 2003, 2005, 2011).

Major Trends In Immigration, 1820–2010

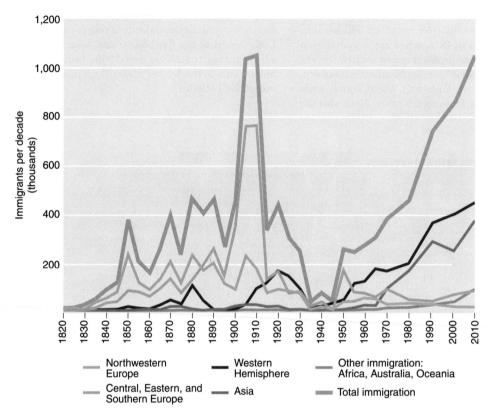

Northwestern Europe

Central, Eastern, and Southern Europe

Western Hemisphere

Asia

Other immigration: Africa, Australia, Oceania

Total immigration

SOURCE: Data from *Historical Statistics of the U.S., Colonial Times to 1970* (1975), *Statistical Abstract of the U.S., 1999* (1999), and *Statistical Abstract of the U.S., 2011* (2011).

Glossary of Historical Vocabulary

A NOTE TO STUDENTS: This list of terms is provided to help you with historical and economic vocabulary. Many of these terms refer to broad, enduring concepts that you may encounter not only in further studies of history but also when following current events. The terms appear in bold at their first use in each chapter. In the glossary, the page numbers of those chapter-by-chapter appearances are provided so you can look up the terms' uses in various periods and contexts. For definitions and discussions of words not included here, consult a dictionary and the book's index, which will point you to topics covered at greater length in the book.

affirmative action Policies established in the 1960s and 1970s by governments, businesses, universities, and other institutions to overcome the effects of past discrimination against specific groups such as racial and ethnic minorities and women. Measures to ensure equal opportunity include setting goals for admission, hiring, and promotion; considering minority status when allocating resources; and actively encouraging victims of past discrimination to apply for jobs and other resources. (pp. 943, 944)

agribusiness Farming on a large scale, using the production, processing, and distribution methods of modern business. Farming became a big business, not just a way to feed a family and make a living, in the late nineteenth century as farms got larger and more mechanized. In the 1940s and 1950s, specialized commercial farms replaced many family-run operations and grew to an enormous scale. (pp. 562, 913)

alliance system The military and diplomatic system formulated in an effort to create a balance of power in pre–World War I Europe. Nations were bound together by rigid and comprehensive treaties that promised mutual aid in the case of attack by specific nations. The system swung into action after the Austrian archduke Franz Ferdinand was assassinated in Sarajevo on June 28, 1914, dragging most of Europe into war. (p. 715)

anarchist A person who rebels against established order and authority. An anarchist is someone who believes that government of any kind is unnecessary and undesirable and should be replaced with voluntary cooperation and free association. Anarchists became increasingly visible in the United States in the late nineteenth and early twentieth centuries. They advocated revolution and grew in numbers through appeals to discontented laborers. Anarchists frequently employed violence in an attempt to achieve their goals. In 1901, anarchist Leon Czolgosz assassinated President William McKinley. (pp. 619, 685, 759)

antebellum A term that means "before a war" and commonly refers to the period prior to the Civil War. (p. 521)

black nationalism A term linked to several African American movements emphasizing racial pride, separation from whites and white institutions, and black autonomy. Black nationalism gained in popularity with the rise of Marcus Garvey and the Universal Negro Improvement Association (1917–1927) and later with the Black Panther Party, Malcolm X, and other participants of the black power movements of the 1960s. (pp. 762, 946)

bloody shirt A refrain used by Republicans in the late nineteenth century to remind the voting public that the Democratic Party, dominated by the South, was largely responsible for the Civil War and that the Republican Party had led the victory to preserve the Union. Republicans urged their constituents to "vote the way you shot." (pp. 524, 587)

***bracero* program** A policy begun during World War II to help with wartime agriculture in which Mexican laborers (*braceros*) were permitted to enter the United States and work for a limited period of time but not to gain citizenship or permanent residence. The program officially ended in 1964. (p. 913)

brinksmanship A cold war practice of appearing willing and able to resort to nuclear war in order to make an enemy back down. Secretary of State John Foster Dulles was the foremost proponent of this policy. (p. 903)

capitalism An economic system in which private individuals and corporations own and operate most means of production. Free-market competition—in which supply and demand is minimally regulated by the state or not regulated at all—determines the prices of goods and services. There are three major aspects of capitalism. First, a capitalist system generally includes many workers who do not own what they produce, but instead perform labor for wages. Second, capitalist societies move beyond local trade to the specialized production of goods for large-scale cash markets. Third, people in a capitalist society internalize a social mentality that emphasizes rationality and the pursuit of profit as the primary goal of economic life. In the United States, most regions made the transition to capitalism by the early nineteenth century. Over the following two hundred years, the United States developed an industrial capitalist system, based on new technologies that allowed for self-sustaining economic growth. (pp. 570, 581, 632)

civil disobedience The public and peaceful violation of certain laws or government orders on the part of individuals or groups who act out of a profound conviction that the law or directive is unjust or immoral and who are prepared to accept the consequences of their actions. Civil disobedience was practiced most famously in U.S. history in the black freedom struggle of the 1960s. (pp. 924, 925)

civil service The administrative service of a government. This term often applies to reforms following the passage of the Pendleton Act in 1883, which set qualifications for U.S. government jobs and sought to remove such jobs from political influence. (pp. 591, 592) *See also* spoils system.

closed shop An establishment in which every employee is required to join a union in order to obtain a job. (p. 752)

cold war The hostile and tense relationship that existed between the Soviet Union on the one hand and the United States and other Western nations on the other from 1947 to 1989. This war was said to be "cold" because the hostility stopped short of armed (hot) conflict, which was warded off by the strategy of nuclear deterrence. (pp. 741, 868, 869) *See also* deterrence.

collective bargaining Negotiation by a group of workers (usually through a union) and their employer concerning rates of pay and working conditions. (pp. 724, 798, 910)

collective security An association of independent nations that agree to accept and implement decisions made by the group, including going to war in defense of one or more members. The United States resolutely avoided such alliances until after World War II, when it created the North Atlantic Treaty Organization (NATO) in response to the threat posed by the Soviet Union. (pp. 753, 873) *See also* North Atlantic Treaty Organization.

communism (Communist Party) A system of government and political organization, based on Marxist-Leninist ideals, in which a single authoritarian party controls the economy through state ownership of production, as a means toward reaching the final stage of Marxist theory in which the state dissolves and economic goods are distributed evenly for the common good. Communists around the globe encouraged the spread of communism in other nations in hopes of fomenting worldwide revolution. At its peak in the 1930s, the Communist Party of the

United States worked closely with labor unions and insisted that only the overthrow of the capitalist system by its workers could save the victims of the Great Depression. After World War II, the Communist power and aspirations of the Soviet Union were held to be a direct threat to American democracy, prompting the cold war. (pp. 740, 779, 802, 886, 1003, 1004, 1005, 1021) *See also* cold war.

conscription Compulsory military service. Americans were first subject to conscription during the Civil War. The Selective Service Act of 1940 marked the first peacetime use of conscription. (p. 718) *See also* draft.

conservatism A political and moral outlook dating back to Alexander Hamilton's belief in a strong central government resting on a solid banking foundation. Currently associated with the Republican Party, conservatism today places a high premium on military preparedness, free market economics, low taxes, and strong sexual morality. (pp. 511, 517, 528, 586, 1004, 1005, 1006, 1007, 1019, 1021, 1025)

consumer culture (consumerism) A society that places high value on, and devotes substantial resources to, the purchase and display of material goods. Elements of American consumerism were evident in the nineteenth century but really took hold in the twentieth century with installment buying and advertising in the 1920s and again with the postwar prosperity of the 1950s. (pp. 755, 758, 799)

containment The U.S. foreign policy developed after World War II to hold in check the power and influence of the Soviet Union and other groups or nations espousing communism. The strategy was first fully articulated by diplomat George F. Kennan in 1946–1947. (pp. 902, 903, 996, 998)

cult of domesticity The nineteenth-century belief that women's place was in the home, where they should create a haven for harried men working in the outside world. This ideal was made possible by the separation of the workplace and the home and was used to sentimentalize the home and women's role in it. (pp. 624, 625) *See also* separate spheres.

culture A term used here to connote what is commonly called "way of life." It refers not only to how a group of people supplied themselves with food and shelter but also to their family relationships, social groupings, religious ideas, and other features of their lives. (pp. 572, 574, 586, 587, 915, 1018, 1059, 1064)

de-industrialization A long period of decline in the industrial sector. The term often refers specifically to the decline of manufacturing and the growth of the service sector of the economy in post–World War II America. This shift and the loss of manufacturing resulting from it were caused by more efficient and automated production techniques at home, increased competition from foreign-made goods, and the use of cheap labor abroad by U.S. manufacturers. (p. 1023)

democracy A system of government in which the people have the power to rule, either directly or indirectly, through their elected representatives. Believing that direct democracy was dangerous, the framers of the Constitution created a government that gave direct voice to the people only in the House of Representatives and that placed a check on that voice in the Senate by offering unlimited six-year terms to senators, elected by the state legislatures to protect them from the whims of democratic majorities. The framers further curbed the perceived dangers of democracy by giving each of the three branches of government (legislative, executive, and judicial) the ability to check the power of the other two. (pp. 505, 513, 529, 564, 1068) *See also* checks and balances.

détente French for "loosening." The term refers to the easing of tensions between the United States and the Soviet Union during the Nixon administration. (pp. 990, 1012)

deterrence The linchpin of U.S. military strategy during the cold war. The strategy of deterrence dictated that the United States would maintain a nuclear arsenal so substantial that the Soviet Union would refrain from attacking the United States and its allies out of fear that the United States would retaliate in devastating proportions. The Soviets pursued a similar strategy. (p. 1066)

disfranchisement The denial of suffrage to a group or individual through legal or other means. Beginning in 1890, southern progressives preached the disfranchisement of black voters as a "reform" of the electoral system. The most common means of eliminating black voters were poll taxes and literary tests. (pp. 528, 704, 760, 810, 879)

domino theory The assumption underlying U.S. foreign policy from the early cold war until the end of the Vietnam War. The theory was that if one country fell to communism, neighboring countries also would fall under Communist control. (pp. 870, 904, 996)

doves Peace advocates, particularly during the Vietnam War. (p. 985)

draft (draftee) A system for selecting individuals for compulsory military service. A draftee is an individual selected through this process. (pp. 718, 835) *See also* conscription.

English Reformation *See* Reformation.

fascism An authoritarian system of government characterized by dictatorial rule, disdain for international stability, and a conviction that warfare is the only means by which a nation can attain greatness. Nazi Germany and Mussolini's Italy are the prime examples of fascism. (p. 790)

federal budget deficit The situation resulting when the government spends more money than it takes in. (pp. 1020, 1022)

feminism The belief that men and women have the inherent right to equal social, political, and economic opportunities. The suffrage movement and second-wave feminism of the 1960s and 1970s were the most visible and successful manifestations of feminism, but feminist ideas were expressed in a variety of statements and movements as early as the late eighteenth century and continue to be expressed in the twenty-first. (pp. 932, 955, 956, 957, 958, 959, 960)

finance capitalism Refers to investment sponsored by banks and bankers and the profits garnered from the sale of financial assets such as stocks and bonds. The decades at the end of the twentieth century are known as a period of finance capitalism because banks and financiers increasingly took on the role of stabilizing markets and reorganizing industries. (p. 581)

franchise The right to vote. The franchise was gradually widened in the United States to include groups such as women and African Americans, who had no vote when the Constitution was ratified. (pp. 516, 652) *See also* suffrage.

free silver The late-nineteenth-century call by silver barons and poor American farmers for the widespread coinage of silver and for silver to be used as a base upon which to expand the paper money supply. The coinage of silver created a more inflationary monetary system that benefited debtors. (pp. 596, 643) *See also* gold standard.

fundamentalism Strict adherence to core, often religious beliefs. The term has varying meanings for different religious groups. Protestant fundamentalists adhere to a literal interpretation of the Bible and thus deny the possibility of evolution. Muslim fundamentalists believe that traditional Islamic law should govern nations and that Western influences should be banned. (pp. 770, 771, 1006)

gender gap An electoral phenomenon that became apparent in the 1980s when men and women began to display different preferences in voting. Women tended to favor liberal candidates, and men tended to support conservatives. The key voter groups contributing to the gender gap were single women and women who worked outside the home. (p. 1026)

globalization The spread of political, cultural, and economic influences and connections among countries, businesses, and individuals around the world through trade, immigration, communication, and other means. In the late twentieth century, globalization was intensified by new communications technology that connected individuals, corporations, and nations with greater speed at low prices. This led to an increase in political and economic interdependence and mutual influence among nations. (pp. 1054, 1056)

gold standard A monetary system in which any circulating currency was exchangeable for a specific amount of gold. Advocates for the gold standard believed that gold alone should be used for coinage and that the total value of paper banknotes should never exceed the government's supply of gold. The triumph of gold standard supporter William McKinley in the 1896 presidential election was a big victory for supporters of this policy. (pp. 597, 641) *See also* free silver.

gospel of wealth The idea that wealth garnered from earthly success should be used for good works. Andrew Carnegie promoted this view in an 1889 essay in which he maintained that the wealthy should serve as stewards and act in the best interests of society as a whole. (pp. 585, 678)

Great Society President Lyndon Johnson's domestic program, which included civil rights legislation, antipoverty programs, government subsidy of medical care, federal aid to education, consumer protection, and aid to the arts and humanities. (pp. 932, 933, 935)

gross domestic product (GDP) A measure of economic production. GDP is the value of all the goods and services produced within a country during a year, regardless of the nationality of the owners of those goods and services. (p. 816)

gross national product (GNP) A measure of economic production. GNP is the value of all the goods and services produced by a country's citizens, regardless of where production takes place. (pp. 814, 915)

guerrilla warfare Fighting carried out by an irregular military force usually organized into small, highly mobile groups. Guerrilla combat was common in the Vietnam War and during the American Revolution. Guerrilla warfare is often effective against opponents who have greater material resources. (pp. 516, 663, 904, 977)

hawks Advocates of aggressive military action or all-out war, particularly during the Vietnam War. (p. 985) *See also* War Hawks.

holding company A system of business organization whereby competing companies are combined under one central administration in order to curb competition and ensure profit. Pioneered in the late 1880s by John D. Rockefeller, holding companies, such as Standard Oil, exercised monopoly control even as the government threatened to outlaw trusts as a violation of free trade. (p. 577) *See also* monopoly; trust.

horizontal integration A system in which a single person or corporation creates several subsidiary businesses to sell a product in different markets. John D. Rockefeller pioneered the use of horizontal integration in the 1880s to control the refining process, giving him a virtual monopoly on the oil-refining business. (p. 577) *See also* vertical integration; monopoly.

impeachment The process by which formal charges of wrongdoing are brought against a president, a governor, or a federal judge. (pp. 514, 1011, 1053)

imperialism The system by which great powers gain control of overseas territories. The United States became an imperialist power by gaining control of

Puerto Rico, Guam, the Philippines, and Cuba as a result of the Spanish-American War. (pp. 525, 537, 543, 544, 545, 667, 668, 669)

iron curtain A metaphor coined by Winston Churchill during his commencement address at Westminster College in Fulton, Missouri, in 1946, to refer to the political, ideological, and military barriers that separated Soviet-controlled Eastern Europe from the rest of Europe and the West following World War II. (pp. 866, 867, 868, 869)

isolationism A foreign policy perspective characterized by a desire to have the United States withdraw from the conflicts of the world and enjoy the protection of two vast oceans. (pp. 658, 753, 825, 826, 873)

Jim Crow The system of racial segregation that developed in the post–Civil War South and extended well into the twentieth century; it replaced slavery as the chief instrument of white supremacy. Jim Crow laws segregated African Americans in public facilities such as trains and streetcars and denied them basic civil rights, including the right to vote. It was also at this time that the doctrine of "separate but equal" became institutionalized. (pp. 519, 588, 704, 705)

Keynesian economics A theory developed by economist John Maynard Keynes that guided U.S. economic policy from the New Deal to the 1970s. According to Keynesians, the federal government has a duty to stimulate and manage the economy by spending money on public works projects and by making general tax cuts in order to put more money into the hands of ordinary people, thus creating demand. (p. 814)

laissez-faire The doctrine, based on economic theory, that government should not interfere in business or the economy. Laissez-faire ideas guided American government policy in the late nineteenth century and conservative politics in the twentieth century. Business interests that supported laissez-faire in the late nineteenth century accepted government interference when it took the form of tariffs or subsidies that worked to their benefit. A broader use of the term refers to the simple philosophy of abstaining from interference. (pp. 585, 586, 640, 654, 674, 788, 789)

land grant A gift of land from a government, usually intended to encourage settlement or development. The British government issued several land grants to encourage development in the American colonies. In the mid-nineteenth century, the U.S. government issued land grants to encourage railroad development and, through the passage of the Land-Grant College Act (also known as the Morrill Act) in 1862, set aside public land to support universities. (pp. 552, 556, 560, 571, 573)

liberalism The political doctrine that government rests on the consent of the governed and is duty-bound to protect the freedom and property of the individual. In the twentieth century, liberalism became associated with the idea that government should regulate the economy and ensure the material well-being and individual rights of all people. (pp. 690, 676, 674, 932, 933, 936, 938, 940, 1013)

manifest destiny A term coined by journalist John O'Sullivan in 1845 to express the popular nineteenth-century belief that the United States was destined to expand westward to the Pacific Ocean and had an irrefutable right and God-given responsibility to do so. This idea provided an ideological shield for westward expansion and masked the economic and political motivations of many of those who championed it. (p. 537)

McCarthyism The practice of searching out suspected Communists and others outside mainstream American society, discrediting them, and hounding them from government and other employment. The term derives from Senator Joseph McCarthy, who gained notoriety for leading such repressive activities from 1950 to 1954. (p. 885)

military-industrial complex A term first used by President Dwight D. Eisenhower to refer to the aggregate power and influence of the armed forces in conjunction with the aerospace, munitions, and other industries that produced supplies for the military in the post–World War II era. (p. 908)

miscegenation The sexual mixing of races. In slave states, despite the social stigma and legal restrictions on interracial sex, masters' almost unlimited power over their female slaves meant that liaisons inevitably occurred. Many states maintained laws against miscegenation into the 1950s. (p. 588)

monopoly Exclusive control and domination by a single business entity over an entire industry through ownership, command of supply, or other means. Gilded Age businesses monopolized their industries quite profitably, often organizing holding companies and trusts to do so. (pp. 568, 571, 577, 581, 583, 596) *See also* holding company; trust.

nationalism A strong feeling of devotion and loyalty toward one nation over others. Nationalism encourages the promotion of the nation's common culture, language, and customs. (pp. 947, 972, 973)

nativism Bias against immigrants and in favor of native-born inhabitants. American nativists especially favor persons who come from white, Anglo-Saxon, Protestant lines over those from other racial, ethnic, and religious heritages. Nativists may include former immigrants who view new immigrants as incapable of assimilation. Many nativists, such as members of the Know-Nothing Party in the nineteenth century and the Ku Klux Klan through the contemporary period, voice anti-immigrant, anti-Catholic, and anti-Semitic sentiments. (p. 680)

New Deal The group of social and economic programs that President Franklin Roosevelt developed to provide relief for the needy, speed economic recovery, and reform economic and government institutions. The New Deal was a massive effort to bring the United States out of the Great Depression and ensure its future prosperity. (pp. 786, 790–792, 795, 801, 809, 810)

New Right Politically active religious conservatives who became particularly vocal in the 1980s. The New Right criticized feminism, opposed abortion and homosexuality, and promoted "family values" and military preparedness. (p. 1012)

New South A vision of the South, promoted after the Civil War by Henry Grady, editor of the *Atlanta Constitution*, that urged the South to abandon its dependence on agriculture and use its cheap labor and natural resources to compete with northern industry. Many Southerners migrated from farms to cities in the late nineteenth century, and Northerners and foreigners invested a significant amount of capital in railroads, cotton and textiles, mining, lumber, iron, steel, and tobacco in the region. (pp. 587–588)

North Atlantic Treaty Organization (NATO) North Atlantic Treaty Organization (NATO) A post–World War II alliance that joined the United States, Canada, and Western European nations into a military coalition designed to counter the Soviet Union's efforts to expand. Each NATO member pledged to go to war if any member was attacked. Since the end of the cold war, NATO has been expanding to include the formerly Communist countries of Eastern Europe. (pp. 864, 867, 1046)

oligopoly A competitive system in which several large corporations dominate an industry by dividing the market so each business has a share of it. More prevalent than outright monopolies during the late 1800s, the oligopolies of the Gilded Age successfully muted competition and benefited the corporations that participated in this type of arrangement. (pp. 550, 583)

plutocracy A society ruled by the richest members. The excesses of the Gilded Age and the fact that just 1 percent of the population owned more than half the real and personal property in the country led many to question whether the United States was indeed a plutocracy. (p. 614)

pogrom An organized and often officially encouraged massacre of an ethnic minority; usually used in reference to attacks on Jews. (p. 608)

Populism A political movement that led to the creation of the People's Party, primarily comprising southern and western farmers who railed against big business and advocated business and economic reforms, including government ownership of the railroads. The movement peaked in the late nineteenth century. The Populist ticket won more than 1 million votes in the presidential election of 1892 and 1.5 million in the congressional elections of 1894. The term *populism* has come to mean any political movement that advocates on behalf of the common person, particularly for government intervention against big business. (p. 656, 657, 659)

predestination The idea that individual salvation or damnation is determined by God at, or just prior to, a person's birth. The concept of predestination invalidated the idea that salvation could be obtained through either faith or good works. (p. 98) *See also* Calvinism.

progressivism (progressive movement) A wide-ranging twentieth-century reform movement that advocated government activism to mitigate the problems created by urban industrialism. Progressivism reached its peak in 1912 with the creation of the Progressive Party, which ran Theodore Roosevelt for president. The term *progressivism* has come to mean any general effort advocating for social welfare programs. (pp. 614, 640, 643, 1072)

Protestantism A powerful Christian reform movement that began in the sixteenth century with Martin Luther's critiques of the Roman Catholic Church. Over the centuries, Protestantism has taken many different forms, branching into numerous denominations with differing systems of worship. (p. 587)

reform Darwinism A social theory, based on Charles Darwin's theory of evolution, that emphasized activism, arguing that humans could speed up evolution by altering the environment. A challenge to social Darwinism, reform Darwinism condemned laissez-faire and demanded that the government take a more active approach to solving social problems. It became the ideological basis for progressive reform in the late nineteenth and early twentieth centuries. (p. 683) *See also* laissez-faire; social Darwinism.

republicanism The belief that the unworkable model of European-style monarchy should be replaced with a form of government in which supreme power resides in the hands of citizens with the right to vote and is exercised by a representative government answerable to this electorate. In Revolutionary-era America, republicanism became a social philosophy that embodied a sense of community and called individuals to act for the public good. (pp. 899–900)

scientific management A system of organizing work, developed by Frederick Winslow Taylor in the late nineteenth century, to increase efficiency and productivity by breaking tasks into their component parts and training workers to perform specific parts. Labor resisted this effort because it de-skilled workers and led to the speedup of production lines. Taylor's ideas were most popular at the height of the Progressive Era. (p. 683)

separate spheres A concept of gender relations that developed in the Jacksonian era and continued well into the twentieth century, holding that women's proper place was in the world of hearth and home (the private sphere) and men's was in the world of commerce and politics (the public sphere). The doctrine of separate spheres eroded slowly over the nineteenth and twentieth centuries as women became more and more involved in public activities. (pp. 588, 761) *See also* cult of domesticity.

social Darwinism A social theory, based on Charles Darwin's theory of evolution, that argued that all progress in human society came as the result of competition and natural selection. Gilded Age proponents such as William Graham Sumner and Herbert Spencer claimed that reform was useless because the rich and poor were precisely where nature intended them to be and intervention would retard the progress of humanity. (pp. 583–586, 686) *See also* reform Darwinism.

social gospel movement A religious movement in the late nineteenth and early twentieth centuries founded on the idea that Christians have a responsibility to reform society as well as individuals. Social gospel adherents encouraged people to put Christ's teachings to work in their daily lives by actively promoting social justice. (pp. 677, 678–679)

socialism A governing system in which the state owns and operates the largest and most important parts of the economy. (pp. 351, 611, 622, 643, 779, 802)

social purity movement A movement to end prostitution and eradicate venereal disease, often accompanied by the censorship of materials deemed "obscene." (p. 677)

spoils system An arrangement in which party leaders reward party loyalists with government jobs. This slang term for *patronage* comes from the saying "To the victor go the spoils." Widespread government corruption during the Gilded Age spurred reformers to curb the spoils system through the passage of the Pendleton Act in 1883, which created the Civil Service Commission to award government jobs on the basis of merit. (pp. 525, 586) *See also* civil service.

states' rights A strict interpretation of the Constitution that holds that federal power over the states is limited and that the states hold ultimate sovereignty. First expressed in 1798 through the passage of the Virginia and Kentucky Resolutions, which were based on the assumption that the states have the right to judge the constitutionality of federal laws, the states' rights philosophy became a cornerstone of the South's resistance to federal control of slavery. (pp. 507, 508, 699)

strict constructionism An approach to constitutional law that attempts to adhere to the original intent of the writers of the Constitution. Strict construction often produces Supreme Court decisions that defer to the legislative branch and to the states and restrict the power of the federal government. Opponents of strict construction argue that the Constitution is an organic document that must be interpreted to meet conditions unimagined when it was written. (p. 1008)

suffrage The right to vote. The term *suffrage* is most often associated with the efforts of American women to secure voting rights. (pp. 500, 554, 683, 703–704, 760) *See also* franchise.

Sun Belt The southern and southwestern regions of the United States, which grew tremendously in industry, population, and influence after World War II. (pp. 909, 912–915)

supply-side economics An economic theory based on the premise that tax cuts for the wealthy and for corporations encourage investment and production (supply), which in turn stimulate consumption. Embraced by the Reagan administration and other conservative Republicans, this theory reversed Keynesian economic policy, which assumes that the way to stimulate the economy is to create demand through federal spending on public works and general tax cuts that put more money into the hands of ordinary people. (p. 1021) *See also* Keynesian economics.

temperance movement The reform movement to end drunkenness by urging people to abstain from the consumption of alcohol. Begun in the 1820s, this movement achieved its greatest political victory with the passage of a constitutional amendment in 1919 that prohibited the manufacture, sale, and transportation of alcohol. That amendment was repealed in 1933. (pp. 589–590, 652–653)

third world Originally a cold war term linked to decolonization, *third world* was first used in the late 1950s to describe newly independent countries in Africa and Asia that were not aligned with either Communist nations (the second world) or non-Communist nations (the first world). Later, the term was applied to all poor, nonindustrialized countries, in Latin America as well as in Africa and Asia. Many international experts see *third world* as a problematic category when applied to such a large and disparate group of nations, and they criticize the discriminatory hierarchy suggested by the term. (pp. 605, 606, 874)

trickle-down economics The theory that financial benefits and incentives given to big businesses in the top tier of the economy will flow down to smaller businesses and individuals and thus benefit the entire nation. President Herbert Hoover unsuccessfully used the trickle-down strategy in his attempt to pull the nation out of the Great Depression, stimulating the economy through government investment in large economic enterprises and public works such as construction of the Hoover Dam. In the late twentieth century, conservatives used this economic theory to justify large tax cuts and other financial benefits for corporations and the wealthy. (pp. 775, 1024)

Truman Doctrine President Harry S. Truman's assertion that American security depended on stopping any Communist government from taking over any non-Communist government—even nondemocratic and repressive dictatorships—anywhere in the world. Beginning in 1947 with American aid to help Greece and Turkey stave off Communist pressures, this approach became a cornerstone of American foreign policy during the cold war. (p. 870)

trust A corporate system in which corporations give shares of their stock to trustees, who coordinate the industry to ensure profits to the participating corporations and curb competition. Pioneered by Standard Oil, such business practices were deemed unfair, were moderated by the Sherman Antitrust Act (1890), and were finally abolished by the combined efforts of Presidents Theodore Roosevelt and William Howard Taft and the sponsors of the 1914 Clayton Antitrust Act. The term *trust* is also loosely applied to all large business combinations. (pp. 568, 577, 595) *See also* holding company.

vertical integration A system in which a single person or corporation controls all processes of an industry from start to finished product. Andrew Carnegie first used vertical integration in the 1870s, controlling every aspect of steel production from the mining of iron ore to the manufacturing of the final product, thereby maximizing profits by eliminating the use of outside suppliers or services. (p. 576)

welfare capitalism The idea that a capitalistic, industrial society can operate benevolently to improve the lives of workers. The notion of welfare capitalism became popular in the 1920s as industries extended the benefits of scientific management to improve safety and sanitation in the workplace as well as institute paid vacations and pension plans. (p. 754) *See also* scientific management.

welfare state A nation or state in which the government assumes responsibility for some or all of the individual and social welfare of its citizens. Welfare states commonly provide education, health care, food programs for the poor, unemployment compensation, and other social benefits. The United States dramatically expanded its role as a welfare state with the provisions of the New Deal in the 1930s. (pp. 804–812)

Yankee imperialism A cry raised in Latin American countries against the United States when it intervened militarily in the region without invitation or consent from those countries. (p. 1041)

yeoman A farmer who owned a small plot of land that was sufficient to support a family and was tilled by family members and perhaps a few servants. (pp. 518, 527–528)

Spot Artifact Credits

Abington School District v. Schempp
(1963), 940
ABMs. *See* Antiballistic missiles
Abolition and abolitionism, Lincoln and,
501
Abortion and abortion rights, 960, 963,
1009, 1027, 1028(i)
Abraham Lincoln Brigade, 827
Abstract expressionism, 920, 920(i)
Abu Ghraib prison abuse, 1068
Abundance. *See also* Consumers;
Prosperity; Wealth
culture of, 915–920
Accommodation
by Indians, 541
Washington, Booker T., and, 705, 706
Acheson, Dean, 870, 880, 888–889, 986
Activism. *See also* Protest(s); Revolts and
rebellions
civil rights, 925(i), 940
environmental, 962–963
feminist, 955–960
gay and lesbian, 955
Latino, 948–949
Native American, 947–948
of New Left and Counterculture,
949–954
ADA. *See* Americans with Disabilities
Act
Addams, Jane, 676(i), 698
Hull House and, 675–676, 677(i), 680
woman suffrage and, 683
World War I and, 730
Adding machine, 618
Administrative Reorganization Act (1938),
815
Advanced Research Projects Agency
(ARPA), 1057
Adventures of Huckleberry Finn,
The (Twain), 570
Adventures of Ozzie and Harriet, The
(TV program), 918(i)
Advertising
in 1920s, 755, 755(i), 758–759(b)
on television, 918
Aerospace industry, 912
AFDC. *See* Aid to Families with Dependent
Children

Affirmative action. *See also* African
Americans
Bakke case and, 1009
critics of, 1025
Johnson, L. B., executive order for
(1965), 943–944
Nixon and, 963
for women, 956–957
Affluent society. *See also* Wealth
Galbraith on, 909
in 1950s, 909
Afghanistan, 1065(m)
Soviets and, 1017–1018, 1033
stabilization of, 1068
Taliban in, 1064
U.S. aid to rebels in, 1032
U.S. in, 1045(m), 1069
AFL. *See* American Federation of Labor
AFL-CIO, 910
Africa, 605
third world nations in, 874
African Americans. *See also* Civil rights;
Civil rights movement; Freedmen;
Race and racism; Race riots; Rights;
Slaves and slavery
accommodationism and, 705, 706
affirmative action for, 943–944
in armed forces, 718–719, 720, 835,
835(i), 838, 880
black codes and, 508
as buffalo soldiers, 552, 553(i)
Carter appointments of, 1014
in cities, 609–610, 613
civil rights and, 877–878, 879, 880,
881(i), 920–926, 940–946
Clinton and, 1050
Colfax massacre against, 528
college enrollments by, 877, 915
Colored Farmers' Alliance and, 642
as cowboys, 560
discrimination against, 845, 846, 877,
878, 880
education for, 705
election of 1960 and, 933
employment of women and, 911
feminism and, 958–959
in Great Depression, 776, 779, 779(i)
Great Society and, 938–939

Harlem Renaissance and, 763–764
housing segregation and, 766–767(b)
Jim Crow laws and, 588
labor unions and, 622
lynchings of, 588–589, 609, 879
median income in 1999, 1054
migrations by, 740–741, 742(i), 845,
877–878, 910
Montgomery bus boycott and, 881(i)
New Deal and, 801(i), 809–810
"New Negro" and, 761–764
Niagara movement and, 706
in 1950s, 898
Obama and, 1068
People's Party and, 655–656
in political office, 943
poverty of, 902
in Progressive Era, 704–706
racism against, 879, 880
in Republican Party, 516–517
segregation of, 877, 879, 880, 881(i)
sharecropping and, 779, 797, 801(i)
in South, 739–740
as strikebreakers, 737
in suburbs, 912, 912(i)
terrorism against, 528
in Vietnam War, 981–982, 987, 987(i)
voting rights for, 512, 513, 515, 588,
940–942, 943(i), 944(m)
in West, 552
westward movement by, 913
women and, 521, 521(i), 589, 617, 726,
958–959
in workforce, 617
in World War I, 718–719, 720, 740–742
after World War I, 742
in World War II, 835, 835(i), 838, 845–846
after World War II, 880
African Methodist Episcopal Church, 503
Afrikaners. *See* Boers
Afro hair style, 947(i)
Age. *See* Elderly
Agencies. *See also* Government (U.S.);
specific agencies and departments
in World War I, 724
Agent Orange, 977, 983, 997
Agnew, Spiro T., 988, 1011
Agrarianism, transformation of, 564

Columbus, Christopher, 535, 544
Comanche Indians, 540, 541, 546
Comanchería, 541
Combine (farm machine), 562
Coming of Age in Mississippi (Moody), 941(i)
Comintern, 738
Commerce. *See* Business; Trade
Commerce and Labor Department, 686
Commercial agriculture, 561, 562–564
Commercial banking, 794
Commercialization, of leisure, 625(i), 626
Commission on the Status of Women (UN), 956, 958(b)
Commission on Training Camp Activities (World War I), 719
Committee for Industrial Organization, 808
Committee on Civil Rights (1946). *See* President's Committee on Civil Rights (1946)
Committee on Fair Employment Practices (1941), 845
Committee on Public Information (CPI), 730
Commodity Credit Corporation, 797, 816
Commodity loans, 797
Common laborers, 615
Communication(s)
　railroads and, 573
　telephone and, 579
Communications technology, 1056–1057
Communism
　in Cambodia, 992
　in China, 903–904
　conservatives and, 1005
　in Cuba, 905
　in Czechoslovakia, 871
　in Eastern Europe, 859, 866, 867(m), 1046
　in East Germany, 866
　Graham, Billy, on, 916–917
　in Great Depression, 779
　Greece, Turkey, and, 870
　in Italy, 873
　Johnson, L. B., and, 978–982
　in Middle East, 906
　national liberation movements and, 874
　Popular Front of, 813
　"Red-baiting" and, 883
　Red scare and, 864, 884, 886
　refugees from, 1060
　in third world, 874
　Truman Doctrine and, 870
　in Vietnam, 903–904, 976–977
　after World War I, 740–741(b)
Communist bloc, 867(m)
Communist Party, 740(b)
　New Deal and, 802
　prosecution of, 886
　Scottsboro Boys and, 779
Communities, African American, 552
Community Action Program (CAP), 935
Competition
　antitrust laws and, 595
　Morgan and, 582
　in petroleum industry, 577
　in railroad industry, 573
　unfair, 700
Compromise of 1877, 529
Compulsory free labor, 502
Comstock, Anthony, 702
Comstock, Henry, 549

Comstock Lode (Nevada), 549–552, 551(i)
Concentration camps
　in Cuba, 664
　in Holocaust, 848–849, 848(m)
Coney Island, New York, 625(i), 626, 631
Confiscation Act
　of 1861, 502
　of 1862, 502
Congress (U.S.). *See also* Congressional Reconstruction; Elections
　"Billion Dollar," 595
　Eisenhower and, 899
　election of 1876 and, 529
　ex-Confederates in, 508, 510
　Gingrich and, 1050–1051
　intelligence agency oversight by, 1012
　Johnson, L. B., and, 935
　override of presidential vetoes, 510
　Reconstruction and, 525–526
　Red scare and, 738–739
　southern congressional delegations (1865–877), 519(f)
　Wilson's address to, 700
Congressional Reconstruction, 510–515
Congress of Industrial Organizations (CIO), 624, 808
　AFL merger with, 910
Congress of Racial Equality (CORE), 846, 924, 940–942
Conkling, Roscoe, 591, 592
ConocoPhillips, 577, 756(i)
Conscientious objectors
　in Vietnam War, 983
　in World War I, 718
Conscription. *See* Draft (military)
Conservation. *See also* Environment
　of energy, 1015
　Hetch Hetchy Valley and, 692–693(b)
　New Deal programs and, 795–796, 795(i), 796(m)
　Roosevelt, T., and, 690–694, 691(m)
　Taft and, 696
Conservatives and conservatism, 1004
　Bush, G. W., and, 1062–1064
　courts, Congress, and, 1025
　in education, 1006–1007(b)
　Eisenhower and, 899–900
　laissez-faire and, 788–789
　New Deal and, 812, 813, 815
　Nixon and, 1004, 1005–1009
　Reagan and, 1004, 1019–1029
　of Supreme Court, 586, 814
Consolidation, of business, 572, 580, 581, 583, 586
Constitution
　Cuban, 668
　Hawai'ian, 660
　reconstruction, in South, 508, 512, 518–519
Constitution (U.S.). *See* Supreme Court (U.S.); specific amendments
Consumer culture
　advertising and, 755, 755(i), 758–759(b)
　Columbian Exposition and, 631, 633(b)
　critique of, 918–919
　in Gilded Age, 619
　in 1920s, 754–756
　in 1950s, 897–898, 915–920
　women in, 761
Consumer goods, 844, 876, 876(i)
　credit and, 756
　production of (1921–1929), 757(f)
　revolution in, 754
Consumers

Great Depression and, 792, 797
　in 1920s, 754–755
　passive, 755
　prices and farm income (1865–1910), 642(f)
　safety for, 937
　after World War II, 876, 876(i), 877
Consumption
　inequality of wealth and, 773
　mass production and, 755
　underconsumption and, 792
Containment policy, 996, 998
　Eisenhower and, 897, 902–903
　Kennan and, 867, 871, 872
　Kennedy and, 971, 972
　Korean War and, 888, 889
　Nixon and, 990
　Reagan and, 1032
　six-pronged strategy for, 871–873
　Truman and, 870, 888, 889
　toward Vietnam, 903–904
Contraception. *See also* Birth Control
　defined, 702
Contract labor
　freedmen and, 502
　Populists and, 644
Contras, in Nicaragua, 1032–1033
Cooke, Amos Starr, 660
Coolidge, Calvin, 736, 750, 751, 752–753
"Coolie labor," 553
Cooperatives, farmers', 642–643
Coral Sea, Battle of (1942), 840, 852
CORE. *See* Congress of Racial Equality
Corliss, Alonzo B., 516(b)
Corporate consolidation, 583, 586
Corporate liberalism, 690
Corporations. *See also* Business
　assembly line and management changes in, 754
　foreign-owned in U.S., 1059–1060
　pensions and, 808
　Rockefeller and, 577
　Supreme Court and, 586
Corruption
　in city government, 629, 631
　in Gilded Age, 591
　under Grant, 524, 525(i)
　under Harding, 752
　in southern Republican governments, 520
Costa Rica, 663
Cotton and cotton industry
　sharecropping and, 524
　in Texas, 561
Cotton Club, 764, 764(i)
Coughlin, Charles, 803
Council of Economic Advisers, 876
Counterinsurgency strategy, in Iraq, 1067(i)
Coups, against Diem, 977
Court-packing plan, of Roosevelt, Franklin D., 814
Courts. *See* Supreme Court (U.S.)
Covert operations, of CIA, 897–898, 984, 1012
Cowboys, 557, 560, 561
　industrial, 563
Cox, Archibald, 1010–1011
Cox, James M., 743, 744(m), 751, 787
Coxey, Jacob S., 654
Coxey's army, 654–655, 655(i)
Craft unions, 622
Crashes (financial). *See* Depressions (financial); Panics

ATLAS OF THE TERRITORIAL GROWTH OF THE UNITED STATES

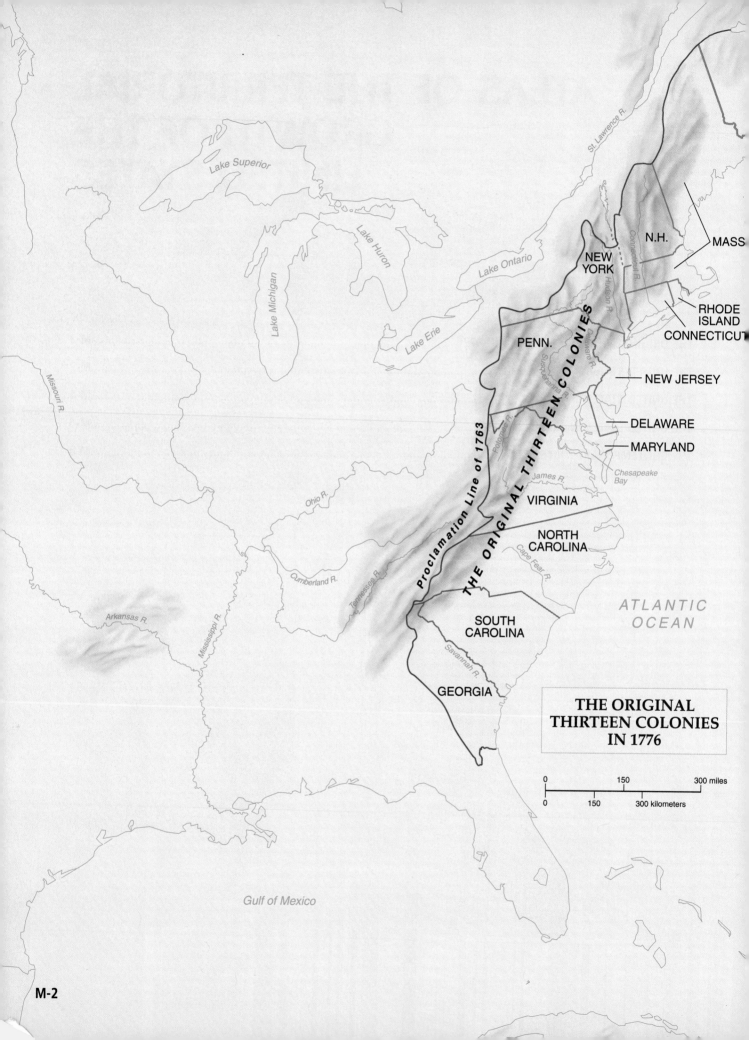

Lake Superior

Lake Michigan

Lake Huron

Lake Ontario

Lake Erie

St Lawrence R.

Missouri R.

Ohio R.

Cumberland R.

Tennessee R.

Mississippi R.

Arkansas R.

N.H.

NEW YORK

Connecticut R.

MASS

RHODE ISLAND

CONNECTICUT

PENN.

Hudson R.

Delaware R.

Susquehanna R.

NEW JERSEY

DELAWARE

MARYLAND

Potomac R.

Chesapeake Bay

James R.

VIRGINIA

Proclamation Line of 1763

THE ORIGINAL THIRTEEN COLONIES

NORTH CAROLINA

Cape Fear R.

ATLANTIC OCEAN

SOUTH CAROLINA

Savannah R.

GEORGIA

THE ORIGINAL THIRTEEN COLONIES IN 1776

0   150   300 miles

0   150   300 kilometers

Gulf of Mexico

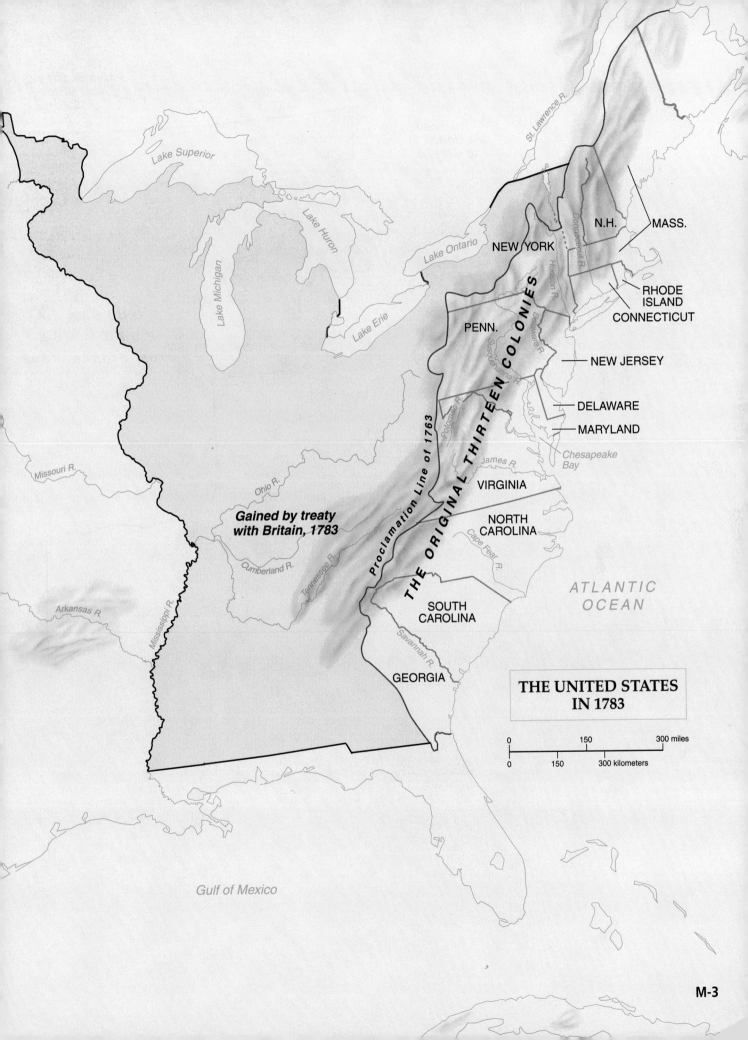

Lake Superior

Lake Huron

Lake Michigan

Lake Ontario

Lake Erie

St. Lawrence R.

Connecticut R.

N.H.

MASS.

NEW YORK

RHODE ISLAND

CONNECTICUT

Hudson R.

PENN.

Delaware R.

NEW JERSEY

Susquehanna R.

DELAWARE

MARYLAND

Missouri R.

Ohio R.

Potomac R.

Chesapeake Bay

James R.

THE ORIGINAL THIRTEEN COLONIES

Gained by treaty with Britain, 1783

Proclamation Line of 1763

VIRGINIA

NORTH CAROLINA

Cape Fear R.

Cumberland R.

Tennessee R.

Arkansas R.

Mississippi R.

ATLANTIC OCEAN

SOUTH CAROLINA

Savannah R.

GEORGIA

THE UNITED STATES IN 1783

| 0 | 150 | 300 miles |
| 0 | 150 | 300 kilometers |

Gulf of Mexico

M-3

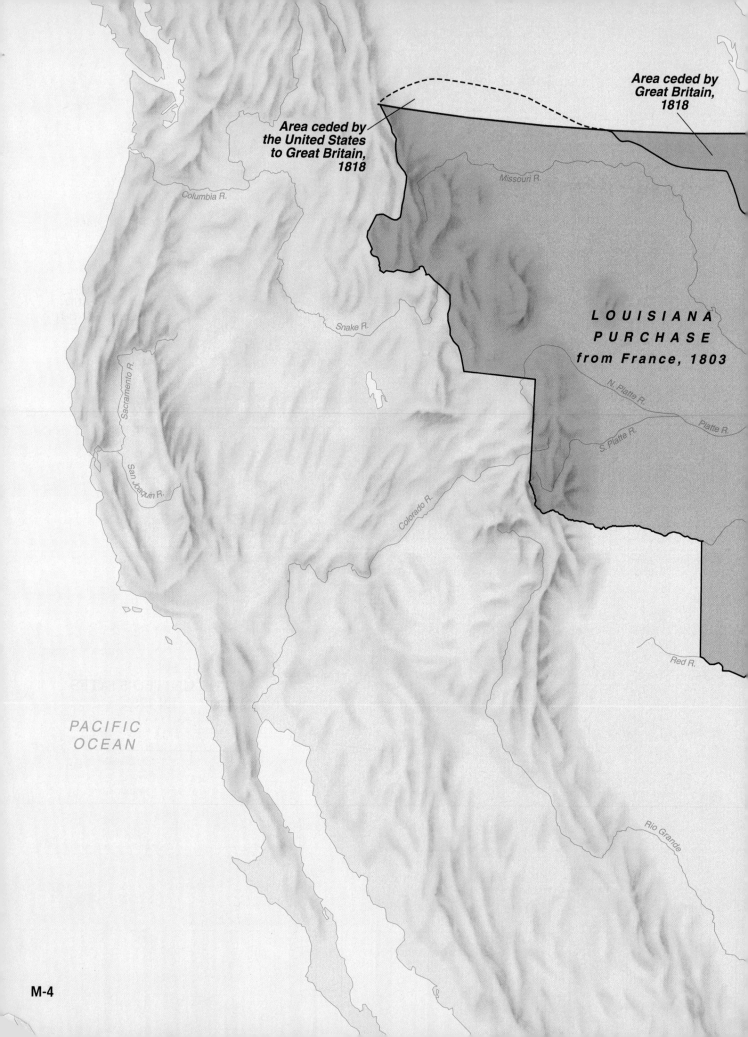

Area ceded by
the United States
to Great Britain,
1818

Area ceded by
Great Britain,
1818

Columbia R.

Missouri R.

Snake R.

LOUISIANA
PURCHASE
from France, 1803

Sacramento R.

N. Platte R.

Platte R.

San Joaquin R.

S. Platte R.

Colorado R.

Red R.

PACIFIC
OCEAN

Rio Grande

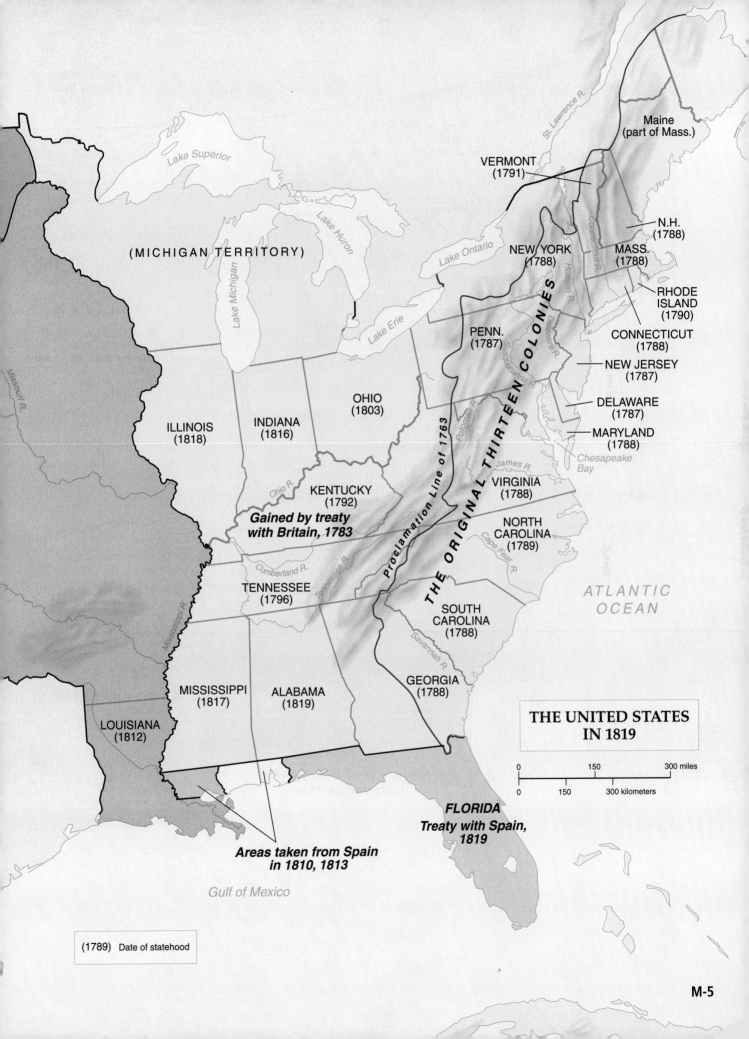

Maine
(part of Mass.)

VERMONT
(1791)

N.H.
(1788)

Lake Superior

(MICHIGAN TERRITORY)

Lake Huron

Lake Michigan

Lake Ontario

Lake Erie

NEW YORK
(1788)

MASS.
(1788)

St. Lawrence R.

Connecticut R.

Hudson R.

RHODE
ISLAND
(1790)

CONNECTICUT
(1788)

NEW JERSEY
(1787)

DELAWARE
(1787)

MARYLAND
(1788)

PENN.
(1787)

Delaware R.

Susquehanna R.

THE ORIGINAL THIRTEEN COLONIES

Proclamation Line of 1763

Potomac R.

Chesapeake
Bay

OHIO
(1803)

ILLINOIS
(1818)

INDIANA
(1816)

Missouri R.

Ohio R.

KENTUCKY
(1792)

Gained by treaty
with Britain, 1783

Cumberland R.

Tennessee R.

TENNESSEE
(1796)

James R.

VIRGINIA
(1788)

NORTH
CAROLINA
(1789)

Cape Fear R.

ATLANTIC
OCEAN

Mississippi R.

MISSISSIPPI
(1817)

ALABAMA
(1819)

SOUTH
CAROLINA
(1788)

Savannah R.

GEORGIA
(1788)

LOUISIANA
(1812)

THE UNITED STATES
IN 1819

0   150   300 miles

0   150   300 kilometers

Areas taken from Spain
in 1810, 1813

FLORIDA
Treaty with Spain,
1819

Gulf of Mexico

(1789)   Date of statehood

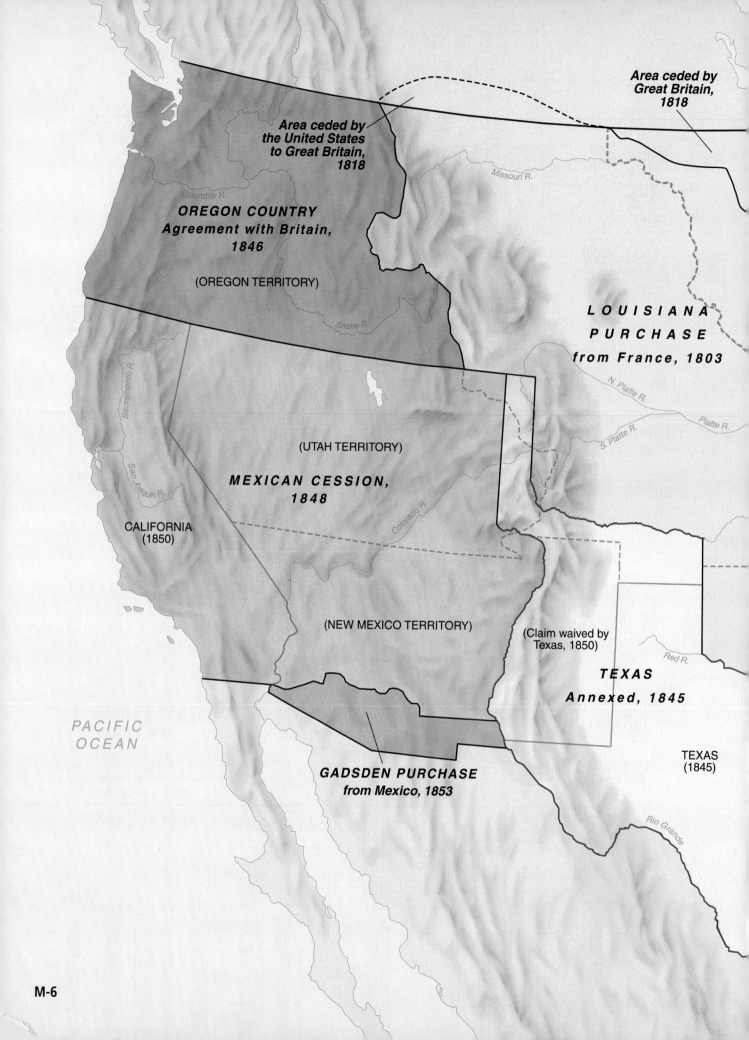

Area ceded by
Great Britain,
1818

Area ceded by
the United States
to Great Britain,
1818

Missouri R.

OREGON COUNTRY
Agreement with Britain,
1846

Columbia R.

(OREGON TERRITORY)

L O U I S I A N A
P U R C H A S E
from France, 1803

Snake R.

Sacramento R.

(UTAH TERRITORY)

N. Platte R.

Platte R.

S. Platte R.

MEXICAN CESSION,
1848

San Joaquin R.

CALIFORNIA
(1850)

Colorado R.

(NEW MEXICO TERRITORY)

(Claim waived by
Texas, 1850)

Red R.

TEXAS
Annexed, 1845

P A C I F I C
O C E A N

TEXAS
(1845)

GADSDEN PURCHASE
from Mexico, 1853

Rio Grande

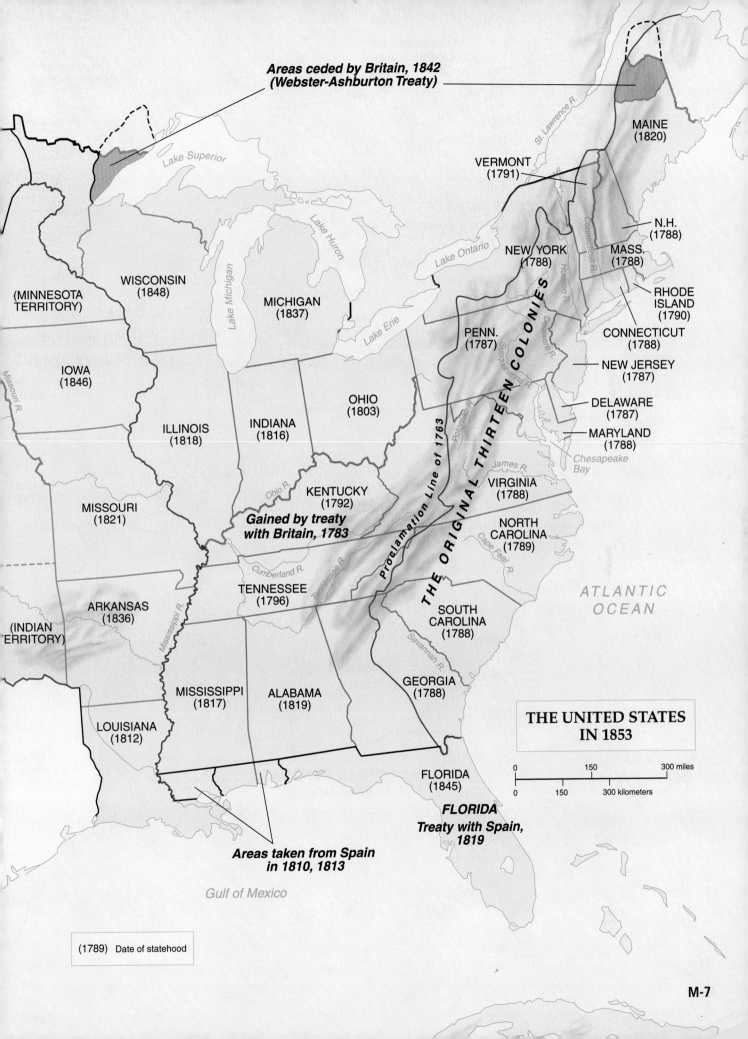

Areas ceded by Britain, 1842
(Webster-Ashburton Treaty)

St. Lawrence R.

MAINE
(1820)

Lake Superior

VERMONT
(1791)

N.H.
(1788)

NEW YORK
(1788)

MASS.
(1788)

Lake Huron

Lake Ontario

Hudson R.

RHODE
ISLAND
(1790)

Connecticut R.

(MINNESOTA
TERRITORY)

WISCONSIN
(1848)

Lake Michigan

MICHIGAN
(1837)

Lake Erie

PENN.
(1787)

Susquehanna R.

Delaware R.

CONNECTICUT
(1788)

NEW JERSEY
(1787)

IOWA
(1846)

OHIO
(1803)

DELAWARE
(1787)

Missouri R.

ILLINOIS
(1818)

INDIANA
(1816)

Potomac R.

MARYLAND
(1788)

*Chesapeake
Bay*

Ohio R.

KENTUCKY
(1792)

James R.

VIRGINIA
(1788)

MISSOURI
(1821)

**Gained by treaty
with Britain, 1783**

Proclamation Line of 1763

NORTH
CAROLINA
(1789)

ATLANTIC
OCEAN

Cumberland R.

Tennessee R.

Cape Fear R.

ARKANSAS
(1836)

TENNESSEE
(1796)

THE ORIGINAL THIRTEEN COLONIES

(INDIAN
TERRITORY)

Mississippi R.

SOUTH
CAROLINA
(1788)

Savannah R.

MISSISSIPPI
(1817)

ALABAMA
(1819)

GEORGIA
(1788)

**THE UNITED STATES
IN 1853**

LOUISIANA
(1812)

0   150   300 miles

0   150   300 kilometers

FLORIDA
(1845)

**Areas taken from Spain
in 1810, 1813**

FLORIDA
**Treaty with Spain,
1819**

Gulf of Mexico

(1789)   Date of statehood

M-7

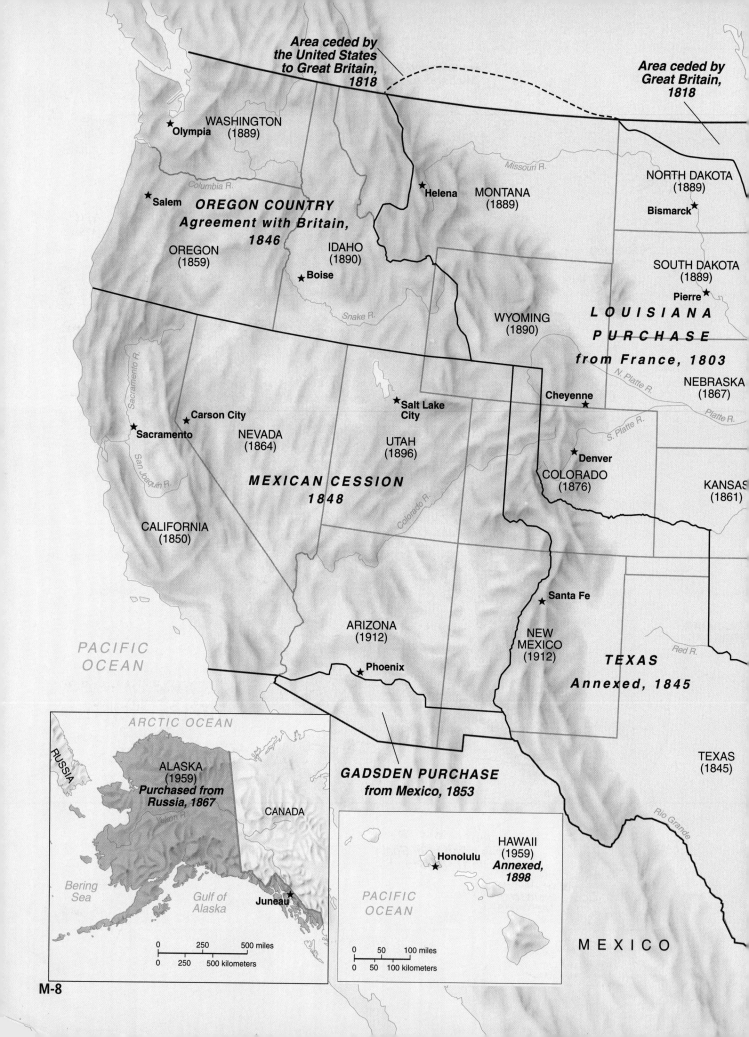

Area ceded by
the United States
to Great Britain,
1818

Area ceded by
Great Britain,
1818

WASHINGTON
(1889)
★ Olympia

Missouri R.

★ Helena   MONTANA
(1889)

NORTH DAKOTA
(1889)

Bismarck ★

Columbia R.

★ Salem   **OREGON COUNTRY**
Agreement with Britain,
1846

OREGON
(1859)

IDAHO
(1890)
★ Boise

SOUTH DAKOTA
(1889)

Pierre ★

Snake R.

WYOMING
(1890)

L O U I S I A N A
P U R C H A S E
from France, 1803

N. Platte R.

NEBRASKA
(1867)

Platte R.

Sacramento R.

★ Salt Lake
City

Cheyenne ★

S. Platte R.

★ Carson City

NEVADA
(1864)

UTAH
(1896)

Denver ★

COLORADO
(1876)

KANSAS
(1861)

★ Sacramento

San Joaquin R.

MEXICAN CESSION
1848

Colorado R.

CALIFORNIA
(1850)

ARIZONA
(1912)

Santa Fe ★

NEW
MEXICO
(1912)

TEXAS
Annexed, 1845

Red R.

PACIFIC
OCEAN

★ Phoenix

TEXAS
(1845)

GADSDEN PURCHASE
from Mexico, 1853

Rio Grande

ARCTIC OCEAN

RUSSIA

ALASKA
(1959)
Purchased from
Russia, 1867

CANADA

Yukon R.

*Bering
Sea*

*Gulf of
Alaska*

Juneau ★

HAWAII
(1959)
Annexed,
1898

Honolulu ★

PACIFIC
OCEAN

M E X I C O

| 0 | 250 | 500 miles |
| 0 | 250 | 500 kilometers |

| 0 | 50 | 100 miles |
| 0 | 50 | 100 kilometers |

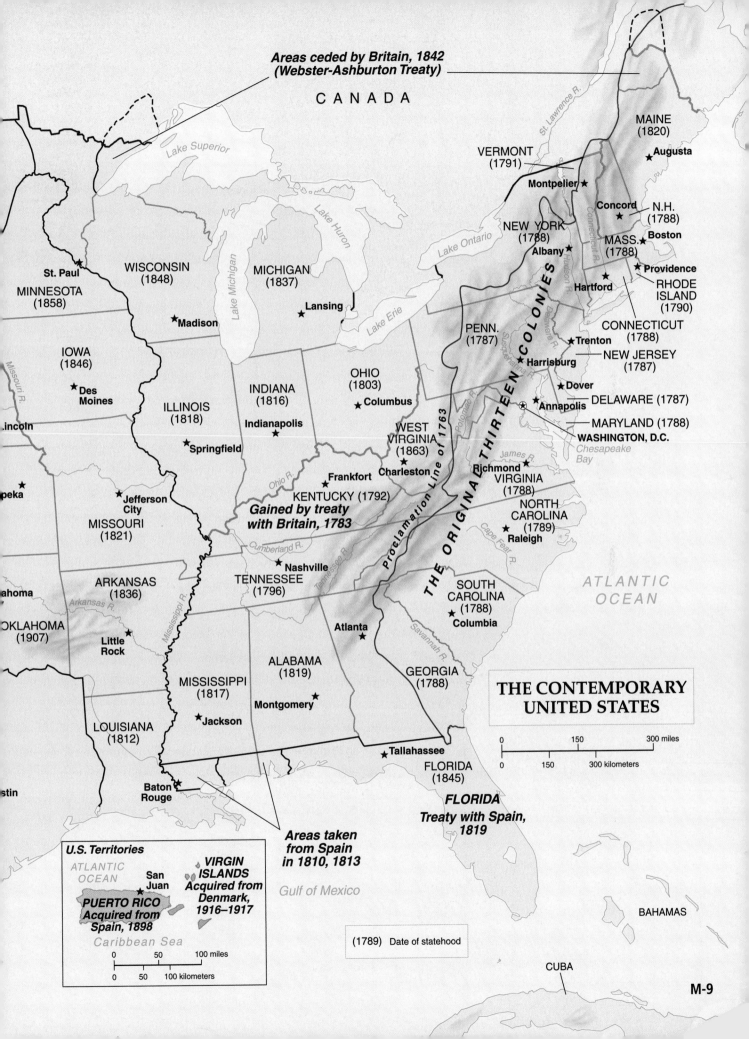

Areas ceded by Britain, 1842
(Webster-Ashburton Treaty)

CANADA

St. Lawrence R.

MAINE
(1820)

★ Augusta

VERMONT
(1791)

Montpelier ★

Concord
★

N.H.
(1788)

Lake Superior

NEW YORK
(1788)

Albany ★

Connecticut R.

MASS.
(1788)

★ Boston

★ Providence

RHODE
ISLAND
(1790)

Hudson R.

Hartford ★

St. Paul
★

WISCONSIN
(1848)

MICHIGAN
(1837)

Lake Huron

Lake Michigan

PENN.
(1787)

Susquehanna R.

Delaware R.

CONNECTICUT
(1788)

MINNESOTA
(1858)

★ Trenton

NEW JERSEY
(1787)

Harrisburg ★

Lake Ontario

Lansing ★

Lake Erie

★ Madison

IOWA
(1846)

OHIO
(1803)

★ Dover

DELAWARE (1787)

⊛ Annapolis

MARYLAND (1788)

WASHINGTON, D.C.

Potomac R.

★ Des
Moines

INDIANA
(1816)

Columbus ★

WEST
VIRGINIA
(1863)

Missouri R.

ILLINOIS
(1818)

Indianapolis ★

Richmond ★

James R.

*Chesapeake
Bay*

incoln

Springfield ★

Charleston ★

VIRGINIA
(1788)

THE ORIGINAL THIRTEEN COLONIES

peka

Jefferson
City ★

Ohio R.

Frankfort ★

Proclamation Line of 1763

NORTH
CAROLINA
(1789)

Cape Fear R.

KENTUCKY (1792)

Raleigh ★

MISSOURI
(1821)

**Gained by treaty
with Britain, 1783**

Cumberland R.

Nashville ★

Tennessee R.

ahoma

ARKANSAS
(1836)

TENNESSEE
(1796)

SOUTH
CAROLINA
(1788)

Arkansas R.

OKLAHOMA
(1907)

Little
Rock ★

Mississippi R.

Columbia ★

ATLANTIC
OCEAN

Atlanta ★

Savannah R.

stin

ALABAMA
(1819)

GEORGIA
(1788)

**THE CONTEMPORARY
UNITED STATES**

MISSISSIPPI
(1817)

Montgomery ★

LOUISIANA
(1812)

★ Jackson

0   150   300 miles

0   150   300 kilometers

★ Tallahassee

Baton
Rouge ★

**Areas taken
from Spain
in 1810, 1813**

FLORIDA
(1845)

**FLORIDA
Treaty with Spain,
1819**

Gulf of Mexico

U.S. Territories

*ATLANTIC
OCEAN*

San
Juan
★

**VIRGIN
ISLANDS**
Acquired from
Denmark,
1916–1917

BAHAMAS

PUERTO RICO
Acquired from
Spain, 1898

Caribbean Sea

0   50   100 miles

0   50   100 kilometers

(1789)   Date of statehood

CUBA

M-9